# Twentieth-Century Literary Criticism

# Guide to Gale Literary Criticism Series

| For criticism on | Consult these Gale series |
|---|---|
| Authors now living or who died after December 31, 1999 | *CONTEMPORARY LITERARY CRITICISM (CLC)* |
| Authors who died between 1900 and 1999 | *TWENTIETH-CENTURY LITERARY CRITICISM (TCLC)* |
| Authors who died between 1800 and 1899 | *NINETEENTH-CENTURY LITERATURE CRITICISM (NCLC)* |
| Authors who died between 1400 and 1799 | *LITERATURE CRITICISM FROM 1400 TO 1800 (LC)* <br><br> *SHAKESPEAREAN CRITICISM (SC)* |
| Authors who died before 1400 | *CLASSICAL AND MEDIEVAL LITERATURE CRITICISM (CMLC)* |
| Authors of books for children and young adults | *CHILDREN'S LITERATURE REVIEW (CLR)* |
| Dramatists | *DRAMA CRITICISM (DC)* |
| Poets | *POETRY CRITICISM (PC)* |
| Short story writers | *SHORT STORY CRITICISM (SSC)* |
| Literary topics and movements | *HARLEM RENAISSANCE: A GALE CRITICAL COMPANION (HR)* <br><br> *THE BEAT GENERATION: A GALE CRITICAL COMPANION (BG)* <br><br> *FEMINISM IN LITERATURE: A GALE CRITICAL COMPANION (FL)* <br><br> *GOTHIC LITERATURE: A GALE CRITICAL COMPANION (GL)* |
| Asian American writers of the last two hundred years | *ASIAN AMERICAN LITERATURE (AAL)* |
| Black writers of the past two hundred years | *BLACK LITERATURE CRITICISM (BLC)* <br><br> *BLACK LITERATURE CRITICISM SUPPLEMENT (BLCS)* <br><br> *BLACK LITERATURE CRITICISM: CLASSIC AND EMERGING AUTHORS SINCE 1950 (BLC-2)* |
| Hispanic writers of the late nineteenth and twentieth centuries | *HISPANIC LITERATURE CRITICISM (HLC)* <br><br> *HISPANIC LITERATURE CRITICISM SUPPLEMENT (HLCS)* |
| Native North American writers and orators of the eighteenth, nineteenth, and twentieth centuries | *NATIVE NORTH AMERICAN LITERATURE (NNAL)* |
| Major authors from the Renaissance to the present | *WORLD LITERATURE CRITICISM, 1500 TO THE PRESENT (WLC)* <br><br> *WORLD LITERATURE CRITICISM SUPPLEMENT (WLCS)* |

ISSN: 0276-8178

Volume 377

# Twentieth-Century Literary Criticism

**Criticism of the
Works of Novelists, Poets, Playwrights,
Short-Story Writers, and Other Creative Writers
Who Lived between 1900 and 1999,
from the First Published Critical
Appraisals to Current Evaluations**

Jonathan Vereecke
*Editor*

Produced in association with
Layman Poupard Publishing

GALE
A Cengage Company

Farmington Hills, Mich • San Francisco • New York • Waterville, Maine
Meriden, Conn • Mason, Ohio • Chicago

**Twentieth-Century Literary Criticism,
Vol. 377**

Layman Poupard Publishing, LLC

Editorial Director: Richard Layman

Editorial Production Manager: Janet Hill

Permissions Manager: Kourtnay King

Quality Assurance Manager:
Katherine Macedon

Content Standards Editor: Connor Towle

Senior Editors:
Dennis Poupard, Eric Bargeron, Hollis Beach

Editors:
DeAnna Ellis, Christina Petrides,
Darien Cavanaugh

Bibliographer/Editor: Kevin Kyzer

Content Conversion, Data Coding,
Composition: Apex CoVantage, LLC

Advisors to LPP:
Ward Briggs
Robert C. Evans
James Hardin
Joel Myerson
Andrew S. Rabin

Volume Advisors:
Douglas S. Kern, University of Maryland,
College Park (for "James Baldwin")
Linda Wagner-Martin, The University of
North Carolina at Chapel Hill
(for "Theodore Dreiser")

For product information and technology assistance, contact us at
**Gale Customer Support, 1-800-877-4253.**
For permission to use material from this text or product,
submit all requests online at **www.cengage.com/permissions.**
Further permissions questions can be emailed to
**permissionrequest@cengage.com**

*Gale*
27500 Drake Rd.
Farmington Hills, MI, 48331-3535

LIBRARY OF CONGRESS CATALOG CARD NUMBER 76-46132

ISBN-13: 978-1-4103-8288-7

ISSN: 0276-8178

Printed in Mexico
1 2 3 4 5 6 7 23 22 21 20 19

# Contents

Preface vii

Acknowledgments xi

# Preface

S ince its inception *Twentieth-Century Literary Criticism* (*TCLC*) has been purchased and used by some 10,000 school, public, and college or university libraries. *TCLC* has covered more than 1000 authors, representing over 60 nationalities and nearly 50,000 titles. No other reference source has surveyed the critical response to twentieth-century authors and literature as thoroughly as *TCLC*. In the words of one reviewer, "there is nothing comparable available." *TCLC* "is a gold mine of information—dates, pseudonyms, biographical information, and criticism from books and periodicals—which many librarians would have difficulty assembling on their own."

## Scope of the Series

*TCLC* is designed to serve as an introduction to authors who died between 1900 and 1999 and to the most significant interpretations of these author's works. The great poets, novelists, short-story writers, playwrights, and philosophers of the period are frequently studied in high school and college literature courses. In organizing and reprinting the vast amount of critical material written on these authors, *TCLC* helps students develop valuable insight into literary history, promotes a better understanding of the texts, and sparks ideas for papers and assignments. Each entry in *TCLC* presents a comprehensive survey of an author's career or an individual work of literature and provides the user with a multiplicity of interpretations and assessments. Such variety allows students to pursue their own interests; furthermore, it fosters an awareness that literature is dynamic and responsive to many different opinions.

Volumes 1 through 87 of *TCLC* featured authors who died between 1900 and 1959; beginning with Volume 88, the series expanded to include authors who died between 1900 and 1999. Beginning with Volume 26, every fourth volume of *TCLC* was devoted to literary topics. These topics widen the focus of the series from the individual authors to such broader subjects as literary movements, prominent themes in twentieth-century literature, literary reaction to political and historical events, significant eras in literary history, prominent literary anniversaries, and the literatures of cultures that are often overlooked by English-speaking readers. With *TCLC* 285, the series returned to a standard author approach, with some entries devoted to a single important work of world literature and others devoted to literary topics.

*TCLC* is part of the survey of criticism and world literature that is contained in Gale's *Contemporary Literary Criticism* (*CLC*), *Nineteenth-Century Literature Criticism* (*NCLC*), *Literature Criticism from 1400 to 1800* (*LC*), *Shakespearean Criticism* (*SC*), and *Classical and Medieval Literature Criticism* (*CMLC*).

## Organization of the Book

A *TCLC* entry consists of the following elements:

■ The **Author Heading** cites the name under which the author most commonly wrote, followed by birth and death dates. If the author wrote consistently under a pseudonym, the pseudonym will be listed in the author heading and the author's actual name given in parentheses on the first line of the biographical and critical introduction. Also located here are any name variations under which an author wrote, including transliterated forms for authors whose native languages use nonroman alphabets. Uncertain birth or death dates are indicated by question marks. Single-work entries are preceded by a heading that consists of the most common form of the title in English translation (if applicable) and the author's name (if applicable).

■ The **Introduction** contains background information that introduces the reader to the author, work, or topic that is the subject of the entry.

■ The list of **Principal Works** is ordered chronologically by date of first publication and lists the most important works by the author. The genre and publication information of each work is given. In the case of works not published in English, a translation of the title is provided as an aid to the reader; the translation is a published translated title or a free translation provided by the compiler of the entry. As a further aid to the reader, a list of **Principal English Translations** is provided for authors who did not publish in English; the list focuses primarily on twentieth-century translations, selecting those works most commonly considered the best by critics. Unless otherwise indicated, plays are dated by first performance, not first publication, and the location of the first performance is given, if known. Lists of **Representative Works** discussed in the entry appear with topic entries.

- Reprinted **Criticism** is arranged chronologically in each entry to provide a useful perspective on changes in critical evaluation over time. The critic's name and the date of composition or publication of the critical work are given at the beginning of each piece of criticism. Unsigned criticism is preceded by the title of the source in which it appeared. All titles by the author featured in the text are printed in boldface type. Footnotes are reprinted at the end of each essay or excerpt. In the case of excerpted criticism, only those footnotes that pertain to the excerpted texts are included. Criticism in topic entries is arranged chronologically under a variety of subheadings to facilitate the study of different aspects of the topic.

- A complete **Bibliographical Citation** of the original essay or book precedes each piece of criticism. Citations conform to recommendations set forth in the Modern Language Association of America's *MLA Handbook*, 8th ed., 2016.

- Critical essays are prefaced by brief **Annotations** describing each piece.

- An annotated bibliography of **Further Reading** appears at the end of each entry and suggests resources for additional study. In some cases, significant essays for which the editors could not obtain reprint rights are included here. Boxed material following the further reading list provides references to other biographical and critical sources on the author in series published by Gale.

# Indexes

A **Cumulative Author Index** lists all of the authors who have appeared in a wide variety of reference sources published by Gale, including *TCLC*. A complete list of these sources is found facing the first page of the Author Index. The index also includes birth and death dates and cross references between pseudonyms and actual names.

A **Cumulative Topic Index** lists the literary themes and topics treated in *TCLC* as well as in *Classical and Medieval Literature Criticism, Literature Criticism from 1400 to 1800, Nineteenth-Century Literature Criticism, Contemporary Literary Criticism, Drama Criticism, Poetry Criticism, Short Story Criticism,* and *Children's Literature Review.*

A **Cumulative Nationality Index** lists all authors featured in *TCLC* by nationality, followed by the numbers of the *TCLC* volumes in which their entries appear.

An alphabetical **Title Index** accompanies each volume of *TCLC*. Listings of titles by authors covered in the given volume are followed by the author's name and the corresponding page numbers where the titles are discussed. English translations of titles published in other languages and variations of titles are cross-referenced to the title under which a work was originally published. Titles of novels, plays, nonfiction books, and poetry, short-story, or essay collections are printed in italics, while individual poems, short stories, and essays are printed in roman type within quotation marks. All titles reviewed in *TCLC* and in the other Literary Criticism Series can be found online in the *Gale Literary Index*.

## Citing *Twentieth-Century Literary Criticism*

When citing criticism reprinted in the Literary Criticism Series, students should provide complete bibliographic information so that the cited essay can be located in the original print or electronic source. Students who quote directly from reprinted criticism may use any accepted bibliographic format, such as Modern Language Association (MLA) style or University of Chicago Press style. Both the MLA and the University of Chicago formats are acceptable and recognized as being the current standards for citations. It is important, however, to choose one format for all citations; do not mix the two formats within a list of citations.

The examples below follow recommendations for preparing a works cited list set forth in the Modern Language Association of America's *MLA Handbook*, 8th ed., 2016. The first example pertains to material drawn from periodicals, the second to material reprinted from books:

Cardone, Resha. "Reappearing Acts: Effigies and the Resurrection of Chilean Collective Memory in Marco Antonio de la Parra's *La tierra insomne o La puta madre.*" *Hispania,* vol. 88, no. 2, pp. 284-93. *Twentieth-Century Literary Criticism,* edited by Thomas J. Schoenberg and Lawrence J. Trudeau, vol. 206, Gale, 2008, pp. 356-65.

Kuester, Martin. "Myth and Postmodernist Turn in Canadian Short Fiction: Sheila Watson, 'Antigone' (1959)." *The Canadian Short Story: Interpretations,* edited by Reginald M. Nischik, Camden House, 2007, pp. 163-74. *Twentieth-Century Literary Criticism,* edited by Thomas J. Schoenberg and Lawrence J. Trudeau, vol. 206, Gale, 2008, pp. 227-32.

The examples below follow recommendations for preparing a bibliography set forth in *The Chicago Manual of Style,* 16th ed., 2010. The first example pertains to material drawn from periodicals, the second to material reprinted from books:

Cardone, Resha. "Reappearing Acts: Effigies and the Resurrection of Chilean Collective Memory in Marco Antonio de la Parra's *La tierra insomne o La puta madre.*" *Hispania* 88, no. 2 (May 2005): 284-93. Reprinted in *Twentieth-Century Literary Criticism.* Vol. 206, edited by Thomas J. Schoenberg and Lawrence J. Trudeau, 356-65. Detroit: Gale, 2008.

Kuester, Martin. "Myth and Postmodernist Turn in Canadian Short Fiction: Sheila Watson, 'Antigone' (1959)." In *The Canadian Short Story: Interpretations,* edited by Reginald M. Nischik, pp. 163-74. Rochester, N.Y.: Camden House, 2007. Reprinted in *Twentieth-Century Literary Criticism.* Vol. 206, edited by Thomas J. Schoenberg and Lawrence J. Trudeau, 227-32. Detroit: Gale, 2008.

# Suggestions Are Welcome

Readers who wish to suggest new features, topics, or authors to appear in future volumes, or who have other suggestions or comments, are cordially invited to call, write, or fax the Product Manager:

Product Manager, Literary Criticism Series
Gale
A Cengage Company
27500 Drake Road
Farmington Hills, MI 48331-3535
1-800-347-4253 (GALE)
Fax: 248-699-8884

# Acknowledgments

The editors wish to thank the copyright holders of the criticism included in this volume and the permissions managers of many book and magazine publishing companies for assisting us in securing reproduction rights. Following is a list of copyright holders who have granted us permission to reproduce material in this volume of *TCLC*. Every effort has been made to trace copyright, but if omissions have been made, please let us know.

## COPYRIGHTED MATERIAL IN *TCLC*, VOLUME 377, WAS REPRODUCED FROM THE FOLLOWING PERIODICALS:

*American Literary Realism 1870-1910,* vol. 3, no. 3, Summer 1970. Copyright © 1970 *American Literary Realism 1870-1910.* Reproduced by permission of the publisher.—*Arizona Quarterly,* vol. 70, no. 1, Spring 2014 for "James Baldwin's Post-Sentimental Fiction: From 'Previous Condition' to *Another Country*" by Adam T. Jernigan. Copyright © 2014 Adam T. Jernigan. Reproduced by permission of the author.—*Ball State University Forum,* vol. 18, no. 2, Spring 1977. Copyright © 1977 *Ball State University Forum.* Reproduced by permission of the publisher.—*Bucknell Review,* vol. 18, no. 1, Spring 1970. Copyright © 1970 Associated University Presses. Reproduced by permission of the publisher.—*CLA Journal,* vol. 33, no. 4, June 1990; vol. 56, no. 1, September 2012. Copyright © 1990, 2012 *CLA Journal.* Both reproduced by permission of the publisher.—*The Commonweal,* vol. 64, no. 9, 1 June 1956. Public domain.—*Current Opinion,* vol. 63, 3 September 1917; vol. 66, 3 March 1919. Both public domain.—*The Dreiser Newsletter,* vol. 11, no. 1, Spring 1980. Copyright © 1980 International Theodore Dreiser Society. Reproduced by permission of the editor.—*Dreiser Studies,* vol. 22, no. 2, Fall 1991; vol. 32, no. 2, Fall 2001. Copyright © 1991, 2001 International Theodore Dreiser Society. Both reproduced by permission of the editor.—*Journal of the Association for the Interdisciplinary Study of the Arts,* vol. 1, no. 1, Autumn 1995 for "Love and Death Reconsidered: The Union of Lovers in *Another Country*" by Susan Amper. Copyright © 1995 Susan Amper. Reproduced by permission of the author.—*The Library Chronicle,* vol. 33, 1967. Copyright © 1967 *Library Chronicle.* Reproduced by permission of the publisher.—*Masses and Mainstream,* vol. 8, no. 12, December 1955. Public domain. —*Michigan Academician,* vol. 20, no. 2, Spring 1988. Copyright © 1988 Michigan Academy of Science, Arts, and Letters. Reproduced by permission of the publisher.—*The Midwest Quarterly,* vol. 42, no. 3, Spring 2001. Copyright © 2001 *The Midwest Quarterly.* Reproduced by permission of the publisher.—*The Monthly Review,* vol. 7, no. 4, August 1955. Public domain.—*The Nation,* vol. 162, 20 April 1946. Public domain.—*Negro American Literature Forum,* vol. 6, no. 4, Winter 1972. Copyright © 1972 *African American Review.* Reproduced by permission of the publisher.—*The New Republic,* 3 May 1919. Public domain.—*The New York Times Book Review,* 29 April 1945. Public domain.—*The New Yorker,* vol. 24, no. 8, 17 April 1948. Public domain.—*The North American Review,* vol. 186, no. 623, October 1907. Public domain.—*PMLA,* vol. 55, no. 1, March 1940; vol. 67, no. 2, March 1952; vol. 78, no. 5, December 1963. All public domain; vol. 124, no. 3, May 2009. Copyright © 2009 Modern Language Association of America. Reproduced by permission of the publisher.—*The Quarterly of Film, Radio, and Television,* vol. 6, no. 4, Summer 1952. Copyright © 1952 University of California Press. Reproduced by permission of the publisher.—*The Sewanee Review,* vol. 34, no. 4, October-December 1926. Public domain. —*Southwest Review,* vol. 31, no. 4, 1946. Public domain.—*University of Pennsylvania Library Chronicle,* vol. 17, 1950. Public domain.—*Yale University Library Gazette,* vol. 25, no. 3, January 1951. Public domain.—*Zeitschrift für Anglistik und Amerikanistik,* vol. 27, no. 3, 1979 for "The Dream of Success in Dreiser's *A Gallery of Women*" by Yoshinobu Hakutani. Copyright © 1979 Yoshinobu Hakutani. Reproduced by permission of the author.

## COPYRIGHTED MATERIAL IN *TCLC*, VOLUME 377, WAS REPRODUCED FROM THE FOLLOWING BOOKS:

Beer, Janet. From *Soft Canons: American Women Writers and Masculine Tradition,* edited by Karen L. Kilcup, University of Iowa Press, 1999. Copyright © 1999 University of Iowa Press. Reproduced by permission of the publisher.—Butler, Robert. From *Theodore Dreiser and American Culture: New Readings,* edited by Yoshinobu Hakutani, University of Delaware Press, 2000. Copyright © 2000 Associated University Presses. Reproduced by permission of the publisher.—Gerber, Philip. From *Theodore Dreiser and American Culture: New Readings,* edited by Yoshinobu Hakutani, University of Delaware Press, 2000. Copyright © 2000 Associated University Presses. Reproduced by permission of the publisher.—Goodfellow, Donald M. From *Six Novelists: Stendhal, Dostoevski, Tolstoy, Hardy, Dreiser, Proust,* Carnegie Press, Carnegie Institute of Technology, 1959. Public domain.—Grebstein, Sheldon Norman. For "*An American Tragedy*: Theme and Structure" in *The Twenties: Poetry and*

# *Another Country*
## James Baldwin

American novelist, essayist, short-story writer, nonfiction writer, playwright, and poet.

The following entry provides criticism of Baldwin's novel *Another Country* (1962). For additional information about Baldwin, see *CLC*, Volumes 1, 2, 3, 4, 5, 8, 13, 15, 17, 42, 50, 67, and 127, and *TCLC*, Volumes 229, 376; for additional information about the short story "Sonny's Blues," see *CLC*, Volume 90.

## INTRODUCTION

*Another Country*, the third novel by James Baldwin (1924-1987), is in a sense a continuation of the themes of his first two. In *Go Tell It on the Mountain* (1953), Baldwin had written semiautobiographically about his intellectual and emotional coming of age as a black writer. *Giovanni's Room* (1956), remarkable for its time, treated homosexual relationships with a poignancy and depth often lacking in earlier literature. In *Another Country*, Baldwin built on his earlier work by chronicling the lives of several New York musicians, actors, and authors, whose relationships span the societal fault lines of race, gender, and sexual identity. The characters were based loosely on Baldwin's friends and associates in New York, many of whom were writers and artists. Like its predecessors, *Another Country* was a commercial success, even though—characteristically of Baldwin's fiction—it broached topics that were still deemed scandalous in the United States of the 1960s, including interracial relationships and bisexuality. Professional and academic critics were, however, sharply divided in their reviews. One notable detractor was Eldridge Cleaver, who in his 1966 essay "Notes on a Native Son" (see Further Reading) condemned the novel as a permissive portrayal of African American subservience. Baldwin's longtime rival Norman Mailer (1963; see Further Reading) offered similarly harsh commentary on the novel's style, declaring *Another Country* "an abominably written book." Twenty-first-century critics have not entirely set aside the categories of race, gender, and sexuality on which earlier criticism tended to fixate. Rather, they have emphasized the ways in which Baldwin's novel undermines these categories and gestures toward the possibilities of unity and understanding. Latter-day readings have also analyzed details of novelistic craft in what has gradually come to be seen as an underappreciated work. Baldwin's motivic use of jazz—especially bebop—music, for example, has garnered critical attention, as has his careful arrangement of secondary characters in a novel whose initial protagonist is largely absent.

## PLOT AND MAJOR CHARACTERS

*Another Country* is divided into three books, the first of which concerns jazz drummer Rufus Scott. Strikingly, the book begins just before Rufus takes his own life by leaping from the George Washington Bridge, sketching out the causes of his suicide retrospectively. To some extent, the malaise that Rufus finds inescapable is a part of the New York environment, present in the impersonal heft of its buildings and the alienating pace of life. In a more acute sense, Rufus is the victim of a deep self-hatred that, Baldwin hints, is actually a form of internalized racism. Rufus's relationship with Leona, a white woman whom he meets at a show, is censured by his sister, Ida, as a sign of low self-esteem. Ida's rejection of the relationship fuels Rufus's abusive behavior toward Leona and his irrational conviction that she is trying to destroy him. Leona, who has a history of mental illness, is tipped over the edge into a nervous breakdown and subsequently committed to a psychiatric institution.

Rufus leaves behind him a complicated network of friends and lovers, whose lives are the principal concern of the novel's second and third books. In Rufus's absence, the role of protagonist is fulfilled by his friend Vivaldo Moore, an Italian American novelist from a working-class background. Struggling to publish his first book, Vivaldo finds himself in a rivalry with his mentor, Richard Silenski, who was Rufus's English teacher years earlier. Ida, notwithstanding her attitude toward her brother's interracial relationship, becomes romantically involved with Vivaldo, but the relationship is strained by infidelities on both sides. Ida, a singer, conducts an affair with television producer Steve Ellis on the understanding that he will assist her rise to stardom. Upon his return from overseas, Eric Jones, Rufus's onetime lover, pursues an affair with Richard's wife, Cass, and also has a brief tryst with Vivaldo. The encounter leaves Vivaldo with new ideas about love and masculinity, along with a bittersweet clarity about his relationship with Rufus. Late in the novel, something like a truce is established among the central characters. Eric returns to his longtime lover, Yves, whom he met in France; Vivaldo and Ida admit their respective affairs and reaffirm their love for each other. The novel closes on an uncertain but not altogether pessimistic note, as Vivaldo recognizes the fatuousness of viewing the world in terms of black and white.

## MAJOR THEMES

The "other country" of the novel's title has been interpreted in various ways, most often with reference to the racial discrimination still widely and openly practiced in Baldwin's time. Although they live in the same city, the black and white characters in *Another Country* are often depicted as coming from different worlds and having quite different expectations of life. The white characters, including the numerous policemen who appear in various scenes, in many cases look on their black counterparts with contempt. Fear, suspicion, and fascination are mutual, as Vivaldo's sincere but simplistic attitude toward Ida demonstrates. Moreover, attempts to bridge the black and white "worlds" via any connection beyond platonic friendship are looked on with hostility, as exemplified by the backlash to Rufus's relationship with Leona. In his earlier nonfiction, Baldwin had often written about the sense of cultural isolation that stems from racial prejudice against black people. He sketched out elements of it in his first novel, *Go Tell It on the Mountain,* and wrote of it poignantly in the essay "Letter from a Region in My Mind," published the same year as *Another Country.*

The novel's "other country" may also point to sexual "otherness," encompassing forms of sexuality and gender identity that were viewed at the time of the novel's writing as existing outside societal conventions. Several of the male characters in the novel are behaviorally bisexual, even if they do not outwardly identify as such. All of them find themselves caught between their sexual desires and the social norms of their time. Rufus, as his violent rejection of Eric suggests, labors under an idea of manhood that leaves him with little capacity to express love for other men, whether physically or through any display of emotion. Eric, when he first appears in the novel, is ashamed of his sexual desires and struggles to hide and repress them. To escape Rufus's abuse, he literally flees to another country, France, where Baldwin himself found the emotional distance to write candidly about his life. Eric's chosen country of refuge, however, might also be construed as a sort of offstage haven from the pressures of a rigid masculine code. He seems to bring a piece of it back with him to the United States—and even to impart some of it to the belatedly self-accepting Vivaldo.

Whatever insight the novel's characters achieve is, however, hard-won. Jealousy, not only between lovers but also between artistic rivals, is a common thread in their interactions. Richard and Vivaldo, to name a prominent example, are jealous of each other's literary careers: Vivaldo bitterly envies Richard's success, while Richard secretly chides himself as a sellout and grudgingly admires Vivaldo for adhering to the ideal of the struggling, principled artist. A further twist to the two men's rivalry arises from Richard's mistaken belief that it is Vivaldo, not Eric, who is carrying on an affair with his wife. Part of the staying power of Vivaldo and Ida's relationship, it is hinted, comes from their ability to endure or surmount jealousy and to find a way of coping with the racial animus that surrounds them on both sides. The question at the novel's close is whether such an emotional commitment can last.

## CRITICAL RECEPTION

At the time of its publication *Another Country* received a mixed critical response. While it was a financial success and received largely positive notices in the black press, Baldwin's third novel, like *Giovanni's Room* before it, shocked and outraged some readers for depicting what were then considered taboo subjects. Some critics felt that *Another Country* strayed from Baldwin's earlier views, expressed in works such as his 1949 essay "Everybody's Protest Novel," which deprecated sentimentality in literature and questioned the validity of many of the black protest novels of the day. Boyd M. Berry (1966; see Further Reading) evaluated *Another Country* in light of those early essays and suggested that the novel's black characters should be read as flawed rather than as fueled by racial injustice.

In the last quarter of the twentieth century, Baldwin increasingly fell out of favor with many scholars, who judged his later writings—among which included *Another Country*—as inferior; still, some thoughtful commentary was produced. Two studies of *Another Country* from that period—by Barry Gross in 1972 and D. Maureen Thum in 1988—focused on Baldwin's literary techniques. Gross closely analyzed the patterns of images in the novel, stressing "that much of the imagery is based on color—specifically, black and white—and light and dark." Thum elucidated Baldwin's narrative technique in the first book of *Another Country,* which depicts the last hours of Rufus's life, declaring that it is "Baldwin's subtle analysis and presentation of time—the interplay of past and present—which reveals the protagonist as a convincing, authentic individual, a character of uncommon depth, sensitivity, and intelligence."

Like Thum, Alfred R. Ferguson (1977), in his thematic comparison of *Another Country* and Richard Wright's

*The Outsider* (1953), emphasized Rufus's unsuccessful struggle to fully realize his identity. Ferguson maintained that the protagonists of both novels "strive for and fail to achieve their humanity, the full realization or integration or definition of the self." The "quest for humanity [is] undertaken" by Rufus in Baldwin's novel and Cross Damon in Wright's, Ferguson asserted, "not merely because they happen to be black, but because they are simply trying to be." Susan Amper (1995) explored themes of separation and union in the novel, declaring that "*Another Country* represents a breakthrough in American literature, reversing the separation of lovers that has so characterized our fiction." Baldwin's goal in the novel, she argued, "is to find a solution, a reconciliation that will work, not only on a personal level, but on a social level, that will bring together not only the polarities of male and female but those of black and white and gay and straight."

Amper's assessment can perhaps be seen as an early example of the modern scholarly reappraisal of Baldwin and his influence on the African American canon, a process that has led to a revaluation of *Another Country* as a masterpiece. Twenty-first-century critics have attended to the complexities of the novel's depictions of race and sexuality, with much of the focus being placed on Rufus. Ernesto Javier Martínez (2009) explored what he called the novel's "suicidal sensibility," arguing that "*Another Country* is motivated less by the tragedy of Rufus's suicide early in the novel than by the ethical imperative faced by all the characters to risk their sense of self (to figuratively commit suicide) in order to better understand their lives. They need to be willing to die, as it were, to come to know more fully." Ben Robbins (2013) sought "to demonstrate . . . a point of common ground" between Baldwin and William Faulkner, observing that in their works both "utilize transgressive sex, in which alternative, challenging modes of sexuality disregard normative sociosexual practices to question—and even destroy—preexisting social boundaries."

In 2014, Adam T. Jernigan mounted a defense of Baldwin against those critics who charged that his novels are guilty of the same sentimentalism that he attacks in his essays. Jernigan countered that "a close analysis of Baldwin's early stories and novels reveals that his critique of sentimentalism enabled him to rework the formal dimensions of his fiction, and in particular to develop new kinds of characters, scenes, and plots." Jernigan declared *Another Country* to be "the clearest example of the author's post-sentimental aesthetic."

Michael J. Hartwell

Academic Advisor: Douglas S. Kern,
University of Maryland, College Park

# PRINCIPAL WORKS

*Go Tell It on the Mountain.* Alfred A. Knopf, 1953. Print. (Novel)

*\*Notes of a Native Son.* Beacon Press, 1955. Print. (Essays)

*Giovanni's Room.* Dial Press, 1956. Print. (Novel)

*Nobody Knows My Name: More Notes of a Native Son.* Dial Press, 1961. Print. (Essays)

*Another Country.* Dial Press, 1962. Print. (Novel)

*†The Fire Next Time.* Dial Press, 1963. Print. (Essays)

*Blues for Mister Charlie: A Play.* Dial Press, 1964. Print. (Play)

*Nothing Personal.* Atheneum Publishers, 1964. Print. (Nonfiction)

*Going to Meet the Man.* Dial Press, 1965. Print. (Short stories)

*The Amen Corner: A Play.* Dial Press, 1968. Print. (Play)

*Tell Me How Long the Train's Been Gone.* Dial Press, 1968. Print. (Novel)

*A Rap on Race.* With Margaret Mead. J. B. Lippincott, 1971. Print. (Dialog)

*No Name in the Street.* Dial Press, 1972. Print. (Essay)

*One Day When I Was Lost: A Scenario Based on* The Autobiography of Malcolm X. London, Michael Joseph, 1972. Published as *One Day When I Was Lost: A Scenario Based on Alex Haley's* The Autobiography of Malcolm X. Dial Press, 1973. Print. (Screenplay)

*César: Compressions, l'homme et la machine* [César: Compressions, Man and Machine]. With Françoise Giroud. Translated by Yvonne Roux. Paris, Hachette, 1973. Print. (Nonfiction)

*A Dialogue.* With Nikki Giovanni. J. B. Lippincott, 1973. Print. (Dialog)

*If Beale Street Could Talk.* Dial Press, 1974. Print. (Novel)

*The Devil Finds Work: An Essay.* Dial Press, 1976. Print. (Essay)

*Little Man, Little Man: A Story of Childhood.* Dial Press, 1976. Print. (Children's novel)

*Just above My Head.* Dial Press, 1979. Print. (Novel)

*Jimmy's Blues: Selected Poems.* London, Michael Joseph, 1983. Print. (Poetry)

*The Evidence of Things Not Seen.* Holt, Rinehart and Winston, 1985. Published as *Evidence of Things Not Seen.* London, Michael Joseph, 1986. Print. (Nonfiction)

*The Price of the Ticket: Collected Nonfiction, 1948-1985.* St. Martin's, 1985. Print. (Nonfiction)

*Gypsy and Other Poems.* Gehenna Press, 1989. Print. (Poetry)

*Sonny's Blues and Other Stories.* London, Penguin Books, 1995. Print. (Short stories)

*James Baldwin: Collected Essays.* Edited by Toni Morrison. Library of America, 1998. Print. (Essays)

*James Baldwin: Early Novels and Stories.* Edited by Morrison. Library of America, 1998. Print. (Novels and short stories)

*The Cross of Redemption: Uncollected Writings.* Edited by Randall Kenan. Pantheon Books, 2010. Print. (Essays)

*James Baldwin: The Last Interview and Other Conversations.* With Quincy Troupe et al. Melville House, 2014. Print. (Interviews)

*James Baldwin: Later Novels.* Edited by Darryl Pinckney. Library of America, 2015. Print. (Novels)

*Includes "Everybody's Protest Novel," first published in the 16 June 1949 issue of *Partisan Review.*

†Includes "Down at the Cross: Letter from a Region of My Mind," first published as "Letter from a Region of My Mind" in the 17 November 1962 issue of *The New Yorker.*

---

# CRITICISM

## Barry Gross (essay date 1972)

SOURCE: Gross, Barry. "The 'Uninhabitable Darkness' of Baldwin's *Another Country*: Image and Theme." *Negro American Literature Forum,* vol. 6, no. 4, Winter 1972, pp. 113-21.

[*In the following essay, Gross closely studies the patterns of images in* Another Country, *stressing "that much of the imagery is based on color—specifically, black and white— and light and dark." His investigation of the clusters of meanings associated with these images leads him to conclude that the novel's climax comes with Vivaldo's "realization that black is not black and white is not white, that dark is not dark and light is not light."*]

**Another Country** is a big novel. It crosses an ocean, color lines, sex lines. It sprawls over four hundred and thirty six pages. Yet it is impressively tight. Much of the unity is achieved through the interactions of the various characters, the intersecting lines of contact, the points at which so many of the lives touch one another. A more subtle, but no less significant unity is achieved through Baldwin's imagery which grows out of the characters, as all good imagery should. Given Baldwin's subjects, it is not surprising that much of the imagery is based on color— specifically, black and white—and light and dark. What may be surprising is that the imagery ultimately becomes a vehicle for judgment.

That is a strong statement and I'd best explain what I mean. At the end of the novel, Vivaldo stares "into his cup, noting that black coffee was not black, but deep brown. Not many things in the world were really black, not even the night, not even the mines. And the light was not white, either, even the palest light held within itself some hint of its origin, in fire."[1] I take this to be the climax of **Another Country,** the realization that black is not black and white is not white, that dark is not dark and light is not light. I take it that this is the understanding, the epiphany, which Baldwin means his characters to achieve, and that their individual successes are to be measured by how close they come to this realization. However, those who fail are not to be condemned; such an epiphany can only be arrived at with great struggle and great pain,

> such secrets, the secrets of everyone, were only expressed when the person laboriously dragged them into the light of the world, imposed them on the world, and made them a part of the world's experience. Without this effort, the secret place was merely a dungeon in which the person perished; without this effort, indeed, the entire world would be an uninhabitable darkness.
>
> (112)

Clearly, some are not capable of such laborious effort, for whatever reasons. They perish in the dark dungeon.

For Rufus, the light of the world defines only black and white, and there are no other colors. "Under the lights, ... white people showed teeth to each other, ... vanished ... into the blackness of side streets" (4). Newsstands are "like small black blocks" (4). He sees "frantic black people" (4), "a white couple, laughing" (5). "Pale, unlovely lights" emphasize "the blackness of the Jersey shore" (11). When "the lights ... go down ... the party would change character and become very pleasant and quiet and private ... the shadows of the room would be alive" (16). A boy who looks at him "with hatred" is "splashed by the sun falling through the trees" (30). Lights are "a great shock" (47), "very bright and hot" (54), "hideous" (54). They illuminate "a policeman, ... phoning in" (72), "two girls and two boys, white,

... a young white boy in a ... black leather jacket" (84). "The bright lights of 125th Street" illuminate "the black people, ... the white people" (86).

His memories are the same. He remembers "the white policeman who had taught him how to hate" (6), "the white policeman and the money they made on black flesh" (7). In his mind's eye, he sees a "boy dead from an overdose on a rooftop in the snow" (6)—black on white—"The shoe of a white officer against his mouth. He was in his white uniform" (12). He recalls a drowning, the "small group of people" coming "into the sun, one man in the middle, the boy's father, carrying the boy's unbelievably heavy, covered weight" (17). He cannot forget Leona and "the halls of the hospital: white; and the uniforms and the faces of the doctors and nurses, white on white" (78). Doctors and nurses are, "first of all, up-right, clean-living, white citizens" (34).

It is no different with the people he is closest to. Leona has a "damp, colorless face, the face of the Southern poor white, and ... straight, pale hair" (9). In the darkness, "her face ... gleam[ing] ... like alabaster" (21), "nothing could have stopped him, not the white God himself. ... Under his breath he cursed the milk-white bitch. ... He beat her with all the strength he had and felt the venom shoot out of him, enough for a hundred black-white babies" (22). When she tells him "that there was nothing wrong in being colored, he answered, 'Not if you a hard-up white lady'" (53). She is, forever after, "the raped white woman" (53). Vivaldo, his one friend—black or white—is "the liberal white bastard" (24). He wonders if Vivaldo is like "most white men" who were "likely to betray his friend for a woman, ... especially if the friend were black" (36). He unable to think of Vivaldo as an individual: about Vivaldo's sex life, he thinks, "So that's the way white boys make it" (69); he includes him under the heading of "all you white boys" who have "a big thing about how us spooks was making out" (70); at a table with Vivaldo and Jane, he regards the empty chairs as "a chasm now between [himself] and the white boy and the white girl" (82). Jane is "that white chick" (69); her face is "white and terrified" (36). He hates "all those white sons of bitches out there ... the miserable white cocksuckers" (67). He has "to fight with the landlord because the landlord's white! ... with the elevator boy because the motherfucker's white! Any bum on the Bowery can shit all over you because maybe he can't hear, can't see, can't walk, can't fuck—but he's white!" (68).

On his last night of life a white man with an "ice-cold, ice-white face" (42) tries to pick him up. He wanders through streets that are "black" (44), past buildings that are "black"

(44). On the subway, "a white man leaned on a strap near him. Rufus felt his gorge rise" (86). The subway provides a final, apocalyptic vision of "many white people and many black people, chained together in time and in space, and by history. ... The train, ... as though protesting the proximity of white buttock to black knee, groaned, lurched, ... rushed into the blackness with a phallic abandon, into the blackness which opened to receive it" (86). It is the same blackness Rufus rushes to, the same blackness which opens to receive him: "he was black and the water was black" (87).

Only briefly is Rufus able to break away from the black-white dichotomy, only at moments of love. In Ida, he sees for the first time "the beauty of black people," a beauty not of blackness but of "the colors of the shawl, the colors of the sun. ... Watching her dark face in the sunlight, softened and shadowed by the glorious shawl, it could be seen that she had once been a monarch" (7). In his first flush of passion for Leona, before her face gleams like alabaster, he sees that her breasts are "mounds of yellow cream," her nipples "brown" (21). With Eric, he sees "their hands together, ... the red and the brown" (45). But otherwise, Rufus is unable to see that not many things in the world are really black, that the light is not white either. For him, the entire world remains an uninhabitable darkness.

Ida is very much her brother's sister, but more so. "Somewhat darker than Rufus" (98), she rebukes him about Leona: "You'd never even have looked at that girl, Rufus, if she'd been black. But you'll pick up any white trash just because she's white. What's the matter—you ashamed of being black?" (28). After Rufus' death, her face becomes "a dark mask behind which belligerence battled with humility. ... Her eyes ... were always ready, within a split second, to turn black and lightless with contempt" (144). Like Rufus, Ida condemns the whole white world, but more intensely "proud" of being Negro, she does so with more vehemence. She is "not about to be bugged by any more white jokers who still can't figure out whether [she's] human or not" (279). She is convinced that "there's no way in the world" a white person can know "what it's like to be a black girl in this world, and the way white men, and black men, too, baby, treat you" (347). She accuses "the filthy, white cock suckers" (351). She remembers

the way white men watched me ... all dressed up in their damn white skin, and their clothes just so, and their little, weak, white pricks jumping in their drawers. ... They wanted to do something dirty and they knew that you knew how. All black people know that. ... I used to wonder what in the world they did in bed, white people I mean, between themselves, to get them so sick.

(419)

She is sure she knows "all about white people, ... what they were like," because she has been with them "alone, where only a black girl could see them, and the black girl might as well have been blind as far as they were concerned. Because they knew they were white ... and they ruled the world" (423).

Like Rufus, she is unable to distinguish individual whites. About Leona she bitterly comments, "There's nothing like a Southern white person, especially a Southern *woman,* when she gets her hooks into a Negro man. ... She's still living, the filthy white slut, and Rufus is dead" (265). About Cass and Eric she comments, "She can't find anything *better* to do than start screwing some poor white faggot from Alabama. I swear, I don't understand white folks worth a damn" (323). She tells Cass, "There's no way in the world for you to know what Rufus went through, not in this world, not as long as you're white" (351). More seriously, she fails to separate Vivaldo, who loves her, from the white mass. She tells him, "All you white bastards are the same" (169). When she complains to him that she will "never understand white people," he can only reply, "I am not *white people!*" (262). After telling Vivaldo "all you white boys make me sick" (277), she calls him "white motherfucker! ... big white liberal asshole" (280). "Goddamn your white prick" (280), she curses him:

> Every damn one of your sad-ass white chicks think they get a cunt for peeing through, and they don't piss nothing but the best ginger ale, and if it wasn't for spooks wouldn't a damn one of you white cock suckers *ever* get laid

(280)

Because she's "black," she knows "how white people treat black boys and girls," knows that her being together with Vivaldo "doesn't change the world" and that if it does for him, it's because he's "white," to which Vivaldo can only respond, "It's not my fault I'm white. It's not my fault you're black" (324). She is convinced "Vivaldo didn't want to know [Rufus] was dying because he doesn't want to know that [Rufus] would still be alive if he hadn't been born black" (351) and she tells Vivaldo he "didn't know anything about Rufus ... because he was black" (415).

But there is some hope for Ida, despite her bitterness. Unlike Rufus, "she always been afraid of the dark" (139). At her best moments—when she is singing, for instance—she is identified with the light:

> Ida was wearing a tight, white, low-cut dress, and her shoulders were covered with a bright shawl. On the little finger of one hand, she wore a ruby-eyed snake ring; on the opposite wrist, a heavy, barbaric-looking bracelet, of silver. Her hair was swept back from her forehead, piled high, and gleaming, like a crown. ... Her heavy silver earrings caught the light.

(249)

This is, indirectly, the result of love, Rufus's gift of the shawl, Eric's gift to Rufus of the cufflinks which have become Ida's earrings. She is saved from the dungeon Rufus dwells in by Vivaldo. She is forced to admit, despite all her hatred, that "if any *one* white person gets through to you, it kind of destroys your—single-mindedness" (350) and Vivaldo has gotten through to her, although she fights him all the way.

Although it takes the whole novel for Vivaldo to realize that not many things in the world are really black or really white, he has intimations of that truth throughout. He is both black and white, his "eyes, his eyebrows, and his hair ... like so many streaks of charcoal on a dead white surface" (99), dressed "emphatically in black and white: white shirt, black tie, black suit, black shoes, black coat; and black hair, eyes, and eyebrows, on a dead-white bone-dry face" (109), "dressed, as he almost always was, in black and white" (344). But in Vivaldo black and white exist in uneasy and unsatisfying conjunction. They produce gray, a non-color, a non-existence. Although he tells himself that in Harlem "there were the same kids on the block that used to be on my block—they were colored but they were the same, really the same," that "they're colored and I'm white but the same things have happened, really the *same* things" (113), Cass is right to point out the "difference": "they didn't ... happen to you *because* you were white. They just happened. But what happens up here ... happens *because* they are colored" (113-114). In a sense, then, Ida is right: Vivaldo *is* white people. He uses Harlem, uses Negroes parasitically, vicariously, to solve his own identity crises:

> For several years it had been his fancy that he belonged in those dark streets uptown precisely because the history written in the color of his skin contested his right to be there. He enjoyed this, his right to *be* being everywhere contested; uptown, his alienation had been made visible and, therefore, almost bearable.

(132)

He is in flight from himself, trying to lose himself in the black jungle; that is why "he sometimes seemed to surprise in the dark faces which watched him a hint of amused and not entirely unkind contempt. ... He was just a poor white boy in trouble and it was not in the least original of him to come running to the niggers" (133).

Vivaldo's use of Negroes is usually sexual; indeed, Baldwin suggests that this relationship is always sexual. As

Richard says, he has "always had a thing about colored girls" (156). He cannot forget the "very dark" man who caught him a Negro prostitute: "Where was you thinking of putting that, white boy? ... You'd be a mighty sorry white boy if you had. You wouldn't be putting that white prick in no more black pussy, I can guarantee you that ... What I don't understand ... is why you white boys always come uptown, sniffing around our black girls. You don't see none of us spooks downtown, sniffing around you white girls" (62-64). Nor can he forget the time

> he and a colored buddy had been drunk, and on leave, in Munich. They were in a cellar someplace, it was very late at night, there were candles on the tables. There was one girl sitting near them. Who had dared whom? Laughing, they had opened their trousers and shown themselves to the girl. To the girl, but also to each other. The girl had calmly moved away, saying that she did not understand Americans. But perhaps she had understood them well enough. She had understood that their by-play had very little to do with her. But neither could it be said that they had been trying to attract each other—they would never, certainly, have dreamed of doing it that way. Perhaps they had merely been trying to set their minds at ease; at ease as to which of them was the better man. And what had the black boy thought then? But the question was, what had *he* thought? He had thought, Hell, I'm doing all right. There might have been the faintest pang caused by the awareness that his colored buddy was doing possibly a little better than that, but, indeed, in the main, he had been relieved. It was out in the open, practically on the goddamn table, and it was just like his, there was nothing frightening about it.
>
> He smiled—*I bet mine's bigger than yours is*—but remembered occasional nightmares in which this same vanished buddy pursued him through impenetrable forests, came at him with a knife on the edge of precipices, threatened to hurl him down steep stairs to the sea. In each of the nightmares he wanted revenge? Revenge for what?
>
> (134)

For using him as a sort of yardstick, for fearing that the Negro's penis wasn't just like his, that there was something frightening about it, for thinking in those terms at all. The Negro buddy of his dream is the personification of his other Negro buddy, Rufus. He seeks revenge for Rufus as well as for himself because "somewhere in his heart Vivaldo had feared and hated Rufus because he was black" (134). Vivaldo's identity crisis is also a sexual crisis. He suppresses a strong sexual attachment for Rufus, whom he also wishes to use. His love for Ida is, at first, merely a transference, an acting out of the love—lust—he felt for her brother. He can be free to love Ida as Ida only when he consummates his love for Rufus, which he is finally able to do with Eric, who also loved Rufus.

So Vivaldo is neither black nor white; he's gray. And he sees the grayness around him, "these houses which time

and folly had so blasted and darkened, the cornices ... sulking in shame, all tarnished and despised" (114), the "gray houses leaning forward to cut out the sky," the "long, gray street" (115), the "gray sheet" (66) on Rufus' bed, "the gray light, coming in through the monk's-cloth blinds, ... with the malice of the noncommittal, ... examining every surface, corner, angle, of the unloved room" (130).

But he is forced to see black, to know black. Ida is "very, very dark" (144), her eyes "very large and dark" (171), her head "dark" (171). Entering her is like "traveling up a savage, jungle river, looking for the source which remained hidden just beyond the black, dangerous, dripping foliage" (177). He will find that source—"even the palest light held within itself some hint of its origin, in fire" (430)—but painfully, only after he is made to see the black and white he thought made no difference. He begins to see things as Rufus saw and Ida sees them, "the black-and-white couples, defiantly white, flamboyantly black" (297), Jane, her face "illumined and horribly distorted" by "the light," "so that her eyes looked like coals of fire" (298), taunting him,

> "If I was as liberal as my friend, Vivaldo, here ... why, I wouldn't be with *you,* you poor white slob. I'd be with the biggest, blackest buck I could find!" ... were watching them. ... The blacks now suspected him of being an ally—though not a friend, never a friend!—and the whites, particularly the neighborhood Italians, now knew that he could not be trusted. ... The Italians heard the laughter of the black men; the black men remembered that it was a black girl Vivaldo was screwing.
>
> (298-299)

He hears Rufus snicker, "You don't be careful, motherfucker, you going to get a *black* hard on" (301). From Harold, "the prince of darkness" (311), he hears about "Romeo and Juliet today, only she's black and he's white" (304). He is made to see black and white because Ida, whom he loves, "never lets me forget I'm white, she never lets me forget she's colored" (340).

In his sleep, "he dreamed of a baby boy who had Ida's mouth and eyes and forehead, his hair, only curlier, his build, *their* color. What would that color be?" (341). That is the question Vivaldo must answer. He cannot answer that question satisfactorily until he comes to grips with his past, with his guilt, until he understands his love-hate relationship with Rufus and, consequently, with Negroes in general. Eric provides him the means for that encounter. With Eric, who loved Rufus sexually and has admitted it, Vivaldo comes face to face with that moment he and Rufus almost became lovers: "it was as dark in that room, then, as it is in this room, now" (342). In a dream, he experiences his sexual murder of Rufus, "watched Rufus' blood run down, bright over the black spikes" (382). And he wakes to find Eric loving him and asking to be loved. At the moment Vivaldo and Eric reach their climaxes, they both lay Rufus' ghost to rest. Vivaldo is free to think, "unwillingly, of all the whores, black whores, with whom he had coupled, and what he had hoped for from them, and he was gripped in a kind of retrospective naused" (426-427). Admitting that he did think in terms of black and white, that he used Negroes—men and women—as things, as means for his own particular satisfactions, Vivaldo can now find an answer to that question.

What would that color be? Not gray, that hypothetical blend in which white loses its whiteness and black loses its blackness. Vivaldo has intimations of what that color will be throughout the novel; indeed, it is his occasional ability to perceive colors—rather than black and white, rather than just drab gray—that spells the hope in *Another Country.* In Harlem, he sees "the beautiful children in the street, black-blue, brown, and copper" (114). More importantly, in Ida he sees "a dull, mahogany sheen" (173), "reddish-brown nipples" (174), "the honey and the copper and the gold and the black of her" (176). "her blue-black hair and . . . her Aztec brow" (382). Although Ida, who is trapped in the black-white dichotomy, insists that she is "the same old color all over," Vivaldo knows better: "I love your colors. You're so many different, crazy colors. . . . You can't see yourself all over. But I can. Part of you is honey, part of you is copper, some of you is gold—. . . part of you is black, too, like the entrance to a tunnel" (175). To see oneself and, hence, to see others—that is the goal. At the end of the novel, Vivaldo is able—entitled—to tell Ida that "suffering doesn't have a color" (417). He is able to see, finally and in earnest, that "not many things in the world were really black, not even the night, not even the mines. And the light was not white, either, even the palest light held within itself some hint of its origin, in fire" (430). Vivaldo has laboriously dragged the dark secrets into the light of the world, has imposed them on his world, has made them a part of its experience. For him and for Ida, the world will not be an uninhabitable darkness.

In many important respects, Eric is the key to this novel: he is the link between Vivaldo and Rufus and, consequently, between Vivaldo and Ida. He is the common denominator, as in the film his "face operated, in effect, as a footnote to the twentieth-century torment" (330). He can be this because he had dragged his secrets into the light of the world. His vehicle for self-discovery is Yves and it is no accident that Eric sees Yves more as Negro than as white, what with his "long, wiry body . . . brown as bread" (184), his "grave, brown, affectionate face" (190), his "eyes . . . black and bright" (214), "dark and enormous" (222), "his teeth gleam[ing]" (224). When they first meet and Eric tells

him he is from Alabama, Yves replies, "Then you are a raciste. . . . I have many African friends and I have noticed that Americans do not like that" (216-217). On the contrary, Eric likes that very much. Indeed, "there was something in Yves which reminded him of Rufus" (192). Like Vivaldo, Eric must face his love for Rufus and his relationships with Negroes before he can illuminate the darkness:

> It had taken him a long while to realize that one of the reasons Yves had so stirred his heart, stirred it in a way he had almost forgotten it could be stirred, was because he reminded him, somehow, on the eve of his departure, to begin to recognize that part of Rufus' great power over him had to do with the past which Eric had buried in some deep, dark place; was connected with himself, in Alabama, *when I wasn't nothing but a child*; with the cold white people and the warm, black people, warm at least for him, and as necessary as the sun which bathed the bodies of himself and his lover now. Lying in this garden now, so warm, covered, and apprehensive, he saw them on the angular, blazing streets of his childhood, and in the shuttered houses, and in the fields. They laughed differently from other people, so it had seemed to him, and moved with more beauty and violence, and they smelled like good things in the oven.
>
> (193-194)

"He had loved the cook, a black woman named Grace" (197). And he had loved her husband Henry, thinking "it was wrong because Henry was a grown man, and colored, and he was a little boy, and white" (198), not because they were both male. When he is older, he learns that "it was wrong" because it is homosexual. He discovers it on "a hot day. . . . The trees along the walks gave no shade. The white houses, with their black front doors, their blackly shadowed porches, seemed to be in battle with the sun, laboring and shuddering beneath the merciless light" (201). He discovers it with Leroy, "very tall and very black" (201): "his knowledge clamored in him and fell all around him, like the sun, and everything in him was aching and yearning for the act" (203). "A cream-colored roadster, bearing six young people, three white boys and three white girls (204), passes by, but such a white world is not for Eric. For Eric there is Leroy, "staring at [him], with a terrible expression on his black face. . . . He reached out and pulled Eric against him, under the shadow of the leaves" (205). Eric must learn that, like Vivaldo, "he was just a poor white boy in trouble and it was not in the least original of him to come running to the niggers" (133). Or to use them. That is the truth Eric must face:

> But had he ever loved Rufus? Or had it simply been rage and nostalgia and guilt? Was it the body of Rufus to which he had clung, or the bodies of dark men, seen briefly, somewhere, in a garden or a clearing, long ago, sweat running down their chocolate chests and shoulders, their

voices ringing out, the white of their jock-straps beautiful against their skin, one with his head tilted back before a dipper—and the water splashing, sparkling, singing down!—one with his arm raised, laying an axe to the base of a tree? Certainly he had never succeeded in making Rufus believe he loved him. Perhaps Rufus had looked into his eyes and seen those dark men Eric saw, and hated him for it.

(194)

Hated him because he saw himself as just another dark man, not as Rufus, as with Vivaldo Ida sees herself as just another black woman and not as Ida.

But recognition of the truth is no guarantee that the secret place will not remain a dungeon. What is needed is the laborious effort of *dragging* the secrets into the light of the world, *imposing* them on the world, *making* them a part of the world's experience. He has done that here, but it has been relatively easy in permissive France. Can he do it in restrictive America?

> Now that his flight was so rigorously approaching its end, a light appeared, a backward light, throwing his terrors into relief. And what were these terrors? They were buried beneath the impossible language of the time, lived underground where nearly all of the time's true feeling spitefully and incessantly fermented. Precisely, therefore, to the extent that they were inexpressible, were these terrors mighty; precisely because they lived in the dark were their shapes obscene. And because the taste for obscenity is universal and the appetite for reality rare and hard to cultivate, he had nearly perished in the basement of his private life.

(197)

In the darkness of that dungeon, where "lonely men . . . had used him, . . . wrestled with him, caressed him, and submitted to him, in a darkness deeper than the darkest night" (210-211), "the shameful, the punishing dark" (211)— dark because "the dark submission was the shadow of love—if only someone, somewhere, loved them enough to caress them this way, in the light, with joy!" (212).

As he loves Yves and Yves loves him? Perhaps. The night they become lover, they take a room when "the sun was setting and great streaks of fire and dull gold were splashed across the still, blue sky" (220). In the town, "the walls of the houses were all black"; they walk "through great patches of blackness between one far-off street to another" (221). But "the trees and the tables and chairs and the water were lit by the moon" (221) and "in the violet moonlight . . . he slowly pulled the covers away from Yves" (222). Eric fears both the light and the dark; he fears "the morning, when the moon and stars would be gone, when this room would be harsh and sorrowful with sunlight" (225); he fears "the grave darkness around him, . . . the black distance"

(228). But such darkness is "lit up, at intervals," by "Yves' eyes, like a searchlight of the Eiffel Tower or the sweep of a lighthouse light" (228). This light is "his only frame of reference and his only means of navigation" (228).

At the end of the novel, Eric is able to love Yves in the light, and, therefore, illuminate the uninhabitable darkness. By laying Rufus' ghost to rest with Vivaldo, he has learned to live with both the light and the dark: "darkness was beginning to fall. The lights of the city would soon begin to blaze; it would not be long, now, before these lights would carry his name" (408). Yves arrives "at dawn. . . . Naturally" (429). He steps from the plane into "the light, hard and American" (434), "the sun glared at him, and everything wavered in the heat" (435), the harsh, sorrowful sunlight Eric feared. But there is Eric, leaning "on the rail of the observation deck, grinning" (435). This is "a new and healing light" (435).

Of all the characters in the novel, Cass is the "whitest," and, as a characterization, the least successful. Perhaps Baldwin is simply unable to see her whole. Whatever the reason, she is the only character in the novel who resembles the characters in Vivaldo's:

> He did not seem to know enough about the people in his novel. They did not seem to trust him. They were all named, more or less, all more or less destined, the pattern he wished them to describe was clear to them. He could move them about but they themselves did not move. He put words in their mouths which they uttered sullenly, unconvinced. . . . He begged them to surrender up to him their privacy. And they refused . . .

(127)

For me, Cass never does surrender up her privacy. I never know enough about her, perhaps because Baldwin does not. And what I do know does not quite add up to whatever pattern it is that Baldwin wishes her to describe.

She is too keenly aware of black and white. She sees herself as "one, small, lone, white woman hurrying along 125th Street on a Saturday morning" (117). She tells the Negro saleslady she would "like to get a scarf. Black"—and "how the word seemed [to Cass] to roll through the shop" (118). At Rufus' funeral, she is acutely aware that, in addition to Vivaldo, she is "the only other white person . . . in the place" (118). The Negro girl who eulogizes Rufus "twisted a white handkerchief, the whitest handkerchief Cass had ever seen" (119). When Vivaldo tells her he wants to make Ida "know that the world's not as black as she thinks it is," she says "dryly," "Or . . . as white" (125). And she senses that Vivaldo "was refusing to react to her tone" (125).

"Glad of the darkness but not protected by it" (283), she seeks light in Eric; "there's a king of light around you" (239), she tells him. But not too much light: "afraid of what unanswerable and unimaginable riddles might be uncovered in so merciles a light, she switched off the lamp at the head of the bed and watched him come to her in the gloom" (291). I am not sure that the riddles ever do come to light. In a nightclub, she is attracted to a "large, ginger-colored boy dancing with a tall, much darker girl" (354), aware of "her barely conscious wish to have the ginger-colored boy . . . make love to her" (355-356). Maybe that is the answer to the riddle of Cass: she fears too much light, she fears too much darkness. Would she have been attracted by someone much darker than the ginger-colored boy? I don't think so. "Huddled in the darkness" (361) of a taxi-cab, she is attracted to the Puerto Rican driver, "uncomfortably aware of . . . his shoulders, his untried face, his color, and his soft, dark eyes. . . . She thought again, unwillingly, of the ginger-colored boy" (362). When Richard beats her for her infidelity, "his face . . . went and white and ugly," "she thought of the ginger-colored boy and the Puerto Rican" (371). Of all the characters, she alone ends up empty-handed, perhaps because she lacks the strength to drag her secrets—whatever they are—into the light of the world. She remains in the dungeon of her *barely* conscious wishes, never quite brave enough to make them part of the world's experience. If her world is not exactly an uninhabitable darkness, it is a dismal gloom.

*Another Country* makes no easy assertions, proposes no simple solutions. It is hard to realize that black is not really black and white not really white, that the dark is not really dark and the light not really light. Only when man drags his secrets into the light of the world, imposes them on the world, and makes them a part of the world's experience can he escape his private dark dungeon. But before he can do any of this, he must acknowledge to himself what these secrets are, must come face to face with his personal and collective guilts, must, as Ida says, pay his dues. That such exertion is strenuous and difficult goes without question. But it also goes without question that such an effort must be undertaken as a matter of life and death. James Baldwin vividly and movingly demonstrates in *Another Country* that "without this effort, the secret place was merely a dungeon in which the person perished; without this effort, indeed, the entire world would be an uninhabitable darkness."

### Note

1. James Baldwin, *Another Country* (New York: The Dial Press, 1962), p. 430. All page references are from this edition.

### Alfred R. Ferguson (essay date 1977)

SOURCE: Ferguson, Alfred R. "Black Men, White Cities: The Quest for Humanity by Black Protagonists in James Baldwin's *Another Country* and Richard Wright's *The Outsider*." *Ball State University Forum*, vol. 18, no. 2, Spring 1977, pp. 51-58.

[*In the following essay, Ferguson details how the protagonists of* Another Country *and* The Outsider *both "strive for and fail to achieve their humanity, the full realization or integration or definition of the self." The "quest for humanity [is] undertaken" by Rufus Scott in Baldwin's novel and Cross Damon in Wright's, Ferguson asserts, "not merely because they happen to be black, but because they are simply trying to be."*]

Two black protagonists in two novels, *The Outsider* by Richard Wright and *Another Country* by James Baldwin, strive for and fail to achieve their humanity, the full realization or integration or definition of the self. In the case of Baldwin's protagonist, Rufus, the attempt at self-realization is made within the context of traditional values of the community, in the widest possible sense to denote the plexus of ethics and values derived from the Greco-Judeo-Christian traditions of Western civilization. In the case of Wright's protagonist, Cross Damon, the attempt at self-definition is made in antithesis to the community and its value structure.

The struggle of both protagonists for self-realization takes place in the confines of the city—New York in the instance of Rufus; Chicago and New York in the case of Cross Damon. In both novels the values or the lack of values of the city are imaged by the moral and social outlines and physical shape of the city. The two protagonists' different responses to the city constitute the differing nature of their quest—a quest for humanity undertaken by them not merely because they happen to be black, but because they are simply trying to be.

The composite image of the city in the two novels differs markedly in accordance with the theme each novel develops. The intensive conflict in *Another Country* is between what Baldwin assumes man historically is—or has been—but cannot be or finds difficulty in being because of the malforming pressures of the city. The extensive conflict in *The Outsider* revolves around the question, "What *is* man?" Wright's protagonist could realize the potentials of being within a historical framework, but he initially rejects historical potentials; they are in his terms "veils of illusion"—self-limiting, restrictive of the autonomy of his will, and irrelevant to his perception of the existential quidditas of the self. Stripped of the commonly definitive values, commitments, responsibilities—his "veils of illusion"—he launches himself on a voyage of the self to explore the naked potential of being through a Nietzschean transvaluation of all historical values.

Wright's city is a metaphorical repository of accumulated human history against which the alienated protagonist as outsider pits himself in an attempt at self-definition. Wright's outsider exists not as a black man in particular, not as a man with particular needs and values the city cannot provide for or sustain: he exists as an alien presence that is nothing in particular—and as such stands outside all law, all tradition, all values.

Baldwin reverses these poles: it is the city as it now organically and socially manifests itself which presents an alien, unhistorical, pathological, and primordial environment. The conflict in his novel is between the city and the protagonist who possesses in spite of the city or is prevented from possessing through defeat by the city the traditional values of the Greco-Judeo-Christian ethos: the perception of order in reality, a communal regard for the integrity of a differentiated and inviolable self, and a relationship with human reality, the "other," based on love or agape or, in the Sartrian sense, acts done in good faith.

"Pride in Industrialism" is a painting by DuBuffet depicting two people in a car. The people are static, mannequin-like. But the lines of the car are fluid, organic—suggestive of an amoeba-like, aggressive vitality. Baldwin's city has the same primordial, quasi-organic quality as DuBuffet's car, and the people imprisoned in his image of the city while propelled by its force are immobile mannequins—frozen, unimaginative stereotypes of one another. Baldwin's protagonist, Rufus, in his Daedalus-like wandering about the city perceives it as a primitive, alien presence. It is created by men; yet it is inhuman. It is structured by men; yet it is beyond human scale. And it bears down with a crushing weight on all men who walk its streets:

> The great buildings, unlit, blunt like the phallus or sharp like the spear, guarded the city which never slept. ... Beneath them Rufus walked, one of the fallen—for the weight of this city was murderous—one of those who had been crushed on the day, which was every day, these towers fell. Entirely alone, and dying of it, he was part of an unprecedented multitude.

A typical greeting among blacks in Harlem is, "How you making it?" Expressed in pretentious diction, this means: "What device are you using to accommodate yourself to your environment?" Or, "What method are you using to get a share of whatever satisfactions your environment affords?" Rufus, though a talented jazz drummer, cannot "make it" because his identity has been consumed by the city. He has descended from a height of moderate acclaim,

comfort, and success to wander the streets accompanied only by the urgency of selling his body for the price of the food necessary to sustain it. From this point Baldwin reveals in a series of flashbacks the pressures the city has exerted on Rufus to bring him to this lower—or lowest—depth. It is an apposite device, for while Rufus has a past he has no future; he is figuratively dead because of that past and will shortly become literally so.

Baldwin is clear about Rufus' loss of identity being the particular result of his being black—a black and alien presence in a white city. But the cause of this effect is the wholesale importation by the urban North of racist stereotypes fostered by the rural South. He is impaled by these stereotypes which the city, as Baldwin images it, does nothing to mitigate. The two chances Rufus has to establish a genuinely human contact and thus escape the self-alienation which drives him to suicide are destroyed because of these stereotypes: the stereotype of superior sexuality of blacks, the concomitant stereotype of white jealousy of this easy superiority, and the fatally destructive image of black manhood these stereotypes superimpose on Rufus' imagination. Rufus cannot accept Eric's redemptive love for him because his notion of manhood cannot include Eric's love, or Eric's own manhood:

> He had despised Eric's manhood by treating him as a woman, by telling him how inferior he was to a woman, by treating him as nothing more than a hideous sexual deformity.

Rufus turns this same viciousness on Leona, whose love he destroys through transferrence of stereotyped white envy of black sexuality to Leona's innocent passion for him: "'You know all that chick knows about me? The *only* thing she knows?' He put his hand on his sex, brutally, as though he would tear it out. ...'"

The sexual stereotype imposed on Rufus not only destroys his love for Eric and Leona, it also destroys his own self-regard. The reduction of his identity to a black phallus, in terms of the stereotype, fills him with self-hatred and disgust; a self-hatred shared by those, white or black, consumed by the distorted, loveless sexuality fostered by the city and its readily accessible stereotypes of easy gratification; a self-hatred mirrored by the pathetic graffiti on the wall of a public toilet:

> It smelled of thousands of travelers, oceans of piss, tons of bile, vomit and shit. He added his stream to the ocean, holding that most despised part of himself loosely between two fingers of one hand. ... He looked at the horrible history splashed furiously on the walls ... cocks, breasts, balls, cunts, etched into these walls with hatred. *Suck my cock. I like to get whipped. I want a hot stiff prick*

*up my ass. Down with the Jews. Kill the niggers. I suck cocks.*

The city is nondiscriminatory in this sense: Its oppressive weight bears mercilessly on black and white alike. Rufus dies a literal death; but there are many modes of death in Baldwin's city. The city demands the negation of self as *something in particular,* and a consequent rape of integrity; it demands the fashion of the day, the stereotyped, predictable mode of expression, and an atavistic "incoherent homogeneity" which Herbert Spencer ascribed to the lower, prehistoric forms of nonhuman life. Rufus' friend Richard is the epitome of the New England WASP, one of the fortunate few on whom one would expect the city to bestow its blessings. And it does, in a sense: Richard enjoys a quick and easy success with his writing because his work matches the city's demand for stylized behavior and stereotyped responses. But as a result of his success his integrity as an artist and as a man is destroyed, and he is alienated from his wife, Cass:

> I score him . . . for being second-rate, for not having any real passion, any real daring, any real thoughts of his own. . . . He doesn't have any real work to do, that's his trouble . . . the trouble with this whole unspeakable time and place. . . .

The stereotyped mode of Richard's popular writing is reflected in the "icy and angular" walls of the Guggenheim Museum, where the walls blare like "frozen music":

> Before them was a large and violent canvas in greens and reds and blacks, in blocks and circles, in dagger-like exclamations; it took a flying leap, as it were, from the wall, poised for the spectators' eyeballs; and at the same time it seemed to stretch endlessly and adoringly in on itself, reaching back into unspeakable chaos.

This painting is probably an example of the arty moderne and Kultural Kitsch with which many galleries often fill their walls. But whether this painting and innumerable others like it are aesthetically good or bad art is irrelevant. Baldwin's point is that this art is a totally accurate representation of the city—where it is all but impossible to do real work, where actions and responses have the empty, masturbatory, chaotic movement of form without content, of ritual without meaning, of isolation without differentiation, of purpose without imagination.

Baldwin's city prevents the complete extrusion of the individual personality through a successful quest for identity because it is an inhuman country generating a pathological environment peculiarly remote from life-enhancing values. Stereotyped art, stereotyped sex, stereotyped personalities, ritualistic action . . . Baldwin's city is a cash nexus unconcerned with an imaginative provision for human needs or values. **Another Country** could be read as another Romantic literary denigration of the city—a *fortissimo* accompaniment to the anti-urban roar produced by eighteenth and nineteenth-century Romantic nature worshippers. But to do so is to do violence to Baldwin's theme in the novel and his general intellectual position. As does any Romantic, Baldwin views the city—its incoherent plan and physical impact—as beyond human scale; as a place where definition of the self in a genuinely human context is nearly impossible; as a vast repository of alienation, hostility, and unconcern; as the enemy, per se. But it is an enemy to be conquered, not abandoned. The anti-urbanism of the eighteenth and nineteenth-century Romantics such as Jefferson and Thoreau defined the individual outside of any communal context—positing the individual as a unique atom of enlightened self-interest in a functional relationship with nature, or Nature, rather than in a communitarian context. Baldwin's position in the novel harkens to a tradition far earlier than Romantic individualism—to a traditional value of Western civilization: Christian love, or agape, coupled with a sensitive awareness of the moral responsibility of individuals for the human condition in the context of the urban community.

In contrast to Baldwin, Wright's protagonist in *The Outsider* does not see the city as the enemy per se. To him it simply is; it exists as a historical presence in which Cross dwells not as an alienated man in the context of society, but as an alienated presence outside of any context at all:

> Cross's opportunistic rejection of his former life had been spurred by his shame at what a paltry man he had made of himself. . . . His consciousness of the color of his skin played no part in it. . . . His own inner life had made him too concerned with himself to cast his lot wholeheartedly with Negroes in terms of racial struggle. Practically he was with them, but emotionally he was not of them. . . . His character had been so shaped that his decisive life struggle was a personal fight for the realization of himself. . . . He had long yearned to be free of all responsibilities of any sort. . . . What had irked him about his past responsibilities had been their dullness, their tenuity, their tendency to simply bore him. . . .

The problem of Baldwin's protagonist, Rufus, is his struggle to be what the city will not permit him to be—sentient, perceptive, complete, capable of love—all values within a traditional context. The struggle of Wright's protagonist, Cross Damon, is the existential struggle for self-identification outside of any social, cultural, or historical context, or scheme of values. To both Wright and Baldwin the city is a trap and a determinant force that imprisons and buries consciousness. But in *The Outsider* it is not the city's unnerving pressure exerted by physical objects and relentless stereotypes which shatters the individual's integrity. It is, rather, the sanctions imposed on the individual will by the city that constitutes the enemy; that is, the city as the representative of historical process entailing accumulated values and human relationships, or what Harvey Cox has called in *The Secular City* the "intersection of social forces." Baldwin's rebels wish to restructure the city along the line of traditional humanistic values; they want to be able to express love—to impose on the will the capacity to love. Wright's rebel questions the value of all values that impose a determinate definition of man external to the will.

At the beginning of the novel Cross is entangled in a web of human relationships and commitments. He has taken to bed a girl who is underage. She is pregnant by him and threatens to have him arrested for statutory rape unless he marries her. He cannot marry her—and has no wish to as he no longer loves her—because his wife will not give him a divorce. But neither does he care for his wife; he finds the responsibilities of personal commitment to her and his three sons a destructive, onerous burden. And he is indifferent to his mother, because he detects incestuously tinged feelings in her response to him, a response masked by Puritanical piety. He is hedged in by the demands of what he perceives as a crazy world, a world veiled with illusion:

> Weren't there somewhere in this world rebels with whom he could feel at home, men who were outsiders not because they had been born black and poor, but because they had thought their way through the many veils of illusion?

The opportunity to break out of his trap is presented to Cross in a brilliantly constructed image with a double meaning. Cross is in a subway accident; he escapes serious injury but is pinned in the wreckage (symbolizing the city and all it represents as a trap); he cannot free himself because another passenger, possibly dead but possibly only unconscious, is also pinned in the wreckage and blocks his way. The only way out for him is to force the man's body out of the wreckage. But he cannot. The man's head is wedged in too tightly. It must be forced. Cross carries a gun which he has been considering using on himself as an escape from his trap. With the butt of this gun he hammers the man's face until its features dissolve into a morass of bludgeoned tissue: "He looked; the mangled face was on the floor; most of the flesh had been ripped away. He had done it; he could move his leg."

By a brutal act, what had been a trap for Cross becomes a means of escape. The image of the subway wreck is a pivotal one, for it dramatizes Cross' former condition, his former enslavement, and what he must do to achieve freedom. It foreshadows the brutality to which he will become committed—a committal which, ironically, automatically

limits his freedom by imposing a condition on him he has not consciously chosen. He wishes to escape from commitment, but he destroys the end he wishes to achieve by the means—a commitment—he must use to achieve that end.

Through Cross' accidentally leaving his overcoat containing identification in the wrecked train, the authorities are misled into believing the dead man, whose features are now unidentifiable and who had no identification of his own, is Cross. Thus his escape is total, or nearly so. But his new freedom engenders loneliness along with relief. He takes up with a prostitute, living with her long enough to precipitate a tacit commitment between the two of them and to enable a fellow employee of Cross' visiting the hotel to recognize him. Once again he is trapped, and his escape mirrors his escape from the wrecked train. He deceives the prostitute and murders his former friend. His main regret is not for murder or the deceit, but for having permitted his feelings to interfere with his freedom: "He had thought he was free. But was he? He was free from everything but himself."

His next step toward freedom is an attempted denial of the self through the interposition of his will between himself and any spontaneous feelings or normal human responses. As he leaves Chicago for New York he embarks on a journey of self-exploration for the purpose of creating—or recreating—his total being as ultimate will. But he knows that he will fail in this attempt:

> The outside world had fallen away from him now and he was alone at the center of the world of the laws of his own feelings. And what was this world he was? ... The dreary stretches of Chicago passed before his window; it was a dim, dead, dumb, sleeping city wrapped in a dream, a dream born of his frozen impulses. ... He recalled that pile of steaming garbage, the refuse the world had rejected; and he had rejected himself and was bowed, like that heap of garbage, under the weight of endurance and time.

Yet he is compelled to continue on what he himself will later call this "long, bloody, twisting road" through a messiah-like impulse: "Could he awaken this world from its sleep?" As did Raskalnikoff and Nietzsche's Zarathustra before him he asks: "What crazy fool had thought up these forms of human relations? Or had men and women just drifted blindly through the centuries into such emotional arrangements?"

Wright effects a transition from the outsider as Negro to an outsider of another color, the hunchback Houston, whom Cross meets on the train. Houston, like Cross, has thought his way through the "many veils of illusion": "This damned hump has given me more psychological knowledge than all the books I read at the university." But unlike Cross he functions within the framework of the polis—both literally and figuratively: he is the District Attorney for New York. He plays the police inspector to Cross' Raskalnikoff; he knows Cross is guilty as only one who stands outside the illusory claims of guilt could know: "All my life I've been haunted by the notion that this life we live is a pretense. . . ."

If Houston recognizes Cross for what he is, that recognition cuts two ways. For Cross instinctively senses Houston's nature: "How cleverly the man had worked out his life. . . . He could experience vicariously all destructive furies of the murderer, the thief, the sadist, without being held to accountability."

Being as pure will is impossible for Cross, ex post facto, because he is never able to rid himself completely of human responses to the god-like, imperious actions he commits—actions which stem from his willful rejection of a rationale for existence, an illusion of meaning in life, a pretense for being human:

> He passed the train's huge engine and longed to become as uncaring and passively brutish as that monster of steel. But, no; he was to feel all of those anxieties in his shivering flesh. . . . To swap the burden of this sorry consciousness for something else! To be a God who could master feeling! If not that, then a towering rock that could feel nothing at all!

Shortly after Cross' arrival in New York he allows himself to be used by the Communist Party as a foil in an attempt to integrate an apartment building. It amuses him to observe the humanitarian pretenses of the party's totalitarian adherents and functionaries, each of whom is really committed only to the tyranny over others by the self, who bend their will to the party for the sake of being able to bend the will of others to their own. He is fascinated by the practice of bad faith as a way of life, the mobilization of the hopes and dreams and anxieties of other men for selfish ends. And Cross knows he is like them, to that extent. But he reserves for himself this difference: he believes he possesses the "perilous subjective tension that spells the humanity of man." But, of course, as we are aware though Cross is not, he has surrendered his humanity to his will. It is an awareness he himself shortly comes to.

He is instructed to move into an all-white apartment building in the Village, owned by a self-proclaimed Fascist. Ultimately his being there precipitates a grotesque fight between Herndon, the owner, and Gil, a highly placed party factotum. Cross comes on the two of them when they have beaten each other nearly senseless—and casually crushes their skulls. Herndon is killed first, and then: "He was not through. The imperious feeling that had impelled him to action was not fulfilled. . . . Yes, this other insect had to be crushed, blotted out of existence. . . ." The subsequent

shock of this god-like, imperious action brings Cross to full realization of the thing he has become: "Their disease had reached out and claimed him. . . . He had become what he had tried to destroy, had taken on the guise of the monster he had slain."

Eva, Gil's wife, has been used brutally by the party: Gil's marriage to her—as she later discovered—was essentially a public relations gesture by the party, a means of accruing to its ranks an artist of international reputation. Thus in her defiled innocence she instinctively reaches out to Cross because she believes he too is innocent. But Cross of course is not innocent. The peeling away of illusion has left him with a clarity of vision such as that of Kurtz in *The Heart of Darkness*—a vision so clear it precipitates a paralysis of will and a failure of imagination. He cannot superimpose on reality any mitigating condition, such as love for Eva. This possibility does not exist because love is an imaginative illusion, and in his attempt at self-definition he has rejected the claims of illusion. He is left only with the horror, and a view of reality contained in his description of the city as a colossal symbol of a world that mirrors the psychic disintegration and alienation of his own soul:

> The slaves of today are those who are congenitally afraid of the new and untried, who fall on their knees and break into a deep sweat when confronted with the horrible truth of the uncertain and enigmatic nature of life. . . . Keep that point in mind while I remind you of what is happening in the great cities of the earth today—Chicago, Detroit, Pittsburgh, London, Manchester, Paris, Tokyo, Hong Kong, and the rest. These cities are, for the most part, vast pools of human misery, networks of raw, human nerves exposed without benefit of illusion or hope to the new, godless world wrought by industrial man. Industrial life plus a rampant capitalism have blasted the lives of men in these cities; those who are lucky enough to be hungry are ridden with exquisite psychological sufferings.

This is a different image of the city than was given us through the protagonist's perception earlier in the novel. It is a perception similar to that of Baldwin's rebel. And like Rufus there is no chance for Cross to discover that "other country," but for a completely different reason. Cross' Nietzschean transvaluation of values leads him deeper into the necessity for violent action. He is forced to kill again, but this time not as a result of a motion stemming from an autonomous decision of his imperious will. He has discovered that the total freedom of identity which found expression earlier in his compulsive, imperious acts has, ironically, bound him to a paralyzing, iron-clad necessity completely external to his identity. And this act in turn soon precipitates another—Eva's death by suicide—for which he is responsible but over which he has utterly no control. So far has his denial of the claims of illusion taken him that he is now at the mercy of his alienation. Eva ultimately discovers the magnitude of his willful violence, and in an agony of disgust and hatred hurls herself out of a sixth story window:

> It was over for him. Eva was gone; she had slipped through his clutching, clumsy fingers. He had botched it and Eva's crushed, mute face told him that this was hell: this swooping sense of meaninglessness, this having done what never could be undone. ... He had in him the full feeling that had sent him on this long, bloody, twisting road: self-loathing. ...

And with her is gone any possibility of redemptive love. He has destroyed God, peeled away the layers of illusion, but he could not rid himself of that part of himself from which God and other illusions spring—the hard, central core of reality, of human reality, which is the "perilous subjective tension that spells the humanity of man." Indeed, the denial of this reality has destroyed him by leading him to an idolatrous, totalitarian, absolute service of the self. In the name of freedom of the self he has ineluctably gravitated to a bondage of the self. In the substitution of violence for imagination he has found his imagination and the options it might otherwise provide consumed by violence. He is aware of this, but he cannot return to that which he might have been:

> Cross kept on to the end of the block. He was moving again among people. But how could he ever make a bridge from him to them? To live with them again would mean making promises, commitments. But he had strayed so far that little commitments were now of no avail. He would have to start all over again. And it was impossible to do that *alone. ...*

Cross dies in the closing scene of the novel, shot by a Communist agent because, ironically, he has not fit into the party's totalitarian, absolutist scheme, just as all values, all commitments, all promises—all illusions—have not fit into his. His counterpart, Houston, is with him. Cross' death scene remarks to Houston spell the *Dies Irae* of the alienated man, and of the alienated race, whether it be that 20 percent in America that is dark skinned, or that 20 percent in the world that is white:

> "Tell me, why did you choose to live that way?"
>
> "I wanted to be free ... to feel what I was worth ... what living meant to me. ..."
>
> "And what did you find?"
>
> "Nothing. ... The search can't be done alone. ... Never alone ... alone a man is nothing. ..."
>
> "How was it with *you*, Damon?"
>
> "It ... it was ... horrible. ..."

## D. Maureen Thum (essay date 1988)

SOURCE: Thum, D. Maureen. "Rufus' Journey to Suicide in James Baldwin's *Another Country*." *Michigan Academician*, vol. 20, no. 2, Spring 1988, pp. 211-20.

[*In the following essay, Thum elucidates Baldwin's narrative technique in the first book of* Another Country, *which depicts the last hours of Rufus's life, declaring that it is "Baldwin's subtle analysis and presentation of time—the interplay of past and present—which reveals the protagonist as a convincing, authentic individual, a character of uncommon depth, sensitivity, and intelligence."*]

In their rather brief analyses of **Another Country,** critics and reviewers have concentrated on the underlying themes, the social issues, and the characters. At least equally important, however, is Baldwin's narrative structure. The first chapter of the novel—the story of Rufus Scott, a Black jazz musician—clearly illustrates certain important stylistic aspects of Baldwin's work, and may be seen virtually as a self-contained novella.

In this eighty-eight page chapter, more than one-fifth of the entire novel, the author portrays in detail the last five or six hours of Rufus' life. But the mere narration of events is not the primary focus: it is rather Baldwin's subtle analysis and presentation of time—the interplay of past and present—which reveals the protagonist as a convincing, authentic individual, a character of uncommon depth, sensitivity, and intelligence.

In its conventional sense the term "flashback" signifies little more than a stylistic means to flesh out the story at hand. As Baldwin employs it, this complex interplay of different periods in Rufus' life is more than a mere technique to interrupt and complement the narrative. The author transforms it into a mirror for the mental processes it is designed to express. Baldwin's style in itself becomes a significant—if not the principal—factor in his analysis of Rufus' character, reflecting the workings of the jazz musician's mind in the form of concrete, vivid images. Rufus' dilemma and his agony are revealed in his perception of time; the significance of his past experiences is examined in relationship to a present which appears to have lost its well-defined contours, and to have become an incomprehensible and frightening web of uncertainties.

Thus, only about one-third of the first chapter deals with the actual present, with the final hours of Rufus' life. The remaining two-thirds consist of scenes from the past relived with such an emotional intensity that they have the power to displace or to superimpose themselves on the present. This experience of time plays an important role in Rufus' eventual decision to commit suicide.

In his portrayal, Baldwin traces the gradual encroachment of images from the past upon the objective reality of the present. As the painful memories become more and more overwhelming, Rufus slips into them almost unawares and without transition. The past becomes unmanageable.

The protagonist loses control over his memories because he refuses to acknowledge their implications. Instead of recalling previous events deliberately, in order to understand and come to terms with them, he resists his past experiences, which nonetheless surge up in his mind in a series of stark, disturbing pictures. He is forced to confront these images constantly, but fails to discover fully the significance they hold for his present state of agony and degradation.

If, from time to time, he reaches a point of objective assessment, he withdraws, or tries to withdraw, almost immediately. Thus the feelings of despair, bitterness, guilt, regret, and rage associated with these fearful pictures are not resolved, but intensified. Eventually the chaotic flood of remembrances causes such a mental disorientation that the present appears to lose its objective reality. It becomes instead another picture in Rufus' mind, a terrible, destructive vision of an evil, depersonalized city, which drives him to his final act of despair and self-destruction.

Although Rufus' experiences cannot be divorced from his individuality, they have universal validity. The following comment of Baldwin on the human condition could be seen as a reflection on his protagonist's personal dilemma:

> ... the barrier between oneself and one's knowledge of oneself is high indeed. There are so many things one would rather not know! We become social creatures because we cannot live any other way. But in order to become social, there are a great many other things that we must not become, and we are frightened, all of us, of those forces within us that perpetually menace our precarious security. Yet the forces are there; we cannot will them away. All we can do is learn to live with them. And we cannot learn this unless we are willing to tell the truth about ourselves, and the truth about us is always at variance with what we wish to be.[1]

In the opening pages of the novel, Baldwin's technique is illustrated in a manner almost axiomatic for the remainder of the chapter. Past and present are interwoven in a series of time frames which provide insight into the mental state of the main character while situating him within a specific social context.

The author introduces Rufus at the most critical point in his life, just before his downfall. He has lost every contact with his friends and relatives, and is in a state of utter degradation, walking the streets of down-town New York, penniless, filthy, shivering and in despair. As he emerges from a movie theater and begins to walk along Seventh Avenue, he finds himself in a city which seems foreign to him. He has already entered "another country," the strange, threatening mental environment expressed in the title of the novel, a place which is no longer home, even though the physical surroundings are the supposedly familiar ones. Rufus begins to realize that New York City is a place peopled by strangers who do not seem to share his inner torment, or if they do, then they suffer like him, alone and in darkness:

> At corners, under the light, near drugstores, small knots of white, bright, chattering people showed teeth to each other, pawed each other, whistled for taxis, where whirled away in them, vanished through the doors of drugstores or into the blackness of sidestreets ... A sign advertised the chewing gum which would help one to relax and keep smiling. A hotel's enormous neon name challenged the starless sky ... The great buildings, unlit, blunt like the phallus or sharp like the spear, guarded the city which never slept.[2]

Rufus begins to experience the city as a place of alienation, but since he never reaches a full—i.e. lucid—perception of his suddenly strange surroundings, he becomes progressively unable to cope with a world which he still wishes to see as familiar. In this "other country," the smile, normally a gesture of fellow-feeling which underlies and strengthens social bonds, appears only as a vicious baring of teeth. Advertisements underline the bleakness of a society whose panaceas—chewing gum to help keep one smiling and relaxed—bear no relationship to the very real problems which they offer to "resolve." Buildings are reflections of an impersonal, materialist credo: the neon sign challenges a sky that holds no answers. God is silent in this black and starless firmament. And the buildings themselves are enormous, threatening battlements of a fortress which is always guarded against the entrance of any outsider. The power these structures exude is frightening and emasculating.

Baldwin consciously abstains from adopting the role of the impersonal, omniscient author who sketches merely an objective backdrop for his main character. Instead, he portrays this scene and subsequent scenes in downtown New York not simply as the reflection of an objective, physical reality. They are just as much—if not more so—the projections of Rufus' present state of mind. Thus, we experience the city through Rufus' eyes as a dehumanized, almost autonomous entity, in which individuality is denied, and human beings appear as anonymous, frightening masks for an underlying emptiness:

> Now he stood before the misty doors of the jazz joint, peering in, sensing rather than seeing the frantic black people on the stand and the oblivious, mixed crowd at the bar. The music was loud and empty, no one was doing anything at all, and it was being hurled at the crowd like a malediction in which not even those who hated most deeply any longer believed.
>
> (pp. 4-5)

Only after introducing the reader to this frightening cityscape and the state of mind it expresses does Baldwin begin to probe the past in order to bring to light the constitution of the present. Rufus is in an alley, relieving himself, ashamed and humiliated. Suddenly the scene dissolves, as he is overwhelmed by recollections from the past, agonizing images which he attempts without success to reject. And now the highly overcharged present reveals itself at least in part to be a product of the past, both collective and individual.

At first these images from the past appear to be nothing more than random, disjointed scenes from the protagonist's childhood and youth. Yet they soon reveal a thematic pattern—a motif—which announces, if faintly at first, the subsequent episodes, both actual and remembered. An unforgotten phrase of his father holds his attention, running through his mind clearly not for the first time: "A nigger... lives his whole life, lives and dies according to a beat" (p. 6). This sentence seems to have assumed an awesome and destructive power, suggesting an overwhelming, suprapersonal fatality which rules the life of Rufus as it governs the lives of most men living in Harlem. It does not refer to the main character alone, but to a race and a class. It is "the beat of Harlem," "the beat of his own heart" (p. 7). Baldwin indicates that Rufus is not alone in his experience. His perceptions are symptomatic for at least one aspect of a collective consciousness which seems, on the surface at least, to have become a mental prison.

Baldwin now focuses more strongly on the individual expression of this experience as a scene from the more recent past displaces the apparently random memories. The time is seven months previous to the present, when Rufus was still apparently happy. He was a drummer for a small jazz band, playing the last evening of a gig in a Harlem night spot. The connection with the previous memories becomes clear, as the theme of fatality reappears almost immediately, this time in the figure of a saxophone player. Here the determinism is clearly demonstrated in the life of one individual. As Rufus relives the episode, he sees in his fellow band member a reflection of himself. During a long, emotional solo, the saxophonist expresses his suffering, and hints at the same seemingly inexorable forces from the past which dictate his own individual suffering in the present. It

seems to Rufus at this point as if, some time in his earlier life, the saxophonist "had received a blow from which he never would recover" (p. 9).

This deep injury in all its variations is the focus of the next time frame: a remembered occurrence which may be seen as a doorway, perhaps even the principal entrance to Rufus' past. Implicit in these scenes is Rufus' growing fear of—if not obsession with—an unavoidable, crushing fatality, a fatality which he regards as a force intent on destroying first his fellow musician and now himself. Now the past becomes self-revelation, but also an expression of the ills afflicting an entire society. The social conflict has become so deeply internalized in its manifestations that "inside" and "outside" are inextricably entangled in a web of paradox and contradiction.

The key event—the blow—which precipitates the subsequent, seemingly unavoidable chain of events in Rufus' life is his chance encounter with Leona, a poor, white woman from the South. Even though she is thin, considerably older than he, and not particularly attractive, Rufus finds himself drawn to her. Baldwin's portrayal emphasizes that the attraction lies at first not so much in her physical appearance as in her symbolic value, as a representative of Southern white society. Rufus initial sexual encounter with Leona on the balcony of a Black singers expensive apartment appears at first to the protagonist as a triumph over the reversals of his existence. Somehow he sees himself as reasserting his manhood in his conquest of a white woman. As he is about to make love to her, "he seemed to be standing on a cliff in the wilderness, seeing a kingdom and a river which had not been seen before. He could make it his, every inch of the territory ..." (p. 20). Not only is he reasserting his manhood. In some dark way, he feels that by humiliating and subduing this Southern white woman he has "evened the score" against a white boot-camp officer from the South who had victimized him in the past. During the episode with Leona, he directs toward her all of his understandable rage at white society a rage crystallized in the remembered image of the officer's boot, kicking him in the mouth as he lay in the dust, powerless to protest or to exact revenge (pp. 12-13).

But Baldwin takes great pains to show that precisely what appears to be an assertion and a triumph has another, more sinister dimension. Here, in this sexual scene, Rufus expresses a cruelty and brutality in which reside the seeds of his later self-destruction. His violence and hatred are directed as much toward himself as toward Leona, even though they are expressed primarily in an outward form, as hostility toward his lover.

Rufus has forgotten in his rage—and Baldwin emphasizes this omission in his portrayal of Leona herself—that Leona does not belong to the class of white boot-camp officers, and is certainly not among the overt practitioners of racism. Instead, she herself has been the object of a brutality which, while not racially motivated, has determined her life and harmed her deeply. She, too, has been a victim. Thus, Rufus' anger at Leona, the individual, while understandable, is at best misplaced.

And yet, Baldwin does not portray Rufus merely or even chiefly as a brutal, merciless man. Despite the violence and anger expressed in his thoughts and gestures during the sexual episode, there is another, completely different side to Rufus' character which is at odds with the cliché of the conquering, vengeful Black male. It is an aspect just as important as the self-imposed stereotype, if not more so.

This is Rufus, the individual: Rufus in search of another human being who will love him, and whom he can love in return. The longing Rufus feels is much more than the mere desire for a bed partner, which had characterized his past relationships, when he was "making it with any chick he wanted" (p. 5). The two parts of Rufus' dual personality—the cruel, angry seeker of vengeance for past and present wrongs, and the pleading, vulnerable lover—are engaged in a terrible conflict. Although Rufus relives his inner struggle in these pictures from the past, he is unable to distance himself from their immediate, blinding impact and to read their message in order to take control of his present and future. Thus the inner division finds its "resolution" with tragic necessity only in Rufus' destruction and death.

On the surface, chance appears to play a strong role. Rufus' accidental meeting with Leona has precipitated his fall. But in the course of the chapter, through the recurring memories which continue to haunt his protagonist, Baldwin reveals that a critical mental state, a certain predisposition was already there, latent, before Leona's arrival. Leona resurrected something. She exacerbated a mental inclination which had already been acted out in at least one previous relationship, also with a white Southerner—a homosexual named Eric.

In the case of Eric, Rufus had excused his own merciless behavior on the grounds that he was dealing with what he perceived to be a sexual aberration. With Leona, even this justification—in which he does not believe himself—is absent:

> He had despised Eric's manhood ... by treating him as nothing more than a hideous sexual deformity. But Leona had not been a deformity. And he had used against her the very epithets he had used against Eric, and in the very

same way, with the same roaring in his head, and the same intolerable pressure in his chest.

(p. 46)

Leona is a catalyst. Were Rufus differently predisposed, this relationship could not have led to his destruction. Although his mental predisposition compels him to see her as a cliché and as a stereotype, he cannot deny Leona's individuality and humanity as the woman whom he loves. His attempt to keep both images—the stereotype and the individual—simultaneously before his mind's eye is unsuccessful. However tenacious his efforts, he cannot impose upon her the ready, racial cliché. He knows that it does not fit her individuality. He knows that it cannot adequately explain their relationship, and he knows that she does not resemble the white oppressor, since she too has been brutally victimized without being able or willing to retaliate. The polarity resulting from this mental conflict leads to an almost unbearable tension which expresses itself in anger and violence. Rufus, the individual, the vulnerable human being, looks on in horror at his own behavior, all the while telling himself that he has no choice, and that his course has been determined from the beginning by forces beyond his individual control.

While it is true that Rufus is surely a victim, and that his rage is understandable, it is just as true that Rufus has now assumed the very role which he had so detested in the white racists he had encountered. And he has adopted this stance not toward those who have treated him cruelly, but toward those who have accepted him as their fellow human being. He mistreats those who are vulnerable and are victims, in many ways, like himself: Eric, whose homosexuality alienates him from his own past; and Leona, whose husband beat and misused her. Nor does he spare his best friend, Vivaldo, whom he loves deeply, and who at first appears to be a wholly unlikely target. Again, the images of the past are the key to the present. But since Rufus cannot decipher the hidden meaning of these memories, he is unable to understand his present state of alienation and despair. The barriers which he has erected between himself and his knowledge of himself are, in Baldwin's words, "high indeed."[3]

The question of fatality in all its variations runs like a leitmotif through Rufus' memories, insistently present in all the recollections which overwhelm him and from which he attempts to escape. Less overt is its counterpart: the theme of responsibility and the question of consciousness—Rufus' consciousness of his own role in, and his own contribution to the apparently irresistible flow of events which seem to have such power over his life. In the course of the chapter, the author leads the reader as well as his protagonist to the increasingly clear perception of two different yet intertwined destinies: that of the victim—a very real victim of circumstance and racial prejudice—and that of the individual who, while limited in his course of action, is nevertheless an agent who has the power to act freely.

The silent question repeated with each variation on this dual theme is whether or not Rufus will, or can, bring himself to the point of seeing his own role, of understanding that when he assumes the stance of those who have mistreated them, he destroys not only those whom he hurts, but above all, himself. Again, the answers Rufus seeks lie within the images he relives in these last hours, and in their relationship to the present.

In the final scenes before his death, Rufus knows darkly that everything he has attempted to uphold previously has proved inadequate to help him through the present crisis. During a last desperate attempt to escape the implications of his past experiences and to suppress his own self-knowledge, he is talking to his friend, Vivaldo, while listening to a Bessie Smith record. As his memories, the reality of the present, and the sounds of Bessie Smith's blues weave a pattern of interrelated pictures in his mind, he fastens suddenly on a line from her song, as if it might hold a new meaning for him: "My house fell down and I can't live there no mo'" (p. 49). He recognizes in her words his own sense of abandonment, the breakdown of an entire world picture. His former view is bankrupt. He senses this loss with a very real terror, and wonders to himself "how others moved beyond the emptiness and horror which faced him now" (p. 49).

Rufus does not succeed in moving beyond this void. He refuses to come to terms with the past, to accept his own role in his downfall, to understand that his attempt to stereotype others is at least a partial source of his agony.

In the final few minutes of his life, as he walks up the steps of the subway station into the empty streets leading to Washington Bridge, he sees the same alien, guarded and threatening city of the opening scene, the place which used to be his home:

> Tall apartment buildings, lightless, loomed against the dark sky and seemed to be watching him, seemed to be pressing down on him. The bridge was nearly over his head, intolerably high, but he did not yet see the water. He felt it, he smelled it. He thought how he had never before understood how an animal could smell the water...
>
> Then he stood on the bridge, looking over, looking down. Now the lights of the cars on the highway seemed to be writing an endless message, writing with awful speed in a fine, unreadable script. There were muted lights on the

Jersey shore and here and there a neon flame advertising something somebody had for sale.

(p. 87)

Rufus knows the message is there, but he cannot read it. He cannot accept responsibility for a fate which seems to him to have been imposed by an external fatality, by a force beyond his control. Desperately, he clings to his role of judge and, as he is about to commit his last, desperate act, he widens the blame to include God himself, the basis of all order.

> He stood at the center of the bridge and it was freezing cold. He raised his eyes to heaven. He thought, You bastard, you motherfucking Bastard. Ain't I your baby, too? He began to cry. Something in Rufus which could not break shook him like a rag doll and splashed salt water all over his face and filled his throat and nostrils with anguish. He knew the pain would never stop. He could never go down into the city again. He dropped his head as though someone had struck him and looked down at the water. It was cold and the water would be cold.

(p. 87)

His final thoughts reflect the same polarity which has driven him to self-destruction: they express the hatred but also the tenderness he feels for Eric, Leona, Vivaldo, and all his friends. Projecting these conflicting feelings on God, he ends his life with both an accusation and a plea:

> ... and then the wind took him, he felt himself going over, head down, the wind, the stars, the lights, the water, all rolled together, *all right*. He felt a shoe fly off behind him, there was nothing around him, only the wind, *all right, you motherfucking Godalmighty bastard, I'm coming to you.*

(pp. 87-88)

These last words are a paradox. He is saying, in effect, "I hate you Lord but please take me into your arms and forgive me as I have been unable to forgive myself." And the wind takes him.

Despite Rufus' brutality, cruelty, and destructiveness, Baldwin does not condemn him. The author withholds judgment because Rufus really is a victim. Baldwin's insistence on the need for our compassionate assessment is reflected in the words of Reverend Foster, who speaks at the funeral:

> Someone we loved is dead. Someone we loved and laughed with and talked with—and got mad at—and prayed over—is gone ... He had a hard time getting through this world, and he had a rough time getting out of it. When he stand before his Maker, he going to look like a lot of us looked when we first got here—like he had a rough time getting through the passage. It was *narrow*.

(p. 120)

Rufus, the individual, and Rufus "everyman"—the representative for a collective experience—becomes in his despair and death more than a mere sociological or psychological "case." His search for consciousness, although unsuccessful, is a pattern for all human beings who seek to come to terms with the painful events of their past and present. In the long flash of light which illuminates his protagonist's fate, Baldwin examines the human condition.

Baldwin's technique—the skillful interplay and justaposition of past and present—shows that our human experience of time, at least *in extremis,* is far more complex than we would ordinarily assume. In Baldwin's characters, the experience of time is not to be understood as unilinear progression. It is not a mere continuum. In fact, this way of viewing time reveals itself to be a fiction. The past is not dead and gone. In *Another Country,* the past reasserts itself, showing that it is part of the present. It cannot with impunity be shelved, forgotten or disregarded, since the present discloses its meaning only in view of and because of past occurrences, whether they be social, economic, historical, or psychological. Through the portrayal of Rufus, Baldwin shows that if the individual fails to come to terms with past events, and thus fails to distance himself from them by understanding their implications for his present life, then he will remain their prisoner. They will haunt him, and they may even—as in the case of Rufus—destroy him.

In *Another Country,* the author demonstrates that the fabrications of the past—the clichés, the stereotypes, the "untruths" of former times—have as great a power as objective reality. If we choose to subordinate objective reality to such delusions, the delusions themselves may prove to be stronger than reality itself.

*Notes*

1. "Creative Dilemma" *Saturday Review* 8 Feb 1964, p. 58.

2. Cited from James Baldwin's *Another Country* (New York: The Dial Press, 1972), p. 4. All quotations in this paper have been cited from this edition of the novel. The page numbers will be given in parentheses directly in the text.

3. "Creative Dilemma," p. 58.

**Susan Amper (essay date 1995)**

SOURCE: Amper, Susan. "Love and Death Reconsidered: The Union of Lovers in *Another Country." Journal of the Association for the Interdisciplinary Study of the Arts,* vol. 1, no. 1, Autumn 1995, pp. 103-11.

[*In the following essay, Amper maintains that "Another Country represents a breakthrough in American literature, reversing the separation of lovers that has so characterized our fiction." Baldwin's goal in the novel, she argues, "is to find a solution, a reconciliation that will work, not only on a personal level, but on a social level, that will bring together not only the polarities of male and female but those of black and white and gay and straight."*]

The final union of Eric with Yves and Vivaldo with Ida in ***Another Country*** represents a breakthrough in American literature, reversing the separation of lovers that has so characterized our fiction. Time and again, as Leslie Fiedler has pointed out, the women in our stories, from Cooper's Judith Hutter to Hawthorne's Beatrice Rappaccini and Faith Brown to James's Daisy Miller and Maria Gostrey are found to be fatally flawed in some way or another, and the men, unable to accommodate themselves to their lovers' shortcomings, bound to withdraw into isolation.

Baldwin adopts this conceptual framework. His goal is to find a solution, a reconciliation that will work, not only on a personal level, but on a social level, that will bring together not only the polarities of male and female but those of black and white and gay and straight. Baldwin's *context,* then, is the "Fiedler dilemma," the theme of separation of male and female. The *structure* of his solution is the story of Adam and Eve; the *content* of that solution is existentialism.

The first problem to examine is the isolation of the hero, which is conceived as a kind of sin. "Eric sat naked in his rented garden" (183), writes Baldwin, launching book 2. The paragraph then quickly introduces Eric's lover, appropriately named Yves. This Adam-and-Eve imagery is part of a pattern of references that root the novel in the Biblical story of the Fall. Indeed, "falling" is itself a recurring motif. Eric fears that he is "falling, falling out of the world" (407). And Rufus, the novel's Satan character, is introduced as "one of the fallen" (4). He falls literally, from the George Washington Bridge, cursing God as he falls.

A good way to begin exploring the nature of the fall in the novel is by asking a logical first question: If Eric is compared to Adam, what is his transgression? This proves a suitably complex question, for on examination we can discern two quite different sins.

Eric's "original" sin is homosexuality. This is his primal sin, committed at an early age, "in the fiery shadow of a tree" (205). It is explicitly described as a transgression:

Nothing could have moved him out of LeRoy's arms, away from his smell, and the terrible, new touch of his body; and yet, in the same ways that he knew that everything he had ever wanted or done was wrong, he knew that this was wrong, and he felt himself falling.

(205)

Contemporary readers are likely to respond that homosexuality is no sin, but merely a taboo imposed by a sexually repressed, and repressive, society. Nevertheless, Eric clearly regards it as a sin. His homosexuality is bound up with "everything he had ever wanted or done"; it is his nakedness, his vulnerability, and it is consistently referred to as an evil. Rufus describes Eric's admission of homosexuality as a "confession," and it "delivered him into Rufus's hands" (45). Eric himself calls it an "infirmity" that "made him the receptacle of an anguish which he could scarcely believe was in the world" (211).

Homosexuality in the novel is to be regarded quite literally as *original* sin, which by its nature is a pre-existing condition. Human beings do not commit original sin; we are born with it. It is in this sense that it is not really a sin. Homosexual or heterosexual, we are all born naked. Southern or northern, black or white, we are born with a hunger for love. Our real sins come later.

Of these later sins the greatest is the sin of isolation, of separation from others. This sin comes after and in response to the original sin; it is, at its simplest, a hiding of the original sin. Eric's reaction to his encounter with Henry, for example, is that he "knew that what he felt was somehow wrong, and must be kept a secret" (198). In fact, "by this time he knew that everything he did was wrong in the eyes of his parents, and in the eyes of the world, and that, therefore, everything must be lived in secret" (199). Eric's redemption, when it comes, will consist of his overcoming not the original sin of homosexuality, but the reactive sin of denial. It is in embracing and affirming his original sin that he will redeem both his own life and those of his lovers.

The two-sin, two-step view of man's fall closely parallels the Adam and Eve story, especially as Milton handles it in *Paradise Lost*. Here, as in *Another Country,* there is an original sin and a subsequent, reactive one. The immediate consequence of Adam and Eve's eating the forbidden fruit is that they become aware of their nakedness. Their nakedness exposes their need, their vulnerability, and it makes them ashamed. Their response is to hide their nakedness behind fig leaves, just as Eric hides his homosexuality, just as his "army of lonely men," vulnerable and ashamed, hide in darkness:

[T]he need they brought to him was one they scarcely knew they had, which they spent their lives denying, which overtook and drugged them, making their limbs as heavy as those of sleepers or drowning bathers, and which could only be satisfied in the shameful, the punishing dark, and quickly, with flight and aversion as the issue of the act. They fled, with the infection lanced but with the root of the infection still in them. Days or weeks or months might pass—or even years—before, once again, furtively, in an empty locker room, or an empty stairway or a roof, in the shadow of a wall in the park, in a parked car, or in the furnished room of an absent friend, they surrendered to the hands, to the stroking and fondling and kissing of the despised and anonymous sex. ... They came, this army, not out of joy but out of poverty, and in the most tremendous ignorance. Something had been frozen in them, the root of their affections had been frozen, so that they could no longer accept affection, though it was from this lack that they were perishing.

(211-12)

Adam and Eve compound their alienation from each other through endless bouts of mutual recrimination (Milton 9.1187-89). Their behavior stands as a model for the abuse Eric experiences: from the ignorant army of lovers in general, and from Rufus in particular. The model applies as well to the bitter acrimony between Rufus and Leona and between Vivaldo and Ida.

Baldwin's counterpoint between original sin and the greater sin of isolation connects *Another Country* to a long tradition in American fiction. It connects Baldwin to his paragon, Henry James, for example, and back to James's paragon, Hawthorne. Indeed, the interplay of the two types of sin may well be the most prominently recurring story device in Hawthorne's fiction. We find it in the contrast in *The Scarlet Letter* between Hester's acknowledged adultery and Dimmesdale's and Chillingworth's secret sins; in the opposition in "Rappaccini's Daughter" between the poison in Beatrice and the poisonous suspicions of Giovanni; in the way Rev. Hooper's black veil begins as a sign of *universal* sin and ends as an emblem of his own alienation; and so on.

Hawthorne and Baldwin not only agree in viewing isolationism as worse than the original sin; they agree in identifying it as the consequence of the original sin. In story after story, Hawthorne's characters recognize sin and recoil from it, isolating themselves in the process. Most of these characters, including Rappaccini and Giovanni, Chillingworth, and Aylmer in "The Birthmark," are either scientists or other learned men, and their behavior is consistently depicted as a mental act: the pursuit of an idea at the expense of reality, the elevation of head over heart. From here it is but the shortest of steps to Baldwin's existentialism. Merely substitute essence for head and existence for heart, and Hawthorne meets Sartre.

Before discussing this, let me outline what I see as Baldwin's broader answer to the broader dilemma. If isolation is the sin unto death, for Baldwin as for his predecessors, then the answer—the counterpoint to the army of lonely men—is articulated by Cass. One's secrets, she says, must be laboriously dragged into the light and imposed on the world's experience. "Without this effort, the secret place was merely a dungeon in which the person perished; without this effort, indeed, the entire world would be an uninhabitable darkness" (112). The darkness that symbolizes isolation pervades the novel. The story begins past midnight, with the fallen Rufus wandering through Times Square. Later he plunges to his death framed against a dark sky and an even darker abyss of black water. Likewise the stormy encounters between Vivaldo and Ida nearly always take place at night. Even in the daytime there is dark: Eric's departure from France takes place "in the deep black shadow" of a train station" (228); when he receives the news of Rufus's death, it is pouring rain and all is "wavering and gray" (192); when he visits Cass and Richard, Bessie Smith sings, "it's raining and it's storming on the sea"; and his final meeting with Cass takes place in a torrential storm. By contrast, the resolution, when it comes, will be awash in light.

The light for Baldwin, throughout his work, is the light of love. Love is, he says in his dialogue with Nikki Giovanni, the "key" to unlocking the "mysterious endeavor" that constitutes life (35). But Baldwin's love is painful and powerful; it involves suffering and sorrow and sharing. He says that we must "realize that [our] suffering does not isolate [us], but instead is our bridge" (*A Dialogue* 74). David in *Giovanni's Room* ultimately reaches such a realization, for after he has failed to love and save Giovanni, the end of the story finds him "walking toward the waiting people" (224), a suggestion that he now sees that his pain connects him to others. In *If Beale Street Could Talk,* Fonny comes to see his link to a community that includes not only him and Tish and their families, but also the white lawyer Hayward, the Italian grocer, Pedrocito and the other Spanish waiters, and the Jewish landlord.

Nikki Giovanni and Baldwin discuss many things during their dialogue ranging from politics, to writing, to the future of black Americans, but Baldwin keeps returning to the subject of love. When Giovanni repeatedly addresses what she regards as the interpersonal failure of the black man, Baldwin's response is subtle yet persuasive; he does not directly disagree with her, but insists that she "understand" the history of oppression and humiliation and pov-

erty that leaves the black man in "such an awful pain and rage" that he cannot reach out to those who love him. Yet Baldwin's love extends beyond black men and women—encompassing white, yellow, red, gay, straight, man, woman, rich and poor—all of us, whom he sees as "terrified" of life, and desperately needing to bridge the gulf of terror by sharing it. It's an inspiring conversation, in which Baldwin seems to practice what he preaches by accepting all of Giovanni's frustration and anger. I see her as demurring at every point he makes until finally she concludes, "We agree. Love is a tremendous responsibility."

The resolution in *Another Country,* as I have said, uses the structure of the creation story; its content is existentialism. The way Baldwin brings together these seemingly disparate perspectives is as simple as it is surprising. I, for one, would not have pegged Milton as an existentialist. Yet the fit, on inspection, is remarkable. For the existentialist, the "knowledge of good and evil" is the awareness that such terms are inescapably subjective. Coming to this awareness is unavoidable; it is what defines the human condition. And it brings us to bitter anguish: separating us from an external God, expelling us from a universe of another's design, and sending us forth sorrowing to make our own way in the world.

The "creation story" is, from an existentialist viewpoint, aptly named, for it is the story not merely of God's creation of Adam and Eve, but of their creation of themselves. The story seeks to explain how humans came into being; in the most important sense, however, Adam and Eve did not *become* truly human until they *left* the garden. At that point, Milton writes in his famous final lines:

> Some natural tears they dropp'd, but wip'd them soon;
> The World was all before them, where to choose
> Their place of rest, and Providence their guide:
> They hand in hand with wand'ring steps and slow,
> Through Eden took their solitary way.
>
> (12. 645-649)

While existentialists would balk at the concept of "Providence" as guide, the term might conceivably be stretched to apply to the self as the author of one's own actions. With this exception, Milton's words seem astonishingly in tune with existential thought, pinpointing in just five lines all the most prominent concepts of existential theory: the anguish; the sense of the world as uncreated; the primacy of human choice; and the responsibility of the individual for his or her choice.

From an existential perspective, the denial of original sin, the hiding of our nakedness, is the attempt to escape from our knowledge that meaning does not exist outside us. The escape path is a belief in essences, that is to say categories of existence, which presume to give order to our world, but which have no real existence, being only constructs of the mind. We escape into essentialism whenever we adopt sexual or racial stereotypes, sign onto society's behavioral or ethical norms, or experience ourselves, or others, as types, rather than as immediate, uniquely existing beings.

In *Another Country* the sin of essentialism is the existential face of the sin of isolation. It is centered most of all in the tragic figure of Rufus. Rufus is a black hole of isolation, introduced to us as "entirely alone and dying of it" (4). Loved by Eric and by Leona, but ashamed of his need for their love, he drives them away. And he does it by reducing them to types. He despises Eric for being a Southerner and a white, and abuses him "by treating him as a woman" (46). Rufus treats Leona the same way, even using the same epithets. His distance from his lovers *depends* on his refusal to see them as individuals. When Leona starts offering specific details about herself, he sees it as a threat: "Something touched his imagination for a moment, suggesting that Leona was a person and had her story and that all stories were trouble" (13).

Eric comes to recognize that loving people is incompatible with typing. "Had he ever loved Rufus?" he wonders: "Was it the body of Rufus to which he had clung, or the bodies of dark men, seen briefly, somewhere, in a clearing, long ago, sweat running down their chocolate chests and shoulders, their voices ringing out, the white of their jockstraps beautiful against their skin ..." (194). Whether I associate my partner, as Rufus does, with a group I hate, or as Eric does, with a group I love, the central fact remains: if I regard someone in terms of any category, then my emotion is not love. The love that alone can save us from the chaos of isolation must be individual, immediate, and personal: in other words, existential.

Rufus's rejection of Eric and Leona continues the long tradition in American literature of rejecting the fallen woman (where "fallen" is understood in a far more general sense than that of common parlance) but ultimately Eric, and Vivaldo, succeed in breaking out. As Adam characters, they hark back to an even older tradition, in which the fallen female is emphatically embraced. Adam, approached fruit in hand by a fallen Eve, faces the most existential of choices. And he makes his choice on strikingly existential grounds:

> How can I live without thee, how forgo
> Thy sweet Converse and Love so dearly join'd,
> To live again in these wild Woods forlorn?
> Should God create another Eve, and I

> Another Rib afford, yet loss of thee
> Would never from my heart. ...

(9.908-913)

Milton's hero certainly engages heavily throughout the poem in sexual typing; at this critical juncture, however, he emerges as pointedly uninterested in womanhood or the idea of woman. For once he sees Eve as an irreplaceable individual, not a representative of her sex, and he makes an authentic choice based not on concepts, but on his immediate, specific, situation.

Adam's choice is very much like the paradigmatic one of the young man in Sartre's essay "Existentialism," who must choose between staying with his mother in France or going to England and joining the war effort (1197-98). And Adam's choice, like the young man's, is one that not only proceeds from love, but *actualizes* that love: gives it reality through concrete action. Adam's decision, an affirmation of his need for love, is therefore both his fall and his redemption. It separates him from God and thus brings him anguish, but at the same time it defines his humanity.

The same analysis applies to Eric. His homosexuality is his original sin, and his affirmation of his homosexuality is his salvation. "If only someone, somewhere," thinks Eric, reflecting on his ignorant army of past lovers, "loved them enough to caress them this way, in the light, with joy!" (212). Loving in the light is the redemptive act that Eric finally comes to: the affirmation of his homosexuality and his need for love. It is the understanding that love consists in loving; that it is not limited by society's sexual norms, nor confined within the bounds of a "lasting relationship." Eric breaks off his relationship with Cass, a relationship based on his attempt to deny his homosexuality. In the subsequent scene with Vivaldo, he comes to terms also with his future with Yves. Before, he had feared that on the day Yves left him he would "drop back into chaos" (210). Now he realizes that he can and must eventually let Yves go. Eric's face now gleams in the yellow light, and presently the light of dawn comes up behind the window and, Baldwin says, "insinuate[s] itself into the room" (289). Eric's affirmation is redemptive not only for him and Yves, but through him, for Cass, and even more clearly Vivaldo and Ida.

Vivaldo and Ida, too, are likened to Adam and Eve, as is clear from Rufus's effect on them (including his gift to Ida of the snake ring) and their bouts of mutual recrimination, which strongly resemble those between Adam and Eve. The ultimate reconciliation of Vivaldo and Ida closely parallels the episode in book 10 of *Paradise Lost* in which Eve, responding to Adam's railing at her, professes her love and elicits in turn a similar profession from him.

Immediately after Vivaldo tells Ida he loves her, they embrace:

> They stared at each other. Suddenly, he reached out and pulled her to him, trembling, with tears starting up behind his eyes, burning and blinding, and covered her face with kisses, which seemed to freeze as they fell. She clung to him; with a sigh she buried her face in his chest. . . . Her long fingers stroked his back, and he began, slowly, with a horrible, strangling sound, to weep, for she was stroking his innocence out of him.
>
> (431)

The tone here of mixed sorrow and joy matches perfectly the tone at the end of *Paradise Lost*. For Adam and Eve the pain of expulsion from paradise is assuaged by their love, the sentence of death offset by the promise of eternal life. Existentially, our anguish, too, is counterbalanced by the affirmation that authentic choice entails. The Vivaldo and Ida scene is the midpoint of an arc that begins with the tearful and rainy departure of Cass, who has just begun the anguished acceptance of existential responsibility, and ends in the reunion of Eric and Yves. Here, finally, the rain that has pervaded the novel ceases (431), and in the next paragraph, at the start of the final chapter, the light at last emerges:

> The sun struck, on steel, on bronze, on stone, on glass, on the gray water far beneath them, on the turret tops and the flashing windshields of crawling cars, on the incredible highways, stretching and snarling and turning for mile upon mile upon mile, on the houses, square and high, low and gabled, and on their howling antennae, on the sparse, weak trees, and on those towers, in the distance, of the city of New York.
>
> (432)

The union of male and female, so persistently rejected in American fiction, is finally found in Eric's acceptance of himself.

## Works Cited

Baldwin, James, and Nikki Giovanni. *A Dialogue*. Philadelphia: Lippincott, 1973.

Baldwin, James. *Another Country*. New York: The Dial Press, 1962.

Milton, John. *Paradise Lost. Complete Poems and Major Prose*. Ed. Merrit Y. Hughes. New York: Macmillan, 1957.

Sartre, Jean Paul. "Existentialism." *The Norton Reader: An Anthology of Expository Prose*. Ed. Arthur M. Eastman. New York: Norton, 1988. 1193-1202.

## Ernesto Javier Martínez (essay date 2009)

SOURCE: Martínez, Ernesto Javier. "Dying to Know: Identity and Self-Knowledge in Baldwin's *Another Country*." *PMLA*, vol. 124, no. 3, May 2009, pp. 782-97.

[*In the following essay, Martínez contends that* "Another Country *is motivated less by the tragedy of Rufus's suicide early in the novel than by the ethical imperative faced by all the characters to risk their sense of self (to figuratively commit suicide) in order to better understand their lives." He proposes to "explore this epistemological and ethical feature of* Another Country *by interrogating what I call the novel's suicidal sensibility."*]

> [B]ecause I am an American writer my subject and my material inevitably has to be a handful of incoherent people in an incoherent country. And I don't mean incoherent in any light sense. . . . It's a kind of incoherence that occurs, let us say, when I am frightened, I am absolutely frightened to death, and there's something which is happening or about to happen that I don't want to face.

James Baldwin, **"Notes for a Hypothetical Novel"**

One of the most unsettling features of James Baldwin's 1962 novel ***Another Country*** is that while it emphasizes the need to challenge the racist and homophobic status quo of the American 1950s, it simultaneously presents a series of characters who are rarely successful in bringing about any kind of change.[1] The characters who would most benefit from a revamping of social norms find themselves confused and unable to actualize even minor changes in their own lives. Those involved in interracial relationships frequently mistrust and hurt one another; the men in same-sex relationships are perpetually troubled by a fear of fleetingness, if not utter untenability; and the ghostly protagonist, Rufus Scott, positioned at the intersection of these two lines of social conflict, ominously commits suicide because of his deep-seated loneliness and desperation. Confusion and incoherence are thus thematically central to Baldwin's vision, but it is their chronic presence that makes ***Another Country*** a particularly difficult novel to read. Early critics of Baldwin's fiction dismissed such an emphasis as symptomatic of Baldwin's own "incoherent" identity.[2] Recent critics have been prompted to impose narrative and thematic resolutions.[3] But just about every reader is left with questions about the logic of a novel that so consistently depicts its major characters in states of deep confusion, incapable of reaching even preliminary conclusions about the nature of their predicaments.[4]

***Another Country*** is preoccupied with incoherence and confusion as epistemically significant states and needs to be read as an extended meditation on the peculiar difficulty of gaining self-knowledge in oppressive social contexts. The difficulty that Baldwin explores is not just intellectual or cognitive in nature, for it refers to the difficulty of living differently, living in ways that either imply or lead to new self-knowledge. Baldwin shows how self-knowledge frequently involves more than simply "opening one's eyes" and how it often requires complex acts that themselves have significant social, psychological, and epistemic effects. The novel's preoccupation with confusion and incoherence can be understood, then, as having both epistemological and ethical dimensions. What Baldwin's characters can *know* about themselves and their social contexts is intimately related to what they are willing to *do* in the social domain.

I explore this epistemological and ethical feature of *Another Country* by interrogating what I call the novel's suicidal sensibility.[5] This sensibility involves an attentiveness to imminent action that is deliberate, seemingly irrevocable, and self-menacing, and it lies at the conceptual center of Baldwin's novel. Through it Baldwin examines how self-knowledge in oppressive contexts often depends on people making extreme shifts in their conception of self—of who they are in relation to their society. These shifts are experienced as states of what Baldwin in the epigraph above calls incoherence, as destabilizing and dangerous, because they register the complexity of opposing a social order in which one is implicated and enmeshed. Baldwin understands this incoherence to be a distinctly American affliction and compares it to the terror associated with purposeful evasiveness and impending doom ("when . . . I am absolutely frightened to death, and there's something which is happening or about to happen that I don't want to face").[6]

*Another Country* is motivated less by the tragedy of Rufus's suicide early in the novel than by the ethical imperative faced by all the characters to risk their sense of self (to figuratively commit suicide) in order to better understand their lives. They need to be willing to die, as it were, to come to know more fully.[7] Ironically, *Another Country* rarely depicts successful instances of this figurative suicide. Indeed, it boldly foregrounds characters who seem unable or unwilling to risk their sense of self. This emphasis in Baldwin's text is uncompromising testimony to the often deeply menacing process of acquiring self-knowledge in oppressive contexts.

Baldwin's view on self-knowledge is supported by an implicit thesis about identities and their epistemic value. In the novel, identities are often depicted as impediments that one would do best to discard. But if discarding them appears self-menacing, it is because Baldwin also understands identities as necessary for making sense of the world. Identities, for Baldwin, entail not only multiple ways of life but

also multiple modes of knowing. Instead of simply thinking of identities as impediments (as social constructs we would do better without), Baldwin thinks of them as practices of interpretation and interaction for which we need to be increasingly more responsible and through which we might better understand our social world. Thus the novel focuses on the fear of shedding identities only as testimony to the difficulty of taking responsibility for one's identity in oppressive contexts; Baldwin's novel ultimately argues that something new and epistemically more adequate must be worked toward and put in their place.[8]

This nuanced emphasis in Baldwin's novel shares affinities with the recent work of philosophers and literary theorists developing "realist" approaches to identity, experience, and knowledge.[9] Like Baldwin, contemporary realist theorists understand identities as potential resources that, to lesser and greater degrees of accuracy, offer us access to aspects of the social world. The access that identities offer us is not self-evident, but it is, as realists argue, achievable, because identities are neither arbitrary fictions nor inexplicable essences. Identities are more like lived theories that have a complex, causal relation to the social world and its organization. They can be limiting, but they can also be rethought and redeployed to explain aspects of the social world and our experiences in it. Baldwin not only anticipates basic realist theoretical principles but also provides a provocative version of realist ideas. If, as realists argue, identities are like theories and can be evaluated (examined for degrees of epistemic value), Baldwin provides indispensable phenomenological detail regarding the enormous difficulty of actualizing that potential in oppressive contexts.[10]

### SUICIDAL RUMINATIONS ON "RESPONSIBILITY"

Rufus Scott's unexpected suicide ninety pages into Baldwin's novel is the narrative premise that sets in motion the tense interracial and homosexual relationships in the novel. However, Rufus's suicide also insinuates itself into the novel's epistemology and ethics, becoming one of its conceptual frames. A suicidal sensibility forms a central part of the novel, since how and what the characters know is intimately tied to the manner in which they come to terms with the moral and mortal risks of acting outside the normative codes of conduct. Rufus's decision to kill himself—an act of desperation arising out of a compelling identity crisis and loneliness—looms heavily over attempts in the novel to explore more figural, but no less dangerous, losses of self. These attempts are often cast in terms of what it might mean to take responsibility for one's self (and one's identity) in contexts of intense ideological violence and interpersonal conflict, particularly when the possibility of unscripted action (action that transcends and challenges the norms of one's community) is obstructed by self-doubt, confusion, and fear.

The characters in **Another Country** face constitutive difficulties in understanding their emotions and articulating their motivations.[11] These perceptual and communicative entanglements, I want to suggest, should be understood in the way that philosophical realists like Susan Babbitt ("Moral Risk") and Satya Mohanty ("Epistemic Status") have outlined, as typical of activities where the acquisition of knowledge about oppressions—and one's place in relation to them—are central. Coming to better understand systemic forms of oppression, Babbitt argues, deserves recognition as a particular kind of learning process, one that is often disorienting because it stresses who people understand themselves to be, where and among whom they find themselves located, and what they see from that location. Because their interactions are socially unsanctioned (sexual encounters with the same gender, interracial relationships) and intimate, Baldwin's characters are on the verge of knowing something fundamental about how oppression in the United States functions in their lives. Assimilating such knowledge, however, is particularly difficult for these characters not simply because they are learning about previously unfathomed networks of power but because the prospect of acquiring knowledge about their lives is fundamentally tied to who they understand themselves to be and, more important, whom they are willing to risk losing and becoming.

One of the main African American characters of the novel, Ida Scott, exemplifies the complexity of such a suicidal sensibility. For instance, Ida finds it hard to grasp how she can be in love with a white man (Vivaldo, the "sweetest man" she's ever known [344]) and still feel a sense of impossibility at the thought of making a life together with him. While her anxiety is partly explained as the inability to clearly foresee what their life together, as an interracial couple, might be like, it is also accounted for as a consequence of her ability to *correctly* discern constitutive features of her social world. Ida understands that Vivaldo's dismissive disposition toward questions of racist oppression (i.e., his all too anxious persistence that race should not matter) prevented him from coming to the aid of her brother, Rufus, when he was most in need. Even though Ida cannot see, or is simply unwilling to see, some factors (like Vivaldo's queer sexuality) that kept him from treating Rufus with integrity, she is able to perceive that Vivaldo's underexamined attitude toward questions of race made him act irresponsibly with Rufus. Ida intimates as much when she states to one of Vivaldo's friends, "Well, you know, Vivaldo was his best friend—and Rufus was *dying,* but Vivaldo didn't know it. And I was miles away, and I *did*!" From

her vantage point, Ida concludes that she could never marry Vivaldo. A partnership with him would be a contract of mutual self-destruction: "it would be the end of him and the end of me" (347).

The idea that committing to spending her life with Vivaldo is, in essence, committing suicide is a provocative declaration. It not only undermines the liberal humanist notion that love can transcend all obstacles but also reinscribes the trauma of Rufus's suicide into the way Ida conceptualizes her actions and circumstances.[12] Ida's association of interracial marriage with suicide might be understood, by some, as a consequence of her inability to think and behave in ways unscripted by the racialized tensions of the 1950s. Such a perspective, however, mischaracterizes the predicament that Ida seems to be in, especially in terms of the multiple structures of domination she is running up against and the distinctly praxical and deeply personal manner in which they are coming to light. An alternative account of Ida's suicidal reflections would interpret them less as an effect of racialized tensions and more as the thoughts of a conflicted agent in the midst of negotiating these tensions. From this perspective, Ida is relatively clear about her abilities to act in an unprecedented fashion, but she deeply fears the consequences. That is to say, Ida discerns correctly that a "true" commitment to staying with Vivaldo may not mean a literal death but would require Vivaldo and Ida to rethink their relationship significantly, thereby challenging the sociopolitical circumstances that undergird it. To the extent that these circumstances form key aspects of their own self-conceptions and interpretive horizons, committing to a life together in this radical way would imply, in certain instances and to certain degrees, ending their former ideas of self. Suicide, in this sense, is not so much hyperbole as it is the mark of integrity and responsibility for themselves (and for their identities) in an interracial relationship.

Taking responsibility for one's self and one's identity in this suicidal manner constitutes a monumental difficulty for the characters in Baldwin's novel, in terms of what they see themselves capable of knowing and how they conceptualize their possibilities for action. This is so, in part, because taking responsibility for one's self and one's identity often consists, as the literary theorist Paula Moya notes, of a commitment not only to exploring the correlations between what one knows and where and who one is but also to distinguishing between "better" and "worse" frameworks for understanding the self.[13] For characters like Ida, however, the ability to discern how some frameworks are more significant than others lies in the adoption of, and responsibility for, new ones. One cannot, in other words, simply imagine the value, efficacy, or durability of an identity but must manifest that identity in the world and "stand behind it," as Babbitt (drawing on the work of Claudia Card) puts it, in such a way that its possibilities in the social can have consequences ("Moral Risk" 236-42). Here, it is important to note what Ida's identity would be if, as an African American woman in the 1950s, she were married to a white man and to consider the speculation one could make about what constitutes the psychology, emotions, and epistemic consequences of that positionality—something one might never fully know without inhabiting that social location. To take up a stigmatized identity and lifestyle in this way, one must develop a disposition toward the self that is, on the one hand, experimental (challenging oppressive norms) and, on the other, relatively stable (not easily swayed from counterhegemonic stances). The difficulty inherent in developing such a disposition, the novel seems to suggest, is that identities are not simply lenses through which one sees the world, nor are they easily acquired or discarded. As the example of Rufus and his suicide illustrates so poignantly, identities often structure how we are emplaced in the world and what we experience from that location. Our identities, in other words, are intimately connected to our knowledge *and* sociality, not only influencing our values but, more precisely, determining whom we find ourselves living, learning, and loving among. Consequently, as the novel shows, taking responsibility for one's self and one's identity implies reconceptualizing one's relation not only to one's self but to one's community and belief systems. Taking responsibility in this way means that to know the world and one's relation to it—to know them better—one might have to adopt new senses of one's self, new identities that, in any given circumstance, might contradict former self-conceptions and community values.

If Baldwin's novel can be seen as promoting dialogue on the need to take responsibility for oneself and one's identity in contexts of systemic oppression, why is such a dialogue overburdened with failures and trauma, with pain and uncertainty? Indeed, one of the most disconcerting features of Baldwin's *Another Country* is that even as the novel posits the need for social change, it depicts a series of characters who rarely succeed in bringing about that change. In the light of such unsettling outcomes, it is no wonder that critics have been recently characterized as eager to read the novel as transcending sexual confusion and the failure of interracial harmony. According to Kevin Ohi, commentators as varied as Emmanuel Nelson, Michael Lynch, Terry Rowden, and William Cohen have misread the novel by stressing moments of resolution and self-awareness at the expense of understanding why confusion figures so prominently alongside moments of

sought-after clarity. As Ohi notes, moments of sought-after transcendence and self-revelation unquestionably occur in the novel, but instead of representing states of achieved clarity these moments exist as nonrevelations, as experiences determined by confusion and self-doubt.

Ohi's point is well-taken. Unfortunately, his own answer to the question of why incoherence figures so prominently in the novel does not do justice to the novel's complex understanding of identity and knowledge. Whereas previous criticism may be faulted for evading the novel's peculiar engagement with incoherence, Ohi can be faulted for underreading its epistemological, ethical, and indeed referential significance. Ohi concludes that every instance of confusion in the novel plays a purely "structural" role[14] and that—other than providing instantiations of the narrative difficulty of knowing—the novel has little to say that is in conversation with "a concept of political intervention modeled on representational politics" (263). With its theoretical overemphasis on the indeterminacy of meaning and its undervaluing caricature of "representational politics," Ohi's claim is unsupported by the text. Ohi particularly overstates the case when he claims that the "traumatic opacity" that prevails in *Another Country* is "as incommensurable as it is inconsolable and as incomprehensible as it is essential" (264). The opacity prevalent in the novel is "incommensurable" not as a point of fact but to the extent that characters in the novel prove themselves incapable of taking responsibility for how they understand themselves in the world, refusing to assimilate the possibility that their identities seriously hinder (and, at times, substantially help) them objectively understand the circumstances around them (i.e., the interracial and homosexual friendships they foster and the mechanisms of power that permeate them). In other words, moments of incoherence in *Another Country* might be most usefully theorized as social, rather than as purely narrative, phenomena. In this sense, one might come to see the novel's thematization of incoherence as referencing a paradigmatic feature of systemic oppression and as the epistemic and communicative crisis that Baldwin seeks to render intelligible.

Attending to Baldwin's own recollections of living in Greenwich Village in the 1940s, one can detect correlations between the confusing racial and sexual politics that Baldwin was experiencing personally and those he chose to write about in the novel. In fact, Baldwin began writing *Another Country* in Greenwich Village in 1948. Consider the similarity between the following two passages as just one example of how crucial Baldwin's observations are to an analysis of his novel. In **"Here Be Dragons,"** Baldwin writes:

At bottom, what I had learned was that male desire for a male roams everywhere, avid, desperate, unimaginably lonely, culminating often in drugs, piety, madness or death. It was also dreadfully like watching myself at the end of a long, slow-moving line: Soon I would be next. All of this was very frightening. It was lonely and impersonal and demeaning.

(683)

Now, compare this to what Baldwin writes in *Another Country*:

He remembered the army of lonely men who had used him, who had wrestled with him. ... They were husbands, they were fathers, gangsters, football players, rovers; and they were everywhere. ... Days or weeks or months might pass—or even years—before, once again, furtively, in an empty locker room, on an empty stairway or a roof, in the shadow of a wall in the park, in a parked car, or in the furnished room of an absent friend, they surrendered to the hands, to the stroking and fondling and kissing of the despised and anonymous sex.

(210-11)

I want to suggest not that the meaning of Baldwin's novel lies in reference to the author's biography but rather that Baldwin's treatment of the thematic issues central to the novel (desire, confusion, and a suicidal attitude toward the self) is motivated by an understanding of society and is not fully explained in terms of textual indeterminacy. Baldwin was unequivocal during his lifetime about the necessary and even "inevitable" presence of incoherence in his writing (**"Notes"** [**"Notes for a Hypothetical Novel"**] 238), because he understood the United States to be in a profound state of incoherence (regarding race relations in particular), and he saw it as his life's work to engage that incoherence in a purposeful manner.

Ohi is correct to emphasize the impossibility of achieving transparent self-knowledge in the novel, but he is wrong to associate a lack of transparency with a lack of intelligibility in any and all cases. The following section examines crucial passages in the novel that further prove how incoherence, far from being a *purely* structural feature of the novel, is actually central to the novel's embedded thesis on the relations among identity, experience, and knowledge. Specifically, I address some pivotal moments in the lives of two characters (Eric and Vivaldo) that help to constitute the novel's conclusions about social fragmentation and the need for people to risk, at times, their sense of self in an effort to better understand it.

## RISKING (DIS)ORDER

Toward the end of the novel, when Eric and Vivaldo are finally able to have some time alone—away from their lovers and mutual friends—a powerful conversation takes place that has implications for understanding the relations among identity, oppression, and incoherence. It is at this moment that Eric and Vivaldo finally broach the subject of their sexual desires for both men and women (Eric from the perspective of a self-identified homosexual man and Vivaldo from a primarily heterosexual perspective), sharing a deep sense of frustration and confusion about what their desires mean for their current and future relationships. This confusion is interesting not as an "incommensurable" and "inconsolable" fact but as an issue entirely dependent on the forms of oppression that both men are subject to and the risks they are willing to take to see themselves, and the world in which they live, differently.

Eric, for example, having recently made love with his close female friend Cass, begins to openly question his sense of himself as a homosexual man (335). Vivaldo, without fully understanding the value of working through his confusion, advocates for circumventing altogether the issue of his sexual identity—referring to his own sexuality as an ambivalent one and arguing that he and Eric both need to accept the constitutive uncertainty of their bisexual predicament: "*I* can't be sure ... that one fine day, I won't get all hung up on some boy—like that cat in *Death In Venice*. So *you* can't be sure that there isn't a woman waiting for you, just for you, somewhere up the road" (336). In a manner consistent with Vivaldo's privilege as a heterosexually identified man, Vivaldo takes for granted a correspondence between Eric's sexual uncertainty and his own and then passes off his own lack of responsibility for his identity (i.e., his easy assumption that his sexual practices and sexual desires have no purchase on his heterosexual identification) as an inevitable mode of operation. The reference to Thomas Mann's novel *Death in Venice* further shows that for Vivaldo love and relationships are not about how one identifies oneself but about impulse and desire in the abstract. Love and desire, for Vivaldo, are simply things that happen to one, not phenomena that are constrained by one's self-identifications and social location. Of course, Vivaldo could not be further from the truth on this issue. How one identifies oneself and how one is seen in the world indeed influence how one desires and how one practices that desire with others, and the novel goes to great lengths to demonstrate this.

Responding to Vivaldo, Eric accepts that he may never achieve certainty about his desires but does not allow this to excuse postponing processes of self-reflection and self-critique about his identity: "Indeed ..., I can't be sure. And yet I must decide. ... I mean, I think you've got to be truthful about the life you have. Otherwise, there's no possibility of achieving the life you want ... or think you want"

(336). Eric cannot be certain whom he will end up loving, a man or a woman, and yet he "must decide" on a way of life to see that particular possibility through. He must be "truthful" about the uncertainty that constitutes his sexual desire, but he must "stand behind" his nonheteronormative behavior to fully understand the consequences of that behavior. Eric seems to understand, in other words, that how he chooses to identify himself and, consequently, how he chooses to lead his life and to be seen in the world have ramifications for the types of experiences and knowledge he will acquire. Given this understanding of the value of self-identification for knowledge production, it seems clear why Eric would distrust Vivaldo's desire to leave the question of identity undecided, as if it had no implications for one's practice in, and perspective on, the world. Furthermore, Eric's response to Vivaldo does not do away with the uncertainty of his desires for both men and women (the uncertainty does not simply vanish because Eric makes choices about his identity) but acknowledges that his uncertainty about his sexuality and sexual identity is more than a matter of psychological interiority or individual sexual preference. His uncertainty is, in fact, shaped by social forces. Therefore, Eric's response implies an understanding that the indecision he feels about identifying himself as heterosexual or homosexual has to be evaluated in regard to the ways these two identities are not equally valued options, how they are decidedly unequal modes of identification and how one often functions at the great expense of the other.

Eric's response to Vivaldo holds an embedded epistemological thesis: that to know even complicated things like desire one needs to make decisions that, in one form or another, amount to sustained personal and social commitments—sustained lines of inquiry—that have a stronger purchase on one's life than one intends. By this I mean that, as Babbitt has pointed out, the situations in which we take total control over outcomes infrequently constitute the types of learning experiences needed to radically reinterpret our lives ("Feminism"). This is particularly true in contexts of systemic social oppression, for in these contexts one often exists, consciously and unconsciously, as a mode for its perpetuation. In other words, what one is able to comprehend as being good for oneself may in fact be good for the perpetuation of oppression and may not facilitate a more accurate account of how one often thinks and strategizes, desires and feels, in relation to oppressive regimes of power.

Take, as a brief example, Vivaldo's suggestion that he can have sexual relations with men as a favor to them, as an acknowledgment of their need for him, but not with any sense of being changed by the encounter. In Vivaldo's eyes,

this benevolence toward homosexuals may be liberating but does not implicate him in the logic of homosexuality (337). Eric, of course, opposes Vivaldo's characterization of himself in this way and responds by associating responsibility for one's identity with intellectual and emotional labor, with personal risk. He tells Vivaldo, "If you went to bed with a guy just because he wanted you to, *you* wouldn't have to take any responsibility for it; *you* wouldn't be doing any of the work. *He'd* do all the work. And the idea of being passive is very attractive to many men, maybe to most men" (337). Eric implies that what Vivaldo understands as good is primarily a way for Vivaldo to avoid questioning his sense of self. He exposes the true purpose Vivaldo's benevolence serves—it minimizes personal risk and maintains the heterosexual status quo. Eric further demystifies the notion that one's ability to objectively understand oppression, and one's relation to it, lies simply in intent. Likewise, he clarifies how understanding oppression often requires stamina and courage, a sustained awareness that comfort may signal stagnation and that fear and anxiety may signal potential growth and breakthrough.

Taking responsibility for one's self in the manner suggested by Eric—as a risky, against-the-grain, sustained line of inquiry—is the novel's thematic core. Yet, the novel does not represent the process through which one *successfully* takes responsibility for one's self. It addresses the ways in which one can lose track of that possibility. In fact, the novel concerns itself with characters that have not been able to understand how their social location impinges on, as much as it informs, their horizon of possibility. One of ***Another Country***'s most interesting explorations of the relation between social location and knowledge makes this feature of the novel more explicit. This example shows that at the same time the novel emphasizes incoherence, its formative subtext stresses the process by which even utterly confused characters can gain more or less accurate understandings of their social predicament.

Close to the end of the novel, an unusual scenario unfolds. Vivaldo experiences an unexpected "revelation" vis-à-vis a particularly queer sexual attraction to an unknown woman at a bar:

> He looked at the blonde again, wondering what she was like with no clothes on. ... He wondered about her odor, juices, sounds; for a night, only for a night; then abruptly, with no warning, he found himself wondering how Rufus would have looked at this girl, and an odd thing happened; all desire left him, he turned absolutely cold, and then desire came roaring back, with legions. *Aha,* he heard Rufus snicker, *you don't be careful, motherfucker, you going to get a* black *hard on.* He heard again the laughter which had followed him down the block. And something in him was breaking; he was, briefly and horribly, in a

region where there were no definitions of any kind, neither of color, nor of male and female. There was only the leap and the rending and the terror and the surrender. . . . What order could prevail against so grim a privacy? And yet, without order, of what value was the mystery?

(301-03)

In the midst of an otherwise unremarkable contemplation of this woman's "odor, juices, [and] sounds" and momentary longings to be with her "for a night, only for a night," Vivaldo suddenly, and without warning, finds himself wondering how Rufus (if he were alive) might have reacted to this woman. To his surprise, Vivaldo's queries take the form of an out-of-body experience. Vivaldo briefly loses all desire (shocked at his unexpected recollection of Rufus), only to have it come "roaring back, with legions" when he suddenly finds himself *inside* Rufus's body. Shocked at the ambiguous source (and force) of his sexual arousal, Vivaldo imagines Rufus snickering: *"aha . . . , you don't be careful, motherfucker, you going to get a* black *hard on."* The remarkable awakening of desire that results from merging with Rufus's body positions Vivaldo "briefly and horribly, in a region where there [are] . . . no definitions of any kind, neither of color, nor of male and female. There [is] . . . only the leap and the rending and the terror and the surrender." This is a peculiarly evocative moment in the novel because the experience is understood simultaneously as a dreaded, intersubjective manifestation of (queer) racialized desire by Vivaldo and as a chaotic "region" where race and gender have little relevance. Because this region is described as stripped of the circumstances that led to Rufus's sense of isolation and death, Vivaldo's menacing revelation of the desire that overtakes him when he merges with Rufus, into Rufus, represents a distinctive moment of convergence for the novel. Indeed, the allusions to Rufus's suicide (through words like "leap," "rending," "terror," and "surrender") suggest that the trauma Vivaldo undergoes in this new location has implications for what readers are to believe the novel is saying about both Rufus's and Vivaldo's experiences of self-knowledge.

This is apparent when the novel shifts its attention from Vivaldo's shock at finding himself in a region with no definitions to the consequences of being there. In a profound culminating moment of free indirect interior monologue, the novel asks, "What order could prevail against so grim a privacy? And yet, without order, of what value was the mystery?" These questions seem to reflect the notion that when queer desire is taken seriously, no prior gendered or racial system of ordering the world can remain intact. More important, however, without some alternative way of reconceptualizing the world according to this formerly suppressed reality, there is no use in the revelation.

The implications of these two questions for Vivaldo's actions are crucial but require some unpacking. Vivaldo makes sense to himself through the logic of heteronormativity and moral individualism. These two ways of ordering the world are placed into crisis by the shocking revelation of his racialized desire through and for Rufus and through and for other men and women. While Vivaldo experiences confusion and fear, the true dilemma is that he does not risk adopting an alternative way of conceptualizing this new and uncomfortable reality. Because no new order is ventured to replace the previous one, Vivaldo understands the instability as chaotic rather than generative.

As the novel clarifies, this is a pattern of complacency with terrible consequences, for "when people no longer knew that a mystery could only be approached through form . . . , they perished" (302). Vivaldo experiences desire (through Rufus) as chaotic because the "order" through which Vivaldo is accustomed to seeing the world obscures the complexities of (queer) racialized desire. The novel's conviction that a "mystery" can only be approached through "form," then, emphasizes the importance of risking alternative ways of life, of risking the disorder necessary to sustain alternative social orders. Understanding one's relation to structures of oppression, as the novel suggests, involves unraveling forms of identification—indeed, it involves ending some forms of identification—but not in indiscriminate ways and certainly not by leaving a vacuum in their stead. Risking identities in this manner, far from implying that Baldwin rejects identity, suggests that identities can actually reference and illuminate (to varying degrees of accuracy and comfort) aspects of the social world. Seen in this way, feelings of incoherence and chaos are not examples of textual indeterminacy but are cognitive and affective registers that have liberatory potential.

### IDENTITY, REFERENCE, AND THE "REAL": A FINAL NOTE ON SUICIDAL RESPONSIBILITY

This reading of Baldwin on identity raises vital questions for contemporary literary and social theory. Principally, it stresses the necessity of situating identities in nuanced and less alarmist relations to social constructivist theses. For example, the suicidal account of knowledge acquisition in Baldwin's novel grants complexity to the relation between identity and knowledge (going so far as to assert the necessity of "dying"—of ending certain forms of identification—in order to know) without claiming that all identities are thoroughly and always suspect forms of subjection. Some identities, like Vivaldo's, get in the way of solidarity and comprehension precisely because of the function that identities serve as means of making sense of the social world *in particular ways*. Identities are profoundly mediated (socially constructed) realities. Still, it is of no advantage to render all identities suspect simply on these grounds. Such an emphasis obscures not only the differences in mediated realities but also the prospect that some identities have greater epistemic and political value than others—and that they gain this value not in self-evident, transhistorical ways but contextually and through the great effort and self-reflexivity of people and communities working toward a more just world.

Underlying this argument is a realist concern similarly articulated by the feminist political theorist Lois McNay, a concern regarding the still-fashionable theorization of subjecthood solely from within "negative" paradigms of knowledge production, paradigms where violence is ascribed to any and all forms of normative claims and subjecthood is only and always a form of subjection.[15] A realist approach to the emphasis on subjecthood as subjection notes the rigidity of this equation, arguing that it erases difference by attributing to all forms of subjecthood a pernicious origin and hence necessitates its subversion. When one reduces all identities to forms of subjection that one must subvert, one cannot for example begin to ascertain why Vivaldo's decision to leave the question of his sexual identity open-ended might in fact be wrong, or why the taking up of a publicly nonheteronormative identity could in fact help him to understand features of the social that would otherwise remain unintelligible to him because of his privileged identity as a heterosexually identified white man. It may be that Vivaldo needs to end his sense of self. However, an indiscriminate imperative to subvert identity does not fully capture the difficult moral and emotional work, the decision making and moral risk taking, that people like Vivaldo (situated at the intersection of ideological, historical, and material circumstances) will undertake when deciding how best to subvert identities. Critics might say that Vivaldo subverts heterosexuality by keeping his sexual options as a heterosexual man open, but such a reading would have to erase the novel's emphasis on the ways that pernicious forms of masculinity remain intact, and are even fostered, when men have sex with men.

Related to this account of identity (and its reformulation of the subjecthood-as-subjection model) is another realist concern regarding projects that attribute a linguistic indeterminacy and contingency of meaning to all texts. While these projects may be thought provoking and often illuminating, they fail to some extent to theorize a complex account of reference. Ohi's approach, for example, makes apparent certain aspects of linguistic representation that go unnoticed in other conceptual frames—and for this reason projects like his are important as part of the repertoire for critical social inquiry. Yet such readings may not be sufficient for

understanding what any particular indeterminacy, in any given context, might mean. Additionally, philosophical realists have argued that indiscriminate approaches to highlighting the indeterminacy of meaning in texts are often guilty of epistemological denial, of occluding their own epistemological foundations to make other approaches particular or ideological so theirs, in rhetorical contrast, come across as universal and true—all without having to substantiate why and on what grounds the truth value of their claims regarding the indeterminacy of meaning should be believed.[16] My argument bears repeating: insight garnered from, say, deconstructive reading strategies must be tempered with the understanding that these forms of reading may foreground aspects of a narrative that are overlooked by other approaches but will not sufficiently explain the function of indeterminacy in any given context. This is so because they remain unwilling to differentiate between kinds of indeterminacy and because they seem reluctant to theorize what Mohanty (drawing on the philosophers Charles Sanders Peirce and Richard Boyd) refers to as "degrees of epistemic access" ("Dynamics" 233-34; see also *Literary Theory* 198-253 and "Can Our Values?").

The deconstructive practice of attending to the indeterminacy of meaning in texts reflects a more general disposition toward knowledge and the social that often shirks away from questions of reference. According to Mohanty, such questions are associated with the now outdated claims of epistemological foundationalism (i.e., "the view that knowledge and inquiry should ultimately be grounded in a privileged class of beliefs, or a method, which are themselves uniquely resistant to falsification through new evidence, to changes in knowledge" ["Dynamics" 231]). Mohanty argues that the critique of epistemological foundationalism, while valuable, only partially succeeds as a springboard for contemporary social theory, because it erroneously attributes to theories of reference and objectivity a reductive politics—a "nostalgic desire to seek extra-textual certainty and to avoid epistemic complexity" (*Literary Theory* 2). But theorizations of reference and objectivity need not be associated with the illusion of error-free "certainty" for them to be meaningfully used in social analysis. For example, if Marxist projects do not, for any number of reasons, accurately describe our world or effectively promote the needs of the people they claim to represent, we need not evacuate from these social movements the "degrees of epistemic access" they offer us through their approaches, successes, and failures.

To situate a critique of epistemological foundationalism is, on the one hand, to acknowledge its importance and, on the other, to show where an extreme skepticism goes wrong. In this way, social inquiry can shift to address complex questions pertaining to political criticism and social change—How do texts, in fact, reflect reality? Who are our own people? How do we learn from experience?[17] The shift does not mean that these questions are now easily answered but that the prospect of error is no longer seen as opposing the possibility of objectivity and reference. The emphasis is on degrees of access and on remaining self-reflective about the mediated quality of experiences and identities.

At stake here is the extent to which texts like Baldwin's can be said to reference the social world, offering degrees of epistemic access. Put differently, at issue is the degree to which we believe that discussions of reference simply rehearse a "nostalgic desire . . . to avoid epistemic complexity." What I have tried to show is that epistemic complexity is exactly what hangs in the balance when critics undertheorize the novel as a form of social analysis and when they exaggerate claims to the indeterminacy of meaning in Baldwin's text. Rehabilitating reference is not an attempt to avoid epistemic complexity. In fact, attending to reference opens up difficult questions regarding politics and objectivity.[18] For instance, consider Eldridge Cleaver's claim that *Another Country* risks being an irresponsible novel because the characters it portrays do not represent the "real" black experience of social resistance. While I do not share Cleaver's conclusion that Baldwin's novel is unrepresentative, I want to stress that developing a compelling counterresponse does not solely involve proving the representativeness of the text (by showing how it represents the ways "real" people act). One important answer to the question of *Another Country*'s unrepresentativeness lies outside a narrow definition of representation. In the pages that remain, I will make some concluding suggestions about the role unrepresentative narratives play in acquiring crucial knowledge about the world.

In a brief philosophical reading of Samuel Delany's autobiography, *The Motion of Light in Water*, Susan Babbitt makes a series of important observations regarding the relation between knowledge and narration. She writes:

> Delany notices that he was never able to remember some incidences of his life *until he began to tell a story of a certain sort, motivated by a commitment to a direction of thought and action.* He claims that he had to develop a certain orientation, in theory and practice, in order to understand some things about his life that were actually part of his conscious memories and experience. There were things that he remembered and knew that he had experienced, but to which he could not give appropriate significance.

("Moral Risk" 240; my emphasis)

Drawing, first, on Delany's assertion that his own capacity to know depended literally on the kinds of stories he was capable of telling—some of which cognitively excluded events and emotions because the stories could not give them "appropriate significance"—Babbitt goes on to emphasize Delany's even more radical understanding of the epistemic significance of storytelling. Delany places the epistemic value of storytelling in its germinative capacity and not, strictly, its representative one. Delany resists the naive understanding of narration as simply representing reality and dares to complicate knowledge acquisition by highlighting the always theory-laden (i.e., situated, partial) nature of what and how we know. Babbitt adds a crucial qualification to Delany's important claims: she distinguishes Delany's nonfoundationalist account of knowledge from its potential coherence with radical postmodern skepticism. She distinguishes, in other words, between the postmodern notion that discourses construct reality and the realist notion that discourses are always somehow impinging on and impinged upon by reality. The point, however, is not to make a too strict separation between narration and "the real" but to acknowledge that the real is not simply what is thought about it and that some narratives, because they highlight certain features of the social as opposed to others, give us the necessarily *interested* possibility of understanding our lives—and all the ideologies and experiences that constitute them—in a particular way. This understanding of the relation between knowledge and narration, Babbitt reminds us, differs from philosophical perspectivism or radical postmodern skepticism, because it recognizes that narrating reality in different ways does not, strictly speaking, change reality with each perspectival shift. The important realist claim, here, is that narratives will organize and influence the social but never completely determine it.

Building on the foregoing realist account of the relation between knowledge and narration, I would say that Cleaver's concerns about representativeness in Baldwin's novel can be challenged without making use of traditional understandings of representation. If the black characters in the novel are not recognized as representing real black experience, such a question of referential accuracy needs to be problematized with an acknowledgment that narratives need not be representative to be epistemically useful. This is not to say that all unrepresentative narratives are useful but to acknowledge the germinative, as opposed to the strictly representative, quality of narrative. Indeed, based on Babbitt's insights, this concluding account of *Another Country* might be ventured: perhaps what Baldwin wanted to say about the very real experiences of resisting racial and sexual oppression could not be fully accounted for until he was disposed to write something with a critical objective in mind and with a new and distinctive story to tell—a novel that staged the death of an African American protagonist early on, for example, and prompted white characters and a black character to think deeply about race and sexuality, together (in proximity to each other), but with great cognitive and experiential distances to overcome. Baldwin's novel might not be representative—in the sense of documenting what has already been—but his story might still be germinative in a way that helps elucidate what many of us, for better or worse, have been dying to know: that the possibility for human flourishing is both founded on and mired by the identities that we have made and that have been made of us; that the task in front of us, then, is not to avoid this fact but to engage it and to do so with the only resources we have, our capacity for self-reflection and our courage to change. The consequences of not doing so, Baldwin would add, are plainly for us to find out, for it is an all too present, all too tangible reality that "people pay for what they do, and, still more, for what they have allowed themselves to become. And they pay for it very simply: by the lives they lead" (**"No Name"** [**"No Name in the Street"**] 386).

*Notes*

1. Set primarily in New York City, *Another Country* follows the racially strained and sexually intertwined lives of a group of bohemian artists. Early in the novel, one of them—Rufus, an African American jazz drummer with an ambiguous sexual orientation—unexpectedly commits suicide, initiating a crisis among those who surround him. After Rufus's death, his sister, Ida, begins a relationship with one of his closest friends, a struggling Italian American writer named Vivaldo. Ida loves Vivaldo but resents his privileges and holds him responsible for Rufus's untimely death. Vivaldo loves Ida but is encumbered by his own identity and haunted by a fear that he could have done more to save Rufus. Toward the end of the novel, Vivaldo has a soul-searching sexual encounter with Eric, another member of this group of friends. Eric is an actor recently returned from France and one of Rufus's former lovers. These relationships, in turn, are entangled with those of other characters in the circle of friends, and the racial and sexual tensions remain unresolved at the novel's foreboding end.

2. See, for example, Bone 236; Cleaver; Kazin 223-24; Hyman 27. For a summary of critical responses to *Another Country,* see Cohen.

3. On this tendency, see Ohi.

4. Baldwin's commitment to documenting the contradictions of living in an age of heightened social unrest and racial conflict is one reason critics experience difficulty reading him. However, Baldwin was also subject to pressures that necessarily impacted his writing and ideas. For biographical details regarding Baldwin's own formative existential crisis during the writing of *Another Country,* see Campbell; Kenan; Baldwin, "Art." For an analysis of Baldwin's seemingly wavering public support of sexual identity politics, see McBride on the pressures of being a racial spokesperson. For an analysis of the anticommunist climate that saturated public discourse and impacted Baldwin's writing, see Corber, *Homosexuality*; Murphy.

5. For other readings of suicide, see Cleaver; Fryer; Ohi; Ross; Rowden; Ryan.

6. For a discussion of incoherence and white liberalism, see Baldwin, "White Man's Guilt"; Aanerud 64-65.

7. My argument recalls two recent studies of death and black identity. Its resemblances to Abdul JanMohamed's *The Death-Bound Subject* have less to do with his insightful theorization of the "imminent threat of death" that encompasses black subjectivity than with the attention JanMohamed gives to how black subjects "might 'free' themselves by overcoming their fear of death and redeploying it as a ground for their struggle" (291-300). My argument shares with Sharon Holland's *Raising the Dead* a cautionary approach to the ostensibly liberating process of ending certain pernicious identities and assimilating "better" ones (124-48).

8. This understanding of Baldwin on identity differs from the early-1990s work of Henry Louis Gates, Jr., and William Cohen. As Robert Corber notes, Gates and Cohen mistakenly interpret Baldwin's distress over the narrowly defined identity categories available in his lifetime "as evidence that he thought the classification of individuals by their race, class, gender, and sexuality was [in and of itself] dehumanizing" ("Everybody" 167).

9. As noted by Satya Mohanty, the "return to realism" in recent years can best be understood as a corrective to the dominance of postmodern skepticism as an epistemological position in the academy ("Realist Theory" 97). Realists share with postmodernists a basic commitment to the idea of social construction but are less cynical about the attainability of nonpositivist object knowledge. Realists argue that objective knowledge is realizable not as indefinite certainty but through degrees, careful revision, and by taking

background theories seriously. Since the mid-1990s, realists have expanded this view on knowledge and argued against a purely constructivist view of identity, noting among other things that what matters is not whether identities are constructed but "what difference different kinds of construction make" (Alcoff and Mohanty 6). Against the tendency to associate the constructedness of identities and experiences with epistemic unreliability, realists have sought a more elaborate account of how identities make possible better and worse knowledge about the world. For more on realism, see Alcoff, "Who's Afraid?" and *Visible Identities*; Alcoff et al.; Babbitt, "Feminism" and "Moral Risk"; Hames-García, "'Who Are Our Own People?'" and *Fugitive Thought*; Macdonald and Sánchez-Casal; Mohanty, "Epistemic Status" and *Literary Theory*; Moya, *Learning*; Moya and Hames-García; Siebers; Teuton. For critiques of realism, see Aldama; Foley; LaCapra; Saldívar.

10. Baldwin's novel may be an important mediating text for scholars like Dominick LaCapra and Ramon Saldívar, scholars who, although largely in agreement with realists, feel that experience and identity are more complicated than realists have so far theorized.

11. The epigraph to *Another Country* emphasizes the conceptual centrality of confusion: "They strike one, above all, as giving no account of themselves in any terms already consecrated by human use; to this inarticulate state they probably form, collectively, the most unprecedented of monuments; abysmal the mystery of what they think, what they feel, what they want, what they suppose themselves to be saying."

12. Susan Feldman writes, "The conventional approach among scholars has been to read Baldwin's treatment of love and sexuality as evidence of the novelist's faith in the promise of liberal individualism, and to thus maintain that in Baldwin's fiction the sexual and the political, the private and the public, are bipolar opposites" (101).

13. This emphasis on adjudication and the epistemic value of identity is based on a corollary claim that identities have the power to motivate or impinge on resistance to oppressive networks of power. "Some identities," writes Moya, "because they can more adequately account for the social categories constituting an individual's social location, have greater epistemic value than some others that the same individual might claim" (*Learning* 85).

14. Ohi writes, "*Another Country* speaks repeatedly of 'revelation' and of the revelation of secrets, but the content of the secrets revealed is nowhere specified; the secret seems to occupy a purely structural place in the novel" (264).

15. McNay writes, "If, following Michel Foucault, the process of subjectification is understood as a dialectic of freedom and constraint—'the subject is constituted through practices of subjection, or, in a more autonomous way, through practices of liberation, of liberty'—then it is the negative moment of subjection that has been accorded theoretical privilege in much work on identity construction" (2-3).

16. On epistemological denial, see Alcoff, "Politics"; Creech; Roof; Moya, *Learning*; Mohanty, *Literary Theory*.

17. These questions are raised in the work of the realist theorists Hames-García, Mohanty, and Moya. While not the first to seek answers for these questions, these scholars are unique in their collective attempt to make this line of inquiry speak to the theoretical weaknesses of some of the most referenced and theoretically dominant approaches in literary and cultural criticism.

18. For realist accounts of representation, see, among others. Alcoff, "Problem"; Hames-García, "Which America?"; Hau; Mohanty, "Identity"; Moya, "Postmodernism."

*Works Cited*

Aanerud, Rebecca. "Now More than Ever: James Baldwin and the Critique of White Liberalism." *James Baldwin Now.* Ed. Dwight A. McBride. New York: New York UP, 1999. 56-74. Print.

Alcoff, Linda Martín. "The Politics of Postmodern Feminism, Revisited." *Cultural Critique* 36 (1997): 5-27. Print.

———. "The Problem of Speaking for Others." *Cultural Critique* 20 (1991-92): 5-32. Print.

———. *Visible Identities: Race, Gender, and the Self.* Oxford: Oxford UP, 2006. Print.

———. "Who's Afraid of Identity Politics?" Moya and Hames-García 312-44.

Alcoff, Linda Martín, and Satya Mohanty. Introduction. Alcoff et al. 1-9.

Alcoff, Linda Martín, et al. *Identity Politics Reconsidered.* New York: Palgrave, 2006. Print.

Aldama, Frederick Luis. "Poststructuralist Sand Castles in Latin American Postcolonial Theory Today." *Latin American Research Review* 37.3 (2002): 201-16. Print.

Babbitt, Susan E. "Feminism and Objective Interests: The Role of Transformational Experiences in Rational Deliberation." *Feminist Epistemologies.* Ed. Linda Alcoff and Elizabeth Potter. New York: Routledge, 1993. 245-64. Print.

———. "Moral Risk and Dark Waters." *Racism and Philosophy.* Ed. Babbitt. Ithaca: Cornell UP, 1999. 235-54. Print.

Baldwin, James. *Another Country.* New York: Vintage, 1992. Print.

———. "The Art of Fiction No. 78." *Paris Review* 91 (1984): 51. Print.

———. "Here Be Dragons." Baldwin, *Price* 677-90.

———. "No Name in the Street." *James Baldwin: Collected Essays.* Ed. Toni Morrison. New York: Lit. Classics of the US, 1998. 349-476. Print.

———. "Notes for a Hypothetical Novel." Baldwin, *Price* 237-44.

———. *The Price of the Ticket.* New York: St. Martin's, 1985. Print.

———. "White Man's Guilt." Baldwin, *Price* 101-06.

Bone, Robert A. *The Negro Novel in America.* New Haven: Yale UP, 1965. Print.

Campbell, James. *Talking at the Gates: A Life of James Baldwin.* Berkeley: U of California P, 2002: 128-32. Print.

Cleaver, Eldridge. "Notes on a Native Son." *Soul on Ice.* New York: McGraw, 1968. 122-37. Print.

Cohen, William A. "Liberalism, Libido, and Liberation: Baldwin's *Another Country.*" *The Queer Sixties.* Ed. Patricia Juliana Smith. New York: Routledge, 1999. 201-22. Print.

Corber, Robert J. "Everybody Knew His Names: Reassessing James Baldwin." *Contemporary Literature* 17.1 (2001): 166-75. Print.

———. *Homosexuality in Cold War America: Resistance and the Crisis of Masculinity.* Durham: Duke UP, 1997. Print.

Creech, James. "From Deconstruction." *Closet Writing/ Gay Reading: The Case of Melville's* Pierre. Chicago: U of Chicago P, 1993. 3-43. Print.

Feldman, Susan. "Another Look at *Another Country*: Reconciling Baldwin's Racial and Sexual Politics." *Reviewing James Baldwin: Things Not Seen.* Ed. D. Quentin Miller. Philadelphia: Temple UP, 2000. 88-104. Print.

Foley, Barbara. Rev. of *Reclaiming Identity: Realist Theory and the Predicament of Postmodernism,* ed. Paula M. L. Moya and Michael Hames-García. *Cultural Logic: An Electronic Journal of Marxist Theory and Practice* 4.2 (2001): n. pag. Web. 6 Mar. 2009.

Fryer, Sarah Beebe. "Retreat from Experience: Despair and Suicide in James Baldwin's Novels." *Journal of the Midwest Modern Language Association* 19.1 (1986): 21-28. Print.

Gates, Henry Louis, Jr. "The Welcome Table." *English Inside and Out: The Places of Literary Criticism.* Ed. Susan Gubar and Jonathan Kamholtz. New York: Routledge, 1993. Print.

Hames-García, Michael. *Fugitive Thought: Prison Movements, Race, and the Meaning of Justice.* Minnesota: U of Minnesota P, 2004. Print.

———. "Which America Is Ours? Martí's 'Truth' and the Foundations of 'American Literature.'" *Modern Fiction Studies* 49.1 (2003): 19-53. Print.

———. "'Who Are Our Own People?' Challenges for a Theory of Social Identity." Moya and Hames-García 102-32.

Hau, Caroline. "On Representing Others: Intellectuals, Pedagogy, and the Uses of Error." Moya and Hames-García 133-204.

Holland, Sharon. *Raising the Dead: Readings of Death and (Black) Subjectivity.* Durham: Duke UP, 2000. Print.

Hyman, Stanley Edgar. *Standards: A Chronicle of Books for Our Time.* New York: Horizon, 1966. Print.

JanMohamed, Abdul. *The Death-Bound Subject: Richard Wright's Archaeology of Death.* Durham: Duke UP, 2005. Print.

Kazin, Alfred. *Bright Book of Life: American Novelists and Storytellers from Hemingway to Mailer.* Notre Dame: U of Notre Dame P, 1980. Print.

Kenan, Randall. *James Baldwin.* New York: Chelsea, 1994. Print.

LaCapra, Dominick. "Identity and Experience." Alcoff et al. 228-45.

Macdonald, Amie A., and Susan Sánchez-Casal. "Feminist Reflections on the Pedagogical Relevance of Identity." Introduction. *Twenty-First-Century Feminist Classrooms: Pedagogies of Identity and Difference.* Ed. Macdonald and Sánchez-Casal. New York: Palgrave-Macmillan, 2002. 1-30. Print.

McBride, Dwight A. "Can the Queen Speak? Racial Essentialism, Sexuality, and the Problem of Authority." *Callaloo* 21.2 (1998): 363-79. Print.

McNay, Lois. *Gender and Agency: Reconfiguring the Subject in Feminist and Social Theory.* Malden: Blackwell, 2000. Print.

Mohanty, Satya P. "Can Our Values Be Objective? On Ethics, Aesthetics, and Progressive Politics." *New Literary History* 32.4 (2001): 803-33. Print.

———. "The Dynamics of Literary Reference: Narrative Discourse and Social Ideology in Two Nineteenth-Century Indian Novels." *Thematology: Literary Studies in India.* Ed. Sibaji Bandyopadhyay. Calcutta: Jadavpur U, 2004. 230-48. Print.

———. "The Epistemic Status of Cultural Identity: On *Beloved* and the Postcolonial Condition." *Cultural Critique* 24 (1993): 41-80. Print.

———. "Identity, Multiculturalism, Justice." *Literary Theory and the Claims of History: Postmodernism, Objectivity, Multicultural Politics.* Ithaca: Cornell UP, 1997. 198-253. Print.

———. *Literary Theory and the Claims of History: Postmodernism, Objectivity, Multicultural Politics.* Ithaca: Cornell UP, 1997. Print.

———. "Realist Theory." *International Encyclopedia of the Social Sciences.* 2nd ed. Ed. William Darity, Jr. Vol. 7. New York: Macmillan Ref., 2007. 97-100. Print.

Moya, Paula M. L. *Learning from Experience: Minority Perspectives, Multicultural Struggles.* Berkeley: U of California P, 2002. Print.

———. "Postmodernism, 'Realism,' and the Politics of Identity: Cherríe Moraga and Chicana Feminism." *Feminist Genealogies, Colonial Legacies, Democratic Futures.* New York: Routledge, 1997. 125-50. Print.

Moya, Paula M. L., and Michael Hames-García. *Reclaiming Identity: Realist Theory and the Predicament of Postmodernism.* Berkeley: U of California P, 2000. Print.

Murphy, Geraldine. "Subversive Anti-Stalinism: Race and Sexuality in the Early Essays of James Baldwin." *English Literary History* 63.4 (1996): 1021-46. Print.

Ohi, Kevin. "'I'm Not the Boy You Want': Sexuality, 'Race,' and Thwarted Revelation in Baldwin's *Another Country.*" *African American Review* 33.2 (1999): 261-81. Print.

Roof, Judith. "Lesbians and Lyotard: Legitimation and the Politics of the Name." *The Lesbian Postmodern.* Ed. Laura Doan. New York: Columbia UP, 1994. 47-66. Print.

Ross, Marlon. "White Fantasies of Desire: Baldwin and the Racial Identities of Sexuality." *James Baldwin Now.* Ed. Dwight A. McBride. New York: New York UP, 1999. 13-55. Print.

Rowden, Terry. "A Play of Abstractions: Race, Sexuality, and Community in James Baldwin's *Another Country.*" *Southern Review* 29.1 (1993): 41-50. Print.

Ryan, Katy. "Falling in Public: Larsen's *Passing,* McCarthy's *The Group,* and Baldwin's *Another Country.*" *Studies in the Novel* 36.1 (2004): 95-119. Print.

Saldívar, Ramon. "Multicultural Politics, Aesthetics, and the Realist Theory of Identity: A Response to Satya Mohanty." *New Literary History* 32.4 (2001): 849-54. Print.

Siebers, Tobin. "Disability in Theory: From Social Constructionism to the New Realism of the Body." *American Literary History* 13.4 (2001): 737-54. Print.

Teuton, Sean. *Red Land, Red Power: Grounding Knowledge in the American Indian Novel.* Durham: Duke UP, 2008. Print.

## W. Lawrence Hogue (essay date 2012)

SOURCE: Hogue, W. Lawrence. "The Blues, Individuated Subjectivity, and James Baldwin's *Another Country.*" *CLA Journal,* vol. 56, no. 1, Sept. 2012, pp. 1-29.

[*In the following essay, Hogue examines "how Baldwin in* Another Country *painstakingly describes Rufus' demise, and how that demise serves as a catalyst" for the novel's "other characters to confront their conscious and/or unconscious past, to challenge their social labels and categories, to recognize and acknowledge their human needs and desires, their otherness, to take risks, to grow, and to find freedom and fulfillment in the midst of the turbulent, angst-filled, racially balkanized, capitalist, and spiritually empty world of New York City."*]

James Baldwin's ***Another Country*** was published in 1962 and, though commercially successful, is considered his literary masterpiece.[1] Set in New York City (and France) among artists, writers, actors, and musicians, and told in the third person by an omniscient narrator who has a blues cadence in his voice, ***Another Country*** is the story of the bohemian, jazz drummer Rufus Scott who commits suicide because he could not find his way in a Eurocentric, Puritan, infantile, masculinist American society. The text uses his suicide to examine the pre-requisite for survival, for living whole in the midst of the American whirlwind. To do this, ***Another Country*** interrogates naturalized but repressive and stifling American categories such as race, sex, class, region, and gender, as it offers/imagines a social world where racial identity, sexuality, gender identity, and subjectivity are much more fluid, multiple, open, dynamic, and becoming.

Writing about the nature of identity formation or individuated subjectivity in **"Everybody's Protest Novel,"** Baldwin states,

> We have, as it seems to me, in this most mechanical and interlocking of civilizations, attempted to lop creature (human being) down to the status of a time-saving invention. He is not, after all, merely a member of a Society or a Group or a deplorable conundrum to be explained by Science. He is ... something more than that, something resolutely indefinable, unpredictable. In overlooking, denying, evading this complexity ... we are diminished and we parish; only within this web of ambiguity, paradox, this hunger, danger, darkness, can we find at once ourselves and the power that will free us from ourselves. It is this power of revelation which is the business of the novelist.
>
> (29)

The novelist James Baldwin believes fiction should not be a "pamphlet" to protest a "Cause" (28, 29), but instead it should get at the truth of this complex, indefinable, and unpredictable subjectivity. In this article, I examine how Baldwin in *Another Country* painstakingly describes Rufus' demise, and how that demise serves as a catalyst for other characters to confront their conscious and/or unconscious past, to challenge their social labels and categories, to recognize and acknowledge their human needs and desires, their otherness, to take risks, to grow, and to find freedom and fulfillment in the midst of the turbulent, angst-filled, racially balkanized, capitalist, and spiritually empty world of New York City.

Although individuals are socialized into and are imprisoned by racial, gender, and class categories, argues Baldwin, these categories do not capture the totality of their complex existence. "Our passion for categorization, life neatly fitted into pegs," states Baldwin, "has led to an unforeseen, paradoxical distress; confusion, ... a breakdown of meaning" (**"Everybody's"** [**"Everybody's Protest Novel"**] 31). Categories might provide us with the illusion of safety and security, but they are limited and ineffective in defining the individual. Ultimately, categories end up oppressing, stifling, and destroying our plural subjectivity, our free flow of desires.

For Baldwin, the issue of identity formation is further complicated because, although these racial, gender and class categories limit and cage individuality, causing repression in the psychic, they are also an inescapable part of one's individuality. Individuals internalize social norms and categories, which try to keep their identity static, but they also defy them, struggle against them, as competing and sometimes contradictory desires and/or needs (for love) disrupt or challenge these norms.

To find ourselves and the power that will free us from the boundaries, which diminish us of our socially constructed selves, we have to liberate our desires. In characterizing his American characters, particularly his white American characters, Baldwin, to liberate them from naturalized forms of particularized white American power, reverses the gaze, forcing them to recognize and transcend their limited, white categories. Instead of whites defining blacks, Baldwin, a black who has the experiences of racial oppression and otherness and the knowledge of America as a white, Eurocentric society, allows whites to experience themselves as he perceives them and their history. In Baldwin's reversed gaze, if they are to find themselves and be free, these characters must become conscious of themselves as racial, sexual, and/or gendered whites.

In Baldwin's another country, there is a privileging of the free flow of desire, in the Deleuzian sense.[2] But it is not a flow of desire that leads to utopia, but to a blues flow that accepts, as the norm, the good and the bad, the ugly and the beautiful, the spectrum of life. To survive, to be healthy in Baldwin's another country, everyone has to recognize the trap of society to tell him or her who she is. Yet, he can only save himself by letting his "void" demand "a new act of creation" against the oppressive rules of society (**"Everybody's"** 32). He has "to come to terms with the moral and mortal risks of acting outside the normative codes of conduct" (Martinez 784). Everyone has to find one's self in the midst of social forces, of suffering and pain, in the void of his unknown self, and within the web of ambiguity, darkness, and paradox.

In *Another Country,* Baldwin uses Rufus Scott, who cannot successfully escape/transcend the violence of his own racial, gender, and sexual categorization, both internally and externally, as a catalyst for other characters to breakout of certain social, sexual, and racial categories, to become alive. Rufus' death raises the question of the condition of possibility for other characters to survive. The other characters' "subsequent narratives," argues Stephanie Dunning, "are framed and informed by Rufus' life and his death" (104). Rufus undergoes an apotheosis through his violent end, becoming a kind of angry ghost that haunts the conscience and consciousness of the other primary characters. Each of the primary characters uses his life and death as an excuse to ask questions about his or her life and to seek transformation, to successfully find one's self.

As the novel opens, Rufus Scott, who is in his late twenties, is in the final weeks of his life, where he has been reduced to wandering the streets, sexually prostituting himself with men in order to get money for food and shelter. He has been in hiding for "nearly a month" (4). The loss of his job, of his sense of self, and of Leona has driven him to the brink of disintegration. As with Eric, Rufus had a simultaneous attraction to and hatred of Leona, who is white and who has come to New York to make a new life for herself. But she is "lost" in New York. Refus knows her history. There are rare moments—like when she tells him about leaving the South—when he sees her as a person. But most of the times, Rufus cannot see beyond her white skin, her white history, or beyond his experience of racism during boot camp in the South.

Although she is marginal and can empathize with Rufus, Leona is unable or refuses to accept the difference between her own life experience and Rufus'. Denying Rufus' difference, Leona believes "people are just people as far as [she is] concerned" (13), telling Rufus that there is "nothing wrong with being colored" (52).[3] Although Leona loves Rufus, her liberal white sentiment fails to impact Rufus, who is not capable of receiving her love, of appreciating her "tenderness" (21). Therefore, for Rufus, Leona becomes the object of his scorn, contempt, humiliation, and abuse, as he violently uses her, as he did Eric, to get back at white people for what he thinks they have done to him. Therefore, he destroys her, causing a psychological breakdown and forcing her into a mental institution. We last see Leona "one freezing night, half-naked, looking for her baby" (71). Now, in his final weeks, Rufus is tortured and tormented by her loss and the subsequent guilt stemming from the way he treated her.

But Rufus has other problems. First, he has failed to become an American success. When people had heard him play, they would "come up to him to bawl their appreciation and to prophesy that he would do great things" (77). But this does not happen. Second, adding to his burden, Rufus is estranged from his past, his conventional Harlem family, and his village community because of his bohemian, musician lifestyle and his white mistress. Now, he is separated from both blacks and whites by his relationship with Leona. His sister Ida and the whites on the streets have a particular response to their presence. Ida wants to know why he cannot find a black woman, and whites bitterly stare at him and Leona. When he and Leona walk down the streets the first time, the world "stared unsympathetically out at them from the eyes of the passing people" (27). The Italian adolescent on the street "looked at him with hatred; his glance flicked over Leona as though she were a whore" (30). Everybody is against his interracial relationship with Leona, and he is having problems psychologically surviving it. Third, Rufus' final attempt to connect with

another, with "the only friend he had left in the city, or maybe the world" (3), Vivaldo, fails because Vivaldo cannot engage Rufus' raw pain and suffering, which are due partially to racism. More important, he cannot reciprocate Rufus' request/desire for human touch.

Fourth and finally, Rufus cannot call upon his music to save him, to help him face life. Until the night he quits playing his music, music helped him to survive. "For a brief interlude," writes Marlene Mosher, "Rufus ... was able—through his music—to help both himself and his listeners deal with the daily horrors of life in New York City" (11). Without his music and with his troubling interracial relationship with Leona, Rufus cannot find an anchor. At the end, music seems to be ineffectual. In his final visit to Vivaldo's apartment, Rufus listens to the lines—*"There's thousands of people . . . ain't got no place to go . . . cause my house fell down and I can't live there no 'mo"*—from Bessie Smith's *Backwater Blues* and "wonder[s] how others had moved beyond the emptiness and horror which faced him now" (49). But he does not come up with an answer. Rufus is not saved by one of the things, black music, which African Americans have historically relied on for survival.

Rufus' death results from his inability to escape oppressive racial, social, religious, gender, and sexual categories and the refusal of society to allow his unacknowledged and unrecognized complex, fluid, multiple, and dynamic subjectivity to exist and thrive. Therefore, he denies, overlooks, and/or evades aspects of his plural subjectivity and sexuality. Society diminishes him, "boomerang[ing him] into chaos" (**"Everybody's"** 31).

Yet, to survive, ultimately, Rufus must be able to face the past, must be able or prepared to become existential or a bluesman. But, he is not prepared to "really dig down into [himself] and [to] re-create [him]self. . . . [He is not able or is not sufficiently strong enough] to *decide* who [he is] and force the world to deal with" him (Terkel 5, 6). Therefore, after looking within himself and his surroundings, realizing that there is no help for him, and knowing that the "pain would never stop" (87), Rufus decides that death is the only option. Here, with Rufus not facing his past, argues Susan Feldman, "Baldwin demonstrates the terrible cost of such escape, the dangerous and deadly consequences that result from self and social avoidance" (91). In the end, he thinks that he is a worthless human being and that white people are trying to kill him.

But Rufus' death allows Baldwin in *Another Country* to ask the question: what are the conditions of possibility for other characters to survive, to freely desire, to recognize and live their complex subjectivity and sexuality in the midst of a Eurocentric, hetero-patriarchal American society? In Vivaldo, Eric, Cass, and Ida, we are given a vast section of the American experience that incorporates various strata of class, race, sexuality, gender, and regions. Because of their artistic bent, which allows them to be more aware and sensitive to their surroundings, they are in exile/refugees in New York City. In being in exile from "the world around them," they are in "perpetual danger of being forever banished from any real sense of [themselves]" (316). While they belong to certain hegemonic social, racial, gender, and sexual categories, these mostly white, liberal characters are not strictly defined by these categories. In *Another Country,* Baldwin finds a way for these characters to be in these categories and yet take the risk and transcend them. As the title of the third book suggests, all the characters, except Richard, are moving toward Bethelhelm to be born,[4] as they find their own existential or blues existence in the U S.

Baldwin uses a blues vision or paradigm, which embodies an African American experience, to get these characters to Bethelhelm, to allow them to transcend their various limited, stifling categories. In **"The Uses of the Blues,"** Baldwin argues that the blues refers to "the experience of life" (57), which includes accepting "the reality of pain, of anguish, of ambiguity, [and] of death" (64). Accepting suffering, and knowing that other people have suffered, is "what makes life bearable for any person, because every person, everybody born, ... is certain of one thing: he is going to suffer. There is no way not to suffer" (**"Uses"** 59). Suffering brings self-knowledge, self-awareness, and higher consciousness.[5] The knowledge that everyone suffers lets you know that you are not alone. Hopefully, with this knowledge, you will suffer less. For Baldwin, life is not about safety and happiness, it is about taking risks, growing, accepting one's uncanny strangeness, and accepting life's spectrum. "If you can accept the worst, ... then you can see the best; but if you think life is a great, big, glorious plum pudding, ... you'll end up in the madhouse" (19). In Baldwin's world, the characters who live and thrive are those who learn this blues philosophy, who question and transcend racial, class, gender, and sexual categories, who confront their repressed foreignness or secrets, who take risk and act on desires, and who, despite the odds, existentially re-create and re-invent (renew) themselves.[6]

Now, I want to discuss how the characters Eric Jones and Vivaldo Moore come from two different sexual categories but end up in the same fluid space, as Baldwin troubles their self-identified, sexual identities. But, first, I want to discuss Baldwin's position on sexual categories, or sexual identity politics. Baldwin believes that heterosexuality and homosexuality are not exclusive, natural categories, that they are socially constructed. Underneath these categories, he thinks, sexuality is fluid and open. Writing in **"Here Be Dragons,"** Baldwin argues that "[w]e are all androgynous ... because each of us, helplessly and forever, contains the other—male in female, female in male, white in black and black in white" (690). It is clear that Baldwin does not believe in identity politics as it pertains to sex or gender, or think individuals are born one way or another. For Baldwin, everyone is homosexual.

With Eric and Vivaldo, Baldwin begins with two subjects who sexually belong to two different social/sexual categories: ostensibly Eric is a self-identified homosexual who comes from an upper-middle family in Alabama and Vivaldo is a self-identified heterosexual who comes from a working-class family in Brooklyn. By undermining their social/economic classes and their constructed identities and by putting them in situations where they have experiences that allow them to take risk and get to know their "unknown selves" (**"Everybody's"** 32), Baldwin allows both to arrive in another country where there are no significant labels and definitions, and where they can *choose* to live according to their complex desires, their many selves.

As a young boy in Alabama, Eric learns very early that there was something wrong with the source of his human touch and, therefore, it had to be kept secret. Never feeling "real" love from his parents, who felt that everything he did was wrong in their eyes, Eric receives love from the Other, Grace, the black cook, "who fed him and spanked him and scolded and cuddled him, and dried the tears which scarcely anyone else in the household ever saw" (197). But even more, Eric comes to love Grace's husband, Henry, who was the first man to touch him. Later, as a teenager, Eric realizes that his desire for a black boy, Le Roy, in whose arms he finds a healing transformation, was unacceptable to the folkways of southern racism and homophobia. He asks, "Why can't people do what they want to do" (205)? Rather than capitulate to the social mores of the South and accept himself as a repressed, closeted homosexual, who cannot freely desire, Eric extricates himself from the South because there he cannot do what he wants to do, love whom he wants to love, and befriend whom he wants to befriend. But during his short stay there, Eric has the experience of knowing the Other, the African American.

Moving to New York City, Eric meets Rufus with whom he hopes to recapture that touch and love and to express his desires openly. But Rufus, who is blinded by hatred for whites and his own homophobia, by his own inability to touch/love another, cannot return Eric's love/touch. Instead, he despises Eric because he believes heterosexuality is absolute and all other forms of sexualities are deviant.

Eric's homosexual presence disturbs Rufus, for it mirrors what Rufus denies in himself, thus exposing the weakness of compulsory heterosexuality and challenging the myth of masculinity. Understanding Rufus' hatred of him, but not fully understanding Rufus, and having Rufus make him pay for being white, Eric flees to Europe.

In France, for three years, Eric grows up; he learns to touch and be touched by another person, to live and love openly with the Frenchman Yves, who reminds him of Rufus. Just before he returns to New York to star in a Broadway play, he, unlike Rufus, confronts and acknowledges his past, the darkness and the pain, the suffering and the terror that had been buried in his unconscious:

> They [the terrors] were buried beneath the impossible language of the time, lived underground where nearly all of the time's true feeling spitefully and incessantly fermented. Precisely, therefore, to the extent that they were inexpressible, were these terrors mighty; precisely because they lived in the dark were their shapes obscene. And because the taste for obscenity is universal and the appetite for reality rare and hard to cultivate, he had nearly perished in the basement of his private life.
>
> (197)

Confronting the darkness, the unknown, the foreignness within himself, Eric achieves a perspective on life, outside the rules and mores of society, that allows him to persevere in life's troubles, demanding a new act of creation, which can save him. He is ready to exist in and cope with the desperate ambiguities of life, the danger, the paradox, the pain and suffering, the frustration, realizing that his homosexual desire is one of many obstacles he has to contend with.

To maintain and test all that he has gained in France, Eric needs to move forward by going home and risking it all. He needs to know that he can withstand the forces that caused him to flee America. The director of the French film captures the mature Eric. In the film, Eric, who has a small part, has the face of "a tormented man. ... There was great force in the face, and great gentleness. But, as most women are not gentle, nor most men strong, it was a face which suggested, resonantly, in the depths, the truth about our natures" (330). It is a face that cannot be genderly categorized or labeled, that is fluid and unpredictable, which is how Baldwin defines subjectivity. In France, then, Eric interprets his tumultuous relationship with Rufus as a kind of rite of passage that allows him to engage his personal secrets, to transcend his southern white past, to renew himself, and to find peace of mind and love with Yves.

But the Eric who is in a loving, homosexual relationship with Yves also has another self, the forgotten self, in addition to the buried one he reclaims in France, which undermines/complicates (and shows the limitation of) the representation of him as a self-identified homosexual. Human desires are capable of flowing unpredictably in all directions. Therefore, during his remembrances of his past with Cass in New York City, he thinks about and recalls "that other side of himself" (239), the heterosexual self who had "a few girls hanging around," who was thinking of getting married. His thought makes it clear that these girls were "unloved, but not wholly undesired" (239). Here, we see how desires do not adhere to or are not completely defined by social and sexual categories. Desires cannot be legislated.

Although Eric has become a mature person, he does not live an utopian life. He continues to experience pain and suffering, to grow, and to become. There are moments when he does not feel safe in New York. When Cass tells him about Rufus' last days, he feels his safety threatened by the pain. As he walks through the park with Ida, Vivaldo, and Ellis, a "sea of memory washes over him, again and again, and each time it receded another humiliated Eric was left writhing on the sands" (261). But he is not afraid of this pain, these memories and experiences. The difference now is that, he knows and accepts pain and suffering and risk as part of life, as having "become a part of him" (238). After confronting successfully the complexities inherent in the human condition, Eric is finally able to maintain "equilibrium despite precarious circumstances" (Murray, *Stomping* 251), to approach life with grace and dignity.

It is precisely because of his ability to come to terms with himself, to know that growth entails discovery and recognition of limitations, to approach life with equanimity, and to view life in a totally new way that he becomes so attractive to his friends. Cass is attracted to him because he is "sure of himself" (236). Upon seeing him for the first time, Vivaldo "beamed on Eric as though Eric were his pride and joy" (251). And because he is open, fluid, and multiple emotionally and sexually and is not weighed down by puritan morality, he is able to violate the self-identified homosexual/gay category and have a fulfilling heterosexual affair with Cass.

Eric has a serious affair with Cass, which further "awaken[s] something in him, an animal long caged" (292). When Cass first visits his apartment, Eric tells her she "makes him feel things [he] didn't think [he'd] ever feel again" (287), indicating a plural sexuality, an "expression of sexuality [or desire] going in all directions" (Guattari, *Soft* 45-46). Because he has no desire to defend "conventional morality," with Cass, Eric is willing to accept the flow, to take the risk of other and "trust it" (288). For Eric, love and desire flow; they defy categories, though he does make it clear to Cass that his lover Yves is coming to New York City and he loves him very much. Here, as it is drawn out in his conversation with Vivaldo about the *Death In Venice,* Eric, through risk and struggle, has come to admit and accept that he has complex, unpredictable, diverse desires, that he has many selves. But even with the acceptance of this knowledge, he still has to "decide [about the life he wants]. ... you've got to be truthful about the life you *have*" (336). At this moment, Eric has decided to live a homosexual life with Yves. But, this decision does not guarantee safety and security; it does not assure happiness. Something else can still happen. He can still fall in love with someone else or encounter a "woman waiting for [him], just for [him] somewhere up the road" (336). Therefore, Eric expects the best but prepares for the worst. For the blues sensible Eric, fulfillment cannot be charted. Eric is the kind of honest subject that Baldwin defines as challenging, as transcending stifling social categories, as being "undefinable and unpredictable."

Whereas Eric begins in the self-identified homosexual category and ends in a fluid, multiple, and dynamic social and sexual space, Vivaldo begins in a working-class, compulsory hetero-patriarchal, white category and moves to a fluid, multiple, and dynamic social, sexual and racial space. Vivaldo is "condemned to women" (385), though he fails to become intimate with any of them except Ida, hinting at the insecurities within his masculine identity. There is the affair with the older Jane, but Vivaldo spends a lot of time running "after the [black] whores" up in Harlem (61), never thinking about what Trudier Harris calls, "the political, racial, or moral implications of his actions" (108). In fact, Cass accuses him of getting "involved with impossible women—whores, nymphomaniacs, drunks ... in order to protect [himself] from anything serious. Permanent" (96). With these women, Vivaldo does not have to touch them or be touched by them. He and the women "clung to a fantasy rather than to each other" (131). At this stage of his development, Vivaldo is not capable of touching another person, though he does come to establish a complicated emotional bond with Ida.

In addition, neither Vivaldo nor Rufus can deal honestly with the homosexuality of the heterosexual. They cannot consciously and openly accept and acknowledge their homosexual selves/desires, indicating that they "have internalized their culture's homophobia" (Feldman 97). Because they have what Baldwin calls a "terror of the flesh, ... a terror of being able to be touched" (Goldstein 182), they end up repressing, excluding their homosexual desire, or allowing it to emerge in a twisted, negative way. When Rufus asks Vivaldo if he is queer, Vivaldo responds, "I used to think maybe I was. Hell, I think I even wished I was. ... But I'm not. So I'm stuck" (51). Interestingly, we

later learn that Vivaldo has secretly had sexual relations with other men, which he represses—"My time with boys was a long time ago" (315). When Vivaldo is in Germany, he has a homoerotic moment with his black buddy, which he also represses. Rather than acknowledge the homoerotic moment, the two read the situation into the heterosexual, masculine norm. "Perhaps they had merely been trying to set their minds at ease; at ease as to which of them was the better man" (134). In all of the above instances, Baldwin is troubling Vivaldo's self-identified, heterosexual identity, showing all these emotional and sexual places he cannot go. This is what Hélène Cixous calls "men's loss in phallocentrism" (83).

Likewise, Rufus refuses to take overt, sexual risk, or to accept his homosexual self. His complex, plural sexuality is displayed in his encounter with Eric, with whom he is uncomfortable. When Eric reaches for Rufus' hand and Rufus says, "I don't go that way," the socially constructed heterosexual Rufus is speaking. But, with Eric's touch, another unknown or secret self within Rufus emerges, which he responds to but does not and cannot acknowledge. "[W]ith his hands on Eric's shoulders, affection, power, and curiosity all knotted together in him—with a hidden, unforeseen violence which frightened him a little; the hands that were meant to hold Eric at arm's length seemed to draw Eric to him; the *current that had begun flowing* he did not know how to stop" (46 emphasis added). In this instance, repressed desires emerge and take over, allowing Baldwin to unmask Rufus' compulsory heterosexuality. Neither Vivaldo nor Rufus can accept the flow of desire.

In many ways, Vivaldo comes from a background similar to Rufus. With prodding from Cass, Vivaldo recalls that upon his earlier visit to Rufus' house, he saw something that was familiar. "I walked through that block and I walked in that house and all seemed—I don't know— *familiar.* ... they were colored but they were the same, really the same—and, hell, the hallways have the same stink, and everybody's well, trying to make it but they know they haven't got much of a chance. The same old woman, the same old men—maybe they're a little bit more *alive*—and I walked into that house and they were just sitting there" (98-99). But Vivaldo has rejected this past, leaving "something of himself back there on the streets of Brooklyn which he was afraid to look at again" (111). Though different racially, the two have similar backgrounds.

Although Vivaldo and Rufus might have similar backgrounds, they are different racially. Vivaldo's problem is that he is not capable or is not ready to deal with Rufus' bout with American racism. In fact, Vivaldo refuses to recognize race/racism. The narrator tells us, "He had refused to see it [race/racism], for he had insisted that he and Rufus were equals. They were friends, far beyond the reach of anything so banal and corny as color" (133). In refusing to deal with race, Vivaldo is validating the "white perspective that everything is okay" (Wise 21). He is refusing to deal with the consequences of race, particularly white privilege, white racism, and black hatred. Like Leona, Vivaldo refuses to admit that because of racism Rufus' life experiences and existence might be different from his. Although this friendship between Vivaldo and Rufus is "erotically charged," writes Cohen, it is "racially and sexually blocked" (210). Vivaldo refuses to deal with Rufus' racial difference, and their racial and sexual differences are compounded by the fact that they have competing masculinities.

It is only after Rufus' death that Vivaldo begins to make connections between Rufus' suffering and his own, begins to discern his failure as a friend, and finally begins to confront his own unconscious past. Working in a bookstore and trying to write "serious" fiction, Vivaldo undergoes growth and transformation. En route to Rufus' funeral with Cass, Cass's questioning forces him to stare "at the high, hard wall which stood between himself and his past" (113). He begins to deal with his secrets. "Perhaps such secrets, the secrets of everyone were only expressed when the person laboriously dragged them into the light of the world, imposed them on the world, and made them a part of the world's experience" (98). Bringing secrets into the light makes for a more complex subjectivity and reality. It also makes for a more fulfilling life. Somehow the vague feelings of guilt for the part he played in Rufus' death is beginning to work its way into his consciousness. "I know I failed him, but I loved him, too" (99). Vivaldo feels his lost friend's presence largely as an overwhelming sense of guilt that hangs over his head like the sword of Damocles. But guilt does not bring about change if it remains unexamined.

Initially, Vivaldo believes that he can redeem himself by having a relationship with Rufus' sister. He thinks "love" can overcome "the wrongs done by the history of racism" (Cohen 204). But "[l]ove was a country he knew nothing about" (296). In the beginning, Ida sees her relationship with Vivaldo and others as an opportunity to make them assume responsibility for Rufus' suicide. Upon the death of her brother, whom she idealized, Ida moves from her church-centered family in Harlem into the bohemian circle of white liberals in the Village who were friends of Rufus. Because she grew up black and female, she is not innocent, being fully aware of the violence of sexual and racial oppression. Like Rufus, her hatred of white people has made her bitter, which means in a blues sense she cannot face life. Because she allows her anger, hatred, and dream of ven-

geance to dominate her life, Ida, like Rufus, loses her normal capacity for love, for connection to other people. Since she is forced to hold her head high in order not to destroy her self with hate, argues Jacqueline E. Orsagh, she develops a "sense of self so profound and so powerful that it does not so much leap barriers as reduce them to atoms" (254). She is trapped by the bitterness.

Embittered by the death of her brother, on whom she had counted to save her from the streets of Harlem, and having taken the risk and become romantically involved with Vivaldo, a white man, Ida finds herself in a difficult position. Although she falls in love with Vivaldo, she, as with Rufus in his relationships with Eric and Leona, cannot commit herself to the relationship because he is white. Having grown up in America, Ida knows the reality of race, knows about whites' inability or refusal to deal with racism. She knows the gulf between the races. Speaking to Cass, Ida states, "I'll never marry Vivaldo. ... Sure, I love [him]; he's the sweetest man I've ever known. And I know I've given him a rough time sometimes. I can't help it. But I can't marry him, it would be the end of him, and the end of me" (346-47). Although Vivaldo tells her that he loves both her and Rufus, Ida is fully aware that he does not know them or their past. "How can you say you loved Rufus when there was so much about him you didn't want to know? How can I believe you love me? ... How can you love somebody you don't know anything about? You don't know where I've been. You don't know what life is like for me" (325). Vivaldo thinks love can solve all of the problems.

But although the relationship between Vivaldo and Ida is wrought with all of the hatred and anger that comprise the relationship between Rufus and Leona, blacks and whites in the U S, there is, at the end, a glimmer of hope for Ida and Vivaldo and race relations. In her final scene, Ida reveals to Vivaldo that she has betrayed him and used sex with Ellis as a means to promote her career. Ida now knows that she did not win but is the victim of this tactic. Here, it becomes clear that her anger, and her thirst for revenge have acted as corrosive forces on her own life. We see Ida confronting and acknowledging the extent of the rage she carries as a result of the racial oppression she and those she loves have experienced in America. With this self-knowledge, Ida can give up the bitterness and, perhaps, become a mature person who can live Vivaldo.

Yet there is a counter-current to Ida's rage. Near the conclusion of this final scene, Ida and Vivaldo look at each other and "an unnameable heat and tension flash violently alive between them, as close to hatred as it was to love" (431). Ida confronts Vivaldo with the intensity of her love and hatred of him, and for white America. In so doing, she forces Vivaldo to become aware of his constructed white "self." For a while, Vivaldo resists his past, his unconscious, the "void where anguish lived and questions crouched" (305). But, in the bar, with Ida absent and in the midst of an "aimless, defeated, and defensive bohemia," (317), Vivaldo begins to challenge his internalized social definitions and to engage his void, acknowledging racial difference and his country's racial history. "You wouldn't want to be colored here" (307), he says. He thinks of Ida, of his tormented mystery, and "of his own white skin" (308), thereby dislodging his privileged white position. He becomes aware of the reversed gaze and conscious of his white self, asking what did Ida see "when she looked at [me]" (308).

In the wake of Vivaldo's confrontation with Ida's betrayal and "the recognition that Ida's betrayal of his love is undeniably connected to his betrayal of Rufus, to America's betrayal of its black populations" (Feldman 100), the boundaries of his white male identity are problematized. As Vivaldo stands in the kitchen while Ida cries, his "heart began to beat with a newer, stonier anguish, which destroyed the distance called pity and placed him, very nearly, in her (Ida's) body, beside that table, on the dirty floor" (426). Vivaldo begins to know, understand, and empathize with Ida for the first time and she becomes a part of him. Vivaldo at least cannot escape the truth that his fate is inextricably tied to Ida's fate, just as the fate of white and black Americans are tied together, just as the fate of men and women are tied together. Afterward, the two embrace and Vivaldo accepts the fact that life is not innocence, that anguish is a part of life. "Her long fingers strokes his back, and he began, slowly with a horrible, strangling sound, to weep, for *she was stroking his innocence out of him*" (431 emphasis added). This is the self-willed and deceptive 'innocence' that Baldwin "has said is the burden and insulation" of white Americans (Thelwell 190). Here, Vivaldo suffers, experiences anguish, and gains self-knowledge, finding himself amidst his complex American history. Now, he can become a "serious" writer.

In this final scene between them, Vivaldo and Ida are forced to interrogate and reconsider their own identities and actions. Both confront their past and learn more about themselves. But something powerful has passed between Vivaldo and Ida, and yet the consequences of this revelation are not entirely clear. The scene ends with a physical gulf separating the two characters, seemingly brought on by the violent and antagonistic racial history of which they both belong. They are in love with each other, but "they remained so locked away from one another" (296). Ida's last act is to "turn in her sleep and call his (Vivaldo's) name" (431).

Vivaldo does not go to her, but instead walks to the window and looks out at the sky. Just previous to this moment, we also learn that Vivaldo "had at last got what he wanted, the truth out of Ida, or the true Ida; and he did not know how he was going to live with it" (430). In this instance, even as Baldwin emphasizes the redemptive power of love, he also suggests its limitations. That is to say, Baldwin's vision of redemption is not utopian, in which recognition signifies resolution. Rather it is a blues vision of redemption, where individuals accept the good with the bad, the best and the worst. It is a situation where both Ida and Vivaldo can proceed with life "in spite of, and even in terms of, the ugliness and meanness inherent in the human condition" (Murray, *Hero* 36). Both Vivaldo and Ida racially have moved toward a fuller knowledge of themselves and each other. If they remain together, it will be in a new way.

Although he racially grows in his relationship with Ida, Vivaldo, in his brief relationship with Eric, becomes a more sexually and emotionally mature person, causing him to challenge another repressive, social category. As with Ida, in a conversation with Eric, Vivaldo is able to finally implicate himself in Rufus' death. He recalls sleeping with Rufus the night before his death, and he gains the courage to articulate that guilt which remains pent up inside him.

> I had the weirdest feeling that he wanted me to take him in my arms. And not for sex, though maybe sex would have happened. I had the feeling that he wanted someone to hold him, to hold him, and that, that night, it had to be a man. I got in the bed and I thought about it and I watched his back, it was as dark in that room, then, as it is in this room, now, and I lay on my back and I didn't touch him and I didn't sleep. I remember that night as a kind of vigil.
>
> (288)

But even now, as he talks to Eric, Vivaldo is afraid that if he had taken Rufus in his arm that night, Rufus "wouldn't understand that it was—only love" (342). Here, Vivaldo is still not completely ready to touch and be touched by anybody.

But in contrast to Vivaldo and Rufus' final night together, Vivaldo and Eric's night together ends differently. Initially, Vivaldo comes to touch/love Eric, allowing Baldwin to show a non-sexual, non-erotic, intimate, touching relationship between two men. Eric and Vivaldo move around Eric's apartment, drinking and "watching the light come up behind the window and insinuate itself into the room" (343). At one point, Eric touchingly takes Vivaldo's "face between his hands and kisse[s] him, a light, swift kiss, on the forehead" (343), allowing intimacy to exist in their lives. After getting more ice from the kitchen, Eric returns with two glasses and the two touch glasses. Then they sat comfortably together, side by side, on Eric's bed within an inch of each other, as Vivaldo's uptight masculinity melts away. At this moment, neither has the desire to control himself nor dominate the other, developing an intersubjective relationship. They stare at each other and outward "because they were beginning to look inward. And Eric felt, for perhaps the first time in his life, the key to the comradeship of men" (344). Sitting there with their elbows nearly touching, as Eric listens to the rise and fall of Vivaldo's breath, "[t]hey were like soldiers, resting from battle, about to go into battle again" (344). Their feelings are express and their needs for the other are taken care of. Finally, they finish their drinks, take off their shoes, stretch out beside each other in bed, and Eric puts his head on Vivaldo's chest and falls asleep. The two are vulnerable and dependent upon each other, becoming emotionally open and physically tactile. Unlike in the Rufus and Vivaldo's final scene, this scene between Vivaldo and Eric has touching, intimacy, love, but no sex, though maybe sex could have happened. In this moment, Eric and Vivaldo "disturb the actual power relations that reproduce the gender system" and transcend the terror of being able to touch (Rutherford 46).

But sex does happen between Eric and Vivaldo in the Bethlehelm section of *Another Country.* Baldwin brings the self-identified homosexual Eric into a fluid and multiple space (another country) with the self-identified heterosexual Vivaldo, as the two connect emotionally and sexually and transcend racial and gender and sexual boundaries. "[T]here is only one sexuality," writes Guattari in *Soft Subversions,* "it is neither masculine, nor feminine, nor infantile; it is something that is ultimately flow" (47). In the Bethlehelm scene, Vivaldo struggles to accept the flow, a space already occupied by Eric. Vivaldo has already experienced the masculine, and now he is prepared to experience the feminine of the masculine, thereby challenging and undermining traditional gender/sexual categories.

> [H]e knew that he was condemned to women. What was it like to be a man, condemned to men? He could not imagine it and he felt a quick revulsion, quickly banished, for it threatened his ease. But at the very same moment his excitement increased: he felt that he could do with Eric whatever he liked. Now, Vivaldo, who was accustomed himself to labor, to be the giver of the gift, and enter into his satisfaction by means of the satisfaction of a woman, surrendered to the luxury, the flaming torpor of passivity, and whispered in Eric's ear a muffled, urgent plea.
>
> (385)

After struggling between his masculine and feminine desires, Vivaldo surrenders completely to the flow of his feminine desire, opening up to the role of passivity. In the sexual scene, Vivaldo imagines that he is making love to Rufus, that Eric is making love to him, and that he is Rufus making love to Eric. In the sexual moment between Vivaldo and Eric, in which Rufus is invoked, one can see where Vivaldo exists "in a region where there were no definitions of any kind, neither of color, nor of male and female. There was only the leap and the rending and the terror and the surrender" (301-302). Here, Vivaldo is visited with a vision of the world in which race, sex, and gender are social constructions.

Here, in this sexual moment, desire is completely liberated, existing outside of any repressive system or category. Yet, the relationship does not culminated into utopia. We are told that a repeat of the sexual encounter between the two might not happen again. "[I]f they should never lie in each other's arms again, there was a man in the world who loved him" (387), thinks Vivaldo. Although Vivaldo now knows that he is capable of loving and touching anyone, man or woman, black or white, he, as with Eric and his decision to live a homosexual life, *decides,* at this moment, that he wants to live a heterosexual life. And then, of course, anything can still happen, for life is resolutely indefinable and unpredictable. One day he can "get all hung up on some boy" (336).

Vivaldo's subjectivity becomes all of his experiences and encounters, including his unconscious (foreign) ones. "By recognizing *our* uncanny strangeness," writes Kristeva in *Strangers To Ourselves,* "we shall neither suffer from it nor enjoy it from the outside. The foreigner is within me, hence we are all foreigners. If I am a foreigner, there are no foreigners" (192), which means there is no Other. When the borders of Vivaldo's white male identity, as he knows it, become blurred and porous, and his conscious and unconscious desires, his secrets are accepted, Baldwin makes us understand the possibility of another way of existing, of conceiving of our subjectivity. Such moments emphasize the socially constructed nature of many of the categories that human beings use to define themselves and others— including, but not limited by race, sex, class, and gender.

Finally, Cass Silenski also undergoes a transformation, which allows her to enter Baldwin's another country. Cass comes from an upper-middle-class, New England family, which she rebels against by marrying Richard, the son of a Polish carpenter who wants to be a writer. As a result, she is condemned to live in social exile from her aristocratic, New England family and society, which is mostly white. In the beginning of the marriage, she is an innocent, childlike figure who is content being a wife, with her family being her only life. She lives what she thinks is a liberal, bohemian life in New York City, hanging out with writers and artists and musicians. But it is an insulated, patriarchal, white life.

But, later, Cass becomes slightly uncomfortable knowing that her needs and desires have become Richard's.

> He had been absolutely necessary to her—or so she had believed; ... and so she had attached herself to him and her life had taken shape around him. She did not regret this for herself. *I want him,* something in her had said, years ago. And she had bound him to her; he had been her salvation; ... She did not regret it for herself and yet she began to wonder if there were not something in it to be regretted, something she had done to Richard which Richard did not see. ... *I had to try to fit myself around [Richard] and not try to make [Richard] fit around me.*
>
> (107-108)

To accommodate Richard's desires, Cass has repressed her own desires and needs, creating a void within herself. In discovering this disturbing void, Cass realizes and admits that the image of Richard, which she has fashioned, is a false one. She begins to acknowledge, finally, that she has loved Richard as a child and that her true personality has been sublimated to his needs. As she awakens to her own needs and desires and Richard's literary success increases, she realizes he is more of a stranger to her.

But it is in her two trips to Harlem and her affair with Eric that Cass's small town white past, her marriage, and her liberal, aimless bohemian white world are seriously challenged, allowing her to begin to grow and mature, to begin to accept a blues perspective on life. Needing a scarf to attend Rufus' funeral in Harlem, Cass goes out on 125th street, looking for a store. Encountering Harlemites, Cass is "threatened by the existence of [their] otherness," becoming "afraid of these [black] people, these streets, the chapel to which she must return" (117). They offer her an alternative way to be, which she fears. Here, Cass is forced to see the limits of her white, liberal narrative, how it has insulated her from the world, forcing her to devalue people who are different. Reflecting on this trip, Cass thinks to herself, "You're so juvenile. ... You know so little ... about life. About women" (126). But, rather than seek self-knowledge, she retreats to her liberal, white world.

On her second trip to Harlem with Ida, Cass continues to be racially challenged. She reminds Ida that she lived a "sheltered life" in a small, New England town with very few blacks. But, Ida forces Cass to confront and understand the impact of racial oppression, the life and "the world" that "Rufus went through" (351). Cass wants to resist Ida in the same way that she wanted to resist Eric when he tells her about cops violently beating up homosexuals in Paris. Because of her white privilege, Cass has

never had to "deal with policemen in her life, and it had never entered her mind to feel menaced by one" (290). Also because of her white privilege, she has never had to contemplate her racial position, remaining "gleefully ignorant of the role of race" in society (Wise 23).

But, forcing Cass to deal with her internalized social mores and definitions about being white, a wife and mother, Ida gives Cass a lesson in the blues, assuring Cass that she can experience pain and suffering, that, in leaving Richard for Eric, she takes the risk of losing her children, her husband, and her home. Cass's safety is threatened. Later at *Small's Paradise* with Ida watching her, Cass, who feels exposed and in danger at *Small's,* becomes aware of the reversed gaze, of seeing herself through the eyes of a black woman. She "sensed, for the first time in her life, the knowledge that black people had of white people—though what, really, did Ida know about her, except she was lying, was unfaithful, and was acting"? (357) Although Ida's perception of Cass might be wrong, Cass, psychologically imagining the different space of the African American, becomes conscious of herself, causing her to turn the gaze around and look at and question her invisible, normalized (white) space. Here, Cass begins to shatter what Jacqueline Orsagh calls her "tight and idyllic" white world (59).

In experiencing some suffering of her own and in understanding and empathizing with the pain and suffering that Rufus endured, Cass intellectually is beginning to realize what Vivaldo and Eric already know—that suffering and pain are aspects of one's life, one's identity. "I am beginning to think ... that growing just means learning more and more about anguish" (405). With this knowledge, she can acknowledge and proceed with the world despite all its problems, knowing that the "misery in the world ... will never end because we're what we are" (406). To mature, to grow, to know one's self is to come to accept this dimension of life.

But it is in her affair with Eric that Cass's sexual and emotional growth and transformation really begins. Unhappy in her marriage, Cass decides to take a risk, jeopardizing everything. She visits Eric's apartment and begins a sexual affair where she connects sexually and emotionally with him, with the clear knowledge and understanding that the relationship does not have a future. But Cass is willing to transcend America's puritan morality and to accept the "tenuous nature of all human existence" (Murray, *Omni-Americans* 89), accepting the fact that life is never certain and secure. After having sex with Eric, Cass was "relieved to discover that she was apprehensive, but not guilty. She really felt that a weight had rolled away, and that she was herself again, in her own skin for the first time in a long time" (292). She becomes emotionally alive with Eric, feeling herself being "carried back to an unremembered, unimaginable time and state ... when she had not been weary, when love was on the road but not yet at the gates" (291). Unlike with her and Richard, Cass feels that she and Eric are "oddly equal" (291). When Eric tells her their affair, but not their friendship, is over, Cass thanks him for doing "something very valuable" for her (407), helping to liberate her from a dead life and marriage. Now, Cass is free to decide who she wants to be. We last hear that she is thinking about visiting New England with her boys. Seemingly, Cass, at thirty-four years of age, is going home to face her buried past, which is, for Baldwin, a prerequisite for moving forward.

In the end, all of the characters in **Another Country,** except Richard and Leona, and with Rufus as a catalyst, are moving toward Bethlehelm, as the title of Book Three suggests. Having engaged their buried past, having troubled traditional categories of family, race, class, region, and religion, having disturbed sexual identities, these characters—as they demand the creation of a complex subjectivity—have accepted the pain and suffering and anguish that is a part of the world, allowing them to empathize with others. Now they must decide who they are, and what they want to do, with the clear knowledge that this decision is also risky. Life is still unpredictable. These characters do not move into utopia. Instead, they exist in the world, living moment to moment and doing the best they can under any circumstances. They wish for the best and expect the worst. With this understanding, they are progressing toward a discovery of their own "indefinable, unpredictable" subjectivity, which ultimately hold the promise of a new and total understanding of themselves and of their subjectivities. They also signal another (blues) way to live in the world, beyond the categories that limit human desires and human affection.

### Notes

1. Though violently attacked by what Mike Thelwell calls the "New York literary establishment" for what Norman Podhoretz calls Baldwin's novel's "militancy and cruelty of its vision of life," I have no desire or inclination to defend Baldwin's *Another Country* against critics who hate the novel because of its subject matter. I suspect what ultimately spooked the New York critics was Baldwin putting homosexuality in non-traditional/non-stereotypical places. The critics, perhaps, would have been much more comfortable had homosexuality stayed in its traditional role in material drag queens. For those who need that defense, see Podhoretz's "In Defense of James Bald-

win," Mike Thelwell's "*Another Country*: Baldwin's New York Novel," and Fred L. Standley's "*Another Country,* Another Time."

2. Deleuze defines subjectivity not as a physical body but as a network of desires that flow in all direction, as in a machinic way.

3. In "The Uses of the Blues," Baldwin makes it clear that the blues is a metaphor for a particular life experience, a life experience that accepts pain and suffering and anguish. Therefore, in *Another Country,* he would accept a reading of both Leona and Eric as blues characters.

4. Baldwin takes the title of this third section from Yeats's poem "The Second Coming," which deals with the emergence of a new order, a new person.

5. James Baldwin was a great fan of Dostoevsky who also had similar notion of suffering. Dostoevsky believed that suffering, experienced in the depth of despair, can help to heal oneself.

6. In an interview with Eve Auchincloss and Nancy Lynch, Baldwin puts forth the argument that the African American experience is the only thing possible that can save the United States. He states, "If the Negro doesn't save this country, then nobody else can. ... I don't mean the Negro as a person; I mean the Negro as an experience—a level of experience American deny" (208).

### Works Cited

Auchincloss, Eve and Nancy Lynch. "Disturber of the Peace: James Baldwin." *The Black American Writer Vol. I: Fiction.* Edited by C. W. E. Bigsby. Baltimore, Maryland: Penguin Books, Inc., 1969: 199-215.

Baldwin, James. *Another Country.* New York: Vintage International, 1993.

———. "Everybody's Protest Novel." *The Price of the Ticket: Collected Nonfiction, 1948-1985.* New York: St. Martin's, 1985: 27-33.

———. "Here Be Dragons." *The Price of the Ticket: Collected Nonfiction, 1948-1985.* New York: St. Martin's. 1985: 677-690.

———. "The Uses of the Blues." *The Cross of Redemption: Uncollected Writings.* Edited by Randall Kenan. New York: Pantheon Books, 2010: 57-66.

Cohen, William A. "Liberalism, Libido, Liberation: Baldwin's *Another Country*." *The Queer Sixties.* Edited by Patricia Juliana Smith. New York: Routledge, 1999: 201-222.

Cixous, Hélène and Catherine Clement. *The Newly Born Woman.* Trans. Betsy Wing. Minneapolis: University of Minnesota Press, 1986.

Dunning, Stephanie. "Parallel Perversions: Interracial and Same Sexuality in James Baldwin's *Another Country.*" *MELUS* 36.4 (2003): 95-112.

Feldman, Susan. "Another Look at *Another Country*: Reconciling Baldwin's Racial and Sexual Politics." *Re-Viewing James Baldwin.* D. Quentin Miller, ed. Philadelphia: Temple University Press, 2000: 88-103.

Goldstein, Richard. "'Go the Way Your Blood Beats': An Interview with James Baldwin. *James Baldwin: The Legacy.* Edited by Quincy Troupe. New York: A Touchstone Book, 1989: 173-185.

Guattari, Felix. *Chaosophy: Soft Subversions.* Trans. David L. Sweet and Chet Wiener. New York: Semiotext(e), 1996.

Harris, Trudier. *Black Women in the Fiction of James Baldwin.* Knoxville: The University of Tennessee Press, 1985.

Kristeva, Julia. *Strangers to Ourselves.* Trans. Leon S. Roudiez. New York: Columbia University Press, 1991.

Martinez, Ernesto J. "Dying to Know: Identity and Self-Knowledge in Baldwin's *Another Country.*" *PMLA: Publications of the Modern Language Association of America* 124.3 (2009): 782-797.

Mosher, Marlene. "James Baldwin's Blues." *Critical Essays on James Baldwin.* Edited by Fred L. Standley and Nancy V. Burt. Boston: G. K. Hall & Co., 1988: 111-120.

Murray, Albert. *The Hero and the Blues.* New York: Vintage, 1973.

———. *The Omni-Americans: New Perspective on Black Experience and American Culture.* New York: Avon, 1970.

———. *Stomping the Blues.* New York: Da Capo, 1976.

Orsagh, Jacqueline E. "Baldwin's Female Characters: A Step Forward?" *James Baldwin: A Critical Evaluation.* Edited by Therman B. O'Daniel. Washington, D.C.: Howard University Press, 1977: 56-68.

Podhoretz, Norman. "In Defense of James Baldwin." *Five Black Writers: Essays on Wright, Ellison, Baldwin, Hughes, and Le Roi Jones.* Edited by Donald B. Gibson. New York: New York University Press, 1970: 143-147.

Rutherford, Jonathan. "Who's That Man." *"Male Order": Unwrapping Masculinity.* Edited by Rowena Chapman and Jonathan Rutherford. London: Lawrence & Wishart, 1988: 21-67.

Standley, Fred L. "*Another Country,* Another Time." *Studies in the Novel* 4.3 (Fall 1982): 504-512.

Terkel, Studs. "An Interview with James Baldwin." *Conversations with James Baldwin.* Edited by Fred L. Standley and Louis H. Pratt. Jackson: University Press of Mississippi, 1989: 3-23.

Thelwell, Mike. "*Another Country*: Baldwin's New York Novel." *The Black American Writer. Vol. I: Fiction.* Edited by C. W. E. Bigsby. Baltimore, Maryland: Penguin Books, Inc., 1969: 181-198.

Wise, Tim. *White like Me: Reflections on Race from a Privileged Son.* Revised and updated. Brooklyn: Soft Skull Press, 2008.

## Ben Robbins (essay date 2013)

SOURCE: Robbins, Ben. "Dangerous Quests: Transgressive Sexualities in William Faulkner's 'The Wild Palms' and James Baldwin's *Another Country.*" *Faulkner and the Black Literatures of the Americas: Faulkner and Yoknapatawpha, 2013,* edited by Jay Watson and James G. Thomas, Jr., UP of Mississippi, 2016, pp. 147-60.

[*In the following essay, originally presented at a conference in 2013, Robbins seeks "to demonstrate . . . a point of common ground" between Baldwin and Faulkner, observing that in their works both "utilize transgressive sex, in which alternative, challenging modes of sexuality disregard normative sociosexual practices to question—and even destroy—preexisting social boundaries."*]

In Baldwin's **"Autobiographical Notes,"** which prefaces his first essay collection from 1955, *Notes of a Native Son,* the author credits Faulkner as being one among a handful of writers who have begun to grapple with the question of black identity in America contextually, this "context being the history, traditions, customs, the moral assumptions and preoccupations of the country."[1] Baldwin names Faulkner alongside Robert Penn Warren and—most significantly for him among newly emerging writers—Ralph Ellison as the key literary figures making progress in this regard. Baldwin praises Faulkner for providing his generation of writers with a base from which it is possible to write about race in a way that encompasses its multiple contexts within American life and society. Revealing here is that Baldwin does not situate himself within a black writers' tradition, a northern black man instead seeing himself as the successor (along with Ellison) to two white southern writers. This demonstrates that the writer is a mobile subject, free to identify imaginatively across racial (and geographic) lines, gathering from the breadth of American literary tradition autonomously.[2] It is also a rhetorical gesture on Baldwin's part as we see him sidestepping his possible categorization as a successor to another Mississippi writer from Faulkner's generation, Richard Wright; as such, Baldwin refutes the essentialist notion of a black succession of literary heirs.

However, Baldwin's sense of debt to Faulkner does not preclude points of conflict in the literary relationship. In his essay **"Faulkner and Desegregation,"** published in 1956, Baldwin attacks Faulkner's statement that the process of racial integration in the South should "go slow." Baldwin opens the essay with a challenge:

> Any real change implies the breakup of the world as one has always known it, the loss of all that gave one an identity, the end of safety. And at such a moment, unable to see and not daring to imagine what the future will now bring forth, one clings to what one knew, or thought one knew; to what one possessed or dreamed that one possessed. Yet, it is only when a man is able, without bitterness or self-pity, to surrender a dream he has long cherished or a privilege he has long possessed that he is set free.[3]

Baldwin argues here that there are two possible responses to the dangerous processes of social reorganization—resistance and surrender—but only through the latter is one liberated. The passage reveals Baldwin's frustrations with Faulkner on the level of the social but also by implication on the level of the literary. Elsewhere, Baldwin credits Faulkner with the progressive—even courageous—exploration of race in his art through characters who wrangle with categories of identity; he comments in his 1972 memoir-cum-essay collection, *No Name in the Street,* that Faulkner's black characters are infused with "the torment of their creator."[4] In **"Faulkner and Desegregation,"** though, Baldwin expresses his anger that Faulkner fails to carry that work into his public statements on race, clinging instead to retrograde demarcations. Faulkner appears across Baldwin's essays as a split self—alternately progressive and backward, forward-thinking and restrictively traditional, his voice vacillating between the private realm of literature and the public realm as self-appointed spokesman for the national consciousness. When Baldwin accuses Faulkner of lacking courage, he successfully highlights how Faulkner's novels explore forms of social change and development that the same author publically advocates retreating from.

I am conscious that this may seem like a one-sided verbal exchange between Baldwin and Faulkner. Aside from Baldwin's prominence as a public intellectual in the late 1950s, Faulkner would likely have been aware of Baldwin's **"Faulkner and Desegregation"** essay, which appeared in *Partisan Review* in the fall of 1956. The journal was influential from the late 1930s to the early 1960s, a period during which it served as home to some of Faulkner's fellow modernists, publishing two of T. S. Eliot's *Four Quartets* (1943) and Clement Greenberg's high-profile essay on the cultural divide, "Avant-Garde and Kitsch" (1939). Faulkner also had a copy of Baldwin's debut semiautobiographical novel, *Go Tell It on the Mountain* (1953), in his library at Rowan Oak.[5] Faulkner's was a first-edition copy, which raises the tantalizing possibility that he had read the novel by the time **"Faulkner and Desegregation"** was published in 1956.

It is within Faulkner's fiction that the older author lives up to Baldwin's charge to face "the loss of all that gave one an identity, an end of safety." In the two novels I will consider, Faulkner's *If I Forget Thee, Jerusalem* (1939) and Baldwin's *Another Country* (1962), both authors use sex and sexuality as the tool that motivates and effects this loss of stable selfhood in the formation of a new social order. Baldwin has been recognized as an important writer on issues of race and sexuality in the twentieth century, but critics have approached these two areas of study separately until relatively recently. Dwight A. McBride, in his introduction to a collection of essays on the author, *James Baldwin Now* (1999), charges that scholarship has tended to relegate Baldwin to one or the other of the identity categories to which he can be said to belong, but that at the beginning of the twenty-first century, it is time for reassessment, since with the insights afforded by cultural studies models of analysis, we need not locate Baldwin as "exclusively gay, black, expatriate, activist, or the like but as an intricately negotiated amalgam of all of those things, which had to be constantly tailored to fit the circumstances in which he was compelled to articulate himself."[6]

The ability of Baldwin's work to transcend borders of race, gender, and sexuality is a crucial aspect of his ideological project that I am keen to demonstrate as a point of common ground with Faulkner. Both authors utilize transgressive sex, in which alternative, challenging modes of sexuality disregard normative sociosexual practices to question—and even destroy—preexisting social boundaries. Baldwin's novel, *Another Country,* is set in New York in the late 1950s and focuses principally on a group of Greenwich Village and Harlem bohemians: musicians, artists, actors, and writers among them. It radically addresses many sexual taboos of the time: homosexuality and bisexuality, interracial couples, and extramarital affairs. Baldwin himself moved to the Village in 1944, initially staying with his artist friend Beauford Delaney, who introduced him to the art world, along with blues and jazz, new genres of music to him at the time. The novel studiously imagines all its central male characters within equivalent and plural erotic configurations, as the three principal protagonists all engage in both homosexual and heterosexual sexual affairs with both black and white partners, creating a complex web of transgressive alliances. These couplings critique the American ideal of sexuality that, for Baldwin, has created absurdly fixed polarities, leaving us with "cowboys and Indians, good guys and bad guys, punks and studs, tough guys and softies, butch and faggot, black and white," as he writes in his essay **"Freaks and the American Ideal of Manhood,"** first published in *Playboy* magazine in 1985.[7]

To combat this, Baldwin gives us a vision of New York through the eyes of a mobile subject in search of sexual adventure. This motion is not simply a joyous surrender to new erotic possibilities, though; it is an often-painful flight from prescribed and imprisoning social identities. During the composition of *Another Country,* Baldwin himself was also engaged in a period of intense mobility; during the time he worked on the novel, between 1956 and 1961, he crossed the Atlantic by sea at least six times, traveling extensively within both Europe and North America. The novel was consequently written during the most transatlantic period in Baldwin's career up to that point. Baldwin had initially moved to Europe in 1948, urgently feeling the need to leave America in order to transcend the fatal social role he felt was thrust upon him as a black man in postwar New York; he felt he would have ultimately killed himself had he remained in the city, as his friend Eugene Worth did in the winter of 1946 by jumping from the George Washington Bridge.[8]

The pressures of the American metropolis that spurred Baldwin's restless movements are reflected in *Another Country.* We are presented with different phases of Baldwin's life story through two characters: a black jazz musician, Rufus, who stays in New York but is ultimately driven mad by the city and commits suicide, and Eric, a white gay southerner and actor, who leaves New York for Paris. Baldwin places these two characters in a sexual relationship before Rufus's suicide and Eric's journey to Europe, which results in a violent clash between alternate versions of the author. Eric senses that Rufus despises him as a southerner and has had sex with him to explore that hatred; comprehending this, Eric flees to Europe.[9] The consequences of their sexual relationship reveal how high the stakes are in the erotic landscape of Baldwin's novel: sex can be the catalyst for self-destruction or self-imposed exile. James A. Dievler demonstrates how Baldwin uses sex as a means to escape narrow identity categories in the sexual culture of the American postwar period, arguing that Baldwin is "advocating a postcategorical, poststructural concept of sexuality that we might call 'postsexuality.'"[10] He goes on to argue that Baldwin's emigration from America was necessary for his characters to express their own sense of being exiled, and as such the author prescribes this

state "as an almost necessary way of coming to terms with an exclusive culture."[11] While I similarly explore the link between sex and motion in *Another Country,* I see exile as but one form of generative motion the novel explores. Particularly in the character of Eric, we see the threat of total disconnection from one's native culture that might result from exile; when Eric is offered a role in a Broadway play while still in France he faces a dilemma as he realizes that "to accept it was to bring his European sojourn to an end; not to accept it was to transform his sojourn into exile" (184). Eric does return to New York to take up the role, ultimately seeing exile as a poor solution to his troubled relationship with the country of his birth. Baldwin came to the same decision in 1957 when he returned to the United States to witness the growth of the civil rights movement firsthand. Baldwin's characters actively fight against disconnection and an attendant erosion of resistance by seeking points of contact with the Other. My focus is on productive and dangerous acts of transgression that critique the way power polices the boundaries of social division. Such acts find multiple avenues of expression, most prominently, for Baldwin and Faulkner, in sex and art.

Between the extreme options of death or exile, Baldwin, in an attempt to explode social demarcations, drives the novel's bohemian crowd frenetically between zones of the city in pursuit of sexual adventure: white men seek adventures with black women uptown and black men with white women downtown. This reflects the way geographic space can become racialized in Faulkner's work; in *Light in August* (1932), for example, Joe Christmas journeys north to become black, leaving his southern white upbringing behind him.[12] Baldwin explores the motivation of eroticized movement through the character of the young artist and working-class Italian American, Vivaldo—himself an admirer of Faulkner's craft and work ethic—who makes frequent journeys to Harlem to sleep with prostitutes:

> For several years it had been his fancy that he belonged in those dark streets uptown precisely because the history written in the color of his skin contested his right to be there. He enjoyed this, his right to *be* being everywhere contested; uptown, his alienation had been made visible, and therefore, almost bearable. It had been his fancy that danger, there, was more real, more open, than danger was downtown and he, having chosen to run these dangers, was snatching his manhood from the lukewarm waters of mediocrity and testing it in the fire. He had felt more alive in Harlem, for he had moved in a blaze of rage and self-congratulation and sexual excitement, with danger, like a promise, waiting for him everywhere. . . . His dangerous, overwhelming lust for life had failed to involve him in anything deeper than perhaps half a dozen extremely casual acquaintanceships in about as many bars.

(135)

This passage demonstrates the manner in which characters seek out experiences loaded with perceived deviance. The sexual danger that Vivaldo explores in Harlem is double-edged: he relishes how his otherness in uptown New York contests his sense of belonging anywhere in the city as a stable subject, but his casual sexual encounters there are essentially superficial since the risks involved are low. Though charged with adventure, they are a mask for the deeper reorganization of self that is necessary; Vivaldo avoids confronting the "clash and tension of the adventure proceeding inexorably within" by "taking refuge in the outward adventure" (136), a subject adrift in the sexual territories of the modern metropolis. Baldwin makes us aware that a deeper engagement with the perceived Other and the geographical space in which one encounters otherness is required for personal and social progress.

On a similarly double-edged quest are the two central lovers of "The Wild Palms" sections of *If I Forget Thee, Jerusalem*. Faulkner once stated that Harry Wilbourne and Charlotte Rittenmeyer are looking in the novel "to escape from the world."[13] This need for escape takes them from New Orleans to Chicago, to a cabin in the Wisconsin woods, to a mining camp in Utah, on to Texas, back to New Orleans, and finally to the Gulf Coast. It is a utopian journey as the lovers attempt to craft an idealized union seemingly incommensurate with the world around them (and also wholly outside Yoknapatawpha). In the novel, the lovers' flight is presented as a joint attempt to liberate themselves from bourgeois constraints in New Orleans: Charlotte from her husband and children, Harry from his training to become a doctor. Charlotte's desire to escape from the orthodox configuration of the nuclear family is also a desire for constant motion in the pursuit of sexual intensity:

> [Charlotte] grasped [Harry's] hair again, hurting him again though now he knew she knew she was hurting him. "Listen: it's got to be all honeymoon, always. Forever and ever, until one of us dies. It cant be anything else. Either heaven, or hell: no comfortable safe peaceful purgatory between for you and me to wait in until good behavior or forbearance or shame or repentance overtakes us."[14]

Charlotte wants to put distance between herself and what she perceives as the static "purgatory" of marriage, the family unit, and the attendant framework of erotic inertia and control. She replaces these qualities with a new mode of sexual dialogue with Harry—hard, spontaneous, frank, and unchecked—which is the initial motor for their quest. Flight in both novels then is initially sexually motivated, as characters like Vivaldo and Charlotte seek a more productive, creative relationship to the Other, and to themselves, through erotic journeys fueled by a sense of transgressive (and potentially fatal) danger. Their attempts to forge alternative, challenging modes of sexuality result in flux and flight within and away from the inhospitable metropolis: New York for Baldwin, New Orleans and Chicago for Faulkner.

It is in this mobile state that these characters hope to fashion a new social identity through transgression against limiting demarcations of gender and race. Both Faulkner and Baldwin explore fears connected to this mode of being, but realize somewhat different conclusions. Baldwin shows how racial and gender antagonism can be confronted by engaging personally and intimately with all its points of contact, even when this inspires anxiety. In *Another Country*, Vivaldo enters into a deep and painful relationship with Ida, a black woman from Harlem, an affair far more challenging than any of his previous "casual acquaintance-ships" in that part of the city. Baldwin is frank about the destructive emotions this interracial union provokes in both lovers: fear in Vivaldo and anger in Ida. Late into the novel, after his long affair with Ida, Vivaldo experiences an epiphany. The insight he gains into how far he has come from his days of running Harlem is provoked by his superficial assessment of the sexual availability of a blonde woman in the bar in which he is sitting: "Something in him was breaking; he was, briefly and horribly, in a region where there were no definitions of any kind, neither of color, nor of male and female. There was only the leap and the rending and the terror and the surrender" (297).

Vivaldo has shifted into another territory beyond unchallenging promiscuity, a space without clear sexual polarities. Ida struggles to separate her generalizations about white people from the particular reality of her love for Vivaldo, illustrated when she confesses that "if any *one* white person gets through to you, it kind of destroys your—single-mindedness. They say that love and hate are very close together. Well, that's a fact. ... Wouldn't you hate all white people if they kept you in prison here?" (343-44) Through these lovers' difficulties in reconciling themselves to one another, Baldwin seeks to show how profound sexual engagement manifests, beyond mere sexual pleasure and the pursuit of orgasm, all of what he calls "the terrors of life and love" in his 1961 essay, **"The Black Boy Looks at the White Boy."**[15]

In "The Wild Palms," Charlotte's erotic life is spontaneous, unaffected, and productively linked to her creativity as an artist, but her androgyny and unselfconscious sexual desires result in her lover Harry's fear that he will be emasculated and engulfed by her. John Duvall names this dynamic a "counterhegemonic alliance" in which male dominance is subverted through its occupation of a passive position to the female.[16] Harry is a virgin when he enters the relationship with Charlotte, and he fears that her strength and relative sexual experience will unman him; he jokes, among many similar expressions, that Charlotte's courage makes her "a better man than I am" (586). The quip masks Harry's deeper anxiety about his disempowerment as a man within a union in which gendered roles have been subjected to flux. Metropolitan Chicago transforms under Harry's gaze into a feminine territory that threatens to consume him. In a Chicago department store in which Charlotte temporarily works, he observes a nightmare of "charwomen [who] appeared on their knees and pushing pails before them as though they were another species just crawled molelike from some tunnel or orifice leading from the foundations of the earth itself" (577). This image is part of the novel's critique of commerce and wage labor, in which, as Richard Godden argues, "Man appears just as an instrument of passage for the circulation of commodities," a world which the fugitive lovers attempt to escape in search of authentic experience.[17] However, Harry's view of commodity culture is clearly aligned with his sexual fears, what Anne Goodwyn Jones calls the novel's "patriarchal oxymoron" of masculine anxiety: Harry may place the twin specters of the feminine and commercial culture in a position of alterity, but the fear that accompanies this gesture undermines his relative position of patriarchal mastery.[18] In accord with his vision of the department store, Harry later describes his loss of virginity to Charlotte as the moment when you "feel all your life rush out of you into the pervading immemorial blind receptive matrix, the hot fluid blind foundation—grave-womb or womb-grave, it's all one" (589). Harry views the commercial metropolis through the same frame as his disproportionate and melodramatic response to a sexual act. The Chicago department store is conversely a world in which Charlotte feels at comparative ease; it is the market for her art objects, which she produces with an erotic charge. It would appear that Faulkner therefore wishes us to view Harry's emotional state critically as a consequence of his character's inability to manage his sexual relation to Charlotte productively. Where Charlotte's flight seems motivated by a search for increased sexual dynamism, Harry appears to run from the sight of his exaggerated fears. As such, Harry sabotages any possibility of purging the gender antagonism between them.

The aspect of the lovers' experience in "The Wild Palms" with which Faulkner most explicitly sympathizes is Charlotte's vital engagement with her art as an expression of sexual freedom. Charlotte produces a series of small, marionette-like sculptures that playfully depict compromised mock-heroic figures. Her work exhibits a deft blending of high and low imagery as she traverses categories of cultural distinction in a wild medley of visual referents not too dissimilar from the allusive practice of a high modernist work like *The Waste Land*:

> a Quixote with a gaunt mad dreamy uncoordinated face, a Falstaff with the worn face of a syphilitic barber and gross with meat (a single figure, yet when [Harry] looked at it he seemed to see two: the man and the gross flesh like a huge bear and its fragile consumptive keeper . . .), Roxane with spit curls and a wad of gum like the sheet music demonstrator in a ten cent store, Cyrano with the face of a low-comedy Jew in vaudeville.

(556-57)

Charlotte ambitiously references the Spanish, English, and French literary canons in her work, producing a cubist Quixote, a Falstaff that evokes the popular entertainment form of the bear fight, a commercially framed Roxane and a vaudevillian Cyrano de Bergerac. The troubling racism of this last image can perhaps be explained by the influences Charlotte gathers into her practice. Her ailing Falstaff alludes to Harry's first job in Chicago as a laboratory assistant in a charity hospital "making routine tests for syphilis" (552). The anti-Semitism of her Cyrano may also have been gleaned from Harry's own racist comments about his patients' sexual health: he claims that he doesn't need a microscope or any other medical method to diagnose them, because "all you need is enough light to tell what race they belong to" (552). It should also be noted that our view of Charlotte's art is mainly focalized through Harry's consciousness, so he may bring his own xenophobic interpretations to bear on her work. Her high-low fusions do not signal dumbing down but rather her mastery of a breadth of seemingly antagonistic influences. Charlotte's art insistently flattens out and reformulates high/low distinctions, a divide frequently coded along gender lines, as argued most influentially by Andreas Huyssen, who demonstrates how mass culture has been insistently gendered as female within patriarchal structures, associated with the rise of first-wave feminism's mass movements, which challenged and threatened male-dominated culture.[19] Working through Huyssen's ideas in relation to Faulkner's fiction, Jones sees Charlotte as an exception to Faulkner's codification elsewhere in his work of popular culture as a promiscuous and threatening woman because Charlotte maintains her sexual autonomy and integrity within a novel that broods on modes of cultural distinction.[20] Additionally, though, for a female artist whose integrity in the face of the market is continually questioned to produce such artful modernist objects shows how a woman can transcend prescribed positions within cultural practice and shatter oppositions within hierarchies of cultural taste.

***Another Country*** also shows how art has the potential to transcend cultural boundaries. Ida performs in a jazz bar in the East Village, which attracts an "unorthodox" (244) and racially diverse downtown crowd. Vivaldo worries about the power dynamic of "rank and color and authority" within which his role as audience member positions him in relation to the black jazz musicians (249). As if to counter Vivaldo's consciousness of hierarchical relations, Baldwin describes Ida's voice as having a quality that "involves a sense of the self so profound and so powerful that it does not so much leap barriers as reduce them to atoms ... it transforms and lays waste and gives life, and kills" (250). Ida's voice violently overcomes the racial and class divisions of the audience as she merges with the audience's collective identity by generating affect and emotional identification. I should acknowledge here that Harry's melodramatic "voice" is also an affective mode designed to generate emotional identification. But Harry's overwrought emotional register distances him from the communities of the novel and alienates the reader; we anxiously watch Harry turn material realities into threatening spectacles resulting in crippling states of mind, an imaginative journey we may recognize but on which we do not wish to accompany him. The important factor is the "sense of self" that Ida's voice retains; by powerfully asserting themselves through their art, characters such as Ida and Charlotte are able to shatter cultural boundaries that divide along lines of gender and race.

Vivaldo and Ida's relationship concludes in the narrative with a moment of intense physical identification in which the boundaries of the body are exploded: "His heart began to beat with a newer, stonier anguish, which destroyed the distance called pity and placed him, very nearly, in her body, beside that table on the dirty floor. ... He went to her, resigned and tender and helpless, her sobs seeming to make his belly sore" (416). Vivaldo shares Ida's physical and emotional pain and almost enters her body through the experience in a form of profound intimacy that is more metaphysical than sexual. This moment occurs simultaneous to Vivaldo's experience of intense feelings of anger, fear, and shame, stemming from Ida's confession that she has been having an affair with her manager. The experience as a whole, however, has a transformative effect on Vivaldo, leading him first to a moment of intense creative insight when a much-sought-after detail for his novel falls "neatly and vividly, like the tumblers of a lock, into place in his mind ... [which] illuminated, justified, clarified everything" (417). In addition, he experiences a calm postracial epiphany, now perceiving that "not many things in the world were really black, not even the night. ... And the light was not white, either, even the palest light held within itself some hint of its origins, in fire" (419-20). Finally, when Vivaldo weeps and Ida comforts him near the end of the passage, the text states that "she was stroking his

innocence out of him" (420) as he realizes a new maturity. Collectively, these developments point to a remolding of Vivaldo's consciousness.

While their relationship is left unresolved in its enduring tension between the liberatory and the traumatic, Baldwin sees the productive potential of the transmutative processes of transgressive sex. Baldwin elsewhere writes of the central gay couple in the novel, Eric and Yves, that "each was, for the other, the dwelling place that each had despaired of finding" (184). Though more anguished in nature, Vivaldo and Ida experience a similar realization, moving toward inhabiting one another's bodies as they exit from the novel. It becomes apparent that the other "country" Baldwin alludes to in the novel's title is not geographical but corporeal—the body of a lover with whom one has transgressed against social constraints. For Baldwin, one can find a home in the other through a painful, yet ultimately necessary, explosion of the boundaries of the self. Such a process reveals Baldwin's fierce advocacy of utopian discoveries of identity in new, nonnormative, or taboo forms of sexual practice. The utopian effect is of course slippery as it expresses an imaginative investment in a perfect place or state of mind that may not actually exist. The impalpable nature of social utopia achieved through sex is reflected in the unintelligibility of Baldwin's prose; it is an "unnameable heat and tension ... as close to hatred as it [is] to love" (420) that Vivaldo and Ida share in their final dramatic scene in the novel. Utopia gestures beyond the real; as Karl Mannheim argues, the utopian "state of mind" is "incongruous with the state of reality within which it occurs," and as such, in its orientation it aims to transcend reality.[21] Additionally, when such utopian orientations "pass over into conduct, [they] tend to shatter, either partially or wholly, the order of things prevailing at the time."[22] We recognize Baldwin looking toward what may lie beyond the borders of the individual body with a utopian mindset but finding it difficult to fully locate that idealized space of collective identity in the imagination as it transcends the real. Baldwin nevertheless forcefully asserts that attempting to locate such a space is of great social importance. As he argues at the close of his essay **"Down at the Cross,"** an important milestone in the author's increasingly active and vocal engagement with the civil rights movement published just five months after *Another Country* in November 1962,

> If we—and now I mean the relatively conscious whites and the relatively conscious blacks, who must, *like lovers,* insist on, or create, the consciousness of the others—do not falter in our duty now, we may be able, handful that we are, to end the racial nightmare, and achieve our country, and change the history of the world.[23]

Vivaldo senses that he is "very nearly" in Ida's body, tantalizingly close, yet still at some indecipherable degree of remove. This nevertheless represents a necessary step within Baldwin's utopian vision: merging consciousness with the racial Other with whom one engages as a lover.

This ultimate dissolution of self is one that Faulkner's characters do not realize. Where Baldwin gives us a final metaphysical merging of identities, at the close of "The Wild Palms," Harry's distance from Charlotte's body is emphasized. After Charlotte's death by the botched abortion she demands that Harry perform on her, Harry is imprisoned. His state at the conclusion of the novel demonstrates his resistance to some of the more drastic courses of action that Baldwin's characters pursue. First, he refuses flight from America when Rittenmeyer, Charlotte's husband, offers him money to jump bail and run to Mexico or some other faraway destination. Second, he rejects suicide as a way to end the pain of his incarceration, taking the cyanide tablet Rittenmeyer gives him after he rejects the money and crushing it against the bars of his cell window. Though Harry does thereby manage to refuse those paths of escape that eradicate or defer fully confronting the self's relationship to a hostile world in which social and sexual identity threaten to become warped, his rejection of suicide or flight does not strike the reader as noble in the same way as does Vivaldo and Ida's ongoing struggle with their identities and relation. In the end, Harry pays homage to a mere phantom, his imagination resurrecting the memory of Charlotte, "remembering, the body, the broad thighs and the hands that liked bitching and making things" (715). From his cell on the Gulf Coast, Harry attempts to reanimate the sensual charge of Charlotte's body by masturbating. Harry wishes to engage in erotically motivated productive grief, but the gesture does not compensate for the fear that he had of Charlotte as a sexual subject while she was alive. Harry idealization of the vitality of Charlotte's body and her creativity arrives too late to signal progression.

One may account historically for this discrepancy between the two writers' visions of the social potential of aberrant sexual culture. Faulkner wrote "The Wild Palms" in the late 1930s, at a time when the gender and sexual revolutions of the 1920s had been curtailed by the Great Depression. As John D'Emilio and Estelle B. Freedman argue, although American society was moving toward sexual liberalism in the 1920s, during the Depression "the consumerism and commercialized amusements that gave play to sexual adventure temporarily withered. Sobriety and gloom replaced the buoyant exuberance of the previous decade."[24] In a potentially ironic hangover from the Roaring Twenties, Chicago, one of the cultural hubs of that excessive decade, proves in the text to be particularly inhospitable to Harry

and Charlotte's sexual desires in the 1930s. Baldwin, however, published *Another Country* at the dawn of the sexual revolution of the 1960s. This potentially allowed him to see more clearly how the transgressive register of his fiction could effect tangible social change in the near future, hence his relative optimism. At the close of **"Faulkner and Desegregation,"** Baldwin advocates an urgent casting off of the constraints that society places on the individual, challenging the public Faulkner of the 1950s that "there is never time in the future in which we will work out our salvation. The challenge is in the moment, the time is always now."[25] Faulkner was able to channel this spirit of urgency into the potentially fruitful, and socially disruptive, erotic wanderings of Harry and Charlotte in "The Wild Palms," but it took Baldwin to visualize some two decades later what transcendent outcome such a traumatic sexual quest might produce.

*Notes*

1. James Baldwin, "Autobiographical Notes," in his *Collected Essays* (New York: Library of America, 1998), 9.

2. Such identification with Faulkner is, however, not without its dangers. Baldwin later wrote in *No Name in the Street* (1972) that Faulkner's situation as a canonical author within the white patriarchal tradition of history renders his work problematic for the black subject. Baldwin advocates the discovery of an autonomous black identity unshackled from white history, a move that for the black writer may entail a new relationship to his own influences, potentially resulting in a temporary rejection of Faulkner (Baldwin, *Collected Essays,* 380-82).

3. James Baldwin, "Faulkner and Desegregation," in his *Collected Essays* (New York: Library of America, 1998), 209.

4. James Baldwin, *No Name in the Street,* in his *Collected Essays* (New York: Library of America, 1998), 381.

5. Joseph Blotner, *William Faulkner's Library: A Catalogue* (Charlottesville: University Press of Virginia, 1964), 16.

6. Dwight A. McBride, introduction to *James Baldwin Now,* ed. Dwight A. McBride (New York: New York University Press, 1999), 2. In addition to this collection of essays, D. Quentin Miller, ed., *Re-Viewing James Baldwin: Things Not Seen* (Philadelphia: Temple University Press, 2000), and Douglas Field, ed., *A Historical Guide to James Baldwin* (Oxford: Oxford

University Press, 2009), have done much to foster critical engagement with Baldwin's work from the perspective of both race and sexuality.

7. James Baldwin, "Freaks and the American Ideal of Manhood," in his *Collected Essays* (New York: Library of America, 1998), 815.

8. Jordan Elgraby, "James Baldwin: The Art of Fiction No. 78," *Paris Review* 91 (Spring 1984), http://www.theparisreview.org/interviews/2994/the-art-of-fiction-no-78-james-baldwin.

9. James Baldwin, *Another Country* (1962; repr., London: Penguin, 2001), 53. Subsequent references to this edition will appear parenthetically in the text.

10. James A. Dievler, "Sexual Exiles: James Baldwin and *Another Country*," in *James Baldwin Now*, ed. Dwight A. McBride (New York: New York University Press, 1999), 163.

11. Ibid., 168.

12. William Faulkner, *Light in August*, in *Novels 1930-1935*, ed. Joseph Blotner and Noel Polk (New York: Library of America, 1985), 564-65.

13. Frederick L. Gwynn and Joseph L. Blotner, eds., *Faulkner in the University* (Charlottesville: University of Virginia Press, 1995), 178.

14. William Faulkner, *If I Forget Thee, Jerusalem*, in *Novels 1936-1940* (New York: Library of America, 1990), 551. Subsequent references to this edition will appear parenthetically in the text.

15. James Baldwin, "The Black Boy Looks at the White Boy," in *Collected Essays* (New York: Library of America, 1998), 277.

16. John N. Duvall, *Faulkner's Marginal Couple: Invisible, Outlaw, and Unspeakable Communities* (Austin: University of Texas Press, 1990), xiv.

17. Richard Godden, *Fictions of Labor: William Faulkner and the South's Long Revolution* (Cambridge: Cambridge University Press, 2007), 203.

18. Anne Goodwyn Jones, "'The Kotex Age': Women, Popular Culture, and *The Wild Palms*," in *Faulkner and Popular Culture: Faulkner and Yoknapatawpha, 1988*, ed. Doreen Fowler and Ann J. Abadie (Jackson: University Press of Mississippi, 1990), 146.

19. Andreas Huyssen, *After the Great Divide: Modernism, Mass Culture, Postmodernism* (Bloomington: Indiana University Press, 1986), 47.

20. Jones, "'Kotex Age,'" 145.

21. Karl Mannheim, *Ideology and Utopia: An Introduction to the Sociology of Knowledge* (1929), trans. Louis Wirth and Edward Shils (1936; repr., London: Routledge and Kegan Paul, 1949), 173.

22. Ibid.

23. James Baldwin, "Down at the Cross," in his *Collected Essays* (New York: Library of America, 1998), 346-47; emphasis added.

24. John D'Emilio and Estelle B. Freedman, *Intimate Matters: A History of Sexuality in America* (New York: Harper & Row, 1988), 241-42.

25. Baldwin, "Faulkner and Desegregation," 214.

## Adam T. Jernigan (essay date 2014)

SOURCE: Jernigan, Adam T. "James Baldwin's Post-Sentimental Fiction: From 'Previous Condition' to *Another Country*." *Arizona Quarterly*, vol. 70, no. 1, Spring 2014, pp. 173-201.

[*In the following essay, Jernigan mounts a defense of Baldwin against critics who have charged that his novels are guilty of the same sentimentalism that he attacks in his critical essays. He finds* Another Country *to be "the clearest example of the author's post-sentimental aesthetic."*]

One of the ironies of modern-day literary criticism is that the scholars who identify with the sensibility found in James Baldwin's essays frequently distance themselves from the author's fiction. The most recent enactment of this irony comes from Henry Louis Gates, Jr. and Hollis Robbins, who use their editorial introduction in *The Annotated Uncle Tom's Cabin* (2006) to undertake a "reassessment both of the novel and of James Baldwin's critique, itself now part of the canon" (xiii). Although Gates and Robbins state that their objective is to establish the transcendence of Stowe's novel over Baldwin's critique, their method is not, as might be expected, to refute the critique itself. Instead, they turn from Baldwin's essays to his literary output, and seek to show that Stowe's sentimental opus profoundly influenced Baldwin's fiction. Focusing on the "novels about race" that Baldwin wrote in the 1960s (xxviii), they argue that the "Manichean simplicity" which Baldwin diagnosed in *Uncle Tom's Cabin* (1852) would become the "central flaw" in works like **Another Country** (1962) and **Tell Me How Long the Train's Been Gone** (1968) (xxvi). Alleging that the characters in these novels "seem to exist as set pieces for ideological diatribes rather than nuanced explorations of their full humanity," they determine that Baldwin was never able "to extricate himself from sentimentality" (xxvi, xxx). Ultimately, then, it is a "reassessment" of Baldwin's fiction that enables Gates and Robbins to affirm the resilience of Stowe's novel. They close with the provocative suggestion that the essayist who was Stowe's most acute critical executor would also become the novelist who was her "twentieth-century literary heir"—amounting to little more than "Stowe in blackface" (xxx).[1]

Of course, Gates and Robbins were not the first critics to offer up Baldwin's fiction at the altar of his essays. As early as 1963, Irving Howe determined that while Baldwin had "secured his place as one of the two or three greatest essayists this country has ever produced," he had "not yet succeeded . . . in composing the kind of novel he counterposed to the work of Richard Wright" (362). In 1970, Albert Murray lamented that Baldwin's fiction had not lived up to the "assumed promise" of his early essays on aesthetics, and concluded that *Another Country* did not reflect the "sensibility of the novelist" any more than the "polemical essay, *The Fire Next Time*" (145, 148). Indeed, several years before Gates and Robbins weighed in with their critique, Lawrie Balfour observed that "much of the critical attention generated by **'Everybody's Protest Novel'** has focused on whether or not Baldwin's own novels escape his complaints about protest fiction" ("Finding" 75).

Despite being exposed to such negative assessments fairly early in his writing career, however, Baldwin persisted in thinking of himself primarily as a fiction writer. Baldwin's commitment to his artistic medium seems to have been motivated by his belief that it was not essays and speeches but novels and short stories that had the capacity to improve race relations in the United States. During the early 1960s, when he was frequently asked to speak on behalf of the Civil Rights Movement, Baldwin resisted being hailed as a spokesperson, observing that "it is impossible to be a writer and be a public spokesman, too, because the line which you have to use, really, in polemics, is to my point of view, just a little . . . too simple" ("James Baldwin, as Interviewed" 13). By the late 1960s, when his nuanced approach to race relations was being drowned out by polarized integrationist and separatist positions, Baldwin would have cause to reaffirm his fidelity to fiction: "I am *not* a public speaker. I *am* an artist." ("Disturber" 81). If Baldwin was optimistic about the prospect of improving U.S. race relations, it was because he believed in the transformative potential of a certain literary aesthetic.[2]

My aim in the present essay is not to adjudicate whether Baldwin's fiction can be found guilty of sentimentality, but rather to illuminate aspects of his fiction that have been occluded by the critical fixation with that question. More specifically, my aim is to inquire into what Baldwin's fiction might reveal about the forms and functions of a post-sentimental literary aesthetic. A close analysis of Baldwin's early stories and novels reveals that his critique of sentimentalism enabled him to rework the formal dimensions of his fiction, and in particular to develop new kinds of characters, scenes, and plots. Writing in an intellectual climate that Eric Porter has referred to as "the first post-racial moment" (3), Baldwin seems to have been hopeful that a post-sentimental aesthetic might light a path toward a post-racial society.[3] But what would a post-sentimental literary text look like? And what might such a text do? How would it operate on the world? What might it change?

Understanding how and why Baldwin sought to pioneer a post-sentimental aesthetic will require examination of not just his assessment of literary sentimentality but, more important, his analysis of the widespread cultural formation that we might call "sentimentalism." In early essays like **"Everybody's Protest Novel"** (1949), Baldwin argued that sentimentalism amounted to a dominant structure of feeling that was being reinforced by sentimental and anti-sentimental fiction alike. Marlon Ross was the first scholar to use Raymond Williams's concept of "structures of feeling" when discussing Baldwin's analysis of U.S. race relations. Writing about the construction of whiteness in *Giovanni's Room* (1956), Ross explains that Baldwin reframed the "race problem" as a problem inhering in the structure of feeling that sustains white security: "Baldwin makes the central problem of the twentieth century the strange meaning of being white, as a structure of feeling within the self and within history—a structure of felt experience that motivates and is motivated by other denials" (25). Building on Ross's analysis, the present essay examines how Baldwin used his fiction to interrogate the emotion system that underpins hegemonic whiteness in both its conservative and liberal manifestations.

On one level, then, Baldwin's early essays focused on how efforts to depart from literary sentimentality had bound novelists like Richard Wright ever more tightly to a moral-sentimental structure of feeling.[4] Yet Baldwin's larger purpose seems to have been to shed light on how his contemporaries might surpass the deadlock between the sentimental and the anti-sentimental—and begin to dissolve the dominant feeling structure. Indeed, I would venture that what has sustained scholarly interest in Baldwin's reassessment of Wright—and what differentiates it from scholarly reassessments of Baldwin—is that Baldwin rounded out his critique with a conceptual reformulation of sentimentality intended to light a path toward a post-sentimental literary aesthetic. In short, where Baldwin diagnosed an unwitting inheritance, he strove to create the conditions for a mindful departure.

Although most scholars have assumed that Baldwin's critique of sentimentalism was first elaborated in the essays just mentioned, I will show that Baldwin's critique was actually launched in his first published short story, **"Previous Condition"** (1948). By focusing the first section of this essay on **"Previous Condition,"** I hope to clarify why Baldwin thought it was so important to foster a post-sentimental literary tradition. Written when he was just twenty-four, Baldwin's semiautobiographical story offers a compelling account of how a sentimental structure of feeling could keep Americans invested both in the practice of racial ascription and in the enforcement of ascriptive hierarchies. The story interrogates how white Americans are able to generate a felt sense of security and self-possession by projecting economic and bodily insecurity onto black Americans. As its title suggests, **"Previous Condition"** constitutes both an homage to literary predecessors like Stowe and Wright and an explanation of why Baldwin found it necessary to renounce their aesthetic strategies.

In the second section of this essay, I will turn to Baldwin's third novel, ***Another Country,*** which I take to be the clearest example of the author's post-sentimental aesthetic. My claim in the second section will be that Baldwin's insights about sentimentalism motivated his attempts, throughout the 1950s and 1960s, to forge a post-sentimental literary mode that I refer to as "affective realism." In Baldwin's view, the best way to liberate Americans from their reliance on racial stereotypes was to help them confront and accept the disquieting sides of their affective lives. In novels like ***Another Country,*** I argue, Baldwin reworked the formal dimensions of his fiction in hopes of encouraging a closer attention to the reverberations of affect within and between bodies. Whereas some critics have dismissed Baldwin's fiction for its dalliance with polemics, I aim to uncover the understated, antipolemical, connective side of the author's aesthetic.

### I. THE SAFETY OF SENTIMENTAL SCRIPTS: "PREVIOUS CONDITION"

Published in *Commentary* in October of 1948, **"Previous Condition"** could almost be described as a work of literary criticism. As the story opens, readers learn that the narrator-protagonist, a twenty-five-year-old black actor named Peter, has just returned to New York City from a theatrical production in which he starred as "a kind of intellectual Uncle Tom, a young college student working for his race" (**"Previous"** 83). Toward the end of the story, Peter will joke with his white girlfriend, Ida, that his casting agency

has just landed him "the lead in *Native Son*" (95). These allusions to *Uncle Tom's Cabin* and *Native Son* set the stage for Baldwin to explore how a repertoire of familiar character types could impact the lives of black Americans like Peter. On the most obvious level, Baldwin's story constitutes a critique of the state of national theater in the 1940s, when talented black actors could only find work in a limited number of conventional roles. On a deeper level, however, the story offers an analysis of why, outside the theater, white Americans persisted in attributing certain character traits to black Americans. As we will see, the plot of **"Previous Condition"** turns on its protagonist's epiphany about the psychological forces underpinning such attributions. Because **"Previous Condition"** is semiautobiographical, I will suggest that a similar revelation may have been what propelled Baldwin to devote the greater part of his writing career to elaborating a mode of post-sentimental fiction.

Although **"Previous Condition"** opens as its protagonist is waking up in his Greenwich Village apartment, the first few pages serve primarily to apprise readers of significant events in the protagonist's childhood. Peter tells of being raised by his mother in the black section of a racially segregated town in New Jersey. Feeling hemmed in by the "old shack" in which his mother resided, he spent many afternoons "wandering by [him]self" through the rest of the town (85). "I hated my mother for living there," Peter recalls. "I hated all the people in my neighborhood. ... When the landlord came around they paid him and took his crap" (85). Several years later, he and his friends "formed gangs" and continued to wander through town, occasionally meeting with "white boys and their friends" to throw "rocks and tin cans at each other" from "the opposite sides of fences" (87). As a teenager, however, Peter began to notice that, despite their adolescent rebelliousness, his friends were about to capitulate to the same system that had exploited the members of their parents' generation. In Peter's memory, this series of events takes on the quality of scenes in a drama whose *dénouement* is all but predictable. "They were going to settle down and ... pay the same rents for the same old shacks and it would go on and on" (87). Refusing to play a part in that drama, the sixteen-year-old protagonist decided to "run away" from both his mother and the town (85).

Proceeding to discuss his early adulthood, Peter tells of spending a number of years "running around" in cities across the continental United States (88). "I'd knocked about through St. Louis, Frisco, Seattle, Detroit, New Orleans, worked at just about everything" (85). Although he shares few details about what happened to him during those years, he does mention that he "learned a few things" about the judgments that others would make about his character.

I'd learned never to be belligerent with policemen, for instance. ... What might be accepted as just good old American independence in someone else would be insufferable arrogance in me. After the first few times I realized that I had to play smart, to act out the role I was expected to play. ... When I faced a policeman I acted like I didn't know a thing. ... I looked as humble as I could and kept my mouth shut and prayed.

(88-89)

Here, significantly, Baldwin invokes the motif of acting to capture the way in which interactions between whites and blacks often seem to be mediated by a repertoire of fantasmatic roles and scripts. What Peter "learned" from his first few encounters with police officers was that when he exercised his citizenship rights, those officers perceived him as a "belligerent" Bigger Thomas. What he learned from subsequent encounters was that in order to preempt this perceptual bias, he had to assume the "expected" role of a "humble" Uncle Tom. In this way, the first pages of **"Previous Condition"** treat the protagonist's early recognition of how a person can become caught in the double bind of antithetical yet mutually reinforcing stereotypes.

The protagonist's experiences in New Jersey and elsewhere should be sufficient to explain why, on the first page of **"Previous Condition,"** Peter can be found lying on his back in a cold sweat, recovering from a "nightmare" whose contents he cannot remember—though he knows he "had been running" (83). Yet those early experiences also constitute the backstory for the central plot in **"Previous Condition,"** which turns on Peter's attempts to achieve a felt sense of belonging in New York City. Like many other artists of his generation, Peter rents an apartment in the bohemian neighborhood of Greenwich Village. Having realized that some landowners in the Village would be unwilling to lease an apartment to a black man, he entreated a white friend, Jules, to secure a room for him.[5] On the morning of his third day in the apartment, however, Peter is summoned from his bed by the sound of his landlady's footsteps on the stairs. When he opens the door, the landlady wastes no time in evicting him, asserting, "I can't have no colored people here" (91). As the landlady explains that her female tenants are "afraid to come home nights," Peter becomes aware that she too appears "frightened to death" (91). Witnessing the intensity of her emotions, Peter realizes that it would be nearly impossible to shake the image of him that she has brought to their encounter. Unsurprisingly, his insistence that the other tenants "ain't gotta be afraid of me" comes as little reassurance to the landlady. "You get outa my house!" she shrieks. "Why don't you go on uptown, like you belong?" (91).[6]

In this way, Baldwin uses the first half of **"Previous Condition"** to address a social problem that would have been familiar to most readers of *Commentary*: namely, the problem of racial stereotypes. During the nineteenth century, the word "stereotype" referred to the metal plates used by printers to duplicate text or imagery onto a page. In the early 1920s, however, Walter Lippmann applied the word to the sphere of everyday life. In *Public Opinion* (1922), Lippmann argued that individuals rely upon abstract "picture[s] in their heads" to respond efficiently to external stimuli (4). Describing how people make recourse to stereotypes in their encounters with new persons and environments, he explained that "we notice a trait which marks a well known type, and fill in the rest of the picture by means of the stereotype we carry about in our heads" (89). Whether or not Baldwin was familiar with Lippmann's work, his analysis of American race relations came to be shaped by a similar understanding of the ways in which mental images could premediate how people approach one another in the real world.[7] For black Americans, the persistence of racial stereotypes has meant that "a great deal of one's energy is expended in reassuring white Americans that they do not see what they see" (**"The White Man's Guilt"** 722).[8]

Yet if the first half of **"Previous Condition"** focuses on its protagonist's exhaustion with the typed roles that he has been made to play both inside and outside the theater, the second half focuses on the protagonist's dawning realization that he and his girlfriend have been activating those same roles in order to maintain a sense of emotional security within their relationship. After he has been evicted from his Village apartment, Peter becomes aware that the pitying "concern" proffered by his white girlfriend, Ida, functions less to mitigate his feelings of vulnerability than to shore up her own feelings of security and virtue (**"Previous"** 96). At the same time, Peter comes to perceive that he has been trading on Ida's "subterranean Anglo-Saxon guilt"—and trading on his own "value as forbidden fruit"—in order to elicit certain responses from her (89). He perceives that he has been wielding his symbolic identity "like a knife," and that he has been "twist[ing]" the knife to "get his vengeance" (89). Put differently, Peter begins to realize that he has been "us[ing] his color like a shield" in order to "get what he wants" (89).

In the second half of the story, then, Peter comes to realize that he and Ida have been trafficking in images that serve to shore up their own sense of emotional security, images that keep each insulated from the vulnerability of self and other. It is at this point that the protagonist arrives at what his author would refer to as a revelation. "I knew these things long before I realized that I knew them and in the beginning I used them, not knowing what I was doing. Then, when I began to see it, I felt betrayed" (89). Peter's realization of how he has "used" racialized images and scripts is what leads him to joke with Ida that he has been offered "the lead in *Native Son*" (95). But he promptly adds that he "turned it down," explaining, "Type casting, you know. It's so difficult to find a decent part" (95). Recognizing the irony in Peter's voice, and riffing on the absurdity of refusing such a part, Ida replies, "The very *idea* of offering you *Native Son!* I wouldn't stand for it" (95). While this exchange amounts to a moment of levity between the characters, it also carries an acknowledgment of the gravity of their predicament. For Peter's reference to *Native Son* reflects his awareness that if he and Ida were to continue to traffic in defensive emotions such as pity and guilt, they might end up inflicting injuries not unlike the ones that Wright's characters perpetrate against one another. Notwithstanding his feelings about the security operations of white people, it dawns on Peter that his own pursuit of emotional security threatens to become his most acute personal danger. "I'm not worried about that miserable little room," he exclaims; "I'm worried about what's happening to me, *to me,* inside" (93).

In this way, Baldwin uses the second half of **"Previous Condition"** to reveal how a moral-sentimental structure of feeling could underpin the existence of racialized images and roles. Contravening the common sense about the genesis of stereotypes, Baldwin suggests that their origins lie not in literary and cultural texts, much less in direct observations or experiences, but rather in a feeling structure that relies upon morally coded images as moorings for sentimental emotions. Although Baldwin would never organize an entire essay around the topic of stereotypes, his early stories and reviews amount to an extended meditation on why it was that, in the theater of the white imagination, blacks were often cast as victims and perpetrators, sinners and saints. In Baldwin's view, the moral predication of black Americans as victims and perpetrators, exemplified by figures like Uncle Tom and Bigger Thomas, had come to play such an important role in organizing the sense that white Americans had of themselves—of their own virtue and vulnerability—that it prevented liberals and conservatives alike from perceiving black Americans in all their complexity, and hence from entering into complex relations with them.

Baldwin offers a similar analysis in the early literary review, **"The Image of the Negro"** (1948), for example, in which he suggests that the white majority have been able to disavow their vulnerability to economic and bodily volatility by projecting such volatility onto unconscious "images" of black Americans. By conjuring images of black Americans in the charged space of unconscious fantasy, white Americans are able to replace affects related to the contin-

gencies of their own lives with stabilizing emotions organized around fixed and familiar images of others. Put more concretely, whites are able to replace decompositional affects like economic anxiety and erotic desire with sentimental emotions like pity and guilt, fear and fascination. Although these racialized images reside largely in unconscious fantasy—its own affectively charged fictional space—they exert real effects upon U.S. social and political life. In the first place, the dependence on such images results in the pernicious tendency to associate blacks with poverty, violence, sexuality, and so on. In the second place, the dependence keeps people invested in the enforcement of ascriptive hierarchies. In an essay suggestively titled **"The White Problem"** (1964), Baldwin explains: "What it means to be a Negro in this country is that you represent, you are the receptacle of and the vehicle of, all the pain, disaster, sorrow which white Americans think they can escape. This is what is really meant by keeping the Negro in his place" (78).[9]

In sum, while the first half of **"Previous Condition"** demonstrates how stereotypes can impact the everyday lives of black Americans like Peter, the second half of the story asks where these stereotypes come from and why they have been so resilient. The answers to these questions emerge not from any new information about how the white characters treat the protagonist, but from the latter's reflexive insights about his own recourse to stereotypes. If readers identify with Baldwin's protagonist, they do so not because he is constructed, like the protagonist of a sentimental novel, as a morally innocent or virtuous character, but rather because he is a morally complex character who relinquishes his attachment to his own innocence just enough to experience a personal revelation that pushes him toward self-transformation.

But if **"Previous Condition"** turns on a series of revelations that suggest Peter has acquired a good deal of critical insight about his predicament, the story also acknowledges that he has yet to discover a new mode of being in the world that would enable him to connect in fulfilling ways with others. Toward the story's end, Peter decides not to audition for any more sentimental stage dramas and resolves to leave the liberal mecca of midtown. He boards an uptown train and makes his way to a "rundown" Harlem blues bar (**"Previous"** 99). Yet Peter will not feel any more "in his element" in Harlem than he had in the Village; for he experiences this return to a predominantly black neighborhood as a capitulation to the white world's attempts to keep him "in his place" (100). "I longed for some opening, some sign, something to make me part of the life around me. But there was nothing except my color" (100). Commenting on his outsider status in the worlds of both whites and blacks, he concludes, "I didn't seem to have a place" (100).[10] Finding himself with nowhere else to go, however, the protagonist attempts to create an "opening" by offering to buy a drink for a woman who appears to be a regular patron of the bar (100). Ironically, Baldwin's story comes to a close when, accepting this offer, the woman invites the protagonist to tell her about himself: " 'Baby,' said the old one, 'what's your story?' " (100). Absorbed by the voice of Ella Fitzgerald on the jukebox, and startled by the reverberant "shaking" of his body, Peter can only reply, "I got no story, Ma" (100).

By concluding his first published story with the protagonist's admission that he has "no story," Baldwin may have been acknowledging that he too had yet to develop a literary aesthetic of his own. If the author of **"Previous Condition"** was resolved, like his protagonist, to turn the page on literary sentimentality, what kind of aesthetic would he develop instead? Throughout the 1950s and early 1960s, Baldwin would pioneer a post-sentimental realist aesthetic intended to help readers move beyond racialized images and scripts. In his magnum opus, *Another Country,* Baldwin attempts to dissolve such images through a particular articulation of song and story. In **"Many Thousands Gone"** (1951), Baldwin suggests that the surest way to dispense with racial stereotypes is to tell, as it were, the "story" of the black American: "To tell his story is to begin to liberate us from his image and it is, for the first time, to clothe this phantom with flesh and blood" (**"Many"** 34). The title of **"Many Thousands Gone"** is taken from a nineteenth-century spiritual whose melody would eventually be adapted into the Civil Rights anthem, "We Shall Overcome." Lest the significance of his title be lost on readers, Baldwin opens the essay by observing, "It is only in his music ... that the Negro in America has been able to tell his story" (19). In the next section, then, I will explore how Baldwin's critique of literary sentimentality, together with his discovery of a post-sentimental strain in early African-American blues music, pushed him to rework the formal dimensions of his fiction.

## II. DEVELOPING A POST-SENTIMENTAL AESTHETIC: *ANOTHER COUNTRY*

In the sentimental novel, it is the sanctity of the self and the home—evidenced by access to stabilizing conventions of emotional response—that serves as the ground for expanding the bounds of fellow feeling. As scholars of nineteenth-century literature have observed, sentimental novelists constructed the family as the locus of privileged emotional attachments, and they presumed those attachments to be similar across all families. At the same time, by codifying a set of expressive conventions, sentimental novelists rendered the emotions of characters instantaneously legible to other characters and readers. These presumptions and conventions set the stage for virtuous protagonists to sympathize with the anguish felt by characters who had been separated from their family members—thereby modeling a sympathetic responsiveness that could be emulated by readers. Yet insofar as sentimental fiction trained the reader to reach out, from a position of relative security, to the members of other families in need, it risked predicating the virtue of the reader upon the vulnerability of socially differentiated others. What's more, pity, guilt, and other stabilizing emotions could function as defense mechanisms not only against acknowledging one's own vulnerability but against apprehending the vulnerability of others.

In the 1950s and 1960s, Baldwin sought to pioneer a post-sentimental aesthetic in which the subject's exposure to volatility would be taken as the default human condition as well as the basis for reimagining life in common. Each of Baldwin's early novels might be said to open with the protagonist's exposure to a destabilizing condition or event, and then to build dramatic tension around the question of how the protagonist will respond. In *Go Tell It on the Mountain* (1953), for example, fourteen-year-old protagonist John Grimes meets with the upheaval of puberty, and he flees to the sanctuary provided by the church. In *Giovanni's Room,* twenty-something protagonist David confronts his desire for another man, and he retreats to the safe haven of a culturally sanctioned form of intimacy. In Baldwin's third novel, *Another Country,* vulnerability is generalized as the everyday condition of a black man who loses his job and his income, and is threatened with losing his home and his social moorings. If the sentimental novel was grounded in the sanctity of the self and the home, Baldwin's third novel treats the struggles of a protagonist who has, in the words of Bessie Smith, "*no place to go*"—who has neither a stable home nor a family that he can turn to (*Another* 49). Influenced by early female blues singers like Smith, Baldwin constructs the characters of *Another Country* as sonorous subjects whose internal tensions will only be mitigated when they can accept the "shaking" and "trembling" of the body, let their vulnerabilities resound within an audiosocial space, and discover various affective harmonies with others.

The first chapter of *Another Country* is a lesson in just how quickly a person can lose his job, lose his apartment, and—having lost his self-esteem in the process—find himself too ashamed to appeal for help. The character at the center of this chapter is a talented jazz drummer who has been without a home for more than a month and without a gig for almost half a year. When the novel opens, the character has just emerged from a grindhouse cinema, where he had sequestered in hopes of settling a sleep deficit. It is not until the second paragraph of the book that readers learn the character's name: Rufus Scott. This deferral of nominal reference serves to reinforce Baldwin's portrayal of his character's phenomenological disorientation. For if readers are not provided with the point of reference comprised by the protagonist's proper name, it is because Rufus has begun to lose his own sense of locality and directionality.

Readers approaching **Another Country** for the first time may be equally disoriented by the frequency with which Rufus's movements are interrupted by involuntary memory. Realizing that he might know some of the musicians at a nearby jazz club, Rufus heads north on Seventh Avenue in hopes that one of the guys on the stand might "lay enough bread on him for a meal" (4). Upon approaching the club, however, he is curbed by the thought that the regulars who knew him as a successful musician will now look at him "with pitying or scornful or mocking eyes" (5). At the same time, the recollection of a period in his life when he had felt in charge—"on the stand or in the crowd, sharp, beloved, making it with any chick he wanted"—triggers a second memory that is located not so much in the mind as in the visceral depths of the body (5). "He remembered Leona. Or a sudden, cold, familiar sickness filled him and he knew he was remembering Leona" (6). Baldwin will use the next thirty pages to familiarize readers with the events that have solidified Rufus's relationships with both his girlfriend, a working-class white woman named Leona, and his best friend, a twenty-eight-year-old Italian American named Vivaldo Moore. At the same time, by allowing the forward movement of the narrative to be all but taken over by the backward movement of memory, Baldwin is able to steep readers in the interference pattern that makes up the present tense of Rufus's life.

If layering multiple histories and temporalities creates an affective field that implicates the reader, it also deepens the reader's understanding of Rufus's implication in his own demise. For although Rufus is on the skids, he is not constructed as the kind of innocent victim common to sentimental fiction. When Rufus finds that he has become dependent on the money that Leona brings home from her job as a waitress, he defends against his feelings of dependency and guilt by displacing them onto her. Suspecting that her attraction to him is based largely on "his sex," and observing that she seems to credit blacks with harboring a "sexual secret," Rufus begins to accuse Leona of sleeping with other black men behind his back (68, 53). Soon enough, their defensive suspicions spiral into acts of aggression. "They fought each other with their hands and their voices and then with their bodies" (53). When Rufus

realizes that these transactions leave him "utterly unsatisfied," he begins to flee into bars, where a mixture of "triumph" and "guilt" pushes him "to pick fights with white men" (53).[11]

Gates and Robbins justify their assessment that the "central flaw" of **Another Country** inheres in characters who "seem to exist as set pieces for ideological diatribes" by citing a brief passage from Baldwin's novel in which Rufus meets Leona for the first time. Gazing into the face of this Southern white girl, Rufus is struck by a memory of being stepped on by a white drill sergeant in the South: "He remembered, suddenly, his days in boot camp in a Southern boot camp in the South and felt again the shoe of a white officer against his mouth" (12).[12] Finding fault with the way in which this passage elicits emotion from readers, Gates and Robbins offer the following gloss on its emotional pragmatics: "See that white girl, feel that boot!" ("Introduction" xxix). They complain that Baldwin is too heavy-handed in "telling" readers how they "should feel about the novel's action" (xxvii). But far from playing up the subjective dimensions of Rufus's experience, Baldwin describes only the physical actions of the protagonist and the drill sergeant. Nor does he use language that would invite a strong emotional response from readers. Indeed, where Gates and Robbins use the evocative word "boot," Baldwin uses the more neutral "shoe."

The part of Gates and Robbins's analysis that I find constructive is their account of how Rufus's experience of racialized violence shapes his interactions with white people in the present. The paragraph in which Rufus is reminded of the drill sergeant's shoe comes to a close when Rufus acknowledges that his attacker had "vanished ... beyond the reach of vengeance" (**Another** 13). Picking up on Rufus's desire for "vengeance," Gates and Robbins observe that Rufus will fulfill this desire by taking advantage of the Southern white girl: "When Rufus takes Leona, Rufus is exacting Uncle Tom's revenge" (xxix).

Although I suspect that Gates and Robbins may be right to draw attention to the sentimental dimension of the early encounters between Rufus and Leona, they neglect to add that the scenes they focus on take the form of memories recounted in the first twenty pages of the novel. In subsequent pages, Rufus will make an effort to move beyond the sentimental scripts that organize his interactions with Leona. Indeed, while Baldwin may use the early pages of his novel to thematize the sentimentalism that pervades American culture, the greater part of **Another Country** treats the efforts of various characters to move beyond the sentimental feeling structure that mediates relations between them. In that sense, the central focus of Baldwin's novel is not the "big-booted oppressions of bigotry"—to borrow a phrase from Patricia Williams—but rather the "small aggressions of unconscious racism" (61).

In the sentimental novel, characters are framed as worthy of sympathetic identification in part because they are endowed with the moral purity that comes with being deprived of agency—deprived, that is, of the ability to improve their situation, and of the ability to harm others. In post-sentimental novels like *Another Country,* by contrast, characters become worthy of sympathetic identification because they endeavor to build a life in a world full of volatility, and they struggle to avoid taking out their frustrations on others. Characters like Rufus are neither bereft of agency nor imputed with privileged insight and moral authority. My own interpretation of Rufus comes closest to the one offered by James Campbell, who ventures that "Rufus Scott is probably Baldwin's most fully realized black character after Peter in **'Previous Condition'**" (155). In interviews, Baldwin refers to Rufus as a character who "had never appeared in fiction before" (**"James Baldwin Interviewed"** 104). He observes that Rufus is not imputed with the innocence of a sentimental victim like Uncle Tom: "There are no antecedents for him. He was in the novel because I didn't think anyone had ever watched the disintegration of a black boy from that particular point of view. Rufus was partly responsible for his doom, and in presenting him as partly responsible, I was attempting to break out of the whole sentimental image of the afflicted nigger driven that way (to suicide) by white people" (104).

Of course, if it would be a mistake to read Rufus as another Uncle Tom, it would also be a mistake to read him as another Bigger Thomas. Some literary critics have suggested that scenes like the one in which Rufus fights with Leona justify a strong moral evaluation of his character. For example, Houston Baker has concluded that Rufus is a "raging, screaming, sexually-aggressive Black creator pleading for the white world's acceptance" ("The Embattled" 68). In my reading, however, both Rufus and Leona amount to morally complex characters whose recourse to "raging" and "pleading" is part of a larger struggle to admit their vulnerabilities and see one another through. Rufus's abuse of Leona might be taken as an example of what Balfour refers to as one of the "most insistent points" of Baldwin's fiction, namely, that "the experience of victimization does not exhaust the experience or identity of individuals who suffer systematic oppression; nor can it be disentangled from the experience or identity of individuals who are privileged by such oppression" (*Evidence* 103).

In their introduction for *The Annotated Uncle Tom's Cabin,* Gates and Robbins also argue that in ***Another Country,***

Baldwin's obligation to "show or to dramatize" gets trumped by his temptation to "tell us ... the way that we should feel about the novel's action" (xxvii). My claim is that while the characters' memories and flashbacks may be mediated by a prominent narrative voice, Baldwin minimizes the narrative voice when dramatizing action in the present. He does this in order to reopen the question of how characters and readers might feel within the unfolding present. Balfour makes a similar point: "As a writer, Baldwin strains for the words that will move his readers without making them conscious of his efforts or presuming to control exactly how they will respond" (*Evidence* 119).

Finding himself "bowed down with the memory of all that had happened" during those months, Rufus is eventually driven to the doorstep of his best friend, Vivaldo (***Another*** 49). Rufus is astonished by the warm reception he receives from Vivaldo. "You've had us all scared to death, baby. We've been looking for you everywhere" (47). The expression of concern, even coming from his best friend, hits Rufus with a force that might as well be physical. "It was a great shock and it weakened Rufus, exactly as though he had been struck in the belly. He clung to Vivaldo as though he were on the ropes" (47). Here, Baldwin invokes the metaphor of boxing to convey the depth of the affective connection between Rufus and Vivaldo. The metaphor also reverberates with the history that has solidified their friendship. For one year earlier, when Vivaldo's girlfriend, Jane, had made an inflammatory remark in an Irish American bar, and Rufus had found himself confronted by one of the bar's imposing patrons, Vivaldo had been willing to put his body on the line for his friend in what would become a full-blown brawl. The fight sent Vivaldo to the hospital with a "great gash in his skull," but it also consolidated an unspoken trust between the two friends (35). While Rufus and Vivaldo "never spoke of this night," readers learn that "from that time on" the two friends had "depended on and trusted" one another as they did no one else (35-36).[13]

Yet while Vivaldo has demonstrated his loyalty to Rufus through a show of strength, it remains unclear whether he will be able to sustain the receptive embrace that he provides on the doorstep. The dynamic that unfolds between the two characters after Vivaldo invites Rufus into his apartment becomes a crucial test of their relationship. The inconclusive nature of the unfolding interaction is crucial to Baldwin's portrayal of the risks that go with making oneself available to another. In earlier passages treating Rufus's memories of his interactions with Leona, Baldwin made use of indirect discourse to convey the nature of the couple's verbal and physical exchanges. By utilizing metapragmatic frames that captioned the performative force of such exchanges, he left readers with little doubt about the injuries that those characters had been attempting to inflict.[14] By contrast, when Baldwin describes Rufus's interactions in the ongoing present—as in the following exchange between Rufus and Vivaldo—the author limits himself to direct discourse and is extremely sparing in his use of metapragmatic description.

> "Did you ever have the feeling," he asked, "that a woman was eating you up? I mean—no matter what she was like or what else she was doing—that that's what she was *really* doing?"
>
> "Yes," said Vivaldo.
>
> Rufus stood. He walked up and down.
>
> "She can't help it. And you can't help it. And there you are." He paused. "Of course, with Leona and me—there was lots of other things, too——"
>
> Then there was a long silence. They listened to Bessie.
>
> "Have you ever wished you were queer?" Rufus asked, suddenly.
>
> Vivaldo smiled, looking into his glass. "I used to think maybe I was. Hell, I think I even *wished* I was." He laughed. "But I'm not. So I'm stuck."
>
> Rufus walked to Vivaldo's window. "So you been all up and down that street, too," he said.
>
> "We've all been up the same streets. There aren't a hell of a lot of streets. Only, we've been taught to lie so much about so many things, that we hardly ever know *where* we are."
>
> Rufus said nothing. He walked up and down.
>
> Vivaldo said, "Maybe you should stay here, Rufus, for a couple of days, until you decide what you want to do."
>
> "I don't want to bug you, Vivaldo." ... Again he felt that he was smothering.
>
> (51-52)

Throughout this scene, Baldwin frames the dialogue between Rufus and Vivaldo with speech verbs—such as "said" and "asked"—that have minimal metapragmatic valence. At the same time, his account of the characters' movements is so restrained that it reads as stage direction, as in "He walked up and down." In this way, Baldwin deprives readers of the cues that normally indicate what the characters intend and/or accomplish by saying the things that they say, or by moving in the ways that they move. That is, he deprives readers of the cues that endow speech and movement with their social consequentiality. And by doing as much, Baldwin charges readers with interpreting what each interlocutor is really asking of the other, how each is responding to the other's proposals, and what kind of interactional event they are co-constructing. At the same time, and perhaps more important, he is able to steep readers in the ambiguities and tensions that suffuse the two characters' attempts to arrive at interpersonal harmony.

It is in this same scene that Baldwin first utilizes direct discourse to immerse readers in the aural ambience shared by the characters. As in much of Baldwin's fiction, stretches of both ambient sound and silence comprise their own rich semiotic medium and convey at least as much as the dialogue does about the communications between characters. In the above passage, it is Rufus who stands, walks to Vivaldo's window, and then repeatedly walks "up and down." Interspersed between the dialogue, his movements may reflect a desire to build more space—perhaps even to build more "streets"—into their relationship. By contrast, Vivaldo seems unsettled by what is described as "the silence that hung in the room"; and in an effort to fill it, he rises to flip through his record collection (48). When he sits back down, the plaintive tones of Bessie Smith's "Backwater Blues" (1927) begin to echo through the sparsely furnished apartment. *"There's thousands of people ... ain't got no place to go"* (49).

Earlier in the novel, Rufus had attended a party with Charlie Parker's music playing in the background (14). But the scene with "Backwater Blues" is the first time that music insinuates itself directly—mimetically rather than diegetically—into the text. The lyrics move Rufus to wonder how others have leveraged themselves out from a similar state of desolation. "Now that Rufus himself had no place to go—*'cause my house fell down and I can't live there no mo',* sang Bessie—he heard the line and the tone of the singer, and he wondered how others had moved beyond the emptiness and horror which faced him now" (49). To the extent that the content of his conversation with Vivaldo constellates around friendship and hospitality, the answer may already be in the air. Alternatively, or simultaneously, the answer may be in the music—in its dialectic of content and form. For between Bessie Smith and pianist James Pete Johnson, there develops a relation of witnessing—in the antiphonal structure and harmonic holding—that serves to lighten the loneliness in the song's lyrics. "The piano bore the singer witness, stoic and ironic" (49).

In this crucial scene, Baldwin constructs the affective field as an audiosocial space in which flows of affect alternately harmonize and dissonate in the manner of sound waves, causing bodies to vibrate and resound like so many instruments or resonance chambers. In *Listening* (2007), Jean-Luc Nancy has used music to theorize a kind of subject that achieves its identity not through any substantive internal properties but rather through its difference or distance from itself, and through its being continually returned to itself by others—which makes subjectivity not only resonant but rhythmic. "It is a question," writes Nancy, "of going back from the phenomenological subject, an intentional line of sight, to a resonant subject, an intensive spacing out of a rebound that does not end in any return to self without immediately relaunching, as an echo, a call to that same self" (27). In Baldwin's fiction, the body is similarly presented as the locus of internal tensions that seek opportunities to resonate with other bodies, objects, and scenes.

Whereas Richard Wright had constructed the body of Bigger Thomas on the model of a furnace—as the locus of internal tensions that sought release—Baldwin constructs the bodies of his protagonists as so many resonance chambers whose internal vibrations seek to harmonize with their surroundings. In works like **"Sonny's Blues"** (1957) and *Another Country,* physical "shaking," "shuddering," and "trembling" are the signs that the characters remain open, that they can still be touched, that they have mustered the courage to approach the precipice of their own experience. Indeed, if Baldwin chose to narrate that crucial scene with minimal metapragmatic description, he may have done so in hopes of enabling unspoken thoughts as well as affective inrushes and outflows—of expectancy, hesitation, desire—to resound more clearly. In *Of Hospitality* (2000), Jacques Derrida reminds readers that *"reticence,* as you know, is the figure of a deliberate *keeping-quiet* so that more than eloquence can be heard in it" (95).

During his early years in Europe, Baldwin listened incessantly to the female singers of the "classic" blues era: Bessie Smith, Gertrude "Ma" Rainey, Billie Holiday, and others. It was his way of maintaining a connection with his homeland and of uncovering another country within that homeland. At the same time, however, Baldwin took Bessie Smith's blues as a model for the aesthetic he hoped to achieve in his fiction. In recent years, scholars of black culture have argued that the blues fulfill a number of important functions within the African American community. Houston Baker interprets the blues as a locus for collective self-definition; Henry Louis Gates, Jr., interprets it as a vernacular for coded critique of the dominant culture; and Angela Davis interprets it as a propaedeutic for more overt social and political protest.[15] But these dimensions of blues music were not the ones that motivated Baldwin's interest in the genre. What drew Baldwin to the blues was the directness with which it addressed people's vulnerability to structural and contingent misfortunes, as well as the urgency of its appeal for a deeper sense of social entanglement and mutual responsibility.

In an interview with Studs Terkel just before the publication of *Another Country,* Baldwin explains that he had been drawn to the secular realism—or what he calls the "sense of tragedy"—that he perceived in the blues: "It is the ability to look on things as they are and survive your losses, or . . . to know that your losses are coming. To know they are coming is the only possible insurance you have, a faint insurance that you will survive them" (**"An Interview"** [**"Disturber of the Peace: James Baldwin—An Interview"**] 22). In the spirituals, the sorrow songs, and other musical forms that emerged under slavery, the geospatial compass of African American music had been oriented toward the proverbial drinking gourd and the pole star—if not toward a more directly celestial deliverance. By contrast, the blues took shape as a secular realist aesthetic that was grounded in an acknowledgment of people's material and relational vulnerability—and did not presume to plot an escape from that condition.[16] What's more, the blues was a musical form in which a provisional sense of power or pleasure could be derived, however paradoxically, from the admission of vulnerability. In the lexicon of 1920s blues singers like Ma Rainey and Bessie Smith, words like "wandering" and "rambling" functioned as ciphers for an approach to the world premised on the acknowledgment and acceptance of such vulnerability.

If any respite from the condition of vulnerability were possible, it would take the form, in Baldwin's view, of horizontal and often evanescent connections with others. Baldwin believed that it was only by accepting limitations that people could find freedom. Thus, when Bessie Smith testifies on behalf of the lonely multitude who have no "place" to go, she is referring not to a physical location, but to a social, interpersonal refuge. In an essay appropriately titled **"Nothing Personal,"** Baldwin makes this point bluntly: "I have always felt that a human being could only be saved by another human being" (**"Nothing"** 700). The blues, as Baldwin knew it, could offer not just a spatial home but a temporal one as well, giving people both locations to dwell in and techniques for dwelling on.

In this way, Baldwin perceived that the blues could inculcate an ethos that took dispossession or homelessness as the basis for our being in common. But he also believed that insofar as the blues nourishes an emotional stance that allows individuals to acknowledge and accept their vulnerability, it functions as a homeopathic aesthetic that can help them to survive such vulnerability:

> Now I'm trying to suggest that the triumph here—which is a very Un-American triumph—is that the person to whom these things happened watched with eyes wide open, saw it happen. So that when Billie or Bessie or Leadbelly stood up and sang about it, they were commenting on it, a little bit outside it; they were accepting it. And there's something funny—there's always something a little funny

in all our disasters, if one can face the disaster. So that it's this passionate detachment, this inwardness coupled with outwardness, this ability to know that, all right, it's a mess, and you can't do anything about it . . . so, well, you have to do something about it. You can't stay there, you can't drop dead, you can't give up, but all right, OK, as Bessie said, "Picked up my bag, baby, and I tried it again."

(**"The Uses"** [**"The Uses of the Blues"**] 59; ellipsis orig.)

Baldwin understood that the "ironic" or "double-edged" relation to pleasure evidenced in the blues stemmed from the recognition that pleasure has no guarantees, that it may be here today and gone tomorrow. While the title character in **"Sonny's Blues"** has been able to subdue the internal turbulence that had driven him to heroin, he acknowledges that "it can come again" (135). At the same time, this insight about the impermanence of pleasure was reversible, as evidenced by blues lyrics such as "Well, if we don't today, we will tomorrow night" (Baldwin, **"Down"** [**"Down at the Cross"**] 311). That's what Bessie Smith meant when she sang of searching for a lost friend: "Picked up my bag, baby, and I tried it again" (Smith). To Baldwin's mind, this ironic sensibility was one source of the much-touted "tenacity" of black Americans (**"Down"** 311). In all of these ways, Baldwin perceived that the blues could mediate what Baker has referred to as the subject's "experiencing of experience" (*Blues* 7).[17] Baldwin developed a dialectical aesthetic whose purpose was to help readers perceive that personal security is a danger, willed innocence is a crime, and vulnerability is a key to freedom.

In the aforementioned scene from *Another Country,* Rufus and Vivaldo seem to approach the harmonic rapport that is evidenced between Bessie Smith and James Pete Johnson. "The most impenetrable of mysteries moved in this darkness for less than a second, hinting of reconciliation" (*Another* 54). In the end, however, they fail to establish such a rapport. Vivaldo's nervous energy moves him to pour another drink, turn over the record, disburse the tension: "He stood over Rufus for yet another moment, then he said, 'I'm going to take you out and buy you a pizza'" (54). By the end of the first chapter, Rufus will find himself alone on the street again. Not unlike the experience of falling, Rufus's feeling of isolation—his fall into himself—is made all the more agonizing by the feeling of being powerless to stop it. Later that night, Rufus will allow his body to drop from the George Washington Bridge into the Hudson River. His fate echoes that of Baldwin's best friend, Eugene Worth, who had committed suicide at the age of twenty-four in December 1946. Remembering this friend in an essay written toward the end of his life, Baldwin wrote, "I would have done anything whatever to have been able to hold him in this world" (**"Price"** [**"The Price of the Ticket"**] 833).

III. BALDWIN'S FUTURES

One year after Baldwin published *Another Country,* Norman Podhoretz sought to defend Baldwin's novel against a string of patronizing reviews. Podhoretz argued that what reviewers failed to see was that the novel's banality was part of its radical efficacy:

> Whites coupled with Negroes, heterosexual men coupled with homosexuals, homosexuals coupled with women, none of it involving casual lust or the suggestion of neurotic perversity, and all of it accompanied by the most serious emotions and resulting in the most intense attachments—it is easy enough to see even from so crude a summary that Baldwin's intention is to deny any moral significance whatever to the categories white and Negro, heterosexual and homosexual.

(247)

In the years since Baldwin's death in 1987, the moralism that Americans had long brought to the topic of race has made its way into debates about same-sex marriage, single parenting, immigration, abortion, and other topics. At a time when public discourse increasingly takes the form of a struggle to capture the high ground of moral innocence, what seems particularly relevant about Baldwin's literary practice is his attempt to forge an aesthetic that might help Americans to move beyond the moralism of a sentimental culture. Oddly enough, in *The Annotated Uncle Tom's Cabin,* Gates and Robbins lavish praise upon Stowe for having anticipated the "hot-button cultural and political concerns" of the twenty-first century: concerns such as "marriage, sexual orientation, class, language, and religion" (xiii). What Gates and Robbins do not mention is that the sentimental structure of feeling reinforced by Stowe's novels may have been partially responsible for making those issues so "hot." As shown here, Baldwin's analyzes how the moral heat that Americans are capable of bringing to such issues can have detrimental effects on all manner of social relations. Because he understood that racial stereotypes were rooted in a moral-sentimental structure of feeling, Baldwin was able to perceive that the most effective technique for counteracting stereotypes might not be to launch a campaign of moral condemnation. His fiction suggests that the best way to draw down the drama around issues like race and sexuality might be to find ways of helping Americans to accept the vicissitudes of their affective lives. My hope is that shifting critical discourse away from questioning whether Baldwin was guilty of the sins that he condemned in his predecessors may increase focus on whether and how his aesthetic innovations might help to usher in another country—one less preoccupied with guilt and sin.

## Notes

1. Given the extent to which Baldwin's early essays on aesthetics have influenced Gates's literary criticism, it may come as little surprise that Gates does not engage them directly. In a recent interview, Gates affirms that "the consistent theme of [his] literary criticism" derives from an idea that he first encountered in those early essays: namely, "the idea that there's a difference between an aesthetic and a polemical statement" ("Q&A"). Even Gates's characterization of Baldwin-the-novelist as "Stowe in blackface" might be seen as a nod to Baldwin-the-essayist. For in "Everybody's Protest Novel," Baldwin used the trope of unwitting inheritance when he argued that Richard Wright's anti-sentimental *Native Son* (1940) made its author into the heir of Stowean sentimentality: "Bigger is Uncle Tom's descendent, flesh of his flesh, so exactly opposite a portrait that, when the books are placed together, it seems that the contemporary Negro novelist and the dead New England woman are locked together in a deadly, timeless battle" ("Everybody's" 18). By turning Baldwin's critical apparatus against his fiction, Gates is able to redeem the object of Baldwin's critique while figuring himself as the heir of Baldwin's critical mantle.

2. Few scholars have examined Baldwin's literary output for clues to the transformative potential that the author envisioned in fiction. Nor have scholars queried the particular form of fiction that Baldwin sought—regardless of whether or not he was successful—to engender. In an introduction to an anthology on Baldwin's fiction, McBride observes that while a "Baldwin revival" seems to have been fomenting since the 1990s, there has been a "paucity of real critical treatment of Baldwin's work in favor of the more biographical portraitures of the man" ("Introduction" 8). And in a recent bibliographic essay on Baldwin scholarship, Henderson similarly observes that while a "Baldwin Renaissance" seems to be under way, the vast majority of Baldwin's literary output "still remains unjustly overlooked" (240, 234).

3. While the presidency of Barack Obama has ushered the United States into a second "post-racial moment," I would not want my use of that phrase to imply that I believe a post-racial society has been achieved. Rather, the phrase is meant to index a historical period when the prospect of bringing about a post-racial society comes to hold a prominent place in the collective imaginary as well as to motivate the work of race scholars. In *The Problem of the Future World,* Porter focuses on how, during the 1950s, the prospect of bringing about such a society came to motivate the late writings of W. E. B. Du Bois—though Porter might as easily have focused on the writings of scholars like Ralph Bunch, Oliver Cox, or Baldwin himself.

4. For a cogent analysis of the "post-sentimental" as it is manifested in Baldwin's essays as well as in works of fiction by contemporary authors like Morrison, see Berlant, "Poor Eliza."

5. Campbell notes that in 1945, Baldwin's experiences with landlords and property agents in the Village drove him out of the city to upstate New York. "It would not be unusual, for example, for a friend of Baldwin's to rent a place and move in first, establishing a confident relationship with the superintendent; only then would Baldwin follow. The superintendent might or might not object; or the neighbors might protest directly to the owner. If so, then Baldwin would have to leave" (30).

6. As Patricia Williams might put it, the landlady's "fight [is] not really about whatever the fight is about" (47). Rather, the landlady's altercation with Peter needs to be understood as an internal psychological confrontation "between the real and the imagined, the remembered and the fantasized, the likely and the outrageous" (47).

7. For an astute argument about how ideological images and scripts premediate human perceptions and experiences of the world, see Grusin, *Premediation.*

8. For a recent account of the energy that many people expend when dealing with "stereotype threat," see Steele, *Whistling Vivaldi.*

9. In the foregoing paragraphs, I have followed Baldwin in using the phrase "white Americans." But it may be worth noting that Baldwin recodes "whiteness" in terms of a sensibility that keeps people invested in the downward social constitution of others. In a 1968 interview with *Esquire,* Baldwin observed that whiteness "is not a color, it's an attitude. You're as white as you think you are. It's your choice" ("How Can We" 52). See also Baldwin's comments on whiteness in Baldwin and Mead, *A Rap on Race* 179.

10. In one of the few scholarly essays to take up "Previous Condition," Bluefarb asserts that "the core of the

story" lies in Peter's assertion that he "didn't seem to have a place" (28). Bluefarb's main argument is that "Peter's inability to identify with either group—black or white—represents of course the true source of his alienation, as a Negro in the white society and as an Artist-Intellectual in the black" (28). Campbell makes a similar argument when he observes that the final scene in "Previous Condition" dramatizes the "dilemma in which its author was then trapped: between two hemispheres, one black and one white" (42).

11. Because I have already discussed how their respective histories inform the intimate relations between Peter and Ida, I will not elaborate upon how those same forces inform the dynamic between Rufus and Leona. But readers interested in such an analysis might consult Feldman, "Another Look" 93-95.

12. Questioning the historical plausibility of this passage, Gates and Robbins ask, "After all, how many black soldiers could actually have been physically abused by white officers in boot camp even in the South of the 1930s and 1940s?" (xxix). Although data on such abuse may be hard to come by, Baldwin does seem to have based the scene on historical testimony, having received letters from his brother Wilmer in which the latter described being mistreated by a white officer in the army.

13. For an account of how Baldwin and his white friend Engin Cezzar were attacked in a bar called the Village Paddock, see Leeming, *James Baldwin* 161.

14. For an extended analysis of the metapragmatic dimensions of reported speech, see Hickmann, "The Boundaries."

15. For an account of how the blues has served as a locus for reflexive cultural self-definition, see Baker, *Blues*. For how the blues has served as a kind of encryption algorithm—or a vehicle for indirection and double-voicing—within the African American speech community, see Gates, *The Signifying Monkey*. For how the blues has served as a propaedeutic for social protest, see Davis, *Blues Legacies*.

16. Angela Davis may have been the first to observe that the blues was characterized by a nonteleological vision and an ambivalent emotional tonality. Discussing Gertrude "Ma" Rainey's "Lost Wandering Blues" (1924), Davis writes, "Although, contrary to popular belief, there is no all-consuming pessimism in the blues, blues consciousness also eschews the optimism so evident in the spirituals. ... The lyrics of 'Lost Wandering Blues' articulate a commitment to undertake an emotional journey, regardless of what the risks may be and despite the fact that the destination cannot be precisely conceptualized" (112-13).

17. Here is Baldwin's eloquent description of how the blues can remediate experience in a manner that lends a margin of maneuverability: "I'm talking about the recreation of experience, you know, the way it comes back. Billie Holiday was a poet. She gave you back your experience. She refined it, and you recognized it for the first time because she was in and out of it and she made it possible for you to bear it. And if you could bear it, then you could begin to change it. That's what a poet does" ("*The Black Scholar*" 155).

*Works Cited*

Baker, Houston A., Jr. *Blues, Ideology, and Afro-American Literature: A Vernacular Theory.* Chicago: U of Chicago P, 1984. Print.

———. "The Embattled Craftsman: An Essay on James Baldwin." *Critical Essays on James Baldwin.* Ed. Fred L. Standley and Nancy V. Burt. Boston: Hall, 1988. 62-77. Print.

Baldwin, James. *Another Country.* New York: Dial, 1962. Print.

———. "*The Black Scholar* Interviews James Baldwin." 1973. *Conversations with James Baldwin* 142-58.

———. *Conversations with James Baldwin.* Ed. Fred L. Standley and Louis H. Pratt. Jackson: UP of Mississippi, 1989. Print.

———. *The Cross of Redemption: Uncollected Writings* Ed. Randall Kenan. New York: Pantheon Books, 2010. Print.

———. "Disturber of the Peace: James Baldwin—An Interview." 1969. Conducted by Eve Auchincloss and Nancy Lynch. *Conversations with James Baldwin* 64-82.

———. "Down at the Cross." 1963. *James Baldwin: Collected Essays* 296-347.

———. "Everybody's Protest Novel." 1949. *James Baldwin: Collected Essays* 11-8.

———. *Going to Meet the Man.* 1965. New York: Vintage Books, 1995. Print.

———. "How Can We Get the Black People to Cool It?" *Esquire* 70.1 (1968): 49-53. Print.

————. "The Image of the Negro." *James Baldwin: Collected Essays* 582-87.

————. "An Interview with James Baldwin." 1961. Conducted by Studs Terkel. *Conversations with James Baldwin* 3-23.

————. *James Baldwin: Collected Essays.* Ed. Toni Morrison. New York: Penguin, 1998. Print.

————. "James Baldwin Interviewed." 1970. Conducted by John Hall. *Conversations with James Baldwin* 98-107.

————. "James Baldwin, as Interviewed by François Bondy." *Transition* 3.12 (1964): 12-19. Print.

————. "Many Thousands Gone." 1951. *James Baldwin: Collected Essays* 19-34.

————. "Nothing Personal." 1964. *James Baldwin: Collected Essays* 692-706.

————. "Previous Condition." 1948. *Going to Meet the Man* 81-100.

————. "The Price of the Ticket." 1985. *James Baldwin: Collected Essays* 830-42.

————. "Sonny's Blues." 1957. *Going to Meet the Man* 101-41.

————. "The Uses of the Blues." 1964. *The Cross of Redemption* 57-66.

————. "The White Man's Guilt." 1965. *James Baldwin: Collected Essays* 722-27.

————. "The White Problem." 1964. *The Cross of Redemption* 72-79.

Baldwin, James, and Margaret Mead. *A Rap on Race.* Philadelphia: Lippincott, 1971. Print.

Balfour, Lawrie. *The Evidence of Things Not Said: James Baldwin and the Promise of American Democracy.* Ithaca: Cornell UP, 2001. Print.

————. "Finding the Words: Baldwin, Race Consciousness, and Democratic Theory." McBride, *James Baldwin Now* 75-99.

Berlant, Lauren. "Poor Eliza." *American Literature* 70.3 (1998): 635-68. Print.

Bluefarb, Sam. "James Baldwin's 'Previous Condition': A Problem of Identification." *Negro American Literature Forum* 3.1 (1996): 26-29. Print.

Campbell, James. *Talking at the Gates: A Life of James Baldwin.* Berkeley: U of California P, 1991. Print.

Davis, Angela. *Blues Legacies and Black Feminism: Gertrude "Ma" Rainey, Bessie Smith, and Billie Holiday.* New York: Pantheon, 1998. Print.

Derrida, Jacques. *Of Hospitality.* 1997. Stanford: Stanford UP, 2000. Print.

Feldman, Susan. "Another Look at *Another Country*: Reconciling Baldwin's Racial and Sexual Politics." *Re-Viewing James Baldwin: Things Not Seen.* Ed. D. Quentin Miller. Philadelphia: Temple UP, 2000. 88-104. Print.

Gates, Henry Louis, Jr. "Q&A Henry Louis Gates Jr." Conducted by Harvey Blume. *Boston Globe* 12 Nov. 2006. Web. 25 Aug. 2011. <http://www.boston.com/news/globe/ideas/articles/2006/11/12/qa_henry_louis_gates_jr>.

————. *The Signifying Monkey: A Theory of Afro-American Literary Criticism.* New York: Oxford UP, 1988. Print.

Gates, Henry Louis, Jr., and Hollis Robbins. "Introduction." *The Annotated Uncle Tom's Cabin.* Ed. Henry Louis Gates, Jr., and Hollis Robbins. New York: W. W. Norton, 2006. xi-xxx. Print.

Grusin, Richard. *Premediation: Affect and Mediality after 9/11.* New York: Palgrave Macmillan, 2010. Print.

Henderson, Carol E. "Bibliographic Essay: The Price of the Ticket: Baldwin Criticism in Perspective." *A Historical Guide to James Baldwin.* Ed. Douglas Field. Oxford: Oxford UP, 2009. 233-52. Print.

Hickmann, Maya. "The Boundaries of Reported Speech in Narrative Discourse: Some Developmental Aspects." *Reflexive Language: Reported Speech and Metapragmatics.* Ed. John A. Lucy. Cambridge: Cambridge UP, 1993. 63-90. Print.

Howe, Irving. "Black Boys and Native Sons." *Dissent* 10.4 (1963): 353-68. Print.

Leeming, David. *James Baldwin: A Biography.* New York: Knopf, 1994. Print.

Lippmann, Walter. *Public Opinion.* New York: Harcourt, Brace and Company, 1922. Print.

McBride, Dwight A. "Introduction: 'How Much Time Do You Want for Your Progress?': New Approaches to James Baldwin." *James Baldwin Now* 1-12.

————, ed. *James Baldwin Now.* New York: New York UP, 1999. Print.

Murray, Albert. *The Omni-Americans: New Perspectives on Black Experience and American Culture.* New York: Outbridge, 1970. Print.

Nancy, Jean-Luc. *Listening.* New York: Fordham UP, 2007. Print.

Podhoretz, Norman. "In Defense of James Baldwin." *Doings and Undoings: The Fifties and After in American Writing.* Farrar, 1964. 244-50. Print.

Porter, Eric. *The Problem of the Future World: W. E. B. Du Bois and the Race Concept at Midcentury.* Durham: Duke UP, 2010. Print.

Ross, Marlon. "White Fantasies of Desire: Baldwin and the Racial Identities of Sexuality." McBride, *James Baldwin Now* 13-55.

Steele, Claude M. *Whistling Vivaldi: How Stereotypes Affect Us and What We Can Do.* New York: Norton, 2010. Print.

Smith, Bessie. "Long Old Road." Rec. 11 Jun. 1931. Columbia. Phonograph (10-inch single).

Williams, Patricia J. *Seeing a Color-Blind Future: The Paradox of Race.* New York: Farrar, 1997. Print.

---

# FURTHER READING

## Bibliographies

Elam, Michele, editor. *The Cambridge Companion to James Baldwin.* Cambridge UP, 2015.

> Provides an in-depth list of works by Baldwin, along with a brief but helpful guide to further reading regarding Baldwin, including biographies, select critical studies, interviews, international receptions, and select video recordings.

Standley, Fred L., and Nancy V. Standley. *James Baldwin, a Reference Guide.* G. K. Hall, 1980.

> References major works by and about Baldwin.

## Biographies

Field, Douglas. *All Those Strangers: The Art and Lives of James Baldwin.* Oxford UP, 2015.

> Navigates the various journeys of Baldwin's life and career by connecting significant features of his major work to his political and spiritual development.

Leeming, David. *James Baldwin: A Biography.* Alfred A. Knopf, 1994.

Details a thorough cradle-to-grave narrative of Baldwin's personal and professional relationships and life as a political activist, poet, essayist, novelist, social critic, and playwright.

## Criticism

Bell, Matt. "Black Ground, Gay Figure: Working through *Another Country,* Black Power, and Gay Liberation." *American Literature,* vol. 79, no. 3, 2007, pp. 577-603.

> Clarifies *Another Country*'s influence on, and connections to, the burgeoning gay liberation and black power movements.

Berry, Boyd M. "Another Man Done Gone: Self-Pity in Baldwin's *Another Country." Michigan Quarterly Review,* vol. 5, 1966, pp. 285-90.

> Evaluates *Another Country* in light of Baldwin's early essays that challenged black protest novels. Berry suggests that the novel's black characters should be read as flawed, rather than as fueled by racial injustice. Though now outdated, Berry's claim provides an example of a response to Baldwin written around the time of the novel's publication.

Cleaver, Eldridge. "Notes on a Native Son." *Ramparts,* June 1966, pp. 51-58.

> Condemns *Another Country* as a permissive portrayal of African American subservience.

Fisher, Laura R. "Possible Futures and Grammatical Politics in James Baldwin's *Another Country." Journal of Modern Literature,* vol. 41, no. 1, Fall 2017, pp. 137-55.

> Argues that Baldwin's experimental grammars expressed throughout the novel gesture toward a possible utopia, free of racial and sexual oppression.

Mailer, Norman. "Norman Mailer versus Nine Writers: Some Children of the Goddess." *Esquire,* July 1963, pp. 63+.

> Condemns nine writers' novels, including Baldwin's *Another Country,* which Mailer declares is "an abominably written book."

Odhiambo, David N. "James Baldwin's *Another Country* as an Abstract Machine." *Pacific Coast Philology,* vol. 52, no. 1, 2017, pp. 69-87.

> Asserts that *Another Country* simultaneously represents both protest literature and an "asubjective" text.

Omry, Keren. "Baldwin's Bop 'n' Morrison's Mood: Bebop and Race in James Baldwin's *Another Country* and Toni Morrison's *Jazz." James Baldwin and Toni Morrison: Comparative Critical and Theoretical Essays,* edited by Lovalerie King and Lynn Orilla Scott, Palgrave Macmillan, 2006, pp. 11-35.

Contends that both Morrison's *Jazz* and Baldwin's *Another Country* use music in their texts to link to the conceptualization of bebop—both work to reconsider and reconceive notions of race, just as bebop worked to deconstruct preconceived notions of race within music.

Quinn, Laura. "'What Is Going on Here?': Baldwin's *Another Country*." *Journal of Homosexuality,* vol. 34, nos. 3-4, 1998, pp. 51-65.

Explores two separate experiences regarding the teaching of *Another Country* to survey the novel's critical history as well as its relationships to sexuality and race.

Reddinger, Amy. "'Just Enough for the City': Limitations of Space in Baldwin's *Another Country*." *African American Review,* vol. 43, no. 1, Spring 2009, pp. 117-30.

Frames Rufus as *Another Country*'s absent protagonist to argue that urban and domestic space within the text should be read as a system of meanings.

---

**Additional information on Baldwin's life and works is contained in the following sources published by Gale:** *African American Writers,* Eds. 1, 2; *American Writers Retrospective Supplement,* Vol. 2; *American Writers Supplement,* Vol. 1; *Authors and Artists for Young Adults,* Vols. 4, 34; *Beacham's Encyclopedia of Popular Fiction: Biography and Resources,* Vol. 1; *Black Literature Criticism,* Vol. 1; *Black Literature Criticism: Classic and Emerging Authors since 1950,* Vol. 1; *Black Writers,* Ed. 1; *Children's Literature Review,* Vol. 191; *Concise Dictionary of American Literary Biography: 1941-1968; Concise Major 21st-Century Writers; Contemporary American Dramatists; Contemporary Authors,* Vols. 1-4R, 124; *Contemporary Authors Bibliographical Series,* Vol. 1; *Contemporary Authors New Revision Series,* Vols. 3, 24; *Contemporary Literary Criticism,* Vols. 1, 2, 3, 4, 5, 8, 13, 15, 17, 42, 50, 67, 90, 127; *Contemporary Novelists,* Eds. 1, 2, 3, 4; *Contemporary Popular Writers; Dictionary of Literary Biography,* Vols. 2, 7, 33, 249, 278; *Dictionary of Literary Biography Yearbook,* 1987; *DISCovering Authors; DISCovering Authors: British Edition; DISCovering Authors: Canadian Edition; DISCovering Authors Modules: Most-Studied Authors, Multicultural Authors, Novelists,* and *Popular Fiction and Genre Authors; DISCovering Authors 3.0; Drama Criticism,* Vol. 1; *Drama for Students,* Vols. 11, 15; *Encyclopedia of World Literature in the 20th Century,* Ed. 3; *Exploring Short Stories; Gale Contextual Encyclopedia of American Literature,* Vol. 1; *Literature and Its Times,* Vol. 5; *Literature Resource Center; Major 20th-Century Writers,* Eds. 1, 2; *Major 21st-Century Writers; Modern American Literature,* Ed. 5; *Nonfiction Classics for Students,* Vol. 4; *Novels for Students,* Vol. 4; *Reference Guide to American Literature,* Ed. 4; *Reference Guide to Short Fiction,* Ed. 2; *Short Stories for Students,* Vols. 2, 18, 44; *Short Story Criticism,* Vols. 10, 33, 98, 134, 199; *Something about the Author,* Vols. 9, 54; *Twayne's United States Authors; Twentieth-Century Literary Criticism,* Vols. 229, 376; and *World Literature Criticism,* Vol. 1.

# Theodore Dreiser
## 1871-1945

(Born Theodor Herman Albert Dreiser) American novelist, short-story writer, essayist, journalist, playwright, and autobiographer.

The following entry provides criticism of Dreiser's life and works. For additional information about Dreiser, see *TCLC,* Volumes 10, 18, and 35; for additional information about the novel *An American Tragedy,* see *TCLC,* Volume 83; for additional information about the novel *Sister Carrie,* see *TCLC,* Volumes 277 and 377.

## INTRODUCTION

Best known for his novels *Sister Carrie* (1900) and *An American Tragedy* (1925), Theodore Dreiser created detailed and often bleak portrayals of the various institutional and social forces shaping human lives in modern industrial society. He is frequently cited with Frank Norris as a leading American practitioner of naturalism, a school of writing promoted in the nineteenth century by French author Émile Zola that was marked by an emphasis on gritty realism and a tendency to present the fate of a character as largely predetermined by biological and socioeconomic forces beyond his or her control. Controversial during his lifetime because of the perceived amorality of some of his characters and story lines, Dreiser was also criticized for his prose style, which many commentators found plodding and syntactically awkward. Nonetheless, his frank and comparatively nonjudgmental depiction of the underpinnings of American life exerted a profound influence on later authors, and today he is regarded as a central figure in early-twentieth-century American literature.

## BIOGRAPHICAL INFORMATION

Dreiser was born on 27 August 1871 in Terre Haute, Indiana, the ninth of the ten surviving children of John Paul Dreiser, a frequently unemployed German immigrant, and Sarah Maria Schänäb, the daughter of Mennonite farmers of Moravian-German background. Dreiser's upbringing was heavily influenced by his family's precarious financial situation, as well as by his father's dogmatic Catholicism, against which Dreiser and his siblings often rebelled. At the age of sixteen, he moved to Chicago, where he worked at various menial jobs until 1889, when he began attending Indiana University with the financial assistance of a former high school teacher. He dropped out after a year and returned to Chicago, where he eventually began a career as a newspaper reporter. His journalistic endeavors later took him to St. Louis, Pittsburgh, and New York City. During this period he also became familiar with the writings of the French novelist Honoré de Balzac and the English philosopher Herbert Spencer, both of whom greatly influenced his literary sensibility.

In 1898 Dreiser married Sara Osbourne White, a schoolteacher. By this time he was making a living as a freelance magazine writer, and the following year his friend Arthur Henry encouraged him to begin work on his first novel. Dreiser completed *Sister Carrie* in March 1900, and it was accepted for publication by Doubleday, Page and Company on the enthusiastic recommendation of the novelist Frank Norris. Not everyone at Doubleday thought highly of the novel, however, and it was published but not promoted. It received mixed reviews and sold poorly, though a British edition published the following year garnered a more positive reception. After a period of severe depression that lasted for about two years, Dreiser spent several months working as a railroad day laborer before resuming his writing career. In 1907 he became editor of the *Delineator,* the most popular women's magazine of the era, but he was fired three years later for pursuing a romantic relationship with the teenage daughter of an assistant editor. He also separated from his wife around this time.

Meanwhile, public opinion regarding *Sister Carrie* had improved significantly following a 1907 reissue of an edited version of the novel. The warm reception given his second novel, *Jennie Gerhardt* (1911), further encouraged Dreiser to concentrate on his literary endeavors. During the following fifteen years he produced a large quantity of fiction, drama, travel writing, essays, and autobiography, which culminated in 1925 with the publication of his most acclaimed work, *An American Tragedy.* In 1919 he met his distant cousin Helen Patges Richardson, who became his principal romantic partner, though he continued to pursue various short-term affairs. He did not marry Richardson until 1944, following the death of his first wife, to whom he had remained legally married. In the later decades of his career, Dreiser focused his energies on social and political activism, and much of his work from this period consists of nonfiction writings in support of various liberal causes. Eventually, this advocacy began to overshadow his reputation as a fiction writer, though in his final years he devoted much of his time to completing two novels he had begun long before. Dreiser died of heart failure in Hollywood, California, on 28 December 1945. He was buried in Glendale, California. His last two novels, *The Bulwark* and *The Stoic,* were published in 1946 and 1947, respectively.

## MAJOR WORKS

*Sister Carrie* prefigures much of his subsequent output in its focus on the "American Dream" of prosperity and social mobility. The novel describes the experiences of a young woman, Caroline (Carrie) Meeber, who leaves her home in rural Wisconsin to make her way in Chicago, where she initially lives with her older sister and brother-in-law. Over time, Carrie rises in social status and becomes a famous actress. Her ascent is facilitated in part through romantic relationships with two men, one of whom—an affluent bar manager with a wife and children—experiences a corresponding decline in social and material success and eventually takes his own life in a flophouse. The novel is often cited as a pioneering departure from moralistic Victorian literary conventions, particularly in its occasionally sordid realism and its failure to punish the title character for her sexual improprieties.

Dreiser's second novel, *Jennie Gerhardt,* is also a tale about a poor, young Midwestern woman who becomes intimately involved with much wealthier men, but it differs from *Sister Carrie* in that its protagonist is generous, loyal, and self-effacing, rather than ambitious and self-interested. *The Financier* (1912) inaugurated a novel series known as the Cowperwood trilogy, or the Trilogy of Desire, which also includes *The Titan* (1914) and *The Stoic.* The series chronicles the socioeconomic ventures and romantic entanglements of Frank Cowperwood, an unscrupulous financier whose character Dreiser modeled on that of transportation magnate Charles Yerkes, as Philip Gerber (2000) detailed. *The "Genius"* (1915), an account of the life of a talented Midwestern painter, is rarely cited as one of Dreiser's best works, but it became a major rallying point in public conversations about artistic censorship after the New York Society for the Suppression of Vice attempted to have it banned on grounds of obscenity.

Dreiser's greatest critical and commercial success was *An American Tragedy,* which centers on an ambitious but feckless young man, Clyde Griffiths, who, after attracting the romantic interest of a wealthy heiress, considers murdering his poor, pregnant fiancée. The latter ultimately dies in a boating accident, from which Clyde chooses not to rescue her. Eventually, he is arrested, charged with murder, convicted, and executed. *The Bulwark* depicts the travails of a devout Quaker businessman amid the materialism of twentieth-century American life. Dreiser's works outside the novel genre tend to attract relatively little attention, though some, including the European travelog *A Traveler at Forty* (1913) and the essay collection *Hey Rub-a-Dub-Dub* (1920), are of interest to scholars because of the insight they provide into both Dreiser's own experiences and the sociopolitical and philosophical convictions informing his fiction.

## CRITICAL RECEPTION

Early- to mid-twentieth-century critics often mentioned that Dreiser's literary style was problematic, yet they disagreed markedly on the extent to which this affected the quality of the material he produced. M. A. (1919), writing for *The New Republic,* complained that Dreiser's *Twelve Men* (1919), an early collection of a dozen short biographical sketches, exhibits a "lack of style." In *The Sewanee Review,* E. M. K. (1926) asserted that the "authentic and inevitable" power of Dreiser's "genius" for nonjudgmental observation far surpasses any technical defects in his storytelling. On the other hand, Lionel Trilling (1946) described *The Bulwark* as a "moralizing" testament to an extant "weakness" in the writer, declaring that Dreiser "is precisely literary in the bad sense; . . . he is full of flowers of rhetoric and he shines with paste gems," and his "ideas are inconsistent or inadequate," notwithstanding his much-lauded "reality and great brooding pity." Seymour Krim (1956) celebrated Dreiser's role in broadening "the scope of the American conscience" but deplored "the deformed sprawl of his mind and works" evidenced in his "often dreary . . . literary style." For some critics, like Randolph Bourne, quoted in a 1917 *Current Opinion* essay, Dreiser's "largeness of utterance," was part of his flouting conventional ideas "of optimism and redemption." James T. Farrell (1945) contradicted the contention that Dreiser is "merely heavy-handed and careless" in his reliance on detail. William L. Phillips (1963) also opposed the idea that Dreiser "had no awareness of the resources of image and metaphor," examining the ways in which he used imagery in five of his novels.

The character of Dreiser and the degree to which his writings reflect his own experience, his observations, and variations in his philosophy have played an important role in assessments of his work. M. A. attributed Dreiser's stylistic shortcomings to "a general and real lack of philosophy" in the author, who had allegedly not "fought free" of conventional repressions. Charles Child Walcutt (1940) showed "how, in three distinct stages he has taken three different [philosophical] attitudes" based on the six novels Dreiser published in his lifetime. Roger Asselineau (1961; see Further Reading) linked Dreiser to the nineteenth-century Transcendentalists; he admitted the strong naturalist strain in Dreiser's work but saw that balanced by an almost mystical belief system. John T. Flanagan (1946) recalled Dreiser's personal familiarity with poverty, which imbued him with "pessimism and bitterness" and began his lifelong quest as a "fighter for free and full expression of all facets of human experience, . . . [and] as a ruthless critic of exploitation and injustice and special privilege." John Lydenberg (1955) described Dreiser as a literary "bulldozer" determined to unmask "the realities of life." Phillips noted how Dreiser's use of imagery changed over time in line with his "philosophical preoccupations." Sheldon Norman Grebstein (1966) focused on differences between *An American Tragedy* and the characters and circumstances of the real-life legal case on which it was partly based, finding aspects of Dreiser's life interwoven in them.

More recent criticism has tended to approach Dreiser within the broader context of the society in which he wrote. Renate von Bardeleben (1991; see Further Reading) contemplated the effects of Dreiser's German-Slavic ethnicity on his literary output and career in the United States and abroad, and the later formation of "his personal view" relative to this inheritance based on his midlife travels to Europe. Shawn St. Jean (2000) discussed Dreiser's Trilogy of Desire in terms of the writer's standard American semiclassical education. Laura Hapke (2003) positioned "Dreiser and his taxonomy of paid work within a literary naturalism of social protest" and compared the writer's working-class depictions of white people "in a landscape of relative privilege" to academic studies of the socio-ethnically stratified labor market in American cities of the time and to Dreiser's own journalistic knowledge of the ethnic makeup of the working classes.

Other scholars have focused on the author's differing treatment of men and women subjects. Yoshinobu Hakutani (1979) examined the characterization of the American woman in Dreiser's 1929 *A Gallery of Women,* with which early readers were disappointed. Hakutani found that the portraits in the book are motivated more by internal psychology that by the external social factors which "determined the characters" in *Twelve Men.* According to Hapke (2000), Dreiser deplored "the sanitizing of women wage earners," yet he devised strategies so that his characters Carrie and Jennie did not remain long in that class. Dreiser depicted men caught in dire poverty as dull and depleted. In contrast, said Hapke, he created women untouched by extended poverty and displayed "ambivalence" toward characters, especially women, who must be a part of the workforce.

James Overholtzer

Academic Advisor: Linda Wagner-Martin,
The University of North Carolina at Chapel Hill

## PRINCIPAL WORKS

*Sister Carrie.* Doubleday, Page, 1900. Print. (Novel)

*Jennie Gerhardt.* Harper and Brothers, 1911. Print. (Novel)

\**The Financier.* Harper and Brothers, 1912. Rev. ed. Boni and Liveright, 1927. Print. (Novel)

*A Traveler at Forty.* Century, 1913. Print. (Travel essays)

\**The Titan.* John Lane, 1914. Print. (Novel)

*The "Genius."* John Lane, 1915. Print. (Novel)

*A Hoosier Holiday.* John Lane, 1916. Print. (Travel essays)

*Plays of the Natural and the Supernatural.* John Lane, 1916. Enlarged ed. *Plays, Natural and Supernatural.* London, Constable, 1930. Print. (Plays)

*Free and Other Stories.* Boni and Liveright, 1918. Print. (Short stories)

*The Hand of the Potter.* Boni and Liveright, 1918. Print. (Play)

*Twelve Men.* Boni and Liveright, 1919. Print. (Sketches)

*Hey Rub-a-Dub-Dub: A Book of the Mystery and Wonder and Terror of Life.* Boni and Liveright, 1920. Print. (Essays)

*A Book about Myself.* Boni and Liveright, 1922. Published as *Newspaper Days: A History of Myself.* Horace Liveright, 1931. Print. (Autobiography)

*The Color of a Great City.* Boni and Liveright, 1923. Print. (Sketches)

*An American Tragedy.* Boni and Liveright, 1925. 2 vols. Print. (Novel)

*Moods: Cadenced and Declaimed.* Boni and Liveright, 1926. Enlarged ed. *Moods: Philosophic and Emotional, Cadenced and Declaimed.* Simon and Schuster, 1935. Print. (Poetry)

*The Carnegie Works at Pittsburgh.* Privately printed, 1927. Print. (Essay)

*Chains: Lesser Novels and Stories.* Boni and Liveright, 1927. Print. (Short stories)

*Dreiser Looks at Russia.* Horace Liveright, 1928. Print. (Travel essays)

*Epitaph.* Heron Press, 1929. Print. (Poetry)

*A Gallery of Women.* Horace Liveright, 1929. 2 vols. Print. (Sketches)

*My City.* Horace Liveright, 1929. Print. (Prose poem)

*Fine Furniture.* Random House, 1930. Print. (Short story)

*Dawn.* Horace Liveright, 1931. Print. (Autobiography)

*Tragic America.* Horace Liveright, 1931. Print. (Essays)

*America Is Worth Saving.* Modern Age Books, 1941. Print. (Nonfiction)

*The Bulwark.* Doubleday, 1946. Print. (Novel)

*The Best Short Stories of Theodore Dreiser.* Edited by Howard Fast. World Publishing, 1947. Print. (Short stories)

*\*The Stoic.* Doubleday, 1947. Print. (Novel)

*Letters of Theodore Dreiser.* Edited by Robert H. Elias. U of Pennsylvania P, 1959. Print. (Letters)

*Letters to Louise: Theodore Dreiser's Letters to Louise Campbell.* Edited by Louise Campbell. U of Pennsylvania P, 1959. Print. (Letters)

*Selected Poems.* Edited by Robert Palmer Saalbach. Exposition Press, 1969. Print. (Poetry)

*Notes on Life.* Edited by Marguerite Tjader and John J. McAleer. U of Alabama P, 1974. Print. (Nonfiction)

*Theodore Dreiser: A Selection of Uncollected Prose.* Edited by Donald Pizer. Wayne State UP, 1977. Print. (Essays and journalism)

*American Diaries, 1902-1926.* Edited by Thomas P. Riggio. U of Pennsylvania P, 1982. Print. (Diaries)

*An Amateur Laborer.* Edited by Richard W. Dowell. U of Pennsylvania P, 1983. Print. (Autobiography)

*Selected Magazine Articles of Theodore Dreiser.* Edited by Yoshinobu Hakutani. Fairleigh Dickinson UP, 1985-87. 2 vols. Print. (Journalism)

*Dreiser-Mencken Letters: The Correspondence of Theodore Dreiser and H. L. Mencken, 1907-1945.* Edited by Riggio. U of Pennsylvania P, 1986. 2 vols. Print. (Letters)

*Journalism: Newspaper Writings, 1892-1895.* Edited by T. D. Nostwich. U of Pennsylvania P, 1988. Print. (Journalism)

*Theodore Dreiser's "Heard in the Corridors" Articles and Related Writings.* Edited by Nostwich. Iowa State UP, 1988. Print. (Prose)

*Fulfilment and Other Tales of Women and Men.* Edited by Nostwich. Black Sparrow Press, 1992. Print. (Short stories and sketches)

*Dreiser's Russian Diary.* Edited by Riggio and James L. W. West III. U of Pennsylvania P, 1996. Print. (Diary)

*Theodore Dreiser's "Ev'ry Month."* Edited by Nancy Warner Barrineau. U of Georgia P, 1996. Print. (Essays and reviews)

*Collected Plays of Theodore Dreiser.* Edited by Keith Newlin and Frederic E. Rusch. Whitston Publishing, 2000. Print. (Plays)

*Art, Music, and Literature, 1897-1902.* Edited by Hakutani. U of Illinois P, 2001. Print. (Essays and interviews)

*Theodore Dreiser's Uncollected Magazine Articles, 1897-1902.* Edited by Hakutani. U of Delaware P, 2003. Print. (Journalism)

*Interviews.* Edited by Rusch and Pizer. U of Illinois P, 2004. Print. (Interviews)

*Political Writings.* Edited by Jude Davies. U of Illinois P, 2011. Print. (Prose)

*The Titan: The Critical Edition.* Edited by Roark Mulligan. Winchester UP, 2016. Print. (Novel)

\*These works are collectively referred to as the Cowperwood trilogy, or the Trilogy of Desire.

---

# CRITICISM

## *Current Opinion* (essay date 1917)

SOURCE: "Dreiser's Novels as a Revelation of the American Soul." *Current Opinion*, vol. 63, 3 Sept. 1917, p. 191.

[*In the following essay, the writer reflects on Randolph Bourne's assessment of Dreiser as among the first American writers "to achieve a largeness of utterance," flouting conventional ideas "of optimism and redemption."*]

The struggle to make something artistic out of the chaotic materials that lie around us in American life is, for Randolph Bourne, the fundamental motive of the novelist Theodor Dreiser. Mr. Bourne thinks that most readers have not yet awakened to the real significance and importance of a writer whom Edgar Lee Masters has called a "soul-enrapt demiurge, walking the earth, stalking life," and whom John Cowper Powys regards as an epic philosopher of the "life-tide." We have not so many great American novelists that we can afford to forget or depreciate any of them. Mr. Dreiser, as Randolph Bourne sees him, is complicated, but he is complicated in a very understandable American way, the product of the uncouth forces of small-town life and the vast disorganization of the wider American world. "As he reveals himself, it is a revelation of a certain broad level of the American soul." Mr. Bourne continues (in the Chicago *Dial*):

> In spite of his looseness of literary gait and heaviness of style, Dreiser seems a sincere groper after beauty. It is natural enough that this should so largely be the beauty of sex. For where would a sensitive boy, brought up in Indiana and in the big American cities, get beauty expressed for him except in women? What does mid-Western America offer to the starving except its personal beauty? A few landscapes, an occasional picture in a museum, a book of verse perhaps! Would not all the rest be one long, flaunting offense of ugliness and depression? **"The 'Genius,'"** instead of being that mass of pornographic horror which the Vice Societies repute it to be, is the story of a groping artist whose love of beauty runs obsessingly upon the charm of girlhood. Through different social planes, through business and manual labor and the feverish world of artists, he pursues this lure. Dreiser is refreshing in his air of the moral democrat, who sees life impassively, neither praising nor blaming, at the same time that he realizes how much more terrible and beautiful and incalculable life is than any of us are willing to admit. It may be all *apologia,* but it comes with the grave air of a mind that wants us to understand just how it all happened. **"Sister Carrie"** will always retain the fresh charm of a spontaneous working-out of mediocre, and yet elemental and significant, lives. A good novelist catches hold of the thread of human desire. Dreiser does this, and that is why his admirers forgive him so many faults.

For all who care to speculate about personal and literary qualities that are specifically American, Dreiser, Mr. Bourne remarks, should be as interesting as any one now writing in America. He is revealed in his books as a hopelessly unorientated, half-educated boy who had to struggle for his place in the world and who had to discover his own sincerity. In this his experience has been typical. "Talent in America," Mr. Bourne says, "flowers very late because it takes so long to find its bearings. It has had almost to create its own soil, before it could put in its roots and grow. It is a grueling and tedious task, but those who come through it contribute, like

Vachel Lindsay, creative work that is both novel and indigenous." The process can be more easily traced in Dreiser than in almost anybody else. As Mr. Bourne puts it:

> **"A Hoosier Holiday"** not only traces the personal process but it gives the social background. The common life, as seen throughout the countryside, is touched off quizzically, and yet sympathetically, with an artist's vision. Dreiser sees the American masses in their commonness and at their pleasure as brisk, rather vacuous people, a little pathetic in their innocence of the possibilities of life and their optimistic trustfulness. He sees them ruled by great barons of industry, and yet unconscious of their serfdom. He seems to love this countryside, and he makes you love it.

> Dreiser loves, too, the ugly, violent bursts of American industry,—the flaming steel-mills and gaunt lakesides. **"The Titan"** and **"The Financier"** are unattractive novels, but they are human documents of the brawn of a passing American era. Those stenographic conversations, webs of financial intrigue, bare bones of enterprize, insult our artistic sense. There is too much raw beef, and yet it all has the taste and smell of the primitive business-jungle it deals with. These crude and greedy captains of finance with their wars and their amours had to be given some kind of literary embodiment, and Dreiser has hammered a sort of raw epic out of their lives.

Not only in his feeling for themes of crude power and sex and for the American common life is Dreiser interesting. His emphases, Mr. Bourne concludes, are those of a new America which is latently expressive and which must develop its art before we shall really have become articulate.

> For Dreiser is a true hyphenate, a product of that conglomerate Americanism that springs from other roots than the English tradition. Do we realize how rare it is to find a talent that is thoroly American and wholly un-English? Culturally we have somehow suppressed the hyphenate. Only recently has he forced his way through the unofficial literary censorship. The *vers-librists* teem with him, but Dreiser is almost the first to achieve a largeness of utterance. His outlook, it is true, flouts the American canons of optimism and redemption, but these were never anything but conventions. There stirs in Dreiser's books a new American quality. It is not at all German. It is an authentic attempt to make something artistic out of the chaotic materials that lie around us in American life. Dreiser interests because we can watch him grope and feel his clumsiness. He has the artist's technique. That is one of the tragedies of America. But his faults are those of his material and of uncouth bulk, and not of shoddiness. He expresses an America that is in process of forming. The interest he evokes is part of the eager interest we feel in that growth.

In an illuminating essay published in *The Seven Arts,* H. L. Mencken, the foremost champion of our most disputed novelist, points out the peril confronting Theodore Dreiser. The war that has been waged against his books may, fears Mr. Mencken, convert him into a "professional revolutionary, spouting stale perunas for all the sorrows of the world." He hopes Theodore Dreiser will not take up causes and remedies:

> The peril that Dreiser stands in is here. He may begin to act, if he is not careful, according to the costume forced on him. Unable to combat the orthodox valuation of his place and aim, he may seek a spiritual refuge in embracing it, and so arrange himself with the tripe-sellers of heterodoxy, and cry wares that differ from the other stock only in the bald fact that they are different. ... Such a fall would grieve the judicious, of whom I have the honor to be one.

### *Current Opinion* (essay date 1919)

SOURCE: "The Secret of Personality as Theodore Dreiser Reveals It." *Current Opinion,* vol. 66, 3 Mar. 1919, pp. 175-76.

[*In the following essay, the writer contemplates Dreiser's recent remarks on the necessity of "inherent capacity" in individual achievement of distinction.*]

During recent years the Emersonian doctrine that every man is a potential genius has had a wide vogue in America. Against this idea, Theodore Dreiser, the novelist, sets his conviction that "all good things are gifts" and that it is impossible for an individual to develop an especial and remarkable capacity unless it is already inherent in him at birth. Mr. Dreiser reaches this conclusion in an article in *Pearson's* (New York), and he cites, in support of his argument, some of the great names of the ages.

In the last analysis, he tells us, personality appears to be a sense of power resting on a feeling of wisdom and usefulness or right to be. Or, perhaps, this may be reversed for some and it be said that it is a sense of usefulness which springs from inherent wisdom and power. "At best, it is inexplicable to the individual himself. He does not know where it comes from, why he has it, why he of all people should have it and so many other billions not, why his thoughts should be so large where those of others are so small, his cunning or subtlety great where those of so many others is obviously less."

> "Why should I be born with a great mind," Caesar, or Shakespeare, or Hannibal, or Leonardo might well have asked himself, "whereas so many have little ones? Why is my frail bark speeded by winds of destiny or chance over favorable seas to power, where so many are beached or foundered *en route?* Did I make myself? Did I foreknow all?" Where so profound an egotist, even with a minute brain, to claim as much?

> The truth is, all good things are gifts—a voice, strength of body, vigor of mind, vision, the power to lead, as in war,

any art, beauty, charm. This is not to say that these things may not be technically improved, and are; but this, if you please (improvement of primary capacities), is the business with which mediocrity is chiefly concerning itself.

> The man of personality or destiny realizes the guidance, enmity or favor of not necessarily higher, we will say, but different, powers. (I am not for saints, guardian *angels,* Buddhas, Christs—perfect gods all.) He realizes all too keenly the element of chance, luck, unpropitious as well as propitious hours. Sometimes, in spite of himself and to his wonder, he notes that his affairs prosper. 'There is a tide.' At other times (and who has not realized this?) that try as he will, he had better lay aside all effort and disappear. Fortune will have none of him. Whatever his personal merits or seeming qualities, life will have none of him. The furies hover over his path. Harpies beset him.

It is easy to cite the old-time virtues of honesty, stability, truthfulness, fair-dealing, etc., as proving the value of character and the power of any one, however weak or defective, to achieve it. But how about magnetism, courage, assurance? These are not ethical or truthful things necessarily, but they make for success just the same. Mr. Dreiser notes that youth admires color, flare, pugnacity. Middle age respects knowledge of sorts, aggressiveness, endurance, success. Old age prefers wisdom, generosity, humility. Very few of these qualities are strictly ethical. In the quiet halls of learning or reflection some of the tabulated virtues may be extolled, but to whom does the world pay attention, to whom has it paid attention? Darius, Artaxerxes, Alexander, Caesar, Hannibal, Attila, Alaric, Peter the Hermit, Napoleon, possessing what of all these virtues? Caesar, kind, patient, honest, truthful? Napoleon the same? Antony the same? "Not even the popes, the preachers, the founders of religion," Mr. Dreiser asserts, "were so. Always craft, force, diplomacy, but little of the sacrificial media so extolled and commended to the rank and file."

Mr. Dreiser welcomes the tendency in America to-day to emphasize personality rather than character. He is glad that we are beginning to recognize, "all the copybook maxims to the contrary notwithstanding," that "there are certain things which we cannot do—make, even, as we go along—wisdom, strength, genius, or even skill in many fields and professions." We hear less nowadays of being Napoleons all, of adding inches to our stature by taking thought, and more of plain effort according to our especially inherited abilities or capacity. "It is a sad truth for most Americans when they discover it (for most men perhaps), but it is nevertheless an economic and helpful one. Men do better once they realize their genuine limitations and cease reaching after the moon." Mr. Dreiser proceeds:

> I have often wondered why it is that the word 'common,' in its sense of being plentiful and therefore indifferent, has

not struck home to the many of us for what it is—an expression of contempt—and that 'uncommon,' 'extraordinary,' denote approbation. Why, if this is not true, should everything that is common be held so lightly of the mass, whereas that which is special or individual, inherited or no, is of such intense interest to it? For example, the individual skill or personal traits of the actor, painter, writer, sculptor, the exceptionally talented in any field?

The truth is that the average man, dull as he is, realizes quite well that a creature who has little or nothing that is different to millions of his kind is of small import here or anywhere. There is no especial demand for what he has to offer. If he wishes to stand out above his fellows, he must bring something new, and this he cannot provide by mere wishing or thinking. There is something more than that— inherent capacity. He also knows that nature sends bubbling up from her inexhaustible springs an infinitude of creatures who are, however, of small import, because they have no inherent power wherewith to develop very special characteristics, or, better yet, very individual impulses—in other words, personality. They cannot, and are not asked to, create them after they arrive here. They must have them to begin with, or they are not important, cannot make their way easily—*vide* Napoleon, Goethe, Shakespeare, Lincoln. It is obviously quite right that a creature which has no qualities except those of the species should have to confine its claim to an existence entirely within the limits of the species, and live a life conditioned by them. If nature wishes one to rise above the conditions wherewith he finds himself surrounded at birth, she usually provides him with the equipment for so doing during gestation, or before.

The upshot of the argument is that that which places one being over another and sets differences between man and man is not alone intellect or knowledge, as some would have us believe, but these "plus the vital energy to apply them or the hypnotic power of attracting attention to them— in other words, personality." Mr. Dreiser concludes:

> Whatever else you do, believe nothing in regard to the individual's ability to develop an especial and remarkable capacity, unless it is already inherent in him at birth. Nature works in no other way. It is not true—a passing illusion. Another thing: Life cannot do without brains, however much disassociated from beatific virtues these may be, but these are a gift and can no more be created here than you can add to your height by taking thought. What life does is to develop and train especial inherent capacities—an eye, a hand, a taste, a smell perhaps. But the instinct and the ability to foreknow, do, appreciate, understand—these things are not taught in schools. Schools labor with them to improve, polish, give them a special turn or bent—little more and little less.

## M. A. (review date 1919)

SOURCE: M. A. "Theodore Dreiser." Review of *Twelve Men,* by Theodore Dreiser. *The New Republic,* 3 May 1919, pp. 30-31.

*[In the following review, the critic complains that Dreiser's* Twelve Men *exhibits a "lack of style" which can be attributed to Dreiser's "general and real lack of philosophy," and although he is a "conscientious and competent observer," he has not "fought free" of the conventional repressions which bind him.]*

A fairly respectable biography of Theodore Dreiser might be concocted with no other bibliography than his ***Twelve Men*** and an American Who's Who. For the round dozen of them are manifestly real folk the author has known more or less intimately at different stages of his career, and we glimpse him through his contacts with them. We learn, for example, that he grew up in a stringently moral home in the middle west, and that his coming to New York was hastened by the undeniable fame and fortune his brother Paul was accumulating there as the foremost writer of popular songs. It comes as news that Theodore (and not Paul) wrote the first stanza and the chorus of On the Banks of the Wabash just to show his brother how these things should be managed. It would be possible to piece together the facts of his connection with many newspapers and magazines, the details of a "psychic breakdown" necessitating a sanatorium, an adventure in labor as a member of a railroad gang, and an astonishing prestige as editor of magazines for women, such as the Delineator.

The style of ***Twelve Men*** differs from that of ***The "Genius"*** in being fairly simple, with only occasional inextricable meanings. It lacks as did The Genius and all its predecessors, the finish that might have given resonance and carrying quality to what is said. Only a man as thoroughly sophisticated as Anatole France could use a medium of expression so loose as this without drifting once in a while into inanity. And he would not use it. But Mr. Dreiser is not sophisticated. He is easily disgusted, easily moved to tears. He writes "my dear brother" a little too often, and regrets Paul's eastern burial in the sentence, "It was so cold and dreary there, horrible."

The most acid realism may sometimes represent nothing more than a self-conscious sentimentalism dodging itself, if one judge from the following, hard to ascribe to any realist: "Ah, Broadway! Broadway! And you, my good brother! Here is the story that you wanted me to write, this little testimony to your memory, a pale, pale symbol of all I think and feel. Where are the thousand yarns I have laughed over, the music, the lights, the song? Peace, peace. So shall it soon be with all of us. It was a dream. It is. I am. You are. And shall we grieve over or hark back to dreams?"

But this lack of style, whether it be flaw or virtue, is only one angle of a general and real lack of philosophy.

Theodore Dreiser is a conscientious and competent observer, but an observer galled and limited in range by strands of old repressions, angered to find himself bound by an inculcated morality in an age when others have fought free. He is constantly at war against his Puritanical instincts, with the result that he is never sure of his own boundaries. He can assume no consistent attitude, can put no coherence into the way he says his say about American life.

There is, strangely enough, a kind of consistency in the lives of the twelve men he has chosen to represent. No less than six of them were men of great promise who died without achieving the things they seemed fitted to do. And four, perhaps five, can be put down as minor philanthropists, men who, because of some religious or personal bias, have found their happiness in serving others. For Dreiser it is a remarkable collection. In all of them the element of selfishness is reduced to a minimum; it is as if he had said to himself that he had been confined too closely to the hopeless, that he would now make a study of the creative spirit and eternal kindliness in men. He succeeds rather indifferently with the humanitarians. For them he seems to have only a mild and artificially exaggerated sympathy; and his misunderstanding of them verges in some instances on complete bewilderment. With the young journalists, artists and publicists he was in closer touch; catalogues of peculiarities occur, but vivified by inner acquaintance. Peter, who opens the book, assumes life and charm from the beginning.

It was evidently Peter who first woke Theodore Dreiser from his middle-western sleep to a realization that the world and its possibilities were wider than had been allowed to appear on the surface, and much wider than his education. With Peter he went about St. Louis for the first time.

> As I view myself now, I was a poor, spindling, prying fish, anxious to know life, and yet because of my very narrow training very fearsome of it, of what it might do to me, what dreadful contagion of thought or deed it might open me to! Peter was not so. To him all, positively *all,* life was good. ... When I look back now upon the shabby, poorly lighted, low-ceiled room to which he led me 'for fun,' the absolutely black or brown girls with their white teeth and shiny eyes, the unexplainable, unintelligible love of rhythm and the dance displayed, the beating of the drum, the sinuous, winding motions of the body, I am grateful to him. He released my mind, broadened my view, lengthened my perspective. For as I sat with him, watching him beat his drum or play his flute, noted the gayety, his love of color and effect, and feeling myself *low,* a criminal, disgraced, the while I was staring with all my sight and enjoying it intensely, I realized that I was dealing with a man who was 'bigger' than I was in many respects, saner, really more wholesome. I was a moral coward.

There are many instances of their common adventures, told with the same directness, and indicating in a similar fashion the influence of Peter in opening the eyes of his companion, not only to the dives of the city, but to the religions, arts, and philosophies of the earth. Probably it was these peregrinations that temporarily smothered the sentimentalist—the song-writer—in Dreiser.

As an experiment in literary form the book is only a passable success. Interesting as many of the figures are, they interest only in themselves, and not in the sketches to follow. There is nothing in Peter to prepare us for the sudden change of atmosphere in **"A Doer of the Word,"** and though the autobiographical thread exists it runs in tangled convolutions. There comes a time when the momentum is insufficient to carry over. To be sure there will be those who overcome the inertia, and turn the page, remembering that this man Dreiser never puts his best foot forward, never seems to be going to get anywhere, and yet somehow, after a good deal of fuss and bungling, sometimes does.

## E. M. K. (review date 1926)

SOURCE: E. M. K. Review of *An American Tragedy,* by Theodore Dreiser. *The Sewanee Review,* vol. 34, no. 4, Oct.-Dec. 1926, pp. 495-97.

*[In the following review, the critic admits that Dreiser's style is "unbeautiful" but asserts that the "authentic and inevitable" power of Dreiser's "genius" for nonjudgmental observation far surpasses any technical defects in his storytelling.]*

After ten years of silence, Dreiser has returned from themes of high finance to populated towns and streets he loved to explore in the earlier days of **Sister Carrie** or **Jennie Gerhardt.** His new novel, **An American Tragedy,** is the bulkiest among his bulky works, and it has all the familiar defects of size, formlessness, and clumsiness of style. And one hears again the echoes of familiar but thoughtless complaining that he is so unbeautiful. We do not like the springless wagon-ride behind oxen on rutted country roads. There is no speed, no glamor, no humor, no cadence, no crushed perfume, and no cool refuge for the heart's refinement in Dreiser's style. But as for me, he holds me steadfast to the end, fascinated, this steadfast ox-cart driver with his story so authentic and inevitable, so complete of integrity with itself and the materials, so tragic in its nerveless gestures. It is not a story of smiling cultivated fields and of trim secluded garden-plots, nor of a land with tamed, channeled rivers sparkling in the springtime sun. His is primitive prairie; a dark continent; a muddy, sprawling, untameable

Mississippi, carrying the life of farm and forest on its vast expanse, unmoving if one watches it at one point, yet majestic, rude in its passion, and steady in its power and magnitude if one looks at it, Father of Waters, from the north to the Gulf. Then it seems no longer still and muddy; then it has color, persuasiveness, ease of force.

A dark continent. A brutish, planless life of cities, grand hotels, factories, clubs. The inheritance of lawless traditions of getting on in the blood. Predatory man, with murder in his heart, unassimilating the symmetry and beautiful ordering of his delicate machinery, and so breaking and ravishing the root-ends and the root-needs of life. Passionate, personal success. Mawkish sentiment. Optimism. And the human wolf-cub fed on hypocrisy, squalid ambitions, and the vulgar pap of evangelism, avid for ready cash and the things cash buys. Clyde Griffith—one of millions spawned of a vast industrialism, trivial bits of humanity living extinguished lives before the sun is at mid-day, left with nothing save the ambition to get on and to possess, dreaming of the beauty of girls and money, money which will buy position and beauty and meaning of life perhaps. Clyde is legion—wolf-weaklings entangled in little sins and desirings, committing murder in their hearts every day; wolf-weaklings who can neither wholly will nor act, whom passion finds defenceless and unprepared, but leading them on just the same and just as inevitably to kill the dead unstruggling prey. A lawless order, strong in possessions. A lost, bewildered man-cub. Murder. ... Who is the murderer?

Millions murdered of spirit, and millions murdering at heart, this is the American tragedy, the universal tragedy of a sweating, on-getting, incoherent, moralistic industrialism, the muddy current of our untamed and chaotic existence. The claws of the beast are in our souls. And Dreiser is touched by the tragic failure of our being in its innermost relationships, moved by the strangeness of life, and the sanctities of our human contacts floundering in the brutal mass of matter. He loves life, insatiably, in all its significances and irrelevancies, the whole wealth of life he cherishes, the mighty current surging around and under all the agitated particles of mankind carried resistlessly on, massive, always terrible. Whither? There is no answer. We move darkly on the boundless current of life—victims, victims all: Clyde, his mother, Roberta, Sondra, doctor, factory hands, foremen, bellhops, the powerful collar-magnate, the frail and the competent, all unimportant, without the strength to put meaning in life, and so without the truth of life by which man lives. Occasionally a gleam of beauty and tenderness—O Clyde and O Roberta in the brief moment of love under the dark-blue sky—and then swallowed by darkness and driven to inevitable doom; again unmeaningness, again helplessness. And humbly, kindly,

helplessly, the genius of Dreiser is looking on, touching every one with his pity, condemning no one, ridiculing nothing. And what he sees he tells honestly, brokenly, as a man reeling and befuddled by the terror of things seen. Murder, in fact, and greater murdering of the human spirit. Here one goes puzzled to die in the electric chair; one will return to preaching on street-corners; one to the manufacturing of more collars, more collars. ... And the heart trembles in the unrelenting grasp of some ancient god. ...

### Charles Child Walcutt (essay date 1940)

SOURCE: Walcutt, Charles Child. "The Three Stages of Theodore Dreiser's Naturalism." *PMLA,* vol. 55, no. 1, Mar. 1940, pp. 266-89.

[*In the following essay, Walcutt traces "the development of Dreiser's naturalism" through the six novels he published during his lifetime, "showing how, in three distinct stages he has taken three different [philosophical] attitudes."*]

The naturalism of Theodore Dreiser may be approached through a study of his personality, the sort of experiences he had in his formative years, and the philosophical speculations which grew from his experiences and his reading. A warm, boundless human sympathy;[1] a tremendous vital lust for life with a conviction that man is the end and measure of all things in a world which is nevertheless without purpose or standards;[2] moral, ethical, and religious agnosticism;[3] contact with the scientific thought of the late nineteenth century which emphasized the power and scope of mechanical laws over human desires;[4] belief in a chemical-mechanistic explanation of the human machine—an explanation which substantiates his materialism while it does full justice to the mystery of consciousness and the vital urge;[5]—these are the elements which Dreiser brings to the Creation of his novels.[6] It must be emphasized that his awareness of the shifting, cyclical quality of human and natural affairs arises as much from experience as from his contact with literary models or scientific thought. His determinism, again, loses its force because he is more interested in the mystery and terror and wonder of life itself than in tracing those forces which might account for and so dispel the mystery. Science is not, to him, the wonderful high priest of benign Nature, because he has seen too many of the evils of industrialism and the malignancy of natural forces. But life is eternally seeking, searching, striving, throbbing—life is the single positive element in a cosmos of ruthless flux. And the pathetic fortunes of people in this cosmos of purposeless change are the main concern of Dreiser's novels.

The present study will trace the development of Dreiser's naturalism through his six novels, showing how, in three distinct stages he has taken three different attitudes toward the body of ideas just described, which have resulted in three kinds of naturalistic novels.

### I

In the first stage he was expounding his conviction of the essential purposelessness of life and attacking the conventional ethical codes which to him seemed to hold men to standards of conduct that had no rational basis in fact, while they condemned others without regard to what Dreiser thought might be the real merits of their situations. The first half of this program—expounding the purposelessness of life—is the backbone of his first novel, *Sister Carrie,* published in 1900. Through a queer juxtaposition of incidents, and with only small regard for the worthiness of their impulses, one character achieves fame and comfort while another loses his social position, wealth, pride, and finally his life.

Into this novel Dreiser has brought all the vivid reality of his own experience with the dreary, beaten, downtrodden life of those who have no money, no background, no sophistication, and no especial talent. With a deep compassion that never assumes the right to pass moral judgment upon the actions of his characters, he shows Carrie Meeber coming to Chicago from the country, drearily passing from one ill-paid and health-breaking job to another, and at length, jobless and depressed at the thought of having to return defeated to the country, falling in and setting up housekeeping with one Drouet, a "drummer" whom she had met on the train as she first entered the city.

At this crucial instance begins Carrie's rise in the world. As a "fallen woman" she is in no wise judged; and even more astonishing, Drouet is shown to be flashy, crude, essentially shallow, but nevertheless at the antipodes from villainy. He is good-hearted and generous; in fact he has every intention of marrying Carrie—although he does not ever do so. With this social and financial advance over the miserable narrowness that characterized the home life of the sister with whom she had been living Carrie begins to recognize class differences, to long for better things, even to sense that Drouet is not on the heights of sophistication and culture. Drouet's friend Hurstwood represents the next higher level of poise, wealth, and understanding. He is manager of a prosperous saloon, he owns a fine house, and his family is eagerly climbing the social ladder. When he meets Carrie he falls desperately in love with her and, in what almost amounts to an abduction, abandons

his family, steals $10,000 from his employers, and flees with her through Canada and into New York.

From this point the fall of Hurstwood and the rise of Carrie are depicted in antiphonal relationship. Hurstwood's degeneration is a marvelous representation of the meaningless, almost unmotivated sort of tragedy that art had, until then, conspired to ignore. His wife's grasping jealousy and pettiness impel him towards Carrie, and his being seen with her gives his wife grounds for a divorce action. It is by the merest chance that he finds the safe open on the very night when he had planned to disappear. His theft of the $10,000 results from a nervous impulse which he is too weak to resist. He is later forced to return the money, but he never recovers his self-esteem. In New York he takes a half interest in a second-rate saloon and after a time loses his investment. Then he dawdles, first looking for jobs, finally sitting in hotels instead of looking; at length he stays at home, reading newspapers endlessly and hoarding the little money he has left. The change in his character from an affluent good-fellow to a seedy miser is as convincing as it is tragical.

> Some men never recognize the turning in the tide of their abilities. It is only in chance cases, where a fortune or a state of success is wrested from them, that the lack of ability to do as they did formerly becames apparent. Hurstwood, set down under new conditions, was in a position to see that he was no longer young.[7]

Carrie stays with him as long as she can; but when she gets a place in a stage chorus she leaves him in order to room with a girl who is dancing in the same chorus. Hurstwood goes down and down—to poverty, destitution, begging, starvation, and finally suicide. The story of his downfall is perhaps the most moving one that Dreiser has written.

Carrie, on the other hand, rises rapidly from the moment she leaves Hurstwood. She graduates from the chorus to a minor rôle:

> Evidently the part was not intended to take precedence as Miss Madenda [Carrie] is not often on the stage, but the audience, with the characteristic perversity of such bodies, selected for itself. The little Quakeress was marked for a favourite the moment she appeared, and thereafter easily held attention and applause. The vagaries of fortune are indeed curious.[8]

The last sentence of this newspaper account of Carrie's first step forward on the stage emphasizes the major theme of the book—how curious are the vagaries of fortune. As Hurstwood is drawing nearer to his sordid death, Carrie climbs rapidly until she is earning what was to her an unheard of salary, living in one of the finest hotels in the city, and receiving countless proposals and attentions from men as far superior to Hurstwood at his best as he had been to the flashy Drouet. "Even had Hurstwood returned in his original beauty and glory, he could not now have allured her."[9] The book ends on a note of uncertainty. Carrie is not to be thought of as having attained any final goal. She is still longing and wondering—

> an illustration of the devious way by which one who feels rather than reasons, may be led in the pursuit of beauty. Though often disillusioned, she was still waiting for that halcyon day when she should be led forth among dreams become real.[10]

Shocking to contemporary readers—or reviewers, for there were few if any readers at first—was the amoral attitude from which *Sister Carrie* was written.[11] Nowhere is there a moral pointed. There is no inevitable punishment for transgression, no suggestion that there ought to be. In one passage Dreiser even appeals to Nature as against conventional moral standards and intimates that the only evil in what is ordinarily considered sinful comes from the codes which call it evil, rather than from the deed itself:

> He [Drouet] could not help what he was going to do. He could not see clearly enough to wish to do differently. He was drawn by his innate desire to act the old pursuing part. He would need to delight himself with Carrie as surely as he would need to eat his heavy breakfast. He might suffer the least rudimentary twinge of conscience in whatever he did, and *in just so far he was evil and sinning*. But whatever twinges of conscience he might have would be rudimentary.[12]

What is perfectly natural or spontaneous is good: the brooding mind makes sin. Morals may thus be rigid, unrealistic; but they do reflect a life force which goes deeper than the simple mechanist is willing or able to perceive. To Dreiser some such mystical principle represents the force which perhaps lies behind the wonder and terror and mystery of life. It is the recognition of this urge that makes life so positive and wonderful to him and that makes him doubt the rigidly "scientific" approach to problems of human conduct:

> For all the liberal analysis of Spencer and our modern naturalistic philosophers, [he writes], we have but an infantile perception of morals. There is more in the subject than mere conformity to a law of evolution. It is yet deeper than conformity to things of earth alone. It is more involved than we, as yet, perceive. Answer, first, why the heart thrills; explain wherefore some plaintive note goes wandering about the world, undying; make clear the rose's subtle alchemy evolving its ruddy lamp in light and rain. In the essence of these facts lie the first principles of morals.[13]

Elsewhere[14] Dreiser has been shown to distrust the concept of purpose or ethical design in the universe; yet such passages as that just quoted betray him in the characteristically naturalistic action of substituting the compelling, vital mystery of Nature for the failing God of orthodox religion. Here is the naturalistic affirmation in full force—springing equally from Dreiser's temperament and from the intellectual climate of the day. Conventional standards are set aside, but the richness of life is magnified rather than ignored. It must, of course, be recognized that the "affirmation" is not as strong with Dreiser, who has come to see the impossibility of reducing all phenomena to orderly laws, as it was with those earlier devotees of science who transferred their religious zeal directly to Nature, never doubting that the answers to all men's problems were to be found by patient searching through Her domain.

A consciously scientific use of detail appears when Dreiser brings chemical physiology to the explanation of Hurstwood's mental condition as he is beginning his final downward plunge:

> Constant comparison between his old state and his new showed a balance for the worse, which produced a constant state of gloom or, at least, depression. Now, it has been shown experimentally that a constantly subdued frame of mind produces certain poisons in the blood, called katastates, just as virtuous feelings of pleasure and delight produce helpful chemicals called anastates. The poisons generated by remorse inveigh against the system, and eventually produce marked physical deterioration. To these Hurstwood was subject.[15]

This, in small compass, is a clear-cut instance of the influence of science upon Dreiser's method: he is approaching his problem with a new set of instruments. The chemical explanation of mental conditions is of a piece with the amoral outlook and the change of focus away from ethical plot-conflict toward the dispassionate *observation* of life. This latter problem, which brings one to the heart of what is new in the form of *Sister Carrie,* may now be considered.

The novel has a carefully worked out structural form consisting of the two life cycles which are opposed to each other in studied balance. What *Sister Carrie* exhibits that is most characteristically naturalistic is the complete absence of ethical plot-complication. The movement of the novel does not depend upon acts of will by the central figures. There is no suspense waiting for resolution upon a decision which will be judged in terms of absolute ethical standards. The movement is the movement of life—skilfully selected and represented by the artist, to be sure, but still a movement which has little resemblance to the typical plot that begins with a choice or a crucial action and ends with the satisfaction of all the forces and the passions set in motion by that choice. The difference is fundamental. The novels of such writers as Thackeray and Trollope have complication, climax, and dénouement in every instance. *Sister Carrie* has no such movement. There is never any suspense created because the art of the novelist is directed by an entirely different motive. Dreiser is not manipulating a portion of life; he is observing it. It is the quality of the lives represented that moves the reader, not the excitement of what the characters do ... And most wonderful and mysterious of all is the ceaseless change which is the sign of life, change which is the outstanding characteristic of Nature. Thus, having deprived his novel of the conventional structure, Dreiser supplies the two cycles: Carrie's rise and Hurstwood's descent. These two cycles embody the principle of change which, to repeat, Dreiser finds fundamental to all life and all natural process.

Here a reservation must be made, for this statement of the case obscures the fact that Dreiser is primarily a novelist, a student of humanity, and, in his novels at least, only incidentally a philosopher. Human values are always first with him, and philosophical implications second. *Sister Carrie* is more important as a story than for the ideas it contains. The reader is interested in Carrie as a person who faces problems comparable to his own; and if the reader is not to be offended by the course of the story, the successes and failures of the characters must in some way answer to the reader's notion of their worth as human beings. Carrie's rise, even though accidental and not, by conventional standards, deserved, is welcome because she is an appealing character; and Hurstwood's degeneration, distressing though it may be, is not unbearably offensive because Hurstwood has qualities which cause him to lose some of the reader's sympathy. The philosopher in Dreiser makes concessions to the novelist because his heart is in league with humanity. This fact is inescapable. It is the people who struggle with cosmic purposelessness who interest him, and being one of them he cannot entirely abandon them to the haphazard buffetings of fate which his intellect would undoubtedly tell him were perfectly possible. One cannot write stories in which, just as the crisis is approaching, the hero is killed by a falling meteor. Things like that happen in life, but they cannot in novels, which, as artistic units, must exhibit design and organization that transcend the perfectly possible accidents of reality. With these reservations, which depend upon the fact that the novelist is "in league with humanity" and cares more for human suffering than for the demonstration of the principle of cosmic indifference, we may return to the assertion that *Sister Carrie* is organized to demonstrate the essential purposelessness of life. The plot structure of conventional fiction is abandoned for the new organization that answers to Dreiser's view of reality. But, though he recognizes the operation of external force, he is not, in *Sister Carrie,* concerned with an experi-

mental demonstration of the nature of that operation. Rather he is concerned with the pathos of human life and with the constant inscrutable change by which it is attended.

We come, in the last analysis, to a matter of emphasis: one may study the way external forces operate upon man, attempting to lay bare all the secrets of their action; or one may see life through the eyes of the objects of these forces, with all the wonder and terror of the changes unexplained. Dreiser does a little of both: he shows clearly enough how Hurstwood and Carrie change as they do; but mostly he is concerned with bringing out the shifting, uncertain, mysterious nature of life as it appears when being acted upon by forces which it cannot fathom and which have no purpose that can be related to the purposes of men.

Dreiser, to conclude, believes in a determinism which destroys or modifies the moral view of conduct. He is, further, impressed by the inscrutability of fortune, the lack of meaning and purpose in the action of external force. Between these two smothering convictions flourishes his affirmation—his belief in the vitality and importance of life. It is upon the latter that one's attention is directed in *Sister Carrie.* The inscrutable variations of fortune serve chiefly to underline the positive quality of living. Throughout the book it is this quality of life—shifting, elusive, unaccountable—that holds our attention, rather than the spectacle of carefully analyzed forces operating under "experimental" conditions.[16]

The human will is not denied in *Sister Carrie*; nor is there any effort made to demonstrate the elements of which that "fiction" is composed. Dreiser is concerned with people first of all, and he sees them as acting according to their individualities, behind which he does not usually try to penetrate.[17] But on the other hand Dreiser does show clearly how the will is thwarted, dominated, lured astray by all the social forces among which it lives. Best of all, perhaps, he shows how the will can, for lack of purpose or conviction, lose control so that the individual drifts from situation to situation without knowing just why he does so. In this sense Dreiser does show how the individual is dominated by his environment. He does make a convincing presentation of the way circumstantial[18] influences can combine with weakness of will to take a character's fate out of his own hands. Something of this sort is done with both Carrie and Hurstwood. What happens to such people does not prove any cosmic generalizations. It does not seem to explain the operation of determinism. It merely shows how the freedom of the will is conditioned by a multitude of pressures and circumstances, forces which work changes in the lives of those who are passive, just as they nullify the efforts of those who plan.[19]

The generalizations applied to *Sister Carrie* are also true of *Jennie Gerhardt* (1911). The difference between the two books which is of importance to this study is a difference of emphasis. In *Sister Carrie* conventional ethical codes are *assumed* to be invalid or at least impractical for evaluating life as it is, while the story is largely pointed toward *demonstrating* the unpredictable purposelessness of all things. In *Jennie Gerhardt* this emphasis is reversed. Ceaseless and unintentioned change has become an accepted hypothesis with Dreiser, while the story is devoted to a consideration of the moral and ethical standards according to which society (supposedly) operates. The previous assumption that they are unreal here becomes the point at issue, the material of Dreiser's thesis in so far as he has one. He shows how the life of a "kept woman" is blighted by society's treatment of what it considers her immorality. The criticism is pointed by the heroine's being a rich and lovely character (which illustrates again the contention that Dreiser is primarily a novelist, in league with humanity), and the effect of the story is to show how utterly inadequate are standard Christian ethics for the judgment or guidance of conduct in a world that does not, as Dreiser sees it, correspond to the notion of reality upon which that ethical code is based.

Jennie Gerhardt is the daughter of a stupidly devout German glass-blower. She is one of a large family that lives in the poor district of Columbus, Ohio, at a bare subsistence level. She is not a semi-moron (as one critic has said) but a girl rich and direct in feeling—the sort of person whose feelings take the place of thoughts:

> There are natures born to the inheritance of flesh that come without understanding, and that go again without seeming to have wondered why. Life, so long as they endure it, is a true wonderland, a thing of infinite beauty, which could they but wander into it wonderingly, would be heaven enough. ... From her earliest youth goodness and mercy had molded her every impulse.[20]

At the hotel where she scrubs floors, Senator Brander is impressed by her beauty, decides to marry her, and presently seduces her.

The Senator dies suddenly, before he is able to carry out his intention of marrying Jennie, leaving her with child. After it is born, the disgraced family moves to Cleveland, where Jennie presently meets the man who is to be the center of her thoughts for the rest of her life. Lester Kane comes from a wealthy Cincinnati family of carriage-makers. He is generous, forceful, direct, and the slightest bit coarse-grained. In spite of his wealth and good breeding, the reader is made to feel that he is, emotionally, less beautifully constructed than Jennie, though he is capable of appreciating her fine

nature and is, indeed, worlds beyond her culturally. Most of the book is devoted to their changing relations. He keeps her in various apartments, supplying her liberally with money, always half intending to marry her but never quite making his mind up to disturb the comfortable *status quo*. Jennie's most pressing concern, after her love for Lester, is to keep her little girl near without having Lester, whom she has foolishly kept in ignorance, learn of the child's existence. She is happy in her love for him and in being able to help her impoverished family with money. Lester's discovery of the child precipitates a crisis, and he thinks of leaving her. But he has become so attached to her goodness that he cannot bear the thought of separation. When his family discovers the connection and tries to break it, he defiantly installs Jennie in a large house in Chicago, and a period of precarious happiness follows.

Then forces conspire to take Lester away from her. His father dies, leaving Lester's inheritance contingent upon his abandoning Jennie. His family brings all its persuasive force to bear. And, to sweep aside the last hesitation, Lester is attracted by a cultivated and wealthy widow who is deeply in love with him. Again in the matter of this choice, Jennie is wholly unselfish in wanting Lester to do what is best for himself—and it is he who is uncertain which way to turn, drawn at once by loyalty to Jennie, fascination for Mrs. Gerald, the desire to retain his accustomed wealth and to be active in his father's business, and the influence exerted by his family and the polite society which wants him to become finally "respectable."

> But he did not want to do this. The thought was painful to him—objectionable in every way. Jennie was growing in mental acumen. She was beginning to see things quite as clearly as he did. She was not a cheap, ambitious, climbing creature. She was a big woman and a good one. It would be a shame to throw her down, and besides she was good-looking. ... It is an exceptional thing to find beauty, youth, compatibility, intelligence, your own point of view—softened and charmingly emotionalized—in another.[21]

The reader cannot entirely blame Lester when he finally gives Jennie up, for he understands the many subtle pressures—which Dreiser so masterly depicts—that condition his exercise of volition. Lester could choose readily enough if he knew exactly what he wanted. What makes the influence of external forces credible is the wealth of careful documentation that Dreiser presents so that the reader may actually *see* all the influences that work upon Lester and paralyze his will. Social ostracism, combined with the loss of a large part of his independent fortune, which makes his need for a share in his father's estate more pressing, finally turns the balance against Jennie—though it is she who urges him to go.

At a subsequent meeting he tries to explain his feelings:

> "I was just as happy with you as I ever will be. It isn't myself that's important in this transaction apparently; the individual doesn't count much in the situation. ... All of us are more or less pawns. We're moved about like chessmen by circumstances over which we have no control. ...
>
> "After all, life is more or less of a farce," he went on a little bitterly. "It's a silly show. The best we can do is to hold our personality intact. It doesn't appear that integrity has much to do with it."[22]

Stricken with a fatal illness, he calls her to his death bed, where he tells her:

> I haven't been satisfied with the way we parted. It wasn't the right thing, after all. I haven't been any happier. I'm sorry. I wish now, for my own peace of mind, that I hadn't done it. ... It wasn't right. The thing wasn't worked out right from the start; but that wasn't your fault. I'm sorry. I wanted to tell you that. I'm glad I'm here to do it.[23]

The story ends with Jennie at the station for a last glimpse of the coffin. Nowhere has Dreiser matched the pathos of these closing lines:

> Before her was stretching a vista of lonely years down which she was steadily gazing. Now what? She was not so old yet. There were those two orphan children to raise. They would marry and leave after a while, and then what? Days and days in endless reiteration, and then————?[24]

A novel with a "kept woman" for its central figure would be somewhat unusual, but when that kept woman is presented as good and admirable, as possessing positive virtues which raise her quite above the general run of socially minded people, then we recognize a novel in which an unusual approach is taken to the problem of man in society.

This approach constitutes the philosophy of the novel. As in *Sister Carrie* it can be stated as a belief in determinism accompanied by a conviction that the appointed course of events has neither purpose nor an order that is accessible to man's intellect. What strikes the reader again and again is the unreasonable way in which events pile up to direct the lives of the characters. Luck is more important than careful planning, and "goodness" does not necessarily appeal to the unknown controllers of destiny. The novel presents a long sequence of "controlled" events in a way that convinces anyone who reads. The evidence is there and cannot be gainsaid: a thousand circumstances enfold man in their invisible garment of steel; and no one is capable of seeing the pattern according to which the garment is woven; one only feels the pressures which check or direct him in particular movements.

The same kind of thinking is extended to Dreiser's idea of the human will. He recognizes will as a function of what he might call personality. His people act from apparently autonomous impulses. Jennie's goodness, for example, he regards as something which need not and indeed cannot be accounted for; it can only be described. But at the same time, by the approach outlined in the preceding pages, Dreiser shows that the will is not free to operate independently, that it has not the power to bring its impulses to fulfillment. Thus instead of attempting to go behind the will and identify the components of its apparently free volitions, he follows these impulses into the world and shows us precisely why and how they are thwarted by social and economic forces. We might say that he admits free will with reference to volition but denies it with reference to action. One can wish freely, but one cannot freely carry out one's wishes.

In a world so envisaged, good intentions do not necessarily bear good results. Nor is what is conventionally called evil punished. Hence standard ethics are discredited because they do not, in Dreiser's eyes, represent a realistic interpretation of social relations. They do not constitute the genuine forces which make for social cohesion and regulate the conduct of civilized man. It would be useless to blame someone for conditions beyond his control. This assumption is fundamental in *Jennie Gerhardt.* As Lester says, "The best we can do is to hold our personality intact." Jennie's goodness is valued more highly than the society which destroys her chance for happiness. Dreiser does not show that there may be extenuating circumstances to pardon the sinfulness of the "fallen woman." He denies that she is sinful; he deplores the moral codes which, failing to restrain her first slip, inflict a consciousness of guilt upon her ever after; he considers her good and beautiful, and the reader is led to conclude that Lester Kane was foolish (or very unlucky) not to have married her. These conclusions grow naturally from Dreiser's conviction that, since human feeling is the one real value in a cosmos of purposeless change, any social pressures which blight the fullest satisfaction of that feeling are of questionable benefit to mankind.

All these abstract notions depend for their conviction upon the emotional weight which Dreiser is able to attach to the personality of Jennie. That he succeeds with his "message" is due to his complete success in making of her a rich and lovely woman, a creature who is all good and whose simple heart is capable of endless devotion. Jennie is undoubtedly his richest creation. The reader's sympathies are entirely with her. Her misfortunes are truly heart-rending. Indeed her sufferings are so real that the reader is not aware of an auctorial "message," for he reaches the conclusions here described through his emotional response to the events of the story. This point is important, for it shows that the pathos of Jennie's life is the outstanding fact of the novel, the fact upon which depend any ideas that the reader may gather. As a work of art *Jennie Gerhardt* is, therefore, successful; for the ideas upon which it is based serve first of all to create a certain aesthetic effect and do not obtrude themselves in the way of that effect. It is too bad that Jennie should suffer, and the system is to be deplored for making her suffer, but that is not tantamount to saying that the institution of marriage, for example, should be rejected. It would indeed detract from the pathos of Jennie's situation if the author were crusading for change. The conditions which crush her must, for the purposes of the novel, be regarded as unchangeable.

## II

In the second stage of his development Dreiser added another element to the two main ideas which we have described as constituting the first phase of his naturalism. That was the idea of the superman. When one had found that life was meaningless and morals absurdly inadequate, the next step was to conclude that the only good lay in exercising one's will to power. The philosophy of the superman was conveniently available to enable Dreiser to take this step; and he wrote three novels about the activities of supermen in the modern world. Nietzsche's philosophy saw in the superman the only hope for the betterment of mankind. Dreiser may have known this aspect of Nietzsche's thought, he may even have begun *The Financier* with the intention of demonstrating some such idea, but his study of the activities of one of the Robber Barons of the late nineteenth century seems finally to have drawn him away from the notion that the financial superman was an indispensable agent in the development of a capitalistic society.

Dreiser's **"Trilogy of Desire,"** of which *The Financier* (1912) and *The Titan* (1914) have been published,[25] represents his effort to set forth the life of a modern financial superman. Although written from the point of view of the superman and begun as a celebration rather than an indictment of him, these novels virtually accomplish Jack London's avowed but unfulfilled purpose in writing *The Sea-Wolf*—to show that "the superman cannot be successful in modern life ... ; he acts like an irritant in the social body."[26] This cannot be called Dreiser's purpose, however, for he has never arrived at that degree of conviction which would permit him to organize a portion of the social scene and write about it as if he had thought his way through to a final conclusion about its meaning. Indeed it is the planlessness and inconclusiveness of life that interest Dreiser.

On the other hand, nearly all critics have ceased accusing him of being merely a patient recorder who copies his books tediously from newspaper records. He organizes his material without seeking to organize life into a "perfect round."

*The Financier* and *The Titan* contain perhaps the greatest mass of documentation to be found in any American novels in the naturalistic tradition. They are records of an epoch of American life. The career of Charles T. Yerkes, traction magnate of Philadelphia and Chicago, supplied Dreiser with the materials for his two books. Yerkes is transformed into Frank Algernon Cowperwood, and the novels record his economic and amorous affairs in minutest detail. *The Financier* takes Cowperwood from boyhood up to the panic of 1873. A "superman" devoid of ethical restraints, he goes from business to business, gaining control of the Philadelphia street-railway network and becoming involved with political graft. He becomes a millionaire and is laying plans to make a billion when the Chicago fire of 1871 causes a panic which wipes out his fortune. Because he has tampered with the daughter of the political boss, he is at this time abandoned by those in control and made a scapegoat to appease an indignant populace. After thirteen months in prison he is pardoned just in time to regain his fortune by selling short in the panic of 1873. Here ends *The Financier.*

*The Titan* is longer and more detailed. It tells how Cowperwood moves to Chicago and, through bribes and cleverness, gains a number of franchises for the distribution of suburban gas. After this coup he launches into a long fight to gain control of all the Chicago street railways. The novel presents the great struggle in all its complexity, showing how banks, local politicians, legislators, governors, and newspapers are drawn into the vortex of the conflict— and how Cowperwood is finally defeated in his efforts to buy or control the entire State legislature and obtain from them a fifty-year franchise on Chicago street-railway transportation. The details of all these transactions are given so fully that the reader is convinced of their authenticity: he comes from the books feeling that he has seen the whole picture, presented more minutely—and far more effectively—than it could have been presented in the best historical or economic treatise available. The facts are all there, vividly realized and brought to life. And since the affairs of Cowperwood are part and parcel of this vast economic complex, the recording of its intricacies is documentation in the best naturalistic tradition. It is as intimately united with the story as the documentation in Zola's *L'Assommoir* or *Germinal*. It is setting, condition, and material for the novel; none of it is extraneous, none gratuitous, because it is all a part of Cowperwood's career.

Interlarded with Cowperwood's business dealings throughout the two novels are his amorous intrigues and domestic difficulties. One critic has described *The Titan* as a "huge club-sandwich composed of slices of business alternating with erotic episodes,"[27] and the description is an apt one, although it gives less attention than it might to the close relationship between the two sides of Cowperwood's life. His amorous escapades round out his "business" personality; they also cause violent repercussions in his various business transactions, for the women he knows quite naturally are connected with the men whom he deals with in the world of politics and finance.

It has been shown in the discussion of both *Sister Carrie* and *Jennie Gerhardt* that Dreiser's determinism is determinism *after the fact*. That is, he does not pretend to go behind an act of so-called will and show all the conditions and pressures of which it is composed.[28] He does not pretend to set down a perfect chain of causal relationships that account for the fiction known as free will; but, admitting that fiction, he does show how in its actions it is swayed and guided by "deterministic" forces outside of it—so that in effect it is relatively helpless.[29]

In *The Financier* and *The Titan* there is the same attitude toward man and society, but the situation is greatly altered by a change in one of the factors of the problem. That factor of course is Frank Algernon Cowperwood. Instead of being relatively weak like Carrie, Hurstwood, Jennie, and Lester Kane, Cowperwood is a financial superman. He is born to conquer, and he knows it. At the age of eighteen he receives a five-hundred dollar Christmas bonus from the grain brokers to whom he has been "apprenticed" without salary to learn the business. Already he is indispensable—and perfectly confident:

> On the way home that evening he speculated as to the nature of this business. He knew he wasn't going to stay there long, even in spite of this gift and promise of salary. They were grateful, of course; but why shouldn't they be? He was efficient, he knew that; under him things moved smoothly. It never occurred to him that he belonged in the realm of clerkdom. Those people were the kind of people who ought to work for him, and who would. There was nothing savage in his attitude, no rage against fate, no dark fear of failure.[30]

He is selfish because his own concerns are paramount with him. In another paragraph his nature is carefully described:

> Cowperwood was innately and primarily an egoist and intellectual, though blended strongly therewith was a humane and democratic spirit. We think of egoism and intellectualism as closely confined to the arts. Finance is an art. And it presents the operations of the subtlest of the intellectuals and of the egoists. Cowperwood was a finan-

cier. Instead of dwelling on the works of nature, its beauty and subtlety, to his material disadvantage, he found a happy mean, owing to the swiftness of his intellectual operations, whereby he could, intellectually and emotionally, rejoice in the beauty of life without interfering with his perpetual material and financial calculations. And when it came to women and morals, which involved so much relating to beauty, happiness, a sense of distinction and variety in living, he was but now beginning to suspect for himself at least that apart from maintaining organized society in its present form there was no basis for this one-life, one-love idea.[31]

Toward the end of *The Titan* he is still strong; "he seemed a kind of superman, and yet also a bad boy—handsome, powerful, hopeful ... impelled by some blazing internal force which harried him on and on."[32] He is the apotheosis of individualism, the man who moves the mass, which "only moves forward because of the services of the exceptional individual." He answers to the wish "that the significant individual will always appear and will always do what his instincts tell him to do."[33]

At the end of *The Financier* Cowperwood, the financial superman, has asserted himself stupendously and yet, like Jennie and Lester Kane and Hurstwood, has been swept back and forth by the surge of environing forces more powerful than even his intelligence and resolution. Being a larger figure, he moves in a more elaborate complex of forces; but the forces elude his brilliant foresight and generalship and temporarily strip him of freedom and fortune.

At the end of the great struggle related in *The Titan,* when Cowperwood is temporarily defeated by the enmity his power has evoked (a situation which is a better example than London could produce of how the financial superman "acts like an irritant in the social body"), Dreiser expatiates upon the spectacle of his superman's career:

> Rushing like a great comet to the zenith, his path a blazing trail, Cowperwood did for the hour illuminate the terrors and wonders of individuality. But for him also the eternal equation—the pathos of the discovery that even giants are but pygmies, and that an ultimate balance must be struck. Of the strange, tortured, terrified, reflection of those who, caught in his wake, were swept from the normal and the commonplace, what shall we say? Legislators by the hundred were hounded from politics into their graves; a half-hundred aldermen of various councils who were driven grumbling or whining into the limbo of the dull, the useless, the commonplace.[34]

These sentences repeat the philosophy which was outlined at the beginning of this analysis of Dreiser's work and which was found in *Sister Carrie* and *Jennie Gerhardt.* What distinguishes *The Financier* and *The Titan* from the two previous novels is, as we have seen, the different weight given in them to the human factor in Dreiser's equation of change. Cowperwood is a greater force than Dreiser's earlier characters, but his position in the cosmos is essentially the same.

In conclusion we may consider the ethical import of these books. Hearing about them, one's reaction is that Dreiser must have composed them as an indictment of the business methods of the Robber Barons—to show that they were social menaces who should have been extirpated. Doubtless some such conclusion comes to the reader after he has finished the novels; but so long as he is reading them Cowperwood is the hero. His morals may not be held up as exemplary for American society, but his intelligence and energy make him the center of attention and concern. The reader sees the struggle through Cowperwood's eyes; he cannot avoid lending his sympathy to the owner of those eyes. He is attracted, as people always are in reality, to a man with the personal force to affect the lives of thousands of people. Further than this, Dreiser is frequently at pains to cast doubt upon the judgments which condemn Cowperwood. Early in **The Financier,** young Cowperwood gets his first lesson in the law of tooth and fang by watching a lobster devour day-by-day a squid that was placed in a tank with him in a store window.[35] The same novel ends with a parable about the Black Grouper, which survives by virtue of its ability to change color and so deceive enemy and prey alike. We are asked,

> What would you say was the intention of the overruling, intelligent, constructive force which gives to Mycteroperca this ability? To fit it to be truthful? To permit it to present an unvarying appearance which all honest life-seeking fish may know? Or would you say that subtlety, chicanery, trickery, were here at work? An implement of illusion one might readily suspect it to be, a living lie, a creature whose business it is to appear what it is not, to simulate that with which it has nothing in common, to get its living by great subtlety, the power of its enemies to forefend against which is little. The indictment is fair.

> Would you say, in the face of this, that a beatific, beneficent, creative, overruling power never wills that which is either tricky or deceptive?[36]

The conclusion is that Christian ethics are illusory, that people should not be blamed for disobeying a code which, if followed, would render them unfit to survive. Indeed, he found, as Burton Rascoe writes, "an epic quality in the rise of individuals to merciless and remorseless power through the adaptation of their combative instincts to the peculiar conditions of the American struggle for existence."[37] In the same spirit Dreiser interpolates a disquisition on monogamy, his point being that Christian moral standards do not answer to human needs.[38] Again,

he questions the idea of divine guidance and the relation of man to nature:

> How shall we explain these subtleties of temperament and desire? Life has to deal with them at every turn. They will not down, and the large, placid movements of nature outside of man's little organisms would indicate that she is not greatly concerned. We see much punishment in the form of jails, diseases, failure, and wrecks; but we also see that the old tendency is not visibly lessened. Is there no law outside of the subtle will and power of the individual to achieve? If not, it is surely high time that we knew it— one and all. We might then agree to do as we do; but there would be no silly illusions as to divine regulation.[39]

It does not follow from this denial of conventional ethics that a Cowperwood is a boon to society. He may "move the mass" but Dreiser's own story shows that he does not move it to any good end. There is no paradox here. The point is that Dreiser is thinking in terms of the individual without sufficiently considering his social function. Cowperwood cannot reasonably be condemned to hellfire for following his natural bent, but his social value is another matter. If Dreiser had studied it, he would unquestionably have recognized society's need to restrain such individuals. And he has done so since then. Indeed, his adoption of a more social point of view may explain his inability to complete **The Stoic** (see below, note 42). He undoubtedly began the series with the conviction that the Nietzschean superman was an instrument of social betterment, but he was open-minded enough to let the facts change this conviction.

Dreiser does not point his remarks upon conventional ethical codes further than to show that they are incapable of coping with modern problems, that most successful people disregard them, and that their application to the human animal under any conditions is a dubious procedure. He does not, on the other hand, suggest that modern society is perfect or that nothing can be done to improve it. But although he hopes for social improvement, Dreiser's purpose in these novels is to deal with life as it is lived under modern social and economic conditions. His art is devoted to a study of things as they are—which is to say that he is a successful novelist rather than a pseudo-scientist or propagandist.

**The "Genius"** (1915) is cut from the same block as **The Financier** and **The Titan**. Both in form and ideology it resembles those novels so closely that an extended analysis of it is unnecessary. Eugene Witla, the hero of **The "Genius,"** is a superman like Cowperwood. He is an artist rather than a financier, but otherwise he is much the same sort of person. Like Cowperwood, again, he is set loose in the turbulence of modern life and permitted to exercise his superior cunning untrammeled by moral restraints. Like Cowperwood he has his successes and his failures, the forces which thwart his intentions frequently being the combinations of weaker people who unite in defiance of his superman self-assertion. And again, Witla's amours occupy a large portion of the story, represent the super-abundance of his artistic "genius," and are responsible for several of his misfortunes. Like *The Financier* and *The Titan, The "Genius"* consists of a loosely connected sequence of events related by chronology and by the fact that Eugene Witla participates in them all. The book, furthermore, ends upon the note of wonder and uncertainty which we have found to be characteristic of Dreiser's attitude toward life. And finally, the superman hero is the center of reference and attention throughout the story. His effect upon society is not considered, for Dreiser is still brooding over the place of the individual in his meaningless cosmos.

### III

The third stage in Dreiser's naturalism is marked by his conversion to socialism. Here the ideas that signalized his first stage remain, but instead of advocating individual anarchy, as he tended to do under the aegis of Nietzsche, he has come to believe that something can be accomplished toward the amelioration of social evils if men will unite in a concerted attack upon those evils. *An American Tragedy* is founded upon this point of view, although the reader must remember that this, like Dreiser's other novels, is first of all a human story.

*An American Tragedy* recounts the life of Clyde Griffiths. He is first seen in Kansas City, the child of itinerant street preachers, singing on a corner with them. He becomes a bell-boy in a lavish hotel and there acquires a longing for all the comforts and luxuries which his family can not provide. He soon goes to Chicago where, still working as a bell-boy, he meets his rich uncle Samuel, a collar manufacturer in Lycurgus, New York. The uncle later has Clyde come to Lycurgus and starts him at the bottom of his business, with every opportunity to work his way to the top. But Clyde is not accepted socially by his wealthy relatives until the fascinating Sondra Finchley takes him up—out of spite—and introduces him to the highest social set of Lycurgus. In the meantime Clyde had been sharing his loneliness with Roberta Alden, a simple country girl who was working under him in the factory. Now when he sees a promising future before him, it transpires that Roberta is with child. In desperation, after weeks of torturing worry, he plans to take her boating in the country and "accidentally" drown her. At the final moment he is too weak to tip the boat over, but Chance—or the situation produced by the two personalities in their particular relation—completes the design in another way: Seeing his despairing and horrified expression, Roberta comes to-

ward him in the boat. He strikes out desperately to fend her off and hits her with a camera unconsciously held in his hand; the boat capsizes, striking Roberta as she falls into the water, and Clyde refrains from saving her.[40]

The rest of the story is devoted to the apprehension, trial, conviction, and execution of Clyde for the murder of Roberta. As the passage referred to above indicates, Clyde himself is not perfectly sure whether or not he is guilty. Before Roberta arose and came toward him in the rowboat, he had certainly decided that he would not commit the crime he had planned. On the other hand, he instituted the expedition with murder in his heart—a fact which exerted much influence upon the final decision of the jury. The prosecution brings dozens of witnesses and traces Clyde's movements minutely. Clyde's only defense is his last minute change of heart for which there is no evidence and which is easily counterbalanced by the absolute proof of his murderous intentions.

The peculiar way in which the "murder" of Roberta occurred is one of the most important facts in the novel. Clyde's inability to commit the deed in cold blood is indicative of his general weakness of will. But when some kind of chance, which might be described by an omniscient psychologist as the inevitable reaction of Roberta to Clyde's horrified expression, enters the action and the boat is capsized, Clyde is given a shock which enables him to refrain from rescuing her. The effect of this careful description of the incident is to show that Clyde is not the master of his fate, that only under particular conditions is he able to "choose" the "evil" course that he desires to carry out. He does not really "choose" to abandon Roberta; it would be more accurate to say that he is conditioned by his weeks of planning so that when the situation enables him to overcome his scruples (equally the product of long training) he is carried along by the impetus of this conditioning to commit the act he has planned. Thus from an objective point of view, one can hardly blame Clyde for an action in which he was largely a helpless participant. Clyde did not wilfully produce the painful dilemma which called forth his unhappy attempt to resolve it. His craving for wealth and social position can be understood—like his complementary lack of ethical standards—in the light of his upbringing. His weakness is contemptible to some readers, but Dreiser certainly does not contemn it. Clyde has a certain power of choice, to be sure, which Dreiser does not reduce to its ultimate chemical constituents as the first naïve naturalists thought they might finally be able to do; but that power of choice, though accepted as a factor in the problem, is shown to be conditioned by the many forces among which it exists. Jennie Gerhardt and Lester Kane had "wills" that were impotent, because of external pressures, to fulfill their desires. The same generalization holds for Clyde Griffiths. In both books Dreiser's attitude toward the relation between personal will and conditioning pressures is the same, and that attitude has been sufficiently described in the preceding pages.

In *An American Tragedy,* however, there is a difference of emphasis which is intimately associated with the structure of the novel. To begin with, Clyde is doubtless the weakest of Dreiser's heroes; he has least of the inexplicable inner drive which makes a commanding personality. He begins, further, with a pitifully meager background and a narrow view of life. He is no Cowperwood or Witla superman—he has not even the charm of Carrie or Jennie. And as the novel proceeds there is so careful an attention to detail and so complete a delineation of the various experiences which add to Clyde's miserable store of ideas and ideals that the reader seems to be gaining a full insight into the forces which account for the nature of Clyde's personality. This statement involves a good deal of oversimplification—for indeed Clyde has a certain amount of personality from the beginning which is never explained as the product of any known forces. It is, further, only a literary convention which permits the novelist to appear to be presenting all the facts of a situation. Dreiser, to be sure, presents more documentary facts perhaps than any other novelist has ever gathered about a comparable problem; and so the illusion of completeness achieved is less "illusory" than in any other novel which seeks to create the same illusion. The effect on the reader is to make him understand the Clyde who commits the crime in terms of the growth through which Dreiser has conducted him in the first half of the novel. The characters in *Sister Carrie* and *Jennie Gerhardt* begin, so to speak, in mid-career; they enter the story with attributes behind which Dreiser has not time to explore. They have, further, more of that charm or personality which creates the impression of free will and ethical independence. Thus we illustrate the truism that only with simple characters—who usually live under sordid conditions—can the naturalistic method succeed in appearing to present the external pressures which control the characters' lives and which account to a considerable degree for what they are as well as what they do. It is because of the simplicity of Clyde's character and the narrowness of his initial outlook that Dreiser is able apparently to go so much further behind the phenomenon of his will and explain its constituents. Of course the ultimate vital principle is as mysterious as ever, but the elements which condition its growth are presented more fully than elsewhere.

This is a striking difference between the naturalism of *An American Tragedy* and of Dreiser's earlier novels. But even so it is a difference only in degree, for in spite of his mass of evidence Dreiser is still unable to find purpose or organization in the ceaseless ebb and flow of life. He pretends to explain Clyde's character more fully in terms of heredity and especially milieu than he has done before—but he is still bound to the conviction that the changes of fate are too inscrutable ever to be finally understood by man.

Having offered these generalizations, we must hasten to qualify them in another respect. *An American Tragedy* differs greatly in structure from the earlier novels. In all of them we have discerned a formlessness which seemed to answer to Dreiser's conception of reality. Carrie was left in mid-career with a question. Lester and Jennie were buffeted about, but not through any sharply articulated dramatic sequence of events. The structure of *The "Genius"* and *The Titan* is Dreiser's assertion that real life is not made up of beautifully organized patterns but of ceaseless fluctuations about a norm which is hidden or even non-existent. *An American Tragedy,* on the contrary, is completely unified by the fact that every event in the novel is related to the central crisis of Roberta's murder. Book One presents Clyde's early years and his development. Book Two deals with his life in Lycurgus, his affair with Roberta, and the complications brought about by Clyde's love for Sondra Finchley—ending with the murder. Book Three contains the apprehension, trial, and execution of Clyde. What would have been a tawdry and wandering life is given meaning by the great central event of the murder. By making the last two books of the novel specifically the story of the murder—as they must be, since Clyde has committed it—Dreiser is able to have his action single and unified. Doubtless this unity is characteristic of tragedy, which can occur even in a naturalist's world and give a principle of organization to what might otherwise be a meaningless life. This change in structure then, arises from a change in the content of the novel, not from a change in Dreiser's naturalism. But there is a difference between the philosophy of *An American Tragedy* and the earlier novels, which justifies the assertion that it marks a third distinct stage in Dreiser's naturalism. In *The Financier, The Titan,* and *The "Genius"* Dreiser saw life through the eyes of a "superman," to whom it appeared as a welter of forces among which he must try somehow to work out his individual salvation. The careers of Cowperwood and Witla are seen as individuals' struggles, without particular social implications.[41] In Clyde Griffiths' progress, on the contrary, social implications abound. Dreiser had been converted to socialism[42] since writing *The "Genius"*; his American tragedy is a tragedy brought about by the society in which we live. That society is responsible, as the immediate cause, for Clyde's actions. This social consciousness marks the third stage of Dreiser's naturalism.

This is not to say that *An American Tragedy* is an indictment of our social order. It is first of all a work of art, the tragedy of Clyde Griffiths, a picture of a life that is tragic because the protagonist is at once responsible (as any human being feels another to be) and helpless (as the philosopher views events). ... Clyde's tragedy is a tragedy that depends upon the American social system. It shows the unfortunate effects of that system more, for example, than did the defeat of Cowperwood at the end of *The Titan*. In the latter instance a "superman" was battling with the opposition aroused by his will to power. In Clyde's case the whole of the American social order, in its normal activity, is brought into the picture.

*An American Tragedy* is naturalistic because Clyde's downfall is presented as inevitable. In the final analysis Clyde is not deemed morally responsible in the slightest degree. Dreiser's deep compassion records the story and broods over the pity of it. And again the artist triumphs over the propagandist in presenting the tragedy as inevitable. This triumph makes the work naturalistic and it makes of it a great tragedy.[43] The reader's being led to wonder about the rightness of the social order is, like his doubts about the social value of Cowperwood, an activity subsequent to the aesthetic experience of the tragedy itself. Dreiser the artist deals with things as they are. Dreiser the socialist demonstrates the evils of our society in a way that may lead the reader some time to think about correcting them. But this socialistic purpose—if it may be called a purpose—does not become part of the movement of the novel; it does not contaminate the tragedy; it does not, in short, prevent Dreiser from being, still, a naturalist.

## Notes

1. "I was never tired of looking at the hot, hungry, weary slums." (*A Book about Myself* [New York, 1922], p. 210) "I was honestly and sympathetically interested in the horrible deprivations inflicted upon others, their weaknesses of mind and body, afflictions of all sizes and sorts, the way so often they helplessly blundered or were driven by internal chemic fires ..." (*Ibid.,* p. 140.) Dreiser experienced poverty as well as observed it in his youth, yet never developed a cynical indifference to suffering. Indeed, "it was the underdog that always interested me more than the upper one, his needs, his woes, his simplicities." (*Ibid.,* p. 370)

2. He tells of

   finding both Old and New Testaments to be not compendiums of revealed truth but mere records of religious experiences ... and then taking up *First Principles* and

discovering that all I deemed substantial—man's place in nature, his importance in the universe, this too, too solid earth, man's very identity save as an infinitesimal speck of energy or a 'suspended equation' drawn or blown here and there by larger forces in which he moved quite unconsciously as an atom—all questioned and dissolved into other and less understandable things, I was completely thrown down in my conceptions or non-conceptions of life.

   (*Ibid.,* pp. 457-458)

   Elsewhere he tells of his eagerness for life: "Soon the strength time, the love time, the gay time, of color and romance, would be gone, and if I had not spent it fully, joyously, richly what would there be left for me then? The joys of a mythical heaven or hereafter played no part in my calculations. When one was dead one was dead for all time. Hence the reason for the heartbreak over failure here and now; the awful tragedy of a love lost, a youth never properly enjoyed. Think of living and yet not living in so thrashing a world as this, the best of one's hours passing unused or not properly used." (*Ibid.,* p. 198.)

3. See note 2, and such a statement as the following: "The world, as I see it now, has trussed itself up too helplessly with too many strings of convention, religion, dogma. ... Is it everybody's business to get married and accept all the dictates of conventional society—that is, bear and rear children according to a given social or religious theory?" (*Ibid.,* p. 326.)

4. To him the universe is characterized by eternal, purposeless flux. The vast patterns of cosmic change were doubtless comprehensible to a being sufficiently omniscient to see all the particles at once; but even so the pattern would reveal no moral or ethical purpose: "Indeed the rough balance or equation everywhere seen and struck between element and element, impulse and impulse ... really indicates nothing more than this rough approximation to equation in everything—force with matter, element with element—as an offset to incomprehensible and, to mortal mind, even horrible and ghastly extremes of disorder; nothing more." (*Hey Rub-A-Dub-Dub: A Book of the Mystery and Terror and Wonder of Life* [New York, 1919], pp. 157-158)

5. Of one's ideals, struggles, deprivations, sorrows and joys, it could only be said that they were chemic compulsions, something which for some inexplicable but unimportant reason responded to and resulted from the hope of pleasure and the fear of pain. Man was a mechanism, undevised and uncreated, and a badly and carelessly driven one at that. ... There was of course this other matter of necessity, internal chemical

compulsion, to which I had to respond whether I would or no. ... With a gloomy eye I began to watch how the chemical—and their children, the mechanical—forces operated through man and outside him.

*(A Book about Myself,* p. 458)

Dreiser does not pretend to comprehend the workings of the mind, but he is, apparently, sure that there is nothing transcendental in it. He hides part of its mystery behind the term "chemic."

6. He describes the literary influence of Balzac (*Ibid.,* p. 412) and of a Zolaësque novel written by one of his fellow-newspaper men (*Ibid.,* pp. 126 and 131-133), but he has admitted that he had not read anything by Zola before writing *Sister Carrie*; see Dorothy Dudley, *Forgotten Frontiers: Dreiser and the Land of the Free* (New York, 1932), p. 95. Literary influences are clearly secondary.

7. *Sister Carrie* (New York, 1900; ed. 1917), p. 362.

8. *Ibid.,* p. 494.

9. *Ibid.,* p. 557.

10. *Idem.*

11. American reviewers were also offended by its treatment of lives which they deemed too sordid for genteel readers. See D. Dudley, *Forgotten Frontiers,* p. 186.

12. *Sister Carrie,* p. 85.—The italics are added.

13. *Ibid.,* p. 101.

14. Above, note 2.

15. *Sister Carrie,* p. 362.

16. The gap between Dreiser's work and the experimental novel of Zola is a wide one, for Dreiser does not make even a pretense of controlling his conditions and discovering truths about the nature of human psychology and physiology. Just where Zola, for example, would theoretically put most emphasis—i.e., on the extraction of laws about human nature— Dreiser is most uncertain and most sure that no certainty can be attained. To him such laws would be fruitless for the very reason that external conditions cannot ever be controlled—a fact of which all his experience had convinced him.

17. We here assume that the central element of what is known as a personality is the existence of will. The moment a character comes alive and achieves individuality the reader becomes conscious of a will which is the new force that has come into being. A perfectly naturalistic character might—though it would be at once monstrous and uninteresting—be so completely "explained" that it would have neither personality nor will. But Dreiser believes in individuality, and apparently he accepts it as a final reality behind which he cannot penetrate. For him will—as life-impulse and the power to make ethical choices— exists. Dreiser, however, would not recognize any ethical absolutes; nor would he free this power of "ethical" choice from those influences which have determined what the individual recognizes as good and bad.

18. A circumstance is an influence so removed from its causal sequence that it appears accidental.

19. George Eliot (who was respected in her day as a psychologist) shows how the will operates in the midst of all the conditions and pressures of modern life. With her, however, the will to make ethical choices does operate among all these conditions: it is implicit in her writing that the will represents the divinity in man, his contact with God. Dreiser on the other hand shows how the will is operated upon. He admits the empirical fact of its autonomy, but he thinks of it as a product of "chemic" reactions. His metier is not a psychological study of how the will operates, but a study of how it is controlled and influenced. For Dreiser moral responsibility is not so important as the study of forces. For George Eliot moral responsibility is of tremendous importance; it is a concept which her study of the mind in action does not impair, for her novels are built around choices which are, though never so carefully documented, seen as free and hence judgeable.

20. *Jennie Gerhardt* (New York, 1911; ed. 1926), pp. 15-16.

21. *Ibid.,* pp. 290-291.

22. *Ibid.,* pp. 400-401. This passage is notable as the most explicit statement of belief in the novel. It comes from Lester, but it represents Dreiser's own attitude because it is virtually the thesis of his novel.

23. *Ibid.,* p. 422.

24. *Ibid.,* p. 431.

25. Volume III, *The Stoic,* has been announced, but apparently it will not be published. See below, p. 289 and note 42.

26. Quoted in Charmian London, *The Book of Jack London* (New York, 1921), II, 57.

27. Stuart P. Sherman, *On Contemporary Literature* (New York, 1917), p. 98.

28. See note 17, above.

29. Dreiser comments as follows upon the "meaning" of life:

> I can make no comment on my work or my life that holds either interest or import for me. Nor can I imagine any explanation or interpretation of any life, my own included, that would be either true—or important, if true. Life is to me too much a welter and play of inscrutable forces to permit, in my case at least, any significant comment. One may paint for one's own entertainment, and that of others—perhaps. As I see him the utterly infinitesimal individual weaves among the mysteries a floss-like and wholly meaningless course—if course it be. In short I catch no meaning from all I have seen, and pass quite as I came, confused and dismayed.

> ("Statements of Belief," *The Bookman,* LXVIII [September, 1928], 25)

30. *The Financier* (New York, 1912; ed. London, 1927), p. 35.

31. *The Financier,* p. 140.

32. *The Titan* (New York, 1914; ed. London, 1928), p. 461.

33. *Hey-Rub-a-Dub-Dub,* p. 89; quoted from Harry Hartwick, *Foreground of American Fiction* (New York, 1934), p. 97. These ideas, expressed in 1919, show Dreiser touched by the Nietzschean philosophy; they precede his conversion to socialism. Mr. Hartwick, however, goes on to insist that they prove Dreiser to have admired and condoned the behavior of Cowperwood as valuable to society. This cannot be entirely true, for the course of the novels does not show Cowperwood to have been socially useful. The ethical implications are considered further below.

34. *The Titan,* p. 542.

35. *The Financier,* pp. 9-12.

36. *Ibid.,* p. 510.

37. *Theodore Dreiser* (New York, 1925), p. 78.

38. *The Financier,* pp. 152-153. "That the modern home is the most beautiful of schemes, when based upon mutual sympathy and understanding between two, need not be questioned. And yet this fact should not necessarily carry with it a condemnation of all love not so fortunate as to find so happy a denoue-ment. Life cannot be put in any mould, and the attempt might as well be abandoned at once."

39. *Ibid.,* p. 147.

40. *An American Tragedy* (2 vols., New York, 1925), II, 78-80.

41. Dreiser's repeated questioning of moral codes is a criticism of society for its effects upon the individual—not a recognition of the effect of the individual on society.

42. This doubtless accounts for his inability to complete *The Stoic* and round out his "Trilogy of Desire." That novel, in order to preserve the unity of tone of the other two, would have also to be written from the viewpoint of the superman—a very difficult task for a socialist.

43. We cannot deal at length with the problem of whether such a book can be called a tragedy at all. Certain obvious modifications, indeed, must be made in the Aristotelian definition if it is to cover *An American Tragedy,* but they are not intolerable modifications. The hero is not noble, his will—and hence his tragic flaw—are minimized; but the protagonist is destroyed by forces beyond his control. That Clyde is a sordid rather than a noble character—a condition which violates the Aristotelian definition—and yet his tragedy is compelling rather than contemptible to a modern audience.

## James T. Farrell (essay date 1945)

SOURCE: Farrell, James T. "Some Aspects of Dreiser's Fiction." *The New York Times Book Review,* 29 Apr. 1945, p. 7+.

[*In the following essay, Farrell contradicts the critical contention that Dreiser is "merely heavy-handed and careless" in his reliance on detail and proposes that Dreiser illuminates the passions driving his characters, who do not tend to undergo "real moral and intellectual growth" in the course of his stories.*]

The sensational murder story involving sex has—thanks to the practices of many newspapers—become an American commonplace. And this kind of material has been frequently used by writers as a means to get rich quick, to produce some piece of writing which promises to bring big rewards. The material of life that is furnished us in the tabloids is, in fact, a fairly common source for motion picture scenarists, playwrights, novelists, detective story writers, radio writers and others. But rarely is such material used for novels, plays, pictures with an effort toward intensifying and en-larging our comprehension of contemporary American life, our grasp of some of the operational meanings, implica-tions and human consequences in contemporary American life which flow from the so-called American dream. This material is usually exploited for sensational purposes and then the sensational purposes are often masked in hypocrit-ical moral banalities that stress the lesson that crime does not pay and that the wages of sin is death. Considering these commonplaces of the American social and cultural scene, one is struck doubly by the sincerity which motivates Theodore Dreiser's **"An American Tragedy."**

This novel was first published in 1925, and was a best seller. It is considered by many critics and readers to be Dreiser's "best" book. However, although Dreiser's name often appears in critical writings and reviews, and although at present he is continually criticized and attacked as a realist, a naturalist, an apostle of blind determinism and pessimism, it is rare that efforts are really made to analyze and discuss his writings. All of his novels are lumped together as if they were of one piece, and the same banal criticisms of him are made, almost ad nauseam. It is wor-thy of note that those who use his novels as the major target for attack in their current campaign against naturalism, realism, pessimism, determinism and the like, do not at all analyze what he has written; usually they do not even attempt to pose such questions as should inevitably occur after any study or re-study of his fiction.

\* \* \*

Novels such as **"The Financier"** and **"The Titan"** can appropriately be described as works of fiction which em-body a viewpoint of Social-Darwinism. Dreiser's Frank Cowperwood has an outlook on life that is decidedly to be characterized by this phrase. He takes what he wants, and he has no qualms as to his methods and his means of achieving his goals and his desires. In these novels, as well as in other of Dreiser's works, character is presented in terms of a biological perspective. Dreiser accepted gener-alizations from nineteenth-century materialism as scientif-ic, and these generalizations, given a biologic turn, are at the root of his characterizations. In the Dreiserian world, man reveals a lack of balance between passion and instinct, on the one hand, and reason on the other. The former has a biologic basis. The biological basis of man is counterposed to the social ideals and social conventions of American life of the time of the novels, and of the milieu of the respective characters.

The world recreated is one of the strong and the weak, the rich and the poor, the successful and the unsuccessful. The weak disintegrate, are crushed, become losers in the strug-gle for existence, for the satisfaction of passions, for the attainment of wealth which permits this satisfaction; the strong seek and usually manage to attain position, the means of gratification of the needs of their natures. But even then, they remain unslaked. Satisfaction, success, only leave them with yearning, sometimes with bewil-dered yearning.

\* \* \*

Generally speaking, it is this feature of Mr. Dreiser's work which is referred to when it is characterized as determin-istic, as mechanistic in orientation and perspective. Withal, Mr. Dreiser's determinism is not so simple as the critics make it out to be. For besides this biological determinism in his work, there is also a social determinism which is to be seen as a consequence of the operation of social laws. Now when we look back on the production of so-called realistic and naturalistic writing over a period of many decades, it should be clear that this literary tradition has been evolving toward the end of seeking to understand, to image, to recreate a sense of the lives of human beings, of the patterns of human destiny in terms of the operation of what are called laws, scientific laws on the one hand and social laws (which also are or can be scientifically formu-lated) on the other hand.

More important, more revealing than Dreiser's biologi-cism is his social determinism. By and large, his biologi-cism, his references to mysterious chemisms are auctorial and explanatory. Frequently, in both "The Titan" and "The Financier," it can be observed that in the instance of many specific appeals to and reliances on "chemisms" as the explanation of many actions of his characters, especially of Cowperwood, the actions thereby explained are caused by unconscious motivations and can be more adequately explained by the use of Freudian conceptions than by the biologicisms of Mr. Dreiser. In addition, Mr. Dreiser is not always a consistent naturalist or mechanist, as witness occasional lapses of his into affirmations of telepathy. So much for this. His social determinism is presented, not in any mere auctorial manner, but rather by actions and char-acterizations; it is reflected, revealed, embodied concretely in his stories.

\* \* \*

Involved in all of Mr. Dreiser's fiction is the story of youth trying to make its way in America. Cowperwood, Eugene Witla and Clyde Griffiths are all, when first met, boys or youths; Carrie Meeber is a girl. All of these characters are set off from one another by the precise nature of their needs. In one way or another, all of them want more of life than life seems to promise them as it is lived in their times. They all must make their way in the world. Desire is stronger in all of them than it is in the case of many with whom they come in contact. Thus, while there are differences among them, they also have something in common. Cowperwood is a man of force, energy, will, and from youth onward he is capable of ruthless and determined action. Witla's sensibilities predict the career of an artist early in his life. Carrie is passionate, romantic, yearning, and possessed of a certain fiber of character which saves her from being spoiled when she lives the life of a kept woman. All three are, thereby, more endowed than Clyde. What Clyde has in common with them is a restlessness, based on the romantic needs of his nature, which sends him seeking, seeking something.

\* \* \*

It is interesting to note that Carrie is a poor girl from the country who wants more than life can give her in her native locale, and that she goes into the world in search of a better life. Carrie succeeds as an actress. Like Clyde, she is exposed to what are called the temptations of the world and the occasions of sin; like him, she contravenes the conventional middle-class moral code and the tenets of religion which are embodied in that code. In her case, the wages of sin is not death. Her course in life is, in some ways, more difficult than that of Clyde. She is a girl, seeking her way in a man's world. But Carrie, in the latter part of the nineteenth century, succeeds and becomes a famous actress. Clyde, a boy of the twentieth century, living in a period when American economy has continued to expand, when the nation is richer than it was even in the days of Carrie, fails.

The contrast in the end of Carrie, on the one hand, and of Clyde, on the other, is dialectical. This contrast is further marked by observations on the careers of Dreiser's young people. The road to success for Carrie, for Eugene Witla, for Cowperwood is one which permits them to use the best potentialities which they have latent within themselves. Carrie has the makings of an actress in her; Eugene, the capacity to be an artist; Frank Cowperwood, a genius in the realm of manipulation. Clyde, less gifted than these, has few doors of opportunity open to him. Clyde, in order to try to get on in the world must not develop his best traits. He must be more socially deceitful than his predecessors and this on a petty scale. These differences, this dialectical contrast, have the merit of corresponding with changes in the character of American social relationships which have come in the wake of the expansion of American economy. In time span, the various novels of Mr. Dreiser run from the period of the Civil War on into the present century. Clyde, then, lives in a richer America than did the chief protago-

nists of the previous Dreiser novels; but in this richer America the doors to opportunity are less open. Unlike his predecessors, the real door to opportunity for Clyde lies solely in social climbing, and by getting the aid of rich relatives. Uneducated and with no specially marked talents, what other doors of opportunity can there be open to him?

\* \* \*

Also this dialectical contrast is further to be seen by comparisons of other Dreiserian characters. Consider the rich girl, Aileen Butler, who marries Cowperwood, and Sondra Finchley, whom Clyde loves. Not only is Aileen more spirited than Sondra, but also she is willing to take more social risks. Equally as selfish as Sondra, she is capable of loving with greater passion. Objectively, she has more to lose by taking social risks, because she is not accepted in the highest social circles of her city, whereas Sondra is in hers. And although Aileen's father is a man of stronger character than is Sondra's father, Aileen will defy him, and even more openly, than will Sondra her parents.

\* \* \*

In consonance with the more widespread social stratification revealed in "An American Tragedy" than in Dreiser's earlier novels, the important characters here are more concerned with social conventions, and they show less willingness to take social risks than did their predecessors, and their capacities for love, for passion, seem watered down. And these contrasts suggest how, over a span of decades, Dreiser mirrored the story of American ideals, and recounted in tragic fiction important aspects of the patterns of American destinies lived in the time of the aegis of the "American Dream." In addition, they suggest the important aspect of his determinism—his social determinism.

Mr. Dreiser's characterizations are social in the sense that his characters are recreated in terms of their environment and the social roles they play in society. It is this fact which helps to explain his copious reliance on details. He is not, as some critics aver, merely heavy-handed and careless in his selectivity. On the contrary, he is often highly illuminating. What his major characters have in common is need, based on passions. But each of these, feeling this need to a more or less acute degree, is then characterized in accordance with the kind of social role he or she plays. Driven only onward, they must expand, they must rise in the world, they must find something. The conditions of their environment demand that they seek and find through social change, social rise, social expansion. Rise in the world, change in social status, acquisition in order to satisfy needs, impulses, passions—herein is the theme in his novels.

\* \* \*

It is singular in his work that there is little of what can be called real moral and intellectual growth. Because of this, I suspect, some critics overemphasize his determinism. His characters, even when they have will, as does Cowperwood, more or less possess the coloring of their environment, in either a positive or a negative sense. In their life histories, they do not overcome themselves. If they change, the basic change within them is that of the opening out or unfolding of passion and impulse. The social changes observable in "An American Tragedy" buttress this treatment of theme. For the operational play of ideals and ambitions, the increasing stratification of social relationships mirrored in the novel do not stimulate growth.

By and large, the themes of moral growth, of self-discovery and awareness drop out of realistic American writing with the generation at the end of the last century. In place of this, we have themes relating to change of social status, and to the results of social stratification on character. In practice the life of the American middle-class in particular, and of most Americans in general, has been lived on a plane that can be described as Benthamism in this century. The "American Dream" is not a dream of moral growth but of social rise, and positively and negatively it has been the main thematic concern of American literature in this century.

## Lionel Trilling (essay date 1946)

SOURCE: Trilling, Lionel. "Dreiser and the Liberal Mind." *The Nation,* vol. 162, 20 Apr. 1946, pp. 466-72.

[*In the following essay, Trilling concludes that Dreiser "is precisely literary in the bad sense; . . . he is full of flowers of rhetoric and he shines with paste gems," and his "ideas are inconsistent or inadequate," notwithstanding his much-lauded "reality and great brooding pity." Trilling describes Dreiser's posthumous novel* The Bulwark *as a "moralizing" testament to an extant "weakness" in the writer.*]

We are all a little tired of Henry James—or, rather, we are tired of the Henry James we have been creating by all our talk about him, by those intense and bitter conversations in which he existed as a symbol so glowingly but so passively, the martyr-hero of a certain kind of culture. It is now time, surely, to let him go back into privacy, releasing him from the deadly public life of polemic, to read him again in quiet. And yet I cannot help detaining him for a moment longer in

the life-in-death of argument by mentioning him in connection with Theodore Dreiser, whose name has again been so much with us since his death and the appearance of his posthumous novel, **"The Bulwark"** (Doubleday).

James and Dreiser: with that juxtaposition we are immediately at the dark and bloody crossroads where culture and politics meet. One does not go there gladly, but I found that I was there perforce, for as I read the new Dreiser novel my thoughts kept recurring to a pronouncement on James which I had come on some months ago. The passage had then struck me as so representative of a certain aspect of American intellect that I had saved it. Robert Gorham Davis is commenting on the belief, held by some, that there is a kind of political value in James's awareness, in his moral perceptiveness. Mr. Davis says, "Unfortunately, it is a little too late for this . . ." and then goes on:

> There has been a tremendous increase in our cultural awareness and achievement in recent decades, and American intellectuals need feel no inferiority before European culture or the ghost of Henry James. But these same decades have taught us that delicacy of perception, knowledge, a refinement of relationships within limited groups can coexist with the grossest evils and dangers and do almost nothing to counter them. The disasters that we have just barely escaped and the disasters that are certain to threaten demand a kind of self-committal, a going forth to battle with Apollyon and Giant Despair that James's experience, emotional and metaphysical, simply cannot help us with. . . .

Mr. Davis, as we know, is not the kind of critic who brushes aside delicacy of perception and knowledge—on the contrary, he is notable in his own work for these very qualities. And as the rest of Mr. Davis's review shows, he has great respect for James and takes no delight in throwing him to the wolves of political fate. He only wants to warn us that the moral and intellectual qualities which he and James have in common are not to be counted on in moments of crisis.

American intellectuals, especially when they are being American or political, are remarkably quick to warn us that perception and knowledge, although somehow valuable—"American intellectuals need feel no inferiority before European culture"—will never get us through gross dangers and difficulties. We are still haunted by a kind of social fear of intellect, the same uneasiness that Tocqueville observed in us more than a century ago.

This uneasiness is the more intense when intellect works as intellect ideally should, when its processes are vivacious or complex and its results are interesting and brilliant. It is then that we like to confront it with gross difficulties and dangers and challenge it to save us from disaster. What I suppose was meant by the idea Mr. Davis is commenting on, the political value of James's qualities, was not that they will set up an umbrella against the atomic bomb or solve political contradictions but that, within the natural limit of the art that contains them, they can suggest the moral and intellectual qualities that might save us and that certainly make salvation worth while. When intellect is awkward and dull, we do not put it to the question of ultimate or immediate practicality—no liberal critic would go out of his way to remark that "unfortunately it is a little too late" for what Dreiser gives us. James's style, characters, subjects, and especially his manner of personal life are looked upon with a hostile eye, no quarter given. But Dreiser's faults, we have always been given to understand, are essentially virtues. Parrington established the formula for the criticism of Dreiser by calling him a "peasant." When Dreiser thinks stupidly, it is because he has the slow stubbornness of a peasant; when he writes badly, it is because he is impatient of the literary gentility of the bourgeoisie. It is as if wit and flexibility of mind, as if perception and knowledge, were to be equated with aristocracy, while dulness and stupidity must naturally suggest a virtuous democracy, as in the old plays.

The liberal judgment of Dreiser and James goes back of politics, goes back to the moral assumptions that make politics. It is the fear of mind, much more than any explicit political meaning that can be drawn from the works of the two men, that accounts for the unequal justice they have received from our progressive critics. If it could be conclusively demonstrated—say, by documents in James's holograph—that James intended his books as pleas for cooperatives, labor unions, better housing, more equitable taxation, and closer relations with Russia, the American critic in his liberal and progressive character would, one feels, still be worried by James because his work shows so many of the electric qualities of mind. And if the opposite were proved of Dreiser, it would be brushed aside—as his anti-Semitism has in fact been brushed aside—because his books have the awkwardness, the chaos, the heaviness which we associate with "reality." In the American metaphysic, reality is always material reality, hard, resistant, unformed, impenetrable. And that work of mind is felt to be trustworthy which most resembles this reality by reproducing the sensations it affords.

Professor Beard in "The Rise of American Civilization" gives an ironic account of James's career and implies that we have the clue to its irrelevance when we know that James was "a whole generation removed from the odors of the shop." Or Granville Hicks in "The Great Tradition" comments on James's stories about artists and makes the point that such artists as James portrays, so concerned

about art and their integrity in art, do not really exist. "Who has ever known such artists? Where are the Hugh Verekers, the Mark Ambients, the Neil Paradays, the Overts, Linberts, Dencomes, Delaways?" The question, Mr. Hicks admits, had occurred to James himself, but how had James answered it? "If the life about us for the last thirty years refused warrant for these examples," James said, "then so much the worse for that life. ... There are decencies that in the name of the general self-respect we must take for granted, there's a rudimentary intellectual honor to which we must, in the interest of civilization, at least pretend." And to this Mr. Hicks, shocked beyond argument, replies, "But this is the purest romanticism, this writing about what ought to be rather than what is!" James was a traitor to the reality of the odors of the shop. He betrayed the reality of *what is* for the projection of *what ought to be*. Dare we ever trust him again?

To Mr. Hicks, Dreiser is "clumsy" and "stupid" and "bewildered" and "crude in his statement of materialistic monism"; and in his personal life—which perhaps is in point because James's personal life is always supposed to be so much in point—not quite emancipated from "his boyhood longing for crass material success," showing "again and again a desire for the ostentatious luxury of the successful business man." The judgment is true, and so far as it is personal it is based on Dreiser's own statements. But Dreiser's faults are the sad, lovable, honorable faults of "reality" itself, or of America itself—huge, inchoate, struggling toward expression, caught between the dream of power and the dream of morality.

Or again: "The liability in what Santayana called the genteel tradition was due to its being the product of mind apart from experience. Dreiser gave us the stuff of our common existence, not as it was hoped to be by any idealizing theorist, but as it actually was in its crudity." The author of this statement is a writer who certainly cannot be accused of any lack of feeling for what James represents; yet how easily Mr. Matthiessen, in his *Times* review of Dreiser's novel, falls into the liberal cliché which establishes as the criterion of Dreiser's value his difference from some "idealizing theorist," his opposition to the genteel tradition. This is the line on which has proceeded the long, wearisome defense of Dreiser's prose style. Everyone is aware that Dreiser's prose is full of roughness and ungainliness, and the critics who admire Dreiser tell us it does not matter. Of course it does not matter. No reader with a right sense of style would suppose it does matter, and he might even find it a virtue. But it has been taken for granted that the ungainliness of Dreiser's style is the only possible objection to be made to it, and that whoever finds any fault at all in it wants, instead, a prettified genteel style.

For instance, Edwin Berry Burgum, in a leaflet on Dreiser put out by the Book Find Club, tells us that Dreiser was one of those who used—or, as he says, utilized—"the diction of the Middle West, pretty much as it was spoken, rich in colloquialism and frank in the simplicity and directness of the pioneer tradition"—a diction substituted for "the literary English, formal and bookish, of New England provincialism that was closer to the aristocratic spirit of the mother country than to the tang of everyday life in the new West." This is mere fantasy. Quite apart from the fact that Hawthorne, Thoreau, and Emerson were all remarkably colloquial—wrote, that is, in their own speaking tones—and specifically American in quality and quite simple and direct in manner, Dreiser is far from writing in the diction of the Middle West: If we are to talk of bookishness, it is Dreiser who is bookish; he is precisely literary in the bad sense; at hundreds of points his diction is not only genteel but fancy; he is full of flowers of rhetoric and he shines with paste gems.

Charles Jackson, the novelist, telling us, in the same leaflet, that Dreiser's style does not matter, reminds us how much still comes to us when we have lost by translation the stylistic brilliance of Thomas Mann or the Russians or Balzac. He is in part right. And he is right too when he says that a certain kind of conscious, supervised artistry is not appropriate to the novel of large dimensions. Yet it is the fact that the great novelists have usually written great prose, and what comes through even a bad translation is exactly the power of mind that made the well-hung sentence of the original text. In literature style is so little the mere clothing of thought—need it be said at this late date?—that we may say that from the novelist's prose spring his characters, his ideas, and even his story itself.

To the extent that Dreiser's style is defensible, his thought is also defensible. That is, when he thinks like a novelist, he is worth following—when by means of his rough and ungainly but effective style he creates rough, ungainly, but effective characters and events. But when he thinks like, as we say, a philosopher, he is likely to be not only foolish but vulgar. He thinks as the modern crowd thinks when it decides to think: religion is nonsense, "religionists" are fakes, tradition is a fraud, what is man but matter and impulses, mysterious "chemisms"?—"What, cooking, eating, coition, job holding, growing, aging, losing, winning, in so changeful and passing a scene as this, important? Bunk! It is some form of titillating illusion with about as much import to the superior forces that bring it all about as the functions and gyrations of a fly. No more. And maybe less." Thus Dreiser at sixty. And yet there is for him always the vulgarly saving suspicion that maybe there is Something Behind It All. It is much to the point of his vulgarity

that Dreiser's anti-Semitism was not merely a social prejudice but an idea, a way of dealing with things.

No one, I suppose, has ever represented Dreiser as a masterly intellect. It is even a commonplace to say that his ideas are inconsistent or inadequate. But once that admission has been made, his ideas are hustled out of sight while his reality and great brooding pity are spoken of. (His pity is to be questioned—pity is to be judged not by amount but by kind.) Why has no one ever said that it was "unfortunately a little too late" for Dreiser's awkward, dim speculation, a little too late for so much self-pity, for so much lust for "beauty" and "sex" and "living" and "life itself"? With us it is always a little too late for mind, but never too late for honest stupidity; always a little too late for understanding, never too late for righteous, bewildered wrath; always too late for thought, never too late for naive moralizing. We seem to like to condemn our finest, but not our worst, qualities by pitting them against the exigency of time. It is perhaps not wholly accidental that the article on Literature in that compendium of liberal thought, the Encyclopedia of the Social Sciences, should be by Max Lerner, who gave us the phrase "It is later than you think," and that it should tell us that "literature faces ... continually the need for rebarbarization."

What we will be patient of and find time for when we confront disasters is of course a matter of taste. But like every matter of taste, it is eventually a practical matter as well. It has its consequences and its issue. Their nature is suggested by Dreiser's posthumous novel—a work of some years back but revised and concluded recently—and by the reception given to it.

**"The Bulwark"** is a work not merely of piety but of pietism. It is a simple, didactic story recommending a simple Christian belief, the virtues of self-abnegation and self-control, of belief in and submission to the purposes of higher powers, those "superior forces that bring it all about," once, in Dreiser's opinion, so indifferent, now somehow benign. This is not the first occasion on which Dreiser has shown a tenderness toward religion. **"Jennie Gerhardt"** and the figure of the Reverend Duncan McMillan in **"An American Tragedy"** are in a way forecasts of the avowals of **"The Bulwark."** Yet they cannot prepare us for the blank pietism of the new novel, not after we have remembered how salient in Dreiser has been his long surly rage against the "religionists" and "moralists," the men who presume to think that life can be given any law and who dare to believe that faith or tradition can shape the savage and beautiful entity that Dreiser liked to call "life itself." For to Dreiser now nothing can be simpler than the control of life. For the safe conduct of the personal life we have only to follow the Inner Light according to the regimen of the Society of Friends, or, presumably, according to some other godly rule.

To find an analogue to **"The Bulwark,"** we must go back to the moralizing novels of the eighteenth or early nineteenth century. Everything in the story is subordinated to the moment when the Quaker Solon Barnes sees that life has an obscure purpose and justification. Barnes's childhood and youth, his marriage of deep love, his business success in Philadelphia, the alienation of his children and the inadequacy and tragedy of their lives after they have rejected the Quaker faith, are all given in merest summary, with none of that often excessive circumstantiality that makes Dreiser's earlier novels so ineradicably memorable. All details of drama and development are rigorously suppressed to hasten the book toward the moment when Solon Barnes experiences faith and affirmation and his daughter turns from her life of free sexual experience to a chaste sadness for life itself.

I must not be taken to mean that the novel is wholly without power. After all, we cannot follow the life of a man up to the moment of his reconciliation and death without a sense of the majestic significance of the happening. But to take the book and its message in any other serious way than as a fact in Dreiser's biography is, I am sure, impossible.

Dreiser's mood of "acceptance" in the last year of his life is not a thing to be submitted to the tests of intellectual validity. It consists of a feeling of cosmic understanding, an overarching sense of reconciliation to the world with its evil as well as its good. Any reader of nineteenth-century literature will be perfectly familiar with it and, very likely, perfectly sympathetic. It is no more to be quarreled with or reasoned with than love itself—indeed, it is a form of love, not so much love of the world as love of oneself in the world. It is often what is meant by peace. Perhaps it is either the cessation of desire or the perfect balance of desires. If it was Dreiser's own emotion in the end of his life, who would not be happy that he achieved it? I am not even sure that our civilization and our political action would not be the better if more of us knew and cultivated such emotions of grave felicity.

Yet, granting the personal validity of the emotion, the book of which it is the issue and the point is a failure. In the light of Dreiser's past ideas, it is even an offensive failure. On the whole, our liberal critics have been willing to accept it. Mr. Matthiessen accepts it and warns us of the attack that will be made upon it by "those who believe that any renewal of Christianity marks a new 'failure of nerve.'" Life does not look to me the way it looks to the contributors to

the "Failure of Nerve" symposium in the *Partisan Review,* and I am not inclined to make such a simple diagnosis as Mr. Matthiessen predicts. The failure of the book does not derive from a failure of nerve but from a failure of heart and mind.

I measure the resolution of **"The Bulwark"** by "Candide," and know that in the light of the Lisbon earthquake or any more recent catastrophe or holocaust no mood of reconciliation or acceptance can be rationalized into a social doctrine. Or I measure it by works more sympathetic to the religious mood—Ivan Karamazov's "giving back his ticket," his admission to the "harmony" of the universe, suggests that **"The Bulwark"** is not morally adequate; we dare not, as Solon Barnes does, "accept" the suffering of others; and from "The Book of Job" I know that it does not include enough in its exploration of evil and is not stern enough.

When I say that the book is a failure of thought and feeling I naturally do not mean that Dreiser got old and weak in his mind and heart. The weakness was always there. And in a sense it is not Dreiser who failed but a whole movement of ideas in which we have all been involved. Our liberal, progressive culture found the time to tolerate the vulgar materialist denial, the cry of "Bunk"; and now, almost as a natural consequence, it has given, and is willing to receive and find time for, this pietistic mood of reconciliation in all its thinness.

Dreiser, of course, was stronger than the culture that accepted him. He *meant* his ideas. But we, when it came to his ideas, talked about his great brooding pity and shrugged the ideas off. We are still doing it. Robert Elias, who is writing the biography of Dreiser, tells us (in the Book Find leaflet) that "it is part of the logic of [Dreiser's] life that he should have completed **'The Bulwark'** at the same time that he joined the Communists." Just what kind of logic this is we learn from Mr. Elias's further statement: "When he supported left-wing movements and finally, last year, joined the Communist Party, he did so, not because he had examined the details of the party line and found them satisfactory, but because he agreed with a general program that represented a means for establishing his cherished goal, greater equality among men." Dreiser was perhaps following the logic of his own life, but certainly he was also following the logic of the progressive criticism that accepted him so heedlessly and so happily—the progressive criticism that first establishes the ultimate social responsibility of the writer and then goes on to say that he is not really responsible for anything, even his ideas. Ideas are but "details," and for details we have no time. With a "cherished goal" before our eyes dare we stop for piddling distinctions and discriminations? And is this not the moment, spiritually and politically, when it is so very late and men are gasping in their inequalities, to learn to accept without quibble the ultimate wisdom of the "superior forces"?

## John T. Flanagan (essay date 1946)

SOURCE: Flanagan, John T. "Theodore Dreiser in Retrospect." *Southwest Review,* vol. 31, no. 4, 1946, pp. 408-11.

[*In the following essay, Flanagan recalls Dreiser's personal familiarity with poverty, which imbued him with "pessimism and bitterness" and began his lifelong quest as a "fighter for free and full expression of all facets of human experience, . . . as a ruthless critic of exploitation and injustice and special privilege."*]

In Dreiser's posthumous novel **The Bulwark,** a certain character, the daughter Etta, weeps at her father's funeral. Her brother rebukes her for shedding tears on an occasion for which he holds her partly responsible. And she answers: "Oh, I am not crying for myself, or for Father—I am crying for *life*."

Probably Theodore Dreiser never expressed better anywhere, certainly not more simply, his basic philosophy. During a long and productive life he constantly assailed a society which stacked the cards against the frail and the weak and the poor. The capitalism which allowed speculators like Frank Cowperwood to exploit the public ruthlessly, and which likewise permitted innocents like Jennie Gerhardt and Clyde Griffiths to be victimized by an implacable and omnipotent enemy, he regarded as vicious. To the end of his life Dreiser pictured this uneven struggle, with capitalism sucking away the life of the worker or tantalizing him by depriving him of success (as in the case of Clyde Griffiths) just when he thought he had achieved it. In his very first novel, *Sister Carrie,* Dreiser exposed the purposelessness of life and the inadequacy of the prevailing moral codes. Subsequently he toyed with the idea of a superman, creating a buccaneer like Cowperwood who shouldered his way through to personal success and moral chaos. Finally, Dreiser's official joining of the Communist party in the last year of his life suggests his solution of the individual's problem in a socially antagonistic world.

In the early novels it is the characters themselves who bring about the final catastrophe through their own frailty and spinelessness. In **The Bulwark** (most of which was written some years before Dreiser's death) it is the sons and daughters of Solon Barnes whose errant ways produce the collapse of this respectable and orthodox Quaker. But throughout his fiction Dreiser consistently portrayed the disintegration of human figures who at the beginning were neither depressed nor depraved.

Dreiser's pessimism and bitterness were firmly grounded in his own experience. He knew what it meant to be born on the wrong side of the railroad tracks in a small town and to be the child of a woman who did washing and took in boarders. He knew poverty and insecurity from the time he and his brothers used to pick up coal from the railroad right-of-way to supply the family stove. He knew the pitiful scarcity which sometimes kept the Dreiser children at home because they lacked the money to buy respectable clothes in which to appear at school. And wherever he lived as a young man, in Indiana small towns, in Chicago, in St. Louis, in Pittsburgh, he knew the life of the slums and the underprivileged.

Following graduation from high school at Warsaw, Indiana, and a year of college at Indiana University, Dreiser worked on various middlewestern newspapers. Sheer persistence brought him a reportorial job on the *Chicago Globe* in the days when Eugene Field was the most celebrated journalist in the Windy City, and gradually he advanced from writing obituaries and notices of visitors to dramatic criticism and feature articles. His journalistic experience implemented the early impressions he had gained of social and economic inequality, and generally embittered him. Probably his Pittsburgh sojourn was especially significant, because there he found the misery and filth of the mining section all around him and at the same time he became aware of more philosophical attacks on predatory capitalism. Years afterward he wrote: "I was never tired of looking at the hot, hungry, weary slums." Before his Pittsburgh residence Dreiser had *felt* deeply the plight of the worker in his one-sided battle; thereafter he began to *think* about it and *brood* over it.

This period of gestation continued through his early New York days when he was doing free-lance writing and seeing something of his brother Paul. After the stillbirth of **Sister Carrie** in 1900 Dreiser relinquished the novel for several years and worked for various periodicals, at one time being editor of the *Delineator.* But he never stopped observing, storing innumerable details in his patient brain, and learning enormously about an economic system which he savagely arraigned in later books.

It is curious, incidentally, that Dreiser never became the satirist of social conditions that the majority of his fellow writers of the Middle West turned out to be. He lacked, of course, the biting humor that Sinclair Lewis turned upon Main Street and George F. Babbitt, and he was equally incapable of the poetic mysticism which prevented

Sherwood Anderson's sketches of the *Winesburg, Ohio* people from becoming corrosive. The caustic concision of Masters' *Spoon River* epitaphs was as little his forte as Vachel Lindsay's tubthumping for the village improvement parade. But probably the main reason Dreiser was not a satirist lay in his deep-rooted sympathy for the victims of a bad economic order, his compassion and pity for the toilers. Thus his method in fiction was not satire in deft, swift strokes, but a patient accumulation of documentary detail that frequently bore down the reader by its dead weight while at the same time it etched an unforgettable picture of injustice and selfishness. The technique of the naturalist is obviously not that of the satirist, and Dreiser was always better at collection and enumeration than he was at selection.

In fact his very piling up of details, although these were often relevant and revealing, became one of his major faults—this, and his style. Among contemporary novelists only Thomas Wolfe rivaled Dreiser in his capacity for inclusiveness, and Wolfe sometimes evinced a sensuousness which Dreiser utterly lacked. The naturalist, of course, tends to overwrite his thesis, and to this rule Dreiser was no exception. As for his stylistic faults, they have been noted and assailed by every critic who ever discussed his fiction, although probably few would agree with Ludwig Lewisohn that Dreiser is the worst writer of his eminence in the entire history of literature. Certain it is that bad grammar, false connotations, misuse of words, and generally poor taste in the selection of language (note his fondness for words like chic, trig, and swell) were weaknesses he never outgrew. Yet it must not be forgotten that Dreiser could also write simple, vigorous English. See, for example, much of *The Bulwark* and the second half of *An American Tragedy.*

To balance the numerous strictures one can concede very strong merits. Dreiser was an accurate and meticulous reporter, and this native quality was strengthened by a long journalistic apprenticeship. H. L. Mencken, in his introduction to the new edition of *An American Tragedy,* retells the familiar story of the inception of Dreiser's longest and most ambitious novel. There actually was a Clyde Griffiths, under a different name, who murdered his sweetheart because she got in the way of a subsequent attachment, and who was sent to the electric chair for his crime. As Mencken acutely observes, Dreiser was the most matter-of-fact novelist who ever lived, almost suffocating with facts directly observed, and willing to pack his stories with details which often were neither interesting nor important. To him a street name, the exact hour of a train departure, the procedure of a court trial, the plan of an opera house were in themselves significant items which must be faith-

fully observed and recorded. Often these facts got in the way of the narrative, sidetracking it or prolonging it unmercifully. Dreiser never took as many pages as did Thomas Wolfe to describe a train journey, but surely there are no longer accounts of court trials in fiction than the prosecution of Clyde Griffiths.

Yet this obsession with details did not prevent Dreiser from becoming a successful storyteller. Oddly enough his stories do move—sometimes with surprising velocity, like an elephant running. Despite the huge girth and deliberate background of his novels, they still retain the reader's interest as narratives. Dreiser could paint a large canvas with extraordinary skill and could build up suspense and climax with surprising adroitness. One is never particularly eager to learn what happens to Sinclair Lewis' Babbitt; it is enough to watch his mind function, his reactions ossify. But the reader wants to know the end of the chain of events in which a Cowperwood is enmeshed. Plot for Dreiser is never static.

Another strong point in Dreiser's favor is his ability to characterize sharply and memorably. If his gallery of people is not extensive, it is strongly individual. All three of the major figures in *Sister Carrie* are fully conceived and projected: the innocent country girl who enters into two liaisons and emerges at the end of the novel a stage success; the traveling salesman Drouet, brash and ostentatious; the absconding tavern manager Hurstwood. American naturalism has not seen a more perfect example of character disintegration—moral and physical—than this same Hurstwood. And probably for this very reason, not to mention Dreiser's choice of an amoral heroine whom he grants material success, James Farrell has selected *Sister Carrie* as one of the major American novels of the twentieth century.

Nor is Dreiser's success in portraiture limited to his first novel. Jennie Gerhardt, meek and undemanding mistress of two men, and loyal to the second despite his subsequent marriage, is also made real. The lengthy account of Frank Cowperwood, the predatory traction magnate who is aggressive and unscrupulous in matters both of business and of love, runs through two volumes, *The Financier* and *The Titan.* And to these I should most certainly add Solon Barnes, the hero of *The Bulwark* and Dreiser's only example of a thoroughly admirable and respectable if benighted protagonist.

It is singular that all of Dreiser's chief figures, with the exception of Solon Barnes, are failures, material or moral, or both; there is no success story in the Dreiser canon. But the explanation is not far to seek. First of all, Dreiser was writing during the most blatantly materialistic period in

American history; all around him he saw spiritual values debased in the mad rush for money and power. Again, his characters were less imagined than copied, and he chose his models to a large extent from the small town backwaters, the city slums, the journalistic eddies which he best knew. Moreover, his preoccupation with the lower classes and his naturalistic philosophy limited his human material. A typical Dreiser character is a young man or woman from a small community, rootless and without prospects, who is attracted to the city as the typical moth is to the flame. Despite weakness, innocence, even some social adversity, the protagonist achieves some small success, only to experience the final catastrophe which is the inevitable result of internal frailty and external pressure. Dreiser's people, like the Tilbury Town figures of Edwin Arlington Robinson, are weaklings who come to a futile end; but where the poet is sardonic and cynical, the novelist is deeply compassionate.

I should like to suggest that Dreiser will be remembered for more than his fiction. While no novel appeared from 1925 to his death, he published a stream of sketches, verse, short stories, and reminiscences. Much of this material took the form of biography and autobiography. And together with earlier works like *Twelve Men* and *A Hoosier Holiday* these volumes are often as significant as his fiction.

Writers of the Middle West have been extremely prolific and often distinguished in autobiographical writing. And Theodore Dreiser revealed qualities in describing himself which he rigidly excised from his novels. *Twelve Men* contains thinly disguised portraits of the journalists and artists whom Dreiser knew personally, and they are depicted with intimate but usually tender frankness. *A Hoosier Holiday* has both nostalgia and charm, traits not commonly identified with its author, and it describes an Indiana countryside which even James Whitcomb Riley would have liked. *Dawn* and *Newspaper Days* are as frank and uninhibited as they are egocentric. I have often thought that Carl Sandburg has as much chance to be remembered as the biographer of Lincoln as he has as a poet. It is not inconceivable that Dreiser's biographical volumes will be accorded the same recognition in the future that his novels have won today.

We are still, of course, too close to Dreiser's achievements to judge them fairly. He was a shaggy genius with obvious faults and striking merits. If some critics still belabor him for his clumsiness of style, his lack of a sense of humor or a sense of proportion, such partisans as James Farrell still praise him to the skies for his courage, his naturalism, his social criticism, his candor. In American literary history the name of Theodore Dreiser is already written in large

letters. Even those future critics who will reduce his stature aesthetically will also admit his salience and his influence. Considered only as a fighter for free and full expression of all facets of human experience, considered only as a ruthless critic of exploitation and injustice and special privilege, Dreiser is a great figure. And of one thing we may be certain: American fiction would not have flowered when and as it did if Theodore Dreiser had never lived.

## H. L. Mencken (essay date 1948)

SOURCE: Mencken, H. L. "The Life of an Artist." *The New Yorker,* vol. 24, no. 8, 17 Apr. 1948, pp. 64-71.

[*In the following essay, Mencken recalls his relationship with Dreiser and the latter's interactions with admirers and with critics who attempted to prevent the sale of his more controversial works.*]

Down to World War I, the late Theodore Dreiser, the novelist, lived a strictly bourgeois life in the horse latitudes of upper Broadway, a region then chiefly inhabited by white-collar workers who were slightly but not much above the rank of slaves. His modest quarters were in an apartment house with bumpy ornaments of terra cotta outside and a friendly smell of home cooking within. The somewhat grand entrance was flanked by a delicatessen to one side and an up-and-coming drug-store to the other. It was a place almost as remote to me, a chronic stranger in New York, as the Jersey Meadows, but I made the trip to it often, for Dreiser, in those days, was being strafed unmercifully by the Comstocks, and I was eager to give him some aid. Besides, I liked him very much and greatly enjoyed hearing him discourse in his ponderous, indignant way, suggesting both the sermons of a Lutheran pastor and the complaints of a stegosaurus with a broken leg.

His remarks, to be sure, sometimes set my teeth on edge, for I was a born earthworm and he had an itch for such transcendental arcana as spiritualism, crystal gazing, numerology, and the Freudian rumble-bumble, then a scandalous novelty in the world. Once, landing in his den on a rainy night, I found him nose to nose with an elderly female who undertook to penetrate the future by scanning the leaves in a teacup. She predicted in my presence that he was about to be railroaded to jail by the Comstocks, and added that he'd be lucky if he got off with less than five years in Sing Sing. Inasmuch as he was then sweating away at two books and eager to finish the manuscripts and collect advances, this threw him into a considerable dither, and it took me an hour to restore him to normalcy after I had shooed the sorceress out.

But in realms less unearthly we got on quite well. He believed, and argued with some heat, that the human race was the damnedest collection of vermin in the sidereal universe, and against this I could think of nothing to say. If we differed on the point, it was only because he excepted all ruined farm girls and the majority of murderers, whereas my own bill of exceptions was confined to the classical composers, Joseph Conrad, and a bartender in Baltimore named Monahan. Dreiser believed that every politician alive, including especially the reformers, should be hanged forthwith, and I went along without cavil. The same for social workers, with stress on the so-called trained ones. The same for all persons having any sort of connection with Wall Street. The same for pedagogues of all ranks. The same for the rev. clergy of every known persuasion. The same for hundred-per-cent Americans. When it came to authors, we again differed slightly, for there were then, besides Conrad, half a dozen whom I admired more or less—as artists, if not as men. But Dreiser, in my hearing, never praised any save Frank Norris, who had whooped up Dreiser's own first novel, **"Sister Carrie,"** and Harris Merton Lyon, a young short-story writer, now forgotten. He also had some respect for Balzac, but not much; I recall that he once declared that all Frenchmen were too ornery for so humane a mortuary tool as the guillotine. He read the Russians but denounced them unanimously as psychopaths of marked homosexual and homicidal tendencies. Dickens he consigned to the bilge deck of his private Gehenna, along with Howells, Henry James, and H. G. Wells. Even when it came to Arnold Bennett, who, on landing in New York, had told the gaping reporters that **"Sister Carrie"** was one of the greatest novels of all time, the most he would concede was that Bennett was probably tight or full of dope at the time, and hence not up to the customary viciousness of an Englishman.

What caused this highly orthodox citizen, almost between days, to throw off the shroud of correctness and precipitate himself into Greenwich Village is more than I can tell you, though I knew him well and pondered the question at length. The Village in that era had a very dubious reputation, and deserved it. Nine-tenths of the alleged writers and artists who infested it lived on women, chiefly from the small towns of the Middle West, and I never heard of one who produced anything worth a hoot. Whenever, in the pursuit of my duties as a literary critic, I denounced the whole population as fraudulent and nefarious, the elders of the community always threw up Eugene O'Neill and (later) Dreiser himself as shining disproofs, but O'Neill had actually made off at sight of the first refugee from Elwood, Indiana, and Dreiser was a famous man before he moved to Tenth Street. The typical Village ménage was

made up of a Cubist painter who aspired to do covers for pulp magazines and a corn-fed gal who labored at an erotic novel and paid the bills. This gal, in the standard case, was the daughter of a rural usurer who had died leaving her three thousand dollars a year in seven-per-cent farm mortgages. Until her father's executors cabbaged the money, she was a rich woman, and a rich woman, in Schmidtsville, was a target of intolerable scandal and contumely. If her I.Q. was above 7 or 8, it inevitably occurred to her, soon or late, that her dreadful experiences would make a powerful novel, so she entrained for New York and sought the encouragement of aesthetic society. She got it without delay, for the resident bucks heard of her the moment she crossed Fourteenth Street, and fought for her ferociously. If she was above the average in guile, she made the winner marry her, but this was seldom necessary, and when it happened, the marriage did not outlast her money.

Dreiser, moving to Tenth Street, found himself in a dense mass of such Little Red Riding Hoods and their attendant wolves. They swarmed in all the adjacent courts and alleys, and spilled out into the main streets and even into Washington Square. He had no more than unpacked his quills and inkhorn and hung up his other suit when they began to besiege him, for the gals all believed that his word was law with magazine editors, and their parasites were well aware that he knew every art director in New York. They barged in on him at all hours, but chiefly between 10 P.M. and 3 A.M., and the gals all brought manuscripts for him to read. I once found him with his desk surrounded by a breastwork of such scripts at least three feet high, and in a corner was a stack of canvases showing women with purple hair, mouths like the jaws of Hell, gem-set umbilici, and three or four vermilion and strabismic eyes. He was then virtually a teetotaller, but soon he had to lay in booze for the entertainment of his guests. Their tastes, it appeared, ran to liqueurs of the more exotic kinds, and they were not slow to ask for them. He then made his first acquaintance with such fancy goods as mescal, arrack, Danziger Goldwasser, and slivovitz, and had to take to massive nightcaps of bicarbonate of soda. Once, a lady poet induced him to try a few whiffs of marijuana, and his sensations were so alarming that he preached a crusade against it for years afterward.

All this cost him more money than he could afford, for the Comstockian assault had cut off his book royalties, and his magazine market was much depleted. Moreover, his working hours were invaded by his visitors, many of whom stayed a long while, and there were days when he couldn't write a line. He was a very kindly man, and the memory of his own early difficulties made him push tolerance of neophytes to the edge of folly. One night, a bulky pythoness from the Western Reserve of Ohio broke into his studio, helped herself to half a bottle of *crème de violette,* and proceeded to read to him the manuscript of a historical novel running to four hundred and fifty thousand words. He got rid of her only by what the insurance policies call an act of God. That is to say, a fire broke out in one of the art-and-love warrens across the street, and when the firemen came roaring up and began fetching aesthetes down their ladders, the pythoness took fright and ran off. The next day, he had an extra lock put on his door, which opened directly into the street, but it worked so badly that it often locked him in without locking the Village literati out. After that, he shoved an armchair against the door, but they soon learned how to climb over it.

Toward the end of 1916, the Comstocks closed in on Dreiser with psalteries sounding and tom-toms rolling, and many of his fellow-authors began to take alarm, for if he could be suppressed for a few banal episodes of calf love in his latest book, **"The 'Genius,'"** then the whole fraternity might find itself facing an idiotic and ruinous censorship. Accordingly, a manifesto was circulated protesting against the attack on him, and a number of bigwigs signed it. William Dean Howells, Hamlin Garland, and a few lesser old fellows of the prissier sort refused to do so, but most of the other authors of any consequence stepped up eagerly, and in a little while the paper had a hundred or more important signatures. But then Dreiser himself took a hand in gathering them, and the first list he turned in threw the committee into a panic. For all the quacks of the Village, hearing what was afoot, rushed up to get some publicity out of signing, and their new neighbor was far too amiable to refuse them. This list and those that followed day by day were really quite extraordinary documents, for a good half of the signers had never had anything printed in magazines above the level of the pulps, and the rest had never seen print at all. The nascent Communists of the time—they were then thought of as harmless cranks—were all there, and so were the poetical advocates of free love, the professional atheists, and the great rabble of yearning females from the Cow States. The Harlem poets signed unanimously. Not a few of the hand-painted-oil-painter signatories were being pursued by the indignant mothers of runaway daughters, and several of the etchers were under police scrutiny for filling the Village art shoppes with aphrodisiacal steals from Anders Zorn.

When Dreiser began sending in the signatures of psycho-analysts—they were then called sexologists, and their books had a great undercover sale—the committee howled in earnest, and there ensued an unseemly wrangle between the beneficiary of the manifesto and its promoters. The latter had common sense on their side, but Dreiser was too adamantine a man to be moved by any such consider-

ation. All his fellow-Villagers, of course, leaped up to defend him and themselves, and one night when I waited on him in Tenth Street I found him palavering with a delegation that insisted that he insist on retaining the signature of a Buddhist writer from Altoona, Pennsylvania, who had been collared that very day for contributing to the delinquency of a minor; to wit, a psychopathic free-verse poetess from the Upper Peninsula of Michigan. It made me dizzy to see how easily they fetched him. They had not got out a hundred words before he was pledging his life, his fortune, and his sacred honor to the Buddhist, who had got out on bail and was present in person, in a mail-order suit of clothes, with a towel wrapped around his head. I slunk out much depressed, determined to advise the committee to disband at once and tear up its manifesto, but that, happily, was never necessary, for soon afterward the Comstocks began to flush other game, and Dreiser was forgotten.

As I have said, his flat was on the ground floor of the old house he lived in, and its door opened directly upon the street. It was comfortable enough during the first six months of his occupancy, but then excavations began for the Seventh Avenue subway, and the eastern edge thereof ran along his wall. The tearing down of the house next door did not bother him much, for in the throes of literary endeavor he had a high power of concentration, but when the gangs of workmen got down to the rocks underlying Manhattan Island and began rending them with great blasts of explosives, he sometimes made heavy weather of it. More than once, his whole collection of avant-garde art came tumbling from his walls, and on several occasions he was bounced out of bed in the middle of the night. Such adventures gave him nightmares, and even when no dynamite was going off, he dreamed of being pursued by hyenas, lawyers, social workers, and other authropophagi. But the most curious of his experiences in those days did not have to do with detonations but with a quiet neighbor who occupied the basement under his apartment. In the New York fashion, Dreiser had had no truck with this neighbor, and, in fact, didn't know his name, but now and then the man could be seen ducking in or out of the areaway at the front of the house. He operated some sort of machine downstairs, faintly audible between blasts in the larval subway, and Dreiser assumed that he was a tailor, and so gave him no thought.

One day, there was a ring at the front door, and when Dreiser opened it, three men wearing derby hats brushed past him into his apartment. An ordinary author might have been alarmed, but Dreiser was an old newspaper reporter, and hence recognized them at sight as police detectives. Keeping their hats on, they got down to business at once. Who was the man who lived below? What was his name? What sort of trade did he carry on? Did he ever have any visitors? If so, who were they, and at what time of day did they visit him? Dreiser replied that he knew nothing about the fellow and couldn't answer. He had seen and heard no visitors, though the place might be swarming with them without his knowledge. Well, then what sound *did* he hear? Dreiser mentioned an occasional subdued thumping, as of a sewing machine. Was that in the morning, in the afternoon, or in the evening? Dreiser, urging his memory, replied that he had heard it at all hours. After midnight? Probably not after midnight. After eleven o'clock? Perhaps. After ten o'clock? Yes. Was it loud or soft? Soft. How long did it go on at a stretch? Sometimes half an hour; sometimes less; sometimes more. Did he hear any heavy weights being thrown about? No. Any clank or clink of metal? He couldn't recall any. Did the neighbor look suspicious when he used the areaway? Did he peer up and down the street? Did anyone ever meet him? What sort of clothes did he wear? Did he ever carry packages?

By this time, Dreiser was growing tired of his callers, and invited them to go to hell. They showed no resentment but did not move. Instead, they became confidential. The man below, they revealed in whispers, was a counterfeiter—one of the leaders of the profession. He made half dollars out of solder melted from old tin cans, and what seemed to be his sewing machine was a contraption for casting them. The dicks said that they were preparing even now to raid and jug him. Half a block down the street, two federal agents waited with a truck, and he would be taken with all his paraphernalia. Of the three cops now in attendance, one would guard the areaway and the two others would climb down through the subway excavation and rush him from the rear. As for Dreiser, he was instructed on pain of prosecution to keep his mouth shut and maintain complete immobility. If he so much as walked into his rear bedroom, it might scare the culprit off. Meanwhile, a few last questions. Had the counterfeiter ever tried to work off any bogus half dollars on him, or proposed that he help work them off on others? Had Dreiser ever smelled burning lead? Had he ever noticed any glare of flame at night? Had there been any excessive heat, as from a furnace? Had he heard any banging, bumping, booping, or bubbling?

Dreiser now renewed his invitation to his visitors to go to hell, and this time they departed. He waited a few minutes and then peeped out of the bedroom window that gave onto the yard in the rear. The two cops of the storming party were having a hard time crawling and stumbling through the subway crater, but eventually they made it and began thumping on the basement's rear door. When they got no answer, they borrowed a scantling from a subway foreman and proceeded to batter the door down. Once they were

inside, Dreiser began to see copy for one of his novels in the affair and took to the excavation himself. By the time he got to the door, muddy and bruised, the dicks were preparing to depart. While they had been sweating him upstairs, the counterfeiter had made tracks, and not only had made tracks but had taken his machine with him, and not only his machine but also his spare clothes (if any) and all his secret documents. There was nothing left save half a dozen defective counterfeit coins on the floor and a note on the table. It was written in a good, round hand and read:

> Please notify the Gas Company to shut off the gas.

### Robert H. Elias (essay date 1950)

SOURCE: Elias, Robert H. "The Library's Dreiser Collection." *University of Pennsylvania Library Chronicle,* vol. 17, 1950, pp. 78-80.

[*In the following essay, Elias summarizes the contents of the University of Pennsylvania Library's large collection of Dreiser's personal and professional papers.*]

The continuing controversy over the artistic merits of the work of Theodore Dreiser is possibly sufficient evidence that Dreiser's importance as an American writer has become itself a fact beyond controversy. The man whose **Sister Carrie** in 1900 ushered in the literature of twentieth-century America and whose **An American Tragedy** in 1925 contributed a popular phrase to our language is now a figure in the history of our culture. Growing up late in the nineteenth century under circumstances that made him receptive to post-Darwinian philosophy, Dreiser brought into our fiction a religious regard for nature and its processes that challenged the then complacent notion that man's will is invincible in all its enterprises and that provided later writers with the inspiration to portray life more faithfully and more somberly, though no less affirmatively, than most nineteenth-century American authors had felt themselves at liberty to do. A member of no clique or coterie or "school," a leader without mere disciples for followers, he usually struggled alone; yet he faced the problems that characterize the life of the society of his time, 1871-1945, whether that meant the problem of the proper limits of fiction, the issues of justice in a free society, or the question of man's position in the universe. An insight into the career of the American people may be provided by an understanding of Theodore Dreiser's career.

Most scholars in American literature now know that the materials for such an understanding are in the Library of the University of Pennsylvania. Since the spring of 1942, when Dreiser shipped his first boxes of correspondence eastward from his home in Hollywood, the Library staff and graduate students in American Civilization have been arranging and cataloguing a collection of Dreiser's books and papers so extensive that the letters and manuscripts alone must by now easily number twenty or thirty thousand items. Letters to Dreiser, letters or copies of letters from Dreiser, publishers' contracts, royalty statements, and legal documents constitute the bulk of the collection. But in addition there are the original manuscripts of almost all the major stories, novels, essays, poems, the uncompleted and unpublished as well as the completed and published—the latter accompanied by notes, typescripts, and the usual proofs; there are clippings from newspapers and magazines—too many ever to count—of articles, speeches, and interviews by and about Dreiser; and there are shelves of first editions, foreign editions, and translations of Dreiser's works, together with books presented to Dreiser by fellow authors. The collection may not be entirely unique in character, but it is certainly both a remarkably concentrated and a remarkably comprehensive assemblage of source materials for the study of a single writer—additionally remarkable in that the writer was a contemporary who made it possible for his own time to begin to study him before he died.

The value of most of the items is evident enough not to require explanations. Besides the bibliographical interest that the books satisfy, there is the evidence they help provide of Dreiser's popularity and reputation both here and abroad. When the news stories and critical notices are included in the account, we have material for a chapter in the history of American taste. The manuscripts, of course, are invaluable to biographers and critics alike for what they reveal of Dreiser's intellectual development and artistic growth. The various drafts of **The Bulwark,** begun before World War I in the days of **The "Genius"** and the novels about Charles T. Yerkes, and not finished until 1945, are, for example, indispensable in tracing Dreiser's progress from objective determinist through active social reformer to reverent, mystical believer in an ordered universe. And the letters, with the many complex relationships that correspondence implies, place before us Dreiser in terms of both his personal and his public problems. Whether one wishes to examine the correspondence with Frank Doubleday and Frank Norris to understand the publisher's "suppression" of **Sister Carrie** in 1900, or follow the years of exchanges with H. L. Mencken to define the critical challenge of literary naturalism in the first quarter of the century, or read the numerous letters to and from leftist organizations or committees in the '30's to see how a sensitive hater of injustice could become involved in communism, the boxes and filing cabinets offer rewarding treasure. Sherwood Anderson and Edgar Lee Masters;

Floyd Dell and Arthur Davison Ficke; George Jean Nathan, H. G. Wells, and James T. Farrell; Earl Browder, John L. Lewis, and Franklin D. Roosevelt—they are all there. Even if one wishes answers only to why Dreiser slapped Sinclair Lewis, or what led to his throwing a cup of coffee in Horace Liveright's face, or how toothpicks were used to indict Dreiser for adultery in the Kentucky coal fields, the correspondence is important—important to anyone concerned with the literary life of the times or with the radical political currents that have swept up many contemporary writers.

Why did Dreiser give his papers to the University of Pennsylvania? He had come to know the University as a place where vigorous work in American literature was encouraged, where he was already being studied disinterestedly, where free inquiry was hampered by no religious or political dogma—where, in short, the spirit of Benjamin Franklin was alive. When Professor Sculley Bradley and I described those conditions to Dreiser, he, wishing both to keep his literary estate intact after he died and to assure an honest critical accounting, gave the collection to the Library.

Since Dreiser's death the collection has been added to, occasionally by purchase but usually by gifts from generous friends of the Library or of Dreiser's, and plans are now complete for making available by publication some of the more significant items in the collection, beginning with the correspondence. To be sure, use has already been made of the files. I had access to almost everything when writing my own biographical study a few years ago, and the late Professor F. O. Matthiessen also consulted them when working on his volume forthcoming in the *American Men of Letters* series. Graduate students, too, have benefitted. Plans to publish the correspondence, however, will make more generally available what is at present within the physical reach of too few, and then the value that must be accepted only through the words of interpreters or accounts such as this one will be disclosed in its proper form.

### Carl Van Vechten (essay date 1951)

SOURCE: Van Vechten, Carl. "Theodore Dreiser as I Knew Him." *Yale University Library Gazette,* vol. 25, no. 3, Jan. 1951, pp. 87-92.

[*In the following essay, Van Vechten recalls his acquaintance with Dreiser, whom he first met while the latter was editing the* Broadway Magazine, *and notes that his appreciation for Dreiser's writing has increased over time.*]

Theodore Dreiser was perhaps the second major novelist I encountered (the first was Robert Herrick, with whom I took courses at the University of Chicago) and if we were not extremely intimate, at least I met him shortly after the publication of **Sister Carrie** and I knew him all through his career. I had come to New York to look for a job after I had been discharged from the *Chicago American* for "lowering the tone of the Hearst papers." At any rate this was the Managing Editor's euphemism in his final note to me. Some one, I have forgotten who now, told me that the *Broadway Magazine* was looking for a journalist to write an article about Richard Strauss's "Salome," soon to be produced at the Metropolitan Opera House.

Music was very much in my line at that period (indeed, eventually I obtained the job of assistant music critic under Richard Aldrich on the *New York Times*). So I called on the editor of the *Broadway Magazine,* who happened to be the then not very well known Theodore Dreiser. He must have immediately commissioned the article. At any rate I wrote it. My contacts on the magazine were mostly with James Keating and Harris Merton Lyon ("De Maupassant, Jr." in *Twelve Men*), but occasionally I enjoyed audience with the walrus-jawed Mr. Dreiser. The principal memory I retain of these meetings is of his habit of folding and refolding his handkerchief until it was a nest of tiny squares. When this objective was attained, he appeared to be satisfied. He would then unfold the handkerchief and begin the process again. This habit he clung to all through life.

The article, profusely illustrated, appeared in the January, 1907, issue of the *Broadway Magazine.* My copy, plentifully interlarded with subsequent comment by the editor, may be located with my books and manuscripts in the New York Public Library. In the meantime "Salome" had been taken off the Metropolitan Opera House boards, after a single performance (a dress rehearsal), and was heard of no more until Mary Garden discovered its possibilities.

Meanwhile I had captured a job on the *New York Times.* Also Mr. Dreiser had commissioned another article on which I worked long and laboriously under the tutelage of Annie Nathan Meyer and James Keating. This was to be about Barnard College but, although my father had studied law at Columbia University, this subject did not appeal to me and as a matter of fact the article was not accepted or even finished. I believe no trace of it exists today.

It was probably fifteen years before I saw Dreiser again, although occasionally I ran into one of his girl friends, Florence Deshon or another. Our paths lay in different directions. I worked in musical circles and he continued to edit magazines, most successfully in the case of the *Delin-*

*eator.* I have recently been reading Robert Elias's *Theodore Dreiser* and rereading Dorothy Dudley's *Forgotten Frontiers,* and was amazed to discover how successful Dreiser had been as editor. He might have made a comfortable fortune at that job alone. At the time nothing interested me less than big-shot magazines and the manner in which they are run. I was interested in Allen Norton's *Rogue,* in Donald Evans's Claire-Marie Publishing Company, in Marcel Duchamp's journalistic experiments and his ready-mades, in Walter Arensberg's growing collection of paintings, in Fania Marinoff's contributions to the moving-picture world, in the *Little Review,* in "291," Stieglitz's early contribution to the world of art, in the Provincetown Theatre, and in Alexander's Ragtime Band. I was dimly aware that the author of **Sister Carrie** was going places, but I did not much care to know what these places might be.

Looking over my Dreiser collection, recently, preparatory to sending it to Yale, I was amazed to discover how complete it was. Most of the early "difficult" books, everything, indeed, but some of the pamphlets and a few of the late volumes, is included. This despite the fact that I did not admire his writing (who does?) and seldom read him. I appreciate his work, today, indeed, more than I did then. He was, however, a friend and acquaintance from 1906 until the day he died.

Our second meeting may have been in the Gotham Book Mart, where we thought it was funny to write in a copy of the Bible lying on the counter, "With the compliments of the Author." Maybe God himself did consider it funny. Certainly, today, I do not; but I recall we had quite a ribald laugh after this silly performance.

Dreiser was responsible for my withdrawal from the Authors' League, for when, due to the action of the censor, **The "Genius"** got into trouble, that august body refused to come to the author's assistance. I was indignant about this and resigned from the society, and I have never rejoined the League. Not that I liked **The "Genius"** so much; as a matter of fact I have never read it, but I thought it was the business of the Authors' League to protect its members, especially its important members, as Dreiser had become in many eyes, on occasions like this.

Dreiser once gave a party at his apartment in St. Luke's Place which has been described by several writers, never quite accurately. Mencken, Boyd, and I dined on the way to the party, very probably at the Brevoort, where we were joined by Scott Fitzgerald, then in his early prime. He expressed great admiration for Dreiser, said that he would rather meet him than any one else he could think of, and admitted he was most envious of us others who had been invited to the great man's house. Despite this special pleading, we did not ask him to accompany us.

The party wasn't much. There was nothing to drink but beer. We, reinforced by T. R. Smith and a few others, whose names I have forgotten, sat stiffly and soberly in a circle, "All silent and all damn'd!" There was little conversation, surprisingly little considering the names of those present, but it must be remembered that the literati of that period often depended on external moisture to open their lips. Anyway in the midst of this nothingness there was a distraction. The doorbell rang and Dreiser answered it himself. The door opened into the large bare room where we sat so quietly, and there was Scott with a bottle of champagne under one arm. I shall never forget his boyish charm, of which he had a plenty in those days, or the sweet gesture with which he handed the bottle to Dreiser, who accepted it with thanks, and invited Scott in. Our host put the bottle on ice (the refrigerator was also visible from where we sat) and we never saw it again. Soon after the party broke up.

On another occasion, Dorothy Dudley, who was engaged in writing *Forgotten Frontiers,* asked me to dinner with the subject of her book. I had a reason for wanting to see him and accepted the invitation with alacrity. Formerly it was my custom (perhaps it was even a superstition) to have my contracts witnessed by some one to whom the book was dedicated or at any rate by some one connected in some way with the subject of the novel. I wanted Dreiser to witness the contract for *The Tattooed Countess* and I carried it with me to Dorothy's. She was living in Nyack at the time, near the River, and we dined in a grape arbor on a table extravagant with its fiascos of Chianti, colored glass, and splendid nappery. Dreiser and I signed the contract on this table.

A great deal later, when Dreiser occupied the huge studio at 200 West 57th Street, he gave a party every month. He had become easier in manner and his bank account was larger, and he could invite pretty nearly any one in New York with the assurance he would turn up, if not otherwise engaged. However these parties did not come off much better than the earlier one I have described. He was not by nature a party giver. Anita Loos reported to me once that in the midst of one of his soirées, with the rooms crowded with people, she had missed Dreiser and, searching for him, discovered him in the butler's pantry, dissolved in tears, shed no doubt for the sorrows of the world.

In spite of this behavior, he was actually perverse enough to enjoy the company of people, and one of his chief pleasures was to ask questions of all and sundry. I brought Max Ewing with me one night. This was during the winter

of 1927-28. Dreiser as usual was concerned with an idea. He wanted to find out what became of handsome men. What, he demanded, would become of Max in ten years? He made Max and me agree to tell him. Alas, in barely three years from that date, Max, poor devil, killed himself.

Dreiser often visited our apartment on East 19th Street. He even came to our apartment at 150 West 55th Street, opposite Mecca Temple, but I do not recall seeing him at 101 Central Park West. The letters remain to remind me that Helen Richardson asked us to a dancing party for May 31, 1928, and withdrew the invitation later because she was unsuccessful in securing the guests she desired. The author of *Jennie Gerhardt* was not fitted by nature to practise the rites of Terpsichore, but nevertheless he enjoyed them.

Having suffered the slings and arrows of outrageous fortune, and being actually poor most of his youth, Dreiser was not of the "giving" kind, but he actually presented me with the French translation of *Twelve Men, Douze Hommes,* and it was characteristic of him that he inscribed it more warmly than he had the books I asked him to inscribe when he came one night to my apartment on East 19th Street, along with Tom Smith. We had enjoyed a bibulous dinner and he was fairly ribald on this occasion, as one or two of the books, now at Yale, will bear testimony. Later, inserting a clipping for *Douze Hommes,* he wrote me inquiringly, "Why can't you two frogs agree?" I had assured him that the book was well translated. The clipping asserted that the translation was bad.

He professed to admire Henry Fuller as an early realist, but he seemed to possess none of his books. I sent him some; also some volumes by T. F. Powys, a favorite of mine. Powys did not agree with him. Fuller did not agree with Miss Cather to whom I was also sending books at this period. She decided he was "old-fashioned."

On March 21, 1927, Dreiser wrote me from Reading, Pennsylvania (where Bobby Clark's celebrated roué came from), inviting me to join him in a walking tour. The invitation was not accepted. I had a feeling that Dreiser and I would be an odd pair of walking-tour mates. Walking, indeed, is scarcely one of my major pastimes.

In 1930 Hugh Walpole expressed a wish to meet Dreiser. I couldn't exactly contemplate with pleasure the idea of bringing these two men together. Probably no two more uncongenial souls could have been discovered among fiction writers. However, an idea occurred to me which I thought would make the encounter more possible. I invited Long Lance, a Blackfoot Indian, very popular at the period, who spoke English perfectly, to join us at lunch.

Dreiser wrote me: "Dear Van Vechten, The thought of lunching with three indians appeals to me. Therefore on Feb 12 I shall pass my breakfast & make the Crillon at one. I have black feet myself."[1] This letter, of course, is pure Menckenese, and is much lighter in tone than Dreiser usually managed to achieve. For instance, let me quote the following example of his disastrous and elephantine attempt at humor:

> I wouldst have come—and gladly [*it must have been a reply to some invitation*]—but I had a previous engagement with Chomias Oppenheim & his wife at Washington Square South & couldn't. But another time, God willing, I will post-haste—de facto and de jure—similia simillibus—or is it simile-ebus. Anyhow—well.
>
> And I missed all the drinks. God, what a tragedy.
>
> The Author of Deuteronomy

Admittedly this is pretty awful, but no worse than certain passages in *Hey Rub-a-Dub-Dub.*

I recall an evening at the psychiatrist's, Dr. Berg's, with Dreiser, Mabel Dodge Luhan, and a few others. All specialists interested him because he could ask them questions, but on this occasion his principal subject was drugs and anesthetics. He had recently been experimenting with these in an attempt to discover if they had any value for the writer. He found out, for instance, that laughing gas apparently puts you in touch with the secrets of the universe, but when its effects depart, which they do almost immediately, no whit of this remains in your consciousness and anything you attempt to write is gibberish.

When I began to make photographs, Dreiser was one of the first authors I invited to pose. He had a wonderful head for photography and my pictures of him are superb. He came to me in the morning on his way to a train. He was in great good humor and joked all through the sitting. Indeed, one of the best pictures shows Dreiser laughing, a rare shot, which is published in Elias's biography. Dreiser's last letter to me in 1938 refers to these photographs.

*Note*

1. Dreiser's letters are quoted by permission of his wife, Helen Richardson Dreiser, and of the Yale University Library to which they now belong.

## Joseph J. Kwiat (essay date 1952)

SOURCE: Kwiat, Joseph J. "Dreiser's *The "Genius"* and Everett Shinn, the 'Ash-Can' Painter." *PMLA,* vol. 67, no. 2, Mar. 1952, pp. 15-31.

[*In the following essay, Kwiat considers Dreiser's relationship to Shinn, of the New York realist school of painters, and refers to Shinn's commentary on* The "Genius," *for which he may have served as the model.*]

I

During the period in which Theodore Dreiser wrote his first five novels, *Sister Carrie, Jennie Gerhardt, The Financier, The Titan,* and *The "Genius,"* the novelist indicated a particularly strong interest in those American painters who interpreted the city scene. And it was the so-called New York Realists—Robert Henri, John Sloan, William J. Glackens, George Luks, and Everett Shinn—who made the greatest appeal to him from approximately 1899 to 1915.[1] Several reasons may be suggested for Dreiser's sympathy for this particular group of painters. First, the newspaper and magazine careers of the artists, with the exception of Henri, closely paralleled Dreiser's own career; and both Dreiser and the graphic artists eventually utilized this common background for their more ambitious work as novelist and as painter. Second, with Henri leading the attack, the group of painters emerged as the most aggressive force in the artistic revolt against the domination of the tradition-bound National Academy when they became known as the notorious "Ash-Can school" and "apostles of ugliness" soon after the turn of the century. Dreiser, of course, served a similar function in his challenge to the Genteel Tradition, the literary equivalent of the Academy in the United States. Third, the Ash-Can painters not only believed, as Dreiser did, that an artist must be an honest and truthful recorder and interpreter of the life he saw and knew, but it was in their depiction of these "truths" of city life, its violence and brutality *and* its beauty, that their relationship to Dreiser is most clearly seen.

Dreiser was in a strategic position to exploit his interest in the artistic portrayal of the city when he edited *Broadway Magazine* from 1906 to 1907 and, for a time, also wrote a column. This column, "The Month in New York," closely paralleled the subject matter that captured the interest of the Ash-Can artists. Dreiser, however, also took pains to call to the attention of his readers what he considered to be the significance of these particular painters of the New York scene. Using Henri as the center for his discussion, he wrote:

> New York has a painter whose work is found in almost every gallery and salon in Europe, whose name is respected in every Continental studio, and who, in spite of this, is scarcely known in his own city and country by what has been kindly termed "the people at large."
>
> But if New York does not know Robert Henri the reverse cannot be said. Henri does know his New York and he has

a school of followers who go with him to the tenements and alleyways to paint—Glackens, Sloan, Shinn, to name a few of them. "New York is better than Paris for artists," says Henri; and "Stop studying water pitchers and bananas and paint every day New York life—a Hester Street pushcart is a better subject than a Dutch windmill."

But Dreiser's greater interest in Everett Shinn, of all the Ash-Can painters, gradually emerges. The novelist-editor also suggested articles for his magazine. One of these, on a group of artists' wives, included a discussion of Mrs. Shinn. Everett Shinn was already known to Dreiser as a collaborator and colleague on magazines, and the editor's hand is apparent in the digression on Mrs. Shinn when reference is made to her husband's paintings as "broadly interesting pictures, many of which are scenes of New York life in its most modern aspect—skyscrapers, fire engines, typical street scenes, and the like."[2]

Dreiser referred once again to Shinn in a sketch written before 1915, the year *The "Genius"* was published. The sketch was Dreiser's attempt to paint an "inspired picture" of an oil refinery, and it represents his brilliant effort to translate the technique of the graphic artist in capturing the spirit of an industrial scene:

> This region is remarkable for the art, as for the toil of it, if nothing more. A painter could here find a thousand contrasts in black and gray and red and blue, which would give him ample labor for his pen or brush. These stacks are so tall, the building from which they spring so low. Spread out over a marshy ground which was once all seaweed and which now shows patches of water stained with iridescent oil, broken here and there with other patches of black earth to match the blacker buildings which abound upon it, you have a combination in shades and tones of one color which no artist could resist. A Whistler could make wonderful blacks and whites of this. A Vierge or Shinn could show us what it means to catch the exact image of darkness at its best. ... It is a great world of gloom, done in lines of splendid activity, but full of the pathos of faint contrasts in gray and black.[3]

This passage illustrates Dreiser's general indebtedness to painters for invaluable lessons in "seeing." But it has a more immediate significance: it refers to Shinn and his selection of unconventional subject matter; it serves to remind us of Dreiser's familiarity with Shinn's work and his aesthetic intentions; and it suggests how the literary man identified his own artistic efforts with that of his friend working in another artistic medium.

## II

Everett Shinn has also given evidence of his personal and artistic relationship to Dreiser. He has done this in conversations and correspondence with me, and in his heretofore unpublished annotations in my copy of Dreiser's novel, *The "Genius."*[4] A letter by Shinn establishes the fact that he knew Dreiser during their respective magazine writing and illustrating days and testifies to his conviction that he was Dreiser's model for the career of the painter Eugene Witla, the fictional hero of *The "Genius."* The following is an excerpt from the most relevant passages in Shinn's letter:

> In compliance with your wish I have carefully read Theodore Dreiser's book, *The "Genius,"* and have carefully made such marginal notes that touched on my art activities, incidents and almost precise identification of some of my pictures that were fresh in the minds of Dreiser and in my own during a close office friendship where we both talked of our individual work, and our hopes for further success.
>
> That period that marked the start of any public notice extended to me was of that same period where I enjoyed Dreiser's friendship. We started on *Ainslee's Magazine* together. I had just left the Art department of the New York *World* to be free to work for magazines.
>
> Dreiser's mention of the periodical *Truth*[5] fits the time I came over from Philadelphia, monthly visits, and sold several drawings to Mr. MacArthur, the art editor, who gasped at my nerve in showing them, but nevertheless bought them because he said, "They are so damned different." I also drew for all the magazines that Dreiser mentions in his book. My center pages in *Harper's Weekly* and in color and those in *Harper's Bazaar* fit Dreiser's descriptions [of] the city streets and theatre crowds.
>
> The art gallery that Dreiser overlays with another name is obviously that of Knoedler. One of my earliest exhibitions was held in that gallery when the gallery was at the corner of 34th St. and 5th Avenue. Pictures described in that gallery at one of my shows fit the things I made.
>
> I made illustrations for Dreiser when he was the editor of *Hampton's Magazine.* We were friends and talked much about ourselves. I remember a row of wooden boxes back of his desk that he said contained the plates of his novel, either *Sister Carrie* or *Jenny Gerhardt.* Not making a literary disturbance he had decided to use the plates to republish the book.
>
> I see myself in many places and feel that as I was alone in interpreting New York as he describes it ... and with no wish to claim Witla as being something of me I nevertheless feel that Dreiser looked on my work and the magazines I worked for as fitting material for his character, the artist, Witla.
>
> Beyond the actual art expression I am in no way related to Witla the artist in Dreiser's book, *The "Genius."* His emotional side is far and away from mine. That side of Witla's character is presumably the emotional unrest of Dreiser himself.[6]

Everett Shinn was born in Woodstown, New Jersey, in 1876, five years before Dreiser. For a time he was a student of mechanical drawing at Spring Garden Institute and then a drafting room worker in a lighting fixtures factory where he was found idly sketching in the margins, whereupon his employer advised him to forsake the T-square for art. Shinn then became a Philadelphia newspaper illustrator in 1893 for the *Inquirer* and in 1896 for the *Press.* Dreiser, it will be recalled, began his work on newspapers in Chicago in 1892. Among Shinn's fellow artists on the Philadelphia newspapers were John Sloan, William J. Glackens, and George Luks. Robert Henri, a painter, encouraged Shinn and the other newspaper artists to continue their rather desultory art studies at the Pennsylvania Academy; they also banded together for stimulating talks which were led by Henri, whose more formal art studies had been carried on in Philadelphia and abroad and whose knowledge of the world of ideas and books was much more extensive than that of the others. Finally, around the turn of the century, Shinn preceded the other Philadelphians to New York, where he worked for the *Journal,* the *Herald,* and also the *World.*[7]

Newspaper work was for Shinn, as for Dreiser, a stepping stone to magazine work. And many of the magazines to which he contributed his drawings, in black and white and in color, were the magazines which carried Dreiser's name as an editor or as a writer of articles and short stories. These included *Truth, Ainslee's, Harper's Weekly, Harper's Bazaar, Hampton's* and *Broadway Magazine, McClure's, Century, Scribner's, Everybody's, Cosmopolitan,* and *Delineator.*[8] From 1899 on, Shinn's black and white studies, pastels, and water colors were exhibited in public and private art galleries in Philadelphia, Boston, and New York.

Shinn's historical distinction was climaxed in 1908 when he became a member of the notorious "Eight" Group, under the leadership of Henri, in the now-famous show at the Macbeth Gallery in New York. With the five Philadelphians (Shinn, Sloan, Glackens, Luks, and Henri) as the nucleus,[9] the "Eight" Show marked a revolutionary turning point in American art. For in its insistence upon the essential dignity of any subject matter, whether "respectable" or "ash-can," and the necessity for honesty, sincerity, and integrity of vision and purpose by the artist, it represented the spirit of revolt in twentieth-century American painting.[10]

### III

There is no doubt, then, that Dreiser and Shinn knew each other. But, as we have already seen, their relationship has an additional interest. For when Dreiser came to write his first draft of the manuscript for *The "Genius"* in 1911, only three years after the highly publicized and controversial "Eight" Show, he chose as his central character a painter, Eugene Witla. And although Witla's story in the book is essentially Dreiser's story, it is significant that the novelist selected Everett Shinn to serve as the model for the fictional painter and, in something of a Dostoievskyan sense, as his own "double."

Shinn's annotations in this single copy of *The "Genius"* are, to be sure, a most interesting literary curiosity. But they also suggest something of the way in which Dreiser manipulated his central image of a creative artist and transformed the raw materials of reality for his artistic ends. And, finally, the annotations give valuable insights into the way in which Dreiser identified his own artistic efforts and intentions with that of a kindred artist, a painter of the unconventional Ash-Can school.

Briefly, then, *The "Genius"* deals with the amorous adventures of Witla, an artist, who comes from a small town in Illinois, studies art in Chicago, and distinguishes himself as an illustrator in New York. His strenuous living results in a nervous collapse, he recovers, and he becomes a financially successful art director and managing publisher of a chain of magazines. His wife dies in childbirth and Witla returns to his painting. The novel ends in the artist's search for genuine and permanent values.

Shinn's annotations indicate the personal resemblances which he detects between the fictional characterization of Witla and himself.[11] When, for example, Witla gravitates toward New York and sets himself up in a studio in Waverly Place with two friends, Shinn notes: "I lived at 112 Waverley Place for 14 years and knew Dreiser before and after living there. I built a large studio in the rear. There I painted and also gave my 3 plays: 'More Sinned Against than Usual,' 'Wronged from the Start' and 'The Prune Hater's Daughter.'"[12] Witla's grandiose dreams of having his pictures hanging in Fifth Avenue galleries and even in the Metropolitan Museum along with Corot, Daubigny, Rousseau, Turner, and Watts, elicit a caustic comment from Shinn: "This boob, Witla, has no reserve, no doubts of his genius. ... Idiot. My picture bought from Knoedlers Art Gallery produced at the time a particular elation but I didn't entertain a belief that I was in any way as good as Winslow Homer that hung on the right of my picture and one by Whistler on the left" (p. 223). And Witla's travels to London and Paris not only parallel Shinn's own European experiences, but the painter recalls that his Parisian studio was very similar to the one described in the novel (pp. 242-243).

Shinn has commented also upon certain resemblances between Witla's career as an art student in Chicago with his own student days in Philadelphia. The fictional hero's admiration for the dramatic war pictures of Verestchagin and a "great, warm tinted nude" by Bouguereau leads Shinn to remark that he too saw the Russian painter's pictures "and felt their extravagant and harrowing reality," but that he hated the French painter "for his boneless, cosmetic smoothe-powdered lust" (p. 51). When the art instructor in the novel emphasizes the idea that a general plan of the drawing is necessary before the details can be worked out, Shinn detects a reference to the influence of the Munich School of painting, one to which he had been haphazardly exposed.[13]

Witla's career as a newspaper artist in Chicago and as a magazine illustrator in New York was, in broad outline, similar to Shinn's experiences in Philadelphia and in New York. Two newspaper artists in the novel, Howe and Mathews, impress young Witla with their connoisserurship of pen and ink illustration, particularly in their awareness of Steinlen and the "whole rising young school of French poster workers" and such "radical" European art journals as *Jugend* and *Simplicissimus*. Shinn comments that two men in the art department of the Philadelphia *Press* had also been trained in painting abroad, Luks in Munich and Howe[14] in Paris, and that Steinlen was "much admired by me" (p. 89).

When Witla arrives in New York and attempts to show his pictures at the offices of the *Century, Harper's* and *Scribner's,* he is overawed by the drawings created by the leaders in the illustration world which he sees hanging on the walls of the art and editorial rooms of the magazines. Shinn was reminded of his similar feelings, and writes: "I, too, looked at framed illustrations in the offices of these same magazines by C. D. Gibson, W. T. Smedley, Rhinehart [sic], Wenzell, Andre Castaigne and others and felt my presumptuousness in imagining one of mine hanging on the walls" (p. 105). After many rebuffs, Witla is surprised and delighted when he sells a drawing of an East Side street scene of working girls at six o'clock to a weekly magazine, *Truth,* which uses it as a double-page spread. Shinn indicates that his own first published drawings in New York also appeared in *Truth,* and that they were "just people, streets, crowds" (pp. 110-111). During the same year, Witla makes the acquaintance of the editor of *Craft,* a magazine "devoted to art subjects." Shinn identifies the magazine as the *Craftsman,* which, as he indicates, printed several articles about his early work (p. 113). And when Witla finally makes his appearance in *Harper's Magazine,* his confidence increases and he deliberately sets out to "make" the other top-flight periodicals, *Scribner's* and the *Century* (p. 136). Shinn points out that he worked for all of these magazines.[15]

Shinn's comments upon Witla's experiences with the National Academy are revealing since this institution repre-sented the same conservative and sterile forces in American art for the Ash-Can painters as the leaders of the Genteel Tradition in literature did for Stephen Crane, Frank Norris, and Dreiser himself. When Witla early in his art school career is considerably impressed by the distinction of his instructors, for they were men who were "N.A.'s," Dreiser remarks that the young student "little knew with what contempt this honor was received in some quarters, or he would not have attached so much significance to it." Shinn's comment merely reads: "All the 'Eight' hated the staff at the N.A." (p. 54). Much later, however, after Witla achieves recognition as a magazine illustrator in New York, he decides to send the original of his East Side picture, "Six O'clock," which had appeared in *Truth,* to the National Academy of Design exhibition. But his decision is based upon cynical motives, since Witla's attitude toward the "N.A." is now anything but respectful.

> To have a picture accepted by this society and hung on the line was in its way a mark of merit and approval, though Eugene did not think very highly of it. . . . Eugene had thought the first two years he was in New York that he was really not sufficiently experienced or meritorious, and the previous year he had thought that he would hoard all that he was doing for his first appearance in some exhibition of his own, thinking the National Academy commonplace and retrogressive. The exhibitions he had seen thus far had been full of commonplace, dead-and-alive stuff, he thought. It was no great honor to be admitted to such a collection. Now, . . . because he had accumulated nearly enough pictures for exhibition at a private gallery which he hoped to interest, he was anxious to see what the standard body of American artists thought of his work. They might reject him. If so that would merely prove that they did not recognize a radical departure from accepted methods and subject matter as art. The impressionists, he understood, were being so ignored. Later they would accept him. If he were admitted it would simply mean that they knew better than he believed they did.
>
> (pp. 219-220)[16]

Although Shinn also felt Witla's contempt for the National Academy, he too had sent pictures to them. After three consecutive years of rejection, seven of his pictures were accepted for hanging and, what was even more surprising, they were requested by that august body. But, Shinn emphasizes, this invitation *followed* several successful private shows. Thus the National Academy, ever-cautious, did not recognize an original talent until the artist had succeeded in winning a certain amount of popular applause and approval (p. 213). Shinn's dissatisfaction with the "N.A.'s" artistic timidity and dictatorial powers contributed significantly toward his alignment with fellow artists who revolted against its domination in the "Eight" Show in 1908 under Robert Henri's leadership.

IV

Dreiser, however, did not content himself with merely describing various phases of Shinn's personal life, his art student days, his career as a newspaper artist and as a magazine illustrator, and his hostility toward that symbol of conservatism and tediousness, the National Academy. For, even more significantly, Dreiser described many of Shinn's specific drawings and paintings and something of the artistic intentions motivating them. Witla's unconventional and even revolutionary theory and practice characterized Shinn *and* the group of which he was a member, the scorned Ash-Can artists. And Dreiser, as we have seen, knew the work and admired the historic role of Shinn and his colleagues, Henri, Sloan, Glackens, and Luks. He borrowed, undoubtedly, numerous suggestions from the work of these painters for his descriptions of Witla's artistic efforts. But it is Shinn who serves as Dreiser's central image in his portrayal of the unorthodox and genuinely interesting and live American artist around the turn of the twentieth century, a crucial period which promised in so many ways that this country was finally coming of age.

Both Witla and Shinn, like Dreiser himself, are thrilled by the dramatic spectacle of the city. To Witla, drawing the city while working as a newspaper artist in Chicago "seemed a beautiful privilege and he loved the thought of making the commonplace dramatic. It was all dramatic to him—the wagons in the streets, the tall buildings, the street lamps—anything, everything." Shinn comments: "Certainly this was my intention—all dramatic" (p. 89). Dreiser later describes Witla's first wanderings in New York and his fascination with its life, and he points out that the city had a special appeal for the artist when it was wet or white. "He saw Fifth Avenue once in a driving snowstorm and under sputtering arc lights, and he hurried to his easel next morning to see if he could not put it down in black and white." Shinn's comment is: "I made all these" (p. 108). In an unpublished manuscript by Shinn in my possession, dated 8 September 1948, the artist has indicated at greater length how he too was captured by the special quality of snow and rain in the city.[17] And many of Shinn's drawings and paintings that I have seen in the original and in reproduction are sufficient proof of his affinity with Witla on this score.

The esthetic appeal of unconventional subject matter, railroad yards, dumps, the East River, which are to be found in Shinn's work, also inspired Witla early in his life. When Witla arrives in Chicago, he is described as responding to scenes "that he felt sure he could, when he had learned to draw a little better, make great things of,—dark, towering factory-sites, great stretches of railroad yards laid out like a puzzle in rain, snow, or bright sunlight; great smoke-stacks throwing their black heights athwart morning or evening skies." Shinn comments that he made all these scenes in Philadelphia (pp. 48-49). A railroad yard scene catches Witla's eye during this period in Chicago, and he is enthralled by its artistic possibilities: "... big black engines throwing up clouds of smoke and steam in a grey, wet air; great mazes of parti-colored cars dank in the rain but lovely. At night the switch lights in these great masses of yards bloomed like flowers. He loved the sheer yellows, reds, greens, blues, that burned like eyes. Here was the stuff that touched him magnificently. ..." Shinn indicates that this scene also attracted him and that he made many freight yard scenes for newspapers in Philadelphia and later in color for magazines (p. 76). Witla's response to Goose Island in the Chicago River, with its "little tumble-down huts and upturned hulls of boats used for homes," reminds Shinn that he "also haunted and painted the dumps" in Philadelphia (p. 78). And when he arrives in New York, Witla makes tentative sketches of things he sees: "... a large crowd in the dark at 34th Street; a boat off 86th Street in the East River in the driving rain; a barge with cars being towed by a tug." Shinn remembers that he painted all these: "East River—crowds—slush" (p. 103).

But Shinn has also been able to identify many of his own individual pictures from Dreiser's descriptions of Witla's work. Dreiser was, of course, familiar with Shinn's magazine illustrations in black and white and in color. And he was aware of the artist's original pastel drawings which were to serve as illustrations for a book, never completed, by William Dean Howells on various phases of New York City life in 1899.[18] But Dreiser had other opportunities to see Shinn's work; for the originals of the magazine illustrations, the water-colors, and the pastels for the book with Howells were exhibited in public and private galleries in New York, Philadelphia, and Boston from 1899 on. A mere listing of some representative titles from the body of Shinn's work at this time will give an idea of the range of his subject matter and will, in addition, anticipate the subject matter of many of Witla's own pictures as described by Dreiser in this novel. Some of Shinn's titles include: "South Ferry Slip," "East River," "Fifth Avenue at Thirty-Fourth Street," "Crush at Brooklyn Bridge," "Roof Garden," "The Snow Plough," "A Summer Night—Tenements," "Chinese Restaurant," "An Eviction," "Salvation Army," "Ambulance Call," "Downtown Saloon," "Gramercy Park," "Bowery Side-Show," "Cabs on the Fifth Avenue Side of Madison Square," "Street Fight," "The Haymarket," "Broadway, Late in the Afternoon," "Saloon Musicians," "Grand Central Station—Midnight Train," "Broadway Theatre District," "Rag Picker," "Fleischman's Bakery—

Free Distribution of Bread and Coffee,"[19] and various rain and snow scenes in the city.

One of Witla's first artistic successes is with "Six O'clock." It had been his first magazine illustration and Dreiser describes it as Witla's attempt to portray "a mass of East Side working girls flooding the streets after six o'clock. There were dark walls of buildings, a flaring gas lamp or two, some yellow lighted shop windows, and many shaded half seen faces—bare suggestions of souls and pulsing life" (p. 110). Witla eventually sends the original of the picture to an exhibition given under the auspices of the National Academy—and it is accepted; he confides at the time that he expects to have a show of his own very soon. Shinn indicates that he had made a picture, in color, with an identical title.[20] Another one of Shinn's pictures that I have seen, "The Tenements at Hester Street," is similarly concerned with the dramatic quality of East Side life.

Witla's drawing of a Greeley Square scene in a sopping drizzle is seen by the fictional artist with an eye for contrasts, "picking out lights and shadows sharply, making wonderful blurs that were like colors in precious stones, confused and suggestive." Shinn comments that he made a corresponding drawing of Greeley Square on a snowy night.[21] With extraordinary effectiveness Dreiser succeeds in catching the pictorial qualities in "Fifth Avenue in a Snow Storm," a scene which also appealed to Shinn. Dreiser describes the picture as it is seen for the first time by the director of an art gallery: "... he paused struck by its force. He liked the delineation of swirling, wind-driven snow. The emptiness of this thoroughfare, usually so crowded, the buttoned, huddled, hunched, withdrawn look of those who traveled it, the exceptional details of piles of snow sifted on to window sills and ledges and into doorways and on to the windows of the bus itself, attracted his attention" (p. 227). Shinn's "Fifth Avenue at Thirty-Fourth Street in 1900," "Cabs on the Fifth Avenue Side of Madison Square," and "Broadway, Late in the Afternoon" have striking pictorial similarities to Dreiser's description.

Dreiser briefly describes other pictures by Witla. These also resemble Shinn's work and remind the painter of them. One of these is "The Bowery by Night," with the L train rushing overhead (p. 113). Shinn's "Elevated Railroad" and "A Fire Beyond the Elevated" also make use of the elevated motif for its value as a picturesque background in the life of the city. Another of Witla's paintings is "East River," and the analysis of this picture by the art director actually represents an acute and sensitive awareness of Shinn's flair for the dramatic quality of his subject matter: "M. Charles passed on ... to the steaming tug coming up the East River in the dark hauling two great freight barges. He

was saying to himself that after all Eugene's art was that of merely seizing upon the obviously dramatic. It wasn't so much the art of color composition and life analysis as it was stage craft. The man before him had the ability to see the dramatic side of life" (p. 228). An excellent illustration of this quality in a work by Shinn which treats a similar subject is "East River, Sunset."

Dreiser's description of "Engines Entering a Freight Yard" reveals the novelist's sympathy for Witla's (and Shinn's) portrayal of the "beauty-in-ugliness" theme in the life of the city, and his ability to visualize the scene with a painter's eye for color tones, composition, and mood. "It was the three engines entering the great freight yard abreast, the smoke of the engines towering straight up like tall whitish-grey plumes, in the damp, cold air, the sky lowering with blackish-grey clouds, the red and yellow and blue cars standing out in the sodden darkness because of the water. You could feel the cold, wet drizzle, the soppy tracks, the weariness of 'throwing switches.' There was a lone brakeman in the foreground, 'throwing' a red brake signal. He was quite black and evidently wet" (p. 231). Freight yard scenes were for Shinn, and the other Ash-Can painters, a popular subject matter. Another of Witla's depictions of the city's manifold life, "After the Theatre," reminds Shinn of his own "Metropolitan Opera House" (pp. 232-233). Witla's work is described by Dreiser as "a painting full of the wonder and bustle of a night crowd under sputtering electric lamps." It is strikingly reminiscent of many of Shinn's pictures of crowds emerging from a theatre; his "Metropolitan Opera House" and his untitled magazine illustration for *Town Topics* (1900) of an audience descending the brownstone steps of Daley's Theatre are examples of this phase of his work.

Witla later paints his pictures in Paris and London for a brief period and Shinn notes that this also corresponds to his own career (pp. 246, 272). In Paris, Witla is attracted toward the scenes that attracted Shinn: not only the Apache district and summer parties at Versailles, but also "factory throngs, watchmen and railroad crossings, market people, market in the dark, street sweepers, newspaper vendors, flower merchants" (p. 246). Representative titles from some of Shinn's pictures in Paris suggest their kinship to Witla's work in the selection of subject matter: "Versailles Garden," "The Flower Market," "Early Morning, Paris," "Matinee, Paris Music Hall," "Scavengers on the Seine," and "Opening Shop—Paris." The strong similarities in Witla's and Shinn's mood and attitude toward their materials can, of course, only be realized by actually examining Shinn's pictures. "Early Morning, Paris" and "Opening Shop—Paris," for example, emphasize the image of the ash-can and the human scavenger of its contents; these pictures of human misery are sketched over against a back-ground of bleakness in nature and loneliness in the complete absence of other men or, when they are present, in their indifference to the suffering which permeates the pictures.

The fictional director of a New York art gallery, M. Charles, is the counterpart, according to Mr. Shinn, of one of the members of the Knoedler Gallery.[22] Both the fictional and the real director give the artist his opportunity to exhibit his work. When M. Charles attempts his first appraisal of Witla's pictures, originally executed as maga-zine illustrations,[23] he wracks his memory for the "influ-ences." "Of whose work did it remind him—anybody's? He confessed to himself as he stirred around among his numerous art memories that he recalled nothing exactly like it. Raw reds, raw greens, dirty grey paving stones—such faces! Why this thing fairly shouted its facts. It seemed to say: 'I'm dirty, I am commonplace, I am grim, I am shabby, but I am life.' And there was no apolo-gizing for anything in it, no glossing anything over. Bang! Smash! Crack! came the facts one after another, with a bitter, brutal insistence on their so-ness" (p. 231).

The connoiseur finally recognizes that not only is Witla highly individual in his technique and in his attitude to-ward his subject matter but that his vision of the life of the city is all-inclusive.

> He saw that Eugene had covered almost every phase of what might be called the dramatic spectacle in the public life of the city and much that did not appear dramatic until he touched it—the empty canyon of Broadway at three o'clock in the morning; a long line of giant milk wagons, swinging curious lanterns, coming up from the docks at four o'clock in the morning; a plunging parade of fire vehicles, the engines steaming smoke, the people running or staring open-mouthed; a crowd of polite society figures emerging from the opera; the bread line; an Italian boy throwing pigeons in the air from a basket on his arm in a crowded lower West-side street. Everything he touched seemed to have romance and beauty, and yet it was real and most grim and shabby.

(p. 232)

Shinn's magazine drawings, and particularly his thirty-six illustrations in pastel for the unfinished book on New York by night, to be written by William Dean Howells, were undoubtedly in Dreiser's mind when he wrote this passage. A picture by Shinn to parallel each word-sketch by Dreiser can be identified without any difficulty. Finally, Mr. Shinn states that the art director representing the Knoedler Gallery reacted to his pictures as did M. Charles to Witla's pictures.

The parallel between the artistic careers of Witla and Shinn is continued in the judgment upon their work by the critics.

The two fictional criticisms of Witla's first show echo to an astonishing extent the judgments of Shinn's work, as well as that of the other Ash-Can painters. Dreiser describes in detail one picture by Witla which, apparently, represents the general subject matter and attitude of his other draw-ings. The central subject is a negro.

> He was standing in a cheap, commonplace East Side street. The time evidently was a January or February morning. His business was driving an ash cart, and his occupation at the moment illustrated by the picture was that of lifting a great can of mixed ashes, paper and garbage to the edge of the ungainly iron wagon. His hands were immense and were covered with great red patched woolen and leather gloves. ... His head and ears were swaddled about by a red flannel shawl or strip of cloth. ... He was looking purblindly down the shabby street, its hard crisp snow littered with tin cans, paper, bits of slop and offal. Dust—gray ash dust, was flying from his upturned can. In the distance behind him was a milk wagon, a few pedestrians, a little thinly clad girl coming out of a delica-tessen store. Over head were dull small-paned windows, some shutters with a few of their slats broken out, a frowsy headed man looking out evidently to see whether the day was cold.

(p. 236)

One critic for a conservative publication makes a sweeping indictment of Witla's artistic ability and integrity. He denies that Witla is an American Millet: "The great Frenchman was a lover of humanity, a reformer in spirit, a master of drawing and composition. There was nothing of this cheap desire to startle and offend by what he did. If we are to have ash cans and engines and broken-down bus-horses thrust down our throats as art, Heaven preserve us. ... Broken window shutters, dirty pavements, half frozen ash cart dri-vers, over-drawn, heavily exaggerated figures of police-men, tenement harridans, beggars, panhandlers, sandwich men—of such is *Art* according to Eugene Witla."[24] But another critic applauds Witla's works for the very same reasons the previous critic damns them: "A true sense of the pathetic ... the ability to indict life with its own gross-ness, to charge it prophetically with its own meanness and cruelty in order that mayhap it may heal itself; the ability to see wherein is beauty—even in shame and pathos and degradation. ... There is no fear here, no bowing to tradi-tions, no recognition of any of the accepted methods."[25]

## V

This study establishes that Dreiser not only knew and admired the artistic aims and work of the entire Ash-Can school of painters, but that he had a special interest in and knowledge of Everett Shinn. It also demonstrates that Shinn knew Dreiser as a friend and as a colleague on mag-azines. And although Witla's story in the novel is largely

Dreiser's own story, Shinn's annotations in the copy of *The "Genius"* reveal the ways in which the novelist identifies his fictional character with the graphic artist. Various phases of Shinn's personal life, his art student days, his career as a newspaper artist and magazine illustrator, and his hostility toward the National Academy are retold in Witla's own career. And the similarities between Witla and Shinn are extended to include their parallel artistic theory and practice. Both, for example, are thrilled by the dramatic spectacle of the city and both "loved the thought of making the commonplace dramatic" by responding to what was considered to be unconventional subject matter: railroad yards, dumps, city crowds, and lower East Side scenes. The parallel between Witla and Shinn is continued in Dreiser's description of specific pictures: "Six O'clock," "Fifth Avenue in a Snow Storm," "The Bowery by Night," "East River," "Engines Entering a Freight Yard," "After the Theatre," "Greeley Square," and the London and Paris drawings. Finally, there is a striking similarity in Witla's and Shinn's experiences with the director of a private art gallery in New York and in the ridicule and defense of their pictures by the art critics.

The broader implications of Dreiser's substitution of a painter for a writer, since *The "Genius"* is obviously autobiographical, may be suggested. Dreiser's selection of a painter instead of a writer for his central character serves a strategic function. It may have permitted him to objectify his own situation; but as soon as Dreiser exhausts his material on the rise and fall of Eugene Witla as a graphic artist and becomes immersed in his personal problems, the novelist loses control of his materials. The novel becomes, from this point, neither good autobiography nor effective fiction. Whether Dreiser might not have been more successful if he had continued to deal with the original problem—the hazards confronting an original and serious artistic talent in the United States after the turn of the century—is conjectural. But the substitution of a painter for a writer also serves as Dreiser's positive act of *identification* with Shinn and the other members of the Ash-Can group in common artistic aims, common artistic practices, and common critical fate. When Dreiser sympathizes with their belief in the inherent dignity and character of an honest and living art which portrays every aspect of the city and which seeks for "commonplace beauty" and the possibilities for "beauty-in-ugliness," Dreiser is also sharing the painters' artistic credo. When Dreiser admires their pictures for their persistence in depicting the city scene with an eye for detail, with directness and brusqueness and power, with raw and undecorated masses, and with solidity of effect, he is also striving for these technical accomplishments in his own fiction. And when Dreiser records the critical contro-

versy which rages when the painters exhibit their work, he expresses his awareness of the hazards which confronted those courageous souls who stood firm against the tide of gentility and fashionableness in favor of an honest and truthful portrayal of the American scene.

*Notes*

1. The significance of Dreiser's relationship to these and other artists is discussed in greater detail in my article, "Dreiser and the Graphic Artist," *American Quarterly,* III (Summer 1951), 127-141.

2. *Broadway Magazine,* XVII (March 1907), 589, 736.

3. Dreiser, *The Color of a Great City* (New York, 1923), p. 199.

4. This copy of *The "Genius,"* annotated by Shinn during August 1947, is the World Publishing Co. edition (Cleveland, 1946). All references to Mr. Shinn's annotations in my text or notes and to Dreiser's text will be to this edition. I wish here to acknowledge my indebtedness and gratitude to Mr. Shinn, whose wholehearted cooperation made this study possible.

5. Shinn's comic illustrations for *Truth* were slight endeavors which served no more purpose than to give point to the humorous caption. As far as I could ascertain in checking the files, they appeared only in Vols. 17 and 18 for 1898. But it is interesting to note that on the opposite page of an illustration by Shinn for Vol. 17 (26 Sept. 1898) there appeared an article by Dreiser, "The Haunts of Hawthorne"; and Vol. 18 of *Truth* ran a series of articles by Dreiser on painters.

6. Shinn to Kwiat, 7 Sept. 1948. Dreiser himself confirmed the use of Shinn as a prototype; see Robert H. Elias, *Theodore Dreiser: Apostle of Nature* (New York, 1949), p. 328, n. 12.

7. Dreiser had also had connections with the *World* several years earlier.

8. Furthermore, the nature of the relationship between a magazine editor and his contributors probably threw Dreiser and Shinn together even more intimately than the artist suggests in his previously cited letter.

9. The other three artists were Maurice Prendergast, Ernest Lawson, and Arthur B. Davies.

10. Commenting upon the impact of the "Eight" in 1908, Oliver Larkin writes: "What shocked the world of art was a preoccupation with types, localities, and incidents to which Americans were conveniently deaf and blind. A degree of strenuousness could be forgiven in

the days of Teddy Roosevelt; but to paint drunks and slatterns, pushcart peddlers and coal mines, bedrooms and barrooms was somehow to be classed among the socialists, anarchists, and other disturbers of the prosperous equilibrium." *Art and Life in America* (New York, 1949), p. 336.

11. He also indicates some personal differences. Witla, during his early days in Chicago, neither drinks nor smokes; Shinn says that he smoked but did not drink (*The "Genius,"* annotated copy, p. 72). Witla is described as "big"; Shinn's comment: "I was *never* big" (p. 78).

12. Ibid., p. 187. It is interesting to note that Shinn began to use his studio as a little theater about 1912, producing his burlesques as good-natured slaps at the insipid dramas then appearing in Broadway theaters. This was, as Albert Parry points out, the first Little Theater in Greenwich Village, "even though Shinn did not suspect the import of his fun." *Garrets and Pretenders* (New York, 1933), p. 277.

13. The following passage in the novel is the one which caught Shinn's eye: "'A plan! A plan!' said his instructor, making a peculiar motion with his hands which described the outline of the pose in a single motion. 'Get your general lines first. Then you can put in the details afterward'" (p. 69).

14. Note that this person's name is identical with that of Dreiser's character. See also p. 174.

15. Shinn specifies, however, that he worked for *Harper's Weekly* and *Harper's Bazaar* but never for *Harper's Monthly.*

16. Shinn comments directly on this passage: "Nor had I any respect for the National Academy, a sepulcher with a smell of the embalmed. Its opening receptions held the quiet hush of funereal respect. Not that the Academicians felt the chill of their artistic arteries but that social poise and quiet low-voiced discourse made its appeal to the diamond splashed chatelaines of private art galleries who felt in the sight of a well trimmed Van Dyke beard a metamorphosis of that great painter and a murmuring lion in their drawing rooms."

17. An anecdote in this MS. illustrates Shinn's artistic attitude. He states that at one time he was commissioned by an art dealer to paint a picture of a rich client's home, one built in the medieval French style. "On my first visit to make my sketch I was disturbed by the lack of pictorial interest. ... Here ... there was no rain to dazzle the surface in reflections, no snow to track down and weave with traffic lanes, no leaves to drift across the street from the park trees to lay down islands of color." Working in midsummer, and coming to grips with the problem before him, Shinn recalls: "To 'turn in a thing of beauty' I set about making what I believed was my idea of beauty. Lavishly I applied the snow, sifting the slanting roofs and chimneys ... laying it on window sills and knobby ornament. A bus careened in its uneven weight of passengers and scudded close to a hansom cab. Plodding folk spotted the foreground, others in swishing skirts and buttoned coats wavering insecure in their footing in the shadow of floundering horses. A dog leaped a drift to gain a path where a bent figure toiled half hidden in a drift." The activity, human and otherwise, engendered by snow and rain contributed in Shinn's estimation to a picture's "pictorial interest" and his "idea of beauty." It may not be an anticlimax to note that Shinn's aesthetics was not shared by his agent. The painting was indignantly rejected for being an incongruous depiction of a wealthy man's home.

18. Page 219, insert. See Howells' reference to Shinn in his letter to his daughter Mildred, 5 March 1900: "Mamma says I must tell you something of the young artist, Everett Shinn, who came this morning to make an appointment to pastel me. ... He is the most unaffected charming boy I've seen in a long time; has an exhibition at Bussod and Voladen's [sic]: 'Of course, I can't *sell* anything so queer, but the papers have treated me well.'" *Life in Letters of William Dean Howells,* ed. Mildred Howells (New York, 1928), II, 127. Shinn's relationship to Howells will be developed in a forthcoming article.

19. This picture offers an interesting parallel to Dreiser's description of the Fleischman bread line which Hurstwood knows so intimately toward the end of his tragic career in *Sister Carrie.*

20. Page 114. A painting with a similar title, "Six O'Clock, Winter," was made by John Sloan in 1912. *The "Genius"* was being written at this time, and it is possible that Dreiser had Sloan's painting in mind.

21. Pages 112 and 174. Dreiser adds another description of the Greeley Square picture: "Eugene by some mystery of his art had caught the exact texture of seeping water on gray stones in the glare of various electric lights. He had caught the values of various kinds of lights, those in cabs, those in cable cars, those in shop windows, those in the street lamp—

relieving by them the black shadows of the crowds and of the sky" (p. 228).

22. Shinn's pastel drawings were exhibited at the galleries of M. Knoedler & Company after the turn of the century. The catalogue for the exhibition from 9 to 21 March 1903, for example, advertised pastels of "New York and Paris types." The painting, "Fifth Avenue at 34th Street," here reproduced by permission of M. Knoedler & Company, portrays the former Knoedler shop on the right (it is now the corner on which Altman's is built).

23. Note that Shinn, like Witla, used the originals of his magazine work as a means for exhibiting his pictures. Shinn also believed that this phase of his career was to be considered seriously for its artistic merits.

24. Page 237. The anonymous art critic for *Town Topics* attacked the "Eight" Show in this vein in 1908: "Does it represent a new school, or even superior work on old lines? Bosh! It is technique ... and as an offset poor drawing and an unhealthy, nay even coarse and vulgar point of view. Vulgarity smites one in the face at this exhibition, and I defy you to find anyone in a healthy frame of mind. ... Is it true art to exhibit our sores? ... Bah! The whole thing creates a distinct feeling of nausea."

25. Pages 237-238. Giles Edgerton wrote a sympathetic interpretation of the "Eight" Show for the *Craftsman* in 1908: "If they [The 'Eight'] will talk about their work at all, any one of them will tell you that just now there is no civilization in the world comparable in interest to ours; none so meteoric, so voluble, so turbulent, so unexpected, so instinct with life, so swift of change, so full of riotous contrast in light or shade. We have vivacity and bleakness, subtle reserve and brutal frankness, gorgeous color and pathetic dreariness. ... We are enthusiastic and fickle, and we are just beginning to understand our power, our beauty and our blunders and the fact that we have just as good a right to regard ourselves as a source of inspiration as of revenue only." The *Craftsman,* it will be recalled, was referred to as the *Crafts* in *The "Genius."*

## Irving Pichel (essay date 1952)

SOURCE: Pichel, Irving. "Revivals, Reissues, Remakes, and 'A Place in the Sun.'" *The Quarterly of Film, Radio, and Television,* vol. 6, no. 4, Summer 1952, pp. 388-93.

[*In the following essay, Pichel reflects on the 1951 film* A Place in the Sun, *a remake of the first screen adaptation of* An American Tragedy, *and the differences among the novel and the two filmed versions.*]

By the odd illogic of many polls, the recent vote by the Academy of Motion Picture Arts and Sciences determined that George Stevens was the best director of the year and that the Michael Wilson-Harry Brown screenplay, *A Place in the Sun,* was the best screenplay of the year, but that the best director directing the best screenplay did not produce the best picture of the year. This anomolous situation merits no further comment, but it is noteworthy that Stevens won his award with a new version of a story that had been filmed before. It is impossible to recall any other instance of a film so made which was more successful than the earlier version. This is the more noteworthy in the light of the fact that the first version was not a particularly successful film. Remakes are ordinarily made in the hope of recapturing an earlier success. It may be that only Stevens wanted to make the picture and that only he believed a successful film could be made from a story which had been a comparative failure. And it is common knowledge that Paramount believed it had another failure on its hands and withheld the release of the picture for some time.

It is no discredit to the film industry that it does not know what to do about its failures but it is generally unresourceful about what to do with its successes. Its common practice is to saturate the country and squeeze the revenue out of a successful film in as short a period as possible. Second, it imitates its own successes, creating cycles which are forcing-beds for failures. And, third, it "remakes" earlier successes without quite knowing how to better them. Superficially, it would appear that if Stevens' example is a guide, old failures should provide the material for current successes, provided, of course, that writer and director know what they are doing as well as Stevens does, and that the values they find in a story are those which were overlooked in the first telling. If the understressed values happened to be the enduring ones rather than those of contemporary interest, there is a good chance of rescue. But, in effect, this will be making the film for the first time, not remaking it. To a large degree, this is what Stevens has done.

A sound work of literature—or any other representative art—becomes a fixed point of reference of any survey of the time in which it was produced. The best of today's films will be of exceptional value to future students who seek to visualize mid-twentieth-century society and its value concepts, its preoccupations, and its mores. But we have no assurance that any one of such films, projected to an audience a hundred years from now, will have more than historical interest or will receive an emotional response comparable to that received from an audience of today. The few works in the theater that retain this magic power after the passage of a century or twenty centuries are, of course, classics. They are little suns in the center of the odd orrery called theater, the fixed point about which revolve in eccentric motion the planets—the audience, the players, the production. These planetary bodies are not only nonconstant by reason of their motion; they have the same mortality that besets the minds and bodies of men. Film is able to endow two of them, the players and the production (but not the audience), with a kind of semipermanence. But films have been in existence too short a time for us to know whether the actors of today and the manner of presentation of today will, along with our stories, have more than a curiosity value for the audience of the far-off future.

In the short span of film history, only a handful of films achieve revival, mostly by film societies and other nontheatrical interests. The comedies of Chaplin alone have shown theatrical survival value and remain comic although the society they lampoon has greatly altered. Over and above everything in them that is of a time and place there is something universally and eternally humorous and touching.

During the recent period of production dearth, the film industry has reissued a considerable number of films, too recent to be remade with new casts and not old enough to be regarded as revivals. Many of these are costume pieces, set in a remote period, and so relieved of any obligation to fashion in dress or timeliness of custom. Such reissues do not often get bookings comparable in number to those of the original release, but since the cost of reissue involves only new prints and press material they commonly show some profit.

More often the industry tries to recapture former success by remaking stories with new casts, new productions, and such story changes as the producers feel will make them more acceptable to the new audiences they are to entertain. A current example is *I'll Never Forget You,* a drearily emotional retelling of John Balderston's *Berkeley Square.* This will be remembered as a charming and diverting fantasy on the theme of time. It juggled past and present so that hindsight became foresight with a resultant play of anachronism from which the late Leslie Howard extracted delightful comedy and a rueful romance. The current version abjures humor so that the anachronistic vision of the hero becomes merely the basis for peril from which he can escape only into the present, his own time. The film seems to have been made for no other reason than to correct the reaction of an audience which Howard, were he living

today, might mislead into finding something wryly amusing in the plight of a man who revisits a past time.

*A Place in the Sun* is a different matter. As a remake of *An American Tragedy,* it is not only exceptional in being more successful than the first film, it is also the first remake of which I have knowledge which is made as though for the first time. It tells essentially the same story as the earlier film but with a totally different emphasis and perspective. It moves organically and gives no sense of being managed by writers or director. Its characters have an immediate reality that all but absorbs the recognized personalities that play them. Its events sum up to a tragic irony which provides all the theme and thesis the story needs. This is the more remarkable since Theodore Dreiser wrote his novel to prove a case. He had read newspaper accounts of a story that supported his analysis of certain social conditions of the period during which the events took place. The characters were, in his view, pawns moved by rules of a game they did not understand and were powerless to alter. He wrote *An American Tragedy* not merely as a tragic tale which happened in America but as one which could happen only in America or in a country which like America presented great contrasts of wealth and poverty, inherent in its economic system and its social structure. He predicated a villain outside his cast of characters, impersonal and implacable. He asked forgiveness for Clyde Griffith's guilt, which he found, at worst, technical and irresponsible.

We may be certain that none of Dreiser's sociology interested Paramount when it bought the screen rights to the novel and to the successful play which had been made from it.[1] We may be equally certain that it was exactly this that interested the late Sergei Eisenstein when, brought to Hollywood by Paramount in 1930, he selected it from among the studio's story properties and made a treatment in collaboration with Ivor Montagu. We may understand as readily the studio's rejection of the script, just as it had rejected an earlier script he had prepared telling the story of Johan Sutter and the discovery of gold in California. The studio was not looking for allegorical diagnoses of the ills of capitalistic society but for solid melodramas and, whatever else it might be, *An American Tragedy* was a story of crime, its detection and punishment. Eisenstein's contract was terminated and the story was handed to Joseph von Sternberg. The screen play was written by the late Samuel Hoffenstein and held with fidelity to Dreiser's story.

Von Sternberg was at the time Paramount's outstanding director. He had already made *Blue Angel* and *Morocco* and so had thus begun the association with Marlene Dietrich which was to occupy him for several years to come. But he had also directed a series of films with George

Bancroft, at the end of the silent era, including *The Docks of New York* and *Underworld.* This latter film was to remain, until the appearance of *Scarface,* the best film of its genre. Von Sternberg had qualified as an expert not only in the formalized sensuality which was to make Dietrich into a legendary symbol of sex but also as a master of the crime story. And *An American Tragedy,* as he presented it, was above all a story of crime, detection, and retribution. The story of Clyde and Roberta was treated fully and sympathetically, but Sondra, the wealthy girl, intervened as a virginal seductress, a plot complication which precipitated the planned murder and led Clyde to the courtroom. Here the real drama was enacted and everything which preceded it was a long exposition, the spinning of a web of circumstance from which the hero was unable to extricate himself. The story became that of a boy who had planned a crime so well that, although he did not carry out his plan and accident took over, his plan convicted him. The courtroom sequence, following the catatonic actions that led up to it, had suspense and vitality, but Clyde Griffith seemed more the helpless victim of a vengeful and self-righteous prosecutor than of a society which had made his predicament inevitable.

Twenty years later, when George Stevens looked at the story, Dreiser's thesis had lost much of its validity. More than that, the social climate has so altered that even a moderately doctrinaire rationalization of Clyde Griffith's downfall would be, to put it mildly, unwelcome. Stevens may have asked himself whether such a story, having happened nearly thirty years ago, might still happen today and whether, having happened because of conditions Dreiser described, it might still happen when those conditions no longer apply with the same force. If we can feel that we know anything of a director's mind from his work, we know of Stevens that he sees people as individuals and that he is interested in character as it is found, not as it is determined or conditioned. People as he sees them act from root motives and drives, however these motives may be complicated by circumstance. In other words, he is now a determinist but simply an observer. He may not be the most objective of observers since he sees through the lens of his own humor, his sentiment, his sincere but often somewhat ingenuous warmth, but he does observe closely and sympathetically. He may not see the economic and social pressures which, in Dreiser's view, bear down upon a Clyde Griffith, but he does see Griffith, his loneliness, his need for love, his feckless lack of guile which make him the victim of his desires and aspirations.

*A Place in the Sun,* as Stevens tells the story, is not a tale, then, of crime and detection and retribution. The trial is not the climax of the story but a coda, a conclusion to a series of events for which there is no other end. His characters are not victims of some particular system but of their own common humanity and their fates are determined by their inherent needs as they seek to fulfill themselves in a world of chance.

This may not be the story Dreiser wrote, but it is what remains today of the novel. *An American Tragedy,* by Dreiser, is a point of reference in a consideration of the America of 1925 as seen by Dreiser. The film made in 1951 may be less completely a view of what might have happened in 1951, but it may also be more completely a view of what might have happened in that year or in any other year and, perhaps, in any other country. It extracts from its events that which *may* be permanent, which *may* be universal, which *may* be the kind of constant to give the film and its story survival value and elicit from future audiences the kind of response it has found today.

Stevens remarked once, in a talk to his colleagues, that the weakness of the film industry lies in the fact that it makes film for markets and not for people. This is an error he has not fallen into in making *A Place in the Sun.*

### Note

1. *An American Tragedy* was published in 1925 and Patrick Kearney's dramatization was produced in October, 1926.

## John Lydenberg (essay date 1955)

SOURCE: Lydenberg, John. "Theodore Dreiser: Ishmael in the Jungle." *The Monthly Review,* vol. 7, no. 4, Aug., 1955, pp. 124-36.

[*In the following essay, Lydenberg celebrates the seemingly intractable nature of Dreiser, whom he describes as a literary "bulldozer" determined to unmask "the realities of life."*]

"I was an Ishmael, a wanderer." So Dreiser spoke of himself during his homeless newspaper days in the 1890s. Did he think of himself as an outcast, too? As the daughter of Hagar, the slave girl, instead of Sarah, the proper wife? Whether he did or no, his birth on the wrong side of the Terre Haute tracks marked him as drastically as did Ishmael's birth in the wrong tent. America does not cast out the sons of its servant girls to wander in the desert, but in the 1870s it did not readily accept them as priests in its Back Bay or Fifth Avenue temples. If not an outcast, Dreiser was at least an outsider.

At one time the outsider seemed about to push his way in. Only a few years after he had stood on the banks of the East

River so lonely and disheartened that he planned to jump in, he was a $10,000-a-year editor of the Butterick publications. Flashily dressed, confident behind his shiny desk, he fashioned articles that would please the new-rich ladies who sought culture and chic in the slick pages of the *Delineator.* Dreiser had the force, the ability, and the drive to make his way in, and he could have stayed in and huckstered his way ever onward and upward like a good American.

But stronger than the allure of success was something in this outsider which made him reject respectability, or even sheer unrespectable power. Dreiser was by instinct a loner, an *"isolato,"* to use Melville's term, like so many of our great writers. As an outsider he wanted to get in, to glitter among the strong, the rich, the admired. But he could never *be* one of them; he could never wholemindedly accept their ways or their views. So having proved that he could force his way across the tracks, he withdrew, not to his natal place on the wrong side, but to the tracks themselves, where he could stand alone, exposed, and observe both the sides that he knew so well from experience and sympathy.

The term "rugged individualist" is peculiarly appropriate for Dreiser not merely because of the ironic implications of applying it to him, but because it is literally so apt. His pictures show him rough, solid, and hard despite sagging flesh, bigboned and forbidding. Anecdotes reveal him alone and aloof at parties, shy and a trifle wistful, but withdrawn chiefly because he chose to remain outside, wondering and watching. Society could not soften him; nor could either hostile critics or friendly guides polish him. He was immobile and unmalleable. He was what he was—not pretty or pleasing, not a good writer by most standards, not even very intelligent, but integral, a whole man.

In *My Life with Dreiser,* Helen Richardson shows how little even the love of one he loved could tame or mold him. She lived with him most of the time from about 1920 until he died, marrying him in 1942 after the death of his long-estranged wife. She had to learn to take him as he was and to endure his desertions, his moods, and his tempers, for he could not be changed, only escaped, and she would not escape at the price of losing him. His friend, admirer, and defender, H. L. Mencken, tells of the "gigantic steadfastness" with which Dreiser ignored all his attempts "to entice him in this direction or that, fatuously presuming to instruct him in what would improve him and profit him." Mencken's flinty barbs could not even scratch Dreiser's adamant. Muckrakers, reformers, radicals of all sorts tried to entice him into their camps where each was so sure that Dreiser belonged. But they were no more successful than Mencken: Dreiser would write as he pleased. Of course the

genteel critics and all the respectable defenders of the purity of the American Girl and the happiness of the American Way flung taunts, arrows, and stinkbombs at him continuously from *Sister Carrie* in 1900 until his death. He was impervious to the Methodists as to Mencken.

The latter described Dreiser as the Hindenburg of the American novel. Today a bulldozer might provide a more appropriate image. Caring nothing for shouts or shots, unable to see or to save the flowers of the tender saplings, he drove his bulldozer over the whole terrain, shattering the old buildings and pushing aside the rubble until the ground was cleared and the foundations laid bare. He demolished not out of hatred but out of a feeling that the structures, with their conventional fronts or painted with familiar slogans, served to hide the realities of life, and these he had to uncover at any cost.

Instead of steel or ice in his heart, there was only bewilderment and wonder and pity. This was the quality that Sherwood Anderson chose to emphasize in the foreword of *Horses and Men,* which he dedicated to Dreiser:

> Long ago when he was editor of the *Delineator,* Dreiser went one day, with a woman friend, to visit an orphan asylum. The woman once told me the story of that afternoon in the big, ugly grey building with Dreiser, looking heavy and lumpy and old, sitting on a platform, folding and refolding his pocket-handkerchief and watching the children all in their little uniforms, trooping in.
>
> "The tears ran down his cheeks and he shook his head," the woman said, and that is a real picture of Theodore Dreiser. He is old in spirit and he does not know what to do with life, so he tells about it as he sees it, simply and honestly. The tears run down his cheeks and he folds and refolds the pocket-handkerchief and shakes his head.

Dreiser's position in American literature is very special. He was the first important writer to come from a non-Anglo-Saxon, lower-class background. It was not simply a matter of coming from relatively poor or humble folk— that was indeed more usual than unusual among American writers: witness for example, Thoreau, Whitman, Twain, Howells, and Crane. Nor was it a matter merely of feeling isolated; we have only to think of others like Poe, Hawthorne, Melville. The difference was that all of these "belonged" in a most essential respect. They came from the old settlers; they were of the great white Protestant middle class that dominated 19th-century America and its literature, and that determined what was orthodox and genteel. Whatever their personal or psychological problems, however they might intellectually or emotionally reject the standards of their society, they were insiders. They scarcely knew of the existence of that strange new society that was growing unrecognized beneath the crust of the old America.

Both Dreiser's parents were German immigrants, his father a fiercely puritanical Catholic and his mother a Mennonite whose original piety had become overlaid with a pagan mysticism. Dreiser was one of eleven children. His family's attempt to rise in the American way had ended with an accident to his father shortly before Theodore's birth. Thereafter, the father's work was intermittent and never such as to support the family. The younger children stole coal from the Terre Haute railroad yards in the winters, and the older sisters took up with men who could offer them temporary financial security if not matrimony. When Theodore was eight, the mother took him and the three younger children off—not to seek anyone's fortune, but as Dreiser would say, in a vagrom search for a less uncomfortable life, somewhere.

In Vincennes, Indiana, they lived with a friend over the fire station until they discovered that the rest of the quarters were being used as a bawdy house. In Sullivan, Indiana, they moved into a barren box of a house adjacent to the railroad yards; there the mother took in washing and rented out a scarcely-spare room. Then one day the glamorous older brother Paul—already famous as songwriter Paul Dresser—turned up and suggested they move to Evansville where he had a pleasant cottage for them. This he rented from his mistress—a local madam and the original of "My Gal Sal"—until the affair broke up and the Dreisers had to move on again. After a year in Chicago they went to Warsaw, in northern Indiana, where for the first time, at thirteen, Theodore was permitted to go with Protestants to a public school instead of to a Catholic school, and where also he heard the local sports crack wise about the difference between his sisters and the nice middle-class girls they would later marry.

Dreiser was brought up properly to believe in the standard American moralities. Good and evil could be distinguished readily according to the rules taught in schools, Sunday and weekday; the rewards for following the good and scorning the evil were clear, and the punishments for doing otherwise were certain.

In glaring contrast to the morality he was taught was the life he observed and lived. His kind, patient, beloved mother said nothing and held the family together as best she could: when a virginal daughter handed her $10 proffered by a local lawyer, she took it and bought food without a word to condemn the coming loss of "virtue." "Proper" morals came from those he had no love for. They came through his broken father, who would turn up at their latest home, sick,

hungry, jobless, but not too cowed to shout imprecations at his daughters for their immoral ways and to warn them of the vast punishments they were heaping up for themselves. They came through his respectable acquaintances in Warsaw who looked up to their own protected sisters and down upon the sisters they casually ruined across the tracks. Paul rose in the artistic demi-monde, brother Rome dropped down through gambling and drink. Rome may have been "bad" but Paul certainly was not "good." What mattered, as far as Theodore could see, was not their morality or immorality; the significant difference was that Paul, like his mother, was always kind and generous, Rome boastful, unfeeling, and selfish. On the porch of the Sullivan rooming house old men rocked away their lonely last years; did their fate have any relation to their virtues?

The world he was taught about had a nice clear-cut meaning; his experience showed him a world which denied that meaning and seemed to have no other. What, possibly, could the defeat of these helpless old men be said to mean? Where did one see the working out of the principle that virtue was rewarded and only vice punished? People did what they had to do, what they could do. They survived. What grounds could there be for praise or blame? Certainly none were to be found in any of the official moralities. In the last analysis all that remained was "goodness of heart," the quality Dreiser attributed to Jennie Gerhardt and knew in his mother.

He did not formulate his thoughts this way at the time. He was simply bewildered, dreamy, unhappy, but thrilled and excited by the life of the big city to which he returned, on his own, in 1887. He drifted through odd frustrating jobs for a few years and then into reporting in 1892. Newspaper work was the training ground for many authors from the nineties on, and the breeding ground *par excellence* of cynicism. At no time was life in America more raw; never did the disparities between precepts and practices gape more widely and openly; and no experience was as effective as the journalist's in preventing a man from comfortably ignoring the raw disparities. It was only too easy to conclude with one of Dreiser's first editors that "Life is a god-damned stinking, treacherous game, and nine hundred and ninety-nine men out of every thousand are bastards."

The adoption of that attitude would have provided one solution for Dreiser—and had he accepted it, we would never have heard of him. Happily he couldn't, for he was too much a child of his time, the young man from the country, fascinated at the shiny fruit dangled before him, bright-eyed at the wonders of the city, enthralled by the men and women in their fine clothes and handsome carriages, the grand gay hotels, the wonderful insolence of the powerful. For all he was an outsider, he was also the typical American with the conventional goals: "My eyes were constantly fixed on people in positions far above my own. Those who interested me most were bankers, millionaires, artists, executive leaders, the real rulers of the world." "No common man am I," he said then of himself as he dreamed of a Horatio Alger rise from rags to riches.

But he had neither the cynicism nor the blindness needed for one who would successfully follow that dream. The ultimate effect of his newspaper experience, superimposed upon that of his youth, was to make him not a cynic but a skeptic, a questioner, a seeker. Like Lincoln Steffens, he saw a world made up of the strong and the weak instead of the good and the bad. The strong were successful, and success brought its rewards, but these were scarcely the rewards of virtue, however much the conventionally pious would like to think it so. Nor were the rewards the Devil's brand, as some reformers would have it; the sentimentalist's equation of strong with bad and weak with good was simply the converse of the orthodox view and no less inapplicable to the real American jungle. One could only say that people were what they were, that victory in the battles was sweet but impermanent, that defeat was more common, and that it was a pity the world had to be so:

> For myself, I accept now no creeds. I do not know what truth is, what beauty is, what love is, what hope is. I do not believe any one absolutely and I do not doubt any one absolutely. I think people are both evil and well-intentioned.

This, then, was the Dreiser who at the age of twenty-eight sat down to write his first novel. The life he had experienced was neither gracious nor moral. He had succeeded as a free-lance writer in the great New York city that had so frightened and appalled him at first. He had learned that the fight was as ruthlessly ungloved in the publishing world as in that of the new industrialists whose life stories he had been writing. And he had made his way up in that world so that in 1899 he was sufficiently well known for the first edition of *Who's Who in America* to include his name, listing him as "Journalist-Author."

"Author" was, as a matter of fact, a misnomer. Though in his early newspaper days the example of some of his colleagues had led him to attempt a few plays and short stories, he had done so only half heartedly and he quickly gave up. He was as exceptional among American authors in his lack of literary training and ambitions as in his family background. The other novelists who had started out as newspapermen had, with few exceptions, seen their journalism as preparation for "serious" writing. They rec-ognized a literary tradition and sought to be "writers" within that tradition.

Dreiser had a call, as do all great authors, but it was not a call to "write." What he had to do was simply *describe* the America he had experienced, tell how he felt about the life he had known, point out the bewildering, contradictory, unadmitted truths. No other important American author showed such a lack of concern for the craft of writing. Paradoxically, this was for him a source of strength as well as a weakness. Scorning the tricks of fine writing, he never succeeded in developing grace or beauty or even facility, but by the same token he never succumbed to the temptation to follow one or more of the roads to popularity. When *Sister Carrie* failed, instead of trying to find a manner that would satisfy readers, critics, and publishers, he simply abandoned fiction and responded again to the siren call of success. But at the *Delineator* desk his own personal call soon came back again, louder, irresistible; and he gave up editing to be an author, cost what it might. Like Thoreau, whom he later came to admire greatly, he marched to a drummer that no one else heard; like Emerson and Thoreau, he found that he must follow his own genius, wherever it led, that to be a man and a writer he must be a nonconformist however much the world might whip him with its displeasure.

In *Newspaper Days* (1922), Dreiser tells how his budding desires to write short stories had been nipped by his reading of the magazines.

> I set to examining the current magazines. ... I was never more confounded than by the discrepancy existing between my own observations and those displayed here, the beauty and peace and charm to be found in everything, the almost complete absence of any reference to the coarse and the vulgar and the cruel and the terrible. ... But as I viewed the strenuous world about me, all that I read seemed not to have so very much to do with it. Perhaps, as I now thought, life as I saw it, the darker phases, was never to be written about. Maybe such things were not the true province of fiction anyhow. I read and read, but all I could gather was that I had no such tales to tell, and, however much I tried, I could not think of any. The kind of thing I was witnessing no one would want as fiction.

Yet he had tried a few short stories while vacationing with Arthur Henry, an old newspaper friend from Toledo. Then in the fall of 1899, only half in earnest, he responded to Henry's insistence that he should try a novel. According to his account, he put the words "Sister Carrie" atop a blank page of paper, with no idea of what he was going to say, and then went on to write the first half of the novel with no planning and little difficulty.

He was able to do that because he was simply recording his own experiences and emotions instead of trying to tell a tale that would belong to the "true province of fiction." Indeed, one could say that in *Sister Carrie* Dreiser was not writing a novel at all; he was simply transcribing a part of his version of the American experience. Although taken scene by scene or character by character almost everything in it could have been found in preceding novels, taken as a whole it was unique as a social novel. Its uniqueness lay in the fact that Drouet, Carrie, and Hurstwood were facets of their author; whereas in other novels the drummer, the poor girl from the country who fell to the wiles of the city slicker, the flashy front-man who absconded with the cash and paid with his soul or his life, these were either stock figures or at their best characters observed from above with varying degrees of condescension or sentimentality. If Dreiser could not write popular magazine fiction because he was outside the official American culture and the conventional literary circles, he could write something different and true and lasting because he was inside the jungle of the new urban, industrial society.

Henry James and Edith Wharton wrote about their American aristocrats from intimate acquaintance. Howells and a multitude of now-unread minor novelists described with authority the life of the old middle class. Train, and after him Howe, Frederic, Garland, gave authentic accounts of the rural societies they had grown up in. All of them sensed the changes in postbellum America, and most of them tried in one way or another to show these changes in their books. But none of them could deal directly, from firsthand experience, with what was most distinctive about the new society. Novelists had, of course, already written about the ignorant, destitute immigrants from southern and eastern Europe, about tenements and saloons and sweatshops, about jobless workers, radicals, labor organizers, prostitutes, industrialists, political bosses; and between *Sister Carrie* and *Jennie Gerhardt* a spate of muckraking novels exposed in ever more odorous detail the great American Augean stables. Most of these were righteous, indignant novels describing the evils in lurid detail, and implicitly or explicitly urging the good people to do something, to throw out rascals or rescue the perishing or care for the falling. And most—possibly all—were written by the old insiders who could only see from the outside this world across the tracks.

Howells' streetcar strike is viewed from an easy-chair, not from the carbarns and the strikers' saloons as is Dreiser's. Crane, the rebel against his respectable Protestant background, observes Maggie the girl of the slums and the streets sardonically, ironically, and so unsentimentally as to shock his friends; but Carrie is Dreiser's sister. It is significant that Howells liked *Maggie,* ignored *Sister Carrie.* McTeague's disintegration is depicted with a fine use of

symbolic actions selected by Norris with care (and remembrance of Zola); Hurstwood's decline is that of the old men Dreiser had known, and it is given added poignance by the fear never far from the surface of Dreiser's heart that he might one day join the Hurstwoods in breadlines and flophouses. One might claim a similarity between Dreiser and Robert Herrick, in the fact that Cowperwood—the subject of a trilogy, *The Financier* (1912), *The Titan* (1914), *The Stoic* (1917)—was modeled closely after a real tycoon, Yerkes, as Herrick's American citizen, Van Harrington, the hero of *The Memoirs of an American Citizen* (1905), was based on the careers of the great meat-packers. But the difference is more significant: Professor Herrick could never have been his Van Harrington, whereas, in at least a part of him, Dreiser was Cowperwood, sharing his drive for power and his love of ostentation and luxury, his inability to accept official views of right and wrong, and his disdain for the *unco guid* who hid their weaknesses behind a cloak of reformist morality. Clyde Griffiths in *An American Tragedy* (1925), was but another part of Dreiser—his background and his longings; and as Clyde stole money to buy his teasing Hortense a coat, so Dreiser himself had once "borrowed" $25 from his employer that he might be more nattily attired. Of all his novels we can say, paraphrasing Whitman, Dreiser was the man, he was there, he suffered.

Dreiser was as alone and as integral in his art, if such we can call it, as in his life. Where other novelists adopted a literary theory and tried to make their fiction fit it, or introduced a particular subject matter because they thought it should be dealt with, Dreiser wrote only about what he knew, as he knew it. Traditionless himself, he was unable or unwilling to adopt the traditions, literary or social, of the genteel arbiters of the thought of his day. And so, all unwittingly, simply because he looked at the world about him with untrained, uncultured eyes and insisted on being himself, he brought a revolution to American literature.

As he accepted no literary formulas, so he adopted no political or social formulas—at least as far as his fiction was concerned. T. S. Eliot's observation about Henry James that "he had a mind so fine that no idea could violate it" is possibly even more applicable to Dreiser, at least if for "fine" we substitute "honest" or "stubborn." At first glance this assertion may seem absurd, for Dreiser was continually being seduced by plausible theories. Indeed he fancied himself a Thinker and went around arguing the Big Questions with anyone he thought had a new idea. He even published several volumes in which he essayed to formulate the philosophical or social theories that currently attracted him, dreary writings that merely express in pseudo-intellectual terms his inability to "understand."

Understanding of this sort was not his forte. Lionel Trilling in a righteous Columbiad has cited Dreiser's intellectual failings as symbolic of the degeneration of the liberal imagination. Such an attitude is almost as perverse as the simple moralism of Stuart Sherman, literary critic of the 1920s, that supporters of Dreiser regularly use to show the myopia of his contemporaries. For one thing, Dreiser was no more of a "liberal" than Thoreau. More important, the power of his novels lies precisely in the fact that they were not illustrations of any political ideas or social theories. When he introduces his jejune philosophizing into his novels, we hurry ashamedly over the turgid, pretentious passages, ignoring them as intrusions. His strength lies not in his thought but in his observation of the social milieu, his feeling for the way people lived and dreamed and despaired. His account of the American experience of his time, of the lure of wealth and power and the fear of poverty and defeat, of tawdry dwellings and gaudy hotels, of the weak and the strong, the seeker and the sought, is unsurpassed because in his novels his mind did remain inviolate and he saw his American scene not as revealing any dialectical process, or endorsing any moral or political theory, but simply as being Life, wonderful, terrible, very mysterious.

Until he had finished all his major novels, Dreiser resisted the blandishments of the Left as firmly as he did the admonitions of Comstockery. In 1916, Floyd Dell appealed to him in the old *Masses*: "Life at its best and most heroic is rebellion. All artists, big and little, are in their degree rebels. You yourself are a rebel. . . . Why do you not write the American novel of rebellion?" But Dreiser stubbornly insisted that he was an observer and an artist. Alongside his sympathy for the downtrodden lay his empathy for those who strove greatly and successfully for power. Much as he would have liked to see a better world, he did not see how it could be brought into being, nor could he imagine what it would be like—except, vaguely, that it should contain less suffering and more goodheartedness. When tempted to explain his views he would sometimes castigate American ideals and institutions and hypocrisies as the source of social injustices, implying that changes should be made. More often he would assert that the world's ills were ineradicable because some men were born strong and some weak, and suffering lay in the nature of things. In *A Traveller at Forty* (1913), he wrote:

> There are those who still think that life is something which can be put into a mold and adjusted to a theory, but I am not one of them. I cannot view life or human nature save as an expression of contraries—in fact, I think that is what life is. . . . I cannot see how there can be great men without little ones; wealth without poverty. . . .
>
> I did not make my mind. I did not make my art. I cannot choose my taste except by predestined instinct. . . . I indict

nature here and now, as I always do and always shall do, as being aimless, pointless, unfair, unjust. I see in the whole thing no scheme but an accidental one—no justice save accidental justice.

He insisted that he cared more for the spectacle of contending forces than for any permanent good that might come out of them. "I like labor leaders," he wrote in the same book. "I like big, raw, crude, hungry men who are eager for gain—for self-glorification." Over a decade later, when he was working in Los Angeles on the tragedy of Clyde Griffiths' America, he gave a reporter an interview which showed him little changed:

> I want to be back where there is struggle. . . . I like to wander around the quarters of New York where the toilers are. . . . That's health. I don't care about idlers or tourists, or the humdrum, or artistic pretenders that flock out here, or the rich who tell you—and that is all they have to tell— how they did it. They would have interested me when they were struggling. . . .
>
> It is wrong and can't be righted. When you know that, the unalterableness isn't going to cause you any tears. I don't worry about it. One could lose his mind if he took it to heart.
>
> I don't care a damn about the masses. It is the individual that concerns me.

Despite the element of pose in that public statement, it suggests the essential character of Dreiser's social views as they informed his fiction. He was concerned above all with the individual. He enjoyed struggle and admired the victors. But he did not think for a minute that the mighty were right. If he pretends sometimes to amorality, he here shows his real feelings by characterizing the outcome of the struggle as "wrong." Only when he denies that it causes him any tears is he really disingenuous. No tears in the *American Tragedy*?

The popular success of *An American Tragedy* (no other novel of Dreiser's came close to being a best seller) brought him increased attention from reformers of all sorts. The Soviet Union invited him to visit the country as a guest, promising, on his insistence, that he would be free to see what he wanted and say what he thought. He was interested in Russia because of "its change, its ideals, its dreams," skeptical about it because he was an individualist. On leaving, he publicly criticized many aspects of the new society, concluding that "more individualism and less communism would be to the great advantage of this mighty country." But at home he defended the Soviets against what he considered complacent or dogmatic American criticisms. Communists were outsiders as he had been, and he would stand up for them against the smug insiders. There were also important things to say in favor of Russia: for all her poverty, she had no unemployed and no breadlines as did the rich United States even during the boom of the 1920s.

With the coming of the depression, Dreiser found himself pulled more and more into political controversies, until finally they came to occupy almost his entire attention. The reasons for the shift were many: his passive sympathy for the poor turned into an active insistence that something had to be done to stop the rapidly increasing misery; the social consciousness and political involvement of writers of the thirties was so pervasive and so pressing that few could remain aloof; after *An American Tragedy* Dreiser was for the first time relatively free from financial worries and the pressure to publish; and apparently he felt a growing need to escape from his loneliness.

It would be easy to say that the Communists got their ring through his nose and led him along their twisting line from 1930 until his death in 1945. Nor would it be entirely inaccurate. For he did follow along their line. Yet, like the led bull, he was not the tame creature of his leaders; he conceded to them none of his integrity or spirit of independence. By the early thirties, Dreiser had become a signer and a joiner. He would give his name to any good cause; he soon learned to speak in public, something he had always dreaded and avoided; and reporters could now get from him impassioned, partisan, newsworthy statements where formerly they had simply been told that life was unknowable and social forces uncontrollable. If it was Communist guidance that he most often seemed to take, that was partly because the Communists, typically, were most assiduous in wooing him, and partly because he saw them both as maligned victims of all the American reactionaries, and as clear-sighted, open-minded (so it really seemed to Dreiser and to many others then) analysts of the middle-class hypocrisies and illusions. But he was not a party man; he was still his old self, and on occasion he resigned from an organization that he decided was really Communist-dominated and following paths he did not wish to take.

But while he was fighting alongside the Communists for the Scottsboro boys, the Spanish Loyalists, nonintervention during the days of the Nazi-Soviet Pact and a second front almost immediately thereafter, he was at the same time pursuing another, apparently divergent, course. The mysticism that had always lurked behind his materialism came increasingly to the fore. Having rejected the conventional absolutes of American orthodoxy, he sought restlessly for an absolute of his own. The outcome of this search appears in his post-humous books, on which he had worked intermittently between *An American Tragedy* in 1925 and his death. *The Stoic,* last volume of the **Cowperwood trilogy,** ends with the heroine's rather soggy

conversion to Yoga. *The Bulwark* much more convincingly depicts a Quaker's doubts and his ultimate reconciliation to religion as he comes to recognize the beneficence of the life force working through all things.

On Good Friday of 1945, Dreiser took communion in a Congregational church. In the fall he joined the Communist Party, issuing a statement written for him by his Communist friends, but insisting that he still remained his own master and would continue to speak his own mind.

Failure of nerve? Betrayal of radicalism? Possibly both, in a sense. But neither action was entirely inconsistent with his earlier attitudes, and neither was a denial of his integrity. Despite his constant excoriation of religionists and moralists, he had always had a strong religious, mystical strain. He had always wanted to discover final answers to the whys of existence. He had always longed to find some all-embracing meaning to his life of wandering and the struggles and heartbreaks of his fellows. If, toward the end, he found some peace in the mysticisms of Eastern religion, or the mystery of the sharing of Christ's body and blood, or the symbolism of world brotherhood in Communism, this did not mean that he had fallen into acceptance of his father's puritan moralism or Russia's totalitarianism.

And in the last analysis these two acts did not matter, just as his writings since 1925 do not matter much now. This Ishmael had, in his old age, tried on the mantle of Isaac, but what we will remember and cherish is the bitter fruit of his days as Ishmael the outcast, wandering alone in the desert, telling the truths that the orthodox and well-born saw not or dared not tell.

Dreiser's books seem to have been hewed out of stone. Uncouth and often ugly, so bold that they were hard to read, they were ignored or derided when Dreiser was erecting them on the foundations he had laid bare. But they last. The paint flakes off the fashionable wooden structures built on sand, and the boards rot and fall off. Who now reads David Graham Phillips or Robert Herrick or our American Winston Churchill? Garland, Frank Norris, even Howells as social realist, have faded. And it is not at all unlikely that Dos Passos and Steinbeck will shortly recede as Sinclair Lewis is already doing.

Dreiser was a radical in the great, and much dishonored, American tradition because he insisted on being himself. He resisted the admonitions and cajoleries of the critics; he saw through all the creeds of the orthodox and accepted none from the reformers. Because he had the courage, the stubbornness, the lack of literary sensitivity to write as he did, Dreiser built far better than he or his contemporaries knew. No novelist today would think of using his fiction as a model. But none will write social novels with such lasting power unless he has Dreiser's essential qualities of integrity and independence, wonder and pity.

## Seymour Krim (review date 1956)

SOURCE: Krim, Seymour. "Dreiser and His Critics." Review of *The Stature of Theodore Dreiser: A Critical Survey of the Man and His Work,* edited by Alfred Kazin and Charles Shapiro, *The Commonweal,* vol. 64, no. 9, 1 June 1956, pp. 229-31.

[*In the following review, Krim celebrates Dreiser's role in broadening "the scope of the American conscience" but criticizes "the deformed sprawl of his mind and works" evidenced in his "often dreary . . . literary style."*]

What should we do with Theodore Dreiser today—build him a statue, read him, use him as spiritual inspiration? Probably all three if we believe, as I do, that he has enlarged the scope of the American conscience. But there is still a problem. The phenomenon of Dreiser remains almost as puzzling now as when he was alive. He is not specifically relevant today in spite of his great chaotic independence and unremitting dedication to the truth. Yet he looms above, making many of our present writers seem like peevish children and establishing alp-like heights for other novelists to aim at. In this sense he is always relevant even while being, at times, literally impossible to read if one has even a minimum sensitivity to language.

Still another complicating fact in trying to fix Dreiser's position in literature—and he is always breaking through or around what we mean by "art" and even "the novel"—is that it is hard not to become personal about the man since his writing is so self-revelatory. Several articles in the present book[1] pulse with frustrated love under a crust of fact, and a few others with an equally personal distaste, although this is mainly the reserve of academic critics. Yet even in their articles a bit of fascination with this strange figure peeps through. The simple heroism of Dreiser's helplessness, confusion, ingenuousness and refusal to be sidetracked challenges these writers to hurt him harder than they would another novelist, yet by doing so they acknowledge him.

It is hard to see how they couldn't, in some degree, for our literary history in this century shows that Dreiser was a tremendous pioneer, beginning with the publication of **Sister Carrie** in 1900, a perfect symbolic date. But to return to our first thought—what shall we do with this pioneer now? The biggest obstacle to Dreiser's staying alive is the often hackneyed way in which he expressed himself, and the boredom which he can arouse in even the most sympathetic reader. There was something of the hack-writer about Dreiser, a man who did all kinds of commercial and undistinguished writing to support himself, and who in his young manhood was prey to many conflicting desires which were never resolved; these took him down to the depths as man and writer as well as to heights rarely matched by an American prose writer in this century.

The depths, the gluttony, carelessness, the very literary prostitution and opportunism which soiled his pen and which only the demands of a great soul could transcend even in spasms, are not really considered by many of his good-willed admirers in the present book. These include James T. Farrell, John Chamberlain, Malcolm Cowley, H. L. Mencken and others. In Mencken's case it is understandable that while he was aware of Dreiser's sins he did not talk much about them in print; his hands were full trying to get Dreiser a hearing, a task that is hard for young people fully to appreciate today when every kind of iconoclasm seems to have its place in the modern scene. But perhaps the other critics have more of a responsibility, precisely because of Dreiser's greatness, to look more closely at his wastefulness as a writer and not leave it to unsympathetic writers who wish to see only that. It is this reviewer's personal opinion that unless some of Dreiser's books are sensitively edited—a task that some publisher might consider—they may, in the future, go completely unread.

Such is the fate of much that is remarkable in its own time but that out of simple human inability to cope with all of life must take itself "too" seriously in order to do justice to living experience; if the artist or writer stops to gauge how the standards of the next generation are going to measure his work he may—we have the evidence all around us today—become a critical ruler instead of a genuine creator. Nevertheless, and as some of the writers in this book suggest, the more time departs from Dreiser the more it unmasks the deformed sprawl of his mind and works, as if the curtain had been pulled back from a grounded whale. His books were heroic improvisations, epic in reach and intention, even in a comprehensiveness of the recreation of life which rivals Proust, but undeveloped in form—inert crates of matter, often. Thus one would say that it is unrealistic in spite of the highest respect to persist in praising the dross in even his best books when Dreiser's accomplishment shows itself more objectively in a succession of parts rather than in complete wholes. Even a prehistoric writing animal like this genuine hero couldn't successfully bull his way through the invisible laws of proportion that civilization has constructed on the experience of many generations.

\* \* \*

Dreiser, like many of the most alive Americans, often wrote as if the world began with his birth and might end with his death, and his engorgement made a joke of selectivity and even defied sanity. And yet the peculiar conditions of this country have logically led to the individual's straining the possibilities of reality, and Dreiser was a menacing incarnation of the sophomore-genius type in that sense, which is no more to be sneered at if you are an American than the houses you live in, the music you hear, etc. He is likely "juvenile" in the sense that Henry James said his old countrymen were. But he is also powerful and grave in a way that James never characterized Americans, and that can exalt a reader's mind to spare mountain-peaks of universal truth like the noblest symphonies.

This book makes clear, from anecdote and personal reminiscence, that it was impossible for Dreiser to write without using his actual experience as the ultimate test for the truthfulness of his imagination. Fancy he had, but it was always weighted and even sacrificed by the characteristic experience of the masses of "typical" people of his generation. He identified with these people strongly because all his life he dreamed their dreams and suffered their betrayals, his lower middle-class past being an active part of his mind and his emotions for the course of his entire life.

As John Berryman points out in one of the essays in this book—a refreshingly frank and personal one—what distinguished Dreiser from his contemporaries was "a kind of stupidity, a kind of unself-consciousness" that kept him immune from any kind of fancy superficiality or even improvement of his often dreary (and often moving, when the subject had a dimension that words could not harm) literary style. For all his receptivity and Balzacian association of blazing city lights with fame, fortune and beautiful women, it is never the flash of local color that dazzles Dreiser. Consequently there is less concern over immediate effects—often not enough concern in the sense of shaping a scene to bring out its full significance—and the persistent tread of Dreiser's larger conception soon takes on the solemnity of a religious service, with the reader, in Dreiser's best works, yielding up all minor irritations to the spell of the writer's complete absorption in recreating life on the page.

\* \* \*

This present assessment of Dreiser is welcome in general, interesting, balanced, and missing only some of Burton

Rascoe's honest, early criticism to have done its entire duty. It is divided into three main sections: personal reminiscences by such men as Edgar Lee Masters, Ludwig Lewisohn, and Ford Madox Ford; early newspaper and magazine criticism of Dreiser, both pro and con; and finally more extended studies of several of his books by such critics as Malcolm Cowley, James T. Farrell, Alfred Kazin, the late F. O. Matthiessen and others. Almost all of these essays are interesting if you are concerned about Dreiser, including those written out of the "enemy camp," which can be divided into the independents, the neo-humanist group, and Mr. Trilling's "mature liberalism" approach.

This last section includes penetrating critics, such as Thomas K. Whipple, Robert Shafer and Stuart Sherman—unfamiliar names that take one back thirty years when Irving Babbitt and the Humanists were an intellectual force in America and were defending respectable medievalism in modern dress from assaults by Goths like Dreiser. The approach of these critics is sober and high-minded, as befits a group of men oriented to the classics and holding a rigid Christian view of man, but they pelt Dreiser's crudities and "animalization" of human life without honest public recognition of his intention. Ibsen once said: "Zola goes down into the sewer to bathe; I go down to scour it." Never having forgiven Zola, the neo-humanist critics would not admit that Dreiser "went down" with a heavy heart not to exploit but to mother life's victims. In essence their work is ivory-tower criticism, bitter about any change that doesn't embrace their philosophy and turning away from all creative images of the present which exist by their own vitality. Beneath their criticism runs the graver conflict that orthodox Christian critics have had with "naturalism," but it is characteristic of such criticism that it often abandons art completely, as the neo-humanists did, because it is ultimately interested in propagandizing a point of view more than seeing another for what it is.

I find Lionel Trilling's pique with Dreiser's mental slovenliness and general grossness—his "vulgar materialism," in Mr. Trilling's words—also somewhat prissy and unrealistic for all its enlightened air. Mr. Trilling's essential point, made in the course of a long essay on the "easiness" of liberal thinking, is that the liberal critics never dissected Dreiser's vague generalizations about life as they should have, that they sentimentally honored his "honest stupidity" instead of demanding intelligence, clarity and responsibility from him in regard to his ideas. No one wants to quarrel with this as an abstract ideal, but Mr. Trilling, cross-planting T. S. Eliot and the *Nation,* seems to want all the fruits of the spirit hanging from a single tree—that of his own critical taste and cultivation plus the political implications of liberal thought. He wants to reduce

Dreiser's philosophizing to its inadequacy as moral precept, and becomes indignant because none of his liberal predecessors have exposed the tatters before.

There is a lack of warmth and charity in this attitude, but apart from that a reluctance on the critic's part to realize that he is privileged to be able to synthesize what is best in several points of view just because there were certain original writers like Dreiser (or Mr. Eliot) who found a commanding vision of truth when Mr. Trilling was a student fighting his way through books. Such truth may need a much more sophisticated or time-dominated revision now, but that would entail a wider respect for the harsher aspects of American life than Mr. Trilling gets into the high brow of his writing. It is all too other-worldly to stick as sharp, permanent criticism of a major writer who certainly deserves acute illumination, but not from the upper stratosphere. Implicit in all the sensible things Mr. Trilling appears to say is the absence of what one must appreciate before one can judge Dreiser, that he is a writer who brought something new into being.

*Note*

1. *The Stature of Theodore Dreiser: A Critical Survey of the Man and His Work.* Edited by Alfred Kazin and Charles Shapiro. Introduction by Mr. Kazin. Indiana University Press.

## Donald M. Goodfellow (essay date 1959)

SOURCE: Goodfellow, Donald M. "Theodore Dreiser and the American Dream." *Six Novelists: Stendhal, Dostoevski, Tolstoy, Hardy, Dreiser, Proust,* Carnegie Press, Carnegie Institute of Technology, 1959, pp. 53-66.

[*In the following essay, Goodfellow explores Dreiser's perspective on and experience of the contrast between the wealthy and the poor in America and his efforts to fight "the prudishness of American literary taste."*]

When Theodore Dreiser, then twenty-two, arrived in Pittsburgh, he hoped to find nothing more than a job as a reporter on one of the newspapers. A quarter of a century later he wrote: "Of all the cities in which I ever worked or lived, Pittsburgh was the most agreeable. Perhaps it was due to the fact that my stay included only spring, summer, and fall, or that I found a peculiarly easy newspaper atmosphere, or that the city was so different physically from any I had thus far seen; but ... certainly no other newspaper work I ever did seemed so pleasant, no other city more interesting."

Undoubtedly Dreiser's pleasant recollections were due in part to the opportunity to attempt something for the Pittsburgh *Dispatch* more literary than he had been permitted to do for Chicago and St. Louis papers—"a series of mood or word pictures about the most trivial matters—a summer storm, a spring day, a visit to a hospital, the death of an old switchman's dog, the arrival of the first mosquito." These little sketches gave him his "first taste of what it means to be a creative writer." And one afternoon, having nothing else to do, he wandered into the Allegheny Carnegie Library and by the merest chance picked up one of Balzac's novels. As he began reading, "a new and inviting door to life" was suddenly thrown open to him. "Not only for the brilliant and incisive manner with which Balzac grasped life and invented themes whereby to present it, but for the fact that the types he handled with most enthusiasm and skill—the brooding, seeking, ambitious beginner in life's social, political, artistic and commercial affairs—were, I thought, so much like myself." In that characterization of Balzac's types are summarized the types that Dreiser was to portray in his novels—types that were so much like himself, no matter from what walks of life they came or what heights or depths they attained.

Equally important in directing Dreiser's thoughts during his Pittsburgh days were the writings of Huxley, Tyndall, and Spencer, which he also discovered in the library. "Up to this time," he wrote,

> there had been in me a blazing and unchecked desire to get on and the feeling that in doing so we did get somewhere; now in its place was the definite conviction that spiritually one got nowhere, that there was no hereafter, that one lived and had his being because one had to, and that it was of no importance. Of one's ideals, struggles, deprivations, sorrows and joys, it could only be said that they were chemic compulsions, something which for some inexplicable reason responded to and resulted from the hope of pleasure and the fear of pain. ... With a gloomy eye I began to watch how the chemical—and their children, the mechanical—forces operated through man and outside him, and this under my very eye.

Also before his eyes "were always those regions of indescribable poverty and indescribable wealth" which led him to write: "Never in my life, neither before nor since, in New York, Chicago, or elsewhere, was the vast gap which divides the rich from the poor in America brought so vividly home to me. ... True, all men had not the brains to seize upon and make use of that which was put before them, but again, not all men of brains had the blessing of opportunity as had these few men." Then came this self-analysis, only part of which was to prove prophetic: "How to get up in the world and be somebody was my own thought now, and yet I knew that wealth was not for me.

The best I should ever do was to think and dream, standing aloof as a spectator." A spectator Dreiser was throughout his life, but he was also an observer; and as soon as he began to record his observations, he became a novelist. As for wealth—although he would never be another Carnegie, Frick, or Rockefeller, thirty years later, following the publication of his sixth novel, he had what was to him a fortune: about $25,000 in royalties for the first six months' sale of the book and $90,000 for the motion picture rights. *An American Tragedy,* though never on the best-seller list, was far more popular than any of his other novels had been on publication.

More significantly, reviewers and critics who had not been favorably disposed toward Dreiser's earlier books found something praiseworthy in this one. After a quarter-century during which he had stood his ground in spite of disheartening attacks from almost all sides, he was "somebody"—he had got "up in the world." And what he had risen from, what he had seen and felt and thought on his way up—the themes, the types of people, the events that make up his novels—we find touched on in the following passages from the first two pages of *An American Tragedy.*

> Dusk—of a summer night. And the tall walls of the commercial heart of an American city of perhaps 400,000 inhabitants—such walls as in time may linger as a fable. And up the broad street, now comparatively hushed, a little band of six,—a man of about fifty, short, stout, with bushy hair protruding from under a round black felt hat, a most unimportant-looking little person, who carried a small portable organ such as is customarily used by street preachers and singers. And with him a woman perhaps five years his junior, taller, not so broad, but solid of frame and vigorous, very plain in face and dress, and yet not homely, leading with one hand a small boy of seven and in the other carrying a Bible and several hymn books. With these three, but walking independently behind, was a girl of fifteen, a boy of twelve and another girl of nine, all following obediently, but not too enthusiastically, in the wake of the others. ... As they sang, [the] nondescript and indifferent street audience gazed, held by the peculiarity of such an unimportant-looking family publicly raising its collective voice against the vast skepticism and apathy of life.

The "little band of six" provide an interesting example of Dreiser's way of fusing elements from his own background and elements drawn from observation. The father, modeled in part on a street preacher seen years before in Kansas City, where *An American Tragedy* opens, also calls to mind his own overreligious father, whose appearance "bespoke more of failure than anything else." Mrs. Griffiths reminds the reader of Dreiser's mother; and her boy Clyde is what Dreiser describes himself as having

been: a "mother child." The elder Dreisers had appeared previously in *Jennie Gerhardt,* as had other members of the family, including one of Theodore's sisters, whom we see again here as Hester Griffiths. Both the Dreiser and the Griffiths families were "always hard-up, never very well clothed, and deprived of many comforts and pleasures which seemed common enough to others." It was partly this sense of deprivation that developed in Clyde Griffiths the same longing that Dreiser had experienced: "... the gay pairs of young people, laughing and jesting, and the 'kids' staring, all troubled him with a sense of something different, better, more beautiful than his ... life."

One of Dreiser's own early characteristics is represented in this opening chapter of *An American Tragedy,* not by Clyde's reaction, but by that of members of the street audience. "Some were interested or moved sympathetically by the rather tame and inadequate figure of the girl at the organ, others by the impractical and materially inefficient texture of the father. ..." From childhood, Dreiser had longed for better things for himself; but at the same time that he envied and admired the wealthy and the strong, he sympathized with the poor and the weak. In one of his autobiographical volumes he recalls his childish pity for his mother when he noticed her worn and broken shoes. "That," he said, "was the birth of sympathy and tenderness in me." In St. Louis just prior to his departure for Pittsburgh, he was looking at everything about him with a covetous eye, depressed by the thought that he would never know prosperity and fame. He was also "filled with an intense sympathy for the woes of others, life in all its helpless degradation and poverty, the unsatisfied dreams of people ... the things they were compelled to endure. ..."

A further passage from the first page of *An American Tragedy* will lead us into a consideration of Dreiser's most significant novels: "And the tall walls of the commercial heart of an American city. ..." From boyhood, Dreiser had been fascinated by cities—first Chicago, then St. Louis, later Pittsburgh, and still later New York. In the opening chapter of *Sister Carrie* he recalls the thrill of his first visit to Chicago, and the setting of that novel is urban throughout. The action in *Jennie Gerhardt* takes place in Columbus, Cleveland, and Chicago. The first two volumes of the "trilogy of desire"—*The Financier* and *The Titan*—have Philadelphia and Chicago as their settings. And it is Kansas City and Chicago that start Clyde on his way in *An American Tragedy.* In the first two and the last of these five novels Dreiser makes plain the isolation of the individual surrounded by the "tall walls." But it is against the "commercial heart" not only of the city but of America that he is inveighing in all his major novels.

Dreiser was not the first American novelist to focus his attention on post-Civil War urbanization and its attendant corruptions. Henry Blake Fuller had dealt with Chicago in *The Cliff-Dwellers* and *With the Procession,* and Frank Norris had presented detailed pictures of parts of San Francisco in *McTeague* and *The Octopus* and of Chicago in *The Pit.* More important than these writers, however, because of his influence on youthful readers, was the man who promised the inevitable rise to fame and fortune of any boy, provided that he arrived in the city equipped with pure heart and a full set of copybook maxims, worked hard, remained honest, and saved the life of a millionaire's daughter. Jed the Poorhouse Boy, Paul the Peddler, Julius the Street Boy, Phil the Fiddler, Tom the Bootblack, Ragged Dick—all these Horatio Alger heroes helped to promote the tradition that arose out of the success of Fisk, Gould, Carnegie, Vanderbilt, and Rockefeller. Between 1866 and the end of the nineteenth century, about 130 Alger titles attained an aggregate sale of between sixteen and seventeen million copies. And the majority of these books, though warning against the pitfalls of urban life, held out the hope of success to American boyhood.

As a boy in Evansville, Indiana, Dreiser had read Alger's *Brave and Bold, Luck and Pluck, Work and Win,* as well as Hill's *Manual of Etiquette and Social and Commercial Forms,* in which he found "pictures of cities and great buildings and of men who began as nothing in this great sad world but rose by honesty and industry and thrift and kind thoughts and deeds to be great." As an adolescent in Chicago, he was burning to use the brain that an older man of considerable knowledge assured him he had, so that he "might share in the material splendors which everywhere, as I saw, men were struggling for." Some time later, while employed as a bill collector for a household furnishings company, he realized that he could not satisfy his dreams on $14.00 a week. "I had to take them out in longing or derive some way of raising the money." Desiring especially an overcoat with satin lining, the better to fit in his dream world, he withheld surplus payments collected from customers, intending to repay gradually the amount thus "borrowed." But he was soon discovered and discharged. Such an experience, though it stopped far short of murder, must have given him some insight into the Clyde Griffiths who would come into being about thirty-five years later.

By this time Dreiser was "nearly hypochondriacal on the subjects of poverty, loneliness, the want of the creature comforts and pleasures of life. The mere thought of having enough to eat and to wear and to do had something of paradise about it." Experience had marked him with a horror of being without work; but he soon obtained the first of a succession of reportorial assignments on Chicago newspapers. From Chicago he was to proceed by way of St. Louis to Pittsburgh, where he first tried his hand at creative writing, and where, as he later told Burton Rascoe, he decided to become a novelist and to use as a subject one of the industrial or business geniuses of the period.

For about five years after his Pittsburgh experiences, Dreiser was an editor and a free-lance writer of magazine articles in New York. Before finding an opportunity of any kind, he lived precariously and fearfully on the edge of poverty. As he sat one wintry day on a park bench, he sensed anew the overwhelming contrast between the world of the unemployed and destitute whom he saw around him and the world of success symbolized by the tall buildings near at hand. While writing **Sister Carrie** in 1899 he was to remember this experience.

What happened to Dreiser's first novel is a commentary on American culture. **Sister Carrie** had been accepted for publication by Frank Norris, the reader for Doubleday, and Dreiser had signed a contract with the publisher. But the story goes that Doubleday handed a copy to his wife; she read it; and the trouble began. Mrs. Doubleday found the novel so shocking that her husband, prompted by her reaction, issued only enough copies to abide by the contract, and advertised the book not at all. What impressed Mrs. Doubleday and some other early readers as immoral was the fact that Carrie Meeber, an innocent young woman from a farm, was permitted to rise to fame unpunished in spite of having lived, without benefit of clergy, for a short time with Drouet, then for three years with Hurstwood. Dreiser's first contribution to the development of the American novel was his refusal to pretend that a girl who had Carrie's experiences inevitably paid for her misdemeanors while the man went on his merry way. Only eight years before the first printing of **Sister Carrie,** Stephen Crane's *Maggie,* the brief story of a girl driven to prostitution, had shocked the few who read it; but the fact that Maggie ended her life by drowning should have satisfied those whose moral views demanded that the wages of sin must be death. Carrie Meeber was not made to suffer because Dreiser based her story on the experience of his own sister, deceived by a man who, like Hurstwood, had stolen from his employers and taken her with him to New York. Dreiser knew that his sister's irregular behavior did not end in degradation or death.

There are few more gripping chapters in fiction than those tracing the decline of Hurstwood. When Carrie meets him, he is the successful, well-to-do, respected manager of a Chicago restaurant. But once the couple are in New York, Carrie's fortunes rise and Hurstwood's steadily sink: loss of work, dwindling funds, apathy, loneliness, beggary, and then his last appearance in the small, close room that he has rented for fifteen cents, obtained by begging. "After a few moments, in which he reviewed nothing, but merely hesitated, he turned the gas on again, but applied no match. Even then he stood there, hidden wholly in the kindness that is night, while the uprising fumes filled the room. When the odour reached his nostrils, he quit his attitude and fumbled for the bed. 'What's the use?' he said weakly, as he stretched himself to rest." Our minds go back to the man who, as he rubbed elbows with the destitute in a New York City park, shuddered with a fear of what might be ahead for him. It was at that moment, Dreiser said, "that Hurstwood was born." And in the words of F. O. Matthiessen, it was "with Hurstwood" that "Dreiser began his chief contribution to American literature."

For seven years after its first publication, *Sister Carrie* was almost completely unknown to American readers. Dreiser's frustration over the fate of his first novel (from which he had netted less than $100) led to a severe breakdown; he was unable to work, except sporadically, for three years. Eventually he obtained editorial employment, and for six years, while producing potboilers for periodicals, he was connected with various magazines that published the unrealistic kind of fiction which he could not bring himself to write. Nothing seems more incongruous than the Naturalistic author of *Sister Carrie,* complete with pince-nez and "nobby" clothes, serving as the editor of *The Delineator,* a magazine for properly domesticated women. His secretary said he looked "Not as I had expected an editor to look. More like a College professor." In spite of that handicap, Dreiser was a most successful editor; the wonder is that throughout this period the spirit and feeling that had caused him to write *Sister Carrie* survived. When his connection with the Butterick publications was severed, he settled down to work on *Jennie Gerhardt.*

In the early part of this novel, Dreiser drew heavily upon the predicament of his family during his childhood. The experience of Jennie, an unwed mother, is based upon that of one of his sisters, but in her sweetness of character she is modeled upon his mother. Whereas in *Sister Carrie,* Hurstwood seems to be the chief character, here Jennie is really the heroine. For many years the mistress of a rich man, she cannot become his wife because of their difference in station. Although Dreiser does not gloss over the illicitness of their relationship, he refrains from creating scenes of passion. In both *Sister Carrie* and *Jennie Gerhardt* he is reticent about physical love. He no more intended to pander to the taste of those who desired a vicarious and salacious thrill than he intended to represent the attraction of men and women for each other as

leading to a sexless relationship. He was presenting the truth as he saw it and knew it.

If in his next two novels—*The Financier* and *The Titan*—Dreiser places greater emphasis on sex (though here too his scenes of physical passion seem quite restrained today), he does so because his "hero," Frank Cowperwood, must behave as did his original, Charles Yerkes. Dreiser chose Yerkes from among the financial buccaneers of nineteenth-century America because he needed a central character different from most of the robber barons, who have been characterized as discreet and well controlled, their strongest lust their appetite for money. Yerkes was very much a man of flesh and blood, as the entry in the *Dictionary of American Biography* will show. This biographical account of the man who gained control of the transit systems in Philadelphia and Chicago proves how closely Dreiser followed the facts. Yet Cowperwood is not merely an academic representation of Yerkes; to a degree, in his sexual drive, he is Dreiser himself. Speaking of his brother Paul, Dreiser once remarked: "I have never known a man more interested in women from the sex point of view (unless perchance it might be myself). ..." Perhaps for this reason he is able to be objective and never condemnatory in treating Cowperwood's affairs. But more important than this slight resemblance is the significance of Cowperwood as a symbol at once of the kind of success that the young Dreiser had dreamed about and of the injustice practiced on the weak by the strong and clever.

Whereas the history of Hurstwood had been an Alger story in reverse, *The Financier* gets under way in typical Alger fashion. Frank Cowperwood is not poor; but it is largely on his own initiative that he scores his first successes; and because of the promise he shows, he wins the approval and help of his superiors. In the first chapter, however, he adopts a philosophy that can hardly be considered Horatian, basing his conclusion on a drama that he has witnessed. On his way to and from school he passed a fish market, at the front of which stood a tank containing a squid and a lobster. Day by day, little by little, the lobster preyed upon the squid, until finally the squid was no more. Young Frank began to analyze the incident. "'How is life organized?' he asked himself. 'Things lived on each other—that was it. Lobsters lived on squids and other things. What lived on lobsters? Men, of course! ... And what lived on men? ... Was it other men? ... Sure, men lived on men.'" And with this decision, the boy's feet are set on the path not of Paul the Peddler but of the ruthless financiers of the Gilded Age. He is on the way to becoming a Naturalistic strong man; like Jack London's physical brutes, he will illustrate the meaning of the Darwinian-Spencerian phrase "the survival of the fittest."

Since both *The Financier* and *The Titan* are biographical, the plot line was laid down for Dreiser in advance. By reading all the newspaper reports of the life of Yerkes, he obtained the major incidents. As for the character of the man, it is said that for all his crimes against American cities, there was something fresh and ingratiating about Yerkes, possibly because he was not hypocritical. "The secret of success in my business," he frankly stated, "is to buy old junk, fix it up a little, and unload it upon the other fellows." When attacked for not making available more seats in trolleys, he remarked, "It is the strap-hanger who pays the dividend." Cowperwood is not so plainspoken, nor does he win the reader's sympathy. But Dreiser tries to make him understandable. Cowperwood's motto is, "I satisfy myself." In applying this motto to his sexual behavior, he explains his motivation in terms of the "chemic compulsions" or "chemisms" that Dreiser mentioned so frequently after reading Spencer. And this behavior among businessmen and politicians is what we should expect of a man who sees life in terms of the relations between squids and lobsters.

If *The Financier* and *The Titan* are read in succession, the second seems hardly more than a duplication of the first. Stuart P. Sherman's characterization of *The Titan* might apply equally well to its predecessor: a "huge club-sandwich composed of slices of business alternating with erotic episodes." Both contain a wealth of detail which make them good social history. The American businessman had been pictured in various guises by a number of novelists including William Dean Howells and Frank Norris. But Cowperwood dwarfs all others as a ruthless financial pirate, a character stranger than fiction because founded on fact. Once we have acknowledged the historical significance of these two novels, we must admit they are not lively reading. Dreiser manages to create a certain amount of suspense in *The Financier,* and there are melodramatic scenes in *The Titan*; but the average reader will find both less fascinating than *Sister Carrie* and *Jennie Gerhardt,* perhaps because of lack of sympathy for Cowperwood.

During the remaining twenty-one years of his life Dreiser was to complete only three more novels. One, *The Bulwark,* was published posthumously. (*The Stoic,* volume three of the "trilogy of desire," was also published after his death, though unfinished.) The two which appeared during his lifetime are *The "Genius"* and *An American Tragedy.* The first of these is considered by many to be the weakest of his novels, perhaps because it is too autobiographical. The fact that the New York Society for the Suppression of Vice banned *The "Genius"* temporarily in 1916 is of interest chiefly because it emphasizes Dreiser's unique contribution to American literature. From 1900 he had been fighting what amounted to a one-man battle against the prudishness of American literary taste. He steadfastly refused to omit or change a situation or a detail which he had experienced or observed and therefore knew to be true. He would not falsify to please the Mrs. Doubledays or the John S. Sumners. Some later writer would have fought such a battle if Dreiser had not done so; but no one before him had dared or had lived to press the fight. The Hemingways, Dos Passoses, Faulkners, Farrells have Dreiser to thank for having won for them the right to present life honestly.

Soon after the publication of *The "Genius"* Stuart P. Sherman, a fairly conservative critic, wrote of the Dreiser novels that had thus far appeared: "These five works constitute a singularly homogeneous mass of fiction. I do not find any moral value in them, nor any memorable beauty . . . but I am greatly impressed by them as serious representatives of a new note in American literature. . . ." This "new note" Sherman discusses at some length, concluding: "It would make for clearness in our discussions of contemporary fiction if we withheld the title of 'realist' from a writer like Mr. Dreiser, and called him, as Zola called himself, a 'naturalist.' . . . A naturalistic novel is based upon a theory of animal behavior. Since a theory of animal behavior can never be an adequate basis for a representation of the life of man in contemporary society, such a representation is an artistic blunder. . . . And so one turns with relief from Mr. Dreiser's novels to the morning papers."

Ten year later Sherman opened his review of *An American Tragedy* as follows:

> Youngsters who think to shelve Dreiser with the retiring title of 'the grand old man of realism' reckon without his large, stolid, literary ambition, which to my mind, is his most salient and admirable moral characteristic. As a novelist he has been silent these ten years. And now with his familiar huge plantigrade tread he comes lumbering down the trail with a massive 800-page American tragedy which makes the performances of most of his rivals and successors look like capering accomplishments of rabbits and squirrels. . . . I do not know where else in American fiction one can find the situation here presented dealt with so fearlessly, so intelligently, so exhaustively, so veraciously, and therefore, with such unexceptionable moral effect.

Undoubtedly Sherman had grown in tolerance and understanding during the World War I period. And following the war, as a book reviewer he could hardly wave aside the novels that were coming from the pens of Sinclair Lewis, Dos Passos, and numerous writers, more popular in their day than now, all of whom revealed at least traces of the Naturalism of which Sherman had formerly disapproved. At the same time, it must be admitted that *An American Tragedy* is different from Dreiser's previous novels in one important respect. Ironically enough, what raised it so high in Sherman's estimation was the fact that it is, in its objectivity, the most Naturalistic novel that Dreiser ever wrote. In each of the preceding novels, editorializing or philosophizing comments are numerous. The improvement in Dreiser's technique Sherman noted; but he attributed it to a change from "barbaric naturalism" to "tragic realism." Actually, objectivity had always been the first desideratum of the American Naturalists, though probably none before this had so completely attained it.

When Sherman after reading *The "Genius"* turned "with relief ... to the morning papers," he was going to the source—the objective source—from which Dreiser drew much of his material not only for the Cowperwood novels but for his greatest work, *An American Tragedy.* Not that he was waiting for a sensational news story that would furnish a plot. His problem was to choose from among at least sixteen murder cases which had been reported at length during the preceding thirty years the one that would best suit his theme. Ever since becoming a newspaperman, he had noticed how frequently a certain type of crime was committed: the murder of a socially and financially inferior girl by a lover who hoped, by removing her, to be free to marry a wealthy girl of higher social station. In each instance, as Dreiser saw it, the guilty man was himself a victim—a victim of the American Dream. The only kind of success recognized in America was that measured by money and social position. Perhaps because he found the material easily accessible, Dreiser decided to concentrate on the case of Chester Gillette, who had been electrocuted on March 20, 1908, for the drowning of a girl named Grace Brown in Big Moose Lake.

The story of *An American Tragedy* can be briefly summarized. Clyde Griffiths, the son of street-corner evangelists, has already begun at the age of twelve to think of how he may better himself. After a short period in his early teens as a helper in a drugstore, he obtains a job as a bellboy in a leading Kansas City hotel. He finds his first taste of worldly life most exciting. But this experience ends suddenly following an automobile accident in which a child is killed; although Clyde was not the driver of the borrowed car, he fears punishment and disgrace, and flees. In Chicago, while working as bellboy in the Union League Club, he meets the wealthy uncle of whom he has often heard his parents speak, and whom he impresses so favorably that he is eventually offered employment in the uncle's collar and shirt factory in New York state. At this point, Horatio Alger

seems to be winning. But Clyde finds that his wealthy relatives are not disposed to pay much attention to him. Once they have entertained him at dinner, they consider their social obligation ended. He does not enjoy his work, he has no friends, and he finds his days dull and depressing, even after he is promoted to a foremanship. He yearns for companionship, especially feminine; but without the help of his relatives he has no way of meeting other young women than those in the factory, and company rules forbid showing an interest in them.

One week end, seeking entertainment at a near-by park, he comes upon Roberta Alden, the only girl by whom he has been attracted at the factory. Ironically, in view of what is to follow, they spend a happy, innocent hour rowing on the lake. After this, Clyde and Roberta continue to meet after working hours; but the coming of cold weather, when parks are closed and long walks in the country are out of the question, raises a problem. Eventually, now much in love with Clyde, Roberta allows him to visit her in her rooms and becomes his mistress. Shortly after, Sondra Finchley, one of the Griffiths set, invites Clyde to a social function, chiefly to annoy his cousin Gilbert, who dislikes Clyde. This incident leads to a succession of invitations from other members of the socially elite, and it encourages Clyde to think of a possible future with Sondra, who represents beauty, wealth, and social prestige. About the time it becomes apparent that Sondra is in love with him, Roberta tells him that she is pregnant and demands that he provide for her. From the beginning, Clyde has been determined not to let his relationship with Roberta lead to marriage; now that his prospects with Sondra and her world are so bright, he persuades Roberta to try certain drugs and then to appeal to a doctor to perform an illegal operation. These attempts are unsuccessful. When it is obvious that Roberta will expose him to his relatives unless he marries her, he is stirred by a newspaper story to plan an "accidental" drowning. Rowing to an isolated spot on an Adirondack lake, he finds himself at the crucial moment afraid to carry out his plan; but as Roberta gets to her feet and moves toward him, he raises his hand, and, not actually intending to do so, throws her off balance. The boat capsizes; and as Roberta sinks beneath the surface, Clyde swims to shore. Within a few hours he is apprehended. Following a lengthy trial, in which the political ambition of the district attorney plays a more important part than a desire to see justice done, Clyde is convicted of murder and goes to the electric chair.

Although Dreiser read the published accounts of the Chester Gillette case, especially the report of the trial, he made some changes and additions. The opening section of *An American Tragedy* was undoubtedly suggested by the early life of Dreiser himself. Clyde as a bellboy is modeled upon a bellboy whom Dreiser had encountered in Chicago. Various details connected with the drowning scene are changed. And the period is the twenties instead of the first decade of the century. What is most important is that whereas Gillette actually committed murder, Clyde accidentally strikes the blow that sends Roberta to her death. Thus, as has been said, "the evidence is of a crime against Christian morals rather than against written law." This change makes it possible for Dreiser to label Clyde a mental and moral coward rather than a killer. Whether Clyde's weakness entitles him to pity is a matter which the individual reader must decide. Certainly, though we are told that Sondra and most of her crowd found Clyde "charming," we see little evidence of his charm; we have been with him since childhood days and know him to have no definite character, but only a vague desire to rise in the world in accordance with American standards. To quote Carl Van Doren, "Nobody tells him what to be. Everybody tells him what to have."

If we compare Clyde with the central characters in the other novels, we observe that though he is the least qualified to succeed, he is motivated by the same incentive as Carrie Meeber and Frank Cowperwood. Carrie, a poor girl from the country, was looking for something better than she had known. She stepped outside the recognized moral code to get her start, and after Hurstwood's fortunes began to decline, she would undoubtedly have gone the way of Crane's Maggie to prostitution and death if she had not possessed some talent as an actress. Frank Cowperwood, as a boy from a family that was reasonably well off, had a better chance than Carrie at the outset; and having a sharp intelligence, no conscience, and the determination to satisfy himself, he was bound to succeed. Clyde, with no gift or talent, and certainly no strength of character, could only trust to luck. Without attempting to influence the reader to judge Clyde, Dreiser follows him with underlying pity from his beginnings as a seemingly good-hearted boy to his end as a seeming murderer. His luck had been against him. And even though his own weakness was ultimately responsible for his downfall, yet with a different start in life, better educational opportunities, a few more dollars each week in his pay envelope, but most of all, a different criterion of success, what might his life have been? That the dividing line is thin is suggested by the fact that Dreiser received many letters from people who wrote: "Clyde Griffiths might have been me."

But also deserving of pity is Roberta Alden, whom most critics seem to ignore. Her background was no better than Clyde's—or, for that matter, than Carrie Meeber's or Jennie Gerhardt's—and she had the same dreams. The irony of her situation is that as she sees her association with

Clyde as a step up the social ladder, he himself is frustrated because he cannot attain the status of his uncle's family and their circle. The awful aloneness of Roberta after she senses that Clyde no longer really loves her Dreiser handles with tenderness and understanding. It is more of an American tragedy—tragedy for America, perhaps a tragedy for which America was responsible—that Roberta, an attractive, sweet-natured, kind-hearted girl, who had once shown the potentiality of realizing her dreams, should go to her lonely death because of the mores and rules of her society, than that Clyde should be driven to plan her death because of his desire to improve himself. She is both a more winning and a more living character than Clyde.

The same cannot be said of the other girl. When Dreiser attempted to deal with a social group outside his own orbit, he was not successful. Sondra Finchley and her gay circle speak and behave like characters in a travesty on life among the Four Hundred. Perhaps Dreiser's lack of sympathy with such people made it impossible for him to bring them to life, but the fact that he had never mingled in that society is probably an adequate explanation. His other leading characters and the numerous minor middle-class figures are realistically conceived. In the creation of those in subordinate roles, Dreiser uses countless details to good effect. Typical is the introduction of the country coroner, who "was lethargically turning the leaves of a mail-order catalogue for which his wife had asked him to write. And while deciphering from its pages the price of shoes, jackets, hats, and caps for his five omnivorous children, a greatcoat for himself of soothing proportions, high collar, broad belt, large, impressive buttons chancing to take his eye, he had paused to consider regretfully that the family budget of $3,000 a year would never permit of so great a luxury this coming winter, particularly since his wife, Ella, had had her mind upon a fur coat for at least three winters past." In a novel of lesser proportions this material might seem superfluous, but by the time we are two-thirds through *An American Tragedy,* we are not surprised to find such a passage. A reader of Dreiser recognizes the accumulation of details as part of his method of making the reader believe that something *is.*

How necessary and effective a part of Dreiser's method it is can be appreciated from a reading of his posthumous novel *The Bulwark,* which at times gives the impression of being a skeleton of a novel, lacking the flesh that Dreiser's documentation had always before provided. But if in this respect the method is somewhat changed, the same cannot be said so unreservedly of the style. The ineptitudes for which Dreiser had been criticized ever since he began to write novels are evident in *The Bulwark.* The deficiencies of his style are so obvious as to call for no special comment: the passages that I have quoted contain illustrations of those faults. But in his best novels Dreiser rises above his style; and if the first principle of success in literature is sincerity, then in spite of his style he must be judged a success. As Sherwood Anderson said, "If you look for word-love in his book you'll get left. Love of human beings you'll find. It's a finer attribute in the end."

Near the close of *The Bulwark,* Solon Barnes, the central character, while walking in his garden, observes the behavior of a green fly, and ponders.

> Why was this beautiful creature, whose design so delighted him, compelled to feed upon another living creature, a beautiful flower? . . . And now so fascinated was he by his meditations on this problem that he not only gazed and examined the plant and the fly, but proceeded to look about for other wonders. . . . Then, after bending down and examining a blade of grass here, a climbing vine there, a minute flower, lovely and yet as inexplicable as his green fly, he turned in a kind of religious awe and wonder. Surely there must be a Creative Divinity, and so a purpose behind all of this variety and beauty and tragedy of life.

Whether Solon Barnes, approaching the end of his days, is here expressing a conclusion that Dreiser himself had reached is a matter for conjecture. Whatever may have been his personal thought, the view of life presented at the conclusion of *The Bulwark* is vastly different from that at the beginning of *The Financier.* In replacing the squid and the lobster with the flower and the fly, Dreiser closes his career as a Naturalistic writer.

## William L. Phillips (essay date 1963)

SOURCE: Phillips, William L. "The Imagery of Dreiser's Novels." *PMLA,* vol. 78, no. 5, Dec. 1963, pp. 572-85.

[*In the following essay, Phillips contradicts the general critical idea that Dreiser "had no awareness of the resources of image and metaphor," examining the ways in which he used imagery in five of his novels, and how this changed over time in line with his "philosophical preoccupations."*]

### I

The fiction of Theodore Dreiser has often been praised for its fidelity to the facts of ordinary experience, its massive accumulation and arrangement of incidents, and its criticism of bourgeois America. It has seldom been praised as skillful writing, however; and with almost the sole exception of F. O. Matthiessen, critics have dismissed Dreiser as a poor manipulator of the language, whose effects are achieved in spite of his style. It is usually suggested, fur-

thermore, that beyond a recurring use of clothing as symbols, Dreiser had no awareness of the resources of image and metaphor. It is said that his efforts at comparison were likely to be hackneyed and incredibly jumbled, as in a passage in *The Financier* about men who fade into poverty: "They were compelled by some devilish accident of birth or lack of force or resourcefulness to stew in their own juice of wretchedness, or to shuffle off this mortal coil—which under other circumstances had such glittering possibilities—*via* the rope, the knife, the bullet, or the cup of poison."[1]

Nevertheless, a close reading of Dreiser's novels reveals complex patterns of imagery, sometimes the result, apparently, of conscious manipulation and sometimes of an unconscious compulsion to say things in a particular way, a way which occasionally runs counter to the overt content of the novel. These patterns have the effect of drawing into a larger context the figurative clichés which are ineffective or even painful when they stand alone, and they contribute to the ultimately rich effect of Dreiser's novels, which often puzzles a reader who has been disturbed by the ineptitude of individual passages. Nor are the image patterns drawn from the chemical-physical conception of life which Dreiser preached in a number of essays. One may find allusions to "chemic conditions," "magnetic impulses," and "electric glances" if he searches for them; but they are rare compared to the extensive manipulation of a more conventional literary imagery drawn from three traditional sources—water (the sea, the lake, the stream), animal life, and tales of magic. This traditional imagery provides the moral undercurrent which the reader often senses in Dreiser's novels in spite of his frequent protests that he never judged or condemned.

This study will examine the dominant image patterns of five novels, *Sister Carrie, The Financier, The Titan, An American Tragedy,* and *The Bulwark*; demonstrate by extensive quotation the ways in which Dreiser's imagery enriches the total effect of the novels and helps to discriminate individual incidents and characters; and point out the ways in which Dreiser's use of his major groups of images shifted with his changing philosophical preoccupations and the changing intentions of his novels.

### II

The largest and most obvious group of images in *Sister Carrie* is that clustering around the sea, which was for the early Dreiser the symbol of modern urban life. This image is introduced at the end of the first chapter when Carrie's situation is summarized: She is "alone, away from home, rushing into a great sea of life and endeavor . . . a lone figure in a tossing, thoughtless sea."[2] The hydrography is soon laid out: "the entire metropolitan centre possessed a high and mighty air calculated ... to make the gulf between poverty and success seem both wide and deep" (p. 16). The most terrifying quality of Dreiser's society-sea, however, is not the width of the gulf between poverty and success, but the suggestions that those who attempt a crossing are without power to advance or to remain anchored, that each traveller makes more perilous the plight of another, and that the port of success constantly shifts.

The powerless travellers in this sea *drift* (the word is repeated at least a dozen times in the novel) on the tide; we are told that Carrie "felt the flow of the tide of effort and interest—felt her own helplessness without quite realizing the wisp on the tide that she was" (p. 26). Indeed, one survives in this sea only if he does not have too acute an idea of his condition of helplessness. Drouet clowns his way through the novel, "assured that he was alluring all, that affection followed tenderly in his wake" (p. 114), although Carrie seems "ever capable of getting herself into the tide of changes where she would be easily borne along" (p. 278). Whether or not Dreiser consciously intended the pun on Carrie's name, it is clear that he conceives of her as *carried* along by the sea, not moving by the exertions of her will. Hurstwood, on the other hand, is destroyed by his nagging awareness that in taking the money from the safe of Fitzgerald and Moy he has cut himself off from security. In Chicago, Hurstwood strikes Carrie as one who easily controls the life around him; his apparent solidity and strength draw her to him. It soon appears that "in an ocean like New York," however, he is only "an inconspicuous drop" (p. 265); there he finally becomes a derelict, one "of the class which simply floats and drifts, every wave of people washing up one, as breakers do driftwood upon a stormy shore," and he ends as a nameless corpse carried to his grave on "a slow, black boat setting out from the pier at Twenty-seventh Street" (pp. 440, 453).

Not only is life in general characterized by the ceaseless motion and the relentless tides of the sea; individuals in their desires for a secure harbor make perilous the condition of others. Hurstwood, forty, and weary of a marriage which had lost all its meaning, is attracted by Carrie's youth and grace; Carrie, by his promise of a new security. Yet, when they first meet alone in her parlor, his gaze makes her weak and insecure; "The little shop-girl was getting into deep water. She was letting her few supports float away from her."[3] When Hurstwood first proposes that she leave Drouet, Carrie feels "a wave of feeling sweep over her" (p. 137). Later when Hurstwood urges her more strongly, the scene again is filled with water images: "[Hurstwood] wanted to plunge in and expostulate with

her. ... He looked at her steadily for a moment, slowing his pace and fixing her with his eye. She felt the flood of feeling. 'How about me?' he asked. This confused Carrie considerably, for she realized the floodgates were open ... 'I don't know,' returned Carrie, still illogically drifting and finding nothing at which to catch. ... What should she do? She went on thinking this, answering vaguely, languishing affectionately, and altogether drifting, until she was on a borderless sea of speculation. ... He turned on her such a storm of feeling that she was overwhelmed."[4]

If the figure of life as a turbulent sea is the commonest metaphor in **Sister Carrie,** the comparison of life to a world of struggling animals is also important. In a passage often quoted, and often seen as related to the interest in animal evolution among the literary naturalists of the 1890's, the comparison is made explicit: "Our civilization is still in a middle stage, scarcely beast, in that it is no longer wholly guided by instinct; scarcely human, in that it is not yet wholly guided by reason. ... We see man far removed from the lairs of the jungles. ... He is becoming too wise to hearken always to instincts and desires; he is still too weak to always prevail against them. As a beast, the forces of life aligned him with them; as a man, he has not yet wholly learned to align himself with the forces. In this intermediate stage he wavers ..." (pp. 70-71). Incidental animal imagery runs through the novel, although the animals specified are as often domestic as wild. Carrie fears the coming of winter, like "the sparrow on the wire, the cat in the doorway, the draw horse tugging his weary load"; poverty hangs around her "like a hungry dog at her heels" (pp. 87-88, 57). Mrs. Hurstwood is "a pythoness in humour" who, "animal-like," turns on her husband, and scents his disaffection "as animals do danger, afar off" (pp. 197-198, 188). Fitzgerald and Moy's restaurant is an "insect-drawing, insect-infected rose of pleasure" (p. 46). Drouet is "the old butterfly" (p. 448). Lola Osborne, the chorus girl, clings "with her soft little claws to Carrie" in "a sort of pussy-like way" (p. 388). Hurstwood begins his involvement with Carrie by "merely spinning those gossamer threads of thought which, like the spider's, he hoped would lay hold somewhere" (p. 99); when he is presented with $10,000 in an open safe, he wavers between his desire for the money and a fear comparable to "the animal's instinctive recoil at evil" (p. 238); and when he arrives in swarming New York, "the sea was already full of whales. A common fish must needs disappear wholly from view— remain unseen. In other words, Hurstwood was nothing" (pp. 99, 238, 265). New York is not only an ocean; it is an animal world where angry strikers surround Hurstwood "like a small swarm of bees," as contrasted to the "hive of peculiarly listless and indifferent individuals" in the theater where Carrie searches for work (pp. 380, 341-342); where hungry men wait at a mission door "like cattle" and oppose Hurstwood with an "animal feeling of opposition" (pp. 440-441) when he moves to the head of a bread line; and where the face of a starving derelict may be "as white as drained veal" (p. 449) and men only look "sheepish . . . when they fall" (p. 447).

Out of context, such a word as "sheepish" may seem no longer to evoke any sense of the animal from which it derives; yet in the context of Hurstwood's decline the worn figure is refurbished. In addition to the truly functional animal imagery in the novel, there are many animal clichés: "a snail's pace" (p. 10), "moths . . . in the light of the flame" (pp. 45, 60), "the grapeless fox" (p. 107), the fly in the spider's net (p. 113), "birds of fine feather" (pp. 90, 173, 255) and "money-feathers" (p. 275), thoughts "upon eagles' wings" (p. 177), and "a dog's life" (p. 382). Even such common comparisons as these, the staple of the journalism of the 1890's, tend to regain some luster when they are embedded in the total texture of the imagery: after it occurs to Hurstwood that he is leading "a dog's life" his condemnation of others who oppose him as "the little cur!" (p. 382), "God damned dog!" (p. 446), and "damned old cur" (p. 446) has an ironic force. Although sometimes Dreiser clumsily piles together unrelated conventional figures seemingly aiming at decoration and achieving only imprecision, as in the quotation in the first paragraph of this article, he often effectively combines sea and animal imagery. An example occurs in the final scene of the book, as Hurstwood waits in the snow among a crowd of derelicts to enter the Bowery lodginghouse where he expects to commit suicide. The men "looked at [the closed door] as dumb brutes look, as dogs paw and whine and study the knob. . . . Then the door opened. It was push and jam for a minute, with grim, beast silence to prove its quality, and then it melted inward, like logs floating, and disappeared. There were wet hats and wet shoulders, a cold, shrunken, disgruntled mass, pouring in between bleak walls" (pp. 450-451).

Life is a sea; life is a jungle; reality is outside, wet, cold, snarling, swarming, and dark (much of the action takes place at night, and time is marked off by the passing of winters). What is inside, dry, warm, comforting, and light, is only illusion, an *Arabian Nights* tale which man invents to keep himself from suicide, "a door to an Aladdin's cave . . . delights which were not . . . lights of joy that never were on land or sea" (p. 411). Someone has remarked that the characteristic stance for Dreiser's characters is that of the outsider looking in upon comfort and luxury. More specifically, in the early novels it is that of the outsider gazing into Aladdin's cave, which he imagines holds the life of delight. The pathos of Carrie's struggles arises from the contrast between the delights which she envisages from outside her various caverns and the disappointment which she inevitably feels once she is inside and the genie proves inadequate: "she encountered a great wholesale shoe company, through the broad plate windows of which she saw an enclosed executive department, hidden by frosted glass. Without this enclosure, but just within the street entrance, sat a grey-haired gentleman at a small table, with a large open ledger before him. . . . 'Well, young lady,' observed the old gentleman, looking at her somewhat kindly, 'what is it you wish?' 'I am, that is, do you—I mean, do you need any help?' she stammered. 'Not just at present,' he answered smiling. 'Not just at present'" (p. 19).

Her escape from the factory chambers is only to the chambers of Drouet, however; under his protection she is "safe in a halcyon harbour" (p. 86), and within his rooms she sits in her rocking-chair, endlessly rocking, in an ironic likeness to the sea she thinks she has escaped. Beyond Drouet's chambers are others more promising for Carrie. There are the mansions on Lake Shore Drive, which Carrie subconsciously connects with Hurstwood: "Such childish fancies as she had had of fairy palaces and kingly quarters now came back. She imagined that across these richly carved entranceways, where the globed and crystalled lamps shone upon panelled doors set with stained and designed panes of glass, was . . . happiness" (p. 107). Most compelling for Carrie is "the fascinating make-believe of the moment"—the theater; for her a role in a hackneyed melodrama in an Elks' Club is "A Glimpse through the Gateway." The theater and "all the nameless paraphernalia of disguise . . . took her by the hand kindly, as one who says, 'My dear, come in.' It opened for her as if for its own. . . . She had come upon it as one who stumbles upon a secret passage, and, behold, she was in the chamber of diamonds and delight!" (p. 158). Ironically, Drouet is the "witless Aladdin" who opens for Carrie these chambers more exciting than his own. Although Carrie escapes from poverty through the theater, she finally recognizes, in a chapter which Dreiser titles "And This Is Not Elfland," that still "the door to life's perfect enjoyment was not open" (p. 413), and Bob Ames soon appears to "unlock the door to a new desire" (p. 437), the career in serious drama which Carrie ponders at the close of the novel as she sits in her rocking chair, dreaming by a window.[5]

Hurstwood's career, as has been often remarked, traces a descending line contrasting to Carrie's ascent; in terms of the sea and chamber imagery, while Carrie begins as "a lone figure in a tossing, thoughtless sea" (p. 11) and ends in "comfortable chambers at the Waldorf" (p. 447), Hurstwood begins in the illusory elegance of Fitzgerald and Moy's "bubbling, chattering, glittering chamber" (p. 45) and ends as a corpse in the sea. The rooms which he inhabits become progressively more depressing until he reaches the dingy room in which he commits suicide, in a pathetic parody of Aladdin's lamp: "A small gas-jet furnished sufficient light for so rueful a corner. ... He arose and turned the gas out, standing calmly in the blackness, hidden from view. After a few moments ... he turned the gas on again but applied no match. Even then he stood there, hidden wholly in that kindness which is night, while the uprising fumes filled the room. When the odour reached his nostrils, he quit his attitude and fumbled for the bed. 'What's the use?' he said, weakly, as he stretched himself to rest."[6]

### III

*Sister Carrie* established the basic opposition of image groups upon which Dreiser was later to play extensive variations—the indifferent sea and the animal world, which exist as uncomfortable fact, and the appealing harbour-chambers of illusion, magic, and the supernatural, in which man seeks comfort, love, and beauty.[7] However different in some respects Carrie Meeber and Frank Cowperwood may be, the alternatives open to them are essentially the same: struggling in a sea-jungle or retreating to an illusory harbor-chamber.

In the first two novels of the **Cowperwood series,** *The Financier* and *The Titan,*[8] the animal becomes dominant and the sea imagery secondary. From the earliest reviews of *The Financier* to the present, critics have taken the incident in Chapter One in which young Frank Cowperwood watches the battle of a lobster and a squid as pointing an important, if obvious, parallel to the fiercely competitive philosophy which the young man takes as his guide to life. In literary histories of the period, this incident has frequently been quoted to show Dreiser's acceptance of the Darwinian struggle as a fundamental principle of life.[9] The attention paid it, however, has diverted attention from the very extensive and varied animal imagery in the remainder of the novel, and in its immediate sequel, *The Titan.* In *The Financier,* one finds metaphors drawn from sea animals: seahorse, squid, lobster, fish, oyster, clam, herring, Black Grouper, and jellyfish; from among predatory land animals: wildcat, bear, leopard, tiger, lion, fox, wolf, and beaver; and many others: bird, partridge, hawk, gull, pigeon, chicken, duck, drake, dog, puppy, Newfoundland, collie, hound, cattle, bull, pig, horse, sheep, lamb, snake, cat, rat, mouse, insect, spider, moth, bee, fly, and worm. In *The Titan,* half of these recur, augmented by another thirty: eel, barnacle, sponge, walrus, clam, shark, octopus; lynx, rhinoceros, hyena, ferret, gray wolf; eagle, owl, ostrich, buzzard, goose, rooster; mastiff, bulldog, terrier; cow, ox,

swine, donkey, ass; pussy, kitten; chameleon, butterfly, wasp, and scorpion.[10]

Dreiser's theme is forced home: however civilized and ordinary the activities of businessmen and politicians may seem to be on the surface, they have at bottom the ferocity and the irrationality of animal life. Near the end of *The Titan,* in describing the Illinois legislature, Dreiser makes clear his theme, as well as his fictional method: "The surface might appear commonplace—ordinary men of the state of Illinois going here and there ... yet a jungle-like complexity was present, a dark, rank growth of horrific but avid life—life at the full, life knife in hand, life blazing with courage and dripping at the jaws with hunger" (*T* [*The Titan*], p. 516). He is aided by the dead metaphors of animal life which are a part of business and political talk: "wildcat banks," "bulls" and "bears" of the market, a "stalking horse," "small-fry politicians," "one-horse banks," "watch-dogs" of treasuries, "political sharks," and politicians "waiting to get their noses in the trough" (*F* [*The Financier*], pp. 34, 41, 350, 453, et passim; *T,* pp. 366, 421, 514, 534). The conversations of Cowperwood and his associates are full of commonplace animal comparisons like "It's a case of dog eat dog in this game."[11] Dreiser develops and extends this traditional similarity with fresh, precise variations. Traders on the stock exchange are "like a lot of gulls or stormy petrels, hanging on the lee of the wind, hungry and anxious to snap up any unwary fish" (*F,* p. 43); and at Chicago's Union Club the luncheon table is ringed by "eyes and jaws which varied from those of the tiger, lynx, and bear to those of the fox, the tolerant mastiff, and the surly bulldog."[12] As each character enters Cowperwood's career, Dreiser sketches his appearance, very often in animal terms: Warden Desmas has "even-edged, savage-looking teeth, which showed the least bit in a slightly wolfish way when he smiled" (*F,* p. 444). Occasionally, through carelessness or unrestrained enthusiasm for the method, he makes a character a multi-animal: Laughlin "had a thick growth of upstanding hair looking not unlike a rooster's comb ... [and] a slightly aquiline nose. ... His eyes were as clear and sharp as those of a lynx. ... His one companion was a small spaniel, simple and affectionate, a she dog, Jennie by name, with whom he slept" (*T,* p. 23). Often, however, the comparisons are apt and ingenious: the first Mrs. Cowperwood's mind is described as "oyster-like in its functioning, or, perhaps better, clam-like, [with] its little siphon of thought-processes forced up or down into the mighty ocean of fact and circumstance" (*F,* pp. 244-245).

Dreiser forces the reader's attention to the animal-man comparison not only by beginning *The Financier* with the lobster-squid battle but also by ending it with a little sermon about *Mycteroperca Bonaci,* the Black Grouper, a huge fish capable of simulating its surroundings by controlling its pigmentation. Because it has been created "tricky and deceptive" to "all honest life-seeking fish," it suggests to Dreiser that "the constructive genius of nature . . . is not beatific," and that Man's "feet are in the trap of circumstance; his eyes are on an illusion" (*F,* pp. 501-502). This treatise, "Concerning *Mycteroperca Bonaci,*" is an awkward addition to the novel, an attempt to foreshadow the disillusionment yet to come to Cowperwood, even though he leaves the novel full of "youth and wealth and a notable vigor of body" (*F,* p. 499). As in a similar essay at the end of **The Titan** ("In Retrospect"), Dreiser here seems to recognize that he has not adequately objectified his argument that Cowperwood, in spite of his dreams of power and beauty and his intense animal energy, is doomed to disillusionment and failure at last. Dreiser has created a Cowperwood on such a grand scale that he dwarfs the puny men who surround him, just as F. Scott Fitzgerald drew Gatsby so large in comparison to the Tom Buchanans that the reader may not sufficiently understand Gatsby's serious flaws.

Bound to the Charles Yerkes story as he was, Dreiser could, through the major incidents, only show Cowperwood with temporary defeats at the conclusions of **The Financier** and **The Titan.** He relies upon his manipulation of the animal imagery, however, to imply the ambiguity of Cowperwood's character, his position, and his ultimate success; for Cowperwood, like the Black Grouper, takes on a variety of appearances. To the business rivals who hate him, he is "a ravening wolf," "slippery as an eel," with "the heart of a hyena and the friendliness of a scorpion"; and when Dreiser pictures him as fighting his lonely battles with his competitors, he calls him "a wolf prowling under glittering, bitter stars in the night, . . . looking down into the humble folds of simple men" and "a canny wolf prowling in a forest of trees of his own creation" (*F,* pp. 380, 495; *T,* 220, 286, 398). Although even Cowperwood's business rivals must admire his courage and speak of him as "A very lion of a man. . . . A man with the heart of a Numidian lion" (*T,* p. 437), in the Philadelphia prison where he spends more than a year his most savage activity is trapping the rats that infest his cell (*F,* pp. 436 ff.).

In his numerous love affairs, Cowperwood's fortunes are no more stable, and their instability suggested in shifting animal metaphors. When Cowperwood first meets Aileen, she reminds him of "a high-stepping horse without a check-rein" (*F,* p. 89). A man like Cowperwood who "could not endure poor horse-flesh" (*T,* p. 19) might be expected to tire of Aileen as she ages; "You'd like to turn me off like an old horse," she charges (*T,* p. 503), and she is

right. But ironically Cowperwood soon finds in Berenice Fleming another "likely filly [with] the signs and lineaments of the future winner of a Derby . . . the air, the grace, the lineage, the blood . . . and she appealed to him . . . as no other woman before had ever done" (*T,* p. 358). Berenice herself, however, is an ambiguous animal; she has "cat-like eyes," moves with "cat-like grace," can affect the languid air of "a chilly cat," and catches fish with her hands; but when she catches a young baby sparrow she insists to Cowperwood that the mother bird will not mind because "'She knows I am not a cat,' . . . The word 'cat' had a sharp, sweet sound in her mouth" (*T,* pp. 351, 361, 394, 396, 550).[13]

Although animal imagery is more fully exploited in the Cowperwood novels than in **Sister Carrie,** the imagery of the stormy sea and the tossing ship are also continued strongly. Life is a "mighty ocean of fact and circumstance" (*F,* p. 245) where "there is no tracing to the ultimate sources all the winds of influence that play upon a given barque—all the breaths of chance that fill or desert our bellies or our sagging sails" (*T,* p. 188), for "the impediments that can arise to baffle a great and swelling career are strange and various. In some instances all the cross-waves of life must be cut by the strong swimmer. With other personalities there is a chance, or force, that happily allies itself with them; or they quite unconsciously ally themselves with it, and find that there is a tide that bears them on" (*T,* p. 251). This tide, however, which seemed to carry the will-less Carrie Meeber through her life, now begins in the **Cowperwood books** to be attached in Dreiser's mind to a transcendental vision of ultimate order, foreshadowing his preoccupation with the mystical experience in **The Bulwark.** Nature itself displays an "instinct" toward wholeness and order, to be perceived "in the drifting of sea-wood to the Sargasso Sea, in the geometric interrelation of air-bubbles on the surface of still water . . . as through the physical substance of life—this apparition of form which the eye detects and calls real—were shot through with some vast subtlety that loves order, that is order" (*F,* pp. 363-364). Dreiser's language takes on the confidence of the early Emerson when he extends this instinct toward order to the individual: "The atoms of our so-called *being,* in spite of our so-called *reason*—the dreams of a mood—know where to go and what to do. They represent an order, a wisdom, a willing that is not of us" (*F,* p. 364). Although Cowperwood doubts "the existence of a kindly, over-ruling Providence" because of "the unheralded storms out of clear skies—financial, social, anything you choose—that so often brought ruin and disaster to so many" (*F,* p. 226), he fails to recognize that his activities are responsible for at least some of "the ruffled surface of the angry sea that he had blown to fury" (*T,* p. 548), and that these activities are themselves the means by which "God, or the life force" maintains itself as "an equation." "In the end a balance is invariably struck wherein the mass subdues the individual or the individual the mass—for the time being. For behold, the sea is ever dancing or raging … without variation how could the balance be maintained?" (*T*, p. 551).

The animal imagery and the sea imagery are occasionally combined in passages which, although individually distracting and ineffective, demonstrate the connection in Dreiser's mind between the animal world and the sea. He speaks of a "storm of wildcat money which was floating about" and a jury of "assorted social fry which the dragnets of the court, cast into the ocean of the city, bring to the surface" (*F*, pp. 2, 330). Cowperwood's "curiously leonine glare which went over [Aileen] like a dash of cold water" (*T*, p. 109) indicates the fading of his love for her, which was "to leave her high and dry on land, as a fish out of its native element, to take all the wind out of her sails—almost to kill her" (*T*, pp. 109, 145). These well-worn metaphors suggest again the base of popular figurative language, here particularly the language of business, upon with Dreiser built his imagery. Cowperwood and his associates "float" schemes, and when there is trouble, they "trim sails" or "shorten sail" (*T*, pp. 41, 103, 400). But the humble origins of Dreiser's imagery are not so important as the great numbers of variations which he plays upon them. His unfortunate attachment to such words as "trig" and "chemic" have often been noticed by his critics, but the word of which he is fondest in the Cowperwood novels is neither of these; it is "storm." On the level of diction at least, ***The Financier*** and ***The Titan*** are as stormy as *Moby Dick*. Cowperwood, caught in the panic raised by the Chicago fire, tries to "weather the storm" (*F*, p. 190), thinking that "this storm would surely blow over" (*F*, p. 169), but when the clamor increases, he seeks "any port in a storm" (*F*, p. 373). He convinces the city treasurer Stener that "it's a case of sink or swim" for both of them (*F*, p. 203), and to try to save himself, commits a crime involving the city's "sinking fund" (*F*, p. 232), for which he is sent to prison. There he welcomes the sympathy of his cell overseer as "any straw to a drowning man."[14]

Like ***Sister Carrie,*** Cowperwood betrays his fear of the stormy world of finance by trying to construct quiet chambers where he may escape into an illusion of success and peace. In this tendency he is aided by Aileen, whose seduction is not accompanied so much by a desire to share Cowperwood's struggles as by a desire to find with him a relief from the storm; her dream is "a yacht on the sea with him, a palace somewhere—just they two" (*F*, p. 144). This palace of escape from struggle is, as in ***Sister Carrie,*** often given an *Arabian Nights* flavor. Dreiser describes the first liaison

of the two thus: "There was a cold, snowy street visible through the interstices of the hangings of the windows, and gas-lamps flickering outside. He had come in early, and hearing Aileen, he came to where she was seated at the piano. She was wearing a rough, gray wool cloth dress, ornately banded with fringed Oriental embroidery in blue and burnt-orange. … On her fingers were four or five rings, far too many—an opal, an emerald, a ruby, a diamond—flashing visibly as she played" (*F*, p. 137). Nor is Aileen the only one of Cowperwood's women to whom he is drawn because of "all the Orient richness she represented" (*T*, p. 37). When he tires of Aileen, he finds Stephanie Platow who is "like something out of Asia" (*T*, p. 212), and when he discovers Stephanie nude and "curled up in the corner of a suggestive oriental divan" with a newspaper reporter, he thinks that "in an older day, if they had lived in Turkey, he would have had her strangled, sewn in a sack, and thrown into the Bosporus. As it was, he could only dismiss her" (*T*, pp. 237-239). Later he is drawn to Berenice Fleming, "as charming a figure as one would have wished to see—part Greek, part Oriental" (*T*, p. 457), who can translate him "as by the wave of a fairy wand, into another realm" (*T*, pp. 393, 397). To her he holds out the possibility of a beautiful house to overcome the social stigma of her procuress mother, "almost an Arabian situation," as she thinks of it, "heightened by the glitter of gold" (*T*, p. 497).

However stormy the sea outside may be, the inside of Cowperwood's palaces are keyed to a painting which he purchased for his Chicago mansion—"A particularly brilliant Gerôme, then in the heyday of his exotic popularity—a picture of nude odalisques of the harem, idling beside the highly colored stone marquetry of an oriental bath" (*T*, p. 68). The palatial chambers which Cowperwood builds for his wives and mistresses, however, are not so much Levantine as Mediterranean, and his make-believe role is not so much master of a harem as a Renaissance merchant prince.[15] Yet none of Cowperwood's mansions finally gives him shelter from the storms of life. The treasures in his Philadelphia house are sold, and the palaces which await him are the battlemented towers of Moyamensing Prison (*F*, p. 366), and later the Eastern District Penitentiary of Pennsylvania, "not at all unlike the palace of the Sforzas at Milan" (*F*, 427). At the end of *The Titan* he is forced out of his New York mansion to come back to Chicago to defend himself in the Chicago city hall, a "large, ponderous structure of black granite … suggesting somewhat the somnolent architecture of ancient Egypt" which contains not isolated luxury but "a sea of unfriendly faces" and "as hungry and bold a company of gray wolves as was ever gathered under one roof" (*T*, pp. 542, 543). Like Hurstwood and Carrie, Cowperwood has been the dupe of a false Aladdin; the stormy waves and the cries of animal life enter even into his chambers, and he has "no ultimate peace, no real understanding, but only hunger and thirst and wonder" (*T*, p. 552). He discovers that he is "quite as other men, subject to the same storms, the same danger of shipwreck. Only he was a better sailor than most" (*T*, p. 166).

## IV

For all its apparent concern with the workings of American society and legal machinery, *An American Tragedy* is, with the possible exception of *The "Genius,"* more an "interior" novel than anything which Dreiser had written up to this time. It is documentary, but it documents the internal states of Clyde Griffiths, rather than the risings and fallings of the public fortune of a man like Cowperwood. The symbolic structure of *An American Tragedy* is also significantly different. The conflict which gave *Sister Carrie* and the Cowperwood novels their central unity—the conflict between the seemingly impersonal, inhuman workings of an indifferent universe and the yearning of the individual for a realization of beauty and security—was presented in two opposing sets of images, the universe as a sea or a jungle and the world of dreams as a magic harbor or chamber. Now in *An American Tragedy* the animal imagery becomes so infrequent and diffuse that most of the examples seem to be the result of habit rather than of conscious intent; the few really functional instances are the concentration of references to Clyde as a harried animal in the short time between Roberta's death and his seizure by the agents of the law. Furthermore, the imagery of the sea and the tempest has almost entirely disappeared, or rather has been transformed into the more restricted images of a lake or a pool. What remains constant in Dreiser's imagery is the motif of *The Arabian Nights*. Although one may suspect that the *Arabian Nights* imagery of the early books derived from an unconscious imitation of nineteenth-century pseudo-romances and popular plays, Dreiser in *An American Tragedy* developed it more fully than in any of the earlier novels and used it to provide the central fable of Clyde Griffiths' life. In place of the tension between the actuality of a turbulent sea and the illusion of a secure chamber which provided the central contrast of the earlier novels, Dreiser has in *An American Tragedy* substituted the theme of the ambiguity of reality, symbolized by the glittering lake which is transformed into a pool of death, and an Aladdin's cave which is transformed into a tomb.

The imagery of *The Arabian Nights* provides the symbolic structure for *An American Tragedy.* Late in Clyde's trial, his defense attorney points to this structure most directly when he speaks of Clyde's attraction to Sondra as "a case

of the Arabian Nights, of the ensorcelled and the ensorcellor ... a case of being bewitched ... by beauty, love, wealth, by things that we sometimes think we want very, very much, and cannot ever have."[16] Although Clyde does not understand what the lawyer means, and the lawyer himself is merely indulging in rhetoric for the jury, he has provided the key to Dreiser's dominant image of Clyde. Throughout its 800 pages the novel is permeated with the quality of Scheherazade's tales, from the beginning description of Clyde as a twelve-year old boy with "a certain emotionalism and exotic sense of romance" and a "vivid and intelligent imagination" (I, 10) to the end in the death house, where Clyde is given a gift of a copy of *The Arabian Nights* by a man condemned to death "for poisoning an old man of great wealth" (II, 362, 369). Again the language with which Dreiser explores Clyde's personality is less the language of science than the language of romance; "chemisms" are spoken of much less frequently than "dreams," the key word of this novel. Clyde has "wishes," "phantasies," and "visions"; he sees and hears "apparitions," "genii," "effrits," "ghosts," "giants," "ouphes," "barghests," and "ogres"; and he and the other characters are "ensorcelled," "enchanted," "enslaved," "infatuated," "entranced," and "transported" by "witchery" and by dreams which are "mysterious" and "insubstantial," and visions which "materialize."[17]

More particularly, three stories of *The Arabian Nights* sequence are relevant to the life of Clyde Griffiths—"The History of Aladdin, or the Wonderful Lamp," "The History of the Barber's Fifth Brother," and "The History of the Fisherman." As in *Sister Carrie,* it is the first of these stories which is most frequently mentioned, but here the parallels are more explicit. Like Aladdin, Clyde is a poor boy who disregards the advice of his parents; and like Aladdin, he is conducted into a cavern by a long-lost uncle, who tries to keep him imprisoned until he discovers the magic ring and lamp which provide him wealth, social position, and a beautiful wife. Clyde's imagination is his own genie of the lamp, however. Coupled with his inexperience, it is capable of transforming vulgarity and gaudiness into exotic beauty. When he first visits a house of prostitution, "having pushed through the curtains of heavy velvet ... Clyde found himself in a bright and rather gaudy general parlor or reception room, the walls of which were ornamented with gilt-framed pictures of nude or seminude girls and some very high pier mirrors. ... It was really quite an amazing and Aladdin-like scene to him" (I, 63, 65). The hotel in which he works, however gauche Dreiser and the reader may find it, is to Clyde a wonder of his world: "[through] a green-marbled doorway ... he beheld a lobby ... more arresting, quite, than anything he had seen before. It was all so lavish. Under his feet was a checkered black-and-white marble floor. Above him a coppered and stained and gilded ceiling. And supporting this, a veritable forest of black marble columns as highly polished as the floor—glassy smooth. ... He gazed about in awe and amazement" (I, 29-30). Later Dreiser carefully poses Clyde at the doorway to the Griffiths factory and then the Griffiths house in an attitude of awe at an excitingly new world (I, 189-190, 219-220), and magically these doors respond to his "Open, Sesame!" It must be remembered that many of Clyde Griffiths' dreams are accomplished. His dreams of a job as bell-boy at the Green-Davidson are fulfilled, and he is ecstatic in his delight: "Kind Heaven! What a realization of paradise! What a consummation of luxury!" (I, 33, 37); each tip is "a mysterious and yet sacred vision" (I, 41). His dream of an outing with Hortense Briggs is made possible by the sudden appearance of a Packard which belonged to "an elderly and very wealthy man who at the time was traveling in Asia" (I 123). Later in Chicago his uncle, imagined as "a king of Croesus, living in ease and luxury there in the east" (I, 14), suddenly appears at the Chicago Union League Club to offer him a new opportunity just after Clyde had "wished and wished that he could get into some work where he could rise and be somebody" (I, 175). Still later we find Clyde canoeing on Crum Lake, lonely and wishing that Roberta Alden were with him, when she appears on the shore; Clyde's face is "lit by the radiance of one who had suddenly, and beyond his belief, realized a dream," while to Roberta, Clyde is "a pleasant apparition suddenly evoked out of nothing and nowhere, a poetic effort taking form out of smoke or vibrant energy" (I, 265). And finally Clyde, as the result of an accidental meeting at night before the gates of a Wykeagy Avenue palace, is taken up by Sondra Finchley, "a princess" (I, 315), a "goddess in her shrine of gilt and tinsel" (I, 323), "a star, a paragon of luxury and social supremacy" (I, 374), whose glances "enslave" him (I, 315, 323, 341, 374). Some of Clyde's wishes and dreams are indeed "materialized."

The successful Aladdin, however, was only one of the poor youths in *The Arabian Nights* sequence; Alnashar, the Barber's Fifth Brother, is in some respects closer to Clyde Griffiths. Alnashar, it may be remembered, is a lazy, imaginative, and talkative youth who inherits 100 drachms of silver, and invests his inheritance in a stock of bottles and glass objects which he displays for sale on a tray. While waiting for customers he dreams of how he will sell his glasses, reinvest his profits in more glasses, and so on until he has 100,000 drachms, which enable him to dress like a prince, give gifts to the grand vizier, and demand his beautiful daughter as a bride. Then after his marriage he will pretend to lose interest in his bride, and

when she and her mother come to plead for his favor, he will push them away violently. At this point Alnashar's dream becomes so real to him that he thrusts out his foot and knocks his tray of glasses to the street, where they lie in fragments. Although Dreiser mentions Alnashar at only one point in the novel (I, 317), he describes Clyde's Alnashar dreams many times: "To be able to wear such a suit with such ease and air! To be able to talk to a girl after the manner and with the sang-froid of some of these gallants! ... And once he did attain it—was able to wear such clothes as these—well, then was he not well set upon the path that leads to all blisses? ... The friendly smiles! The secret handclasps, maybe—an arm about the waist of someone or another—a kiss—a promise of marriage—and then, and then!"[18] Furthermore, Clyde is like Alnashar, who continued to be victimized throughout his life because of his impractical dreaming, in that he never really *learns*. The "dream" just quoted comes when Clyde is fifteen; another, equally Alnashar-like, comes when he is twenty-one. Between the two he has had his dream of securing Hortense Briggs shattered by a discovery of her vulgar self-centeredness, his dream of rising in the hotel business shattered by a procession of unrewarding jobs, his dream of rising rapidly in the Griffiths factory shattered by the drudgery which his relatives prescribe for him, and his dream of having Roberta as lover without any responsibility for her shattered by the discovery of her pregnancy. Critics who emphasize society's responsibility for Clyde's failure forget how really foolish Clyde is. Mason, the district attorney who solves Clyde's murder plot and takes him into custody in less than four days time, contemptuously calls Clyde "a dunce" (II, 150), and Dreiser frequently underlines Clyde's thoughtlessness with phrases like "no thought," "none of the compulsion of the practical," "no serious consideration," "no more plan than this," "he hadn't really thought about that," "he had not even stopped to look," and "he had never thought of them" (II, 5, 8, 17, 61, 129, 135). Clyde's lack of practical wisdom cannot be explained by his limited childhood training, however unrelated his parents' religious teachings seem to be to "the world." Like Alnashar, he "had a soul that was not destined to grow up. He lacked decidedly that mental clarity and inner directing application that in so many permits them to sort out from the facts and avenues of life the particular thing or things that make for their direct advancement" (I, 174). The seeming inevitability of Clyde's failure depends upon our accepting the fact that he never learns from his experience, that he remains the adolescent dreamer into his twenties.

The third story of *The Arabian Nights* which has relevance to the novel is the "History of the Fisherman" who on the third cast of his nets into the sea brings up a jar from which, when it is unsealed, a black smoke issues into the shape of a genie, or efrit. The efrit has power to reward the fisherman for releasing it, but unaccountably proceeds to threaten the fisherman with death; finally the fisherman tricks the efrit into returning to the jar for a moment, and stoppers the jar with Solomon's seal forever. Clyde is neither so suspicious nor so resourceful as the fisherman. He is faced with a need to rid himself of Roberta Alden, who blocks his acquisition of Sondra as "the central or crowning jewel to so much sudden and such Aladdin-like splendor" (II, 8). Then he reads a newspaper account of a double drowning in another state just before he drives to a lake with Sondra and her friends. The conjunction of these three events is enough to bring forth "as the genii at the accidental rubbing of Aladdin's lamp—as the efrit emerging as smoke from the mystic jar in the net of the fisherman—the very substance of some leering and diabolic wish or wisdom concealed in his own nature" (II, 48). Dreiser combines the language of *The Arabian Nights,* Freudian psychology, and Christian theology as he personifies Clyde's "darker or primordial and unregenerate nature" and "his darkest and weakest side" as a "Giant Efrit . . . the Efrit of his own darker self," speaking in the "sealed and silent hall" of his brain in language ambiguously like that of the inscriptions on the walls of his parents' mission, "Behold! I bring you a way. It is the way of the lake" (II, 49-56). Before this "genii of his darkest and weakest side" Clyde seems powerless to stopper the jar of his secret wishes or to drive them away with his will.

Because he suggests "the way of the lake" (II, 53), the ambiguity of this genie is all the more terrifying. The life of the turbulent sea which surrounded Carrie and Cowperwood was unambiguous; it was a dangerous actuality, however unpredictable. Clyde, however, tries not so much to find a safe harbor from stormy seas as to find a place on a lake which will not change its character beneath him. It will be noticed that Clyde's love affairs are frequently prosecuted on water. He comes nearest to intimacy with Hortense Briggs (whose dream is a beaver coat) on the ice of a river near Excelsior Springs. When he arrives in Lycurgus, he soon begins to feel that his position as a Griffiths raises him above dancing to "Dream Boat" with Rita Dickerman and Zella Shuman, and he learns to swim, dive, and manage a canoe so that he will have the accomplishments valued by the Griffiths and their friends. As he paddles his canoe alone on Crum Lake, he discovers Roberta Alden on the shore and takes her into his canoe to pick water lilies, but even while he is on Crum Lake with Roberta he thinks that "had fortune favored him in the first place by birth, he would now be in some canoe on Schroon or Racquette or Champlain Lake with Sondra Finchley or

some such girl" (I, 263). Sondra, unlike Roberta, is literally at home on the lake, in her family's new bungalow on Twelfth Lake, "right down at the water's edge" (I, 153), and she appears in a Lycurgus parade as an Indian maiden in a flower-covered canoe on the Mohawk (I, 241). To Clyde, Roberta soon comes to symbolize everything associated with his unhappy past—poverty, naiveté, sensuality warring with an uncertain primness, at best Crum Lake; Sondra, on the other hand, suggests wealth, sophistication, an easy confident manner, the social climate of Twelfth Lake. Dreiser catches this opposition in a single image: outside the Griffiths factory where Roberta stamps collars and where Clyde is assistant foreman is the river; "through the many open windows that reached from floor to ceiling could be seen the Mohawk swirling and rippling . . . always [seeming] to hint of pleasures which might be found by idling along its shores" (I, 243).

How is Clyde to rid himself of Roberta and get Sondra? "Because of his own great interest in . . . any form of water life" (II, 23), he is attracted to the newspaper story of the accidental drowning of a couple on Pass Lake, Massachusetts. Some days later, after a trip to Big Bittern Lake with Sondra and her friends, Clyde meets his "genii," the embodiment of his overwhelming desire to do away with Roberta: "Would you escape from the demands of Roberta that but now and unto this hour have appeared unescapable to you? Behold! I bring you a way. It is the way of the lake—Pass Lake" (II, 49). The way of Pass Lake, enacted on Big Bittern Lake, will be, Clyde thinks, the way for him to pass forever from Crum Lake to Twelfth Lake.

As Clyde, the witless Aladdin, stumbles toward a seeming solution to his troubles, taking Roberta up the Mohawk to Utica, then on to Grass Lake, and finally to Big Bittern Lake, his life becomes more nightmare than actuality. He leaves such obvious clues behind him that a country lawyer can arrest him forty-eight hours from the time that Roberta's body is discovered. It is not simply that Clyde is stupid or inept (he has considerable success in his relationships with Sondra and her friends); rather he is moving *in* a dream and *toward* a dream of release and oblivion. When he takes Roberta into the boat on Big Bittern Lake, he recalls the details of their first outing on Crum Lake, but *this* lake and *this* Roberta are unreal: "an almost nebulous figure, she now seemed, stepping down into an insubstantial rowboat upon a purely ideational lake." The lake itself is magically shifting in shape. Behind an island the lake seemed to contain another lake within it, "an especially arranged pool or tarn to which one who was weary of life and cares—anxious to be away from the strife and contentions of the world, might most wisely and yet gloomily repair . . . where there was no end of anything—no plots—

no plans—no practical problems to be solved—nothing . . . the water itself looking like a huge black pearl cast by some mighty hand, in anger possibly, in sport or phantasy maybe" (II, 70, 74).

The Way of the Lake proves illusory for Clyde. The Big Bittern is a real lake, composed of real water which remains on his suit even when he carries it in his bag to Twelfth Lake. The lake does not accept Roberta into nothingness, but gives her up on a grappling hook along with Clyde's camera containing the snapshots that he had taken of her just before her drowning. The Way of the Lake does not make Sondra secure for Clyde: he never sees her again after his arrest, and the few hours he has with her before his arrest are filled with suffering as he watches her play at drowning in her boat on Twelfth Lake. Clyde's trial is not so much an unjust dispensing of "justice," as some of Dreiser's critics have suggested, as it is an indication of how inexorably the world moves on, how far it is removed from a fairy tale. Clyde's killing of Roberta was an actual killing, not a magic way to success. His world was a world in which his actions were related to others, not merely existing in isolation. "How people seemed to remember things," Clyde marvels during his trial, "more than ever he would have dreamed they would have" (II, 229).

## V

If the epigraph for **Sister Carrie** might have been "She was . . . a lone figure on a tossing, thoughtless sea," that of **The Bulwark** might have been "He leadeth me beside the still waters." The world of **The Bulwark** is no longer that of the turbulent sea or the savage jungle, no longer that of the ambiguous lake, but one in which the lion and the lamb finally lie down together along a quiet stream. Lever Creek, clear, cool, and quiet, meanders through the novel, lacing together the various episodes which take place upon it, introducing the major motifs, and providing the central image for the transcendental wisdom which Solon Barnes finally attains. It is a source of inspiration for Solon's father, who, when he comes to Thornbrough, sets about restoring the banks of the stream from "neglect and decay" to make them "not sinful or wasteful ever—just gay and clean."[19] His improvements to the arbor, the benches, and the paths along the stream lead Rufus Barnes to resolve the conflict between his Quaker desire for simplicity and his love of comfort; convinced that his accumulation of property is evidence of a stewardship intended by God, he has the motto "He leadeth me beside the still waters" painted on his bedroom wall (p. 26). It is beside the creek that Solon confesses his love for Benecia, who becomes his wife, and the creek becomes a symbol to them of the blessed, protected existence which they want for their children.

Nevertheless, the episode in which the young Solon, his future wife Benecia, and his cousin Rhoda catch the minnows in the Thornbrough pool with dip nets foreshadows the trials which later come to the Barnes family. Rhoda, who years later will assist two of Solon's children to escape the restrictions their father has placed upon them, sees the fishing merely as good sport: "We'll have some fun," she says. "See if we can't outwit some of these minnows" (p. 69). Benecia, whose later concern and affection for her children shows itself only in sentimental gestures, says "I don't want to keep any of the little fishes out of the water too long. . . . If I do catch any, I'll put them right back. That'll teach them to be more watchful" (p. 70). Solon's reply, "Teaching minnows to be careful will certainly keep thee busy," foreshadows his later role as law-giver, when he comes to believe that life is "a series of law-governed details [and] . . . that those who were caught in the nets of evil paid dearly in this world or the next, or both" (pp. 70, 90).

As Solon and his children leave Lever Creek, they enter the world of **Sister Carrie, The Financier,** or **An American Tragedy** with the characteristic violent sea and lake imagery of those novels. It is on the beach of a lake that the boy Solon first meets violence in the person of Walter Hokutt, the town bully; and it is on the beach sands of Atlantic City that Solon's son Stewart is initiated into sex and later is involved in the seduction and death of a young girl, in a manner reminiscent of Clyde Griffiths' actions on the New York lakes. Solon's children share the dreams of success, longings for beauty, and strong sexual desires with Dreiser's earlier characters. His son Orville becomes a Gilbert Griffiths and his daughter Dorothea a Sondra Finchley, their Quaker upbringing adding only a certain blandness to their social-climbing. Isobel and Etta are college-educated Carries, filled with longings for beauty and excitement not to be found at Thornbrough. Stewart, as we have said, re-enacts Clyde Griffiths' entrapment by sexual desire and panic, and commits suicide while awaiting trial for his part in the death of a young girl. Solon himself is drawn into the Cowperwood world of finance, where he finds that the directors of his bank value him chiefly as a respectable front behind which they may manipulate their investments.[20]

Shocked by his own failure and the failures of his children, Solon leaves the bank in Philadelphia for the banks of Lever Creek. "Lift up your heads, you that have come through and beyond all outward washings, unto the Lamb of God, that your robes may be washed white in His Blood; that thereby you may overcome and then sit down in the Kingdom with weary Abraham, thoroughly tried Isaac, and wrestling Jacob," says a sermon given him by a friend (p. 296). If it is not literally true that Solon finds the Lamb of God near the Creek, he does regain through a mystical experience the love for "all people and things" which "raised him out of the black shadow of grief that had all but removed him from life itself, and now caused his sympathy and interest to reach out again—to [Etta] and Isobel, to the flowers and insects and the fish in Lever Creek" (p. 331).

Two incidents lead this "thoroughly tried Isaac" to humility and a new sense of the superiority of love over law. First, Solon sees "an exquisitely colored and designed green fly" eating the small bud of a plant; "why was this beautiful creature, whose design so delighted him, compelled to feed upon another living creature, a beautiful flower? ... Which was intended to live—the fly, the bud, or both?" (pp. 316-317). This scene is an obvious parallel to that in *The Financier* when the young Cowperwood watches the lobster devour the squid and finds in that elemental struggle a rationale for his own ruthless rise to power. But Dreiser's animal world is no longer a savage jungle; it is a peaceable kingdom. If the Quaker teachings of John Woolman, George Fox, and Rufus Jones provided many of the ideas of *The Bulwark*,[21] the paintings of the Quaker primitive, Edward Hicks, could have provided the imagery. Instead of turning from Lever Creek to immerse himself again in the financial world of Philadelphia, as Cowperwood would have done, Solon Barnes goes on to examine the habits of fish, birds, butterflies, vines, flowers, and grass. He experiences "a kind of religious awe and wonder" recognizing that "surely there must be a Creative Divinity, and so a purpose, behind all of this variety and beauty and tragedy of life" (p. 317). In this mood of wonder and resignation, Solon later steps near a puff-adder, vicious and threatening in its appearance, but amenable to evidences of Solon's good intentions toward it. As the snake quietly turns from its attitude of hostility and crosses over Solon's feet, Solon's sense of divine purpose becomes more explicit; not only is there a Creative Divinity with a purpose, but this purpose is good: "Good intent is of itself a universal language, and if our intention is good, all creatures in their particular way understand, and so it was that this puff-adder understood me just as I understood it. ... And now I thank God for this revelation of His universal presence and His good intent toward all things—all of His created world. For otherwise how would it understand me, and I it, if we were not both a part of Himself?" (p. 319).

This peaceable kingdom in which snakes discover good intentions and flies eat flowers for the good of both is as far removed from the Philadelphia financial world and the prison in which Solon's son commits suicide in despair as the world of *The Arabian Nights* was from the everyday world of Carrie Meeber or Clyde Griffiths. But now the

fairy land has become the *real* world, and the world of struggle and torment only illusory. Even Etta, temporarily guilt-ridden by her disloyalty to her father's teachings, is caught up in the experience of divine love, and she regains her childhood wisdom—a "wisdom that is related to beauty only, that concerns itself with cloud forms and the wild vines' tendrils, whose substance is not substance, but dreams only, and those dreams are entangled with the hopes and the yearnings of all men" (p. 130). For the Dreiser of *The Bulwark*, as for the boy Stewart Barnes, no longer was there need for "fairy tales of Jack and the Beanstalk, Bluebeard, or Sinbad the Sailor" to distract one from an actual world of struggle. "This mystic, colorful world was fairy-land enough" (p. 142).

His primary groups of symbols—of water, animals, and fairyland—have shifted in their suggestions through the course of his career and have traced the central meaning of his novels. The water is first the turbulent sea of society, then the lake of private guilt, and finally the still stream of the Inner Light; the animals first inhabit a jungle but later a peaceable kingdom; and the hopes and desires of men turn out not to be false promises of a genie before Aladdin's Cave but the transcendental knowledge of the goodness of things which one discovers as he walks along Lever Creek. Dreiser's relentless questioning has taken him from the "external" naturalism of **Sister Carrie** and the **Cowperwood books,** through the "internal" naturalism of *An American Tragedy,* to the transcendental acceptance of *The Bulwark.*

### Notes

1. *The Financier* (New York, 1927, rev. ed.), p. 135. F. O. Matthiessen, *Theodore Dreiser* (New York, 1951) and Alexander Kern, "Dreiser's Difficult Beauty," *Western Review,* XVI (Winter 1952), 129-136, find some merit in Dreiser's style. The common view is still that of Thomas K. Whipple, *Spokesmen: Modern Writers and American Life* (New York, 1928), pp. 71, 73: "His style is atrocious, his sentences are chaotic, his grammar and syntax faulty; he has no feeling for words, no sense of diction. ... [His writing lacks] any sort of beauty—beauty of form, of imagery, of rhythm."

2. *Sister Carrie,* ed. Kenneth S. Lynn (New York, 1957), pp. 10, 11. Further references to *Sister Carrie* are made to this edition, and will be incorporated into the text. In his introduction to this edition Kenneth Lynn briefly discusses the sea imagery of *Sister Carrie,* as does Matthiessen, pp. 83-84.

3. When Hurstwood speaks of his own dissatisfaction with life, Carrie pities him: "To think ... that he

needed to make such an appeal when she herself was lonely and without anchor" (p. 119). When Drouet inquires about the frequency of Hurstwood's visits, Carrie lies to him because she is "all at sea mentally" (p. 125). Hurstwood himself is not immune to storms of feeling. When he watches Carrie play the role of "a cold, white, helpless object" in an amateur drama, he "blinked his eyes and caught the infection. The radiating waves of feeling and sincerity were already breaking against the farthest walls of the chamber. The magic of passion which will yet dissolve the world, was here at work" (p. 166).

4. Pp. 184-186. Hurstwood's relationship to his wife is also charted in terms of water. Because of his attraction to Carrie, the "river of indifference" (p. 128) which ran between Hurstwood and his wife is soon flooded by a storm, which approaches slowly; their arguments are "really precipitated by an atmosphere which was surcharged with dissension. That it would shower, with a sky so full of blackening thunderclouds, would scarcely be thought worthy of comment" (p. 188). Searching for something to justify her jealousy, Mrs. Hurstwood awaits "the clear proof of one overt deed ... the cold breath needed to convert the lowering clouds of suspicion into a rain of wrath" (p. 190). When she learns merely that Hurstwood has been seen riding with a strange woman, the incident is not conclusive enough. "Only the atmosphere of distrust and ill-feeling was strengthened, precipitating every now and then little sprinklings of irritable conversation, enlivened by flashes of wrath" (p. 191). But when the storm finally comes, with Mrs. Hurstwood's announcement that she has discovered enough about her husband to enable her to dictate terms to him her manner is so cool and cynical that "somehow it took the wind out of his sails. He could not attack her, he could not ask her for proofs. ... He was like a vessel, powerful and dangerous, but rolling and floundering without sail" (p. 198).

5. Kenneth Lynn has observed the degree to which *Sister Carrie* is theatrical: "the theatrical world was to Dreiser a microcosm of the glamorous city, a quintessence of its artificial splendors" (p. xii). Though this is to some extent true, it misses the point. In *Sister Carrie* the shoe factory, the West Side flat, the street-car line, and the Bowery flophouse are closer to Dreiser's conception of the quintessence of the city; the theater is rather an escape from the city's ugly reality. It is the fairy tale world of illusion, an "elf land" toward which Carrie drifts to escape "the grim world without" (p. 341). The theater in

which she first appears professionally is a "large, empty, shadowy playhouse, still redolent of the perfumes and blazonry of the night, and notable for its rich oriental appearance" (p. 345), and her first minor success comes as she plays "one of a group of oriental beauties who ... were paraded by the vizier before the new potentate as the treasures of his harem" (p. 386) in a comic opera called "The Wives of Abdul." As her popularity increases, there are stage-door genii to offer her whatever she wants: "I could give you every luxury. There isn't anything you could ask for that you couldn't have ... I love you and wish to gratify your every desire," and her $150 a week seems to be "a door to an Aladdin's cave" (pp. 410, 411).

6. Pp. 451-452. Hurstwood is "shut out from Chicago—from his easy, comfortable state" (p. 250) by having stolen money from Fitzgerald and Moy's; and no longer "subject to the illusions and burning desires of youth" (pp. 265-266), he is unable to conceive of himself as re-entering the gaudy chamber, which seems to him to be "a city with a wall about it. Men were posted at the gates. You could not get in. Those inside did not care to come out to see who you were. They were so merry inside there that all those outside were forgotten, and he was on the outside" (p. 297). His attempts to escape from the turbulent sea are mockeries. First he seeks refuge as a chairwarmer, "shielding himself from cold and the weariness of the streets in a hotel lobby" (p. 331); next he tries to escape into an illusion of activity, as in his rocking-chair he "buried himself in his papers. ... What Lethean waters were these floods of telegraphed intelligence!" (p. 311); then there is the poker room where "visions of a big stake floated before him" before he loses half his money and walks out into the "chill, bare streets" (pp. 330, 332).

7. In addition to passages already cited, allusions to water, the sea, tides, storms, ships, and harbors may be found on pp. 9, 73, 74, 76, 110, 111, 145, 169, 188, 190, 193, 198, 206, 211, 213, 231, 252, 254, 255, 263, 273, 308, 314, 333, 356, 363, 380, 395, 402, 430, and 438. Additional allusions to chambers, caves, the theater, magic, and *The Arabian Nights* may be found on pp. 7, 9, 12, 14, 16, 17, 18, 22, 24, 26, 28, 30, 39, 41, 46, 52, 59, 65, 69, 72, 74, 76, 95, 102, 127, 140, 148, 162, 170, 200, 223, 225, 228, 255, 280, 281, 284, 287, 288, 289, 290, 294, 312, 314, 334, 397, 407, and 445. Carrie's preoccupation with clothes, which Matthiessen sees as representing her "craving for pleasure" (p. 70) and the

"expression of 'pecuniary culture'" (p. 83), may also be seen as coverings from the weather, and thus allied to the "chamber" imagery. Allusions to clothing in the novel may be found on pp. 6, 7, 22, 23, 33, 39, 42, 48, 53, 58, 60, 61, 65, 72, 94, 251, 270, 278, 280, 285, 321, 343, and 394.

8. *The Financier* (New York, 1912; revised, 1927); *The Titan* (New York, 1914). Further references to *The Financier* and *The Titan* are made to these editions and will be incorporated into the text, with the titles indicated by "*F*" or "*T*." Although Dreiser revised *The Financier* extensively, the revisions of the imagery studied here were insignificant, and the greater accessibility of the revised edition argues for its use in this study.

Any extended consideration of *Jennie Gerhardt* (New York, 1911) must be omitted here. Written between *Sister Carrie* and *The Financier,* its major imagery is, as we might expect, divided equally between the sea and the animal world. For references to water, the sea, storms, and ships in that novel, see pp. 16, 17, 18, 90, 95, 99, 172, 177, 239, 274, 299, 364, 373, 398, 403, 417, and 419. For references to the animal world, see pp. 10, 35, 88, 100, 126, 130, 131, 133, 189, 190, 201, 203, 219, 223, 236, 238, 239, 277, 286, 295, 327, 370, 378, 404, 414, and 415.

9. See, for example, Harlan Hatcher, *Creating the Modern American Novel* (New York, 1935), p. 50; Kenneth S. Lynn, *The Dream of Success* (Boston, 1955), p. 52; and Charles C. Walcutt, *American Literary Naturalism, A Divided Stream* (Minneapolis, Minn., 1956), p. 204.

10. References to these animals, as well as to animal life in general, may be found in *F,* pp. 2, 3, 5, 9, 17, 21, 34, 41, 42, 43, 69, 89, 101, 108, 123, 124, 125, 127, 128, 137, 140, 141, 150, 154, 164, 185, 189, 198, 199, 200, 202, 203, 205, 211, 214, 215, 220, 229, 244, 251, 253, 254, 255, 270, 298, 323, 327, 328, 332, 338, 350, 357, 359, 364, 376, 380, 393, 431, 436, 439, 441, 444, 464, 468, 471, 473, 485, 489, 493, 495, 501, and 502; and in *T,* pp. 7, 10, 19, 23, 24, 28, 30, 32, 45, 46, 47, 51, 60, 66, 67, 68, 70, 77, 83, 85, 101, 108, 109, 113, 114, 116, 120, 127, 128, 138, 139, 144, 145, 147, 148, 149, 150, 152, 155, 156, 157, 160, 162, 164, 167, 187, 188, 203, 206, 220, 221, 222, 230, 239, 248, 253, 262, 286, 303, 304, 316, 326, 331, 332, 338, 343, 351, 352, 355, 356, 357, 358, 361, 366, 374, 375, 386, 389, 393, 394, 396, 398, 406, 408, 410, 414, 419, 421, 432, 436, 437, 441, 458, 473, 479, 482, 489, 494, 501,

503, 508, 513, 514, 515, 516, 521, 532, 533, 534, 535, 539, 542, 544, and 550.

11. *F,* p. 202. Cf. "Might as well be tried for stealing a sheep as a lamb" (*F,* p. 339); "There is more than one way to kill a cat" (*T,* p. 303); "They're all as crooked as eels' teeth" (*T,* p. 47); and "... jumping around like a cat in a bag" (*T,* p. 331).

12. *T,* p. 10. In Philadelphia, "the city treasury and the city treasurer were like a honey-laden hive and a queen bee around which the drones—the politicians—swarmed in the hope of profit," and rival financiers have a regard for each other "as sincere as that of one tiger for another" (*F,* pp. 150, 185).

13. Cowperwood fancies himself to be quite a gay dog, and after several episodes of "puppy love" (*F,* p. 21), he meets Aileen Butler and thinks "some lucky young dog [will] marry her pretty soon" (*F,* p. 89). He pursues her much as he has followed his first business venture, like a "young hound on the scent of game" (*F,* p. 17); to Aileen, one of his most attractive features is his eyes, "as fine as those of a Newfoundland or a Collie and as innocent and winsome" (*T,* p. 7). These comparisons and others add an ironic force to the melodramatic clichés with which Aileen's father denounces him ("dirty dog") and which Aileen herself hurls at him again and again as their marriage crumbles: "You dog! you brute!" (*T,* pp. 145 ff.).

14. *F,* p. 438. Besides the storms of financial difficulty which Cowperwood constantly arouses and the "storm of words" which his schemes sometimes raise in the newspapers (*T,* pp. 255, 526), there are the tempests which his many love affairs engender. Aileen Butler's father is aroused to the pitch of a storm by Cowperwood's making her his mistress (*F,* p. 319); so is her brother Callum later (*F,* p. 477); meanwhile the first Mrs. Cowperwood's soul "rages" like a "tempest" (*F,* p. 406). Later, Cowperwood's involvement with Rita Sohlberg, although it fails to precipitate the "storm of public rage" which Cowperwood fears (*T,* p. 151), leads to "storms of disaster" (*T,* p. 160) in his union with Aileen, leading particularly to her "emotional storm" when she discovers that Cowperwood has had other mistresses than Mrs. Sohlberg (*T,* pp. 247, 248), as well as to "a storm of protest" in the home of Caroline Hand, one of the mistresses (*T,* p. 265).

15. The exterior of his office in Philadelphia is "early Florentine in its decorations" with a door panel

featuring "a hand ... holding aloft a flaming brand ... formerly ... a moneychanger's sign used in old Venice"; and inside the gas lights are "modeled after the early Roman flame-brackets" (*F*, pp. 104, 105). He fills his house with bronzes of the Italian Renaissance and bits of Venetian glass (*F*, p. 453). For Aileen, then his mistress, he builds a secret meeting place which is "a veritable treasure-trove" (*F*, p. 161), and later a mansion in Chicago, the "Florence of the West" (*T*, p. 6), where the dining room is "rich with a Pompeian scheme of color" and "aglow with a wealth of glass" (*T*, p. 71), and the gallery contains Pinturicchio's portrait of Caesar Borgia, in whose career Cowperwood has recently begun to take an interest, befitting his reputation among his associates who think of him as "devil or prince, or both" (*T*, p. 164) and "a prince of politicians" (*T*, p. 220). Yet when Cowperwood, like Hurstwood, finds that it is easier to build his reputation in Chicago than in New York, where in spite of his wealth and power "he was not yet looked upon as a money prince," he decides that what he needs to fulfill his conception of himself is a new mansion built to imitate "the Italian palaces of medieval or Renaissance origin which he had seen abroad" and "a union, morganatic or otherwise, with some one who would be worthy to share his throne" (*T*, pp. 438-439). When the house is completed, a newspaper account of its exaggerates only a little the surroundings of this self-made Borgia: "his court of orchids, his sunrise room, the baths of pink and blue alabaster, the finishings of marble and intaglio. Here Cowperwood was represented as seated on a swinging divan, his various books, art treasures, and comforts piled about him. The idea was vaguely suggested that in his sybaritic hours odalesques [sic] danced before him and unnamable indulgences and excesses were perpetrated" (*T*, pp. 541-542).

The "ideal ... a wraith, a mist, a perfume in the wind, a dream of fair water" (*T*, p. 201) for which Cowperwood searches is symbolized by the fountains which he installs in each of his houses, culminating in the "sunrise room" where "in a perpetual atmosphere of sunrise were ... racks for exotic birds, a trellis of vines, stone benches, a central pool of glistening water, and an echo of music" (*T*, p. 440).

16. Theodore Dreiser, *An American Tragedy* (2 vols.; New York, 1925), II, 274. Further references to *An American Tragedy* are made to this edition, and will be incorporated into the text. Matthiessen, pp. 194 and 200, briefly treats the *Arabian Nights* theme in the novel. Dreiser's acquaintance with *The Arabian Nights* probably dates from his early childhood, but it was continued in the theaters and music halls of Chicago; see Robert H. Elias, *Theodore Dreiser: Apostle of Nature* (New York, 1949), p. 25. His interest in Eastern legend is to be seen not only in the frequent use of Oriental imagery in his major novels but also in his unfortunate excursions into such pseudo-Oriental tales as "Khat" and "The Prince Who Was a Thief" in *Chains* (New York, 1927).

17. I, 48, 175, 265, 331, 341, 376; II, 42, 48, 49, 56, 65, 118, 233, 274, 381. References to Clyde's dreams are found in I, 33, 84, 116, 136, 138, 175, 192, 228, 230, 309, 427, 428; II, 5, 16, 27, 31, 50, 133, 221, 229, 383, 385, 392, 405.

18. I, 26. A similar Alnashar dream is stimulated by Sondra Finchley: "Sondra, Twelfth Lake, society, wealth, her love and beauty. He grew not a little wild in thinking of it all. Once he and she were married, what could Sondra's relatives do? What, but acquiesce and take them into the glorious bosom of their resplendent home ... he to no doubt eventually take some place in connection with the Finchley Electric Sweeper Company. And then would he not be ... joint heir with Stuart to all the Finchley means" (II, 8).

19. Theodore Dreiser, *The Bulwark* (New York, 1946), p. 9. Further references will be incorporated into the text.

20. Dreiser worked on the novel which became *The Bulwark* at various times from 1912 until his death in 1945, and the middle portion of the completed novel was "largely a merging of three early, pre-*American Tragedy* typescripts" (Gerhard Friedrich, "A Major Influence on Theodore Dreiser's *The Bulwark*," *American Literature*, XXIX, May 1957, 189). It is therefore understandable that the incidents and imagery of the middle portion of the novel should recall those of the earlier books, and that the first and the last chapters should contain the bulk of the references to benign animals and to Lever Creek.

21. Friedrich, op. cit., and Gerhard Friedrich, "Theodore Dreiser's Debt to Woolman's *Journal*," *American Quarterly*, VII (Winter 1955), 385-392.

## Sheldon Norman Grebstein (essay date 1966)

SOURCE: Grebstein, Sheldon Norman. "*An American Tragedy*: Theme and Structure." *The Twenties: Poetry and Prose; 20 Critical Essays,* edited by Richard E. Langford and William E. Taylor, Everett Edwards Press, 1966, pp. 62-66.

[*In the following essay, Grebstein focuses on* An American Tragedy *as "one of the enduring novels of our century," noting differences between the novel and the characters and circumstances of the real-life legal case on which it was partly based and finding aspects of Dreiser's own experience interwoven in them. Grebstein also observes that the "social content" of the work is similarly multidimensional.*]

With every passing year it becomes further apparent that there is a greatness in Dreiser which overleaps his defects and his limitations, his bunglings, contradictions, and intrusions. The greatness reached its apogee in ***An American Tragedy*** which, four decades after its publication in 1925, impresses us more and more as one of the enduring novels of our century. Such distinguished men of letters as Robert Penn Warren pay it homage, and it continues to provoke the most careful and respectful critical commentary, even from those who find Dreiser vulgar or irreverent. Because ***An American Tragedy*** is so large a novel and so far from a simple one, it might prove instructive to turn our scrutiny once again to this work which has already declared itself more than a curiosity, more than a document of the jazz age (although in part it is that, too), and attempt to explore some of its complexities of theme and structure.

Thematically, ***An American Tragedy*** is a resonant work which, like all enduring literary creations, reverberates on multiple levels of meaning, at one and the same time bearing individual, social, and universal implication. We need look no farther than the novel's title for an outline of its themes, each word in the title signifying a thematic dimension: "An"—a single but not singular tale; "American"—a tale somehow representative not only of a particular nation but also, as the word increasingly connotes, a social structure, an experience, a life-style; "Tragedy"—a tale which concerns the end of man and its import.

On the individual level, or the simple one-to-one application of the content of a literary work to some aspect of real life within the reader's actual (or potential) experience, Dreiser employed, as is widely known, the records of an actual crime as the basis for his novel. This was the case of Chester Gillette, nephew and employee of a wealthy shirt manufacturer of Cortland (Lycurgus), New York, in which Gillette was convicted for the murder of his pregnant sweetheart, Grace Brown, and executed March 29, 1908, after appeals had delayed the death penalty for almost two years. Although Dreiser's use of this material is of considerable interest, an exhaustive account of the matter is not pertinent here. Suffice it to say that Dreiser relied heavily upon documentary materials, altering fact in two significant areas, however, to better serve the purposes of fiction:

1. The details of the real crime are changed so that the crime in *An American Tragedy* has a stronger element of the accidental. To name only one important difference, in the Gillette case five doctors agreed that drowning was *not* the primary cause of Grace Brown's death; the murder weapon was allegedly a tennis racket carried into the boat by Gillette and later found with all its strings broken.

2. More important, Clyde Griffiths only partly resembles Chester Gillette. He is less athletic and physically effectual (Gillette's photographs show him a bull-necked, deep-chested young man—also, Gillette admitted during the trial that he had initiated sexual relations with Grace Brown by force); less poised and self-contained (if contemporary newspaper accounts can be believed, Gillette did not lose his nerve under stress of indictment and trial); less well-equipped intellectually (Gillette had attended Oberlin for two years and seems to have been quick-witted, or at least glib). Finally, in contrast to Clyde's passion for Sondra, it is doubtful that Gillette was enamoured of any one girl in the wealthier class to which, like Clyde, he had gained access.

Much of what is different from the novel's Clyde Griffiths and life's Chester Gillette was supplied by Dreiser himself, from the raw materials of his own youth. The moving from place to place; the shame at the poverty and ineffectuality of the parents, especially the father; the sister who was made pregnant and then deserted; the young Dreiser's burning sexual hungers frustrated yet intensified by parental thou-shalt-nots and his own fears of inadequacy; the lust for beauty which expressed itself in a fascination with fine things, money, prestige, and which became inextricably interwoven with Dreiser's sexual appetites; the pervasive guilt for all desires and deeds not consonant with the iron doctrines of the devoutly Catholic father—all this was Dreiser and was to become Clyde Griffiths. This transubstantiation does much to explain the peculiar poignancy of Clyde's characterization.

The total effect of Dreiser's alterations of Chester Gillette, conjoined with the projection of his own experience, is cumulatively much stronger than the individual changes themselves would seem to suggest. They result in a character who is far weaker than one might expect a murderer to be, yet who is more sympathetically and credibly motivated because he kills, or plans to kill, not only for money but for beauty and love. As Dreiser himself remarked in a letter protesting the diluted and cheapened film version which had been made of his novel, Clyde's affair with Roberta is not wholly sordid: "As they [the film's producers] picture it, there is nothing idyllic about it, and there should be—there must be. Until Sondra comes into his life, Clyde is content, more or less happy in his love life with Roberta." We recall, too, that as Clyde languishes in the death house for nearly two years the one element of his past he does not repudiate, the one element in the whole complex of factors leading to his fate which he continues to affirm and which sustains him almost to the end, is the vision of Sondra's beauty and the thrilling memory of her kisses. For better or worse he loves her more than he has loved anyone and to the limit of his capacity to love, and if his discrimination can be questioned, the fact of his feelings cannot. It is a fact which recommends Clyde to the reader's heart, if not to his approving judgment.

Just as the individual or personal thematic level of *An American Tragedy* is hardly simplistic, so its social content has at least two dimensions.

First, the novel is the fictional but not fictitious treatment of an all too common situation in American life, that in which some desperate young man kills his poor (and usually pregnant) sweetheart in order to marry his way up the social scale. It might be called the tragedy of the aspiring young man, the pregnant working girl, and the debutante. Although Dreiser chose the Gillette-Brown murder case as the basis for his story, he had dozens of similar episodes at his disposal. As a boy Dreiser had immersed himself in potboiling fiction, one of whose staples was the poor-boy-gets-rich-girl theme, and he had early concluded, both from his reading and experience that money, not achievement, was the chief American ideal. Moreover, as a young reporter in various cities Dreiser encountered at first hand similar cases, some of them involving murder. And when, Helen Dreiser tells us, many years later he was formulating plans for the book first titled "Mirage" and then "An American Tragedy," he studied fifteen such incidents before finally deciding on the Gillette case. Not only did the Gillette case conform to his thoughts, it had been so well publicized that it was still being discussed into the 1920's and its records were readily accessible.

To Dreiser, then, the story of Chester Gillette and others like him became symbolic of certain dominant forces in American life, and in the characters and events of *An American Tragedy* he dramatized trends that had been true for generations: the worship of the goal of success, together with the refusal to condone the methods and consequences it engendered; the excitation and prurient display of sexuality in all forms of entertainment, billboards, magazines, popular literature, yet the stern legal repression of all but the narrowest forms of sexual expression (in marriage for the purpose of procreation only); the pretense of democratic egalitarianism, yet the existence of rigid class stratification; the absurd idealization of women; the stifling influence of intrinsically false but powerfully institutionalized religious creeds—these were elements which for Dreiser had tarnished the once-luminous Amer-

ican Dream. And all this shapes the social purpose of *An American Tragedy.* In addition to its depiction of these broad issues, (and much of Dreiser's triumph in *An American Tragedy* is that he depicts rather than editorializes), the novel indicts the legal system which could condemn and slaughter a youth whose real sin was weakness and real crime that of illicit sexual pleasure. The trial itself is vividly dramatized, with Dreiser demonstrating persuasively how Clyde becomes as much a victim of rigged evidence, political ambition, and public opinion as of "Justice"; *e.g.,* at one point in the proceedings a spectator speaks out in the voice of the people when he interjects: "Why don't they kill the God-damned bastard and be done with him?" Throughout, Dreiser is remarkably objective, but at moments toward the conclusion of his narrative, unable to restrain himself, he drops the guise of novelist and speaks with missionary fervor directly to the reader about the brutality of prisons, the death house, and by implication, the concept of justice which could tolerate such practices. Some critics would find this a flaw in the novel; nevertheless, there is probably no more trenchant argument against capital punishment in American literature.

Despite the weight of its social burden, *An American Tragedy* is much more than a tract, much more than a problem novel. Rather, it is a chronicle of American life. In the handling of his material Dreiser once again simply but effectively transformed history into art by means of a skillful manipulation of time. His main strategem was to move the time of the action forward about ten years, or just enough to make the book's composition and publication parallel the events it narrates. That is, unlike its documentary source the story begins sometime during the 'teens and ends in the '20's, rather than in the period before 1910, when the Zeitgeist belonged to the 19th century, not the 20th. Thus, as F. O. Matthiessen has noted, the novel occurs in and conveys a generalized atmosphere of the era following the end of the first World War, the historic moment parent to much of what we are now living. Although *An American Tragedy* is perhaps the most sober book of the decade, its cast nevertheless includes a number of authentic sheiks and flappers, of both high and low class, who dash around in automobiles, carry hip flasks, dance to jazz music, and neck—or worse. Even that elite group of young people of Lycurgus who comprise the Olympian company to which Clyde aspires display a freedom from parental restraint and a mobility unknown before the war. Certainly Hortense Briggs, one of the novel's minor triumphs of characterization and a girl best described in the parlance of the time as a tease and a gold-digger, could not have existed before 1920 as an accepted member of society.

In this respect it could even be said that *An American Tragedy* tells another part of the story Fitzgerald recorded in *The Great Gatsby*. The analogy need not be carried too far, but Clyde Griffiths and Jay Gatsby have kinship, as do Sondra Finchley and Daisy Buchanan. Clyde and Gatsby pursue the same dream, the dream of an orgiastic future embodied in a beautiful girl with a voice like the sound of money; both pursue it passionately but illicitly, and with similarly disastrous results. There the comparison of the two books should probably end, but clearly it is more than a coincidence that two novels so superficially different yet thematically so alike should be published in the same year and should come to the same mordaunt conclusions about American life.

It has already been remarked how *An American Tragedy* functions on the individual and social levels; it remains to be seen how the book fulfills the third and most profound thematic dimension—the universal—or, in brief, how it functions as tragedy. Here Dreiser has fused an individual but representative instance and a social milieu into the larger saga of what happens to any man whose desires exceed both his capacity to satisfy them and his ability to avoid retribution, since satisfaction can only come at the expense of others. On this level Dreiser is no longer a meliorist concerned with changing certain attitudes toward poverty or sex or crime. Rather, he is a tragedian, a tragic ironist, who confronts the problem of human destiny and demonstrates what can happen in a cosmos indifferent to human suffering but inhabited by humans who persist in finding meaning in their suffering. In *An American Tragedy* he gives us a synthesis of the two basic tragic situations of western literature, the tragedy of frustrated love and the tragedy of thwarted ambition, as played by a proletarian hero and as written by a compassionate agnostic.

The source of Clyde's anguish (and, we may conjecture, Dreiser's as well) is that he belongs neither to the old theistic world, with its assurance of certain certainties, however harsh, nor in the new existential one, in which man (like Mersault, also a condemned criminal, in Camus's *The Stranger*) can stoically accept and even find a sense of happiness in the benign indifference of the universe. Man's law has declared Clyde guilty but few of the men who judge him have been so fiercely afflicted by the same desires. Belknap, Clyde's lawyer, is one of the few who can be honestly sympathetic because he, too, had once gotten a girl into trouble. Like one of Dreiser's earlier characters, the hero of the play *The Hand of the Potter,* Clyde could well cry out as his only defense, "I didn't make myself, did I?" Consequently, Clyde can feel none of the guilt whose admission his fellows wish to exact from him, and although just before his execution he signs a

Christian testimonial-warning to errant youth, he does so only to repay his mother and the Reverend McMillan for the love and spiritual labor they have lavished upon him. It is grimly ironic that Clyde goes to his death still unconvinced in his heart of his guilt, while the Reverend McMillan, closest to him at the end, leaves the death house both convinced of Clyde's guilt and shaken in his belief in the efficacy of his own Christian mission.

Although in his refusal to confirm Clyde's guilt, or to confirm the fact of human guilt at all, Dreiser has risked the approval of much of his audience—for most of us believe that without guilt tragedy can have no moral value and consequently result in no catharsis—his tough-mindedness and his refusal to compromise his position invoke our admiration. If he has rejected the Christian or moralistic solution to man's dilemma, the promise of redemption and salvation through suffering, he refuses equally to take comfort from the science-inspired creeds of Naturalism or Determinism, which imply that all problems, including evil, are soluble once we learn enough about them. Instead, Dreiser persists in employing as his tragic formula that which has never been quite compatible to western man: the tragedy of humans overwhelmed by an omnipotent external fate. Accordingly, he does not permit Clyde even that dignity which is the agnostic, humanistic substitute for redemption. In his very weakness Clyde Griffiths becomes a metaphor of human frailty, and in his refusal to accept guilt he signifies the futility of human thought and endeavor in the context of life's essential meaninglessness. The result could easily have been stark nihilism, yet somehow, perhaps because of the indefinable quality of what has been called Dreiser's brooding pity, Clyde's story is meaningful and poignant.

Purists in tragedy might argue that Clyde's fate is not tragic because his weakness does not permit sufficient struggle. Dreiser provides the basis for a reply. The death house is populated with others wiser and stronger than Clyde, *e.g.,* Nicholson, the lawyer, who has had all the advantages Clyde lacked; these are men of different races, religions, backgrounds—a Negro, an Oriental, Italians, a Jew, Irish—and all share the same fate. Obviously the death house is another of Dreiser's metaphors of the human condition. It is the place, the metaphor implies, where all men, wise or stupid, weak or strong, meet because all are condemned to a common fate not because they have sinned but because they are men. To their credit, most of them—including Clyde—leave life more nobly than they have lived it.

To assert, then, as a number of critics have recently, that Dreiser's treatment of tragedy is inferior because of some supposed flaw in his tragic vision, his employment of inadequate heroes, his denial of free will, is neither to comprehend Dreiser's position fully nor to judge it fairly on its own terms, but really to disagree with it. Granting Dreiser his premises and placing him in the appropriate tradition of tragedy, one can only say that one prefers some other tradition, not that Dreiser fails. It is also likely that Dreiser's hostile critics have confused his world-view with his workmanship, attributing to one a defect of the other, for if Dreiser falls short he does so as a stylist rather than a tragedian (I speak here, of course, specifically about *An American Tragedy*). That is, we have always had difficulty distinguishing between the tragic situation and the writer's treatment of it and his mode of utterance. To western audiences, consequently, the most splendid and moving tragedies are those most splendidly and movingly written, whether the idiom be Shakespeare's high rhetoric or Hemingway's colloquial cadences, and in Dreiser we find neither the soaring magnificence nor purged intensity of language which strikes the reader as the proper vehicle for tragedy.

Here, too, there is the tendency toward an unjust appraisal of *An American Tragedy*; for although Dreiser fails to overwhelm us with his eloquence, he persuades us by means of his novel's exceedingly durable and tight structure and by his use of ironic parallels, juxtapositions, and foreshadowings, which effectively emphasize the tragic irony of its theme.

Structurally, *An American Tragedy* is by far the most carefully planned of Dreiser's novels, each "Book" of the novel's three-part division is deliberately matched to a major aspect of its situations and themes. Although the three "books" vary in length, they achieve considerable symmetry, the first two dealing with cause and the third with effect. Further, Books I and II together comprise about two-thirds of the novel, with Roberta's death occuring almost exactly at the two-thirds mark. To use an analogy from drama, Book I is like the first act of a three-act play. It is relatively short, quick in movement and action, and it sets out the main lines of characterization as well as the basis for the conflict. (Note: in Dreiser's original manuscript Book I was considerably longer, containing nine chapters detailing Clyde's boyhood and offering additional documentation for his sense of inferiority). In Book II the conflict between sex and ambition is established, intensified by complications which produce a crisis (Roberta's pregnancy) and which result in a climax, the "murder." Book III provides a long dénouement, the trial, imprisonment, and execution, in which matters are settled but, as we have already observed, not resolved. That is, *An American Tragedy* is an open-ended drama. Within this general framework Clyde's tragic career may be described as an arc rather than a rise and fall. Just at the midpoint of his climb, when he has become a member of the smart set, has accompanied Sondra home for a midnight snack and declared his love for her, and she responds—a scene which occurs almost exactly midway in the novel—Roberta tells Clyde she is pregnant. For a time his momentum continues to carry him forward to greater social prestige and romantic success with Sondra, but to the observer, if not to Clyde himself, it is clear that the only possible movement is downward.

This deliberateness in structure carries over into Dreiser's use of various devices for ironic emphasis, devices thickly but not obtrusively deployed throughout the novel. By far the most obvious is the similarity of scene with which the novel begins and ends. Despite the passage of twelve years, the disgrace of a daughter and the execution of a son, the Griffiths continue to loft their prayers and hymns to a just and merciful God against the tall, indifferent walls of a commercial city, as a symbolic darkness descends. Everything Mother Griffiths has learned can be summed up in the dime for ice cream she gives Esta's illegitimate child, Clyde's replacement in the group of street evangelists; it is her way of forestalling another American tragedy. And the door through which the group disappears into the mission house reminds us of the door through which Clyde had passed to the electric chair. Another such parallel concludes both Book I and Book II. At the close of Book I Clyde flees, in darkness, from an accident in which a girl has been killed; at the end of Book II Clyde flees, once more in darkness, from the scene of a second girl's death. A somewhat similar device is Dreiser's detailed reproduction of religious mottoes and fragments of scripture at just those moments when the bitter facts of life are most shockingly apparent, especially in Books I and III. Note, for example, the heavy irony in the last few pages of Chapter xvii of Book III, where each stage of Mother Griffiths' anguish at hearing of Clyde's indictment for murder is interlined with fragments from the Psalms.

There are still other ironic techniques, only a few of which will be set down here. One of the more subtle is Dreiser's use of season and weather. Clyde's job at the Green-Davidson Hotel, a crucial experience in the shaping of his desires for sex, money, and position, begins in the fall (a better season for endings than beginnings; that, too, is intentional). Likewise, Clyde's sexual intimacy with Roberta begins in the fall, and his trial for murder takes place in the fall. Winter is an even gloomier Dreiserian season, for Clyde runs away from Kansas City in the winter, Roberta announces her pregnancy to Clyde in the winter, the judge passes sentence on Clyde in the winter, and Clyde's execution is carried out in the winter—and in darkness.

Finally, Dreiser stages a series of suggestive word-plays and scene-parallels which serve both to foreshadow and intensify the action. Just after coming to Lycurgus Clyde admires the Griffiths' stately home, which has as its lawn decorations a fountain in which a boy holds a swan (would Clyde have let Sondra drown?), and an arrangement of statuary in which dogs pursue a fleeing stag. Soon after this Clyde finds himself in the company of an all-too-willing girl named Rita (whom he has met at a church social), and in his efforts to remain on his feet and avoid risky sexual entanglements he dances with her to a tune called "The Love Boat." When, a few months later the lonely and now less cautious Clyde encounters Roberta on the shores of a nearby lake, he persuades her to come into his canoe, assuring her, "You won't be in any danger. . . . It's perfectly safe. . . . It won't tip over." Shortly after this, when they meet on the street (in darkness) for their first rendezvous, Clyde says presciently, "We have so little time." Later still, just after Roberta has determined that Clyde must either arrange an abortion or marry her, Dreiser shifts focus momentarily to Sondra, whose romantic daydreams of Clyde include fancied episodes in which she and Clyde are alone in a canoe on some remote, idyllic lake. And after Roberta's death, when an inwardly hysterical Clyde has rejoined the gay vacation group at Twelfth Lake, Sondra says to a boy steering a boat in which she, Clyde, and others are riding, "O, say, what do you want to do? Drown us all?"

Is it now not obvious that any judgment of *An American Tragedy* which has been made solely or largely on the basis of its "style" (always the same word) must be a narrow and capricious judgment? This is too big, too significant, too serious a book to permit an assessment of the writer's diction and command of sentence structure to stand as the last word; the strength and dimensions of its architecture tower over whatever defects may appear in the facing. In any case, *An American Tragedy* has already survived virtually a half-century of critical winnowing. It seems safe to predict that it will continue to grow in our esteem, and that in time it will join that all-too-small group of permanent books we call American classics.

### Richard W. Dowell (essay date 1970)

SOURCE: Dowell, Richard W. "'You Will Not Like Me, I'm Sure': Dreiser to Miss Emma Rector; November 28, 1893, to April 4, 1894." *American Literary Realism 1870-1910*, vol. 3, no. 3, Summer 1970, pp. 259-70.

[*In the following essay, Dowell presents "five tentatively romantic letters" Dreiser wrote to a female childhood friend at the outset of his literary career.*]

In the fall of 1893, when Dreiser was a reporter for the St. Louis *Republic,* he was seized by "a letter-writing fever," during which he poured out his hopes and dreams, sorrows and frustrations, to Sara Osborne White, ultimately his first wife. Years later, when recalling his literary apprenticeship in *Newspaper Days* (1931), Dreiser referred to those love letters as his "first and easiest attempt at literary expression, the form being negligible and yet sufficient to encompass and embody without difficulty all the surging and seething emotions and ideas which had hitherto been locked up in me, bubbling and steaming to the explosion point. Indeed the newspaper forms to which I was daily compelled to confine myself offered no outlet, and in addition, in Miss W—— I had found a seemingly sympathetic and understanding soul, one which required and inspired all the best that was in me."[1] Unfortunately, these "long, personal, intimate accounts" by the twenty-two-year-old Dreiser are not available to scholars interested in his formative years;[2] however, a series of five tentatively romantic letters, concurrent with the earliest White correspondence and possessing the same introspective quality, have recently been donated to the Lilly Library at Indiana University by the recipient, Emma (Rector) Flanagan, a Linton, Indiana, school teacher at the time of the correspondence.[3]

Miss Rector and Dreiser had been childhood acquaintances during his family's residence in Sullivan, Indiana (1879-1882). The Dreiser children had visited the Rector farm frequently, and the eldest son, Paul, had lived there for several months during a period of estrangement from his father. For Paul and his sister Claire, this affection for the Rectors lasted a lifetime.[4] Theodore also retained fond memories of the association. Miss Emma, he recalled in a letter of December 28, 1893, had been "a jolly playmate and a good fellow generally." "Your house and yourself," he continued, "are connected with a few of these happier moments [of his childhood] and if you knew how dear they are to me you would feel too that they are sacred." Twelve years had passed since he had last seen Emma, and during that time, Dreiser speculated, she had "grown graceful and pretty with dark brown hair and large lustreful eyes to match." Thus, when his brother Ed wrote that the Rector girls had visited the Dreisers in Chicago during the 1893 World's Fair, Theodore decided to renew his acquaintance with Emma, his engagement to Sara White notwithstanding.[5]

In *Newspaper Days,* Dreiser described himself at twenty-two as a "half-baked poet, romancer, dreamer," vacillating constantly between rapture at the beauty and prosperity around him and despair at his inability to partake of it.[6] He longed to travel, see the world, be recognized and applauded; yet, his sensitivity to life's inequities was steadily convincing him that these hopes would never be realized. "Spiritually," Dreiser later wrote, "I was what might be called a poetic melancholiac, crossed with a vivid materialistic lust of life. ... Love of beauty as such—feminine beauty first and foremost, of course—was the dominating characteristic of all my moods: joy in the arch of an eyebrow, the color of an eye, the flame of a lip or cheek, the romance of a situation, spring, trees, flowers, evening walks, the moon ... spring odors, moonlight under the trees, a lighted lamp over a dark lawn—what tortures have I not endured because of these! My mind was riveted on what love could bring me, once I had the prosperity and fame which somehow I foolishly fancied commanded love; and at the same time I was horribly depressed by the thought that I should never have them, never. ..."[7]

This emotional response to life gave Dreiser's writing "a mushy and melancholy turn" and allowed him to "discolor the most commonplace scenes as to make one think that [he] was writing of paradise."[8] "Indeed," he later confessed, "I allowed my imagination to run away with me at times and only the good sense of the copy reader or the indifference of a practical-minded public saved the paper from appearing utterly ridiculous."[9] The Dreiser-Rector correspondence tends to validate these self-evaluations made more than twenty-five years later.

In editing Dreiser's letters, I have remained faithful to the text, making no attempt to emend or indicate the numerous and rather obvious mechanical errors.

\* \* \*

The Southern[10]
St. Louis Nov. 28 1893

Miss Emma Rector,

I suppose upon the strength of such old memories as I possess of you and your family relatives I should be justified in addressing you as dear friend. I have long been interested in the welfare of the Rector family and have always delighted in hearing of the pleasent occurences that go to make your home existence a happy one. Recently when my brother Ed wrote me that you had visited Chicago I was much interested. A postscript that he added however to the effect that a letter from myself to you would not prove wholly unacceptable was the most charming part of it all. In accordance with the suggestion and the hope of renewing what I remember as a pleasent childish acquaintance I post this short note, trusting that it will find you.

Im not sure of your address and so will only suggest that if you should receive it, you should also be kind enough to give me your correct address and such other family information as may be. I am at present connected with the St. Louis Republic as traveling correspondent. Sometimes I

travel east, but so far have never touched near Dugger.[11] I should be more than pleased to hear from you, if you feel so inclined. Please excuse the manner in which this missive is gotten up. Opening letters are awful hard to write especially to young ladies of whom one can never be certain even after years of acquaintence.

You would perhaps find that another letter—in answer—would be more readable and let us hope more agreeable.

I beg to remain

Sincerely Yours
Theodore Dreiser

\* \* \*

Office. - Night.

St Louis, Dec 13th 93.

My dear Miss Rector,

Your answer—dispaired of—came today and I address you with more of that bon homme freedom than you grant me, "My dear Miss." Of course I will say right here that I was pleased to hear from you and to think that my letter had not been so egregiously flat after all as to have discouraged you at the very outset. Now let us both hope that the exchange will be, say, of mutual benefit. I know that I shall be improved and I can only hope that you will. Do you know you write exactly like someone else that I know.[12] You would be astonished to see how much they look alike. The other person has not the charm of diction that your latest missive shows. You delight do you in recieving letters from persons once held near and dear. What a pity it was that I didnt remain near and dear—then you wouldnt have cause to write me and recieve my answers in the mood retrospective. But thats neither here nor there. To be candid I remember ever so faintly a few particulars about our old acquaintenceship. I remember that I was given to considering you a jolly playmate and a good fellow generally but I cant remember just how pretty you were. Ill wager a goodly sum that you have grown graceful and pretty with dark brown hair and large lustreful eyes to match. I cant say now why but I imagine you must have. You see I'm reckoning without a picture. Your in Linton now. Somehow I know something about Linton. I had a friend once by the name of Brandon who either lived in Linton or had a young lady friend on whom he dated and who resided there. Im talking about college days now at Bloomington. Another person, I cant exactly call him a friend for I never did like him, one William Yokey either lived in Linton or called there as did Brandon. Yokey was of the stripe belligerent, entirely to enthusiastic and very passe to say the least. I feel as though I cared very little to hear anything about him. I heard very recently again of Miss Maggie and Miss Jennies[13] visit to Chicago. I erred when I thought that you had been there. Chicago is an ideal city, very swift, very new and very satisfying. I enjoyed working there but now that I am away I really believe that it will be years, if ever, before I return to it.[14] I dispised St. Louis at first, then learned to tolerate it and now I like it. Ive picked up a number of acquaintences and so Im content in a measure. Im thinking seriously of going east though. New York is my objective point and probably in time to come I'll reach there. New Yorks the place for special writers and literary effusions are my strong "fast ball" as our Indiana friends often say, so that I think I must go. Not now however. I'm a newspaper man at present with all the untoward instincts of one and not until I have achieved a certain status of perfection will I be able to throw of the shell as they say and spring out into that other much desired sphere. Do you know that often I look back over the years of labor that I have endured and cast in to the mold of my making with a feeling alive to sorrow almost disgust. I long at times to be young again and to appreciate the beauties of life again with the vivid fancy and facination of a child. Your house and yourself are connected with a few of these happier moments and if you knew just how dear they are to me you would feel too that they are sacred. One of the happiest mornings of my existence I spent on your fathers farm near Dugger, while on a visit there. I remember seeing the gorgeous sun rising over one of the neighboring hill crests bathed with that early dew which is pearly and casting its molten arrows aslant the medow and the stream that ran near your house. I went fishing that morning in that dainty little rivulet whose waters were no deeper then a knee and as clear as crystal. You came with me I believe and we improvised tackle of plain tree branches, twine and pins, fishing most excellently with the same. I used to see the sun rise very frequently then, but now I must confess I have not seen the sun rise in a year or more. I never get up until 10 A.M.

I believe I'm leading you into these dry newspaper facts and fancys of my life that are of no interest. Im writing away here until I positively feel that this letter is becoming outrageously extensive and a burden. You will have no objection then to my drawing these opinions of mine to a close and awaiting another opourtunity. I hope that now I address you at Linton you will not be long in answering. I know I shall be delighted to hear from you and besides very soon I have a favor to ask of you which will be facillitated by a better understanding.

Will you kindly give my regards to your relatives—those who remember me, and allow me to remain—

Sincerely your friend,
Theodore Dreiser

* * *

Republic
Saturday, Feb. 18th 1894

Miss Emma Rector,

My Dear Friend:

Your curt little note, filled with righteous indignation came today, or rather late last night. It was a revelation to me for it brought me the knowledge that I had recieved a letter from you and had been ungentlemanly enough not to answer. I know that before your note, I had been wondering why you didnt write, and had concluded that my last letter, away back in December some time, had proved distasteful. Now comes your letter and rebukes for not answering something I never recieved. Its really embarassing to me and I'm lost for an explanation. Surely Miss Emma you would not accuse me of deliberately neglecting a correspondence that was begun at my own solicitation and with the most pleasureable sensations. I dont believe you do, else you never would have written your inquiry. You must have imagined the letter went astray or something and took this method of informing me; or am I to sanguine in my explanation. Anyhow I'm sorry—I'm awfully sorry. I would give a great deal to get the letter even now, and a great deal more to make you understand just how I feel upon the subject of your accusation.

How could you think that your inquiry would be offensive? Hereafter you must pin your faith to the gentlemanly instincts of your old acquaintence and never doubt once that he would show the slightest irregularity that might in anyway irritably affect a young lady—and a pretty young lady at that.

You say, "Why have I not heard from you"? How shall I tell you? Part of the time since I wrote you last (and maybe just at the time your letter came) I was out of the city. I've been away, once two weeks, once five days and a third time three days. A half dozen times I've been away one and two days at a time. It must have failed to reach the Republic or if it came it may have got mixed with the counting room or the typographical department mail. Several times in the past I have missed letters and found them dust covered and forsaken lying upstairs, belonging supposedly, to some errant printer, who had come and gone like a thousand others. Such mishaps are rare though and its just my luck to have the very identical letter I most longed for go astray and fail to reach me. I've instituted a serch. The two departments shall be rumaged and if that letter comes to light I'll answer it, even at this late day. Meanwhile wont you write me? Tell me the news of your pleasent home and the college boys I once knew. If your other letter had come I had intended asking (begging) you in this for your picture. I believe I told you that I had something to ask of you—a great, great favor. I want to see "who you are" anyway, and to revive my recollection of such a dear old playmate as you once were. If you think not—if I'm to bold or its not exactly proper, why then I'll forego my wish and try to look demure, and just as though I didn't want it at all;—but I do. I'll do, or say, or give most anything in my poverty-stricken possession to get it and if you have one, for the sake of old family acquaintencship give it to me.

But maybe your angry? Maybe your disgusted with the miserable trend events have taken and intend, as soon as your wounded pride is allayed, to stop writing and count the explanation sufficient. Dont do it! Answer again just as though nothing had happened and I promise that barring mishap my answers will always come soon and as neat as I can make them. Then if I dont hear from you for a long time I'll take it for granted that the letters gone astray and write you anyhow. Now, how is that?

Mr. Paul[15] was here week before last in the Danger Signal.[16] He had a lot of lovely new songs he's composing to sing to me and lots of very droll stories to tell. He inquired of me whether I ever heard anything of the Rector family and I mournfully told him, no. He said he expected, maybe, that next summer he would pay a visit to southern Indiana and to his dear old friend Jesse Rector,[17] especially. Have you recieved any word from Chicago? Who all writes to you?

I hope that you have become mollified now and that you aren't angry. I hope to that youve decided to write me a nice long letter telling me that I'm forgiven and that I'm going to receive a picture of you. Then I'll smoke right up and be ever so grateful and happy and we'll get along after the fashion of "ye ancient fairy tale" very happily ever afterwards.

With the kindest wishes and a whole heart full of regrets I'm

Faithfully yours
Theodore Dreiser

\* \* \*

Republic

Thursday Mch 1st, 94

My dear Miss Rector;

Today has been so fair and cool, so brilliant in the glory of all its sunshine and blue sky, that I have felt much more like writing you an answer in rhyme, than in this dull prose strain. Surely March has entered like a lamb, soft and meek. Let us hope, you and I, that it remains so and does not retire the ferocious, proverbial lion, all changed as though the worlds iniquities had transformed it.

And by the way, I often feel as though the world were making a lion of me in temperament, so wearied am I, at times, and so disgusted; and that sometime, I too shall retire snarling, a cynic and a dissembler—but this is no conversation for so fair a day. Your letter came this A. M; a part of the delight of the day to me. It began with a delightful little odour of vindicativeness that read as though you were still uncertain whether you had not best punish me for my not recieving your letter anyhow; and wound up with mellowed kindness, that charmed me beyond measure. How pleased I shall be to have your picture! and how sure I am that I shall prize it very highly! If mine be of any interest to you, why certainly you shall have one. I shall proceed forwith to have some new ones taken. Still that will require two to three weeks you know. Before then I hope to have yours.

Your letter has been found. I have it. It is very pleasent, but not so good as the one I just received. In writing this I answer both. So my friend Brandon sends his regards. I thank him. I liked Brandon. Rather a frank, unassuming fellow, I thought; open and generous. Will you kindly remember me to him, and hope that he will be all well in the future. As for Mr. Yokey, he was not so much of a friend. I remember him as a boisterous, hair-brained athe-

letic fellow, with unbalanced ideas and a warm heart, sadly offset however by a belligerent attitude on all questions, and a dominant desire to rule. I never imagined for one instant that he liked me, or would remember me at all. Since my memory is not defiled, I surely ought to be grateful, and am. For all of his mentioned generosity, please return my regards. It is my thanks—nothing more. These gentlemen would not think much of me now as I am. The worldly experience of mine has shattered the ideals that were reflected in my eyes those days. Still ambitious, until my very heart aches, and filled with the knowledge of the endless good about, I am modified in temperament and void of that wild enthusiasm, that in those dear old college days made every silvery cloud a fairy legend; and every song birds voice, a poem, sung by the great Master of All. I dream now of lesser conquests and my visions have narrowed down. Perhaps though all this is for the best and I am to be happier in the end. If I did not trust beyond my heart however, I should not believe it. But I weary you. I was thinking this morning what would be the end of this correspondence; friendship, or the sorrowful knowledge that we had met just one more person in the world, whom we could not like. You know how such things go: First curiosity—a continued desire to know of the life and environment of the newcomer; then satisfaction and weariness; and lastly a bonded feeling and sentiment, or a most discouraging remembrance, that you would much prefer not to have at all. You do not know me, nor I you. I cannot even imagine from your words, how you look. Perhaps when I see your picture, I shall discover a physiological tracing of thought upon your countenance, that I could not like—then I should wish to cease writing. When you look at mine, you will see egotism written in every lineament; a strong presentment of self love in every expression. I have a semi-Roman nose, a high forehead and an Austrian lip, with the edges of my teeth always showing. I wear my hair long, and part it in the middle, only to brush it roughly back from the temples. Then I'm six feet tall, but never look it, and very frail of physique. I always feel ill, and people say I look cold and distant. I dislike companionship, as far as numbers go, and care only for a few friends, who like what I like. I prefer writing to reading and would rather see for myself, than hear or read all the knowledge of the world. You will not like me, Im sure. Here is another fact. Girls of strong personality invariably dislike me. Girls of much egotism in regard to the exquisitely womanly things of their character, like me, for I adore the womanly traits, when confined, and not roughened by the world. If you can lecture 40 minutes on Greek history, or have a weakness for discussion, you cannot possibly hope to ever get along with me. I never discuss, and yet am thoroughly self opinionated. Above all I am of a gloomy disposition, and a dreamer, to whom everything romantic appeals, and everything (in fact nothing but the) natural in real action, satisfys. Can you imagine now? However I must close this outrageously extensive letter. Write me a long letter. Tell me about Emma Rector alone. If ever I pass near Linton I shall visit you.

Faithfully Yours
Theodore Dreiser

Use same size envelope each time.
I shall save your letters. T.D.

\* \* \*

Boody House[18]

Toledo, O., Wed. Apr 4<u>th</u> 1894

My dear Miss Rector,

I will wager ever so much that you are angry with me, in daring to drift along so monotonously and not answer your delightful letter, which I received in St. Louis sometime since. Well I am out on the road.[19] I have been to Detroit and Cincinnati very recently and once I must have passed within 60 mile of Linton, anyhow for I came from St. Louis to Toledo, over the Clover Leaf route. That passes Kokomo Ind and ever so many other towns but I cant recall their names now. Tonight I leave for Cleveland Ohio, and have reason to believe I shall be in Buffalo N.Y. by Sunday. If not I shall travel even farther east—perhaps Pittsburg and Philadelphia. If you answer you had best address me care of the Cleveland Plain Dealer, editorial room. No—I'll take that back. You had better address me care of Arthur Henry, city editor of the Blade, here in Toledo, and he will forward it to me wherever I may be.[20] Since March has gone lovely weather has prevailed here. There has been ever so much of warm flooding sunshine and pleasant spring breeze. I traveled up the beautiful Maumee river here, for 30 miles of its winding course and never saw fairer hillsides, nor more beautiful farm lands. The water of the river is not deep, but wide spread, and hurrys along over the coolest and mossiest of all stones.[21] I was pleased beyond measure and have felt ever so rested. If I come west shortly, and I do so much want to run back St. Louis I am coming to Linton, to see you. I shall pass near you, and instead of doing so I will climb down and run over. Will I be at all welcome after this long delay? Well if you were I, and found yourself brushed around from place to place, you would forgive yourself for not writing letters, and so I trust my country school ma'm will forgive her erratic friend and condone one of the most apparent and flagrant faults of the profession—poor letter writing. I sincerely trust that a letter will come soon and relieve me upon this score. I owe you a picture. Shortly you shall have it.[22]

Faithfully yours
Theo. Dreiser

*Notes*

1. Theodore Dreiser, *Newspaper Days* (NY: Liveright, 1931), p. 319.

2. The earliest Dreiser-White correspondence has presumably been lost; however, seventy-one letters from Dreiser to Sara White, dated May 1, 1896, through September 6, 1898, have become the property of the Lilly Library at Indiana University. At the request of Miss White's heirs, this file is at present inaccessible to scholars.

3. The Rector letters are apparently the earliest Dreiser correspondence thus far discovered. Robert Elias, Neda Westlake, and Donald Pizer have indicated that they know of none extant dated before November 28, 1893.

4. Claire and Paul Dreiser (Dresser) maintained a correspondence with the Rector family throughout their lifetimes. These letters are also the property of the Lilly Library.

5. Dreiser indicated that he became engaged to Miss White in the fall of 1893 (*Newspaper Days*, pp. 322-330).

6. Ibid., p. 9.

7. Ibid., pp. 106-107.

8. Ibid., p. 183.

9. Ibid., pp. 183-184.

10. Consistent with Dreiser's confessed tendency to exaggerate his own importance during his early manhood, the opening letter was written on the stationary of the Southern Hotel, the finest in St. Louis but not where Dreiser was living. See *Newspaper Days*, pp. 10-11, 100, 127-128.

11. The Rector farm was near Dugger, Indiana, about eight miles from Sullivan, Indiana.

12. This reference in all probability is to Miss Sara Osborne White, with whom Dreiser was also corresponding during this period.

13. Jennie and Maggie were Emma Rector's younger sisters.

14. Actually Dreiser had spent two weeks in Chicago during the previous summer when he chaperoned a REPUBLIC-sponsored tour for local school teachers to the World's Fair. It was on this tour that he met Sara White. See *Newspaper Days*, pp. 235-266.

15. Dreiser was referring to his brother Paul Dresser.

16. Paul was in the road company of DANGER SIGNAL, a farce.

17. Jesse Rector was Emma's father.

18. Dreiser left the REPUBLIC on March 5, intending to buy half-interest in a Grand Rapids, Ohio, newspaper. When that venture failed, he had begun working his way from city to city toward New York. See

*Newspaper Days,* pp. 361-381; also, see W. A. Swanberg, DREISER (NY: Scribner's, 1965), pp. 52-55.

19. The final letter was written on the stationery of the Boody House, Toledo, Ohio.

20. For Dreiser's initial response to Arthur Henry, his long-time friend, see *Newspaper Days,* pp. 372-374.

21. The beauty of the Maumee River made such an impression on Dreiser that twenty-five years later he recalled it in *Newspaper Days,* pp. 362-364.

22. Dreiser apparently sent the picture, for one was included among the papers presented to the Lilly Library. No correspondence, however, remains after March 4, 1894.

## Yoshinobu Hakutani (essay date 1979)

SOURCE: Hakutani, Yoshinobu. "The Dream of Success in Dreiser's *A Gallery of Women*." *Zeitschrift für Anglistik und Amerikanistik,* vol. 27, no. 3, 1979, pp. 236-46.

[*In the following essay, Hakutani examines the characterization of the American woman in Dreiser's* A Gallery of Women, *with which early readers were disappointed. Hakutani finds that the portraits in the book are motivated more by internal psychology that by the external social factors which "determined the characters" in* Twelve Men, *published ten years earlier.*]

### I

Although Theodore Dreiser is often regarded as a pioneer among modern American novelists for the characterization of woman, very little critical attention has been paid to *A Gallery of Women* (1929). Upon its publication, this collection of fifteen semi-fictional portraits was compared to his *Twelve Men* (1919), a well-received volume of biographical portraits. Despite his disclaimers to the contrary, Dreiser did not have the same intimate knowledge of his women as he did of his men. Undoubtedly Dreiser portrayed women whom he had come across in his career, but his portraits lack conviction. Critics agree that the best portraits in *Twelve Men* are those of his brother Paul and his father-in-law Arch White, or men like Peter McCord and William Louis Sonntag, Jr., both most inspirational in his early journalism. Dreiser's readers had thus expected as much authenticity in *A Gallery of Women* as in *Twelve Men,* but they were disappointed.[1] And yet later readers still persisted in the same expectation. Considering *A Gallery of Women* as the companion volume to *Twelve Men,*

F. O. Matthiessen, for instance, looked for Dreiser's technique in differentiating women characters but concluded that such skills "deserted him when he tried to handle details that must have seemed to him more intimate."[2]

But the comparison was grossly unfair. The cool reception that has attended *A Gallery of Women* might have resulted not so much from Dreiser's treatment as from his subject-matter. Readers in twentieth-century America have shown a tendency to minimize the importance of woman in fiction. Only recently have Kate Chopin's short stories attracted serious attention; *Sister Carrie* was suppressed for seven long years. Such a tendency is hard to understand, for in the late nineteenth century the public accepted as a matter of course the greater freedom in the selection of themes in fiction than before. Needless to say, James' *The Portrait of a Lady* (1881) is a monumental work concerned with the problem of an American woman. A realist like Howells, too, responding to the libertarians' attack on the socially enforced misery of marriage, successfully treated a divorce for his subject in *A Modern Instance* (1882). In modern times, there has been no question about American novelists' willingness to deal with the woman question.

The difficulty, however, lies with the reading public. Ironically, even H. L. Mencken, Dreiser's staunch supporter, dismissed *A Gallery of Women* as a work inferior to *Twelve Men*:

> ... if the collection is not quite as interesting as its forerunner, then that is probably because women themselves are considerably less interesting than men. Not one of them here is to be mentioned in the same breath with Dreiser's brother Paul, the shining hero of **"Twelve Men"**. ... The rest are occasionally charming, but only too often their chief mark is a pathetic silliness. What ails most of them is love. They throw away everything for it, and when they can't get the genuine article they seem to be content with imitations. And if it is not love, real or bogus, that undoes them, then it is some vague dream that never takes rational form—of puerile self-expression, of gratuitous self-sacrifice, of something else as shadowy and vain.[3]

Moreover, what disappointed many early readers was the lack of variability they felt in Dreiser's characterization. For a reviewer who had expected to find as great a variety of preoccupations in women as in men, *A Gallery of Women* left the impression that "Mr. Dreiser believes there is one kind of woman—the one who is over-troubled with sex."[4] But this is far from true, for many of the heroines are not even remotely concerned with sex. Ernita, for example, is an American revolutionary who has voluntarily joined the communist movement in Siberia and is not at all tormented by sex.[5] If she is over-troubled by her life, it is not because of sex, but because she immerses herself in the ideology of communism. If Dreiser's ideal woman calls for an equilibrium of mind and heart, Ernita serves as an example of the woman who lacks heart. After an unwilling experience with what Dreiser calls "free love," in which she fails to satisfy herself, Ernita finally decides to return to her lawful husband. She confides to Dreiser: "I walked the floor, suffering because of my mind—this unescapable Puritan conscience of mine."[6] In Dreiser's denouement, Ernita, if anything, is "under-troubled" with the problem of sex.

The same holds true of the portraits of the fortuneteller Giff and an invincible ghetto woman named Bridget Mullanphy. Both are the types that are untroubled with sexual problems of any kind, and they are the ones who survive the most persecuting tyranny of life itself. In that world, however, as one critic observes, Dreiserian women are temperamental rather than intellectual; "so inevitably, as they strive to escape a dilemma not truly of their own making, they fare badly."[7] This dilemma destroys an ill-prepared woman like Esther Norn, who lets her lovers exploit her. But such a predicament is not what distresses other women in the same book. Under the circumstances, stoic women such as Bridget and Albertine fare magnificently because they are the types of women that Dreiser knew are endowed with unusual strength of character. Their success in life, furthermore, is demonstrated in terms of the qualities of mind and heart that make those of men glaringly inferior and shameful.

Whether heroines in *A Gallery of Women* fare well or not thus depends upon their individual merits and faults. For some, their lovers are wealthy and only seek sexual enjoyment in them; for others, their lovers are sexually content but only interested in their money. Being women, they are all subjected to various predicaments, but their ultimate success or failure in life is determined not by their circumstances but by themselves. In case after case, Dreiser's portraits suggest not a seemingly meaningless and ferocious struggle for existence, but an affirmation of individual worth. Always sympathetic with his heroine's potential as an individual being, Dreiser strives to present her in the best light. In their quest for success, Dreiser's women are unmistakenly drawn here to emphasize their own special needs for fulfillment. In brief, his intention was not a rehash of social determinism.

Thus, what distinguishes *A Gallery of Women* from a book like *Twelve Men* is that Dreiser's attitude toward his material is more psychological than social. The character traits that fascinated him in *A Gallery of Women* are not defined in terms of the social patterns that determined the characters in *Twelve Men.* The idiosyncrasies of Dreiser's

women seemed more internal to him than those of men. This was perhaps why Mencken, commenting on Dreiser's difficulty with *A Gallery of Women,* argued that women in general "remain more mysterious and hence more romantic."[8] Even though Giff appeared strangely nebulous in her intellectual outlook, or Olive Brand seemed only vaguely motivated by her sexual freedom, Dreiser did not fill in his abstract moral equations with the kind of realistic detail expected of a naturalist writer. Rather, he left the mystery inscrutable to the last.

Dreiser's attempt to be a "romantic" writer, however, did not result in ambiguities in his characterization. He made the best of his material, and of his knowledge about woman. He was persistent in search of truths about feminine temperament and what he understood to be woman's fate. His method was thus analytical, and to some of the portraits he adopted a psychological, if not consistently psychoanalytical, approach. For revelation of feminine secrets, Dreiser was occasionally preoccupied with Freudian theory, which was already fashionable in the 1920s. But here, too, Dreiser was curious rather than convinced, openly experimental rather than theoretical. Dreiser's open-mindedness about his subject and treatment in *A Gallery of Women* was thus indicated by his mention of the project as early as 1919. "God, what a work!" he told Mencken, "if I could do it truly—The ghosts of Puritans would rise and gibber in the streets."[9]

## II

One of the major themes that bind together the various portraits in *A Gallery of Women* is the American dream of success. Dreiser's women regard themselves as protagonists in their battle for success among male antagonists. In many of the stories, however, the heroine craves for success in her profession not so that she can rise superior to men, but so that she can achieve pride and peace of mind as an individual. By the time Dreiser planned to formulate these portraits, the dream of success for men had been so finely engrained in American life that it had become an essential part of the American psyche. Dreiser was only expected to modify this tradition as it would have applied to women. Unlike the characterization of the hero in a success story—in which the author's avowed emphasis was on the man's natural survival tactics in society—Dreiser's focus in *A Gallery of Women* was upon the heroine's personal motives and actions rather than the social and economic forces that would also determine her life.

Despite the variety of women portrayed in the book, and its length, the details of social and familial contexts that mark a Dreiserian novel are indeed scarce. This is a clear departure from Dreiser's use of imagery and symbolism derived from the concrete details of the character's reality—streets, houses, rooms, furniture, and clothes—as in *Sister Carrie* or a short story like **"The Second Choice."** Instead his portraits abound in verbal impressions, conversations, confessions, points of view, and abstract authorial explanations of various kinds. The successful portraits are those in which Dreiser effectively structures these details to show how his heroines are trying to fit their temperaments to their struggles despite repeated failures. In particular, Dreiser's primary interest lies in an exposé of the intricate and complex relationships which a woman writer, painter, or actress holds with her husbands, lovers, and gigolos. In the most successful of his portraits, such as **"Esther Norn,"** Dreiser's denouement creates pathos, since the heroine's "pursuit of happiness" is constantly hindered by the turn of the events that stem from her own errors in judgment.

Dreiser's portraits of the women professionals derive in large part from his own experiences in Greenwich Village in the twenties. He was fascinated by their lives, as he says at the beginning of each tale, because they were young and beautiful and they appeared intellectually competent. But as the story develops, the narrator—in most cases Dreiser himself—gradually informs the reader with some hesitation that the woman in question lacks the qualities of mind necessary for the realization of her dream. Clearly, Dreiser is dealing here with a "second-rate" personage in a particular profession. It is interesting that Dreiser as a magazine writer in the 1890s was convinced of the gift and originality attributed to many a woman professional—artist, writer, composer, lawyer, musician, singer.[10] Perhaps Dreiser of the twenties was a much more severe critic of woman's abilities than Dreiser of the nineties.

In any event, *A Gallery of Women* as a whole suggests that the dream of success in fields like art and writing could be realized only by independent, strong-willed women. This implication does have some relationship with Dreiser's latent prejudice against woman's intellectual abilities. In 1916 Dreiser told his first biographer, Dorothy Dudley Harvey, a graduate of Bryn Mawr, that he had found it difficult "to name one woman of any distinction or achievement out of the twenty-five years of that institution."[11] Later in **"Life, Art and America,"** included in *Hey Rub-a-Dub-Dub,* Dreiser thus declared:

> There is not a chemist, a physiologist, a botanist, a biologist, an historian, a philosopher, an artist, of any kind or repute among them; not one. They are secretaries to corporations, teachers, missionaries, college librarians, educators in any of the scores of pilfered meanings that may be attached to that much abused word. They are curators, directors, keepers. They are not individuals in the true

sense of that word; they have not been taught to think; they are not free. They do not invent, lead, create; they only copy or take care of, yet they are graduates of this college and its theory, mostly ultra conventional, or, worse yet, anæmic, and glad to wear its collar, to clank the chains of its ideas or ideals—automatons in a social scheme whose last and final detail was outlined to them in the classrooms of their alma mater. That, to me, is one phase, amusing enough, of intellectual freedom in America.[12]

What ultimately prevents Ellen Adams Wrynn, one of the heroines in *A Gallery of Women,* from becoming a successful painter is the lack of independence and freedom in her character. Although Dreiser emphasizes at the outset how this "young, attractive, vigorous, and ambitious" blonde will benefit the free spirits and creativity associated with the bohemian life of the Village, he predicts that "her enthusiasm would not last the numerous trials and tribulations of those who essay illustration and painting in general" (*Gallery,* I, 134). Ellen marries Walter Wrynn, a young broker, for "the delight of sex as well as the respect and material prosperity and social advancement that sometimes went with marriage for some." The marriage is obviously doomed and Dreiser uses Jimmie Race, a novice in painting much like Ellen, to serve as a foil to Walter. Dreiser's argument is that there is nothing wrong with a young woman's—much less an artist's—being a "varietist." More significantly, Ellen's problem is caused by her attitude toward sex; she takes sex lightly and lets her success dream preempt her desire for fulfillment. Despite her innate beauty and intelligence, she deliberately seeks the habits and mores antithetical to those one must acquire as an artist. For the benefit of her husband, she functions merely as a form of "sex worship" (I, 139); for Race, her first lover, she remains a listener to his sophormoric discourse on art and poetry.

Ellen's static personality, shown by the lack of spiritual communion with her sexual partner, is also reflected in her work. Though she travels to Paris and studies first hand the Post-Impressionists by living with one painter after another, she fails to be recognized for her work. One of her most influential lovers and mentors is a Scotish painter, Keir McKail, whose workmanship gives a clue to what is lacking in hers. While Dreiser admires the exotic color and thought in her painting, he notices the internal solidity behind the paint in McKail's work. "Naturally," Dreiser comments, "he avoided with almost religious austerity any suggestion of the sterile eccentricities that spoiled so much of the work of others . . . whereas beneath her surfaces was no real depth" (I, 160-61).

Another flaw in her character is reflected in a rigid and extreme relationship she establishes with her lover. She either dominates him or lets herself be dominated by him. Domination, in Dreiser's scheme for this story, means some compensation for the one who is dominated. Thus Ellen, dominated by McKail, learns a great deal from him about painting, and her workmanship improves. The irony is that from the other men she has dominated, she gains nothing but what she does not need for purposes of her art. From her husband she gets his physically strong manhood and their unwanted child; from Race, his complaints and lectures on abstract subjects. The most significant point is that Ellen lacks an independently motivated discipline of art. This initial deficiency in her character is proved by the fact that as soon as McKail leaves her, her workmanship declines and she is once more doomed to be a failure.[13]

Another heroine in *A Gallery of Women* who fails in her career is an Hollywood actress named Ernestine De Jongh.[14] She later commits suicide in New York at twenty-nine. At the close of the story, Ernestine relates to Dreiser another tragic story in which an actress she knew in Hollywood went downhill and committed suicide. Dreiser listens to her observation that Hollywood actresses "counted the years from sixteen to twenty-eight as the best of those granted to woman. After them came, more than likely, the doldrums" (*Gallery,* II, 562). Ernestine's account here not only points to the age phobia from which many women in that profession suffered but more significantly reveals the lack of confidence underlying her own character. As in Ellen Adams Wrynn's career, Ernestine always encounters the problem of identity. She is an actress as anyone recognizes, but she does not take advantage of her own beauty and "sex appeal"—the undeniable assets in her that Dreiser emphasizes.

The most serious problem Dreiser discovers, however, in Ernestine's career as in that of any other woman here is the lack of development in her character. It is true that Ernestine's becoming the mistress of Varn Kinsey, a poet and an altruistic intellectual of the community, enables her to reject the tinsel world of Hollywood. She recognizes through him, for example, that the order of the day in Hollywood is an orgy of self-satisfaction totally oblivious of art and creativity. And yet she deliberately seeks fame and power in that world by succumbing to an incompetent director whose main interest is in sexual orgies rather than in film-making. Despite her gift and ingenuity, she always remains secondary to a leading actress. Ironically, "she was looked upon as rather serious ... and directors desired and required types which were all that youth and beauty meant but without much brains" (II, 55). In Dreiser's assumption, then, she is neither brilliant nor ignorant; she is neither accomplished nor innocent. Like Ellen Adams Wrynn, Ernestine is denied possible success because of a dilemma: although she has sufficient intelligence to reach the top of her profession,

given the guidance of a lover like Kinsey, she can never reach her goal, nor is she content to take a secondary role in her profession.

In Dreiser's conception of the success dream, the lack of flexibility and growth in the woman's training for her profession has a direct corollary to the degree of her failure. Ernestine's failure, unlike Ellen's, is tragic not because of her suicide, but because there has been less interaction in her relations to her lovers than in the case of Ellen. The problem Ernestine faces in her life with Kinsey is thus more serious than that of Ellen in her relations with McKail. Ellen can gain artistic insights from her domineering lover; for Ernestine, however, her lover's dictatorial demeanor does shut off the channels of intellectual and artistic influence which she desperately needs. Even though Ernestine, like Ellen, displays her sympathy and admiration for her lover's noble spirits, she must dictate her own code of behavior and thus ruin her meaningful relationship with him. This naiveté is also evident in her sexual life. Ernestine's attitude toward sex is immature, for her beauty and physical appeal are used only for self-satisfaction and for mercenary gain.[15] Dreiser suggests that she is guilty of isolating her sexual life from the meaningful communion between man and woman. For she makes sex the touchstone of her own pleasure and, in particular, her vanity in quest of success.

Ernestine's attitude toward sex thus contrasts with Albertine's. Albertine is a strong-willed but graceful woman—a wife, a mother, and the mistress of a sculptor. Dreiser admires Albertine because she is capable of making sex grow beyond the realm of the physical. For her, unlike Ernestine, sex represents a search for human relatedness, a way out of her otherwise meaningless social and economic struggle. Besides saving herself from loneliness and isolation, she gives birth to an illegitimate child whose identity is kept only to themselves. Ernestine's way of life, on the contrary, is sterile. For Ernestine, the call of sex is not transformed in character since it is not supported by a genuine feeling of love and responsibility. In short, Ernestine's sexual life neither enriches her life nor improves her talent as an actress.

The weaker qualities of mind and heart exhibited in the failures these heroines have faced in their careers can be related to their backgrounds. Except for Esther Norn, all of the women in search of success in their chosen fields come from wealthy, conservative families. In the case of Emanuela, her family's Puritan heritage—despite her broad education in literature—has made her sexually frigid for life. Failing to seduce her at a crucial point in their relations, Dreiser bluntly tells her: "You're suffering from an inhibition of some kind against sex, your normal relationship to men and life" (*Gallery,* II, 708). Isabel Archer in *The Portrait of a Lady,* who seems to live with a fear of over-sexed men, is nevertheless capable of feeeling the power of sex as shown in her final encounter with Goodwood.[16] If Isabel is considered a morally and sexually independent spirit, as she is by most critics, Emanuela in *A Gallery of Women* is clearly a pathological case. At the final moment in her encounter with Dreiser—who has by then lost all his passion for her—she confesses: "Oh well, you may be right, I don't know. I'm not going to try to explain or adjust myself now" (II, 709). Ernestine De Jongh's background is equally conservative and affluent: she is the daughter of a prosperous dairyman in America's northwest. Although she is not sexually inhibited as Emanuela is, her family education has not helped her become a free spirit. The irony in her life is that her most esteemed lover is involved in many liberal causes—woman suffrage, child labor, and publication of radical magazines.

Thus, Dreiser's women professionals like Emanuela and Ernestine share their common family backgrounds that are intellectually stifling and detrimental to their growth and development. Esther Norn, on the other hand, does not come from such a family, but she is handicapped in another way. Losing her mother in her youth, she was raised by her father. Because he was often unemployed, as in many of Dreiser's stories as well as in his own life, Esther was forced to subject herself to a series of menial jobs. Like Sister Carrie, she manages to obtain a small part in a play and thus begins her career to realize her dream. She falls in love with a young poet of the Village—"an on-the-surface eccentric and clown or court-jester" (II, 732). As this relationship wears off, another self-styled poet, Doane, comes into her life. Though she marries him, Doane turns out to be financially dependent upon her. The significant point in her character, however, is that her actions of sacrifice for the benefit of her husband are not caused by his inability or unwillingness to secure a livelihood for them, but derived from her own upbringing. The reader is constantly reminded of the fact that Esther's father, like her lovers, has always been what Dreiser calls a "loafer" and "woman-chaser." This image in her girlhood was so strongly imprinted in her mind that she takes her father's way of life for that of all men. Unlike Hurstwood, who falls a victim in a similar predicament, Doane can instead prey on Esther. For example, Doane encourages Esther, his lawful wife, to be sexually involved with a theatre manager so that she may succeed on the stage. Dreiser's advice against such an adventure for Esther's sake suggests that not only is Doane a moral coward, but also that she is destined to be a failure as well.

In *A Gallery of Women,* then, the loss of self-confidence an heroine suffers in seeking success seems to result partly from her early life. The respective backgrounds of Esther and Ernestine, for example, represent two extreme cases of family influence. Esther's life is perverted by the ever-present parasitic way of life led by her father; Ernestine's is misdirected by the cloistered existence in her early life. Each in her own way struggles to lead an independent life in spite of the earlier influences and experiences which are detrimental to her new spirit. Some women, such as Ellen, come close to the realization of their dreams. In fact, Ellen does reach a point of excellence in her career. But she cannot maintain that excellence, let alone go beyond, without the help of a superior artist and philosopher who also serves as her lover.

This pattern of failure, however, applies to Dreiser's heroines who are deliberately seeking success in the professions formerly monopolized by men. There are no such dreams cherished by women like Bridget and Albertine. Bridget, a wife and mother, is the virtual head of a household inhabited by her drunken husband, an old daughter with an illegitimate child, and relatives; and yet she succeeds in putting her family together and survives with dignity. Albertine is the loyal wife of a businessman who is bankrupt and charged with a fraud, but she too survives the ordeal and successfully raises her children. For the woman whose function in life is to be a wife and mother, her dream of success is survival. But for the woman whose dream is to achieve success in a man's world, she is necessarily handicapped, and no matter how bravely she pursues her goal she fails to reach it.

Why is it that a woman professional fails in America despite her promising potential? Dreiser attempts to answer this central question in *A Gallery of Women.* The international critic of women who appears in **"Ernestine"** describes American women in a lengthy commentary:

> These American girls are astonishing, really. They are not always so well equipped mentally, but they have astounding sensual and imaginative appeal as well as beauty and are able to meet the exigencies of life in a quite satisfactory manner, regardless of what Europe thinks. ... By that I mean that your American girl of this type thinks and reasons as a woman, not as a man, viewing the problems that confront her as a woman, studying life from a woman's viewpoint and solving them as only a woman can. She seems to realize, more than do her sisters of almost any other country to-day, that her business is to captivate and later dominate the male, with all his special forces and intelligence, by hers, and having done that she knows that she has bagged the game. Now I do not count that as being inferior or stupid. To me it is being effective.

(II, 532)

However, what is finally lacking in a woman like Ernestine De Jongh is a stable and independent philosophy that transcends the narrow confines of feminine mentality. Dreiser's prediction, stated before her story unfolds, is that she is "too much inclined, possibly, to look for worth in others—too little to compel it in herself" (II, 529). Dreiser's conclusion, therefore, is just opposite of the European observer's view: the way in which an American woman of Ernestine's type is prepared in her quest for success is simply *not effective.*

### III

There is no doubt about Dreiser's compassion for these ill-prepared heroines in *A Gallery of Women,* just as one is reminded that Dreiser has shown more sympathy for Jennie Gerhardt than Carrie Meeber. *A Gallery of Women,* moreover, exhibits a consciously developed pattern in which the less self-reliant the heroine is the higher price of injury she has to pay for the battle of life. Because she is not mentally well equipped, she develops a tendency to rely on men for spiritual and financial securities. Because she has a limited vision and understanding of her lover's worth, she can be swiftly exploited by him. All this happens to Ernestine, Emanuela, and Ellen with equal intensity.

The most complex pattern Dreiser weaves into the success stories in *A Gallery of Women* is that of Esther Norn. It bears a structural resemblance to *Sister Carrie.* Both women, under twenty, start out in a huge, friendless city, looking for employment but in vain. Then they are both rescued by men. Esther's first lover is, like Drouet, a good, carefree man "in search of pleasure and things to interest him" (II, 729), and he maintains a bachelor apartment on the borders of the Village. Esther's second lover is Doane, who is, like Hurstwood, more sophisticated than his rival in every way. Once Esther and Doane are married, Doane's infatuation with Esther wears off and Doane, like Hurstwood, becomes financially dependent upon his wife who can make more money in the theatre. Unlike Carrie, however, Esther lets Doane take advantage of her livelihood. The third man who appears on the scene for Esther is a liberal social worker named J. J. As in Carrie's relationship to Ames, Esther is greatly fascinated by J. J.'s intellectual abilities but avoids any emotional, much less sexual, involvement with him. The most important difference between the two heroines is obvious: while Carrie is "bright"[17] to begin with and able to cultivate a free spirit in her development,[18] Esther is not.

Dreiser's conception of the success dream in *A Gallery of Women* is thus crystalized in the story of Esther Norn. For Esther figures as a clear antithesis to what Carrie stands for in a woman's struggle for success in the modern world.

Esther is not motivated by honorable intentions as Carrie is; financially Esther becomes the mistress of her fate as Carrie does not. From the beginning Esther falls in love with a well-intentioned rich man only for security, but she does not possess a temperament, a vital spirit, that must serve as proof against the wheel of life. As her consumptive health well demonstrates, her striving for success is set back by every change of fortune; Esther is the type of woman that cannot fulfill ever higher potentialities of being. Each of her affairs, unlike Carrie's, does not serve to facilitate her emotional and artistic growth. Even when Doane becomes unemployed and his character begins to degenerate, she fails to take over and dominate him. She has none of Carrie's resourcefulness and eagerness to face up to and venture into all that life has to offer. Most pathetically, while Carrie at the end of the novel is on her way to "success" in her profession, Esther dies in a sanatorium only wondering about her husband who has long neglected her.

The most serious failing Dreiser finds in the women who cherish the dream of success is their dependence upon men. This idea which pervades *A Gallery of Women* is based on Dreiser's conviction that success attends only those truly liberated women who can resist men's intellectual and economical influences. Marguerite Tjader, who perhaps knew Dreiser more than anyone else living today, writes:

> Women's characters and experiences interested Dreiser endlessly. He loved to question them about themselves, their impressions, their reactions to this and that. He was never tired of studying the likes and dislikes that made up, what was to him, the mystery of feminine behavior. ... Women were tremendously stimulated by him, because he always wanted to build them up to whatever superior qualities they might have, wanted them to be their best, most daring, selves.
>
> At the same time, he had come to be afraid of making commitments to any woman who might want to depend on him too much.[19]

Such testimony by a woman reader clarifies the places of various heroines in Dreiser's feminism. A woman of Esther's type that immediately reminds us of Jennie Gerhardt is a battered heroine of beauty and gentleness, thus generating our pity and sympathy. But the character of such a woman is decidedly inferior to the contrasting stature of Carrie, whom Dreiser calls a "little soldier of fortune" (*Sister Carrie,* p. 67). Carrie is better armed for the battle of life, can outlast any man placed in a similar predicament. And, in the end, even after breaking the conventions of society—in which "All men should be good, all women virtuous" (p. 101)—by becoming the mistress of one man after the other, she is still too strong to suffer any anguished pangs of remorse as a Jennie or an Esther is not. It is understandable that genteel American readers could swallow neither Carrie's success at the close of the novel nor her indifference to society's so-called "moral" laws. From the standpoint of liberated women, however, Dreiser's ending of **Sister Carrie** could have elicited nothing but their admiration and respect. Given a male point of view, on the other hand, it is not difficult to understand why the stories of Jennie and Esther can bring in the reader not only compassion but a deluded sense of relief and satisfaction.

### Notes

1. Critics' misunderstanding of Dreiser's intention in *A Gallery of Women* stemmed partly from Dreiser himself. With an eye for promoting a greater sale of his books under a single imprint, Dreiser wrote on March 30, 1922, to Arthur Carter Hume, a legal consultant: "It is a work about woman à la *Twelve Men*. It will be as frank and direct and sincere as *Twelve Men*" (*Letters of Theodore Dreiser,* ed. Robert H. Elias, Philadelphia 1959, II, 393). Dreiser, however, privately admitted that *A Gallery of Women* was clearly more fictional than otherwise and that at its planning stage it was not equated with *Twelve Men*. Thus, he had earlier told William C. Lengel, his secretary: "Anyhow, each paper is a study of a woman, not always young, not always old, sometimes a relative, sometimes a friend, sometimes merely a woman whom I have observed from a distance but relative to whom I have the data" (*Letters*, I, 349).

2. F. O. Matthiessen, *Theodore Dreiser,* New York 1951, p. 182.

3. H. L. Mencken, "Ladies, Mainly Sad," *American Mercury,* 19 (February 1930), 254-55, in Jack Salzman, ed. *Theodore Dreiser: The Critical Reception,* New York 1972, p. 579.

4. Rollo Walter Brown, "Fifteen Women," *Saturday Review of Literature,* 6 (February 8, 1930), 707-08, in Salzman, p. 582.

5. Ernita's prototype is Emma Goldman. Dreiser remembered her role in the assassination attempt against Henry Clay Frick during the Homestead strike in 1892, when he was a newspaper reporter in St. Louis. His personal relationship with Goldman dates as early as from 1910, when both attended the Anarchists' Ball in New York. Sinclair Lewis, who attended the same ball, wrote in a letter to a friend: "Emma Goldman has never been married, living openly with the man of her choice. She is so violent a radical that a U.S. soldier was given three years in the military prison at Leavenworth for merely attending one of her lectures and then shaking hands with her. ... And this bomb-thrower proved to be a stout, plain faced, eye-glassed woman like a Jewish haus-frau with a little education. ... She got into a discussion of the advancement of anarchism, with Theodore Dreiser. ... Dreiser, seated next me, waggled his scrawny forefinger, and looked superiority through his heavy, gold rimmed, scholastic eye glasses; but Emma sent back hot shot—speaking as quietly as the haus-frau she seemed to be; yet tremendous in her conviction that a complete and immediate emancipation of individuality from all the old bonds of religion and government and prejudice and ignorance is at hand." See Mark Schorer, *Sinclair Lewis: An American Life,* New York 1961, p. 179; cf. Hakutani, "Sinclair Lewis and Dreiser: A Study in Continuity and Development," *Discourse,* 7 (Summer 1964), 254-76. Dreiser also wrote to Goldman in 1928 asking for more information on her life to be included in *A Gallery of Women*; see *Letters,* II, 483-84.

6. *A Gallery of Women,* I, New York 1929, 343-44; hereafter referred to as *Gallery.*

7. John J. McAleer, *Theodore Dreiser: An Introduction and Interpretation,* New York 1968, p. 28.

8. Mencken in Salzman, p. 580.

9. See Dreiser's letter of April 5, 1919, to Mencken in *Letters,* I, 264.

10. In "A High Priestess of Art," *Success,* 1 (January 1898), 55, Dreiser attempted to destroy the widely held favoritism for women artists by quoting Alice Barber Stephens: "Neither girl nor boy can succeed without aptitude and the hardest kind of work, but girls are rather novel in the field, and their work may receive slightly more gentle consideration to begin with. It would not be accepted, however, without merit." In a similar article on Mrs. Kenyon Cox, a painter herself and wife of a well-known American painter in the nineties, Dreiser recognized a controversy over "the fitness and originality of women in other branches of art work" but was convinced of her distinction and achievement in the field of decoration. The future novelist was impressed not only by Mrs. Cox's illustrative technique but by a profound philosophy underlying her successful paintings; see

"Work of Mrs. Kenyon Cox," *Cosmopolitan,* 24 (March 1898), 477.

11. Dorothy Dudley, *Dreiser and the Land of the Free,* New York 1946, p. 363.

12. See Dreiser, *Hey Rub-a-Dub-Dub,* New York 1920, pp. 260-61.

13. Dreiser discussed a screenplay of "Ellen Adams Wrynn" prepared by an Hollywood writer: "I do not say that hers [Ellen's art] deteriorated, but certainly it did not improve once she was separated from him [McKail]. It is a phase that might well be dramatically developed." See Dreiser's letter of March 17, 1934, to I. E. Chadwick in *Letters,* II, 675.

14. This story had previously appeared under the title "Portrait of a Woman" in *The Bookman,* 66 (September 1927), 2-14.

15. The orgiastic life of Hollywood is satirized in this portrait with considerable detail:

> Then, more than now, the grandees and magnificoes of this realm—the male portion at least, to say nothing of a heavy percentage of the women themselves—were determined to satiate themselves at any cost. Rules were even made that no young married woman of any shade of loyalty to her vows need apply for advancement in this field, and no unmarried woman of any great beauty or physical appeal need apply unless willing to submit herself, harem-wise, to the managers and directors, and even principals. For in nearly all cases at this time the principals were able to say with whom, or without whom, they would work. And if a girl were young and attractive she had to be hail-fellow-well-met with every Tom, Dick and Harry from prop-boy and office-scullion to director, casting director and president. She had to "troop," be "a regular fellow."

> (*Gallery,* II, 548-49)

16. In the revised version James describes Goodwood's kiss as "white lightning, a flash that spread, and spread again, and stayed; and it was extraordinarily as if, while she took it, she felt each thing in his hard manhood. ..." See *The Novels and Tales of Henry James,* New York 1908, IV, 436. Cf. Stephen Reid, "Moral Passion in *The Portrait of a Lady* and *The Spoils of Poynton,*" *Modern Fiction Studies,* 12 (Spring 1966), 24-43.

17. In Dreiser's initial depiction of Carrie, "She was eighteen years of age, bright, timid, and full of illusions of ignorance and youth" (*Sister Carrie,* New York 1900, p. 1).

18. Readers of *Sister Carrie* have responded somewhat differently to Carrie's development and, in particular, the final scene of Carrie rocking in her chair. Philip Gerber, in *Theodore Dreiser,* New York 1964, p. 63, points out that "successful but unhappy, accomplished but unfulfilled, she dreams of further conquests which will—*must*—bring her lasting joy." I have suggested that the "hopeful tone" in which the scene is rendered indicates her strength of will and hence her free spirit, "*Sister Carrie* and the Problem of Literary Naturalism," *Twentieth Century Literature,* 13 (April 1967), 15. Louis Auchincloss, in "Introduction" to the facsimile edition of *Sister Carrie,* Columbus 1969, p. x, maintains: "I do not see why it is so bad to dream such happiness, and ... it had not occurred to me that Carrie *was* that kind of dreamer." Donald Pizer, in *The Novels of Theodore Dreiser: A Critical Study,* Minneapolis 1976, p. 346, regarding the scene "as a constant flux of momentary delight and prolonged dissatisfaction," argues that she would "lose the happiness she had temporarily gained, and that this cycle is never-ending."

19. Marguerite Tjader, *Theodore Dreiser: A New Dimension,* Norwalk, Conn. 1965, p. 12.

## Miriam Gogol (essay date 1990)

SOURCE: Gogol, Miriam. "*The "Genius"*: Dreiser's Testament to Convention." *CLA Journal,* vol. 33, no. 4, June 1990, pp. 402-14.

[*In the following essay, Gogol argues that* The "Genius" *exhibits "the problems inherent in Dreiser's naturalistic fiction," and that the novel actually depicts a world in which "free will in effect does not exist."*]

*The "Genius"* (1915) is one of Dreiser's least known and yet most significant novels. I think it is Dreiser's most misread, most misunderstood work. Upon publication, it was wrongly attacked by the New York Society for the Suppression of Vice. They called it obscene and said that it promoted licentious behavior. It hardly does that. Eugene Witla, the protagonist, is struck down by a disease, "locomotor ataxia," for every moment of what Dreiser calls his sexual "over-indulgence." It has been wrongly defended, in contrast, by critics who see in the novel a plea for the artist and the artist's special need for freedom outside the conventions of society. And it has been wrongly ignored—hence this article. Perhaps *The "Genius"* is as great a novel as *An American Tragedy.* Certainly, in my estimation, it is greater than *Sister Carrie*—in any of its forms. It is one of the best explorations of a marriage gone wrong in the annals of American fiction. Dreiser himself declared it his "best" novel.

*The "Genius"* reveals a great deal about Dreiser's perception of the role of the artist in American society and, by implication, about his view of each individual's role in society. In the course of this discussion, I might sound quite critical of the novel—which is not my intention. My intention is to point out the problems inherent in Dreiser's naturalistic fiction, and since *The "Genius"* exemplifies what can and does go wrong in such fiction, I chose it as my subject.

The novel begins in the 1880s; the central character, Eugene Witla, is from a midwestern, middle-class family described as "typically American."[1] He goes to Chicago and then to New York, where he becomes a famous painter, hence the title, *The "Genius."* He reluctantly marries Angela Blue, a country girl, because he feels it his duty. (She had threatened suicide if he refused, after their long courtship.) The marriage is so horrendous that, in one of the novel's milder passages, Eugene describes their union as a "galling yoke" (p. 352). His problem (and his wife's) is that he craves other women, and so has a series of affairs, including one with an eighteen-year-old girl, for whom he loses his home and his prestigious job. By the end of the novel, his wife has died in childbirth, he himself has had two nervous breakdowns, and he is left gazing at the stars, "hardened" and "tempered for life and work" (p. 714).

On this outline of the plot, I think the critics and I can agree. Also, we agree that the novel deals primarily with Eugene's demand for special privileges and special freedoms (such as freedom from the obligations of marriage, freedom to live with young girls, freedom from establishing any enduring relationships). But that is as far as our agreement goes. R. N. Mookerjee, for example, says that the novel "makes a strong plea for the *special recognition* of the artist who is not governed and judged by the same moral and ethical code as ordinary human beings, especially in the matter of . . . relationship[s] [*sic*] between the sexes" (emphasis mine).[2] Philip Gerber also believes that Dreiser advocates "the natural right of the artist to absolute freedom. [Dreiser] protests with vehemence . . . the dark prejudices and empty ideals of society which curb the creative genius."[3] I could go on and on, citing many critics who applaud Eugene as a model of individuality and who deplore—along with Dreiser they presume—the society that tries to curb him.

Much to the contrary is my belief that *The "Genius"* is one of the strongest and most frightening arguments ever put forth in fiction for how we all must conform to the conventions of middle-class American society. This novel argues forcefully and unrelentingly that there is no alternative to the status quo, except unmitigated suffering, spiritual and physical, for those who violate its codes. For his excessive sexual appetite, Eugene suffers the most acute physical pain (aches in the groin) and mental anguish (two nervous breakdowns). He ultimately learns to modify his behavior and serve society.

Critics usually regard Dreiser as a "subversive" who calls America to account for the inequities of its ways. In *The "Genius,"* Dreiser is and must be, in spite of himself, a proponent of the American political system. In his fiction, he is a proponent of capitalism (that is, free enterprise, a competitively viable meritocracy) and the middle-class norms that support it—the values, symbols, beliefs, and rituals designed to keep the system going—by that I mean competition, individualism, belief in will power and character, belief in the naturalness of individual ambition.[4] The narrative never endorses those characters who try to oppose social norms and conventions. To the extent that they oppose those norms, they are punished by events. Dreiser is engaged in an essentially conservative form of rhetoric that does not allow for significant dialectical challenges to American social realities. Granted, again and again he does try to challenge the prevailing social system, but each time he retreats, for he commands neither the vocabulary, the fictional strategies, nor the values to articulate an "un-American" set of ideals. In effect, Dreiser's fiction is governed by a series of evasions, which are not intentional on Dreiser's part. They result from the influence of cultural norms on his fictional imagination.

I am obviously suggesting that *The "Genius"* only seems naturalistic, if by "naturalistic" we mean a novel that uses the method of empiricism and espouses the philosophy of determinism, a novel whose characters are shaped by impersonal social, economic, and biological forces, where free will in effect does not exist. Such a novel would in effect be antithetical to American ideological thought. From the beginning of *The "Genius,"* we see the characteristic middle-class cast of Dreiser's imagination in his unquestioning assumption of the universe as essentially a natural marketplace. The American dream of material success comes true again and again for Eugene. He rises to the top in two different fields—advertising and art—because he is the most gifted and ambitious. But in contrast to Dreiser, Émile Zola, who is regarded as the founder of literary naturalism, focuses not on individual ambition but on overpowering economic and biological forces that create circumstances beyond the individual's control or influence. Thus, someone like Gervaise in Zola's *L'Assommoir,* despite heroic efforts, can never escape the Paris ghetto in which we first glimpse her. And Catherine and Etienne in *Germinal* remain part of an oppressed community of miners trapped in a struggle between labor and capital. Ultimately Zola blames the social order, and he suggests the alternative possibility of organized labor.

Like a naturalistic novel, ***The "Genius"*** focuses on Eugene's need to defy society. The central question debated throughout the novel's 700-odd pages is whether Eugene can live by "private law." Can he be "a ravening wolf of indifference to convention"? The debate is dramatized by Eugene's tumultuous marriage to Angela Blue. As a social institution, marriage carries with it rules and constraints representative of the society-at-large. By defying these rules and constraints, Eugene demonstrates his desire to protest marriage's validity and meaning and that of society as well. The fact that Eugene expresses his defiance by insisting on sexual freedom is of particular importance, for sex in the novel is characterized as a "raging lion." When it becomes "master," Eugene follows "its behest blindly, desperately, to the point almost of exposure and destruction" (p. 172). Since sex may and later does lead almost to destruction, built into the debate is a foregone conclusion about the danger of freedom if taken to excess.

Eugene perceives himself as "not an ordinary man" (because he is a genius) and thus refuses "to live an ordinary life" (p. 555). He wants to live as "a law unto himself" (p. 632), that is, he wants to do anything he pleases, which, in his case, of course, means the constant pursuit of other women before, during, and after his marriage to Angela. Openly defiant, he seems to provide an example of another way of life outside of conventional society that satisfies his needs. Most of the novel focusses on his refusal to "settle down," on his judgment of marriage as an abnormal state. Through his affairs, he raises questions about the validity of monogamy, the family, and, by extension, the social order they preserve. This seeming challenge to the status quo is, I believe, what leads some critics to see in ***The "Genius"*** an indictment of society that ultimately does not materialize.

Contrary to general opinion, Dreiser is not opposed to the status quo. He really endorses social constraints, law and order, and conformity to social roles, and that can be seen by looking at the results of Eugene's efforts to flout society. To the extent that Eugene and other of Dreiser's characters (Hurstwood, Jennie, Clyde, Stewart, and Etta) attempt to live by their own rules, they are drummed out of society and forced to make due reparations. Neither Eugene nor these others can enjoy the privilege of "private law." To Dreiser, law is *by definition* like Hawthorne's in *The Scarlet Letter*: One cannot stand in radical opposition

to society and survive in that society. One's act cannot have, as Hawthorne puts it, a "consecration of [its] own."[5]

The actual plot of the story reads like a tract on moral rectitude. Dreiser's underlying vision is the same as that of James 1:15: "When lust hath conceived, it bringeth forth sin: and sin, when it is finished, bringeth forth death." In ***The "Genius,"*** Eugene begins to endure a living death. Overindulgence in sex destroys his business instinct and his artistic ability! The narrator tells us so: Sex can "rob talent of its finest flavor, discolor the aspect of the world for [Eugene] ... and hamper effort with nervous irritation and make accomplishment impossible" (p. 238). It is remarkable that Dreiser, one of the first American writers to introduce explicit sex into the mainstream of American fiction, should also condemn it.

The only recourse for Eugene until he recovers from his nervous breakdown is sexual abstinence—which suggests the degree to which Dreiser fears the dangers of bodily desires. But Eugene refuses to abstain. Dreiser's story sounds like Jonah's in the Old Testament: Eugene repeatedly flees from God (or "Truth") and is visited by divine retribution, in this case by two nervous collapses. During these periods, he perceives sin as all around him. His world begins to resemble Milton's description of hell in *Paradise Lost*: Dreiser describes Eugene as surrounded by "lust, dishonesty, selfishness, envy, hypocrisy, slander, hate, theft, ... dementia, insanity, inanity ... no light anywhere. Only a storm of evil and death" (p. 260). Like the religious melancholiac in William James's *The Varieties of Religious Experience,* Eugene suffers from anhedonia, a loss of appetite for all life's pleasures and rewards—as he must—for that condition, followed by a gnawing, carking, questioning and anguished search for philosophic relief, is a prerequisite to salvation.[6]

As long as Eugene persists in this state of sinful willfulness, he perceives the external world as hateful and grim; he has been endowed

> with the ability to turn this terrible searchlight of intelligence ... [on] the deep as with a great white ray ... It revealed ... how the big fish fed upon the little ones, the strong ... [upon] the weak. ... Good was not always rewarded—frequently terribly ill-rewarded. Evil was seen to flourish beautifully at times. It was all right to say that it would be punished, but would it?
>
> (p. 348)

This perception of unpunished evil as flourishing and triumphant is central to the novel's meaning. Eugene has been granted a prophetic glimpse of the overwhelming malevolence, cruelty, and injustice of a world forsaken.

He confronts the depths of lust, madness, and degradation in order to understand better whether life has any moral significance. If this viewpoint had been corroborated in the novel, *The "Genius"* would no doubt be a powerful indictment of life, particularly American life, since the evil and inequality of which Eugene speaks ("The big fish feeding upon the little," "The good that was ill rewarded") are based upon his own experiences here.

But this catastrophic view contends with another one, which is beneficent and affirmative. Eugene has the ability to "tear himself up by the roots in order to see how he was getting along" (p. 346). By examining his own inner processes, he learns that he is not "going as a true man should" (p. 346), that there is a universal standard to which he is not measuring up. Repeatedly, Dreiser makes references to this "true man," to this "real" (p. 353) or "ideal" self that can provide Eugene and others with a sense of purpose and direction, and with the means to regeneration. This "true" self always stands, as we will see, in concert with "all forceful society" (p. 379), which is a power beyond the influence of any individual who tries to defy it. My point here is that such references to "ideal" selves complying to universal standards of good that corroborate society's sanctions have no relation to naturalism's basis in empiricism. In fact, such assertions are in direct contradiction to naturalism's espousal of detachment from any assumed truths.

These conflicting views of universal evil and of universal good warred with each other in Eugene's mind until the end of the novel. At that time, we learn that his pessimistic view serves a specifically punitive and corrective function: it helps teach him what not to do, what not to think. Significantly, his external world is created by and exists only as a reflection of his own level of moral behavior. He sees in it only what he sees in himself at that point. Dreiser says, "As a man thinketh so is he" (p. 286), but here we see that as a man thinketh, so is the world. If he is righteous and "clean," he perceives the world as such. He is, then, in this particular sense, responsible for the world as well as for his own personal destiny. For the universe reflects his moral state which—as the end of the novel suggests—is always remediable. Dreiser encourages us to see the gap between what is and what should be in this didactic novel. We, too, are urged to "tear ourselves up by the roots" to see if we are meeting the universal standards of good.

I think that one of the reasons many critics interpret the novel as anticonvention and antimarriage is that convention and marriage seem to be epitomized in Angela, Eugene's long-suffering, repressive wife whom Dreiser appears to abhor. She is neither self-directed nor self-controlled. She is held up to comparison with formidable women like the artists Miriam Finch and Christina Channing, who "reach experience and understanding of how the world is organized and what they . . . have to do to succeed" (p. 139). Dreiser openly celebrates these women, for he is interested in characters, particularly women who can "get on" in this world. Since Angela binds Eugene in marriage, refuses divorce, and spouts all kinds of "conventional" ideas *ad nauseam,* it is easy to label her the enemy and her values the source of Eugene's problems and thus interpret the novel as opposed to convention. But Angela is not in touch with her "true" or ideal self, which is brought out in the juxtaposition of her with these other "liberated" women. She conforms to society merely out of fear, without development of her intellectual and artistic self which, if developed, would invariably accord with higher truths that reinforce the values of family, order, and society.

Society, as it stands, is a reflection of "those principles which govern the universe" (p. 125). Although our motives might not be pure, we still uphold that which is for the best. Dreiser explains in the novel:

> Our social life is so organized, so closely knit upon a warp of instinct, that we almost always *instinctively* flee that which does not accord with custom, usage, preconceived notions and tendencies—those various things which we in our littleness of vision conceive to be dominant. Who does not run from the man who may because of his deeds be condemned of that portion of the public which we chance to respect? Walk he ever so proudly, carry himself with what circumspectness he may, at the first breath of suspicion all are off—friends, relations, business acquaintances, the . . . social fabric in toto.

(p. 666)

That sounds like typical Dreiser, criticizing the hypocrisy of people. But Dreiser then says, and this is the important part, that "it seems *a tribute to that providence* which shapes our ends, *which continues perfect in tendency* however vilely we may overlay its brightness with the rust of our mortal corruption, however imitative we may be" (p. 666). My point, or rather Dreiser's unironic point, is that regardless of our motives in disdaining "non-standard" behavior, nonetheless a "perfect" providence is supporting and countenancing its effect (which is to alienate those with nonstandard modes of behavior), and Dreiser salutes the wisdom of this providence.

Near the end of the novel, the issues that Dreiser set out to analyze are evaded. The last fifty-odd pages turn from Eugene's actual problems (breakdown, unemployment, lust) to an exegesis of Christian Science and other metaphysical beliefs. No pragmatic solutions are ever offered for Eugene's problems; instead, the problems are elevated to a spiritual plane where pragmatic solutions lose all significance. How strange for a naturalistic novel to end with spiritual concerns.

For spiritual refuge, Eugene reads Emerson, Huxley, Russell Wallace, and finally Christian Science's Mary Baker Eddy, who believes that a true comprehension of spirit can drive away mortal ills and that "everything that is is for the best" (p. 706). Eugene thus reasons that if it is right to cease living with his wife, Angela, it will happen. And if he does what is right, he will have peace and happiness (p. 671).

Eugene learns that all things, including his own sense of self, are based on ideas. And being a "perfect and indestructible" idea in God, he can *will* himself to do anything he chooses. As the narrator says: "'As a man thinketh so is he' and so also is the estimate of the whole world at the time he is thinking of himself thus—not as he is but as he thinks he is" (p. 286). This belief in will power, so crucial to Eugene's self-restoration, is, of course, antithetical to naturalism's foundation in determinism. But it is fundamental to Dreiser and his interpretation of American life. Much of what he says about will power might have come not from Zola but from a contemporary American self-help tract that espouses traditional middle-class beliefs: "Will it and it is thine. . . . No longer grovel as though the hand of fate were upon thee. Stand erect. Thou art a man, and thy mission is a noble one."[7]

This notion of self-creation floods Eugene with a sense of "positive liberty" (p. 533)—of his and every man's inalienable right to follow the unbridled aspirations of his heart and understanding. This sense dominates the latter part of the novel and promises an enormous freedom. Yet, significantly, Eugene does not put these principles to the test of dramatic resolution. (He does not, for example, run away with his eighteen-year-old girlfriend. He inexplicably complies with her mother's demands, even though he knows that they signal the end of the relationship, a relationship for which he risked and lost his wife, his home, and his high-powered job.) Nor does Eugene apply these principles pragmatically to the problems of his life. And neither does Dreiser. He holds out the promise of freedom for Eugene and then drops it, as the novel attempts to answer all questions metaphysically.

By the close of the novel, Eugene is taught the lesson that he must change his ways. According to Dreiser, he had not followed "the course of righteousness" (p. 666) espoused by the Old Testament prophets. Dreiser says that this in one of the most astonishing passages in the text. He compares Eugene to those whom God *made examples of* because of their follies. The following quotation is so shocking in light of false assumptions about Dreiser's naturalistic allegiances, that I need to quote it at length. Dreiser says:

> The prophets of the Old Testament . . . were forever pronouncing the fate of those whose follies were in opposition to the course of righteousness and who were made examples of by a beneficent and yet awful power. . . . Eugene was in a minor way an exemplification of this seeming course of righteousness. His kingdom, small as it was, was truly at an end.

(p. 665-66)

But this is not the end for Eugene. His punishment has been a "corrective affliction," and he emerges with a deeper sense of piety. He has gained a new "responsibility to that abstract thing, society" (p. 705). He learns to combine his artistic talent with civic duty, painting murals in banks and other public places. And through the birth of his daughter, "the child of conscience" (p. 702), he becomes further accountable for his actions, for he now sees himself as a father, a model, and a provider.

Dreiser's portrait of Eugene's decline and rise implies that the proper attitude toward life is to be realized by living in accord with what Dreiser elsewhere calls the "Equation Inevitable,"[8] a "law" in nature that strikes a balance between conflicting elements, causing the wrong to be made right, sinners to be punished, and justice to prevail.

In *The "Genius,"* he suggests that individuals such as Eugene must be made fully aware of their responsibility to society and must act in accordance with what is good for all. If the individual benefits society, he will benefit himself as well. Through this exclusive focus on the individual's own moral responsibility to himself and to those around him, Dreiser circumvents any analysis of the problems intrinsic to society itself.

Yet, remarkably, Dreiser does not regard the "Equation Inevitable" as necessarily a "moral" law. On this issue, he retreats into an agnostic reticence, echoing the conflict of Eugene, his central character. Dreiser asks: Is there a "Supreme Being who is all-just, all-truthful, all-merciful, all-tender?" Or is there only an indifferent mechanism—an amoral "system of minor arrangements, reciprocations, and minute equations, which have little to do with the aspects of much larger forces?"[9] Dreiser posits a universal law that seems to create a moral order. He then refuses to acknowledge its moral significance. But in his fiction the connection is made. He creates a character who is subjected to moral correction by being punished for his sins and who responds by making reparations to society.

All of Dreiser's own ostensibly contradictory beliefs—in Christian Science, in Transcendentalism, in Russell Wallace's evolutionary theism—are absorbed into this cosmology of the "Equation Inevitable." It amounts to a cosmic justification of the values of middle-class American society. By relegating final justice and equality to this "mechanical force," Dreiser evades the very problems that he set out to study.

So we see in *The "Genius"* that even the artist who, after all, is usually portrayed in fiction as a rebel, as an outspoken contester of society, does not, in Dreiser, ultimately move at cross-purposes with society at all but actually supports its norms. Although Dreiser did not practice this conformity in his own life, in his fiction we see it with the force of a moral imperative. Far from going beyond naturalism, Dreiser indeed reverts to the Puritan currents within American culture.

### Notes

1. Theodore Dreiser, *The "Genius"* (New York; New American Library, 1967), p. 9. Hereafter cited parenthetically in the text.

2. R. N. Mookerjee, *Theodore Dreiser: His Thought and Social Criticism* (Delhi: National, 1974), p. 58.

3. Philip Gerber, *Theodore Dreiser* (New York: Twayne, 1964), p. 114.

4. Special gratitude to Sacvan Bercovitch, who is the source of much of the underlying argument in this article. Bercovitch analyzed the origins of the allegiance to middle-class norms in America. The Massachusetts Bay emigrants, who were drawn mainly from the entrepreneurial and professional middle classes in England, set up a comparatively fluid society in colonial New England. The ideology that emerged—that is, the values, symbols, and beliefs characteristic of this group—became a consensus that served as a way of sustaining and molding the social order. See Sacvan Bercovitch, "The Rites of Assent," *The American Self,* ed. Sam B. Girgus (Albuquerque: Univ. of New Mexico Press, 1981), pp. 5-42. Myra Jehlen also was particularly helpful. She applies this theory of consensus to the American nineteenth-century novel which, she argues, avoids meaningful political analyses. Whereas the European novel regards the internal organization of society as its "problem," the American novel accepts the status quo as simply natural and instead focusses on the difficulties of individual conformity. She emphasizes that basic assumptions about American culture are involved in creating this difference and not any conscious choice on the part of individual writers. See Myra Jehlen, "New World Epics: The Novel and the Middle-Class in America," *Salmagundi,* 36 (Winter 1977), 49-68.

5. Nathaniel Hawthorne, *The Scarlet Letter* (New York: New American Library, 1959), p. 140.

6. William James, *The Varieties of Religious Experience* (New York: New American Library, 1958), p. 128.

7. John Taylor, *Money for the Million: Or, Straw for the Tale of Bricks* (London: Tallant and Allen, 1857), p. 58.

8. Theodore Dreiser, *Hey, Rub-A-Dub-Dub* (New York: Modern Age Books, 1941), p. 157.

9. Ibid.

### Claire Preston (essay date 1999)

SOURCE: Preston, Claire. "Ladies Prefer Bonds: Edith Wharton, Theodore Dreiser, and the Money Novel." *Soft Canons: American Women Writers and Masculine Tradition,* edited by Karen L. Kilcup, U of Iowa P, 1999, pp. 184-201.

[*In the following essay, Preston explores "the development of the money novel," citing the books in the Cowperwood trilogy as examples along with other novels of the early 1900s.*]

> Social conditions as they are just now in our new world, where the sudden possession of money has come without inherited obligations, or any traditional sense of solidarity between the classes, is a vast & absorbing field for the novelist, & I wish a great master could arise to deal with it.[1]

"Undine Spragg," the name of the protagonist of *The Custom of the Country,* glares like a neon sign amid Edith Wharton's more traditional, natural nomenclature. As the book's first phrase, it seems to enter the fictional room like an indiscriminately applied scent, before its owner. The disagreeable ungainliness of the syllable "Spragg" begins with an assailing consonant cluster, plosively suggesting the embouchure of spitting or of disdain, and it ends in a rhyme with "nag," "gag," and "slag." But those initial consonants also recall "sprite," the famous folkloric bearer of the name "Undine."[2] An attempted pronunciation of "sprite," it seems, has swerved disastrously off the tongue. And when to "Spragg" is added "Undine"—hard to know how to pronounce, delicately feminine, probably foreign—

we are further disconcerted. Is she "undeen," "undīne," or "oondeen," and on which syllable is the name accented? Her hapless mother calls her "Undie," which may or may not be authoritative. The mystery and instability of pronunciation, the irksome yoking of the adamantine "Spragg" with the sinuous and ethereal "Undine," are also features of the girl herself.

To Ralph Marvell the name suggests the motion of waves and an improbable allusion by the Spragg parents to Montaigne;[3] Wharton, too, notices Undine's irritating rippling effects and ceaseless posing. What is actually being commemorated in her christening, however, is the successful hair-waving formula invented by her father and patented in the week of her birth, a substance so-called because—as Mrs. Spragg explains—"of *un*doolay ... the French for crimping."[4] The product is named not for sprites or for aqueous disturbances but for a hairdressing technique; so the daughter, who is named for the chemical. She could as well be called Marcel, or Blondine, or Clairol. By name and by nature, Undine is a product, genetic and commercial, and she roams the novel like a traveling saleswoman. A ruthless, fluctuating self-promoter and self-merchandizer, her name is an exact account of all that she is.

In 1907 the foundation of the Harvard School of Business Studies dismayed Edith Wharton: "[it] plunged me into ... depth[s] of pessimism ... skyscrapers don't symbolize a lifting of the soul. ... Alas, alas!"[5] In spite of this she herself was engaged at that moment, as were many of her contemporaries, in the creation of a money novel, a novel rich in the culture of business and skyscrapers, *The Custom of the Country.* The American money novel of the period 1870-1930 is, like the study of business, primarily interested in the mechanics of getting rich, which it discovers in the technicalities of finance, commerce, consumption, labor relations, and social mobility. Often it figures such themes in the career of a stratospheric entrepreneur, who might be a thinly veiled portrait of a Vanderbilt, a Morgan, a Yerkes, a Rockefeller, Frick, Belmont, Gould, or Cooke,[6] embodiments of what William Dean Howells called "the American poetry of vivid purpose."[7] Mark Twain's *The Gilded Age* (1873) and Howells's *The Rise of Silas Lapham* (1885) and *A Hazard of New Fortunes* (1890) were the first models in the genre; Frank Norris's *The Octopus* (1901) and *The Pit* (1902), charting railroad battles and wheat wars, derive their texture and surface from the ebb and flow of market transactions; Upton Sinclair was writing *The Metropolis* (1908) and *The Money Changers* (1909), muckraking satires of Wall Street; Theodore Dreiser was establishing the poetics of upward mobility in Frank Cowperwood—in the so-called **"Trilogy of Desire," *The Financier*** (1912), ***The Titan*** (1914), and ***The Stoic*** (post-

humous, 1947). Later, Sinclair Lewis's *Babbitt* (1922; dedicated to Wharton) satirized boosterism and salesmanship; Booth Tarkington's *The Plutocrat* (1927) showed the business titan at play; and John Dos Passos's *USA* trilogy (including *The Big Money* [1936]) was built around high finance and heroic industrial development. Near the end of this era, Fitzgerald's *The Great Gatsby* (1926) evoked the potential tragedy of the self-made man. Both Harvard and the money novelists, in other words, were giving their imprimatur to the art and science of profit.

The "primary" money-novel era of Twain and Howells is, distinctively, morally conservative. *The Gilded Age* imagines financial desire as a kind of malady. Like the heirs in *Bleak House,* everyone in the book is corroded and finally destroyed by the dreams of avarice prompted by the vast but worthless tract of Tennessee land at the center of the story. One young man is prematurely aged, his father loses his wits, his sister dies of heart disease, their patron is publicly humiliated. Silas Lapham, unlike Twain's pipe dreamers, has actually discovered, dug, mixed, manufactured, and marketed his best-selling mineral paint; it is his misguided but admirable refusal to take advantage of business adversaries that brings about his downfall, with a slippery former partner functioning in the Lapham business chronicle like a family curse from a Greek tragedy.

The subsequent development of the money novel—and this may be a symptom of the modernist shift from romance to realism[8]—prefers to leave ethics aside, to allow that avarice and its psychological conditions, unembellished by moral consequences, is itself a fit subject for the novelist. These later novels, especially those by Dreiser and Norris, tend to replicate the addictive rhythm of money operations at the expense of characters, who become bland and null in comparison with the fascinating power they wield. It is a blandness articulated with special power in a related money narrative—what we might call "woman-on-the-make," a genre well known since Defoe but suddenly enjoying an energetic reflorescence at the beginning of the twentieth century. Among these are Dreiser's ***Sister Carrie*** (1900) and ***Jenny Gerhardt*** (1911); Robert Grant's *Unleavened Bread* (1900) (perhaps the single most important influence on *The Custom of the Country*);[9] Robert Herrick's *One Woman's Life* (1913); Louis Joseph Vance's *Joan Thursday* (1913); Winston Churchill's *A Modern Chronicle* (1910); and Anita Loos's *Gentlemen Prefer Blondes* (1925). The heroines of these romances are not, of course, tycoons, nor could they be;[10] instead, they reinvent the dynamic aggrandizing impulses of the upwardly mobile, greedy, financially cunning, traditionally male money figures in forms of personal, sexual, or aesthetic transaction. These novels show that the pathology of the financier is not sex-specific. The female money figure shares the financier's incessant and insatiable appetite for gain, but like him she cannot be satisfied by anything money can buy; she has his enigmatic, or merely vacant, insubstantial quality; and her story, like his, is open ended and unfinished. The pathology is neatly formulated in the motto of Dreiser's Frank Cowperwood: "I satisfy myself"[11] has the grammatical reflexivity of Undine's Spragg's self-absorption. The genre that in 1912 had yielded a Cowperwood, the essential male money figure, had by the same moment discovered his female equivalent in Undine.[12]

Among Wharton's surviving papers from the period 1910-1914 is the outline of a money story in which a panic on the markets provoked by the serious illness of an important financier is supposed to be averted by the secret substitution of his cousin, a near double. The cousin, overwhelmed by the strain of publicity, has a fatal heart attack, and the real financier must be displayed on his sickbed to calm the markets; but the punters, confused and imposed upon, panic anyway. The story's central conceit is an act of substitution that mimics the transactions of commerce, the transactions that Undine herself will promote in her career of upward trading. Wharton ends this note with the tantalizing question, "*Après?*"[13] This "*après?*" might be the watchword of the money novel she did write, the word encapsulating the appetite that impels it and the narrative structure that contains it.

"In America," Paul Bourget wrote, "all men in society have been and still are business men. They were not born to social status; they have achieved it."[14] Dreiser was fascinated by the ability of those known to the chroniclers of wealth as "nature's noblemen" (Howells, *Silas Lapham,* 21) to *achieve*—money, status, possession—by means of their astonishing, imperial appetite and energy for financial acquisition and conquest. In spite of the New York *World*'s conviction that the careers of such men could not be written by any living novelist,[15] hardly any money novel in this period is so abandoned to the minutiae of transaction as ***The Financier.*** The descriptions of Cowperwood's complex and arcane share dealings and loan hypothecations, the cunning manipulations of his companies, holding companies, sinking funds, and deposit accounts, have the salaciousness and relentless monotony of pornography. Only Frank Norris and Upton Sinclair pitch transactional energy as fervently: in *The Pit,* the lunacy of the trading floor is electrifyingly poeticized; Sinclair, by contrast, surrenders to the tragic, epic inevitability of Wall Street, "where they fought out the battle of their lives … the cruel waste and ruin of it, the wreckage of the blind, haphazard strife."[16] These writers are more ravished by wheeling and dealing, triumph and disaster, in the

money arena than by the fruits of finance. Norris's Jadwin buys houses, yachts, and paintings that are pointedly dreary and pompous; Sinclair gleefully burdens his plutocrats with lists and descriptions of their vulgarities. The truth is that their possessions cannot sustain the attention of the financier or his creator for long; only the market unfailingly stimulates and summons him. Notably remote from goods, Dreiser is much more interested in the physical laws of greed, which best demonstrate themselves in financial activity, and he is careful to detach Cowperwood from any profound connection to his collections of art and women; these are rendered clinically, almost insouciantly, because *things* are only the epiphenomena of transaction.

Wharton's entrepreneurial capitalist is a woman whose ferocity of acquisition must partly displace the ferocity of transaction, and her portrait of Undine's possessions is, unlike Dreiser's, rich and enthusiastic. The novel's texture is overburdened not just with deals but with *things,* a plenitude almost as extravagant as Cowperwood's precipices of debt and unlimited leverage, partly because no extravagance of daring or of possession can ever still her appetite, but mainly because Undine herself is unimaginable, incomprehensible, and is only intelligible in her acquisitions.

Navigating new worlds and laying them low with commercial cunning, or through arcane, often abstract, operations in the fiscal arena, the money figure is a kind of frontiersman, that valiant, wily conqueror of the howling American wilderness who arrives (usually solitary) in unsettled territory, a "young giant out of the East"[17] who subdues wild beasts and hostile aboriginals to his will and establishes a state or a city or a family fortune by destroying what he finds in the name of profit and glory. Like him, the financial frontiersman rarely has identifiable roots; any that he has are indistinct, onomastically western—places with names like Apex, Opake, Euphoria, or Deposit. Even if he *has* established mines, oil fields, railroads, and manufacturing empires, this frontiersman immediately heads *east,* not further west, to subjugate the financial landscape of the major metropolises (principally New York) with the cash laboriously acquired. He was modeled on the multitude of Civil War profiteers who converted their earnings into houses, parties, wardrobes, yachts, and art collections, and proceeded to translate their financial success into social prestige; the numbers of millionaires in postwar America increased by an order of magnitude.[18] The social sanctuary simultaneously breached is the domain of the female money figure: Undine is new and heroic, quite unlike the demure daughter of the established elite, vigorously and intrepidly in command of her own material and matrimonial destiny. She too heads east, and, armed with male earnings and her own energy and ambition, she vanquishes the swollen monsters of social exclusivity, as the financier demolishes the barriers erected by its capital.

In twentieth-century money novels, the struggles of the money titans rock New York: "Swift, imperious, terrible, trampling over all opposition ... Wall Street had reeled in the shock of the conflicts" (Sinclair, 192). The plutocrat is likened to "a passage in Homer, or in some Gothic poem ... some great scarlet-robed Carthaginian ... Hamilcar or his gorgeous son Hannibal";[19] his books on banking and credit promise "to unfold the shining secrets that only Midas and Morgan and Maecenas knew";[20] he is an overreacher, "a great personage of the Elizabethan order" (***Titan,*** 245), hailed as the Weird Sisters hail Macbeth (***Financier,*** 448). "Everything stopped when he raised a finger; everything leaped to life with the fury of obsession when he nodded his head ... no Czar, no satrap, no Caesar ever wielded power more resistless" (149).[21]

Even Wharton's Elmer Moffatt recites his business battles with "Homeric volume" (145); his exploits are "like the long triumph of an Asiatic conqueror" (303). Indeed, Moffatt's epic (Ralph Marvell wants to write a book about him) is the mighty underpinning of the more frivolous but narratively primary tale of Undine, a strong obbligato theme of financial ebb and flow in the form of shady land deals, insider trading, bubbles and booms, blackmail, and bought evidence, which is never straight-forwardly—only laconically and indirectly—delivered. Moffatt is a financial magician whose tricks rely on numerical legerdemain, hype, and low cunning rather than on solid investment or production.[22] Neither exact nor public, Moffatt's career and the story of it are like one of those "shadowy destructive monsters beneath the darting small fry of the surface" (*Custom,* 149).

This "epic effrontery" (146) belongs also to Undine Spragg, the social and financial pirate.[23] With her financier's temperament, appetite, and initiative, and her own acquisitive cunning, Undine's character and behavior are replicated by the surface of the novel, Wharton's most energetic and febrile. Like the seventeenth- and eighteenth-century buildings she so admired, with their Vitruvian, Palladian cadences and stately rhythms, her best stories are usually measured, almost architecturally patterned, entirely governed by their design, with scant room for extraneous detail or episode. But *The Custom of the Country* simulates an upward trajectory with no hint of gravity in it, no corresponding downward path. The novel and the career of its protagonist are more like the detested skyscraper than the Italian villa.

Despite this scale there are, perhaps oddly, no epic similes for Undine. Instead, she attracts two other kinds of image: the fluid and liquid (she has the name of a water sprite; she ripples and glitters; she is launched into New York society on the profits of the Pure Water Move), and the adversarial, the umbrageous, the bellicose (she thinks always in terms of "getting even," of dominating, of "running the show"). Constitutionally (even onomastically) in transit and full of fluctuations, Undine is like Curtis Jadwin of *The Pit,* the man unable to sit out the contention in futures, or Frank Cowperwood, who cannot take his eyes off the market even in prison, or in love. Money figures are incapable of rest; and Undine ripples in company, is ceaselessly *mouvementée*; her restlessness is both geographical and social. Even if Undine Spragg Moffatt Marvell de Chelles Moffatt, as she is at the end of the novel, is never actually likened to Tamburlaine, she collects husbands and patronymics the way Tamburlaine collects kingdoms, and the litany of her momentary American locales reads like Sherman's march through Georgia—Apex, Deposit, Skog Harbor, Potash Springs, New York City, Dakota—in a progress that uses up a good half of the American continent. Like those conquerors, she leaves behind a trail of social and financial wreckage. Undine arises, like a force of nature, out of the soil of the Midwest, a creature without history or tradition, autochthonous, autonomous, relentless. Hers is a heroic narrative on a par with any Wall Street titan: she rampages through countries and continents, families and neighborhoods, never satisfied, always, like her classical counterparts, looking for new domains to conquer. As Moffatt boasts, "Nobody can stop me now if I want anything" (301), so the object of Undine's gigantic and exhaustless appetites is, "Why, *everything!*" (57). *The Custom of the Country* is the heroic account of getting it.

Although Undine originates in the dismal boomtown of Apex City, to say she is *from* anywhere in particular is too sentimental a reading of her origins, just as it is sentimental to imagine that her name has any traditional or intended symbolic significance. Apex is a name as opportunistic as "Undine," an unmeant booster joke (like the real place in Illinois hopefully called "Hometown"), a place invented every day by shady boomers like Undine's father even as Undine invents herself. But Undine's placelessness is as necessary as it is typical: like the financier, she can only aggregate by ceaseless motion: as stasis is fatal to the stock market, where fortunes are made from transaction on movement in either direction, so Undine is never still. The joke-name "Apex," like "*après*?" is, in other words, perfectly serious after all; Apex is simultaneously everywhere and nowhere: it is only the temporary pinnacle from which Undine surveys a loftier, beckoning eminence. A kind of Faustian ubiquism, "Apex" is the word for everything Undine wants, achieves, and immediately puts behind her: "She had everything she wanted," Undine muses, "but she still felt, at times, that there were other things she might want if she knew about them" (333). This, the most terrifying sentence in the book, is also its most typical.[24] Although Undine deploys her personal capital with the shrewdness of an investor, she is caught up in "a nightmare of perpetually renewable choice and decision ... her amusement at any cost and in any quantity that suits her she *will* have, let who will pay."[25]

Like Undine's beauty, Frank Cowperwood's brilliance is apparently coercive, the source of infinite means. The son of a middling bank clerk, he follows a seemingly inexorable upward trajectory in Philadelphia financial circles, always moving on to ever more arcane operations until, having reached the purest (and most lucrative) forms of finance in the abstract arithmetic of discount bonds, arbitrage, market manipulations, and leveraged buyouts, rather than the messier transactions involving commodities, real estate, and stock, he is ruined by the far-reaching consequences of the Chicago fire of 1871. Bankrupt and in prison for financial improprieties, and friendless for having appropriated the daughter of a powerful machine politician, on his release he nevertheless quickly recoups and outstrips his old prosperity in the panic that follows the Northern Pacific Railroad failure of 1873. In *The Titan* and *The Stoic* he goes to Chicago and London and founds street railways, becoming one of the richest men in the United States.

In his analysis of modes of wealth, Thorstein Veblen makes a distinction between "worthy" and "unworthy" employments, which he calls, respectively, "exploit" and "industry."[26] Industry is deemed in the social code of leisure to be the necessary but "unworthy" activity that creates new things out of brute material; it is associated, primitively, with agriculture or manufacture but could in a more modern form include certain services. Industry, comprising work and effort of all descriptions, is essentially dishonorable. Exploit, by contrast, is the peremptory *seizing* of others' goods or energies. Exploit is removed from sources or means of production; it represents instead the higher exercise of force over others. Exploit, in Veblen's scheme, is "worthier" than industry.

Cowperwood, Moffatt, and Spragg are hard to contain within these definitions. In Veblen's scheme, the most honorable kind of wealth is passively, unlaboriously acquired in the form of inherited money. But these three have little or no inherited funds; instead, they commit great energy to acquisition, as if they were industrious, and yet they are nonproductive (they manufacture nothing, usually provide no goods or services); they specialize— on Wall Street or Fifth Avenue—in covert and transgressive exploit in the form of the financial killing or the social conquest. If industry yields "earnings" (a morally loaded word), exploit consists of "takings"; and the vocabulary of finance is violent and abrupt, with words like "killing," "hit," "takeover," and the "big steal" evoking its combat. Veblen comments that "in the life of the barbarian, prowess manifests itself in ... force and fraud" (273); exploit in its most refined form is financial deception, the exemplary behavior that appropriates the possessions of others with least cost to the predator. Undine, Moffatt, and Cowperwood are, paradoxically, industrious *and* exploitative: without hereditary wealth, they are energetic in the pursuit of money. Cowperwood's exploits, like Moffatt's, are rarefied in numbers and pure cash, away from goods and chattels, particularly in the form of fraud. Undine's power over money is more rarefied still; she has long since abandoned anything like industry (Ralph imagines her as a child having made only foolish items of cork and cigar wrappers) for the imperious grabbing of men, jewels, and transatlantic junkets. Undine's cunning is not the conscious art of the financiers—she cannot, ironically, understand why all her entitlements "come to her as if they had been stolen" (275); nevertheless, with her indistinct but potent sexual allure, she too is a fraudster. She is not interested in sex but in acquisition; she cuts deals with men to whom she never delivers her part of the bargain. Her desirability is snake oil or a junk bond—a false product or at best a high-risk investment. "Everything in Wall Street is stolen," says Upton Sinclair (*Metropolis,* 214); her history, even if she cannot see its resemblance to Moffatt's and Cowperwood's, is a tale of steals rather than of deals.

Undine and Cowperwood share an unreflecting, disturbing boldness, a casual disregard for the subtle social arrangements and obligations that stand in the way of desire. She truculently reflects upon her French husband's devotion to the abstract and immaterial concept of Family, a concept symbolized by needlework—the embroidery carried out by the women of the de Chelles cousinage for the ancestral chateau, and the great Louis Quinze Boucher tapestries, the family's chief hereditary treasure. Their "industrious" behavior (significantly, traditional "women's work") and their familial solidarity (so much nonliquid capital tied up in a relic) are faintly dishonorable, and certainly stupid, because not self-serving, and attract only her scorn. This reaction emblematizes that of the exploiting individual about toil in the service of remote, disembodied, and selfless ideas such as "heritage." Her attempt to have the world-famous tapestries appraised pits exploit against industry, expedience against tradition. It characteristically seeks to put a price tag on what is priceless, invaluable to de Chelles. As an exploiter, she wants to know what the tapestries might be converted into (cash or dresses or central heating) as a way of finding out what can be "got out of" her husband.

But this appraisal represents an act of appetite rather than of imagination, and in this Undine is essentially distinct from her male counterparts. Moffatt does not care about the de Chelles tradition any more than Undine does, but he covets the tapestries as art objects. Undine, by contrast, is outraged, bewildered, or ignorant of everything not already hers or within her horizon of wants; to her the tapestries are merely "old and faded." "Passionately imitative" (14), her desires are uninflected by taste or opinion. Moffatt looks at the tapestries and calculates how much money will buy these priceless objects; Undine looks at them and calculates how much they will yield. Money figures are characterized by their extraordinary appetites: Moffatt, as billionaire railroad emperor, has driven up prices on the international art markets with the volume of his buying. Cowperwood has a collection ranging from the Old Masters to the Pre-Raphaelites. Like Lorelei Lee in the book described by Wharton as "*the* great American novel,"[27] Undine needs only to hear of something unattainable to discover an instant need to own it. As instantly, she will find a man to buy it for her. With inchoate, impatient appetites, these young women do not know what they want until they are confronted with it; they have no long-term outlook; they could never be futures traders.

Elmer Moffatt and Frank Cowperwood, however, are specific embodiments of the inventive acquisitive imagination; they understand the similitude of railroads and Rembrandts,[28] and quickly learn discrimination equivalent to their wallets. They have plans—and patience. Moffatt's rapidly developing taste and discernment are as carefully charted as his business exploits. His personal and ethical grossness and the subtle delicacy of such descriptions (of a crystal, a leather binding, a piece of Phoenician glass) produce a fascinating and unexpected counterpoint typical of the man. His sophistication as a collector, famous for his Persian carpets and Chinese porcelain, is acknowledged in the same breath as his financial skill. Although Cowperwood is rather more detached from his extensively described collections, Dreiser takes care to suggest the discrimination of such acquisitions, which include a portrait of Cesare Borgia, significantly rich with "rumor of his crimes and machinations" (*Titan,* 117). Exploiters are quick learners and use this faculty to get their possessions, like their money, out of the blue. In this respect, Undine qualifies as a money figure only in the ruthlessness of her acquisition; she fails to live up to the exploiter's inventiveness in her imaginative poverty.

In their creative unpredictability Cowperwood, Moffatt, and Undine epitomize the supple cunning, flexibility, and protean potential of the money character, whose very livelihood depends on the ability to take creative advantage of market opportunities, especially to get something for nothing or for as little as possible. As Cowperwood takes advantage of a sudden panic, Undine ripplingly converts herself into the sort of woman likely to attract the man of the moment. In her person Undine combines at once the financier and the funds he wields, agent and medium. "'The American girl,'" said Wharton in *The Buccaneers,* is "the world's highest achievement,"[29] like American steel and wheat; but the young women of that novel are manipulated commodities, the pawns of two mutually beneficial systems (of capital and of honors); in *The Custom of the Country* both systems are at the mercy of the self-commodified Undine. Undine's financial philosophy is summed up by Lorelei Lee in *Gentlemen Prefer Blondes*: "When a girl looks at Mrs. Nash and realizes what Mrs. Nash has got out of gentlemen, it really makes a girl hold her breath" (78). Lorelei and Undine are gold diggers in almost the literal sense of the term: they are excavating to see what can be "got out of" men.

Any number of American financial magicians might provide models for the male money figure. Jay Gould, the so-called "Mephistopheles of Wall Street," wrecked a railroad and left only its "financially lifeless body" (Josephson, *The Robber Barons,* 137). Wrecking railroads and wrecking homes are compared in *The Custom of the Country*; and, indeed, Undine wrecks homes in the way that railroads are wrecked. She makes preemptive strikes by preventing more credible marriages (between, say, Ralph and Harriet Ray, or between de Chelles and some resident of the faubourg). She maneuvers in romantic intrigues as "Mr. Spragg might have ... at the tensest hour of the Pure Water Move" (168); she loots marriages as Moffatt might loot a corporation. She is an asset stripper; she leaves the debilitated or lifeless corpses of disillusioned men scattered about the social landscape.

Like Cowperwood and Moffatt, Undine makes and forfeits several fortunes—hers in the marriage market, theirs in the stock market. After their first scandalous union and hasty divorce in the Midwest, Undine and Moffatt trace nearly parallel careers of boom and bust, only occasionally intersecting. At the end of the book, they merge once more. The consistently offensive, transgressive Moffatt once managed to carry away the teenaged Undine to an illicit marriage in Nebraska, a primitive version of the more rarefied financial combat and wealth grabbing in which he later specializes. Moffatt's truly inconceivable riches subsequently defy the principles of social exclusion because those riches, and he, are predatory: there is no art, no property, safe from his purchasing ability, just as there is, apparently, no social ethos proof, or any man secure, against Undine's predations.

But Moffatt is softer than Undine: he is moved by art, by young children; she merely uses them. She successfully "exploits" her own family in the exact Veblenian sense, seizing their wealth for the same reason that she demands her child from them: because she *can*. Like the chateau, tended by ancillary family members, little Paul Marvell is a treasure selflessly nurtured by all his grandparents, even the Spraggs. But selflessness is outside his mother's philosophy: she needs him in order to furbish up her respectability. Undine's ability to exploit her parents is apparently inherited, the nearest thing to "tradition" in the Spragg family. By the time the novel opens, Mr. Spragg, a quondam exploiter and fraudster, is being efficiently despoiled in turn by his even more ruthless daughter, whose genetic inheritance seems to include not only his active business sense but also his taste and talent for "steals."

"What were you going to do about the so-called morals and precepts of the world?" Cowperwood muses. "There were people who believed in some esoteric standard of right ... they were never significant, practical men who clung to these fatuous ideals" (*Financier*, 225-226). Cowperwood's amorality is never made to seem reprehensible, because the money novel is necessarily located in the strangely colorless world of abstract monetary operations, a world either divorced entirely from the acquisitive rewards of great wealth or at least emotionally distanced from those rewards. The process of accrual, dealing, and fraud is dense and hypnotic; however, the details of material or social gain, although finely tuned by someone like Dreiser, are strangely remote from the intensity of the trading floor, obligatory and off-hand, rather than essential to our understanding of the financier. The substantial rewards of money dealing cannot, it seems, compete with the fascinating labor that acquires them, and Dreiser's severe naturalism maintains this detachment in its scientific, carefully reportorial neutrality, which mimics in the transparent and unimpassioned account of his possessions the blankness of Cowperwood's personality. Although we are privy to such specificities as his middle name, the layout of his house, and the richness of his silk underwear, the subject of the novel is money and its operations, and thus he is instantiated (but never substantiated) only in his net worth, his stockholdings, or his possessions. Barely a personality, he is the construction of his money, the physical representation of its abstract and unstable value; like his money, he is a man of quantities but not qualities. An embodiment only of crude desire, he can sustain no further detail; Frank Cowperwood

is a character of whom there is ("frankly") nothing to infer. Although the narrative voice of *The Custom of the Country* is rich and intrusive, it is nonetheless distant and superior to Undine herself, whom her creator, like Raymond de Chelles, seems not to recognize as a member of her own species.

Cowperwood is a fascinating cipher: a magnetic personality whose authority and argument seem to seduce men and women alike, he is nonetheless terrifyingly empty. His attitude to all but the principle of self-aggrandizement is offhand: slavery, the West, panics, the sanctity of the home, right and wrong, the theory of evolution do not concern him; such abstrusities are "the toys of clerics, by which they made money." His earliest understanding is of "money as a medium of exchange" (*Financier*, 240, 11); he "subscribes to nothing" and instead can "fit himself in with the odd psychology of almost any individual" (*Titan*, 8, 21). Dreiser concludes *The Financier* with an emblematic essay about *mycteroperca bonaci*, a fish with "an almost unbelievable power of simulation ... power to deceive" (*Financier*, 447). All self-made fictional financiers—Gatsby, Jadwin, Wharton's own Beaufort and Rosedale—are powerfully enigmatic in this way. Elmer Moffatt is a cipher, a man known by his schemes, tastes, possessions, and exploits, but ultimately mysterious and unaccountable, never viewed from anything but a great distance. When in *The Great Gatsby* Nick Carraway asks of Gatsby, "Who is he?" he is told, "He's just a man named Gatsby" (50). In truth, financiers are like Gatsby, "platonic conceptions of themselves" (95).

But it is Undine who possesses this psychological blankness in highest measure: she is vacant but for her trimmings. Like Frank Cowperwood, she too is a vacuum: although her beauty is painted out in bold strong colors, a beauty able to withstand the strongest, harshest illumination, a beauty not appropriate to the half-tones of Old New York or faubourg interiors, yet like Cowperwood she has no *innate* qualities. Her beauty is her wealth, the currency in which she trades up. When her divorce from Ralph Marvell temporarily relegates her to the society of the unfashionable, "her one desire was to get back an equivalent of the precise value she had lost in ceasing to be [his] wife. Her new visiting-card, bearing her Christian name in place of her husband's, was like the coin of a debased currency testifying to her diminished trading capacity" (205). Articulation more elaborate than this she—and every money figure—lacks: Moffatt is extremely laconic; Cowperwood repudiates all political conviction; beyond a few conventional exclamations of amazement and consternation, Undine herself has nothing to say: when she speaks, she seems to disappear. She has only "deep-seated wants for which her acquired vocabulary had no terms" (302); her linguistic capacity is primitive and unnuanced: she understands simply that "every Wall Street term had its equivalent in the language of Fifth Avenue" (303).[30]

While still a boy Cowperwood is asked by an uncle what he is interested in. "Money!" Frank replies. "The financial mind partakes largely of the thing in which it deals" (*Financier,* 15, 347), says Dreiser, and Cowperwood and Undine are just like money. Undine, who reads little, who has no ideas, who is merely imitative, whose paltry stock of conversation makes her beauty fade from view, masks her emptiness with her dazzling and flickering surface, which is finally recognized by Ralph as "the bareness of a small half-lit place" (86). Scruple-free, unreflective, morally and psychologically empty, such characters make the way clear for a narrative driven by transaction and profit, by event and process, rather than by development of character. Wharton noted that "the novel of situation . . . forces [characters] into the shape which its events impose."[31] Greed or desire becomes their signal and single property.

*The Custom of the Country* is in a sense an unfinished, and unfinishable, novel, as is Dreiser's narrative: like Tamburlaine, who dies not in battle but in bed, Cowperwood's bathetic failure is not in spectacular financial collapse but in age and Bright's disease. In the last page of *The Custom of the Country,* Undine querulously rages against the rule that prevents her being an ambassador's wife; but there is an inevitability here quite unlike Cowperwood's: by triumphant money logic, Undine *will* become an ambassador's wife. Either she will find a way around the rule, or she will leave Moffatt for an ambassador (with a huge settlement to back her). Indeed, in the original outline of the story, Undine was to ditch Moffatt for the newly made Ambassador Jim Driscoll, son of Moffatt's old employer and enemy.[32] The open-endedness with which Wharton eventually chose to conclude the novel is more frightening; it is an eternity of conquest, "a nightmare of perpetually renewable choice" that other writers found in industry, commerce, and the market.

## Notes

1. Wharton to Dr. Morgan Dix, 5 December 1905, *The Letters of Edith Wharton,* ed. R. W. B. Lewis and Nancy Lewis (New York: Simon and Schuster, 1988), 99. All second and subsequent references to this and other sources are cited in the text.

2. Thomas L. McHaney, "Fouqué's *Undine* and Edith Wharton's *The Custom of the Country*," *Revue de Littérature Comparée* 45 (1971): 180-186.

3. "*Diverse et ondoyant,*" from Montaigne's essay "Par divers moyons on arrive á pareille fin" on the theme of unpredictable and erratic behavior. See Montaigne, *The Complete Essays,* trans. M. A. Screech (Harmondsworth: Penguin, 1987), 5.

4. *The Custom of the Country* (1913; reprint, Harmondsworth, England: Penguin, 1987), 48.

5. Edith Wharton to Sally Norton, 23 June 1907, Edith Wharton Archive, in Yale Collection of American Literature, Beinecke Rare Book and Manuscript Library, Yale University (hereafter "Yale").

6. See Matthew Josephson, *The Robber Barons: The Great American Capitalists, 1861-1901,* 2d ed. (New York: Harcourt, Brace and World, 1962); Charles Francis Adams and Henry Adams, *Chapters of Erie and Other Essays* (New York: Henry Holt, 1886); Thomas William Lawson, *Frenzied Finance: The Crime of Amalgamated* (London: William Heinemann, 1906).

7. William Dean Howells, *The Rise of Silas Lapham* (1885; reprint, Oxford: Oxford University Press, 1996), 82.

8. On this distinction, see Walter Benn Michaels, "Romance and Real Estate," in *The American Renaissance Reconsidered: Selected Papers from the English Institute, 1982-3,* n.s., 9, ed. Walter Benn Michaels and Donald E. Pease (Baltimore: Johns Hopkins University Press, 1985), 156-157.

9. Edith Wharton to Robert Grant, 25 July 1900, Yale.

10. See Elaine Showalter, "*The Custom of the Country*: Spragg and the Art of the Deal," in *The Cambridge Companion to Edith Wharton,* ed. Millicent Bell (Cambridge: Cambridge University Press, 1995), 90.

11. *The Financier* (1912; reprint, New York: New American Library, 1967), 121. Cornelius Vanderbilt's famous *mot* is almost a motto ("What do I care for the law? Haint I got the power?"). Had she the patience for such things, Undine's motto would be "Go steady, Undine!" (17). William Mulholland, the California water-baron whose career may have provided Wharton with details for the Spragg water dealings at Apex, claimed the motto "Take it" (see Mike Davis, *City of Quartz: Excavating the Future in Los Angeles* [London: Verso Press, 1990], 379-382).

12. Dreiser began *The Financier* (1912) in 1911; Wharton began *The Custom of the Country* (1913) in 1907.

13. Wharton, "Donnée Book" (1910-1914), 9 (Yale).

14. Paul Bourget, *Outre-Mer: Impressions of America* (London: T. Fisher Unwin, 1895), 55.

15. New York *World,* 4 February 1906.

16. Upton Sinclair, *The Metropolis* (London: T. Warner Laurie, 1908), 173.

17. Theodore Dreiser, *The Titan* (1914; reprint, London: John Lane/The Bodley Head, 1915), 223.

18. Ray Ginger, *The Age of Excess: The United States from 1877-1914* (New York: Macmillan, 1965), 93.

19. Booth Tarkington, *The Plutocrat* (Garden City, N.Y.: Doubleday, Page, 1927), 112, 342.

20. F. Scott Fitzgerald, *The Great Gatsby* (1926; reprint, Harmondsworth, England: Penguin, 1990), 10.

21. Frank Norris, *The Pit* (1902; reprint, Harmondsworth, England: Penguin, 1994), 302.

22. Moffatt's complex financial career is scattered within the novel, but it is completely coherent if pieced together, which makes Alfred Kazin's opinion surprising: "what a subject lay before Edith Wharton in that world, if only she had been able, or willing, to use it!" ("Two Educations: Edith Wharton and Theodore Dreiser," in *On Native Grounds: An Interpretation of American Literature* [New York: Harcourt, Brace and World, 1942], 79). Stephen Orgel agrees: "The new American world of capitalist enterprise is ... nearly ... opaque to Wharton" (*The Custom of the Country,* ed. Stephen Orgel [Oxford: Oxford University Press, 1995], x).

23. Cynthia Griffin Wolff dismisses the female money novel: "Horatio Alger's myth in all its manifestations was for men, not for women" (*A Feast of Words: The Triumph of Edith Wharton,* 2d ed. [New York: Oxford University Press, 1995], 221).

24. Silas Lapham—for comparison—is worried that there may be things his money *cannot* buy (149). Undine has no such doubt. Pure appetite, by the era of the modernist money novel, has become equivalent to means.

25. These are Henry James's words about Wharton herself. James to Howard Sturgis (no date given), cited in R. W. B. Lewis, *Edith Wharton: A Biography* (New York: Harper and Row, 1975), 262.

26. Thorstein Veblen, *Theory of the Leisure Class,* ed. John Kenneth Galbraith (1899; reprint, Boston: Houghton Mifflin, 1973), 25.

27. Anita Loos, *Gentlemen Prefer Blondes* (1925; reprint, Harmondsworth, England: Penguin, 1992) 58. See Lewis, ed., *Letters,* 491 n.

28. Josephson, *The Robber Barons* (quoting Henry Frick), 343.

29. Edith Wharton, *The Buccaneers* (1938; reprint, London: Everyman, 1993), 24.

30. Wharton would later transpose this vacancy onto May Welland, the "nice" girl in *The Age of Innocence,* whose transparency is foil for a terrible cunning.

31. *Character and Situation in the Novel,* unpublished ms., Yale, p. 2a.

32. Ms. and notes for *The Custom of the Country,* Yale.

## Philip Gerber (essay date 2000)

SOURCE: Gerber, Philip. "Jolly Mrs. Yerkes Is Home from Abroad: Dreiser and the Celebrity Culture." *Theodore Dreiser and American Culture: New Readings,* edited by Yoshinobu Hakutani, U of Delaware P, 2000, pp. 79-103.

[*In the following essay, Gerber recounts the history of the controversial celebrity businessman Charles T. Yerkes, Jr., and Dreiser's use of sensational newspaper stories about Yerkes, Yerkes's wife, and Yerkes's mistress, to furnish material for his novels* The Financier, The Titan, *and* The Stoic.]

To begin with, she was anything but jolly. She had very little to be jolly about. And to say that she had come "home" was to suggest that she had a "home" to come to. What she had was a house, albeit a grand one, a palace of a house, in fact, superbly situated on a northeast corner lot along Millionaires Row in Manhattan. She was childless, and her husband had long been a husband in name only. It was a second marriage for him, and Mary Adelaide, after a glorious, passionate beginning soaring with hopes for their bright future, had not been able to climb social heights for him any more adeptly than had his first wife, so her husband, being imperious as well as ambitious, was doing his best to rid himself of her. His original bride, Susanna, had been older than he and ineffective as a social hostess in Philadelphia. She had produced five children (two had survived), but aside from that her usefulness had come to an end. Now it was Mary Adelaide's turn to go—if he could manage it, if only she would be more cooperative, consider his imperative needs.

So,—no, Mrs. Yerkes could not accurately be described as a happy woman. Happy or unhappy, however, that was of small consequence to the New York newspapers (though in truth unhappy people did seem to make better copy, by and large). What did matter very much was that as surrogate for her husband Mrs. Yerkes had claim to immense wealth. It mattered also that Charles T. Yerkes, Jr., himself, had been a headline-maker for decades, more often than not as a scoundrel. For better or worse—that scarcely was the point. For he was a Celebrity. A very big one. And so was she—a Celebrity-by-Association, if you will and by virtue of that connection, eminently worth watching.

As a raw teenager during the 1880s, Theodore Dreiser was already watching. First, through the newspapers, which had paid much attention to the costly downtown tunnel on LaSalle Street through which Yerkes's streetcar lines passed; they said that in a shady political deal he had all but stolen it from the city. And then there had come the great strike against the Yerkes streetcar lines in 1888, bringing scenes of street violence which Dreiser had watched from curbside with bewildered and uncomprehending young eyes. The newspapers laid all of the fault at the doorstep of the intransigent owner, the haughty, arrogant Capitalist known as Baron Yerkes when not called a Buccaneer or simply slurred as The Philadelphian, a snide innuendo reminding readers that Yerkes in his native city had raided the treasury, been caught with his greedy hand in the till, been tried, convicted, and incarcerated there in Eastern Penitentiary for his crime.

## I

By the early 1890s, while young Dreiser got his journalistic toes wet serving as a bottom-of-the-totem-pole reporter on local newspapers, it was apparent to any perceptive citizen that Charles T. Yerkes had worn out his welcome in Chicago. The financier himself expressed puzzlement. In his eyes, he had done all the right things. He had built up an imposing collection of Old Masters (thereby sending out the calculated suggestion that his personality contained another, altogether nicer and more altruistic side), and he had lent his favorite paintings, including that of his wife by Jan Van Beers, to the city for exhibition at its great fair, The World's Columbian Exposition, in 1892 and 1893. He had erected in Lincoln Park, hard by Lake Michigan, a mammoth electric fountain. A rainbow of colors played onto jets that shot fifty feet into the air before dropping back to earth in showers of diamonds. This was his magnanimous gift to the city. But—could anyone please Chicago? Apparently not. Yerkes was a plague, cried one columnist; he'd done Chicago as much harm as the cholera epidemic. The man was not well liked, no, not by businessmen, not by newspaper editors, not by the streetcar-riding public. But few denied that he possessed a certain something that

made watching his every move addictive. You had to smile at the sheer effrontery with which he approached the world. He was always good for a story, and so the reporters loved him. He was charismatic in the extreme, and he lived like an emperor. He smiled enigmatically, was a master of the one-line put-down. The rapt newsmen took copious notes and hustled back to their smoke-filled newsrooms to write up their copy. For them, Charles T. Yerkes was the Celebrity par excellence.

But those with firm footholds in the Chicago social world would have none of Yerkes or of his socially ambitious wife, who quite naturally was assumed to be the man's co-conspirator and counterpart. His sharp business practices poisoned the well. He was treading on too many prominent toes. As the 1880s merged into the 1890s, anyone interested in Celebrities might notice in reading the Chicago Society pages that Mary Adelaide Yerkes's name was not likely to be listed anymore among those ladies invited to join Chicago's numerous bicycling clubs, lately the rage. Her name was conspicuously absent also from the published list of guests at the fashionable "bicycling teas" at which society ladies raised money for charity. Nor did the name of Yerkes appear among published lists of invited guests at dinners given by important Chicagoans such as the Marshall Fields, the R. S. McCormicks, the Potter Palmers, the Marvin Hughitts, the S. W. Allertons, and the Philip Armours. However much a power Charles Yerkes might be in business, he had become a social pariah, *persona non grata*.

As for Mrs. Yerkes, Chicago seemed to have tamed her since that day in 1880 when she had swept into town as the financier's second wife with a take-over manner that seemed to announce: "I'm here. Follow me!" In her staid Philadelphia neighborhood, as a girl, the fiery Mollie Moore had set tongues wagging even at age sixteen and seventeen, not long before she became infatuated with the thirty-one-year-old Yerkes. Friends of childhood days remembered Mollie's graceful figure, her raven eyes, her striking mass of black hair, but most of all they recalled the rebellious spirit that encouraged her to drive the streets of the Quaker City, not as a passenger in the usual sedate family brougham coach, but in a carriage drawn by four coal-black horses in gold harness—and in lieu of coachman, she herself controlling the reins. Disapproving voices could be heard behind the lace curtains: "There goes that wild Moore girl again, the young one, Mollie. Right up in the coachman's seat! What can her mother be thinking of? Why don't her parents *do* something about her!"

But with Mollie, passion came first, even if it meant a break with her parents and her big family of siblings (eight brothers and sisters). By the time Yerkes divorced his first wife, Susanna—anathema in the Philadelphia social set—the headstrong girl was branded in polite circles as a homebreaker. The financier, out of prison a half-dozen years, his fortunes now resurgent, suggested to his young mistress that they relocate, make a new start in Chicago. Mollie was quite prepared for the change. They would make a new beginning in the West, where so many were newcomers that to be an *arriviste* was the common and expected thing. So many had left the East under a cloud, it was considered impolite to inquire too deeply into anyone's past, for who knew when tit for tat might cause the tables to be turned? In Chicago, the family responsibilities were to be divided. Charles was to find a way of commanding a top spot in the financial world; while Mary Adelaide was to be the wedge that would break a path for them into the very best and topmost rungs of local society.

If Charles Yerkes before too long was disappointed by his second wife's inability to garner that coveted spot for him atop the Chicago social heap, he retained common sense enough not to discard her on that basis alone, for he recognized that their social *declassement* was based on jealousy and, even more than that, grounded in revenge. Who did these hypocritical meatpackers and drygoods merchants think they were? Had he not played his civic role to the hilt? Had he not presented their new University with the greatest telescope in the world—and a splendid observatory to house it? And had it not been his skill and determination and *imagination* that had built the Union Loop, ringing their downtown business area with streetcars that brought the housewives flocking in from the increasingly far-flung suburbs to shop all day for clothes and household trinkets at Carson, Pirie, and Scott, The Fair, and Marshall Field's new department stores? He couldn't figure these Chicagoans out. What did they resent? And the newspaper editors—who could please them? He'd gone to great expense to cater to the swelling rage for technological innovation, electrifying his lines, and building power plants all over the city to supply the new alternating current that ran his underground cables. But what was his thanks for getting rid of the smelly horse teams that had hitherto fouled the streets? One curt blast after another, front-page stories carping that his smokestacks rained oily black flakes of coal-snow over Chicago! And now, after everything he had done for the city, its councilmen (whose votes had cost him a good $20,000 apiece) did not find it politically expedient to grant him a lifetime monopoly. On top of this, the Illinois state legislature had had the effrontery to nix his bid for a fifty-year streetcar franchise.

Yerkes was ready by the mid-1890s to quit Chicago entirely, as soon as he could unload his well-worn equipment on the next fellow. Chicago was a big town, all right, but he was ready for the Metropolis. In fact, being usually a step or two in advance of his detractors, Yerkes by the end of the 1880s was letting it be known on visits to New York that while he considered Chicago a fine place to make money, he thought New York the best place to spend it. Early in the 1890s he began planning for his mansion on the southeast corner of Fifth Avenue and Sixty-eighth Street, just across the asphalt from Central Park. A good neighborhood, full of Astors and Vanderbilts. The Havemeyers, with a great fortune based on sugar, had built just across the street to the north. Like him, they were collectors of art, kindred spirits, it seemed, and he was planning for a spacious and up-to-the-moment gallery to be attached to his own new home, a room where his own growing collection might be displayed to guests advantageously. Who knew? Perhaps some day, if everything went right, that stone palace and gallery might preserve his name to posterity as one of the great benefactors of society by becoming the Charles T. Yerkes, Jr., Museum of Art, open to the public and second only to the Metropolitan. He'd like that.

When word of Yerkes's plans leaked back West and he was questioned by reporters, he pooh-poohed the rumors, declaring his eternal fidelity to the city that had provided his fortune, and with a straight face explaining that his place in Manhattan would never be more than a *pied a terre,* just a handy out-of-town cottage to be used on his frequent business trips or for short stays prior to or following his and his wife's trips to Europe, a continent they found it convenient to visit more and more frequently now as he built up his collection of old masters. He might have added that it gave the two of them something productive to do during their summers, when they were not welcome in most of the fashionable watering spots popular with Chicago society such as Lake Forest or Oconomowoc. Yerkes had given a good deal of thought to his eastern move and, in fact, had already built his final resting place, again in a very posh neighborhood, on Cypress Avenue in Brooklyn's Woodlawn Cemetery, not far from the tomb of the Whitney family. There he had erected a vault of white Vermont granite, in the Greek style, reminiscent of the Parthenon (but more modest in scale, of course, only 50 feet by 23). Behind its massive bronze doors he had caused to be placed, side by side, beneath an iron-grilled window of stained glass, a suitable pair of sarcophagi, outer cases of polished marble, inner of bronze.

Within these the encoffined bodies of himself and Mary Adelaide would one day be placed, there to rest side by side like some happily bonded couple, perpetually. Over the portal, among the grille work and lions' heads (his chosen totem, they would be carved into the stone of his mansion as well) the name YERKES, chiseled deep into the stone in clean-cut Roman letters that rain or storm could never obliterate. For the spot must be well marked for posterity. Again, who could say? Perhaps in some future time the mausoleum would become a shrine, visited by his admirers and honor paid, for he had made up his mind now to be remembered as a very important philanthropist, dreaming of a great charity hospital that, bearing his proud name, might, as a supplement to his art gallery, just do the trick.

To accomplish this ambitious aim, the financier needed not only to preserve his considerable fortune but see that it multiplied. And he needed to gain socially what had not been possible in that western boondock, Chicago. He had to create a lasting niche for himself in New York society. More than that, he must command a place in the hearts of New Yorkers high and low, young and old. It was love that Yerkes yearned for—the group love of the streetcar-riding populace, whose rain of nickels and dimes had filled his pockets. In seeking immortality as a philanthropist, Yerkes knew it was imperative that he avoid the many mistakes he and Mary Adelaide had made in Chicago. By the time his new home was ready, in 1894, he had determined that this time around he would take pains not to step on the toes of men who could retaliate. Power did have its privileges, he'd learned that lesson.

## II

Theodore Dreiser by now was settled in New York himself. He had left Chicago during the early 1890s to begin ascending the journalistic ladder, one eye, like Yerkes's, ever on a move to the Metropolis. His big brother Paul, already in full career as a Broadway song-and-dance man, helped him to get established in Manhattan, and before long Dreiser had a position with the Joseph Pulitzer's New York *World,* ideally situated for Yerkes-watching. New York was already considerably ahead of Chicago so far as taking note of Celebrities was concerned. Nothing even vaguely approaching such modern Celebrity-driven publications as *People* magazine existed, not to mention its lower-browed counterparts *National Enquirer* or *Star,* or any of their TV avatars like *American Journal,* but a bare-bones beginning had been made in gossip publications such as *Town Topics.* Among newspapers, when it came to sensationalism, the *World* stood in the vanguard.

Dreiser, like Yerkes, was ambitious to become Somebody. His goals and methods were quite different, naturally. He was looking on the newspaper game as possibly serving for no more than a temporary haven, a fine spot in which to hone his natural talents as a writer by learning from his aspiring colleagues and by closely observing the jungle of

life as it whirled on its daily course around him in all its manic phases, from politics to the morgue. New developments in high-speed printing were encouraging the growth of slick-paper monthly magazines, and he took notice that these pages were beginning to provide something resembling steady work for freelancers. Beyond all this lay areas that an untested young writer from the provinces as yet might only dream about. So many of his reporter friends were trying their hands at novels—those of Frenchman Zola, books like *Nana* and *Germinal,* scandalous though they were said to be, popped up as favorite models.

Dreiser must have felt that destiny was somehow at work when he learned that the Charles Yerkeses were abandoning Chicago for the East. He had long been fascinated by the tumultuous career of the streetcar-king and by the runaway rumors concerning the couple's precarious marriage. Yerkes himself seemed such an outrageously outsized figure, a chameleon, a cat that always landed on its feet. He was so much bigger than life, really. Dreiser had packed a thousand Yerkes items away in his memory and carried them with him to New York, and he was ever on the alert for more. From his own Chicago years he had retained scores of fresh recollections. They would provide a good foundation to build on . . . when the time came. His reportorial nose advised him to keep track of both of these Yerkeses. Meanwhile, Yerkes's reputation had preceded him. Much concerning his activities was to be found in the daily pages of the *World* itself, for while the Chicago editors had been rather highly moralistic, determined to blame Yerkes, brand him as an outlaw, and drive him from Illinois, the New York papers were considerably less attuned to making judgments, and more interested in the color of life—in Celebrity, as such.

As the Charles Yerkes mansion was readied for occupancy in 1894, Dreiser seems already to have initiated his practice of scissoring juicy items from the papers. He noted, for his own reference, that sometime around 1893, Yerkes was beginning an open campaign to establish his wife in New York society. And someone at the papers kept—or was kept—abreast on a daily basis of progress with the Fifth Avenue palace, the dollar amounts of what it was costing, with what rarities it was being furnished, and, most vital of all, what type of grand social affairs might be expected soon to occur within its walls.

Contrary to expectations, very few of these looked-for galas occurred. The New York social "400" was notoriously difficult to break into. Money by itself rarely possessed the power to purchase entry for an otherwise unsavory newcomer. As Dreiser would express it in his first book, New York was a sea full of whales, and a man who had dominated other, lesser waters might count for no more than a minnow in Manhattan. In addition, Yerkes was a divorced man, and divorce carried a powerful stigma. A twice-divorced man would be twice-damned. It might well drop him into pariah status. The upshot of this was knowledge that he badly needed Mary Adelaide to be at his side, playing her essential role as Trophy Wife, bedecked in Paris gowns, in diamond chokers and strands of pearls, in feathers and furs. She and his lavish house must become synonymous, the grandeur of one mirroring the splendor of the other. His mansion was to be a marble stage on which great social dramas might be enacted; as Hostess, Mrs. Yerkes was to be the star in these performances, charming everyone. As recompense, engraved cards surely would be delivered by private coachmen, reciprocal invitations to other great houses, other newsworthy parties, up and down the full length of Fifth Avenue.

In his mid-fifties at the time he moved East, Yerkes still stood arrow-straight, six feet tall, his dark, wavy pompadour well greyed, but his dark eyes as piercing as ever. A commanding presence. In Chicago he had been regarded as a man with phenomenal sex appeal and a legendary influence on women (a gift the self-deprecating young Dreiser would have killed for). There had been any number of women in the fellow's life. The Yerkes paramours came and they went, but always there was someone, young, beautiful, perhaps even talented—always talented, of course, in the arts of love, or if not to begin with, then mentored in them by the grand master.

As the twentieth century dawned, the New York financial world was rife with rumors that Charles Yerkes, American monopolist and creator of the Chicago Loop was conniving for control over transportation in London. It was quite true: Yerkes was planning to invade the London Underground field. But he had a second abiding interest in London, for Mrs. Yerkes, as the old century waned, was challenged by a serious new rival for her husband's affections. The ascendant was a Kentucky beauty, Emilie Grigsby, rumored (truthfully) to be the daughter of a society-whorehouse madam whom Yerkes had met at an opulent establishment in Louisville. The daughter, not yet out of her teens, was spectacular. With a cloud of auburn hair and skin like the finest alabaster, Emilie charmed Yerkes, and he fell hard. In no time at all he had brought her to New York along with her mother and her brother, Braxton, whom he employed in his enterprises. Yerkes could not bear to be parted from his new love. If he traveled to Europe, to further his Underground scheme or to visit artists' studios on a buying spree with Mary Adelaide, Emilie and her mother (acting as cover) were sure to have cabins booked for them on the next big liner setting out.

In New York, at the Hotel Grenoble, it was surmised that the Grigsby trio must have access to unlimited cash. Although no one knew quite who they were at first, they occupied an elaborate suite of rooms, staffed by their own personal servants, and kept a stable of saddlehorses and carriages at their disposal. Everyone wondered upon first seeing Emilie, "Who can she be?" Who, indeed! It came out quickly enough, although not publicly, of course. Yerkes had unloaded his rusting streetcar lines in Chicago for twenty million dollars, and a portion of this new wealth went into a place for his Emilie on Park Avenue at 67th Street, a house, if not as spacious as his own, fully as grand, and, audaciously, not more than three blocks away. Sometimes, as if relishing the risk he was taking, Yerkes arranged for the Grigsbys to be entertained at dinner in "Hotel Yerkes," as he mirthfully referred to his grand palace at 864 Fifth Avenue. Mary Adelaide was happy to have them; they were such congenial company, Emilie so strikingly pretty, for she had not had any remarkable luck at breaking into the divine circle whose circumference was both described and delimited by the *Social Register*. Even the purchase of a box at the Metropolitan Opera had not quite done the trick of throwing open the "right" doors. Because Yerkes's reputation was badly stained, and his wife was considered to be a "climber," the gates to social prominence never really opened. They found themselves relegated to a secondary position, relying more and more upon *arrivistes* like themselves or, even more so, to the not quite acceptable new stratum of Celebrities who were eagerly easing their way into notoriety by way of other venues, notably the entertainment world: singers and actors and directors and playwrights. The comic actress Ada Rehan, then at the peak of her popularity, her photograph appearing in widely circulated magazines such as *McClure's,* became one of Mary Adlaide's favorites. The pair became fast friends and, after Rehan had her portrait painted by the society painter John Singer Sargent, Mary Adelaide had her own picture done wearing the same costume in which Rehan had trod the boards in her most famous role, that of Lady Teazle in Sheridan's "A School for Scandal."

So Mrs. Yerkes was glad for the Grigsbys' company—for a time. A full year after Emilie's appearance in Manhattan, a society bachelor at a dinner party, when asked by Mrs. Yerkes whether he had managed to meet the young, pretty, and single Miss Grigsby, replied that she had been pointed out to him at the opera as a magnificent beauty, yes, but was, apparently, the kind of girl of whom everyone may be aware but whom no one should know. Mary Adelaide was aghast. Infinitely more shattering was the revelation, determined after a few inquiries, concerning the reason that Emilie was considered to be *declasse,* the crushing truth that the flow of dollars maintaining the Grigsbys in baronial splendor flowed from the open purse of her husband.

Once Mary Adelaide understood what the rest of New York had long since been aware of, the bronze doors of HOTEL YERKES snapped shut, never to reopen to her rival. No matter. Emilie was comfortably ensconced among her own Aubusson tapestries, diamonds, cameos, cabinets of jades, carved chairs, and $85,000 piano. She would not really miss her intimate little parties on Fifth Avenue all that much. But the unmasking of Emilie Grigsby did serve to snap the threadbare strands of the Yerkes marriage even though on the surface, for public consumption, the couple persisted in their loving-couple charade. On this point the newspapers were silent, perhaps recalling an oft-recounted story from Chicago days, that Yerkes had once discovered an unsavory story-in-the-making that revealed too much about his wife's past and had threatened the reporter so convincingly with death by gunfire that the story never appeared in print.

The nineteenth century passed. Charles Yerkes became a near-total stranger to his official residence. In its place, he maintained a private suite further down Fifth Avenue in the Waldorf. Defeated at heart, Mrs. Yerkes's spirit flagged, and no amount of Jolly Mrs. Yerkes press notices were likely to revive her. She maintained a glacial stoicism, clinging to the only thing of real worldly value she had left, her legal status as Yerkes's wife. No more tears. Instead, she became a fury.

### III

Theodore Dreiser had tracked Yerkes since the 1880s when, as a sixteen-year-old *parvenu* he had observed from the curbside with some wonderment the violence of the strike against the Yerkes streetcar companies in Chicago. By the mid-1890s both Yerkes and Dreiser had relocated to Manhattan and Dreiser, now a budding novelist, had a grandstand seat for observing Yerkes's thwarted attempts to break into New York society. When Yerkes died in December 1905, Dreiser made a note to himself concerning the ironical nature of life as he preserved his thought that Yerkes the multimillionaire had died in an ordinary hotel room. That was the artist at work, of course, altering actuality and waxing hyperbolic to suit his own purposes, for the death chamber was no ordinary hotel room at all, but the same elaborate Waldorf suite which Yerkes had occupied for some years. Bright's Disease, for which there was no cure then (or now) had made quick work of the transportation king.

But hotel bedroom or not, there were ironies aplenty for Dreiser to take note of, for Yerkes had perished while poised on the brink of carrying off the greatest financial coup of his career, control of the London Underground system, a fact that before long would lead to a carnival of lawsuits from creditors who piled in like a famished armada of buzzards ready to tear gobbets of flesh from the Yerkes estate. Another was the sudden emergence of tiny five-foot-three Mrs. Yerkes as a central actor in the unfolding drama. After 1905 Dreiser found himself—along with the rest of New York—inundated with new Yerkes stories as revelations withheld by editors out of propriety or because of the quite real fear of retaliation now became the stuff of everyday headlines—headlines that Dreiser was busily snipping out of the *World* and the *Herald* and squirreling away for future reference, because by this time Dreiser was quite certainly on the verge of beginning an important novel that would be based on Yerkes's life. With Yerkes safely deposited across the river in his magnificent tomb in Woodlawn, the newspapers felt easier about revealing such details of Yerkes-Grigsby connection as were known, including the news that as long ago as 1898 the financier had given Emilie the title to her splendid house on Park Avenue. What other private financial settlements had quietly been made for her would never be known for certain, of course, but suffice to say that the mistress was very well fixed for life, all her expensive toys intact.

Would that life were going as easily for Mary Adalaide Yerkes. During the 1905 summer, it could now be told, the financier, even though mortally ill, was in England to push his Underground scheme, doggedly determined to direct his own destiny. He had secured the services of an unnamed but prominent Manhattan attorney to approach his wife regarding the possibility of a divorce. For years and with reason aplenty, Mary Adelaide had distrusted her wayward spouse, knowing that her presence constituted a rankling obstacle to his happiness and fearful that he would make a sneak attack with some tricky legal maneuver that would oust her from her position and rob her of her legal rights. Yerkes's attorney, said the papers, had apparently been over zealous, exceeding his instructions. He had endeavored to persuade Mrs. Yerkes to vacate 864 Fifth Avenue, threatening, when she balked, to have lights and water shut off. When she stood pat, he then exacerbated the situation by causing her to believe that the financier might leave her unprovided-for in his will. In this manner, it was said, he hoped to provoke her into asking her own attorneys to file for a divorce with a satisfactory financial settlement.

During the autumn of 1905, motivated by intimidation and overweening curiosity, Mary Adelaide Yerkes summoned workmen to the mansion and put them to drilling her absent husband's private safe. Inside she found a bill of sale, dated 1896, which legally transferred to her all of the couple's household goods, furniture, paintings, and other valuables. But knowing her husband's wily nature, this discovery did little to put her mind at rest. And the huge house itself terrified her. It embodied her disastrous social failure and now was staffed by servants she suspected of being no more than her husband's minions. Amid a king's ransom in art, she became a prisoner, terrified that should she leave the house, Yerkes's spy-servants would lock the doors to prevent her return. She barred herself in. Only a small handful of trusted intimates were allowed entry. A guard was stationed outside her private quarters. Emissaries from anyone even remotely connected with Charles T. Yerkes, Jr., were shunned. Mrs. Yerkes tottered dangerously near collapse.

The metropolitan newspapers bided their time, waiting, watching, then reporting. All of this cloak-and-dagger action had the incipient signs of great drama buried in it somewhere. Readers were showing great interest. The story was growing daily more complicated with current legal developments and biographical revelations out of Yerkes's checkered past. Dreiser had been as fascinated, as any other habitue of Celebrity news, as the final chapter in Yerkes's life story approached. In November 1905, returning from London aboard a great liner, the financier had needed to be carried by ambulance directly from the dock to his private apartments in the Waldorf Astoria. His spin doctors released a story explaining that he could not be taken to 864 Fifth Avenue because the place was undergoing extensive remodeling of the art gallery. Few were fooled, and it was noted that the revamping of the mansion in no way rendered the house uninhabitable for Mrs. Yerkes. Public curiosity was piqued by the sudden arrival of the financier's son, Charles E. Yerkes, who had been in Chicago handling what remained of his father's enterprises there. Yerkes's daughter, Mrs. Rondinella, also appeared. Clearly a vigil was underway, and the reporters gathered. The circumspect arrival at the Waldorf of Emilie Grigsby was spotted by alert journalists. But Mary Adelaide remained at home, not venturing out to the Waldorf or anywhere else. Eventually, both Yerkes's major attorney, Louis Owsley, and his financial secretary, Clarence A. Knight, called in person at 864. They struggled to convince Mrs. Yerkes that she had been the victim of a plot designed to embitter her against her husband. But she remained adamant against visiting the man whose audacious verve for life had supplied the supreme thrill of her youth. She seemed fearful now that a simple act of mercy might well prove her undoing. Owsley and Knight met the reporters who stood waiting on her pavement and gave them to understand that Mrs. Yerkes would happily have visited her husband were she not indisposed.

The financier sank rapidly. More and more, a persistent battalion of reporters besieged the mansion. Via her butler Mrs. Yerkes sent out a clarifying message to them: She had not been to the hotel; she did not intend going to the hotel; she was not indisposed; and she absolutely would not discuss her reasons for her actions. From her cunning and imperious husband she had learned a good deal about handling journalists. Soon after taking this bold stand, however, Mary Adelaide Yerkes relented in response to urgent messages from her stepson. A cab was called, and she was driven to the Waldorf posthaste. Because no one expected that Mrs. Yerkes under any circumstances would make a deathbed visit, the watchers' diligence had relaxed. Emilie Grigsby was thrown off her guard. The wife and mistress met face to face at the door of the sickroom. Mary Adelaide was infuriated, raised her voice, and the furor caused inquisitive guests in nearby suites to scurry from their rooms. Eventually, hotel detectives escorted Emilie to her carriage.

Reporters outside the Waldorf accosted Mrs. Yerkes as she left, accompanied by her sister, Mrs. Haywood. Had she seen Mr. Yerkes? Were the couple undergoing a reconciliation? Not at all, said Mary Adelaide: "He treated me shamefully." Mrs. Haywood declared that there was no reason for deathbed forgiveness. Mr. Yerkes had never known how to value his wife, and he quite obviously had learned nothing from his illness. Her sister was through with him. It was Christmas week, but Mrs. Yerkes had long since ceased being sentimental. Asked for permission to have the corpse brought to 864 Fifth Avenue to lie in state, she refused. Even so, on New Year's eve, Yerkes's bronze casket lay in the imposing two-storied reception hall of his marble palace. Friendly reporters confided to Dreiser their discovery that during the wee hours of the night servants had been bribed to open the doors for the undertaker.

Soon the papers were full of news concerning the intended bequest of the Yerkes art treasures to the city of New York. Beyond that, there was to be erected in the Bronx an immense, endowed charity hospital bearing the financier's name to posterity. So, complained the cynical, Yerkes intended to achieve the impossible dream: to pick the public's pocket and make them love him for it. As the press, during January, glutted itself on scandalous disclosures regarding Emilie Grigsby, including the revelation that her mother had been the madam of a brothel, Mrs. Yerkes's attitude took a strange turn. In an abrupt about-face, she now announced that she was seeking consolation in single-minded devotion to her late husband's plans. The idea of the Yerkes Hospital, she said, had been as much her dream as her husband's, and she intended devoting the remainder of her life to seeing that the dream was realized.

The breaking story seemed now to have reached its natural conclusion, but as January 1906 came to a close, there filtered through the news media a rumor too incredible to be believed. It tossed everyone's beliefs and expectations into a cocked hat, and Theodore Dreiser, hearing the rumor, must have wondered what could be happening to the story that had appeared to be winding down so neatly, all of its plot threads finishing, and its giant themes taking shape, including Death as the Great Leveller and the Evanescent Quality of Fame. Now it was said that the Widow Yerkes had remarried. If true, this had to be the first page in an entirely new and unexpected chapter. The precipitate haste of the wedding—supposing there had been one, cast a lurid, Hamlet-like unnaturalness over the death of the financier. But news even more bizarre lay just ahead. The wedding had been secret. What was more, the bridegroom was twenty years Mrs. Yerkes's junior, a Broadway wannabe from the Celebrity circles whose daily companionship she had relied upon in her loneliness.

To the reporters who flocked anew to 864 Fifth Avenue, following leaks from circles close to the putative groom, it all seemed too patently false, at best a sad, sorry joke, certainly not at all a funny prank to play on a poor, bereaved woman. And who was this groom, this Mr. Wilson Mizner, anyway? Mrs. Yerkes, when she eventually showed herself in answer to the newsmen's clamor, seemed near to hysteria. She branded the whole wedding story false, a malicious report advanced by her enemies. Of course she had not married Mr. Wilson Mizner—or anyone else! It was just too ridiculous. Her intention was never to marry again, had she not made the clear?

The reporters located Wilson Mizner at his Broadway digs. He laughed long and loud. Of course the wedding had taken place! In fact, the ceremony had been performed at the Yerkes mansion on 30 January, the one-month anniversary of the financier's demise, Reverend Andrew Gillies of St. Andrews officiating. Mizner was the soul of credibility as he cited times, details, names of witnesses. After the ceremony, the small wedding party had been served refreshments by the Yerkes servants. Then Mizner drove to the Seymour hotel to have sandwiches with some pals while the new bride went out to visit a friend. Later he had called for her, escorted her back to 864, and then returned to his bachelor pad at the Astor.

Word spread immediately to Chicago, where Charles E. Yerkes was initiating the probate of the Yerkes will. A telegram arrived from Mary Adelaide: Story Is Simply Ridiculous, and armed with this, the financier's son denied the Mizner claim. But the telegram was ambiguous. Chicago newspaper joined the New York press in pointing out that the word *ridiculous* might be an attempt to characterize the sensational headlines of recent days, nothing more. Repor-

ters continued to dig. They located another Mizner, Addison, then an antique dealer, but soon to achieve fame as the designer of Spanish-style homes in the very newest of celebrity watering spots, Boca Raton and Miami Beach. Addison Mizner confirmed what his brother had said, and eventually, under pressure, Mary Adelaide dropped her pretense, admitting that indeed she was Mrs. Mizner. "I thought she had more sense," said Charles E. Yerkes, in a dour comment. Did he know Wilson Mizner? Yes, they had met, that was about all. What was he like? How would Charles E. Yerkes characterize him? The younger Yerkes begged off. Hadn't the fellow's own prolixity and the pressure he had put on Mrs. Yerkes stamped his character clearly enough for anyone to see? Surely, the man was a cad.

At age twenty-nine (his bride was fifty) Wilson Mizner now became an instant Celebrity, the press using his own words to dub him a "gentleman of the wide, wide world." Like many men unused to celebrity, Mizner talked altogether too much, telling long-winded stories of his adventures in Central America and the Klondike while puffing on a brown-paper cigarette, all the while nursing a drink in one of Yerkes's best silver goblets. He had come to New York with some vague ambitions to become a playwright, had struck up friendships with theatrical folk, joined the Bohemian Club, and figured in some amateur entertainments. In this company he had become acquainted with the widow Yerkes. The press pegged him "an ambitious Broadway promenader." Sensing his craving for publicity, the reporters dogged his trail, allowing him to swagger a bit and brag until his energy flagged, then writing up the story. Not too much slanting had to be employed, for Mizner, his own worst enemy, set up his own pillory.

On 2 February, on Mizner's invitation, a flock of reporters penetrated the mansion, from which Yerkes had always barred them. Mizner asked the press corps to cool their heels in the Japanese Room off the grand reception hall while he went off in search of his bride. Soon she appeared at a balcony overlooking the foyer, her hair hastily arranged, still gowned in her silk wrapper. She was nervous, her hand gripping and ungripping the marble balustrade as she braced herself to look at the heads turned upward toward her. What did she have to tell them? "All I can say is that I am married to Mr. Mizner. And I hope you will say that I am not fifty but eighty." She seemed confused, at a loss. A bit later the reporter from the *American* was able to speak with her alone and, somewhat more coherently. She told how Mizner had befriended her, supplying help and sympathy while she had lived in the mansion alone, deserted, friendless, and terrified. They had found that they shared certain interests—art, books, reading. She was certain they would be happy. Later in the day, the new master of the house escorted the parade of reporters on a tour of the Italian-garden room and the famous art gallery, where Old Masters were stacked three-deep on the walls. He stopped before a huge oil showing a group of medieval pages playing at dice: "We'd say 'newsboys shootin' crap,' wouldn't we?" Giggles arose from the circled men. The press played up the balcony scene, calling Mizner Romeo and former Mrs. Yerkes a balcony Juliet with a good-looking bank account. Charles T. Yerkes would have known how to handle such brazen audacity from reporters, but he was in his grave. With no protector, his widow was at their mercy. And the presses were hungry.

Reviewing materials for what he now thought held the fine potential for the final pages of his novel-to-be, Theodore Dreiser wrote another note to himself reflecting his dismay at the nastiness overwhelming the journalistic world: "It should be noted in speaking of Mrs. Yerkes the flippant, shameless newspaper accounts—coarse and vulgar." Dreiser's surprise may have sprung from the fact that for so many years the press had handled the Yerkes story with kid gloves. He knew, of course, that a good deal of that reticence had stemmed from fear of massive retaliation. But with the financier safely out of the way, his widow and Mizner seemed literally to beg for it. Of course, the yellow sheets and the tabloids could be expected to exploit this idiotic behavior. But only a few years in the past, when the theft of Mrs. Yerkes's calling-card case and purse had served as a trigger for questionable stories, the staid New York *Times* had rushed to her defense, declaring that a paper that printed gossip without the consent of the victim should be ready to face charges of invasion of privacy. The *Times* itself had been the soul of restraint on the subject of Emilie Grigsby, as an example, although the mistress's story had long been known. But this sad Yerkes-Mizner affair! Even the *Times* was impelled to hoot.

## IV

From 1906 onward Mrs. Yerkes-Mizner knew little peace. Within three weeks rumors spread that the newlyweds had quarreled and separated. On a tip, reporters flocked to Coney Island and dug like dachshunds in the sands of that seaside resort until they located Mizner sparring with boxer Jimmy Britt in an effort, he told them, to regain his lost strength and repair his wasted features. Questioned about a potential reconciliation, Mizner said that he had "slung the slumber mitt" on his dreams of bliss and, gave an answer in two words: "Nothin' doin'." This prognosis notwithstanding, when Mary Adalaide in June 1906 reopened her Chicago house, ostensibly to be available during probate of her dead husband's will, Mizner followed, reg-

istered at the Auditorium Hotel, and called on her, offering a spin in an automobile. Instead, Mary Adelaide remained in Chicago to establish legal residence for a divorce, her attorney (who formerly had guided the financier) gathering evidence to prove that his client had been drugged at the time of the marriage and remembered nothing of the ceremony but what other had told her about it. Mizner countered by producing the Reverend Gillies, who would testify that Mrs. Yerkes had been rational, sufficiently to pledge him to keeping the marriage secret for as long as he could manage. In May 1907 an amicable divorce was granted, Mary Adalaide resuming the name of Yerkes, and Mizner withdrawing from her life. Reports of a million-dollar settlement were denied.

Dreiser wondered how any such settlement could have been possible, given the sad shape in which the Yerkes estate found itself, besieged by creditors. Yerkes's wealth had been estimated at some twenty million dollars (perhaps two hundred million in 1998 dollars), but some months after his death no more than eight million could be located, and his debts amounted to at least five million. Maintenance of the mansion and the army of servants who staffed it cost a small fortune, and the house was still under mortgage. Yerkes's wealth existed primarily in shares of the Chicago Traction Company and the London Underground Railway. But the London subway had not yet been completed; Yerkes's plan to monopolize the Underground still hung precariously in the balance at the time of his death. A plague of lawsuits followed, four years of litigation and legal warfare. Disgusted with the Mizner debacle, Charles E. Yerkes attempted to oust Mary Adelaide from 864 Fifth Avenue, and she in turn attempted to dismiss Louis Owsley as executor of the will, he opposing her wish to claim her dower rights. The dower rights would give her a third of all property; her alternative was to wait for a full share upon eventual settlement of the estate, a prospect that appeared more and more to exist far off in the dim future. The longer she waited, the less worthwhile it seemed, and finally she sued for the dower rights and they were granted.

The implications were immense. For one thing, the Yerkes possessions had to be liquidated in order to determine the dower rights and produce the cash to satisfy them. In consequence, Mary Adelaide must forfeit her right to occupy 864 Fifth Avenue. Plans proceeded rapidly to sell the house and its contents. Everything in Mrs. Yerkes's room was to remain hers, as well as certain canvases from the collection. Otherwise, all personal effects were to go on the auctioneer's block. In December 1909 everything was transferred to the Receiver, Mr. Burlingame: mansion, stables, art gallery, paintings, sculptures, and the famed collection of oriental carpets. Mrs. Yerkes naively had relied to the end on the bill of sale she had found in her husband's private safe, and when the courts finally declared it to be invalid, she was dazed to learn that she would in fact be dispossessed. Guards were stationed in the mansion to prevent her removing so much as a vase; they wore rubber-soled sneakers to protect floors, stairs, and carpets, and this made Mrs. Yerkes ill at ease, despite the fact that the 24-hour surveillance supposedly was designed so as not to interfere with her leaving or entering the home.

The newspapers offered their readers a running account of events, allowing the public to "eavesdrop" while agents of the auction company entered 864 at will. The house that had lacked for visitors was now overrun with men tagging hundreds of paintings, bronzes, and rare carpets according to their placement in the elaborate catalog that was being readied. Collectors, art experts, and dealers joined them, sauntering about the mansion as if they owned it, openly speculating upon values, eyes alert for potential bargains. Even Mrs. Yerkes's boudoir was invaded, and, suffering from neuralgia, she was in a gloomy mood as the work progressed. Theodore Dreiser just then was a busy man, running the Butterick magazines from a limed-oak office and preoccupied with his attempted seduction of eighteen-year-old Thelma Cudlipp, daughter of an employee. But the onrushing show on Fifth Avenue captivated him as well, and he followed the spectacle day by day, learning when the wagons arrived to begin the task of carting three hundred paintings by such as Rembrandt, Hals, Corot, Watteau, Van Dyck, Holbein, Turner, and Rubens to the American Galleries on 23rd Street. Eventually, followed by sixty trunks and a retinue of servants, Mary Adelaide Yerkes left Fifth Avenue for temporary quarters at the new Plaza Hotel before moving to a more permanent home she was leasing at 861 Madison Avenue. Learning from the papers that her new house was considered to be puny compared with the mansion she was leaving, Dreiser jotted down the appropriate thematic comment, in line with the ironic cast that was to characterize the closing pages of his novel-to-be: "And that, after her $50,000 pink marble bath!"

Then, on 5 April 1910, the great Yerkes sale opened to overflow crowds. A $1.00 admission charge during the pre-auction exhibition had not dissuaded many, but only served to whet the appetites of those who wanted to attend the auction and, if not to bid, certainly to be there, to occupy a seat where they might see and be seen. The fact that his copy of the auction catalog was saved among his papers suggests strongly that Theodore Dreiser was among that crowd—and who had a better right or more pressing motive than the man who was now planning somehow to cram all of this American spectacle between the covers of a novel? What an unexpected bonanza this

was! What unlooked-for drama was unfolding in this plot that Life was laying out before him? It was like some grand, appetizing buffet of delicacies! On the first evening of the sale, paintings by Innes, Bouguereau, Israel, Burne-Jones, and Alma-Tadema were knocked down for $162,225. That this sale was going to set an American record seemed certain. On the second evening, any doubts were dispelled as the total ran well past the $400,000 brought by the record-making Mary J. Morgan sale. On the third evening another half million was added to the take with the sale of pictures such as Rembrandt's "Portrait of a Rabbi" and Frans Hals's "Portrait of a Woman" (now in New York's Frick Collection). By the end of the evening the receipts had marched past the two-million-dollar mark.

The auctioneer paused for the weekend. On Monday the auction moved to the mansion, which was to be sold along with the remaining treasures it housed, such as Mrs. Yerkes's Louis XV bedstead of palisander, ormolu, and bronze, and Rodin's marble "Cupid and Psyche." The Celebrity-adoring public at last were enabled to enter the great double bronze doors, free to wander at will up and down the grand central staircase, through the library, into the conservatory, the Japanese Room, the Italian Gardens, to marvel for themselves at the panoply of Success in America, perhaps even to bid on some of the 1300 items tagged for auction—chairs the great Celebrity may have sat in, lamps that had lighted his dinner table. Outside the mansion, on the pavement of Fifth Avenue, a perceptive reporter from the *World* spied a carriage passing slowly, a number of times, the horse pacing first north, then south. He recognized the lone passenger. It was Mary Adelaide Yerkes. When he wrote up his minor scoop, the headline attached to it read: In Brougham, Mrs. Yerkes Sees Crowd Throng Home. Mary Adelaide Moore Yerkes Mizner Yerkes, the life-hungry girl who so long ago had run in company with her Titan husband like a pair of leopards intent on subduing Chicago and the world, now had little left to live for. Her husband was lost, irretrievably, his fabled wealth vanished like a mirage, her own money melting away by the minute. Expecting many millions, she realized a paltry $163,362 after the lucrative sale and the payment of debts. Her health failed along with her expectations. During the fall of 1910 she suffered badly from an attack of grippe; another attack, in February of 1911, finished her off. She died in her rented house on Madison Avenue.

Mary Adelaide had never canceled her plan to rest beside Yerkes in his marble mausoleum out at Greenwood. One final irony—as her funeral cortege wound its slow way through Manhattan toward the Brooklyn Bridge, it was bound to skirt the Forty-Second-Street neighborhood where the Lyric Theatre was presenting *The Deep Purple,* the first smash hit by the heralded new Broadway playwright Wilson Mizner.

By the time that Mrs. Yerkes was laid in the mausoleum at Greenwood, Theodore Dreiser was anticipating publication of his second novel, ***Jennie Gerhardt.*** The manuscript had been completed in the aftermath of the great auction of Yerkes's art collection, and the subsequent sale of the mansion. (The man who bought it denied that he intended tearing it down in order to build a huge apartment building on the site—but of course, New York being what it is, he did precisely that, and as soon as possible.) In ***Jennie Gerhardt*** Dreiser accelerated his use of urban newspapers as plot devices, intensifying his focus upon reporters driven by an ardor for Celebrities. In these pages he made immediate practical use of much that he had learned about current journalistic practices from his attention to the coverage given Mrs. Yerkes's troubles, and in his new novel, reporters, sniffing out a scandal surrounding the love nest that Lester Kane has set up for Jennie Gerhardt and himself, lie in wait for the girl. They stalk her, really, dodging behind shrubbery in order to shoot clandestine film of her daily comings and goings; and newspapers then run soap-opera headlines such as: Sacrifices Millions For His Servant-Girl Love and This Millionaire Fell In Love With This Lady's Maid, headlines which are directly reminiscent of those run in New York during the revelations concerning Yerkes and Emilie Grigsby. These intrusions add immeasurably to Jennie's misery, and Dreiser's criticism of them reflects his own sympathetic response to Mrs. Yerkes in her time of trial, as well as his disgust with intrusive reporters out to "get the story" whatever the cost.

Dreiser was only about twenty years older than the brash young newsmongers of the post-1910 era, but he felt himself to be of another and distant generation entirely, so fast was social change occurring in America. He thought himself to have been bold and even aggressive in tracking down reluctant interviewees during the years surrounding the turn of the century, but his methods could in no way be compared with the voracity of the bloodthirsty young men who had hounded the widow of the financier. Dreiser's reticence was out of date. There were old-fashioned limits beyond which he would not transgress, and these included attacks upon the living. So long as Yerkes lived and his wife survived, Dreiser contented himself with piling up data against the day when he might be freed legitimately to begin composing his epic story. He lived in a muckraking era but was not at heart a member of that clan. He was a novelist. It was strange, though. He'd never written a novel in this manner.

Data was accumulating on a daily basis, it seemed, a new surprise arriving with each dawn. He didn't know anyone else who may have composed a novel in his manner, either. It was all quite peculiar, but extremely exciting.

When both of his principals were safely in their graves, even then the Yerkes saga refused to bring itself to an easy finish. In some ways it appeared only to be getting a good start, for legal hyenas descended upon the scene with a series of lawsuits filed by late-coming creditors and would-be creditors who were intent upon chewing what bones of the estate were left to be gnawed on. These developments, as engrossing as they were appalling, underscored for Dreiser the deep irony of the financier's life and the bubble quality of all of his dreams and brave endeavors. But Dreiser had to move on, because others besides himself were captivated by the story, and it would not wait long for a teller. Already, one of the great new slick magazines, *Everybody's,* had run a summary piece entitled "What Availeth It?" and told much of the tale, complete with photographs. But before he published, Dreiser felt that he needed to do more in site investigation of Yerkes's origins in Philadelphia, read more books on that amazing era in American finance (crib from them if it came to that), and, best of all, take to the road in search of the mysterious essence of his financier. Arguing that he couldn't very well write about a millionaire without learning first-hand how a millionaire had lived, he proposed to sail for Europe and dog Yerkes's footsteps until he came to a full comprehension of what his man's life had been like when he had bulled his way through Paris and London as a famous American Celebrity, gambled for big stakes at Monte Carlo, and purchased expensive art directly from the studios of famous painters. Late in 1911, temporarily setting aside the pages that were fast accumulating for the big novel he was now calling ***The Financier,*** Dreiser boarded the princely liner *Mauretania* in search of the data that would allow him to sail with confidence through Yerkes's later years. Coming home, in April 1912, Dreiser would argue strongly for permission to arrange westbound passage on the maiden voyage of the fabled new liner *Titanic,* the ship he felt sure that Yerkes would have taken, given opportunity. Fortuitously, as it turned out, his impatient publisher refused to support the extravagance.

Meanwhile, the third point of the Yerkes love triangle, the principal figure that Dreiser sometimes lost sight of, had complicated the tale by making her reappearance in New York and moving to center stage. Emilie Grigsby, now popular in exclusive circles in London, where she was rumored to have been the guest of Princess Mary during the coronation of Edward VII, walked down the gangplank of

*Titanic*'s sister ship, *Olympic,* in September 1911, dressed elegantly in black (with a white veil blurring her features) and carrying a bouquet of fresh flowers from a new admirer. Customs officials showed little interest in Emilie's ten trunks, but the man from the *Herald* saw them concentrating instead on the leather bag entrusted to one of her maids. It was opened before the eyes of passengers. Inside, her jewels glittered in the light: diamond tiaras, emerald brooches, a pendant ruby of great size, chokers and ropes of perfectly matched pearls. $800,000 was the value attached. Emilie was disdainful. She invited the officials to examine the settings with care. They would see that her treasures were of *American* design and workmanship, thus not subject to a single red cent of import duty. This was the kind of news that was making the headlines now. Emilie was taking her turn as The Celebrity.

V

When Dreiser returned to New York, Harper and Brothers were screaming for his manuscript, promised so long ago. Dreiser envisioned his fictional account of the Yerkes story as a single volume, admittedly a pretty thick one. He already had written more than a thousand pages, yet his manuscript went no further so far than the Philadelphia years of Frank Algernon Cowperwood, which was the name that he had conjured up for the Yerkes persona. That part of the story had been simple, adhering at most points to the framework established by Yerkes's life and activities. But the parallel account of Mary Adalaide Moore Yerkes required a good deal more work and imagination. Dreiser could have followed either of two paths. He might have cast the second Mrs. Yerkes in a distinctly minor role, obscured by her husbands's gigantic shadow. That would have been advantageous, perhaps, in highlighting the titanic figure of Cowperwood as Dreiser envisioned him, for he surely was to be the motivating center upon whom the plot turned. Another path—the path Dreiser chose—would throw the spotlight upon Mrs. Cowperwood as well and provide her character with a role almost as large and significant as her husband's.

The danger lay in diluting the attention paid to Cowperwood, in possibly creating a second and competing center of dramatic interest. In choosing to go this direction, Dreiser increased his work significantly, for relatively little ready-made material existed concerning the family of Mollie Moore. They were not public figures on whom the newspapers kept tabs. But in a burst of inventiveness that gave the lie to those who carped that he could only report, never invent, Dreiser managed to conjure up for Mollie Moore a celebrity background that rivaled Cowperwood's own. He gave her a wholly new Philadelphia family: two brothers, a sister, an acquiescent mother, and a powerful civic-leader father. It was fictional family cut from whole cloth, yet suggested strongly enough by the mid-nineteenth-century American-big-city milieu as not to violate the sense of actuality that was the lifeblood of Dreiser's story. The family would be headed by Edward Malia Butler, a Philadelphia garbage collector whose shrewdness has assisted him toward a power position in Philadelphia and who works in cahoots with Cowperwood as he bilks Philadelphia of millions.

The Butler character is one of Dreiser's most significant additions to the Yerkes record, a major creation in its own right. But Dreiser's eye is on Butler's daughter, Aileen, the persona through whom Mary Adelaide Moore is reincarnated as a beautiful and headstrong girl whose position as a Butler allows for a convenient and convincing method for her and Cowperwood to become acquainted. Cowperwood first visits the Butler home when Aileen is fifteen. Dreiser has given her a full cosmetic makeover, abolishing Mollie Moore's dark hair and eyes and substituting in their place red-gold locks and blue eyes. Cowperwood is struck by her beauty and her outgoing personality but regards her as a child. Over the next three years Aileen matures, Dreiser introducing another and highly significant physical alteration; rather than remain at Mollie Moore's height of five-foot-three, Aileen has grown to be "nearly" the same height as Cowperwood (who stands five-foot-ten). There is no doubt in my mind that Dreiser here was vitally affected by the publicity given to Mrs. Yerkes after her husband's death; the time period of composition coincides with the years during which the novelist was formulating definite plans to transmute the Yerkes story into fiction. Knowing that in the pages of his novel Mrs. Yerkes-Copwerwood must become something of her husband's equal—in the aftermath of his demise she must stand alone at the center of the action—he took the steps that seemed essential to writing an effective conclusion for his story. Readers have generally assumed that the title of that eventual third portion of the trilogy, **The Stoic,** refers to Cowperwood. But it is Aileen Butler Cowperwood who is the stoic forced to endure silently whatever blows her unkind destiny rains down upon her.

Frank and Aileen Cowperwood are birds of a feather, ideally mated, rather equally ambitious, handsome, amoral creatures of passion. Dreiser in describing Aileen employs terminology that otherwise would be reserved for his hero. She is "vigorously young," "intensely alive," full of "raw, dynamic energy" and "burning vitality," both "fiery" and "intense." At the grand ball celebrating the opening of new side-by-side houses for Cowperwood and his father, the sparks of romance are first struck, Cowperwood crying out, "You're like fire and song." In dramatic terms, these early scenes set the stage appropriately for the future and for its ironic aftermath. At times, in his own rush of enthusiasm for the reified Aileen character (perhaps also to relieve himself of excessive direct authorial adulation of his financier), Dreiser adopts Aileen's point of view, allowing her to depict the Frank Cowperwood she is smitten by. She has been searching for a man whose "love of life" tallies with her own, and in Frank she finds him: "Love! Love! That was the greatest thing in the world. And Frank Cowperwood was the loveliest, most wonderful, most beautiful man that ever was." The lovers do not hesitate at duplicity. As a practical solution to the question of a trysting place, they meet in suburban parks. Here Dreiser expanded inventively upon the single source-note he possessed concerning Mollie Moore's passion for horses. Against tradition, Aileen drives her own pair of spirited bays to the rendezvous, or else dons a riding skirt and rides western style. She averts suspicion for the simple reason that for years she has habitually driven or ridden during her afternoons. The neighbors are accustomed to it. Later, as the love affair matures, Cowperwood sets up a house for clandestine meetings in Tenth Street, furnishing it with treasures from his expanding collection of art works and antique furniture.

Dreiser's plot is served well by this alliance. He arranges for Edward Malia Butler to become a major backer of Cowperwood, supporting him in his risky maneuver to profit (along with the Philadelphia city treasurer) while he uses city funds for his own speculative purposes during interim periods. When the rug is pulled from beneath Cowperwood's feet by the sudden economic crunch that follows the great Chicago fire of 1871, Butler is persuaded by political cronies—but even more so by an anonymous letter exposing Cowperwood's seduction of his beloved daughter—to let the financier twist in the wind. Thus Cowperwood's ruination is linked intimately with the love affair. And following Frank's pardon and release from Eastern Penitentiary, Dreiser again tampers with the actual record as he eliminates the half-dozen and more years during which Yerkes had unsuccessfully attempted to reestablish his reputation in Philadelphia; instead, he causes his locally disgraced lovers to depart for Chicago within six months. One result of these changes in the record is to bind Frank and Aileen together more strongly, to influence the reader to see them as necessary partners in a common fate. Their subsequent social failure, then, and Aileen's predicament when ultimately she is abandoned by Frank, are rendered all the more poignant.

There were many decisions yet to be made by Dreiser. Clearly, the role played by Emilie Grigsby (whom he would dub Berenice Fleming) was going to be a large

and important one, how much so was not clear even in 1910 and 1911, for many revelations were yet to come, including the sale of Emilie's Park Avenue home and her quite improbable (but factually accurate) conversion to the simple life through a trip to India. He hardly dared allow Emilie to become as significant in fiction as she had become in life. But at least, once the financier was dead, the way had been cleared for Aileen to emerge as a believable replacement for Frank at the center of the novel. What to do about the Widow Yerkes's marriage to Mizner was a real puzzle. Its inherent flamboyance held the potential for wrecking Dreiser's otherwise rather neat plot-from-life. Was his story of the financier to be outdone, perhaps swamped, by the outrageous color of that affair? It was a point for serious consideration.

As it happened, such decisions did not need to be made at once, for Harpers, concerned over Dreiser's continual delays in delivering a finished manuscript, acted aggressively. The argument was put to him that his Cowperwood story would never fit between the covers of a single novel. A thousand pages of manuscript had already been examined at the publisher's offices, and it appeared that, with the lovers' departure from Philadelphia, one discrete action had been completed. How would Dreiser feel about allowing Harpers to publish this section under his original title for the whole saga, *The Financier,* both for its own sake and as a drumbeater for two sequels? *The Financier* could be advertised as the opening portion of a trilogy. Three books for one! Dreiser bought the argument. Happily. He gained time; Harpers gained a Dreiser novel for their fall 1912 list. Dreiser then cut his manuscript at the appropriate spot, added a coda which he larded with hints of what was to come, and on 15 October of that year, bulking up at 780 pages and dressed in the same mottled blue binding used in 1911 for *Jennie Gerhardt,* Dreiser's huge story of a businessman as American Celebrity was officially released for sale.

Immediate reactions were mixed; that was not unexpected, given the unorthodoxy of the novel's central players and their deviation from the prevailing social proprieties. But over the long haul, after critical passions had cooled, the novel would be recognized as constituting a superior piece of fiction. In 1959 Ellen Moers declared that *The Financier* and its sequels constituted the best fiction about the world of business that had been published in America;[1] and Maxwell Geismar, in his *Rebels and Ancestors,* confirmed the rightness of Dreiser's decision regarding Aileen, declaring it a "brilliant accomplishment" and saying further that eventually "it was Aileen, the suffering woman, rather than Cowperwood, the perfect operator, who became the central figure in the story of their growing estrangement."[2]

*Notes*

Most of the data in the essay rely upon the thousands of manuscript notes that Dreiser compiled as he prepared to write *The Financier.* These are preserved in the Dreiser collection, University of Pennsylvania.

1. Ellen Moers, *Two Dreisers,* xii.

2. See Maxwell Geismar, *Rebels and Ancestors.*

*Bibliography*

Geismar, Maxwell. *Rebels and Ancestors: The American Novel 1890-1915.* Boston: Houghton Mifflin/Cambridge: Riverside Press, 1953.

Moers, Ellen. *Two Dreisers.* New York: Viking, 1969.

## Laura Hapke (essay date 2000)

SOURCE: Hapke, Laura. "Men Strike, Women Sew: Gendered Labor Worlds in Dreiser's Social Protest Art." *Theodore Dreiser and American Culture: New Readings,* edited by Yoshinobu Hakutani, U of Delaware P, 2000, pp. 104-14.

[*In the following essay, Hapke places Dreiser's works into a political-labor context, referencing his journalism. According to Hapke, Dreiser "deplored the sanitizing of women wage earners," yet he devises strategies so that Carrie and Jennie did not remain long in that class. Dreiser depicts men caught in dire poverty as dull and depleted. In contrast, says Hapke, he creates women untouched by extended poverty; she views Dreiser as ambivalent about characters, especially women, who must be a part of the workforce.*]

Theodore Dreiser was as apt a student of the literary marketplace as Carrie Meeber was of fortune's ways.[1] Yet he deplored the sanitizing of women wage earners central to virtually every popular tale of urban tenement life excepting Stephen Crane's explosive *Maggie: A Girl of the Streets* (1893), which he praised for its realism. While steering clear of the issue of streetwalking, his own "kept woman" novels, **Sister Carrie** (1900) and **Jennie Gerhardt** (1911), subverted the cultural fantasy of proletarian womanhood promulgated in the Laura Jean Libbey dime-novel mode, in which the virtuous lower-class girl is rewarded by marriage to a merchant prince.

Yet Dreiser's ability to transcend the gender discourse of his time was mired in a lingering Victorianism. Astute critical labels such as "Victorian vamp" and "purified fallen woman" suggest the compromised radicalism of his invented narratives of blue-collar female sexuality. Within the cultural parameters available to one who so craved success, the creator of Carrie and Jennie articulated as detailed an analysis of the intersection of labor-class women and capitalism as the era's most "proletarian" text, Upton Sinclair's *The Jungle* (1906). Dreiser's "saving hands" (**SC** [*Sister Carrie*] 1981: 3) approach to feminine economic exploitation, however, reveals the strengths and limitations of his gendered labor vision.

To examine his representation of labor-class women, it is necessary to understand Dreiser's disappointing male proletarians, personified in his novels by the sullenly ambitious stockyard railway worker Hanson in **Sister Carrie** and in his prose writings by the mindless coworkers of his unfinished, autobiographical **An Amateur Laborer** (1904). Working-class men appear in his nonfiction more often than their female counterparts, though rarely as organized-labor militants. Perhaps this ambiguous vision of the masculine worker is the reason little attention has been paid to his gendered approach to class struggle (although, as an author who was fascinated by supermen capitalists and the seductions of upward mobility, class struggle is not a term he would have employed.) In this essay I argue that the sexual segregation in the labor worlds of Dreiser's art and the full extent to which he mirrored his era's prejudices about wage-earning women are illuminated by a look at the connections between Dreiser's journalism and fiction on labor. I thus urge a careful rereading of **An Amateur Laborer**; **"Fall River,"** his unpublished 1899 account of New England loom workers; his assorted articles on factory work, from pieces in the mainstream magazine *Cosmopolitan* to those in the short-lived little magazine *1910* and in the socialist *New York Call*; his retrospective **Newspaper Days** (1922), a description of a mid-1890s visit to a crushed, post-steel strike Homestead, Pennsylvania; and his 1894 *Toledo Blade* piece on a violent local railway strike. Not only does he draw on the beliefs informing the above pieces in the labor-protest section of **Sister Carrie,** but such journalism is crucial for a comprehension of why, for instance, Hurstwood is thrust into the era's real labor turmoil, albeit as a strike-breaker, and Carrie and Jennie are not.

In the labor writings noted above, Dreiser routinely laments the passivity of a lumpenproletariat and occasionally associates embattled working-class manhood with industrial anger. Most often he constructs a work world of men for whom his sympathy is diluted by a certain scorn. As a class-conscious "amateur" in this blue-collar world, he admires the skill involved in some of the most menial construction work. Yet he characterizes his fellow workers as "dull to the ordinary matters of importance in life."[2] He underscores the point in a portion of the manuscript later published in *McClure's* as **"The Mighty Burke"** (1911), in which he praises a foreman at the expense of his crew. Nor can he defend hands at a cotton sheeting plant—"these people are human beings" (177)—without maligning them as "hopeless inadequate to the task of living well" (176).[3] It is true that in **"Three Sketches of the Poor"** (1913), the socialistic Dreiser of the *New York Call* preaches to the converted that the baker's day is one of working hard for little. Yet, returning to a more characteristic stance in his **"Transmigration of the Sweatshop"** (1900), he finds a solution to labor exploitation in enlightened if paternalistic employers who design villages to "rid . . . industry of the smirch of the sweat shop" (499). Curiously, his *Cosmopolitan* piece on the female-fueled workplace bypasses work conditions entirely in favor of the fascinations of the mechanized assembly line.[4]

In his most extended journalistic sortie into a company town, Dreiser's unpublished Fall River essay pinions the mill workforce as "deadly poor in body and soul" (**"Fall River,"** 5). The men and—described more cursorily, the women—depress him by their ill health, mechanical movements, and air of defeat. Cruder than the vulgar shoe-factory workforce that so repels Carrie Meeber, the population is reminiscent of Crane's bellicose Bowery, where drink, profanity, dirt, and family rows prevail. As a major Massachusetts textile town, Fall River was the site of much trade unionism among the more skilled weavers in the years prior to the Dreiser visit; yet he chose to visit the poorest tenement districts, where militance was less visible. There, as at the mills, he deplores the area's spineless workingmen. In the kind of bi-gender approach to workers that he employs in his two classic working-girl novels, he stresses how unattractive the workingwomen are. They are at best, in his important words, "shapeless" and "colorless" (**"Fall River,"** 2). At their worst, they are "slatterns" (6).

Dreiser does give male proletarians respect when they rise up against an oppressive corporate structure. Visiting the Pennsylvania company town of Homestead two years after a momentous, if failed, strike against the Carnegie steel mills, he deplores the crushing defeat. Homestead was one of the most dramatic in a lengthy series of violent confrontations between business and the organized labor movement, and the defeat of the Amalgamated Association of Iron, Steel, and Tin Workers (AAISW) sent shock waves through the American Federation of Labor (AFL), forcing a new policy of pragmatic business unionism and marking relations in basic industry for a decade.[5] While Dreiser focuses on the lowest rung of workers affected by the strike rather than the skilled workers, he does ask whether a democratic nation can suppress its workforce, deny them decent wages, and, by implication, crush the union activity that was at the core of the Homestead expe-

rience.[6] Furthermore, he finds legitimate class rage in the violence of urban Ohio workers following the hiring of streetcar scabs. Interestingly, his *Toledo Blade* piece paints the union men in a positive light, downplaying the tumultuous nature of the protest and focusing on their inability to reclaim their jobs after the strike was settled.

As James L. W. West III notes, Dreiser could sympathize but not identify with workingmen (*SC* 1981: xxx). In **Sister Carrie,** this ambivalence about labor-class effectiveness complicates the portrait of an unwilling proletarian, Hurstwood. In the novel's revised strike scenes, the understandable anger of the Toledo protesters (and, notes Donald Pizer, that of Brooklyn streetcar workers who went on strike in 1895) is now blind, unreasoning fury, disturbing but powerful enough.[7] Yet the energetic wrath of the strikers only makes a scab more sympathetic. Dreiser's journalistic empathy for the played-out Homestead steelmen, who rose but to be crushed by the forces of Carnegie and Frick, is now displaced onto the strikebreaking Hurstwood, a fallen bourgeois morally superior to the working mass in general and Carrie's psychically shrunken brother-in-law, Hanson, in particular. Moreover, little of Dreiser's later compassion for the used-up Harlan County coal miners emerges in the martyrdom of the once-entrepreneurial Hurstwood. Rather, in the scab scenes the potentially anarchic anger of thwarted breadwinners coexists uneasily with the equally thwarted bourgeois individualism of Carrie's downwardly mobile lover. The very drama of Hurstwood's downward trajectory to mendicancy and suicide seems more filled with passion than the Fall Riverite loomworkers' listless anonymity.

Looking at Dreiser's work in the light of women's position in the turn-of-the-century workforce, though, his divided attitude toward collective protest against blue-collar passivity acquires a quite different meaning. In his two "fallen woman" novels that most directly protest inequitable wages and labor-class exploitation, feminine economic oppression, which was far greater than men's, fuels none of the real-life laborite rage evident, for example, among the decade's female textile, clothing trades, and shoe-stitching workers in upstate New York, in New England, or on the Lower East Side. The Fall River Young Ladies' Union of Spoolers, Warper-Tenders, and Drawing-in Girls, prominent in Fall River's 1889 and 1894 strikes, have no more part in his two novels than in his article on his visit there,[8] or than his 1906 *Broadway* magazine interview with firebrand Elizabeth Gurley Flynn in the eponymous **Jennie Gerhardt,** completed a few years after he met with Flynn.[9]

Dreiser knowingly chronicles the twined urban industrial dangers of women's sexual harassment or their dubious "escape" from sweated work through sexual favors to middle- or upper-class men. In his careful attention to the factual realities of salary, work conditions, restrictions, and social relations, as well as to Drouet, Hurstwood, and Lester Kane, men who pay for sex and live with women outside of wedlock, his novels provide fictive counterparts of key sections of Progressive-era documentary classics like the economist Elizabeth Beardsley Butler's *Women and the Trades: Pittsburgh, 1907-1908* (1909). That work appeared under the aegis of the ambitious Pittsburgh Survey, the first systematic effort in the United States to analyze industrial life, including the inequities of sex segregation. Butler's massive industrial study "virtually documented the absence of [non-sex-trade] occupational mobility among wage-earning women" in an early-twentieth-century city comparable to Chicago and New York.[10] Her ambitious examination ranges from scrutinizing the physical characteristics of factories to detailing the laundress's tasks, the sexual division of labor in leading industries, and the health conditions of workingwomen, all subjects treated in the Dreiser novels, taken together. Butler matter-of-factly provides many capsule case histories of women who bartered sexual services for the possibility of ascension. Butler includes her own "Jennie," a small-town Akron girl unable to ascend as a Pittsburgh salesgirl, who "consented to be kept in an apartment" (306). A number of her other subjects even send money home from their new jobs in houses of prostitution (304-6).

What is implicit in Butler is explicit in Dreiser, for he mounts a situational ethics argument that all but transforms the sexual "falls" of Carrie Meeber and Jennie Gerhardt into self-protective feminine economic activity. Yet in a symbolic attempt to shield the labor-class woman from another form of cultural behavior deemed unfeminine, he removes working-class womanhood from the labor fray, and thus from the possibility of a political culture with feminine institutions and networks.

It could certainly be argued that laboring women's actual militance prior to the Depression era was circumscribed indeed, though there was an added erasure of such protest by both the wider culture and unenlightened male trade unionists. Yet the years roughly between the publication of *Sister Carrie* and *Jennie Gerhardt* saw a period in American labor history in which more women engaged in or spearheaded strikes than at any earlier time. However, only three percent of working women, at most, actually belonged to unions, owing in part to discouragement from male trade unionists fearful of female competition for jobs. Certainly those women who were active were visibly so. In 1903, a few years before Dreiser interviewed Flynn, 35,000 women marched in the Labor Day parade in Chicago—the

city where the task of organizing women was taken up more successfully than in any other American city, and where large portions of *Jennie Gerhardt,* which ignored events of this nature, were set. Also in 1903, the Women's Trade Union League, the first national body dedicated to organizing women workers, began its operations in Chicago and New York. Between 1905 and 1915, 100,000 women in the clothing factories of those cities joined workers in Philadelphia, Rochester, and Cleveland and walked off their jobs. Massachusetts textile workers, San Francisco tobacco strippers, Boston telephone operators, and collar starchers in Troy, New York, all agitated for improved working conditions in the face of, at best, lukewarm AFL support and a publics perception of them as the most unwomanly of women.[11]

Carrie Meeber's experiences among female sewing machine operators in a Chicago shoe factory mirror those of the women who created political cultures out of sweatshop toil. But her response to these experiences reasserts Dreiser's need to gentrify her in order to justify her presence in the workplace. From the moment she enters that sex-segregated work site—the skilled male workers are spatially separated from the unskilled females—Dreiser focuses on her revulsion at the "common" women (*SC* 1981: 53) she meets there. To her eyes, they are too familiar with the men, who joke and even touch them playfully. Indeed, these implicitly promiscuous women realize the period's worst fears about the workplace, for they are "free with the fellows ... and [exchange] banter in rude phrases which at first shocked her" (53). Certainly their manners and language are worlds away from her own, as Dreiser is at pains to emphasize. He deplores the fact that the workmate at her right speaks to Carrie "without any form of introduction" (37). Through the bad grammar of the girl at her left, also unnamed, he suggests that she too is vulgar and uncouth. The implication is that these girls are members of an army of women, not worth dignifying by name, who inhabit a verbal world characterized by questions like "Say ... what jeh think he said?" (38). Sexual innuendo and the rowdy giggling with which it is received further brand Carrie's work peers as part of a community of women she does not wish to join. Dreiser summarizes Carrie's response sympathetically: she "felt bad to have to listen to the girl next to her, who was slangy and rather hardened by experience" (53).

Had Carrie met these women's overtures of friendliness with anything more than aloofness, they might well have included her in the jaunts to dance halls and saloons of which they gossiped and which, as Kathy Peiss tells us in *Cheap Amusements,* their real-life counterparts certainly frequented (89-93). Insisting on her separateness from the brazen workplace women, who personify something "hard and low" (*SC* 1981: 40), he casts her as a princess among the serfs.

Even if he makes no link to reactive trade unionism, Dreiser is too much the realist to deny that these women's behavior is an adaptation to the grueling conditions of the workplace. Acknowledging that "[n]ot the slightest provision had been made for the comfort of the employés" (*SC* 1981: 39), Dreiser suggests that the women, routinely addressed by the foreman as "you," must endlessly repeat mechanical movements in a stifling atmosphere at a pace directed by the owner. Dreiser's observation that the work speed turned men and women alike into "clattering automatons" (36)—a term he uses for the machines of Fall River, incidentally— is borne out by autobiographies by garment-trades women such as Elisabeth Hasanovitz and Rose Cohen.

As in many actual factories of the period, the women are used routinely to train apprentices like Carrie, an assignment that takes unpaid time from their own work; they are also denied access to skilled "men's jobs" and treated rudely by bosses and male workers. They are even forbidden to talk on the job because it was believed to lower feminine productivity. Given this dehumanizing taboo against conversing, like their real-life counterparts, they band together to circumvent both ruling and punishment by talking animatedly about their recreational activities and warning one another when the foreman is in listening range. Their work culture, as described by one modern historian of women's work, this fashion, "organize[s] workroom social life around the interests and experiences shared by most young women."[12] Although part of his scorned the low intellectual level on which these women functioned, Dreiser knew that such gossip reflected the interests of young working-women. When in a reminiscence he recalled his own sisters, who worked in low-paying jobs in Chicago in the 1880s, he said they talked constantly of "[c]lothes and men."[13]

Furthermore, if the shoe factory women are attuned to the sexuality of their male coworkers' familiarities, much like the rather wayward Dreiser girls themselves, they also exemplify a consideration for one another, including newcomers like Carrie. The historian Leslie Tentler finds in the turn-of-the-century feminine workplace countless instances of a "supportive work group … embodying an oblique protest" (66) against the demands of incessant productivity. So too among the women Carrie encounters. The very girl whom Dreiser brands as unmannerly for not introducing herself also gives Carrie tips on conserving her energy for the afternoon's sewing. All try to slow up their work so that the inexperienced new girl can better learn her

machine. And they try to initiate her into workplace mores. "Don't you mind. … He's too fresh" (*SC* 1981: 40), one says to comfort her when a young man prods a mortified Carrie in the ribs.

Yet in the end Dreiser still buries the issue of their hard, unremunerative work by decoupling women and work. He uses the providential male rescue to separate his atypical shop girl from the toughened types who try to befriend her. Carrie, it is true, is not able to marry the freewheeling Drouet, and Hurstwood's union with her, though she cultivates ignorance about it, is a bigamous one. But unlike the average lower-class woman of the time, who could expect to work seven years before marriage, Carrie enters a series of semimarital relationships that provide her with much greater economic and emotional rewards than a Hanson for a mate.

Carrie's male protector, however, is not the final resolution of her problems. First one man then another supports her financially. But by encouraging her early attempts at acting and not meeting her needs or insuring her security, both plant the seeds of interest in a career. Her fairly rapid rise to theater fame and financial independence is both her escape from working-girl status and the moral compromises that tarnish her for middlebrow audiences. Even her new work has little to do with the shoe-factory drudges of her erasable past. No arduous climb that involves learning her craft or engaging in endless chorus-line work, Carrie's overnight success is that lucky accident, largely independent of her own efforts, for which she had wished. For, having left Hurstwood and returned to the ranks of wage earners, Carrie does not really reenter the workforce. Just as when she left the vulgar women of the shoe factory, Dreiser undercuts her identity as a working girl. Indeed, given his prejudice against unchaste workingwomen, his refusal to include Carrie, "fallen" or not, in that morally suspect group is a way of defending her innate purity. Sheldon Grebstein, analyzing Carrie's sexual relationships, argues convincingly that Dreiser sanitizes her by playing on associations with "innocence, purity and helplessness" (545). Thus, Dreiser depicts a Carrie, ever demure and wistful, who "sins chastely" (551), quite unlike the brazen women of the city workplace.

A decade later, Dreiser again quickly removed a labor heroine from a worker's life and a Flynn-like militancy. To do so, *Jennie Gerhardt* chronicles a cross-class love affair in which a toiling protagonist, remarkable for beauty and family self-sacrifice, escapes waged work through rescue by a romantic capitalist. In many ways, Dreiser offers the same fairy tale as do the more conservative authors of female labor novels of the 1900s, which replaced the tenement story as the favored working-girl fiction of middlebrow audiences. Unlike these writers, Dreiser criticizes the snobbery that prevents Jennie from marrying Lester Kane. Yet if the plutocratic Lester is unwilling to marry a working woman, Dreiser, ever protective of his heroines, demonstrates his own kind of condescension toward laboring women: he is reluctant to permit his heroine even a transient identification with consciousness of her class situation, and thus with workers' militance.

As early as 1906, laundresses in San Francisco, rebelling against their notoriously ill-paid work, successfully struck for overtime and reduction of the workweek (Foner, 309). Although their striking counterparts in other cities, such as New York, were less successful, the image of the militant laundress had established itself to a certain extent. So, by the time of *Jennie Gerhardt,* had the woman who sewed the clothes that a Senator Brander might send for Jennie to launder. Addressing readers for whom Dreiser himself sometimes wrote, Theresa Serber Malkiel's *Diary of a Shirtwaist Striker* (1910), first serialized in the 1910 *New York Call,* acquainted that audience with the convictions fueling Uprising of the 20,000, as the 1909-10 New York City Shirtwaist Strike was called: "[W]orking people won't be ground to dust much longer. ... [T]heir ever rising fury is bound to break out any day" (204-5).

Dreiser's vision of the female worker, in contrast, is one of complete self-containment. He keeps her from contact with women in the trade, dissatisfied or otherwise. To demonstrate her probity (and thus bolstering his defense of her later dealings with Senator Brander and Lester Kane), Dreiser focuses on Jennie's gratitude for the work. Historian Meredith Tax observes that immigrant and first-generation women often expressed appreciation for the most wretched sweatshop work, comparing it with the poverty of their European lives (28-29). But in distinct contrast to the unreflective Jennie, these women at least had a work consciousness, a sense of what Tax calls "their money-earning capacity" (29). Furthermore, by the second decade of the twentieth century, these were the women who would transform passive gratitude into solidarity and even revolt.

When, early in *Jennie Gerhardt,* Dreiser comments that his title character is too beautiful to have to work with her hands, he both reflects the curiously antilabor bias of the labor romance and demonstrates the impulse to protect his working heroine that characterizes *Sister Carrie.* Like Carrie, Jennie enters the world of work as if she had just come to the city. Both are vulnerable—unused to the splendor of urban places patronized by the affluent, given to blushing when interested men stare, and easily manipulated by ostentatiously successful men who act

kindly and press money into their hands. But in his later novel Dreiser seems even less interested in locating his heroine in a work milieu. Though the Gerhardt women are city dwellers at least seasoned enough to take on cleaning work outside the home at an opulent Columbus hotel, Jennie soon settles for piecework at home, a throwback to women's tasks in the domestic economy of a preindustrial age. She apparently does not think to seek permanent wage-earning work as a hotel laundress. Women routinely held such full-time jobs in large urban centers, as Dreiser, a laundry-wagon driver attracted by the women he worked with in 1890s Chicago, well knew.[14] But his very awareness of the public perception of these women may have prompted him to keep Jennie apart from them.

In her study of laundresses in nineteenth-century French culture, Eunice Lipton argues that middle-class culture insisted on seeing such women "in exclusively sexual ... terms" (302). The fantasy, which bore some relation to reality, was that women who worked in intense heat in semi-clothed conditions, who reinforced each other's need for alcohol to cope with their work, and who delivered men's garments to them in their rooms, were among the most immoral of the female working class. In 1904, Dorothy Richardson, who worked for a time in a New York laundry, gave a less racy description of American laundresses, but one that emphasized their slovenliness, their love of drink, and, to her unsympathetic eyes, a work culture characterized by slang, shouting, and complaints (229-49).

Although he uses Jennie's laundry work as a symbol of the fate of unskilled, impoverished women like her mother and herself, Dreiser censors Jennie's involvement in it. He does not even give it the few pages of description allotted to Carrie's shoe-factory labors. Rather than dignifying Jennie's work, her creator almost calls up the fantasy of the sexually available laundress. To soften the harsh truth that, to make any money, Jennie has only herself to sell, Dreiser emphasizes that she is "barren of the art of the coquette."[15] She does not "fully understand [Senator Brander's] meaning" (37) when he proposes a liaison, and though she accepts his proposal, "enjoy[s] it all innocently" (43)—the second of Dreiser's chaste Chicago sinners.

The dominant late-Victorian trope of the sexually vulnerable woman needing protection against a predatory economic world and her own frailties generated images of deserted streetwalkers in the works of writers even less involved in labor issues than Dreiser, such as Crane's title character in *Maggie* and Frank Norris's Trina in *McTeague* (1899). Lacking male protectors, these working-class women die, it could be argued, of carnal knowledge. (Trina's greed and masochistic sexuality are frequently linked in the Norris text.) Yet whether they perish or, like Carrie and Jennie, endure and ascend, immersion in what the labor historian Francis Couvares calls the "plebeian sea" of worker culture is denied them (36).

Given the real but circumscribed feminine working-class protest during the 1890s and early 1900s, Dreiser's placement of men only in the dialectic between collectivity and competitive individualism compromises the otherwise ardent defense of breadwinning womanhood at the core of **Sister Carrie** and **Jennie Gerhardt.** Consciously or not, he distances himself from what the new labor historians term "woman's work culture," the workingwoman's response both to her female peers and her employer's rules and strictures.[16] Divided between compassion for and condescension toward the typical working woman, between locating their heroines in the feminine workplace and rescuing them from its coarsening influence, Dreiser's novels illustrate his ambivalence about wage-earning women. He has a profound vision of the economic, social, and psychological forces shaping them. But like the sentimental slum tales and romantic labor novels that "explained" working women to middle-class America, Dreiser's fiction draws back from exploring the feminine work experience. If to a certain extent he transcends such fiction, he also shares the prejudices that permeate it. The shelter from female proletarianism he offers is removal from both the industrial working class and the labor movement that rose to defend its interests.

### Notes

1. Dreiser, "The Literary Shower," *Ev'ry Month* (February 1, 1896): 10.

2. Dreiser, *An Amateur Laborer,* 1904, ed. Richard W. Dowell and James L. W. West III, 117.

3. Dreiser, "The Factory," 1910, rpt. in *Theodore Dreiser: A Selection of Uncollected Prose,* ed. Donald Pizer, 175-80.

4. Dreiser, "Scenes in a Cartridge Factory," 322.

5. Ronald L. Filippelli, "Homestead Strike," in *Labor Conflict in the United States: An Encyclopedia,* ed. Filippelli, 241.

6. Dreiser, *Newspaper Days,* ed. T. D. Nostwich, 500.

7. Donald Pizer, "The Strike," in *Sister Carrie,* ed. Pizer (New York: Norton, 1970), 416.

8. Filippelli, "Fall River Textile Strikes," in *Labor Conflict,* 176-77.

9. Hapke, *Tales of the Working Girl: Wage-Earning Women in American Literature, 1890-1925,* 88.

10. Maurine Weiner Greenwald, "Introduction: Women at Work through the Eyes of Elizabeth Beardsley Butler and Lewis Hine," in Butler, *Women and the Trades: Pittsburgh, 1907-1908,* ix.

11. See Philip S. Foner, *Women and the American Labor Movement from Colonial Times to the Eve of World War I,* ch. 17; and Meredith Tax, *The Rising of the Women: Feminist Solidarity and Class Conflict, 1880-1917,* ch. 1.

12. Leslie Woodcock Tentler, *Wage-Earning Women: Industrial Work and Family Life in the United States, 1900-1930,* 69.

13. Dreiser, *Dawn,* 69.

14. Richard Lingeman, *Theodore Dreiser: At the Gates of the City, 1871-1907,* 86.

15. *Jennie Gerhardt,* 1911, (New York: Penguin, 1989), 35.

16. Patricia A. Cooper, *Once a Cigar Maker: Men, Women, and Work Culture in American Cigar Factories, 1900-1919,* 2.

### Bibliography

#### WORKS BY DREISER

*BOOKS*

*A Book about Myself* (*Newspaper Days*), 1922. Greenwich: Fawcett, 1965.

*Dawn.* New York: Horace Liveright, 1931.

*SHORT WORKS*

*The Factory,* 1910, no. 5, n. p. Rpt. in *Theodore Dreiser: A Selection of Uncollected Prose,* ed. Donald Pizer, 175-80.

"Scenes in a Cartridge Factory." *Cosmopolitan* 25 (July 1898): 321-24.

#### WORKS BY OTHERS

Butler, Elizabeth Beardsley. *Women and the Trades: Pittsburgh, 1907-1908.* New York: Charities Publication Committee, 1909. Rpt. with intro. Maurine Weiner Greenwald. Pittsburgh: University of Pittsburgh Press, 1984.

Cooper, Patricia A. *Once a Cigar Maker: Men, Women, and Work Culture in American Cigar Factories, 1900-1919.* Urbana: University of Illinois Press, 1987.

Filippelli, Ronald L. "Fall River Textile Strikes." In *Labor Conflict in the United States: An Encyclopedia,* ed. Ronald L. Filippelli. New York: Garland, 1990, 175-79.

————. "Homestead Strike." In *Labor Conflict in the United States: An Encyclopedia,* ed. Ronald L. Filippelli, 241-46.

Foner, Philip S. *Women and the American Labor Movement from Colonial Times to the Eve of World War I.* New York: Free Press, 1979.

Greenwald, Maurine Weiner. "Introduction: Women at Work through the Eyes of Elizabeth Beardsley Butler and Lewis Hine." In Butler, *Women and the Trades: Pittsburgh, 1907-1908,* 1984, vii-xlv.

Hapke, Laura. *Tales of the Working Girl: Wage-Earning Women in American Literature, 1890-1925.* New York: Twayne / Macmillan, 1992.

Lingeman, Richard. *Theodore Dreiser: At the Gates of the City, 1871-1907.* vol. 1. New York: Putnam, 1986.

Tax, Meredith. *The Rising of the Women: Feminist Solidarity and Class Conflict, 1880-1917.* New York: Monthly Review Press, 1980.

Tentler, Leslie Woodcock. *Wage-Earning Women: Industrial Work and Family Life in the United States, 1900-1930.* New York: Oxford University Press, 1979.

**Shawn St. Jean (essay date 2000)**

SOURCE: St. Jean, Shawn. "Dreiser and American Literary Paganism: A Reading of the Trilogy of Desire." *Theodore Dreiser and American Culture: New Readings,* edited by Yoshinobu Hakutani, U of Delaware P, 2000, pp. 203-13.

[*In the following essay, St. Jean discusses Dreiser's Cowperwood trilogy, which includes his less studied novels*—The Financier, The Titan, *and the long-delayed and posthumously published* The Stoic—*in terms of the writer's semiclassical education, finding in them qualities long associated with ancient classical literature.*]

The penultimate paragraph of *The Titan* (1914) is Dreiser's prose-poetic tribute to the tradition of bards who had before him pondered the questions of human existence:

> What thought engendered the spirit of Circe, or gave to a Helen the lust of tragedy? What lit the walls of Troy? Or prepared the woes of an Andromache? By what demon counsel was the fate of Hamlet prepared? And why did the weird sisters plan ruin to the murderous Scot?
>
> (552)

That the incantation of *Macbeth*'s weird sisters, "Double, double toil and trouble, / Fire burn and cauldron bubble"

which Dreiser further quotes may itself be an allusion to Homer, "Greed and folly double the suffering in the lot of man" (*Odyssey* I. 50-51), demonstrates the eternal nature of such questions. What are the true relationships of fate to free will, suffering to desire?

Like so many American writers who came of age in the nineteenth century, Dreiser drew on a ranging classical education that provided him with both the standards and the perspective with which to interrogate modern humankind.[1] *The Titan*'s final pages are the culmination of a sustained, modern narrative relying extensively on allusive systems based in Greek mythology, Shakespeare's canon, and the Bible. Not only are allusions used as passing literary devices designed to align the author with a tradition of literary philosophy, but they reveal something of the deep structure of Dreiser's novels.

These allusive systems have not yet been adequately explored by Dreiser scholars (or Emerson or Thoreau scholars) for the insight they lend readings of the American masterworks. Reasons for this neglect may include the seeming datedness of the approach in the face of twentieth-century shifts in reading strategies and the rise of literary theory, or what might be hastily judged as the superficiality of the systems themselves or the traditional method of explication. Whatever the objection, I hope to help set it to rest by demonstrating how well consideration of some major works (in this case Dreiser's *Trilogy of Desire*) through the lens of one body of sources, Greek tragedy, functions to clarify one of the most problematic issues in Dreiser studies.

This issue has been blanketed by the term *literary naturalism.* For nearly a century critics have complained that Dreiser's leanings toward the "school" of naturalism have been heavy-handed embarrassments, detracting from the better features of his works and showing little evidence of coherence or consistency. But a more considered position would be that this "school" meets under a house of cards, that authors like Crane, Norris, Dreiser, and Wright do not share enough philosophy or technique to be heaped together in an attempt to ignore the complex questions they raise and relegate them to an eccentric corner of the canon.

Let us begin to navigate this mire in a new way first by considering the broadest definition of (Dreiser's) naturalism and some compelling specific charges by critics. We can then discover how well these subissues can be recontextualized by Dreiser's "pagan" view of the world.

Naturalism is the embodiment of a theory which holds that the lives of human beings are determined by forces external to themselves. Specifics have been appended to this broad definition, such as the extent of determination and naming of forces (heredity and environment are the most popular.) I use the most liberal definition in order to be fair to Dreiser, and yet some would still contend that elements of his works cannot be contained within it and that his system breaks down. For example, Lee Clark Mitchell asserted in 1989 that

> voluntarism and determinism are opposed metaphysical systems that depend upon mutually exclusive categories. When we act as if they are not—assuming for instance, that people are determined yet free, or that some people are determined while others are not—we simply show how powerful are projective moral attitudes.
>
> (137)

This charge of inconsistency undoubtedly refers, at least generally, to what has become one of the most-quoted, notorious, and yet ill-considered passages in Dreiser's canon: the opening of *Sister Carrie*'s Chapter VIII, in which man is equated with "a wisp in the wind" and "wavers" in a "jangle of free will and instinct" (*SC* [*Sister Carrie*] 1981: 73). In 1970 Donald Pizer cited the same passage as evidence of Dreiser's "false or superficial discursive grasp of the meaning of [the] events" in his own novel, "an apology for Carrie's impending choice of an immoral life with Drouet."[2] Both of these critics represent a host of others who would prefer to read the passage as "part of Dreiser's characterization of Carrie" than as "relevant to the themes of the novel as a whole."[3] A converse critical move (but similar in its implications) is to invest such passages as above, those that contain narrative philosophy, with total overriding thematic significance, as Walter Benn Michaels does with a famous scene from *The Financier*:

> Nothing about Dreiser is better known than his susceptibility to Spenserian "physico-chemical" explanations of human behavior. And nothing in Dreiser's work provides a better example of this susceptibility than the allegory of the lobster and the squid. ... The moral of this story, as Cowperwood and Dreiser come to see it, is the irrelevance of anything but strength in a world "organized" so that the strong feed on the weak. Such a moral is ... curiously inapplicable to the events of *The Financier* itself, which persistently exhibit nature not primarily as an organizing force dedicated to survival of the fittest, but as the ultimate measure of life's instability. ...[4]

These three critics, while pursuing different agendas of their own, share preconceived notions about the way literature should work that Dreiser did not. He was trained in an older system that had many congruities to his beliefs and that he readily adapted for his own purposes. These congruities are easily demonstrated. William Chase Greene, in an Aristotelian vein, declared in 1944, just a year before Dreiser's death, that

> It is often asserted that Greek tragedy is fatalistic,—that all events are predestined, that the characters are helpless in the grip of fate, ... [but] any sweeping statement of this sort is fallacious. ... What is true is that a part, great or small, of the action in most of the plays is considered to proceed from cause beyond the control of the characters. ... Conversely, as fate sinks into the background, human character emerges and controls, or seems to control, the situation; in such a case, the struggle of a will to overcome obstacles, or a struggle between two or more wills, provides the chief interest. But the finest and most profound tragic effect comes when the poet is not content merely to set forth external events, nor even the fact of guilt, but exhibits also the moral attitude of his protagonist toward events and toward his own action. He answers the call of honor, come what may; he endures what fate or the gods send. His act may have caused his downfall, but his will remains noble; he learns by suffering; and there may be a final vindication of the sufferer, though of an unexpected kind.[5]

This statement provides some invaluable standards by which to evaluate literary naturalism in general and Dreiser's novels in particular. But for the moment, it helps us take the long view of the previous critical assessments of Dreiser's shortcomings.

Greene claims that the tragic work presents a continuum between fate and character on which the actions shift. Logically, the strength of a character's reactions will effect the force of fate upon him or her in such a model. Just such an insight must have prompted Heraclitus's famous adage (repeated by Emerson) "A man's character determines his fate." As I will show, Dreiser's characters behave according to this model, explaining precisely *how*, in Mitchell's terms, "people [can be] determined yet free," and how "some people are determined yet others are not." Far from being inconsistent, Dreiser's naturalism revives an ancient ideology that explained human existence for a millennia.

Meanwhile, Pizer's reaction to Dreiser as trying to excuse Carrie's immoral behavior is shown to be, in light of Greene's commentary, an importation of ethical standards foreign to those by which the work was created.

Finally, Michaels's astute observation that nature is "unstable" in *The Financier* is voided by his assertion that Dreiser failed to recognize the world he himself created, and that the author discerned no different a "moral" from the lobster and squids' battle than his own preteen character. To lump Dreiser's and young Cowperwood's powers of moral insight together is a fatal error, and can only lead to an erroneous conclusion: that the author has failed to match the events of his novel with his intended theme. The problem is that the theme has been decided beforehand by the critic, not Dreiser, who maintains a varying detachment from his characters and the (at times) philosophic narrator. Failure to employ the basic reading strategy of recognizing this disparity of author, narrator, and character has continued to mar what otherwise might be productive Dreiser criticism.

What is notable about Greene's observations on tragedy is that they could almost as well describe Dreiser's fiction. Many of his characters operate on a sliding scale between free will and total determinism, and, as with tragedy, this crucial insight is easily overlooked even by sharp-eyed critics who have been reared amidst modernist notions of consistency engendered by the scientific and industrial revolutions.[6] However, Greene and Dreiser would seem to part company when Greene speaks of the profoundest spectacle showing characters who endure what fate sends. But Greene is for the moment referring only to characters like Orestes. Equally profound in interest, and more plentiful, are those like the title characters of *Agamemnon* and *Oedipus Rex* who resist rather than endure fate and suffer doubly for it.[7]

This distinction brings us to the key connection between Dreiser and the Greeks, one far more useful than simple surveying of allusions. It is concerned rather with structural and thematic alignments. And when we realize that, just as much as Dreiser, the fifth-century tragedians were social critics, all the pieces fit together. Dreiser's novels are loosely based on the model of Greek tragedy with regard to dramatic movement and character exploration, but they adapt and incorporate a mode of social criticism suited to turn of the century *American* culture. This agenda is readily seen in the title of Dreiser's great work, **An American Tragedy,** the implications of which have been ignored or blurred by critics who insist on defining tragedy in American terms instead of vice versa.[8] Dreiser, throughout his canon, defines America in tragedic terms.

Tracing the manifestations of this agenda is a messy business, bearing in mind that the author discursively drew on other, equally strong models like Shakespeare. But a clear example of structural alignment should demonstrate my point.

Dreiser's so-called **Trilogy of Desire** examines the life of Frank Cowperwood, his rises and falls. Not only does this trilogy emulate Greek tragedy in general, but it is based on the specific myth of Prometheus and on Aeschylus's trilogy in particular. Greene succinctly outlines those works:

> The *Prometheus Bound,* probably the first part of the trilogy, shows us the punishment of Prometheus for having raised man from brutishness to civilization by the gift of fire and the arts, in defiance of Zeus. The *Prometheus Unbound,* of which scanty fragments remain, must have shown the reconciliation of Prometheus and Zeus and the setting free of the Titan. In *Prometheus the Firebringer,* of which hardly more than the title is preserved, and which probably came last, it is likely that the poet dealt with the introduction into Attic cult of the festival of Prometheus, as a fire god ...
>
> (117)

Now beyond the obvious reference of the titles **The Titan** to Prometheus and **The Stoic** to that group of Greek philosophers, what is the structural connection? If Greene is correct in his assignment of chronology, and if Dreiser shared similar knowledge, then **The Financier** (1912) would roughly correspond to *Prometheus Bound.* Of course, the two other source texts were lost long before the nineteenth century and it makes sense that Dreiser would choose the extant drama on which to base his new novel. Notably, the first edition of **The Financier** does not contain any reference to a **Trilogy** [**Trilogy of Desire**], as that of **The Titan** does. The first part may have been conceived as a stand-alone narrative, and it is that. Similarly, the *Prometheus Bound* flashes back and forward, sketching the entire Prometheus myth. The final pages of **The Financier** allude to the rest of Cowperwood's life, leaving a sense of closure in case the other parts were never written. Aeschylus probably saw value in a similar approach: even though tragedies were performed in threes, there is no evidence that any of the trilogies (the *Oresteia,* the *Oedipus* plays) were composed or performed together, and much that suggests otherwise.

In effect, Dreiser's **Trilogy** tells the story of a man who rises, through being the underling of others more powerful, to Titan-like status (critics have been fond of calling Cowperwood a Nietzschian "superman"). When he begins to usurp the power of other financial giants, and, refusing to bow to their efforts to keep him "in his place," threatens them, he is imprisoned and stripped of all power. After regaining his freedom through compromise, he embarks on a career to regain power in another land. His efforts to do so meet with resistance everywhere.

The Prometheus myth has all of these elements. After turning against his fellow Titans and assisting Zeus in ascension over his father Chronos, Prometheus is cast aside by the new regime. The Titan, fearing that Zeus will make good on his threat to destroy flawed humankind and replace them with a more perfect race, steals fire and the arts and gives them to humanity, assisting with their survival by practical means and simultaneously enabling them to act. For this he is chained to a mountain peak and tortured daily. Eventually he is freed by Heracles acting under Zeus's orders.

More interesting than the parallels here are the ways in which Dreiser transforms them to suit his critique of American culture and society. Most notably, Cowperwood's philanthropy is more Machiavellian than Promethean: he maintains its *appearance,* but his services to humanity (street railway systems, the gift of a $300,000 telescope to a local university, and, ironically, orchestration of the failure of the monopolistic American Match Company) mask an anti-promethean lust for personal power:

> The thing for him to do was to get rich and hold his own— to build up a seeming of virtue and dignity which would pass muster for the genuine thing. Force would do that. Quickness of wit. And he had these. Let the world wag. "I satisfy myself," was his motto. . . .

*(F [The Financier],* 244)

Of course, the passage also demonstrates Cowperwood's closest tie to the Titan: his self-characterized "Promethean defiance" to the power and opinions of his society (*T [The Titan]*, 528). Unfortunately, this trait is the source of downfall for both characters. A Titan is something less than a god and more than a man, and Prometheus's refusal to divulge information about Zeus's demise to his punisher, coupled with the original bestowal of divine gifts on humankind, represents a double impiety amounting to *hybris.* He insists upon reaching beyond his sphere. Cowperwood, a man, is guilty of the same crime against society. His actions, incidentally, endear him to women, as represented in these reflections by Berenice Fleming:

> As she thought of him—waging his terrific contests, hurrying to and fro between New York and Chicago, building his splendid mansion, collecting his pictures, quarreling with Aileen—he came by degrees to take on the outlines of a superman, a half-god or demi-gorgon. How could the ordinary rules of life or the accustomed paths of men be expected to control him? They could not and did not.

*(T,* 527)

Instead of gods, other financial "Titans" are the figures who undertake the duty of checking Cowperwood. In a chapter significantly titled "Mount Olympus," they confer together and summon Cowperwood to appear. They intend on calling Cowperwood's loans, thereby ruining him for his manipulation of American Match, an endeavor that threatens to make him richer at their expense. Cowperwood responds to the summons, and after hearing out Hosmer Hand's and others' polite overtures to eviscerate his career, he responds plainly:

"I know why this meeting was called. I know that these gentlemen here, who are not saying a word, are mere catspaws and rubber stamps for you and Mr. Schryhart and Mr. Arneel and Mr. Merrill. . . . You can't make me your catspaw to pull your chestnuts out of the fire, and no rubber-stamp conference can make any such attempt successful. . . . If you open the day by calling a single one of my loans before I am ready to pay it, I'll gut every bank from here to the river. You'll have panic, all the panic you want. Good evening, gentlemen."

*(T,* 434)[9]

He leaves the others enraged but intimidated by his bluff, and escapes only for a greater eventual fall. Compare the scene to one in *Prometheus Bound,* in which the Titan is confronted by Zeus's agent Hermes:

Pr:

> Do I seem to thee
> To fear and shrink from the new gods?
> Nay, much and wholly I fall short of this.
> The way thou cam'st go through the dust again;
> For thou wilt learn nought which thou ask'st of me.

Her:

> Aye, by such insolence before
> You brought yourself into these woes.

Pr:

> Plainly know, I would not change
> My ill fortune for thy servitude,
> For better, I think, to serve this rock
> Than be the faithful messenger of Father Zeus.
> Thus to insult the insulting it is fit.

Her:

> Thou seem'st to enjoy thy present state.

Pr:

> I enjoy? Enjoying thus my enemies
> Would I see; and thee 'mong them I count.

(959-73)

Refusal to act as underling and declaration of open hostility mark the speeches of both protagonists. In both cases this is taken for insolence by superior-positioned opponents. And both encounters degenerate into veiled threats on each side. These are contests that can at best be only temporarily won by the protagonists against overwhelming odds.

Greene hypothesizes that a kind of reconciliation is reached, after due punishment, between Prometheus and Zeus in a later part of the trilogy. Cowperwood also manages a kind of alignment with the "powers that be" in the third city to which he visits his financial wizardry, London.

Despite resistance to American influence over their public utilities, Cowperwood befriends (as opposed to bribes) the right people, notably Johnson and Lord Stane, and smoothes the way. Instead of fighting the forces arrayed against him, he attempts to join with them. This would appear to be a change in Cowperwood's philosophy key to the themes of *The Stoic*: "Take things as they come and make the best of them," he reminds himself in various ways (*S* [*The Stoic*], 20, 47, 94, 148, 224, 228). In Greene's words:

> What must be, must be; but man, by his insight, may will to do what must be done, and so may act in harmony with nature; or, again, he may resist. The result, considered externally, will be the same in either case, for man cannot overrule Nature, or Fate; but by willing cooperation, by making its law his law, he can find happiness, or by resignation he can at least find peace. ... To live "according to nature": that is the phrase, often repeated by the Stoics, which sums up their ethical ideal. ... This is man's whole business; it leads to self-preservation; it involves action, not mere contemplation; it is attended by pleasure, though that is a by-product, not in itself the goal.
>
> (340-41)

Prometheus himself adopts an attitude of stoicism. Enchained by Zeus's agent Hephaistos, he declares "The destined fate / As easily as possible it behoves [me] to bear, knowing / Necessity's is a resistless strength" (103-5). Through this same philosophy Cowperwood comes as close to happiness as the *Trilogy* ever takes him: so far that "I satisfy myself" transforms into real philanthropy, such as plans for endowments of a public art museum and a free hospital for the poor after his death (*S*, 256).

However, tragedy dictates that wisdom is never unaccompanied by loss, and Cowperwood has learned his lessons too late. His estate is plundered after his death and the great bequests fail to materialize because in life he had failed to meet contemplation with action, or at least the right kind of action. The denouement of the *Trilogy* approximates only in sadly parodic fashion *Prometheus the Firebringer*: no cult or worship grows up around the figure of Cowperwood; indeed, the newspapers question the worth of all his endeavors in the face of the posthumous dissipation of his fortune (*S*, 303).

The Prometheus myth shows that everyone—god and man—has limits that are imposed by more powerful forces rarely understood. Rex Warner, a modern translator, explains

> that nature, and what the Greeks called "necessity," do not proceed in accordance with human standards of justice and morality and, so Aeschylus seems to suggest, a failure to recognise this is a dangerous and unjustifiable form of pride.
>
> (*Prometheus Bound*, 4)

Cowperwood's attempts to transcend his own limits by undermining external forces must fail regardless of the morality of his intentions (which improves with time), just as the Titan's do. After creating (and in a sense relating, since Cowperwood's life was so closely modeled on that of Charles Tyson Yerkes) these events, themes emerge *from* them,[10] one of which Dreiser's narrator ponders:

IN RETROSPECT

> The world is dosed with too much religion. Life is to be learned from life, and the professional moralist is at best but a manufacturer of shoddy wares. At the ultimate remove, God or the life force, if anything, is an equation, and at its nearest expression for man—the contract social—it is that also. Its method of expression appears to be that of generating the individual, in all his glittering variety and scope, and through him progressing to the mass with its problems. In the end a balance is invariably struck wherein the mass subdues the individual or the individual the mass—for the time being. For, behold, the sea is ever dancing or raging.
>
> In the mean time there have sprung up social words and phrases expressing a need of balance—of equation. These are right, justice, truth, morality, an honest mind, a pure heart—all words meaning: a balance must be struck. The strong must not be too strong; the weak not too weak. But without variation how could the balance be maintained? Nirvana! Nirvana! The ultimate, still, equation.
>
> (*T*, 550-51)

Dreiser is not interested in chasing down the true source of this "ultimate equation," whether it be morality in a Christian God, feuding among the pagan gods, consciousless Fate, or balance in nature. He is concerned, rather, with tracing its effects in individual human lives throughout his work. Variation and individualism are necessary components for the growth of the world, yet their transformative powers are meager in themselves and can only work slowly and in concert with the world. Different characters are worth examining to see this dynamic at work. The theory also goes far in explaining what might be called variable determinism throughout his novels.[11] Characters who steadfastly refuse to act for themselves, like Lester Kane and Clyde Griffiths, are acted upon or for by the forces of balance. Conversely, Frank Cowperwood attempts to act with too much force of his own and is checked by "Fate." Whatever its name, this cosmic power operates according to a sole principle which, from the perspective of people caught up in their own lives and ambitions, is unfathomable. And because we cannot understand even the standards of "balance" by which this force operates according to human terms, stoicism (an attitude Carrie Meeber, Jennie Gerhardt, and the older Cowperwood seem to share) seems the only viable option. Even the vantage point of auditor of the literary work seems no protection. We see characters as free as any of us bowed under the same pressures we seek to evade in our own lives. Dreiser's fiction is thus rightly experienced as untidy and unpredictable, and so discomforting to readers and critics.

Henry James argued in "The Art of Fiction" (1884) that "The only reason for the existence of a novel is that it does attempt to represent life" (166).[12] If life for the realist writer is what he can observe, then life for his "naturalist" counterpart might include speculations about those observations. But such distinctions as these obviously involve a great deal of fluidity, and as time continues to pass, the critical constructs of romanticism, realism, and naturalism may become more important as icons of critical history than as functioning critical tools. Dreiser seems to be a writer on whom these convenient terms are already well-exhausted. His novels represent life alternately as he saw it, read about it, deplored it, wished it could be. He imported to American life the moral and theological perspective of a past civilization, abandoning those of his own milieu. The apparent disjunction of all this will certainly fail "to represent life" for many, who, like the fell sergeant who came for dying Hamlet, are strict in their arrest. Yet we must try to understand, as James says, "the truth . . . that *he* [not the critic] assumes, the premises that we must grant him, whatever they may be" (167, emphasis added) of a writer, if, like Horatio, we are to report him and his cause aright to the unsatisfied.

### List of Abbreviations

The following abbreviations parenthetically refer to Dreiser's books.

| | |
|---|---|
| *F* | *The Financier* |
| *SC* | *Sister Carrie* |
| *S* | *The Stoic* |
| *T* | *The Titan* |

### Notes

1. I have not determined the formality of this education as yet, though the internal evidence is overwhelming.

2. See *Sister Carrie,* ed. Donald Pizer, 583-85.

3. Ibid., 586-87.

4. See Walter Benn Michaels, "Dreiser's *Financier*: The Man of Business as a Man of Letters," 288-89.

5. See William Chase Greene, *Moira: Fate, Good, and Evil in Greek Thought,* 91.

6. For a pertinent example of how scientific criteria can come to dominate the thinking of humanists, see Emile Zola, *The Experimental Novel.* This important work has had a long-range influence on naturalist criticism, with the unfortunate side effect of shutting down avenues such as the one pursued in the present investigation. For example, Zola makes a distinction between determinism and fate: the former is limited to observable criteria like heredity and environment, while fate cannot be contained in such ways and is thus beyond the province of the novelist. Definitions like this one have served to devalue the work of those "naturalists," like Dreiser, whose characters are acted upon by less quantifiable forces.

7. These characters may or may not ultimately learn from their suffering. Dreiser, undoubtedly in the service of his social criticism, often dramatized the contrast between both types. For example, Carrie Meeber perseveres while George Hurstwood ends his life in despair, murmuring "What's the use" (*SC* 1981: 499).

8. Philip Gerber relates, in *Theodore Dreiser,* that consternation [engendered by misunderstanding, in my view] about the title began before the book even saw publication:

> Sections of the book were already being set up in type and proofs circulated privately among selected readers. Opinions began coming in. Some damned, some praised. Some questioned the title, which Dreiser had changed from *Mirage* to *An American Tragedy.* How arrogant! Pompous, really. "How in the world can Dreiser call a book *An American Tragedy*?" asked Thomas Smith, Liveright's closest literary adviser. The author held firm.
>
> (132)

Although Gerber does not speculate as to Dreiser's insistence, I believe it must have been to preserve the mythic dimension he was, by then, intentionally crafting into his canon.

9. Gerber has shown that this scene occurred in the real life of Charles Tyson Yerkes, the Chicago street-railway magnate whom Dreiser used as a source for Cowperwood (105).

10. A key to Dreiser's realism is his extensive borrowing from the events of real lives like Yerkes's and Chester Gillette's. It seems strange that critics have widely recognized the author's genius in doing this, but in general have resisted his interpretations of what those events mean to the human condition.

11. See my article, "Social Deconstruction and *An American Tragedy*," for a full explication of the term.

12. See Henry James, "The Art of Fiction."

*Bibliography*

This bibliography contains only those items cited in the text. A year after a work indicates the year in which the work was originally published.

WORKS BY DREISER

*BOOKS*

*The Financier.* New York: Harper and Brothers, 1912.

*The Stoic.* Garden City: Doubleday Company, 1947.

*The Titan.* New York & London: John Lane, 1914.

WORKS BY OTHERS

Aeschylus. *Prometheus Bound,* trans. Henry D. Thoreau. *The Dial* 3. 3 (1843).

Gerber, Philip L. *Theodore Dreiser.* New York: Twayne, 1964.

Greene, William Chase. *Moira: Fate, Good, and Evil in Greek Thought.* Cambridge: Harvard University Press, 1948.

James, Henry. "The Art of Fiction." In *The Art of Criticism: Henry James on the Theory and the Practice of Fiction,* eds. William Veeder and Susan M. Griffin, 165-83. Chicago: University of Chicago Press, 1986.

McCall, Dan. *The Example of Richard Wright.* New York: Harcourt, Brace, 1969.

Mitchell, Lee Clark. *Determined Fictions: American Literary Naturalism.* New York: Columbia University Press, 1989.

Pizer, Donald. "The Problem of Philosophy in the Novel." *Bucknell Review* 18 (March 1970): 53-62.

St. Jean, Shawn. "Social Deconstruction and *An American Tragedy.*" *Dreiser Studies* 28 (Spring 1997): 3-24.

## Yoshinobu Hakutani (essay date 2000)

SOURCE: Hakutani, Yoshinobu. "Wright, Dreiser, and Spatial Narrative." *Theodore Dreiser and American Culture: New Readings,* edited by Hakutani, U of Delaware P, 2000, pp. 248-73.

[*In the following essay, Hakutani compares the urban visions of Dreiser and of African American writer Richard Wright, asserting that "among all the writers in English, Dreiser had the strongest influence on Wright's mode of understanding American history and culture."*]

I

As African Americans found the rural South a living hell and dreamed of overcoming racial prejudice and living in northern cities, their writers were intent upon conveying their pains and dreams. The mode of their writing was diametrically opposed to that of nineteenth-century American novelists who often described the mood of pastoral idyl inspired by a longing for simpler agrarian society. This type of fiction was written largely as a reaction to the disharmony and friction that occurred among rugged individualists, strong-willed white men, living in urban society. The new kind of white man was not only able to live in harmony with nature, he would find a bosom friend in the stranger, a dark-skinned man from whom he learned the values of life he had not known. Natty Bumppo in Cooper's leather-stocking novels strikes up friendship with Chingachgook and Hard-Heart, noble savages of the wilderness. Ishmael in *Moby-Dick* is ritualistically wedded to Queequeg, a pagan from the South Seas. Huck Finn discovers a father figure in Jim, a runaway slave.

In twentieth-century American literature, however, a substantial reversal of the antiurban sentiment is found in both European American and African American writings, a new literary tradition often critical of the values expressed in earlier American literature. In ***Jennie Gerhardt,*** for example, Dreiser described the city as a site of freedom and subjectivity. A realistic modernist like Dreiser, who intimately knew the squalor and corruption city life brought on, used the urban environment as a space in which to dramatize individual liberty and pursuit of happiness. For both men and women, the city was envisioned as a site of confluence between the individual and society, a space which was fluid and wide enough to enable citizens and workers to interact with an industrialized culture.

Much important African American literature which has emerged since the Depression has also been largely urban in character. Although never hesitant to criticize the negative aspects of city life, it has only rarely suggested that pastoral alternatives to the city exist for African Americans. This large and significant body of literature, moreover, contains some surprising celebrations of city life. One way to explain this positive image of the city is to examine the historical experience of African Americans. From the very onset, African Americans were denied imaginative access to a pre-urban homeland in Africa because the institution of slavery did everything possible to stamp out the memory of that world.[1] And the actual experience of slaves in America did not permit them the luxury of romantically imagining the non-urban settings which are so mythically prominent in nineteenth-century American fiction by such writers as Cooper, Melville, and Twain. As Huck Finn and Jim sadly discovered, the territories ahead could be truly liberating only for European Americans. In the era following the literal end of slavery, new strategies for reinslavement were devised in the South where codes of segregation and the practice of sharecropping were to make it impossible for African Americans to establish a positive image of rural life which could serve as a counterbalance to the pull of urban life.

For Richard Wright, Chicago was split between wonder and terror, but it was always preferable to the southern environment he had so categorically rejected. What is remarkable about his impression of Chicago was its dichotomous vision:

> Then there was the fabulous city in which Bigger lived, an indescribable city, huge, roaring, dirty, noisy, raw, stark, brutal; a city of extremes: torrid summers and sub-zero winters, white people and black people, the English language and strange tongues, foreign born and native born, scabby poverty and gaudy luxury, high idealism and hard cynicism! A city so young that, in thinking of its short history, one's mind, as it travels backward in time, is stopped abruptly by the barren stretches of wind-swept prairie! But a city old enough to have caught within the homes of its long, straight streets the symbols and images of man's age-old destiny, of truths as old as the mountains and seas, of dramas as abiding as the soul of man itself![2]

Not only did Chicago in the 1930s and 40s present itself as the center of a powerful industrialized economy, but it was also a striking representation of a modern civilization buttressed by multiculturalism. Small wonder Chicago produced, besides Wright, Margaret Walker, Gwendolyn Brooks, and a host of American writers whose cultural legacies were other than Anglo-Saxon and mostly ethnic, such as Dreiser, James T. Farrell, Nelson Algren, and Saul Bellow.[3]

Farrell was one of the earliest American writers who championed Wright's narrative for an unusual intermixture of realism and lyricism. He wrote in *Partisan Review* that *Uncle Tom's Children* serves as an exemplary refutation for those who wished to write "such fancy nonsense about fables and allegories." In response to such reviewers as Granville Hicks and Alan Calmer, who wanted Wright to pace more steadily in his narrative and delve more deeply into his material, Farrell argued that Wright effectively

uses simple dialogue "as a means of carrying on his narrative, as a medium for poetic and lyrical effects, and as an instrument of characterization."[4] By contrast, as if in return for Wright's unfavorable review of her novel *Their Eyes Were Watching God*, Zora Neale Hurston categorized *Uncle Tom's Children* as a chronicle of hatred with no act of understanding and sympathy. As did some other critics, she opposed Wright's politics, arguing that his stories fail to touch the fundamental truths of African American life.[5]

For Wright, however, what enabled his narrative to convey the truth about African American experience was not an application of literary naturalism but a creation of perspective. Almost a decade earlier than James Baldwin's review of *Native Son*, Wright had posited a theory of African American narrative in "Blueprint for Negro Writing," published in *New Challenge*. This narrative, whether in fiction or in nonfiction, as he argued, must be based on fact and history and cannot be motivated by politics or idealism. African American writing, then, does not assume the role of protest: "even if Negro writers found themselves through some 'ism,'" he asks, "how would that influence their writing? Are they being called upon to 'preach'? To be 'salesmen'? To 'prostitute' their writing? Must they 'sully' themselves? Must they write 'propaganda'?" The inquiry is "a question of awareness, of consciousness; it is, above all, a question of perspective." This perspective, Wright defines, is "that part of a poem, novel, or play which a writer never puts directly upon paper. It is that fixed point in intellectual space where a writer stands to view the struggles, hopes, and sufferings of his people."[6]

Substantiating perspective with "intellectual space," Wright further posits that perspective must not be allied with "world movements" and must be established by the self. Because perspective is "something which he wins through his living," it is "the most difficult of achievement" ("Blueprint" 45-46). This intellectual space comprises, on the one hand, a writer's complex consciousness deeply involved in African American experience and, on the other, a detachment from it. By a detachment Wright means a reflection accomplished in isolation, in a space where neither those afflicted nor those sympathetic to their plight, such as Marxists, are allowed to enter. "The conditions under which I had to work," Wright recalls in *American Hunger,* "were what baffled them [members of the Communist party in Chicago]. Writing had to be done in loneliness."[7]

His attempt to establish perspective and provide it with intellectual space accounts for his lifelong commitment to a narrative by which he is able to convey his own vision of life. His entire work has shown that he was a remarkably resilient thinker and writer. At the outset of his career his writing was deeply influenced by Marxism, but later, as he came to establish his own point of view, he used only the doctrine of Marxist theory on class struggle, which made sense to African American life, but rejected much of the practice, which suppressed freedom and subjectivity.

Although some critics have regarded Wright's work as a product influenced by earlier American and European literary movements, he never considered himself belonging to any of them. In 1941 he told Edwin Seaver: "Dreiser could get his sociology from a Spencer and get his notion of realism from a Zola, but Negro writers can't go to those sources for background ... In fact, I think in many cases it is good for a Negro writer to get out on his own and get his stuff first hand rather than get it through the regular educational channels" (*Conversations,* 46).

Whatever philosophy Wright had earlier come across, he adamantly adhered to his own theory of narrative. Whether he was interested in Marxism, Zolaesque naturalism, and French existentialism, none of them taught him how to attain his perspective and intellectual space. The Marxist doctrines of class struggle against capitalism proved less relevant to African American life than they did to American life in general. Literary naturalism, based on the concepts of heredity and social environment, would not have applied to African American narrative, for such concepts had less to do with African Americans than they did with European Americans. Racism alone, ever-present in American society, made the social environment of African Americans vastly differ from that of European Americans. By the same token, existentialism, as originally conceived for European society, would not have provided Wright's narrative with the perspective and intellectual space it entailed.

Not only did "Blueprint for Negro Writing," published in 1937, give a clear definition, but Wright also provided a remarkable illustration for his theory. Perspective, he wrote,

> means that a Negro writer must learn to view the life of a Negro living in New York's Harlem or Chicago's South Side with the consciousness that one-sixth of the earth surface belongs to the working class. It means that a Negro writer must create in his readers' minds a relationship between a Negro woman hoeing cotton in the South and the men who loll in swivel chairs in Wall Street and take the fruits of her toil.
>
>                            ("Blueprint," 46)

Focusing on the relationship between African American women workers in the South and European American

businessmen in the North, Wright sounded as though he were giving a demonstration of American racial problems. But the perspective he urged the African American writer to achieve does not merely apply to African Americans, it signifies "the hopes and struggles of minority peoples everywhere that the cold facts have begun to tell them something" ("Blueprint," 46).

## II

Of his reading in the Chicago period, the recently published *Conversations with Richard Wright* confirms that he paid his utmost attention to such influential American novelists in the twentieth century as Dreiser, Faulkner, and Hemingway.[8] Of the three, Wright was least inspired by Hemingway. In a radio discussion of the New York Federal Writers' Project broadcast in 1938, he said: "I like the work of Hemingway, of course. Who does not? But the two writers whose work I like most today are André Malraux and William Faulkner. I think both of them in their respective fields are saying important things" (*Conversations,* 10). Despite Hemingway's reputation, established by such novels as *The Sun Also Rises,* Wright realized that a Hemingway novel makes a great impression on the reader's mind not for establishing perspective but for creating style. Wright also realized that a Hemingway novel thrives on action, a technique lacking in French novelists like Sartre and Camus.[9] In the 1930s, Wright felt that he belonged to the latest literary generation, which included both Hemingway and Faulkner. He paid a greater tribute to Faulkner because he thought Faulkner's fiction conveys a judicious point of view. In particular, he recognized Faulkner's importance in developing the American novel, in which the "unhappiness" of the American people was realistically described (*Conversations,* 109).

Among all the writers in English, Dreiser had the strongest influence on Wright's mode of understanding American history and culture. "The first great American novelist I came across," Wright said in retrospect shortly before his death, "was Theodore Dreiser. Thanks to him, I discovered a very different world in America" (*Conversations,* 214). As early as 1941, Wright said, "I never could get into Dickens ... He reeks with sentimentality. Theodore Dreiser ... is the greatest writer this country has ever produced. His ***Jennie Gerhardt*** is the greatest novel" (*Conversations,* 38). Toward the end of *Black Boy* he wrote:

> I read Dreiser's ***Jennie Gerhardt*** and ***Sister Carrie*** and they revived in me a vivid sense of my mother's suffering; I was overwhelmed. I grew silent, wondering about the life around me. It would have been impossible for me to have told anyone what I derived from these novels, for it was nothing less than a sense of life itself. All my life had

shaped me for the realism, the naturalism of the modern novel, and I could not read enough of them.[10]

Wright's affinity with Dreiser has conventionally been understood in terms of naturalism, but Wright never considered himself a naturalist.[11] That Wright made no distinction between realism and naturalism in reading Dreiser's novels suggests a predilection for the fiction that mirrors social reality, the writing that not only expresses the sentiments of the socially oppressed but also thrives upon the unalloyed feelings of individuals. This subjectivity on the part of the writer, which Wright deemed the most difficult to achieve, constitutes what he called "perspective" and "intellectual space," the twin elements indispensable to his narrative.

One of the chief reasons why *Jennie Gerhardt* had a strong affinity for Wright is that Dreiser's novel is not a naturalistic novel as is, for example, Stephen Crane's *Maggie: A Girl of the Streets.* As an American realist, Dreiser took pains to deal with young women's search of happiness in the city. Just as the young Wright, finding the rural South a living hell, escaped to Chicago, as so poignantly portrayed in *Black Boy,* Jennie, suffering social ostracism in small Ohio communities, moves to a happier life in Chicago, where she faces less prejudice of class and gender. Unlike Maggie in Crane's novel, to whom the "shutters of the tall buildings were closed like grim lips ... the lights of the avenues glittered as if from an impossible distance,"[12] Jennie finally finds in Chicago not only privacy and subjectivity but the gay, energetic spirit of life that frees her from oppressive social conventions. Given a slum section of the city and a self-centered family situation, on the contrary, Crane's portrayal of Maggie's life becomes utterly predictable. Growing up in such a family, Maggie has little desire to leave the slum life or to better herself. Although she is described as "blossomed in a mud puddle" and "a most rare and wonderful production of a tenement district, a pretty girl" (141), she is deprived of any sense of autonomy and vision.

In *Jennie Gerhardt* Dreiser achieves what Wright calls "perspective" by gauging the relationship between Jennie and Lester Kane, two individuals placed poles apart in society just as Wright urged his fellow novelists to envision the distance between a black woman cotton picker in the South and a white businessman in Wall Street. Even though Lester is heir to a millionaire business tycoon, he is attracted with great compassion to Jennie, a daughter of poor immigrants, who helps her mother scrub hotel floors in Columbus. Far from a victim of social environment, Lester is described as "a naturally observing mind, Rabelaisian in its strength and tendencies." From Jennie's vantage point, "the multiplicity of evidences of things, the vastness of the panorama of life," of which he is conscious, makes her quest for liberation from class oppression less painful (125). As she moves from Cleveland to Chicago, the multiple and panoramic vision of urban life intensifies. "Yes, Chicago was best," Dreiser declares. "The very largeness and hustle of it" made the concealment of Lester's liaison with Jennie "easy" (173).

Unlike Maggie and her family, who forever remain victims of the big city slum environment, Jennie and her family are endowed with abilities to circumvent the situation and create space for themselves. While Maggie is trapped and her movement is circular at best, Jennie, like the narrator of *Black Boy,* who went from Natchez, Mississippi, to Memphis and then to Chicago, moves from smaller cites to larger ones, from Columbus to Cleveland, and to Chicago. And just like the mature Wright, who later went to New York to broaden his horizon, Jennie is also able to visit the metropolis. Unlike Maggie's brother Jimmie, who cares only about his own life, Jennie's brother Bass, although early on he cares very little for his family, becomes not only concerned about the family's welfare but feels a great sympathy for his sister. In an immigrant family, the oldest son, being young and most acculturated to the American way of life, served as the catalyst for the success of his family.

Most significantly, Wright was inspired by Dreiser's spatial narrative, through which the city in Jennie's ordeal becomes her savior. In Dreiser's narrative, living in a city not only separates her from the restrictive past dominated by class and gender prejudices but gives her the fluid, indeterminate space in which to gain her subjectivity. Furthermore, the spirit of freedom the city inspires in Jennie is also shared with Lester. Whether she succeeds in her search for liberation has a corollary in what happens to his life in Chicago. In *Maggie,* on the contrary, the Bowery life, which is extremely confined, does not allow for the residents' mobility, let alone their travels.

In *Jennie Gerhardt,* the idea and excitement of travel is expressed throughout the novel. As the Gerhardt children walk to the railroad tracks to steal coal, they watch luxurious trains pass by. "Jennie, alone, kept silent," Dreiser remarks, "but the suggestion of travel and comfort was the most appealing to her of all" (28). After his father's death Lester decides to leave the wagon factory owned by his family and departs on a European tour with Jennie, as Wright, while living in exile in Paris, extended his travels to Pagan Spain, West Africa, and Southeast Asia. Jennie, Dreiser writes, "was transported by what she saw and learned":

> It is curious the effect of travel on a thinking mind. At Luxor and Karnak—places Jennie had never dreamed existed—she learned of an older civilization, powerful,

complex, complete. . . . Now from this point of view—of decayed Greece, fallen Rome, forgotten Egypt, and from the notable differences of the newer civilization, she gained an idea of how pointless are our minor difficulties after all—our minor beliefs.

*(JG [Jennie Gerhardt] 1992: 307)*

Although Lester is portrayed initially as an animalistic man, he turns out to be "a product of a combination of elements—religious, commercial, social—modified by the overruling, circumambient atmosphere of liberty in our national life which is productive of almost uncounted freedoms of thought and action" (126). Despite her lack of education and experience, Jennie is also inspired by the same spirit of freedom Lester attains.

In contrast to Crane's deterministic portrayal of Maggie, the fluid, spatial narrative that informs Jennie's liberation had profound influence upon Wright's mode of understanding American history. Dreiser's heroine is a victim of gender prejudice and social, economic oppression. At the outset of his career in Chicago, Wright attempted to acquire his own perspective and intellectual space through the John Reed Club. As he told Edward Aswell, he had a strong affinity for Marxism at that time: "I was a member of the Communist Party for twelve years ONLY because I was a Negro. Indeed the Communist Party had been the only road out of the Black Belt of Chicago for me. Hence Communism had not simply been a fad, a hobby; it had a deeply functional meaning for my life."[13] As Wright also wrote for the *Daily Worker* in 1937, the aim of Marxist African American writers like him was "to render the life of their race in social and realistic terms. For the first time in Negro history, problems such as nationalism in *literary perspective,* the relation of the Negro writers to politics and social movements were formulated and discussed" (emphasis added).[14]

At the very inception of his Chicago period, Wright was indeed intent upon subverting the traditional, hierarchical discourse in American writing, a hegemonic, racist mode of expression. Such a mode of understanding American history was rigid and antithetical to the spirits of freedom and democracy, the twin ideals of American culture. In place of the traditional narrative, Wright wanted to create a spatial model of amelioration. While he lived in Chicago, Marxist writing indeed served his initial purpose: his early writing, and *Uncle Tom's Children* in particular, vividly demonstrated Marxist conceptions of history as the forums in which power relations are understood.

### III

"Big Boy Leaves Home," the first story in the 1938 and 1940 editions of *Uncle Tom's Children,* features a young black boy's escape from his violent southern community.[15] Four innocent, happy-go-lucky black boys are discovered naked by a white woman while they are swimming in a pond and later drying their bodies on a white man's premises. When she screams, her male companion without warning begins shooting and kills two of the boys. Big Boy manages to overcome the white man and accidentally kills him. Now the two surviving boys must take flight: Bobo gets captured, but Big Boy reaches home and is told by black church leaders to hide in a kiln until dawn, when a truck will come by to take him to Chicago. While hiding, he poignantly watches Bobo lynched and burned. Witnessing such an event gives Big Boy not only a feeling of isolation, terror, and hatred but a sense of self-awareness and maturity.

Not only is "Big Boy Leaves Home" based upon Wright's personal experience, but the sexual taboo that precipitates this tragedy originates from the fact both black and white people in the South knew so well. The white woman who suddenly appears near the swimming hole, as the story unfolds, is closely guarded and protected by the white world. "In that world," as Blyden Jackson has noted, "at least when 'Big Boy Leaves Home' was written, all Negro males, even young and with their clothes on, were potential rapists. And so this woman screams, and screams again, for someone named Jim, and Jim himself, a white man from her world, comes apace, with a rifle in his hands."[16]

Instead of a comparison between what happens in "Big Boy Leaves Home" and the facts of racism in America, the story has been compared to an ancient myth.[17] In Ovid's *Metamorphoses,* the myth of Actaeon and Diana is told this way:

> Actaeon and his companions are out hunting at midday when Actaeon calls an end to the chase since "Our nets and spears / Dip with the blood of our successful hunting." Nearby, in a grotto pool nestled in a valley, the goddess Diana, herself tired from hunting, disrobed and disarmed, bathes with her maidens. Quite by accident, Actaeon, now alone, comes upon the idyllic scene. Finding no weapon nearby, Diana flings a handful of the pond's water on the hapless hunter, taunting, "Tell people you have seen me, / Diana, naked! Tell them if you can!" He flees from the scene, by stages transformed into a stag, a metamorphosis he does not comprehend (though he marvels at his own speed) until he pauses to drink. Then he "finally sees, reflected, / His features in a quiet pool 'Alas!' / He tries to say, but has no words." Stunned he hears his hounds approach. "The whole pack, with the lust of blood upon them / Come baying . . . Actaeon, once pursuer / Over this very ground, is now pursued . . . He would cry / 'I am Actaeon . . .' / But the words fail." The hounds set upon him "And all together nip and slash and fasten? Till there is no more room for wounds." Meanwhile, his companions arrive, call for him, and rue that he is missing the

good show. "And so he died, and so Diana's anger / Was satisfied at last."

(Atkinson, 251-52)

The parallels between Wright's story and this classical myth are indeed striking. Both tales begin with idyllic scenes before the plot focuses on an initial encounter between the opposite sexes. Big Boy, the leader of the group, and three friends, who are supposed to be at school, walk through the woods, laughing, beating vines and bushes as if they are hunting anything that interests them. As Big Boy, accompanied by his sidekicks, are pursuing his avocation in a most enjoyable environment, Actaeon, too, with his companions, is hunting in good weather. Before the unexpected appearance of a woman, both Actaeon and Big Boy are at rest, Actaeon tired with hunting and Big Boy warming his body after swimming in the cold pond. Another point of similarity is the hero's fleeing the scene. Before seeing Diana, Actaeon is alone now that his companions have retired from hunting; upon seeing her, he flees the scene. Similarly, Big Boy flees the scene alone since two of his friends are killed and Bobo takes a separate rout and eventually gets captured. Finally, both protagonists sustain serious wounds during their flight. It is, furthermore, significant that the wounding of the hero occurs in two stages. Actaeon suffers what Michael Atkinson calls "the transformative sprinkling with pondwater, which removes his humanity, and the obliterative tearing by the dogs' teeth, which destroys the last form and vestige of life."[18] In Wright's tale, Big Boy first suffers the loss of Buck and Lester, whose blood is sprinkled over him, and secondly he suffers from watching Bobo's body mutilated.

But the points of difference between the tales are equally striking and significant. While in the Roman myth the male protagonist alone encounters a goddess, in Wright's story a group of young boys see an adult woman. However accidental it might be, it is Actaeon who comes upon the scene where Diana is already bathing with her maidens in a secluded pond. The circumstances under which Wright's story begins are reversed: it is the lady who comes upon the scene where Big Boy is already swimming with his friends. The initial setting Wright constructs in "Big Boy Leaves Home" thus poses a serious question whether boys under age should be judged morally wrong when they are seen naked, while swimming, by an adult woman. In the Actaeon myth, given the tradition of privacy behind it, Actaeon is deemed clearly guilty of watching a naked goddess surrounded by her maids. If Big Boy were Actaeon, Big Boy would be arrested as a Peeping Tom in any society. Even if Big Boy were Actaeon, Big Boy's punishment would be only blindness as legend tells that Peeping

Tom looked at Lady Godiva riding naked through Coventry and was struck blind. But blindness, the price Peeping Tom paid for his offense, is a far cry from the psychological wounds Big Boy and all other black boys in America indeed suffered: the shooting death of Buck and Lester caused by an army officer on leave and the lynching of Bobo perpetrated by a white mob.

It is also significant that unlike Actaeon, none of the black boys in Wright's story is alone when a member of the opposite sex appears on the scene. The woman in question, moreover, is fully protected by an adult male companion with a shotgun which could legally be used should she be molested and raped by the unarmed black boys. In the myth, however, the goddess is protected neither by those who can overcome a potential seducer nor by any kind of weapon save for her flinging of a few drops of magical pondwater. In terms of crime and punishment, those who are guilty in Wright's story, the lynch mob and the woman who screams, go unpunished, whereas those who are innocent, the four black boys, are physically or psychologically destroyed. In the myth, Actaeon, the only one who is guilty, meets his death while all the innocent, Diana, her maids, and Actaeon's companions all survive the ordeal. If the Actaeon myth and the legend of Peeping Tom tell us anything significant about an ancient system of justice which meted out punishment for humankind, then the system of justice Wright condemns in "Big Boy Leaves Home" is not only unjust but fundamentally corrupt.

While "Big Boy Leaves Home" and the classical myth of Actaeon and Diana are thematically different, Wright's treatment of the sexual theme in this story has a closer resemblance to Dreiser's **"Nigger Jeff."**[19] It is quite likely that before writing "Big Boy Leaves Home" Wright read **"Nigger Jeff."** Dreiser's story, in which a white mob lynches a black youth, deals with the same problems of race and miscegenation in America as does Wright's. In **"Nigger Jeff,"** one day a white cub reporter named Elmer Davies is sent out by the city editor to cover the lynching of an alleged black rapist, Jeff Ingalls. Jeff is first captured by a sheriff to await trial, but later taken away by a mob of white men led by the brother and father of a white woman, the supposed rape victim, and finally hanged from a bridge over a stream. After learning the circumstances of the rape, Jeff's behavior, his family's grief, and above all the transcending beauty and serenity of nature against the brutality and criminality of the mob, Davies realizes that his sympathies have shifted.

At the outset of each story, the author stresses the peace and tranquillity of the setting where people, black and white, are meant to enjoy their lives in harmony with nature. In Wright's story, the four innocent, happy black youths, as mentioned earlier, roam about the woods and pasture, laughing, chanting, smelling sweet flowers. "Then a quartet of voices," Wright describes, "blending in harmony, floated high above the tree tops" (*Uncle Tom's Children*, 17). In Dreiser's story, a young impressionable man comes upon the setting on a lovely spring day in the beautiful countryside of Pleasant Valley. As Big Boy and his friends are happy not only with themselves but with the world, Davies, as Dreiser describes, "was dressed in a new spring suit, a new hat and new shoes. In the lapel of his coat was a small bunch of violets . . . he was feeling exceedingly well and good-natured—quite fit, indeed. The world was going unusually well with him. It seemed worth singing about" (*Free* [*Free and Other Stories*], 76). Under such circumstances no one would expect violence to occur and destroy peace and harmony.

Both stories are told through the protagonist's point of view. In the beginning both Big Boy and Elmer Davies are young and naive, but the violence and injustice they witness make them grow up overnight. In the end, Big Boy, though stunned and speechless, is determined to tell the world what he has learned. As *Black Boy* suggests, Big Boy was modeled after the young Richard Wright himself growing up in the twenties. Dreiser's *A Book about Myself,* one of the finest autobiographies in American literature as *Black Boy* is, also suggests that Elmer Davies was indeed the young Dreiser himself when the future novelist was a newspaper reporter in St. Louis in the early 1890s. As Wright fled the South for Chicago to write his early short stories, Dreiser left the Midwest for New York to write his.

In both stories, the plot, which does not hinge upon a conflict of social forces, thrives on a progression of vision. Each story opens with pastoral idylls, moves through the visions of violence and injustice, and reaches the hero's losing his relative state of innocence. Both writers take much pains to show that the point of view character, the protagonist, rather than society, the antagonist, is capable of vision. The climactic scene in Wright's story, where the victim is hanged and mutilated, is presented with bright firelight. The mob is situated so close to the scene of violence that they cannot see what is transpiring. By hiding in the dark in a kiln, creating space, and establishing perspective, Big Boy can see it far better than can the mob. "Big Boy," Wright says, "shrank when he saw the first flame light the hillside. Would they see im here? Then he remembered you could not see into the dark if you were standing in the light" (48). From his own perspective Dreiser, too, presents the climax for Elmer Davies to see rather than for the mob to see, as Dreiser describes the scene: "The silent company, an articulated, mechanical and therefore

terrible thing, moved on. . . . He was breathing heavily and groaning. . . . His eyes were fixed and staring, his face and hands bleeding as if they had been scratched or trampled upon. . . . But Davies could stand it no longer now. He fell back, sick at heart, content to see no more. It seemed a ghastly, murderous thing to do" (103-4). Seeing an asinine murder makes Davies feel as though he became a murderer himself and seems to retard the progression of the story, but the pace of the revelation increases as Dreiser portrays the scene.

In Wright's story, too, Big Boy remains in the kiln through the night after the mob departs and becomes the victim's sole companion. Just as morning comes for a truck to deliver Big Boy to Chicago, dawn breaks for Davies to return to his office. After the crowd depart, Davies thinks of hurrying back to a nearby post office to file a partial report. But he decides against it since he is the only reporter present, just as Big Boy is, and because "he could write a fuller, sadder, more colorful story on the morrow" (105), just as Big Boy could have when he left for Chicago in the morning. This momentary delay in Davies's action gives his revelation a heightened effect.

Moreover, Dreiser's description of dawn in **"Nigger Jeff,"** as that of the opening scene, is tinged with a transcendental vision: "As he still sat there the light of morning broke, a tender lavender and gray in the east. Then came the roseate hues of dawn, all the wondrous coloring of celestial halls, to which the waters of the stream responded." During the lynching, Davies sees the signs of evil on the struggling body, the black mass, and black body hanging limp. The images of the dark are intermingled in his mind with those of the light that suggest hope: "the weak moonlight," "the pale light," "the glimmering water," "the light of morning," "a tender lavender and gray in the east," "the roseate hues of dawn," "[t]he white pebbles [shining] pinkily at the bottom" (*Free,* 105-6). As the story progresses toward the end, signifiers for hope increasingly dominate those for despair.

The same pattern of imagery is also created toward the end of Wright's story. During the night Big Boy has to protect himself from cold wind and rain as well as a persistent dog. Even though morning arrives with the warm sunlight and brightened air, he is still reminded of "a puddle of rainwater" and "the stiff body" of the dead dog lying nearby. "His knees," Wright describes, "were stiff and a thousand needlelike pains shot from the bottom of his feet to the calves of his legs. . . . Through brackish *light* he saw *Will's truck* standing some twenty-five yards away, *the engine running.* . . . On hands and knees he looked around in the *semi-darkness.* . . . Through *two long cracks* fell *thin blades of daylight. . . .* Once he heard *the crow of a rooster.* It made him think of *home,* of *ma* and *pa*" (*Uncle Tom's Children,* 51-52, italics for emphasis). At the final scene the nightmare that has tormented Big Boy throughout the night is now chased out of his mind and destroyed by the blades of the sun: "The truck swerved. He blinked his eyes. The blades of daylight had turned brightly golden. The sun had risen. The track sped over the asphalt miles, sped northward, jolting him, shaking out of his bosom the crumbs of corn bread, making them dance with the splinters and sawdust in the golden blades of sunshine. He turned on his side and slept" (*Uncle Tom's Children,* 53).

In the ending of **"Nigger Jeff"** as well, Dreiser still makes the hero's consciousness move back and forth between hope and despair as if the images of light and dark were at war. When Davies visits the room when the body is laid and sees the victim's sister sobbing over it, he becomes painfully aware that all "corners of the room were quite dark. Only its middle was brightened by splotches of silvery light." For Davies, another climactic scene of his experience takes place when he dares to lift the sheet covering the body. He can now see exactly where the rope tightened around the neck. The delineation of the light against the dark is, once more, focused on the dead body: "A bar of cool moonlight lay just across the face and breast" (*Free,* 109-10). Such deliberate contrasts between the light and the dark, good and evil, suggest that human beings have failed to see "transcending beauty" and "unity of nature," which are merely illusions to them, and that they have imitated only the cruel and the indifferent which nature appears to signify.

At the end of the story, Davies is overwhelmed not only by the remorse he feels for the victim, as Big Boy does, but also his compassion for the victim's bereft mother he finds in the dark corner of the room:

> Davies began to understand. . . . The night, the tragedy, the grief, he saw it all. But also with the cruel instinct of the budding artist that he already was, he was beginning to meditate on the character of story it would make—the color, the pathos. The knowledge now that it was not always exact justice that was meted out to all and that it was not so much the business of the writer to indict as to interpret was borne in on him with distinctness by the cruel sorrow of the mother, whose blame, if any, was infinitesimal.

> (*Free,* 110-11)

The importance of such fiction is not the process of the young man's becoming an artist—as Big Boy or the young Richard Wright is surely not trying to become merely an artist. It is the sense of urgency in which the protagonist living in American society is compelled to act as a reformer. In such a narrative, Dreiser and Wright are both able to create their space and perspective. With his final proclamation, "I'll get it all in" (*Free,* 111), Davies's revelation culminates in a feeling of triumph. Although, to Dreiser as well as to Wright, human beings appear necessarily limited by their natural environment and by their racial prejudice, both writers in their respective stories are asserting that human beings are still capable of reforming society.

Indeed, protest fiction, the term critics have assigned "Big Boy Leaves Home," becomes successful literature only if it is endowed with a universal sense of justice as "Big Boy Leaves Home" and **"Nigger Jeff"** are exemplars. Such a narrative, moreover, must address an actual and pressing social issue, whether it is a lynching a European American writer witnessed in a border state in the 1890s or a problem of race and miscegenation an African American writer encountered in the deep South of the 1920s. As both stories show, great social fiction can be created not so much with the artistry the writer can put into it—much of which is taken for granted in these stories—as with the writer's moral space and perspective the subject matter demands. In "Big Boy Leaves Home," this urgency does not come from the quality of Big Boy's will, nor is it anything to do with the collective will of African Americans. Rather, it comes from the conscience of humanity, the collective will of decent individuals living anywhere. It is a revelation given to Big Boy, as it is given to Elmer Davies. And through the protagonist and with the skill of a gifted writer, it is disseminated to the modern world at large.

### IV

Except for the obvious issues of race, Wright and Dreiser shared quite similar experiences before they became novelists. Since their boyhood both had been economically hard pressed; they were always ashamed that they had grown up on the wrong side of the tracks. As boys they witnessed struggling and suffering and felt excluded from society. They grew up hating the fanatic and stifling religion practiced at home. In both lives, the family suffered because of the father's inadequacies as a breadwinner; the son inevitably rebelled against such a father, and the family was somehow put together by the suffering mother. Under these circumstances, their dream of success was merely survival; they tried to hang on to one menial job after another. As a result, both had nurtured a brooding sensibility. At twelve, Wright held "a notion as to what life meant that no education could ever alter, a conviction that the meaning of living came only when one was struggling to wring a meaning out of meaningless suffering" (*Black*

*Boy,* 112), a statement which also echoes in *Dawn,* Dreiser's autobiography of youth.

It would seem that both authors, being literary realists, used authentic court records in writing *An American Tragedy* and *Native Son.* Dreiser drew on the Gillette murder case in upstate New York; Wright on the Leopold and Loeb kidnap-murder as well as the Robert Nixon murder trial and conviction in Chicago. Both titles strongly imply that Clyde and Bigger are the products of American culture and that society, not the individuals involved in the crimes, is to blame. But doesn't such a narrative *always* create tensions in the life of the hero, growing out of an environment over which he has no control and about which he understands very little and, therefore, by which he is *always* victimized. If so, *Native Son* does not exactly fit into this genre. While Dreiser and Wright share the perspective of an disadvantaged individual, the characterization of the individual in his or her respective society considerably differs.

It is true that both novels employ crime as a thematic device. In *Native Son,* the murder of Bessie is the inevitable consequence of Mary Dalton's accidental death; in *An American Tragedy,* Clyde's fleeing the scene of the accident which kills a child leads to his plotting of murder later in the story. Without the presence of crime in the plot neither author would have been able to make significant points about his protagonist. But the focus of the author's idea differs in the two books. Wright's center of interest, unlike Dreiser's, is not crime but its consequences—its psychological effect on his hero. Before committing his crime Bigger is presented as an uneducated, uninformed youth; indeed he is portrayed as a victim of white society who grew up in the worst black ghetto of the nation. We are thus surprised to see him gain identity after the murder. The crime gives him some awareness of himself and of the world of which he has never been capable before. We are surprised to learn that after the murder Bigger is well versed in world affairs. "He liked to hear," Wright tells us, "of how Japan was conquering China; of how Hitler was running the Jews to the ground; of how Mussolini was invading Spain" (*Native Son,* 110). By this time he has learned to think for himself. He is even proud of Japanese, Germans, and Italians, because they "could rule others, for in actions such as these he felt that there was a way to escape from this tight morass of fear and shame that sapped at the base of his life" (109-10).

Despite a death sentence handed down by his white rulers, Bigger now proclaims his own existence. Even Max, who has taken a sympathetic attitude toward the racially oppressed, is bewildered by Bigger's deep urges for freedom and independence. "I didn't want to kill," Bigger tells Max.

"But what I killed for, I *am!*" (391-92). Having overcome white oppression, Bigger now stands a heroic exemplar for the members of his race. His brother Buddy, he realized, "was blind ... went round and round in a groove and did not see things." Bigger sees in Buddy "a certain stillness, an isolation, meaninglessness" (103). And he finds his sister and mother to be equally weak individuals. "Bigger," says Wright, "was paralyzed with shame; he felt violated" (280).

In both *Native Son* and *An American Tragedy* a preacher appears before the trial to console the accused. But in *Native Son* the black preacher is described in derogatory terms. Bigger immediately senses that the Reverend Hammond possesses only a white-washed soul and functions merely as an advocate of white supremacy. Wright offers this explanation: "The preacher's face was black and sad and earnest. ... He had killed within himself the preacher's haunting picture of life even before he had killed Mary; that had been his first murder. And now the preacher made it walk before his eyes like a ghost in the night, creating within him a sense of exclusion that was as cold as a block of ice." (*Native Son,* 264)

During his act of liberation, too, Bigger is consciously aware of his own undoing and creation. To survive, Bigger is forced to rebel, unlike Clyde, who remains a victim of the tensions between individual will and social determinism. In rebelling, Bigger moves from determinism to freedom. Bigger knows how to escape the confines of his environment and to gain an identity. Even before he acts, he knows exactly how Mary, and Bessie later, has forced him into a vulnerable position. No wonder he convinces himself not only that he has killed to protect himself but also that he has attacked the entire civilization. In *An American Tragedy,* Dreiser molds the tragedy of Clyde Griffiths by generating pity and sympathy for the underprivileged in American society. In *Native Sons,* however, Wright departs from the principles of pity and sympathy which white people have for black citizens. In "How 'Bigger' Was Born," Wright admits that his earlier *Uncle Tom's Children* was "a book which even bankers' daughters could read and weep over and feel good about."[20] In *Native Son,* however, Wright would not allow for such complacency. He warns readers that the book "would be so hard and deep that they would have to face it without the consolation of tears."[21]

The meaning of *Native Son* therefore derives not from crime but from its result. Dreiser's interest in *An American Tragedy,* on the other hand, lies not in the result of crime but in its cause. While Bigger at the end of his violent and bloody life can claim his victory, Clyde at the end of his life remains a failure. *Native Son* thus ends on an optimistic note; *An American Tragedy* as a whole stems from and ends on the dark side of American capitalism. F. O. Matthiessen is right in maintaining that the reason for Dreiser's use of the word *American* in his title "was the overwhelming lure of money-values in our society, more nakedly apparent than in older and more complex social structures."[22] Furthermore, Helen Dreiser seems to confirm Dreiser's central thought in interpreting materialism as the cause of Clyde's tragedy. Commenting on Dreiser's choice of the Chester Gillette murder case for fictionalization, Helen Dreiser writes:

> This problem had been forced on his mind not only by the extreme American enthusiasm for wealth as contrasted with American poverty, but the determination of so many young Americans, boys and girls alike, to obtain wealth quickly by marriage. When he realized the nature of the American literature of that period and what was being offered and consumed by publishers and public, he also became aware of the fact that the most interesting American story of the day concerned not only the boy getting the girl, but more emphatically, the poor boy getting the rich girl. Also, he came to know that it was a natural outgrowth of the crude pioneering conditions of American life up to that time, based on the glorification of wealth which started with the early days of slavery and persisted throughout our history.[23]

Dreiser's fascination with this subject resulted in his treatment of Clyde as a victim of the American dream. Bigger, too, a product of the same culture, cherishes a dream of his own. Like anyone else, he reads the newspapers and magazines, goes to the movies, strolls the crowded streets. Bigger is intensely aware of his dreams: "to merge himself with others ... even though he was black" (*Native Son*, 226). Unlike Dreiser, Wright must have clearly recognized his hero's sense of alienation from the rest of the world. It is an alienation that Wright himself, not Dreiser, often experienced as a boy and as a man. But it never occurs to Bigger that he can pursue such a dream. Indeed, throughout the text Wright amply documents the prevailing social mores, economic facts, and public sentiments to prove that Bigger's actions, attitudes, and feelings have already been determined by his place in American life. It is understandable for James Baldwin to say of *Native Son* that every black person has "his private Bigger Thomas living in the skull."[24] Given such a determined state of mind, Bigger would not be tempted to pursue his dreams. Ironically, the racial oppression and injustice in fact enhance his manhood. To Clyde Griffiths, however, the flame of temptation is brighter and more compelling. He is easily caught, and he thrashes about in a hopeless effort to escape the trap. Under these circumstances, "with his enormous urges and his pathetic equipment,"[25] as Dreiser once characterized the plight of such an individual in America, there is no way out for Clyde but to plot murder.

The central meaning of *An American Tragedy* thus comes from the economic and social forces that overpower Clyde and finally negate his aspirations. Where a Bigger Thomas before liberation must always remain an uninformed, immature youth, a Clyde Griffiths is the one whose mind is already ingrained with that glorious pattern of success; one must climb the social ladder from lower to middle to upper class. Money is necessarily the barometer of that success. At the beginning of the story Dreiser creates social space and perspective by directly showing how the family's mission work in which Clyde is compelled to take part looks contrary to his dreams. Dreiser at once comments that "his parents looked foolish and less than normal—'cheap' was the word. ... His life should not be like this. Other boys did not have to do as he did."[26] A basically sensitive and romantic boy, he cannot help noticing the "handsome automobiles that sped by, the loitering pedestrians moving off to what interests and comforts he could only surmise; the gay pairs of young people, laughing and jesting and the 'kids' staring, all troubled him with a sense of something different, better, more beautiful than his, or rather their life" (*AAT* [*An American Tragedy*], 10). This scene functions in the story as a great contrast to a similar scene in *Native Son*. Near the beginning Bigger goes to the movies and sees double features. *The Gay Woman*, portraying love and intrigue in upper-class white society, quickly loses his attention, and *Trader Horn*, in which black men and women are dancing in a wild jungle, shows him only life in a remote world. Bigger is thus placed in no-man's-land; he is only vaguely aware that he is excluded from both worlds. Unlike Wright, however, Dreiser places his hero in *An American Tragedy* at the threshold of success and achievement.

The two novelists' divergent attitudes toward the problem of guilt are reflected in the style and structure of their books. *Native Son* is swift in pace and dramatic in tone, and displays considerable subjectivity, involving the reader in experiences of emotional intensity. The thirties were hard times for both white and black people, and it was not possible to take a calm and objective view of the situation. Wright himself was a victim of the hard times and he could speak from his heart. Moreover, Bigger Thomas is a conscious composite portrait of numerous black individuals Wright had known in his life. As indicated in "How 'Bigger' Was Born," all of them defied the Jim Crow order, and all of them suffered for their insurgency.[27] As in the novel, Wright had lived in a cramped and dirty flat. He had visited many such dwellings as an insurance agent.[28] In Chicago, while working at the South Side Boys' Club, he saw other prototypes of Bigger Thomas—fearful, frustrated, and violent youths who struggled for survival in the worst slum conditions.[29]

The twenties, the background of Dreiser's novel, however, had not of course erupted into the kind of social strife witnessed a decade later. Unlike the hostile racial conflicts dramatized in *Native Son,* what is portrayed in *An American Tragedy* is Clyde Griffiths' mind, which is deeply affected by the hopes and failures of the American dream. A later reviewer of *An American Tragedy* accused Dreiser of scanting, "as all the naturalists do, the element of moral conflict without which no great fiction can be written, for he fobbed the whole wretched business off on that scapegoat of our time, society."[30] But the depiction of such a conflict was not Dreiser's intention for the novel in the first place. Rather the poignancy of Clyde's tragedy comes from his helpless attraction and attachment to the dream which society had created. Dreiser defines this essential American psyche in an essay:

> Our most outstanding phases, of course, are youth, optimism and illusion. These run through everything we do, affect our judgments and passions, our theories of life. As children we should all have had our fill of these, and yet even at this late date and after the late war, which should have taught us much, it is difficult for any of us to overcome them. Still, no one can refuse to admire the youth and optimism of America, however much they may resent its illusion. There is always something so naive about its method of procedure, so human and tolerant at times; so loutish, stubborn and ignorantly insistent at others, as when carpetbag government was forced on the South after the Civil War and Jefferson Davis detained in prison for years after the war was over.[31]

In contrast to Bigger's violent life, Clyde's mind can only be conveyed by a leisurely pace and undramatic tone. Dreiser's approach is basically psychological, and this allows us to sympathize with the character whose principal weakness is ignorance and naivete. Consequently we become deeply involved with Clyde's fate. Above all, the relative calmness and objectivity in which Clyde's experience is traced stem from a mature vision of the tribulations shared by any of us who have ever dreamed.

The lack of dramatic tone in *An American Tragedy* is also due to change of setting. Dreiser's restless protagonist begins his journey in Kansas City, flees to Chicago, and finally reaches his destination in upstate New York. In contrast, Wright achieves greater dramatic intensity by observing a strict unity of setting. All of the action in *Native Son* takes place in Chicago, a frightening symbol of disparity and oppression in American life. Wright heightens the conflict and sharpens the division between

the two worlds earlier in the novel. In the beginning, the Thomases's apartment is described as the most abject place imaginable, while the Dalton mansion suggests the white power structure that ravages black people and destroys their heritage. The conflict is obvious throughout, and the descriptions of the two households present ironic contrasts. Whereas everything at the Thomases' is loud and turbulent, at the Daltons' it is quiet and subdued. But the true nature of the racial oppressor is later revealed: Mr. Dalton, real estate broker and philanthropist, tries to keep African American residents locked in the ghetto and refuses to lower the rents. During the trial, the prosecutor, the press, and the public equally betray the most vocal racial prejudice and hatred. Thus the central action of Book III is for the defense to confront and demolish this wall of injustice before Bigger could be spared his life.

The narrative pattern in *An American Tragedy* is entirely different. Although the novel is divided into three parts as is *Native Son,* Dreiser's division is based upon change of time, space, and characters. Each part has its own complete narrative, and one part follows another with the same character dominating the central scene. Each unit is joined to the other not only by the principal character but by the turn of events that underlies the theme of the novel. Book I begins with Clyde's dreams of success but ends in an accident that forebodes a disaster. This narrative pattern is repeated in Book II, beginning with a portrayal of the luxurious home of Samuel Griffiths in Lycurgus and ending with the murder. Book III opens with a depiction of Cataraqui County, where Clyde is to be tried and executed. Clyde's defense, resting upon the most sympathetic interpretation of his character as a moral and mental coward, clearly indicates the possibility of hope but nonetheless ends on a note of despair. The death of a child caused by an automobile accident at the end of Book I does not make Clyde legally guilty, but his fleeing the scene of the accident makes him morally culpable. This pattern is also repeated at the end of Book II, where he willfully ignores Roberta's screams for help, an act of transgression for which he is tried and punished. Such a narrative pattern is not given to the death of Mary and Bessie in *Native Son,* since one murder is necessarily caused by the other. Despite the fact that Bessie's death is caused by a premeditated murder, Bigger's crime does not raise the same moral issue as does Clyde's.

In *An American Tragedy* the author's voice is relatively absent. In *Sister Carrie* Dreiser is noted for a lengthy philosophical commentary inserted at every significant turn of event, as well as for a strong tendency to identify with his characters, especially his heroine. But in *An American Tragedy* Dreiser's comments are not only few but short.

Despite Clyde's resolution to work hard and steadily once he has reached the luxurious world of the Green-Davidson, Dreiser's comment is devastatingly swift: "The truth was that in this crisis he was as interesting an illustration of the enormous handicaps imposed by ignorance, youth, poverty and fear as one could have found" (*AAT*, 384).

In contrast to *Native Son*, Dreiser in *An American Tragedy* also reduces the author's omniscience by relying upon the method of indirect discourse. When Clyde is helplessly trapped between his loyalty to Roberta and his desire for Sondra, the insoluble dilemma is rendered through his dreams involving a savage black dog, snakes, and reptiles. About the possibility of Roberta's accidental murder, Dreiser depicts how Clyde is trying to dismiss the evil thought but at the same time is being enticed to it. Clyde's actual plot to murder, suggested by the newspaper article, now thrusts itself forward, as the narrator says, "psychogenetically, born of his own turbulent, eager and disappointed seeking." This crucial point in Clyde's life is explained in terms of a well-known myth: "there had now suddenly appeared, as the genie at the accidental rubbing of Aladdin's lamp—as the efrit emerging as smoke from the mystic jar in the net of the fisherman" (*AAT*, 463). The immediate effect of such a passage for the reader is to create compassion for the character whose mind is torn between the two forces with which the character is incapable of coping. Given Clyde's weaknesses, then, the reader is more likely to sympathize with than despise such a soul.

On the contrary, Bigger's manhood—which is as crucial a point in his life as Clyde's dilemma in his—is rendered through direct discourse. It is not the narrator's voice but the character's that expresses his inner life—the newly won freedom. His murder of a white girl makes him bold, ridding him of the fear that has hitherto imprisoned him. In the midst of describing Bigger's intoxication over his personal power and pleasure, Wright shifts the tone of the narrative to let Bigger provide a lofty voice of his own. While preparing a ransom note, Bigger utters: "Now, about the money. How much? Yes; make it ten thousand. *Get ten thousand in 5 and 10 bills and put it in a shoe box. . . .* That's good. . . . He wrote: *Blink your headlights some. When you see a light in a window blink three times throw the box in the snow and drive off. Do what this letter say*" (*Native Son*, 167). Even more remarkable is Bigger's final statement to Max:

> "What I killed for must've been good!" Bigger's voice was full of frenzied anguish. "It must have been good! When a man kills, it's for something. . . . I didn't know I was really alive in this world until I felt things hard enough to kill for 'em. . . . It's the truth, Mr. Max. I can say it now, 'cause I'm going to die. I know what I'm

saying real good and I know how it sounds. But I'm all right. I feel all right when I look at it that way. . . ."

(*Native Son*, 392)

Bigger's utterance, in fact, startles the condescending lawyer. At this climactic moment Max, awe-stricken, "groped for his hat like a blind man" (*Native Son*, 392). Interestingly enough, Dreiser's presentation of Clyde in the same predicament is given through indirect discourse:

> He walked along the silent street—only to be compelled to pause and lean against a tree—leafless in the winter—so bare and bleak. Clyde's eyes! That look as he sank limply into that terrible chair, his eyes fixed nervously and, as he thought, appealingly and dazedly upon him and the group surrounding him.
>
> Had he done right? Had his decision before Governor Waltham been truly sound, fair or merciful? Should he have said to him—that perhaps—perhaps—there had been those other influences playing upon him? . . . Was he never to have mental peace again, perhaps?

(*AAT*, 811)

In contrast to this portrait of Clyde, who is largely unaware of his guilt and his manhood, the final scene of *Native Son* gives the ending its dramatic impact. Despite his crimes and their judgment by white society, Bigger's final utterance elicits from readers nothing but understanding and respect for the emerging hero.

The sense of ambiguity created by Dreiser's use of portraits, dreams, and ironies in *An American Tragedy* is thus suited to the muddled mind of Clyde Griffiths. Bigger Thomas, however, can hardly be explained in ambivalent terms, for he has opted for the identity of a murderer. Clyde is presented as a victim of the forces over which he has no control, and Dreiser carefully shows that Roberta's murder—the climax of the book—has inevitably resulted from these forces. The principal interest of the novel, centering upon this crime, lies in Clyde's life before the murder and its effect on him. In Book III, Clyde is depicted not merely as a victim of society but more importantly as a victim of his own illusions about life. In the end, then, he still remains an unregenerate character as Dreiser has predicted earlier in the story.

## V

Like Clyde, Bigger in *Native Son* is presented in the beginning as an equally naive character, and his life is largely controlled by fear and hatred. He kills Mary Dalton because he fears his own kindness will be misunderstood. He hates in turn what he fears, and his violence is an expression of this hatred. But unlike Clyde, he has learned through his murders how to exercise his will and determination. Each of the three sections of *Native Son* is built on its own climax, and Book III, "Fate," is structured to draw together all the noble achievements of Bigger's life. Significantly enough, each of the changes in Bigger's development is also measured by his own language. The difference in characterization between the two Americans is therefore reflected in the style and structure of the novels. Granted, both novelists deal with similar material, but their treatments of a young man's crime and guilt in American society differ in ideology and in discourse.

In some respect, earlier American writers provided Wright with models for conveying his painful vision. Hawthorne and James, who dealt with the woman's search for freedom and subjectivity, represented by such figures as Hester Prynne and Isabel Archer, focused on an older, more rigid society. But such materials were far removed from what appealed to Wright's endeavor. Twain, who dramatized the relation of European and African Americans in *Huck Finn* and *Pudd'nhead Wilson,* satirized racist society. But his assailing of American life might have sounded quite benign, as Van Wyck Brooks thought that Twain's seriousness about American society was "arrested" by his humor.[32] Despite his high regard for Twain's skills as a humorist, Dreiser, too, was critical of Twain's fictional discourse. As Dreiser noted, Twain's mode of writing diverts its author "almost completely from a serious, realistic, and ... Dostoevskian, presentation of the anachronisms, the cruelties, as well as the sufferings, of the individual and the world which, at bottom, seem most genuinely to have concerned him."[33]

The closest model that appealed to Wright's understanding of American life was shown by Dreiser, especially by ***Jennie Gerhardt*** and **"Nigger Jeff."** It is not surprising that Wright considered Dreiser the greatest writer American culture had produced. It is indeed Chicago that provided the young Richard Wright, as it did Jennie Gerhardt, with ample space in which to move about freely, cherish dreams, and fulfill desires. Having recovered from the first economic depression the nation experienced, Chicago in the 1910s to Dreiser was a throbbing city with space and energy. Wright's Chicago two decades later was similarly a volatile, fluid city, what Wright called "the fabulous city."[34] And, interestingly enough, the nexus of Wright and Dreiser was characterized by mutual admiration. Only recently has it come to light that Dreiser shortly before his death regarded *Black Boy* as a model of writing, "an honest forth right book."[35] In any event, American literary history will record that *Black Boy* is not only one of the greatest autobiographies ever written by an American author but also the greatest achievement of the Chi-

cago Renaissance, a literary movement which would not have flourished without Dreiser's precedence and influence.

*List of Abbreviations*

AAT     *An American Tragedy*

JG      *Jennie Gerhardt*

*Notes*

1. Among African American works, perhaps the most successful effort to fictionalize that memory was made by Toni Morrison in *Beloved* (1987).

2. Wright, "How 'Bigger' Was Born," in *Native Son,* xxvi.

3. Dreiser, a son of a poor immigrant, spoke only German in his early childhood. Farrell, who grew up in the Irish-American neighborhoods of Chicago, drew on his early experience in *Studs Lonigan*; both Farrell and Wright were influenced by Dreiser as they influenced each other. Algren, who was also closely associated with Wright, wrote *Never Come Morning,* which Wright said, "deals with Polish life": praising Algren's work, Wright called it "as hard hitting a realistic piece of writing as you will ever read." Bellow, born of Russian immigrant parents in Canada, was raised in Chicago in a multicultural (English, French, and Jewish) household. See Wright, *Conversations with Richard Wright,* eds. Keneth Kinnamon and Michel Fabre, 46. Subsequent references will parenthetically appear in the text as *Conversations.*

4. James T. Farrell, "Lynch Patterns."

5. Zora Neale Hurston, "Stories of Conflict."

6. Wright, "Blueprint for Negro Writing," rpt. in *Richard Wright Reader,* ed. Ellen Wright and Michel Fabre, 45. The essay was originally published in *New Challenge* 2 (Fall 1937): 53-65. Further references to the essay are to *Richard Wright Reader* and are given in the text as "Blueprint."

7. Wright, *American Hunger,* 123.

8. In ranking modern novelists writing in English, as compared with the three Britons, Meredith, Hardy, and the early H. G. Wells, Allen Tate wrote in 1948: "I am convinced that among American novelists who have had large publics since the last war, only Dreiser, Faulkner, and Hemingway are of major importance." See Allen Tate, "Techniques of Fiction," *Visions and Revisions in Modern American Literary Criticism,* ed.

Bernard S. Oldsey and Arthur O. Lewis, Jr., 86. Tate's essay first appeared in Tate, *Collected Essays,* 1948.

9. In response to a question of the influence of American novelists on French novelists, Wright said, "Sartre and Camus show that. French writers realized that action was lacking in their novels, at least in the raw, rapid, sure form that characterizes the good American writers (Hemingway, Caldwell, Lewis, and others). We should make clear that this only concerns the focus of some chapters in which the fiction is presented in vivid terms, without apparent style, to lay out a very intense impression. Now, in philosophical and conceptual matters, the influence is null" (*Conversations,* 137).

10. Wright, *Black Boy: A Record of Childhood and Youth,* 274.

11. In a *New York Post* interview in 1938, Wright stated: "I wanted to show exactly what Negro life in the South means today … I think the importance of any writing lies in how much felt life is in it." The interviewer stated: "From reading Mencken in Memphis, Richard Wright branched out in Chicago to Henry James and Dostoievsky, to Hemingway, Malraux, Faulkner, Sherwood Anderson and Dreiser, writers of 'the more or less naturalistic school,' although he lays no claims to being, or even wanting to be, a 'naturalistic' writer" (*Conversations,* 4).

12. Stephen Crane, *Great Short Works of Stephen Crane,* 183. Textual references to *Jennie Gerhardt* are to *Jennie Gerhardt,* ed. James L. W. West III (Philadelphia: University of Pennsylvania Press, 1992), and are subsequently given in parentheses.

13. Qtd. in Michel Fabre, *The Unfinished Quest of Richard Wright,* 542.

14. Qtd. in Fabre: 129.

15. Page references to Wright's "Big Boy Leaves Home" are to *Uncle Tom's Children,* 1940.

16. Blyden Jackson, "Richard Wright in a Moment of Truth," 172. Jackson's essay originally appeared in *Southern Literary Journal* 3 (Spring 1971): 3-17.

17. Michael Atkinson, "Richard Wright's 'Big Boy Leaves Home' and a Tale from Ovid: A Metamorphosis Transformed."

18. Ibid., 257.

19. Page references to "Nigger Jeff" are to *Free and Other Stories* and are parenthetically given in the text as *Free.*

20. Wright, "How 'Bigger' Was Born," in *Native Son,* xxvii.

21. Ibid.

22. F. O. Matthiessen, *Dreiser,* 203.

23. Helen Dreiser, *My Life with Dreiser,* 71-72.

24. James Baldwin, "Many Thousands Gone," in *Notes of a Native Son,* 33. The essay first appeared in *Partisan Review* 18 (November-December 1951): 665-80.

25. Qtd. by Matthiessen in *Dreiser,* 189.

26. Dreiser, *An American Tragedy,* 1925 (New York: New American Library, 1964), 12. Page references to this edition are given in the text.

27. Wright, "How 'Bigger' Was Born," in *Native Son,* xii.

28. Wright, "The Man Who Went to Chicago," in *Eight Men,* 210-50.

29. See Keneth Kinnamon, *The Emergence of Richard Wright,* 120.

30. J. Donald Adams, "Speaking of Books."

31. Dreiser, "Some Aspects of Our National Character," in *Hey Rub-A-Dub-Dub,* 24.

32. Although Brooks recognized in Twain a genius and a "tortured conscience," he thought Twain's dedication to humor, "[the] spirit of the artist in him," diluted his philosophy of humankind. See Van Wyck Brooks, "From *The Ordeal of Mark Twain,*" in *Adventures of Huckleberry Finn,* eds. Scully Bradley, et al., 295-300.

33. Dreiser, "Mark the Double Twain," 621.

34. Wright, "How 'Bigger' Was Born," in *Native Son,* xxvi.

35. In a letter of 10 July 1945, to Yvette Eastman, one of Dreiser's young mistresses who had a literary ambition, Dreiser wrote:

> Yvette Dear:
>
> Such a poetic, Lovely letter from you this morning July 10th. You are off on a hill somewhere—up near Brewster, and you fairly sing of the heavens and the earth which considering all you have to do and your unchanging sense of duty always impresses me. I marvel that you dont at least verbally rebel against the conditions that have almost always made you earn your own way. So often I feel that it might be a relief to you if you were to write an honest forth right book like *Black Boy* and in it have your say concerning all the things you have had to endure and so what you think of life. It would be colorful and more dramatic

and I feel it would sell, yet not only the data but because of the beauty of your prose. Why not.

See Yvette Eastman, *Dearest Wilding: A Memoir with Love Letters from Theodore Dreiser,* ed. Thomas P. Riggio, 211.

## Bibliography

### WORKS BY DREISER

#### BOOKS

*Free and Other Stories.* New York: Boni and Liveright, 1918.

#### SHORT WORKS

"Mark the Double Twain." *English Journal* 24 (October 1935): 615-27.

"Some Aspects of Our National Character." In *Hey Rub-A-Dub-Dub,* 24-59. New York: Boni and Liveright, 1920.

"Theodore Dreiser's Letter to Yvette Eastman," 10 July 1945. In Yvette Eastman, *Dearest Wilding: A Memoir with Love Letters from Theodore Dreiser,* ed. Thomas P. Riggio, 211. Philadelphia: University of Pennsylvania Press, 1995.

### WORKS BY OTHERS

Adams, J. Donald. "Speaking of Books." *New York Times Book Review* (16 February and 6 April 1958).

Baldwin, James. "Many Thousands Gone," 1951. In *Notes of a Native Son,* 18-36. New York: Bantam, 1968.

Brooks, Van Wyck. "From *The Ordeal of Mark Twain.*" In *Adventures of Huckleberry Finn,* eds. Scully Bradley, et al, 295-300. New York: Norton, 1977.

Crane, Stephen. *Great Short Works of Stephen Crane.* New York: Harper and Row, 1965.

Dreiser, Helen. *My Life with Dreiser.* Cleveland: World, 1951.

Eastman, Yvette. *Dearest Wilding: A Memoir with Love Letters from Theodore Dreiser.* Ed. Thomas P. Riggio. Philadelphia: University of Pennsylvania Press, 1995.

Fabre, Michel. *The Unfinished Quest of Richard Wright,* New York: William Morrow, 1973.

Farrell, James T. "Lynch Patterns." *Partisan Review* 4 (May 1938): 57-58.

Hurston, Zora Neale. "Stories of Conflict." *Saturday Review of Literature* 17 (2 April 1938): 32.

Jackson, Blyden. "Richard Wright in a Moment of Truth." In *Modern American Fiction: Form and Function,* ed. Thomas Daniel. Baton Rouge: Louisiana State University Press, 1989.

Kinnamon, Keneth. *The Emergence of Richard Wright.* Urbana: University of Illinois Press, 1972.

Matthiessen, F. O. *Theodore Dreiser.* New York: William Sloane, 1951.

Morrison, Toni. *Beloved.* New York: Plume, 1987.

Tate, Allen. "Techniques of Fiction," 1948. In *Visions and Revisions in Modern American Literary Criticism,* eds. Bernard S. Oldsey and Arthur O. Lewis, Jr., 81-96. New York: E. P. Dutton, 1962.

Wright, Richard. *American Hunger.* New York: Harper and Row, 1979.

———. *Black Boy: A Record of Childhood and Youth,* 1945. New York: Harper and Row, 1966.

———. "Blueprint for Negro Writing," 1937. Rpt. in *Richard Wright Reader,* eds. Ellen Wright and Michel Fabre, 36-49. New York: Harper and Row, 1978.

———. *Conversations with Richard Wright,* eds. Keneth Kinnamon and Michel Fabre. Jackson: University Press of Mississippi, 1993.

———. "How 'Bigger' Was Born," 1940. In *Native Son,* vii-xxiv. New York: Harper and Row, 1966.

———. *Native Son,* 1940. New York: Harper and Row, 1966.

## Laura Hapke (essay date 2003)

SOURCE: Hapke, Laura. "No Green Card Needed: Dreiserian Naturalism and Proletarian Female Whiteness." *Twisted from the Ordinary: Essays on American Literary Naturalism,* edited by Mary E. Papke, U of Tennessee P, 2003, pp. 128-43.

[*In the following essay, Hapke positions "Dreiser and his taxonomy of paid work within a literary naturalism of social protest" and compares the writer's working-class depictions of white people "in a landscape of relative privilege" to academic studies of the socioethnically stratified labor market in American cities of the time and to Dreiser's own journalistic knowledge of the ethnic makeup of the working classes.*]

Over the past few decades, scholars have moved well beyond previous paradigms of American literary naturalism in general and Dreiser studies in particular.[1] The classic scholarship of the past drew the naturalist as an American

Zola who dramatized the collision of environment and heredity with the America *idée fixe* of the success ethic. Dreiserian texts in particular were said to overlay this quasi-mechanistic model with both the primacy of desire and a compassion for the working poor. Now the cutting-edge scholarship includes recent deconstructions by Christophe Den Tandt, Walter Benn Michaels, and Amy Kaplan; and essay collections edited by James L. West as well as Miriam Gogol. Looking at Dreiser and his fellow naturalists and realists, Den Tandt finds that naturalism, "using the plurivocal approach to an unrepresentable social world" (xi), exists in a dialogic interplay with the romantic sublime. No less revisionist rereadings find *Sister Carrie, Jennie Gerhardt,* and other Dreiser texts to be consumerist narratives "embracing the ethos of capitalism which values excess over restraint" (Michaels, qtd. in Kaplan 142). The "new" Dreiserian naturalism is further viewed as an attempt to manage the contradictions of a society that prospers by marketing unfulfilled materialist desires (Kaplan 143) or, simply, as an account of the endless process and contradictions of a "convulsive" capitalism (Zayani 18).

Read within such contexts, *Sister Carrie*'s emphasis on monotony in an age of mechanical reproduction exists in tension with the restlessness, desire, and unsettledness that erupt in the novel's adulteries, strikes, and financial reversals. No Dreiserian character can experience contentment within a system that is inherently unstable and that exhibits such a twinned commodification of fantasy and lack of fulfillment.

In this startling shift of critical discourse, what remains curiously repressed is the issue of Dreiser's relationship to capitalism's "hard contract" (*Sister Carrie* 40). For different reasons, in all of these recent studies he remains the writer who allied himself with *Success* magazine, who ambivalently admired titans and financiers, and who sought far more to explain than to muckrake class stratification and ethnic, racial, and gender segregation. As a scholar with a focus on labor fiction, I reposition Dreiser and his taxonomy of paid work within a literary naturalism of social protest. As Carla Cappetti aptly notes, the decades after the McCarthy era saw the scholarly mainstream's denigration of naturalism as inherently "proletarian." Denied too was a straight line of influence from Dreiser to the proletarian authors, like Mike Gold (who praised Dreiser), James T. Farrell, Jack Conroy, and Nelson Algren, who lapsed into postwar obscurity and disrepute. To join a renewed labor studies conversation about literary naturalism as an early form of industrial realism, I (re)trace the Dreiserian intersection of capital and labor (Wixson 349), but rather than reinscribe the title characters of Dreiser's woman-centered early novels in the masculin-

ist tradition of the proletarian bildungsroman, I build on the groundwork laid by Shelley Fisher Fishkin, Miriam Gogol, and others who have studied Dreiser's gendered presentation of turn-of-the-century workers. Recent surveyors of Dreiser bibliography have noted that the historical truth of Dreiser's accounts of working women's lives offers new possibilities in labor studies (Orlov and Gogol 15).

There is an added dimension, however, to a class and gender analysis of literary naturalism. As Mary Papke astutely observes, there are few black, Jewish, immigrant, or other minority writers readily accepted as naturalist, whereas Frank Norris, despite his hardly ambiguous white supremacist views and classism, is constantly invoked. Dreiser may not be as conscious of that agenda as Norris, but he certainly buys into it. Yes, this "labor Dreiser" widens the naturalist discussion of working-class experience but only by positioning white working people in a landscape of relative privilege (Lott; Roediger, *Wages;* Bernardi). Dreiser's racial-ethnic theories remain under-researched; it is my purpose here only to generate discussion and to place Carrie within a still-evolving American delineation of race and the "real" working class.

As a social-protest writer with a residual bitterness about his family's ethnic and economic marginalization, Dreiser intuitively understood the period distinctions between native-born workingmen and everyone else—racial-ethnic men and women in particular. His chapters on menial shoe-factory work as the only kind of job that an unskilled provincial young woman like Carrie can find rest squarely on a comprehension of the hierarchies in the labor movement of his day.

At the top was the "male and pale" skilled artisan who dominated the trade union movement in ways that still endure. This upper tier of the labor movement could even aspire to a bourgeois, pro-capitalist identity—but only as long as it confined its membership to native-born or Anglo-Saxon immigrant whiteness. The majority of ethnic workers were excluded from such affiliations and historically had little opportunity to profit from a labor-class version of acquisitive individualism in the industrial trades.[2] The skilled trades routinely ignored or opposed the job needs of recently freed blacks and newly arrived Slavic and Mediterranean immigrants,[3] and they were loud in vilifying the Chinese, perceived in most quarters as strike-breaking or otherwise wage-deflating emigrants (Miller 175, 195-99, 235n). And the skilled trades were unmoved by a federal Indian policy that turned detribalized Native Americans into reservation-based laborers. In white labor's name, workers demanded attention, forged a certain visibility, and pointed repeatedly to their exclusion from the American Dream (Freeman et al. 30; Montgomery, "Workers' Control"). At the same time, non-union craft workers, even in the increasingly militant carpentry, iron, and steel industries, applied the old artisanal ethic to industrial autonomy.[4]

New social historians have argued in their groundbreaking texts of history from the bottom up that these working-class privileges, as Daniel Bernardi notes, rest on "an ideology of race that positions 'whites' as normal and 'non-whites' as deviant and inferior" (105; Freeman et al.). A recent American Studies Association conference included a panel on "Repudiating Whiteness: The Politics of Passings and Trespassings" that addressed some of Dreiser's colleagues, the Midwestern expatriate Sinclair Lewis chief among them.[5] For students of actual Midwest labor racism, Rich Halpern's investigation of color hierarchies in the Progressive-era Chicago meatpacking industry and beyond is helpful, as is S. J. Kleinberg's survey of Pittsburgh's segregated working-class neighborhoods in the shadow of the steel mills. The most incisive work has been done on the "poor whites" of the American Southwest and West. In *The White Scourge,* Neil Foley finds such constituencies eager to hold on to "the whiteness of manhood" (12). Rather than be spurned as the "bad-gened whites" of eugenicist theory, they pride themselves on being the "purest whites" in Appalachia (6). Writing about the continued white rural sharecropping culture in Texas (where the Ku Klux Klan maintained a presence) prior to the Second World War, Foley posits that the "pore whites" clung to what they were not—black, Mexican, or foreign-born (7). If, at least in this regard, whiteness was a collective identity, sustaining it involved a posture of defiance in regions so impoverished that there were no jobs for either whites or people of color.

Elsewhere too, of course, during the last century's early decades, the racialized presence of African Americans shaped the American landscape whether in the many actual conflicts or the reinvented ones of Dreiser's industrial Midwest and Northeast. Jim Crow attitudes and laws dominated the late-nineteenth-century proletarian landscape; as late as 1898 the AFL suggested mass colonization of African workers (Roediger, *Wages* 141). It can be argued that blackness is the crucial if apparitional racial category in a novel like *Sister Carrie* so devoted to the progress of its lily-white heroine. With its focus on the ethnic workers who people Carrie Meeber's labor sub-world, this paper can only touch on the important issue of the black worker's place in the ethnic color hierarchy. Returning to Dreiser as an imaginer of the laboring classes for the quarter of a century between *Sister Carrie* (1900) and *An American*

*Tragedy* (1925), we should now place these texts within the multiple and conflicting contests of naturalism, wage-earning women's history, and "whiteness studies."

The question, then, is whether Carrie (and to a lesser extent, the sidelined labor figure Roberta Alden) fits the "bad-gened" white trash definition of single womanhood—an uneducated lower-class woman toiling at a dead-end job and not averse to paid sexual encounters. Is Carrie doing what was commonly and nativistically called the "nigger work" that white men would not deign to do? Blacks and ethnic women were absent as yet from the factory floor in the late 1880s, as they still are in small-town America when Clyde Griffiths becomes Roberta's supervisor. Yet there is no doubt that the workplace was sweated labor of the lowest sort.

The phony eugenics at the core of both nativism and racism began its flowering as a dubious science around the turn of the century. Dreiser was born into the largest immigrant group in Chicago, but throughout his life, despite an attraction to High German "Kultur," he presented himself as an American narrator, distanced from the painful ethnicity of his early days. Though the Dreiser family was quite poor, his mother had middle-class aspirations. Germanic origins were not handicaps to skilled industrial work—the construction, furniture, and cigar trades (the last a trade in which blacks occupied the lowest, segregated rung). Irishmen, on the other hand, may have ascended to foreman positions in the steel and railroad trades, but they were consistently presented in bestial images in the pages of American fiction—as Dreiser does in the unfinished *An Amateur Laborer*—their faces often smeared with slum or coal-mining dirt.[6] To an extent, the Germans handily joined others grouped by government surveys as "Caucasians": the Welsh, British, and Scandinavians were the aristocrats of the labor movement in the early union years.[7] This was the same period in which Dreiser was imagining the blue-collar lives of Carrie Meeber, her brother-in-law Sven Hanson, a railroad yard cleaner, and that "underworld of toil" characteristic of Chicago in the year 1889, when Carrie arrives there.

What is clear from the novel's outset is that, as Dreiser wishes us to know, Carrie exhibits neither "bold" nor "vulgar" (read oversexed) behavior, two marks of unprincipled lower-class white work, whether Appalachian or otherwise. In fact, Dreiser offers Carrie's whiteness as a given. When he writes about ethnics, he uses the familiar period labels—at their most extreme in a story written and published the same year he was finishing *Sister Carrie,* **"Nigger Jeff,"** a lynching tale whose attitude is ambiguous at best toward the n-word. In contrast, Carrie occupies what David

Roediger, a well-known scholar in the new "whiteness studies" field, calls a "sort of invisible norm" (qtd. in Newitz and Wray 3) rather than membership in a "racially marked group existing in relation to many other such groups" (Newitz and Wray, 5). It should be remembered, too, that as early as antebellum times the labor movement distinguished white man's labor from "nigger work" (Laurie 27).[8] Into that racist category they poured the various "Hunky" and East European constituencies flocking to steel mills and ethnically segregated company towns—of which Chicago was one. Furthermore, the stigmata of racial difference were applied especially to Jews, whether upwardly mobile or not. A daring new book by Karen Brodkin, *How Jews Became White Folks* (1998), locates this marginalization even as recently as the Second World War.

Carrie herself arrives in Chicago with no understanding of or interest in the remaking of a once white American working class (Takaki 311-24, 201-2; Freeman et al.). She seems to be oblivious to the fact that almost 800,000 new arrivals to the city are immigrants or their children. Not so Dreiser himself. As a proletarian wagon driver and cub reporter, Dreiser was a participant-observer of the "other half" well before he completed *Sister Carrie* in 1899. In the late 1880s and early 1890s, he was a veteran of five successive jobs, including bill collector for cheap curios and clocks. (It is no accident that a sign of the perpetual economic failure of Clyde Griffiths's father is his attempt at clock peddling in the Windy City.) The Chicago and Saint Louis business and factory districts walked wearily by a job-seeking young American girl surely had an ethnic presence in the 1880s, as Dreiser, who drove a laundry wagon for his Jewish employers, well knew. The influx of Jews was heavy enough by 1888 for the Hebrew Immigrant Aid Society to open a Chicago office (Cutler 56), and relative ethnic "haves" like Dreiser's bosses could look back to a Jewish presence in the city of half-a-century. Dreiser's job also took him into the Slavic neighborhoods, "where people were ... bustling over potatoes ... and cabbage," and into the black ghettoized districts, where he negotiated with washerwomen (Lingeman 46). Blacks were routinely imported as strikebreakers in the meat-packing and heavy-industrial districts of the city, an anti-unionist tactic that Dreiser would probably have known about. He certainly could not have missed the Jim Crow operative in Chicago's "Black Belt" (a grim herald of the bloody Race Riot of 1919). He witnessed racial violence, too, when in 1893 he covered a lynching near Valley Park, fifteen miles from Saint Louis, an event that inspired the story **"Nigger Jeff"** (Lingeman 67). Ethnic labor in the city space was also the subject of Dreiser's 1894 pieces written as a cub crime reporter in Saint Louis, Pittsburgh, and Allegheny (Lingeman 87), including **"Fall River"** (c.

1899), a piece on a Gorkyesque cross-ethnic post-strike Homestead.

Midwestern habitat was likewise crucial to the comprehension of immigrant oddity in the work of a major "local color" writer who was well known to mass audiences when Dreiser was still an unknown. When the regionalist author Hamlin Garland was dispatched to post-strike Homestead, he focused on the squalid communities surrounding it, ignoring both the steel-mill experience and the skilled "white" workers' dwellings a short distance from the mill, even those that housed the militant strikers of 1892 themselves. "To give these folk power would unchain strange beasts," he concluded of the newest ethnics (Garland).[9] Other visitors to the sullen Homestead further decried what they perceived as the squalor of the ethnic inhabitants (Dreiser, **"Fall River"**; see also *Sister Carrie*, 498-501).

The urban story successfully offered its hyperactive inner-city ethnics to Garland's middlebrow audience, to whom the working, marginal, and criminal poor, all embodied in the immigrant, were exotic (Giamo 54). Sharing with this book-buying readership a moralism about the metropolitan "lower orders" central to the genteel practitioners of so much pre-1890s portraiture, tenement authors never rejected class ascension or the rags-to-riches credo outright. The social Darwinism of their slum tales implicitly reasserted their own Protestant values. But like their bourgeois readers, they were fascinated by those who neither saw ambition as triumph over adversity nor engaged in the Franklinesque struggle upward. In tenement fare, the very disorder of ethnic laboring life is a tourist attraction.[10] The perceived descent into the immigrant city generates a taxonomy of types. Substituting eccentricity for aspiration, these tales "cloud the conditions and dynamics of poverty by an unfailing reduction to moral individualism, the picturesque, or the dangerous classes" (Giamo 32).

By 1895, a few years before beginning *Sister Carrie*, Dreiser had walked across City Hall Park and visited the infamous Mulberry Bend of Little Italy (Lingeman 94-95); his retrospective location of Carrie's story in Chicago in 1889 was overlaid with his understanding of the cross-ethnic, industrial Midwest and Northeast, both prior to and in the decade following that time. But it was also influenced by his colleague in the industrial Northeast, E. W. Townsend. The subject of Dreiser's hardly complimentary review in *Ev'ry Month* magazine, Townsend's approach was more anti-model than template for serious American writers, naturalistic or not (Dreiser, **"Literary Shower"**). Few authors put the Lower East Side laboring ethnic on parade, transforming the working and borderline poor into an exciting slum show, with more popular success than

Townsend. He struck publishing gold in the early 1890s with the Chimmie Fadden stories. They were a regular feature of the *New York Sun* and in eponymous book forms sold 200,000 copies ("Edward W. Townsend Dies"). All that had repelled a Hamlin Garland about working people—their rough ways, lack of ambition, unrestrained emotion, and slangy inarticulateness—became the stuff of comedy in the person of the truculent Irish street kid Chimmie.[11]

If Chimmie's monologues and observations of the pretensions of the Four Hundred generate a comedy based on the unbridgeability of class gaps, he is as harmless as a stage Irishman. He peddles newspapers, hangs around the settlement house observing the Ladies Bountiful, and accepts tips from the rich for escorting them on saloon tours. "Mr. Paul often says t'me dat he's stuck on de Bow'ry" (177), he observes.[12] In all ways he is a sidewalk gamin asserting his class identity for humorous ends: "Listen. De old mug calls me 'a unregenerate heathen!' Did ye ever hear such langwudge?" (11). To milk the cross-class comedy, Townsend has Chimmie gain the patronage of a society employer, trading his newsie's route for a valet's post (103). But he remains the court jester, returning to his old haunts for new material.

Although Stephen Crane chose to satirize the shallowness of the Townsend model in *Maggie: A Girl of the Streets* (1893), he did not spare the ethnic subject in so doing, as the many anti-Irish passages in the novella demonstrate. Without undermining the nativist racialism of a Stephen Crane or a Frank Norris, Dreiser took another path. Dreiser's knowledge of working-class makeup is at odds with his decision to portray the working class as white. In other words, he fits naturalism to fashion, as did even the period's rare socialist texts, which preferred the skilled native-born or old immigrant worker to the unruly ethnic. For instance, Mrs. Nico Bech-Meyer's 1894 novel *Pullman-town* privileges a German machinist and an American-born carpenter. Both men doubt whether the unskilled new workforce can achieve political awareness.

Dreiser's choice, then, was between the nativist vision and the absent ethnic. If we consider Sven Hanson as the product of a narrow literary choice, we see that this American-born child of a Swede—as Dreiser is careful to note (12)—is a suspect type to be sure: hard to fathom and mean-spirited even though he is a white in the railroad yards, not an Irish or black. But his ambitiousness and parsimony separate him psychically from the Chicago and Homestead ethnics of the otherwise diverse period fare of Garland, Crane, and their contemporaries. What,

then, is blue-collar whiteness, where is it, and how is Carrie its exemplar, even its goddess?

To answer: Carrie never steps out of a white work and leisure world. Even the derelicts are white—her father, the "flour-dusted miller," the "ragged men" in Chicago (145), the "rough, heavy-built" individuals (27) who eye her, Evans the barkeeper (125), and the "poorly-clad girls" (145). The hierarchy of mainstream, presumably non-ethnic whiteness is implicitly underscored by Dreiser's reference to the Irish coal heavers whom Carrie sees on her walk. "Irishmen with picks, coal heavers with great loads to shovel," are proletarians in contrast to other manual workers but also "Americans busy about some work which was a mere matter of strength" (145).

Carrie travels with few clothes but is never without the mantle of racial privilege, as a traveling salesman eyeing her on the train (blacks sat in different cars) attests. Compared to the many "swarthy" and racially suspect immigrant women flocking to the factory floor at the end of the nineteenth century, Carrie is as untarnished by nativist class prejudice as she is unaffected by class consciousness. Her own Americanness, particularly her name and her father's small-town Protestant background (that flour-dusted miller), propels her above the era's many greenhorn strugglers in the Darwinian clothing trades laborscape. Of course we know very little else about Carrie's genealogy, but its very blankness suggests an absence of ethnic ties: the homogeneity of the dominant culture.

Carrie's brief foray into shoe work is suggestive, too. Although by her time the pay had dwindled, shoe work was traditionally a Yankee daughter's trade, and the women in it had often been compared to the Lowell mill girls. By the early decades of the nineteenth century, native-born white women formed a significant portion of the region's workforce in textile New England, with Lowell, Massachusetts, the jewel in the region's manufacturing crown.[13] Moreover, well before the Civil War a female seamstress and laundress workforce was a fixture of shoe factories in New England, collar manufacturers in New York State, and the piecework clothing trade in New York City. Their hopes were evident in organizations like the Ladies' Shoebinders, the United Seamstress Society, and the New York Working Women's Labor Union (Blewett; Turbin; Stein, pts. 1 and 2; see also Siegel 81; Foner 139). Labor sparks even flew, thanks to the Daughters of Saint Crispin, among skilled shoe-factory workers at Lynn agitating before and after the Civil War (Blewett; Cameron, chs. 1-3; Levine, ch. 2).

Chicago, in turn, saw its women factory hands march two decades later, though not in the devolving shoe trades: more than two decades after the Civil War, Carrie's coworkers have, in Dreiser's rendering, clearly debased the principled rebelliousness of the Daughters of Saint Crispin. Yet even the most sex-obsessed girls on her shop floor are native-born, as witnessed by their slangy vernacular. However much her self-absorption walls her off from social or industrial solidarity with them, Carrie Meeber's experiences among female sewing machine operators in a Chicago shoe factory mirror those of the women of the less "political" workplace cultures carved from sweatshop toil: she resents the strictures on her freedom and the monotony of her workday, and she longs for an unspecified lover to take her out of the fray. Only her timorous response to these experiences, evidenced by her initial fear of the masher Drouet, reinforces Dreiser's gentrification of her as a princess among workplace serfs. From the moment she enters the sex-segregated work site—the skilled male workers are spatially separated from the unskilled females—Dreiser focuses on her revulsion at the "common" woman she meets there (*Sister Carrie* 53). To her eyes, they are too familiar with the men, who joke and even touch them playfully. But if these implicitly promiscuous women realize the period's worst fears about the workplace—they are "free with the fellows and exchange ... banter in rude phrases which at first shocked her" (53)—they are Yankees still: the girl at her left may have bad grammar and utter phrases like "Say ... what jeh think he said?" (38), but she is slangily American through and through.

Furthermore, one can contextualize Carrie's reaction within that of the larger white male working-class society. Her innocent habit, for instance, of standing in the doorway of her brother-in-law's house in a white working-class neighborhood raises fears that she will be taken for a prostitute—evidence of the clinging to respectability that was fiercely evident in "borderline" neighborhoods like Van Buren Street.

Carrie's education may be scanty, but her grammar is good (note the correctness of her Dear John letter to Hurstwood later in the novel). She can navigate a white work world: she applies for shop and office jobs and takes factory work only as a last resort (256). The rare black women with clerical skills worked only for black-owned businesses, and Carrie could have beaten them out of the work had she even considered so doing.

The fact, then, that the two men in her life see her as "this lily" (146), and that her employers see her as "pretty," as prettiness is constructed in Dreiser's world—refined, "sweet-faced" (41), she carries herself as one who "felt that she should be better served" (41)—takes on more than clichéd meaning, as does the fact that as a coquette

on the stage in New York she is appealing in the standard American girl mode of the time.

Only in later novels does another hardy young working woman—Jennie Gerhardt (German American rather than East European or Mediterranean) or upstate New York's Roberta Alden—profit from or fail in spite of the invisible privilege her racial identity provides. Reading ***An American Tragedy*** backward from our day, with its intensified focus on racial and gender inequalities in the naturalist text, one finds that Dreiser was here investigating fault lines in the workforce rather than collectivity.

This is particularly the case with his portrayal of female workers. The portrait of Carrie's spiritual cousin, Roberta Alden, in his novel ***An American Tragedy,*** is crucial for an understanding of the way Dreiser's leftist ideology collided with his racial attitudes. Roberta is somewhat of an anomaly at the Lycurgus Collar Factory: a non-ethnic factory hand. With her small-town Protestantism, work ethic, and at least more religious training than Carrie Meeber, she resembles those Yankee daughters who peopled the Lowell mills when the "lady of industry" ideology was developed by manufacturers in search of a cheap, tractable labor force. By the 1860s, all thought of Lowell ladies was gone: Irish and, later, Polish workers in Lycurgus were refashioning the morality and workplace culture of the mill. By the time ***An American Tragedy*** was written, Fordism had taken a viselike hold of assembly lines such as Roberta's. An unknown soldier in a womanly army at the Griffiths factory—one of the "old and weary-looking women who looked more like wraiths than human beings" (248)—she finds no gateway to opportunity, only a future marked by monotonous way stations in what she sees as the dreary journey from one low-level job to the next.

Whiteness once again complicates the matter of Roberta's abdication of ambition. This disappointed daughter of the shabby genteel (but too refined to be quite "poor white") would have settled for a "practical education" in bookkeeping on the lower rungs of white-collardom (246). Her derailed hopes are evident in the factory job she has to take. She becomes so fixated on marital instead of job-site ascension that she ducks training sessions at the home of a coworker for amusement park evenings with her lover, whom she hopes will marry her. Dreiser points to Roberta as one who rechannels her legitimate need for job advancement into an obsessive and Hollywood-fueled interest in wedlock. Viewed in the context of her white Protestant mainstream identity, however, her abdication of ambition reveals something else as well.

The woman from a WASP culture, even a downwardly mobile one, was figuring in period fiction more and more as a vestige. She felt neither at home among the factory oligarchs like the Griffithses nor ethnic or political kinship with the "bread and roses" marchers of venues like the ethnic Lawrence Textile Mill. No wonder that the conservative writer Winston Churchill, in the 1917 bestseller with which Dreiser may have been familiar, *The Dwelling Place of Light,* kills off the American-sounding Janet Bumpus, Roberta's pregnant predecessor. (Janet is a step up from Roberta; as an office worker, she catches the eye of the factory owner, but otherwise plot similarities abound.) Like Roberta after her, she is too ambitious to marry a mere, or non-white, factory hand, and too déclassé to form a part of an industrial elite.

What Marx called the vulnerability of the factory girl to the seduction of her capitalist employer—in Roberta's case, her manager—should not blind us to Roberta's sense of white entitlement. She is no less an ethnic snob than Clyde—even on death row he resents that a fellow prisoner is Chinese. Whatever awe she may have of Clyde in the Lycurgus social pecking order, she is certain of her moral and racial superiority to the girls with accents who work alongside her. However commonplace, even vulgar, Roberta begins to appear to Clyde, she projects her own status vulnerability onto the sensual, in-her-face Poles, Italians, and others who try to wring some joy out of monotony on the line.

Set against the "red scare" climate of the Sacco and Vanzetti 1920s, Roberta, a symbol of the white working class under siege, is as morally unattractive as the Griffiths clan, from the Aladdin-like Clyde to the snide Gilbert. A possessive investment in her own whiteness, replicated in countless period social surveys of the steel town, the dance hall, the department store, and the Lower East Side, is a crucial dimension of her character and one that has too long been overlooked in studies of "proletarian naturalism."

Roberta Alden's racial identity cannot protect her, however, from the murderous greed of a poor boy determined to climb up. Carrie Meeber, in contrast, moves completely from the hard times dominating the lives of white and non-white working-class people alike. Dreiser chose not to tell their New York story. Even if she had had to do sewing work for another decade after relocating to New York, she would never have been among the casualties of the Triangle Shirtwaist Fire, one of the city's worst industrial tragedies. A true workers' event, in contrast to Carrie's quicksilver movement up from and out of manual work, the fire martyred only the immigrant Jews and Italians whose allies would forge the "swarthy" ILGWU. Thus did Dreiser legitimize his lower-middle-class title character, protecting her from tainted associations with unionist ethnicity.

In a larger sense, this racialized vision disrupts Dreiser's association with the social-protest mode as much as does his ambivalent attitude toward monopoly capitalism. To be sure, by the 1930s Dreiser had enlarged his understanding of the disenfranchised among the white working class. He found proletarian whiteness to be no capitalist asset in his tour of strike-torn mining towns in Harlan County; in the next decade, he formally joined the Communist Party. Whatever his evolving vision of the "poor white" workingman, however, his enduring portraits of white workingwomen dissatisfied with their class position neither challenge nor, for that matter, indict the ideology of selective ascension central to the "success ethic." To the end of Dreiser's life, the competitively individualistic heroine Carrie, and her luckless alter ego Roberta, continued to pose troubling questions about his privileging of proletarian female whiteness.

## Notes

1. For an excellent summary of the "old" and "new" in Dreiser studies, see Miriam Gogol's introduction in Gogol (xvii). See also Orlov and Gogol.

2. Ostreicher argues for a "working-class subculture of opposition" (xv). Yet he defines the term in a way that suggests cooperation with one another rather than opposition to the capitalist way: "an interlocking network of formal institutions and informal practices based on an ethic of social equality."

3. Comments Ehrlich, "Throughout the later 1870s and well into the 1880s unskilled jobs were at a premium, and the continued influx of immigrant workmen only served to intensify this problem" (530). By 1865 there were three million immigrants in the United States, and four million African Americans.

4. Fixing output quotas themselves, in some cases they secured privileged positions without union rules or accommodation to employers (Montgomery, "Workers' Control" 489, 492).

5. "Repudiating Whiteness: The Politics of Passings and Trespassings," American Studies Association Conference, Detroit, 13 Oct. 2000. The University of Toronto hosted a conference titled "Defining Whiteness: Race, Class, and Gender in North American History" on Oct. 13-15, 2000.

6. In 1894, for instance, then Police Commissioner of New York City Theodore Roosevelt referred to the "Irish Race." A notable exception is Dreiser's *McClure's* essay, "The Mighty Burke" (1911), in which he praises an Irish foreman at the expense of his (Italian) crew.

7. For the argument that the Germans were no better regarded than the Irish, see Bernardi (105), although he is vague on the time period in the nineteenth century to which he alludes.

8. Laurie, *Artisans into Workers* 27. I found this common racist phrase of the day in an 1844 issue of the craft-connected periodical *The Mechanic* (Roediger, *Wages* 44).

9. Although a few hundred blacks lived in Homestead, Garland apparently did not "see" them. Garland's comment on "strange beasts" is quoted in Taylor (187). So, too, in *The Workers* (1898), the economics professor Walter Wyckoff, a participant-observer of manual laborers, both immigrant and native-born, spends more time describing their lodgings and customs than their work.

10. Good analyses of tenement tales and novels appear in Giamo (54-64) and in Trachtenberg.

11. On one level, Chimmie is the spiritual grandfather of the confrontational toughs of Depression-era gangster films like *Angels with Dirty Faces* (1938) and *The Public Enemy* (1931). On another, he is a clever update of the antebellum Mose figure, with an overlay of Elizabeth Oakes Smith's good-hearted newsboy.

12. A similar character appears in the popular cartoons of the period; see Woolf and Outcault.

13. On Lowell's centrality to women's labor history, see Dublin.

### Works Cited

Bernardi, Daniel. "The Voice of Whiteness: D. W. Griffith's Biograph Films." *Race and the Emergence of U.S. Cinema.* Ed. Bernardi. New Brunswick, NJ: Rutgers UP, 1996. 103-28.

Blewett, Mary H. *We Will Rise in Our Might: Workingwomen's Voices from Nineteenth-Century New England.* Ithaca: Cornell UP, 1991.

Brodkin, Karen. *How Jews Became White Folks and What That Says about Race in America.* New Brunswick, NJ: Rutgers UP, 1998.

Butler, Elizabeth Beardsley. *Women and the Trades: Pittsburgh, 1907-1908.* 1909. Introduction by Maurine Weiner Greenwald. Pittsburgh: U of Pittsburgh P, 1984.

Cameron, Ardis. *Radicals of the Worst Sort: Laboring Women in Lawrence, Massachusetts, 1860-1912.* Urbana: U of Illinois P, 1993.

Cappetti, Carla. *Writing Chicago: Modernism, Ethnography, and the Novel.* New York: Columbia UP, 1993.

Couvares, Francis G. *The Remaking of Pittsburgh: Class and Culture in an Industrializing City, 1877-1919.* Pittsburgh: U of Pittsburgh P, 1984.

Cutler, Irving. *The Jews of Chicago: From Shtetl to Suburb.* Urbana: U of Illinois P, 1996.

Den Tandt, Christophe. *The Urban Sublime in American Literary Naturalism.* Urbana: U of Illinois P, 1998.

Dreiser, Theodore. *An Amateur Laborer.* 1904. Ed. Richard W. Dowell and James L. W. West III. Philadelphia: U of Pennsylvania P, 1983.

———. *An American Tragedy.* 1925. New York: New American Library, 1964.

———. "The Factory." 1910. *Theodore Dreiser: A Selection of Uncollected Prose.* Ed. Donald Pizer. Detroit: Wayne State UP, 1977. 175-80.

———. "Fall River." Unpublished manuscript, [c. 1899]. Theodore Dreiser Papers, Van Pelt-Dietrich Library, U of Pennsylvania.

———. *Jennie Gerhardt.* 1911. New York: Penguin, 1989.

———. "The Literary Shower." *Ev'ry Month* (1 Feb. 1896): 10-1.

———. "The Mighty Burke." *McClure's* 37 (May 1911): 40-50.

———. *Newspaper Days.* 1931. Ed. T. D. Nostwich. Philadelphia: U of Pennsylvania P, 1991.

———. "Nigger Jeff." 1898. *Free and Other Stories.* New York: Boni and Liveright, 1918. 76-111.

———. "Scenes in a Cartridge Factory." *Cosmopolitan* 25 (July 1898): 321-24.

———. *Sister Carrie.* 1900. Ed. James L. West et al. New York: Penguin, 1981.

———. "The Strike To-day." *Toledo Blade* [24 Mar. 1894]: 1, 6. *Sister Carrie: An Authoritative Text, Backgrounds, and Sources.* Ed. Donald Pizer. 2nd ed. New York: Norton, 1991. 417-23.

———. "Three Sketches of the Poor." *New York Call* 23 Nov. 1913: 10.

———. "The Transmigration of the Sweatshop." *Puritan* 8 (July 1900): 498-502.

Dublin, Thomas. *Women at Work: The Tramformation of Work and Community in Lowell, Massachusetts, 1826-1860.* New York: Columbia UP, 1979.

"Edward W. Townsend Dies." *New York Times* 17 and 21 Mar. 1942.

Ehrlich, Richard L. "Immigrant Strikebreaking Activity: A Sampling of Opinion Expressed in the *National Labor Tribune, 1878-1885.*" *Labor History* 15 (Fall 1974): 528-42.

Filippelli, Ronald L. "Fall River Textile Strikes of 1884 and 1889." *Labor Conflict in the United States: An Encyclopedia.* Ed. Ronald L. Filippelli. New York: Garland, 1990. 159-75.

———. "Homestead Strike." Filippelli, *Labor Conflict* 241-46.

Fishkin, Shelley Fisher. "Dreiser and the Discourse of Gender." *Theodore Dreiser: Beyond Naturalism.* Ed. Miriam Gogol. New York: New York UP, 1995. 1-30.

Foley, Neil. *The White Scourge: Mexicans, Blacks, and Poor Whites in Texas Cotton Culture.* Berkeley: U of California P, 1997.

Foner, Philip S. *Women in the American Labor Movement from Colonial Times to the Eve of World War I.* New York: Free Press, 1979.

Freeman, Joshua, et al. *Who Built America?: Working People and the Nation's Economy, Politics, Culture, and Society.* Vol. 2. New York: Pantheon, 1992.

Garland, Hamlin. "Homestead and Its Perilous Trades." *McClure's* 111 (June 1894): 3-20.

Giamo, Benedict. *On the Bowery: Confronting Homelessness in American Society.* Iowa City: U of Iowa P, 1989.

Gogol, Miriam, ed. *Theodore Dreiser: Beyond Naturalism.* New York: New York UP, 1995.

Greenwald, Maurine Weiner. "Introduction: Women at Work Through the Eyes of Elizabeth Beardsley Butler and Lewis Hine." Butler vii-xlvi.

Halpern, Rick. *Down on the Killing Floor: Black and White Workers in* Chicago's *Packinghouses, 1904-1954.* Urbana: U of Illinois P, 1997.

Kaplan, Amy. *The Social Construction of American Realism.* 1988. Chicago: U of Chicago P, 1992.

Kleinberg, S. J. *The Shadow of the Mills: Working-Class Families in Pittsburgh, 1870-1907.* Pittsburgh: U of Pittsburgh P, 1989.

Laurie, Bruce. *Artisans into Workers: Labor in Nineteenth-Century America.* New York: Farrar-Noonday, 1989.

Levine, Susan. *Labor's True Woman: Carpet Weavers, Industrialization, and Labor Reform in the Gilded Age.* Philadelphia: Temple UP, 1984.

Lingeman, Richard. *Theodore Dreiser: An American Journey.* New York: John Wiley, 1993.

Lott, Eric. *Love and Theft: Blackface Minstrelsy and the American Working Class.* New York: Oxford UP, 1993.

Michaels, Walter Benn. *The Gold Standard and the Logic of Naturalism: American Literature at the Turn of the Century.* Berkeley: U of California P, 1987.

Miller, Stuart Creighton. *The Unwelcome Immigrant: The American Image of the Chinese, 1785-1882.* Berkeley: U of California P, 1969.

Montgomery, David. "William Sylvis and the Search for Working-Class Citizenship." *Labor Leaders in America.* Ed. Melvyn Dubofsky and Warren Van Tine. Urbana: U of Illinois P, 1987. 3-24.

———. "Workers' Control of Machine Production in the Nineteenth Century." *Labor History* 17 (1976): 489, 492.

Newitz, Annalee, and Matt Wray. Introduction. *White Trash: Race and Class in America.* Ed. Newitz and Wray. New York: Routledge, 1997.

Orlov, Paul, and Miriam Gogol. "Prospects for the Study of Theodore Dreiser." *Resources for American Literary Study* 24.1 (1988): 1-21.

Ostreicher, Richard Jules. *Solidarity and Fragmentation: Working People and Class Consciousness in Detroit, 1875-1900.* Urbana: U of Illinois P, 1986.

Outcault, R. F. *"The Yellow Kid": A Centennial Celebration of the Kid Who Started the Comics.* Introduction by Bill Blackbeard. Northampton, MA: Kitchen Sink, 1995.

Peiss, Kathy. *Cheap Amusements: Working Women and Leisure in Turn-of-the-Century New York.* Philadelphia: Temple UP, 1986.

Pizer, Donald. "The Strike." Dreiser, *Sister Carrie,* ed. Pizer 416.

Roediger, David. *Towards the Abolition of Whiteness: Essays on Race, Politics, and Working Class History.* London: Verso, 1994.

Roediger, David. *The Wages of Whiteness: Race and the Making of the American Working Class.* London: Verso, 1991.

Siegel, Adrienne. *The Image of the American City in Popular Literature, 1820-1870.* Port Washington, NY: Kennikat, 1981.

Stein, Leon, ed. *Out of the Sweatshop: The Struggle for Industrial Democracy.* New York: Quadrangle-New York Times Book Co., 1977.

Takaki, Ronald. *A Different Mirror: A History of Multicultural America.* Boston: Little, Brown, 1993.

Taylor, Walter Fuller. *The Economic Novel in America.* Chapel Hill: U of North Carolina P, 1942.

Townsend, E. W. *Chimmie Fadden.* 1895. New York: Garrett, 1969.

Trachtenberg, Alan. "Experiments in Another Country: Stephen Crane's New York City Sketches." *Southern Review* 10 (Spring 1974): 265-85.

Turbin, Carole. *Working Women of Collar City: Gender, Class, and Community in Troy, 1864-1888.* Urbana: U of Illinois P, 1992.

West, James L. W., III. Introduction. *An Amateur Laborer.* By Theodore Dreiser. Ed. Richard W. Dowell and James L. W. West III. Philadelphia: U of Pennsylvania P, 1983. xi-lv.

————, ed. *Dreiser's* Jennie Gerhardt*: New Essays on the Restored Text.* Philadelphia: U of Pennsylvania P, 1995.

Wixson, Douglas. *Worker-Writer in America: Jack Conroy and the Tradition of Midwestern Literary Radicalism, 1898-1990.* Urbana: U of Illinois P, 1999.

Woolf, Michael Angelo. *Sketches of Life in a Great City.* New York: G. P. Putnam's Sons, 1899.

Zayani, Mohamed. *Reading the Symptom: Theodore Dreiser, Frank Norris, and the Dynamics of Capitalism.* New York: Peter Lang, 1999.

## Jerome Loving (essay date 2005)

SOURCE: Loving, Jerome. "*Sister Carrie*." *The Last Titan: A Life of Theodore Dreiser,* U of California P, 2005, pp. 140-63.

[*In the following essay, Loving contrasts Arthur Henry's conventional 1900 novel* A Princess of Arcady *with Dreiser's unconventional* Sister Carrie, *also published by Doubleday the same year, noting the origins of the characters and plot of the latter novel in Dreiser's own observations and experiences.*]

*Sister Carrie* is a work of genius and Doubleday belongs to that species of long-eared animals which are not hares.

George Horton to Arthur Henry,
February 9, 1901

Fresh from a summer on the banks of the Maumee, Dreiser took out a piece of yellow paper and changed the course of American letters. As a result, he is called the "Father of American Realism," but that academic saw ignores, of course, the pioneering work of Walt Whitman, whose fifth edition of his indefatigable book was privately published in the year of Dreiser's birth. The next edition of *Leaves of Grass,* and essentially the last, came under fire by Anthony Comstock and his New England Society for the Suppression of Vice, which even attempted to have Whitman's book banned from the U.S. mail. Dreiser, as we shall see, caught the wrath of the second generation of that infamous censorship movement with the publication of *The "Genius,"* but *Sister Carrie* was the first heir to Whitman's fight to tell the truth in literature. Indeed, Dreiser's title may actually come from Whitman's era in the form of a Civil War song of the same name, in which **"Sister Carrie"** (South Carolina) is chastised for leaving home (or the Union).[1] Whitman is the true precursor of American literature in the twentieth century, but he wrote poetry instead of prose—many denied it even the claim to poetry—which kept it out of general circulation among popular readers during his lifetime. But *Sister Carrie* was a novel, a genre more accessible to the average reader, especially women, who made up the great majority of American readers at the end of the nineteenth century. One of them was allegedly Mrs. Frank Doubleday.

Dreiser probably began *Sister Carrie* in late September of 1899, shortly after returning to New York City. Henry returned, too, again leaving Maude and Dottie behind, to resume for the next month or so his residence with the Dreisers, and he either continued or began to write *A Princess of Arcady.* While Henry imagined a conventional romance in which the heroine is sent to a convent school to preserve her innocence until the proper time for marriage, Dreiser began his own fable about an American princess, "two generations removed from the emigrant," who rules only in her dreams and loses her innocence at almost the first opportunity. Henry wrote an idyll about a "nun" whose youthful sexuality is never violated, while Dreiser wrote a novel about a sister who commits adultery. It is generally thought that Dreiser was thinking exclusively of his sister Emma and not even remotely—or ironically—about a nun when he gave his Carrie the title of "Sister" at the top of his page, but Henry's use of nuns and a convent in his book may have had an associative influence. Dreiser's romantic chapter titles, which were added between the first draft and the revision published by Doubleday, suggest the moral contrast and underscore the departure of this gritty tale of two cities from the Victorian fiction of its day.

It is instructive to take a closer look at *A Princess of Arcady*. The story concerns two children, Hilda and Pierre, whom we first meet on Pilliod's Island, a paradise of vineyards and richly colored flowers on the Maumee River. They meet Minot Alexander, who visits the island with its owner (the boy's grandfather, Jean Pilliod), and who feels a strange attachment to the girl in spite of the fact that he is old enough to be her grandfather. The feeling is mutual, and the girl escorts Alexander back to her humble cottage, where her sick mother is slowly dying and her fisherman father drinks too much. The ambiguity of Alexander's feeling for the girl is vaguely associated with a love affair he had had long ago with a woman now lost to the convent, a woman named Betty, whom he still remembers as passionate and beautiful. Alexander returns to the village of Maumee, here elevated to the status of city, where he befriends Christopher Mott and his daughter Primrose, an eccentric and homely woman of thirty, who occupy gardens and greenhouses in the middle of town, one of the last holdouts against urban sprawl. Mott is an impractical man who refuses to give up his precious plants, which he considers more noble than humans. When the bank threatens to foreclose, Alexander quietly pays off the mortgage and tears up the note. In the meantime, Hilda's mother dies, and the child is put into an orphanage. By the time Alexander learns of it, Hilda has escaped and returned to the island. He adopts her on the condition that she will attend a convent school in order to grow into the ideal woman whose charm inspires not merely sexual passion but "achievements which have made epochs and kingdoms famous when the patronage of the throne alone would have failed."[2]

He writes to his old flame, now Mother Superior Pelagia at the Convent of Our Lady of Peace, to get permission to send Hilda to the convent, which is in New York City, across from the Palisades. Before Hilda leaves, however, she visits the island one last time. There she finds young Pierre carrying stones from the water's edge and fantasizing that he is building a palace for the two of them. Hilda goes away to the convent school, returning every summer to the Motts' cottage, which she now considers her permanent home. Interestingly, on her first train ride to the school, she befriends a fellow enrollee named Edna, whose beautiful mother attracts the attention of a "drummer, who wishing to look at her now and then, took a place on a vacant seat behind where she would not notice." Dreiser's *Sister Carrie,* of course, begins on a train with the same kind of "masher" or "drummer," the traveling

salesman Charles Drouet, who befriends Carrie. Alexander also accompanies Hilda to the school upon her enrollment and sees for the first time in forty years his Betty, now a "black-robed figure" and a "little old lady."

Many years later, following Hilda's graduation from the convent school, she learns what has happened to Pierre. Apparently, after losing her he had become a disgruntled and disappointed young man who got into minor scrapes with the law. Hilda returns home to Maumee, where Pierre, now twenty, reformed, and the owner of Pilliod's Island following his grandfather's death, secretly watches over her at the Mott gardens—which thanks to Alexander's financial support have become a sanctuary not unlike the beautiful garden in Hawthorne's "Rappaccini's Daughter." Hilda is not cursed by paternal love in this romance, however, and so she and Pierre are soon reunited and marry to live happily ever after. The novel closes with Mott's saying to Alexander that Hilda had "come to fine flower" under his influence. When Alexander denies any direct influence, Mott agrees but says that he had "done all the best gardeners could do. You provided the good soil and shelter from the storm."[3]

While Henry was writing his novel about true love and eternal romance, he carried on an extramarital affair with Anna T. Mallon, leaving Maude to worry about the upbringing of their daughter and the mortgage on the House of the Four Pillars. Anna, who was several years older than Henry, ran a typing service at 308 Broadway. Dreiser had patronized it for his magazine articles, and Henry apparently went down to the typing pool one day on an errand for either Dreiser or himself and promptly fell in love. His dedication of his book to Anna, whom he would eventually marry, suggests that she influenced the plot of *A Princess of Arcady*: to Anna "on whose attitude toward her own convent life was founded the convent of 'Our Lady of Peace.'" Since the convent scenes cover the second half of the book, this may mean that he was halfway through his novel when he moved in with Anna that fall. Meanwhile, Dreiser was spinning his own romance in the same urban jungle that Hilda is protected against. Indeed, as we learn on his very first page, the city is the seducer as much as any drummer on a train. "The gleam of a thousand lights," he wrote, "is often as effective as the persuasive light in a wooing and fascinating eye."[4]

By the time Henry moved in with Anna, Dreiser had written the first ten chapters of *Sister Carrie.* He wrote "steadily," as he told Mencken, until the middle of October, then quit in disgust, thinking his work was "rotten." He laid the manuscript aside until December, when Henry came back to prod him again. He wrote on until the end of January before quitting once more, just before the climactic scene of the book, where the story will cease to be mainly Carrie's and become primarily Hurstwood's. "Then in February," he told Dorothy Dudley in 1930, "Arthur Henry, off flirting with some girl, came back and read it. He thought there was nothing wrong with it, told me I must go on." Possibly, Dreiser was blocked by his unpleasant memories of the *World* and that fateful day in City Hall Park when the idea of Hurstwood was first born. But if so, he recovered from the blues those memories gave him, "managed to get the thread" of his story back, and "finished it up."[5]

The plot of *Sister Carrie* involves essentially three characters who, true to Dreiser's sense of determinism, are pawns of heredity and environment. Like Henry's tale, it begins hopefully, if not romantically, with a young woman seeking her destiny, but unlike Hilda's fate, which involves nuns, priests, and a garden, Sister Carrie's destiny threatens to become a train ride to hell as she becomes involved with two male predators. The fates of all three intersect first in Chicago and then in New York to send Carrie to stardom on Broadway, Hurstwood to the soup kitchens and flophouses of the Bowery, and Drouet on his merry way, neither hurt nor helped by his interaction with the other two. Knowing nothing of Henry's chivalric code but only self-interest, like any lower creature, they are driven by the gods of money and sex to their fates. Carrie Meeber ("amoeba") moves from the country to the city, exchanging her virginity for material comfort. Her successive lovers, Charles Drouet and George Hurstwood, see her, reciprocally, as a symbol of the pleasure money and power can purchase. Carrie abandons the unmarried Drouet for the married Hurstwood, who in turn leaves his family and his position as manager of a posh Chicago saloon, steals money from his employers, and flees with Carrie to New York. There, as he eventually fails in his new investment, Carrie abandons him as well, and he soon finds himself homeless, sick, and dazed by fate in the winter of 1896.

\* \* \*

It is difficult to see how this plot can be the Siamese twin of *A Princess of Arcady.* Yet these two books, both published by Doubleday in 1900, one an Arcadian romance, the other a grim tale of success and failure, were born together on the Maumee. Indeed, Henry helped cut and revise *Sister Carrie,* and Dreiser later claimed to have finished *A Princess of Arcady.* "At that time," he told Mencken, "Henry's interest in *Sister Carrie* having been so great his own book was neglected and he could not finish the last chapter." This may be an exaggeration or even an outright lie, for by 1916 when Dreiser made the claim, he and his friend had been estranged for many years. Furthermore, the style

throughout the thirteen chapters of *A Princess of Arcady* appears to be uniformly Henry's. What the boast does suggest, aside from an opportunity to undercut the work of a former friend, is that Dreiser was as familiar with Henry's plot as Henry was with *Sister Carrie.* In fact, as he told Mencken, "Since he had told it to me so often and I knew exactly what he desired to say, I wrote it."[6]

*The Princess of Arcady* is also a nature book in the tradition of John Burroughs, "one of the living men," Henry once wrote, "I admire most at a distance." (Ironically, Dreiser once interviewed Burroughs for an article in *Success,* but Henry never met him.) Henry would develop his abilities as a nature writer much more directly in his next two works, *An Island Cabin* (1902) and *The House in the Woods* (1904). They are Thoreauvian recollections of his escapes from the daily grind of the city—first on an island off the coast of Connecticut, which Anna had either purchased or rented, and then in the Catskills, where the couple built a cabin. These books reflect the nineteenth-century idea that even pristine nature cannot help us if we cannot help ourselves. "Let those who think they are unhappy, because of an unfriendly world, retire to a wilderness," he writes in *An Island Cabin,* "and they will discover the source of all their sorrows is in themselves." As nature writers of such self-help books went, he was probably at least as good as most of his competitors. The *Brooklyn Eagle* called his books "delightful nature literature," and *Bookman* stated that "As a result of life so close to nature Mr. Henry brought back a more intangible yet indestructible possession in the form of fresh ideals and hopes."[7] He was a dreamer, just like Dreiser. And like him, he pursued beauty (usually in the feminine form) most of his life. In fact, there is something of Henry in Carrie's daydreamy nature. Dreiser even dedicated *Sister Carrie* to Henry, "whose steadfast ideals and serene devotion to truth and beauty have served to lighten the method and strengthen the purpose of this volume." He withdrew the dedication in later printings, however, and never again formally dedicated a book to anyone, except Grant Richards ("Barfleur") in *A Traveler at Forty* (1913) and his mother in *A Hoosier Holiday* (1916).

Henry, on the other hand, dedicated *An Island Cabin* to his by then ex-wife Maude. And while their separation was brutally sprung on Maude (in the presence of Anna), they remained friends for the rest of their lives. Henry was that lovable, and he attracted Dreiser as much as anybody else who was charmed by the man's cherubic looks and affable way. One gets the sense of his ebullience from reading his books, especially the ones following *A Princess,* where he drops all pretense of the storyteller and aspires to become the Emersonian essayist and poet. Henry had already worked out his idea of the self-reliant life in two essays, "The Doctrine of Happiness" and "The Philosophy of Hope," both utterly derivative of the transcendentalist doctrine. Dreiser's theme in **Sister Carrie** also argues that no island sanctuary exists in life, but in Carrie and Hurstwood's world the romance of self-reliance gives way almost completely to the naturalistic picture of robotic characters true to their basic needs and nothing more. When young Hilda of *A Princess* is asked whether she would like to live in the city, she answers yes, but only out of love and self-respect: "if ever the prince should come and marry me." When Carrie is asked to remain in the city by Drouet, it takes only twenty dollars—"two soft, green, ten-dollar bills" to persuade her.[8]

Dreiser's Chicago and New York experiences in the 1890s meshed to produce this masterpiece of reportorial realism, poetry, family history, and the drama of the city. He knew well the types he wrote about. He had seen many examples of Drouet on his train trips while on magazine assignments. Carrie, of course, springs in part from the character of Emma and from attributes of his other sisters. And Hurstwood, the first unforgettable tragic figure of American literature in the twentieth century and the prototype for such other unforgettable failures as F. Scott Fitzgerald's Jay Gatsby and Arthur Miller's Willy Loman, was based on Hopkins. He was also based—though Dreiser probably wouldn't have admitted it at the time—on his general sense of his father's failure in life. John Paul Dreiser barely lived long enough to be aware of the novel. He died on Christmas Day 1900, a little over six weeks after the book's publication on November 8. He was by then living in Rochester, New York, with Mame and Austin Brennan. (To save money, Dreiser wrote a personal dedication in one of his ten free author copies of **Sister Carrie** to all three of them, with the proviso that "if any of you fail to read and praise, the book reverts to me." The book did come back to him, either after Mame divided up their father's estate or following her own death in 1944, and is now part of the Dreiser collection at the University of Pennsylvania.)[9]

There is no father figure in **Sister Carrie**. Only Carrie's mother is vaguely mentioned in the beginning of the book. Certainly the married Hurstwood is no father figure. Carrie's brother-in-law Hanson, who cleans out refrigerator cars in Chicago, is a doting father but also one of the first to try to cheat her in the big city. There is no God the Father in this naturalistic tale either, only children of desire. This is not any lofty desire for the beautiful, but a basic, primitive desire for clothing, shelter, and sex, elevated to the fantastic level suggested in the magazines of the day, including *Ev'ry Month* with its exotic women. This is first illustrated in Carrie's life with the Hansons and her visions of something so much better. While Carrie looks for a job the first day, she enters one of the new department stores. Dreiser was no doubt thinking of Marshall Field's at the corner of State and Twentieth streets in Chicago, once burnt-out shells of horse-car barns in which Field set up his business after the fire of 1871 and accidentally invented the department store.[10]

As Carrie, with hardly a cent in her purse, passes down the aisles of the store displaying its latest items, she cannot help but feel the claim of every object upon her personally. "There was nothing there which she could not have used—nothing which she did not long to own. The dainty slippers and stockings, the delicately frilled skirts and petticoats, the laces, ribbons, hair-combs, purses, all touched her with individual desire." In spite of his prosperous appearance, Drouet too is intoxicated by such symbols of the good life. He "was as deluded by fine clothes as any silly-headed girl."[11] That and the company of successful men. It is associations above all that count to this salesman, or any salesman for that matter, on the lookout to succeed in the selling of his wares. He dines in the "right" restaurants and takes his nightcap at the "resort" of Fitzgerald and Moy's saloon (originally Dreiser used the real name of Hannah and Hogg's of Chicago, before the revision for Doubleday).

Here we meet George W. Hurstwood, the manager of the saloon and a social notch or two above the drummer Drouet. Everyone in this book is looking to ascend—as in all of Dreiser's novels. Carrie is satisfied with Drouet until the more burnished Hurstwood appears, just as in *An American Tragedy,* Clyde is satisfied with one girl until another more attractive one (both physically and financially) comes along. Hurstwood himself is by now about as high on the social ladder as he will ever get and serves as a sort of social referee who ranks his saloon patrons according to three essential groups in order to hold onto his position. He is a professional "Hail fellow, well met" who knows most of his customers by name. Yet he also knows his place.

> He had a finely graduated scale of informality and friendship, which improved from the "How do you do?" addressed to the fifteen-dollar-a-week clerks and office attachés ... to the "Why, old man, how are you?" which he addressed to those noted or rich individuals who knew him and were inclined to be friendly. There was a class, however, too rich, too famous, or too successful, with whom he could not attempt any familiarity of address, and with these he was professionally tactful, assuming a grave and dignified attitude, paying them the deference which would win their good feeling.[12]

The saloon manager keeps a neat life consisting of horse, house, wife, and two children—until he meets Carrie.

* * *

Hurstwood has risen by perseverance "through long years of service, from the position of barkeeper in a commonplace saloon," but in the manner of Paul Dresser, who often, in the beginning of his career at least, accepted flat fees instead of royalties for his songs, Hurstwood may occupy a fairly imposing managerial position, "but lacked financial control." In other words, he could fall into poverty almost immediately, as Paul would go broke by 1903. This is a world of hangers-on and the sometimes lucky. Dreiser knew about both from personal experience and the American successes he had interviewed during the last two years. Emma's Hopkins had been a cashier in the saloon of Chapin and Gore in Chicago before he fled with her—and his employer's cash. Marshall Field had begun, as he told Dreiser during his interview, as a clerk in a dry goods house on South Water Street, but his luck had been different.

After Carrie has lost her job through illness and is living with Drouet at a three-room flat on Ogden Place, she meets Hurstwood, whom she sees immediately as "more clever than Drouet in a hundred ways."[13] Drouet now seems to her to have no "poetry in him," and in fact Drouet has been losing interest in Carrie until Hurstwood enters the picture. But both Drouet and Hurstwood merely hope to keep Carrie as a paramour—until both men capitulate to a deeper infatuation when they see her in an Elks' production of Daly's *Under the Gaslight* (a play Dreiser had seen during his days as a drama critic in St. Louis). Then, found out by his wife, who threatens to have his wages garnisheed with his employers' approval, Hurstwood is cornered by circumstance. Determined to have Carrie now at any cost, he steals his employers' money and flees like Hopkins to Canada and then to New York.

It is at this point in the plot that Dreiser got stuck once again, but he also became energized, because the Hurstwood section in New York is what gives this novel much of its drama and pathos. We feel a kind of detached sympathy for the bedraggled figures in Crane's "Men in the Storm" or the soldier in Garland's "The Return of the Private," but Hurstwood personifies the prosperity of the American Dream—and he flings it away for the youth and beauty of Carrie. More tragic is the fact that Hurstwood cannot help himself. The scene with the safe is a mechanical demonstration of Spencer's ideas about humans as wisps in the wind, "still led by instinct before they are regulated by knowledge." When the lock to the safe clicks shut, Hurstwood, still contemplating the act of theft, is left holding $10,800 of its funds. Dreiser asks, "Did he do it?"[14] The answer is no, but the consequences of his actions must be accepted. This is no Pilliod's Island or Mott's Garden. The island is New York on the eve of the Panic of 1893.

*Sister Carrie* amplifies the same sense of foreboding that informs Dreiser's earliest short stories. Hurstwood is doomed long before he finds himself tipsy in front of his employer's money. He is programmed for catastrophe. He arrogantly underestimates his wife, into whose hands he has put the legal ownership of everything they have. The first omen of danger comes from his son, who coolly informs his father in his mother's presence: "I saw you, Governor, last night." George, Jr., has seen his father with Drouet and Carrie at McVickar's Theater watching a production of *Rip Van Winkle*. If this isn't his wake-up call, the reader's comes along shortly when "a gaunt-faced man of about thirty, who looked the picture of privation and wretchedness" approaches Hurstwood on the street while he is walking with Carrie and Drouet. Drouet is the first to see him and the only one to sympathize, handing over a dime "with an upwelling feeling of pity in his heart. Hurstwood scarcely noticed the incident. Carrie quickly forgot."[15] Ultimately, Carrie will forget about Hurstwood, as will his wife and two children.

Once Hurstwood and Carrie move to New York, and Hurstwood invests in the Warren Street saloon, Dreiser traces his gradual downfall with painful detail. One way this is accomplished is by watching his money dwindle. Dreiser worried about money, as we know, most of his life, and this phobia is dramatized in the increasing shabbiness of Hurstwood's living quarters. He and Carrie begin uptown in the neighborhood where Dreiser and Jug first lived, then after three years move to the area around Fifteenth Street, where Hopkins and Emma had lived. The money count, beginning with $1,300 following Hurstwood's forced restitution of most of the stolen money, is then at $700, then to $340 after a gambling loss, then tumbling through another card game to $190 on down to $100, $50, $13, and $10. All the while, Carrie's success as a chorus girl nets a salary beginning with $12 a week, rising steadily with the decline of Hurstwood's savings. On her way up to $150 a week, she deserts him to brood by himself.[16]

In chapter 45, which reuses the title "Curious Shifts of the Poor," Hurstwood begins again with $70 after selling their furniture and deserting their flat for "a third-rate Bleecker Street hotel" on the edge of the Bowery. He comes down to his last fifty cents and finds a job sweeping up and doing odd jobs, perhaps as Hopkins did, at the Broadway Hotel near Washington Square. "Porters, cooks, firemen, clerks"—all were higher than the now almost wholly defeated Hurstwood, who gets the lowly position by telling the manager, "I came here because I've been a manager myself in my day." When he falls sick with pneumonia in February of 1896 and loses even this job, he is sent to Bellevue, where Dreiser had one of his last assignments as a reporter on the *World*. It is here that the "Captain" of the *Demorest's* essay enters the story. The fact that Dreiser drew on this article, written before he wrote the novel, confirms his own sense of gloom and doom as he constructed his tale. He not only spliced in parts of the **"Curious Shifts"** [**"Curious Shifts of the Poor"**] essay, but he restored parts that the editors at *Demorest's* had taken out.[17]

The difference between the versions in *Demorest's* and *Sister Carrie* is that one of the figures of "Curious Shifts of the Poor" emerges out of the shadows as George Hurstwood, once utterly oblivious of those whose ranks he has now joined. Although he sees Carrie once more very briefly and gets nine dollars from her, she forgets about him as quickly as she had the beggar to whom Drouet allowed a dime. He tries to see her again by going to the stage door of her theater, where he is pushed into the icy slush by the doorman. The scene shifts to Carrie in her Waldorf Astoria suite, Drouet's unsuccessful attempt to renew relations, and Hurstwood's family comfortably riding in a Pullman car on their way to a ship bound for Rome. At the same moment, Hurstwood is described as standing in a side street waiting to pay fifteen cents for his final night's rest—this scene, too, adapted from one of the vignettes in "Curious Shifts of the Poor." Dreiser originally ended the novel with Hurstwood's suicide, dating the conclusion of his penciled manuscript, "Thursday, March 29, 1900—2:53 P.M."[18]

\* \* \*

Just how Dreiser came to extend this final chapter so that it ends with Carrie in her rocking chair alone dreaming of such happiness as she will never feel is not known, and may never be. Once the original manuscript was typed at Anna Mallon's agency, he, Arthur, and Jug edited it. He told Mencken that they reduced it by almost forty thousand words, and the scholarly editors of the original typescript estimate approximately thirty-six thousand words.[19] Dreiser was from the beginning a prolix writer, and after Dreiser Henry made most of the substantive cuts, while Jug looked after her husband's grammar, spelling, and punctuation. Henry's books show him to have been a better and more economical stylist than Dreiser, though falling well behind his friend in originality and literary substance. Dreiser may have also agreed to the cuts because they both feared it was too long for commercial publication. Henry's *A Princess* is just over three hundred pages in

print; even as revised, *Sister Carrie* would run almost twice that.

Since the book's title was *Sister Carrie,* it no doubt seemed reasonable to end with Carrie somehow, and the basis of what were to be the final words already appeared in the penultimate chapter. Robert Ames (an Edison-like figure who is also a stand-in for the author), urges Carrie to consider applying her talents to serious drama, but she continues blindly as a showgirl, trapped in both the sentimental culture of her class and a lack of education. It is clear that no serious relationship between them will ever work out, because Carrie is simply too intellectually shallow for this electrical engineer. They part, and Carrie is left almost as emotionally needy as she had been in the beginning of the novel. Dreiser originally wrote, perhaps with some help, the following coda in the penultimate chapter:

> Oh, blind strivings of the human heart. Onward, onward it saith, and where beauty leads, there it follows. Whether it be the tinkle of a lone sheep bell o'er some quiet landscape, or the glimmer of beauty in sylvan places, or the show of soul in some passing eye, the heart knows and makes answer, following. It is when the feet weary in pursuit and hope seems vain that the heartaches and the longings arise.

This kind of "nature" writing and florid style could easily have been a part of *A Princess of Arcady,* so much so as to suggest that Henry influenced its composition. We know from internal evidence that Henry helped with the romantic chapter titles, which were penciled into the typescript in both men's hands as they were getting it ready to go to press at Doubleday.[20] The sentimental romantic convention to which the titles subscribe suggests Henry's idealism more than Dreiser's realism, from the first chapter ("The Magnet Attracting: A Waif Amid Forces") to the last ("The Way of the Beaten: A Harp in the Wind"). Other Henryesque titles are "The Machine and the Maiden: A Knight of To-Day" (6), "The Lure of the Beautiful: Beauty Speaks for Itself" (7), "A Witless Aladdin: The Gate to the World" (16), and "An Hour in Elfland: A Clamour Half Heard" (19). The products of what F. O. Matthiessen calls "magazine verse"—and most likely the joint project of two writers who had worked for magazines—the titles serve as a counterpart to the book's harsh naturalism, but they also cloak it to some extent.[21]

But to return to the final chapter of the Doubleday version, in which Carrie is featured following the suicide of Hurstwood. It, too, is written in the florid style of the penultimate chapter and the chapter titles. In fact, the last paragraph of the final chapter is taken almost verbatim from the coda of the penultimate chapter. Dreiser merely shifted it to the end of the Doubleday version of the book, placing "O Carrie! O Carrie" at its beginning, before "blind striving of the human heart." And then he added three more sentences that brought the passage in line with one of the leitmotifs in the novel, the rocking chair into whose arms both Carrie and Hurstwood fall whenever confused or defeated: "Know then, that for you is neither surfeit nor content. In your rocking chair, by your window dreaming, shall you long, alone. In your rocking chair, by your window shall you dream such happiness as you may never feel."[22]

It may be conjectured, therefore, that Henry helped to write the last paragraph in the last chapter of *Sister Carrie.* The paragraph appears to be in Jug's hand; she evidently made a fair copy of the paragraph taken from the original penultimate chapter, in which, as the editors of the original typescript note, she made slight changes. Of course, all these alterations, like any suggestions Henry may have made for the final paragraph, could have been agreed upon orally by Dreiser.[23] But ironically, although Dreiser, as noted earlier, claimed to have written the last chapter of Henry's novel, the opposite may have been true. Whatever the case, the extent of Henry's collaboration may be greater than has been thought. They knew each other's plots intimately, the two books were conceived together on the Maumee, and they both had female protagonists who were in one sense or another "nuns."[24]

Aside from the logic of Dreiser's title, ending the book with Carrie may also have been an effort to placate the Victorian critics by "punishing" her for her adultery in leaving her basically unhappy, if also materially enriched. But that wasn't enough for the censors in 1900. Nor had it been in 1899 when Kate Chopin in *The Awakening* felt obliged to have her adulterous female commit suicide. Only Hester of *The Scarlet Letter,* published a half century earlier, passed America's puritanical code of literature because she became the object of Hawthorne's sermon and final scolding remarks (through Dimmesdale), just as she was the object of the minister's sermon on sin on the scaffold at the beginning of the story. As we shall see, by the time Dreiser had finally written the novel he indicated to Henry he couldn't write, he was prepared to do almost anything to see it in print.

\* \* \*

Once the typescript had been initially edited and its changes spliced in, Dreiser asked Henry Alden of *Harper's Monthly* to read it and advise as to its chances of publication. Alden had sent him a kind letter of rejection for **"The Shining Slave Makers,"** and *Harper's* had just published his article on the railroad. Furthermore, Alden frequently read book manuscripts for the well-established publishing house of Harper and Brothers. Alden told Dreiser it was a capable piece of work and ought to be published, but he doubted whether any publisher would touch it because of the reigning standards of decency. Nevertheless, no doubt at Dreiser's urging, Alden passed the typescript on to Harper and Brothers, who, as Dreiser remembered in his letter to Mencken about the affair, "promptly rejected [it] with a sharp slap." Actually, the reader's report he received from the firm was not a flat-out rejection, but in the first half at least an able and accurate assessment, which finally devolved into a vague argument as to why Harper's dare not publish it.[25]

In the report dated May 2, 1900, the unknown reader or readers called it "a superior piece of reportorial realism— of highclass newspaper work, such as might have been done by George Ade." This may have been part of the "slap," but "reportorial realism" had already been published not only by Crane (albeit privately) but by Garland and even Howells in *A Hazard of New Fortunes.* The report continued to note Dreiser's "many elements of strength— it is graphic, the local color is excellent, the portrayal of certain below-the-surface life in the Chicago of twenty years ago faithful to fact." Furthermore, it found "chapters that reveal very keen insight into this phase of life and incidents that disclose a sympathetic appreciation of the motives of the characters of the story." It seems clear that in declining to publish *Sister Carrie* Harper's made a commercial—and moral—decision, not an aesthetic one. The negative side of the report is less exact in making its arguments, such as the statement that "the author has not risen to the standard necessary for the efficient handling of the theme." The key to their true meaning here comes in the statement that Dreiser's "touch is neither firm enough nor sufficiently delicate to depict without offense to the reader [i.e., 'feminine readers who control the destinies of so many novels'] the continued illicit relations of the heroine." Its parting shot took aim at the alleged weariness of parts of the plot (mainly dealing with Carrie, since the report admired the section on Hurstwood's decline) and Dreiser's uneven or colloquial style.[26] The matter of that "style" would dog him throughout his lifetime—as well as his literary reputation today.

It has been said that Dreiser was crushed by the letter, believing he had written a novel in the tradition of Balzac and Hardy (which he had), but Alden had warned Dreiser that his inclusion of illicit sexual relations would not be tolerated. Dreiser later described himself at the time as being "as green as grass about such matters, totally unsophisticated." He promptly took Alden's advice to try the newer firm of Doubleday and Page—recently reorganized from the firm of Doubleday and McClure, which had published in 1899 a novel almost as challenging to the standards of decency, Frank Norris's *McTeague: A Story of San Francisco*.[27]

Before he did so, **Sister Carrie** very likely went through another round of revisions, this time to cut out or moderate the offensive parts of the book. Henry, whose novel was already in press at Doubleday, was the logical choice for the job. Once this work was done, Dreiser took the typescript to the offices of Doubleday and Page at 34 Union Square and personally handed it to Frank Doubleday. He remembered that Doubleday looked at him "with a kind of condescending, examining smirk." The publisher had a big ego, too big for his former partner Sam McClure (who after their split had formed the house of McClure and Phillips). When he left McClure, Doubleday had taken Walter Hines Page and Frank Norris with him as part of his editorial staff.[28] He now turned over the typescript either to his partner Page or directly to Norris, because he himself was getting ready to go abroad with his wife.

About a week later, Jug's sister Rose White, who was visiting, raved to her brother-in-law about *McTeague*. Dreiser read it and admired it immensely. "It made a great hit with me and I talked of nothing else for months," he later told Mencken. "It was the first real American book I had ever read—and I had read quite a number by W. D. Howells and others." At almost the same time, Frank Norris was reading **Sister Carrie** in a cabin resort in Greenwich, Connecticut, and coming to an equally enthusiastic conclusion about Dreiser's decidedly American book. Although his reader's report is unfortunately lost, he wrote directly to Dreiser that "it was the best novel I had read in M.S. since I had been reading for the firm, and that it pleased me as well as any novel I have read in any form, published or otherwise."[29] If events had played out differently, we might be celebrating this literary intersection as another "shock of recognition" such as what Melville experienced when he crossed paths with Hawthorne or Emerson when he greeted Whitman "at the beginning of a great career."

But there were other players, not only Doubleday, but the second reader on Dreiser's submission, Henry Lanier, the firm's junior partner. While he joined Norris in recommending **Sister Carrie,** Lanier evidently had his reservations about the potential risks to the firm's reputation. For the time being, however, he kept them to himself. Meanwhile Page, who acted as third reader, liked the book almost as much as Norris. He wrote to Dreiser on June 9, "As, we hope, Mr. Norris has informed you, we are very

much pleased with your novel." Congratulating him "on so good a piece of work," Page invited the author to come down to their offices the following Monday afternoon. Dreiser's prospects couldn't have looked better, and after the meeting he felt confident enough about them to leave town and accompany his wife back to Missouri to see her family.

It was about this time—between mid-June and early July—that Frank Doubleday returned from Europe. Just what happened isn't clear, even to this day. Allegedly, Doubleday took the typescript home and shared the enthusiastic reports of the book with his wife, whom Dreiser later described as "a social worker and active in moral reform." According to legend, Mrs. Doubleday read the typescript and strongly advised her husband not to publish it. Mrs. Doubleday's role in the affair, however, has never been verified; all accounts of her involvement as Mrs. Grundy come from Dreiser, who told the story at various points in his life.[30] The actual villain and possibly the catalyst to Doubleday's decision to try to get out of the firm's oral agreement with Dreiser may have been Henry Lanier, whom Arthur Henry described to Dreiser on July 14 as "a good deal of a cad ... [who] knows nothing at all about real life ... [and] is exceedingly conceited."

Since Dreiser was still in Missouri, Henry had gone to see Lanier at Norris's suggestion when the process for publishing Dreiser's book had suddenly and mysteriously stalled. During the interview, he and Lanier had engaged in "a warm argument" over the value of Dreiser's realism in **Sister Carrie.** Lanier insisted that Dreiser was unnecessarily "straining after realism." Interestingly, this had been the same argument his late father, the poet Sidney Lanier, had used against Walt Whitman in *The English Novel and the Principle of Its Development* (1883), where he objected to Whitman's depiction of the "rough" as the ideal or average American. The senior Lanier also stood for form in poetry, thinking "free verse" no more preferable than political anarchy.[31] It appears that Henry Lanier shared this tradition in literature with his father, objecting to Dreiser's focus on the average American who falls short of the ideal in sentimental literature. He could have stomached his colleague Norris's characters in *McTeague* because there the author himself treats them condescendingly (almost humorously) as defectives in the fantasy of Social Darwinism. Dreiser's creations, moreover, were not the kind of people, as Page would soon tell Dreiser, who would interest ladies and gentlemen, or the great majority of their readers.[32] In a word, Lanier thought Dreiser's realism was not only "strained," but false since its view of life failed to uplift the reader morally. While Lanier—as Henry told Dreiser—may have been as surprised as Norris by

Doubleday's decision not to publish *Sister Carrie,* he was certainly prepared to abide by it.

\* \* \*

In a strange twist, Lanier was arguing these points with someone who had upheld the same Victorian standard. Henry had, after all, written *A Princess of Arcady,* for which Lanier had probably been a reader along with his work on *Sister Carrie.* But Henry held his ground on behalf of his friend. Once the real reason for the delay became apparent, Henry urged Dreiser to return to New York at once and hold Doubleday and Page to their decision to publish the book. When he learned from Norris that Page had written a letter dated July 19 to Dreiser saying that they preferred not to publish his book after all, Henry was dumbfounded. "It has dazed me—I am amazed and enraged," he told his friend, "Doubleday has turned down your story. He did it all by himself and to the intense surprise of Norris and Lanier."[33] One has to wonder not only about Lanier's role here but also Norris's, for the author/reader found himself in a tight place. He was financially dependent on the firm for a salary as well as its intention to publish *The Octopus* (1902).

Norris, however, never lost faith in Dreiser's work. As we shall see, he did almost everything he could to promote it once the decision was reluctantly reached to issue the novel. But he does seem to have joined ranks initially with Doubleday and Page to discourage Dreiser from making *Sister Carrie* his first novel, especially at Doubleday. In breaking the bad news about *Sister Carrie* to Henry, Norris told him on July 18 that Page's letter was first held up for Dreiser's return and then dispatched to him for fear that if the firm waited any longer the delay would constitute a commitment. He tried to mollify Henry (and hence Dreiser, as would Page's letter) by suggesting that the firm would do something else in return for Dreiser's decision to yield on the question. "There is much more than a 'turning-down' of Sister Carrie" in Page's letter of July 19, he told Henry. "Page—and all of us—Mr. Doubleday too—are immensely interested in Dreiser and have every faith that he will go far." The publishers expressed faith in him as a writer and wanted to publish his *second* novel, hoping that it would be more acceptable to conventional taste. To vouch for their continued interest, they offered him an editorial position on a new magazine the firm was getting ready to publish—*World's Work.* They also promised to attempt to place *Sister Carrie* with another publisher, though one wonders exactly what firms they had in mind.[34]

At first, upon receiving Henry's letter, Dreiser tried to remain calm. But it was a mere pose, for as he later remembered, the Doubleday affair "proved to be the greatest blow I was ever to have."[35] In fact, he had been actively worried ever since receiving Henry's letter about his meeting with Lanier, even asking the blacks who worked around Arch White's farm in Danville if there was a fortune-teller nearby. He had—he told "Hen" in his letter of July 23—received both Henry's letter and Page's, and he enclosed a copy of his response to Page, which spoke of the enormous embarrassment he faced in the wake of this latest decision. Word of his success was already abroad. He had, for example, received a note of congratulations from the assistant editor of the *Atlantic Monthly,* and a lecture was being arranged for him at the Player's Club on his new kind of realism. "The repute in which your firm is held," he told Page, "the warm and rather extra-ordinary reception accorded my effort by your readers—the number and enthusiasm of those interested in me—all could but combine to engender a state, the destruction of which must necessarily put me in an untoward and very unsatisfactory predicament."[36] In other words, his literary reputation would be in tatters.

Dreiser didn't say he *wouldn't* withdraw the novel, telling Henry privately that he might if he could borrow the manuscript from Doubleday and silently offer it to Macmillan for a "quick consideration." He told Page that he was "willing to rest the matter, leaving for another day my reply to your eventual decision." Perhaps in denial, he simply could not believe what was happening. Any hope of relief was dashed, however, by Page's blunt if lengthy reply of August 2. "You do not say specifically whether you will release us," Page stated, adding cruelly in response to Dreiser's fear of embarrassment over the affair: "After all, other people, even our friends, think much less of our work than we imagine they do!" This should have, and probably did, convince Dreiser that the firm didn't have his best interests at heart. He therefore ignored their offer of August 15 to try to place the novel with another publisher. By now Henry might have already looked into those prospects and found absolutely no interest. He was also convinced that Doubleday and Page couldn't be trusted, telling his friend that while his own story was being "set up," he was sorry he had signed a contract for *A Princess of Arcady,* that he would have held off and used his own book as a bargaining chip for Dreiser's. Henry, however, had another reason for his deep devotion. He considered Dreiser his literary double whom he needed to spur on his own writing. He hoped to move back in with Dreiser and Jug, so that they might write another set of books together. "I am already to begin mine—am only waiting for you," he told him. "I want to be with you when you start yours."[37]

At this point, Dreiser was just as devoted to Henry. In his letter of July 23, he had told his literary collaborator that he was "thoroughly pleased" by his support, saying that it reflected his own distress when things went badly for Henry. "Surely there were never better friends than we. If words were anything I think I would tell you how I feel." He called Henry his doppelgänger—"a very excellent Dreiser minus some of my defects. . . . If I could not be what I am, I would be you."[38] If we didn't understand before exactly why he dedicated his book to Henry, it becomes clear with these words. If it hadn't been for Henry, Dreiser might have given in to the pressure applied not only by Frank Doubleday, whom Henry described to Dreiser as thinking *Sister Carrie* both "immoral and badly written," but by his staff, which quickly closed ranks behind their leader.

Doubleday thought at first that they could simply notify Dreiser of their decision not to publish his book. After talking first with Henry and then with Page, as well as with his attorney, however, Doubleday asked Dreiser through Page to release them from their proclaimed intentions. When it was clear that Dreiser was adamant, a contract was finally drawn up on August 20. Nonetheless, Doubleday sent Dreiser a cold letter of September 4 ("Dear Sir"), which doggedly rehearsed earlier suggestions to change all real names of people and places. It had to be clear to Dreiser that the firm was going to do as little as possible to fulfill its contract, which promised the author royalties on retail sales of 10 percent on the first 1,500 copies sold, 12.5 on the next 1,500, and 15 percent on everything over 3,000 copies. The first and only press run was just 1,008 sets of sheets, of which only 558 sets were initially bound, to be sold for $1.50 apiece. (There was further binding of copies from the 1008 sets, but the exact number is not known.) Norris, who was in charge of publicity at Doubleday, did his best to stimulate sales by sending out an estimated 127 review copies. But Dreiser's first and last royalty check from Doubleday, which tracked sales between November 1900 and February 1902, was a dismal $68.40.[39]

Furthermore, when *Sister Carrie* appeared in the fall of 1900 along with *The Princess of Arcady,* the physical contrast between the two couldn't have been greater. Henry's garden-green cover was imprinted with stalks of flowers, while the flat dull red of Dreiser's book made it—in the words of one biographer—resemble a plumber's manual. It has been said that Doubleday refused to advertise *Sister Carrie.*[40] Yet there is no evidence that the firm advertised *A Princess* either. In fact, if the issues of the *New York Times Saturday Review of Books* between November and January are a reliable gauge, Doubleday didn't advertise any of its books. On the other hand, the competition—Scribner's,

Macmillan, G. P. Putnam's Sons, Harper and Brothers, Houghton, Mifflin, and Company, even McClure, Phillips, and Company—ran full-page advertisements for their fall lists. The November 10 issue of *Saturday Review* would have been the time to strike for *Sister Carrie,* but the only book of lasting value to appear—under review—in the journal that day was the first variorum edition of another book suppressed in its day, *Leaves of Grass.* Some of the reviews of *Sister Carrie* actually commented on the paucity of advertising, among them the review in William Marion Reedy's *Mirror* (which would publish "Butcher Rogaum's Door" in 1902) in its issue of January 3. And on January 16, George Horton of the *Chicago Times Herald,* one of Henry's former colleagues, asked "Why a firm that can get hold of such literature should expend all their resources in pushing such cheap and trite clap-trap as 'An Englishwoman's Love Letters' must remain a puzzle to everybody not in the publishing business."[41]

The Doubleday affair would render Dreiser forever suspicious of publishers. In fact, he prepared to remember and to record it (not always faithfully) from the very beginning. He told Henry when the crisis first surfaced, "If when better known and successful I should choose to make known this correspondence, every scrap of which I have, even to letters of commendation from others, the house of Doubleday would not shine so very brightly." To this end, he accumulated a scrapbook consisting of 245 letters, including copies in his hand of Henry's letters relating to the affair, which in fact are almost the only extant evidence of his friend's assistance.[42] He would also embellish his own artistic role, telling an interviewer for the *New York Herald* in 1907, when the book was first reissued by another publisher, of his heroic struggle to complete it. "The story had to stop, and yet I wanted in the final picture to suggest the continuation of Carrie's fate along the lines of established truths," he was paraphrased as saying. "Finally, with note book and pencil I made a trip to the Palisades, hoping that the change of scene would bring out just what I was trying to express." There, he said, he stretched himself out on one of its ledges. After two hours, the inspiration finally came: "I reached for my note book and pencil and wrote. And when I left the Palisades **'Sister Carrie'** was completed."[43] This account may be a cruel shorthand to both acknowledge and erase Henry's role in the ending, for his "sister" or sisters in *A Princess of Arcady* dwell in a convent facing the Palisades. We will never know what if anything Dreiser changed in transcribing Henry's letters, but this later account left his now ex-friend completely out of the picture. Their falling out in 1902 no doubt contributed to this, but earlier Dreiser may have chafed at the superior treatment Henry had received from Doubleday.

Only Norris remained unscathed, or unrevised, in Dreiser's memory of the affair, and even here he apparently made some comments in 1930 about the writer's conflict of interests. Although Dreiser also wrote a flattering introduction to a reissue of *McTeague* about the same time, their relationship was cut short when Norris died of peritonitis in 1902. A month after the muted appearance of *Sister Carrie,* Dreiser sent Norris an autographed copy, acknowledging his "earliest and most unqualified approval" and claiming that his book was an "offspring" he had "so generously fostered." For his part, Norris reiterated his admiration of Dreiser's book. "I have read most of her again," he told Dreiser in thanking him for the book. "It is a *true* book in all senses of the word."[44]

\* \* \*

Aside from Norris's valiant statements and support, an American novel couldn't have appeared under more unpromising circumstances. The number of review copies Norris actually was allowed to send out may be exaggerated, but it was the only advertisement the book was going to receive. As a result of the Doubleday reversal, word surely got out that *Sister Carrie* was not to be celebrated, or even noticed, in the literary press. No doubt, after his experience with Dreiser, Howells had no qualms about ignoring the book in *Harper's.* Other mainstream journals that might have been expected to do reviews—the *North American Review,* the *Atlantic Monthly,* the *Critic,* the *Arena,* the *Literary Digest,* the *Review of Reviews,* and curiously enough even *Ainslee's,* where Dreiser's friend Richard Duffy was the editor—also ignored it. *Outlook, Current Literature,* and the *Nation* listed the book as published but never reviewed it.[45] Mainly, it was the newspapers that reviewed *Sister Carrie.*

Part of the legend surrounding *Sister Carrie* was that the reviews were overwhelmingly negative, but the fact is that of the handful that the first edition received between November 20, 1900, and March 9, 1901—fewer than thirty— more than a few hinted that despite the book's colloquial language and seamy plot, it was undeniably a rare example of literary genius. "Here, at last, is, in its field," wrote Horton in the *Chicago Times Herald* of January 16, "a great American novel." By "in its field," he undoubtedly referred to naturalism with its focus on the more sordid aspects of American life, such as in *McTeague,* which many condemned for its vulgarity in depicting the bestial natures of the main characters. Interestingly, one of the reasons Doubleday may have shied away from Dreiser's book was because of the adverse reviews of *McTeague* (again for its subject matter, not its power), which he had published when he was still a partner with McClure.

But what struck reviewers of *Sister Carrie* was how Dreiser managed to state his case without either profanity or the use of explicit scenes like those found in the underground literature of its day.

"It is a remarkable book," said the *Louisville Times* of November 20, "strong, virile, written with the clear determination of a man who has a story to tell and who tells it." Its coverage by New York reviewers was almost nil, but the *New York Commercial Advertiser* of December 19 referred to its "extraordinary power" to tell a profound and moving story. Three days later the *Albany Journal* called it "intensely human." Up in New Haven, the *Journal-Courier* of January 12 thought its "depth of insight into human character [had] evidenced . . . a touch of Balzac's strength and penetration." And out West, the *Seattle Post Intelligencer* of January 20 called Dreiser "a new writer with endowments of a most unusual order. It seems not unlikely that, if himself so wills it, he can stand at the head of American novelists." Complaints, sometimes the predominant feature of a review, were aimed at Dreiser's style ("the English is seldom good and frequently atrocious"), the title ("this oddly named story"), and that fact that the story "was not a book to be put into the hands of every reader indiscriminately." Two reviewers recognized Dreiser's borrowing from George Ade.

Two others observed that neither the word "God" nor "Deity" occurred anywhere in its 557 pages, only "the godless side of American life." Generally, reviewers objected to the idea that life had no deeper or higher meaning than the accidental paths that Carrie and Hurstwood follow. Hurstwood's drama was thought to be the greater strength in the book, but ironically its force lay in the fact that the ex-manager falls for no better or worse reason than that by which Carrie rises. He falls down and down and nobody seems to care, not even God. Naturally, Hurstwood drew more sympathy than Carrie. To many reviewers (all male in this case), Carrie was regarded as an irresponsible shopgirl who got lucky, but Hurstwood drew their empathy. The *Hartford Courant* of December 6 thought that there was "nothing more impressive in the year's novel writing" than the description of Hurstwood's last days and death. "There is hardly such another picture anywhere of the man who has lost his grip," wrote the *Seattle Post Intelligencer,* "the man who disintegrates utterly in the face of adversity."

One bright interlude in the publishing history of *Sister Carrie* occurred when the English got to read the novel. Through Norris, a copy of the "banned" book fell into the hands of the British publisher William Heinemann, who was getting a series in American fiction under way with his

"Dollar Library," in which a reprint of an American book was published every month. The book had also been brought to his attention by George A. Brett, an editor at Macmillan who wrote Dreiser an admiring letter about *Sister Carrie.* Heinemann made the offer of publication through Doubleday on May 6, 1901. The only requirement for change was that in order for the book to conform to the length of the other five books already published Dreiser would have to condense the first two hundred pages down to eighty. Heinemann had no intention of expurgating or revising the content of the book, but the end result was to produce a novel with a tighter structure and one in which the dramatic downfall of Hurstwood is more central to the overall plot. Henry once again helped his friend edit *Sister Carrie,* indeed, may have done the job himself to cut material from the first 195 pages, or up to Chapter 18, where Hurstwood, out to the theater one night with Carrie and Drouet, lies that his wife is ill.[46]

The revised novel, which appeared in 1901, sold better than the Doubleday edition, exhausting its first printing of 1,500 copies and netting Dreiser royalties of $150.[47] The bigger pay-off came, however, in the English reviews, which were much stronger than the American ones. Up until the time of Washington Irving, the English had been condescending toward American authors, but they had spent the latter half of the nineteenth century in condescension toward American critics, who seemed to overlook everyone of their countrymen who wrote unlike the English, such as Whitman and Mark Twain. Heinemann suspected a new American School of writers, perhaps thinking of Crane and Garland, with Dreiser as its latest head. "At last a really strong novel has come from America," announced the *London Daily Mail* of August 13, 1901; "Dreiser has contrived a masterpiece." The *Manchester Guardian* of the following day wrote, "Rarely, even in modern work, have we met with characters so little idealised." The *Academy* of August 24 readily admitted its ignorance of this new breed of American writers, "but *Sister Carrie* has opened our eyes. It is a calm, reasoned, realistic study of American life, ... absolutely free from the slightest traces of sentimentality ... and dominated everywhere by a serious and strenuous desire for the truth." The comparison with Zola in the *Athenaeum* of September 7 was quoted in the *New York Commercial Advertiser* of September 18, which had already given the original edition one of its best American reviews. Now the book was hailed as "not only one of the best novels published last year by Doubleday, Page and Company, but one of the strongest and best-sustained pieces of fiction that we have read for a long time." It also noted that while *Sister Carrie* was winning "golden opinions" from the British, it had "curiously enough attracted comparatively little notice in this country."

\* \* \*

By the time of the English edition of *Sister Carrie,* Dreiser had already begun two other new novels. The first, to be called **"The Rake,"** was the story of a sexual adventurer and may have been based either on his sexual exploits as a newspaperman or possibly a "rake" like Frank Cowperwood of *The Financier.* Perhaps fearing the subject offensive to the publishing industry, he turned instead on New Year's Day 1901 to write *Jennie Gerhardt,* originally entitled *The Transgressor.* Richard Lingeman speculates that it was his father's death a week earlier that prompted this novel, based not only on another sister but on his father and mother. He wrote up to forty chapters, then tore up all but the first fifteen, before he ran out of gas. He was emotionally exhausted and began to brood. It was as if his world had come to an end with the old century, collapsing on the eve of the new in a reversal of William Walton's prospects in his short story "When the Old Century Was New." Young Walton has "no inkling" of what the century might bring forth, but he is naively optimistic. His creator could see only "the crush and stress and wretchedness fast treading upon his path."[48] In fact, Dreiser was almost fatally intertwined with his fictional characters and the sense of impending doom that frequently envelops them—so much so that the author of *Sister Carrie* began to turn into the gloomy Hurstwood.

*Abbreviations*

Cornell    Carl A. Kroch Library, Cornell University.

*DML*      *Dreiser-Mencken Letters: The Correspondence of Theodore Dreiser and H. L. Mencken,* ed. Thomas P. Riggio. Philadelphia: University of Pennsylvania Press, 1986, 2 volumes.

*DN*       *Dreiser Newsletter.*

*DS*       *Dreiser Studies.*

*FF*       Dorothy Dudley, *Forgotten Frontiers: Dreiser and the Land of the Free.* New York: Harrison Smith, 1932. Reprinted as *Dreiser and the Land of the Free.* New York: Beechhurst, 1946. Citations are to the 1932 edition.

*Free*     *Free and Other Stories.* New York: Boni & Liveright, 1918.

*L*        *Letters of Theodore Dreiser,* ed. Robert H. Elias. Philadelphia: University of Pennsylvania Press, 1959, 3 volumes.

SC     *Sister Carrie,* ed. Donald Pizer. New York: W. W. Norton, 1991; originally published, 1900.

SCP     *Sister Carrie: The Pennsylvania Edition,* ed. John C. Berkey and Alice M. Winters. Philadelphia: University of Pennsylvania Press, 1981.

SMA     *Selected Magazine Articles of Theodore Dreiser: Life and Art in the American 1890s,* ed. Yoshinobu Hakutani. Rutherford, N.J.: Fairleigh Dickinson University Press, 1985, 1987, 2 volumes.

TD     Theodore Dreiser.

TDCR     *Theodore Dreiser: The Critical Reception,* ed. Jack Salzman. New York: David Lewis, 1972.

*Notes*

1. Allen F. Stein, "*Sister Carrie*: A Possible Source for the Title," *American Literary Realism* 7 (Spring 1974): 173-74.

2. Arthur Henry, *A Princess of Arcady* (New York: Doubleday, Page, & Co., 1900), 17.

3. Henry, *Princess of Arcady,* 170, 307.

4. *SC,* 1; see *SCP* for the uncut original version of *Sister Carrie.*

5. *FF,* 162, where Dreiser is paraphrased to say that he finished the book in May, but the completion date was definitely earlier, possibly as early as March. In an interview with the *St. Louis Post-Dispatch,* January 27, 1902, Dreiser gives March, but in "The Early Adventures of *Sister Carrie,*" (*Colophon,* Part Five [March 1931, unpaginated, 4 pp.]) which is included as a preface to the first Modern Library edition of the novel in 1932, he states that he finished the book in May. The manuscript is dated as having been completed in March (see n. 18 below); the revisions by Jug and Arthur Henry, which included a different ending, no doubt took the process a little longer, but not into May, for by May 2, it had already been rejected by Harper's.

6. *DML,* 1: 233; see also Vrest Orton, *Dreiserana: A Book about His Books* (1929; repr. New York: Haskell House, 1973), 13.

7. Arthur Henry, *An Island Cabin* (New York: McClure, Phillips, & Co., 1902), 213; and *The House in the Woods* (New York: A. S. Barnes, 1904). Henry's statement about Burroughs appears in an undated and unpublished preface intended for a reprinting of *An Island Cabin* in 1903 (Cornell).

8. Henry, *Princess of Arcady,* 10; and *SC,* 48. Maude Wood Henry told Robert H. Elias in a letter dated May 13, 1945, that when Henry announced he was leaving her, "Ann[a] was sitting cross-legged on the floor sewing" (Cornell).

9. See James L. W. West III, "John Paul Dreiser's Copy of *Sister Carrie,*" *Library Chronicle* 44 (Spring 1979): 85-93.

10. Dreiser had interviewed Field two years earlier; see "Life Stories of Successful Men—No. 12," *Success* 2 (December 1898): 78; reprinted in *SMA,* 130-38.

11. *SC,* 17, 49.

12. *SC,* 33-34.

13. *SC,* 72.

14. *SC,* 192-93.

15. *SC,* 84, 103.

16. *SC,* 276-321.

17. See *SC,* 327, 338-39; and *SCP,* 511-12, 538n. See also Ellen Moers, *Two Dreisers* (New York: Viking Press, 1969), 67n., for a slightly different view.

18. The manuscript of *Sister Carrie* is in the Manuscript Division of the New York Public Library.

19. *SCP,* 538n.

20. James L. W. West III, *A Sister Carrie Portfolio* (Charlottesville: University Press of Virginia, 1985), 42-45; and Philip Williams, "The Chapter Titles of *Sister Carrie,*" *American Literature* 36 (November 1964): 359-65. For parallels between Ames and Edison, see Lawrence E. Hussman, Jr., *Dreiser and His Fiction: A Twentieth-Century Quest* (Philadelphia: University of Pennsylvania Press, 1983), 30-32.

21. F. O. Matthiessen, *Theodore Dreiser* (New York: William Sloane Associates, 1951), 71.

22. *SCP,* 517; and *SC,* 369; see also Jerome M. Loving, "The Rocking Chair Structure of *Sister Carrie,*" *DN* 2 (Spring 1971): 7-11.

23. In a 1937 letter otherwise undated Dreiser told Louis Filler, "When I finished the book, I realized it was too long, . . . and marked what I thought should be cut out. Then I consulted with a friend, Arthur Henry, who suggested other cuts, and wherever I agreed with him I cut the book" (Penn).

24. *SCP,* 518.

25. Orton, *Dreiserana,* 13-14; and *L,* 1: 210n. Dreiser's railroad article was "The Railroad and the People," *Harper's Monthly* 100 (February 1900): 479-84.

26. *L,* 1: 210n.

27. *SCP,* 519-20; *DML,* 1: 231; and Orton, *Dreiserana,* 14.

28. *SCP,* 520-22; *DML,* 1: 231; and Richard Lingeman, *Theodore Dreiser* (New York: G. P. Putnam's Sons, 1986), 1: 281-82.

29. *DML,* 1: 231; and Frank Norris to TD, May 28, 1900 (Penn). Most of the correspondence concerning *Sister Carrie* and Doubleday, Page, & Company is published in *L,* 1: 50-65, as well as in *SC.* See *FF,* 169, for Norris's location when he read Dreiser's book.

30. TD, "Early Adventures," 2; see also TD to Fremont Older, November 27, 1923, (*L,* 2: 417-21).

31. Jerome Loving, *Walt Whitman: The Song of Himself* (Berkeley: University of California Press, 1999), 451-53.

32. *SC,* 449; and *L,* 1: 55. See *FF* (170) for further suggestions, if not evidence, of Lanier's negative view towards *Sister Carrie.* There is in the Dreiser collection at Penn an unpublished typescript of an introduction to a later edition of the novel that credits Lanier for standing up for the book. But this introduction is also filled with factual errors and exaggerations.

33. Arthur Henry to TD, July 19, 1900 (Penn).

34. Frank Norris to Arthur Henry, July 18, [1900] (Penn).

35. Theodore Dreiser, "Biographical Sketch," written for *Household Magazine* (1929, Penn).

36. *L,* 1: 57.

37. Arthur Henry to TD, undated but received by Dreiser on July 31, 1900 (Penn); and *L,* 1: 59-60. The fact that Henry's letter is written on Doubleday, Page, & Company stationery suggests Henry's closeness to Norris, whose manuscript of *The Octopus* he had read.

38. *L,* 1: 54.

39. *L,* 1: 63-64; Memorandum of Agreement, August 20, 1900 (Penn); and *SCP,* 528-29.

40. Lingeman, *Theodore Dreiser,* 1: 294; and W. A. Swanberg, *Dreiser* (New York: Charles Scribner's Sons, 1965), 92.

41. *TDCR,* 6-7, 10. Concerning the *Mirror* review, William Marion Reedy told Dreiser on December 26, 1900, that he read *Sister Carrie* in one sitting and thought it was "damned good." Horton's puzzlement over Doubleday's actions was soon cleared up by Henry, whom he told on February 8, 1901: "I am not at all surprised at your version of the Doubleday-Dreiser story. I had fancied something of the kind" (Penn).

42. *L,* 1: 52-53; and Neda M. Westlake, "The Sister Carrie Scrapbook," *Library Chronicle* 44 (Spring 1979): 71-84.

43. "'Sister Carrie': Theodore Dreiser," *New York Herald,* July 7, 1907 (quoted from *SCP,* 584).

44. For TD's 1930 comments on Frank Norris, see *FF,* 168-69. Norris's autographed copy of *Sister Carrie* is in the University of California Library, Berkeley, Calif.; his response is published in the *Collected Letters: Frank Norris* (San Francisco: The Book Club of California, 1986), 144. For the pros and cons on whether Norris remained faithful to *Sister Carrie,* see Jack Salzman, "The Publication of *Sister Carrie*: Fact and Fiction," *Library Chronicle* 33 (Spring 1967): 19-33; Robert Morace, "Dreiser's Contract for *Sister Carrie*: More Fact and Fiction," *Journal of Modern Literature* 9 (May 1982): 305-11; and Joseph R. McElrath, Jr., "Norris's Attitude toward *Sister Carrie,*" *DS* 18 (Fall 1987): 39-42.

45. *TDCR,* from which the review quotations that follow are taken.

46. George A. Brett to TD, September 21, 1901 (Penn). It is not altogether clear whether Dreiser was involved in the revision. See John C. Berkey and Alice M. Winters, "The Heinemann Edition of *Sister Carrie,*" *Library Chronicle* 44 (Spring 1979): 43-52; and *Sister Carrie: An Abridged Edition by Theodore Dreiser and Arthur Henry,* ed. Jack Salzman (New York: Johnson Reprint Corporation, 1969), v-x.

47. Doubleday, Page, and Company to TD, May 6, 1901 (Penn).

48. "When the Old Century Was New," *Pearson's Magazine* 11 (January 1901): 131-40; reprinted and slightly revised in *Free.*

---

## FURTHER READING

### Bibliographies

Boswell, Jeanette. *Theodore Dreiser and the Critics, 1911-1982: A Bibliography with Selective Annotations.* Scarecrow Press, 1982.

Focuses on secondary sources, most with annotations.

Elias, Robert H. "Theodore Dreiser." *Fifteen Modern American Authors: A Survey of Research and Criticism,* edited by Jackson R. Bryer, Duke UP, 1969, pp. 101-38.

Combines critical opinions with secondary source information.

Pizer, Donald, Richard W. Dowell, and Frederick E. Rusch. *Theodore Dreiser: A Primary Bibliography and Reference Guide.* G. K. Hall, 1991.

Includes both extensive primary bibliography as well as equally extensive secondary listings.

**Biographies**

Elias, Robert H., editor. *Letters of Theodore Dreiser: A Selection.* U of Pennsylvania P, 1959.

This three-volume selection of Dreiser's letters is an essential segment of any biographical study.

Lingeman, Richard. *Theodore Dreiser: At the Gates of the City, 1871-1907.* Putnam, 1986. *Theodore Dreiser: An American Journey, 1908-1945.* Putnam, 1990.

An important and informative two-volume biography.

Loving, Jerome. *The Last Titan: A Life of Theodore Dreiser.* U of California P, 2005.

Sorts through one hundred years of arguments about naturalism, the use of journalism in fiction, and the characteristics of Dreiser's largely German family. An excerpt from this biography is included in the entry above.

Swanberg, W. A. *Dreiser.* Scribner, 1965.

A remarkably effective starting point for biographical research of this complex writer.

**Criticism**

Asselineau, Roger. "Theodore Dreiser's Transcendentalism." *English Studies Today: Second Series,* edited by G. A. Bonnard, Bern, Francke Verlag, 1961, pp. 233-43.

Links Dreiser to the nineteenth-century Transcendentalists. As the leading French critic to write about American letters, Asselineau admits the strong naturalist strain in Dreiser's work but sees that balanced by an almost mystical belief system (partly religious, partly psychological), and notes Dreiser's alternation between reliance on the latter and largely scientific references. He illustrates Dreiser's wide-ranging philosophy through his poetry.

Butler, Robert. "Urban Frontiers, Neighborhoods, and Traps: The City in Dreiser's *Sister Carrie,* Farrell's *Studs Lonigan,* and Wright's *Native Son.*" *Theodore Dreiser and American Culture: New Readings,* edited by Yoshinobu Hakutani, U of Delaware P, 2000, pp. 274-90.

Makes impressive points about the differences among *Sister Carrie,* James T. Farrell's *Studs Lonigan* (1960), and Richard Wright's *Native Son* (1940), adapting current criticism about life in cities. Butler seems to prefer Dreiser's treatment, stating that for Carrie the city is promising and frontierlike, and Carrie's adaptability, shown in her acting career, enables her to take advantage of what opportunities appear—whether in Chicago, Montreal, or New York. Both Farrell and Wright admired Dreiser and his writing so that even as they crafted very different cities in their works, they felt that Dreiser's writing had given them the right to draw the city as they saw it.

Grebstein, Sheldon Norman. "*An American Tragedy*: Theme and Structure." *Critical Essays on Theodore Dreiser,* edited by Donald Pizer, G. K. Hall, 1981, pp. 313-21.

Reads *An American Tragedy* as if Dreiser were a modernist, and Grebstein often compares it to F. Scott Fitzgerald's *The Great Gatsby* (1925). By emphasizing technical matters, Grebstein sidesteps the naturalist tendency to read most literary texts as sociology—or, in some cases, as reflections of cultural import. In Grebstein's reading, *An American Tragedy* is Dreiser's classic American novel—not only thematically, as the poor suitor tries to marry up the social ladder, but structurally, when layers of narrative echo ironically and the whole work is tightly crafted. The worship of the goal of success aligns itself with sexuality as a means to that success so that readers will not question Clyde's motivation. What is new in Dreiser's treatment is his basing the novel on a recorded crime while incorporating some of his own biography, and as he broadens the "crime" into universality, he makes changes that give the story more and more resonance.

Lears, Jackson. "Dreiser and the History of American Longing." *The Cambridge Companion to Theodore Dreiser,* edited by Leonard Cassuto and Clare Virginia Eby, Cambridge UP, 2004, pp. 63-79.

Writes the history of the development of American cities in terms of what Lears calls "human longing," and his interpretation of Dreiser's novels rests on this "dimension of desire." Lears notes that Dreiser charted the rise of cities "from the inside out," and made a sometimes unexpressed need—whether sexual or knowledge-based—people's primary motivations. He praises Dreiser for recognizing the power of human longing as "perverse, unpredictable, and sometimes self-defeating, but powerful, persistent."

Pizer, Donald. "American Literary Naturalism: The Example of Dreiser." *Studies in American Fiction,* vol. 5, Spring 1977, pp. 51-63.

Sets up the principles of naturalism and then describes Dreiser's most important texts—*Sister Carrie, Jennie Gerhardt,* and *An American Tragedy*—in relation to those principles. Pizer incorporates relevant biography and also pays attention to Dreiser's *Hey Rub-a-Dub-Dub* and *The Bulwark.*

Salzman, Jack. "The Publication of *Sister Carrie*: Fact and Fiction." *University of Pennsylvania Library Chronicle,* vol. 33, no. 3, Spring 1967, pp. 119-33.

Charts the early reaction to the publication of Dreiser's first novel, both when it appeared in 1900 and then when it was reissued several years later. In this fascinating glimpse into turn-of-the-century culture, each reviewer, each journal, and each newspaper shows its social attitude by the positioning of single comments. Salzman, an early scholar of American studies, wrings surprising depth from his various listings.

Von Bardeleben, Renate. "Personal, Ethnic, and National Identity: Theodore Dreiser's Difficult Heritage." *Interdisziplinarität: Deutsche Sprache und Literatur im Spannungsfeld del Kulturen,* edited by Martin Forstner and Klaus von Schilling, Frankfurt am Main, Peter Lang, 1991, pp. 319-40.

Contemplates the effects of Dreiser's German Slavic ethnicity on his literary output and career in the United States and abroad and on the later formation of "his personal view" relative to this inheritance based on his midlife travels to Europe.

---

**Additional information on Dreiser's life and works is contained in the following sources published by Gale:** *American Writers; American Writers Retrospective Supplement,* **Vol. 2;** *American Writers: The Classics,* **Vol. 2;** *Beacham's Guide to Literature for Young Adults,* **Vols. 15, 16;** *Concise Dictionary of American Literary Biography, 1865-1917; Contemporary Authors,* **Vols. 106, 132;** *Dictionary of Literary Biography,* **Vols. 9, 12, 102, 137, 361, 368;** *Dictionary of Literary Biography Documentary Series,* **Vol. 1;** *DISCovering Authors; DISCovering Authors: Canadian Edition; DISCovering Authors Modules: Most-Studied Authors and Novelists; DISCovering Authors 3.0; Encyclopedia of World Literature in the 20th Century,* **Ed. 3;** *Gale Contextual Encyclopedia of American Literature; Literary Movements for Students,* **Vol. 2;** *Literature and Its Times,* **Vol. 2;** *Literature Resource Center; Major 20th-Century Writers,* **Eds. 1, 2;** *Major 21st-Century Writers; Modern American Literature,* **Ed. 5;** *Novels for Students,* **Vols. 8, 17;** *Reference Guide to American Literature,* **Ed. 4;** *Short Story Criticism,* **Vols. 30, 114;** *Twayne's United States Authors; Twentieth-Century Literary Criticism,* **Vols. 10, 18, 35, 83, 277; and** *World Literature Criticism,* **Vol. 2.**

# Sister Carrie
## Theodore Dreiser

(Full name Theodore Herman Albert Dreiser) American novelist, short-story writer, essayist, journalist, playwright, and autobiographer.

The following entry provides criticism of Dreiser's novel *Sister Carrie* (1900); for additional information about *Sister Carrie,* see *TCLC,* Volume 277; for additional information about Dreiser, see *TCLC,* Volumes 10, 18, 35, and 377; for additional information about the novel *An American Tragedy,* see *TCLC,* Volume 83.

## INTRODUCTION

*Sister Carrie,* the first novel by Theodore Dreiser (1871-1945), is widely regarded as a seminal literary treatment of the social and economic dimensions of urban life in industrialized American society. Inspired by the experiences of Dreiser's sister Emma, the novel chronicles the life of Caroline (Carrie) Meeber, a young country woman who moves to Chicago and gradually ascends the socioeconomic ladder, initially through her romantic involvement with wealthier men, and later as a successful stage actress. The novel proved controversial for its nonjudgmental presentation of Carrie's sexual relationships, which scholars recognized as a departure from the moralism of traditional literature in the Victorian era. Occasionally criticized as stylistically clumsy, *Sister Carrie* has nonetheless been hailed for its detail, verisimilitude, and frank treatment of issues of class that helped usher in the era of modernism in American literature.

## PLOT AND MAJOR CHARACTERS

The novel begins in August 1889 with Carrie leaving her home in rural Wisconsin and boarding a train bound for Chicago, where she plans to live with her married sister Minnie while establishing herself in the city. She gets a job in a shoe factory, but the work is dreary, and she is compelled to give most of her wages in rent to Minnie and Hanson, Minnie's husband. Eventually, Carrie falls ill, loses her job, and is unable to secure another. On the street she encounters an attractive traveling salesman, Charles Drouet, whom she had previously met on the train to Chicago. Drouet provides financial assistance and eventually

convinces Carrie to leave her sister's apartment and move in with him.

Living more comfortably, Carrie is introduced by Drouet to his friend George Hurstwood, the manager of an upscale bar, who begins to pursue her romantically while Drouet is away. Carrie, unaware that Hurstwood is a married man with children, hopes that he will ask her to marry him. Hurstwood's family life deteriorates while his relationship with Carrie progresses. Eventually, Hurstwood promises Carrie that he will marry her. Encouraged by Drouet, Carrie gives an excellent performance in an amateur theatrical production. Shortly thereafter, both Drouet and Hurstwood's wife discover the affair between Carrie and Hurstwood, and Carrie learns of Hurstwood's marriage. After an argument, Drouet leaves Carrie, and she severs her relationship with Hurstwood. Now estranged from his wife, Hurstwood steals $10,000 in cash from a safe in the bar and persuades Carrie to run away with him. He later returns most of the money out of fear and guilt and then settles with Carrie in New York City.

Hurstwood invests in another bar, though he makes less money than before, and the couple is forced to live frugally. Over time their resources dwindle and their relationship deteriorates. Meanwhile, Carrie's discontent with her material circumstances is exacerbated by her friendship with a wealthy neighbor, who exposes her to New York's high society. Hurstwood loses his job and gambles away much of their remaining money. Carrie pursues an acting career with considerable success, as she and Hurstwood become increasingly distant until she leaves him. By the end of the novel, Carrie attains substantial wealth and renown as an actress, but her long-standing sense of dissatisfaction with her life continues. Hurstwood, meanwhile, falls into destitution and homelessness. He ultimately commits suicide by gassing himself in a flophouse.

## TEXTUAL HISTORY

Dreiser completed his manuscript in March 1900 with the help of Arthur Henry. After Harper and Brothers rejected it, Dreiser took it to Doubleday, Page, and Company, where Frank Norris read it in May 1900 and eagerly recommended it to Henry Lanier, the secretary of the firm, for publication. Walter H. Page, vice president of the company, also reportedly approved of the novel, and Dreiser was sent an assurance of publication in letter form. However, by July 1900 Frank Doubleday read the manuscript and decided against publication. Henry worked in Dreiser's defense with the publisher during the dispute while Dreiser was staying in Missouri. He advised Dreiser to hold the company to their initial decision which, though not a contract, Henry insisted was still binding. The company asked Dreiser to release them from the agreement, emphasizing their faith in him as a writer, but arguing that it was to his benefit not to make a work with such sordid content his first publication. Dreiser refused all compromises and a contract was signed in August 1900. In cooperation with Henry, Dreiser changed the names of real people to fictional ones, removed the novel's profanity, and cut various passages totaling around thirty-six thousand words overall. Some cuts may have been made in the interest of propriety, but they are largely seen as efforts to shorten a lengthy work by removing ideas already expressed elsewhere.

The publisher sold less than half of the first edition's one thousand printed copies, for which Dreiser was paid ten percent, per his contract. Disappointed by the entire ordeal, Dreiser began discussing the publisher's effort to suppress the novel in interviews and conversations, adding to his account the notion that Mrs. Doubleday was partly to blame for her husband's antipathy toward the work. Dreiser's account of Norris's and Henry's involvement in the affair also transformed as his relationship with Henry soured and Norris died in 1902. Subsequent publishers and biographers repeated Dreiser's account of the affair, and the story became an almost mythical narrative of the battle between censorship and freedom of expression. Jack Salzman (1967) confirmed the elements of the story that can be verified by letters and documents, and pointed out that the story of Mrs. Doubleday's opposition is unverifiable. The novel was more successful in England, and after the narratives about its suppression became widespread, B. W. Dodge and Company published a second edition in the United States in 1907, in which Dreiser made only one brief change in the first chapter. In 1981, the University of Pennsylvania Press revised and enlarged the novel by reinserting the manuscript's language and historical references and also restoring the massive cuts to the manuscript and the brief passage from the first chapter changed in 1907. This edition is commonly referred to as the Pennsylvania Edition, its subtitle. James L. W. West III (2001) was one of the edition's four editors and explained how the restorative effort provided a balance between prioritizing "authorial intention" in published works and viewing them

as "collaborations" between writer and editor, a struggle that the evolution of *Sister Carrie* manifests vividly.

## MAJOR THEMES

The novel's principal thematic concern is the American Dream of upward social mobility. Carrie's experiences constitute a quintessential "rags to riches" story, as she starts out in life with very little and rises to a position of wealth and prestige. However, many details of Carrie's gradual social ascent—especially her long stint as Hurstwood's mistress and her complicity in his theft—stand in sordid contrast to the Victorian ideals of honest effort and sacrifice. Instead of punishing Carrie for her improprieties, Dreiser implies that her willingness to transgress conventional moral strictures in pursuit of her ambitions is central to her eventual success. Her attempts to make a living through honest drudgery early in the novel bear negligible fruit—the labor is unpleasant, the pay is low, and she is fired after illness forces her to miss work for a few days. Only after she becomes a "kept woman" for Drouet—effectively trading her sexual availability for his financial support—do her living conditions improve.

The novel also calls attention to the unfulfilling nature of the consumerism that often accompanies the pursuit of the American Dream. Although Carrie takes pleasure in the material luxuries that she can afford as she ascends the socioeconomic ladder, she never attains lasting contentment. This sense of internal emptiness amid material wealth is also evident in Hurstwood. At the time Carrie meets him, he has largely achieved the respectability and prosperity that Carrie so desires, but his dissatisfaction with his life leads him to jeopardize both his financial security and his respectability by pursuing an extramarital affair with Carrie. His descent into penury and homelessness contribute to the novel's naturalist tone. Whereas other naturalist works portray characters contending with forces of nature in a dispassionate world, Dreiser's protagonists contend with uncaring forces of market economies that are equally uncaring. Dreiser's characters portray a philosophy of human nature in which people are unable to resist their primal urges. Carrie's financial woes early in the story compel her to take up with Drouet and then Hurstwood. Despite his initial high social standing, Hurstwood proceeds headlong into uncertain situations, unable to stop his decline. Furthermore, his feelings of defeat and failure as he loses his social standing underscore the psychological toll of society's conflation of financial success and human worth: even though Hurstwood was not happy with his existence as an affluent bar manager, his fall into destitution disheartens him to the point of suicide.

The novel's emphasis on the commercial nature of industrialized American life is particularly apparent in the commodification of the characters' relationships with one another. Carrie's relationship with her sister is cordial but not especially close, and it is clear that Minnie's reasons for allowing Carrie to stay in her apartment are partly financial: "She had invited Carrie, not because she longed for her presence, but because the latter was dissatisfied at home, and could probably get work and pay her board here. She was pleased to see her in a way but reflected her husband's point of view in the matter of work." Hanson, in turn, thinks of the arrangement in wholly pragmatic terms: "To him the presence or absence of his wife's sister was a matter of indifference . . . His one observation to the point was concerning the chances of work in Chicago." Carrie's subsequent romantic entanglements are similarly transactional in nature: although she does have genuine feelings for both Drouet and Hurstwood, their principal importance to her lies in their financial prosperity and social mobility. Hence, while her eventual willingness to leave Drouet in favor of Hurstwood is not presented as the product of cold calculation on her part, it is nonetheless an inevitable result of her social ambitions and the relatively shallow nature of her emotional connection with Drouet.

## CRITICAL RECEPTION

*Sister Carrie* was classified by critics as a part of the realist and naturalist movements of the late nineteenth century, due to its matter-of-fact portrayal of overbearing economic forces at work in urban America that limit the characters' ability to exercise their free will. Joseph Hornor Coates (1907) reviewed the second American edition of the novel published by Dodge, characterizing Dreiser as part of "the realist school" and adding that the book is a "study . . . of existing conditions operating on human impulses which are inextinguishable, and often dominating." Dreiser (1928) described in private letters his fatalistic view of the causes of Hurstwood's decline, specifically his "sense of folly" in both "having taken the money of his employers" and "his hypnosis in regard to Carrie." Robert Butler (2000) credited Dreiser with a skillful portrayal of the realities of urban life. Butler argued that Carrie's inward growth is reflected in moments where she is "gazing out of windows into urban settings," and gaining knowledge from her experiences in that urban atmosphere. Shawn St. Jean (2001) analyzed the level of determinism in the novel, anchoring his discussion in a comparison between ancient Greek notions of "the will of the gods" and contemporary understandings of "forces like heredity and social environment." St. Jean explained that the varying degrees of external influence on the novel's

different characters shows Dreiser's intent to portray "varied attempts to live successfully and happily."

The novel evoked a strong ethical reaction from readers. Its portrayal of a woman making questionable choices and still obtaining success challenged accepted conventions regarding women's behavior, criminality, and the role of literature in addressing such issues. Janet Beer (1999) accounted for the negative reviews the novel received initially because of Carrie's intention "to establish an identity at odds with the one" prescribed by her society. James L. W. West III (2000) examined the way editorial changes to the first edition of *Sister Carrie* reflect society's attitudes about alcohol, showing how the novel changes when references to liquor and drinking that were removed in the first edition became reinstated in the Pennsylvania Edition. West surmised that these cuts, and others, may have happened in the interest of removing anything "that might cause trouble with reviewers and public moralists."

James Overholtzer

Academic Advisor: Linda Wagner-Martin,
The University of North Carolina at Chapel Hill

---

## PRINCIPAL WORKS

*Sister Carrie.* Doubleday, Page, 1900. 2nd ed. *Sister Carrie.* B. W. Dodge, 1907. Rev. and enlarged ed. *Sister Carrie: The Pennsylvania Edition.* Edited by John C. Berkey et al., U of Pennsylvania P, 1981. Print. (Novel)

*Jennie Gerhardt.* Harper and Brothers, 1911. Print. (Novel)

*\*The Financier.* Harper and Brothers, 1912. Rev. ed. Boni and Liveright, 1927. Print. (Novel)

*A Traveler at Forty.* Century, 1913. Print. (Travel essays)

*\*The Titan.* John Lane, 1914. Print. (Novel)

*The "Genius."* John Lane, 1915. Print. (Novel)

*A Hoosier Holiday.* John Lane, 1916. Print. (Travel essays)

*Plays of the Natural and the Supernatural.* John Lane, 1916. Enlarged ed. *Plays, Natural and Supernatural.* London, Constable, 1930. Print. (Plays)

*Free and Other Stories.* Boni and Liveright, 1918. Print. (Short stories)

*The Hand of the Potter.* Boni and Liveright, 1918. Print. (Play)

*Twelve Men.* Boni and Liveright, 1919. Print. (Sketches)

*Hey Rub-a-Dub-Dub: A Book of the Mystery and Wonder and Terror of Life.* Boni and Liveright, 1920. Print. (Essays)

*A Book about Myself.* Boni and Liveright, 1922. Published as *Newspaper Days: A History of Myself.* Horace Liveright, 1931. Print. (Autobiography)

*The Color of a Great City.* Boni and Liveright, 1923. Print. (Sketches)

*An American Tragedy.* Boni and Liveright, 1925. 2 vols. Print. (Novel)

*Moods: Cadenced and Declaimed.* Boni and Liveright, 1926. Enlarged ed. *Moods: Philosophic and Emotional, Cadenced and Declaimed.* Simon and Schuster, 1935. Print. (Poetry)

*The Carnegie Works at Pittsburgh.* Privately printed, 1927. Print. (Essay)

*Chains: Lesser Novels and Stories.* Boni and Liveright, 1927. Print. (Short stories)

*Dreiser Looks at Russia.* Horace Liveright, 1928. Print. (Travel essays)

*Epitaph.* Heron Press, 1929. Print. (Poetry)

*A Gallery of Women.* Horace Liveright, 1929. 2 vols. Print. (Sketches)

*My City.* Horace Liveright, 1929. Print. (Prose poem)

*Fine Furniture.* Random House, 1930. Print. (Short story)

*Dawn.* Horace Liveright, 1931. Print. (Autobiography)

*Tragic America.* Horace Liveright, 1931. Print. (Essays)

*America Is Worth Saving.* Modern Age Books, 1941. Print. (Nonfiction)

*The Bulwark.* Doubleday, 1946. Print. (Novel)

*The Best Short Stories of Theodore Dreiser.* Edited by Howard Fast. World Publishing, 1947. Print. (Short stories)

*\*The Stoic.* Doubleday, 1947. Print. (Novel)

*Letters of Theodore Dreiser.* Edited by Robert H. Elias. U of Pennsylvania P, 1959. 3 vols. Print. (Letters)

*Letters to Louise: Theodore Dreiser's Letters to Louise Campbell.* Edited by Louise Campbell. U of Pennsylvania P, 1959. Print. (Letters)

*Selected Poems.* Edited by Robert Palmer Saalbach. Exposition Press, 1969. Print. (Poetry)

*Notes on Life.* Edited by Marguerite Tjader and John J. McAleer. U of Alabama P, 1974. Print. (Nonfiction)

*Theodore Dreiser: A Selection of Uncollected Prose.* Edited by Donald Pizer. Wayne State UP, 1977. Print. (Essays and journalism)

*American Diaries, 1902-1926.* Edited by Thomas P. Riggio. U of Pennsylvania P, 1982. Print. (Diaries)

*An Amateur Laborer.* Edited by Richard W. Dowell. U of Pennsylvania P, 1983. Print. (Autobiography)

*Selected Magazine Articles of Theodore Dreiser.* Edited by Yoshinobu Hakutani. Fairleigh Dickinson UP, 1985-87. 2 vols. Print. (Journalism)

*Dreiser-Mencken Letters: The Correspondence of Theodore Dreiser and H. L. Mencken, 1907-1945.* Edited by Riggio. U of Pennsylvania P, 1986. 2 vols. Print. (Letters)

*Journalism: Newspaper Writings, 1892-1895.* Edited by T. D. Nostwich. U of Pennsylvania P, 1988. Print. (Journalism)

*Theodore Dreiser's "Heard in the Corridors" Articles and Related Writings.* Edited by Nostwich. Iowa State UP, 1988. Print. (Prose)

*Fulfilment and Other Tales of Women and Men.* Edited by Nostwich. Black Sparrow Press, 1992. Print. (Short stories and sketches)

*Dreiser's Russian Diary.* Edited by Riggio and James L. W. West III. U of Pennsylvania P, 1996. Print. (Diary)

*Theodore Dreiser's "Ev'ry Month."* Edited by Nancy Warner Barrineau. U of Georgia P, 1996. Print. (Essays and reviews)

*Collected Plays of Theodore Dreiser.* Edited by Keith Newlin and Frederic E. Rusch. Whitston Publishing, 2000. Print. (Plays)

*Art, Music, and Literature, 1897-1902.* Edited by Hakutani. U of Illinois P, 2001. Print. (Essays and interviews)

*Theodore Dreiser's Uncollected Magazine Articles, 1897-1902.* Edited by Hakutani. U of Delaware P, 2003. Print. (Journalism)

*Interviews.* Edited by Rusch and Pizer. U of Illinois P, 2004. Print. (Interviews)

*Political Writings.* Edited by Jude Davies. U of Illinois P, 2011. Print. (Prose)

*The Titan: The Critical Edition.* Edited by Roark Mulligan. Winchester UP, 2016. Print. (Novel)

*These works are collectively referred to as the Cowperwood trilogy, or the Trilogy of Desire.

---

# CRITICISM

## Joseph Hornor Coates (review date 1907)

SOURCE: Coates, Joseph Hornor. "*Sister Carrie.*" Review of *Sister Carrie,* by Theodore Dreiser. *The North American Review,* vol. 186, no. 623, Oct. 1907, pp. 288-91.

[*In the following review, Coates reviews the 1907 second edition of* Sister Carrie, *crediting Dreiser with* "a power of virile earnestness and serious purpose with unusual faculty of keenly analytic characterization and realistic painting of pictures."]

Quite apart from its intrinsic merit as a work of literary art, **"Sister Carrie"** has, for the discriminating, in a marked degree the special interest which any writer's first novel possesses in proportion to the peculiarly individual power it may show as a promise for the future. In this, Mr. Dreiser's book is especially noteworthy, since rarely has a new novelist shown so singular a power of virile earnestness and serious purpose with unusual faculty of keenly analytic characterization and realistic painting of pictures. His people are real people; he compels you to know them as he knows them, to see the scenes amid which they move as he sees them. He shows absolute sincerity, he plays you no tricks; he is rigidly uncompromising, he scorns to tamper with the truth as he knows it, he refuses any subterfuges or weak dallying with what, to him at least, are the crucial facts of life. One may not always accept his philosophy fully and without reserve, but he himself believes in it. That is the general impression the book creates, and he possesses, therefore, a compelling individuality which is bound to make its mark.

The story is of Caroline Meeber, a girl of eighteen bred in a small country village where her father is a miller, who comes to Chicago to seek an independent livelihood by the work of her hands. She has never been away from home before; she knows nothing about the life of a great city, so strange and marvellous to her inexperienced girlhood. She has come, impelled by some restless but vague and as yet unconscious craving for happiness; and happi-ness in her crude and immature imaginings is confused with pleasure and the sensation of the stir of life, as it is with so many of her brothers and sisters the world over. This impressionable girl, unsuited for any successful struggle with hardship by temperament or training, is thrown into the whirlpool of city life during the years when character is beginning to form; and she is weighted by a soft attractiveness of face and gentleness of heart. In the opening chapter, on her way to Chicago she meets Drouet, a travelling salesman, who greatly influences her career. Later, she met Hurstwood, the manager of a fashionable drinking resort and in his way a man of respectable position. The conditions under which she comes to live are not justified, nor excused, by any acceptable code. But they are not uncommon, and Mr. Dreiser handles them with such delicacy of treatment and in such a clean largeness of mental attitude, that they simply enforce an impressive moral lesson. The inevitable growth of her initial yielding softness into a hard cold selfishness at the last, but which yet fails to escape from the power of unsatisfied longing, is traced with much skill and with a logic which seems unanswerable. And the parallel working out of Hurstwood's character is surely a convincing piece of literary art.

**"Sister Carrie"** is a sombre tale. It does not leave you with a bad taste in the mouth, as one says, but with something very like a heartache; an effect even more pronounced here than in Mrs. Wharton's powerful novel, "The House of Mirth," to which it bears a notable similarity in the underlying theme, although widely different in most else. Mr. Dreiser belongs to the realistic school much more distinctly than Mrs. Wharton; he falls below her in grace and beauty of style and in her own characteristic literary art, but he gains in power and in vividness perhaps. The stories told are not the same, the methods of telling differ, but the *motif* in each is at the root of it essentially the same; the tragedy of human beings who, in our present social order, do not escape the crushing weight of a surrender to primal human impulses. The two books seem inevitably in the same class; they enforce a like moral. One is the complement of the other, with little or no superficial resemblance between them other than that each is of great and sombre power and deals with the same theme—the aberrations of social mankind, in America, in its search for pleasure and in its attempts at some basis for sex relations. In the two books the practical difference is only in the variables, the theme itself is constant. Mrs. Wharton works out her problem on one side, the complex laborious pleasure-seeking cult among that small and comparatively insignificant group, the idle rich; Mr. Dreiser is concerned with the greater and far more important class, the working-people from whose ranks it is that the upper strata of the future are to inherit character; for in this country, at least, the proletary of to-day begets the leader of tomorrow. It is the great lower and middle classes, if there are such things, that count.

Human nature is a tolerably constant quantity; men and women are pretty much alike in all times and places, and in all environments. Class distinctions, so far as the humanity of their elements is concerned, are more apparent than real; men are of the same nature everywhere. To find a great difference in essential quality between the very rich and the very poor, the very good and the very bad, the very cultured and intelligent and the very ignorant and stupid, we must, after all, take our measurements with a micrometric scale, so to speak; if we attempt to gauge these human differences by the finger of God, they are hard to find. No doubt, one bacillus differs from another in length, but you cannot mark it by a yard-stick. So that the "drummer" and the saloonkeeper who are arbiters of destiny for Sister Carrie are essentially of the same sort as the men who riot in "The House of Mirth," except that they appear to have retained more human quality of redemption; and the Lily Barts of the world of fashion are but Sister Carries after all. Indeed, the title of Mr. Dreiser's book is, no doubt, intended to suggest the kinship of the world.

And in these days, perhaps more markedly in America, the process of breaking down the class barriers, of interfusion of the social strata, is taking place with notable distinctness. Not only are the upper social ranks, or what passes for such, being constantly recruited by those who have lately risen from the lower stratum, but the economic change in industrial conditions is more and more bringing all humanity into closer touch; with the result that the high and mighty influence, as never before, the desires and the ambitions, the passions, too, of those who are low in social degree. As Mr. Dreiser puts it:

> The great create an atmosphere which reacts badly upon the small. This atmosphere is easily and quickly felt. Walk among the magnificent residences, the splendid equipages, the gilded shops, restaurants, resorts of all kinds; scent the flowers, the silks, the wines; drink of the laughter springing from the soul of luxurious content, of the glances which gleam like light from defiant spears; feel the quality of the smiles which cut like glistening swords and of strides born of place, and you shall know of what is the atmosphere of the high and mighty. Little use to argue that of such is not the kingdom of greatness, but so long as the world is attracted by this and the human heart views this as the one desirable realm which it must attain, so long, to that heart, will this remain the realm of greatness. So long, also, will the atmosphere of this realm work its desperate results in the soul of man. It is like a chemical reagent. One day of it, like one drop of the other, will so

affect and discolor the views, the aims, the desires of the mind, that it will thereafter remain forever dyed. A day of it to the untried mind is like opium to the untried body. A craving is set up which, if gratified, shall eternally result in dreams and death. Aye! dreams unfulfilled—gnawing, luring, idle phantoms which beckon and lead, beckon and lead, until death and dissolution dissolve their power and restore us blind to nature's heart.

So that, from the sociological point of view, the study presented in this book of existing conditions operating on human impulses which are inextinguishable, and often dominating, is of timely import. There are signs that the future of the race in this country may be more perilous than its past has been; it is possible one of those racial crises which are constantly recurring in the history of mankind, may be on the way. "Sister Carrie" is a book to be reckoned with, just as the social conditions—or defects—on which it rests must be reckoned with.

## Theodore Dreiser (letters date 1928)

SOURCE: Dreiser, Theodore. "Dreiser Discusses *Sister Carrie*." *Masses and Mainstream*, vol. 8, no. 12, Dec. 1955, pp. 20-22.

*[In the following letters, written in 1928, Dreiser corresponds with John Howard Lawson, describing the significance of Hurstwood's decline in* Sister Carrie.]

In 1928, a young and forward-looking Broadway producer, H. S. Kraft, made contracts with Theodore Dreiser and myself for a dramatic presentation of **Sister Carrie.** I went to work on the play, in which Paul Muni was to perform the role of Hurstwood.

The plan fell through, largely because of my inability to provide an effective dramatization of Dreiser's massive and subtle novel. We discussed the use of a symbolic device—a series of interludes in which a tramp, a man destroyed by society and wandering in its lower depths, would give a poetic and prophetic sense of the fate awaiting Hurstwood. Looking back over the years, it seems obvious that the suggestion was artificial, and that it conflicted in mood and method with the naturalistic technique and profound psychological depth of the novel.

It seems to me that Dreiser's letters on the subject are of interest for two reason: they illuminate aspects of the problem of translating a novel into dramatic terms. More importantly, they express the author's feeling concerning the social background and significance of one of his greatest stories.

JOHN HOWARD LAWSON

Aug. 10, 1928

My dear Lawson:

I wished to answer your last note before this but had nothing to contribute. Since then, though, I have thought to the following effect. One of the important things of the book—*the* important thing, really—is the mental and social decay of Hurstwood. This as you know can scarcely be more than hinted at in the last act—though it's the thing that moves all of us to wish to dramatize the story. Now I have a way by which (I believe) Hurstwood's decay can be put over and the story itself strengthened by it. I offer you a choice of two prologues, one to be called *A Lodging for a Night*. This would present the old captain housing his company of bedless bums—as in the book—the house in Madison Square, his solitary presence, the gathering of the bums, his appeal and their being marched off to the Bowery. But no suggestion of any connection with the play proper—just a picture inducing a proper psychic mood for the story that follows.

Or you may take *A Cycle of Decay,* another prologue. In six scenes or eight or ten—ten-second scenes spotted against a black stage. You could show the daily content of a failure with life. He is dumped out of a full bed in a lodging house at 7 A.M. He walks the Bowery, eyes a restaurant, attempts an appeal here and there, rests wearily on a park bench or in doorway of a back street, but is driven off, tries a "mission" for warmth and a handout; does a turn in the workhouse, or begs a night in the police station, or sleeps over a warm subway grating. There is also the breadline, a snow-shoveling brigade—anything, everything. The idea though is a quick series of scenes spotted—and over in three or four minutes—yet running a complete cycle. After such a prologue—but with no direct reference to the play, the play itself might end where Hurstwood stands in the vacant room and says "Left me; left me." The minds of all, I am sure, would return to the prologue and so complete your effect. Let me know your reaction.

My compliments.
My sincere good wishes.

THEODORE DREISER

New York City, Oct. 10, 1928

My dear Lawson:

It does seem to me that you are getting much nearer the drama as well as the spirit of the book. And after a fashion I like the idea of the bum or down-and-out as suggesting what I emphasized—the need of presenting clearly the drama of Hurstwood's decay. But I think you will not get this straight, or be able to present it to the best advantage, until you ask yourself, as I asked myself a long time ago, what was it exactly that brought about Hurstwood's decline? What psychic thing in himself? For most certainly it could not have been just the commonplace knocks and errors out of which most people take their rise. It is not enough to say that he is not a strong man, or that he lacked a first class brain. Granted. And it is obvious from the

book. But there is something more. A distillation not only of his lack of strength and his mediocre brain, but of the day and the city and the circumstances of which, at say forty-odd, he found himself a part. And this is of a twofold character. First—a sense of folly or mistake in him because of his having taken the money of his employers and so having lost not only their friendship and confidence but the, for him, almost necessary milieu of Chicago—its significance as the center of his home, children, friends, connections—what you will. Next the ultimate folly of his hypnosis in regard to Carrie. For as the book shows her charm betrayed him. He erred, as he later saw it, in taking her, because she drifted from him—went her own mental way—did not sustain him. These two things, once he was out of Chicago and so away from all he had known and prized, concentrated to form a deep and cancerous sense of mistake which ate into his energy and force. It was no doubt finally the worm at the heart of his life. And without the power to destroy it he was doomed. And it is that *conviction* which is the thing that is stalking him and that is necessary to symbolize in some way. But how? By your bum who becomes a detective and then a bum again? In part, yes, I am inclined to think so, although I think it might be better if the bum never became a detective.

On the other hand, by some words of Hurstwood's here and there throughout the play—a Hamlet-like meditation, or phrase now and then—it is necessary to indicate the unchanging presence of this cancerous conviction of error—its almost psychic reality—a body and mind of defeat. For I do personally believe that in the super energies of all of us lie amazing powers. We can and do embody in the world without many things which fight or aid us. You, as you go along, will best see where and how the truth of this can be shadowed forth. But once it is in I think your listeners are likely to feel the essential awfulness of the man's fate. And so the real drama of the book. If so we are likely to have a successful play. I hope so. I like the spirit of your present outline very much and only wish I might read the completed play.

THEODORE DREISER

## Jack Salzman (essay date 1967)

SOURCE: Salzman, Jack. "The Publication of *Sister Carrie*: Fact and Fiction." *The Library Chronicle*, vol. 33, 1967, pp. 119-33.

[*In the following essay, Salzman breaks down the narratives surrounding the troubled first edition of* Sister Carrie, *noting what events can and cannot be corroborated by letters and documentation.*]

W. A. Swanberg's recent biography of Theodore Dreiser[1] makes clear the need to re-examine the now legendary story of the publication of *Sister Carrie.* For although Swanberg's account of the novel's publication is the most comprehensive we have had to date, his discussion of "L'affaire

Doubleday" and the "myth" of *Sister Carrie*'s suppression is both incomplete and, at times, inaccurate. Swanberg correctly notes that the legend of the "suppression" of *Sister Carrie* is in part erroneous and that much of the error is traceable to Dreiser himself.[2] But what he fails to point out is that "L'affaire Doubleday," as he calls it, is as much a part of literary legend as is the story of *Sister Carrie*'s suppression. And the errors, in both parts of the legend, are traceable not only to Dreiser, but also to the gullibility of those who have written about the novel, a fault from which Swanberg is not entirely excluded.

In truth, relatively little is known for certain about the publication of *Sister Carrie.* We do know that with the assistance of Arthur Henry,[3] Dreiser finished revising the manuscript of his first novel in April or May of 1900.[4] He then took it to Harper & Bros. and left the manuscript with Henry Mills Alden, editor of *Harper's Magazine.* Alden expressed his approval of the work but doubted whether any publisher would take it. Despite his scepticism, however, Alden turned the manuscript over to the publishing branch of Harper's, which eventually sent word that it would not publish the novel. In the opinion of the Harper reader, *Sister Carrie* was "a superior piece of reportorial realism—of highclass newspaper work, such as might have been done by George Ade." But the novel's many strengths notwithstanding, the reader could not imagine the book's arousing the interest of the feminine audience which "control [led] the destinies of so many novels . . ." and did not recommend it for publication.[5]

Although Harper & Bros. rejected the novel, Alden suggested that Dreiser take it to the firm of Doubleday, Page & Co., in the hope that they might be in a better position to consider publishing it. Dreiser did so, and the manuscript was turned over to Frank Norris, who was then a reader for the firm.[6] So much all scholars and critics seem to agree upon. But from this point on, fact frequently gives way to fiction, and a legend is created.

In "The Early Adventures of 'Sister Carrie,'" written thirty-one years after the fact, Dreiser told the story of "the trials and tribulations attendant upon the publication" of his first novel. According to Dreiser, Norris recommended the novel "most enthusiastically to his employers," and it seemed as if *Sister Carrie* were going to be published. But Mrs. Doubleday happened to read the manuscript and, Dreiser claimed, was horrified by its frankness:

> She was a social worker and active in moral reform, and because of her strong dislike for the book and insistence that it be withdrawn from publication, Doubleday Page decided not to put it in circulation. However, Frank Norris remained firm in his belief that the book should come

before the American public, and persuaded me to insist on the publishers carrying out the contract. Their legal adviser—one Thomas McKee who afterwards personally narrated to me his share in all this—was called in, and he advised the firm that it was legally obliged to go on with the publication, it having signed a contract to do so, but that this did not necessarily include *selling*; in short, the books, after publication, might be thrown into the cellar! I believe this advice was followed to the letter, because no copies were ever sold. But Frank Norris, as he himself told me, did manage to send some copies to book reviewers, probably a hundred of them.[7]

This account has, for the most part, gone unquestioned.[8] H. L. Mencken, Dorothy Dudley, Vrest Orton, James T. Farrell, Robert Elias, and Philip Gerber,[9] among others, give substantially the same version of the book's publication as Dreiser; a few expand upon the villainy of Mrs. Doubleday. But none of the accounts which follow Dreiser's lead is trustworthy. Dreiser's story of his own life is always of primary interest; but fact must be separated from fiction, and, all too often, Dreiser failed to do so.[10] Unfortunately, there seems to be no way of ascertaining exactly what happened after the manuscript of *Sister Carrie* was given to Frank Norris. But an examination of the letters and documents written at the time of the novel's publication gives an account quite different from those previously presented.

In an unpublished article on the suppression of *Sister Carrie,* Arthur Henry relates that Norris took the manuscript of the novel home and "before he had gone three-quarters through had become so enthused that he was telling all whom he met of his wonderful discovery."[11] He conveyed his enthusiasm for the novel to Dreiser in a now-famous letter dated 28 May 1900.[12] Norris told Dreiser that *Sister Carrie* was the best novel he had read in manuscript as reader for the firm and that, in fact, it pleased him as much as any novel he had ever read.[13] He was turning the manuscript over to Henry Lanier to read, and assured Dreiser that "I shall do all in my power to see that the decision is for publication."

Norris' letter of 28 May may have been followed by one from Lanier,[14] son of the American poet and a reader for Doubleday, Page & Co., who, "while not so enthusiastic as his junior, Mr. Norris, affirmed his belief in the power of the story, and added that he also would commend it for publication."[15] Finally, according to Henry's account, came a letter from the junior partner of the firm, Walter H. Page, who "heartily agreed with Mr. Norris that the book was a great book and added that the firm would be pleased to publish it." Page suggested that Dreiser come to his office on Monday, 11 June 1900, and "talk it over" with him. The letter is dated 9 June 1900.[16] In fact, however, Page's letter had been preceded by a second letter from

Norris (dated 8 June 1900).[17] Norris asked Dreiser to come to his hotel on Saturday, 9 June—the Saturday before the Monday on which Dreiser was to meet with Page. Norris did not tell Dreiser why he wanted to see him, but his note had a tone of urgency: "Don't fail if you possibly can help it." Although there is no way of knowing if Dreiser went to Norris' apartment, the letter itself is of considerable interest, for the urgency of Norris' request suggests that the publication of *Sister Carrie* may have already been meeting with opposition. Be that as it may, Dreiser went to Page's office on Monday, 11 June, and was well received; when he left the office, he was confident that *Sister Carrie* would soon be before the public.[18]

By mid-July no word had as yet been heard from the firm; and, because Dreiser and his wife were in Missouri, Arthur Henry went to investigate. On 14 July Henry sent a letter to Dreiser informing him that he had gone to Doubleday, Page & Co. and had spoken to Lanier, who did not know when the novel was going to be published. Henry also spoke to Lanier about Dreiser's "changing the names from those of real people to fictitious ones."[19] Lanier did not want Dreiser to use any actual names. "The fact is," wrote Henry, "that Lenier [sic] is a good deal of a cad. He knows nothing at all of real life—his nature is very shallow, and he is exceedingly conceited. We had a very warm argument on the subject. He said that all those things [the citations of actual names] seemed to him like a straining after realism ... [and] intimated to me that he would be opposed to publishing the book unless these vhanges [sic] were made."[20] At some time between the writing of this letter and 18 July, Frank Doubleday read the manuscript of *Sister Carrie* and decided not to publish it.[21] Consequently, on 19 July, Henry wrote to Dreiser:

> It has dazed me—I am amazed and enraged—Doubleday has turned down your story—He did it all by himself and to the intense surprise of Norris and Lenier [sic].
>
> I don't exactly know the real attitude of Page in the matter but I do know that he is not to be taken seriously—I think he is more suave than honest. Doubleday simply read the story by accident—Norris praised it so highly and talked so much about how great it was that he read it and took a violent dislike to it. I called on Norris last Tuesday evening and he met me with a long face. He blurted out the news as if he were stunned by it.
>
> "Doubleday" he said "thinks the story is immoral and badly written. He dont [sic] make any of the objections to it that might be made—He simply dont [sic] think the story *ought* to be published by any body first of all because it is immoral." ...[22]

Page had prepared a lengthy letter to Dreiser explaining the firm's position, but Norris suggested that Henry hold

on to it until they could get Dreiser an offer from another company.[23] Henry at first approved of the suggestion; but, as he thought the matter out, he decided that Dreiser ought to know about it at once.[24] It suddenly occurred to him, as he told Norris, that Doubleday, Page & Co. could be held to its first agreement; although no contract had been signed, "the story had been accepted by a letter. ..."[25] Norris agreed, and Henry went to see Frank Doubleday, who "finally admitted that if the firm had agreed to publish the book it would have to do so" if Dreiser insisted.[26] Henry quickly wrote to Dreiser, telling him of Doubleday's decision and urging Dreiser not to let the difficulties disturb him too much, for "the story will make all its objectors look small when it gets to the public."[27]

Dreiser received Henry's letter on 22 July; that same afternoon he received the letter Page had written on 19 July, asking Dreiser to release him from the agreement the two had reached on 11 June. "The feeling has grown upon us," Page wrote, "that, excellent as your workmanship is, the choice of your characters has been unfortunate."[28] The "kind" of people Dreiser wrote about in *Sister Carrie* did not interest Page, and he found it "hard to believe that they [would] interest the great majority of readers."[29] Nevertheless, the firm believed "heartily" in Dreiser and indulged the hope of eventually adding his name to its publishing list. But, counseled Page, "If you were to ask my advice, I should without hesitation say that *Sister Carrie* is not the best kind of book for a young author to make his first book ... a book about a different kind of material would be a better first book—even if this should be published afterwards."[30]

Dreiser sent Page's letter to Henry, asking him to hold on to it, "as it frankly acknowledges the agreement and recognizes a possible injury to me."[31] At the same time, he wrote a long letter to Page, saying that he was "loath to believe that the firm of Doubleday & Page would countenance an injury to [him]." Dreiser informed Page that his friends had "seen fit to spread news of the matter in in [sic] such a way that [he] would be looked upon as an object of curious interest if the work now failed to appear." "I should be ashamed," said Dreiser, "to face the literary coterie ... with a story of rejection." Moreover, he was convinced that a rejection of his novel after an agreement had been reached would cause him material injury and suggested, therefore, that Doubleday, Page give the matter thorough consideration before coming to a decision.[32]

Dreiser received a reply from Page dated 2 August 1900. He was told that the firm's wish to be released from their agreement was as much for his literary future as for their own good—"we think we can say even more for your benefit than for ours."[33] Once again, Page stated that his firm hoped eventually to publish Dreiser's novels and was anxious that the development of his literary career be made "in the most natural and advantageous way." The publication of *Sister Carrie* as a first novel would be a decided mistake on Dreiser's part, Page warned; it would identify him in the minds of the public with "the use of this sort of material," and would create an impression which would take years to wipe away. Page concluded his letter by remarking that while the firm believed strongly in Dreiser and had high hopes for his future, it did not believe that "any considerable financial success" could be achieved with *Sister Carrie*.[34]

Dreiser was annoyed with Page's insincerity, and his answer, though calm and dignified on the whole, was sarcastic in parts.[35] Telling Page that he had concluded to ask him to publish the novel as originally planned, Dreiser remarked that "even if this book should fail, I can either write another important enough in its nature to make its own conditions and be approved of for itself alone, or I can write something unimportant and fail, as the author of a triviality deserves to fail." As to the choice of material—"I am willing to abide by your first spontaneous judgment of that. If the public will only make the same general error I shall be highly gratified. Whatever betides on that basis there will be room for contention, which a second novel may well endeavor to dissipate." Despite his disagreement with the firm, Dreiser wanted Page to know that "I have assured myself of your sincerity & good wishes and now only wish to know that you accept my assurances in good faith. ... I hope," he concluded, "that always in the future I may be able to avail myself of your personal judgment and good feeling toward me and that I may live to win your complete approval and friendship."[36]

On 15 August 1900, Doubleday, Page & Co. made one final effort to persuade Dreiser to release them from their agreement.[37] They offered to make an appeal to Appleton, Macmillan, Dodd Mead, Stokes, or Lippincott to publish the novel that fall. If, however, Dreiser refused their offer, they would insist upon his changing several names in the manuscript. Dreiser, of course, did refuse their offer; and, on 20 August 1900, the official "Memorandum of Agreement" was signed.[38] Doubleday, Page did not like "Sister Carrie" as a title; according to Henry, "they think it ought to havea [sic] more imposing and pretensious [sic] name."[39] For this reason, both "Sister Carrie" and "The Flesh & the Spirit" are mentioned as possible titles, one to be chosen at a later date. Aside from this provision, the contract was standard: Dreiser was to receive a royalty of 10% of the retail price ($1.50) on all copies under 1,500;

12½% on the second 1,500; and 15% on all subsequent copies above 3,000.[40]

With the signing of the "Memorandum of Agreement," Doubleday, Page & Co. ended their attempt to gain Dreiser's release and immediately began the process of preparing the novel for publication. On 4 September, Frank Doubleday wrote to Dreiser and told him that the firm now felt that it was essential for the original title—"Sister Carrie"—to be retained and the names of all the real people and places to be changed. They themselves had "taken out profanity which [they] regarded as imperative."[41] For the most part,[42] Dreiser agreed with the suggestions made by Doubleday; and, on 8 November 1900, *Sister Carrie* was published.

This much can be determined from an examination of the relevant documents. Such an examination, however, does not clarify every aspect of the story. Most critics, for example, blame Mrs. Doubleday for her husband's sudden decision not to publish Dreiser's novel.[43] But these accounts are all from a common source and are unsubstantiated. In his letter of 19 July 1900, Henry wrote Dreiser that Doubleday alone had turned down *Sister Carrie*; no mention is made of Mrs. Doubleday. The following year Henry again commented on the incident, but this time he stated that Doubleday had taken the manuscript home and had given it to his wife to read. She "at once conceived a violent dislike for it," Henry wrote. "It was in her estimation, so Mr. Norris reported, vulgar and immoral. She thought that it was the kind of literature which ought not to be published."[44] The shift in emphasis from Frank Doubleday to his wife was due, quite obviously, to the report of Norris. Similarly, Dreiser's contention in "The Early Adventures of 'Sister Carrie'" that it was Mrs. Doubleday who had read the manuscript of his novel and had been horrified by its frankness, was based on a talk he had had with Norris and a later one with William Heinemann. In other words, the story of Mrs. Doubleday's role in the publication of *Sister Carrie* is based almost entirely on Frank Norris' say-so.[45]

Of course, one might reason that Norris' word is sufficient; and no other evidence is necessary. Yet there are certain questions which should be raised. First, there is the urgency of Norris' letter to Dreiser of 8 June 1900.[46] Why, we may wonder, was Norris so anxious to speak with Dreiser before Dreiser spoke to Page? And secondly, there is the letter Norris wrote to Henry on 18 July 1900:

> I have just had a talk with Mr. Page about Dreiser, and it seems that he—Page—has written a long *personal* letter to Dreiser, in which there is much more than a "turning-down" of Sister Carrie.

He thinks—and so do I—that it should go to Dreiser at once so I would not hold it up as we talked of doing last night.

Page—and all of us—Mr. Doubleday too—are immensely interested in Dreiser and have every faith that he will go far. Page said today that even if we waited until T. D. got back it would yet be time for MacMillan [sic] or some other firm to get out Sister Carrie as a fall book.

Mr. Page has some suggestions to make to T. D. and is very anxious to have a talk with him as soon as he gets back.[47]

What is striking about this letter is its professional and almost matter-of-fact tone. Norris does not sound "bitterly disappointed";[48] he does not sound angry. If anything, he sounds as business-like as Page.

Norris, in fact, seems to have been extremely cautious about criticizing the firm's handling of the situation. There are, for example, apparently no extant letters in which he expressed his discontent.[49] Dorothy Dudley, it is true, notes that Norris, in a letter to Dreiser, cursed "the company for planning to withdraw the book: 'In her [Mrs. Doubleday's] absurd opinion it was "vulgar and immoral."'"[50] But there is no evidence that such a letter was written. Rather, it seems more than likely that Norris made the remark to Henry in conversation—"It was in her [Mrs. Doubleday's] estimation, so Mr. Norris reported, vulgar and immoral"[51]—and that Miss Dudley, determined to show that the interference of Mrs. Doubleday was "a symbol of the way Americans have always entrusted to women the matter of art along with the matter of society, as unworthy of their important lives,"[52] failed to check her source. Norris may well have been protecting his position with Doubleday, Page; and it is questionable whether the anger he expressed to Henry and Dreiser was also conveyed to either Frank Doubleday or Walter Page. For whatever his role may have been in the publishing history of *Sister Carrie*—and one can still do little more than speculate—it is clear that Norris was, at the very least, a man of considerable prudence, who could be easily pacified. It is true that, according to Dreiser's account in **"The Early Adventures of 'Sister Carrie,'"** it was Norris who persuaded Dreiser to insist upon the firm's carrying out its agreement. But, as we have seen, it was Henry—not Norris—who suggested that Doubleday, Page & Co. could be forced to publish the novel.[53] And, in fact, before he even had a chance to speak with Norris, Dreiser informed Page that he would insist upon the publishers' keeping their agreement. In short, although Frank Norris was unquestionably an influential force in the publication of *Sister Carrie,* it was Arthur Henry who was the novel's most ardent early champion, and it was to him that Dreiser was most indebted.[54]

The legend surrounding the publication of *Sister Carrie,* then, is an oversimplification of the actual events. Although some aspects of the novel's publication must remain uncertain, we can now see that many of the events comprising the strange history of Dreiser's first novel have been inaccurately presented. Not only have we misunderstood the order of events and various commitments involved in the publication of *Sister Carrie,* but we may have also exaggerated the role played by Frank Norris, while perhaps unjustifiably condemning Mrs. Doubleday. Hearsay and distortion have indeed simplified and made legendary a most complex episode in American literary history.

*Notes*

1. *Dreiser* (New York, 1965).

2. *Dreiser,* p. 91.

3. Henry was city editor of the *Toledo Blade* when he met Dreiser in 1894. In 1900, Doubleday, Page & Co. published both *Sister Carrie* and Henry's novel, *A Princess of Arcady.*

4. The exact date is uncertain. Dreiser claims to have finished revising the manuscript in May 1900, whereupon he submitted it to Harper's. In "The Early Adventures of 'Sister Carrie'" (*The Colophon,* pt. 5 [1931]), he says that Harper's kept the manuscript for three weeks; in a letter to H. L. Mencken, dated 13 May 1916, he says that Harper's "promptly rejected it" (*Letters of Theodore Dreiser: A Selection,* ed. Robert Elias [Philadelphia, 1959], I, 210; hereafter cited as *Letters*). Both of these statements are contradicted by the fact that Harper & Bros. rendered its decision on 2 May 1900 (*Letters,* I, 210, fn. 6).

5. The reader's report exists only in a copy in the Dreiser Collection at the University of Pennsylvania. The report is typed and has the following note in Dreiser's hand: "Criticism from Harpers/Rendered May 2nd 1900/Took novel to Doubleday & Page." The report is reprinted in *Letters,* I, 210, fn. 6.

6. Doubleday & McClure Co. had published Norris' *McTeague* in 1899.

7. "Early Adventures," n.p.

8. See, however, Arthur H. Quinn, *American Fiction: An Historical and Critical Survey* (New York, 1936), p. 646; *Sister Carrie,* ed. Claude Simpson (Boston, 1959), p. x; and Swanberg, pp. 90-93. Max Putzel notes that since Dreiser's retrospective charge against Mrs. Doubleday "is not borne out by Dreiser's

correspondence of the time, it should perhaps be received skeptically" ("Dreiser, Reedy, and 'De Maupassant, Junior,'" *American Literature,* XXXIII [January, 1962], 470, fn. 15).

9. H. L. Mencken, *A Book of Prefaces* (New York, 1917), p. 100; Dorothy Dudley, *Forgotten Frontiers: Dreiser and the Land of the Free* (New York, 1932), pp. 171-179; Vrest Orton, *Dreiserana: A Book About His Books* (New York, 1929), pp. 13-15; James T. Farrell, "Dreiser's *Sister Carrie,*" *The League of Frightened Philistines* (New York, 1945), p. 12; Robert Elias, *Theodore Dreiser: Apostle of Nature* (New York, 1949), pp. 113-114; Philip L. Gerber, *Theodore Dreiser* (New York, 1964), pp. 72-73.

10. Although all accounts of the history of *Sister Carrie* written prior to the publication of *Letters of Theodore Dreiser* had to be based largely on Dreiser's say-so (the Dreiser-Henry-Norris-Doubleday letters not having been previously available), other evidence of Dreiser's occasional unreliability as a witness should have been sufficient warning to scholars not to let his account go unquestioned. In "The Early Adventures of 'Sister Carrie,'" for example, Dreiser claimed that Doubleday, Page & Co. did not sell one copy of his novel. The fact is, however, that 456 copies subject to royalty were sold in the United States, and Dreiser earned $68.40 in royalty fees (see the reports of sales in the Dreiser Collection at the University of Pennsylvania). To be sure, the earnings were negligible; but the book had been sold and Dreiser had been paid. And it is his contention to the contrary that makes it necessary for us to question the accuracy of the rest of his account.

11. Henry's account of the suppression of *Sister Carrie* was written some time before 8 February 1901 and is in the Dreiser Collection at the University of Pennsylvania.

12. The original letter is in the Dreiser Collection at the University of Pennsylvania. Also, see *The Letters of Frank Norris,* ed. Franklin Walker (San Francisco, 1956), pp. 60-61.

13. In his account of *Sister Carrie*'s "suppression," Arthur Henry tells of a meeting between Norris and Morgan Robertson, a writer of sea stories, during which Norris asked Robertson to convey to Dreiser his high regard for *Sister Carrie.* "I hope the house [Doubleday, Page & Co.] publishes it," Norris said. "It is a wonder." Also, see Dudley, p. 168.

14. Although Henry claims that Lanier did send Dreiser a letter, the letter is not among the Dreiser papers at the University of Pennsylvania. It is possible that Henry was actually referring to a talk he had had with Lanier on 13 July 1900 (Arthur Henry to Theodore Dreiser, 14 July 1900 [Dreiser Collection, University of Pennsylvania]).

15. Henry, "Suppression," n.p.

16. Dreiser Collection, University of Pennsylvania.

17. *Letters of Frank Norris,* p. 62.

18. See Elias, *Theodore Dreiser,* p. 112.

19. See fn. 14 above.

20. Henry to Dreiser, 14 July 1900. After telling Dreiser what Lanier had said, Henry added: "I don't believe, however, that he could prevent that. If the book is to be got out this fall, they will have to begin to set it up before long; and if I were you I would get this matter settled at once. Get the MSS. in shape and see that they go at it."

21. Failure to distinguish between the oral agreement of 11 June and the formal "Memorandum of Agreement" of 20 August 1900, has caused most critics to give an inaccurate account of the incident. Elias, for example, claims that the Doubledays read the manuscript of *Sister Carrie* after Dreiser had signed the agreement, which is not the case (*Theodore Dreiser,* pp. 112-113). Similarly, Miss Dudley has written that after Norris and Lanier, Page read the manuscript of *Sister Carrie* and "agreed with the younger men that it was a book to publish, 'a natural,' he called it. A contract was drawn up and signed by the author and these two gentlemen" (p. 170). And although the chronology of events in Swanberg's account is correct, Swanberg accepts without question comments by Thomas McKee and Dreiser, despite the fact that both men speak of a contract which never existed (McKee recalled that in Dreiser's meeting with Doubleday, Dreiser got "'tough' ... declaring that the written contract would be fulfilled, 'or else.'" And Dreiser, in a letter to Kathryn Sayre on 23 October 1929, remembered Frank Doubleday's saying: "We publish one edition as to contract, but we won't do as we would by a book we liked" [Swanberg, p. 90]).

22. Dreiser Collection, University of Pennsylvania.

23. Henry to Dreiser, 19 July 1900.

24. Henry to Dreiser, 19 July 1900. In his letter of 19 July, Henry enclosed a letter from Norris dated 18

July, in which Norris told Henry that he had changed his mind about the advisability of holding up Page's letter and suggested that it "go to Dreiser at once" (Dreiser Collection, University of Pennsylvania; also, see *Letters of Frank Norris,* p. 64). However, in a postscript to his letter, Henry told Dreiser that "the letter from Doubleday and Page has not come—I will forward it as soon as it does."

25. Henry is probably referring to Page's letter of 9 June 1900, which reads: "Dear Sir: As, we hope, Mr. Norris has informed you, we are very much pleased with your novel. If you will be kind enough to call here on Monday—preferably later than two o'clock, we shall be glad to talk it over with you. With congratulations on so good a piece of work, we are very Sincerely Yours, . . ." (Dreiser Collection, University of Pennsylvania).

26. Henry to Dreiser, 19 July 1900.

27. Henry to Dreiser, 19 July 1900.

28. Page to Dreiser, 19 July 1900 (typed copy, unsigned, in the Dreiser Collection, University of Pennsylvania; also, see *Letters,* I, 55-56).

29. Page to Dreiser, 19 July 1900.

30. Page to Dreiser, 19 July 1900.

31. Dreiser to Henry, 23 July 1900 (Dreiser Collection, University of Pennsylvania; also, see *Letters,* I, 51-54). In his letter, Dreiser suggested that Henry and Norris submit the manuscript elsewhere, while he would discuss the matter with Doubleday and Page. "If possible, you get the loan of the mss [sic] & try Macmillan's," Dreiser wrote, "while I argue. They [Doubleday, Page & Co.] put themeslves in a queer position by so strange a move and cast but poor credit upon their three readers—Norris, Lenier [sic], and Page. Are these gentlemen's opinions worth nothing then, when Mr. Doubleday objects[?]"

32. Dreiser to Page, 23 July 1900 (Dreiser Collection, University of Pennsylvania; also, see *Letters,* I, 56-59).

33. Dreiser Collection, University of Pennsylvania; also, see *Letters,* I, 60.

34. Page to Dreiser, 2 August 1900.

35. Dreiser to Page, 6 August 1900 (Dreiser Collection, University of Pennsylvania; also, see *Letters,* I, 61-63). Swanberg regards the letter as being "still polite" (p. 89). However, see Dreiser's letter to Henry,

dated 23 July 1900 (*Letters,* I, 51), in which Dreiser says that Page's letter of 19 July (see p. 123 above), "is the height of insincerity."

36. Dreiser to Page, 6 August 1900.

37. Elias incorrectly dates the letter 16 August 1900 (*Letters,* I, 63).

38. On 22 August 1900, the firm sent Dreiser two copies of the formal contract for him to sign, one of which he was to keep and one of which he was to return to the company. Thus 20 August is probably the date on which the contract was drawn up and witnessed by Frank Norris. Copies of the "Memorandum" are in the Dreiser Collection at the University of Pennsylvania and in the office of Doubleday & Co. For the firm's letter see: Doubleday, Page & Company [typed; initialed] to Dreiser, 22 August 1900 (Dreiser Collection, University of Pennsylvania).

39. Henry to Dreiser, 14 July 1900.

40. "Memorandum of Agreement."

41. Doubleday to Dreiser, 4 September 1900 (Dreiser Collection, University of Pennsylvania; also, see *Letters,* I, 63).

42. Dreiser insisted on retaining the names of Daly, Wallack's, and Delmonico's. He also objected to the suggestion that he use a title other than E. P. Roe's *The Opening of a Chestnut Burr* [sic]. Finally, Dreiser wanted to know "Since when has the expression 'Lord Lord' become profane. Wherein is 'damn,' 'By the Lord' and 'By God.'" (Dreiser to Frank Doubleday, after 4 September 1900 [Dreiser Collection, University of Pennsylvania; also, see *Letters,* I, 64-65].)

43. Elias claims that Frank Doubleday took the proofs of *Sister Carrie* home to read, where his wife discovered them; and "there their doom was pronounced" (p. 113). Miss Dudley, whose account of the novel's rejection is as imaginative as it is inaccurate, speaks of Mrs. Doubleday as "the enemy." The villain of the episode, she writes, is Propriety—only now she is "in the refined and engaging dress of Mrs. Frank Doubleday" (p. 171). And Swanberg, although he does not make Mrs. Doubleday the villain, does comment that "she agreed whole-heartedly with her husband that *Carrie* was evil" (p. 87).

44. "Suppression of *Sister Carrie.*"

45. In her account, Miss Dudley mentions Thomas McKee, the firm's lawyer, and William Heinemann,

the English publisher, as two men who supported her contention that Mrs. Doubleday censored *Sister Carrie*. But Miss Dudley cannot give conclusive proof to verify her argument. McKee, we are told, spoke of Mrs. Doubleday "as the original censor" while gossiping with Dreiser (Dudley, p. 181), and "At ... [a] dinner party—Page and Norris were present—she [Mrs. Doubleday] had asked [Heinemann] how he could have published so 'vulgar and disgraceful' a book ..." (Dudley, p. 182). These two accounts have not been substantiated by any other reports, and were made after Norris' comments to Henry. Indeed, on 23 March 1949 and 12 October 1956, McKee told Elias that Frank Doubleday disliked the book on his own and declined to go against popular taste and what he construed to be an adverse critical tide (*Letters,* II, 420, fn. 11). Moreover, Henry Lanier, much to Miss Dudley's annoyance, apparently insisted that "It was Frank [Doubleday] ... who made the trouble. He hated it enough without other influence, called it 'indecent,' and begged us to break the contract" (Dudley, p. 180). And, finally, S. A. Everitt, a member of the firm of Doubleday, Page & Co., who remembers Mrs. Doubleday imploring her husband not to publish a certain novel, cannot be sure if she was referring to *Sister Carrie* or to Tom Dickson's *Leopard's Spots,* "a libel on the Negro race" (Dudley, p. 181).

46. See p. 121 above.

47. *Letters of Frank Norris,* p. 64. The letter is here reprinted with the permission of The Book Club of California.

48. Dudley, p. 183.

49. Of course, many of Norris' letters were destroyed and their contents must remain unknown. However, in a letter to this writer, dated 3 May 1965, Norris' biographer, Franklin Walker, states that in his opinion Norris did no more than recommend the novel for publication.

50. Dudley, p. 181.

51. "Suppression of *Sister Carrie*."

52. Dudley, p. 181.

53. See p. 123 above. In addition to his letter of 19 July, Henry wrote to Dreiser on 26 July 1900: "Dear Teddie—Hold Doubleday and Page to their agreement. I have talked with Norris several times and I am convinced that this is the best thing for you to do. They admit that they are bound to publish it, if you say so and Norris agrees with me that if they do so Double-

day will soon get over his kick and that it will be a great seller. Norris, who attends to the newspapers, critics & c, will strain every nerve for the book and I know that he will be glad if the house publishes the book after all" (Dreiser Collection, University of Pennsylvania; also, see Swanberg, p. 88).

54. Interestingly enough, the first edition of *Sister Carrie* was dedicated to Arthur Henry, but in subsequent editions the dedication was deleted. Henry and Dreiser had a falling out in 1903-1904 (see Swanberg, p. 109), which explains not only the removal of the dedication, but may also explain why Dreiser exaggerated the role played by Frank Norris at the expense of Henry.

## Donald Pizer (essay date 1970)

SOURCE: Pizer, Donald. "The Problem of Philosophy in the Novel." *Bucknell Review,* vol. 18, no. 1, Spring 1970, pp. 53-62.

[*In the following essay, Pizer considers how philosophical ideas function as metaphors in two modern novels, Frank Norris's* Vandover and the Brute *(1914) and Dreiser's* Sister Carrie.]

My starting point is the unalarming but often ignored premise that there is an important difference between studying a writer's philosophy as a system of ideas and examining a particular novel by him as a philosophical novel—that is, as a work in which an ideology explicitly expressed by the author within the novel serves as a means of explicating and evaluating that novel. In order to illustrate the differences that may exist between an author's philosophy and philosophical statements by that author within a novel, I will describe how philosophical statements in novels by two American naturalists, Frank Norris and Theodore Dreiser, must be approached if these novels are to be properly criticized. The advantage of using examples from American literary naturalism is that the novels of this period, in particular the novels of Norris and Dreiser, often contain authorial quasi-philosophical discourse that is both blatantly intrusive in form and puerile in content. My intention is to demonstrate by means of these gross examples that ideas in fiction are not always what they seem to be and thus to suggest—by analogy—that ideas in contemporary fiction which are more sophisticated in content and form (as in the work of Thomas Mann or D. H. Lawrence) are also not always what they seem to be. In short, my purpose is to cast light on a problem in the analysis of contemporary fiction by discussing this problem in two somewhat earlier novels in which the problem differs in degree but not in kind from that found in recent fiction.

The first point I would like to make about philosophical ideas in fiction is that they can serve as metaphors as well as discursive statements. Ideas of this kind are a special form of "objective correlative"—special because we usually associate that term with the concrete image. Their principal role in a novel is not to articulate a particular philosophy at a particular moment but rather to contribute to an emotional reality in the work as a whole. We have come to realize that ideas have played such metaphoric roles in other literary forms in earlier literary periods. We are no longer likely to discuss Alexander Pope primarily as a spokesman for specific eighteenth-century philosophical or literary beliefs, though these beliefs are expressed by Pope in his poems. Rather, we now recognize that Pope's beliefs represent metaphoric equivalents of certain perennial states of mind and that it is these equivalents which constitute the permanent poetic thrust of his work.

We have not, however, recognized that ideas in the modern philosophical novel can be interpreted as we have interpreted ideas in earlier and different literary forms. Indeed, the fact that there is a sub-genre of modern fiction called "the novel of ideas" implies that ideas in fiction are a special literary phenomenon and that philosophical fiction is thus a special class of fiction. There are several reasons for this failure to recognize the similarity between the role of ideas in fiction and in other literary forms. The ability of the novelist to engage in lengthy philosophical discourse leads us initially to think of his ideas principally as ideas. In addition, the modern novel often expresses ideas which—unlike those of Pope—are either familiar or viable. Thus, when Mann or Lawrence voices an idea about politics or about love, his reader is apt to consider the statement as above all an idea about politics or love. He is less apt to realize that the idea might have the same relationship to the theme and form of the novel as a particular action, character, or setting.

These comments on ideas as metaphors are intended to introduce my first example of ideological expression in fiction, a passage from Frank Norris's *Vandover and the Brute.* The passage occurs at the close of Chapter XIV of the novel. Vandover, a young middle-class artist, has been living a debauched life in San Francisco since his return from Harvard. At this point in the novel, he has just discovered that he can no longer draw. His sensual excesses have caused him to contract the disease of general paralysis of the insane (or paresis), an early symptom of which is the loss of finer muscular coordination. On the night that Vandover discovers his illness, he looks over the roofs of the sleeping city and hears a flood of sound, as though from an immense beast. Norris then comments in his own voice:

> It was Life, the murmur of the great, mysterious force that spun the wheels of Nature and that sent it onward like some enormous engine, resistless, relentless; an engine that sped straight forward, driving before it the infinite herd of humanity, driving it on at breathless speed through all eternity, driving it on no one knew whither, crushing out inexorably all those who lagged behind the herd and who fell from exhaustion, grinding them to dust beneath its myriad iron wheels, riding over them, still driving on the herd that yet remained, driving it recklessly, blindly on and on toward some far-distant goal, some vague unknown end, some mysterious, fearful bourne forever hidden in thick darkness.

The passage is a statement of the idea that life is a struggle for existence. Life and its agent Nature are depicted mechanistically, as an engine which drives humanity forward, crushing the weak in the process. Although this process is ultimately beneficial, since it presses the race "forward," the primary emphasis in the passage is on the terror and awe-inspiring inexorableness of natural force. The meaning of the passage can be extracted from the novel to attribute a "hard" Darwinian philosophy to Norris, or it can be used as a commentary on the theme of the novel—that Vandover, a "laggard" in the herd of humanity because of his self-indulgence, has been caught up in the processes of nature (in this instance a debilitating disease) and will ultimately be destroyed, as indeed he is. In either instance, the passage is viewed principally as "philosophy"—that is, as an indication that Norris subscribes to a particular belief and that this belief is at the heart of *Vandover and the Brute.*

*Vandover and the Brute,* however, is only indirectly or secondarily a novel about the struggle for existence. It is primarily a novel about the choices open to the artist in late nineteenth-century America. On the one hand, Norris associated art with man's "higher" self and with effort; it represents man's ability to pursue energetically the life of the spirit. On the other hand, he believed that the artist is often the victim of excessive sensibility and sensual self-indulgence. Norris's ideal artist is close to that depicted by Browning—a figure of robust spirituality who fronts life directly. But Norris's conception of the artist was also colored by the nineteenth-century myth of the demonic, self-destructive artist as that myth reaches from Byron and Poe to Oscar Wilde and the aesthetes of the 1890's. Both of these views are present in *Vandover and the Brute,* but the novel is informed principally by Norris's deep-seated belief that though the Browningesque ideal exists as ideal, most artists are incapable of reaching it and therefore succumb to their demonic tendencies.

Norris's method of dramatizing this belief in *Vandover and the Brute* was to cast Vandover's decline in the form of a middle-class parable. After being introduced to the pleasures of the city, Vandover commits the heinous sin of seducing, getting pregnant, and not marrying a middle-class girl. He then loses the positive influences of Home and a Good Woman, and falls under the dominion of Drink, Gambling, and Disreputable Women until—a second heinous sin—he gambles and dissipates away his inheritance and is left ravaged by disease and poverty. *Vandover* is thus above all a parable of the Way to Hell available to the young American artist in a late nineteenth-century American city.

It is now clear, I trust, that Norris used the idea or philosophy of the struggle for existence in *Vandover and the Brute* primarily to make concrete the dangers inherent in the career of a self-indulgent, middle-class artist. The struggle-for-existence idea in *Vandover,* in other words, is principally an image of fear. Norris does indeed subscribe to the idea as idea, but the major function of this idea in the novel is not to state the idea but to dramatize the emotion. Its role is to make compelling an emotion which exists independent of the idea, an emotion which Norris might have expressed by some other means. His choice of this particular idea as a metaphor of fear was therefore primarily a product both of the contemporary pervasiveness and vitality of the idea and of its adaptability to his own ends.

Much of the critical attack on Norris in recent years has been concentrated on his simpleminded and overstated philosophical ideas. But ideas of this kind can contribute to a novel if they have principally a metaphoric function. Once it is recognized that fear permeates Norris's depiction of the artist, it is necessary to evaluate his philosophical passages dealing with the artist at least in part on the basis of the metaphoric impact of these passages rather than entirely on the basis of their intrinsic superficiality or melodramatic imagery. The philosophy of these passages may indeed be both superficial and overstated, but it can nevertheless successfully communicate the reality of fear. In all, the philosophy of the struggle for existence in *Vandover* should be viewed as a modern critic might view the pastoralism of a Renaissance poet. It should be considered primarily as a device by which the artist can transform a quasi-philosophical idea into evocative metaphor. The artist's success in this endeavor, whether he be Renaissance poet, naturalistic novelist, or contemporary writer of fiction, is more dependent upon his emotional resources and literary skill than on the permanent validity of the idea which serves as his controlling metaphor.

The second point that I intend to make about philosophical ideas in fiction is that such ideas are often inadequate guides to the interpretation of the novel in which they appear. Although the novelist seems to be supplying in a philosophical passage an interpretive key to the events he is portraying, he may have a false or superficial discursive grasp of the meaning of these events. Since an author's explicit commentary can run counter to the dramatic action of a novel, the function of the critic may be to apply yet another critical truism current in the criticism of other literary forms—that an artist is often an unsatisfactory commentator on the meaning of his own work. Again, it is more difficult to apply this dictum to the criticism of fiction than to the interpretation of other forms. An authorial comment within the work itself—as in a philosophical passage in a novel—appears to have more validity than an authorial comment in a letter or an essay. The first kind of comment seems weighty because of its immediacy; the second—removed from the work in time and place—can be viewed more objectively. But the history of literature abounds in examples of writers who are both great artists and inadequate critics of their own work, and we should not permit the presence of an author's philosophy in his novel to obscure the possibility of authorial myopia when we interpret that novel.

The philosophical passage from the work of Theodore Dreiser which I will examine occurs in *Sister Carrie* at the opening of Chapter VIII. At the close of the previous chapter, Carrie has left the Hansons' Chicago flat to move into a room which Drouet has taken for her. In nineteenth-century sentimental terms, she is soon to decide that a comfortable existence as a fallen woman is preferable to the hard life of a poor but honest working girl. Dreiser begins Chapter VIII with a lengthy philosophical commentary on Carrie's action:

> Among the forces which sweep and play throughout the universe, untutored man is but a wisp in the wind. Our civilization is still in a middle stage, scarcely beast, in that it is no longer wholly guided by instinct; scarcely human, in that it is not yet wholly guided by reason. On the tiger no responsibility rests. We see him aligned by nature with the forces of life—he is born into their keeping and without thought he is protected. We see man far removed from the lairs of the jungles, his innate instincts dulled by too near an approach to free-will, his free-will not sufficiently developed to replace his instincts and afford him perfect guidance. He is becoming too wise to hearken always to instincts and desires; he is still too weak to always prevail against them. As a beast, the forces of life aligned him with them; as a man, he has not yet wholly learned to align himself with the forces. In this intermediate stage he wavers—neither drawn in harmony with nature by his instincts nor yet wisely putting himself into harmony by his own free-will. He is even as a wisp in the wind, moved by every breath of passion, acting now by his will and now by his instincts, erring with one, only to

retrieve by the other, falling by one, only to rise by the other—a creature of incalculable variability. We have the consolation of knowing that evolution is ever in action, that the ideal is a light that cannot fail. He will not forever balance thus between good and evil. When this jangle of free-will and instinct shall have been adjusted, when perfect understanding has given the former the power to replace the latter entirely, man will no longer vary. The needle of understanding will yet point steadfast and un-wavering to the distant pole of truth.

In Carrie—as in how many of our worldlings do they not?—instinct and reason, desire and understanding, were at war for the mastery. She followed whither her craving led. She was as yet more drawn than she drew.

The philosophy of the passage combines Spencerian evolutionary ideas and popular "ethical culture" thought, a combination much in vogue among liberal, non-denominational clergymen in the 1890's. Man is pictured as a dualistic creature. He still responds instinctively to life because of his animal heritage, yet he is also capable of rational choice. Nature ("the forces of life") is the absolute moral norm: if man were entirely instinctive in his actions, he would be in accord with that norm; if by free will he could choose the way of nature, he would also be acting correctly. Evolution is progressing in the direction of complete rational choice of nature's way. But at present man often finds himself divided and misled because of the conflicting demands of instinct and reason.

The passage, as becomes obvious in the concluding short paragraph, is an apology for Carrie's impending choice of an immoral life with Drouet. Carrie will sense the "wrongness" of the decision, Dreiser implies, because of the glimmerings of reason. But she is dominated by her instinctive needs—by the fact that Drouet represents at this point the full, rich life of Chicago which her imagination has pictured, and that he will supply shelter, warmth, clothing, and food (as well as appreciation and a kind of love) on a level far superior to that offered by the Hansons and on a level commensurate with her sensual nature, with her "craving for pleasure" (Chap. IV). These instinctive needs associate Carrie with "the tiger [on whom] no responsibility rests"; but they do not disassociate her actions from moral judgment. Man's "reason" permits him to recognize that Drouet represents an inadequate—that is, immoral—fulfillment of Carrie's instinctive needs. Carrie herself, however, finds her instinctive needs too strong, her reason undeveloped and indecisive, and so she "followed whither her craving led. She was as yet more drawn than she drew."

Dreiser's attempt in the passage is to free Carrie from moral responsibility for her action—to suggest that not only Carrie but most men at this intermediate stage of

evolutionary development are more led (and misled) than leading. But the passage also judges Carrie's action even though it does not judge Carrie herself. Going to live with Drouet—that is, sexual immorality—is not the "way of nature," Dreiser suggests. Some day, when evolution has progressed further, the "ideal" and the "distant pole of truth" will unwaveringly guide man, and the unmistakable implication is that they will not guide him toward sexual promiscuity.

The passage is readily understandable in the context of the late 1890's. Dreiser had just depicted his heroine as about to undertake a promiscuous life; his philosophical comments permitted him to placate the moral values of his age. Indeed, his comments also placated his own moral sense, for Dreiser in 1899 was in many ways still a conventional moralist when publicly judging the actions of others. A problem arises, however, if one attempts to apply the meaning of the passage to an interpretation of the dramatic action of the novel as a whole—that is, if one concludes that the reader is supposed to sympathize and identify with Carrie's instinctive drive toward "happiness" and "beauty" throughout the novel while simultaneously condemning the means she uses to achieve these goals. Such an interpretation of the novel as a whole is false. The three men in Carrie's life—Drouet, Hurstwood, and Ames—represent an upward movement on Carrie's part. Drouet introduces Carrie to a middle-class world of comfort, show, and finery; Hurstwood to a world of personal and social power; and Ames to that of the intellect. Each relationship serves to refine Carrie's response to life, to raise her above her previous values and desires to a higher stage of development and awareness. Happiness and beauty will never be hers, Dreiser tells us at the end of the novel, but it is clear that she is at least seeking them at a higher level with Ames than was possible with the Hansons. Within the dramatic context of the novel, therefore, Carrie's two illicit relationships are the opposite of what Dreiser has suggested about such relationships in his philosophical passage. They are moral rather than immoral, since they contribute to Carrie's "spiritual" development. In the course of the novel Dreiser has unconsciously changed his moral norm from one which explicitly condemns specific acts of immorality to one which implicitly renders these acts as moral if they contribute to a larger good.

Dreiser's philosophical comments in Chapter VIII play a meaningful fictional role at that particular point of the novel. They contribute to the reader's compassion for Carrie ("a wisp in the wind") while disarming his possible moral judgment of her. The comments, in other words, are part of Dreiser's characterization of Carrie. But if we accept these comments as relevant to the themes of the novel as a whole, we will be interpreting and evaluating *Sister Carrie* on a level appropriate to the articulated conventional moral philosophy of Dreiser's day rather than on the level of Dreiser's inarticulate unconventional sense of the meaning of experience, a sense expressed by the dramatic action of the novel. And it is no doubt Dreiser's responses to life rather than his explicit comments on life which are the source of the "power" that many readers acknowledge in his fiction.

I have been attempting to suggest by means of two philosophical passages in American naturalistic novels that criticism of fiction must explicate such passages as complex fictional constructs rather than respond to them solely as ideas. The literal meaning of such passages may represent only a portion of their meaning (as in *Vandover*) or it may be an inadequate meaning (as in *Sister Carrie*). The presence in fiction of ideas of this kind is not, I believe, an immediate sign of aesthetic weakness. Rather, their presence suggests the rhetorical similarities between fiction and other literary forms in which ideas have always been more or less than ideas. All writers are "makers," and an idea in a novel is as much a "made" object as a character or an event. Our difficulty as critics of philosophical novels stems in part from our professional intellectuality, since we tend to assume that writers, as intellectuals, do not make ideas but think them. Our task as critics of philosophical fiction, however, requires that we not only understand an idea in a novel but, in a sense, that we refuse to understand it.

**Robert James Butler (essay date 1980)**

SOURCE: Butler, Robert James. "Movement in Dreiser's *Sister Carrie*." *The Dreiser Newsletter*, vol. 11, no. 1, Spring 1980, pp. 1-12.

[*In the following essay, Butler examines images of movement and mobility in* Sister Carrie, *discussing how the novel explores "the possibilities and limitations of motion."*]

One of the central and most distinctive values in American culture is a desire for pure motion, movement for its own sake. A relatively new and chronically rootless society, America has always placed an unusually high premium on mobility rather than security and stability. It is not surprising, therefore, that American literature is densely populated with heroes and heroines who try "to find in motion what was lost in space"[1]—people on the move who are in quest of settings which are fluid enough to

accommodate their passion for a radical independence and completely open possibilities. As Henry Nash Smith and others have cogently argued, Cooper's West, Melville's ocean, Twain's river and Whitman's open road are the mythic places Americans yearn for. John Steinbeck observed in his own travels at the end of his career that the quintessential American impulse is a reflexive wish simply to *move*:

> I saw in their eyes something I was to see over and over again in every part of the nation—a burning desire to go, to move, to get under way, anyplace, away from any Here. They spoke quietly of how they wanted to go somewhere, to move about, free and unanchored, *not toward something but away from something*. I saw this look and heard this yearning everywhere in every state I visited. Nearly every American hungers to move.[2]

(Italics added)

Constance Rourke in *American Humor* similarly speaks of "that perpetual travel which often seemed the single enduring feature of the country."[3] Indeed, one might validly distinguish American literature from the literature of other Western countries in terms of this quest for pure motion. Whereas, for example, movement in the classic English novel is usually directed toward a definite place, a coherent set of tested values and a secure niche in a stable society, movement in the representative American novel is nearly always *undirected,* an open-ended process. Tom Jones, Joseph Andrews, Oliver Twist and even Robinson Crusoe see their journeys as a necessary evil, a way of working out their identities in a place-oriented society, but Jack Kerouac longs simply to be *on* the road itself, knowing full well that the place at its end will most probably be a disappointment. Odysseus moves consciously and instinctively homeward to a wife and a hierarchical society, but Rip Van Winkle ambles off to the woods so that he can avoid both. Don Quixote leaves his kingdom and Dulcinea always to return, but Huckleberry Finn lights out to the territories and never looks back. At the end of *Heart of Darkness*, Marlowe will settle for the illusion of civilization and will tell the lies necessary to maintain this illusion, but Natty Bumppo holds steadfastly to the integrity he feels is threatened by civilization and moves toward an ever-expanding wilderness.

Significantly too, the American version of *The Divine Comedy*, Whitman's *Leaves of Grass,* never defines in any clear way the exact end of its quest. Unlike Dante, who can imagine, metaphorically at least, a clearly defined Heaven down to its minutest physical and spiritual details, Whitman is intent on giving up impressionistic images of constant motion—travelling an open road, wandering along an indefinite sea coast, searching for an infinite West. The journey he tramps is indeed "perpetual,"[4] a process of becoming rather than a state of being.

\* \* \*

*Sister Carrie* epitomizes this American tradition, for it is in many ways a novel about the possibilities and limitations of motion. The novel's remarkable opening scene is a splendid illustration of this. Carrie Meeber, like Benjamin Franklin and a host of other American protagonists, easily separates herself from family, past and a fixed society and sets herself in motion, pursuing goals she can only vaguely sense. The train ride to Chicago "irretrievably" severs all her connections with "girlhood and home,"[5] bringing her to a world of radically expanded possibilities. It is indeed revealing that the first human relationship she forms in this strange new world is with Drouet, a travelling salesman whose very life consists of constant movement. Like Mrs. Vance, who "can't" stay more than six months in one place" (502), Drouet is "a moth of the lamp" (71), a person who is incapable of living a genuinely settled life. This accounts in no small measure for Carrie's favorable reaction to him. He is a perfect mirror image of her own restless tendencies.

Likewise, most of the other major scenes in the novel envision people in motion. Hurstwood proposed to Carrie while they are walking through Jefferson Park. She makes her most serious commitment to him as the two speed madly to Montreal. And the novel ends with a brilliant collage of motion scenes—"gaunt men shuffling" (543) in front of a mission house as they await a handout, Drouet and an anonymous friend setting out for a night of pleasure in New York, Mrs. Hurstwood and her daughter on their way to a vacation in Rome and Carrie gently rocking as she tries to conceive of a new life for herself. It is no coincidence that Hurstwood commits suicide at the end of the novel only after he has exhausted the possibilities of these forms of movement. Returning to a flophouse after milling about the streets and falling several times in the snow, he pulls off his shoes and "lay down" (554), only to arise a few moments later to turn on the gas. The heavy snow which covers New York on the night of his death is a striking metaphor of the world which has defeated him, a world which denies him the secure foothold necessary for purposeful movement:

> Hopelessly he turned back into Broadway again and slopped onward and away, begging, crying, losing track of his thoughts, one after another, as a mind decayed and disjointed is wont to do.

> It was a truly wintry evening, a few days later, when his one distinct mental decision was reached. Already at four o'clock, the sombre hue of night was thickening the air. A heavy snow was falling—a fine picking, whipping snow, borne forward by a swift wind in long, thin lines. The streets were bedded with it—six inches of cold carpet, churned to a dirty brown by the crush of teams and the feet of men.

(548)

One crucial index to Carrie's sensibility is her emotional response to motion. Movement at many key points in the novel intoxicates her because she senses it as a magical release from the limits of a prior mode of existence. She is easy prey for Drouet in the novel's opening scene partly because the exciting movement of the train has helped to dissolve the moral restraints of her earlier life. She is nearly hypnotized by the protean nature of Chicago because she feels that it is a dynamic world which is always offering fresh possibilities. As she walks to the theatre with Drouet, for example, she is greatly impressed with the lively spectacle of the city at night. The "sputtering" (87) are lights, the strong winds and the constant jostle of people in the streets suggest for her a marvellous world of constant novelty. The city's hypnotic influence" (89) is traceable in no small measure to "the swirl of life" (88) that it represents for her.

While riding on North Shore Drive with Mrs. Hale, Carrie's powerful imagination transforms the scene into a Dreiserian fairy land. The physical motion she experiences here is an appropriate analogue to her equally unsettled feelings:

> She gazed and gazed, wondering, delighting, longing, and all the while the siren voice of the unrestful was whispering in her ear.

(128)

The sequence ends later that night in Carrie's apartment, where she again conjures up the magic of Chicago while she hypnotically rocks and sings:

> The glow of the palatial doors was still in her eye, the roll of the cushioned carriages still in her ears. ... At her window, she thought it over, rocking to and fro, and gazing out across the lamp-lit park toward the lamp-lit houses on Warren and Ashland avenue. She was too wrought up to go down and eat, too pensive to do aught but rock and sing.

(128)

This kind of motion releases "siren voices" which go to the core of her deepest longings. While she experiences such motion, it becomes nearly impossible for Carrie to respond to her world in any clear, rational way. It is significant, therefore, that Hurstwood usually works his romantic charms on her while the two are either walking or riding.

While they are riding through Washington Boulevard, Carrie is unable to resist his declaration of love, partly because the slow, drifting movement of the elegant carriage helps to put her conscious mind to sleep. In a later scene which pictures them lazily walking through Jefferson Park, Dreiser consciously employs the nautical metaphor used throughout the novel to suggest a delicious mental drifting. While they walk, Carrie's psychological "flood-gates" (222) open and we observe her "illogically drifting and finding nothing at which to catch" (222). She fully accepts Hurstwood's bogus proposal on a totally irrational basis, knowing very little about him or the kind of future which is possible for them. She agrees to "come away" (223) with him without ever considering *where* they will go or *what* they will do! In an archetypally American way, Carrie naively assumes that travelling to another place will dissolve their pasts and solve their problems. The scene ends, ironically, with Carrie pictured as "tripping elatedly away" (225).

But by far the best example of the nearly mesmeric effects of motion on Carrie is her extraordinary flight to Montreal. Although it is difficult to account in rational terms for such a "strange pilgrimage" (292), Dreiser makes this pivotal scene altogether plausible in terms of his heroine's deepest subconscious impulses. For Carrie goes to Montreal and New York because her instincts, imagination and heart reflexively equate motion with possibility. At the very beginning of Chapter 29, appropriately entitled "The Solace of Travel: The Boats of the Sea," Dreiser editorially comments on these motives:

> To the untravelled, territory other than their own familiar heath is invariably fascinating. Next to love, it is the one thing which solaces and delights. Things new are too important to be neglected, and mind, which is a mere reflection of sensory impressions, succumbs to the flood of objects. Thus lovers are forgotten, sorrows laid aside, death hidden from view. There is a world of accumulated feelings back of the trite expression—"I am going away."
>
> As Carrie looked out upon the flying scenery she almost forgot that she had been tricked into this long journey against her will and that she was without the necessary apparel for travelling. She quite forgot Hurstwood's presence at times, and looked to homely farmhouses and cosey cottages with wondering eyes. It was an interesting world for her. Her life had just begun. She did not feel herself defeated at all. Neither was she blasted in hope. The great city held much. Possibly she would come out of bondage into freedom—who knows?

(305)

As Dreiser makes abundantly clear here, her principal motive for going to Montreal is not her "love" for Hurstwood, although she still is very much attracted to him. It is ex-

tremely significant that Dreiser tells us that she quite forgets about Hurstwood at times during the journey, so enraptured does she become with a vision of her new life. Such a life is not tied to either a person or a particular place. The "great city" is *any* place of expanded possibility. Carrie's vision of her future centers instead around a process of liberation, a chance to start over and become anything she wants to be. It is the American quest for constant metamorphosis, unlimited personal development.

This is what the flight to Montreal suggests to her, and this explains why Carrie does not get off the train even after she discovers that she has been crudely tricked by Hurstwood. Although she consciously articulates a desire to leave the train, she fails to act on this understandable motive when given the chance to do so. Instead, she soon becomes fascinated by the train's movement, associating it at one very revealing point with a haunting music:

> The train was speeding with steady grace across the fields through patches of wood. The long whistles came with sad, musical effect as the lonely woodland crossings were approached.
>
> Now the conductor entered the car and took up the one or two fares that had been added at Chicago. He approached Hurstwood, who handed out the tickets. Poised as she was to act, Carrie made no move.

(297)

Carrie fails to act on her rational ideas because she has been overwhelmed by the train's motion and the blues-like music it creates. For music has often been associated in Carrie's mind with her deepest, most romantic longings. Her habit of singing while she rocks is used consistently as a kind of incantation which springs forth visions of possibility. The "sad musical effect" of the train whistle, therefore, stimulates Carrie's imagination on its most profound level, causing her to see her journey in strongly positive terms.

Curiously, one of Carrie's most anxious moments in the flight sequence occurs when the train actually stops. This allows her to act rationally, but it also points her backward to a past she has grown dissatisfied with. When the train resumes its "rapid motion" (301), Carrie is relieved because this allows her to act upon dreams which point her toward an open future. "As the train swept on frantically through the shadow to a newer world" (302), Carrie relaxes and feels strangely in control of her destiny.

\* \* \*

It is a commonplace of Dreiser criticism that *Sister Carrie* employs upward and downward movements as a basic structural principle. As Kenneth Lynn has observed:

The world that Dreiser portrays is a ceaseless flux, a fluid, wide-open universe in which people are constantly rising or falling ... In such a world the only reality is movement, the only good is upward movement.[6]

Donald Pizer goes so far as to claim: "To describe *Sister Carrie* appears to be an exercise in stating the obvious: Carrie rises and Hurstwood falls."[7] Although these critics are surely correct when they point out the prominence of such movement as a structural principle in this novel, they oversimplify matters by insisting that it is the *only* important form of movement which gives the novel shape and meaning. For Dreiser was careful to use other forms of motion to enrich and complicate his narrative. He constructs the metaphor of motion so that its complex implications can be seen from a number of revealing angles. Contrasting upward and downward patterns as a a major plot design, he also is very much interested in counterpointing centripetal and centrifugal motion as another major plot device. Furthermore, he assigns rocking movements two distinct and crucial meanings. The net effect of all this is to differentiate Carrie from all other characters in the novel. Ultimately, she is capable of "moving" in ways which enable her to attain a status which is denied Hurstwood, Drouet and Ames.

The opening scene of the novel offers an interesting contrast between centripetal and centrifugal movements. As Carrie moves away from the village, the center of her previous life, she is drawn to another center, Chicago, which the chapter heading tells us is "The Magnet Attracting" (1). Chicago itself is perceived both centripetally and centrifugally. Not only does its commercial power attract people and businesses into itself, but it also expands wildly to bewilderingly empty suburbs:

Street-car lines had been extended far out into the open country in anticipation of rapid growth. The city had laid miles of streets and sewers through regions where, perhaps, one solitary house stood alone—a pioneer of the populous ways to be. There were regions open to the sweeping winds and rain, which were yet lighted throughout the night with long blinking lines of gas lamps, fluttering in the wind. Narrow board walks extended out, passing here a house and there a store, at far intervals eventually ending in the open prairie.

(16-17)

Like many people in the novel, Chicago moves too quickly and uncritically to acquire any genuinely moral character. Incoherently drifting outward and brutally drawing people to its turbulent center, it becomes for Dreiser an image of vast, uncontrolled forces exerting themselves in a disturbingly inhuman way. It is more a bewildering *process* than a stabilizing place.[8]

Hurstwood's conduct in the novel can be seen as a series of mindless movements away from and toward centers. His family and job initially center his life, but these are revealed as mere outward contrivances having little or nothing to do with Hurstwood as a man. Likewise, his attraction to Carrie is grounded in blind impulse and, as his life is drawn towards her, his family and job automatically disintegrate for him. His flights to Montreal and New York are also impelled by strong animal drives which he is powerless to either control or understand. It is noteworthy too that when he settles in New York he is disastrously shut out from the "walled city" (363). Cut off from any real center which might vivify and concentrate his life, he apathetically drifts from one experience to another. Ultimately, he is paralyzed, his powers of magnetic attraction completely neutralized:

All day and all day, here he sat, reading his papers. The world seemed to have no attraction.

(392)

The most important use of movements toward and away from centers, however, is contained in the four vignettes placed at the end of the novel. Inverting the traditional form of the sentimental novel which neatly ties together the various strands of its stories, Dreiser creates an appropriately fragmented ending by keeping the lives of his major characters separate. Just as each of these people had earlier been drawn toward each other, creating circles of warmth and dependence, they now wander off in their own directions, never to see or influence each other again. The final effect of this remarkable series of scenes is to go to the very core of the novel's meaning—a revelation of a world which is always changing, falling apart and reconstituting itself in new ways.

Such a radically unstable world finally destroys Hurstwood because he is unable to find anything to center his life around. Drouet and Mrs. Hurstwood are doomed to lives which are completely lacking in continuity and depth. It is Carrie's triumph, however, to survive in such a protean world without doing violence to herself as a person. For as the life around her swirls in circles of amoral force, she can transcend this outward movement by an inward journey to the self. This centripetal motion, as opposed to mere climbing in a materialistic society, is what Dreiser finally endorses.

Drouet, who is ultimately described as "an old butterfly" (550), will never really achieve anything in life beyond his own comfort, and his best days are quickly passing. He is not exempt from the decay which has claimed Hurstwood. Mrs. Hurstwood and her daughter are likewise portrayed in motion which is outwardly glamorous but tinged with corruption and, quite possibly, failure. On a train speeding for a vacation in Rome, they lead uncentered lives devoid of real feeling and purpose. Jessica, who has recently entered into a loveless marriage and who is shown eyeing a banker's son, could very well repeat her father's mistakes. Although her lavish clothes now hide the fact, Mrs. Hurstwood is growing old and is just as cold and supercilious as her daughter.

But one of the most important contrasts worked out in the novel is the difference between the rocking motions associated with Carrie and those linked with Hurstwood. For the latter person, rocking becomes an obvious manifestation of his psychological inertia and final despair. No longer able to function in the brutally competitive environment of New York (he fails interestingly enough, in his attempt to be a streetcar conductor), he retreats into the rocking chair as an admission of his defeat. Warmed by the radiator and lulled into insensitivity by the hypnotic rocking motion, he can easily indulge in his illusions and create for himself a conveniently romanticized past. The newspapers keep him at a safe remove from actual experience—he vicariously enjoys the life they record without risking his own emotions. By the end of the novel, he is reduced to the state of a small child being rocked. Chewing his fingers as he moves back and forth, he gazes mindlessly down at a blank floor.

Carrie's rocking chair is quite another matter. Although Hurstwood's futile movements in the end reduce themselves to paralysis, Carrie is given a way out of this naturalistic trap. For Carrie's rocking is consistently endowed with creativity. Instead of curling up next to a warm radiator, she characteristically places the chair next to a window which provides her with a fresh vista. In chapter four, for instance, she rocks and looks out onto "the pleasantly lighted street" (32), as her intense imagination conjures up vivid prospects of her future. Her rocking is thus contrasted with the "humdrum mechanical movement" (40) of her sister's household. Whereas Minnie accepts a world of grinding poverty and unrewarding labor, Carrie's superior imagination can lift her well beyond this dreary treadmill.

Carrie's rocking is also an occasion for what little clear thinking she is able to do in the novel. In chapter 12 it steadies her mind as she begins to realistically assess Drouet's limitations. She can also evaluate Hurstwood more clearly as she rocks in chapter 32: "She was rocking and beginning to see" (359).

It is notable too that Carrie is often presented as singing while she rocks—a marked contrast to Hurstwood pursuing the sterile newspapers which deaden his mind. The final image we have of Carrie, therefore, is rich and evocative. Singing and dreaming as she rocks, she is perhaps on the verge of a kind of motion which nobody else in the novel is capable of—a creative and vital centripetal journey into the self.

In the final analysis, Carrie is disillusioned with the nervous, amoral culture which she has moved through and mastered, and she is shown as struggling for something more humane and satisfying:

> In her rocking chair she sat, when not otherwise engaged— singing and dreaming.
>
> Thus in life there is ever the emotional and intellectual nature—the mind that reasons and the mind that feels. Of one come the men of action—generals and statesmen; of the other, the poets and dreamers—artists all.
>
> As harps in the wind, the latter respond to every breath of fancy, voicing in their moods all the ebb and flow of the ideal.

(555)

It is this longing for the ideal that lifts Carrie above all the other characters in the novel. Ames, probably a weakling himself, has at least stimulated Carrie's mind and aesthetic sense to the point where she is capable of genuine inward development. In a world of garish appearances and aimless drifting, Dreiser suggests, Carrie may have found an adequate foundation for human living.

It is therefore of paramount importance that by the end of the novel Carrie has abandoned her faith in outward, spatial movement. She refuses the offer to go on the road as a travelling performer, preferring instead the introspective world of her apartment. One must realize, however, that Dreiser presents all this simply as a possibility. It remains to be seen whether Carrie can in fact act upon this new set of longings. Although she is blessed with a superior imagination that develops greatly in the course of the novel, one still does not know whether this will be her salvation or her undoing. Ames has indeed "pointed out a farther step" (557), but he is not a very impressive embodiment of these ideals himself. Surely, he is another person Carrie will inevitably outgrow. And we also have evidence in the novel that the ideal can delude as well as ennoble. The "big motherly woman" (540) who feeds Bowery derelicts does neither herself nor her clients any real favors by her misconceived generosity. The same can be said of the bizarre captain who arranges for the beds his gathered wanderers will sleep in. As much as Dreiser admires the motives of these two humanitarians, he is forced to admit that the net result of their efforts is negligible. They do little more than forestall the inevitable.

One is never fully convinced either of Carrie's skills as an artist. The roles allotted her as an actress steadily improve, but she still has not demonstrated an ability to transcend the melodrama and low comedy that has made her popular. Then too, it is doubtful whether the aesthetically limited American stage of the 1890's could provide her with the kind of serious work Ames prescribes.

* * *

Dreiser's use of the metaphor of motion, therefore, distinguishes the quality of his naturalism from that practiced by Stephen Crane and Frank Norris. Novels such as *Maggie, A Girl of the Streets* and *McTeague* take an almost perverse pleasure in reducing character movement to inertia and stasis, but Dreiser may finally give his heroine the possibility of humanly meaningful movement. Maggie Johnson's various squirmings inevitably result in her depressing plunge into a filthy river, and McTeague's escape is predictably futile. But Carrie *may* have succeeded in transcending the outward movement which the naturalistic character is usually chained to. Accordingly, she may provide us with convincing proof that human beings may ascend as well as descend the evolutionary ladder. Her "innate refinement" (107) might ultimately have found new and creative channels for development in the pursuit of the ideal and the cultivation of the inner life. Dreiser, after collapsing the American myth of spatial movement in classic naturalistic fashion, suggests that this myth may acquire new vitality if translated into psychological and aesthetic terms.

### Notes

1. Tennessee Williams, *The Glass Menagerie* (New York: 1945), p. 115.

2. John Steinbeck, *Travels with Charley* (New York: 1961), p. 10. Robert Elias made a similar point about Dreiser's early life when he observed: "From almost the day of his baptism he was part of a family that was on the move . . . At no time had he been able to strike roots anywhere: at no time could home remain comfortably associated with one house or city." (*Theodore Dreiser: Apostle of Nature* [New York: 1949], pp. 6-7.) Many other biographers have commented that Dreiser's adult life, especially the period preceding and postdating *Sister Carrie,* was remarkable for its restlessness. Between 1894 and 1903 he lived in a bewildering number of places and assumed a great many roles. Perhaps the most dramatic example of Dreiser's propensity for motion was his attempt to overcome a bout of depression with a three-hundred mile *walk* through Maryland, Dela-

ware and Pennsylvania. (See Moer's *Two Dreisers* [New York: 1969], p. 174.)

Characters in Dreiser's other major novels are inclined to a similar wanderlust. Clyde Griffiths is an incurable drifter who characteristically tries to "solve" problems by running away from them. Frank Cowperwood is also a creature of motion who is temperamentally incapable of accepting any settled mode of existence. He enjoys New York and Chicago because they are turbulent centers of change and open possibility.

3. Constance Rourke, *American Humor* (Garden City, New York: 1931), p. 96.

4. Gay Wilson Allen, ed., *Leaves of Grass* (New York: 1960), p. 120.

5. Louis Auchincloss, ed., *Sister Carrie* (Columbus, Ohio: 1969), p. 1. All subsequent references to the text will be to this edition and page numbers will be in parentheses after the quotation.

6. Kenneth S. Lynn, "*Sister Carrie*: An Introduction" (New York: 1957), p. xv.

7. Donald Pizer, *The Novels of Theodore Dreiser: A Critical Study* (Minneapolis: 1976), pp. 81-82.

8. In this way, Dreiser's Chicago is remarkably like the New York which Jean Paul Sartre describes in "New York, the Colonial City." Unlike the European city which is safely anchored in time and space, New York is indeed "a city in motion" (*Literary and Philosophical Essays* [New York: 1955], p. 120.), a fascinating but bewildering process which offers people expanded opportunities while at the same time stripping away their established identities. Although Sartre is in many ways attracted by New York, he concludes that it is "the world's harshest city" (*Literary and Philosophical Essays,* p. 123).

John Dos Passos, Henry James, Carl Sandburg and many other American writers who have treated the American city share this perception of the city as an open-ended process. Like Dreiser, they are fundamentally ambivalent about this, excited about the opportunities created by the process but also fearful of its radical instability.

## Leonard Cassuto (essay date 1991)

SOURCE: Cassuto, Leonard. "From the 1890s to the 1990s: *Sister Carrie* on the Modern Stage." *Dreiser Studies,* vol. 22, no. 2, Fall 1991, pp. 26-32.

[*In the following essay, Cassuto provides an overview of dramatic adaptations of* Sister Carrie *and considers how the productions relate to Dreiser's original text.*]

When I saw last year's Broadway production of Steinbeck's *The Grapes of Wrath,* I remember being impressed at how remarkably closely the play adhered to the book. How callow I was in those days. The new dramatic production of **Sister Carrie** takes such faithfulness to new heights. The unusual length of the play, which can be seen straight through, or in two parts on separate days, compares in my recollection only to the London/Broadway production of *Nicholas Nickleby* of the early 80s. Playwright Louis Lippa and director Ken Marini follow the text amazingly closely. Lippa has written many pages of commendably credible dialogue, while Marini has staged virtually every significant scene in the novel, plus a few more.

I will have a few things to say later on about those extra scenes and about fidelity to the text in general, but since this is also a review, let me begin by saying that the new production of **Sister Carrie** (by The People's Light & Theatre Company in Malverne, Pennsylvania) is sensational, a treat not only for Dreiserians of all stripes, but for anyone who is willing to commit to its seven-hour length. It's well worth it.

Lippa, Marini, and the rest of the company have collaborated to stage a novel that I had thought was unstageable—and I'm sure I wasn't alone in my misjudgment. Using minimal backdrop scenery, the production evokes urban exteriors through superb choreography. A series of doorframes on casters configures the interiors of apartments and offices. Scene changes—and there are many—take place within the flow of the drama.

The effects can be dazzling. When Carrie comes to Chicago, for example, her sister Minnie picks her up and takes her from the train station onto the bustling avenue, and from there to the poor working class neighborhood where she and Sven reside. The transitions are breathtaking: in the station, the people mill about, suggesting a busy terminal; this crowd gives way to the shopping street, where they march quickly back and forth, now smart shoppers in a great big hurry. Carrie allows herself to be gathered up and swirled about in the arms of one passer-by, beautifully symbolizing her seduction by the lure of the city. The Hansens' neighborhood is evoked by a quick costume change to dark and shabby clothes, and by a series of explosively choreographed sidewalk confrontations among resident toughs. All of this takes place wordlessly to music (which is historically accurate and consistently excellent throughout) within five minutes—and it's astonishing.

This expressionism is more than economical; it stimulates the imagination to recreate what could not have been successfully depicted on stage. The costumes are crucial to the success of this kind of staging, and the designer, Lindsay W. Davis (assisted by P. Chelsea Harriman), rises to the task. Given the minimal scenery, the costumes provide the concrete link to verisimilitude in the production. Davis's costumes range literally from rags to riches, and are convincing through the entire spectrum.

The acting is generally first-rate. Elizabeth Meeker, Tom Teti, and Stephen Novelli give impressive performances as Carrie, Hurstwood, and Drouet. The remaining members of the company all play multiple roles (over a hundred altogether) in a collective tour-de-force of protean portrayals. Worthy of special mention from among this gallery of characters is Ceal Phelan's wonderful performance as stoop-shouldered, world-weary Minnie Meeber Hansen.

\* \* \*

Of course Dreiser readers will wonder how the book holds up on stage. The short answer is that it survives very well, though not in its pristine state. But let me elaborate. All adaptations involve interpretive decisions, and Lippa and Marini make their share. Because of the ambiguity that surrounds the two protagonists, **Sister Carrie** presents more problems for playwright, director, and actors than, say, Steinbeck's *Grapes* did. Lippa and Marini confront them boldly.

Carrie and Hurstwood have fuzzy motivations. (By contrast, Drouet's consistency has made him a relatively easy character to play; recall Eddie Albert's excellent performance in William Wyler's otherwise wretched 1952 film version, **Carrie,** as well as Stephen Novelli's fine work in the present production.) Carrie's and Hurstwood's depth of character makes them fun to talk about, but hard to write and play.

Essentially, this kind of ambiguity doesn't translate directly to the stage. To my mind, Louis Lippa's most challenging task was to create Hurstwood and Carrie on stage as understandable characters—not reflecting surfaces—and render their change over time in a way that would be dramatically interesting without betraying the ambiguity of Dreiser's vision. How sympathetic should Carrie be in success, and Hurstwood in failure? Answering such questions necessarily involves interpreting the novel, and Lippa does not flinch from doing so. The results are always interesting, ambitious, and creative, but they may not be completely satisfying to the Dreiser purist. The majority of the changes fall into two broad and familiar categories: class and gender.

During one of the hourly intermissions, one of my companions said to me, "Karl Marx would be proud of this production." And indeed he would have been: Dreiser comes off sounding like Upton Sinclair at times. Lippa's adaptation augments the novel's social commentary and turns it into a persistent push for class consciousness which simmers throughout the play before Hurstwood's decline enables it to reach a rolling boil in the last hour or two. Carrie's sweatshop experience now includes a scene in which a sidewalk union organizer is beaten by the police. When Hurstwood and Carrie walk in the park during their courtship, they are now interrupted by a labor demonstration. Hurstwood scolds a panhandler for interfering with his enjoyment of public space. The police drive this same homeless man off a park bench in a scene that is repeated during the play, and which thus becomes a leitmotif for the widespread insensitivity of the moneyed classes to the have-nots. This recurring sense of class struggle and activism (and there's more to it than I've recounted here) explicitly prepares the audience for Hurstwood's work as a scab (a brilliantly staged scene) and his eventual assumption into the ranks of the homeless himself.

How would Dreiser have reacted to this frankly left-leaning view of events? Consider what has happened: Lippa has taken the novelist's evident sympathy for the poor—both working and unemployed—and placed it into the context of an established ideology. The problem is that Dreiser never stuck to established ideologies himself, at least not for long. Malcolm Cowley described his mind as being "like an attic in an earthquake, full of big trunks that slithered about and popped open one after another, so that he sometimes spoke as a Social Darwinist, sometimes as a Marxist, sometimes as almost a fascist, and sometimes as a sentimental reformer" (59). Dreiser was clearly not a man to be pinned down, but that is what happens to him here. *Sister Carrie* is certainly no paean to capitalism, as Dreiser wrote it, but neither is it a folk song of the labor movement.

I found the treatment of gender in the play to be even more problematic. Lippa has updated the sexual politics of the novel for twentieth century consumption, but in doing so he has saddled Carrie with so much modern feminist rhetoric that she is unrecognizable at times underneath it.

Put simply, Lippa and Marini make Carrie into a twentieth century career woman—in the 1890s. The difference is not so much in her actions as in the self-awareness that now goes with them. The most significant result is an active,

angry Carrie whose resentment at Drouet's treatment of her could even be called vitriolic. Likewise, when she discovers that Hurstwood is married, she exclaims to him, "You're as bad as Charlie! Both of you have treated me like baggage!"

This righteous indignation doesn't ring true to the character Dreiser created, but it's consistent with a certain view of the world that runs through the play. Mrs. Julia Hurstwood, for example, receives a much more sympathetic portrayal than most readers of *Sister Carrie* might expect. She retains her high-handed imperiousness, but she's also a victim, casually dismissed by her husband and driven to her hostile response. We can even feel sorry for her.

Such sympathy necessarily comes at the expense of her husband. George Hurstwood comes off about as badly as a legitimate reading of the book will allow. He is insensitive, jingoistic, conniving, thoughtless, and lazy: hardly the nineties man, no matter which century we're talking about. One telling instance: when Carrie, caught in the familiar bind, rushes to make dinner after a hard day at work, Hurstwood criticizes her afterwards for not bothering to clear the table. On the day that I attended, the audience hissed him.

In assessing these adjustments to Dreiser's plot, let me backtrack a moment to consider what must have been one of Lippa's most vexing problems, that of Carrie's passivity. However true to the novel they may be, passivity and stasis don't play well on stage. Carrie's oddly placid demeanor is not normally the stuff of tragic heroines.

Lippa solves the problem by giving Carrie motivation. He and Marini do a marvelous job of dramatizing her lust for money and the things it buys. She starts out rosy-cheeked and innocent, dazzled by the wealth of the city and wanting to share in it. She later turns into the calculating material girl we know so well from the book. Her metamorphosis (no other word will do) is fueled by the duplicitous treatment she receives from Drouet and Hurstwood. One important new scene in the play is a furious fight between Carrie and Drouet in which Carrie shows an acute—and not always credible—knowledge of Drouet's sexual conduct. So angry is Drouet at his exposure that he walks out on her. This abandonment leaves her with no home to go to, and therefore with little choice once Hurstwood tricks her onto the train. Economically powerless to fight her virtual abduction, she has nowhere to turn except inside herself.

Carrie consequently hardens, becoming the familiar, sharp-eyed, inscrutable character who cautiously drifts from one situation to another. She tells Hurstwood that she'll accompany him to New York, but she also tells him that she reserves the right to leave him at any time. By this round-about dramatic route—which increases sympathy for the victimized Carrie—we finally reach the character we know. Dreiser makes her recognizable from the beginning; Lippa has her change into herself.

\* \* \*

Lippa's interpretive decisions in his adaptation of the novel are a less extreme version of the ones that have resulted in the recent restagings of Shakespeare which have been set in the wild West and other such anachronistic locations. Directors of such productions argue that they are no more radical than a truly historically accurate presentation would appear in this day and age. Indeed, we never see Shakespeare played with young men in the female roles, even though the role-playing often enhances complexities of the frequent gender-switching in certain scripts. To play it that way now would call a different kind of attention to gender-switching, one that Shakespeare could not have intended. But what did Shakespeare intend? What amounts to a corruption of the original intent? What amounts to an unwarranted interpretive decision?

Directors of adaptations and revivals these days are nearly all "restorers" to some degree. They try to make a play into a contemporary theatrical experience, not an artifact of the time it was written. There's a practical reason for this, of course: most theatergoers are not purists. They are looking for entertainment. Underneath the market argument, though, is the philosophical question of which is more important, the letter of the text or its spirit.

Which brings me back to **Sister Carrie**, which has been the site of one restoration debate already, the one which produced the now-familiar "unexpurgated" edition. In deciding which edition of **Carrie** to use, Lippa and Marini have it both ways. They give us the casually philandering Hurstwood of the unexpurgated (restored) version, but the Carrie of the play owes much to the original published text, including a dramatization of the famous Miss Madenda in her rocking chair at the end. The latter scene is presented on a split stage, simultaneous with Hurstwood's suicide, thereby dodging the problem of which to place first.

In bringing their hybrid version to the stage, Lippa and Marini have chosen the spirit over the letter of the text. But like Shakespeare's modern interpreters, they have had to decide just what that spirit is. Though I hasten to point out that this production is predominantly faithful to the novel (which is not exactly ancient, after all), Lippa and Marini have clearly made some important changes in order to

bring it to the stage. As restorers, they have chosen to adjust some of Dreiser's emphasis. They have therefore taken an interpretive risk.

I think it pays off. First of all, the play is unmistakably Dreiser. The adaptation updates the story, though, and I think that's valuable. No viewer of this **Sister Carrie** will fail to identify with these images of the homeless. Some may even recall the days when belonging to a union was something to be proud of. The sexual harassment of Carrie on the job (nicely brought off by Rozwill Young as her foreman) will ring true to a modern viewer, as will the accent on her subsequent economic powerlessness as a victimized housewife. Speaking as a theatergoer, I thoroughly enjoyed this play. My (somewhat less than purist) sense as a Dreiser scholar is that the script survives these modifications of Dreiser's original vision, though the stridency of the changes makes it a narrow escape in places. The production as a whole is a powerful and memorable day—and night—at the theatre.

Note: At this writing, no final decisions have been made about whether **Sister Carrie** will go on tour. We can only hope that it travels long and far.

WORK CITED

Cowley, Malcolm. *The Dream of Golden Mountains.* New York: Penguin, 1981.

**Janet Beer (essay date 1999)**

SOURCE: Beer, Janet. "*Sister Carrie* and *The Awakening*: The Clothed, the Unclothed, and the Woman Undone." *Soft Canons: American Women Writers and Masculine Tradition*, edited by Karen L. Kilcup, U of Iowa P, 1999, pp. 167-83.

[*In the following essay, Beer explains how the novels* Sister Carrie *and Kate Chopin's* The Awakening *(1899) "seek to expose women unloosed from the coercive power of essentialism" in order to investigate and invalidate female stereotypes.*]

Discussions of Kate Chopin's *The Awakening* (1899) and Theodore Dreiser's **Sister Carrie** (1900) often recount the critical hostility that followed—and even preceded—the publication of the novels. Although the degree and extent to which Kate Chopin was affected by adverse criticism, either personally or professionally, has often been over-stated, the almost wholly negative reviews of her novel[1] communicate to the modern reader, one hundred years later, a clear picture of the specific nature of the outrage committed against prevailing morality. Chopin's overstepping of the boundaries of decorum in the presentation of her heroine gave precisely discernible offense to contemporary reviewers.

I intend not to query these critical responses but rather to concur with the essential validity of readings that viewed Chopin's novel as full of disturbing and "unpleasant truths."[2] The novel was deeply disruptive of prevailing social mores, with Chopin's heroine dissident in every way from received notions of womanly propriety. Chopin built into the text an indirect acknowledgment of how few of her 1899 readers would be able to see beyond the breach of bourgeois morality—in Dr. Mandelet's words to the unhappy Edna toward the end of her life: "I am not going to ask for your confidence. I will only say that if ever you felt moved to give it to me, perhaps I might help you. I know I would understand, and I tell you there are not many who would—not many, my dear" (105). Alongside Chopin's picture of the "soul that dares and defies" (61), I want to examine Dreiser's *Sister Carrie,* which received comparable—though not so consistently denunciatory—reviews. Dreiser never tired of talking up his novel as having had a serious brush with censorship before publication,[3] but, I would contend, the text does not, in essentials, present as significant a challenge to the status quo in its picture of womanhood or relations between the sexes as *The Awakening* does. As Donna Campbell observes, "Edna Pontellier follows a path of sensual self-indulgence similar to that of men like Vandover and Theron Ware, and the end of her naturalistic 'degeneration' is the same as theirs: an excess of unexplored possibilities leads to an end of all possibilities, followed by actual or spiritual death."[4] When Edna Pontellier terminates her performance as wife and mother, Kate Chopin issues her most substantial refutation of any statute of limitation upon the proper province of women's writing.

I intend to scrutinize the manner in which Chopin and Dreiser present their heroines as women who can express something of the confusion and anxiety about the situation of woman in American society at the turn into the twentieth century.[5] Although their location in "the" canon—or in competing canons of masculine and feminine writers—has varied over time, these writers problematize matters, ranging from women's sexuality to women at work, that have been oversimplified; both seek to expose women unloosed from the coercive power of essentialism. Edna and Carrie aim to establish an identity at odds with the one by which they are classified—married or fallen woman—and thus, within both texts, the ontology of female stereotype is interrogated and revised. At the heart of any question of

identity in this social world is essentialism, and Chopin and Dreiser, in releasing their women from stereotype, challenge received notions of the binary opposition of whore or wife—and indeed, in Chopin's case, the binary opposition of male and female sexuality—and replace them with possibility and multiplicity. Both writers acknowledge, within the fabric of the tale, that they are writing for a society that has very particular notions of what the story of a woman's life should look like, but that such a story is unlikely to express either the contingent or the random. To incorporate within their texts a recognition of the inadequacy of the standard narrative is therefore to critique such narratives.

### "I Am Yours Truly": *Sister Carrie*

In *Sister Carrie,* Dreiser supplies his readers with what is, in many ways, a deeply conservative portrait of a woman. However, although an intrinsic part of that conservatism derives from his reliance upon reader familiarity with narratives about the inevitable fate of the fallen woman, he also engages in a dialectic with those narratives that challenges easy assumptions about the destination of the woman who topples from grace and remains unrepentant and, indeed, unpunished. There are a variety of received tales of girls and women at work within the larger narrative sweep of the novel, and the most obvious of these opens the story. As Carrie completes her first train journey, Dreiser tells us that she is approaching not only the great city but the great moral divide in any girl's existence: "Either she falls into saving hands and becomes better, or she rapidly assumes the cosmopolitan standard of virtue and becomes worse. Of an intermediate balance, under the circumstances, there is no possibility."[6] The story seems, therefore, to be closed to other interpretations, for we are offered a narrowly focused moral judgment, not the openness of a tale with the potential for multiple meaning. Carrie's first protector, Drouet, traveling on the same train, is attracted both by the simplicity of this country girl and the concomitant opportunity to make something of her, a desire that she awakens in all those who gaze upon her for any length of time. It becomes obvious, all too soon, that the only "saving hands" extended to Carrie, however, are hands made tired and dull by toil, by mere subsistence, and, most crucially, by an unquestioning adherence to a conventional morality that can express itself only in the clichés of a dream sequence that has Carrie variously falling down mineshafts or into deep water. These are hands that have nothing to offer her except equal or unequal toil. The other beckoning hands are bejeweled and insigniaed, have soft ten-dollar bills to pass from palm to palm, and seduce Carrie with the ease of both acquisition and transfer of assets. The traveling salesman, Drouet, snaps Carrie up as surely as if he had spotted her on sale at a warehouse. She is a doll, a mannequin for him to dress up, for she is "really very pretty. Even then, in her commonplace garb, her figure was evidently not bad and her eyes were large and gentle" (60), and, once he has transformed her, she will pass out of his hands into another's hands. Carrie never refutes ownership; she merely moves, or is carried, onwards, seemingly following the primrose path to perdition but actually arriving at the sumptuously appointed "Aladdin's cave" (456) of the Wellington Hotel, where she is asked to represent fashionable society for its owners.

A further development in the essentialist narrative critiqued within the novel has Carrie following the career trajectory of a prostitute. She comes to the city and is lost, as surely as one of Paul Dresser's sentimentalized country girls. She falls immediately into the arms of a protector who takes her virginity and continuing sexual favors in return for clothing, shelter, and amusement, and who puts her on show to the man who will be her next client or protector: "I'll introduce you" (80). She is then stolen away by this new protector, bundled across state, and indeed, national lines, and is kept by him; she subsequently offers herself on the open market as an actress, having changed her name, as would any prostitute on entry into the brothel, and, ultimately, finds ease and comfort in a friendship with another member of the chorus line, Lola, mirroring the homosocial relationships many prostitutes form with other women in their trade.[7]

Dreiser's picture of Carrie thus conforms to many conventional conditions and developments in the career of the fallen woman, but he absolves her of any of the physical consequences that might be expected to follow from her lifestyle—sexual appetite, pregnancy, sexually transmitted disease—none of these appear to touch her.[8] Dreiser does not portray her as debased by her chosen lifestyle, as sordid or predatory, as victim or victimizer, but as a woman so unaffected by her experiences that she can be described as "quiet and reserved" (478) when at the height of her fame as an actress. In this way he incorporates the standard story of the prostitute's life in his narrative but defuses it by closing down—indeed, throwing out—the morality that had seemed to be the only hermeneutic tool on offer at the beginning of Carrie's journey. The deviant subculture, apparently the location for all those who operate outside the limits of the accepted moral code, is mockingly shown to be a place where the woman operates as a little homemaker, producing rarebits and arranging knickknacks, or reading European naturalist novels, rocking in her chair, the model of quiet domesticity rather than a representative of a defiant or degenerate lifestyle.

The secret of Carrie's success—and, most particularly, her successful pass at respectability once she has embarked upon a career as an actress—is that she is contained easily within the structure of specularity offered by her society: she is orectic, concupiscent in the eye of the beholder. In her first professional speaking part, Carrie Madenda, actress, quondam wife, and mistress, extemporizes the line: "I am yours truly" (431) and thereby confirms her part in the narrative as endlessly contingent upon the demands or feelings of another. Carrie embodies specularity: in reflection she gives back to the male onlooker the answer he is always looking for, the picture of his own desire, not hers. Carrie's active choices have to do with seeking paid work, while all her other actions represent mere compliance. On entry to the city she has to negotiate a number of choices that amount to a choice of life: to become a cowed wife like Minnie or one of the girls Drouet points out as worthy of her admiration. In choosing the latter, she redefines herself merely as the woman who is contemplated, observed as deserving of comment. Her destiny as an actress is sealed at that point because she allows herself to be caught and trapped in specularity alone.

Walter Benn Michaels writes, "What you are is what you want, in other words, what you aren't. The ideal that Ames represents to Carrie is thus an ideal of dissatisfaction, of perpetual desire. And, in fact, in *Sister Carrie,* satisfaction itself is never desirable; it is instead the sign of incipient failure, decay, and finally death."[9] While I concur absolutely with Michaels's description of the contiguities of satisfaction in the novel, I would like to delimit severely the extent to which Carrie can actually be considered to be the perpetually hungry "desireful Carrie" (487) that Dreiser tries to persuade us she is. From first to last Carrie is neutralized, rendered passive, as a creature without appetites beyond the basic ones of food and clothing. She is the ideal soft pornographer's model, having internalized exactly what is required of her: she takes on the role assigned, demonstrating the possibility for desire's fulfillment but never exerting any physical preference herself, except, of course, where it is a sensual response to the imprecations of leather and lace: "'My dear,' said the lace collar she secured from Pardridge's, 'I fit you beautifully; don't give me up'" (98). Carrie is the mediated woman— endlessly described in terms of her appeal to other people and always uncertain of her own authenticity—"what is it I have lost?" (88)—unable to see shame in her mirror but always able to be spotted by the man or in the job that will take her to a place of comfort. As Irene Gammel suggests, despite Dreiser's reputation for having radicalized writing about sex, he was actually a firm adherent of the "gender stereotypical seduction theme,"[10] and in his picture of

Carrie she is always compliant, taking the initiative only insofar as it reinforces the already overt passion of her admirer.

Carrie understands that in order to get what she wants she must respond as if she were completely yielding to the pleasure of the man; indeed, the imitation of devotion, or sexual excitement (for imitation is all that Carrie is capable of), is what ensures her success as ersatz wife or actress. Her response is, above all, disproportionate to what is on offer, as, with that crucial line, "I am yours truly," she makes herself distinct from the rest of the harem but remains a member of the group, there to display collective sexual availability to the man, to simulate excitement when chosen for sexual favors. Carrie in the harem is again the soft pornographer's model, ready to fake sexual excitement and even fulfillment; the fact that she never conceives a child, despite her two sexual relationships, only serves to confirm that she is designed for male pleasure, not for productive or reproductive purposes. However, Carrie's success in specularity—that is, in reflecting what the male onlooker wants to see—is ultimately, Dreiser never lets us doubt, dependent upon the simultaneous sucking away of power from that male. The most reactionary message in the text is that women such as Carrie are monsters, ball-breaking and insatiable in their expectations of material gain, that Hurstwood made a fatal error when he thought that "in the mild light of Carrie's eye was nothing of the calculation of the mistress. In the diffident manner was nothing of the art of the courtezan" (122).

The story of Carrie's meteoric rise to fame is interwoven with the stations of Hurstwood's humiliating journey toward a death that becomes a martyrdom. Hurstwood stands and looks at the evidence, on advertising hoardings, of her ascent, as he descends into the underworld of homelessness and hunger. The prerogative embedded in the relationship has shifted from the once powerful Hurstwood, the shiny, well-dressed, successful showman, to the governed, the once complicit woman whose demands he aroused but can no longer satisfy. The turning point is marked by Dreiser as Carrie returns home: "When she saw him in bed that night, she knew that it imported failure. Coming on top of a further improvement in her own situation which must now be detailed, and as a destroyer of her hope that he had really roused himself, it was a shock. She could only shake her head in despair" (430). The moment of revelation of his insufficiency in enterprise is made confluent with his insufficiency in bed; indeed, his very presence in the bed means "failure," he is un*aroused* whereas she is "on top" and intolerant of his inadequacies. A price is exacted of the man who once invited such as Carrie to perform for him, who took his pleasure on "a

junket that was to last ten days" (86) and in New York took "cognizance of the pleasures of the tenderloin."[11] Once his own part in the transaction begins to falter, once he fails to come up to the standards of vigor and enterprise expected by the woman, the end of the relationship is a foregone conclusion.

Carrie is at first nonthreatening to men because she sits or stands where she is placed; Hurstwood has to carry her away by trickery in order to get her to move, and her body language is endlessly precipitate: "She had a chic way of tossing her head on one side, and holding her arms up as if for action—not listlessly. In front of the line this showed up even more effectually" (401). The telling phrase is "as if for action": there is nothing real about Carrie's preparedness for action; she can simulate energy as well as she can simulate attention to the male onlooker. As Amy Kaplan argues: "Although desire in *Sister Carrie* propels constant motion, it also becomes a substitute for actively changing either the social order or the individuals within it. This form of desire contributes to the paradoxical sense of stasis in the text at the times of greatest motion; Carrie is constantly on the move up the social scale—from one city, one man, one job to the next—yet she always seems to end up in the same place, as the final scene suggests: rocking, and dreaming, and longing for more."[12] Carrie is, in particular, sexually inert; she is only active in pursuit of clothes or material comfort. Although she performs various roles as mistress, wife, and actress, these roles, as Kaplan underscores, give the appearance of action but leave her—and others—untouched in essentials. She performs the drama of class mobility through dressing up and acting up; she likes to work, her dream is "to be rid of idleness and the drag of loneliness—to be doing and rising—to be admired, petted, raised to a state where all was applause, elegance, assumption of dignity" (177). These are, of course, the demands that she makes in return for her compliance, a compliance that is endlessly expectant and therefore exacting, and which, in the end, seals Hurstwood's fate as a man irrelevant to her needs.

Like Kate Chopin, Dreiser is uncritical of his heroine's illicit liaisons, although he does intervene directly to acknowledge at every step of the way the contraventions of his characters against the accepted moral code. Woven into the text—in Minnie's cliché-driven dream of Carrie's fall as well as in Dreiser's direct commentary—is the standard of bourgeois morality breached by Carrie's easy acceptance of money, favors, sexual congress, and bogus or bigamous marriages. Dreiser has an apologetic and often pompous tone in the interpolations that gloss his characters' weakness in the face of temptations both carnal and fiscal: "And whoso is it so noble as to ever avoid evil, and who so wise that he moves ever in the direction of truth?" (91). These special-pleading interruptions in the text serve only, however, to highlight the fact that the most effective means of undermining conventional morality is the portrait of Carrie herself, who, despite living with two different men as their mistress, taking part in a bigamous marriage, and working as an actress, passes for respectable and has a fairly chaste notion of what it means to be a "good time" (444) girl. The best argument against easy acceptance of female stereotyping is the final version of Carrie, who wants, at the close, to do good: "Not applause—not even that—but goodness—labor for others" (486). Dreiser's final irony is that given work, decently paid work from which she derives status and economic independence, the woman is restored to respectability. Carrie becomes a celibate, spurning offers from the stage-door Johnnies who blandish her with tales of great wealth and comfort. No longer interested in being a kept woman, she is given encouragement by Ames to become her own woman, although Dreiser tells us plainly that Carrie does not lose her ability to reflect back at the observer that which he wants to see: "[Ames] looked after her sympathetically. What Mrs. Vance had told him about her husband's having disappeared, together with all he felt concerning the moral status of certain kinds of actresses, fled. There was something exceedingly human and unaffected about this woman—something which craved neither money nor praise. He followed to the door—wide awake to her beauty" (487). This new Carrie is not, however, any more authentic than the earlier Carrie; surrendering endlessly to specularity, to the philanthropist's vision as easily as to the soft pornographer's notion of her purpose, her identity is neither stable nor single nor fixed: "She was the old, mournful Carrie—the desireful Carrie,—unsatisfied" (487). Her very capacity to pass for respectable, to pass for tragic heroine, made possible by Hurstwood's banishment to a separate strand of the narrative, emphasizes the folly of trying to contain the woman within a standard tale. Dreiser thus confirms that economic, sexual, and social boundaries can and will be crossed, and that categorization can only lead to the proliferation of performative fictions of identity, fictions that put some on the stage and put others to bed into a sleep from which they will never awaken.

### "The Inward Life Which Questions": *The Awakening*

Kate Chopin's Edna Pontellier possesses the only voice in *The Awakening* allowed to acknowledge that her behavior might be construed as at odds with the prevailing morality: "By all the codes which I am acquainted with, I am a devilishly wicked specimen of the sex. But some way I can't convince myself that I am" (79). In contradistinction to Dreiser, Chopin refuses to offer moral prescriptions or

judgments to her readers through the authorial voice, leaving Edna, as the author said in her famous "Retraction," free to "[work] out her own damnation."[13] Edna, of course, poses the particular danger to the social order that arises from a woman's having independent financial means. The possession of an inheritance from her mother underscores that she is not forced to perform the role of wife. She need not live in fear of the withdrawal of maintenance, she need not fear a husbandless future for economic reasons; therefore, she fulfills the worst fears of the male-dominated social order: that an economically independent woman will be an uncontrollable woman. This is the really frightening specter in Chopin's novel, not the sexually awakened woman, but the sexually independent woman with a cash base unconstrained by either love or need.

In *The History of Sexuality* Michel Foucault describes the strategic "deployment" of sexuality within the family: "The family is the interchange of sexuality and alliance: it conveys the law and the juridical dimension in the deployment of sexuality; and it conveys the economy of pleasure and the intensity of sensations in the regime of alliance."[14] Edna Pontellier very precisely and deliberately takes her "sexuality" outside the legal and social framework of marriage; indeed, an intrinsic part of her awakening is the recognition that her physical desires cannot be contained within the family unit or, ultimately, in relationship with one man. Chopin shows Edna herself at first bemused by the fact that her newly awakened sexual appetite is indiscriminate, that the first erotically fulfilling encounter of her new life is not with the man with whom she is infatuated and who has been the focus for all her unrequited desire: "She felt as if a mist had been lifted from her eyes, enabling her to look upon and comprehend the significance of life, that monster made up of beauty and brutality. But among the conflicting sensations which assailed her there was neither shame nor remorse. There was a dull pang of regret because it was not the kiss of love which had inflamed her, because it was not love which had held this cup of life to her lips" (80). Edna has been as much a "dupe" (105), as she herself describes it, as other women to the commonly accepted idea of complete romantic fulfillment with one man, whether Robert or one of her earlier fantasy lovers.

Unlike Carrie, Edna does not seek material advantage in taking new sexual partners, for in sleeping with a well-known roué, Alcée Arobin, she is embracing the disreputable, the déclassé. Edna seemingly wants to sleep with men who will worsen her financial security and destroy her respectability, men who are marginal in both social and financial circles. She deliberately relinquishes her secure position as married woman in order to seek physical fulfillment. She declassifies herself, shedding her inhibitions, her class and status, her material wealth, and her clothes in order to become more fully herself. She identifies herself with no other woman, taking herself, instead, outside convention, outside society.

Edna Pontellier goes to her death having failed to find a reflection anywhere in her world of the kind of woman she becomes during the course of the narrative. Where specularity was Carrie's route to survival and success, Edna fails to return the image required of her by husband, family, and friends; where Carrie imitates, Edna deviates and initiates. She can find no one who leads the kind of life she wants to lead; having rejected the roles of mother, wife, and artist, there are no models for her to imitate. Carrie is constantly imitative; she copies those girls that Drouet points out to her as stylish and well-presented, and through her contact with him—and the immaculately turned out Hurstwood— she betters her material status, re-dressing herself in the eyes of the world. Edna Pontellier, however, cannot authenticate herself in the eyes of the world, and eventually she gives up, defeated. She dresses down to the raw; she takes off her clothes in order to recodify herself, seeking physical comfort and freedom, seeking a real self in naturalness, in absence of ceremony, in nakedness. She can find no other reflection of herself in the exterior world than the naked man she herself envisions as a part of her imaginative response to Mademoiselle Reisz's playing. The human creature, naked and unadorned and finally ungendered, is her last—and the only possible—point of identification before she swims to her death.

Edna has not been able to discern any likeness in those that surround her to the woman she wants to be, because the only models on offer are the married woman categorized by Chopin as the "mother-women ... who idolized their children, worshiped their husbands, and esteemed it a holy privilege to efface themselves as individuals and grow wings as ministering angels" (9). Neither Chopin nor Dreiser portrays married love with any zest: the two marriages we see in *Sister Carrie*—Minnie and Sven, Hurstwood and his wife—are either dreary or ill-tempered matches. Chopin does, however, spend a considerable portion of her narrative on her portrait of the Ratignolles: in love and bourgeois contentment, they are compatible, safe, and ultimately dull. What her intimacy with Adèle Ratignolle does for Edna, however, is not to provide her with a role model as perfect wife and mother but to alert her, through the sensual response she makes to her friend, to the indiscriminate and anarchic nature of sexual attraction. Edna regards most of Madame Ratignolle's pursuits with bemused contempt; she joins in with activities such as dressmaking in order not to appear "unamiable and uninterested" (10), because the real

attraction of being in Adèle's company is that Edna is sexually stimulated by her proximity. Madame Ratignolle is described as realizing to perfection ideals of "feminine" beauty in contrast to the "long, clean and symmetrical" (15) lines of Edna's body. Adèle's nearness disturbs Edna's equilibrium: "The excessive physical charm of the Creole had first attracted her, for Edna had a sensuous susceptibility to beauty. Then the candor of the woman's whole existence, which every one might read, and which formed so striking a contrast to her own habitual reserve—this might have furnished a link. Who can tell what metals the gods use in forging the subtle bond which we call sympathy, which we might as well call love" (14-15). The attraction is absolutely sensual, as is Adèle's response to Edna. She is unequal to the challenge of responding to Edna's expressions of confusion about the feelings she is experiencing except with touching and stroking and murmurs of generalized sympathy—"*pauvre chéri*"—and although "the action was at first a little confusing to Edna ... she soon lent herself to the Creole's gentle caress" (17).

It is a sensual awakening to the pleasures of the flesh in the person of Madame Ratignolle that lends the character of anarchy, of "tumult" (14) to Edna's newly realized sexuality. This is the real center of deviance from the norms of the established sexual and social "regime of alliance," in Foucault's words: Edna's awakening is homoerotic and thus disrupts the structure of power and affiliation in sexual as well as economic and social terms. Every time that Edna responds unconventionally—for example, to Robert's expression of his dream that she will become his wife—by saying that she gives herself where she chooses, that she is no one's possession, she is refuting the precept that says that the woman's sexuality must be neutralized by passivity and compliance and expressed only within the family unit. Edna's conduct throws into flux not only preconceptions of female sexuality but the category of woman in its entirety; in Judith Butler's terms, she takes herself out of the "context of the heterosexual matrix"—to the point of fracture. As Butler notes: "When the constructed status of gender is theorized as radically independent of sex, gender itself becomes a free-floating artifice, with the consequence that *man* and *masculine* might just as easily signify a female body as a male one, and *woman* and *feminine* a male body as easily as a female one."[15] Edna Pontellier's rebellion confutes conjugal, maternal, and social structures of womanliness; she unsexes herself, taking to the streets, walking, talking, eating, drinking, smoking, gambling, forming sexual liaisons in the public spaces of New Orleans.

The home of the married woman, after the return of all the vacationing families to New Orleans, becomes the site of this rebellion, of the subversion of all the modes of behavior denoted as normal. Unlike Carrie, with her pathetic attempts at domesticity while in Drouet's establishment, Edna abjures housekeeping, receiving visitors, marital relations, and mothering, and, in removing herself to the pigeonhouse, endeavors to escape from the pigeonhole to which she has been assigned. She pursues the erotic feelings inspired by one woman in a relationship with another, as she demands from Mademoiselle Reisz the sexual charge provided by her music and that she become the representative of Robert, the desired physical presence. In the pianist's attic rooms Edna surrenders her reserve in full as she allows herself to be swept into sensation by the intensity of the emotional atmosphere as well as by the music. The words exchanged between the two women are passionate and much more closely approximate the teasing, ardent language of lovers than any dialogue between Edna and Robert. Mademoiselle Reisz calls Edna "*ma belle*" and "*ma reine*"; she has a declamatory, histrionic tone as she confronts Edna about the nature of physical attraction and disputes with her about the putative reader of Robert's letters: "'Haven't you begged me for them? Can I refuse you anything? Oh! you cannot deceive me" (77). The two woman enact the struggle toward frank expression of desire, which never happens either between Edna and Arobin or Edna and Robert, and it is because of the passionate nature of their engagement that Edna is ready to respond to Arobin and "the first kiss of her life to which her nature had really responded. It was a flaming torch that kindled desire" (80).

Unlike Carrie, Edna Pontellier refuses to keep still and refuses to fake her emotions. She expresses her newfound sense of self in motion, walking through the city, involving herself in the move between houses, climbing ladders, moving furniture, and performing otherwise unexpected exertions in order to reclaim both her body and her living space. In *The Awakening* Chopin refuses to indulge the cultural predisposition to pathologize any behavioral or sexual deviation from the norm; as Butler notes in discussion of Foucault, "The binary reproduction of sexuality suppresses the subversive multiplicity of a sexuality that disrupts heterosexual, reproductive and medicojuridical hegemonies" (19).[16] Indeed, Chopin makes this refusal even more emphatic by making the only man who has any insight into Edna's true condition a doctor, an elderly family doctor at that, who sees beyond the repressive effects of the stereotypical expectations for women's satisfaction to the frustration and pain of an individual case: "The Doctor . . . knew his fellow-creatures better than most men; knew that inner life which so seldom unfolds itself to unanointed eyes. He was sorry he had accepted Pontellier's invitation. He was growing old, and beginning to need rest and an

imperturbed spirit. He did not want the secrets of other lives thrust upon him. 'I hope it isn't Arobin,' he muttered to himself as he walked. 'I hope to heaven it isn't Alcée Arobin'" (68). When the doctor expresses this wish, it is because he recognizes Edna's awakened sexuality, not because he thinks she is especially depraved or debauched; he merely wishes her a better lover than the roué Alcée Arobin, with his practiced, glib charm. In his experience, then, she is actually representative, not exceptional; to Doctor Mandelet the sexually alive woman is a known quantity. This recognition allows Chopin to normalize—albeit in a manner that points to the esoteric nature of the knowledge required—Edna's developing sensuality. Again, it is this very acceptance, this normalization, that would have been one of the most profoundly shocking aspects of the narrative to most of its readers. Women with dissatisfactions, with appetites like Edna's, might not, then, be aberrations or exceptions; such women, women who refuse to be bound by the appearance of conventional morality, are well known to the Doctor in his professional if not in his personal life. In presenting a challenge to the social order, Edna Pontellier fails to externalize a mode of existence that will provide her with a coherent self-definition. From the beginning "she had apprehended instinctively the dual life—that outward existence which conforms, the inward life which questions" (14), but after undermining, even undoing the ontology of her identity as married woman, she has nothing to put in its place except the certainty of total isolation. She has sought to choose her mode of existence, and, as every choice is a recognition of the limits that operate to constrain choice, she finally understands that a life authenticating her newly awakened physical self does not and cannot exist. Finally, to surrender to the close embrace of the sea is her only option.

\* \* \*

The crucial difference between Edna and Carrie ultimately inheres in the distinct economic circumstances that condition their lifestyle choices. Chopin launches her heroine from a position of financial independence; Edna is able to see integrity and wholeness in divesting herself of material possessions, loosening and finally discarding her clothes in order "to realize her position in the universe as a human being, and to recognize her relations as an individual to the world within and about her" (14). Carrie clothes herself in a number of conventional attitudes and poses in order to achieve the material independence that is Edna's from the outset; for Carrie, "the voice of want made answer for her" (90). Carrie ends, however, in defiance of stereotype, surrounded with material comfort, unpunished physically or mentally by promiscuity, and distinguished from the chorus line or harem by her autonomy. Carrie has been more the object of desire than the "desireful Carrie": she has been able to convert illicit into the appearance of licit sex, she moves from the pathetic adoption of the (false) married name to the point where her "name is worth … repute" (451). Edna makes herself subject to desire and thereby removes herself from any world recognizable to those around her; as she tells Robert, "I give myself where I choose" (102), and her "choosing" to give herself to the sea is the only manner in which she can locate a secure self-identity, unclothed and uncompromised.

### Notes

1. See Emily Toth, *Kate Chopin* (London: Century, 1990), 422-425, for a discussion of the myths and misapprehensions that have grown up around the reception of *The Awakening.* See the selection of reviews published in the Norton Critical Edition of *The Awakening,* ed. Margo Culley, 2d ed. (New York: W. W. Norton, 1994), 161-173.

2. See Culley, ed., *The Awakening,* 164 (review in the 20 May 1899 St. Louis *Post-Dispatch*). All second and subsequent references to this and other sources appear in the text.

3. See Ellen Moers, *Two Dreisers: The Man and the Novelist* (London: Thames and Hudson, 1970), part 3, chapter 2.

4. Donna M. Campbell, *Resisting Regionalism: Gender and Naturalism in American Fiction, 1885-1915* (Athens, Ohio: Ohio University Press, 1997). Campbell argues that Edna's career most closely parallels the male protagonists of such naturalist writers as Frank Norris and Harold Frederic (149).

5. For a discussion of American women writers of this period, see Elizabeth Ammons, *Conflicting Stories: American Women Writers at the Turn into the Twentieth Century* (New York: Oxford University Press, 1991). For some other views of the two novels, see Donald Pizer, *New Essays on* Sister Carrie (New York: Cambridge University Press, 1991); David E. E. Sloane, Sister Carrie: *Dreiser's Sociological Tragedy* (New York: Macmillan, 1992); Margit Stange, *Personal Property: Wives, White Slaves, and the Market in Women* (Baltimore: Johns Hopkins University Press, 1998); Cynthia Griffin Wolff, "Un-Utterable Longing: The Discourse of Feminine Sexuality in Kate Chopin's *The Awakening,* in *The Calvinist Roots of the Modern Era,* ed. Aliki Barnstone et al. (Hanover, N.H.: University Press of New England, 1997), 181-197. For a discussion of Chopin's

use of historical discourses of homoeroticism, specifically, her use of the emerging stereotype of the lesbian and her connection to the woman artist, see Kathryn Lee Seidel, "Art Is an Unnatural Act: Homoeroticism, Art, and Mademoiselle Reisz in *The Awakening,"* *Mississippi Quarterly* 46.2 (1993): 199-214; for a more theoretical reading of Edna as "lesbian," see Elizabeth LeBlanc, "The Metaphorical Lesbian: Edna Pontellier in *The Awakening,"* *Tulsa Studies in Women's Literature* 15.2 (1996): 289-307. See also Laurie E. George, "Women's Language in *The Awakening,"* in *Approaches to Teaching Chopin's* The Awakening, ed. Bernard Koloski (New York: MLA, 1988); Emily Toth, *Kate Chopin* (New York: William Morrow, 1990), 438. Readers may also wish to consult the following forthcoming volume: Emily Toth, *Kate Chopin: The Centennial Story* (Jackson: University Press of Mississippi, 1999).

6. Theodore Dreiser, *Sister Carrie* [the unexpurgated edition], ed. N. M. Westlake et al. (New York: Viking Penguin, 1981), 3-4.

7. Ruth Rosen, *The Lost Sisterhood: Prostitution in America, 1900-1918* (Baltimore: Johns Hopkins University Press, 1982), 102-103.

8. For a discussion of Dreiser's desexualization of Carrie, see Laura Hapke, *Tales of the Working Girl: Wage-Earning Women in American Literature, 1890-1925* (New York: Twayne, 1992), 78-82.

9. Walter Benn Michaels, "Sister Carrie's Popular Economy," *Critical Inquiry* 7 (1980): 382.

10. Irene Gammel, "Sexualizing the Female Body: Dreiser, Feminism, and Foucault," in *Theodore Dreiser: Beyond Naturalism,* ed. Miriam Gogol (New York: New York University Press, 1995), 31.

11. Dreiser, 316; see Rosen's enumeration of red-light districts in major U.S. cities, including "New York's Bowery, Five Points and Tenderloin" (78-79).

12. Amy Kaplan, *The Social Construction of American Realism* (Chicago: University of Chicago Press, 1988), 149.

13. Culley (78) cites the "Retraction" printed in *Book News* 17 (July 1899): 612.

14. Michel Foucault, *The History of Sexuality,* vol. 1, trans. Robert Hurley (London: Pelican Books, 1981), 108.

15. Judith Butler, *Gender Trouble: Feminism and the Subversion of Identity* (New York: Routledge, 1990), 5-6.

16. See also Marjorie Garber, *Vice Versa: Bisexuality and the Eroticism of Everyday Life* (New York: Simon and Schuster, 1995).

## James L. W. West III (essay date 2000)

SOURCE: West, James L. W., III. "Alcohol and Drinking in *Sister Carrie*." *Theodore Dreiser and American Culture: New Readings,* edited by Yoshinobu Hakutani, U of Delaware P, 2000, pp. 56-64.

[*In the following essay, West assesses the role of alcohol and other "modern" behaviors in* Sister Carrie. *West points out that both Drouet and Hurstwood drink, whereas Ames does not; he even refuses wine, compelling Carrie to also refuse it, accordingly.*]

Is alcohol a factor in *Sister Carrie*? is it important in any of Dreiser's writings? We don't think of alcohol as significant in his life; until his last years he drank very little. He was never able to match Mencken pilsner for pilsner, nor was he much interested in doing so. And there is the apocryphal story of F. Scott Fitzgerald's showing up one night at a Dreiser soirée with a bottle of champagne which he presented to his host, expecting the older writer to pop the cork and offer libations to those present. Instead Dreiser shoved the bottle in his icebox and saved it to drink later. This was a concept unknown to Fitzgerald.

Dreiser made no serious effort that I'm aware of in his fiction or nonfiction to explore the effects of alcohol on human behavior and personality. Perhaps he felt unqualified; probably the subject didn't interest him in the same way that it did Fitzgerald and Hemingway and Malcolm Lowry—and many other writers who have explored alcohol and alcoholism. Dreiser's characters are driven by forces and compulsions other than drink, most of them economic and social. Lester Kane, for example, dies in part from overindulgence in rich foods and wines, but there is no suggestion that he is an alcoholic. He expires more from weariness with life and bafflement over its meaning and arrangement than from any physical addiction. And no one important in the **Trilogy of Desire,** or in ***An American Tragedy,*** or in the other novels and stories, or in the nonfiction writings such as ***Twelve Men,*** is destroyed by drinking.

The same can be said, for the most part, of *Sister Carrie.* If ever a man had reason to turn to liquor for solace, Hurstwood would be that man, especially after he bottoms out in New York. Certainly liquor has been a part of his life; he manages two saloons in the course of the novel, and he must know that alcohol can be a soothing agent and that

it can help one to forget the past. But there is no hint that Hurstwood is a drinker; he is destroyed by economic and social forces, not by bad personal habits. Likewise with Drouet, who seems to enjoy his tipple, but who is energized by the pursuit of women, not by the pursuit of the bottle.

There are, however, three appearances of alcohol in *Sister Carrie*—in the Pennsylvania text of the novel—that are important, and that I'd like to discuss in this essay. I want to argue that in Dreiser's original conception of *Sister Carrie* these three appearances constitute a pattern, a leitmotif, and that he uses these mentions of alcohol to measure the three major male characters in the novel. Two of these appearances are not present in the first edition, the 1900 Doubleday, Page & Co. text. The third is present in both texts. Dreiser removed one mention from the typescript of the novel, probably between the time he submitted it to Harpers in May 1900 and had it turned down, and the time a few weeks later when he sent it to Doubleday. The other appearance vanished between the setting-copy typescript and the first printing. In preparing the Pennsylvania text, I restored the two passages, reasoning that the cuts must have been made either to take out references to liquor, or simply to remove details so that the plot might move along more swiftly. I'd like now to reexamine my thinking in making those restorations and to speculate about how the novel is changed by the presence or absence of the passages.

All three mentions of alcohol occur within a space of about one hundred pages. The first occurs when Drouet, who has discovered that Carrie has been seeing Hurstwood in the afternoons, goes to their apartment, resolved to confront her with his new knowledge. "The drummer was flushed and excited, and full of great resolve to know all about her relations with Hurstwood," wrote Dreiser in his manuscript. Then comes this detail: "He had taken several drinks and was warm for his purpose" (223).[1]

Drouet proceeds to make a fool of himself. He tells Carrie that Hurstwood is a married man, something she has not known, and she, in a display of emotional illogic, becomes angry with him for not letting her know of Hurstwood's matrimonial status. Drouet has not meant to break off with Carrie; he has not really suspected her of serious wrongdoing. His vanity has been wounded, and he wants to reassert his control over her. But to his surprise she shows considerable spunk. "I won't talk about it," she says. "Whatever has happened is your own fault" (232). Drouet, after whining a little, packs some things in a valise and puts his hand on the doorknob. "You can go to the deuce as far as I am concerned," he tells her in his exit line. "I'm no sucker" (232).

This is an important scene; it sets in motion all else that will happen in the novel. Hurstwood, who has been observed riding in a buggy with Carrie, is facing problems of his own now—an angry, unforgiving wife who is dictating some quite severe financial terms for a divorce settlement. He will shortly steal ten thousand dollars from his employers, lure Carrie (now alone) onto the train to Montreal, and progress from there to New York with her. It is necessary, therefore, that Drouet behave foolishly in his confrontation with Carrie. Certainly those "several drinks" he had taken, in Dreiser's original conception of the scene, should have muddled his judgment. Was Dreiser trying to suggest that Drouet was not foolish enough on his own to botch this showdown with Carrie? Did he need assistance from alcohol?

It's impossible to know exactly what Dreiser thought. What we do know is that the sentence quoted above—"He had taken several drinks and was warm for his purpose."—is present in the typescript (264) but missing from the first printing (242). It must therefore have been cut in galleys or page proofs. But by whom?

Perhaps the cut was made by someone at Doubleday, Page. Perhaps it was made by Dreiser—either under pressure from the publisher, or at the suggestion of someone else, or of his own volition. We do know that Dreiser removed allusions to sex and instances of profanity from the typescript at the publisher's prompting. These passages were queried in blue pencil; Dreiser responded by making the excisions.[2] Might this process have extended into the galley and page-proof stages, where a reference to drinking was targeted? We also know that Dreiser was influenced to make cuts and changes in manuscript and typescript by Arthur Henry, his friend, and Sara White Dreiser, his wife. Some of these changes toned down sexual or otherwise "offensive" passages. Might one of these two persons have suggested that he cut the sentence about Drouet's drinking?

These are possible explanations, but let's assume for now that Dreiser made the cut himself, without pressure or prompting. Why might he have done so? Possibly he did not want Drouet to have alcohol as an excuse for his behavior. Drouet is good hearted but shallow. He is not long on intellect, nor is he the sort of man who would handle himself nimbly or cleverly in a face-off with an angry woman. Perhaps, then, Dreiser wanted to remove any excuse for Drouet. He might have wanted to take alcohol out of this equation and let Drouet make a fool of himself without the assistance of those "several drinks." That sounds plausible, but it's no more provable than the other two propositions.[3]

The next mention of alcohol in *Sister Carrie* is the one that remains unchanged from manuscript to typescript to published book. This is the pivotal scene in which Hurstwood, depressed over his problems with his wife, begins drinking with some patrons at Hannah and Hoggs—several actors, a theatrical manager, and a wealthy rounder of Chicago. In Dreiser's phrase, Hurstwood joins in the drinking "right heartily" and matches his companions "glass for glass." Dreiser notes, "It was not long before the imbibing began to tell" (266). Lubricated by liquor, the men begin telling droll stories of sexual conquests, Hurstwood contributing a few of his own, and they continue drinking.

When closing time comes, at midnight, Hurstwood is "in a very roseate state." His mind, Dreiser tells us, is "warm in its fancies" (266). He retires to his office, counts up the receipts, and discovers the ten thousand dollars in the safe. In these sections, Dreiser reminds us twice more that Hurstwood is still under the influence of drink. "Wine was in his veins," Dreiser says (268). And then, about a page further on, "The imbibation of the evening had not yet worn off. . . . [He] was still flushed with the fumes of liquor" (269). When Hurstwood takes the money, therefore, his reason is beclouded. He loses his head, puts the cash into his satchel, watches the door to the safe close and click shut, then panics and runs.

Dreiser removed none of these references to alcohol between manuscript and typescript or between typescript and print. Here he must have felt that Hurstwood, normally a man of probity (if not actual honesty), would have needed a prod from alcohol to commit an act of thievery. In this way Dreiser was giving Hurstwood, at least in part, an explanation for his bad judgment. Whatever Dreiser's apprehensions (if he had any) about including references to alcohol in his text, he must have felt that these needed to stay. It is also true, however, that these references would have been difficult to remove. There were several of them, scattered throughout a lengthy scene. They were integral to the language and motivation of the section; Dreiser would have had to rewrite from scratch in order to remove the mentions of alcohol.

The third reference to alcohol also comes in an important scene—the one in which Carrie goes to dinner at Sherry's restaurant with Mr. and Mrs. Vance and Robert Ames. This is Carrie's introduction to Ames, and ours as well. Ames will play an important part in what is to come in the novel. He will function as a tutor of sorts for Carrie; he will stand as an example that she will attempt several times to follow. The portly, prosperous Mr. Vance spreads himself in the elegant restaurant, ordering "freely of soup, oysters, roast meats and side dishes." Vance, Dreiser tells us, also has "several bottles of wine brought, which were set down beside the table in a wicker basket." Then follows this exchange:

> Young Ames volunteered the information that they knew he did not drink.
>
> "I don't care for wine either," said Carrie.
>
> "You poor things," said Mrs. Vance. "You don't know what you're missing. You ought to drink a little, anyhow."
>
> "No," said Carrie, "I don't believe I will."
>
> (333)

It has been made clear to us that Ames does not use alcohol; this is almost the first thing we learn about him. Carrie, watching him refuse the wine, decides on the spot to follow his lead, the first of several times she will do so in the narrative. The small exchange begs for interpretation, not least because Ames is generally thought to be Dreiser's representative in *Sister Carrie*. The exterior details of his career are probably taken from the career of the inventor Thomas Edison, but the ideas and the personality seem to be Dreiser's—as Dreiser wanted to see himself. Ames, like Dreiser, is not interested in drink. We know, then, that he will speak with a voice unbefuddled by alcohol. He will operate with reason and will speak with clarity.

About one hundred pages earlier we have seen Drouet—in the Pennsylvania text—make a fool of himself under the influence of whiskey. And about fifty pages after that, Hurstwood has made an even bigger mess of his affairs after drinking too much. Ames, it is obvious, has been placed in the novel to stand in contrast to Drouet and Hurstwood. He is more intelligent and independent than they, mush less dazzled by wealth and material display, infinitely better read and better informed, and more intuitive and sympathetic toward Carrie. In the Pennsylvania text, he has announced that he does not drink alcohol—a trait Carrie seems to like and which she mimics. Is his abstinence another instance of his superiority to Drouet and Hurstwood?

The exchange over wine at Sherry's, however, was cut from the typescript (389) by Dreiser and does not appear in the Doubleday text (355). And here we have evidence that someone, most likely Arthur Henry, suggested the cut to Dreiser, who then made it. We know from Dreiser's later testimony that Henry went through the typescript of *Sister Carrie* and marked passages that he thought could be pruned. We have evidence of Henry's work in the left-hand margins of the typescript sheets. He drew lines bracketing the passages that he recommended for excision. Dreiser came behind and made the cuts, sometimes (but not always) erasing Henry's lines. On this particular typescript sheet,

Henry's marks were erased but are still easily visible around the passage in which Ames and Carrie turn down the wine. It's almost certain, then, that Henry suggested the cut.

What does this mean? One's best guess is that Arthur Henry failed to recognize the point Dreiser was making about alcohol (if indeed he was making such a point) and saw the small exchange about wine as a bit of detail that could be dispensed with. From his other work on the typescript, it appears that one of Henry's chief goals was to streamline the narrative. Dreiser went ahead and made the cut; we can only speculate about *his* motives. Perhaps he had decided that the point about alcohol was not important. Or perhaps he had forgotten the contrast that I believe he was making between Drouet and Hurstwood on the one hand and Ames on the other. Perhaps he was too trusting of Henry's judgment. (It is true that he cut virtually every passage that Henry marked for removal.) Or perhaps he had no point at all to make about the drinking habits of these three men. It is impossible finally to know.

It should be obvious what I have been doing here. I have been constructing small biographical narratives and literary interpretations that will explain the presence of alcohol in three places in *Sister Carrie* and that, more importantly, will give reasons for Dreiser's having removed two of those references. I have in fact wanted to find reasons that will justify my having restored those references to the text of the Pennsylvania edition. Perhaps I should say that *we* have been constructing such narratives, for I would guess that readers of this essay have been doing the same thing as they have followed these speculations, perhaps inventing some alternate motivations for Dreiser or constructing some other interpretations of his text. This is fun: it's what textual editors do all the time. At base it is an exercise in biography. It certainly is not a cold, logical, dispassionate consideration of dry textual evidence—not a turn-the-crank exercise in editorial method. It's a mixture of biography, textual scholarship, and literary interpretation.[4]

I won't spin out the implications of these passages any further, but I would encourage readers to do so. It seems to me, in looking back now almost twenty years to the late 1970s, when I was first trying to make decisions about what to restore to Dreiser's text and what not to restore, that my evidence for restoring the reference to Drouet's "several drinks" was thin and speculative. That doesn't mean that the decision was wrong: only that I took a leap of faith in putting the sentence back into the text. I did so because I conceived of Doubleday, Page as keen to remove as much disreputable behavior as they could from his novel, and of Dreiser as willing to go along a certain distance in order to mollify the firm. The year, after all, was 1900, and representatives of the genteel tradition were still very much in the saddle in the literary world, as editors and critics. What is more, temperance was a large issue in American public discourse of the time. Many temperance advocates watched popular literature closely and attacked authors, and their publishers, if narratives were favorable or even neutral on the subject of alcohol. Dreiser, with his experience in the magazine world, would have known this. Perhaps, in such an atmosphere, Drouet's "several drinks" could be cut from the proofs.

I also restored the reference to Drouet's drinking because I liked the three-part statement about alcohol. Drouet drinks and behaves foolishly; Hurstwood drinks and behaves irrationally; Ames does not drink and behaves well (if a bit stiffly). I thought I discerned a pattern, a statement that Dreiser wanted to make, but I could have been wrong.[5]

I was on firmer ground, I believe, in restoring the lines in which Ames turns down the wine at Sherry's and Carrie follows suit. This is just the sort of small touch that Dreiser was good at. It is also the kind of detail that Henry asked Dreiser to cut at many other points in the typescript. I'm convinced that the restoration of such material to the Pennsylvania *Sister Carrie* makes it a richer, more suggestive and allusive novel than the Doubleday text. And here I have not only my interpretation to rely on but also Henry's marks in the margins, bracketing the passage for removal.

The larger matter that needs to be emphasized is that textual editing of this kind is far from a mechanical process. That's what makes it such an intriguing business. It requires us to think of *Sister Carrie* as an unstable, unsettled text, capable of yielding many variations in interpretation, especially when one knows the origins and textual history of important passages. A game of "What if?" is instructive here. What if the reference to Drouet's drinking were absent but the reference to Ames's abstinence were present? A textual editor could justify such a course. One's opinion of Drouet might change: he might seem even more of a fool (because he is sober and still behaves in a silly way), and Ames might seem simply to be a stuffed shirt who cannot relax and enjoy himself with a little wine at dinner. Or what if, as in the Doubleday text, only Hurstwood drinks and no mention is made either of Drouet's "several drinks" or of Ames's preferences? In that case the novel might be thought to contain a veiled moral lesson: if one imbibes when one must make important decisions, one risks ruin and destruction. Or what if, as in the Pennsylvania text, alcohol is present in all three places? Here my own take is that Dreiser is asking us to judge these three men, all of whom are important in Carrie's life, in part by the ways in which they handle strong drink. Ames wins the contest.

From an editor's point of view, these are really questions of biography. One is speculating about Dreiser's motives and intentions, and about Arthur Henry's and Doubleday, Page's as well. One is constructing roles for people to play (Dreiser as realistic and blunt, though willing to compromise in order to get his novel into print; Henry as facile and shallow, interested primarily in making Dreiser's narrative move along more quickly; Doubleday, Page as keen to remove anything from the text that might cause trouble with reviewers and public moralists). The evidence upon which one is speculating is no weaker or stronger than that used by most biographers—a famously imaginative group of writers. Textual editors, we should therefore realize, are a rather imaginative crew themselves, though they often cloak their speculations and imaginative flights in technical sounding terminology, and they cover themselves with textual tables that are hard to decipher and interpret.

One can raise questions about alcohol in *Sister Carrie* (or about similar conundrums in the text) not only in published essays such as this one, but in classrooms as well, both graduate and undergraduate. In this case, the students might be encouraged to think of *Sister Carrie* as a gambling machine. Pull the lever and only one reference to alcohol appears—but which one? Pull it again, and two references appear—but which two? Pull it once more and all three appear. How does one's interpretation change after each pull? This would not simply be a literary parlor game. An editor could justify any combination in which the references to Hurstwood's drinking remained in the text—and it might be instructive to speculate about the effect on the novel if those references were cut as well.

I hope that teachers of *Sister Carrie* will engage in this kind of exercise, and that they will use the textual apparatus in the Pennsylvania text to ferret out other points at which a restoration changes one's interpretation of the novel, in a small or a large way. That's what textual editors are supposed to do: stir up the silt at the bottom of the pool. Editors shouldn't claim that the text they present is calm, shimmering, and serenely perfect. They should instead muddy things up and stimulate discussion, as I've tried to do here.

*Abbreviation*

*JG*　　*Jennie Gerhardt*

*Notes*

1. References to *Sister Carrie* are to the text of the Pennsylvania edition: Historical Editors, John C. Berkey and Alice M. Winters; Textual Editor, James L. W. West III; General Editor, Neda M. Westlake

(Philadelphia: University of Pennsylvania Press, 1981).

2. See the Pennsylvania *Sister Carrie* 1981: 525, and West's *A "Sister Carrie" Portfolio*, 64-65.

3. An interesting side note here is that in a quite similar scene in *Jennie Gerhardt* (1911), a reference to drinking by Lester Kane was removed. See *Jennie Gerhardt* (New York: Harper and Brothers, 1911), as well as *Jennie Gerhardt*, ed. James L. W. West III. In fact, between manuscript and print, nearly all mentions of alcohol were cut from the text of the novel. In the passage in question, Lester has learned from a distraught Jennie that she has a child—little Vesta, whose existence she has been concealing from him. Vesta's caretaker, however, has come to the apartment that Jennie and Lester are sharing in Chicago and has told Jennie that Vesta is dangerously ill. Jennie rushes away to minister to the child, but not before Lester has extracted from her the information that she has a daughter. While Jennie is away, Lester meditates (rather uncharitably) on Jennie's past history. Almost his first action is to leave the apartment and stop "at the first convenient saloon" for alcohol (*JG* 1992: 208). Thus when he confronts Jennie later, after she returns, he has some of that alcohol in his bloodstream. His demeanor toward her is angry at first, but he is quickly disarmed by the simplicity and honesty of her explanations. The reference to Lester's drinking, however, was cut between manuscript and print. Since the typescript on which the editors at Harper and Brothers worked does not survive, one cannot know certainly whether they or Dreiser removed the reference, but other mentions of drinking, by Old Gerhardt, for example (*JG* 1992: 271), were also removed before the Harpers text was published. I decided that the Harpers editors probably made the cut, and I restored Lester's visit to the saloon to the Pennsylvania *Jennie Gerhardt*.

4. For an elaboration of this idea see West, "The Scholarly Editor as Biographer."

5. See West, "Fair Copy, Authorial Intention, and 'Versioning.'"

### Bibliography

#### WORKS BY DREISER

##### BOOKS

*An Amateur Laborer*, 1904. Ed. Richard W. Dowell, James L. W. West III, and Neda M. Westlake. Philadelphia: University of Pennsylvania Press, 1983.

*An American Tragedy*, 1925. New York: New American Library, 1964.

*A Book about Myself.* New York: Boni and Liveright, 1922.

*A Book about Myself (Newspaper Days)*, 1922. Greenwich: Fawcett, 1965.

*The Bulwark.* New York: Doubleday, 1946.

*Dawn.* New York: Horace Liveright, 1931.

*Dreiser-Mencken Letters.* Ed. Thomas P. Riggio. 2 vols. Philadelphia: University of Pennsylvania Press, 1986.

*The Financier.* New York: Harper and Brothers, 1912.

*Free and Other Stories.* New York: Boni and Liveright, 1918.

*Fulfilment and Other Tales of Women and Men.* Ed. T. D. Nostwich. Santa Rosa: Black Sparrow Press, 1992.

*Hey Rub-A-Dub-Dub: A Book of the Mystery and Terror and Wonder of Life.* New York: Boni and Liveright, 1920.

*A History of Myself: Newspaper Days.* New York: Horace Liveright, 1931.

*A Hoosier Holiday.* New York: John Lane, 1916.

*Jennie Gerhardt.* New York: Harper and Brothers, 1911.

*Jennie Gerhardt,* 1911. New York: Penguin, 1989.

*Jennie Gerhardt.* Ed. James L. W. West III. Philadelphia: University of Pennsylvania Press, 1992.

*Newspaper Days.* Ed. T. D. Nostwich. Philadelphia: University of Pennsylvania Press, 1991.

*Notes on Life.* Ed. Marguerite Tjader and John J. McAleer. University: University of Alabama Press, 1974.

*Selected Magazine Articles of Theodore Dreiser: Life and Art in the American 1890s.* Ed. Yoshinobu Hakutani. 2 vols. Rutherford: Fairleigh Dickinson University Press / London & Toronto: Associated University Presses, 1985, 1987.

*Sister Carrie.* New York: Doubleday, Page & Company, 1900.

*Sister Carrie.* Rpt. of the 1900 ed. Columbus: Charles E. Merrill, 1969.

*Sister Carrie.* Ed. Donald Pizer. New York: Norton, 1970.

*Sister Carrie.* Rpt. of the 1981 ed. New York: Penguin, 1981.

*Sister Carrie.* Ed. James L. W. West III, John C. Berkey, Alice M. Winters, and Neda M. Westlake. Philadelphia: University of Pennsylvania Press, 1981, rpt. 1998.

*Sister Carrie.* Ed. Donald Pizer. New York: Norton, 1970, 2nd ed. 1991.

*The Stoic.* Garden City: Doubleday Company, 1947.

*Theodore Dreiser: The American Diaries, 1902-1926.* Ed. Thomas P. Riggio, James L. W. West III, and Neda M. Westlake. Philadelphia: University of Pennsylvania Press, 1982.

*Theodore Dreiser: A Selection of Uncollected Prose.* Ed. Donald Pizer. Detroit: Wayne State University Press, 1977.

*Theodore Dreiser's Letters to Louise Campbell.* Ed. Louise Campbell. Philadelphia: University of Pennsylvania Press, 1959.

*The Titan.* New York & London: John Lane, 1914.

*A Traveler at Forty.* New York: Century, 1913.

*Twelve Men,* 1919. Philadelphia: University of Pennsylvania Press, 1998.

*UNPUBLISHED MATERIAL*

Aglaia, ms. coll. 30, box 351, folder 1, Dreiser Collection, Van Pelt Library, University of Pennsylvania, Philadelphia.

Fall River, 1899, Dreiser Collection, Van Pelt Library, University of Pennsylvania, Philadelphia.

Manuscript notes for *The Financier,* n. d., Dreiser Collection, Van Pelt Library, University of Pennsylvania, Philadelphia.

Theodore Dreiser's Letters to Suzanne Menahan Sekey, 1929-1930, Dreiser Collection, Van Pelt Library, University of Pennsylvania, Philadelphia.

Theodore Dreiser's Letters to Yvette Szekely and Others, ms. coll. 114, Dreiser Collection, Van Pelt Library, University of Pennsylvania, Philadelphia.

This Madness, Aglaia, ms. coll. 30, box 351, folder 2, Dreiser Collection, Van Pelt Library, University of Pennsylvania, Philadelphia.

*SHORT WORKS*

"A Confession of Faith." In *Theodore Dreiser: A Selection of Uncollected Prose,* ed. Donald Pizer.

"The Factory," 1910, no. 5, n. p. Rpt. in *Theodore Dreiser: A Selection of Uncollected Prose,* ed. Donald Pizer, 175-80.

"... the game as it is played ..." *New York Times* (15 January 1901). Rpt. in *The Stature of Theodore Dreiser,* eds. Alfred Kazin and Charles Shapiro, 59-60. Bloomington: Indiana University Press, 1955.

"Life Stories of Successful Men—No. 10: Philip D. Armour." *Success* 1 (October 1898): 3-4. Rpt. in *Selected Magazine Articles of Theodore Dreiser,* ed. Yoshinobu Hakutani, 1: 120-29.

"Life Stories of Successful Men—No. 12: Marshall Field." *Success* 2 (December 1898): 7-8. Rpt. in *Selected Magazine Articles of Theodore Dreiser,* ed. Yoshinobu Hakutani, 1: 130-38.

"The Literary Shower." *Ev'ry Month* (1 February 1896): 10-11.

"Mark the Double Twain." *English Journal* 24 (October 1935): 615-27.

"The Mighty Burke." *McClure's* 37 (May 1911): 40-50.

"Muldoon, the Solid Man." Rpt. in *Fulfilment and Other Tales of Women and Men,* ed. T. D. Nostwich. Santa Rosa: Black Sparrow, 1992.

"Neurotic America and the Sex Impulse." In *Hey Rub-A-Dub-Dub,* 1920, London: Constable, 1931.

"Nigger Jeff," 1901. In *Free and Other Stories,* 76-111. New York: Boni and Liveright, 1918.

"Preface." In *Sister Carrie.* New York: Modern Library, 1932.

"Scenes in a Cartridge Factory." *Cosmopolitan* 25 (July 1898): 321-24.

"Some Aspects of Our National Character." In *Hey Rub-A-Dub-Dub,* 24-59. New York: Boni and Liveright, 1920.

"The Strike To-day." *Toledo Blade* (24 March 1894): 1, 6. Rpt. in *Sister Carrie,* ed. Donald Pizer, 417-23.

"Theodore Dreiser's Letter to Yvette Eastman," 10 July 1945. In Yvette Eastman, *Dearest Wilding: A Memoir with Love Letters from Theodore Dreiser,* ed. Thomas P. Riggio, 211. Philadelphia: University of Pennsylvania Press, 1995.

"This Madness: Sidonie." *Cosmopolitan* 86 (June 1929): 83-87, 156-68.

"Three Sketches of the Poor." *New York Call* (23 November 1913): 10.

"The Town of Pullman." *Ainslee's* 3 (March 1899): 189-200.

"The Transmigration of the Sweat Shop." *Puritan* 8 (July 1900): 498-502. Rpt. in *Selected Magazine Articles of Theodore Dreiser,* ed. Yoshinobu Hakutani, 2: 214-21.

"True Art Speaks Plainly." *Booklover's Magazine* 1 (February 1903).

### WORKS BY OTHERS

West, James L. W. III. "Fair Copy, Authorial Intention, and 'Versioning.'" *Text: Transactions of Society of Textual Scholarship* 6 (1994): 81-89.

———. *A "Sister Carrie" Portfolio.* Charlottesville: University Press of Virginia, 1985.

———. "The Scholarly Editor as Biographer." *Studies in the Novel* 27 (Fall 1995): 295-303.

### Robert Butler (essay date 2000)

SOURCE: Butler, Robert. "Urban Frontiers, Neighborhoods, and Traps: The City in Dreiser's *Sister Carrie,* Farrell's *Studs Lonigan,* and Wright's *Native Son.*" *Theodore Dreiser and American Culture: New Readings,* edited by Yoshinobu Hakutani, U of Delaware P, 2000, pp. 274-90.

[*In the following essay, Butler contrasts three novels, starting with* Sister Carrie, *in which the main characters contend with the realities of city life, but whose relationships with their urban environments differ greatly.*]

Theodore Dreiser, James T. Farrell, and Richard Wright form an interesting literary triad since they were twentieth-century Chicago novelists who operated within a tradition which may be loosely described as "realistic" and "naturalistic." Moreover, both Farrell and Wright stressed their indebtedness to Dreiser for freeing them from the limitations of conventional fiction, thus enabling them to develop visions and voices which were distinctly modern. Farrell, who greatly admired Dreiser's fiction, knew him personally, and later became his literary confidante and executor, observed in *Reflections at Fifty* that he was awakened as a writer by Dreiser's novels which left an "impression" on him which was both "deep and lasting." Although he was never comfortable with Dreiser's "deterministic vision of man" and also rejected what he felt were his documentary "methods of writing," Farrell was inspired by Dreiser's conception of character and his ability to evoke human experience in a powerful, resonant way. Describing his reading of Dreiser's fiction in his own formative years, Farrell observed:

More than anything else, I felt wonder and awe: I was strengthened in my feeling that human emotions, feelings, desires, aspirations are valuable and precious. I gained more respect for life, more sympathy for people, more of a sense of human thoughts and feelings in this, our common life.[1]

Wright was likewise strongly affected by Dreiser's example and work. In a 1938 interview he stressed that "I value [Dreiser's work] . . . above, perhaps, any American writer." His praise of Dreiser three years later was even stronger, characterizing him as "the greatest writer this country has ever produced." Furthermore, Wright and Farrell shared a long friendship which went back to the early 1930s and lasted to Wright's premature death in 1960. He considered himself as part of the same "literary generation"[2] as Farrell and was clearly influenced by Farrell's novels, particularly *Studs Lonigan.*

Despite these important biographical connections and literary influences, surprisingly little has been written about the extremely fruitful relationship between these three writers.[3] It is my purpose in this essay to probe some important points of similarity and difference between these three writers as they offer fresh images and interpretations of urban experience in three representative novels, ***Sister Carrie,*** *Studs Lonigan,* and *Native Son.* Taken together, these masterworks provide a powerful literary record of Chicago from the turn of the century to the end of the Great Depression. And although they clearly reveal important affinities and continuities, emphatically demonstrating the lessons which Farrell and Wright learned from Dreiser and also from each other, they also are distinctively different in style and vision. In the final analysis, these three remarkable novels reveal their authors' unique experiences in the modern American city and their distinctive manner of portraying these experiences in a fresh and compelling vision of urban life.

Dreiser's enormously vital and energetic urban world in ***Sister Carrie,*** a world which inspires such wonder and terror in its central character, seems at first glance an altogether different literary universe from the unspectacular ethnic neighborhood depicted in *Studs Lonigan* and the frightening ghetto portrayed in *Native Son.* Not only are the social worlds in each novel radically different but the central characters' responses to their respective cities are markedly dissimilar. Because of this, each author employs radically different literary techniques to capture the human experience of these cities. Dreiser relies primarily on naturalistic methods to stress the solidity and dynamism of his large-scale urban environment while Farrell uses a wide range of realistic and impressionistic techniques to bring to life an urban world which is more ordinary and personal. As he revealed in *Reflections at Fifty*:

> I felt closer to Anderson's intimate world than I did to that depicted in Dreiser's massive novels. The neighborhoods of Chicago in which I grew up possessed something of the character of a small town. They were little worlds of their own. Many of the people living in them knew one another. There was a certain amount of gossip of the character that one finds in small towns. One of the largest nationality and religious groups in these neighborhoods was Irish-American and Catholic. I attended a parochial school. Through the school and Sunday Mass the life of these neighborhoods was rendered somewhat more cohesive.[4]

Wright, on the other hand, envisions a city that has deteriorated into a massive ghetto which is anything but an "intimate world" characterized by rituals and institutions making community life more "cohesive." The urban universe of *Native Son* is a painfully alienating environment producing tremendous fear and guilt in its inhabitants. In order to dramatize the terrifying loneliness and estrangement which his central character feels on a daily basis, Wright uses expressionistic and gothic techniques to describe the ghetto as a dark mindscape reflecting the horror of modern urban experience. All three novels can be seen as "seminal" or "paradigmatic" works since they portray the city in powerfully new ways which strongly influence subsequent American literature.

One way to focus sharply on how these novels are both connected and strikingly different in their portrayal of modern urban life is to examine how they use a centrally important motif, the recurrent image of a central character gazing out of windows into urban settings which not only provide epiphanies revealing the nature of urban experience but also clearly reflect the inward lives of these central characters. This motif, which Dreiser perhaps found in his reading of Flaubert's *Madame Bovary*,[5] is used extensively in *Sister Carrie* both as a measure of the social world she must master and also as a reflector of her inward nature and growth. It is used in a similar way in *Studs Lonigan* to reveal Studs's deepest human longings as well as to define the relationship between his personal life and the life of his urban community. *Native Son*, however, brilliantly inverts this motif. When Bigger looks out of windows at the city he is condemned to live in, he perceives neither the dynamic city which triggers Carrie's growth nor does he sense the continuity between the self and neighborhood which often calms and reassures Studs Lonigan. Rather, he perceives himself as doubly trapped, in dilapidated rooms which torment him materially and a fragmented, nightmarish public world which is a grim extension of his ghetto apartment. He feels incarcerated

in both worlds which push his mind to the brink of despair and madness.

## I

*Sister Carrie* is enclosed by scenes in which the central character looks out at windows and is stimulated by a vision of the city which fires her imagination by extending to her limitless possibilities for growth which her questing spirit craves. At the beginning of the novel Carrie eagerly looks out of the window of the train as she enters Chicago, beholding the city in "wonder" and "terror" while realizing how "alone" she is in the "great sea of life."[6] She clearly senses the city as a reflector of her deepest longings, for it is "alive with the clatter and clang of life" (7), a sharp contrast to the stagnant world of the small town in which she was raised. Beholding Chicago in the early evening, which Dreiser describes as "that mystic period ... when life is changing from one sphere or condition to another" (7), Carrie equates the city with liberating change and excitement, a new world of "theatres" and "parties" (7) which promise her new pleasures and imaginative experience. Although she briefly feels some understandable anxiety at being so abruptly separated from home, such feelings quickly pass and never appear for the remainder of the novel. The "threads" which connect her to the "village" and "home" are "irretrievably broken" (1) at the very beginning of the novel because the modern metropolis touches her at the very core of her being, offering her a protean existence in which she can create an indefinite series of new lives by assuming a variety of roles in an ever-changing city. Looking at Chicago from a train window, she is deeply stirred, thinking "I shall soon be free" (7).

Whenever Carrie's "terror" of the city returns as she directly experiences the harsher features of the urban environment, she is quickly revived by looking out of windows from her position in enclosed space and renewing the positive vision of the city which she imagined in the opening chapter. For example, when she becomes depressed by the "steady round of toil" (10) which characterizes life in Minnie's apartment, she refreshes herself by rocking in a chair by "the open window" and looking at the streets in "silent wonder" (11). While Minnie's world is a trap which will force her to relive her parents' grim working-class existence in Columbia City, Chicago's streets are a sharp break from such a bleak past. As Dreiser notes a few pages later, these streets open up into vast spaces providing new life. They are, in fact, passageways leading to an urban equivalent of the American frontier:

> The City had laid miles and miles of streets and sewers through regions where, perhaps, one solitary house stood out alone—a pioneer of the populous ways to be. There

were regions open to the sweeping winds and rain, which were yet lighted throughout the night with long, blinking lines of gas-lamps, fluttering in the wind. Narrow board walks extended out, passing here a house, and there a store, at far intervals, eventually ending on the open prairie.

(12)

The city as frontier not only provides Carrie with outward growth in the form of money, new clothes, and a progressively more lavish lifestyle but it also offers psychological and spiritual development as well. Scenes in which she looks out of windows at urban scenes that become increasingly more elegant dramatize both kings of growth. At a point where Carrie has tired of the comfortable but mediocre life she shares with Drouet, she gazes out of the window of their apartment and is inspired by the tangible and intangible "possibilities" which she sees in Chicago:

> When Drouet was gone, she sat down in her rocking-chair by the window to think about it. As usual, imagination exaggerated the possibilities for her. It was as if he had put fifty cents in her hand and she had exercised the thoughts of a thousand dollars. She saw herself in a score of pathetic situations in which she assumed a tremulous voice and suffering manner. Her mind delighted itself with scenes of luxury and refinement, situations in which she was the cynosure of all eyes, the arbiter of all fates. As she rocked to and fro she felt the tensity of woe in abandonment, the magnificence of wrath after deception, the languour of sorrow after defeat. Thoughts of all the charming women she had seen in plays—every fancy, every illusion which she had concerning the stage—now came back as a returning tide after the ebb.

(117-18)

Carrie's quest for outward "luxury" is stressed in this reverie but her inward development is also noted. As she rocks by the window and contemplates the city, she is imaginatively stimulated by imagining herself in a variety of roles which not only draw attention to her, making her "the cynosure of all eyes," but also endow her life with control, making her "the arbiter of all fates." It is precisely at this point in the novel that Carrie has become seriously involved with acting, an activity which transforms her inwardly because it gives her imaginative experience which meets some of her deepest psychological needs. Her acting also develops her will since it provides her with the means of support and mental development she needs to gain some measure of control over her environment. And acting becomes a model for developing a protean self, one capable of assuming a great variety of roles in a dynamic urban world which is always becoming new things. Carrie, who in the novel's first scene finds the theater one of Chicago's most attractive features, eventually comes to see the city itself as an immense theater, a

glitteringly protean universe which endows her with the imaginative energy she needs to create a new life.

For the remainder of the novel Carrie continues to experience remarkable physical, emotional, and psychological growth, all of which are reflected in scenes where she looks out of windows and contemplates images of the city which become increasingly more dramatic and rich in meaning. Midway through the novel as she and Hurstwood escape to Montreal on a speeding train, she looks out of the window and conjures up romantic images of two new cities which she feels will transform her life: "Montreal and New York! Even now she was speeding toward those great, strange lands, and could see them if she liked" (200). Some readers have puzzled over this scene, having difficulty finding an adequate motive for Carrie eloping to New York. She clearly feels betrayed by Hurstwood's treachery, has no proof of his divorce, and her earlier infatuation with him has cooled to the point where she clearly realizes that she is not in love with him. But the scene is altogether plausible as Dreiser wrote it and is consistent with other important scenes in the novel because Carrie is not motivated by what she sees inside the train car (a greatly reduced Hurstwood), but is instead motivated by what she imagines as she looks out of the window, a vision of two exotic cities which will provide settings for her continued growth. As was the case in the novel's opening chapter, Carrie equates the modern city with growth which can give her "a newer world" (202) of heightened pleasure, increased status, and personal development. As Hurstwood in this scene looks at the train window and can see only his reflection (a poignant foreshadowing of the narcissism which will contribute to his downfall in New York), Carrie looks "out the window" (204), envisioning a "great city" which can bring her from "bondage to freedom" (209).

Although she receives several setbacks in New York, Carrie's faith in herself and the city are ultimately validated by the radically new life which she achieves in New York. But whenever her confidence ebbs, it is revived when she gazes out of windows and contemplates the city as an emblem of freedom and expanded possibility. At times intimidated by New York's "peculiar indifference" (220), Carrie is refreshed when she looks out of her apartment window at the "great city building up rapidly" (220). After Hurstwood loses his business and becomes "addicted" to the "ease" (267) of hanging around the elegant enclosed space of hotel lobbies, Carrie instinctively separates from him and moves directly into the rough but vital city to secure a job as an actress. As she is being interviewed for a position, she quells her anxiety and self-doubt by viewing "the hard rumble of the city" (279) through the office window.

After she leaves Hurstwood and moves into an apartment with Lola, Carrie often takes pleasure in looking "down into busy Broadway" (331) from the vantage point of her penthouse windows.

The considerable human growth which Carrie achieves by the end of the novel is emphasized by the final image of her in the novel sitting in a rocking chair by a window which overlooks a bustling, growing city which can destroy people who lack sufficient imagination and will but rewards her because she has developed these qualities. Her material progress is obviously stressed by the elegance of her apartment. She has finally entered the gates of the walled city which has excluded Hurstwood and is now ready to move steadily upward in American society. And her human growth, which many readers miss, is also sharply signaled in this scene. Intellectually, she has indeed come a long way from the rather shallow "waif" dominated by the various environmental "forces" depicted in the novel's first chapter, for she is reading a novel by Balzac, the same writer who awakened Dreiser's artistic talents and ambitions. Clearly, Ames, who has urged her to drop low comedy roles and pursue more substantial artistic challenges, has "pointed out a farther step" (369) and she is now able to pursue the ideals which he has inspired in her. And Carrie's moral development is also shown when she expresses dissatisfaction to Lola about her outward success and feels genuine compassion for the bums milling below her window as they seek food and shelter. Although Carrie is aware that the city can be a lethal environment, she knows that she has acquired the human traits necessary for success in the city. As she looks at the cold city below her window, she rocks and sings, warmed by the fact that "she saw the city offering more of loveliness than she had ever known" (365).

### II

Farrell's *Studs Lonigan* presents a startling different picture of the modern American city but it borrows this technique from Dreiser of using window reveries to make its urban vision clear and coherent. At key points in the trilogy, Farrell defines his city and uses it to reveal his central character's inward nature in scenes which portray Studs looking out of windows at city scenes. Midway through *Young Lonigan*, for example, the narrator tells us that

> Studs awoke to stare sleepily at a June morning that crashed through his bedroom window. The world outside the window was all shine and shimmer. Just looking at it made Studs feel good that he was alive. And it was only the end of June. He still had July and August. And this was one of the days when he would feel swell; one of his days. He drowsed in bed, and glanced out to watch the sun scatter over the yard. He watched a tomcat slink along

the fence ledge: he stared at the spot he had newly boarded so that his old man wouldn't yelp about loose boards; he looked about at the patches in the grass that Martin and his gang had torn down playing their cowboy and Indian games. *There was something about the things he watched that seemed to enter Studs as sun entered a field of grass; and as he watched, he felt that the things he saw were part of himself, and he felt as good as if he were warm sunlight; he was all glad to be living, and to be Studs Lonigan.*

(Emphasis added)[7]

Farrell's ethnic neighborhood is dramatically different from Dreiser's metropolis in a number of important ways. First of all, it is an extremely familiar world perceived by one who has been inside that world for his entire life rather than a large-scale, dramatic world which is experienced by a newcomer who is fascinated by the city's energy, size, strangeness, and novelty. Studs is completely home in such a place—he feels "swell" when he looks through his bedroom window at a backyard filled with small, familiar objects. It is not a wide-open frontier evoking wonder and terror but a domestic place where the only hint of a frontier are the games of cowboys and Indians which small children play. Secondly, Studs's city is a communal world, a neighborhood populated by his family and friends and other people who share basic beliefs and assumptions about life. This, of course, is a sharp contrast to the city which Carrie gravitates toward, an open space which appeals to her intense individualism by inviting her to develop a unique self which can meet experience on its own terms.

But Farrell the novelist, like Dreiser, uses this window scene to reveal the nature of his character's consciousness and the urban environment which it must interact with. We find out that Studs is not really the cold "tough guy" he appeared to be in the novel's opening scene which describes him glowering into a bathroom mirror as he smokes a forbidden cigarette, but instead is a normal young man with a very "soft" interior nature which delights in the leisure of summer vacation and feels protected and secure in a warm world bathed in sunlight. Moreover, there is a surprisingly poetic quality in Studs which nobody in his social group sees—an imaginative self which regards the things around him as metaphors revealing his true inward nature. In the same way, Carrie's window meditations reveal surprising aspects of her own personality which others are often unaware of—she is not a helpless "waif amid forces" because she is empowered with imagination, intellect, and will, all of which are vividly demonstrated when she transcends the closed space of small rooms by looking out of windows at spacious, growing cities.

Although Studs's urban environment has shrunk to an ethnic neighborhood which is both a place of "spiritual poverty"[8] and a foundation for human growth, it nevertheless reveals his most deeply human qualities when he contemplates it while gazing out various windows. A vivid example of this occurs roughly midway through *Young Lonigan* when Studs returns home after eighth-grade graduation exercises and looks out of his parlor window at a Wabash Street which has been transformed by the dark night and his pensive mood:

> Studs sat by the window. He looked out, watching the night strangeness, listening. The darkness was over everything like a warm bed-cover, and all the little sounds of night seemed to him as if they belonged to some great mystery. He listened to the wind in the tree by the window. The street was queer and didn't seem at all like Wabash Avenue. ... He thought about the fall, and of the arguments for working that he should have sprung on the old man. He thought of himself on a scaffold, wearing a painter's overalls, chewing tobacco, and talking man-talk, with the other painters; and of pay days and the independence it would bring him. He thought of Studs Lonigan, a free and independent working man. ...

(*YL*, 77-78)

Here Studs clearly resembles the city scene he is contemplating. Both are enveloped in "strangeness" because they are caught in moments of change. Just as the normally familiar Wabash Avenue has an element of "mystery" because it has passed from daylight to darkness, Studs's life is now perplexing to him because he is moving from his stable life as a grammar school student in which his experiences have been structured by others to a new phase where he must make his own decisions about either continuing with his education or dropping out of school and going to work. But he sees the city as offering him viable options—his leaving school will not reduce him to poverty but will make him a "free and independent working man."

Significantly, *Young Lonigan* concludes with Studs again looking out the parlor window at a Wabash Avenue mysteriously darkened by night. But this time Studs's mood has changed, along with the urban scene before him. The tree is now "empty" and Studs is caught in a moment of melancholy, comparing himself to "a sad song" (223). He has made the disastrous decision to drop out of school and work for his father as a house painter, a decision which will greatly empty his future life of new possibilities and growth. In the final two books of the trilogy, which chronicle Studs's decline and downfall, he has all-too-few moments where he is able to envision lucidly the relationship between himself and his urban environment as he gazes out of windows. The tendency toward introspection which brings out his deeply human "soft" nature in *Young Lonigan* is repressed by a social world which demands that he be a "hard" guy given to thoughtless outer action which

becomes increasingly more destructive as the trilogy develops. He is typically described therefore in situations which bring out the worst features of his urban environment. In a very real sense, he moves from the role of Carrie in *Young Lonigan,* a youthful aspirant, to the role of Hurstwood in *The Young Manhood of Studs Lonigan* and *Judgment Day,* a pathetic figure crushed by deterministic forces he can neither understand nor control. Accordingly, he is often portrayed in the final two novels as wasting his energy, losing sight of a meaningful future and lapsing into a debilitating melancholy and nostalgia. He is often depicted, therefore, as gazing narcissistically into mirrors, getting drunk in bars, or hanging around on street corners. Like Hurstwood, he becomes addicted to ease, falling into an enervation which saps his energy and gradually destroys his ability to think clearly and act effectively. His death greatly resembles Hurstwood's demise—his health is weakened by bad weather as he desperately searches for work in a city experiencing severe economic distress. Like Hurstwood who finally becomes overwhelmed by "lassitude" (*SC* [*Sister Carrie*] 1900: 317), Studs succumbs to "weakness and lassitude" wishing "only to sleep, to close his eyes and forget everything."[9]

Danny O'Neill, a character Farrell develops consciously as a foil to Studs, bears close resemblance to Carrie Meeber as he uses imagination, intellect, and will to triumph over the negative forces in the urban environment and use the positive energies of the city to spur his growth. And both figures ultimately transform themselves through a commitment to art. Just as the theaters in New York and Chicago provide Carrie with the role of actress which enable her to tap her imaginative talents, Chicago's schools and libraries liberate Danny O'Neill, making him a writer who can use art both to understand his world and create fruitful directions for himself with that world.

At the end of *The Young Manhood of Studs Lonigan,* Danny is pictured at work in a Chicago gas station where he makes the money necessary to pay his university expenses. Like Carrie, who at the end of her novel is reading a book which stirs her imagination and clarifies her vision, Danny is reading a serious book, Veblen's *The Theory of Business Enterprise,* which induces in him the "elation of intellectual discovery."[10] And like Carrie also, he looks out a window at the city while envisioning a vital future for himself. Although his immediate urban environment confronts him with "dreariness," consisting of a "box-like carburetor factory" (*YM,* 370) and a decaying neighborhood, he can call up in his mind a liberating image of his education providing him with "a newer, cleaner world" (*YM* 372). Just as Carrie uses art as a way of learning how to *act* meaningfully in an environment which threatens to strip her of humanity, Danny discovers that by becoming a writer, he can understand and control his life, gaining "a sense of power" (*YM,* 372) over his experiences. Farrell's city, like Dreiser's city, finally is two radically opposed worlds, a harshly deterministic environment which destroys people like Hurstwood and Studs and a liberating space which offers new lives to people like Carrie and Danny. The city for both writers can be an entrapping room or a window of opportunity.

### III

*Native Son,* although set in roughly the same piece of real estate as *Studs Lonigan* and although deeply influenced by Dreiser's vision of life, presents a vastly different urban world. While Dreiser's and Farrell's characters can either be redeemed or damned by the modern American city, Wright's protagonist sees the city in purely negative terms as a prison, hell, or extended nightmare. Dreiser's metropolis and Farrell's ethnic neighborhood become in *Native Son* a teeming ghetto which contains two equally bleak options, slavery or death.

This is made painfully clear at the opening of the novel where Bigger Thomas looks out a window at the city which he and his family are condemned to inhabit. After killing the rat, he is overcome with revulsion for the life he must live in a one-room tenement apartment and seeks relief in the streets. But as he views these streets through the front door window of his apartment building, he is confronted with more images of entrapment:

> He went down the steps into the vestibule and stood looking out into the street through the plate glass of the front door. Now and then a street car rattled past over steel tracks. He was sick of his life at home. Day in and day out there was nothing but shouts and bickering. But what could he do? Each time he asked himself that question his mind hit a blank wall and he stopped thinking. . . . It maddened him to think that he did not have "a wider choice of action. Well, he could not stand here all day like this. What was he to do with himself?[11]

When Carrie Meeber looks out a window at a Chicago Street she envisions a path through a liberating urban frontier. And when Studs Lonigan examines Wabash Street, he is reminded that it is part of a neighborhood of people like himself which form a community. But when Bigger looks out at the nameless street on which his apartment is located, he sees "steel tracks" which remind him of the ghetto which paralyzes his body and traps his mind. Unlike Carrie, whose inward life is stimulated when she observes urban scenes, and Studs whose poetic thoughts are freed when he muses over what he sees in his backyard, Bigger's mind hits a "blank wall" when he observes how the ghetto

has laid out his life on tracks leading nowhere. While the city is a catalyst for Carrie's inward development and her achievement of selfhood, Bigger's city is a fiercely deterministic world which will destroy the self by reducing him to a machine or an animal. Unlike Studs who feels at home in his neighborhood and seldom wishes to venture forth from it, Bigger is "sick of his life at home" because the ghetto rooms in which he lives are an extension of cold, hard city which lay outside his windows. He can experience little but "shouts and bickering" in either place. "Maddened" by the fact that he does not have "a wider choice of action" in either his domestic life or his public life, Bigger feels triply alienated, estranged from American society, his community, and himself.

To dramatize the intensity and breadth of Bigger's alienation from an urban world that is fundamentally strange and threatening to him, Wright decided to reject the essentially mimetic styles employed by Farrell and Dreiser in favor of surrealistic techniques.[12] The city in *Native Son* is typically presented as a gothic mindscape reflecting the fear and guilt of Bigger's life which is a direct result of the lack of connection he feels between himself and his social environment. Because his external world offers him so little and because it often threatens to rob him of a significant inward life, Bigger apprehends the city as a process of fragmentation and dislocation, a strange nether world which threatens to destroy him.

For this reason, *Native Son* describes very little of the objectively real urban settings which are rendered so accurately in Dreiser's naturalistic style and Farrell's realistic techniques. The fully reified cities of **Sister Carrie** and *Studs Lonigan* become a Poe-esque landscape of nightmare in Wright's masterpiece. We are never given a precise idea of the year in which *Native Son* takes places, a sharp contrast to the exact dating which Dreiser and Farrell use to make the fictional worlds appear more "real" and to draw important parallels between the lives of their characters and the historical forces at work in their societies.[13] Nor do we see much of the physical details of Bigger's city. Full, clear and coherent descriptions of streets, houses, stores, schools, and other landmarks are never given. The novel's second scene, which describes Bigger leaving his family's apartment and walking down the street, provides a clear example of Wright's highly selective method of depicting city life which is designed more to project the character's psychological response to the city than to give a literal picture of the city. The few details mentioned—a streetcar on tracks, a plate glass window and a political poster which reads "*If You Break The Law, You Can't Win!*" (16) are clearly designed to suggest what Bigger is thinking and feeling. Shortly after this, when Bigger and Gus meet on the street, the scene is also rendered impressionistically. Observing a high-flying plane and fast-moving automobiles which painfully remind them of the mobility enjoyed by whites but denied to blacks, they realize that black people have been placed in "one corner of the city" that amounts to little more than a "jail" (32). The few details which Wright selects from the external world provide a telling description of the psychological and emotional entrapment which maddens Bigger.

To emphasize further this dislocated quality of Bigger's perceptions, Wright uses Gothic imagery extensively to describe urban reality. This is especially true in Book II where Bigger is overwhelmed by the fears that were triggered in Book I. Going to Bessie's house to draft a ransom note, he perceives the street lamps as "hazy balls of light frozen into motionlessness" (124). After killing Mary, he passes by buildings that appear to him as "skeletons ... white and silent in the night" (171). In the scene immediately following his brutal murder of Bessie, Bigger wanders the streets caught in a nightmarish world where deserted buildings look like "empty skulls" and where the windows of these buildings "gaped blackly, like ... eye-sockets" (216).

Because Farrell's characters are seldom pushed to the physical and emotional extremes that convert Bigger Thomas's Chicago into this darkly surrealistic world, their city is presented much more mimetically and lyrically. Lyrical images of the city, almost completely absent from *Native Son*, are used skillfully in *Studs Lonigan*, often being sharply counterpointed with realistic images of city life. Farrell's city, despite its harsh features, can connect with his character's deepest impulses, thereby endowing Studs's inward life with a genuine sense of possibility. Thus the street corners, pool rooms, and bars that threaten to trap Studs Lonigan are consistently contrasted with the parks that allow him to relax, free his mind, and envision a better life for himself. His street fight with Weary Reilley epitomizes his "tough outside part" (*YL,* 160), while his romantic afternoon with Lucy in Washington Park demonstrates that Studs has "a tender inside part" (*YL,* 160) to which his environment can be responsive. Looking out the window of his bedroom at the end of *Young Lonigan,* Studs can see the city and himself in terms of possibilities altogether denied to Bigger—when he sees his neighborhood he feels part of it and regards his neighborhood's image of him as consistent with his own desires to become "Studs Lonigan, a free and independent working man" (*YL,* 78).

When Bigger Thomas looks out of windows, however, the poetic "strangeness" (*YL,* 77) which fertilizes the imagination of Studs Lonigan and the exotic urban images which intrigue Carrie Meeber, become an alienating strangeness which disorients and frightens him as he sees himself as living out an extended nightmare. When he returns home after nearly killing Gus in an irrational poolroom fight, Bigger immediately goes to the window and looks out "dreamily" (43) at the city. But instead of receiving the epiphanies which enlighten and invigorate Studs and Carrie, Bigger is beset with "confused emotions" (44). He has become "disgusted" (44) with the gang which has centered his life in the present and is strickened with anxiety about his future life as the Daltons' chauffeur. His fears are powerfully confirmed when he takes a closer look at the ghetto as nightfall approaches:

> Outside his window he saw the sun dying over the rooftops in the western sky and watched the first shade of dusk fall. Now and then a street car ran past. The rusty radiator hissed at the far end of the room. All day long it had been springlike; but now the dark clouds were slowly swallowing the sun.
>
> (44)

From this point on, most of the novel's important scenes will be enacted at night when heavy snows blanket Chicago, creating an eerie world which confuses Bigger and forces him into a variety of self-destructive actions which foreclose his future. As the "sun" illuminating his world dies after being swallowed up by "dark clouds," Bigger's life will also darken until it too is swallowed up by a social environment which forces him into murderous activity.

When Bigger rides with Mary and Jan to Ernie's Chicken Shack, he feels deeply anxious about his proximity to white people in such enclosed space and looks out the car window to seek relief but instead views an urban scene which produces equally intense feelings of entrapment. Just as he sees Jan and Mary as "two vast white looming walls," he views the Chicago skyline as "a vast sweep of tall buildings" (68). On the way back, he drives through Washington Park but envisions a world quite different from the sunny, pastoral world which calms Studs Lonigan and brings out his most deeply human self. The park becomes a grim mindscape reflecting Bigger's deepest fears—as he drunkenly races through the "dark park" (78), he becomes dangerously disoriented: "His sense of the city and park fell away; he was floating in the car ..." (78). This disorientation is the first step in a sequence of irrational actions culminating in his killing of Mary in a dark room.

At the beginning of Book II when Bigger awakens in his family's one room apartment the morning after he has killed Mary, he immediately looks out the window and sees "snow falling," another hypnotic image which puts Bigger into "a strange spell" which ensnares him in a "deadlock of impulses" (93). He is caught in an eerie world where the borderline between life and death has been blurred and he is "unable to rise to the land of the living" (93). For the remainder of Book II he inhabits such a twilight zone of fear and anxiety which robs him of clear consciousness and the ability to act in humanly productive ways. Again, when he looks out of windows the external scene in the city simply mirrors his confusion rather than providing him with epiphanies which clarify things for characters like Carrie Meeber and Danny O'Neill. After being grilled by Britten for an extended period of time, Bigger looks out of the window of his second-floor room, seeking relief and clarity of mind but is again overcome with images of chaos, a city caught in a physical blizzard which exactly mirrors the psychological storms boiling in him:

> He went to the window and looked out at the swirling snow. He could hear wind rising; it was a blizzard all right. The now moved in no given direction, but filled the world with a vast white storm of flying powder. The sharp currents of wind could be seen in whirls of snow twisting like miniature tornadoes.

(182)

Interestingly, Bigger will later jump through this window in his attempt to escape from the police after they have discovered Mary's bones in the furnace but his escape is doomed from the beginning by the hostile urban environment into which he runs. First of all, the snow bank he tumbles into causes him to soil himself by urinating in a "spasm of reflex action" (207). Secondly, the "dark city streets" (207) further confuse him and limit his vision, leading him to "a strange labyrinth" (225) of tangles South Side streets, a "chaos" (225) which Bigger is never able to understand or cope with.

In Book III Bigger has very limited access to windows because he spends all of his time in cramped rooms and his energies are directed toward looking into himself rather than contemplating an external world which he knows he can never return to. His external vision is, for the most part, limited to "staring vacantly at the black steel bars" (336) of his cell or gazing at the walls of the inquest room and courtroom. But when he does get glimpses out of barred windows he is emphatically reminded that the city and the social world it represents fail completely to supply him with meaning for his present or future experiences. His only hope is to recoil from this outward world and undertake a journey into self, hoping to find "some road ... to a sure and quiet knowledge" (226).

Max tries to rejuvenate Bigger's faith in social and historical experience which transcends self by urging him to look hopefully at images of the city but he fails miserably. In the novel's final scene:

> Max rose and went to a small window; a pale bar of sunshine fell across his white head. And Bigger, looking at him, saw that sunshine for the first time in many days; and as he saw it, the entire cell, with its four close walls, became crushingly real. He glanced down at himself; the shaft of yellow sun cut across his chest with as much weight as a beam forged in lead. With a convulsive gasp, he bent forward and shut his eyes.

(386)

Sunlight, which is often used in classic American literature as a symbol of religious awakening and personal conversion,[14] is ironically inverted in this scene as it falls violently with the weight of "lead" over Bigger's chest, inducing a "convulsive gasp" and forcing him to close his eyes. He knows that the sun, which has "died" for him in Book I, will not shine for him much longer. What is "crushingly real" to Bigger is not a hopeful urban prospect outside his windows but the "four closed walls" of his cell.

At the very end of the novel Max once more tries to revive Bigger by looking out his cell window at the city but again fails in his efforts. Coaxing Bigger to look at "the tips of sun-drenched buildings in the Loop" (389), Max hopes to use this image in a way that might restore Bigger's faith in a vaguely Marxist vision of the future. Explaining that such buildings are part of a civilization centered in "the belief of men" (389) who constructed them, Max tells Bigger that the civilization symbolized by these skyscrapers is dying but will eventually be replaced by a socialist culture centered in people like him. Bigger, of course, finds Max's vision far too abstract and remote from his own human needs. He can not connect Max's "picture" of proletarian brotherhood with "what he had felt all his life" (390) and, as a result, distances himself from Max by laughing and telling him "I reckon I believe in myself. ... I ain't got nothing else. ... I got to die ..." (391). At this point Max is described as "leaning against the window" (391), blocking its view and, in effect, turning it into a wall.

With this gesture, the image of the window, which was so romantically developed in *Sister Carrie* and realistically revised in *Studs Lonigan* is harshly inverted to suggest the essentially bleak urban world which Bigger must encounter. In the final analysis, the city fails to provide *any* human meaning for him, becoming an absurd world which he must recoil from in order to salvage an existentially human identity before he dies. The "faint, wry, bitter smile" (392) on his face as he peers through the bars of his cell door in the novel's final sentence suggest that he is on his way to constructing a marginalized existential identity because he has dispossessed himself of any illusions about the city and the social world it represents and looks instead inside himself for meaning. Unlike Max who is ultimately described as a "blind man" (392), Bigger has a lucid awareness that the only windows which can provide him with hope are the windows of his soul.

*Abbreviation*

SC      *Sister Carrie*

*Notes*

1. James T. Farrell, *Reflections at Fifty,* 132.

2. Keneth Kinnamon and Michel Fabre, eds., *Conversations with Richard Wright,* 15, 38, 32.

3. See Yoshinobu Hakutani's "*Native Son* and *An American Tragedy*: Two Different Interpretations of Crime and Guilt." Hakutani offers a penetrating analysis of important thematic parallels and differences between these two novels. See also Robert Butler's "Farrell's Ethnic Neighborhood and Wright's Urban Ghetto: Two Visions of Chicago's South Side."

4. *Reflections,* 164.

5. Flaubert brilliantly uses this motif in providing epiphanies of Emma Bovary's experience. Emma is often described as feeling suffocated in rooms which symbolize her entrapment in a society which stifles her deepest human longings but she often finds relief when she looks out of the windows of these rooms and imagines a new life for herself. For example, after an argument with Charles, Emma goes to the window to refresh herself. After the ball at Vaubysard, she leans out of her bedroom window to prolong the illusion of the luxurious life she had experienced at the ball. After Leon goes to Paris, she goes to the window and is refreshed by sunlight as it irradiates her garden.

6. Donald Pizer, ed., *Sister Carrie* (New York: Norton, 1970), 7. All subsequent references to the text are to this Norton Critical Edition and page numbers will be cited parenthetically after the quotation.

7. Farrell, *Young Lonigan* (New York: Avon Books, 1972), 83. All subsequent references to the text are to this edition and page numbers will be cited parenthetically in the text after the quotation.

8. Farrell, *The League of Frightened Philistines,* 86.

9. Farrell, *Judgment Day* (New York: Avon Books, 1973), 404.

10. Farrell, *The Young Manhood of Studs Lonigan* (New York: Avon Books, 1973), 370. All references to the text are to this edition and page numbers will be cited parenthetically after the quotation.

11. Richard Wright, *Native Son* (New York: Harper and Row, 1966), 16. All subsequent references to the text are to this edition and page numbers will be cited parenthetically after the quote.

12. For an excellent discussion of Wright's use of nonrealistic fictional techniques in *Native Son,* see Dan McCall's *The Example of Richard Wright.* McCall argues persuasively that *Native Son* is in the main tradition of gothic fiction established by Poe and Hawthorne since it uses surrealistic techniques to dramatize the "racial nightmare" of American society.

13. For example, Dreiser draws much attention to the fact that *Sister Carrie* opens in 1889, a time when Chicago experienced enormous growth. He also draws our attention to the fact that Hurstwood's business in New York collapses during the financial panic of 1893. Farrell is more elaborate in the dating of the Lonigan trilogy which begins in 1916, a time of apparently great promise for American culture and ends in the late 1920s when America is in the throes of a cultural collapse brought on by the Great Depression. Significantly the turning point of Studs's life in New Year's Eve 1929, a moment when health problems begin which eventually destroy him and when America likewise develops economic, political, and social "health problems" which could lead to its demise.

14. See, for example, Jonathan Edwards's "Personal Narrative" where a beam of sunlight entering his sick room signals his miraculous recovery from a life-threatening illness and becomes a vivid reminder to him of God's grace. Thoreau, likewise, in *Walden* moves from spiritual sickness to spiritual health when a beam of sunlight entering his cabin reinvigorates him by reminding him of the coming spring and the "rebirth" of nature. Natty Bumppo's achievement of a new name and a new life when he slays the Indian in *The Deerslayer* is also symbolized by sunlight suddenly illuminating the scene.

*Bibliography*

WORKS BY DREISER

BOOKS

*An Amateur Laborer,* 1904. Ed. Richard W. Dowell, James L. W. West III, and Neda M. Westlake. Philadelphia: University of Pennsylvania Press, 1983.

*An American Tragedy,* 1925. New York: New American Library, 1964.

*A Book about Myself.* New York: Boni and Liveright, 1922.

*A Book about Myself* (*Newspaper Days*), 1922. Greenwich: Fawcett, 1965.

*The Bulwark.* New York: Doubleday, 1946.

*Dawn.* New York: Horace Liveright, 1931.

*Dreiser-Mencken Letters.* Ed. Thomas P. Riggio. 2 vols. Philadelphia: University of Pennsylvania Press, 1986.

*The Financier.* New York: Harper and Brothers, 1912.

*Free and Other Stories.* New York: Boni and Liveright, 1918.

*Fulfilment and Other Tales of Women and Men.* Ed. T. D. Nostwich. Santa Rosa: Black Sparrow Press, 1992.

*Hey Rub-A-Dub-Dub: A Book of the Mystery and Terror and Wonder of Life.* New York: Boni and Liveright, 1920.

*A History of Myself: Newspaper Days.* New York: Horace Liveright, 1931.

*A Hoosier Holiday.* New York: John Lane, 1916.

*Jennie Gerhardt.* New York: Harper and Brothers, 1911.

*Jennie Gerhardt,* 1911. New York: Penguin, 1989.

*Jennie Gerhardt.* Ed. James L. W. West III. Philadelphia: University of Pennsylvania Press, 1992.

*Newspaper Days.* Ed. T. D. Nostwich. Philadelphia: University of Pennsylvania Press, 1991.

*Notes on Life.* Ed. Marguerite Tjader and John J. McAleer. University: University of Alabama Press, 1974.

*Selected Magazine Articles of Theodore Dreiser: Life and Art in the American 1890s.* Ed. Yoshinobu Hakutani. 2 vols. Rutherford: Fairleigh Dickinson University Press / London & Toronto: Associated University Presses, 1985, 1987.

*Sister Carrie.* New York: Doubleday, Page & Company, 1900.

*Sister Carrie.* Rpt. of the 1900 ed. Columbus: Charles E. Merrill, 1969.

*Sister Carrie.* Ed. Donald Pizer. New York: Norton, 1970.

*Sister Carrie.* Rpt. of the 1981 ed. New York: Penguin, 1981.

*Sister Carrie.* Ed. James L. W. West III, John C. Berkey, Alice M. Winters, and Neda M. Westlake. Philadelphia: University of Pennsylvania Press, 1981, rpt. 1998.

*Sister Carrie.* Ed. Donald Pizer. New York: Norton, 1970, 2nd ed. 1991.

*The Stoic.* Garden City: Doubleday Company, 1947.

*Theodore Dreiser: The American Diaries, 1902-1926.* Ed. Thomas P. Riggio, James L. W. West III, and Neda M. Westlake. Philadelphia: University of Pennsylvania Press, 1982.

*Theodore Dreiser: A Selection of Uncollected Prose.* Ed. Donald Pizer. Detroit: Wayne State University Press, 1977.

*Theodore Dreiser's Letters to Louise Campbell.* Ed. Louise Campbell. Philadelphia: University of Pennsylvania Press, 1959.

*The Titan.* New York & London: John Lane, 1914.

*A Traveler at Forty.* New York: Century, 1913.

*Twelve Men,* 1919. Philadelphia: University of Pennsylvania Press, 1998.

UNPUBLISHED MATERIAL

Aglaia, ms. coll. 30, box 351, folder 1, Dreiser Collection, Van Pelt Library, University of Pennsylvania, Philadelphia.

Fall River, 1899, Dreiser Collection, Van Pelt Library, University of Pennsylvania, Philadelphia.

Manuscript notes for *The Financier,* n. d., Dreiser Collection, Van Pelt Library, University of Pennsylvania, Philadelphia.

Theodore Dreiser's Letters to Suzanne Menahan Sekey, 1929-1930, Dreiser Collection, Van Pelt Library, University of Pennsylvania, Philadelphia.

Theodore Dreiser's Letters to Yvette Szekely and Others, ms. coll. 114, Dreiser Collection, Van Pelt Library, University of Pennsylvania, Philadelphia.

This Madness, Aglaia, ms. coll. 30, box 351, folder 2, Dreiser Collection, Van Pelt Library, University of Pennsylvania, Philadelphia.

SHORT WORKS

"A Confession of Faith." In *Theodore Dreiser: A Selection of Uncollected Prose,* ed. Donald Pizer.

"The Factory," 1910, no. 5, n. p. Rpt. in *Theodore Dreiser: A Selection of Uncollected Prose,* ed. Donald Pizer, 175-80.

"... the game as it is played ..." *New York Times* (15 January 1901). Rpt. in *The Stature of Theodore Dreiser,* eds. Alfred Kazin and Charles Shapiro, 59-60. Bloomington: Indiana University Press, 1955.

"Life Stories of Successful Men—No. 10: Philip D. Armour." *Success* 1 (October 1898): 3-4. Rpt. in *Selected Magazine Articles of Theodore Dreiser,* ed. Yoshinobu Hakutani, 1: 120-29.

"Life Stories of Successful Men—No. 12: Marshall Field." *Success* 2 (December 1898): 7-8. Rpt. in *Selected Magazine Articles of Theodore Dreiser,* ed. Yoshinobu Hakutani, 1: 130-38.

"The Literary Shower." *Ev'ry Month* (1 February 1896): 10-11.

"Mark the Double Twain." *English Journal* 24 (October 1935): 615-27.

"The Mighty Burke." *McClure's* 37 (May 1911): 40-50.

"Muldoon, the Solid Man." Rpt. in *Fulfilment and Other Tales of Women and Men,* ed. T. D. Nostwich. Santa Rosa: Black Sparrow, 1992.

"Neurotic America and the Sex Impulse." In *Hey Rub-A-Dub-Dub,* 1920, London: Constable, 1931.

"Nigger Jeff," 1901. In *Free and Other Stories,* 76-111. New York: Boni and Liveright, 1918.

"Preface." In *Sister Carrie.* New York: Modern Library, 1932.

"Scenes in a Cartridge Factory." *Cosmopolitan* 25 (July 1898): 321-24.

"Some Aspects of Our National Character." In *Hey Rub-A-Dub-Dub,* 24-59. New York: Boni and Liveright, 1920.

"The Strike To-day." *Toledo Blade* (24 March 1894): 1, 6. Rpt. in *Sister Carrie,* ed. Donald Pizer, 417-23.

"Theodore Dreiser's Letter to Yvette Eastman," 10 July 1945. In Yvette Eastman, *Dearest Wilding: A Memoir with Love Letters from Theodore Dreiser,* ed. Thomas P. Riggio, 211. Philadelphia: University of Pennsylvania Press, 1995.

"This Madness: Sidonie." *Cosmopolitan* 86 (June 1929): 83-87, 156-68.

"Three Sketches of the Poor." *New York Call* (23 November 1913): 10.

"The Town of Pullman." *Ainslee's* 3 (March 1899): 189-200.

"The Transmigration of the Sweat Shop." *Puritan* 8 (July 1900): 498-502. Rpt. in *Selected Magazine Articles of Theodore Dreiser,* ed. Yoshinobu Hakutani, 2: 214-21.

"True Art Speaks Plainly." *Booklover's Magazine* 1 (February 1903).

WORKS BY OTHERS

Butler, Robert. "Farrell's Ethnic Neighborhood and Wright's Urban Ghetto: Two Visions of Chicago's South Side." *MELUS* 18 (Spring 1993): 103-11.

Farrell, James T. *Reflections at Fifty.* New York: Vanguard, 1954.

Hakutani, Yoshinobu. "*Native Son* and *An American Tragedy*: Two Different Interpretations of Crime and Guilt." *Centennial Review* 23 (Spring 1979): 208-26.

Kinnamon, Keneth, and Michel Fabre, eds. *Conversations with Richard Wright.* Jackson: University Press of Mississippi, 1993.

McCall, Dan. *The Example of Richard Wright.* New York: Harcourt, Brace, 1969.

**Shawn St. Jean (essay date 2001)**

SOURCE: St. Jean, Shawn. "'Aye, Chance, Free Will, and Necessity'": *Sister Carrie's* Literary Interweavings." *The Midwest Quarterly,* vol. 42, no. 3, Spring 2001, pp. 240-56.

[*In the following essay, St. Jean points out the varying influence of deterministic forces on the major characters of* Sister Carrie, *arguing that through their diverse outcomes, Dreiser "emphasizes the crucial role of free will in engaging the machineries of fate and chance."*]

As we approach the twentieth-century novel, scholars will take stock of where the study of major literary figures has gone and where it has yet to go. What opportunities have been missed? For example, according to literary myth, Theodore Dreiser began his first novel, **Sister Carrie** (1900), at his friend Arthur Henry's insistence by spontaneously setting down the title and proceeding without a plan. The story's source is Dreiser himself, as he recalled the book's genesis in a letter to H. L. Mencken (qtd. in Swanberg, 82). Even when controverted by documentary evidence, myths like this one have an inexplicable staying power. Speculating as to why leads to unique insights about the novel's construction.

Years later Dreiser would become famous for the painstaking research and preparation that went into novels like *The Financier* (1912) and *An American Tragedy* (1925). These later works have unmistakably crafted plot structures and specific thematic concerns. But *Sister Carrie,* though by no means an aesthetically inferior work, and, indeed, the one for which the author is today best known, appears to meander through intellectual issues much as its protagonist wanders the streets of Chicago seeking employment. Although filled with intrusive disquisitions by the narrator on all manner of topics, the work poses more questions than answers, and its predominent question is the archetypal one: What forces influence (or control) the lives of human beings? It is perhaps best to believe that Dreiser did not steer his book toward predetermined conclusions, that he struggled along with his protagonists with the meta-question. For one thing, such a view allows us to circumvent a major critical mire: whether the overt philosophy peppered throughout Dreiser's novel forms a consistent or even coherent system of thought and provides a reliable index to its themes. *Sister Carrie* more closely follows Emerson's model of organicism, in which thoughts grow naturally from events and are spoken in hard words today though they may be contradicted by everything one says tomorrow.

In pursuing his profound life-questions by this method, one natural enough for the intellectual yet inexperienced novelist, Dreiser drew on a self-acquired background in the classics, a tradition in which the finest minds of the past pursued the same object as he. And while *Sister Carrie* is not patterned in a sustained way after any specific myths or classical works, Dreiser relies heavily on tropes learned from the classical literary tradition and carried on by writers of all subsequent ages. The view of human life that emerges from the novel "stems directly ... from the Greeks" (Mencken, 21), according to terms described by midcentury classicist William Greene:

> The problem of fate, good, and evil, then, is not one that admits of any final intellectual solution; it remains partly, to be sure, within the realm of human activity and human suffering, but it lies partly on the knees of the inscrutable gods. That is what Homer and Greek tragedy have said, once and for all. Man is free, but within limits; therefore life demands of him the patient endurance of evil, the hand of compassion for fellow sufferers, and the smile of irony at fortune's ways. Above all, it demands the performance of God's will, which works through us, and which is the source, if not of worldly success (for chance has a part in that), at least of human good and human happiness.
>
> (Greene, 396)

Although the novel deals scarcely at all with "God's will" in a religious form, it has an updated equivalent in the deter-minism to which Dreiser often (but not wholly) subjects his characters. What the Greeks sometimes called the *Moirea* (fates), anthropomorphized goddesses under which even Zeus was subject, and other times called *moira* (the will of the gods) is really analogous, from the perspective of mortals without access to divine intentions, to the forces like heredity and social environment identified by the nineteenth century. In all cultures in all times people have recognized external forces that limit their freedom—thus even nonworshipping peoples have their "gods."

Beyond those forces, human beings are often profoundly affected by change (*tyche*), which lies halfway between fate and human will. *Tyche* can refer to events completely beyond any form of divine or human control, or to a realm of man's self-determination, as when Tiresias warns Creon that his decision about Antigone's punishment will determine his own future (Green, 146). Thus human will holds the third part in this cosmic scheme, allowed to operate when the other forces do not and often at crucial moments. Herman Melville poetically described the interaction of these forces; Ishmael's fanciful depiction of the swordmat he and Queequeg weave in *Moby-Dick* anticipates the fabric of Dreiserian "naturalism":

> aye, chance, free will, and necessity—no wise incompatible—all interweavingly working together. The straight warp of necessity, not to be swerved from its ultimate course—its every alternating vibration, indeed, only tending to that; free will still free to ply her shuttle between given threads; and chance, though restrained in its play within the right lines of necessity, and sideways in its motions modified by free will, though thus prescribed to by both, chance by turns rules either, and has the last featuring blow at events.
>
> (215)

Dreiser's novels have been the occasions for protracted debates over literary naturalism because of their highly variable reliance on determinism. What twentieth-century critics, who have been less and less rigorously trained in the classics than their nineteenth-century counterparts, have failed to recognize is that close comparative study of authors and their classical influences yields invaluable insight into otherwise baffling problems. Through our eyes a writer like Dreiser appears woefully inconsistent in his philosophy. Adding to the confusion in the case of *Sister Carrie,* three major characters are (partially) determined by three kinds of external force: Carrie Meeber by poverty, Charles Drouet by desire, and George Hurstwood by social convention. Examining in detail the dynamics of each life here represented demonstrates Dreiser's use of archetypes to expose varied attempts to live successfully and happily.

From the moment Carrie arrives in Chicago from her parents' home in Columbia City she is set to the task of obtaining money. At her sister's home she must earn her keep: "Anything was good enough so long as it paid, say, five dollars a week to begin with. A shop girl was the destiny prefigured for the newcomer" (15). Later, after losing her job because of sickness and reencountering Drouet (both chance events), the drummer insists on giving her two ten-dollar bills upon which Dreiser immediately begins the next chapter:

> The true meaning of money yet remains to be popularly explained and comprehended. When each individual realizes for himself that this thing primarily stands for and should only be accepted as a moral due—that it should be paid out as honestly stored energy and not as a usurped privilege—many of our social, religious and political troubles will have permanently passed. As for Carrie, her understanding of the moral significance of money was the popular understanding, nothing more. "Money: something everybody else has and I must get," would have expressed her understanding of it thoroughly.
>
> (62)

Both the narrator's socialistic linking of unequal distribution of money to societal ills and the parody of the "popular," the one circular and the other mindless, pursuit of it reveals Carrie's energies as woefully misdirected. Since she has neither the leisure nor the intellectual proclivity to see beyond immediate goals, she imagines that money equals happiness rather than that money may provide a means to happiness—hence her expectations are disappointed later. In fact, her longings are repeatedly undercut by Dreiser. As she reaches each new plateau of wealth and success, she finds something lacking that only more wealth can provide and so imagines happiness to be just one level away: "She would live in Chicago, her mind kept saying to itself. She would have a better time than she ever had before—she would be happy" (29); "It cut her to the quick, and she resolved that she would not come here [Broadway] again until she looked better. At the same time she longed to feel the delight of parading here as an equal. Ah, then she would be happy" (324); "[The playhouse] was above the common mass, above idleness, above want, above insignificance. People came to it in finery and carriages to see. It was ever a centre of light and mirth. And here she was of it. Oh, if she could only remain, how happy would be her days" (389).

Modern commentators have called such works *bildungsromans* or *erfahrungsromans* because the protagonist learns through experience. Arguably, however, Carrie learns very little. It might be more accurate to say that she is on a quest since she has the final goal of happiness in mind but lacks the knowledge of how or where to seek it. The quest is a universal archetype, and psychologists like Carl Jung have recognized that its object varies greatly but is not as pertinent as the quest itself, which is a desire to fill a void of basic human insecurity. For example, in *The Odyssey* Telemachus goes on a quest for news of his father Odysseus, who has been missing for nearly twenty years. He doesn't know his father (who left for Troy when Telemachus was an infant) and so doesn't love him or even miss him. And even though Athena knows Odysseus will soon return and so Telemachus's dangerous journey is technically unnecessary, she sends him on the quest for the sake of his own manhood: "let him find news of his dear father where he may and win his own renown about the world" (*Od.* I. 120-22). The youth had been complaining:

> Were his death known, I could not feel such pain—
> if he had died of wounds in Trojan country
> or in the arms of friends, after the war.
> They would have made a tomb for him, the Akhaians,
> and I should have all honor as his son.
> Instead, the whirlwinds got him, and no glory.
> He's gone, no sign, no word of him; and I inherit
> trouble and tears—and not for him alone,
> the gods have laid such other burdens on me.
>
> (*Od.* I. 281-89)

The overriding goal of manhood in this epic society is *kleos* (glory), and Telemachus has none of his father's and none of his own so long as his mother's suitors occupy his home. Though he surely wishes for Odysseus's return, any number of solutions would satisfy his real need, which is a secure place for himself. Quests for the missing father, for hidden treasure, for a holy object, to return home or find a new one, all add up to the same thing in terms of archetypal psychology. Similarly, Carrie seeks a substitute for her true goal of happiness and security, the thing *her* society values above all else, money.

All quests involve obstacles. These can take the form of tests of strength, intellect, endurance, or will. Often they build character (as when Telemachus escapes the suitors' ambush at sea), or help a person see previous error, as when Odysseus speaks to Tiresias in the Underworld and learns that Poseidon hates him for the blinding of his son, the cyclopean Polyphemus. In his turn, Dreiser forces us to recognize that the actions of other people can be great impediments and a nearly overwhelming factor of determination, nearly equal to fate itself.

In Carrie's case the two men to whom she becomes mistress pose insidious obstacles since, like *The Odyssey*'s lotus eaters, they appear to represent quick and easy paths to happiness. Drouet tempts Carrie with money, and in extending her "first fall" over several scenes Dreiser masterfully demonstrates how external forces, chance, and will all subtly combine. In fact, the event is so anticlimactic that we may scarcely notice, with Carrie, that she has irrevocably chosen a direction in life. This device was to become a Dreiserian hallmark and a major contribution to literary realism: characters mistake profound decisions as meaningless or minor, and so choose carelessly or without thought at all. In Greek epic and drama, such moments—Oepidus's demanding to know the mystery of his birth or Patroclus requesting to wear Achilles's armor into battle—eventuate in ruin, but force a "late learning"—protagonists and audience see the gravity of error in retrospect of calamity. By no means does this suggest fatalism, since proper consideration of one's decisions at the crucial juncture can always prevent tragedy.

Dreiser's technique of protracting moral failures is an antithesis of the kind of high drama exhibited when Mark Twain's Huck decides not to turn in escaped slave Jim: "It was a close place. I took it [the letter to Jim's mistress] up, and held it in my hand. I was a trembling, because I'd got to decide, forever, betwixt two things, and I knowed it. I studied a minute, sort of holding my breath, and then says to myself: 'All right, then, I'll *go* to hell'—and tore it up" (270-71). Twain punctuates Huck's moral crisis through irony: the reader knows Huck will *not* incur divine wrath—go to hell—and that the crisis has been precipitated only through warped antebellum Southern values. However, it has not been illusory *to Huck,* just as Telemachus never knows that Athena protects him against the suitors' deathtrap. Inner growth occurs regardless of the seeming insignificance of external events.

The difference in Dreiser consists not so much in the scope of events as in the individual's reaction (or lack of) to them. Carrie is hardly equipped to perceive the trap being laid for her, as provincial and beaten down by circumstances as she is. The best she can manage is to waver between desire and some half-formed inhibitions: "He made her take [the twenty dollars]. She felt bound to him by a strange tie of affection now" (61); "She felt ashamed in part to have been weak enough to take it, but her need was so dire, she was still glad" (63); "Carrie finally decided that she would give the money back. It was wrong to take it" (66); "Carrie shook her head. Like all women she was there to object and be convinced. It was up to him to brush the doubts away and clear the path if he could" (68). The pivotal decision of accepting Drouet's money and leaving her sister to live with him is extended over ten pages, though with hardly the concentration that William Dean Howells gave to Lapham's decision between dishonesty and fraud during his overnight vigil. Instead, Dreiser diffuses the significant internal moments,

represented by the brief sentences above, with superficial events—Dreiser's and Carrie's conceptions of Drouet, his light conversation with her, a scene in which Minnie suggests Carrie return to Columbia City, a trip to look at new jackets which is repeated with Drouet, and a dinner date—that deflect our and Carrie's own attention from her dilemma. Indeed, the precise moment of commitment passes without a reflective thought from either the narrator or Carrie:

> The saleswoman helped her on with [the jacket], and by accident it fitted perfectly.
>
> Drouet's face lightened as he saw the improvement. She looked quite smart.
>
> "That's the thing," said Drouet. "Now pay for it."
>
> "It's nine dollars," said Carrie.
>
> "That's all right—take it," said Drouet.
>
> She reached in her purse and took out one of the bills. The woman asked if she would wear the coat and went off. In a few minutes she was back and the purchase was closed.

(70)

Closed as well are Carrie's remaining options. Unemployed and thus paying no board, she cannot bring the jacket home to her sister. Yet she blinds herself to the fact that she has made a contract with Drouet: "The deeper she sank into the entanglement, the more she imagined that the thing hung upon the few remaining things she had not done. Since she had not done so and so yet, there was a way out" (70). But the only alternative is laid out by the drummer: to take her own apartment, subsidized by him. "She thought a long time about this. Finally she agreed" (71). Though this last narrative statement appears to show a moment of decision comparable to Huck's, there is nothing left to think about—Carrie only "imagines" a way out which is already closed. It is as if Huck had already mailed the letter and then sat down to think about the consequences.

It is crucial to notice the interaction of forces that has taken place. Drouet perceives Carrie's untoward circumstances, her narrow life with her sister and her lack of means. Through persuasion and a primitive psychological understanding, he manipulates Carrie into accepting his money. Chance events, her original illness and the "accidental" fit of the jacket, conspire to aid him. Finally, Carrie makes a decision not to accept the money but then spends it voluntarily. There can be no denial of free will at this point, but Carrie yields to desire for instant gratification versus the consideration of long-term consequences. Aeschylus had similarly shown the abdication of will as a source of doom in *Agamemnon.* Upon his triumphant return from Troy,

Agamemnon is begged by his adulterous wife Clytemnestra to walk on a crimson carpet, unwittingly to his death:

CLY:

> Now, my beloved one,
> step from your chariot: yet let not your foot, my lord,
> sacker of Ilium, touch the earth.
> . . . . . . . . . . . . . . . . . . . . . . .

AG:

> Such state becomes the gods, and none beside.
> I am a mortal, a man; I cannot trample upon
> these tinted splendors without fear thrown in my path.
> . . . . . . . . . . . . . . . . . . . . . . . . . . . . . . . . . . . . . . .

CLY:

> O yield! The power is yours. Give way of your own free will.

AG:

> Since you must have it—here, let someone with all speed
> take off these sandals, slaves for my feet to tread upon.
> And as I crush these garments stained from the rich sea
> let no god's eyes of hatred strike me from afar.

*(Agamemnon, 905-47)*

Though Carrie is hardly guilty of the damning *hubris* exhibited here, she has the same opportunity to make her own choice between moral imperative and human persuasion. In the end, however, not even the "late learning" which presumably comes to Agamemnon during his offstage murder lights on Carrie. Unreflectively riding the wave of events, she seldom looks back.

The entire pattern is repeated when Carrie leaves Drouet for Hurstwood. Rather than rehearse what has already been shown, however, it should prove far more useful to reflect on Dreiser's use of the timeless love triangle, also the subject of Aeschylus's drama. Drouet first introduces Carrie into conversation with Hurstwood as an object with which to impress the manager: "Thus was Carrie's name bandied about in the most frivolous and gay of places, and that also when the little toiler was bemoaning her narrow lot, which was almost inseparable from the early stages of this, her unfolding fate" (49). Ironically, it is not her name which has been bandied—Drouet identifies her as "a little peach"—and the two men continue to objectify her in conversation after conversation (80, 108, 134, 166). Though each desires her, the idea is to present the facade of male indifference buttressed by the eternal notion that women are beneath notice. However, fated through Drouet's ambition to cultivate Hurstwood's favor, Carrie meets the manager. He compares favorably to the drummer, an indefatigable flirt who promises to marry Carrie but delivers only material

comfort and spiritual neglect. Hurstwood does the same with his own wife.

During one of Drouet's trips Hurstwood visits Carrie and begins his seduction. One is reminded of Aegisthus, who seduces Clytemnestra while Agamemnon wars at Troy. Like Drouet, Hurstwood uses Carrie's restlessness as a substitute for affection for him:

> "You are not satisfied with life, are you?"
>
> "No," she answered weakly.
>
> He saw he was master of the situation—he felt it. He reached over and touched her hand.
>
> "You mustn't," she exclaimed, jumping up.
>
> "I didn't intend to," he answered easily.
>
> She did not run away, as she might have. She did not terminate the interview, but he drifted off into a pleasant field of thought with the readiest grace. Not long after, he rose to go and she felt that he was in power.
>
> (120)

The same scene has occurred in courtless works in all ages. Here it is significant that Carrie relinquishes her power willingly. She opens the door for the manager to press his suit. For example, Hurstwood contrives, through his social connections, to make Carrie's first stage appearance a success. His acquaintances respond "like Romans to a senator's call" (174). She shines in her performance and the secret rift between the rival men deepens: "He walked away from the drummer and his prize, at parting feeling as if he could slay him and not regret. . . . 'The fool,' he said, now hating Drouet. 'The idiot. I'll do him yet. And that quick. We'll see tomorrow" (194).

Though himself a force over Carrie, Hurstwood too subjects himself to fate and chance through prior choices. As manager of a popular Chicago watering hole, Hurstwood's most important role is to mingle with the affluent clientele. His life is entirely defined by social protocol. Struck in a loveless marriage, he dares not make mistakes:

> He could not complicate his home life, because it might affect his relations with his employers. They wanted no scandals. A man, to hold his position, must have a dignified manner, a clean record, a respectable home anchorage. Therefore he was circumspect in all he did, and whenever he appeared in the public ways of an afternoon on Sunday, it was with his wife and sometimes his children. He would visit the local resorts or those nearby in Wisconsin and spend a few stiff, polished days, strolling about conventional places doing conventional things. He knew the need of it.
>
> (85)

Like Agamemnon about to stroll on the carpet, Hurstwood "deprecate[s] the folly of the thing" that will bring about his own doom. Ironically, he knows of others who have been exposed: "It was all right to do it—all men do those things—but why wasn't he careful? A man can't be too careful. He lost sympathy for the man that made a mistake and was found out" (85). But in his pursuit of Carrie he forgets his objectivity: "That worthy, on the contrary, had formulated no plan of action, though he listened, almost unreservedly, to his desires" (132). Dreiser's narrator explains the unwritten laws with which the manager trifles:

> Many individuals are so constituted that their only thought is to obtain pleasure and shun responsibility. They would like, butterfly-like, to wing forever in a summer garden, flitting from flower to flower, and sipping honey for their sole delight. They have no feeling that any result which might flow from their action should concern them. They have no conception of the necessity of a well-organized society wherein all shall accept a certain quota of responsibility and all realize a reasonable amount of happiness. ... Many such an individual is so lashed by necessity and law that he falls fainting to the ground, dies hungry in the gutter or rotting in the jail and it never once flashes across his mind that he has been lashed only in so far as he has persisted in attempting to trespass the boundaries which necessity sets.
>
> (132)

The repeated word "necessity," a rough equivalent with the Greek *ananke,* connotes those things which are necessary for the greater good and so subject the individual. In the case of transgression, "life has been misunderstood" (133). We have seen that Hurstwood understands well society's rules, and he has hitherto abided by them. His lapse, then, comes not through ignorance nor even some kind of character flaw. It is a miscalculation, a *hamartia*:

> He did not feel that he was doing anything which would introduce a complication into his life. His position was secure; his home life, if not satisfactory, was at least undisturbed; his personal liberty rather untrammeled. Carrie's love represented only so much added pleasure. He would enjoy this new gift over and above his ordinary allowance of pleasure. He would be happy with her and his own affairs would go on as they had—undisturbed.
>
> (133)

His literal *moira,* or "ordinary allowance of pleasure"—a dispensation from the urns of Zeus—fails to satisfy the manager. Many have seen his theft of ten thousand dollars from the tavern safe, the dramatic center of the novel, as the nexus of Hurstwood's decline. Yet it is only the *peripeteia,* the reversal of fortune brought on by this earlier *hamartia,* since he only does it in order to fly with her. His wife has found his affair out; she has locked him out of the house and obtained a lawyer; and she holds most of his assets in her name. He finds he cannot do anything to prevent the turn of events but "think," delay, and "wish over and over that some solution would offer itself" (237). He, in his turn, has become "like a fly in a web" (237). Even at this point there are avenues open to him—like obtaining his own lawyer—yet he does nothing until the fateful night he finds the safe ajar.

We might justifiably wonder if anything besides love or desire brings on Hurstwood's *hamartia.* In his case, the Greek adage "Whom gods destroy they first make mad" provides a clue. He even agrees to marry Carrie (who doesn't yet know he is already married) to convince her to leave Drouet:

> His passion had gotten to that stage now where it was no longer colored with reason. He did not trouble over little barriers of this sort in the face of so much loveliness. ... He would promise anything, everything, and trust to fortune to disentangle him. He would make a try for Paradise, whatever might be the result. He would be happy, by the Lord, if it cost all honesty of statement, all abandonment of truth.
>
> (209-10)

Dreiser's narrator refers several times to Hurstwood's loss of reason (222, 300), expressed here as *ate,* delusion rooted in excess. Try as he might, he cannot induce the same rational loss in Carrie: "She was listening, smiling, approving, and yet not finally agreeing. This was due to a lack of power on Hurstwood's part, a lack of that majesty of passion that sweeps the mind from its seat, fuses and melts all arguments and theories into a tangled mass and destroys, for the time being, the reasoning power" (222). Meanwhile, his lack of reason, or ability to make sound decisions takes on a unique form of determination.

Hurstwood's moment of crisis at the safe is almost painfully drawn out in the novel. As he closes up one night he discovers the safe has been left open by a careless cashier. The temptation to steal the money inside, thus enabling him to fulfill his rebellious fantasies, prompts him to remove the money and transport it back and forth from the safe to his office. The narrator mixes philosophic commentary right in with the spectacle:

> The wavering of a mind under such circumstances is an almost inexplicable thing and yet it is absolutely true. Hurstwood could not bring himself to act definitely. He wanted to think about it—to ponder it over, to decide whether it were best. He was drawn by such a keen desire for Carrie, driven by such a state of turmoil in his own affairs, that he thought constantly that it would be best, and yet he wavered. ...
>
> He went over and restored the empty boxes. Then he pushed the door to for somewhere near the sixth time. He wavered, thinking, putting his hand to his brow.

> While the money was in his hand, the lock clicked. It had sprung. Did he do it? He grabbed at the knob and pulled vigorously. It had closed. . . .
>
> At once he became the man of action.
>
> (271)

If we apply the concepts of the famous passage from Chapter VIII, in which Dreiser's narrator discourses on the power of instinct versus free will, directly to this scene, we see a strange consistency. The most prominent characteristic of both passages is "wavering"; if we take Hurstwood to be representative man here, his "reason," or need "to think it over" is at war with his "desire" for the rewards the money will bring, most notably Carrie. In his paralysis, or inability to act on his own, he becomes a "wisp in the wind" (73), settling where the "forces of life" deposit him. Note the extreme ambiguity of the sequence "the lock clicked. It had sprung. Did he do it?" It is almost as if, in the face of his refusal to act, the "forces of life" deprive Hurstwood of agency and act for him. But on the other hand, we see him decide that "he would do it before he could change his mind." A paragraph later, he says, "I wish I hadn't done that. By the lord, that was a mistake" (271). Hurstwood himself seems to accept responsibility at that moment. But at this crucial juncture, Dreiser's usually overobliging narrator refuses to decide the issue. We get cryptic phrasing and rhetorical questioning, just when we *want* answers.

In the face of such narrative ambivalence, there is nothing for readers to do but reach into their own repertoires, beliefs, and experiences, and extrapolate an answer. The Greeks might compromise by citing *ananke*, necessity—the fate that manifests itself, not remotely like *moira*, but in moments of crisis—as the force at work here, but modern readers have access to no such concept. For the reader that believes in free will and responsibility of the actor, Hurstwood is guilty. For the reader who sees life as ultimately beyond personal control, the manager is innocent. At least, these are the apparent choices, and while readers can afford to defer their decisions indefinitely, most critics do take a side.

But consider again Dreiser's stance in Chapter VIII. He tells us that man is guided sometimes by reason, sometimes by instinct, "erring" and "retrieving" at intervals. It is doubtful, during Hurstwood's apparent surrender to *instinct*, that Dreiser would apply the categories of guilt and innocence to Hurstwood at all, since "on the tiger no responsibility rests." It also seems likely that on another night Hurstwood might just as well have not taken the money, and gone home. As the narrator tells us, "The true ethics of the situation never once occurred to him."

His only fear is whether he will be caught or not. And it is this fear that drives him to flight and the kidnapping of Carrie, and indeed, to his eventual death. At the moment he abdicates choice at the critical juncture (the closing of the safe), his subsequent choices begin to dwindle to the vanishing point. He never even allows himself to consider another course of action. And the fact that he appears determined for the rest of the novel tends to obscure the fact that *choice has at some point been available,* even though the protagonist does not avail himself of it. A third choice, somewhere between guilt and innocence, now becomes available to readers—that the protagonist's deterministic muddle is, in reality, self-imposed. Outside forces don't deprive him of choice, he won't accept choice, the primary manifestation of free will. Thus a kind of "variable" determinism becomes viable: the world goes on even when we refuse to, and can affect us whether we act or not.

After detectives track the fleeing couple and force the ex-manager to return most of the stolen money in exchange for amnesty from prosecution (all without Carrie's knowledge), they settle in New York City. Thus begins Hurstwood's mental and moral decline. He cannot accept that burning his bridges through the original theft has irrevocably lowered his position in society. He rejects the idea of becoming a bartender. Like Agamemnon, he ensures *ate* (ruin) and *nemesis* (retribution) by his *hubris* (pride beyond merit). And like Odysseus returned home, he will eventually be humbled into beggary, though no god intervenes to reserve his transformation. He asphyxiates himself in a fifteen-cent flophouse, repeating the mantra he had learned looking for work, "What's the use?" (361, 387, 499). In other words, he despairs that he can take effectual action any longer and chooses the only option left, a "distinguished decision" to choose the time and manner of his death, thus investing it with some vestige of honor.

In the face of Hurstwood's apathy Carrie realizes that "she herself had been drifting" (376). He even meets her suggestions that she might obtain work as an actress with derision:

> "If I were you I wouldn't think of it. It's not much of a profession for a woman."
>
> "It's better than going hungry," said Carrie. "If you don't want me to do that, why don't you get work yourself?"
>
> There was no answer ready for this. He had got used to the suggestion.
>
> "Oh, let up," he answered.
>
> The result of this was that she secretly resolved to try. It didn't matter about him. She was not going to be dragged into poverty and worse to suit him. She could act.
>
> (378)

Her resolution to act, in the dual sense of the word, marks the parting of their ways, and, more importantly, a major turning point of growth and fortune for Carrie. Even against the painful memories of her job searches in Chicago and repeated rebuffs at agencies and theaters, Carrie obtains a place as a chorus girl. Interestingly, though the play is not named, the chorus girls wear "pink fleshings," "imitation golden helmets," "military accoutrements," and carry short swords and shields (396, 398, 401). Carrie's looks and energy soon earn her the captaincy of the line, complete with "epaulets and a belt of silver." These "new laurels" mark the former country girl-turned-mistress as a warrior in her own right. Her rise to fame and fortune is marked by hard work and chance events. The contrast to Hurstwood's fatalism, his retreat to the "Lethean waters" of newspapers and Carrie's old rocking chair (354), and his lotus-eater-like addiction to ease (373) emphasizes the crucial role of free will in engaging the machineries of fate and chance.

By a creative blurring of disciplinary boundaries, then, of adopting the critical tools of classicists, which were well known to nineteenth and early twentieth-century writers but more and more alien to literary critics today, we can explore the idea that the works of so-called literary naturalists may not be, as has been charged over and over, wildly inconsistent. They may instead follow an ancient paradigm—one that explained human existence for a near-millennium and continued to occupy the likes of philosopher Lequyer, Renouvier, Bosanquet, and Bergson in France and C. S. Peirce and William James in America—and one that fell into disuse only relatively recently with disciplinary shifts and splits in the academy.

*Bibliography*

Aeschylus. *Agamemnon.* Trans. Richmond Lattimore. *Aeschylus I.* Chicago: University of Chicago Press, 1953.

Dreiser, Theodore. *Sister Carrie.* Ed. James L. W. West III. Philadelphia: University of Pennsylvania Press, 1981.

Greene, William Chase. *Moira: Fate, Good, and Evil in Greek Thought.* Cambridge: Harvard University Press, 1948.

Homer. *The Odyssey.* Trans. Robert Fitzgerald. Garden City, New York: Anchor Books, 1963.

Melville, Herman. *Moby-Dick, or The Whale. The Writings of Herman Melville.* Eds. Harrison Hayward, Herschel Parker, and G. Thomas Tanselle. Evanston and Chicago: Northwestern University Press and Newberry Library, 1988.

Mencken, H. L. "The Dreiser Bugaboo." *Seven Arts,* 2 (August 1917), 507-17. Rpt. in Donald Pizer, *Critical Essays on Theodore Dreiser.* Boston: G. K. Hall & Co., 1981: 19-26.

Swanberg, W. A. *Dreiser.* New York: Bantam Books, 1967.

Twain, Mark. *Adventures of Huckleberry Finn. The Works of Mark Twain.* Vol. 8. Eds. Walter Blair and Victor Fischer, Berkeley: University of California Press, 1988.

## James L. W. West III (essay date 2001)

SOURCE: West, James L. W., III. "The *Sister Carrie* We've Come to Know." *Dreiser Studies,* vol. 32, no. 2, Fall 2001, pp. 39-41.

[*In the following essay, West describes the cooperative dilemmas that face writers and editors of published fiction, using as an example his experiences in helping edit the Pennsylvania Edition of* Sister Carrie.]

I'm sometimes asked whether, if I had it to do over, I would again edit the text of **Sister Carrie** as I did for the 1981 Pennsylvania edition. I always answer yes: I would restore the same passages, reinstate the profanity and the real names, drop the chapter titles, and print the original endings for the final two chapters. But I would present the text differently, using an alternative rhetoric, similar to the language with which I presented **Jennie Gerhardt** in 1992 and F. Scott Fitzgerald's *Trimalchio,* an early text of *The Great Gatsby,* in 2000. I would not be as insistent about the virtue of what I was doing.

This requires a short diversion into editorial theory. Speaking very broadly, there are two traditions of editing that operate in the academy today. One, the Greg-Bowers-Tanselle tradition, accepts the idea of authorial intention, values that intention above all else, and relies on editorial judgment. The other, the Peckham-McGann-Reiman approach, insists to the contrary that the culture speaks the text, that all works of literature are collaborations, that they exist in versions that shouldn't be tampered with, and that the modern editor's judgment should be exercised sparingly if at all.

The virtue of the first approach is that the scholarly editor is cast as hero and savior. He or she is the defender of the author's textual rectitude. The vocabulary here is indicative of the moral cast: one does away with "corruption" and "tampering"; one restores a text to the original "purity" of the author's intentions. It's a romantic notion, appealing because it puts the editor in a favorable light. It also delegates to the editor a great deal of authority. The virtue of the second approach is that the scholarly editor cuts a more modest figure: he or she is a presenter or mediator, not a knight-errant. An editor of this persuasion assumes a less confident stance and is reluctant to participate in the creation of an alternative text. Such a reduced role is more attractive to editors hesitant to make aesthetic judgments or to execute emendations; the variant passages are simply presented, and the user of the edition is supposed to contemplate which, if any of them, is preferable to the others. I should add that the labor is the same for editors of both persuasions. We poor, plodding comma-counters must still hunt up the surviving textual forms, collate them one against the other, and present the results in textual tables or electronic lists. (And then wonder whether anyone ever really uses those lists.)

I remain an intentionalist. I would edit *Sister Carrie* again by attempting to recapture, through editorial labor and literary imagination, what I thought to be Dreiser's intentions for his first novel, before he began to listen seriously to advice from his wife Sara and his friend Arthur Henry and before Doubleday, Page required him to expunge profanity, sexual innuendo, and real names. But I now understand that a culture can speak a text too and that the 1900 edition of *Sister Carrie* is as good an example of such a collaborative work of art as we are likely to find in twentieth-century American literature. Texts of this sort are of considerable value; they are worth studying and writing about, just as surely as restored texts (spoken by their own scholarly cultures) are deserving of close attention.

The controversy over the restored *Sister Carrie* helped to bring into the light similar questions about other literary texts. No teacher who stands before a college class today can teach *Sister Carrie* or *Jennie Gerhardt* or *The Great Gatsby* or *Tender Is the Night* or *Sanctuary* or *Go Down, Moses* or "The Yellow Wall-Paper" or *Women in Love* or *Lady Chatterley's Lover* or *Ulysses* or *The Jungle* or *The Sun Also Rises* or *A Farewell to Arms* or *Lie Down in Darkness* or *Black Boy* or *The Floating Opera* or—this list could go on—no one can teach these works responsibly without knowing something about their textual histories and without explaining to the students, undergraduate or graduate, whether the paperback that they hold is a text spoken by a culture or by an author.

I've found my students to be curious about such matters and almost always uninformed about them. The concepts aren't hard to grasp; everyone understands the issues right away. Stories about the composition, editing, bowdlerization, and restoration of texts can be presented effectively with photocopies or slide projectors—or from computer

disks, if the classroom is fitted out with digital equipment. These presentations capture the attention of students, unlike much of what has been coming out of English departments for the past twenty years. Teachers who take the trouble to work up such lectures can use them semester after semester; they can also require something more from their students than (as we used to say in the 1970's), "Read the text, man, and describe your vibes."

I'm glad now that we had a controversy over the text of *Sister Carrie* and that the disagreements haven't gone away. I think we conducted ourselves very well, as opposed, say, to the Joyce scholars with their loud fussing over the text of *Ulysses.* Our controversy made people think about issues of intention and authority; it also helped them to see that a text is not an icon but a process, forever in flux. Texts remain in motion, indeterminate and unstable. Those words are tossed around casually by literary theorists; I like it that we have real, concrete examples of unstable texts—such as *Sister Carrie.*

A final point: I've come to believe that scholarly editing is a species of biography. This insight grew on me while I was writing *William Styron: A Life,* published in 1998. Like biographers, scholarly editors attempt to recapture and describe behavior from the past. Biographers and editors use the same evidence and speculate in the same ways. They also offer moral judgments—or refuse to do so, or pretend not to do so—giving similar reasons for what they are doing or not doing. Editors construct portraits of authors which will legitimize what they mean to do with the texts those authors have written; editors use the methods of biographers to assemble these portraits. Certainly that is what I did with Dreiser and *Sister Carrie.* I meant to present him as a disciplined professional and a serious young artist, not as a poorly educated rube from Indiana who needed chastisement with the blue pencil. I would do it again, but the second time I'd be more aware of my methods and my intentions—for editors have intentions too. I know I did when I edited *Sister Carrie.*

---

## FURTHER READING

### Bibliographies

Boswell, Jeanette. *Theodore Dreiser and the Critics, 1911-1982: A Bibliography with Selective Annotations.* Scarecrow Press, 1982.

A secondary bibliography with annotations.

Elias, Robert H. "Theodore Dreiser." *Fifteen Modern American Authors: A Survey of Research and Criticism,* edited by Jackson R. Bryer, Duke UP, 1969, pp. 101-38.

> Combines critical opinion with secondary listing information.

Pizer, Donald, Richard W. Dowell, and Frederick E. Rusch. *Theodore Dreiser: A Primary Bibliography and Reference Guide.* G. K. Hall, 1991.

> Includes both extensive primary and secondary bibliographic listings.

**Biographies**

Lingeman, Richard. *Theodore Dreiser: At the Gates of the City, 1871-1907.* Vol. 1. Putnam, 1986. *Theodore Dreiser: An American Journey, 1908-1945.* Vol. 2. Putnam, 1990.

> Covers Dreiser's life and career in two parts, the first from early life through the republication of *Sister Carrie* in 1907 and the second throughout his remaining writing career until his death.

Loving, Jerome. *The Last Titan: A Life of Theodore Dreiser.* U of California P, 2005.

> Presents the life of Dreiser in the context of one hundred years of arguments about naturalism, the use of journalism in fiction, and the characteristics of Dreiser's largely German family.

Swanberg, W. A. *Dreiser.* Scribner, 1965.

> Compiles a complete survey of Dreiser's life, separated into six "books" with numerous photographs of Dreiser and his family. Swanberg draws from public knowledge of Dreiser, his publications, and his private notes, letters, and newspaper clippings.

**Criticism**

Fisher, Philip. "The Life History of Objects: The Naturalist Novel and the City." *Hard Facts: Setting and Form in the American Novel,* Oxford UP, 1985, pp. 128-78.

> Takes a New Historicist approach to *Sister Carrie,* comparing the society and politics of the cities to the psychology of the characters. Fisher discusses Carrie's life in New York on the stage, recounting objects and devices pertinent to drama. Fisher contends that Hurstwood drew energy from stealing—both money from his employers and Carrie from Drouet—but because New York is a more formidable setting than Chicago, his energy waned.

Gair, Christopher. "*Sister Carrie,* Race, and the World's Columbian Exposition." *The Cambridge Companion to Theodore Dreiser,* edited by Leonard Cassuto and Clare Virginia Eby, Cambridge UP, 2004, pp. 160-76.

> Comments on the absence of both immigrants and racial minorities in *Sister Carrie* as well as the 1893 World's Columbian Exposition Dreiser visited as a journalist. Gair extends the contrast between the wealthy utopia illustrated by the "White City" segment of the Exposition and the poverty of Chicago, particularly its immigrant population, which is where he places Hurstwood.

Gelfant, Blanche H. "What More Can Carrie Want? Naturalistic Ways of Consuming Women." *The Cambridge Companion to American Realism and Naturalism: Howells to London,* edited by Donald Pizer, Cambridge UP, 1995, pp. 178-210.

> Assesses Carrie's many material desires in light of the deterministic nature of naturalist narratives. Gelfant emphasizes the dual nature of desire as both "ontological and cultural, an innate human condition and the sign of social conditioning."

Griffin, Farah Jasmine. "1900; 1905: *Sister Carrie* and *The House of Mirth.*" *A New Literary History of America,* edited by Greil Marcus and Werner Sollors, Harvard UP, 2009, pp. 459-64.

> Discusses how Carrie's lower-class origins equip her to survive in society. Griffin contrasts Dreiser's Carrie with Edith Wharton's Lily Bart, presenting the latter as weak and bewildered by social strictures. To Griffin, "Carrie makes herself while Lily is made by a society that will also destroy her." Griffin observes that Lily maintains her moral purity, but—in the pattern of earlier American novels—she dies, whereas Carrie not only lives, but succeeds.

Hakutani, Yoshinobu. "*Sister Carrie*: Novel and Romance." *Theodore Dreiser and American Culture: New Readings,* edited by Hakutani, U of Delaware P, 2000, pp. 23-38.

> Takes into account both the 1900 version of *Sister Carrie* and the 1981 Pennsylvania Edition, commenting on Dreiser's initial choices and subsequent revisions. Hakutani also clarifies various uses of the terms "naturalism" and "realism" in relation to *Sister Carrie* and its body of criticism.

Kaplan, Amy. "The Sentimental Revolt of *Sister Carrie.*" *The Social Construction of American Realism,* U of Chicago P, 1988, pp. 140-60.

> Addresses the way Dreiser maintains conventions of sentimental language in *Sister Carrie* but argues that his sentimentalism is "recontextualized" through his "aesthetics of consumption."

Lehan, Richard. "*Sister Carrie:* The City, the Self, and the Modes of Narrative Discourse." *New Essays on Sister Carrie,* edited by Donald Pizer, Cambridge UP, 1991, pp. 65-85.

> Addresses the multiple versions of *Sister Carrie,* always defining the novel as naturalist. Lehan concentrates on what he calls Dreiser's "modes of narrative discourse," creating a rationale for many of Dreiser's changes, particularly between the first version he sent to Doubleday and the 1900 publication.

Markels, Julian. "Dreiser and the Plotting of Inarticulate Experience." *The Massachusetts Review,* vol. 2, no. 3, Spring 1961, pp. 431-48.

> Discusses Dreiser's sometimes ineffective presentation to readers of the ongoing processes in his characters' minds. In the case of Carrie, according to Markels, once she decides to choose Hurstwood over Drouet, she has no further cognition that is relevant; therefore, Dreiser turns his effort to making Hurstwood's decline memorable. Markels sees Dreiser's portraits of Carrie as inconsistent, especially during the latter part of the novel, arguing that Dreiser allows readers to question

her motivation, whether that allowance is intentional or not.

McNamara, Kevin R. "The Ames of the Good Society: *Sister Carrie* and Social Engineering." *Criticism,* vol. 34, no. 2, Spring 1992, pp. 217-35.

> Insists that Carrie's finding a suitable mate might bring her back from her sense of disillusion. McNamara incorporates philosophical views that make Carrie a believable character.

Riggio, Thomas F. "Carrie's Blues." *New Essays on Sister Carrie,* edited by Donald Pizer, Cambridge UP, 1991, pp. 23-41.

> Contends that most readers see *Sister Carrie* as Hurstwood's story, as he declines from a robust, successful businessman to a decrepit man without emotional sustenance. However, Riggio's explanation for Hurstwood's fall stems from Carrie's nearly inexplicable success. Riggio views Carrie as a possible depressive, unable to give of herself to others. Without the presence of her family, according to Riggio, Carrie ends the novel shut away from those who would love her—hence, her "blues."

---

**Additional information on Dreiser's life and works is contained in the following sources published by Gale:** *American Writers*; *American Writers Retrospective Supplement,* **Vol. 2;** *American Writers: The Classics,* **Vol. 2;** *Beacham's Guide to Literature for Young Adults,* **Vols. 15, 16;** *Concise Dictionary of American Literary Biography: 1865-1917*; *Contemporary Authors,* **Vols. 106, 132;** *Dictionary of Literary Biography,* **Vols. 9, 12, 102, 137, 361, 368;** *Dictionary of Literary Biography Documentary Series,* **Vol. 1;** *DISCovering Authors*; *DISCovering Authors: Canadian Edition*; *DISCovering-Authors Modules: Most-Studied Authors* **and** *Novelists*; *DISCovering Authors 3.0*; *Encyclopedia of World Literature in the 20th Century,* **Ed. 3;** *Gale Contextual Encyclopedia of American Literature*; *Literary Movements for Students,* **Vol. 2;** *Literature and Its Times,* **Vol. 2;** *Literature Resource Center*; *Major 20th-Century Writers,* **Eds. 1, 2;** *Major 21st-Century Writers*; *Modern American Literature,* **Ed. 5;** *Novels for Students,* **Vols. 8, 17;** *Reference Guide to American Literature,* **Ed. 4;** *Short Story Criticism,* **Vols. 30, 114;** *Twayne's United States Authors*; *Twentieth-Century Literary Criticism,* **Vols. 10, 18, 35, 83, 277;** **and** *World Literature Criticism,* **Vol. 2.**

# How to Use This Index

## The main references

**Calvino, Italo**
    1923-1985 ....... CLC 5, 8, 11, 22, 33, 39,
                                          73; SSC 3, 48

list all author entries in the following Gale Literary Criticism series:

*AAL* = *Asian American Literature*
*BG* = *The Beat Generation: A Gale Critical Companion*
*BLC* = *Black Literature Criticism*
*BLCS* = *Black Literature Criticism Supplement*
*CLC* = *Contemporary Literary Criticism*
*CLR* = *Children's Literature Review*
*CMLC* = *Classical and Medieval Literature Criticism*
*DC* = *Drama Criticism*
*FL* = *Feminism in Literature: A Gale Critical Companion*
*GL* = *Gothic Literature: A Gale Critical Companion*
*HLC* = *Hispanic Literature Criticism*
*HLCS* = *Hispanic Literature Criticism Supplement*
*HR* = *Harlem Renaissance: A Gale Critical Companion*
*LC* = *Literature Criticism from 1400 to 1800*
*NCLC* = *Nineteenth-Century Literature Criticism*
*NNAL* = *Native North American Literature*
*PC* = *Poetry Criticism*
*SSC* = *Short Story Criticism*
*TCLC* = *Twentieth-Century Literary Criticism*
*WLC* = *World Literature Criticism, 1500 to the Present*
*WLCS* = *World Literature Criticism Supplement*

## The cross-references

See also CA 85-88, 116; CANR 23, 61;
DAM NOV; DLB 196; EW 13; MTCW 1, 2;
RGSF 2; RGWL 2; SFW 4; SSFS 12

list all author entries in the following Gale biographical and literary sources:

*AAYA* = *Authors & Artists for Young Adults*
*AFAW* = *African American Writers*
*AFW* = *African Writers*
*AITN* = *Authors in the News*
*AMW* = *American Writers*
*AMWR* = *American Writers Retrospective Supplement*
*AMWS* = *American Writers Supplement*
*ANW* = *American Nature Writers*
*AW* = *Ancient Writers*
*BEST* = *Bestsellers*
*BPFB* = *Beacham's Encyclopedia of Popular Fiction: Biography and Resources*
*BRW* = *British Writers*
*BRWS* = *British Writers Supplement*
*BW* = *Black Writers*
*BYA* = *Beacham's Guide to Literature for Young Adults*
*CA* = *Contemporary Authors*
*CAAS* = *Contemporary Authors Autobiography Series*
*CABS* = *Contemporary Authors Bibliographical Series*
*CAD* = *Contemporary American Dramatists*
*CANR* = *Contemporary Authors New Revision Series*
*CAP* = *Contemporary Authors Permanent Series*
*CBD* = *Contemporary British Dramatists*
*CCA* = *Contemporary Canadian Authors*

**CD** = Contemporary Dramatists

**CDALB** = Concise Dictionary of American Literary Biography

**CDALBS** = Concise Dictionary of American Literary Biography Supplement

**CDBLB** = Concise Dictionary of British Literary Biography

**CMW** = St. James Guide to Crime & Mystery Writers

**CN** = Contemporary Novelists

**CP** = Contemporary Poets

**CPW** = Contemporary Popular Writers

**CSW** = Contemporary Southern Writers

**CWD** = Contemporary Women Dramatists

**CWP** = Contemporary Women Poets

**CWRI** = St. James Guide to Children's Writers

**CWW** = Contemporary World Writers

**DA** = DISCovering Authors

**DA3** = DISCovering Authors 3.0

**DAB** = DISCovering Authors: British Edition

**DAC** = DISCovering Authors: Canadian Edition

**DAM** = DISCovering Authors: Modules

    **DRAM:** *Dramatists Module;* **MST:** Most-studied Authors Module;

    **MULT:** *Multicultural Authors Module;* **NOV:** Novelists Module;

    **POET:** *Poets Module;* **POP:** Popular Fiction and Genre Authors Module

**DFS** = Drama for Students

**DLB** = Dictionary of Literary Biography

**DLBD** = Dictionary of Literary Biography Documentary Series

**DLBY** = Dictionary of Literary Biography Yearbook

**DNFS** = Literature of Developing Nations for Students

**EFS** = Epics for Students

**EW** = European Writers

**EWL** = Encyclopedia of World Literature in the 20th Century

**EXPN** = Exploring Novels

**EXPP** = Exploring Poetry

**EXPS** = Exploring Short Stories

**FANT** = St. James Guide to Fantasy Writers

**FW** = Feminist Writers

**GFL** = Guide to French Literature, Beginnings to 1789; 1789 to the Present

**GLL** = Gay and Lesbian Literature

**HGG** = St. James Guide to Horror, Ghost & Gothic Writers

**HW** = Hispanic Writers

**IDFW** = International Dictionary of Films and Filmmakers: Writers and Production Artists

**IDTP** = International Dictionary of Theatre: Playwrights

**LAIT** = Literature and Its Times

**LAW** = Latin American Writers

**JRDA** = Junior DISCovering Authors

**MAICYA** = Major Authors and Illustrators for Children and Young Adults

**MAICYAS** = Major Authors and Illustrators for Children and Young Adults Supplement

**MAWW** = Modern American Women Writers

**MJW** = Modern Japanese Writers

**MTCW** = Major 20th-Century Writers

**NCFS** = Nonfiction Classics for Students

**NFS** = Novels for Students

**PAB** = Poets: American and British

**PFS** = Poetry for Students

**RGAL** = Reference Guide to American Literature

**RGEL** = Reference Guide to English Literature

**RGSF** = Reference Guide to Short Fiction

**RGWL** = Reference Guide to World Literature

**RHW** = Twentieth-Century Romance and Historical Writers

**SAAS** = Something about the Author Autobiography Series

**SATA** = Something about the Author

**SFW** = St. James Guide to Science Fiction Writers

**SSFS** = Short Stories for Students

**TCWW** = Twentieth-Century Western Writers

**WLIT** = World Literature and Its Times

**WP** = World Poets

**YABC** = Yesterday's Authors of Books for Children

**YAW** = St. James Guide to Young Adult Writers

# Literary Criticism Series
# Cumulative Author Index

See also DLB 1, 223

**Alcott, Louisa May** 1832-1888 ....... **NCLC 6, 58, 83, 218; SSC 27, 98, 164; WLC 1**
See also AAYA 20; AMWS 1; BPFB 1; BYA 2; CDALB 1865-1917; CLR 1, 38, 109, 195, 196, 222; DA; DA3; DAB; DAC; DAM MST, NOV; DLB 1, 42, 79, 223, 239, 242; DLBD 14; FL 1:2; FW; JRDA; LAIT 2; MAICYA 1, 2; NFS 12; RGAL 4; SATA 100; TUS; WCH; WYA; YABC 1; YAW

**Alcuin** c. 730-804 ................. **CMLC 69, 139**
See also DLB 148

**Aldanov, M. A.**
See Aldanov, Mark (Alexandrovich)

**Aldanov, Mark (Alexandrovich)**
1886-1957 .............................. **TCLC 23**
See also CA 118; 181; DLB 317

**Alden, Jean François**
See Twain, Mark

**Aldhelm** c. 639-709 ...................... **CMLC 90**

**Aldington, Richard** 1892-1962 ....... **CLC 49; PC 134; TCLC 296**
See also CA 85-88; CANR 45; DLB 20, 36, 100, 149; LMFS 2; RGEL 2

**Aldiss, Brian W.** 1925- ........ **CLC 5, 14, 40, 290; SSC 36**
See also AAYA 42; BRWS 19; CA 5-8R, 190; CAAE 190; CAAS 2; CANR 5, 28, 64, 121, 168; CLR 197; CN 1, 2, 3, 4, 5, 6, 7; DAM NOV; DLB 14, 261, 271; MTCW 1, 2; MTFW 2005; SATA 34; SCFW 1, 2; SFW 4

**Aldiss, Brian Wilson**
See Aldiss, Brian W.

**Aldrich, Ann**
See Meaker, Marijane

**Aldrich, Bess Streeter** 1881-1954 ... **TCLC 125**
See also CLR 70; TCWW 2

**Aldrich, Thomas Bailey**
1836-1907 ............................. **TCLC 351**
See also CA 111, 179; DLB 42, 71, 74, 79; SATA 17, 114

**Alegria, Claribel** 1924- ................. **CLC 75; HLCS 1; PC 26, 150**
See also CA 131; CAAS 15; CANR 66, 94, 134; CWW 2; DAM MULT; DLB 145, 283; EWL 3; HW 1; MTCW 2; MTFW 2005; PFS 21

**Alegria, Claribel Joy**
See Alegria, Claribel

**Alegria, Fernando** 1918-2005 ......... **CLC 57**
See also CA 9-12R; CANR 5, 32, 72; EWL 3; HW 1, 2

**Aleichem, Sholom** 1859-1916 .. **SSC 33, 125; TCLC 1, 35**
See also CA 104; DLB 333; TWA

**Aleixandre, Vicente** 1898-1984 ...... **HLCS 1; TCLC 113**
See also CANR 81; DLB 108, 329; EWL 3; HW 2; MTCW 1, 2; RGWL 2, 3

**Alekseev, Konstantin Sergeivich**
See Stanislavsky, Constantin

**Alekseyev, Konstantin Sergeyevich**
See Stanislavsky, Constantin

**Alemán, Mateo** 1547-1615(?) ..... **LC 81, 234**

**Alencar, Jose de** 1829-1877 ......... **NCLC 157**
See also DLB 307; LAW; WLIT 1

**Alencon, Marguerite d'**
See de Navarre, Marguerite

**Alepoudelis, Odysseus**
See Elytis, Odysseus

**Aleramo, Sibilla** 1876-1960 ........ **TCLC 312**
See also DLB 114, 264; WLIT 7

**Aleshkovsky, Joseph**
See Aleshkovsky, Yuz

**Aleshkovsky, Yuz** 1929- ................. **CLC 44**
See also CA 121; 128; DLB 317

**Alexander, Barbara**
See Ehrenreich, Barbara

**Alexander, Lloyd** 1924-2007 .......... **CLC 35**
See also AAYA 1, 27; BPFB 1; BYA 5, 6, 7, 9, 10, 11; CA 1-4R, 260; CANR 1, 24, 38, 55,

113; CLR 1, 5, 48, 227; CWRI 5; DLB 52; FANT; JRDA; MAICYA 1, 2; MAICYAS 1; MTCW 1; SAAS 19; SATA 3, 49, 81, 129, 135; SATA-Obit 182; SSFHW; SUFW; TUS; WYA; YAW

**Alexander, Lloyd Chudley**
See Alexander, Lloyd

**Alexander, Meena** 1951- ........ **CLC 121, 335**
See also CA 115; CANR 38, 70, 146; CP 5, 6, 7; CWP; DLB 323; FW

**Alexander, Rae Pace**
See Alexander, Raymond Pace

**Alexander, Raymond Pace** 1898-1974 ... **SSC 62**
See also CA 97-100; SATA 22; SSFS 4

**Alexander, Samuel** 1859-1938 ....... **TCLC 77**

**Alexander of Hales** c. 1185-1245 ... **CMLC 128**

**Alexeiev, Konstantin**
See Stanislavsky, Constantin

**Alexeyev, Constantin Sergeivich**
See Stanislavsky, Constantin

**Alexeyev, Konstantin Sergeyevich**
See Stanislavsky, Constantin

**Alexie, Sherman** 1966- ... **CLC 96, 154, 312; NNAL; PC 53; SSC 107, 189**
See also AAYA 28, 85; BYA 15; CA 138; CANR 65, 95, 133, 174; CLR 179; CN 7; DA3; DAM MULT; DLB 175, 206, 278; LATS 1:2; MTCW 2; MTFW 2005; NFS 17, 31, 38; PFS 39; SSFS 18, 36

**Alexie, Sherman Joseph, Jr.**
See Alexie, Sherman

**Alexievich, Svetlana Alexandrovna**
1948- ........................................ **CLC 405**

**Al-Fārābī** 870(?)-950 ............ **CMLC 58, 188**
See also DLB 115

**Alfau, Felipe** 1902-1999 .................. **CLC 66**
See also CA 137

**Alfieri, Vittorio** 1749-1803 ........... **NCLC 101**
See also EW 4; RGWL 2, 3; WLIT 7

**Alfonso X** 1221-1284 .................... **CMLC 78**

**Alfred, Jean Gaston**
See Ponge, Francis

**Alger, Horatio, Jr.**
1832-1899 ................. **NCLC 8, 83, 260**
See also CLR 87, 170, 221; DLB 42; LAIT 2; RGAL 4; SATA 16; TUS

**Al-Ghazali, Muhammad ibn Muhammad**
1058-1111 ..................... **CMLC 50, 149**
See also DLB 115

**Algren, Nelson** 1909-1981 ................ **CLC 4, 10, 33; SSC 33; TCLC 359**
See also AMWS 9; BPFB 1; CA 13-16R; 103; CANR 20, 61; CDALB 1941-1968; CN 1, 2; DLB 9; DLBY 1981, 1982, 2000; EWL 3; MAL 5; MTCW 1, 2; MTFW 2005; RGAL 4; RGSF 2

**al-Hamadhani** 967-1007 ............... **CMLC 93**
See also WLIT 6

**al-Hariri, al-Qasim ibn 'Ali Abu Muhammad al-Basri** 1054-1122 ............... **CMLC 63**
See also RGWL 3

**Ali, Ahmed** 1908-1998 ................... **CLC 69**
See also CA 25-28R; CANR 15, 34; CN 1, 2, 3, 4, 5; DLB 323; EWL 3

**Ali, Monica** 1967- ........................ **CLC 304**
See also AAYA 67; BRWS 13; CA 219; CANR 158, 205, 240; DLB 323

**Ali, Tariq** 1943- ..................... **CLC 173, 323**
See also CA 25-28R; CANR 10, 99, 161, 196

**Alifa**
See Rifaat, Alifa

**Alighieri, Dante**
See Dante

**Alkali, Zaynab** 1950- ..................... **CLC 381**
See also CA 172; DLB 360

**al-Kindi, Abu Yusuf Ya'qub ibn Ishaq**
c. 801-c. 873 ........................ **CMLC 80**

**al-Kōnī, Ibrāhīm** 1948- ................... **CLC 397**
See also CA 341; EWL 3

**Allan, John B.**
See Westlake, Donald E.

**Allan, Sidney**
See Hartmann, Sadakichi

**Allan, Sydney**
See Hartmann, Sadakichi

**Allard, Janet** .................................. **CLC 59**

**Allen, Betsy**
See Harrison, Elizabeth (Allen) Cavanna

**Allen, Edward** 1948- ........................ **CLC 59**

**Allen, Fred** 1894-1956 .................... **TCLC 87**

**Allen, Paula Gunn** 1939-2008 ........ **CLC 84, 202, 280; NNAL**
See also AMWS 4; CA 112; 143; 272; CANR 63, 130; CWP; DA3; DAM MULT; DLB 175; FW; MTCW 2; MTFW 2005; RGAL 4; TCWW 2

**Allen, Roland**
See Ayckbourn, Alan

**Allen, Sarah A.**
See Hopkins, Pauline Elizabeth

**Allen, Sidney H.**
See Hartmann, Sadakichi

**Allen, Woody** 1935- ... **CLC 16, 52, 195, 288**
See also AAYA 10, 51; AMWS 15; CA 33-36R; CANR 27, 38, 63, 128, 172; DAM POP; DLB 44; MTCW 1; SSFS 21

**Allende, Isabel** 1942- ... **CLC 39, 57, 97, 170, 264, 350; HLC 1; SSC 65, 209; WLCS**
See also AAYA 18, 70; CA 125; 130; CANR 51, 74, 129, 165, 208; CDWLB 3; CLR 99, 171; CWW 2; DA3; DAM MULT, NOV; DLB 145; DNFS 1; EWL 3; FL 1:5; FW; HW 1, 2; INT CA-130; LAIT 5; LAWS 1; LMFS 2; MTCW 1, 2; MTFW 2005; NCFS 1; NFS 6, 18, 29; RGSF 2; RGWL 3; SATA 163; SSFS 11, 16; WLIT 1

**Alleyn, Ellen**
See Rossetti, Christina

**Alleyne, Carla D.** .......................... **CLC 65**

**Allingham, Margery (Louise)**
1904-1966 ................................ **CLC 19**
See also CA 5-8R; 25-28R; CANR 4, 58; CMW 4; DLB 77; MSW; MTCW 1, 2

**Allingham, William** 1824-1889 ..... **NCLC 25**
See also DLB 35; RGEL 2

**Allison, Dorothy E.** 1949- ............. **CLC 78, 153, 290**
See also AAYA 53; CA 140; CANR 66, 107; CN 7; CSW; DA3; DLB 350; FW; MTCW 2; MTFW 2005; NFS 11; RGAL 4

**Alloula, Malek** ........................... **CLC 65**

**Allston, Washington**
1779-1843 ........................ **NCLC 2, 331**
See also DLB 1, 235

**Almedingen, E. M.** 1898-1971 ........ **CLC 12**
See also CA 1-4R; CANR 1; SATA 3

**Almedingen, Martha Edith von**
See Almedingen, E. M.

**Almodóvar, Pedro** 1949(?)- .. **CLC 114, 229, 427; HLCS 1**
See also CA 133; CANR 72, 151; HW 2

**Almqvist, Carl Jonas Love**
1793-1866 .............................. **NCLC 42**

**al-Mutanabbi, Ahmad ibn al-Husayn Abu al-Tayyib al-Jufi al-Kindi**
915-965 ................................. **CMLC 66**
See also RGWL 3; WLIT 6

**Alonso, Dámaso** 1898-1990 .......... **CLC 14; PC 158; TCLC 245**
See also CA 110; 131; 130; CANR 72; DLB 108; EWL 3; HW 1, 2

**Alov**
See Gogol, Nikolai

**al'Sadaawi, Nawal**
See El Saadawi, Nawal

**al-Shaykh, Hanan**
See Shaykh, Hanan al-

**Angell, Judie**
See Angell, Judie

**Angell, Judie** 1937- .......... **CLC 30**
See also AAYA 11, 71; BYA 6; CA 77-80;
CANR 49; CLR 33; JRDA; SATA 22, 78;
WYA; YAW

**Angell, Roger** 1920- .......... **CLC 26**
See also CA 57-60; CANR 13, 44, 70, 144;
DLB 171, 185

**Angelou, Maya** 1928-2014 ... **BLC 1:1; CLC 12, 35, 64, 77, 155, 389; PC 32; WLCS**
See also AAYA 7, 20; AMWS 4; BPFB 1;
BW 2, 3; BYA 2; CA 65-68; CANR 19,
42, 65, 111, 133, 204; CDALBS; CLR 53,
184; CP 4, 5, 6, 7; CPW; CSW; CWP; DA;
DA3; DAB; DAC; DAM MST, MULT,
POET, POP; DLB 38; EWL 3; EXPN;
EXPP; FL 1:5; LAIT 4; MAICYA 2;
MAICYAS 1; MAL 5; MBL; MTCW 1,
2; MTFW 2005; NCFS 2; NFS 2; PFS 2, 3,
33, 38, 42; RGAL 4; SATA 49, 136; TCLE
1:1; WYA; YAW

**Angouleme, Marguerite d'**
See de Navarre, Marguerite

**Anna Comnena** 1083-1153 .......... **CMLC 25**

**Annensky, Innokentii Fedorovich**
See Annensky, Innokenty (Fyodorovich)

**Annensky, Innokenty (Fyodorovich)**
1856-1909 .......... **TCLC 14**
See also CA 110; 155; DLB 295; EWL 3

**Annunzio, Gabriele d'**
See D'Annunzio, Gabriele

**Anodos**
See Coleridge, Mary E(lizabeth)

**Anon, Charles Robert**
See Pessoa, Fernando

**Anouilh, Jean** 1910-1987 .......... **CLC 1, 3, 8, 13, 40, 50; DC 8, 21; TCLC 195**
See also AAYA 67; CA 17-20R; 123; CANR
32; DAM DRAM; DFS 9, 10, 19; DLB
321; EW 13; EWL 3; GFL 1789 to the
Present; MTCW 1, 2; MTFW 2005;
RGWL 2, 3; TWA

**Anouilh, Jean Marie Lucien Pierre**
See Anouilh, Jean

**Ansa, Tina McElroy** 1949- .......... **BLC 2:1**
See also BW 2; CA 142; CANR 143; CSW

**Anselm of Canterbury**
1033(?)-1109 .......... **CMLC 67**
See also DLB 115

**Anthony, Florence**
See Ai

**Anthony, John**
See Ciardi, John (Anthony)

**Anthony, Peter**
See Shaffer, Anthony; Shaffer, Peter

**Anthony, Piers** 1934- .......... **CLC 35**
See also AAYA 11, 48; BYA 7; CA 200;
CAAE 200; CANR 28, 56, 73, 102, 133,
202; CLR 118; CPW; DAM POP; DLB 8;
FANT; MAICYA 2; MAICYAS 1; MTCW
1, 2; MTFW 2005; SAAS 22; SATA 84, 129;
SATA-Essay 129; SFW 4; SUFW 1, 2; YAW

**Anthony, Susan B(rownell)**
1820-1906 .......... **TCLC 84**
See also CA 211; FW

**Antin, David** 1932- .......... **PC 124**
See also CA 73-76; CP 1, 3, 4, 5, 6, 7; DLB
169

**Antin, Mary** 1881-1949 .......... **TCLC 247**
See also AMWS 20; CA 118; 181; DLB
221; DLBY 1984

**Antiphon** c. 480 BCE-c. 411 BCE .... **CMLC 55**

**Antoine, Marc**
See Proust, Marcel

**Antoninus, Brother**
See Everson, William

**Antonioni, Michelangelo**
1912-2007 .......... **CLC 20, 144, 259**

See also CA 73-76; 262; CANR 45, 77

**Antschel, Paul**
See Celan, Paul

**Anwar, Chairil** 1922-1949 .......... **TCLC 22**
See also CA 121; 219; EWL 3; RGWL 3

**Anyidoho, Kofi** 1947- .......... **BLC 2:1**
See also BW 3; CA 178; CP 5, 6, 7; DLB
157; EWL 3

**Anzaldúa, Gloria (Evanjelina)**
1942-2004 .......... **CLC 200, 350; HLCS 1**
See also CA 175; 227; CSW; CWP; DLB
122; FW; LLW; RGAL 4; SATA-Obit 154

**Apess, William** 1798-1839(?) .......... **NCLC 73; NNAL**
See also DAM MULT; DLB 175, 243

**Apollinaire, Guillaume** 1880-1918 .......... **PC 7; TCLC 3, 8, 51**
See also CA 104; 152; DAM POET; DLB
258, 321; EW 9; EWL 3; GFL 1789 to the
Present; MTCW 2; PFS 24; RGWL 2, 3;
TWA; WP

**Apollonius of Rhodes**
See Apollonius Rhodius

**Apollonius Rhodius**
c. 300 BCE-c. 220 BCE .......... **CMLC 28**
See also AW 1; DLB 176; RGWL 2, 3

**Appelfeld, Aharon** 1932- .......... **CLC 23, 47, 317; SSC 42**
See also CA 112; 133; CANR 86, 160, 207;
CWW 2; DLB 299; EWL 3; RGHL; RGSF
2; WLIT 6

**Appelfeld, Aron**
See Appelfeld, Aharon

**Apple, Max** 1941- .......... **CLC 9, 33; SSC 50**
See also AMWS 17; CA 81-84; CANR 19,
54, 214; DLB 130

**Apple, Max Isaac**
See Apple, Max

**Appleman, Philip (Dean)** 1926- .......... **CLC 51**
See also CA 13-16R; CAAS 18; CANR 6, 29,
56

**Appleton, Lawrence**
See Lovecraft, H. P.

**Apteryx**
See Eliot, T. S.

**Apuleius, (Lucius Madaurensis)**
c. 125-c. 164 .......... **CMLC 1, 84, 182**
See also AW 2; CDWLB 1; DLB 211;
RGWL 2, 3; SUFW; WLIT 8

**Aquin, Hubert** 1929-1977 .......... **CLC 15**
See also CA 105; DLB 53; EWL 3

**Aquinas, Thomas** 1224(?)-1274 ... **CMLC 33, 137**
See also DLB 115; EW 1; TWA

**Aragon, Louis** 1897-1982 .......... **CLC 3, 22; PC 155; TCLC 123**
See also CA 69-72; 108; CANR 28, 71;
DAM NOV, POET; DLB 72, 258; EW
11; EWL 3; GFL 1789 to the Present; GLL
2; LMFS 2; MTCW 1, 2; RGWL 2, 3

**Arany, Janos** 1817-1882 .......... **NCLC 34**

**Aranyos, Kakay** 1847-1910
See Mikszath, Kalman

**Aratus of Soli**
c. 315 BCE-c. 240 BCE .......... **CMLC 64, 114**
See also DLB 176

**Arbuthnot, John** 1667-1735 .......... **LC 1**
See also BRWS 16; DLB 101

**Arbuthnot, John**
See Henry, O.

**Archer, Herbert Winslow**
See Mencken, H. L.

**Archer, Jeffrey** 1940- .......... **CLC 28**
See also AAYA 16; BEST 89:3; BPFB 1;
CA 77-80; CANR 22, 52, 95, 136, 209;
CPW; DA3; DAM POP; INT CANR-22;
MTFW 2005

**Archer, Jeffrey Howard**
See Archer, Jeffrey

**Archer, Jules** 1915- .......... **CLC 12**
See also CA 9-12R; CANR 6, 69; SAAS 5;
SATA 4, 85

**Archer, Lee**
See Ellison, Harlan

**Archilochus** c. 7th cent. BCE .......... **CMLC 44**
See also DLB 176

**Ard, William**
See Jakes, John

**Ardelia**
See Finch, Anne

**Arden, Constance**
See Naden, Constance

**Arden, John** 1930-2012 .......... **CLC 6, 13, 15**
See also BRWS 2; CA 13-16R; CAAS 4;
CANR 31, 65, 67, 124; CBD; CD 5, 6;
DAM DRAM; DFS 9; DLB 13, 245; EWL
3; MTCW 1

**Arenas, Reinaldo** 1943-1990 .......... **CLC 41; HLC 1; TCLC 191**
See also CA 124; 128; 133; CANR 73, 106;
DAM MULT; DLB 145; EWL 3; GLL 2;
HW 1; LAW; LAWS 1; MTCW 2; MTFW
2005; RGSF 2; RGWL 3; WLIT 1

**Arendt, Hannah** 1906-1975 .......... **CLC 66, 98; TCLC 193**
See also CA 17-20R; 61-64; CANR 26, 60,
172; DLB 242; MTCW 1, 2

**Aretino, Pietro** 1492-1556 .......... **LC 12, 165**
See also RGWL 2, 3

**Arghezi, Tudor** 1880-1967 .......... **CLC 80**
See also CA 167; 116; CDWLB 4; DLB 220;
EWL 3

**Arguedas, José María** 1911-1969 ... **CLC 10, 18; HLCS 1; TCLC 147, 359**
See also CA 89-92; CANR 73; DLB 113;
EWL 3; HW 1; LAW; RGWL 2, 3; WLIT 1

**Argueta, Manlio** 1936- .......... **CLC 31**
See also CA 131; CANR 73; CWW 2; DLB
145; EWL 3; HW 1; RGWL 3

**Arias, Ron** 1941- .......... **HLC 1**
See also CA 131; CANR 81, 136; DAM
MULT; DLB 82; HW 1, 2; MTCW 2;
MTFW 2005

**Ariosto, Lodovico**
See Ariosto, Ludovico

**Ariosto, Ludovico** 1474-1533 .......... **LC 6, 87, 206; PC 42, 175**
See also EW 2; RGWL 2, 3; WLIT 7

**Aristides**
See Epstein, Joseph

**Aristides Quintilianus**
fl. c. 100-fl. c. 400 .......... **CMLC 122**

**Aristophanes** 450 BCE-385 BCE ....... **CMLC 4, 51, 138, 164, 176, 180; DC 2; WLCS**
See also AW 1; CDWLB 1; DA; DA3; DAB;
DAC; DAM DRAM, MST; DFS 10; DLB
176; LMFS 1; RGWL 2, 3; TWA; WLIT 8

**Aristotle** 384 BCE-322 BCE .......... **CMLC 31, 123; WLCS**
See also AW 1; CDWLB 1; DA; DA3; DAB;
DAC; DAM MST; DLB 176; RGWL 2, 3;
TWA; WLIT 8

**Arlt, Roberto** 1900-1942 .......... **HLC 1; TCLC 29, 255**
See also CA 123; 131; CANR 67; DAM
MULT; DLB 305; EWL 3; HW 1, 2; IDTP;
LAW

**Arlt, Roberto Godofredo Christophersen**
See Arlt, Roberto

**Armah, Ayi Kwei** 1939- .......... **BLC 1:1, 2:1; CLC 5, 33, 136, 395, 400**
See also AFW; BRWS 10; BW 1; CA 61-64;
CANR 21, 64; CDWLB 3; CN 1, 2, 3, 4, 5,
6, 7; DAM MULT, POET; DLB 117; EWL
3; MTCW 1; WLIT 2

**Armatrading, Joan** 1950- .......... **CLC 17**
See also CA 114; 186

**Armin, Robert** 1568(?)-1615(?) .......... **LC 120**

**Armitage, Frank**
See Carpenter, John

**Armstrong, Gillian** 1950- ............. **CLC 385**
  See also AAYA 74; CA 173
**Armstrong, Jeannette (C.)** 1948- ....... **NNAL**
  See also CA 149; CCA 1; CN 6, 7; DAC;
  DLB 334; SATA 102
**Armytage, R.**
  See Watson, Rosamund Marriott
**Arnauld, Antoine** 1612-1694 ............ **LC 169**
  See also DLB 268
**Arnette, Robert**
  See Silverberg, Robert
**Arnim, Achim von (Ludwig Joachim von**
  **Arnim)** 1781-1831 ................... **NCLC 5,**
  **159; SSC 29**
  See also DLB 90
**Arnim, Bettina von**
  1785-1859 ........................ **NCLC 38, 123**
  See also DLB 90; RGWL 2, 3
**Arnold, Matthew** 1822-1888 ... **NCLC 6, 29,**
  **89, 126, 218, 337; PC 5, 94, 183; WLC 1**
  See also BRW 5; CDBLB 1832-1890; DA;
  DAB; DAC; DAM MST, POET; DLB 32,
  57; EXPP; PAB; PFS 2; TEA; WP
**Arnold, Thomas** 1795-1842 ... **NCLC 18, 323**
  See also DLB 55
**Arnow, Harriette (Louisa) Simpson**
  1908-1986 .......... **CLC 2, 7, 18; TCLC**
  **196, 370**
  See also BPFB 1; CA 9-12R; 118; CANR
  14; CN 2, 3, 4; DLB 6; FW; MTCW 1, 2;
  RHW; SATA 42; SATA-Obit 47
**Arouet, Francois-Marie**
  See Voltaire
**Arp, Hans**
  See Arp, Jean
**Arp, Jean** 1887-1966 ......... **CLC 5; PC 156;**
  **TCLC 115**
  See also CA 81-84; 25-28R; CANR 42, 77;
  EW 10
**Arrabal**
  See Arrabal, Fernando
**Arrabal, Fernando**
  1932- ........... **CLC 2, 9, 18, 58; DC 35**
  See also CA 9-12R; CANR 15; CWW 2;
  DLB 321; EWL 3; LMFS 2
**Arrabal Teran, Fernando**
  See Arrabal, Fernando
**Arreola, Juan Jose** 1918-2001 ..... **CLC 147;**
  **HLC 1; SSC 38**
  See also CA 113; 131; 200; CANR 81;
  CWW 2; DAM MULT; DLB 113; DNFS
  2; EWL 3; HW 1, 2; LAW; RGSF 2
**Arrian** c. 89(?)-c. 155(?) .............. **CMLC 43**
  See also DLB 176
**Arrick, Fran**
  See Angell, Judie
**Arrley, Richmond**
  See Delany, Samuel R., Jr.
**Artaud, Antonin**
  1896-1948 ............. **DC 14; TCLC 3, 36**
  See also CA 104; 149; DA3; DAM DRAM;
  DFS 22; DLB 258, 321; EW 11; EWL 3;
  GFL 1789 to the Present; MTCW 2;
  MTFW 2005; RGWL 2, 3
**Artaud, Antonin Marie Joseph**
  See Artaud, Antonin
**Artemidorus** fl. 2nd cent. ........... **CMLC 129**
**Arthur, Ruth M(abel)** 1905-1979 ... **CLC 12**
  See also CA 9-12R; 85-88; CANR 4; CWRI
  5; SATA 7, 26
**Artsybashev, Mikhail (Petrovich)**
  1878-1927 ........................... **TCLC 31**
  See also CA 170; DLB 295
**Arundel, Honor (Morfydd)**
  1919-1973 ............................... **CLC 17**
  See also CA 21-22; 41-44R; CAP 2; CLR
  35; CWRI 5; SATA 4; SATA-Obit 24
**Arzner, Dorothy** 1900-1979 ............ **CLC 98**
**Asch, Sholem** 1880-1957 ........ **TCLC 3, 251**
  See also AMWS 23; CA 105; DLB 333;
  EWL 3; GLL 2; RGHL

**Ascham, Roger** 1516(?)-1568 ........... **LC 101**
  See also DLB 236
**Ash, Shalom**
  See Asch, Sholem
**Ashbery, John** 1927-2017 .... **CLC 2, 3, 4, 6,**
  **9, 13, 15, 25, 41, 77, 125, 221, 439; PC**
  **26, 159**
  See also AMWS 3; CA 5-8R; CANR 9, 37,
  66, 102, 132, 170, 230; CMTFW; CP 1, 2,
  3, 4, 5, 6, 7; DA3; DAM POET; DLB 5,
  165, 380; DLBY 1981; EWL 3; GLL 1;
  INT CANR-9; MAL 5; MTCW 1, 2;
  MTFW 2005; PAB; PFS 11, 28; RGAL
  4; TCLE 1:1; WP
**Ashbery, John Lawrence**
  See Ashbery, John
**Ashbridge, Elizabeth** 1713-1755 ...... **LC 147**
  See also DLB 200
**Ashdown, Clifford**
  See Freeman, R(ichard) Austin
**Ashe, Gordon**
  See Creasey, John
**Ashton-Warner, Sylvia (Constance)**
  1908-1984 ................................ **CLC 19**
  See also CA 69-72; 112; CANR 29; CN 1, 2,
  3; MTCW 1, 2
**Asimov, Isaac** 1920-1992 ........ **CLC 1, 3, 9,**
  **19, 26, 76, 92; SSC 148, 235**
  See also AAYA 13; BEST 90:2; BPFB 1;
  BYA 4, 6, 7, 9; CA 1-4R; 137; CANR 2,
  19, 36, 60, 125; CLR 12, 79; CMW 4; CN
  1, 2, 3, 4, 5; CPW; DA3; DAM POP; DLB
  8; DLBY 1992; INT CANR-19; JRDA;
  LAIT 5; LMFS 2; MAICYA 1, 2; MAL
  5; MTCW 1, 2; MTFW 2005; NFS 29;
  RGAL 4; SATA 1, 26, 74; SCFW 1, 2;
  SFW 4; SSFS 17, 33; TUS; YAW
**Askew, Anne** 1521(?)-1546 ......... **LC 81, 219**
  See also DLB 136
**Aslam, Nadeem** 1966- .................... **CLC 414**
  See also CA 240; CANR 198, 267
**Asser** -c. 909 ............................... **CMLC 117**
**Assis, Joaquim Maria Machado de**
  See Machado de Assis, Joaquim Maria
**Astell, Mary** 1666-1731 .............. **LC 68, 183**
  See also DLB 252, 336; FW
**Astley, Thea (Beatrice May)**
  1925-2004 ............................ **CLC 41, 332**
  See also CA 65-68; 229; CANR 11, 43, 78;
  CN 1, 2, 3, 4, 5, 6, 7; DLB 289; EWL 3
**Astley, William** 1855-1911 ............. **TCLC 45**
  See also DLB 230; RGEL 2
**Aston, James**
  See White, T(erence) H(anbury)
**Asturias, Miguel Angel** 1899-1974 .... **CLC 3,**
  **8, 13; HLC 1; TCLC 184**
  See also CA 25-28; 49-52; CANR 32; CAP 2;
  CDWLB 3; DA3; DAM MULT, NOV; DLB
  113, 290, 329; EWL 3; HW 1; LAW; LMFS
  2; MTCW 1, 2; RGWL 2, 3; WLIT 1
**Atares, Carlos Saura**
  See Saura (Atares), Carlos
**Athanasius** c. 295-c. 373 ............... **CMLC 48**
**Atheling, William**
  See Pound, Ezra
**Atheling, William, Jr.**
  See Blish, James
**Atherton, Gertrude (Franklin Horn)**
  1857-1948 ................................ **TCLC 2**
  See also CA 104; 155; DLB 9, 78, 186;
  HGG; RGAL 4; SUFW 1; TCWW 1, 2
**Atherton, Lucius**
  See Masters, Edgar Lee
**Atkins, Jack**
  See Harris, Mark
**Atkinson, Kate** 1951- ...................... **CLC 99**
  See also CA 166; CANR 101, 153, 198, 231;
  DLB 267
**'Attar, Farid al-Din Abu Hamid Mohammad**
  1145?-1221? ........................ **CMLC 157**
  See also RGWL 2,3; WLIT 6

**'Attar, Farīd al-Dīn**
  1145?-1221? ........................ **CMLC 157**
  See also RGWL 2, 3; WLIT 6
**Attaway, William (Alexander)**
  1911-1986 ................ **BLC 1:1; CLC 92**
  See also BW 2, 3; CA 143; CANR 82; DAM
  MULT; DLB 76; MAL 5
**Atticus**
  See Fleming, Ian; Wilson, (Thomas)
  Woodrow
**Atwood, Margaret** 1939- ..... **CLC 2, 3, 4, 8,**
  **13, 15, 25, 44, 84, 135, 232, 239, 246, 342,**
  **371, 382; PC 8, 123, 208; SSC 2, 46, 142,**
  **246; WLC 1**
  See also AAYA 12, 47; AMWS 13; BEST
  89:2; BPFB 1; CA 49-52; CANR 3, 24, 33,
  59, 95, 133, 250; CMTFW; CN 2, 3, 4, 5,
  6, 7; CP 1, 2, 3, 4, 5, 6, 7; CPW; CWP;
  DA; DA3; DAB; DAC; DAM MST, NOV,
  POET; DLB 53, 251, 326; EWL 3; EXPN;
  FL 1:5; FW; GL 2; INT CANR-24; LAIT
  5; MTCW 1, 2; MTFW 2005; NFS 4, 12,
  13, 14, 19, 39, 53; PFS 7, 37, 45, 53;
  RGSF 2; SATA 50, 170; SSFS 3, 13, 42;
  TCLE 1:1; TWA; WWE 1; YAW
**Atwood, Margaret Eleanor**
  See Atwood, Margaret
**Aubepine**
  See Hawthorne, Nathaniel
**Aubert, Alvin** 1930-2014 ................... **PC 201**
  See also BW 1, 3; CA 81-84; CAAS 20;
  CANR 26, 82; CP 2, 3, 4, 5, 6, 7; CSW;
  DLB 41
**Aubigny, Pierre d'**
  See Mencken, H. L.
**Aubin, Penelope** 1685-1731(?) ............. **LC 9**
  See also DLB 39
**Auchincloss, Louis** 1917-2010 ...... **CLC 4, 6,**
  **9, 18, 45, 318; SSC 22**
  See also AMWS 4; CA 1-4R; CANR 6, 29,
  55, 87, 130, 168, 202; CN 1, 2, 3, 4, 5, 6,
  7; DAM NOV; DLB 2, 244; DLBY 1980;
  EWL 3; INT CANR-29; MAL 5; MTCW
  1; RGAL 4
**Auchincloss, Louis Stanton**
  See Auchincloss, Louis
**Audelay, John** fl. 1417-1426? .......... **LC 264**
**Auden, W. H.** 1907-1973 ................. **CLC 1,**
  **2, 3, 4, 6, 9, 11, 14, 43, 123; PC 1, 92,**
  **161; TCLC 223; WLC 1**
  See also AAYA 18; AMWS 2; BRW 7;
  BRWR 1; CA 9-12R; 45-48; CANR 5,
  61, 105; CDBLB 1914-1945; CP 1, 2; DA;
  DA3; DAB; DAC; DAM DRAM, MST,
  POET; DLB 10, 20; EWL 3; EXPP; MAL
  5; MTCW 1, 2; MTFW 2005; PAB; PFS 1,
  3, 4, 10, 27; TUS; WP
**Auden, Wystan Hugh**
  See Auden, W. H.
**Audiberti, Jacques** 1899-1965 ......... **CLC 38**
  See also CA 252; 25-28R; DAM DRAM;
  DLB 321; EWL 3
**Audubon, John James** 1785-1851 .. **NCLC 47**
  See also AAYA 76; AMWS 16; ANW;
  DLB 248
**Auel, Jean**
  See Auel, Jean M.
**Auel, Jean M.** 1936- .................. **CLC 31, 107**
  See also AAYA 7, 51; BEST 90:4; BPFB 1;
  CA 103; CANR 21, 64, 115; CPW; DA3;
  DAM POP; INT CANR-21; NFS 11;
  RHW; SATA 91
**Auel, Jean Marie**
  See Auel, Jean M.
**Auerbach, Berthold** 1812-1882 ... **NCLC 171**
  See also DLB 133
**Auerbach, Erich** 1892-1957 ... **TCLC 43, 358**
  See also CA 118; 155; EWL 3
**Augier, Emile** 1820-1889 ................ **NCLC 31**
  See also DLB 192; GFL 1789 to the Present
**August, John**
  See De Voto, Bernard (Augustine)

**Augustine, St.**
354-430 ....... **CMLC 6, 95, 185; WLCS**
See also DA; DA3; DAB; DAC; DAM MST;
DLB 115; EW 1; RGWL 2, 3; WLIT 8

**Aunt Belinda**
See Braddon, Mary Elizabeth

**Aunt Weedy**
See Alcott, Louisa May

**Aurelius**
See Bourne, Randolph S(illiman)

**Aurelius, Marcus** 121-180 ........... **CMLC 45**
See also AW 2; RGWL 2, 3

**Aureoli, Petrus** c. 1280-1322 ...... **CMLC 174**

**Aurobindo, Sri**
See Ghose, Aurabinda

**Aurobindo Ghose**
See Ghose, Aurabinda

**Ausonius, Decimus Magnus**
c. 310-c. 394 ........................ **CMLC 88**
See also RGWL 2, 3

**Austen, Jane** 1775-1817 .......... **NCLC 1, 13,
19, 33, 51, 81, 95, 119, 150, 207, 210, 222,
242, 271, 314, 316; WLC 1**
See also AAYA 19; BRW 4; BRWC 1;
BRWR 2; BYA 3; CDBLB 1789-1832; DA;
DA3; DAB; DAC; DAM MST, NOV; DLB
116, 363, 365, 366; EXPN; FL 1:2; GL 2;
LAIT 2; LATS 1:1; LMFS 1; NFS 1, 14, 18,
20, 21, 28, 29, 33; TEA; WLIT 3; WYAS 1

**Auster, Paul** 1947- ......... **CLC 47, 131, 227,
339, 356**
See also AMWS 12; CA 69-72; CANR 23,
52, 75, 129, 165; CMW 4; CN 5, 6, 7;
DA3; DLB 227; MAL 5; MTCW 2;
MTFW 2005; SUFW 2; TCLE 1:1

**Austin, Frank**
See Faust, Frederick

**Austin, Mary Hunter** 1868-1934 ... **SSC 104;
TCLC 25, 249**
See also ANW; CA 109; 178; DLB 9, 78,
206, 221, 275; FW; TCWW 1, 2

**Avellaneda, Gertrudis Gomez de**
See Gomez de Avellaneda, Gertrudis

**Averroës** 1126-1198 ....... **CMLC 7, 104, 187**
See also DLB 115

**Avicenna** 980-1037 ................ **CMLC 16, 110**
See also DLB 115

**Avison, Margaret** 1918-2007 ............. **CLC 2,
4, 97; PC 148**
See also CA 17-20R; CANR 134; CP 1, 2, 3,
4, 5, 6, 7; DAC; DAM POET; DLB 53;
MTCW 1

**Avison, Margaret Kirkland**
See Avison, Margaret

**Axton, David**
See Koontz, Dean

**Ayala, Francisco** 1906-2009 ............ **SSC 119**
See also CA 208; CWW 2; DLB 322; EWL
3; RGSF 2

**Ayala, Francisco de Paula y Garcia Duarte**
See Ayala, Francisco

**Ayckbourn, Alan** 1939- ................. **CLC 5, 8,
18, 33, 74; DC 13**
See also BRWS 5; CA 21-24R; CANR 31,
59, 118; CBD; CD 5, 6; DAB; DAM
DRAM; DFS 7; DLB 13, 245; EWL 3;
MTCW 1, 2; MTFW 2005

**Aydy, Catherine**
See Tennant, Emma

**Ayme, Marcel (Andre)**
1902-1967 .................... **CLC 11; SSC 41**
See also CA 89-92; CANR 67, 137; CLR 25;
DLB 72; EW 12; EWL 3; GFL 1789 to the
Present; RGSF 2; RGWL 2, 3; SATA 91

**Ayrton, Michael** 1921-1975 ............. **CLC 7**
See also CA 5-8R; 61-64; CANR 9, 21

**Aytmatov, Chingiz**
See Aitmatov, Chingiz

**Azevedo, Angela de** fl. 17th cent. - ... **LC 218**

**Azorin**
See Martinez Ruiz, Jose

**Azuela, Mariano** 1873-1952 ............. **HLC 1;
TCLC 3, 145, 217**
See also CA 104; 131; CANR 81; DAM
MULT; EWL 3; HW 1, 2; LAW; MTCW 1,
2; MTFW 2005

**Ba, Mariama** 1929-1981 .... **BLC 2:1; BLCS**
See also AFW; BW 2; CA 141; CANR 87;
DLB 360; DNFS 2; WLIT 2

**Baastad, Babbis Friis**
See Friis-Baastad, Babbis Ellinor

**Bab**
See Gilbert, W(illiam) S(chwenck)

**Babbis, Eleanor**
See Friis-Baastad, Babbis Ellinor

**Babel, Isaac**
See Babel, Isaak (Emmanuilovich)

**Babel, Isaak (Emmanuilovich)**
1894-1941(?) .............. **SSC 16, 78, 161;
TCLC 2, 13, 171**
See also CA 104; 155; CANR 113; DLB 272;
EW 11; EWL 3; MTCW 2; MTFW 2005;
RGSF 2; RGWL 2, 3; SSFS 10; TWA

**Babits, Mihaly** 1883-1941 ............. **TCLC 14**
See also CA 114; CDWLB 4; DLB 215;
EWL 3

**Babur** 1483-1530 ............................... **LC 18**

**Babylas**
See Ghelderode, Michel de

**Baca, Jimmy Santiago**
1952- ........................... **HLC 1; PC 41**
See also CA 131; CANR 81, 90, 146, 220;
CP 6, 7; DAM MULT; DLB 122; HW 1, 2;
LLW; MAL 5; PFS 40

**Baca, Jose Santiago**
See Baca, Jimmy Santiago

**Bacchelli, Riccardo** 1891-1985 ........ **CLC 19**
See also CA 29-32R; 117; DLB 264; EWL 3

**Bacchylides**
c. 520 BCE-c. 452 BCE ......... **CMLC 119**

**Bach, Richard** 1936- ....................... **CLC 14**
See also AITN 1; BEST 89:2; BPFB 1; BYA
5; CA 9-12R; CANR 18, 93, 151; CPW;
DAM NOV, POP; FANT; MTCW 1;
SATA 13

**Bach, Richard David**
See Bach, Richard

**Bache, Benjamin Franklin**
1769-1798 ................................. **LC 74**
See also DLB 43

**Bachelard, Gaston** 1884-1962 ..... **TCLC 128**
See also CA 97-100; 89-92; DLB 296; GFL
1789 to the Present

**Bachman, Richard**
See King, Stephen

**Bachmann, Ingeborg** 1926-1973 ... **CLC 69;
PC 151; TCLC 192**
See also CA 93-96; 45-48; CANR 69; DLB
85; EWL 3; RGHL; RGWL 2, 3

**Bacigalupi, Paolo** 1973- ................. **CLC 309**
See also AAYA 86; CA 317; SATA 230

**Bacon, Delia** 1811-1859 ............. **NCLC 315**
See also DLB 1, 243

**Bacon, Francis** 1561-1626 .......... **LC 18, 32,
131, 239**
See also BRW 1; CDBLB Before 1660; DLB
151, 236, 252; RGEL 2; TEA

**Bacon, Roger**
1214(?)-1294 ......... **CMLC 14, 108, 155**
See also DLB 115

**Bacovia, G.**
See Bacovia, George

**Bacovia, George** 1881-1957 .......... **TCLC 24**
See Bacovia, George
See also CA 123; 189; CDWLB 4; DLB 220;
EWL 3

**Badanes, Jerome** 1937-1995 ............ **CLC 59**
See also CA 234

**Badiou, Alain** 1937- ....................... **CLC 326**
See also CA 261

**Baena, Juan Alfonso de**
c. 1375-c. 1434 ........................ **LC 239**

**Bage, Robert** 1728-1801 ............. **NCLC 182**
See also DLB 39; RGEL 2

**Bagehot, Walter** 1826-1877 .. **NCLC 10, 322**
See also DLB 55

**Bagnold, Enid** 1889-1981 ............... **CLC 25**
See also AAYA 75; BYA 2; CA 5-8R; 103;
CANR 5, 40; CBD; CN 2; CWD; CWRI 5;
DAM DRAM; DLB 13, 160, 191, 245;
FW; MAICYA 1, 2; RGEL 2; SATA 1, 25

**Bagritsky, Eduard**
See Dzyubin, Eduard Georgievich

**Bagritsky, Edvard**
See Dzyubin, Eduard Georgievich

**Bagrjana, Elisaveta**
See Belcheva, Elisaveta Lyubomirova

**Bagryana, Elisaveta**
See Belcheva, Elisaveta Lyubomirova

**Bai Xianyong** 1937- ....................... **CLC 410**
See also DLB 370; EWL 3

**Bail, Murray** 1941- ....................... **CLC 353**
See also CA 127; CANR 62; CN 4, 5, 6, 7;
DLB 325

**Bailey, Paul** 1937- ........................... **CLC 45**
See also CA 21-24R; CANR 16, 62, 124;
CN 1, 2, 3, 4, 5, 6, 7; DLB 14, 271; GLL 2

**Baillie, Joanna** 1762-1851 ..... **DC 59; NCLC
71, 151; PC 151**
See also DLB 93, 344; GL 2; RGEL 2

**Bainbridge, Beryl** 1934-2010 .......... **CLC 4,
5, 8, 10, 14, 18, 22, 62, 130, 292**
See also BRWS 6; CA 21-24R; CANR 24,
55, 75, 88, 128; CN 2, 3, 4, 5, 6, 7; DAM
NOV; DLB 14, 231; EWL 3; MTCW 1, 2;
MTFW 2005

**Baker, Carlos (Heard)** 1909-1987 ... **TCLC 119**
See also CA 5-8R; 122; CANR 3, 63;
DLB 103

**Baker, Elliott** 1922-2007 .................. **CLC 8**
See also CA 45-48; 257; CANR 2, 63; CN 1,
2, 3, 4, 5, 6, 7

**Baker, Elliott Joseph**
See Baker, Elliott

**Baker, Nicholson** 1957- ........... **CLC 61, 165**
See also AMWS 13; CA 135; CANR 63,
120, 138, 190, 237; CN 6; CPW; DA3;
DAM POP; DLB 227; MTFW 2005

**Baker, Ray Stannard** 1870-1946 ... **TCLC 47**
See also CA 118; DLB 345

**Baker, Russell** 1925- ....................... **CLC 31**
See also BEST 89:4; CA 57-60; CANR 11,
41, 59, 137; MTCW 1, 2; MTFW 2005

**Baker, Russell Wayne**
See Baker, Russell

**Bakhtin, M.**
See Bakhtin, Mikhail Mikhailovich

**Bakhtin, M. M.**
See Bakhtin, Mikhail Mikhailovich

**Bakhtin, Mikhail**
See Bakhtin, Mikhail Mikhailovich

**Bakhtin, Mikhail Mikhailovich**
1895-1975 ................... **CLC 83; TCLC 160**
See Bakhtin, Mikhail Mikhailovich
See also CA 128; 113; DLB 242; EWL 3

**Bakshi, Ralph** 1938(?)- .................. **CLC 26**
See also CA 112; 138; IDFW 3

**Bakunin, Mikhail (Alexandrovich)**
1814-1876 ........................ **NCLC 25, 58**
See also DLB 277

**Bal, Mieke** 1946- .......................... **CLC 252**
See also CA 156; CANR 99

**Bal, Mieke Maria Gertrudis**
See Bal, Mieke

**Baldwin, James** 1924-1987 ........... **BLC 1:1, 2:1; CLC 1, 2, 3, 4, 5, 8, 13, 15, 17, 42, 50, 67, 90, 127; DC 1; SSC 10, 33, 98, 134, 199; TCLC 229, 376, 377; WLC 1**
See also AAYA 4, 34; AFAW 1, 2; AMWR 2; AMWS 1; BPFB 1; BW 1; CA 1-4R, 124; CABS 1; CAD; CANR 3, 24; CDALB 1941-1968; CLR 191; CMTFW; CN 1, 2, 3, 4; CPW; DA; DA3; DAB; DAC; DAM MST, MULT, NOV, POP; DFS 11, 15; DLB 2, 7, 33, 249, 278; DLBY 1987; EWL 3; EXPS; LAIT 5; MAL 5; MTCW 1, 2; MTFW 2005; NCFS 4; NFS 4; RGAL 4; RGSF 2; SATA 9, 54; SATA-Obit 54; SSFS 2, 18, 44; TUS

**Baldwin, William** c. 1515-1563 ... **LC 113, 209**
See also DLB 132

**Bale, John** 1495-1563 ................. **LC 62, 228**
See also DLB 132; RGEL 2; TEA

**Ball, Hugo** 1886-1927 ................... **TCLC 104**

**Ballard, James G.**
See Ballard, J.G.

**Ballard, James Graham**
See Ballard, J.G.

**Ballard, J.G.** 1930-2009 ......... **CLC 3, 6, 14, 36, 137, 299, 431; SSC 1, 53, 146, 232**
See also AAYA 3, 52; BRWS 5; CA 5-8R, 285; CANR 15, 39, 65, 107, 133, 198; CN 1, 2, 3, 4, 5, 6, 7; DA3; DAM NOV, POP; DLB 14, 207, 261, 319; EWL 3; HGG; MTCW 1, 2; MTFW 2005; NFS 8; RGEL 2; RGSF 2; SATA 93; SATA-Obit 203; SCFW 1, 2; SFW 4

**Ballard, Jim G.**
See Ballard, J.G.

**Balmont, Konstantin (Dmitriyevich)** 1867-1943 ................. **PC 149; TCLC 11**
See also CA 109; 155; DLB 295; EWL 3

**Ballantyne, R. M.** 1825-1894 ...... **NCLC 301**
See also CLR 137, 228; DLB 163; JRDA; RGEL 2; SATA 24

**Baltausis, Vincas** 1847-1910
See Mikszath, Kalman

**Balwhidder, Rev. Micah**
See Galt, John

**Balzac, Guez de** (?)-
See Balzac, Jean-Louis Guez de

**Balzac, Honoré de** 1799-1850 ......... **NCLC 5, 35, 53, 153, 273, 311; SSC 5, 59, 102, 153, 244; WLC 1**
See also DA; DA3; DAB; DAC; DAM MST, NOV; DLB 119; EW 5; GFL 1789 to the Present; LMFS 1; NFS 33; RGSF 2; RGWL 2, 3; SSFS 10; SUFW; TWA

**Balzac, Jean-Louis Guez de** 1597-1654 ................................. **LC 162**
See also DLB 268; GFL Beginnings to 1789

**Bambara, Toni Cade** 1939-1995 .... **BLC 1:1, 2:1; CLC 19, 88; SSC 35, 107, 245; TCLC 116; WLCS**
See also AAYA 5, 49; AFAW 2; AMWS 11; BW 2, 3; BYA 12, 14; CA 29-32R; 150; CANR 24, 49, 81; CDALBS; DA; DA3; DAC; DAM MST, MULT; DLB 38, 218; EXPS; MAL 5; MTCW 1, 2; MTFW 2005; RGAL 4; RGSF 2; SATA 112; SSFS 4, 7, 12, 21

**Bamdad, A.**
See Shamlu, Ahmad

**Bamdad, Alef**
See Shamlu, Ahmad

**Banat, D. R.**
See Bradbury, Ray

**Bancroft, George** 1800-1891 ....... **NCLC 359**
See also DLB 1, 30, 59, 243

**Bancroft, Laura**
See Baum, L. Frank

**Bandello, Matteo** 1485-1562 .. **LC 212; SSC 143**

**Banha, 'Ayda Bint**
See Rifaat, Alifa

**Banim, John** 1798-1842 ................. **NCLC 13**
See also DLB 116, 158, 159; RGEL 2

**Banim, Michael** 1796-1874 ............ **NCLC 13**
See also DLB 158, 159

**Banjo, The**
See Paterson, A(ndrew) B(arton)

**Banks, Iain** 1954-2013 ................. **CLC 34, 356**
See also BRWS 11; CA 123; 128; CANR 61, 106, 180; DLB 194, 261; EWL 3; HGG; INT CA-128; MTFW 2005; SFW 4

**Banks, Iain M.**
See Banks, Iain

**Banks, Iain Menzies**
See Banks, Iain

**Banks, Lynne Reid**
See Reid Banks, Lynne

**Banks, Russell** 1940- ........... **CLC 37, 72, 187; SSC 42**
See also AAYA 45; AMWS 5; CA 65-68; CAAS 15; CANR 19, 52, 73, 118, 195, 240; CN 4, 5, 6, 7; DLB 130, 278; EWL 3; MAL 5; MTCW 2; MTFW 2005; NFS 13

**Banks, Russell Earl**
See Banks, Russell

**Banti, Anna** 1895-1985 ................. **TCLC 303**
See also CA 202; DLB 177; WLIT 7

**Banville, John** 1945- ................. **CLC 46, 118, 224, 315**
See also CA 117; 128; CANR 104, 150, 176, 225; CN 4, 5, 6, 7; DLB 14, 271, 326; INT CA-128

**Banville, Théodore (Faullain) de** 1832-1891 ......................... **NCLC 9, 348**
See also DLB 217; GFL 1789 to the Present

**Baraka, Amiri** 1934-2014 ...... **BLC 1:1, 2:1; CLC 1, 2, 3, 5, 10, 14, 33, 115, 213, 389; DC 6, 54; PC 4, 113; WLCS**
See also AAYA 63; AFAW 1, 2; AMWS 2; BW 2, 3; CA 21-24R; CABS 3; CAD; CANR 27, 38, 61, 133, 172; CD 3, 5, 6; CDALB 1941-1968; CN 1, 2; CP 1, 2, 3, 4, 5, 6, 7; CPW; DA; DA3; DAC; DAM MST, MULT, POET, POP; DFS 3, 11, 16; DLB 5, 7, 16, 38; DLBD 8; EWL 3; MAL 5; MTCW 1, 2; MTFW 2005; PFS 9; RGAL 4; TCLE 1:1; TUS; WP

**Baratynsky, Evgenii Abramovich** 1800-1844 ............................. **NCLC 103**
See also DLB 205

**Barbauld, Anna Laetitia** 1743-1825 ....... **NCLC 50, 185; PC 149**
See also CLR 160; DLB 107, 109, 142, 158, 336; RGEL 2

**Barbellion, W. N. P.**
See Cummings, Bruce F.

**Barber, Benjamin R.** 1939- ........... **CLC 141**
See also CA 29-32R; CANR 12, 32, 64, 119

**Barbera, Jack** 1945- ......................... **CLC 44**
See also CA 110; CANR 45

**Barbera, Jack Vincent**
See Barbera, Jack

**Barbey d'Aurevilly, Jules-Amédée** 1808-1889 ... **NCLC 1, 213; SSC 17, 218**
See also DLB 119; GFL 1789 to the Present

**Barbour, John** c. 1316-1395 ......... **CMLC 33**
See also DLB 146

**Barbusse, Henri** 1873-1935 ............. **TCLC 5**
See also CA 105; 154; DLB 65; EWL 3; RGWL 2, 3

**Barclay, Alexander** c. 1475-1552 ..... **LC 109**
See also DLB 132

**Barclay, Bill**
See Moorcock, Michael

**Barclay, William Ewert**
See Moorcock, Michael

**Barclay, William Ewert**
See Moorcock, Michael

**Barea, Arturo** 1897-1957 .............. **TCLC 14**
See also CA 111; 201

**Barfield, Owen** 1898-1997 .......... **TCLC 332**
See also CA 5-8R; CANR 2

**Barfoot, Joan** 1946- ....................... **CLC 18**
See also CA 105; CANR 141, 179

**Barham, Richard Harris** 1788-1845 ................................. **NCLC 77**
See also DLB 159

**Baring, Maurice** 1874-1945 ............. **TCLC 8**
See also CA 105; 168; DLB 34; HGG

**Baring-Gould, Sabine** 1834-1924 ... **TCLC 88**
See also DLB 156, 190

**Barker, Clive** 1952- ................. **CLC 52, 205; SSC 53**
See also AAYA 10, 54; BEST 90:3; BPFB 1; CA 121; 129; CANR 71, 111, 133, 187; CPW; DA3; DAM POP; DLB 261; HGG; INT CA-129; MTCW 1, 2; MTFW 2005; SUFW 2

**Barker, George Granville** 1913-1991 ................ **CLC 8, 48; PC 77**
See also CA 9-12R; 135; CANR 7, 38; CP 1, 2, 3, 4, 5; DAM POET; DLB 20; EWL 3; MTCW 1

**Barker, Harley Granville**
See Granville-Barker, Harley

**Barker, Howard** 1946- ....... **CLC 37; DC 51**
See also CA 102; CBD; CD 5, 6; DLB 13, 233

**Barker, Jane** 1652-1732 ...... **LC 42, 82, 216; PC 91**
See also DLB 39, 131

**Barker, Pat** 1943- ............... **CLC 32, 94, 146**
See also BRWS 4; CA 117; 122; CANR 50, 101, 148, 195; CN 6, 7; DLB 271, 326; INT CA-122

**Barker, Patricia**
See Barker, Pat

**Barlach, Ernst (Heinrich)** 1870-1938 ................................ **TCLC 84**
See also CA 178; DLB 56, 118; EWL 3

**Barlow, Joel** 1754-1812 ... **NCLC 23, 223, 351**
See also AMWS 2; DLB 37; RGAL 4

**Barnard, Mary (Ethel)** 1909- ......... **CLC 48**
See also CA 21-22; CAP 2; CP 1

**Barnes, Djuna** 1892-1982 ......... **CLC 3, 4, 8, 11, 29, 127; SSC 3, 163; TCLC 212**
See also AMWS 3; CA 9-12R; 107; CAD; CANR 16, 55; CN 1, 2, 3; CWD; DLB 4, 9, 45; EWL 3; GLL 1; MAL 5; MTCW 1, 2; MTFW 2005; RGAL 4; TCLE 1:1; TUS

**Barnes, Jim** 1933- .............................. **NNAL**
See also CA 108, 175, 272; CAAE 175, 272; CAAS 28; DLB 175

**Barnes, Julian** 1946- ................. **CLC 42, 141, 315, 434**
See also BRWS 4; CA 102; CANR 19, 54, 115, 137, 195, 310; CMTFW; CN 4, 5, 6, 7; DAB; DLB 194, 377; DLBY 1993; EWL 3; MBL 2; MTCW 2; MTFW 2005; SSFS 24

**Barnes, Julian Patrick**
See Barnes, Julian

**Barnes, Peter** 1931-2004 ............. **CLC 5, 56**
See also CA 65-68; 230; CAAS 12; CANR 33, 34, 64, 113; CBD; CD 5, 6; DFS 6; DLB 13, 233; MTCW 1

**Barnes, William** 1801-1886 ... **NCLC 75, 283**
See also DLB 32

**Barney, Natalie Clifford** 1876-1972 ............................. **TCLC 351**
See also CA 33-36R; DLB 4

**Barnfield, Richard** 1574-1627 .......... **LC 192; PC 152**
See also DLB 172

**Barnivelt, Esdras**
See Pope, Alexander

**Baroja, Pio** 1872-1956 ..... **HLC 1; SSC 112; TCLC 8, 240**
See also CA 104; 247; EW 9

**Baroja y Nessi, Pio**
See Baroja, Pio

**Benedetti, Mario**
1920-2009 .............. **CLC 299; SSC 135**
See also CA 152; 286; DAM MULT; DLB
113; EWL 3; HW 1, 2; LAW

**Benedetti, Mario Orlando Hardy Hamlet Brenno**
See Benedetti, Mario

**Benedetti Farrugia, Mario**
See Benedetti, Mario

**Benedetti Farrugia, Mario Orlando Hardy Hamlet Brenno**
See Benedetti, Mario

**Benedict, Ruth** 1887-1948 ............. **TCLC 60**
See also CA 158; CANR 146; DLB 246

**Benedict, Ruth Fulton**
See Benedict, Ruth

**Benedikt, Michael** 1935- ............. **CLC 4, 14**
See also CA 13-16R; CANR 7; CP 1, 2, 3, 4,
5, 6, 7; DLB 5

**Benet, Juan** 1927-1993 ..................... **CLC 28**
See also CA 143; EWL 3

**Benford, Gregory** 1941- .................. **CLC 52**
See also BPFB 1; CA 69-72, 175, 268;
CAAE 175, 268; CAAS 27; CANR 12,
24, 49, 95, 134; CN 7; CSW; DLBY 1982;
MTFW 2005; SCFW 2; SFW 4

**Benford, Gregory Albert**
See Benford, Gregory

**Bengtsson, Frans (Gunnar)**
1894-1954 ..................... **TCLC 48**
See also CA 170; EWL 3

**Benjamin, David**
See Slavitt, David R.

**Benjamin, Lois**
See Gould, Lois

**Benjamin, Walter** 1892-1940 ... **TCLC 39, 325**
See also CA 164; CANR 181; DLB 242; EW
11; EWL 3

**Ben Jelloun, Tahar** 1944- ...... **CLC 180, 311**
See also CA 135, 162; CANR 100, 166, 217;
CWW 2; EWL 3; RGWL 3; WLIT 2

**Benn, Gottfried**
1886-1956 ........... **PC 35; TCLC 3, 256**
See also CA 106; 153; DLB 56; EWL 3;
RGWL 2, 3

**Bennett, Alan** 1934- ......... **CLC 45, 77, 292**
See also BRWS 8; CA 103; CANR 35, 55,
106, 157, 197, 227; CBD; CD 5, 6; DAB;
DAM MST; DLB 310; MTCW 1, 2;
MTFW 2005

**Bennett, (Enoch) Arnold**
1867-1931 .................. **TCLC 5, 20, 197**
See also BRW 6; CA 106; 155; CDBLB
1890-1914; DLB 10, 34, 98, 135; EWL 3;
MTCW 2

**Bennett, Elizabeth**
See Mitchell, Margaret

**Bennett, George Harold** 1930- ......... **CLC 5**
See also BW 1; CA 97-100; CAAS 13;
CANR 87; DLB 33

**Bennett, Gwendolyn B.** 1902-1981 ... **HR 1:2**
See also BW 1; CA 125; DLB 51; WP

**Bennett, Hal**
See Bennett, George Harold

**Bennett, Jay** 1912- ............................ **CLC 35**
See also AAYA 10, 73; CA 69-72; CANR
11, 42, 79; JRDA; SAAS 4; SATA 41, 87;
SATA-Brief 27; WYA; YAW

**Bennett, Louise** 1919-2006 ........... **BLC 1:1;
CLC 28**
See also BW 2, 3; CA 151; 252; CDWLB 3;
CP 1, 2, 3, 4, 5, 6, 7; DAM MULT; DLB
117; EWL 3

**Bennett, Louise Simone**
See Bennett, Louise

**Bennett-Coverley, Louise**
See Bennett, Louise

**Benoit de Sainte-Maure**
fl. 12th cent. ........................... **CMLC 90**

**Benson, A. C.** 1862-1925 ............. **TCLC 123**
See also DLB 98

**Benson, E(dward) F(rederic)**
1867-1940 ........................... **TCLC 27**
See also CA 114; 157; DLB 135, 153; HGG;
SUFW 1

**Benson, Jackson J.** 1930- ............... **CLC 34**
See also CA 25-28R; CANR 214; DLB 111

**Benson, Sally** 1900-1972 .................. **CLC 17**
See also CA 19-20; 37-40R; CAP 1; SATA
1, 35; SATA-Obit 27

**Benson, Stella** 1892-1933 ............... **TCLC 17**
See also CA 117; 154, 155; DLB 36, 162;
FANT; TEA

**Benet, Stephen Vincent** 1898-1943 ... **PC 64;
SSC 10, 86; TCLC 7**
See also AMWS 11; CA 104; 152; DA3;
DAM POET; DLB 4, 48, 102, 249, 284;
DLBY 1997; EWL 3; HGG; MAL 5;
MTCW 2; MTFW 2005; RGAL 4; RGSF
2; SSFS 22, 31; SUFW; WP; YABC 1

**Benet, William Rose** 1886-1950 .... **TCLC 28**
See also CA 118; 152; DAM POET; DLB
45; RGAL 4

**Bentham, Jeremy**
1748-1832 ..................... **NCLC 38, 237**
See also DLB 107, 158, 252

**Bentley, E(dmund) C(lerihew)**
1875-1956 ........................... **TCLC 12**
See also CA 108; 232; DLB 70; MSW

**Bentley, Eric** 1916- .......................... **CLC 24**
See also CA 5-8R; CAD; CANR 6, 67;
CBD; CD 5, 6; INT CANR-6

**Bentley, Eric Russell**
See Bentley, Eric

**ben Uzair, Salem**
See Horne, Richard Henry Hengist

**Beolco, Angelo** 1496-1542 ................. **LC 139**

**Beranger, Pierre Jean de**
1780-1857 ................ **NCLC 34; PC 112**

**Berceo, Gonzalo de**
c. 1190-c. 1260 ..................... **CMLC 151**
See also DLB 337

**Berdyaev, Nicolas**
See Berdyaev, Nikolai (Aleksandrovich)

**Berdyaev, Nikolai (Aleksandrovich)**
1874-1948 ........................... **TCLC 67**
See also CA 120; 157

**Berdyayev, Nikolai (Aleksandrovich)**
See Berdyaev, Nikolai (Aleksandrovich)

**Berendt, John** 1939- ........................ **CLC 86**
See also CA 146; CANR 75, 83, 151

**Berendt, John Lawrence**
See Berendt, John

**Berengar of Tours** c. 1000-1088 ... **CMLC 124**

**Beresford, J(ohn) D(avys)**
1873-1947 ............................... **TCLC 81**
See also CA 112; 155; DLB 162, 178, 197;
SFW 4; SUFW 1

**Bergelson, David (Rafailovich)**
1884-1952 ............................... **TCLC 81**
See also CA 220; DLB 333; EWL 3

**Bergelson, Dovid**
See Bergelson, David (Rafailovich)

**Berger, Colonel**
See Malraux, Andre

**Berger, John** 1926- .............. **CLC 2, 19, 375**
See also BRWS 4; CA 81-84; CANR 51, 78,
117, 163, 200; CN 1, 2, 3, 4, 5, 6, 7; DLB
14, 207, 319, 326

**Berger, John Peter**
See Berger, John

**Berger, Melvin H.** 1927- ................. **CLC 12**
See also CA 5-8R; CANR 4, 142; CLR 32;
SAAS 2; SATA 5, 88, 158; SATA-Essay 124

**Berger, Thomas** 1924- ........ **CLC 3, 5, 8, 11,
18, 38, 259**
See also BPFB 1; CA 1-4R; CANR 5, 28,
51, 128; CN 1, 2, 3, 4, 5, 6, 7; DAM NOV;
DLB 2; DLBY 1980; EWL 3; FANT; INT
CANR-28; MAL 5; MTCW 1, 2; MTFW
2005; RHW; TCLE 1:1; TCWW 1, 2

**Bergman, Ernst Ingmar**
See Bergman, Ingmar

**Bergman, Ingmar**
1918-2007 ................... **CLC 16, 72, 210**
See also AAYA 61; CA 81-84; 262; CANR
33, 70; CWW 2; DLB 257; MTCW 2;
MTFW 2005

**Bergson, Henri(-Louis)**
1859-1941 ............................... **TCLC 32**
See also CA 164; DLB 329; EW 8; EWL 3;
GFL 1789 to the Present

**Bergstein, Eleanor** 1938- .................. **CLC 4**
See also CA 53-56; CANR 5

**Berkeley, George** 1685-1753 .............. **LC 65**
See also DLB 31, 101, 252

**Berkoff, Steven** 1937- ...................... **CLC 56**
See also CA 104; CANR 72; CBD; CD 5, 6

**Berlin, Isaiah** 1909-1997 .............. **TCLC 105**
See also CA 85-88; 162

**Bermant, Chaim (Icyk)**
1929-1998 ............................... **CLC 40**
See also CA 57-60; CANR 6, 31, 57, 105;
CN 2, 3, 4, 5, 6

**Bern, Victoria**
See Fisher, M. F. K.

**Bernanos, (Paul Louis) Georges**
1888-1948 ..................... **TCLC 3, 267**
See also CA 104; 130; CANR 94; DLB 72;
EWL 3; GFL 1789 to the Present; RGWL 2, 3

**Bernard, April** 1956- ....................... **CLC 59**
See also CA 131; CANR 144, 230

**Bernard, Mary Ann**
See Soderbergh, Steven

**Bernard of Clairvaux**
1090-1153 ..................... **CMLC 71, 170**
See also DLB 208

**Bernard Silvestris**
fl. c. 1130-fl. c. 1160 ............ **CMLC 87**
See also DLB 208

**Bernardin de Saint-Pierre, Jacques-Henri**
1737-1814 ............................... **NCLC 297**
See also DLB 313; GFL

**Bernart de Ventadorn**
c. 1130-c. 1190 ..................... **CMLC 98**

**Berne, Victoria**
See Fisher, M. F. K.

**Bernhard, Thomas** 1931-1989 ......... **CLC 3,
32, 61; DC 14; TCLC 165**
See also CA 85-88; 127; CANR 32, 57;
CDWLB 2; DLB 85, 124; EWL 3; MTCW
1; RGHL; RGWL 2, 3

**Bernhardt, Sarah (Henriette Rosine)**
1844-1923 ........................... **TCLC 75**
See also CA 157

**Berni, Francesco** c. 1497-1536 ......... **LC 210**

**Bernstein, Charles** 1950- .. **CLC 142; PC 152**
See also CA 129; CAAS 24; CANR 90; CP
4, 5, 6, 7; DLB 169

**Bernstein, Ingrid**
See Kirsch, Sarah

**Béroul** fl. c. 12th cent. ......... **CMLC 75, 148;
PC 151**

**Berriault, Gina** 1926-1999 ...... **CLC 54, 109;
SSC 30**
See also CA 116; 129; 185; CANR 66; DLB
130; SSFS 7, 11

**Berrigan, Daniel** 1921- ..................... **CLC 4**
See also CA 33-36R, 187; CAAE 187;
CAAS 1; CANR 11, 43, 78, 219; CP 1,
2, 3, 4, 5, 6, 7; DLB 5

**Berrigan, Edmund Joseph Michael, Jr.**
1934-1983 .................. **CLC 37; PC 103**

See also CA 61-64; 110; CANR 14, 102; CP
1, 2, 3; DLB 5, 169; WP

**Berrigan, Ted**
See Berrigan, Edmund Joseph Michael, Jr.

**Berry, Charles Edward Anderson**
See Berry, Chuck

**Berry, Chuck** 1931- .......................... CLC 17
See also CA 115

**Berry, Jonas**
See Ashbery, John

**Berry, Matilda**
See Mansfield, Katherine

**Berry, Wendell** 1934- .......... CLC 4, 6, 8, 27,
46, 279, 393; PC 28
See also AITN 1; AMWS 10; ANW; CA 73-
76; CANR 50, 73, 101, 132, 174, 228; CP
1, 2, 3, 4, 5, 6, 7; CSW; DAM POET; DLB
5, 6, 234, 275, 342; MTCW 2; MTFW
2005; PFS 30; TCLE 1:1

**Berry, Wendell Erdman**
See Berry, Wendell

**Berry, William**
See Harwood, Gwen

**Berryman, John** 1914-1972 ..... CLC 1, 2, 3,
4, 6, 8, 10, 13, 25, 62; PC 64
See also AMW; CA 13-16; 33-36R; CABS
2; CANR 35; CAP 1; CDALB 1941-1968;
CP 1; DAM POET; DLB 48; EWL 3;
MAL 5; MTCW 1, 2; MTFW 2005; PAB;
PFS 27; RGAL 4; WP

**Berssenbrugge, Mei-mei** 1947- .......... PC 115
See also CA 104; DLB 312

**Bertolucci, Bernardo** 1940- ..... CLC 16, 157
See also CA 106; CANR 125

**Berton, Pierre (Francis de Marigny)**
1920-2004 ............................... CLC 104
See also CA 1-4R; 233; CANR 2, 56, 144;
CPW; DLB 68; SATA 99; SATA-Obit 158

**Bertrand, Aloysius** 1807-1841 ....... NCLC 31
See also DLB 217

**Bertrand, Louis oAloysiusc**
See Bertrand, Aloysius

**Bertran de Born** c. 1140-1215 ....... CMLC 5

**Berwick, Mary**
See Adelaide Anne Procter

**Besant, Annie (Wood)** 1847-1933 ... TCLC 9
See also CA 105; 185

**Bessie, Alvah** 1904-1985 ................. CLC 23
See also CA 5-8R; 116; CANR 2, 80; DLB 26

**Bestuzhev, Aleksandr Aleksandrovich**
1797-1837 ............................. NCLC 131
See also DLB 198

**Bethlen, T.D.**
See Silverberg, Robert

**Beti, Mongo**
1932-2001 ........ BLC 1:1; CLC 27, 380
See also AFW; BW 1, 3; CA 114; 124;
CANR 81; DA3; DAM MULT; DLB
360; EWL 3; MTCW 1, 2

**Betjeman, John** 1906-1984 .......... CLC 2, 6,
10, 34, 43; PC 75
See also BRW 7; CA 9-12R; 112; CANR 33,
56; CDBLB 1945-1960; CP 1, 2, 3; DA3;
DAB; DAM MST, POET; DLB 20; DLBY
1984; EWL 3; MTCW 1, 2

**Bettelheim, Bruno** 1903-1990 ......... CLC 79;
TCLC 143
See also CA 81-84; 131; CANR 23, 61;
DA3; MTCW 1, 2; RGHL

**Betti, Ugo** 1892-1953 ........................ TCLC 5
See also CA 104; 155; EWL 3; RGWL 2, 3

**Betts, Doris** 1932-2012 .. CLC 3, 6, 28, 275;
SSC 45
See also CA 13-16R; CANR 9, 66, 77; CN
6, 7; CSW; DLB 218; DLBY 1982; INT
CANR-9; RGAL 4

**Betts, Doris Waugh**
See Betts, Doris

**Bevan, Alistair**
See Roberts, Keith (John Kingston)

**Bey, Pilaff**
See Douglas, (George) Norman

**Beyala, Calixthe** 1961- ... BLC 2:1; CLC 329
See also EWL 3

**Beyer, Marcel** 1965- ....................... CLC 411
See also CA 244; CANR 216, 254

**Beynon, John**
See Harris, John (Wyndham Parkes Lucas)
Beynon

**Bhabha, Homi K.** 1949- ................ CLC 285

**Bi Shang-guan**
See Shen Congwen

**Bialik, Chaim Nachman** 1873-1934 ... TCLC
25, 201
See also CA 170; EWL 3; WLIT 6

**Bialik, Hayyim Nahman**
See Bialik, Chaim Nachman

**Bickerstaff, Isaac**
See Addison, Joseph; Swift, Jonathan

**Bidart, Frank** 1939- ......... CLC 33; PC 209
See also AMWS 15; CA 140; CANR 106,
215, 268; DLB 372; CP 5, 6, 7; PFS 26

**Bienek, Horst** 1930- ................... CLC 7, 11
See also CA 73-76; DLB 75

**Bierce, Ambrose** 1842-1914(?) .... SSC 9, 72,
124, 169, 244; TCLC 1, 7, 44; WLC 1
See also AAYA 55; AMW; BYA 11; CA
104; 139; CANR 78; CDALB 1865-1917;
DA; DA3; DAC; DAM MST; DLB 11, 12,
23, 71, 74, 186; EWL 3; EXPS; HGG;
LAIT 2; MAL 5; RGAL 4; RGSF 2; SSFS
9, 27; SUFW 1

**Bierce, Ambrose Gwinnett**
See Bierce, Ambrose

**Biggers, Earl Derr** 1884-1933 ....... TCLC 65
See also CA 108; 153; DLB 306

**Bilek, Anton F.** 1919-
See Rankin, Ian
See also CA 304

**Billiken, Bud**
See Motley, Willard (Francis)

**Billings, Josh**
See Shaw, Henry Wheeler

**Billington, Lady Rachel Mary**
See Billington, Rachel

**Billington, Rachel** 1942- ................. CLC 43
See also AITN 2; CA 33-36R; CANR 44,
196, 242; CN 4, 5, 6, 7

**Binchy, Maeve** 1940-2012 ............. CLC 153
See also BEST 90:1; BPFB 1; CA 127; 134;
CANR 50, 96, 134, 208; CN 5, 6, 7; CPW;
DA3; DAM POP; DLB 319; INT CA-134;
MTCW 2; MTFW 2005; RHW

**Binyon, T(imothy) J(ohn)**
1936-2004 ............................... CLC 34
See also CA 111; 232; CANR 28, 140

**Bion** 335 BCE-245 BCE .................... CMLC 39

**Bioy Casares, Adolfo** 1914-1999 ..... CLC 4,
8, 13, 88; HLC 1; SSC 17, 102
See also CA 29-32R; 177; CANR 19, 43, 66;
CWW 2; DAM MULT; DLB 113; EWL 3;
HW 1, 2; LAW; MTCW 1, 2; MTFW
2005; RGSF 2

**Birch, Allison** ................................. CLC 65

**Bird, Cordwainer**
See Ellison, Harlan

**Bird, Robert Montgomery**
1806-1854 ................ NCLC 1, 197, 336
See also DLB 202; RGAL 4

**Birdwell, Cleo**
See DeLillo, Don

**Birkerts, Sven** 1951- ....................... CLC 116
See also CA 128; 133, 176; CAAE 176;
CAAS 29; CANR 151, 243; INT CA-133

**Birney, (Alfred) Earle**
1904-1995 ....... CLC 1, 4, 6, 11; PC 52
See also CA 1-4R; CANR 5, 20; CN 1, 2, 3,
4; CP 1, 2, 3, 4, 5, 6; DAC; DAM MST,
POET; DLB 88; MTCW 1; PFS 8; RGEL 2

**Biruni, al** 973-1048(?) ................... CMLC 28

**Bishop, Elizabeth** 1911-1979 ........... CLC 1,
4, 9, 13, 15, 32; PC 3, 34, 150; SSC 151;
TCLC 121
See also AMWR 2; AMWS 1; CA 5-8R; 89-
92; CABS 2; CANR 26, 61, 108; CDALB
1968-1988; CP 1, 2, 3; DA; DA3; DAC;
DAM MST, POET; DLB 5, 169; EWL 3;
GLL 2; MAL 5; MBL; MTCW 1, 2; PAB;
PFS 6, 12, 27, 31, 44; RGAL 4; SATA-
Obit 24; TUS; WP

**Bishop, George Archibald**
See Crowley, Edward Alexander

**Bishop, John** 1935- .......................... CLC 10
See also CA 105

**Bishop, John Peale** 1892-1944 .... TCLC 103
See also CA 107; 155; DLB 4, 9, 45; MAL
5; RGAL 4

**Bissett, Bill** 1939- ................. CLC 18; PC 14
See also CA 69-72; CAAS 19; CANR 15; CCA
1; CP 1, 2, 3, 4, 5, 6, 7; DLB 53; MTCW 1

**Bissoondath, Neil** 1955- .......... CLC 120, 285
See also CA 136; CANR 123, 165; CN 6, 7;
DAC

**Bissoondath, Neil Devindra**
See Bissoondath, Neil

**Bitov, Andrei (Georgievich)** 1937- ... CLC 57,
361
See also CA 142; DLB 302

**Biyidi, Alexandre**
See Beti, Mongo

**Bjarme, Brynjolf**
See Ibsen, Henrik

**Bjoernson, Bjoernstjerne (Martinius)**
1832-1910 ........................ TCLC 7, 37
See also CA 104

**Blab, W. Epaminondas Adrastus**
See Twain, Mark

**Black, Benjamin**
See Banville, John

**Black, Robert**
See Holdstock, Robert

**Blackburn, Paul** 1926-1971 ......... CLC 9, 43
See also BG 1:2; CA 81-84; 33-36R; CANR
34; CP 1; DLB 16; DLBY 1981

**Black Elk** 1863-1950 ........ NNAL; TCLC 33
See also CA 144; DAM MULT; MTCW 2;
MTFW 2005; WP

**Black Hawk** 1767-1838 ...................... NNAL

**Black Hobart**
See Sanders, Ed

**Blacklin, Malcolm**
See Chambers, Aidan

**Blackmore, R(ichard) D(oddridge)**
1825-1900 .............................. TCLC 27
See also CA 120; DLB 18; RGEL 2

**Blackmur, R(ichard) P(almer)**
1904-1965 ............................ CLC 2, 24
See also AMWS 2; CA 11-12; 25-28R; CANR
71; CAP 1; DLB 63; EWL 3; MAL 5

**Black Tarantula**
See Acker, Kathy

**Blackwood, Algernon**
1869-1951 ....... SSC 107, 220; TCLC 5
See also AAYA 78; CA 105; 150; CANR
169; DLB 153, 156, 178; HGG; SUFW 1

**Blackwood, Algernon Henry**
See Blackwood, Algernon

**Blackwood, Caroline (Maureen)**
1931-1996 ..................... CLC 6, 9, 100
See also BRWS 9; CA 85-88; 151; CANR
32, 61, 65; CN 3, 4, 5, 6; DLB 14, 207;
HGG; MTCW 1

**Blade, Alexander**
See Hamilton, Edmond; Silverberg, Robert

**Blaga, Lucian** 1895-1961 ................. CLC 75
See also CA 157; DLB 220; EWL 3

**Blair, Donovan**
See Neilson, John Shaw

**Blair, Eric**
    See Orwell, George
**Blair, Eric Arthur**
    See Orwell, George
**Blair, Hugh** 1718-1800 .......... **NCLC 75, 368**
    See also DLB 356
**Blair, Robert** 1699-1746 ...................... **PC 204**
**Blais, Marie-Claire** 1939- ........ **CLC 2, 4, 6, 13, 22, 406**
    See also CA 21-24R; CAAS 4; CANR 38, 75, 93; CWW 2; DAC; DAM MST; DLB 53; EWL 3; FW; MTCW 1, 2; MTFW 2005; TWA
**Blaise, Clark** 1940- ... **CLC 29, 261; SSC 225**
    See also AITN 2; CA 53-56, 231; CAAE 231; CAAS 3; CANR 5, 66, 106; CN 4, 5, 6, 7; DLB 53; RGSF 2
**Blake, Fairley**
    See De Voto, Bernard (Augustine)
**Blake, Nicholas**
    See Day Lewis, C.
**Blake, Sterling**
    See Benford, Gregory
**Blake, William** 1757-1827 ............ **NCLC 13, 37, 57, 127, 173, 190, 201, 348; PC 12, 63, 157, 171; WLC 1**
    See also AAYA 47; BRW 3; BRWR 1; CDBLB 1789-1832; CLR 52; DA; DA3; DAB; DAC; DAM MST, POET; DLB 93, 154, 163; EXPP; LATS 1:1; LMFS 1; MAICYA 1, 2; PAB; PFS 2, 12, 24, 34, 40; SATA 30; TEA; WCH; WLIT 3; WP
**Blanchot, Maurice** 1907-2003 ... **CLC 135, 381**
    See also CA 117; 144; 213; CANR 138; DLB 72, 296; EWL 3
**Blanco White, Joseph** 1775-1841 .. **NCLC 305**
**Blasco Ibanez, Vicente** 1867-1928 .............................. **TCLC 12**
    See also BPFB 1; CA 110; 131; CANR 81; DA3; DAM NOV; DLB 322; EW 8; EWL 3; HW 1, 2; MTCW 1
**Blatty, William Peter** 1928- ............. **CLC 2**
    See also CA 5-8R; CANR 9, 124, 226; DAM POP; HGG
**Bleeck, Oliver**
    See Thomas, Ross (Elmore)
**Bleecker, Ann Eliza** 1752-1783 ........ **LC 161**
    See also DLB 200
**Blessing, Lee** 1949- ........................... **CLC 54**
    See also CA 236; CAD; CD 5, 6; DFS 23, 26
**Blessing, Lee Knowlton**
    See Blessing, Lee
**Blessington, Marguerite, Countess of** 1789-1849 ........................ **NCLC 297**
    See also DLB 166
**Blight, Rose**
    See Greer, Germaine
**Blind, Mathilde** 1841-1896 ......... **NCLC 202**
    See also DLB 199
**Blish, James** 1921-1975 ............. **CLC 14; TCLC 358**
    See also BPFB 1; CA 1-4R; 57-60; CANR 3; CN 2; DLB 8; MTCW 1; SATA 66; SCFW 1, 2; SFW 4
**Blish, James Benjamin**
    See Blish, James
**Bliss, Frederick**
    See Card, Orson Scott
**Bliss, Gillian**
    See Paton Walsh, Jill
**Bliss, James L.**
    See Henry, O.
**Bliss, Reginald**
    See Wells, H. G.
**Blixen, Karen** 1885-1962 ......... **CLC 10, 29, 95; SSC 7, 75, 191; TCLC 255**
    See also CA 25-28; CANR 22, 50; CAP 2; DA3; DLB 214; EW 10; EWL 3; EXPS;

FW; GL 2; HGG; LAIT 3; LMFS 1; MTCW 1; NCFS 2; NFS 9; RGSF 2; RGWL 2, 3; SATA 44; SSFS 3, 6, 13; WLIT 2
**Blixen, Karen Christentze Dinesen**
    See Blixen, Karen
**Boll, Heinrich**
    See Boell, Heinrich
**Bloch, Robert (Albert)** 1917-1994 ... **CLC 33**
    See also AAYA 29; CA 5-8R, 179; 146; CAAE 179; CAAS 20; CANR 5, 78; DA3; DLB 44; HGG; INT CANR-5; MTCW 2; SATA 12; SATA-Obit 82; SFW 4; SUFW 1, 2
**Blok, Alexander (Alexandrovich)** 1880-1921 .......... **PC 21; TCLC 5, 335**
    See also CA 104; 183; DLB 295; EW 9; EWL 3; LMFS 2; RGWL 2, 3
**Blom, Jan**
    See Breytenbach, Breyten
**Bloom, Harold** 1930- ....... **CLC 24, 103, 221**
    See also CA 13-16R; CANR 39, 75, 92, 133, 181, 238; DLB 67; EWL 3; MTCW 2; MTFW 2005; RGAL 4
**Bloomfield, Aurelius**
    See Bourne, Randolph S(illiman)
**Bloomfield, Robert** 1766-1823 ... **NCLC 145, 339; PC 160, 204**
    See also DLB 93
**Blount, Roy, Jr.** 1941- ...................... **CLC 38**
    See also CA 53-56; CANR 10, 28, 61, 125, 176; CSW; INT CANR-28; MTCW 1, 2; MTFW 2005
**Blount, Roy Alton**
    See Blount, Roy, Jr.
**Blowsnake, Sam** 1875-(?) ................... **NNAL**
**Bloy, Leon** 1846-1917 ...................... **TCLC 22**
    See also CA 121; 183; DLB 123; GFL 1789 to the Present
**Blue Cloud, Peter (Aroniawenrate)** 1933- ............................................. **NNAL**
    See also CA 117; CANR 40; DAM MULT; DLB 342
**Bluggage, Oranthy**
    See Alcott, Louisa May
**Blume, Judy** 1938- ............ **CLC 12, 30, 325**
    See also AAYA 3, 26; BYA 1, 8, 12; CA 29-32R; CANR 13, 37, 66, 124, 186; CLR 2, 15, 69, 176; CPW; DA3; DAM NOV, POP; DLB 52; JRDA; MAICYA 1, 2; MAICYAS 1; MTCW 1, 2; MTFW 2005; NFS 24; SATA 2, 31, 79, 142, 195; WYA; YAW
**Blume, Judy Sussman**
    See Blume, Judy
**Blunden, Edmund (Charles)** 1896-1974 .............. **CLC 2, 56; PC 66**
    See also BRW 6; BRWS 11; CA 17-18; 45-48; CANR 54; CAP 2; CP 1, 2; DLB 20, 100, 155; MTCW 1; PAB
**Blunt, Wilfrid Scawen** 1840-1922 **TCLC 365**
    See also CA 211; DLB 19, 174; MBL 2
**Bly, Robert** 1926- .............. **CLC 1, 2, 5, 10, 15, 38, 128, 325; PC 39**
    See also AMWS 4; CA 5-8R; CANR 41, 73, 125, 235; CP 1, 2, 3, 4, 5, 6, 7; DA3; DAM POET; DLB 5, 342; EWL 3; MAL 5; MTCW 1, 2; MTFW 2005; PFS 6, 17; RGAL 4
**Bly, Robert Elwood**
    See Bly, Robert
**Boas, Franz** 1858-1942 .................. **TCLC 56**
    See also CA 115; 181
**Bobette**
    See Simenon, Georges
**Bobrowski, Johannes** 1917-1965 ... **TCLC 319**
    See also CA 77-80; CANR 33; DLB 75; EWL 3; RGWL 2, 3
**Boccaccio, Giovanni** 1313-1375 ... **CMLC 13, 57, 140; PC 162; SSC 10, 87, 167**
    See also EW 2; RGSF 2; RGWL 2, 3; SSFS 28; TWA; WLIT 7

**Bochco, Steven** 1943- ...................... **CLC 35**
    See also AAYA 11, 71; CA 124; 138
**Bock, Charles** 1970- ...................... **CLC 299**
    See also CA 274
**Bode, Sigmund**
    See O'Doherty, Brian
**Bodel, Jean** 1167(?)-1210 ..... **CMLC 28, 162**
**Bodenheim, Maxwell** 1892-1954 ... **TCLC 44**
    See also CA 110; 187; DLB 9, 45; MAL 5; RGAL 4
**Bodenheimer, Maxwell**
    See Bodenheim, Maxwell
**Bodin, Jean** 1529/30?-1596 .............. **LC 242**
    See also GFL
**Bodker, Cecil** 1927- ......................... **CLC 21**
    See also CA 73-76; CANR 13, 44, 111; CLR 23; MAICYA 1, 2; SATA 14, 133
**Boell, Heinrich** 1917-1985 ....... **CLC 2, 3, 6, 9, 11, 15, 27, 32, 72; SSC 23; TCLC 185; WLC 1**
    See also BPFB 1; CA 21-24R; 116; CANR 24; CDWLB 2; DA; DA3; DAB; DAC; DAM MST, NOV; DLB 69, 329; DLBY 1985; EW 13; EWL 3; MTCW 1, 2; MTFW 2005; RGHL; RGSF 2; RGWL 2, 3; SSFS 20; TWA
**Boell, Heinrich Theodor**
    See Boell, Heinrich
**Börne, Alfred**
    See Döblin, Alfred
**Boethius** c. 480-c. 524 ... **CMLC 15, 136, 181**
    See also DLB 115; RGWL 2, 3; WLIT 8
**Boff, Leonardo (Genezio Darci)** 1938- ................... **CLC 70; HLC 1**
    See also CA 150; DAM MULT; HW 2
**Bogan, Louise** 1897-1970 ............ **CLC 4, 39, 46, 93; PC 12**
    See also AMWS 3; CA 73-76; 25-28R; CANR 33, 82; CP 1; DAM POET; DLB 45, 169; EWL 3; MAL 5; MBL; MTCW 1, 2; PFS 21, 39; RGAL 4
**Boganey, Frank**
    See Davis, Frank Marshall
**Bogarde, Dirk** 1921-1999 ................ **CLC 14**
    See also CA 77-80; 179; DLB 14
**Bogat, Shatan**
    See Kacew, Romain
**Bogomolny, Robert L.** 1938- .......... **SSC 41; TCLC 11**
    See also CA 121, 164; DLB 182; EWL 3; MJW; RGSF 2; RGWL 2, 3; TWA
**Bogomolny, Robert Lee**
    See Bogomolny, Robert L.
**Bogosian, Eric** 1953- ............... **CLC 45, 141**
    See also CA 138; CAD; CANR 102, 148, 217; CD 5, 6; DLB 341
**Bograd, Larry** 1953- ........................ **CLC 35**
    See also CA 93-96; CANR 57; SAAS 21; SATA 33, 89; WYA
**Bohme, Jakob** 1575-1624 ............... **LC 178**
    See also DLB 164
**Boiardo, Matteo Maria** 1441-1494 ................... **LC 6, 168; PC 180**
**Boileau-Despreaux, Nicolas** 1636-1711 ............................... **LC 3, 164**
    See also DLB 268; EW 3; GFL Beginnings to 1789; RGWL 2, 3
**Boissard, Maurice**
    See Leautaud, Paul
**Bojer, Johan** 1872-1959 ................. **TCLC 64**
    See also CA 189; EWL 3
**Bok, Edward W(illiam)** 1863-1930 .......................... **TCLC 101**
    See also CA 217; DLB 91; DLBD 16
**Boker, George Henry** 1823-1890 ...................... **NCLC 125, 366**
    See also RGAL 4
**Boland, Eavan** 1944- ........ **CLC 40, 67, 113; PC 58**

See also BRWS 5; CA 143, 207; CAAE 207; CANR 61, 180; CP 1, 6, 7; CWP; DAM POET; DLB 40; FW; MTCW 2; MTFW 2005; PFS 12, 22, 31, 39

**Boland, Eavan Aisling**
See Boland, Eavan

**Bolaño, Roberto**
1953-2003 .............. **CLC 294; SSC 248**
See also CA 229; CANR 175

**Bolger, Dermot** 1959- .................... **CLC 442**
See also CA 145; CANR 91; CN 7

**Bolingbroke, Viscount**
See St. John, Henry

**Bolt, Lee**
See Faust, Frederick

**Bolt, Robert (Oxton)** 1924-1995 .... **CLC 14; TCLC 175**
See also CA 17-20R; 147; CANR 35, 67; CBD; DAM DRAM; DFS 2; DLB 13, 233; EWL 3; LAIT 1; MTCW 1

**Bolivar, Simon** 1783-1830 ............ **NCLC 266**

**Bombal, Maria Luisa** 1910-1980 ... **HLCS 1; SSC 37; TCLC 296**
See also CA 127; CANR 72; EWL 3; HW 1; LAW; RGSF 2; SSFS 36

**Bombet, Louis-Alexandre-Cesar**
See Stendhal

**Bomkauf**
See Kaufman, Bob (Garnell)

**Bonaventura** ......................... **NCLC 35, 252**
See also DLB 90

**Bonaventure** 1217(?)-1274 ............ **CMLC 79**
See also DLB 115; LMFS 1

**Bond, Edward** 1934- ....... **CLC 4, 6, 13, 23; DC 45**
See also AAYA 50; BRWS 1; CA 25-28R; CANR 38, 67, 106; CBD; CD 5, 6; DAM DRAM; DFS 3, 8; DLB 13, 310; EWL 3; MTCW 1

**Bonham, Frank** 1914-1989 ............. **CLC 12**
See also AAYA 1, 70; BYA 1, 3; CA 9-12R; CANR 4, 36; JRDA; MAICYA 1, 2; SAAS 3; SATA 1, 49; SATA-Obit 62; TCWW 1, 2; YAW

**Boniface, Saint** c. 675-754 .......... **CMLC 190**

**Bonnefoy, Yves** 1923- ........ **CLC 9, 15, 58; PC 58**
See also CA 85-88; CANR 33, 75, 97, 136; CWW 2; DAM MST, POET; DLB 258; EWL 3; GFL 1789 to the Present; MTCW 1, 2; MTFW 2005

**Bonner, Marita**
See Occomy, Marita (Odette) Bonner

**Bonnin, Gertrude** 1876-1938 ............. **NNAL**
See also CA 150; DAM MULT; DLB 175

**Bontempelli, Massimo**
1878-1960 .............................. **TCLC 352**
See also DLB 264; EWL 3

**Bontemps, Arna** 1902-1973 ......... **BLC 1:1; CLC 1, 18; HR 1:2; TCLC 292**
See also BW 1; CA 1-4R; 41-44R; CANR 4, 35; CLR 6; CP 1; CWRI 5; DA3; DAM MULT, NOV, POET; DLB 48, 51; JRDA; MAICYA 1, 2; MAL 5; MTCW 1, 2; PFS 32; SATA 2, 44; SATA-Obit 24; WCH; WP

**Bontemps, Arnaud Wendell**
See Bontemps, Arna

**Boot, William**
See Stoppard, Tom

**Booth, Irwin**
See Hoch, Edward D.

**Booth, Martin** 1944-2004 ................ **CLC 13**
See also CA 93-96, 188; 223; CAAE 188; CAAS 2; CANR 92; CP 1, 2, 3, 4

**Booth, Philip** 1925-2007 ................. **CLC 23**
See also CA 5-8R; 262; CANR 5, 88; CP 1, 2, 3, 4, 5, 6, 7; DLBY 1982

**Booth, Philip Edmund**
See Booth, Philip

**Booth, Wayne C.** 1921-2005 ........... **CLC 24**
See also CA 1-4R; 244; CAAS 5; CANR 3, 43, 117; DLB 67

**Booth, Wayne Clayson**
See Booth, Wayne C.

**Borchert, Wolfgang** 1921-1947 ......... **DC 42; TCLC 5**
See also CA 104; 188; DLB 69, 124; EWL 3

**Borel, Petrus** 1809-1859 ................. **NCLC 41**
See also DLB 119; GFL 1789 to the Present

**Borges, Jorge Luis** 1899-1986 ..... **CLC 1, 2, 3, 4, 6, 8, 9, 10, 13, 19, 44, 48, 83; HLC 1; PC 22, 32; SSC 4, 41, 100, 159, 170, 183, 187, 191, 215; TCLC 109, 320; WLC 1**
See also AAYA 26; BPFB 1; CA 21-24R; CANR 19, 33, 75, 105, 133; CDWLB 3; DA; DA3; DAB; DAC; DAM MST, MULT; DLB 113, 283; DLBY 1986; DNFS 1, 2; EWL 3; HW 1, 2; LAW; LMFS 2; MSW; MTCW 1, 2; MTFW 2005; PFS 27; RGHL; RGSF 2; RGWL 2, 3; SFW 4; SSFS 17; TWA; WLIT 1

**Borowski, Tadeusz** 1922-1951 ......... **SSC 48; TCLC 9**
See also CA 106; 154; CDWLB 4; DLB 215; EWL 3; RGHL; RGSF 2; RGWL 3; SSFS 13

**Borrow, George (Henry)**
1803-1881 ......................... **NCLC 9, 327**
See also BRWS 12; DLB 21, 55, 166

**Bosch (Gavino), Juan** 1909-2001 .... **HLCS 1**
See also CA 151; 204; DAM MST, MULT; DLB 145; HW 1, 2

**Bosman, Herman Charles**
1905-1951 ............................. **TCLC 49**
See also CA 160; DLB 225; RGSF 2

**Bosschere, Jean de** 1878(?)-1953 ... **TCLC 19**
See also CA 115; 186

**Boswell, James** 1740-1795 .... **LC 4, 50, 182; WLC 1**
See also BRW 3; CDBLB 1660-1789; DA; DAB; DAC; DAM MST; DLB 104, 142; TEA; WLIT 3

**Boto, Eza**
See Beti, Mongo

**Bottomley, Gordon** 1874-1948 .... **TCLC 107**
See also CA 120; 192; DLB 10

**Bottoms, David** 1949- ........ **CLC 53; PC 158**
See also CA 105; CANR 22; CSW; DLB 120; DLBY 1983

**Boucicault, Dion** 1820-1890 ... **NCLC 41, 306**
See also DLB 344

**Boucolon, Maryse**
See Conde, Maryse

**Boullosa, Carmen** 1954- ............... **CLC 350**
See also CA 190; CANR 159

**Bouraoui, Nina** 1967- ................... **CLC 394**

**Bourcicault, Dion**
See Boucicault, Dion

**Bourdieu, Pierre** 1930-2002 ... **CLC 198, 296**
See also CA 130; 204

**Bourget, Paul (Charles Joseph)**
1852-1935 .......................... **TCLC 12**
See also CA 107; 196; DLB 123; GFL 1789 to the Present

**Bourjaily, Vance** 1922-2010 ......... **CLC 8, 62**
See also CA 1-4R; CAAS 1; CANR 2, 72; CN 1, 2, 3, 4, 5, 6, 7; DLB 2, 143; MAL 5

**Bourjaily, Vance Nye**
See Bourjaily, Vance

**Bourne, Randolph S(illiman)**
1886-1918 ............................. **TCLC 16**
See also AMW; CA 117; 155; DLB 63; MAL 5

**Boursiquot, Dionysius**
See Boucicault, Dion

**Bova, Ben** 1932- ............................. **CLC 45**
See also AAYA 16; CA 5-8R; CAAS 18; CANR 11, 56, 94, 111, 157, 219; CLR 3, 96; DLBY 1981; INT CANR-11; MAICYA 1, 2; MTCW 1; SATA 6, 68, 133; SFW 4

**Bova, Benjamin William**
See Bova, Ben

**Bowen, Elizabeth** 1899-1973 ........ **CLC 1, 3, 6, 11, 15, 22, 118; SSC 3, 28, 66, 193; TCLC 148**
See also BRWS 2; CA 17-18; 41-44R; CANR 35, 105; CAP 2; CDBLB 1945-1960; CN 1; DA3; DAM NOV; DLB 15, 162; EWL 3; EXPS; FW; HGG; MTCW 1, 2; MTFW 2005; NFS 13; RGSF 2; SSFS 5, 22; SUFW 1; TEA; WLIT 4

**Bowen, Elizabeth Dorothea Cole**
See Bowen, Elizabeth

**Bowering, George** 1935- ........... **CLC 15, 47**
See also CA 21-24R; CAAS 16; CANR 10; CN 7; CP 1, 2, 3, 4, 5, 6, 7; DLB 53

**Bowering, Marilyn R(uthe)** 1949- .. **CLC 32**
See also CA 101; CANR 49; CP 4, 5, 6, 7; CWP; DLB 334

**Bowers, Edgar** 1924-2000 ................ **CLC 9**
See also CA 5-8R; 188; CANR 24; CP 1, 2, 3, 4, 5, 6, 7; CSW; DLB 5

**Bowers, Mrs. J. Milton**
See Bierce, Ambrose

**Bowie, David** 1947- .......................... **CLC 17**
See also CA 103; CANR 104

**Bowles, Jane (Sydney)**
1917-1973 ........ **CLC 3, 68; TCLC 275**
See also CA 19-20; 41-44R; CAP 2; CN 1; EWL 3; MAL 5

**Bowles, Jane Auer**
See Bowles, Jane (Sydney)

**Bowles, Paul** 1910-1999 ......... **CLC 1, 2, 19, 53; SSC 3, 98, 214; TCLC 209**
See also AMWS 4; CA 1-4R; 186; CAAS 1; CANR 1, 19, 50, 75; CN 1, 2, 3, 4, 5, 6; DA3; DLB 5, 6, 218; EWL 3; MAL 5; MTCW 1, 2; MTFW 2005; RGAL 4; SSFS 17

**Bowles, William Lisle** 1762-1850 .. **NCLC 103**
See also DLB 93

**Box, Edgar**
See Vidal, Gore

**Boyd, James** 1888-1944 ............... **TCLC 115**
See also CA 186; DLB 9; DLBD 16; RGAL 4; RHW

**Boyd, Nancy**
See Millay, Edna St. Vincent

**Boyd, Thomas (Alexander)**
1898-1935 ............................. **TCLC 111**
See also CA 111; 183; DLB 9; DLBD 16, 316

**Boyd, William** 1952- .......... **CLC 28, 53, 70**
See also BRWS 16; CA 114; 120; CANR 51, 71, 131, 174; CN 4, 5, 6, 7; DLB 231

**Boyden, Joseph** 1966- .................... **CLC 393**
See also CA 242; CANR 208, 269

**Boyesen, Hjalmar Hjorth**
1848-1895 ........................... **NCLC 135**
See also DLB 12, 71; DLBD 13; RGAL 4

**Boyle, Kay** 1902-1992 ...... **CLC 1, 5, 19, 58, 121; SSC 5, 102**
See also CA 13-16R; 140; CAAS 1; CANR 29, 61, 110; CN 1, 2, 3, 4, 5; CP 1, 2, 3, 4, 5; DLB 4, 9, 48, 86; DLBY 1993; EWL 3; MAL 5; MTCW 1, 2; MTFW 2005; RGAL 4; RGSF 2; SSFS 10, 13, 14

**Boyle, Mark**
See Kienzle, William X.

**Boyle, Patrick** 1905-1982 ................ **CLC 19**
See also CA 127

**Boyle, Roger** 1621-1679 .................... **LC 198**
See also DLB 80; RGEL 2

**Boyle, T.C.** 1948- ....... **CLC 36, 55, 90, 284; SSC 16, 127**
See also AAYA 47; AMWS 8, 20; BEST 90:4; BPFB 1; CA 120; CANR 44, 76, 89, 132, 224; CN 6, 7; CPW; DA3; DAM POP; DLB 218, 278; DLBY 1986; EWL 3; MAL 5; MTCW 2; MTFW 2005; NFS 41; SSFS 13, 19, 34

**Boyle, T.Coraghessan**
See Boyle, T.C.

**Boyle, Thomas Coraghessan**
See Boyle, T.C.

**Boz**
See Dickens, Charles

**Bozon, Nicole** fl. 14th cent. ......... **CMLC 200**

**bpNichol**
See Nichol, B(arrie) P(hillip)

**Brackenridge, Hugh Henry**
1748-1816 ......................... **NCLC 7, 227**
See also DLB 11, 37; RGAL 4

**Bradbury, Edward P.**
See Moorcock, Michael

**Bradbury, Malcolm** 1932-2000 ... **CLC 32, 61**
See also BRWS 17; CA 1-4R; CANR 1, 33,
91, 98, 137; CN 1, 2, 3, 4, 5, 6, 7; CP 1;
DA3; DAM NOV; DLB 14, 207; EWL 3;
MTCW 1, 2; MTFW 2005

**Bradbury, Ray** 1920-2012 ... **CLC 1, 3, 10, 15,
42, 98, 235, 333; SSC 29, 53, 157; WLC 1**
See also AAYA 15, 84; AITN 1, 2; AMWS 4;
BPFB 1; BYA 4, 5, 11; CA 1-4R; CANR 2,
30, 75, 125, 186; CDALB 1968-1988; CLR
174; CN 1, 2, 3, 4, 5, 6, 7; CPW; DA; DA3;
DAB; DAC; DAM MST, NOV, POP; DLB
2, 8; EXPN; EXPS; HGG; LAIT 3, 5; LATS
1:2; LMFS 2; MAL 5; MTCW 1, 2; MTFW
2005; NFS 1, 22, 29, 42; RGAL 4; RGSF 2;
SATA 11, 64, 123; SCFW 1, 2; SFW 4;
SSFS 1, 20, 28, 37; SUFW 1, 2; TUS; YAW

**Bradbury, Ray Douglas**
See Bradbury, Ray

**Braddon, Mary Elizabeth**
1835-1915 ..................... **TCLC 111, 366**
See also BRWS 8; CA 108, 179; CMW 4;
DLB 18, 70, 156; HGG

**Bradfield, Scott** 1955- ..................... **SSC 65**
See also CA 147; CANR 90; HGG; SUFW 2

**Bradfield, Scott Michael**
See Bradfield, Scott

**Bradford, Gamaliel** 1863-1932 ..... **TCLC 36**
See also CA 160; DLB 17

**Bradford, William**
c. 1590-1657 ........................ **LC 64, 271**
See also DLB 24, 30; RGAL 4

**Bradley, David, Jr.** 1950- ............. **BLC 1:1;
CLC 23, 118**
See also BW 1, 3; CA 104; CANR 26, 81;
CN 4, 5, 6, 7; DAM MULT; DLB 33

**Bradley, David Henry, Jr.**
See Bradley, David, Jr.

**Bradley, John Ed** 1958- ................... **CLC 55**
See also CA 139; CANR 99; CN 6, 7; CSW

**Bradley, John Edmund, Jr.**
See Bradley, John Ed

**Bradley, Marion Zimmer**
1930-1999 ............................... **CLC 30**
See also AAYA 40; BPFB 1; CA 57-60; 185;
CAAS 10; CANR 7, 31, 51, 75, 107; CLR
158; CPW; DA3; DAM POP; DLB 8;
FANT; FW; GLL 1; MTCW 1, 2; MTFW
2005; NFS 40; SATA 90, 139; SATA-Obit
116; SFW 4; SUFW 2; YAW

**Bradshaw, John** 1933- ..................... **CLC 70**
See also CA 138; CANR 61, 216

**Bradshaw, John Elliot**
See Bradshaw, John

**Bradstreet, Anne** 1612(?)-1672 ......... **LC 4, 30,
130; PC 10, 139, 155**
See also AMWS 1; CDALB 1640-1865; DA;
DA3; DAC; DAM MST, POET; DLB 24;
EXPP; FW; PFS 6, 33, 42; RGAL 4; TUS;
WP

**Bradwardine, Thomas**
c. 1295-1349 ........................ **CMLC 196**
See also DLB 115

**Brady, Joan** 1939- ........................... **CLC 86**
See also CA 141

**Bragg, Melvyn** 1939- ....................... **CLC 10**
See also BEST 89:3; CA 57-60; CANR 10,
48, 89, 158; CN 1, 2, 3, 4, 5, 6, 7; DLB 14,
271; RHW

**Bragg, Rick** 1959- .......................... **CLC 296**
See also CA 165; CANR 112, 137, 194;
MTFW 2005

**Bragg, Ricky Edward**
See Bragg, Rick

**Brahe, Tycho** 1546-1601 .................... **LC 45**
See also DLB 300

**Braine, John (Gerard)**
1922-1986 ......................... **CLC 1, 3, 41**
See also CA 1-4R; 120; CANR 1, 33;
CDBLB 1945-1960; CN 1, 2, 3, 4; DLB
15; DLBY 1986; EWL 3; MTCW 1

**Braithwaite, William Stanley (Beaumont)**
1878-1962 .... **BLC 1:1; HR 1:2; PC 52**
See also BW 1; CA 125; DAM MULT; DLB
50, 54; MAL 5

**Bramah, Ernest** 1868-1942 ........... **TCLC 72**
See also CA 156; CMW 4; DLB 70; FANT

**Bramble, Tabitha**
See Robinson, Mary

**Brammer, Billy Lee**
See Brammer, William

**Brammer, William** 1929-1978 ......... **CLC 31**
See also CA 235; 77-80

**Brancati, Vitaliano** 1907-1954 ...... **TCLC 12**
See also CA 109; DLB 264; EWL 3

**Brancato, Robin F.** 1936- ................ **CLC 35**
See also AAYA 9, 68; BYA 6; CA 69-72;
CANR 11, 45; CLR 32; JRDA; MAICYA
2; MAICYAS 1; SAAS 9; SATA 97; WYA;
YAW

**Brancato, Robin Fidler**
See Brancato, Robin F.

**Brand, Dionne** 1953- ....... **CLC 192; PC 205**
See also BW 2; CA 143; CANR 143, 216;
CWP; DLB 334

**Brand, Max**
See Faust, Frederick

**Brand, Millen** 1906-1980 .................. **CLC 7**
See also CA 21-24R; 97-100; CANR 72

**Branden, Barbara** 1929- ................. **CLC 44**
See also CA 148

**Brandes, Georg (Morris Cohen)**
1842-1927 ..................... **TCLC 10, 264**
See also CA 105; 189; DLB 300

**Brandys, Kazimierz** 1916-2000 ....... **CLC 62**
See also CA 239; EWL 3

**Branley, Franklyn M(ansfield)**
1915-2002 .............................. **CLC 21**
See also CA 33-36R; 207; CANR 14, 39;
CLR 13; MAICYA 1, 2; SAAS 16; SATA
4, 68, 136

**Brant, Beth (E.)** 1941- ....................... **NNAL**
See also CA 144; FW

**Brant, Sebastian** 1457-1521 ..... **LC 112, 206**
See also DLB 179; RGWL 2, 3

**Brathwaite, Edward Kamau**
1930- ............ **BLC 2:1; BLCS; CLC 11,
305; PC 56**
See also BRWS 12; BW 2, 3; CA 25-28R;
CANR 11, 26, 47, 107; CDWLB 3; CP 1, 2,
3, 4, 5, 6, 7; DAM POET; DLB 125; EWL 3

**Brathwaite, Kamau**
See Brathwaite, Edward Kamau

**Braun, Volker** 1939- ........................ **CLC 356**
See also CA 194; CWW 2; DLB 75, 124;
EWL 3

**Brautigan, Richard** 1935-1984 ..... **CLC 1, 3,
5, 9, 12, 34, 42; PC 94; SSC 271; TCLC
133**
See also BPFB 1; CA 53-56; 113; CANR 34;
CN 1, 2, 3; CP 1, 2, 3, 4; DA3; DAM NOV;
DLB 2, 5, 206; DLBY 1980, 1984; FANT;
MAL 5; MTCW 1; RGAL 4; SATA 56

**Brautigan, Richard Gary**
See Brautigan, Richard

**Brave Bird, Mary**
See Crow Dog, Mary

**Braverman, Kate** 1950- .................. **CLC 67**
See also CA 89-92; CANR 141; DLB 335

**Brecht, Bertolt** 1898-1956 ... **DC 3; TCLC 1,
6, 13, 35, 169; WLC 1**
See also CA 104; 133; CANR 62; CDWLB
2; DA; DA3; DAB; DAC; DAM DRAM,
MST; DFS 4, 5, 9; DLB 56, 124; EW 11;
EWL 3; IDTP; MTCW 1, 2; MTFW 2005;
RGHL; RGWL 2, 3; TWA

**Brecht, Eugen Berthold Friedrich**
See Brecht, Bertolt

**Brecht, Eugen Bertolt Friedrich**
See Brecht, Bertolt

**Bremer, Fredrika**
1801-1865 ..................... **NCLC 11, 350**
See also DLB 254

**Brennan, Christopher John**
1870-1932 ............................... **TCLC 17**
See also CA 117; 188; DLB 230; EWL 3

**Brennan, Maeve** 1917-1993 ............. **CLC 5;
TCLC 124**
See also CA 81-84; CANR 72, 100

**Brenner, Jozef** 1887-1919 ............. **TCLC 13**
See also CA 111; 240

**Brent, Linda**
See Jacobs, Harriet A.

**Brentano, Clemens (Maria)**
1778-1842 ....... **NCLC 1, 191; SSC 115**
See also DLB 90; RGWL 2, 3

**Brent of Bin Bin**
See Franklin, (Stella Maria Sarah) Miles
(Lampe)

**Brenton, Howard** 1942- ................... **CLC 31**
See also CA 69-72; CANR 33, 67; CBD; CD
5, 6; DLB 13; MTCW 1

**Breslin, James**
See Breslin, Jimmy

**Breslin, Jimmy** 1930- .................... **CLC 4, 43**
See also CA 73-76; CANR 31, 75, 139, 187,
237; DAM NOV; DLB 185; MTCW 2;
MTFW 2005

**Bresson, Robert** 1901(?)-1999 ........ **CLC 16;
TCLC 287**
See also CA 110; 187; CANR 49

**Breton, Andre** 1896-1966 ...... **CLC 2, 9, 15,
54; PC 15; TCLC 247**
See also CA 19-20; 25-28R; CANR 40, 60;
CAP 2; DLB 65, 258; EW 11; EWL 3;
GFL 1789 to the Present; LMFS 2; MTCW
1, 2; MTFW 2005; RGWL 2, 3; TWA; WP

**Breton, Nicholas** c. 1554-c. 1626 ..... **LC 133**
See also DLB 136

**Breytenbach, Breyten**
1939(?)- ....................... **CLC 23, 37, 126**
See also CA 113; 129; CANR 61, 122, 202;
CWW 2; DAM POET; DLB 225; EWL 3

**Bridgers, Sue Ellen** 1942- .............. **CLC 26**
See also AAYA 8, 49; BYA 7, 8; CA 65-68;
CANR 11, 36; CLR 18, 199; DLB 52;
JRDA; MAICYA 1, 2; SAAS 1; SATA 22,
90; SATA-Essay 109; WYA; YAW

**Bridges, Robert (Seymour)**
1844-1930 ..................... **PC 28; TCLC 1**
See also BRW 6; CA 104; 152; CDBLB
1890-1914; DAM POET; DLB 19, 98

**Bridget**
See Robinson, Mary

**Bridie, James**
See Mavor, Osborne Henry

**Brin, David** 1950- ........................... **CLC 34**
See also AAYA 21; CA 102; CANR 24, 70,
125, 127; INT CANR-24; SATA 65;
SCFW 2; SFW 4

**Brink, Andre** 1935- ........... **CLC 18, 36, 106**
See also AFW; BRWS 6; CA 104; CANR
39, 62, 109, 133, 182; CN 4, 5, 6, 7; DLB
225; EWL 3; INT CA-103; LATS 1:2;
MTCW 1, 2; MTFW 2005; WLIT 2

**Brink, Andre Philippus**
See Brink, Andre

**Brinsmead, H. F(ay)**
See Brinsmead, H(esba) F(ay)

**Brinsmead, H. F.**
See Brinsmead, H(esba) F(ay)

**Brinsmead, H(esba) F(ay)** 1922- .... **CLC 21**
See also CA 21-24R; CANR 10; CLR 47;
CWRI 5; MAICYA 1, 2; SAAS 5; SATA
18, 78

**Brittain, Vera (Mary)**
1893(?)-1970 ........ **CLC 23; TCLC 228**
See also BRWS 10; CA 13-16; 25-28R; CANR
58; CAP 1; DLB 191; FW; MTCW 1, 2

**Broch, Hermann**
1886-1951 ...... **TCLC 20, 204, 304, 307**
See also CA 117; 211; CDWLB 2; DLB 85,
124; EW 10; EWL 3; RGWL 2, 3

**Brock, Rose**
See Hansen, Joseph

**Brod, Max** 1884-1968 ......... **TCLC 115, 305**
See also CA 5-8R; 25-28R; CANR 7; DLB
81; EWL 3

**Brodber, Erna** 1940- ...................... **CLC 379**
See also BW 2; CA 143; CN 6, 7; DLB 157

**Brodkey, Harold (Roy)**
1930-1996 ............ **CLC 56; TCLC 123**
See also CA 111; 151; CANR 71; CN 4, 5,
6; DLB 130

**Brodskii, Iosif**
See Brodsky, Joseph

**Brodskii, Iosif Alexandrovich**
See Brodsky, Joseph

**Brodsky, Iosif Alexandrovich**
See Brodsky, Joseph

**Brodsky, Joseph** 1940-1996 ......... **CLC 4, 6,**
**13, 36, 100; PC 9; TCLC 219**
See also AAYA 71; AITN 1; AMWS 8; CA 41-
44R; 151; CANR 37, 106; CWW 2; DA3;
DAM POET; DLB 285, 329; EWL 3; MTCW
1, 2; MTFW 2005; PFS 35; RGWL 2, 3

**Brodsky, Michael** 1948- ................... **CLC 19**
See also CA 102; CANR 18, 41, 58, 147;
DLB 244

**Brodsky, Michael Mark**
See Brodsky, Michael

**Brodzki, Bella** ................................. **CLC 65**

**Brome, Richard** 1590(?)-1652 ... **DC 50; LC 61**
See also BRWS 10; DLB 58

**Bromell, Henry** 1947- ........................ **CLC 5**
See also CA 53-56; CANR 9, 115, 116

**Bromfield, Louis (Brucker)**
1896-1956 .............................. **TCLC 11**
See also CA 107; 155; DLB 4, 9, 86; RGAL
4; RHW

**Broner, E. M.** 1930-2011 ................. **CLC 19**
See also CA 17-20R; CANR 8, 25, 72, 216;
CN 4, 5, 6; DLB 28

**Broner, Esther Masserman**
See Broner, E. M.

**Bronk, William** 1918-1999 ... **CLC 10; PC 178**
See also AMWS 21; CA 89-92; 177; CANR
23; CP 3, 4, 5, 6, 7; DLB 165

**Bronstein, Lev Davidovich**
See Trotsky, Leon

**Bronte, Anne** 1820-1849 ......... **NCLC 4, 71,**
**102, 235**
See also BRW 5; BRWR 1; DA3; DLB 21,
199, 340; NFS 26; TEA

**Bronte, (Patrick) Branwell**
1817-1848 ................................ **NCLC 109**
See also DLB 340

**Bronte, Charlotte** 1816-1855 ......... **NCLC 3,**
**8, 33, 58, 105, 155, 217, 229, 280; SSC**
**167; WLC 1**
See also AAYA 17; BRW 5; BRWC 2;
BRWR 1; BYA 2; CDBLB 1832-1890; DA;
DA3; DAB; DAC; DAM MST, NOV; DLB
21, 159, 199, 340; EXPN; FL 1:2; GL 2;
LAIT 2; NFS 4, 36; TEA; WLIT 4

**Bronte, Emily** 1818-1848 ............. **NCLC 16,**
**35, 165, 244; PC 8; WLC 1**
See also AAYA 17; BPFB 1; BRW 5; BRWC 1;
BRWR 1; BYA 3; CDBLB 1832-1890; DA;

DA3; DAB; DAC; DAM MST, NOV, POET;
DLB 21, 32, 199, 340; EXPN; FL 1:2; GL 2;
LAIT 1; NFS 2; PFS 33, 43; TEA; WLIT 3

**Bronte, Emily Jane**
See Bronte, Emily

**Brontes**
See Bronte, Anne; Bronte, (Patrick) Branwell;
Bronte, Charlotte; Bronte, Emily

**Brooke, Frances** 1724-1789 ... **LC 6, 48, 275**
See also DLB 39, 99

**Brooke, Henry** 1703(?)-1783 ................ **LC 1**
See also DLB 39

**Brooke, Rupert** 1887-1915 ................ **PC 24;**
**TCLC 2, 7; WLC 1**
See also BRWS 3; CA 104; 132; CANR 61;
CDBLB 1914-1945; DA; DAB; DAC; DAM
MST, POET; DLB 19, 216; EXPP; GLL 2;
MTCW 1, 2; MTFW 2005; PFS 7; TEA

**Brooke, Rupert Chawner**
See Brooke, Rupert

**Brooke-Haven, P.**
See Wodehouse, P. G.

**Brooke-Rose, Christine**
1923-2012 ............ **CLC 40, 184, 338**
See also BRWS 4; CA 13-16R; CANR 58,
118, 183; CN 1, 2, 3, 4, 5, 6, 7; DLB 14,
231; EWL 3; SFW 4

**Brookner, Anita**
1928- ............ **CLC 32, 34, 51, 136, 237**
See also BRWS 4; CA 114; 120; CANR 37,
56, 87, 130, 212; CN 4, 5, 6, 7; CPW;
DA3; DAB; DAM POP; DLB 194, 326;
DLBY 1987; EWL 3; MTCW 1, 2; MTFW
2005; NFS 23; TEA

**Brooks, Cleanth** 1906-1994 .. **CLC 24, 86, 110**
See also AMWS 14; CA 17-20R; 145;
CANR 33, 35; CSW; DLB 63; DLBY
1994; EWL 3; INT CANR-35; MAL 5;
MTCW 1, 2; MTFW 2005

**Brooks, George**
See Baum, L. Frank

**Brooks, Gwendolyn** 1917-2000 ..... **BLC 1:1,**
**2:1; CLC 1, 2, 4, 5, 15, 49, 125, 349; PC**
**7, 138; WLC 1**
See also AAYA 20; AFAW 1, 2; AITN 1;
AMWS 3; BW 2, 3; CA 1-4R; 190; CANR
1, 27, 52, 75, 132; CDALB 1941-1968;
CLR 27; CP 1, 2, 3, 4, 5, 6, 7; CWP; DA;
DA3; DAC; DAM MST, MULT, POET;
DLB 5, 76, 165; EWL 3; EXPP; FL 1:5;
MAL 5; MBL; MTCW 1, 2; MTFW 2005;
PFS 1, 2, 4, 6, 32, 40; RGAL 4; SATA 6;
SATA-Obit 123; SSFS 35; TUS; WP

**Brooks, Gwendolyn Elizabeth**
See Brooks, Gwendolyn

**Brooks, Mel** 1926- .................... **CLC 12, 217**
See also AAYA 13, 48; CA 65-68; CANR
16; DFS 21; DLB 26

**Brooks, Peter** 1938- ........................ **CLC 34**
See also CA 45-48; CANR 1, 107, 182

**Brooks, Peter Preston**
See Brooks, Peter

**Brooks, Van Wyck** 1886-1963 ........ **CLC 29**
See also AMW; CA 1-4R; CANR 6; DLB
45, 63, 103; MAL 5; TUS

**Brophy, Brigid** 1929-1995 ......... **CLC 6, 11,**
**29, 105**
See also CA 5-8R; 149; CAAS 4; CANR 25,
53; CBD; CN 1, 2, 3, 4, 5, 6; CWD; DA3;
DLB 14, 271; EWL 3; MTCW 1, 2

**Brophy, Brigid Antonia**
See Brophy, Brigid

**Brosman, Catharine Savage** 1934- ... **CLC 9**
See also CA 61-64; CANR 21, 46, 149, 222

**Brossard, Nicole**
1943- ................... **CLC 115, 169; PC 80**
See also CA 122; CAAS 16; CANR 140;
CCA 1; CWP; CWW 2; DLB 53; EWL 3;
FW; GLL 2; RGWL 3

**Brother Antoninus**
See Everson, William

**Brothers Grimm**
See Grimm, Jacob Ludwig Karl; Grimm,
Wilhelm Karl

**The Brothers Quay**
See Quay, Stephen; Quay, Timothy

**Broughton, T(homas) Alan** 1936- .... **CLC 19**
See also CA 45-48; CANR 2, 23, 48, 111

**Broumas, Olga** 1949- ................. **CLC 10, 73**
See also CA 85-88; CANR 20, 69, 110; CP
5, 6, 7; CWP; GLL 2

**Broun, Heywood** 1888-1939 ........ **TCLC 104**
See also DLB 29, 171

**Brown, Alan** 1950- .......................... **CLC 99**
See also CA 156

**Brown, Charles Brockden**
1771-1810 ....... **NCLC 22, 74, 122, 246,**
**352**
See also AMWS 1; CDALB 1640-1865;
DLB 37, 59, 73; FW; GL 2; HGG; LMFS
1; RGAL 4; TUS

**Brown, Christy** 1932-1981 ............. **CLC 63**
See also BYA 13; CA 105; 104; CANR 72;
DLB 14

**Brown, Claude** 1937-2002 ............ **BLC 1:1;**
**CLC 30**
See also AAYA 7; BW 1, 3; CA 73-76; 205;
CANR 81; DAM MULT

**Brown, Dan** 1964- .......................... **CLC 209**
See also AAYA 55; CA 217; CANR 223;
LNFS 1; MTFW 2005

**Brown, Dee** 1908-2002 .............. **CLC 18, 47**
See also AAYA 30; CA 13-16R; 212; CAAS
6; CANR 11, 45, 60, 150; CPW; CSW;
DA3; DAM POP; DLBY 1980; LAIT 2;
MTCW 1, 2; MTFW 2005; NCFS 5; SATA
5, 110; SATA-Obit 141; TCWW 1, 2

**Brown, Dee Alexander**
See Brown, Dee

**Brown, George**
See Wertmueller, Lina

**Brown, George Douglas**
1869-1902 ................................ **TCLC 28**
See also CA 162; RGEL 2

**Brown, George Mackay**
1921-1996 ..................... **CLC 5, 48, 100**
See also BRWS 6; CA 21-24R; 151; CAAS
6; CANR 12, 37, 67; CN 1, 2, 3, 4, 5, 6;
CP 1, 2, 3, 4, 5, 6; DLB 14, 27, 139, 271;
MTCW 1; RGSF 2; SATA 35

**Brown, James Willie**
See Komunyakaa, Yusef

**Brown, James Willie, Jr.**
See Komunyakaa, Yusef

**Brown, Larry** 1951-2004 ......... **CLC 73, 289**
See also AMWS 21; CA 130; 134; 233; CANR
117, 145; CSW; DLB 234; INT CA-134

**Brown, Moses**
See Barrett, William (Christopher)

**Brown, Rita Mae** 1944- ............ **CLC 18, 43,**
**79, 259**
See also BPFB 1; CA 45-48; CANR 2, 11,
35, 62, 95, 138, 183, 232; CN 5, 6, 7;
CPW; CSW; DA3; DAM NOV, POP; FW;
INT CANR-11; MAL 5; MTCW 1, 2;
MTFW 2005; NFS 9; RGAL 4; TUS

**Brown, Roderick (Langmere) Haig-**
See Haig-Brown, Roderick (Langmere)

**Brown, Rosellen** 1939- ............. **CLC 32, 170**
See also CA 77-80; CAAS 10; CANR 14,
44, 98; CN 6, 7; PFS 41

**Brown, Sterling Allen** 1901-1989 .... **BLC 1;**
**CLC 1, 23, 59; HR 1:2; PC 55**
See also AFAW 1, 2; BW 1, 3; CA 85-88;
127; CANR 26; CP 3, 4; DA3; DAM
MULT, POET; DLB 48, 51, 63; MAL 5;
MTCW 1, 2; MTFW 2005; RGAL 4; WP

**Brown, Will**
See Ainsworth, William Harrison

**Brown, William Hill** 1765-1793 ......... **LC 93**
See also DLB 37

**Cædmon** fl. 658-680 ...... **CMLC 7, 133, 198**
See also DLB 146

**Caeiro, Alberto**
See Pessoa, Fernando

**Caesar, Julius**
See Julius Caesar

**Cage, John (Milton), (Jr.)**
1912-1992 .................... **CLC 41; PC 58**
See also CA 13-16R; 169; CANR 9, 78;
DLB 193; INT CANR-9; TCLE 1:1

**Cahan, Abraham** 1860-1951 ......... **TCLC 71**
See also CA 108; 154; DLB 9, 25, 28; MAL
5; RGAL 4

**Cain, Christopher**
See Fleming, Thomas

**Cain, G.**
See Cabrera Infante, G.

**Cain, Guillermo**
See Cabrera Infante, G.

**Cain, James M(allahan)**
1892-1977 .................. **CLC 3, 11, 28**
See also AITN 1; BPFB 1; CA 17-20R; 73-
76; CANR 8, 34, 61; CMW 4; CN 1, 2;
DLB 226; EWL 3; MAL 5; MSW; MTCW 1;
RGAL 4

**Caine, Hall** 1853-1931 ................... **TCLC 97**
See also RHW

**Caine, Mark**
See Raphael, Frederic

**Caird, Mona** 1854-1932 ............... **TCLC 361**
See also DLB 197

**Calasso, Roberto** 1941- .................... **CLC 81**
See also CA 143; CANR 89, 223

**Calderon de la Barca, Pedro**
1600-1681 .................... **DC 3; HLCS 1;**
**LC 23, 136**
See also DFS 23; EW 2; RGWL 2, 3; TWA

**Caldwell, Erskine** 1903-1987 ........ **CLC 1, 8,**
**14, 50, 60; SSC 19, 147; TCLC 117**
See also AITN 1; AMW; BPFB 1; CA 1-4R;
121; CAAS 1; CANR 2, 33; CN 1, 2, 3, 4;
DA3; DAM NOV; DLB 9, 86; EWL 3;
MAL 5; MTCW 1, 2; MTFW 2005; RGAL
4; RGSF 2; TUS

**Caldwell, Gail** 1951- ....................... **CLC 309**
See also CA 313

**Caldwell, (Janet Miriam) Taylor (Holland)**
1900-1985 ...................... **CLC 2, 28, 39**
See also BPFB 1; CA 5-8R; 116; CANR 5;
DA3; DAM NOV, POP; DLBD 17;
MTCW 2; RHW

**Calhoun, John Caldwell**
1782-1850 ............................ **NCLC 15**
See also DLB 3, 248

**Calisher, Hortense** 1911-2009 ...... **CLC 2, 4,**
**8, 38, 134; SSC 15**
See also CA 1-4R; 282; CANR 1, 22, 117; CN
1, 2, 3, 4, 5, 6, 7; DA3; DAM NOV; DLB 2,
218; INT CANR-22; MAL 5; MTCW 1, 2;
MTFW 2005; RGAL 4; RGSF 2

**Callaghan, Morley** 1903-1990 .... **CLC 3, 14,**
**41, 65; TCLC 145, 292**
See also CA 9-12R; 132; CANR 33, 73; CN
1, 2, 3, 4; DAC; DAM MST; DLB 68;
EWL 3; MTCW 1, 2; MTFW 2005; RGEL
2; RGSF 2; SSFS 19

**Callaghan, Morley Edward**
See Callaghan, Morley

**Callahan, S. Alice** 1868-1894 .......... **NCLC 315**
See also DLB 175, 221; RGAL 4

**Callcott, Lady**
See Graham, Maria

**Callenbach, Ernest** 1929-2012 ............. **CLC 445**
See also CA 57-60; CANR 6, 21; SFW 4

**Callimachus**
c. 305 BCE-c. 240 BCE ......... **CMLC 18, 201**
See also AW 1; DLB 176; RGWL 2, 3

**Calprenede**
See La Calprenede, Gautier de Costes

**Calvin, Jean**
See Calvin, John

**Calvin, John** 1509-1564 .............. **LC 37, 215**
See also DLB 327; GFL Beginnings to 1789

**Calvino, Italo** 1923-1985 ............... **CLC 5, 8,**
**11, 22, 33, 39, 73; SSC 3, 48, 179, 258;**
**TCLC 183, 306, 313**
See also AAYA 58; CA 85-88, 116; CANR
23, 61, 132; DAM NOV; DLB 196; EW
13; EWL 3; MTCW 1, 2; MTFW 2005;
RGHL; RGSF 2; RGWL 2, 3; SFW 4;
SSFS 12, 31; WLIT 7

**Camara Laye**
See Laye, Camara

**Cambridge, A Gentleman of the University of**
See Crowley, Edward Alexander

**Camden, William** 1551-1623 .............. **LC 77**
See also DLB 172

**Cameron, Carey** 1952- ..................... **CLC 59**
See also CA 135

**Cameron, Peter** 1959- ...................... **CLC 44**
See also AMWS 12; CA 125; CANR 50,
117, 188, 239; DLB 234; GLL 2

**Camoes, Luis de** 1524(?)-1580 ....... **HLCS 1;**
**LC 62, 191; PC 31**
See also DLB 287; EW 2; RGWL 2, 3

**Camoens, Luis Vaz de** 1524(?)-1580
See Camoes, Luis de

**Camp, Madeleine L'Engle**
See L'Engle, Madeleine

**Campana, Dino** 1885-1932 ............ **TCLC 20**
See also CA 117; 246; DLB 114; EWL 3

**Campanella, Tommaso** 1568-1639 ..... **LC 32**
See also RGWL 2, 3

**Campbell, Bebe Moore**
1950-2006 .............. **BLC 2:1; CLC 246**
See also AAYA 26; BW 2, 3; CA 139; 254;
CANR 81, 134; DLB 227; MTCW 2;
MTFW 2005

**Campbell, David** 1915-1979 ........ **TCLC 325**
See also CA 97-100; CP 1, 2, 3; DLB 260

**Campbell, John Ramsey**
See Campbell, Ramsey

**Campbell, John W.** 1910-1971 ........ **CLC 32**
See also CA 21-22; 29-32R; CANR 34; CAP
2; DLB 8; MTCW 1; SCFW 1, 2; SFW 4

**Campbell, John Wood, Jr.**
See Campbell, John W.

**Campbell, Joseph**
1904-1987 ............. **CLC 69; TCLC 140**
See also AAYA 3, 66; BEST 89:2; CA 1-4R;
124; CANR 3, 28, 61, 107; DA3; MTCW 1, 2

**Campbell, Maria** 1940- ...... **CLC 85; NNAL**
See also CA 102; CANR 54; CCA 1; DAC

**Campbell, Ramsey** 1946- ... **CLC 42; SSC 19**
See also AAYA 51; CA 57-60, 228; CAAE
228; CANR 7, 102, 171; DLB 261; HGG;
INT CANR-7; SUFW 1, 2

**Campbell, (Ignatius) Roy (Dunnachie)**
1901-1957 ............................ **TCLC 5**
See also AFW; CA 104; 155; DLB 20, 225;
EWL 3; MTCW 2; RGEL 2

**Campbell, Thomas**
1777-1844 ...................... **NCLC 19, 314**
See also DLB 93, 144; RGEL 2

**Campbell, Wilfred**
See Campbell, William

**Campbell, William** 1858(?)-1918 .... **TCLC 9**
See also CA 106; DLB 92

**Campbell, William Edward March**
See March, William

**Campion, Jane** 1954- ............... **CLC 95, 229**
See also AAYA 33; CA 138; CANR 87

**Campion, Thomas** 1567-1620 .... **LC 78, 221;**
**PC 87**
See also BRWS 16; CDBLB Before 1660;
DAM POET; DLB 58, 172; RGEL 2

**Camus, Albert** 1913-1960 .... **CLC 1, 2, 4, 9,**
**11, 14, 32, 63, 69, 124; DC 2; SSC 9, 76,**
**129, 146, 247; TCLC 356; WLC 1**
See also AAYA 36; AFW; BPFB 1; CA 89-92;
CANR 131; DA; DA3; DAB; DAC; DAM

DRAM, MST, NOV; DLB 72, 321, 329; EW
13; EWL 3; EXPN; EXPS; GFL 1789 to the
Present; LATS 1:2; LMFS 2; MTCW 1, 2;
MTFW 2005; NFS 6, 16; RGHL; RGSF 2;
RGWL 2, 3; SSFS 4; TWA

**Can Xue** 1953- ................................ **CLC 412**
See also CA 139; CANR 214; DLB 370

**Canby, Vincent** 1924-2000 ............... **CLC 13**
See also CA 81-84; 191

**Cancale**
See Desnos, Robert

**Canetti, Elias** 1905-1994 ...... **CLC 3, 14, 25,**
**75, 86; TCLC 157**
See also CA 21-24R; 146; CANR 23, 61, 79;
CDWLB 2; CWW 2; DA3; DLB 85, 124,
329; EW 12; EWL 3; MTCW 1, 2; MTFW
2005; RGWL 2, 3; TWA

**Canfield, Dorothea F.**
See Fisher, Dorothy (Frances) Canfield

**Canfield, Dorothea Frances**
See Fisher, Dorothy (Frances) Canfield

**Canfield, Dorothy**
See Fisher, Dorothy (Frances) Canfield

**Canin, Ethan** 1960- .......... **CLC 55; SSC 70**
See also CA 131; 135; CANR 193; DLB
335, 350; MAL 5

**Cankar, Ivan** 1876-1918 .............. **TCLC 105**
See also CDWLB 4; DLB 147; EWL 3

**Cannon, Curt**
See Hunter, Evan

**Cao Zhi** 192-232 ......................... **CMLC 197**
See also DLB 358

**Cao, Lan** 1961- ............................... **CLC 109**
See also CA 165

**Cape, Judith**
See Page, P.K.

**Capek, Karel** 1890-1938 ...... **DC 1; SSC 36;**
**TCLC 6, 37, 192; WLC 1**
See also CA 104; 140; CDWLB 4; DA;
DA3; DAB; DAC; DAM DRAM, MST,
NOV; DFS 7, 11; DLB 215; EW 10; EWL
3; MTCW 2; MTFW 2005; RGSF 2;
RGWL 2, 3; SCFW 1, 2; SFW 4

**Capella, Martianus** fl. 4th cent. ... **CMLC 84**

**Caponegro, Mary** 1956- .................. **SSC 264**
See also DLB 335

**Capote, Truman** 1924-1984 ..... **CLC 1, 3, 8,**
**13, 19, 34, 38, 58; SSC 2, 47, 93; TCLC**
**164; WLC 1**
See also AAYA 61; AMWS 3; BPFB 1; CA
5-8R; 113; CANR 18, 62, 201; CDALB
1941-1968; CN 1, 2, 3; CPW; DA; DA3;
DAB; DAC; DAM MST, NOV, POP; DLB
2, 185, 227; DLBY 1980, 1984; EWL 3;
EXPS; GLL 1; LAIT 3; MAL 5; MTCW 1,
2; MTFW 2005; NCFS 2; RGAL 4; RGSF
2; SATA 91; SSFS 2; TUS

**Capra, Frank** 1897-1991 ................. **CLC 16**
See also AAYA 52; CA 61-64; 135

**Caputo, Philip** 1941- ........................ **CLC 32**
See also AAYA 60; CA 73-76; CANR 40,
135; YAW

**Caragiale, Ion Luca** 1852-1912 .... **TCLC 76**
See also CA 157

**Carballido, Emilio** 1925-2008 ....... **CLC 390**
See also CA 33-36R; CANR 54, 87; CWW
2; DLB 305; DFS 4; EWL 3; HW 1; LAW

**Card, Orson Scott**
1951- ..................... **CLC 44, 47, 50, 279**
See also AAYA 11, 42; BPFB 1; BYA 5, 8;
CA 102; CANR 27, 47, 73, 102, 106, 133,
184; CLR 116; CPW; DA3; DAM POP;
FANT; INT CANR-27; MTCW 1, 2;
MTFW 2005; NFS 5; SATA 83, 127,
241; SCFW 2; SFW 4; SUFW 2; YAW

**Cardenal, Ernesto** 1925- ......... **CLC 31, 161;**
**HLC 1; PC 22**
See also CA 49-52; CANR 2, 32, 66, 138,
217; CWW 2; DAM MULT, POET; DLB
290; EWL 3; HW 1, 2; LAWS 1; MTCW
1, 2; MTFW 2005; RGWL 2, 3

**Castedo-Ellerman, Elena**
See Castedo, Elena

**Castellanos, Rosario** 1925-1974 ..... **CLC 66; HLC 1; SSC 39, 68; TCLC 285**
See also CA 131; 53-56; CANR 58; CDWLB 3; DAM MULT; DLB 113, 290; EWL 3; FW; HW 1; LAW; MTCW 2; MTFW 2005; RGSF 2; RGWL 2, 3

**Castelvetro, Lodovico** 1505-1571 ....... **LC 12**

**Castiglione, Baldassare**
1478-1529 ............................ **LC 12, 165**
See also EW 2; LMFS 1; RGWL 2, 3; WLIT 7

**Castiglione, Baldesar**
See Castiglione, Baldassare

**Castillo, Ana** 1953- ................. **CLC 151, 279**
See also AAYA 42; CA 131; CANR 51, 86, 128, 172; CWP; DLB 122, 227; DNFS 2; FW; HW 1; LLW; PFS 21

**Castillo, Ana Hernandez Del**
See Castillo, Ana

**Castle, Robert**
See Hamilton, Edmond

**Castro (Ruz), Fidel** 1926(?)- ............. **HLC 1**
See also CA 110; 129; CANR 81; DAM MULT; HW 2

**Castro, Guillen de** 1569-1631 ........... **LC 19**

**Castro, Rosalía de** 1837-1885 ... **NCLC 3, 78, 334; PC 41**
See also DAM MULT

**Castro Alves, Antonio de**
1847-1871 ............................ **NCLC 205**
See also DLB 307; LAW

**Cather, Willa** 1873-1947 ..... **SSC 2, 50, 114, 186, 207; TCLC 1, 11, 31, 99, 132, 152, 264, 308, 362; WLC 1**
See also AAYA 24; AMW; AMWC 1; AMWR 1; BPFB 1; CA 104, 128; CDALB 1865-1917; CLR 98; DA; DA3; DAB; DAC; DAM MST, NOV; DLB 9, 54, 78, 256; DLBD 1; EWL 3; EXPN; EXPS; FL 1:5; LAIT 3; LATS 1:1; MAL 5; MBL; MTCW 1, 2; MTFW 2005; NFS 19, 33, 41; RGAL 4; RGSF 2; RHW; SATA 30; SSFS 2, 7, 16, 27; TCWW 1, 2; TUS

**Cather, Willa Sibert**
See Cather, Willa

**Catherine II**
See Catherine the Great

**Catherine, Saint** 1347-1380 .. **CMLC 27, 116**

**Catherine the Great** 1729-1796 ... **LC 69, 208**
See also DLB 150

**Cato, Marcus Porcius**
234 BCE-149 BCE ..................... **CMLC 21**
See also DLB 211

**Cato, Marcus Porcius, the Elder**
See Cato, Marcus Porcius

**Cato the Elder**
See Cato, Marcus Porcius

**Catton, (Charles) Bruce** 1899-1978 ... **CLC 35**
See also AITN 1; CA 5-8R; 81-84; CANR 7, 74; DLB 17; MTCW 2; MTFW 2005; SATA 2; SATA-Obit 24

**Catullus** c. 84 BCE-54 BCE ..... **CMLC 18, 141**
See also AW 2; CDWLB 1; DLB 211; RGWL 2, 3; WLIT 8

**Cauldwell, Frank**
See King, Francis

**Caunitz, William J.** 1933-1996 ....... **CLC 34**
See also BEST 89:3; CA 125; 130; 152; CANR 73; INT CA-130

**Causley, Charles (Stanley)** 1917-2003 ... **CLC 7**
See also CA 9-12R; 223; CANR 5, 35, 94; CLR 30; CP 1, 2, 3, 4, 5; CWRI 5; DLB 27; MTCW 1; SATA 3, 66; SATA-Obit 149

**Caute, (John) David** 1936- ............. **CLC 29**
See also CA 1-4R; CAAS 4; CANR 1, 33, 64, 120; CBD; CD 5, 6; CN 1, 2, 3, 4, 5, 6, 7; DAM NOV; DLB 14, 231

**Cavafy, C. P.**
See Cavafy, Constantine

**Cavafy, Constantine** 1863-1933 ........ **PC 36; TCLC 2, 7**
See also CA 104; 148; DA3; DAM POET; EW 8; EWL 3; MTCW 2; PFS 19; RGWL 2, 3; WP

**Cavafy, Constantine Peter**
See Cavafy, Constantine

**Cavalcanti, Guido** c. 1250-c. 1300 ... **CMLC 54, 162; PC 114**
See also RGWL 2, 3; WLIT 7

**Cavallo, Evelyn**
See Spark, Muriel

**Cavanna, Betty**
See Harrison, Elizabeth (Allen) Cavanna

**Cavanna, Elizabeth**
See Harrison, Elizabeth (Allen) Cavanna

**Cavanna, Elizabeth Allen**
See Harrison, Elizabeth (Allen) Cavanna

**Cave, Nick** 1957- ........................... **CLC 379**
See also CA 303

**Cavendish, Margaret**
1623-1673 ............. **LC 30, 132; PC 134**
See also DLB 131, 252, 281; RGEL 2

**Cavendish, Margaret Lucas**
See Cavendish, Margaret

**Caxton, Pisistratus**
See Bulwer-Lytton, Edward

**Caxton, William** 1421(?)-1491(?) ... **LC 17, 236**
See also DLB 170

**Cayer, D. M.**
See Duffy, Maureen

**Cayrol, Jean** 1911-2005 ................... **CLC 11**
See also CA 89-92; 236; DLB 83; EWL 3

**Cela, Camilo Jose**
See Cela, Camilo Jose

**Cela, Camilo Jose** 1916-2002 ..... **CLC 4, 13, 59, 122; HLC 1; SSC 71**
See also BEST 90:2; CA 21-24R; 206; CAAS 10; CANR 21, 32, 76, 139; CWW 2; DAM MULT; DLB 322; DLBY 1989; EW 13; EWL 3; HW 1; MTCW 1, 2; MTFW 2005; RGSF 2; RGWL 2, 3

**Celan, Paul** 1920-1970 ....... **CLC 10, 19, 53, 82; PC 10, 177**
See also CA 85-88; CANR 33, 61; CDWLB 2; DLB 69; EWL 3; MTCW 1; PFS 21; RGHL; RGWL 2, 3

**Cela y Trulock, Camilo Jose**
See Cela, Camilo Jose

**Celati, Gianni** 1937- ....................... **CLC 373**
See also CA 251; CWW 2; DLB 196

**Celine, Louis-Ferdinand**
1894-1961 ....... **CLC 1, 3, 4, 7, 47, 124**
See also CA 85-88; CANR 28; DLB 72; EW 11; EWL 3; GFL 1789 to the Present; MTCW 1; RGWL 2, 3

**Cellini, Benvenuto** 1500-1571 .............. **LC 7**
See also WLIT 7

**Cendrars, Blaise**
See Sauser-Hall, Frederic

**Centlivre, Susanna** 1669(?)-1723 ...... **DC 25; LC 65, 221**
See also DLB 84; RGEL 2

**Cernuda, Luis** 1902-1963 .... **CLC 54; PC 62; TCLC 286**
See also CA 131; 89-92; DAM POET; DLB 134; EWL 3; GLL 1; HW 1; RGWL 2, 3

**Cernuda y Bidon, Luis**
See Cernuda, Luis

**Cervantes, Lorna Dee** 1954- ........ **CLC 402; HLCS 1; PC 35**
See also CA 131; CANR 80; CP 7; CWP; DLB 82; EXPP; HW 1; LLW; PFS 30

**Cervantes, Miguel de** 1547-1616 ...... **HLCS; LC 6, 23, 93; SSC 12, 108; WLC 1**
See also AAYA 56; BYA 1, 14; DA; DA3; DAB; DAC; DAM MST, NOV; EW 2; LAIT 1; LATS 1:1; LMFS 1; NFS 8; RGSF 2; RGWL 2, 3; TWA

**Cervantes Saavedra, Miguel de**
See Cervantes, Miguel de

**Cesaire, Aime** 1913-2008 ............... **BLC 1:1; CLC 19, 32, 112, 280; DC 22; PC 25**
See also BW 2, 3; CA 65-68; 271; CANR 24, 43, 81; CWW 2; DA3; DAM MULT, POET; DLB 321; EWL 3; GFL 1789 to the Present; MTCW 1, 2; MTFW 2005; WP

**Cesaire, Aime Fernand**
See Cesaire, Aime

**Cha, Louis**
See Jin Yong

**Cha Leung-yung, Louis**
See Jin Yong

**Cha, Theresa Hak Kyung**
1951-1982 ............................ **TCLC 307**
See also CA 217; DLB 312

**Chaadaev, Petr Iakovlevich**
1794-1856 ............................ **NCLC 197**
See also DLB 198

**Chabon, Michael** 1963- ........... **CLC 55, 149, 265; SSC 59**
See also AAYA 45; AMWS 11; CA 139; CANR 57, 96, 127, 138, 196; DLB 278; MAL 5; MTFW 2005; NFS 25; SATA 145; SSFS 36

**Chabrol, Claude** 1930-2010 ........... **CLC 16**
See also CA 110

**Chacel, Rosa** 1898-1994 ............... **TCLC 298**
See also CA 243; CANR 216; CWW 2; DLB 134, 322; EWL 3

**Chairil Anwar**
See Anwar, Chairil

**Challans, Mary**
See Renault, Mary

**Challis, George**
See Faust, Frederick

**Chambers, Aidan** 1934- .................. **CLC 35**
See also AAYA 27, 86; CA 25-28R; CANR 12, 31, 58, 116; CLR 151; JRDA; MAICYA 1, 2; SAAS 12; SATA 1, 69, 108, 171; WYA; YAW

**Chambers, James** ......................... **CLC 21**
See also CA 124; 199

**Chambers, Jessie**
See Lawrence, D. H.

**Chambers, Maria Cristina**
See Mena, Maria Cristina

**Chambers, Robert W(illiam)**
1865-1933 ............... **SSC 92; TCLC 41**
See also CA 165; DLB 202; HGG; SATA 107; SUFW 1

**Chambers, (David) Whittaker**
1901-1961 ............................ **TCLC 129**
See also CA 89-92; DLB 303

**Chamisso, Adelbert von**
1781-1838 .............. **NCLC 82; SSC 140**
See also DLB 90; RGWL 2, 3; SUFW 1

**Chamoiseau, Patrick** 1953- ... **CLC 268, 276**
See also CA 162; CANR 88; EWL 3; RGWL 3

**Chance, James T.**
See Carpenter, John

**Chance, John T.**
See Carpenter, John

**Chand, Munshi Prem**
See Srivastava, Dhanpat Rai

**Chand, Prem**
See Srivastava, Dhanpat Rai

**Chandler, Raymond** 1888-1959 ...... **SSC 23; TCLC 1, 7, 179**
See also AAYA 25; AMWC 2; AMWS 4; BPFB 1; CA 104; 129; CANR 60, 107; CDALB 1929-1941; CMW 4; DA3; DLB 226, 253; DLBD 6; EWL 3; MAL 5; MSW; MTCW 1, 2; MTFW 2005; NFS 17; RGAL 4; TUS

**Chandler, Raymond Thornton**
See Chandler, Raymond

**Chandra, Vikram** 1961- ............... **CLC 302**
See also CA 149; CANR 97, 214; SSFS 16

**Chang, Diana** 1934-2009 ..................... **AAL**
See also CA 228; CWP; DLB 312; EXPP; PFS 37

Chang, Eileen 1920-1995 ...... **AAL; SSC 28, 169; TCLC 184**
See also CA 166; CANR 168; CWW 2; DLB 328; EWL 3; RGSF 2

Chang, Jung 1952- .......................... **CLC 71**
See also CA 142

Chang Ai-Ling
See Chang, Eileen

Channing, William Ellery
1780-1842 ............................. **NCLC 17**
See also DLB 1, 59, 235; RGAL 4

Channing, William Ellery II
1817-1901 ............................. **TCLC 306**
See also CA 215; DLB 1, 223

Chao, Patricia 1955- ..................... **CLC 119**
See also CA 163; CANR 155

Chaplin, Charles Spencer
1889-1977 ................................. **CLC 16**
See also AAYA 61; CA 81-84; 73-76; DLB 44

Chaplin, Charlie
See Chaplin, Charles Spencer

Chapman, George 1559(?)-1634 ....... **DC 19; LC 22, 116; PC 96**
See also BRW 1; DAM DRAM; DLB 62, 121; LMFS 1; RGEL 2

Chapman, Graham 1941-1989 ........ **CLC 21**
See also AAYA 7; CA 116; 129; CANR 35, 95

Chapman, John Jay 1862-1933 ...... **TCLC 7**
See also AMWS 14; CA 104; 191

Chapman, Lee
See Bradley, Marion Zimmer

Chapman, Maile ........................... **CLC 318**

Chapman, Walker
See Silverberg, Robert

Chappell, Fred 1936- ....... **CLC 40, 78, 162, 293; PC 105, 210**
See also CA 5-8R, 198; CAAE 198; CAAS 4; CANR 8, 33, 67, 110, 215, 323; CN 6; CP 6, 7; CSW; DLB 6, 105; HGG

Chappell, Fred Davis
See Chappell, Fred

Char, Rene 1907-1988 ... **CLC 9, 11, 14, 55; PC 56**
See also CA 13-16R; 124; CANR 32; DAM POET; DLB 258; EWL 3; GFL 1789 to the Present; MTCW 1, 2; RGWL 2, 3

Char, Rene-Emile
See Char, Rene

Charby, Jay
See Ellison, Harlan

Chardin, Pierre Teilhard de
See Teilhard de Chardin, (Marie Joseph) Pierre

Chariton fl. 1st cent. (?) .............. **CMLC 49**

Charke, Charlotte 1713-1760 .......... **LC 236**

Charlemagne 742-814 .................. **CMLC 37**

Charles I 1600-1649 ..... **LC 13, 194, 237**

Charrière, Isabelle de
1740-1805 ...................... **NCLC 66, 314**
See also DLB 313

Charron, Pierre 1541-1603 ............. **LC 174**
See also GFL Beginnings to 1789

Chartier, Alain c. 1392-1430 ............. **LC 94**
See also DLB 208

Chartier, Emile-Auguste
See Alain

Charyn, Jerome 1937- ............. **CLC 5, 8, 18**
See also CA 5-8R; CAAS 1; CANR 7, 61, 101, 158, 199; CMW 4; CN 1, 2, 3, 4, 5, 6, 7; DLBY 1983; MTCW 1

Chase, Adam
See Marlowe, Stephen

Chase, Mary (Coyle) 1907-1981 .......... **DC 1**
See also CA 77-80; 105; CAD; CWD; DFS 11; DLB 228; SATA 17; SATA-Obit 29

Chase, Mary Ellen 1887-1973 ......... **CLC 2; TCLC 124**
See also CA 13-16; 41-44R; CAP 1; SATA 10

Chase, Nicholas
See Hyde, Anthony

Chase-Riboud, Barbara (Dewayne Tosi)
1939- ........................................ **BLC 2:1**
See also BW 2; CA 113; CANR 76; DAM MULT; DLB 33; MTCW 2

Chateaubriand, François René de
1768-1848 ............... **NCLC 3, 134, 334**
See also DLB 119, 366; EW 5; GFL 1789 to the Present; RGWL 2, 3; TWA

Chateaubriand, François-Auguste
See Chateaubriand, François René de

Chateaubriand, François-Auguste-René
See Chateaubriand, François René de

Chateaubriand, René de vicomte de
See Chateaubriand, François René de

Chateaubriand, Vicomte de
See Chateaubriand, François René de

Chateaubriant
See Chateaubriand, François René de

Chatelet, Gabrielle-Emilie Du
See du Chatelet, Emilie

Chatterje, Saratchandra -(?)
See Chatterji, Sarat Chandra

Chatterjee, Bankim Chandra
See Chatterji, Bankim Chandra

Chatterji, Bankim Chandra
1838-1894 ...................... **NCLC 19, 345**

Chatterji, Sarat Chandra
1876-1936 .............................. **TCLC 13**
See also CA 109; 186; EWL 3

Chatterton, Thomas 1752-1770 ... **LC 3, 54; PC 104**
See also DAM POET; DLB 109; RGEL 2

Chatwin, Bruce 1940-1989 ... **CLC 28, 57, 59**
See also AAYA 4; BEST 90:1; BRWS 4; CA 85-88; 127; CANR 228; CPW; DAM POP; DLB 194, 204; EWL 3; MTFW 2005

Chatwin, Charles Bruce
See Chatwin, Bruce

Chaucer, Daniel
See Ford, Ford Madox

Chaucer, Geoffrey 1340(?)-1400 ....... **LC 17, 56, 173, 210, 213, 260; PC 19, 58, 155; WLCS**
See also BRW 1; BRWC 1; BRWR 2; CDBLB Before 1660; DA; DA3; DAB; DAC; DAM MST, POET; DLB 146; LAIT 1; PAB; PFS 14; RGEL 2; TEA; WLIT 3; WP

Chaudhuri, Nirad C(handra)
1897-1999 .............................. **TCLC 224**
See also CA 128; 183; DLB 323

Chávez, Denise 1948- ...... **CLC 423; HLC 1**
See also CA 131; CANR 56, 81, 137, 292; CMTFW; DLB 122; FW; HW 1, 2; LLW; MAL 5; MTCW 2; MTFW; MULT

Chaviaras, Strates 1935- ................. **CLC 33**
See also CA 105

Chayefsky, Paddy 1923-1981 .......... **CLC 23**
See also CA 9-12R; 104; CAD; CANR 18; DAM DRAM; DFS 26; DLB 23; DLBY 7, 44; RGAL 4

Chayefsky, Sidney
See Chayefsky, Paddy

Chedid, Andree 1920-2011 ............. **CLC 47**
See also CA 145; CANR 95; EWL 3

Cheever, John 1912-1982 ........ **CLC 3, 7, 8, 11, 15, 25, 64; SSC 1, 38, 57, 120, 243; WLC 2**
See also AAYA 65; AMWS 1; BPFB 1; CA 5-8R; 106; CABS 1; CANR 5, 27, 76; CDALB 1941-1968; CN 1, 2, 3; CPW; DA; DA3; DAB; DAC; DAM MST, NOV, POP; DLB 2, 102, 227; DLBY 1980, 1982; EWL 3; EXPS; INT CANR-5; MAL 5; MTCW 1, 2; MTFW 2005; RGAL 4; RGSF 2; SSFS 2, 14; TUS

Cheever, Susan 1943- ................ **CLC 18, 48**
See also CA 103; CANR 27, 51, 92, 157, 198, 232; DLBY 1982; INT CANR-27

Chekhonte, Antosha
See Chekhov, Anton

Chekhov, Anton 1860-1904 ... **DC 9; SSC 2, 28, 41, 51, 85, 102, 155, 253; TCLC 3, 10, 31, 55, 96, 163; WLC 2**
See also AAYA 68; BYA 14; CA 104; 124; DA; DA3; DAB; DAC; DAM DRAM, MST; DFS 1, 5, 10, 12, 26; DLB 277; EW 7; EWL 3; EXPS; LAIT 3; LATS 1:1; RGSF 2; RGWL 2, 3; SATA 90; SSFS 5, 13, 14, 26, 29, 33; TWA

Chekhov, Anton Pavlovich
See Chekhov, Anton

Chen Jia
See Shen Congwen

Chen Yingzhen 1937-2016 ............. **CLC 438**

Cheney, Lynne V. 1941- ................. **CLC 70**
See also CA 89-92; CANR 58, 117, 193; SATA 152

Cheney, Lynne Vincent
See Cheney, Lynne V.

Chernyshevsky, Nikolai Gavrilovich
See Chernyshevsky, Nikolay Gavrilovich

Chernyshevsky, Nikolay Gavrilovich
1828-1889 ................................. **NCLC 1**
See also DLB 238

Cherry, Carolyn Janice
See Cherryh, C.J.

Cherryh, C.J. 1942- ....................... **CLC 35**
See also AAYA 24; BPFB 1; CA 65-68; CANR 10, 147, 179; DLBY 1980; FANT; SATA 93, 172; SCFW 2; YAW

Chesler, Phyllis 1940- ................... **CLC 247**
See also CA 49-52; CANR 4, 59, 140, 189; FW

Chesnut, Mary 1823-1886 .......... **NCLC 250**
See also DLB 239

Chesnut, Mary Boykin
See Chesnut, Mary

Chesnutt, Charles W(addell)
1858-1932 ....... **BLC 1; SSC 7, 54, 139, 184, 241; TCLC 5, 39**
See also AFAW 1, 2; AMWS 14; BW 1, 3; CA 106; 125; CANR 76; DAM MULT; DLB 12, 50, 78; EWL 3; MAL 5; MTCW 1, 2; MTFW 2005; RGAL 4; RGSF 2; SSFS 11, 26

Chester, Alfred 1929(?)-1971 .......... **CLC 49**
See also CA 196; 33-36R; DLB 130; MAL 5

Chesterfield, Fourth Earl of
See Stanhope, Philip Dormer

Chesterton, G. K. 1874-1936 ... **PC 28, 198; SSC 1, 46, 148; TCLC 1, 6, 64**
See also AAYA 57; BRW 6; CA 104; 132; CANR 73, 131; CDBLB 1914-1945; CMW 4; DAM NOV, POET; DLB 10, 19, 34, 70, 98, 149, 178; EWL 3; FANT; MSW; MTCW 1, 2; MTFW 2005; RGEL 2; RGSF 2; SATA 27; SUFW 1

Chesterton, Gilbert Keith
See Chesterton, G. K.

Chettle, Henry 1560-1607(?) ........... **LC 112**
See also DLB 136; RGEL 2

Chiang, Pin-chin 1904-1986 ........... **CLC 68**
See also CA 118; DLB 328; EWL 3; RGWL 3

Chiang Ping-chih
See Chiang, Pin-chin

Chief Joseph 1840-1904 ..................... **NNAL**
See also CA 152; DA3; DAM MULT

Chief Seattle 1786(?)-1866 ................. **NNAL**
See also DA3; DAM MULT

Ch'ien, Chung-shu
See Qian, Zhongshu

Chikamatsu Monzaemon 1653-1724 ... **LC 66**
See also RGWL 2, 3

Child, Francis James 1825-1896 ... **NCLC 173**
See also DLB 1, 64, 235

Child, L. Maria
See Child, Lydia Maria

Child, Lydia Maria
1802-1880 ................. **NCLC 6, 73, 289**
See also DLB 1, 74, 243; RGAL 4; SATA 67

**Child, Mrs.**
See Child, Lydia Maria
**Child, Philip** 1898-1978 ............. **CLC 19, 68**
See also CA 13-14; CAP 1; CP 1; DLB 68;
RHW; SATA 47
**Childers, Erskine** 1870-1922 ......... **TCLC 65**
See also BRWS 17; CA 113; 153; DLB 70
**Childress, Alice** 1920-1994 ............ **BLC 1:1;**
**CLC 12, 15, 86, 96; DC 4; TCLC 116**
See also AAYA 8; BW 2, 3; BYA 2; CA 45-
48; 146; CAD; CANR 3, 27, 50, 74; CLR
14; CWD; DA3; DAM DRAM, MULT,
NOV; DFS 2, 8, 14, 26; DLB 7, 38, 249;
JRDA; LAIT 5; MAICYA 1, 2; MAICYAS
1; MAL 5; MTCW 1, 2; MTFW 2005;
RGAL 4; SATA 7, 48, 81; TUS; WYA; YAW
**Chin, Frank** 1940- ... **AAL; CLC 135; DC 7**
See also CA 33-36R; CAD; CANR 71; CD
5, 6; DAM MULT; DLB 206, 312; LAIT 5;
NFS 41; RGAL 4
**Chin, Frank Chew, Jr.**
See Chin, Frank
**Chin, Marilyn** 1955- ........................ **PC 40**
See also CA 129; CANR 70, 113, 218;
CWP; DLB 312; PFS 28, 41
**Chin, Marilyn Mei Ling**
See Chin, Marilyn
**Chislett, (Margaret) Anne**
1943- ........................................ **CLC 34**
See also CA 151
**Chitty, Thomas Willes**
See Hinde, Thomas
**Chivers, Thomas Holley**
1809-1858 ............................... **NCLC 49**
See also DLB 3, 248; RGAL 4
**Chiziane, Paulina** 1955- ................ **CLC 415**
See also DLB 367
**Chlamyda, Jehudil**
See Gorky, Maxim
**Chenier, Andre-Marie de** 1762-1794 ... **LC 174**
See also EW 4; GFL Beginnings to 1789; TWA
**Ch'o, Chou**
See Shu-Jen, Chou
**Choi, Susan** 1969- .......................... **CLC 119**
See also CA 223; CANR 188
**Chomette, Rene Lucien** 1898-1981 ... **CLC 20**
See also CA 103
**Chomsky, Avram Noam**
See Chomsky, Noam
**Chomsky, Noam** 1928- ................... **CLC 132**
See also CA 17-20R; CANR 28, 62, 110,
132, 179; DA3; DLB 246; MTCW 1, 2;
MTFW 2005
**Chona, Maria** 1845(?)-1936 ............... **NNAL**
See also CA 144
**Chopin, Kate** 1851-1904 ..... **SSC 8, 68, 110,**
**171, 211; TCLC 127; WLCS**
See also AAYA 33; AMWR 1; BYA 11, 15;
CA 104; 122; CDALB 1865-1917; DA3;
DAB; DAC; DAM MST, NOV; DLB 12,
78; EXPN; FL 1:3; FW; LAIT 3;
MAL 5; MBL; NFS 3; RGAL 4; RGSF 2;
SSFS 2, 13, 17, 26, 35; TUS
**Chopin, Katherine**
See Chopin, Kate
**Chraïbi, Driss** 1926-2007 .............. **CLC 427**
See also CA 151, 259; CWW 2; EWL 3
**Christie**
See Ichikawa, Kon
**Christie, Agatha** 1890-1976 ..... **CLC 1, 6, 8,**
**12, 39, 48, 110; DC 39; TCLC 333**
See also AAYA 9; AITN 1, 2; BPFB 1;
BRWS 2; CA 17-20R; 61-64; CANR 10,
37, 108; CBD; CDBLB 1914-1945; CMW
4; CN 1, 2; CPW; CWD; DA3; DAB;
DAC; DAM NOV; DFS 2; DLB 13, 77,
245; MSW; MTCW 1, 2; MTFW 2005;
NFS 8, 30, 33; RGEL 2; RHW; SATA 36;
SSFS 31, 34; TEA; YAW

**Christie, Agatha Mary Clarissa**
See Christie, Agatha
**Christie, Ann Philippa**
See Pearce, Philippa
**Christie, Philippa**
See Pearce, Philippa
**Christine de Pisan**
See Christine de Pizan
**Christine de Pizan** 1365(?)-1431(?) .... **LC 9,**
**130, 235; PC 68**
See also DLB 208; FL 1:1; FW; RGWL 2, 3
**Chretien de Troyes**
c. 12th cent. ........ **CMLC 10, 135, 180**
See also DLB 208; EW 1; RGWL 2, 3; TWA
**Chrysostom, John, Saint**
c. 349-407 ............................... **CMLC 194**
**Chrysostom, Saint John**
See Chrysostom, John, Saint
**Chuang-Tzu**
c. 369 BCE-c. 286 BCE ..... **CMLC 57, 134**
**Chubb, Elmer**
See Masters, Edgar Lee
**Chudleigh, Lady Mary** 1656-1710 .... **LC 217**
**Chulkov, Mikhail Dmitrievich**
1743-1792 ................................. **LC 2**
See also DLB 150
**Chung, Sonya** ............................... **CLC 318**
See also CA 307
**Churchill, Caryl** 1938- .................... **CLC 31,**
**55, 157; DC 5, 59**
See also BRWS 4; CA 102; CANR 22, 46,
108; CBD; CD 5, 6; CWD; DFS 12, 16,
25, 27, 30; DLB 13, 310; EWL 3; FW;
MBL 2; MTCW 1; RGEL 2
**Churchill, Charles** 1732-1764 ...... **LC 3, 269**
See also DLB 109; RGEL 2
**Churchill, Chick**
See Churchill, Caryl
**Churchill, Sir Winston**
1874-1965 ............................. **TCLC 113**
See also BRW 6; CA 97-100; CDBLB 1890-
1914; DA3; DLB 100, 329; DLBD 16;
LAIT 4; MTCW 1, 2
**Churchill, Sir Winston Leonard Spencer**
See Churchill, Sir Winston
**Churchyard, Thomas** 1520(?)-1604 ... **LC 187**
See also DLB 132; RGEL 2
**Chute, Carolyn** 1947- .............. **CLC 39, 322**
See also CA 123; CANR 135, 213; CN 7;
DLB 350
**Ciardi, John (Anthony)** 1916-1986 .. **CLC 10,**
**40, 44, 129; PC 69**
See also CA 5-8R; 118; CAAS 2; CANR 5,
33; CLR 19; CP 1, 2, 3, 4; CWRI 5; DAM
POET; DLB 5; DLBY 1986; INT CANR-
5; MAICYA 1, 2; MAL 5; MTCW 1, 2;
MTFW 2005; RGAL 4; SAAS 26; SATA
1, 65; SATA-Obit 46
**Cibber, Colley** 1671-1757 ........... **LC 66, 211**
See also DLB 84; RGEL 2
**Cicero, Marcus Tullius**
106 BCE-43 BCE ..... **CMLC 3, 81, 121, 175**
See also AW 1; CDWLB 1; DLB 211;
RGWL 2, 3; WLIT 8
**Cimino, Michael** 1943- .................... **CLC 16**
See also CA 105
**Cioran, E(mil) M.** 1911-1995 ........ **CLC 64;**
**TCLC 365**
See also CA 25-28R; 149; CANR 91; DLB
220; EWL 3
**Circus, Anthony**
See Hoch, Edward D.
**Cisneros, Sandra** 1954- .......... **CLC 69, 118,**
**193, 305, 352; HLC 1; PC 52; SSC 32,**
**72, 143, 187**
See also AAYA 9, 53; AMWS 7; CA 131;
CANR 64, 118; CLR 123; CN 7; CWP;
DA3; DAM MULT; DLB 122, 152; EWL
3; EXPN; FL 1:5; FW; HW 1, 2; LAIT 5;

LATS 1:2; LLW; MAICYA 2; MAL 5;
MTCW 2; MTFW 2005; NFS 2; PFS 19;
RGAL 4; RGSF 2; SSFS 3, 13, 27, 32;
WLIT 1; YAW
**Cixous, Hélène** 1937- ............... **CLC 92, 253**
See also CA 126; CANR 55, 123; CWW 2;
DLB 83, 242; EWL 3; FL 1:5; FW; GLL 2;
MTCW 1, 2; MTFW 2005; TWA
**Clair, Rene**
See Chomette, Rene Lucien
**Clampitt, Amy** 1920-1994 ... **CLC 32; PC 19**
See also AMWS 9; CA 110; 146; CANR 29,
79; CP 4, 5; DLB 105; MAL 5; PFS 27, 39
**Clancy, Thomas L., Jr.**
See Clancy, Tom
**Clancy, Tom** 1947-2013 ........... **CLC 45, 112**
See also AAYA 9, 51; BEST 89:1, 90:1;
BPFB 1; BYA 10, 11; CA 125; 131;
CANR 62, 105, 132; CMW 4; CPW; DA3;
DAM NOV, POP; DLB 227; INT CA-131;
MTCW 1, 2; MTFW 2005
**Clare, John** 1793-1864 .... **NCLC 9, 86, 259;**
**PC 23**
See also BRWS 11; DAB; DAM POET;
DLB 55, 96; RGEL 2
**Clare of Assisi** 1194-1253 ........... **CMLC 149**
**Clarin**
See Alas (y Urena), Leopoldo (Enrique Garcia)
**Clark, Al C.**
See Goines, Donald
**Clark, Brian (Robert)**
See Clark, (Robert) Brian
**Clark, (Robert) Brian** 1932- ........... **CLC 29**
See also CA 41-44R; CANR 67; CBD; CD 5, 6
**Clark, Curt**
See Westlake, Donald E.
**Clark, Eleanor** 1913-1996 ........... **CLC 5, 19**
See also CA 9-12R; 151; CANR 41; CN 1,
2, 3, 4, 5, 6; DLB 6
**Clark, Howard**
See Henry, O.
**Clark, J. P.**
See Clark-Bekederemo, J. P.
**Clark, John Pepper**
See Clark-Bekederemo, J. P.
**Clark, Kenneth (Mackenzie)**
1903-1983 ............................... **TCLC 147**
See also CA 93-96; 109; CANR 36; MTCW
1, 2; MTFW 2005
**Clark, M. R.**
See Clark, Mavis Thorpe
**Clark, Mavis Thorpe** 1909-1999 .... **CLC 12**
See also CA 57-60; CANR 8, 37, 107; CLR
30; CWRI 5; MAICYA 1, 2; SAAS 5;
SATA 8, 74
**Clark, Rev. T.**
See Galt, John
**Clark, Walter Van Tilburg**
1909-1971 ................................ **CLC 28**
See also CA 9-12R; 33-36R; CANR 63, 113;
CN 1; DLB 9, 206; LAIT 2; MAL 5; NFS
40; RGAL 4; SATA 8; TCWW 1, 2
**Clark-Bekederemo, J. P.** 1935- ..... **BLC 1:1;**
**CLC 38; DC 5**
See also AAYA 79; AFW; BW 1; CA 65-68;
CANR 16, 72; CD 5, 6; CDWLB 3; CP 1,
2, 3, 4, 5, 6, 7; DAM DRAM, MULT; DFS
13; DLB 117; EWL 3; MTCW 2; MTFW
2005; RGEL 2
**Clark-Bekederemo, John Pepper**
See Clark-Bekederemo, J. P.
**Clark Bekederemo, Johnson Pepper**
See Clark-Bekederemo, J. P.
**Clarke, Arthur**
See Clarke, Arthur C.
**Clarke, Arthur C.** 1917-2008 ...... **CLC 1, 4,**
**13, 18, 35, 136; SSC 3, 239**
See also AAYA 4, 33; BPFB 1; BYA 13; CA
1-4R; 270; CANR 2, 28, 55, 74, 130, 196;
CLR 119; CN 1, 2, 3, 4, 5, 6, 7; CPW;

DA3; DAM POP; DLB 261; JRDA; LAIT
5; MAICYA 1, 2; MTCW 1, 2; MTFW
2005; SATA 13, 70, 115; SATA-Obit 191;
SCFW 1, 2; SFW 4; SSFS 4, 18, 29, 36;
TCLE 1:1; YAW

**Clarke, Arthur Charles**
See Clarke, Arthur C.

**Clarke, Austin** 1896-1974 ............. **CLC 6, 9; PC 112**
See also BRWS 15; CA 29-32; 49-52; CAP
2; CP 1, 2; DAM POET; DLB 10, 20;
EWL 3; RGEL 2

**Clarke, Austin** 1934- ....................... **BLC 1:1; CLC 8, 53; SSC 45, 116**
See also BW 1; CA 25-28R; CAAS 16;
CANR 14, 32, 68, 140, 220; CN 1, 2, 3,
4, 5, 6, 7; DAC; DAM MULT; DLB 53, 125;
DNFS 2; MTCW 2; MTFW 2005; RGSF 2

**Clarke, Austin Ardinel Chesterfield**
See Clarke, Arthur C.

**Clarke, Gillian** 1937- ....................... **CLC 61**
See also CA 106; CP 3, 4, 5, 6, 7; CWP;
DLB 40

**Clarke, Marcus (Andrew Hislop)**
1846-1881 ....... **NCLC 19, 258; SSC 94**
See also DLB 230; RGEL 2; RGSF 2

**Clarke, Shirley** 1925-1997 ............... **CLC 16**
See also CA 189

**Clash, The**
See Headon, (Nicky) Topper; Jones, Mick;
Simonon, Paul; Strummer, Joe

**Claudel, Paul (Louis Charles Marie)**
1868-1955 .... **DC 56; TCLC 2, 10, 268**
See also CA 104; 165; DLB 192, 258, 321;
EW 8; EWL 3; GFL 1789 to the Present;
RGWL 2, 3; TWA

**Claudian** 370(?)-404(?) .................. **CMLC 46**
See also RGWL 2, 3

**Claudius, Matthias** 1740-1815 ...... **NCLC 75**
See also DLB 97

**Clausewitz, Carl von** 1780-1831 ... **NCLC 296**

**Clavell, James** 1925-1994 ..... **CLC 6, 25, 87**
See also BPFB 1; CA 25-28R; 146; CANR
26, 48; CN 5; CPW; DA3; DAM NOV,
POP; MTCW 1, 2; MTFW 2005; NFS 10;
RHW

**Clayman, Gregory** .......................... **CLC 65**

**Cleage, Pearl** 1948- ......................... **DC 32**
See also BW 2; CA 41-44R; CANR 27, 148,
177, 226; DFS 14, 16; DLB 228; NFS 17

**Cleage, Pearl Michelle**
See Cleage, Pearl

**Cleaver, (Leroy) Eldridge** 1935-1998 ... **BLC 1:1; CLC 30, 119**
See also BW 1, 3; CA 21-24R; 167; CANR
16, 75; DA3; DAM MULT; MTCW 2; YAW

**Cleese, John (Marwood)** 1939- ....... **CLC 21**
See also CA 112; 116; CANR 35; MTCW 1

**Cleishbotham, Jebediah**
See Scott, Sir Walter

**Cleland, John** 1710-1789 ....... **LC 2, 48, 235**
See also DLB 39; RGEL 2

**Clemens, Samuel**
See Twain, Mark

**Clemens, Samuel Langhorne**
See Twain, Mark

**Clement of Alexandria**
150(?)-215(?) .......................... **CMLC 41**

**Cleophil**
See Congreve, William

**Clerihew, E.**
See Bentley, E(dmund) C(lerihew)

**Clerk, N. W.**
See Lewis, C. S.

**Cleveland, John** 1613-1658 ............. **LC 106**
See also DLB 126; RGEL 2

**Cliff, Jimmy**
See Chambers, James

**Cliff, Michelle** 1946- ......... **BLCS; CLC 120**
See also BW 2; CA 116; CANR 39, 72;
CDWLB 3; DLB 157; FW; GLL 2

**Clifford, Lady Anne** 1590-1676 ........ **LC 76**
See also DLB 151

**Clifton, Lucille** 1936-2010 ..... **BLC 1:1, 2:1; CLC 19, 66, 162, 283; PC 17, 148**
See also AFAW 2; BW 2, 3; CA 49-52;
CANR 2, 24, 42, 76, 97, 138; CLR 5; CP
2, 3, 4, 5, 6, 7; CSW; CWP; CWRI 5; DA3;
DAM MULT, POET; DLB 5, 41; EXPP;
MAICYA 1, 2; MTCW 1, 2; MTFW 2005;
PFS 1, 14, 29, 41; SATA 20, 69, 128; SSFS
34; WP

**Clifton, Thelma Lucille**
See Clifton, Lucille

**Cline, Emma** 1989- ...................... **CLC 421**
See also CA 390

**Clinton, Dirk**
See Silverberg, Robert

**Clough, Arthur Hugh**
1819-1861 ....... **NCLC 27, 163; PC 103**
See also BRW 5; DLB 32; RGEL 2

**Clouts, Sydney** 1926-1982 ........... **TCLC 318**
See also CA 207; CP 1, 2, 3; DLB 225

**Clutha, Janet**
See Frame, Janet

**Clutha, Janet Paterson Frame**
See Frame, Janet

**Clyne, Terence**
See Blatty, William Peter

**C. N.**
See Naden, Constance

**Cobalt, Martin**
See Mayne, William

**Cobb, Irvin S(hrewsbury)**
1876-1944 .............................. **TCLC 77**
See also CA 175; DLB 11, 25, 86

**Cobbett, William** 1763-1835 .. **NCLC 49, 288**
See also DLB 43, 107, 158; RGEL 2

**Coben, Harlan** 1962- ...................... **CLC 269**
See also AAYA 83; CA 164; CANR 162,
199, 234

**Coburn, D(onald) L(ee)** 1938- ........ **CLC 10**
See also CA 89-92; DFS 23

**Cockburn, Catharine Trotter**
See Trotter, Catharine

**Cocteau, Jean** 1889-1963 ....... **CLC 1, 8, 15, 16, 43; DC 17; TCLC 119; WLC 2**
See also AAYA 74; CA 25-28; CANR 40;
CAP 2; DA; DA3; DAB; DAC; DAM
DRAM, MST, NOV; DFS 24; DLB 65,
258, 321; EW 10; EWL 3; GFL 1789 to
the Present; MTCW 1, 2; RGWL 2, 3; TWA

**Cocteau, Jean Maurice Eugene Clement**
See Cocteau, Jean

**Codrescu, Andrei** 1946- ........... **CLC 46, 121**
See also CA 33-36R; CAAS 19; CANR 13,
34, 53, 76, 125, 223; CN 7; DA3; DAM
POET; MAL 5; MTCW 2; MTFW 2005

**Coe, Max**
See Bourne, Randolph S(illiman)

**Coe, Tucker**
See Westlake, Donald E.

**Coelebs**
See More, Hannah

**Coelho, Paulo** 1947- ...................... **CLC 258**
See also CA 152; CANR 80, 93, 155, 194;
NFS 29

**Coen, Ethan** 1957- ................. **CLC 108, 267**
See also AAYA 54; CA 126; CANR 85

**Coen, Joel** 1954- ..................... **CLC 108, 267**
See also AAYA 54; CA 126; CANR 119

**Coetzee, J. M.** 1940- ......... **CLC 23, 33, 66, 117, 161, 162, 305, 414, 416**
See also AAYA 37; AFW; BRWS 6; CA 77-
80; CANR 41, 54, 74, 114, 133, 180; CN
4, 5, 6, 7; DA3; DAM NOV; DLB 225,
326, 329; EWL 3; LMFS 2; MTCW 1, 2;
MTFW 2005; NFS 21; WLIT 2; WWE 1

**Coetzee, John Maxwell**
See Coetzee, J. M.

**Coffey, Brian**
See Koontz, Dean

**Coffin, Robert P. Tristram**
1892-1955 ............................... **TCLC 95**
See also CA 123; 169; DLB 45

**Coffin, Robert Peter Tristram**
See Coffin, Robert P. Tristram

**Cohan, George M.** 1878-1942 ....... **TCLC 60**
See also CA 157; DLB 249; RGAL 4

**Cohan, George Michael**
See Cohan, George M.

**Cohen, Arthur A(llen)** 1928-1986 .. **CLC 7, 31**
See also CA 1-4R; 120; CANR 1, 17, 42;
DLB 28; RGHL

**Cohen, Leonard** 1934- ........ **CLC 3, 38, 260; PC 109**
See also CA 21-24R; CANR 14, 69; CN 1,
2, 3, 4, 5, 6; CP 1, 2, 3, 4, 5, 6, 7; DAC;
DAM MST; DLB 53; EWL 3; MTCW 1

**Cohen, Leonard Norman**
See Cohen, Leonard

**Cohen, Matt(hew)** 1942-1999 .......... **CLC 19**
See also CA 61-64; 187; CAAS 18; CANR
40; CN 1, 2, 3, 4, 5, 6; DAC; DLB 53

**Cohen-Solal, Annie** 1948- ............... **CLC 50**
See also CA 239

**Colegate, Isabel** 1931- ...................... **CLC 36**
See also CA 17-20R; CANR 8, 22, 74; CN
4, 5, 6, 7; DLB 14, 231; INT CANR-22;
MTCW 1

**Coleman, Emmett**
See Reed, Ishmael

**Coleridge, Hartley** 1796-1849 ... **NCLC 90, 283**
See also DLB 96

**Coleridge, M. E.**
See Coleridge, Mary E(lizabeth)

**Coleridge, Mary E(lizabeth)**
1861-1907 .............................. **TCLC 73**
See also CA 116; 166; DLB 19, 98

**Coleridge, Samuel Taylor**
1772-1834 .... **NCLC 9, 54, 99, 111, 177, 197, 231; PC 11, 39, 67, 100, 184; WLC 2**
See also AAYA 66; BRW 4; BRWR 2; BYA
4; CDBLB 1789-1832; DA; DA3; DAB;
DAC; DAM MST, POET; DLB 93, 107;
EXPP; LATS 1:1; LMFS 1; PAB; PFS 4, 5,
39; RGEL 2; TEA; WLIT 3; WP

**Coleridge, Sara** 1802-1852 .......... **NCLC 31; PC 197**
See also DLB 199

**Coles, Don** 1928- .............................. **CLC 46**
See also CA 115; CANR 38; CP 5, 6, 7

**Coles, Robert** 1929- ....................... **CLC 108**
See also CA 45-48; CANR 3, 32, 66, 70,
135, 225; INT CANR-32; SATA 23

**Coles, Robert Martin**
See Coles, Robert

**Colette** 1873-1954 ...................... **SSC 10, 93; TCLC 1, 5, 16, 272**
See also CA 104; 131; DA3; DAM NOV;
DLB 65; EW 9; EWL 3; GFL 1789 to the
Present; GLL 1; MTCW 1, 2; MTFW
2005; RGWL 2, 3; TWA

**Colette, Sidonie-Gabrielle**
See Colette

**Collett, (Jacobine) Camilla (Wergeland)**
1813-1895 ............................... **NCLC 22**
See also DLB 354

**Collier, Christopher** 1930- ............... **CLC 30**
See also AAYA 13; BYA 2; CA 33-36R;
CANR 13, 33, 102; CLR 126; JRDA;
MAICYA 1, 2; NFS 38; SATA 16, 70;
WYA; YAW 1

**Collier, James Lincoln** 1928- .......... **CLC 30**
See also AAYA 13; BYA 2; CA 9-12R; CANR
4, 33, 60, 102, 208; CLR 3, 126; DAM POP;

**Crane, R(onald) S(almon)**
1886-1967 .................................. **CLC 27**
See also CA 85-88; DLB 63

**Crane, Stephen** 1871-1900 ... **PC 80; SSC 7,
56, 70, 129, 194, 223; TCLC 11, 17, 32,
216; WLC 2**
See also AAYA 21; AMW; AMWC 1; BPFB
1; BYA 3; CA 109; 140; CANR 84;
CDALB 1865-1917; CLR 132; DA; DA3;
DAB; DAC; DAM MST, NOV, POET;
DLB 12, 54, 78, 357; EXPN; EXPS; LAIT
2; LMFS 2; MAL 5; NFS 4, 20; PFS 9;
RGAL 4; RGSF 2; SSFS 4, 28, 34; TUS;
WYA; YABC 2

**Crane, Stephen Townley**
See Crane, Stephen

**Cranmer, Thomas** 1489-1556 ............. **LC 95**
See also DLB 132, 213

**Cranshaw, Stanley**
See Fisher, Dorothy (Frances) Canfield

**Crase, Douglas** 1944- ....................... **CLC 58**
See also CA 106; CANR 204

**Crashaw, Richard** 1612(?)-1649 ....... **LC 24,
200; PC 84, 190**
See also BRW 2; DLB 126; PAB; RGEL 2

**Cratinus** c. 519 BCE-c. 422 BCE ..... **CMLC 54**
See also LMFS 1

**Craven, Margaret** 1901-1980 .......... **CLC 17**
See also BYA 2; CA 103; CCA 1; DAC;
LAIT 5

**Crawford, F(rancis) Marion**
1854-1909 ................................. **TCLC 10**
See also CA 107; 168; DLB 71; HGG;
RGAL 4; SUFW 1

**Crawford, Isabella Valancy**
1850-1887 ....................... **NCLC 12, 127**
See also DLB 92; RGEL 2

**Crayon, Geoffrey**
See Irving, Washington

**Crayon, Porte**
See Strother, David Hunter

**Crébillon, Claude Prosper Jolyot de (fils)**
1707-1777 ........................... **LC 1, 28, 267**
See also DLB 313; GFL Beginnings to 1789

**Creasey, John** 1908-1973 ................. **CLC 11**
See also CA 5-8R; 41-44R; CANR 8, 59;
CMW 4; DLB 77; MTCW 1

**Credo**
See Creasey, John

**Credo, Alvaro J. de**
See Prado (Calvo), Pedro

**Creeley, Robert** 1926-2005 ...... **CLC 1, 2, 4,
8, 11, 15, 36, 78, 266; PC 73**
See also AMWS 4; CA 1-4R; 237; CAAS
10; CANR 23, 43, 89, 137; CP 1, 2, 3, 4, 5,
6, 7; DA3; DAM POET; DLB 5, 16, 169;
DLBD 17; EWL 3; MAL 5; MTCW 1, 2;
MTFW 2005; PFS 21; RGAL 4; WP

**Creeley, Robert White**
See Creeley, Robert

**Crenne, Helisenne de** 1510-1560 ..... **LC 113**
See also DLB 327

**Crevecoeur, J. Hector St. John de**
1735-1813 ............................. **NCLC 105**
See also AMWS 1; ANW; DLB 37

**Crevecoeur, Michel Guillaume Jean de**
See Crevecoeur, J. Hector St. John de

**Crevel, Rene** 1900-1935 ............... **TCLC 112**
See also GLL 2

**Crews, Harry** 1935-2012 **CLC 6, 23, 49, 277**
See also AITN 1; AMWS 11; BPFB 1; CA
25-28R; CANR 20, 57; CN 3, 4, 5, 6, 7;
CSW; DA3; DLB 6, 143, 185; MTCW 1,
2; MTFW 2005; RGAL 4

**Crichton, John Michael**
See Crichton, Michael

**Crichton, Michael** 1942-2008 ....... **CLC 2, 6,
54, 90, 242**
See also AAYA 10, 49; AITN 2; BPFB 1;
CA 25-28R; 279; CANR 13, 40, 54, 76,
127, 179; CMW 4; CN 2, 3, 6, 7; CPW;
DA3; DAM NOV, POP; DLB 292; DLBY
1981; INT CANR-13; JRDA; LNFS 1;
MTCW 1, 2; MTFW 2005; NFS 34; SATA
9, 88; SATA-Obit 199; SFW 4; YAW

**Crispin, Edmund**
See Montgomery, Bruce

**Cristina of Sweden** 1626-1689 ......... **LC 124**

**Cristofer, Michael** 1945(?)- ............. **CLC 28**
See also CA 110; 152; CAD; CANR 150;
CD 5, 6; DAM DRAM; DFS 15; DLB 7

**Cristofer, Michael Ivan**
See Cristofer, Michael

**Criton**
See Alain

**Croce, Benedetto** 1866-1952 .......... **TCLC 37**
See also CA 120; 155; EW 8; EWL 3; WLIT 7

**Crockett, David**
See Crockett, Davy

**Crockett, Davy** 1786-1836 ...... **NCLC 8, 356**
See also DLB 3, 11, 183, 248

**Crofts, Freeman Wills** 1879-1957 ... **TCLC 55**
See also CA 115; 195; CMW 4; DLB 77;
MSW

**Croker, John Wilson** 1780-1857 ... **NCLC 10**
See also DLB 110

**Crommelynck, Fernand** 1885-1970 .. **CLC 75**
See also CA 189; 89-92; EWL 3

**Cromwell, Oliver** 1599-1658 ............. **LC 43**

**Cronenberg, David** 1943- ............. **CLC 143**
See also CA 138; CCA 1

**Cronin, A(rchibald) J(oseph)**
1896-1981 ................................. **CLC 32**
See also BPFB 1; CA 1-4R; 102; CANR 5;
CN 2; DLB 191; SATA 47; SATA-Obit 25

**Cross, Amanda**
See Heilbrun, Carolyn G.

**Crothers, Rachel** 1878-1958 .......... **TCLC 19**
See also CA 113; 194; CAD; CWD; DLB 7,
266; RGAL 4

**Croves, Hal**
See Traven, B.

**Crow Dog, Mary** (?)- ......... **CLC 93; NNAL**
See also CA 154

**Crowfield, Christopher**
See Stowe, Harriet Beecher

**Crowley, Aleister**
See Crowley, Edward Alexander

**Crowley, Edward Alexander**
1875-1947 ................................. **TCLC 7**
See also CA 104; GLL 1; HGG

**Crowley, John** 1942- ............. **CLC 57, 393**
See also AAYA 57; BPFB 1; CA 61-64;
CANR 43, 98, 138, 177; DLBY 1982;
FANT; MTFW 2005; SATA 65, 140; SFW
4; SUFW 2

**Crowne, John** 1641-1712 .................. **LC 104**
See also DLB 80; RGEL 2

**Crud**
See Crumb, R.

**Cruiser, Benedict**
See Sala, George Augustus

**Crumarums**
See Crumb, R.

**Crumb, R.** 1943- ............................. **CLC 17**
See also CA 106; CANR 107, 150, 218

**Crumb, Robert**
See Crumb, R.

**Crumbum**
See Crumb, R.

**Crumski**
See Crumb, R.

**Crum the Bum**
See Crumb, R.

**Crunk**
See Crumb, R.

**Crustt**
See Crumb, R.

**Crutchfield, Les**
See Trumbo, Dalton

**Cruz, Victor Hernandez** 1949- ........ **HLC 1;
PC 37**
See also BW 2; CA 65-68, 271; CAAE 271;
CAAS 17; CANR 14, 32, 74, 132; CP 1, 2,
3, 4, 5, 6, 7; DAM MULT, POET; DLB 41;
DNFS 1; EXPP; HW 1, 2; LLW; MTCW
2; MTFW 2005; PFS 16; WP

**Cryer, Gretchen (Kiger)** 1935- ....... **CLC 21**
See also CA 114; 123

**Csath, Geza**
See Brenner, Jozef

**Cudlip, David R(ockwell)** 1933- ..... **CLC 34**
See also CA 177

**Cudworth, Ralph** 1617-1688 ........... **LC 257**
See also DLB 252

**Cuervo, Talia**
See Vega, Ana Lydia

**Cullen, Countee** 1903-1946 ... **BLC 1:1; HR
1:2; PC 20; TCLC 4, 37, 220; WLCS**
See also AAYA 78; AFAW 2; AMWS 4; BW
1; CA 108; 124; CDALB 1917-1929; DA;
DA3; DAC; DAM MST, MULT, POET;
DLB 4, 48, 51; EWL 3; EXPP; LMFS 2;
MAL 5; MTCW 1, 2; MTFW 2005; PFS 3,
42; RGAL 4; SATA 18; WP

**Culleton, Beatrice** 1949- ..................... **NNAL**
See also CA 120; CANR 83; DAC

**Culver, Timothy J.**
See Westlake, Donald E.

**Cum, R.**
See Crumb, R.

**Cumberland, Richard** 1732-1811 .... **NCLC 167**
See also DLB 89; RGEL 2

**Cummings, Bruce F.** 1889-1919 ... **TCLC 24**
See also CA 123

**Cummings, Bruce Frederick**
See Cummings, Bruce F.

**Cummings, E. E.** 1894-1962 ... **CLC 1, 3, 8,
12, 15, 68; PC 5; TCLC 137; WLC 2**
See also AAYA 41; AMW; CA 73-76;
CANR 31; CDALB 1929-1941; DA; DA3;
DAB; DAC; DAM MST, POET; DLB 4,
48; EWL 3; EXPP; MAL 5; MTCW 1, 2;
MTFW 2005; PAB; PFS 1, 3, 12, 13, 19,
30, 34, 40; RGAL 4; TUS; WP

**Cummings, Edward Estlin**
See Cummings, E. E.

**Cummins, Maria Susanna**
1827-1866 ............................. **NCLC 139**
See also DLB 42; YABC 1

**Cunha, Euclides (Rodrigues Pimenta) da**
1866-1909 ............................. **TCLC 24**
See also CA 123; 219; DLB 307; LAW;
WLIT 1

**Cunningham, E. V.**
See Fast, Howard

**Cunningham, J. Morgan**
See Westlake, Donald E.

**Cunningham, J(ames) V(incent)**
1911-1985 ............... **CLC 3, 31; PC 92**
See also CA 1-4R; 115; CANR 1, 72; CP 1,
2, 3, 4; DLB 5

**Cunningham, Julia (Woolfolk)** 1916- .. **CLC 12**
See also CA 9-12R; CANR 4, 19, 36; CWRI
5; JRDA; MAICYA 1, 2; SAAS 2; SATA
1, 26, 132

**Cunningham, Michael** 1952- ... **CLC 34, 243**
See also AMWS 15; CA 136; CANR 96,
160, 227; CN 7; DLB 292; GLL 2; MTFW
2005; NFS 23

**Cunninghame Graham, R. B.**
See Cunninghame Graham, Robert Bontine

**Cunninghame Graham, Robert Bontine**
1852-1936 ............................. **TCLC 19**
See also CA 119; 184; DLB 98, 135, 174;
RGEL 2; RGSF 2

3; HGG; INT CANR-17; MTCW 1, 2;
MTFW 2005; RGEL 2; TWA

**Davies, Sir John** 1569-1626 .............. **LC 85**
See also DLB 172

**Davies, Walter C.**
See Kornbluth, C(yril) M.

**Davies, William Henry** 1871-1940 ... **TCLC 5**
See also BRWS 11; CA 104; 179; DLB 19,
174; EWL 3; RGEL 2

**Davies, William Robertson**
See Davies, Robertson

**Da Vinci, Leonardo** 1452-1519 ......... **LC 12,
57, 60**
See also AAYA 40

**Daviot, Gordon**
See Mackintosh, Elizabeth

**Davis, Angela Y.** 1944- .................... **CLC 77**
See also BW 2, 3; CA 57-60; CANR 10, 81;
CSW; DA3; DAM MULT; FW

**Davis, Angela Yvonne**
See Davis, Angela Y.

**Davis, B. Lynch**
See Bioy Casares, Adolfo; Borges,
Jorge Luis

**Davis, Frank Marshall**
1905-1987 ........... **BLC 1:1; TCLC 360**
See also BW 2, 3; CA 123, 125; CANR 42,
80; DAM MULT; DLB 51

**Davis, Gordon**
See Hunt, E. Howard

**Davis, H(arold) L(enoir)** 1896-1960 .... **CLC 49**
See also ANW; CA 178; 89-92; DLB 9, 206;
SATA 114; TCWW 1, 2

**Davis, Hart**
See Poniatowska, Elena

**Davis, Lydia** 1947- ......... **CLC 306, 370, 426**
See also CA 139; CANR 120, 171, 222;
DLB 130

**Davis, Natalie Zemon** 1928- .......... **CLC 204**
See also CA 53-56; CANR 58, 100, 174

**Davis, Rebecca Blaine Harding**
See Davis, Rebecca Harding

**Davis, Rebecca Harding** 1831-1910 ... **SSC 38,
109, 192; TCLC 6, 267**
See also AMWS 16; CA 104; 179; DLB 74,
239; FW; NFS 14; RGAL 4; SSFS 26; TUS

**Davis, Richard Harding** 1864-1916 ... **TCLC 24**
See also CA 114; 179; DLB 12, 23, 78, 79,
189; DLBD 13; RGAL 4

**Davison, Frank Dalby** 1893-1970 ... **CLC 15**
See also CA 217; 116; DLB 260

**Davison, Lawrence H.**
See Lawrence, D. H.

**Davison, Peter (Hubert)** 1928-2004 .. **CLC 28**
See also CA 9-12R; 234; CAAS 4; CANR 3,
43, 84; CP 1, 2, 3, 4, 5, 6, 7; DLB 5

**Davys, Mary** 1674-1732 ........ **LC 1, 46, 217**
See also DLB 39

**Dawe, Bruce** 1930- ........................... **PC 159**
See also CA 69-72; CANR 11, 27, 52, 83;
CP 1, 2, 3, 4, 5, 6, 7; DLB 289; PFS 10

**Dawson, (Guy) Fielding (Lewis)**
1930-2002 ................................. **CLC 6**
See also CA 85-88; 202; CANR 108; DLB
130; DLBY 2002

**Day, Clarence (Shepard, Jr.)**
1874-1935 ............................... **TCLC 25**
See also CA 108; 199; DLB 11

**Day, John** 1574(?)-1640(?) ................. **LC 70**
See also DLB 62, 170; RGEL 2

**Day, Thomas** 1748-1789 ...................... **LC 1**
See also DLB 39; YABC 1

**Day Lewis, C.** 1904-1972 ...... **CLC 1, 6, 10;
PC 11; TCLC 261**
See also BRWS 3; CA 13-16; 33-36R;
CANR 34; CAP 1; CN 1; CP 1; CWRI
5; DAM POET; DLB 77; EWL 3; MSW;
MTCW 1, 2; RGEL 2

**Day Lewis, Cecil**
See Day Lewis, C.

**de Andrade, Carlos Drummond**
See Drummond de Andrade, Carlos

**de Andrade, Mario** (?)-
See Andrade, Mario de

**Deane, Norman**
See Creasey, John

**Deane, Seamus (Francis)** 1940- .... **CLC 122**
See also CA 118; CANR 42

**de Athayde, Alvaro Coelho**
See Pessoa, Fernando

**Deaver, Jeff**
See Deaver, Jeffery

**Deaver, Jeffery** 1950- .................... **CLC 331**
See also CA 204; CANR 30; DLB 18, 156;
RGEL 2; SATA 20

**Deaver, Jeffery Wilds**
See Deaver, Jeffery

**de Beauvoir, Simone**
See Beauvoir, Simone de

**de Beer, P.**
See Bosman, Herman Charles

**Debord, Guy** 1931-1994 ............... **TCLC 348**
See also DLB 296

**De Botton, Alain** 1969- .................. **CLC 203**
See also CA 159; CANR 96, 201

**de Brissac, Malcolm**
See Dickinson, Peter

**de Campos, Álvaro**
See Pessoa, Fernando

**de Chardin, Pierre Teilhard**
See Teilhard de Chardin, (Marie Joseph)
Pierre

**de Conte, Sieur Louis**
See Twain, Mark

**de Crenne, Helisenne**
c. 1510-c. 1560 .................. **LC 113, 218**

**Dee, John** 1527-1608 ........................... **LC 20**
See also DLB 136, 213

**Deer, Sandra** 1940- .......................... **CLC 45**
See also CA 186

**De Ferrari, Gabriella** 1941- ........... **CLC 65**
See also CA 146

**de Filippo, Eduardo** 1900-1984 ... **TCLC 127**
See also CA 132; 114; EWL 3; MTCW 1;
RGWL 2, 3

**Defoe, Daniel** 1660 (?)-1731 ......... **LC 1, 42,
105, 180, 238, 259, 280; PC 179; WLC 2**
See also AAYA 27; BRW 3; BRWR 1; BYA
4; CDBLB 1660-1789; CLR 61, 164; DA;
DA3; DAB; DAC; DAM MST, NOV; DLB
39, 95, 101, 336; JRDA; LAIT 1; LMFS 1;
MAICYA 1, 2; NFS 9, 13, 30; RGEL 2;
SATA 22; TEA; WCH; WLIT 3

**de Gouges, Olympe**
See Gouges, Olympe de

**de Gouges, Olympe** 1748-1793 .. **LC 127, 214**
See also DLB 313

**de Gourmont, Remy(-Marie-Charles)**
See Gourmont, Remy(-Marie-Charles) de

**de Gournay, Marie le Jars**
1566-1645 ............................. **LC 98, 244**
See also DLB 327; FW

**de Hartog, Jan** 1914-2002 .............. **CLC 19**
See also CA 1-4R; 210; CANR 1, 192; DFS 12

**de Hostos, E. M.**
See Hostos (y Bonilla), Eugenio Maria de

**de Hostos, Eugenio M.**
See Hostos (y Bonilla), Eugenio Maria de

**Deighton, Len**
See Deighton, Leonard Cyril

**Deighton, Leonard Cyril** 1929- ... **CLC 4, 7,
22, 46**
See also AAYA 57, 6; BEST 89:2; BPFB 1;
CA 9-12R; CANR 19, 33, 68; CDBLB
1960- Present; CMW 4; CN 1, 2, 3, 4,
5, 6, 7; CPW; DA3; DAM NOV, POP;
DLB 87; MTCW 1, 2; MTFW 2005

**Dekker, Thomas** 1572(?)-1632 .......... **DC 12;
LC 22, 159**
See also CDBLB Before 1660; DAM
DRAM; DLB 62, 172; LMFS 1; RGEL 2

**Delachapelle**
See Claudel, Paul

**de Laclos, Pierre Ambroise Franois**
See Laclos, Pierre-Ambroise Francois

**Delacroix, (Ferdinand-Victor-)Eugene**
1798-1863 .............................. **NCLC 133**
See also EW 5

**Delafield, E. M.**
See Dashwood, Edmee Elizabeth Monica de
la Pasture

**de la Mare, Walter (John)**
1873-1956 ................... **PC 77; SSC 14;
TCLC 4, 53; WLC 2**
See also AAYA 81; CA 163; CDBLB 1914-
1945; CLR 23, 148; CWRI 5; DA3; DAB;
DAC; DAM MST, POET; DLB 19, 153,
162, 255, 284; EWL 3; EXPP; HGG;
MAICYA 1, 2; MTCW 2; MTFW 2005;
PFS 39; RGEL 2; RGSF 2; SATA 16;
SUFW 1; TEA; WCH

**de Lamartine, Alphonse**
See Lamartine, Alphonse de

**Deland, Margaret(ta Wade Campbell)**
1857-1945 ............................... **SSC 162**
See also CA 122; DLB 78; RGAL 4

**Delaney, Franey**
See O'Hara, John

**Delaney, Shelagh** 1939-2011 ... **CLC 29; DC 45**
See also CA 17-20R; CANR 30, 67; CBD;
CD 5, 6; CDBLB 1960 to Present; CWD;
DAM DRAM; DFS 7; DLB 13; MTCW 1

**Delany, Martin Robison** 1812-1885 .. **NCLC 93**
See also DLB 50; RGAL 4

**Delany, Mary (Granville Pendarves)**
1700-1788 ............................... **LC 12, 220**

**Delany, Samuel R., Jr.** 1942- ........ **BLC 1:1;
CLC 8, 14, 38, 141, 313**
See also AAYA 24; AFAW 2; BPFB 1; BW
2, 3; CA 81-84; CANR 27, 43, 116, 172;
CN 2, 3, 4, 5, 6, 7; DAM MULT; DLB 8,
33; FANT; MAL 5; MTCW 1, 2; RGAL 4;
SATA 92; SCFW 1, 2; SFW 4; SUFW 2

**Delany, Samuel Ray**
See Delany, Samuel R., Jr.

**de la Parra, Ana Teresa Sonojo**
See de la Parra, Teresa

**de la Parra, Teresa**
1890(?)-1936 ........ **HLCS 2; TCLC 185**
See also CA 178; HW 2; LAW

**Delaporte, Theophile**
See Green, Julien

**De La Ramee, Marie Louise**
1839-1908 ............................... **TCLC 43**
See also CA 204; CLR 208; DLB 18, 156;
RGEL 2; SATA 20

**de la Roche, Mazo** 1879-1961 ........ **CLC 14**
See also CA 85-88; CANR 30; DLB 68;
RGEL 2; RHW; SATA 64

**De La Salle, Innocent**
See Hartmann, Sadakichi

**de Laureamont, Comte**
See Lautreamont

**Delbanco, Nicholas** 1942- ... **CLC 6, 13, 167**
See also CA 17-20R, 189; CAAE 189;
CAAS 2; CANR 29, 55, 116, 150, 204,
237; CN 7; DLB 6, 234

**Delbanco, Nicholas Franklin**
See Delbanco, Nicholas

**del Castillo, Michel** 1933- .............. **CLC 38**
See also CA 109; CANR 77

**Deledda, Grazia (Cosima)** 1875
(?)-1936 ................................. **TCLC 23**
See also CA 123; 205; DLB 264, 329; EWL
3; RGWL 2, 3; WLIT 7

**Deleuze, Gilles** 1925-1995 ... **TCLC 116, 372**
See also DLB 296

Author Index

**Egoyan, Atom** 1960- ............. **CLC 151, 291**
    See also AAYA 63; CA 157; CANR 151

**Ehle, John (Marsden, Jr.)**
    1925- ................................. **CLC 27, 392**
    See also CA 9-12R; CSW

**Ehrenbourg, Ilya**
    See Ehrenburg, Ilya

**Ehrenbourg, Ilya Grigoryevich**
    See Ehrenburg, Ilya

**Ehrenburg, Ilya** 1891-1967 ... **CLC 18, 34, 62**
    See also CA 102; 25-28R; DLB 272; EWL 3

**Ehrenburg, Ilya Grigoryevich**
    See Ehrenburg, Ilya

**Ehrenburg, Ilyo**
    See Ehrenburg, Ilya

**Ehrenburg, Ilyo Grigoryevich**
    See Ehrenburg, Ilya

**Ehrenreich, Barbara** 1941- ... **CLC 110, 267**
    See also BEST 90:4; CA 73-76; CANR 16,
    37, 62, 117, 167, 208; DLB 246; FW;
    LNFS 1; MTCW 1, 2; MTFW 2005

**Ehrlich, Gretel** 1946- ..................... **CLC 249**
    See also ANW; CA 140; CANR 74, 146;
    DLB 212, 275; TCWW 2

**Eich, Gunter** 1907-1972 ................... **CLC 15**
    See also CA 111; 93-96; DLB 69, 124; EWL
    3; RGWL 2, 3

**Eich, Gunter**
    See Eich, Gunter

**Eichendorff, Joseph**
    1788-1857 ................ **NCLC 8, 225, 246**
    See also DLB 90; RGWL 2, 3

**Eigner, Larry**
    See Eigner, Laurence (Joel)

**Eigner, Laurence (Joel)** 1927-1996 ... **CLC 9**
    See also CA 9-12R; 151; CAAS 23; CANR
    6, 84; CP 1, 2, 3, 4, 5, 6, 7; DLB 5; WP

**Eilhart von Oberge** c. 1140-c. 1195 ... **CMLC 67**
    See also DLB 148

**Ein Russe**
    See Herzen, Aleksandr Ivanovich

**Einhard** c. 770-840 ........................ **CMLC 50**
    See also DLB 148

**Einstein, Albert** 1879-1955 ........... **TCLC 65**
    See also CA 121; 133; MTCW 1, 2

**Eiseley, Loren**
    See Eiseley, Loren Corey

**Eiseley, Loren Corey** 1907-1977 ...... **CLC 7;
    TCLC 310**
    See also AAYA 5; ANW; CA 1-4R; 73-76;
    CANR 6; DLB 275; DLBD 17

**Eisenstadt, Jill** 1963- ...................... **CLC 50**
    See also CA 140

**Eisenstein, Sergei (Mikhailovich)**
    1898-1948 ................................. **TCLC 57**
    See also CA 114; 149

**Eisler, Hanns** 1898-1962 ............. **TCLC 361**
    See also CA 116; IDFW 3, 4

**Eisler, Steve**
    See Holdstock, Robert

**Eisner, Simon**
    See Kornbluth, C(yril) M.

**Eisner, Will** 1917-2005 ................... **CLC 237**
    See also AAYA 52; CA 108; 235; CANR
    114, 140, 179; MTFW 2005; SATA 31, 165

**Eisner, William Erwin**
    See Eisner, Will

**Ekelof, Gunnar** 1907-1968 ... **CLC 27; PC 23**
    See also CA 123; 25-28R; DAM POET;
    DLB 259; EW 12; EWL 3

**Ekeloef, Bengt Gunnar**
    See Ekelof, Gunnar

**Ekeloef, Gunnar**
    See Ekelof, Gunnar

**Ekelund, Vilhelm** 1880-1949 ........ **TCLC 75**
    See also CA 189; EWL 3

**Ekman, Kerstin** 1933- ................... **CLC 279**
    See also CA 154; CANR 124, 214; DLB
    257; EWL 3

**Ekman, Kerstin Lillemor**
    See Ekman, Kerstin

**Ekwensi, C. O. D.**
    See Ekwensi, Cyprian

**Ekwensi, Cyprian** 1921-2007 ........ **BLC 1:1;
    CLC 4**
    See also AFW; BW 2, 3; CA 29-32R; CANR
    18, 42, 74, 125; CDWLB 3; CN 1, 2, 3, 4, 5,
    6; CWRI 5; DAM MULT; DLB 117; EWL
    3; MTCW 1, 2; RGEL 2; SATA 66; WLIT 2

**Ekwensi, Cyprian Odiatu Duaka**
    See Ekwensi, Cyprian

**Elaine**
    See Leverson, Ada Esther

**El Conde de Pepe**
    See Mihura, Miguel

**El Crummo**
    See Crumb, R.

**Elder, Lonne III** 1931-1996 ......... **BLC 1:1;
    DC 8**
    See also BW 1, 3; CA 81-84; 152; CAD;
    CANR 25; DAM MULT; DLB 7, 38, 44;
    MAL 5

**Eleanor of Aquitaine** 1122-1204 ... **CMLC 39**

**Elia**
    See Lamb, Charles

**Eliade, Mircea** 1907-1986 .............. **CLC 19;
    TCLC 243**
    See also CA 65-68; 119; CANR 30, 62;
    CDWLB 4; DLB 220; EWL 3; MTCW
    1; RGWL 3; SFW 4

**Eliot, A. C.**
    See Jewett, Sarah Orne

**Eliot, Alice**
    See Jewett, Sarah Orne

**Eliot, Dan**
    See Silverberg, Robert

**Eliot, George** 1819-1880 ... **NCLC 4, 13, 23,
    41, 49, 89, 118, 183, 199, 209, 233, 340;
    PC 20; SSC 72, 139; WLC 2**
    See also BRW 5; BRWC 1, 2; BRWR 2;
    CDBLB 1832-1890; CN 7; CPW; DA;
    DA3; DAB; DAC; DAM MST, NOV; DLB
    21, 35, 55, 366; FL 1:3; LATS 1:1; LMFS
    1; NFS 17, 20, 34; RGEL 2; RGSF 2;
    SSFS 8; TEA; WLIT 3

**Eliot, John** 1604-1690 ........................ **LC 5**
    See also DLB 24

**Eliot, T. S.** 1888-1965 .......... **CLC 1, 2, 3, 6,
    9, 10, 13, 15, 24, 34, 41, 55, 57, 113; DC
    28; PC 5, 31, 90, 234; TCLC 236; WLC 2**
    See also AAYA 28; AMW; AMWC 1;
    AMWR 1; BRW 7; BRWR 2; CA 5-8R;
    25-28R; CANR 41; CBD; CDALB 1929-
    1941; DA; DA3; DAB; DAC; DAM
    DRAM, MST, POET; DFS 4, 13, 28; DLB
    7, 10, 45, 63, 245, 329; DLBY 1988; EWL
    3; EXPP; LAIT 3; LATS 1:1; LMFS 2;
    MAL 5; MTCW 1, 2; MTFW 2005; NCFS
    5; PAB; PFS 1, 7, 20, 33; RGAL 4; RGEL
    2; TUS; WLIT 4; WP

**Eliot, Thomas Stearns**
    See Eliot, T. S.

**Elisabeth of Schonau**
    c. 1129-1165 .......................... **CMLC 82**

**Elizabeth** 1866-1941 ....................... **TCLC 41**

**Elizabeth I, Queen of England**
    1533-1603 ............................... **LC 118**
    See also BRWS 16; DLB 136

**Elkin, Stanley L.** 1930-1995 ......... **CLC 4, 6,
    9, 14, 27, 51, 91; SSC 12**
    See also AMWS 6; BPFB 1; CA 9-12R; 148;
    CANR 8, 46; CN 1, 2, 3, 4, 5, 6; CPW;
    DAM NOV, POP; DLB 2, 28, 218, 278;
    DLBY 1980; EWL 3; INT CANR-8; MAL
    5; MTCW 1, 2; MTFW 2005; RGAL 4;
    TCLE 1:1

**Elledge, Scott** ................................... **CLC 34**

**Eller, Scott**
    See Shepard, Jim

**Elliott, Don**
    See Silverberg, Robert

**Elliott, Ebenezer** 1781-1849 ............... **PC 96**
    See also DLB 96, 190; RGEL 2

**Elliott, George P(aul)** 1918-1980 ...... **CLC 2**
    See also CA 1-4R; 97-100; CANR 2; CN 1,
    2; CP 3; DLB 244; MAL 5

**Elliott, Janice** 1931-1995 ................. **CLC 47**
    See also CA 13-16R; CANR 8, 29, 84; CN
    5, 6, 7; DLB 14; SATA 119

**Elliott, Julia** 1968- ......................... **CLC 405**
    See also CA 371

**Elliott, Sumner Locke** 1917-1991 ... **CLC 38**
    See also CA 5-8R; 134; CANR 2, 21; DLB 289

**Elliott, William**
    See Bradbury, Ray

**Ellis, A. E.** ...................................... **CLC 7**

**Ellis, Alice Thomas**
    See Haycraft, Anna

**Ellis, Bret Easton** 1964- ........... **CLC 39, 71,
    117, 229, 345**
    See also AAYA 2, 43; CA 118; 123; CANR
    51, 74, 126, 226; CN 6, 7; CPW; DA3;
    DAM POP; DLB 292; HGG; INT CA-123;
    MTCW 2; MTFW 2005; NFS 11

**Ellis, (Henry) Havelock**
    1859-1939 ............................... **TCLC 14**
    See also CA 109; 169; DLB 190

**Ellis, Landon**
    See Ellison, Harlan

**Ellis, Trey** 1962- ............................. **CLC 55**
    See also CA 146; CANR 92; CN 7

**Ellison, Harlan** 1934- ........... **CLC 1, 13, 42,
    139; SSC 14**
    See also AAYA 29; BPFB 1; BYA 14; CA 5-
    8R; CANR 5, 46, 115; CPW; DAM POP;
    DLB 8, 335; HGG; INT CANR-5; MTCW
    1, 2; MTFW 2005; SCFW 2; SFW 4; SSFS
    13, 14, 15, 21; SUFW 1, 2

**Ellison, Ralph** 1914-1994 ....... **BLC 1:1, 2:2;
    CLC 1, 3, 11, 54, 86, 114; SSC 26, 79;
    TCLC 308; WLC 2**
    See also AAYA 19; AFAW 1, 2; AMWC 2;
    AMWR 2; AMWS 2; BPFB 1; BW 1, 3;
    BYA 2; CA 9-12R; 145; CANR 24, 53;
    CDALB 1941-1968; CSW; DA; DA3; DAB; DAC; DAM
    MST, MULT, NOV; DLB 2, 76, 227; DLBY
    1994; EWL 3; EXPN; EXPS; LAIT 4; MAL
    5; MTCW 1, 2; MTFW 2005; NCFS 3; NFS
    2, 21; RGAL 4; RGSF 2; SSFS 1, 11; YAW

**Ellison, Ralph Waldo**
    See Ellison, Ralph

**Ellmann, Lucy** 1956- ....................... **CLC 61**
    See also CA 128; CANR 154

**Ellmann, Lucy Elizabeth**
    See Ellmann, Lucy

**Ellmann, Richard (David)**
    1918-1987 ............................... **CLC 50**
    See also BEST 89:2; CA 1-4R; 122; CANR
    2, 28, 61; DLB 103; DLBY 1987; MTCW
    1, 2; MTFW 2005

**Ellroy, James** 1948- ................. **CLC 215, 412**
    See also BEST 90:4; CA 138; CANR 74,
    133, 219; CMW 4; CN 6, 7; DA3; DLB
    226; MTCW 2; MTFW 2005

**Ellroy, Lee Earle**
    See Ellroy, James

**Elman, Richard (Martin)**
    1934-1997 ............................... **CLC 19**
    See also CA 17-20R; 163; CAAS 3; CANR
    47; TCLE 1:1

**Elron**
    See Hubbard, L. Ron

**El Saadawi, Nawal** 1931- ............. **BLC 2:2;
    CLC 196, 284**

25, 27; DLB 176; LAIT 1; LMFS 1;
RGWL 2, 3; WLIT 8

**Eusebius** c. 263-c. 339 ............... **CMLC 103**

**Evagrius Ponticus** c. 345-c.399 .. **CMLC 203**

**Evan, Evin**
  See Faust, Frederick

**Evans, Caradoc**
  1878-1945 ................ **SSC 43; TCLC 85**
  See also DLB 162

**Evans, Evan**
  See Faust, Frederick

**Evans, Marian**
  See Eliot, George

**Evans, Mary Ann**
  See Eliot, George

**Evaristo, Bernardine** 1959- ........... **CLC 355**
  See also CA 212, 275; CP 7; DLB 347

**Evarts, Esther**
  See Benson, Sally

**Evelyn, John** 1620-1706 .................... **LC 144**
  See also BRW 2; RGEL 2

**Everett, Percival** 1956- ............. **CLC 57, 304**
  See also AMWS 18; BW 2; CA 129; CANR
  94, 134, 179, 219; CN 7; CSW; DLB 350;
  MTFW 2005

**Everett, Percival L.**
  See Everett, Percival

**Everson, R(onald) G(ilmour)**
  1903-1992 ................................. **CLC 27**
  See also CA 17-20R; CP 1, 2, 3, 4; DLB 88

**Everson, William** 1912-1994 ........ **CLC 1, 5,
14; PC 169**
  See also BG 1:2; CA 9-12R; 145; CANR 20;
  CP 1; DLB 5, 16, 212; MTCW 1

**Everson, William Oliver**
  See Everson, William

**Evtushenko, Evgenii Aleksandrovich**
  See Yevtushenko, Yevgenyn

**Ewart, Gavin (Buchanan)**
  1916-1995 ........................... **CLC 13, 46**
  See also BRWS 7; CA 89-92; 150; CANR 17,
  46; CP 1, 2, 3, 4, 5, 6; DLB 40; MTCW 1

**Ewers, Hanns Heinz** 1871-1943 .... **TCLC 12**
  See also CA 109; 149

**Ewing, Frederick R.**
  See Sturgeon, Theodore (Hamilton)

**Ewing, Juliana** 1841-1885 ........... **NCLC 330**
  See also CLR 78; DLB 21, 163; SATA 16;
  WCH

**Exley, Frederick** 1929-1992 ......... **CLC 6, 11**
  See also AITN 2; AMWS 23; BPFB 1; CA
  81-84; 138; CANR 117; DLB 143; DLBY
  1981

**Eynhardt, Guillermo**
  See Quiroga, Horacio (Sylvestre)

**Ezekiel, Nissim (Moses)** 1924-2004 ... **CLC 61**
  See also CA 61-64; 223; CP 1, 2, 3, 4, 5, 6,
  7; DLB 323; EWL 3

**Ezekiel, Tish O'Dowd** 1943- .......... **CLC 34**
  See also CA 129

**Fabius**
  See Dickinson, John

**Fadeev, Aleksandr Aleksandrovich**
  See Bulgya, Alexander Alexandrovich

**Fadeev, Alexandr Alexandrovich**
  See Bulgya, Alexander Alexandrovich

**Fadeyev, A.**
  See Bulgya, Alexander Alexandrovich

**Fadeyev, Alexander**
  See Bulgya, Alexander Alexandrovich

**Fagen, Donald** 1948- ........................ **CLC 26**

**Fagunwa, D. O.** 1903-1963 ......... **TCLC 295**
  See also CA 116

**Fainzil'berg, Il'ia Arnol'dovich**
  See Fainzilberg, Ilya Arnoldovich

**Fainzilberg, Ilya Arnoldovich**
  1897-1937 ............................... **TCLC 21**
  See also CA 120; 165; DLB 272; EWL 3

**Fair, Ronald L.** 1932- ...................... **CLC 18**
  See also BW 1; CA 69-72; CANR 25;
  DLB 33

**Fairbairn, Roger**
  See Carr, John Dickson

**Fairbairns, Zoe (Ann)** 1948- .......... **CLC 32**
  See also CA 103; CANR 21, 85; CN 4, 5, 6, 7

**Fairfield, Flora**
  See Alcott, Louisa May

**Falco, Gian**
  See Papini, Giovanni

**Falconer, James**
  See Kirkup, James

**Falconer, Kenneth**
  See Kornbluth, C(yril) M.

**Falkland, Samuel**
  See Heijermans, Herman

**Falkner, J. Meade** 1858-1932 ...... **TCLC 343**
  See also HGG

**Fallaci, Oriana** 1930-2006 ....... **CLC 11, 110**
  See also CA 77-80; 253; CANR 15, 58, 134;
  FW; MTCW 1

**Faludi, Susan** 1959- ....................... **CLC 140**
  See also CA 138; CANR 126, 194; FW;
  MTCW 2; MTFW 2005; NCFS 3

**Faludy, George**
  See Faludy, Gyorgy

**Faludy, Gyorgy** 1913-2006 ............. **CLC 42**
  See also CA 21-24R; CANR 243

**Fanon, Frantz** 1925-1961 .............. **BLC 1:2;
CLC 74; TCLC 188**
  See also BW 1; CA 116; 89-92; DAM
  MULT; DLB 296; LMFS 2; WLIT 2

**Fanshawe, Ann** 1625-1680 ................ **LC 11**

**Fante, John (Thomas)**
  1911-1983 ................... **CLC 60; SSC 65**
  See also AMWS 11; CA 69-72; 109; CANR 23,
  104; DLB 130; DLBY 1983

**Farah, Nuruddin** 1945- ......... **BLC 1:2, 2:2;
CLC 53, 137, 344**
  See also AFW; BW 2, 3; CA 106; CANR 81,
  148, 243; CDWLB 3; CN 4, 5, 6, 7; DAM
  MULT; DLB 125; EWL 3; WLIT 2

**Fardusi**
  See Ferdowsi, Abu'l Qasem

**Fargue, Leon-Paul** 1876(?)-1947 ... **TCLC 11**
  See also CA 109; CANR 107; DLB 258;
  EWL 3

**Farigoule, Louis**
  See Romains, Jules

**Farina, Richard** 1936(?)-1966 .......... **CLC 9**
  See also CA 81-84; 25-28R

**Farley, Walter (Lorimer)**
  1915-1989 ................................. **CLC 17**
  See also AAYA 58; BYA 14; CA 17-20R;
  CANR 8, 29, 84; DLB 22; JRDA; MAI-
  CYA 1, 2; SATA 2, 43, 132; YAW

**Farmer, Philipe Jos**
  See Farmer, Philip Jose

**Farmer, Philip Jose** 1918-2009 ........ **CLC 1,
19, 299**
  See also AAYA 28; BPFB 1; CA 1-4R; 283;
  CANR 4, 35, 111, 220; CLR 201; DLB 8;
  MTCW 1; SATA 93; SATA-Obit 201;
  SCFW 1, 2; SFW 4

**Farmer, Philip Jose**
  See Farmer, Philip Jose

**Farquhar, George** 1677-1707 ........... **DC 38;
LC 21**
  See also BRW 2; DAM DRAM; DLB 84;
  RGEL 2

**Farrell, J. G.** 1935-1979 .................... **CLC 6**
  See also CA 73-76; 89-92; CANR 36; CN 1,
  2; DLB 14, 271, 326; MTCW 1; RGEL 2;
  RHW; WLIT 4

**Farrell, James Gordon**
  See Farrell, J. G.

**Farrell, James T(homas)**
  1904-1979 ............. **CLC 1, 4, 8, 11, 66;
SSC 28; TCLC 228**
  See also AMW; BPFB 1; CA 5-8R; 89-92;
  CANR 9, 61; CN 1, 2; DLB 4, 9, 86;
  DLBD 2; EWL 3; MAL 5; MTCW 1, 2;
  MTFW 2005; RGAL 4

**Farrell, John Wade**
  See MacDonald, John D.

**Farrell, M. J.**
  See Keane, Mary Nesta

**Farrell, Warren (Thomas)** 1943- .... **CLC 70**
  See also CA 146; CANR 120

**Farren, Richard J.**
  See Betjeman, John

**Farren, Richard M.**
  See Betjeman, John

**Farrugia, Mario Benedetti**
  See Bentley, Eric

**Farrugia, Mario Orlando Hardy Hamlet
Brenno Benedetti**
  See Benedetti, Mario

**Fassbinder, Rainer Werner**
  1946-1982 ................................. **CLC 20**
  See also CA 93-96; 106; CANR 31

**Fast, Howard** 1914-2003 ......... **CLC 23, 131**
  See also AAYA 16; BPFB 1; CA 1-4R, 181;
  214; CAAE 181; CAAS 18; CANR 1, 33,
  54, 75, 98, 140; CMW 4; CN 1, 2, 3, 4, 5,
  6, 7; CPW; DAM NOV; DLB 9; INT
  CANR-33; LATS 1:1; MAL 5; MTCW 2;
  MTFW 2005; NFS 35; RHW; SATA 7;
  SATA-Essay 107; TCWW 1, 2; YAW

**Faulcon, Robert**
  See Holdstock, Robert

**Faulkner, William** 1897-1962 ........... **CLC 1,
3, 6, 8, 9, 11, 14, 18, 28, 52, 68; SSC 1,
35, 42, 92, 97, 191, 200, 204, 209, 222,
224, 228, 231; TCLC 141, 334; WLC 2**
  See also AAYA 7; AMW; AMWR 1; BPFB
  1; BYA 5, 15; CA 81-84; CANR 33;
  CDALB 1929-1941; DA; DA3; DAB; DAC;
  DAM MST, NOV; DLB 9, 11, 44, 102, 316,
  330; DLBD 2; DLBY 1986, 1997; EWL 3;
  EXPN; EXPS; GL 2; LAIT 2; LATS 1:1;
  LMFS 2; MAL 5; MTCW 1, 2; MTFW
  2005; NFS 4, 8, 13, 24, 33, 38; RGAL 4;
  RGSF 2; SSFS 2, 5, 6, 12, 27; TUS

**Faulkner, William Cuthbert**
  See Faulkner, William

**Fauset, Jessie Redmon** 1882-1961 .... **BLC 1:2;
CLC 19, 54; HR 1:2; TCLC 373**
  See also AFAW 2; BW 1; CA 109; CANR
  83; DAM MULT; DLB 51; FW; LMFS 2;
  MAL 5; MAA; SSFS 43

**Faust, Frederick** 1892-1944 .......... **TCLC 49**
  See also BPFB 1; CA 108; 152; CANR 143;
  DAM POP; DLB 256; TCWW 1, 2; TUS

**Faust, Frederick Schiller**
  See Faust, Frederick

**Faust, Irvin** 1924-2012 ....................... **CLC 8**
  See also CA 33-36R; CANR 28, 67; CN 1,
  2, 3, 4, 5, 6, 7; DLB 2, 28, 218, 278;
  DLBY 1980

**Faverón Patriau, Gustavo** 1966- .... **CLC 389**
  See also CA 368

**Fawkes, Guy**
  See Benchley, Robert (Charles)

**Fearing, Kenneth** 1902-1961 ........... **CLC 51**
  See also CA 93-96; CANR 59; CMW 4;
  DLB 9; MAL 5; RGAL 4

**Fearing, Kenneth Flexner**
  See Fearing, Kenneth

**Fecamps, Elise**
  See Creasey, John

**Federman, Raymond** 1928-2009 ... **CLC 6, 47**
  See also CA 17-20R, 208; 292; CAAE 208;
  CAAS 8; CANR 10, 43, 83, 108; CN 3, 4,
  5, 6; DLBY 1980

**Federspiel, J.F.** 1931-2007 .............. **CLC 42**
　　See also CA 146; 257
**Federspiel, Jurg F.**
　　See Federspiel, J.F.
**Federspiel, Juerg F.**
　　See Federspiel, J.F.
**Feiffer, Jules** 1929- .................. **CLC 2, 8, 64**
　　See also AAYA 3, 62; CA 17-20R; CAD;
　　CANR 30, 59, 129, 161, 192; CD 5, 6;
　　DAM DRAM; DLB 7, 44; INT CANR-30;
　　MTCW 1; SATA 8, 61, 111, 157, 201, 243
**Feiffer, Jules Ralph**
　　See Feiffer, Jules
**Feige, Hermann Albert Otto Maximilian**
　　See Traven, B.
**Fei-Kan, Li**
　　See Jin, Ba
**Feinberg, David B.** 1956-1994 ........ **CLC 59**
　　See also CA 135; 147
**Feinstein, Elaine** 1930- .................... **CLC 36**
　　See also CA 69-72; CAAS 1; CANR 31, 68,
　　121, 162; CN 3, 4, 5, 6, 7; CP 2, 3, 4, 5, 6,
　　7; CWP; DLB 14, 40; MTCW 1
**Feke, Gilbert David** ........................ **CLC 65**
**Feldman, Irving (Mordecai)** 1928- ... **CLC 7**
　　See also CA 1-4R; CANR 1; CP 1, 2, 3, 4, 5,
　　6, 7; DLB 169; TCLE 1:1
**Felix-Tchicaya, Gerald**
　　See Tchicaya, Gerald Felix
**Fellini, Federico** 1920-1993 ....... **CLC 16, 85**
　　See also CA 65-68; 143; CANR 33
**Felltham, Owen** 1602(?)-1668 ........... **LC 92**
　　See also DLB 126, 151
**Felsen, Henry Gregor** 1916-1995 ... **CLC 17**
　　See also CA 1-4R; 180; CANR 1; SAAS 2;
　　SATA 1
**Felski, Rita** ........................................ **CLC 65**
**Fenelon, Francois de Pons de Salignac de la**
　　**Mothe-** 1651-1715 .................... **LC 134**
　　See also DLB 268; EW 3; GFL Beginnings
　　to 1789
**Fenno, Jack**
　　See Calisher, Hortense
**Fenollosa, Ernest (Francisco)**
　　1853-1908 ............................... **TCLC 91**
**Fenton, James** 1949- ............... **CLC 32, 209**
　　See also CA 102; CANR 108, 160; CP 2, 3,
　　4, 5, 6, 7; DLB 40; PFS 11
**Fenton, James Martin**
　　See Fenton, James
**Fenwick, Eliza** 1766-1840 ........... **NCLC 301**
**Ferber, Edna** 1887-1968 ........... **CLC 18, 93**
　　See also AITN 1; CA 5-8R; 25-28R; CANR
　　68, 105; DLB 9, 28, 86, 266; MAL 5;
　　MTCW 1, 2; MTFW 2005; RGAL 4;
　　RHW; SATA 7; TCWW 1, 2
**Ferdousi**
　　See Ferdowsi, Abu'l Qasem
**Ferdovsi**
　　See Ferdowsi, Abu'l Qasem
**Ferdowsi**
　　See Ferdowsi, Abu'l Qasem
**Ferdowsi, Abolghasem Mansour**
　　See Ferdowsi, Abu'l Qasem
**Ferdowsi, Abolqasem**
　　See Ferdowsi, Abu'l Qasem
**Ferdowsi, Abol-Qasem**
　　See Ferdowsi, Abu'l Qasem
**Ferdowsi, Abu'l Qasem**
　　940-1020(?) ............................. **CMLC 43**
　　See also CA 276; RGWL 2, 3; WLIT 6
**Ferdowsi, A.M.**
　　See Ferdowsi, Abu'l Qasem
**Ferdowsi, Hakim Abolghasem**
　　See Ferdowsi, Abu'l Qasem
**Ferguson, Helen**
　　See Kavan, Anna

**Ferguson, Niall** 1964- ............. **CLC 134, 250**
　　See also CA 190; CANR 154, 200
**Ferguson, Niall Campbell**
　　See Ferguson, Niall
**Ferguson, Samuel** 1810-1886 ........ **NCLC 33**
　　See also DLB 32; RGEL 2
**Fergusson, Robert** 1750-1774 .......... **LC 29;**
　　**PC 157**
　　See also DLB 109; RGEL 2
**Ferling, Lawrence**
　　See Ferlinghetti, Lawrence
**Ferlinghetti, Lawrence** 1919(?)- .... **CLC 2, 6,**
　　**10, 27, 111; PC 1**
　　See also AAYA 74; BG 1:2; CA 5-8R; CAD;
　　CANR 3, 41, 73, 125, 172; CDALB 1941-
　　1968; CP 1, 2, 3, 4, 5, 6, 7; DA3; DAM
　　POET; DLB 5, 16; MAL 5; MTCW 1, 2;
　　MTFW 2005; PFS 28, 41; RGAL 4; WP
**Ferlinghetti, Lawrence Monsanto**
　　See Ferlinghetti, Lawrence
**Fern, Fanny**
　　See Parton, Sara Payson Willis
**Fernandez, Vicente Garcia Huidobro**
　　See Huidobro Fernandez, Vicente Garcia
**Fernández Cubas, Cristina** 1945- ... **SSC 205**
　　See also CA 211; EWL 3
**Fernandez de Lizardi, Jose Joaquin**
　　See Lizardi, Jose Joaquin Fernandez de
**Fernández Retamar, Roberto**
　　1930- ....................................... **CLC 391**
　　See also CA 131; HW 1
**Fernandez-Armesto, Felipe** 1950- .... **CLC 70**
　　See also CA 142; CANR 93, 153, 189
**Fernandez-Armesto, Felipe Fermin Ricardo**
　　See Fernandez-Armesto, Felipe
**Ferre, Rosario** 1938- ............. **CLC 139, 328;**
　　**HLCS 1; SSC 36, 106**
　　See also CA 131; CANR 55, 81, 134; CWW
　　2; DLB 145; EWL 3; HW 1, 2; LAWS 1;
　　MTCW 2; MTFW 2005; WLIT 1
**Ferrer, Gabriel (Francisco Victor) Miro**
　　See Miro (Ferrer), Gabriel (Francisco Victor)
**Ferrier, Susan (Edmonstone)**
　　1782-1854 ................................... **NCLC 8**
　　See also DLB 116; RGEL 2
**Ferrigno, Robert** 1947- .................... **CLC 65**
　　See also CA 140; CANR 125, 161
**Ferris, Joshua** 1974- ....................... **CLC 280**
　　See also CA 262
**Ferron, Jacques** 1921-1985 ............. **CLC 94**
　　See also CA 117; 129; CCA 1; DAC; DLB 60;
　　EWL 3
**Feuchtwanger, Lion** 1884-1958 ... **TCLC 3, 321**
　　See also CA 104; 187; DLB 66; EWL 3; RGHL
**Feuerbach, Ludwig** 1804-1872 .... **NCLC 139**
　　See also DLB 133
**Feuillet, Octave** 1821-1890 ........... **NCLC 45**
　　See also DLB 192
**Feydeau, Georges** 1862-1921 ......... **TCLC 22**
　　See also CA 113; 152; CANR 84; DAM
　　DRAM; DLB 192; EWL 3; GFL 1789 to
　　the Present; RGWL 2, 3
**Feydeau, Georges Leon JulesMarie**
　　See Feydeau, Georges
**Fichte, Johann Gottlieb**
　　1762-1814 ....................... **NCLC 62, 261**
　　See also DLB 90
**Ficino, Marsilio** 1433-1499 ........ **LC 12, 152**
　　See also LMFS 1
**Fiedeler, Hans**
　　See Döblin, Alfred
**Fiedler, Leslie A(aron)**
　　1917-2003 ....................... **CLC 4, 13, 24**
　　See also AMWS 13; CA 9-12R; 212; CANR
　　7, 63; CN 1, 2, 3, 4, 5, 6; DLB 28, 67; EWL
　　3; MAL 5; MTCW 1, 2; RGAL 4; TUS
**Field, Andrew** 1938- ....................... **CLC 44**
　　See also CA 97-100; CANR 25

**Field, Eugene** 1850-1895 .................. **NCLC 3**
　　See also DLB 23, 42, 140; DLBD 13; MAI-
　　CYA 1, 2; RGAL 4; SATA 16
**Field, Gans T.**
　　See Wellman, Manly Wade
**Field, Kate** 1838-1896 .................. **NCLC 307**
**Field, Michael** 1915-1971 .............. **TCLC 43**
　　See also CA 29-32R
**Fielding, Helen** 1958- ............. **CLC 146, 217**
　　See also AAYA 65; CA 172; CANR 127;
　　DLB 231; MTFW 2005
**Fielding, Henry** 1707-1754 .... **LC 1, 46, 85,**
　　**151, 154, 252; WLC 2**
　　See also BRW 3; BRWR 1; CDBLB 1660-
　　1789; DA; DA3; DAB; DAC; DAM DRAM,
　　MST, NOV; DFS 28; DLB 39, 84, 101; NFS
　　18, 32; RGEL 2; TEA; WLIT 3
**Fielding, Sarah** 1710-1768 ..... **LC 1, 44, 223**
　　See also DLB 39; RGEL 2; TEA
**Fields, James T.** 1817-1881 ......... **NCLC 362**
　　See also DLB 1, 235
**Fields, W. C.** 1880-1946 ............... **TCLC 80**
　　See also DLB 44
**Fierstein, Harvey** 1954- .................. **CLC 33**
　　See also CA 123; 129; CAD; CD 5, 6; CPW;
　　DA3; DAM DRAM, POP; DFS 6; DLB
　　266; GLL; MAL 5
**Fierstein, Harvey Forbes**
　　See Fierstein, Harvey
**Figes, Eva** 1932- .............................. **CLC 31**
　　See also CA 53-56; CANR 4, 44, 83, 207; CN
　　2, 3, 4, 5, 6, 7; DLB 14, 271; FW; RGHL
**Filippo, Eduardo de**
　　See de Filippo, Eduardo
**Finch, Anne** 1661-1720 ....... **LC 3, 137, 277;**
　　**PC 21, 156**
　　See also BRWS 9; DLB 95; PFS 30; RGEL 2
**Finch, Robert (Duer Claydon)**
　　1900-1995 ................................. **CLC 18**
　　See also CA 57-60; CANR 9, 24, 49; CP 1,
　　2, 3, 4, 5, 6; DLB 88
**Findley, Timothy** 1930-2002 ... **CLC 27, 102;**
　　**SSC 145**
　　See also AMWS 20; CA 25-28R; 206; CANR
　　12, 42, 69, 109; CCA 1; CN 4, 5, 6, 7;
　　DAC; DAM MST; DLB 53; FANT; RHW
**Fink, William**
　　See Mencken, H. L.
**Firbank, Louis**
　　See Reed, Lou
**Firbank, (Arthur Annesley) Ronald**
　　1886-1926 ................................. **TCLC 1**
　　See also BRWS 2; CA 104; 177; DLB 36;
　　EWL 3; RGEL 2
**Firdaosi**
　　See Ferdowsi, Abu'l Qasem
**Firdausi**
　　See Ferdowsi, Abu'l Qasem
**Firdavsii, Abulqosimi**
　　See Ferdowsi, Abu'l Qasem
**Firdavsi, Abulqosimi**
　　See Ferdowsi, Abu'l Qasem
**Firdawsi, Abu al-Qasim**
　　See Ferdowsi, Abu'l Qasem
**Firdosi**
　　See Ferdowsi, Abu'l Qasem
**Firdousi, Abu'l-Qasim**
　　See Ferdowsi, Abu'l Qasem
**Firdousi**
　　See Ferdowsi, Abu'l Qasem
**Firdovsi, A.**
　　See Ferdowsi, Abu'l Qasem
**Firdovsi, Abulgasim**
　　See Ferdowsi, Abu'l Qasem
**Firdusi**
　　See Ferdowsi, Abu'l Qasem
**Fish, Stanley** 1938- ................. **CLC 142, 343**
　　See also CA 112; 132; CANR 90; DLB 67

**Fish, Stanley E.**
See Fish, Stanley

**Fish, Stanley Eugene**
See Fish, Stanley

**Fisher, Dorothy (Frances) Canfield**
1879-1958 ................................ **TCLC 87**
See also CA 114; 136; CANR 80; CLR 71;
CWRI 5; DLB 9, 102, 284; MAICYA 1, 2;
MAL 5; YABC 1

**Fisher, Mary Frances Kennedy**
See Fisher, M.F.K.

**Fisher, M. F. K.** 1908-1992 ....... **CLC 76, 87**
See also AMWS 17; CA 77-80; 138; CANR
44, 241; MTCW 2

**Fisher, Roy** 1930- .............. **CLC 25; PC 121**
See also CA 81-84; CAAS 10; CANR 16;
CP 1, 2, 3, 4, 5, 6, 7; DLB 40

**Fisher, Rudolph**
1897-1934 ................ **BLC 1:2; HR 1:2;**
**SSC 25; TCLC 11, 255**
See also BW 1, 3; CA 107; 124; CANR 80;
DAM MULT; DLB 51, 102

**Fisher, Vardis (Alvero)** 1895-1968 ... **CLC 7;**
**TCLC 140**
See also CA 5-8R; 25-28R; CANR 68; DLB 9,
206; MAL 5; RGAL 4; TCWW 1, 2

**Fishman, Boris** 1979- ...................... **CLC 389**
See also CA 362

**Fiske, Tarleton**
See Bloch, Robert (Albert)

**Fitch, Clarke**
See Sinclair, Upton

**Fitch, John IV**
See Cormier, Robert

**Fitzgerald, Captain Hugh**
See Baum, L. Frank

**FitzGerald, Edward**
1809-1883 ........... **NCLC 9, 153; PC 79**
See also BRW 4; DLB 32; RGEL 2

**Fitzgerald, F. Scott** 1896-1940 .... **SSC 6, 31,**
**75, 143, 233; TCLC 1, 6, 14, 28, 55, 157,**
**280, 311; WLC 2**
See also AAYA 24; AITN 1; AMW; AMWC
2; AMWR 1; BPFB 1; CA 110; 123;
CDALB 1917-1929; CLR 176; DA; DA3;
DAB; DAC; DAM MST, NOV; DLB 4, 9,
86, 219, 273; DLBD 1, 15, 16; DLBY
1981, 1996; EWL 3; EXPN; EXPS; LAIT
3; MAL 5; MTCW 1, 2; MTFW 2005;
NFS 2, 19, 20; RGAL 4; RGSF 2; SSFS 4,
15, 21, 25, 36; TUS

**Fitzgerald, Francis Scott Key**
See Fitzgerald, F. Scott

**Fitzgerald, Penelope**
1916-2000 .............. **CLC 19, 51, 61, 143**
See also BRWS 5; CA 85-88; 190; CAAS
10; CANR 56, 86, 131; CN 3, 4, 5, 6, 7;
DLB 14, 194, 326; EWL 3; MTCW 2;
MTFW 2005

**Fitzgerald, Robert (Stuart)**
1910-1985 .............................. **CLC 39**
See also CA 1-4R; 114; CANR 1; CP 1, 2, 3,
4; DLBY 1980; MAL 5

**FitzGerald, Robert D(avid)**
1902-1987 ................................ **CLC 19**
See also CA 17-20R; CP 1, 2, 3, 4; DLB
260; RGEL 2

**Fitzgerald, Zelda (Sayre)**
1900-1948 ...................... **TCLC 52, 355**
See also AMWS 9; CA 117; 126; DLBY 1984

**Flagg, Fannie** 1941- ......................... **CLC 297**
See also CA 111; CANR 40, 238; CPW;
CSW; DA3; DAM POP; NFS 7

**Flaherty, Robert J.** 1884-1951 .... **TCLC 372**
See also CA 115

**Flanagan, Richard** 1961- .............. **CLC 389**
See also CA 195; CANR 169, 213

**Flanagan, Thomas (James Bonner)**
1923-2002 ............................ **CLC 25, 52**

See also CA 108; 206; CANR 55; CN 3, 4,
5, 6, 7; DLBY 1980; INT CA-108; MTCW
1; RHW; TCLE 1:1

**Flashman, Harry Paget**
See Fraser, George MacDonald

**Flaubert, Gustave** 1821-1880 ......... **NCLC 2,**
**10, 19, 62, 66, 135, 179, 185, 251; SSC**
**11, 60, 182, 187; WLC 2**
See also DA; DA3; DAB; DAC; DAM MST,
NOV; DLB 119, 301, 366; EW 7; EXPS;
GFL 1789 to the Present; LAIT 2; LMFS
1; NFS 14; RGSF 2; RGWL 2, 3; SSFS 6;
TWA

**Flavius Josephus**
See Josephus, Flavius

**Flecker, Herman Elroy**
See Flecker, (Herman) James Elroy

**Flecker, (Herman) James Elroy**
1884-1915 ................................ **TCLC 43**
See also CA 109; 150; DLB 10, 19; RGEL 2

**Fleming, Ian** 1908-1964 .............. **CLC 3, 30;**
**TCLC 193**
See also AAYA 26; BPFB 1; BRWS 14; CA
5-8R; CANR 59; CDBLB 1945-1960;
CMW 4; CPW; DA3; DAM POP; DLB
87, 201; MSW; MTCW 1, 2; MTFW 2005;
RGEL 2; SATA 9; TEA; YAW

**Fleming, Ian Lancaster**
See Fleming, Ian

**Fleming, Thomas** 1927- ...................... **CLC 37**
See also CA 5-8R; CANR 10, 102, 155, 197;
INT CANR-10; SATA 8

**Fleming, Thomas James**
See Fleming, Thomas

**Fletcher, John** 1579-1625 .............. **DC 6; LC**
**33, 151**
See also BRW 2; CDBLB Before 1660; DLB
58; RGEL 2; TEA

**Fletcher, John Gould** 1886-1950 ... **TCLC 35**
See also CA 107; 167; DLB 4, 45; LMFS 2;
MAL 5; RGAL 4

**Fleur, Paul**
See Pohl, Frederik

**Flieg, Helmut**
See Heym, Stefan

**Flooglebuckle, Al**
See Spiegelman, Art

**Flournoy, Angela** 1985- ................. **CLC 405**
See also CA 380

**Flying Officer X**
See Bates, H(erbert) E(rnest)

**Fo, Dario** 1926- ... **CLC 32, 109, 227; DC 10**
See also CA 116; 128; CANR 68, 114, 134,
164; CWW 2; DA3; DAM DRAM; DFS
23; DLB 330; DLBY 1997; EWL 3;
MTCW 1, 2; MTFW 2005; WLIT 7

**Foden, Giles** 1967- .......................... **CLC 231**
See also CA 240; DLB 267; NFS 15

**Foer, Jonathan Safran** 1977- ........ **CLC 301**
See also AAYA 57; CA 204; CANR 160;
MTFW 2005; NFS 36

**Fogarty, Jonathan Titulescu Esq.**
See Farrell, James T(homas)

**Fogazzaro, Antonio** 1842-1911 ... **TCLC 355**

**Follett, Ken** 1949- ............................. **CLC 18**
See also AAYA 6, 50; BEST 89:4; BPFB 1;
CA 81-84; CANR 13, 33, 54, 102, 156,
197, 229; CMW 4; CPW; DA3; DAM
NOV, POP; DLB 87; DLBY 1981; INT
CANR-33; LNFS 3; MTCW 1

**Follett, Kenneth Martin**
See Follett, Ken

**Fondane, Benjamin** 1898-1944 ... **TCLC 159**

**Fonseca, Rubem** 1925- ................... **SSC 270**
See also CA 189; CANR 211; DLB 307;
EWL 3

**Fontane, Theodor** 1819-1898 **NCLC 26, 163**
See also CDWLB 2; DLB 129; EW 6;
RGWL 2, 3; TWA

**Fonte, Moderata** 1555-1592 ............. **LC 118**

**Fontenelle, Bernard Le Bovier de**
1657-1757 ................................ **LC 140**
See also DLB 268, 313; GFL Beginnings
to 1789

**Fontenot, Chester** ......................... **CLC 65**

**Fonvizin, Denis Ivanovich**
1744(?)-1792 ............................ **LC 81**
See also DLB 150; RGWL 2, 3

**Foote, Albert Horton**
See Foote, Horton

**Foote, Horton** 1916-2009 .......... **CLC 51, 91;**
**DC 42**
See also AAYA 82; CA 73-76; 284; CAD;
CANR 34, 51, 110; CD 5, 6; CSW; DA3;
DAM DRAM; DFS 20; DLB 26, 266;
EWL 3; INT CANR-34; MTFW 2005

**Foote, Mary Hallock** 1847-1938 ... **SSC 150;**
**TCLC 108**
See also DLB 186, 188, 202, 221; TCWW 2

**Foote, Samuel** 1721-1777 ................. **LC 106**
See also DLB 89; RGEL 2

**Foote, Shelby** 1916-2005 .......... **CLC 75, 224**
See also AAYA 40; CA 5-8R; 240; CANR 3,
45, 74, 131; CN 1, 2, 3, 4, 5, 6, 7; CPW;
CSW; DA3; DAM NOV, POP; DLB 2, 17;
MAL 5; MTCW 2; MTFW 2005; RHW

**Forbes, Cosmo**
See Lewton, Val

**Forbes, Esther** 1891-1967 ................ **CLC 12**
See also AAYA 17; BYA 2; CA 13-14; 25-
28R; CAP 1; CLR 27, 147; DLB 22;
JRDA; MAICYA 1, 2; RHW; SATA 2,
100; YAW

**Forche, Carolyn** 1950- ....... **CLC 25, 83, 86;**
**PC 10**
See also CA 109; 117; CANR 50, 74, 138;
CP 4, 5, 6, 7; CWP; DA3; DAM POET;
DLB 5, 193; INT CA-117; MAL 5; MTCW
2; MTFW 2005; PFS 18, 43; RGAL 4

**Forche, Carolyn Louise**
See Forche, Carolyn

**Ford, Elbur**
See Hibbert, Eleanor Alice Burford

**Ford, Ford Madox** 1873-1939 ........ **TCLC 1,**
**15, 39, 57, 172, 308, 309**
See also BRW 6; CA 104; 132; CANR 74;
CDBLB 1914-1945; DA3; DAM NOV;
DLB 34, 98, 162; EWL 3; MTCW 1, 2;
NFS 28; RGEL 2; RHW; TEA

**Ford, Helen**
See Garner, Helen

**Ford, Henry** 1863-1947 .................. **TCLC 73**
See also CA 115; 148

**Ford, Jack**
See Ford, John

**Ford, John** 1586-1639 .... **DC 8; LC 68, 153**
See also BRW 2; CDBLB Before 1660;
DA3; DAM DRAM; DFS 7; DLB 58;
IDTP; RGEL 2

**Ford, John** 1895-1973 ...................... **CLC 16**
See also AAYA 75; CA 187; 45-48

**Ford, Richard** 1944- ......... **CLC 46, 99, 205,**
**277; SSC 143**
See also AMWS 5; CA 69-72; CANR 11,
47, 86, 128, 164; CN 5, 6, 7; CSW; DLB
227; EWL 3; MAL 5; MTCW 2; MTFW
2005; NFS 25; RGAL 4; RGSF 2

**Ford, Webster**
See Masters, Edgar Lee

**Foreman, Richard** 1937- .................. **CLC 50**
See also CA 65-68; CAD; CANR 32, 63,
143; CD 5, 6

**Forester, C. S.** 1899-1966 ............... **CLC 35;**
**TCLC 152**
See also CA 73-76; 25-28R; CANR 83; DLB
191; RGEL 2; RHW; SATA 13

**Forester, Cecil Scott**
See Forester, C. S.

**Forez**
See Mauriac, Francois (Charles)

**Forman, James**
See Forman, James D.

**Forman, James D.** 1932-2009 ......... **CLC 21**
See also AAYA 17; CA 9-12R; CANR 4, 19, 42; JRDA; MAICYA 1, 2; SATA 8, 70; YAW

**Forman, James Douglas**
See Forman, James D.

**Forman, Milos** 1932- ...................... **CLC 164**
See also AAYA 63; CA 109

**Fornes, Maria Irene** 1930- ....... **CLC 39, 61, 187; DC 10; HLCS 1**
See also CA 25-28R; CAD; CANR 28, 81; CD 5, 6; CWD; DFS 25; DLB 7, 341; HW 1, 2; INT CANR-28; LLW; MAL 5; MTCW 1; RGAL 4

**Forrest, Leon (Richard)**
1937-1997 ...................... **BLCS; CLC 4**
See also AFAW 2; BW 2; CA 89-92; 162; CAAS 7; CANR 25, 52, 87; CN 4, 5, 6; DLB 33

**Forster, E. M.** 1879-1970 ........ **CLC 1, 2, 3, 4, 9, 10, 13, 15, 22, 45, 77; SSC 27, 96, 201; TCLC 125, 264; WLC 2**
See also AAYA 2, 37; BRW 6; BRWR 2; BYA 12; CA 13-14; 25-28R; CANR 45; CAP 1; CDBLB 1914-1945; DA; DA3; DAB; DAC; DAM MST, NOV; DLB 34, 98, 162, 178, 195; DLBD 10; EWL 3; EXPN; LAIT 3; LMFS 1; MTCW 1, 2; MTFW 2005; NCFS 1; NFS 3, 10, 11; RGEL 2; RGSF 2; SATA 57; SUFW 1; TEA; WLIT 4

**Forster, Edward Morgan**
See Forster, E. M.

**Forster, John** 1812-1876 ....... **NCLC 11, 363**
See also DLB 144, 184

**Forster, Margaret** 1938- ................ **CLC 149**
See also CA 133; CANR 62, 115, 175; CN 4, 5, 6, 7; DLB 155, 271

**Forsyth, Frederick** 1938- ........ **CLC 2, 5, 36**
See also BEST 89:4; CA 85-88; CANR 38, 62, 115, 137, 183, 242; CMW 4; CN 3, 4, 5, 6, 7; CPW; DAM NOV, POP; DLB 87; MTCW 1, 2; MTFW 2005

**Fort, Paul**
See Stockton, Francis Richard

**Forten, Charlotte**
See Grimke, Charlotte L. Forten

**Forten, Charlotte L.** 1837-1914
See Grimke, Charlotte L. Forten

**Fortinbras**
See Grieg, (Johan) Nordahl (Brun)

**Foscolo, Ugo** 1778-1827 ... **NCLC 8, 97, 274**
See also EW 5; WLIT 7

**Fosse, Bob** 1927-1987 ...................... **CLC 20**
See also AAYA 82; CA 110; 123

**Fosse, Robert L.**
See Fosse, Bob

**Foster, Hannah Webster**
1758-1840 ...................... **NCLC 99, 252**
See also DLB 37, 200; RGAL 4

**Foster, Stephen Collins** 1826-1864 .. **NCLC 26**
See also RGAL 4

**Foucault, Michel**
1926-1984 ...................... **CLC 31, 34, 69**
See also CA 105; 113; CANR 34; DLB 242; EW 13; EWL 3; GFL 1789 to the Present; GLL 1; LMFS 2; MTCW 1, 2; TWA

**Fountain, Ben** 1958- ...................... **CLC 354**
See also CA 254; CANR 254

**Fouqué, Caroline de la Motte** 1774-
1831 ...................... **NCLC 307**
See also DLB 90; RGWL 2, 3

**Fouque, Friedrich (Heinrich Karl) de la Motte**
1777-1843 ...................... **NCLC 2**
See also DLB 90; RGWL 2, 3; SUFW 1

**Fourier, Charles** 1772-1837 .......... **NCLC 51**

**Fournier, Henri-Alban**
See Alain-Fournier

**Fournier, Pierre** 1916-1997 ............. **CLC 11**
See also CA 89-92; CANR 16, 40; EWL 3; RGHL

**Fourth Earl of Chesterfield**
See Stanhope, Philip Dormer

**Fowles, John** 1926-2005 ....... **CLC 1, 2, 3, 4, 6, 9, 10, 15, 33, 87, 287, 422; SSC 33, 128**
See also BPFB 1; BRWS 1; CA 5-8R; 245; CANR 25, 71, 103; CDBLB 1960 to Present; CN 1, 2, 3, 4, 5, 6, 7; DA3; DAB; DAC; DAM MST; DLB 14, 139, 207; EWL 3; HGG; MTCW 1, 2; MTFW 2005; NFS 21; RGEL 2; RHW; SATA 22; SATA-Obit 171; TEA; WLIT 4

**Fowles, John Robert**
See Fowles, John

**Fox, Norma Diane**
See Mazer, Norma Fox

**Fox, Paula** 1923- ...................... **CLC 2, 8, 121**
See also AAYA 3, 37; BYA 3, 8; CA 73-76; CANR 20, 36, 62, 105, 200, 237; CLR 1, 44, 96; DLB 52; JRDA; MAICYA 1, 2; MTCW 1; NFS 12; SATA 17, 60, 120, 167; WYA; YAW

**Fox, William Price, Jr.**
See Fox, William Price

**Fox, William Price** 1926- ................. **CLC 22**
See also CA 17-20R; CAAS 19; CANR 11, 142, 189; CSW; DLB 2; DLBY 1981

**Foxe, John** 1517(?)-1587 ............. **LC 14, 166**
See also DLB 132

**Frame, Janet** 1924-2004 ... **CLC 2, 3, 6, 22, 66, 96, 237; SSC 29, 127**
See also CA 1-4R; 224; CANR 2, 36, 76, 135, 216; CN 1, 2, 3, 4, 5, 6, 7; CP 2, 3, 4; CWP; EWL 3; MTCW 1,2; RGEL 2; RGSF 2; SATA 119; TWA

**Frame, Janet Paterson**
See Frame, Janet

**France, Anatole** 1844-1924 ............. **TCLC 9**
See also CA 106; 127; DA3; DAM NOV; DLB 123, 330; EWL 3; GFL 1789 to the Present; MTCW 1, 2; RGWL 2, 3; SUFW 1; TWA

**Francis, Claude** ...................... **CLC 50**
See also CA 192

**Francis, Dick**
1920-2010 ............... **CLC 2, 22, 42, 102**
See also AAYA 5, 21; BEST 89:3; BPFB 1; CA 5-8R; CANR 9, 42, 68, 100, 141, 179; CDBLB 1960 to Present; CMW 4; CN 2, 3, 4, 5, 6; DA3; DAM POP; DLB 87; INT CANR-9; MSW; MTCW 1, 2; MTFW 2005

**Francis, Paula Marie**
See Allen, Paula Gunn

**Francis, Richard Stanley**
See Francis, Dick

**Francis, Robert (Churchill)**
1901-1987 ...................... **CLC 15; PC 34**
See also AMWS 9; CA 1-4R; 123; CANR 1; CP 1, 2, 3, 4; EXPP; PFS 12; TCLE 1:1

**Francis, Lord Jeffrey**
See Jeffrey, Francis

**Franco, Veronica** 1546-1591 ............. **LC 171**
See also WLIT 7

**Frank, Anne** 1929-1945 ............... **TCLC 17; WLC 2**
See also AAYA 12; BYA 1; CA 113; 133; CANR 68; CLR 101, 189; DA; DA3; DAB; DAC; DAM MST; LAIT 4; MAICYA 2; MAICYAS 1; MTCW 1, 2; MTFW 2005; NCFS 2; RGHL; SATA 87; SATA-Brief 42; WYA; YAW

**Frank, Annelies Marie**
See Frank, Anne

**Frank, Bruno** 1887-1945 ............... **TCLC 81**
See also CA 189; DLB 118; EWL 3

**Frank, Elizabeth** 1945- ................... **CLC 39**
See also CA 121; 126; CANR 78, 150; INT CA-126

**Frankl, Viktor E(mil)** 1905-1997 .... **CLC 93**
See also CA 65-68; 161; RGHL

**Franklin, Benjamin**
See Hasek, Jaroslav

**Franklin, Benjamin**
1706-1790 ..... **LC 25, 134, 271; WLCS**
See also AMW; CDALB 1640-1865; DA; DA3; DAB; DAC; DAM MST; DLB 24, 43, 73, 183; LAIT 1; RGAL 4; TUS

**Franklin, Madeleine**
See L'Engle, Madeleine

**Franklin, Madeleine L'Engle**
See L'Engle, Madeleine

**Franklin, Madeleine L'Engle Camp**
See L'Engle, Madeleine

**Franklin, (Stella Maria Sarah) Miles (Lampe)**
1879-1954 ...................... **TCLC 7**
See also CA 104; 164; DLB 230; FW; MTCW 2; RGEL 2; TWA

**Franzen, Jonathan** 1959- ....... **CLC 202, 309**
See also AAYA 65; AMWS 20; CA 129; CANR 105, 166, 219; NFS 40;

**Franzos, Karl Emil** 1847?-1904 .. **TCLC 339**
See also DLB 129

**Fraser, Antonia** 1932- ................ **CLC 32, 107**
See also AAYA 57; CA 85-88; CANR 44, 65, 119, 164, 225; CMW; DLB 276; MTCW 1, 2; MTFW 2005; SATA-Brief 32

**Fraser, George MacDonald**
1925-2008 ...................... **CLC 7**
See also AAYA 48; CA 45-48; 180; 268; CAAE 180; CANR 2, 48, 74, 192; DLB 352; MTCW 2; RHW

**Fraser, Kathleen** 1935- ...................... **PC 199**
See also CA 106; CP 1, 3, 4, 5, 6, 7; CWP; DLB 169; PFS 29

**Fraser, Sylvia** 1935- ...................... **CLC 64**
See also CA 45-48; CANR 1, 16, 60; CCA 1

**Frater Perdurabo**
See Crowley, Edward Alexander

**Frayn, Michael** 1933- ............. **CLC 3, 7, 31, 47, 176, 315; DC 27**
See also AAYA 69; BRWC 2; BRWS 7; CA 5-8R; CANR 30, 69, 114, 133, 166, 229; CBD; CD 5, 6; CN 1, 2, 3, 4, 5, 6, 7; DAM DRAM, NOV; DFS 22, 28; DLB 13, 14, 194, 245; FANT; MTCW 1, 2; MTFW 2005; SFW 4

**Fraze, Candida** 1945- ...................... **CLC 50**
See also CA 126

**Fraze, Candida Merrill**
See Fraze, Candida

**Frazer, Andrew**
See Marlowe, Stephen

**Frazer, J(ames) G(eorge)**
1854-1941 ...................... **TCLC 32**
See also BRWS 3; CA 118; NCFS 5

**Frazer, Robert Caine**
See Creasey, John

**Frazer, Sir James George**
See Frazer, J(ames) G(eorge)

**Frazier, Charles** 1950- ... **CLC 109, 224, 396**
See also AAYA 34; CA 161; CANR 126, 170, 235; CSW; DLB 292; MTFW 2005; NFS 25

**Frazier, Charles R.**
See Frazier, Charles

**Frazier, Charles Robinson**
See Frazier, Charles

**Frazier, Ian** 1951- ............................. **CLC 46**
See also CA 130; CANR 54, 93, 193, 227

**Frederic, Harold**
1856-1898 ...................... **NCLC 10, 175**
See also AMW; DLB 12, 23; DLBD 13; MAL 5; NFS 22; RGAL 4

**Frederick, John**
See Faust, Frederick

**Frederick the Great** 1712-1786 ......... **LC 14**

**Fredro, Aleksander** 1793-1876 ........ **NCLC 8**

**Freeling, Nicolas** 1927-2003 ............ **CLC 38**
See also CA 49-52; 218; CAAS 12; CANR
1, 17, 50, 84; CMW 4; CN 1, 2, 3, 4, 5, 6;
DLB 87

**Freeman, Douglas Southall**
1886-1953 ............................... **TCLC 11**
See also CA 109; 195; DLB 17; DLBD 17

**Freeman, Judith** 1946- ..................... **CLC 55**
See also CA 148; CANR 120, 179; DLB 256

**Freeman, Mary E(leanor) Wilkins**
1852-1930 .... **SSC 1, 47, 113, 223, 240;
TCLC 9**
See also CA 106; 177; DLB 12, 78, 221;
EXPS; FW; HGG; MBL; RGAL 4; RGSF
2; SSFS 4, 8, 26; SUFW 1; TUS

**Freeman, R(ichard) Austin**
1862-1943 ............................... **TCLC 21**
See also CA 113; CANR 84; CMW 4; DLB 70

**French, Albert** 1943- ........................ **CLC 86**
See also BW 3; CA 167

**French, Antonia**
See Kureishi, Hanif

**French, Marilyn** 1929-2009 ...... **CLC 10, 18,
60, 177**
See also BPFB 1; CA 69-72; 286; CANR 3,
31, 134, 163, 220; CN 5, 6, 7; CPW; DAM
DRAM, NOV, POP; FL 1:5; FW; INT
CANR-31; MTCW 1, 2; MTFW 2005

**French, Paul**
See Asimov, Isaac

**Freneau, Philip Morin** 1752-1832 ... **NCLC 1,
111, 253; PC 202**
See also AMWS 2; DLB 37, 43; RGAL 4

**Freud, Sigmund** 1856-1939 .......... **TCLC 52**
See also CA 115; 133; CANR 69; DLB 296;
EW 8; EWL 3; LATS 1:1; MTCW 1, 2;
MTFW 2005; NCFS 3; TWA

**Freytag, Gustav** 1816-1895 ........ **NCLC 109**
See also DLB 129

**Friedan, Betty** 1921-2006 ................ **CLC 74**
See also CA 65-68; 248; CANR 18, 45, 74;
DLB 246; FW; MTCW 1, 2; MTFW 2005;
NCFS 5

**Friedan, Betty Naomi**
See Friedan, Betty

**Friedlander, Saul**
See Friedlander, Saul

**Friedlander, Saul** 1932- ................... **CLC 90**
See also CA 117; 130; CANR 72, 214; RGHL

**Friedman, Bernard Harper**
See Friedman, B.H.

**Friedman, B.H.** 1926-2011 ............... **CLC 7**
See also CA 1-4R; CANR 3, 48

**Friedman, Bruce Jay** 1930- ... **CLC 3, 5, 56**
See also CA 9-12R; CAD; CANR 25, 52,
101, 212; CD 5, 6; CN 1, 2, 3, 4, 5, 6, 7;
DLB 2, 28, 244; INT CANR-25; MAL 5;
SSFS 18

**Friel, Brian** 1929- ......... **CLC 5, 42, 59, 115,
253; DC 8, 49; SSC 76**
See also BRWS 5; CA 21-24R; CANR 33,
69, 131; CBD; CD 5, 6; DFS 11; DLB 13,
319; EWL 3; MTCW 1; RGEL 2; TEA

**Friis-Baastad, Babbis Ellinor**
1921-1970 ................................ **CLC 12**
See also CA 17-20R; 134; SATA 7

**Frisch, Max** 1911-1991 .... **CLC 3, 9, 14, 18,
32, 44; TCLC 121**
See also CA 85-88; 134; CANR 32, 74;
CDWLB 2; DAM DRAM, NOV; DFS
25; DLB 69, 124; EW 13; EWL 3; MTCW
1, 2; MTFW 2005; RGHL; RGWL 2, 3

**Frischmuth, Barbara** 1941- .......... **CLC 372**
See also CA 178; DLB 85; SATA 114

**Froehlich, Peter**
See Gay, Peter

**Fromentin, Eugene (Samuel Auguste)**
1820-1876 ...................... **NCLC 10, 125**
See also DLB 123, 366; GFL 1789 to the
Present

**Frost, Frederick**
See Faust, Frederick

**Frost, Robert** 1874-1963 ...... **CLC 1, 3, 4, 9,
10, 13, 15, 26, 34, 44; PC 1, 39, 71, 173;
TCLC 236; WLC 2**
See also AAYA 21; AMW; AMWR 1; CA
89-92; CANR 33; CDALB 1917-1929;
CLR 67; DA; DA3; DAB; DAC; DAM
MST, POET; DLB 54, 284, 342; DLBD
7; EWL 3; EXPP; MAL 5; MTCW 1, 2;
MTFW 2005; PAB; PFS 1, 2, 3, 4, 5, 6, 7,
10, 13, 32, 35, 41; RGAL 4; SATA 14;
TUS; WP; WYA

**Frost, Robert Lee**
See Frost, Robert

**Froude, James Anthony**
1818-1894 ............................ **NCLC 43, 311**
See also DLB 18, 57, 144

**Froy, Herald**
See Waterhouse, Keith

**Fry, Christopher** 1907-2005 ....... **CLC 2, 10,
14; DC 36**
See also BRWS 3; CA 17-20R; 240; CAAS
23; CANR 9, 30, 74, 132; CBD; CD 5, 6;
CP 1, 2, 3, 4, 5, 6, 7; DAM DRAM; DLB
13; EWL 3; MTCW 1, 2; MTFW 2005;
RGEL 2; SATA 66; TEA

**Frye, (Herman) Northrop**
1912-1991 ...... **CLC 24, 70; TCLC 165**
See also CA 5-8R; 133; CANR 8, 37; DLB
67, 68, 246; EWL 3; MTCW 1, 2; MTFW
2005; RGAL 4; TWA

**Fuchs, Daniel** 1909-1993 .............. **CLC 8, 22**
See also CA 81-84; 142; CAAS 5; CANR
40; CN 1, 2, 3, 4, 5; DLB 9, 26, 28; DLBY
1993; MAL 5

**Fuchs, Daniel** 1934-2012 ................. **CLC 34**
See also CA 37-40R; CANR 14, 48

**Fuentes, Carlos** 1928- ...... **CLC 3, 8, 10, 13,
22, 41, 60, 113, 288, 354; HLC 1; SSC
24, 125; WLC 2**
See also AAYA 4, 45; AITN 2; BPFB 1; CA
69-72; CANR 10, 32, 68, 104, 138, 197;
CDWLB 3; CWW 2; DA; DA3; DAB;
DAC; DAM MST, MULT, NOV; DLB
113; DNFS 2; EWL 3; HW 1, 2; LAIT
3; LATS 1:2; LAW; LAWS 1; LMFS 2;
MTCW 1, 2; MTFW 2005; NFS 8; RGSF
2; RGWL 2, 3; TWA; WLIT 1

**Fuentes, Gregorio Lopez**
See Lopez y Fuentes, Gregorio

**Fuentes Macias, Carlos Manuel**
See Fuentes, Carlos

**Fuertes, Gloria**
1918-1998 ................ **PC 27; TCLC 271**
See also CA 178, 180; DLB 108; HW 2;
SATA 115

**Fugard, Athol** 1932- ............... **CLC 5, 9, 14,
25, 40, 80, 211; DC 3**
See also AAYA 17; AFW; BRWS 15; CA
85-88; CANR 32, 54, 118; CD 5, 6; DAM
DRAM; DFS 3, 6, 10, 24; DLB 225;
DNFS 1, 2; EWL 3; LATS 1:2; MTCW
1; MTFW 2005; RGEL 2; WLIT 2

**Fugard, Harold Athol**
See Fugard, Athol

**Fugard, Sheila** 1932- ....................... **CLC 48**
See also CA 125

**Fuguet, Alberto** 1964- ..................... **CLC 308**
See also CA 170; CANR 144

**Fujiwara no Teika** 1162-1241 ...... **CMLC 73**
See also DLB 203

**Fukuyama, Francis** 1952- ....... **CLC 131, 320**
See also CA 140; CANR 72, 125, 170, 233

**Fuller, Charles (H.), (Jr.)** 1939- .... **BLC 1:2;
CLC 25; DC 1**

See also BW 2; CA 108; 112; CAD; CANR
87; CD 5, 6; DAM DRAM, MULT; DFS 8;
DLB 38, 266; EWL 3; INT CA-112; MAL
5; MTCW 1

**Fuller, Henry Blake** 1857-1929 ... **TCLC 103**
See also CA 108; 177; DLB 12; RGAL 4

**Fuller, John (Leopold)** 1937- .......... **CLC 62**
See also CA 21-24R; CANR 9, 44; CP 1, 2,
3, 4, 5, 6, 7; DLB 40

**Fuller, Margaret**
1810-1850 .................. **NCLC 5, 50, 211**
See also AMWS 2; CDALB 1640-1865;
DLB 1, 59, 73, 183, 223, 239; FW; LMFS
1; SATA 25

**Fuller, Roy (Broadbent)**
1912-1991 ............................ **CLC 4, 28**
See also BRWS 7; CA 5-8R; 135; CAAS 10;
CANR 53, 83; CN 1, 2, 3, 4, 5; CP 1, 2, 3,
4, 5; CWRI 5; DLB 15, 20; EWL 3; RGEL
2; SATA 87

**Fuller, Sarah Margaret**
See Fuller, Margaret

**Fuller, Thomas** 1608-1661 ............... **LC 111**
See also DLB 151

**Fulton, Alice** 1952- .......................... **CLC 52**
See also CA 116; CANR 57, 88, 200; CP 5,
6, 7; CWP; DLB 193; PFS 25

**Fundi**
See Baraka, Amiri

**Furey, Michael**
See Ward, Arthur Henry Sarsfield

**Furphy, Joseph** 1843-1912 ............. **TCLC 25**
See also CA 163; DLB 230; EWL 3; RGEL 2

**Furst, Alan** 1941- ........................... **CLC 255**
See also CA 69-72; CANR 12, 34, 59, 102,
159, 193; DLB 350; DLBY 01

**Fuson, Robert H(enderson)** 1927- ... **CLC 70**
See also CA 89-92; CANR 103

**Fussell, Paul** 1924- .......................... **CLC 74**
See also BEST 90:1; CA 17-20R; CANR 8,
21, 35, 69, 135; INT CANR-21; MTCW 1,
2; MTFW 2005

**Futabatei, Shimei** 1864-1909 ......... **TCLC 44**
See also CA 162; DLB 180; EWL 3; MJW

**Futabatei Shimei**
See Futabatei, Shimei

**Futrelle, Jacques** 1875-1912 .......... **TCLC 19**
See also CA 113; 155; CMW 4

**GAB**
See Russell, George William

**Gaberman, Judie Angell**
See Angell, Judie

**Gaboriau, Emile** 1835-1873 .......... **NCLC 14**
See also CMW 4; MSW

**Gadamer, Hans-Georg**
1900-2002 ............................... **CLC 376**
See also CA 85-88, 206; DLB 296

**Gadda, Carlo Emilio** 1893-1973 .... **CLC 11;
TCLC 144**
See also CA 89-92; DLB 177; EWL 3;
WLIT 7

**Gaddis, William** 1922-1998 ..... **CLC 1, 3, 6,
8, 10, 19, 43, 86**
See also AMWS 4; BPFB 1; CA 17-20R;
172; CANR 21, 48, 148; CN 1, 2, 3, 4, 5,
6; DLB 2, 278; EWL 3; MAL 5; MTCW 1,
2; MTFW 2005; RGAL 4

**Gage, Walter**
See Inge, William (Motter)

**Gaiman, Neil** 1960- ........................ **CLC 319**
See also AAYA 19, 42, 82; CA 133; CANR
81, 129, 188; CLR 109, 177, 205; DLB
261; HGG; MTFW 2005; SATA 85, 146,
197, 228; SFW 4; SUFW 2

**Gaiman, Neil Richard**
See Gaiman, Neil

**Gaines, Ernest J.** 1933- ................ **BLC 1:2;
CLC 3, 11, 18, 86, 181, 300; SSC 68, 137**

See also BW 1; CA 120; 124; CANR 79;
  DAM MULT; DLB 345
**Gary, Romain**
  See Kacew, Romain
**Gascar, Pierre**
  See Fournier, Pierre
**Gascoigne, George** 1539-1577 .......... **LC 108**
  See also DLB 136; RGEL 2
**Gascoyne, David (Emery)**
  1916-2001 ................................. **CLC 45**
  See also CA 65-68; 200; CANR 10, 28, 54; CP
  1, 2, 3, 4, 5, 6, 7; DLB 20; MTCW 1; RGEL 2
**Gaskell, Elizabeth Cleghorn**
  1810-1865 .............................. **NCLC 5,**
  **70, 97, 137, 214, 264; SSC 25, 97, 218**
  See also AAYA 80; BRW 5; BRWR 3;
  CDBLB 1832-1890; DAB; DAM MST;
  DLB 21, 144, 159; RGEL 2; RGSF 2; TEA
**Gass, William H.** 1924- ..... **CLC 1, 2, 8, 11,**
  **15, 39, 132; SSC 12, 255**
  See also AMWS 6; CA 17-20R; CANR 30,
  71, 100; CN 1, 2, 3, 4, 5, 6, 7; DLB 2, 227;
  EWL 3; MAL 5; MTCW 1, 2; MTFW
  2005; RGAL 4
**Gassendi, Pierre** 1592-1655 ................ **LC 54**
  See also GFL Beginnings to 1789
**Gasset, Jose Ortega y**
  See Ortega y Gasset, Jose
**Gates, Henry Louis, Jr.**
  1950- ........................... **BLCS; CLC 65**
  See also AMWS 20; BW 2, 3; CA 109;
  CANR 25, 53, 75, 125, 203; CSW; DA3;
  DAM MULT; DLB 67; EWL 3; MAL 5;
  MTCW 2; MTFW 2005; RGAL 4
**Gatos, Stephanie**
  See Katz, Steve
**Gauden, John** 1605-1662 ................ **LC 237**
**Gautier, Theophile** 1811-1872 ........ **NCLC 1,**
  **59, 243, 267; PC 18; SSC 20**
  See also DAM POET; DLB 119, 366; EW 6;
  GFL 1789 to the Present; RGWL 2, 3;
  SUFW; TWA
**Gautreaux, Tim** 1947- ... **CLC 270; SSC 125**
  See also CA 187; CANR 207; CSW; DLB 292
**Gautreaux, Tim Martin**
  See Gautreaux, Tim
**Gay, John** 1685-1732 .. **DC 39, 48; LC 49, 176**
  See also BRW 3; DAM DRAM; DLB 84,
  95; RGEL 2; WLIT 3
**Gay, Oliver**
  See Gogarty, Oliver St. John
**Gay, Peter** 1923- ........................... **CLC 158**
  See also CA 13-16R; CANR 18, 41, 77, 147,
  196; INT CANR-18; RGHL
**Gay, Peter Jack**
  See Gay, Peter
**Gaye, Marvin (Pentz, Jr.)** 1939-1984 .. **CLC 26**
  See also CA 195; 112
**Gebler, Carlo** 1954- ........................ **CLC 39**
  See also CA 119; 133; CANR 96, 186;
  DLB 271
**Gebler, Carlo Ernest**
  See Gebler, Carlo
**Gee, Maggie** 1948- ........................ **CLC 57**
  See also CA 130; CANR 125; CN 4, 5, 6, 7;
  DLB 207; MTFW 2005
**Gee, Maurice** 1931- ........................ **CLC 29**
  See also AAYA 42; CA 97-100; CANR 67,
  123, 204; CLR 56; CN 2, 3, 4, 5, 6, 7;
  CWRI 5; EWL 3; MAICYA 2; RGSF 2;
  SATA 46, 101, 227
**Gee, Maurice Gough**
  See Gee, Maurice
**Geiogamah, Hanay** 1945- ................... **NNAL**
  See also CA 153; DAM MULT; DLB 175
**Gelbart, Larry** 1928-2009 ........ **CLC 21, 61**
  See also CA 73-76; 290; CAD; CANR 45,
  94; CD 5, 6

**Gelbart, Larry Simon**
  See Gelbart, Larry
**Gelber, Jack** 1932-2003 .... **CLC 1, 6, 14, 79**
  See also CA 1-4R; 216; CAD; CANR 2;
  DLB 7, 228; MAL 5
**Gellhorn, Martha** 1908-1998 ..... **CLC 14, 60**
  See Gellhorn, Martha Ellis
  See also CA 77-80; 164; CANR 44; CN 1, 2,
  3, 4, 5, 6 7; DLB 364; DLBY 1982, 1998
**Gellhorn, Martha Ellis**
  See Gellhorn, Martha
**Gellius, Aulus** c. 125-170/180? ... **CMLC 153**
  See also DLB 211
**Genet, Jean** 1910-1986 ............ **CLC 1, 2, 5,**
  **10, 14, 44, 46; DC 25; TCLC 128**
  See also CA 13-16R; CANR 18; DA3; DAM
  DRAM; DFS 10; DLB 72, 321; DLBY
  1986; EW 13; EWL 3; GFL 1789 to the
  Present; GLL 1; LMFS 2; MTCW 1, 2;
  MTFW 2005; RGWL 2, 3; TWA
**Genette, Gérard** 1930- ..................... **CLC 372**
  See also CA 238; DLB 242
**Genlis, Stephanie-Felicite Ducrest**
  1746-1830 ............................. **NCLC 166**
  See also DLB 313
**Gent, Peter** 1942-2011 ..................... **CLC 29**
  See also AITN 1; CA 89-92; DLBY 1982
**Gentile, Giovanni** 1875-1944 ........ **TCLC 96**
  See also CA 119
**Geoffrey of Monmouth**
  c. 1100-c. 1155 ......... **CMLC 44, 164;**
  **PC 140**
  See also DLB 146; TEA
**Geoffrey of Vinsauf**
  fl. c. 1208-1213 .......... **CMLC 129, 201**
**George, Jean**
  See George, Jean Craighead
**George, Jean C.**
  See George, Jean Craighead
**George, Jean Craighead** 1919- ....... **CLC 35**
  See also AAYA 8, 69; BYA 2, 4; CA 5-8R;
  CANR 25, 198; CLR 1, 80, 136; DLB 52;
  JRDA; MAICYA 1, 2; SATA 2, 68, 124,
  170, 226; WYA; YAW
**George, Stefan (Anton)**
  1868-1933 ......................... **TCLC 2, 14**
  See also CA 104; 193; EW 8; EWL 3
**Georges, Georges Martin**
  See Simenon, Georges
**Gerald of Wales**
  c. 1146-c. 1223 ............. **CMLC 60, 144**
**Gerhardi, William Alexander**
  See Gerhardie, William Alexander
**Gerhardie, William Alexander**
  1895-1977 ................................. **CLC 5**
  See also CA 25-28R; 73-76; CANR 18; CN
  1, 2; DLB 36; RGEL 2
**Germain, Sylvie** 1954- ................... **CLC 283**
  See also CA 191
**Gerome**
  See France, Anatole
**Gerson, Jean** 1363-1429 ............. **LC 77, 261**
  See also DLB 208
**Gersonides** 1288-1344 .................. **CMLC 49**
  See also DLB 115
**Gerstler, Amy** 1956- ....................... **CLC 70**
  See also CA 146; CANR 99
**Gertler, T.** ......................................... **CLC 34**
  See also CA 116; 121
**Gertrude of Helfta**
  c. 1256-c. 1301 ..................... **CMLC 105**
**Gertsen, Aleksandr Ivanovich**
  See Herzen, Aleksandr Ivanovich
**Gervase of Melkley**
  c. 1185-c. 1216 ................... **CMLC 121**
**Geyer, Francis**
  See Harwood, Gwen

**Ghalib**
  See Ghalib, Asadullah Khan
**Ghelderode, Michel de** 1898-1962 ... **CLC 6,**
  **11; DC 15; TCLC 187**
  See also CA 85-88; CANR 40, 77; DAM
  DRAM; DLB 321; EW 11; EWL 3; TWA
**Ghiselin, Brewster** 1903-2001 ......... **CLC 23**
  See also CA 13-16R; CAAS 10; CANR 13;
  CP 1, 2, 3, 4, 5, 6, 7
**Ghalib, Asadullah Khan**
  1797-1869 ....................... **NCLC 39, 78**
  See also DAM POET; RGWL 2, 3
**Ghose, Aurabinda** 1872-1950 ........ **TCLC 63**
  See also CA 163; EWL 3
**Ghose, Aurobindo**
  See Ghose, Aurabinda
**Ghose, Zulfikar** 1935- ............. **CLC 42, 200**
  See also CA 65-68; CANR 67; CN 1, 2, 3, 4, 5,
  6, 7; CP 1, 2, 3, 4, 5, 6, 7; DLB 323; EWL 3
**Ghosh, Amitav** 1956- ...... **CLC 44, 153, 300**
  See also CA 147; CANR 80, 158, 205; CN
  6, 7; DLB 323; WWE 1
**Giacosa, Giuseppe** 1847-1906 ........ **TCLC 7**
  See also CA 104
**Giardina, Denise** 1951- .................... **CLC 397**
  See also CA 119; CANR 72, 147, 216
**Gibb, Lee**
  See Waterhouse, Keith
**Gibbon, Edward** 1737-1794 .............. **LC 97**
  See also BRW 3; DLB 104, 336; RGEL 2
**Gibbon, Lewis Grassic**
  See Mitchell, James Leslie
**Gibbons, Kaye** 1960- ......... **CLC 50, 88, 145**
  See also AAYA 34; AMWS 10; CA 151;
  CANR 75, 127; CN 7; CSW; DA3; DAM
  POP; DLB 292; MTCW 2; MTFW 2005;
  NFS 3; RGAL 4; SATA 117
**Gibbons, Stella** 1902-1989 .......... **TCLC 353**
  See also CA 13-16R; 130; CANR 76; CN 1,
  2, 3, 4; DLB 352; MBL 2
**Gibran, Kahlil** 1883-1931 ... **PC 9; TCLC 1,**
  **9, 205**
  See also AMWS 20; CA 104; 150; DA3;
  DAM POET, POP; DLB 346; EWL 3;
  MTCW 2; WLIT 6
**Gibran, Khalil**
  See Gibran, Kahlil
**Gibson, Mel** 1956- ......................... **CLC 215**
  See also AAYA 80
**Gibson, William** 1914-2008 ............. **CLC 23**
  See also CA 9-12R; 279; CAD; CANR 9,
  42, 75, 125; CD 5, 6; DA; DAB; DAC;
  DAM DRAM, MST; DFS 2, 28; DLB 7;
  LAIT 2; MAL 5; MTCW 2; MTFW 2005;
  SATA 66; SATA-Obit 199; YAW
**Gibson, William** 1948- ..... **CLC 39, 63, 186,**
  **192, 333; SSC 52**
  See also AAYA 12, 59; AMWS 16; BPFB 2;
  CA 126; 133; CANR 52, 90, 106, 172,
  229; CN 6, 7; CPW; DA3; DAM POP;
  DLB 251; MTCW 2; MTFW 2005; NFS
  38; SCFW 2; SFW 4; SSFS 26
**Gibson, William Ford**
  See Gibson, William
**Gide, Andre** 1869-1951 ........ **SSC 13; TCLC**
  **5, 12, 36, 177; WLC 3**
  See also CA 104; 124; DA; DA3; DAB;
  DAC; DAM MST, NOV; DLB 65, 321,
  330; EW 8; EWL 3; GFL 1789 to the
  Present; MTCW 1, 2; MTFW 2005; NFS
  21; RGSF 2; RGWL 2, 3; TWA
**Gide, Andre Paul Guillaume**
  See Gide, Andre
**Gifford, Barry** 1946- ....................... **CLC 34**
  See also CA 65-68; CANR 9, 30, 40, 90, 180
**Gifford, Barry Colby**
  See Gifford, Barry
**Gilbert, Frank**
  See De Voto, Bernard (Augustine)

**Godoy Alcayaga, Lucila**
  See Mistral, Gabriela
**Godwin, Gail** 1937- ......... **CLC 5, 8, 22, 31, 69, 125, 331**
  See also BPFB 2; CA 29-32R; CANR 15, 43, 69, 132, 218; CN 3, 4, 5, 6, 7; CPW; CSW; DA3; DAM POP; DLB 6, 234, 350; INT CANR-15; MAL 5; MTCW 1, 2; MTFW 2005
**Godwin, Gail Kathleen**
  See Godwin, Gail
**Godwin, William** 1756-1836 .. **NCLC 14, 130, 287**
  See also BRWS 15; CDBLB 1789-1832; CMW 4; DLB 39, 104, 142, 158, 163, 262, 336; GL 2; HGG; RGEL 2
**Goebbels, Josef**
  See Goebbels, (Paul) Joseph
**Goebbels, (Paul) Joseph**
  1897-1945 .............................. **TCLC 68**
  See also CA 115; 148
**Goebbels, Joseph Paul**
  See Goebbels, (Paul) Joseph
**Goethe, Johann Wolfgang von**
  1749-1832 ........... **DC 20; NCLC 4, 22, 34, 90, 154, 247, 266, 270, 284, 287, 319; PC 5, 147; SSC 38, 141; WLC 3**
  See also CDWLB 2; DA; DA3; DAB; DAC; DAM DRAM, MST, POET; DLB 94; EW 5; GL 2; LATS 1; LMFS 1:1; RGWL 2, 3; TWA
**Gogarty, Oliver St. John**
  1878-1957 ................ **PC 121; TCLC 15**
  See also CA 109; 150; DLB 15, 19; RGEL 2
**Gogol, Nikolai** 1809-1852 .. **DC 1; NCLC 5, 15, 31, 162, 281, 315; SSC 4, 29, 52, 145, 222; WLC 3**
  See also DA; DAB; DAC; DAM DRAM, MST; DFS 12; DLB 198; EW 6; EXPS; RGSF 2; RGWL 2, 3; SSFS 7, 32; TWA
**Gogol, Nikolai Vasilyevich**
  See Gogol, Nikolai
**Goines, Donald** 1937(?)-1974 ....... **BLC 1:2; CLC 80**
  See also AITN 1; BW 1, 3; CA 124; 114; CANR 82; CMW 4; DA3; DAM MULT, POP; DLB 33
**Gold, Herbert** 1924- .............. **CLC 4, 7, 14, 42, 152**
  See also CA 9-12R; CANR 17, 45, 125, 194; CN 1, 2, 3, 4, 5, 6, 7; DLB 2; DLBY 1981; MAL 5
**Goldbarth, Albert** 1948- ............. **CLC 5, 38**
  See also AMWS 12; CA 53-56; CANR 6, 40, 206; CP 3, 4, 5, 6, 7; DLB 120
**Goldberg, Anatol** 1910-1982 .......... **CLC 34**
  See also CA 131; 117
**Goldemberg, Isaac** 1945- ................ **CLC 52**
  See also CA 69-72; CAAS 12; CANR 11, 32; EWL 3; HW 1; WLIT 1
**Golding, Arthur** 1536-1606 ............. **LC 101**
  See also DLB 136
**Golding, William** 1911-1993 .... **CLC 1, 2, 3, 8, 10, 17, 27, 58, 81; TCLC 363; WLC 3**
  See also AAYA 5, 44; BPFB 2; BRWR 1; BRWS 1; BYA 10; CA 5-8R; 141; CANR 13, 33, 54; CD 5; CDBLB 1945-1960; CLR 94, 130; CMTFW; CN 1, 2, 3, 4; DA; DA3; DAB; DAC; DAM MST, NOV; DLB 15, 100, 255, 326, 330; EWL 3; EXPN; HGG; LAIT 4; MBL 2; MTCW 1, 2; MTFW 2005; NFS 2, 36; RGEL 2; RHW; SFW 4; TEA; WLIT 4; YAW
**Golding, William Gerald**
  See Golding, William
**Goldman, Emma** 1869-1940 ......... **TCLC 13**
  See also CA 110; 150; DLB 221; FW; RGAL 4; TUS
**Goldman, Francisco** 1954- ...... **CLC 76, 298**
  See also CA 162; CANR 185, 233

**Goldman, William** 1931- ............ **CLC 1, 48**
  See also BPFB 2; CA 9-12R; CANR 29, 69, 106; CN 1, 2, 3, 4, 5, 6, 7; DLB 44; FANT; IDFW 3, 4; NFS 31
**Goldman, William W.**
  See Goldman, William
**Goldmann, Lucien** 1913-1970 ......... **CLC 24**
  See also CA 25-28; CAP 2
**Goldoni, Carlo**
  1707-1793 ................ **DC 47; LC 4, 152**
  See also DAM DRAM; DFS 27; EW 4; RGWL 2, 3; WLIT 7
**Goldsberry, Steven** 1949- ............... **CLC 34**
  See also CA 131
**Goldsmith, Oliver** 1730(?)-1774 ......... **DC 8; LC 2, 48, 122; PC 77; WLC 3**
  See also BRW 3; CDBLB 1660-1789; CLR 208; DA; DAB; DAC; DAM DRAM, MST, NOV, POET; DFS 1; DLB 39, 89, 104, 109, 142, 336; IDTP; RGEL 2; SATA 26; TEA; WLIT 3
**Goldsmith, Peter**
  See Priestley, J(ohn) B(oynton)
**Goldstein, Rebecca** 1950- .............. **CLC 239**
  See also CA 144; CANR 99, 165, 214; TCLE 1:1
**Goldstein, Rebecca Newberger**
  See Goldstein, Rebecca
**Gombrowicz, Witold** 1904-1969 ...... **CLC 4, 7, 11, 49; TCLC 247**
  See also CA 19-20; 25-28R; CANR 105; CAP 2; CDWLB 4; DAM DRAM; DLB 215; EW 12; EWL 3; RGWL 2, 3; TWA
**Gomez de la Serna, Ramon**
  1888-1963 ................................. **CLC 9**
  See also CA 153; 116; CANR 79; EWL 3; HW 1, 2
**Gomez-Pena, Guillermo** 1955- ...... **CLC 310**
  See also CA 147; CANR 117
**Goncharov, Ivan Alexandrovich**
  1812-1891 .................. **NCLC 1, 63, 328**
  See also DLB 238; EW 6; RGWL 2, 3
**Goncourt, Edmond de** 1822-1896 ... **NCLC 7**
  See also DLB 123; EW 7; GFL 1789 to the Present; RGWL 2, 3
**Goncourt, Edmond Louis Antoine Huot de**
  See Goncourt, Edmond de
**Goncourt, Jules Alfred Huot de**
  See Goncourt, Jules de
**Goncourt, Jules de** 1830-1870 ........ **NCLC 7**
  See Goncourt, Jules de
  See also DLB 123; EW 7; GFL 1789 to the Present; RGWL 2, 3
**Gontier, Fernande** 19(?)- ................ **CLC 50**
**Gonzalez Martinez, Enrique**
  1871-1952 ................................ **TCLC 72**
  See also CA 166; CANR 81; DLB 290; EWL 3; HW 1, 2
**Gonzalez Martinez, Enrique**
  See Gonzalez Martinez, Enrique
**Good Old Papist, A**
  See More, Hannah
**Goodison, Lorna** 1947- ...... **BLC 2:2; PC 36**
  See also CA 142; CANR 88, 189; CP 5, 6, 7; CWP; DLB 157; EWL 3; PFS 25
**Goodman, Allegra** 1967- ............. **CLC 241**
  See also CA 204; CANR 162, 204; DLB 244, 350
**Goodman, Paul** 1911-1972 ... **CLC 1, 2, 4, 7**
  See also CA 19-20; 37-40R; CAD; CANR 34; CAP 2; CN 1; DLB 130, 246; MAL 5; MTCW 1; RGAL 4
**Goodweather, Hartley**
  See King, Thomas
**GoodWeather, Hartley**
  See King, Thomas
**Googe, Barnabe** 1540-1594 ................ **LC 94**
  See also DLB 132; RGEL 2

**Gordimer, Nadine** 1923-2014 ....... **CLC 3, 5, 7, 10, 18, 33, 51, 70, 123, 160, 161, 263, 389; SSC 17, 80, 154; WLCS**
  See also AAYA 39; AFW; BRWS 2; CA 5-8R; CANR 3, 28, 56, 88, 131, 195, 219; CN 1, 2, 3, 4, 5, 6, 7; DA; DA3; DAB; DAC; DAM MST, NOV; DLB 225, 326, 330; EWL 3; EXPS; INT CANR-28; LATS 1:2; MTCW 1, 2; MTFW 2005; NFS 4; RGEL 2; RGSF 2; SSFS 2, 14, 19, 28, 31; TWA; WLIT 2; YAW
**Gordon, Adam Lindsay** 1833-1870 .. **NCLC 21**
  See also DLB 230
**Gordon, Caroline** 1895-1981 ...... **CLC 6, 13, 29, 83; SSC 15; TCLC 241**
  See also AMW; CA 11-12; 103; CANR 36; CAP 1; CN 1, 2; DLB 4, 9, 102; DLBD 17; DLBY 1981; EWL 3; MAL 5; MTCW 1, 2; MTFW 2005; RGAL 4; RGSF 2
**Gordon, Charles William**
  1860-1937 ............................... **TCLC 31**
  See also CA 109; DLB 92; TCWW 1, 2
**Gordon, Lucie Duff**
  See Duff Gordon, Lucie
**Gordon, Mary** 1949- ........ **CLC 13, 22, 128, 216; SSC 59**
  See also AMWS 4; BPFB 2; CA 102; CANR 44, 92, 154, 179, 222; CN 4, 5, 6, 7; DLB 6; DLBY 1981; FW; INT CA-102; MAL 5; MTCW 1
**Gordon, Mary Catherine**
  See Gordon, Mary
**Gordon, N. J.**
  See Bosman, Herman Charles
**Gordon, Sol** 1923- ........................... **CLC 26**
  See also CA 53-56; CANR 4; SATA 11
**Gordone, Charles** 1925-1995 ........ **BLC 2:2; CLC 1, 4; DC 8**
  See also BW 1, 3; CA 93-96; 180; 150; CAAE 180; CAD; CANR 55; DAM DRAM; DLB 7; INT CA-93-96; MTCW 1
**Gore, Catherine** 1800-1861 ........... **NCLC 65**
  See also DLB 116, 344; RGEL 2
**Gorenko, Anna Andreevna**
  See Akhmatova, Anna
**Gor'kii, Maksim**
  See Gorky, Maxim
**Gorky, Maxim** 1868-1936 ............... **SSC 28; TCLC 8; WLC 3**
  See also CA 105; 141; CANR 83; DA; DAB; DAC; DAM DRAM, MST, NOV; DFS 9; DLB 295; EW 8; EWL 3; MTCW 2; MTFW 2005; RGSF 2; RGWL 2, 3; TWA
**Gorriti, Juana Manuela** 1818-1892 ... **NCLC 298**
**Goryan, Sirak**
  See Saroyan, William
**Gosse, Edmund (William)**
  1849-1928 ............................... **TCLC 28**
  See also CA 117; DLB 57, 144, 184; RGEL 2
**Goto, Hiromi** 1966- ...................... **CLC 338**
  See also CA 165; CANR 142
**Gotlieb, Phyllis** 1926-2009 ............. **CLC 18**
  See also CA 13-16R; CANR 7, 135; CN 7; CP 1, 2, 3, 4; DLB 88, 251; SFW 4
**Gotlieb, Phyllis Fay Bloom**
  See Gotlieb, Phyllis
**Gottesman, S. D.**
  See Kornbluth, C(yril) M.; Pohl, Frederik
**Gottfried von Strassburg**
  fl. c. 1170-1215 ...... **CMLC 10, 96, 132**
  See also CDWLB 2; DLB 138; EW 1; RGWL 2, 3
**Gotthelf, Jeremias** 1797-1854 ...... **NCLC 117**
  See also DLB 133; RGWL 2, 3
**Gottschalk** c. 804-c. 866 ............ **CMLC 130**
  See also DLB 148
**Gottschalk, Laura Riding**
  See Jackson, Laura

**Guedes, Vincente**
See Pessoa, Fernando

**Guenter, Erich**
See Eich, Gunter

**Guest, Barbara** 1920-2006 ............. **CLC 34; PC 55**
See also BG 1:2; CA 25-28R; 248; CANR 11, 44, 84; CP 1, 2, 3, 4, 5, 6, 7; CWP; DLB 5, 193

**Guest, Edgar A(lbert)** 1881-1959 ... **TCLC 95**
See also CA 112; 168

**Guest, Judith** 1936- ..................... **CLC 8, 30**
See also AAYA 7, 66; CA 77-80; CANR 15, 75, 138; DA3; DAM NOV, POP; EXPN; INT CANR-15; LAIT 5; MTCW 1, 2; MTFW 2005; NFS 1, 33

**Guest, Judith Ann**
See Guest, Judith

**Guevara, Che** 1928-1967 .. **CLC 87; HLC 1**
See also CA 127; 111; CANR 56; DAM MULT; HW 1

**Guevara (Serna), Ernesto**
See Guevara, Che

**Guibert, Hervé** 1955-1991 ........... **TCLC 332**
See also CA 155; GLL 2

**Guicciardini, Francesco** 1483-1540 ... **LC 49**

**Guido delle Colonne**
c. 1215-c. 1290 ...................... **CMLC 90**

**Guild, Nicholas M.** 1944- ................ **CLC 33**
See also CA 93-96

**Guillaume de Lorris**
13th cent. .................. **CMLC 8, 82, 200**
See also TWA

**Guillemin, Jacques**
See Sartre, Jean-Paul

**Guillen y Alvarez, Jorge**
See Guillen, Jorge

**Guillevic, (Eugene)** 1907-1997 ........ **CLC 33**
See also CA 93-96; CWW 2

**Guillen, Jorge** 1893-1984 ................ **CLC 11; HLCS 1; PC 35; TCLC 233**
See also CA 89-92; 112; DAM MULT, POET; DLB 108; EWL 3; HW 1; RGWL 2, 3

**Guillen, Nicolas** 1902-1989 ........ **BLC 1:2; CLC 48, 79; HLC 1; PC 23**
See also BW 2; CA 116; 125; 129; CANR 84; DAM MST, MULT, POET; DLB 283; EWL 3; HW 1; LAW; RGWL 2, 3; WP

**Guillen, Nicolas Cristobal**
See Guillen, Nicolas

**Guillois**
See Desnos, Robert

**Guillois, Valentin**
See Desnos, Robert

**Guimarães Rosa, João** 1908-1967 ... **CLC 23; HLCS 1; SSC 249**
See also CA 175; 89-92; DLB 113, 307; EWL 3; LAW; RGSF 2; RGWL 2, 3; WLIT 1

**Guiney, Louise Imogen**
1861-1920 .................... **TCLC 41**
See also CA 160; DLB 54; RGAL 4

**Guinizzelli, Guido** c. 1230-1276 .... **CMLC 49**
See also WLIT 7

**Guinizzelli, Guido**
See Guinizelli, Guido

**Guma, Alex La**
See La Guma, Alex

**Gumilev, Nikolai (Stepanovich)**
1886-1921 ............................. **TCLC 60**
See also CA 165; DLB 295; EWL 3

**Gumilyov, Nikolay Stepanovich**
See Gumilev, Nikolai (Stepanovich)

**Gump, P.Q.**
See Card, Orson Scott

**Günderrode, Karoline von**
1780-1806 ........................... **NCLC 338**
See also DLB 90

**Gunesekera, Romesh** 1954- ..... **CLC 91, 336**
See also BRWS 10; CA 159; CANR 140, 172; CN 6, 7; DLB 267, 323

**Gunn, Bill**
See Gunn, William Harrison

**Gunn, Thom** 1929-2004 ........ **CLC 3, 6, 18, 32, 81; PC 26**
See also BRWR 3; BRWS 4; CA 17-20R; 227; CANR 9, 33, 116; CDBLB 1960 to Present; CP 1, 2, 3, 4, 5, 6, 7; DAM POET; DLB 27; INT CANR-33; MTCW 1; PFS 9; RGEL 2

**Gunn, William Harrison**
1934(?)-1989 .......................... **CLC 5**
See also AITN 1; BW 1, 3; CA 13-16R; 128; CANR 12, 25, 76; DLB 38

**Gunn Allen, Paula**
See Allen, Paula Gunn

**Gunnars, Kristjana** 1948- ............... **CLC 69**
See also CA 113; CCA 1; CP 6, 7; CWP; DLB 60

**Gurdjieff, G(eorgei) I(vanovich)**
1877(?)-1949 .......................... **TCLC 71**
See also CA 157

**Gurganus, Allan** 1947- .................... **CLC 70**
See also BEST 90:1; CA 135; CANR 114; CN 6, 7; CPW; CSW; DAM POP; DLB 350; GLL 1

**Gurnah, Abdulrazak** 1948- ........... **CLC 368**
See also CA 179; CANR 153; CN 7; EWL 3

**Gurney, A. R.**
See Gurney, A(lbert) R(amsdell), Jr.

**Gurney, A(lbert) R(amsdell), Jr.**
1930- ............................ **CLC 32, 50, 54**
See also AMWS 5; CA 77-80; CAD; CANR 32, 64, 121; CD 5, 6; DAM DRAM; DLB 266; EWL 3

**Gurney, Ivor (Bertie)** 1890-1937 ... **TCLC 33**
See also BRW 6; CA 167; DLBY 2002; PAB; RGEL 2

**Gurney, Peter**
See Gurney, A(lbert) R(amsdell), Jr.

**Guro, Elena (Genrikhovna)**
1877-1913 .............................. **TCLC 56**
See also DLB 295

**Gustafson, James M(oody)** 1925- ... **CLC 100**
See also CA 25-28R; CANR 37

**Gustafson, Ralph (Barker)**
1909-1995 ............................. **CLC 36**
See also CA 21-24R; CANR 8, 45, 84; CP 1, 2, 3, 4, 5, 6; DLB 88; RGEL 2

**Gut, Gom**
See Simenon, Georges

**Guterson, David** 1956- .................... **CLC 91**
See also CA 132; CANR 73, 126, 194; CN 7; DLB 292; MTCW 2; MTFW 2005; NFS 13

**Guthrie, A(lfred) B(ertram), Jr.**
1901-1991 ............................. **CLC 23**
See also CA 57-60; 134; CANR 24; CN 1, 2, 3; DLB 6, 212; MAL 5; SATA 62; SATA-Obit 67; TCWW 1, 2

**Guthrie, Isobel**
See Grieve, C. M.

**Guthrie, Woody** 1912-1967 ......... **TCLC 337**
See also CA 93-96; 113

**Gutierrez Najera, Manuel**
1859-1895 ............... **HLCS 2; NCLC 133**
See also DLB 290; LAW

**Guy, Rosa** 1925- ........................... **CLC 26**
See also AAYA 4, 37; BW 2; CA 17-20R; CANR 14, 34, 83; CLR 13, 137; DLB 33; DNFS 1; JRDA; MAICYA 1, 2; SATA 14, 62, 122; YAW

**Guy, Rosa Cuthbert**
See Guy, Rosa

**Gwendolyn**
See Bennett, (Enoch) Arnold

**Gyasi, Yaa** 1989- ........................... **CLC 421**

**H. D.**
See Doolittle, Hilda

**H. de V.**
See Buchan, John

**Haavikko, Paavo Juhani** 1931- ... **CLC 18, 34**
See also CA 106; CWW 2; EWL 3

**Habbema, Koos**
See Heijermans, Herman

**Habermas, Jurgen**
See Habermas, Juergen

**Habermas, Juergen** 1929- ..... **CLC 104, 345**
See also CA 109; CANR 85, 162; DLB 242

**Hacker, Marilyn** 1942- .......... **CLC 5, 9, 23, 72, 91; PC 47**
See also CA 77-80; CANR 68, 129; CP 3, 4, 5, 6, 7; CWP; DAM POET; DLB 120, 282; FW; GLL 2; MAL 5; PFS 19

**Hackleskinner, Fred**
See Harwood, Gwen

**Hadewijch of Antwerp**
fl. 1250 .............................. **CMLC 61**
See also RGWL 3

**Hadrian** 76-138 ........................... **CMLC 52**

**Haeckel, Ernst Heinrich (Philipp August)**
1834-1919 ............................. **TCLC 83**
See also CA 157

**Hafiz** c. 1326-1389(?) ......... **CMLC 34, 156; PC 116**
See also RGWL 2, 3; WLIT 6

**Hage, Rawi** 1964- .......................... **CLC 446**
See also CA 269; CANR 266

**Hagedorn, Jessica** 1949- ............... **CLC 185**
See also CA 139; CANR 69, 231; CWP; DLB 312; RGAL 4

**Hagedorn, Jessica Tarahata**
See Hagedorn, Jessica

**Hagendoor, W. W.**
See Harwood, Gwen

**Haggard, H(enry) Rider**
1856-1925 ............................. **TCLC 11**
See also AAYA 81; BRWS 3; BYA 4, 5; CA 108; 148; CANR 112; DLB 70, 156, 174, 178; FANT; LMFS 1; MTCW 2; NFS 40; RGEL 2; RHW; SATA 16; SCFW 1, 2; SFW 4; SUFW 1; WLIT 4

**Hagiosy, L.**
See Larbaud, Valery (Nicolas)

**Hagiwara, Sakutaro** 1886-1942 ........ **PC 18; TCLC 60**
See also CA 154; EWL 3; RGWL 3

**Hagiwara Sakutaro**
See Hagiwara, Sakutaro

**Haig, Fenil**
See Ford, Ford Madox

**Haig-Brown, Roderick (Langmere)**
1908-1976 ............................. **CLC 21**
See also CA 5-8R; 69-72; CANR 4, 38, 83; CLR 31; CWRI 5; DLB 88; MAICYA 1, 2; SATA 12; TCWW 2

**Haight, Rip**
See Carpenter, John

**Haij, Vera**
See Jansson, Tove (Marika)

**Hailey, Arthur** 1920-2004 ............... **CLC 5**
See also AITN 2; BEST 90:3; BPFB 2; CA 1-4R; 233; CANR 2, 36, 75; CCA 1; CN 1, 2, 3, 4, 5, 6, 7; CPW; DAM NOV, POP; DLB 88; DLBY 1982; MTCW 1, 2; MTFW 2005

**Hailey, Elizabeth Forsythe** 1938- ... **CLC 40**
See also CA 93-96, 188; CAAE 188; CAAS 1; CANR 15, 48; INT CANR-15

**Haines, John** 1924-2011 ................. **CLC 58**
See also AMWS 12; CA 17-20R; CANR 13, 34; CP 1, 2, 3, 4, 5; CSW; DLB 5, 212; TCLE 1:1

**Haines, John Meade**
See Haines, John

**Hargrave, Leonie**
See Disch, Thomas M.

**Harington, Donald** 1935-2009 ....... **CLC 412**
See also BPFB 2; CA 13-16R; CANR 7, 55, 109, 160, 194; DLB 152

**Hariri, Al- al-Qasim ibn 'Ali Abu Muhammad al-Basri**
See al-Hariri, al-Qasim ibn 'Ali Abu Muhammad al-Basri

**Harjo, Joy** 1951- ... **CLC 83; NNAL; PC 27**
See also AMWS 12; CA 114; CANR 35, 67, 91, 129; CP 6, 7; CWP; DAM MULT; DLB 120, 175, 342; EWL 3; MTCW 2; MTFW 2005; PFS 15, 32, 44; RGAL 4

**Harlan, Louis R.** 1922-2010 ........... **CLC 34**
See also CA 21-24R; CANR 25, 55, 80

**Harlan, Louis Rudolph**
See Harlan, Louis R.

**Harlan, Louis Rudolph**
See Harlan, Louis R.

**Harling, Robert** 1951(?)- ................. **CLC 53**
See also CA 147

**Harmon, William (Ruth)** 1938- ...... **CLC 38**
See also CA 33-36R; CANR 14, 32, 35; SATA 65

**Harper, Edith Alice Mary**
See Wickham, Anna

**Harper, F. E. W.**
See Harper, Frances Ellen Watkins

**Harper, Frances E. W.**
See Harper, Frances Ellen Watkins

**Harper, Frances E. Watkins**
See Harper, Frances Ellen Watkins

**Harper, Frances Ellen**
See Harper, Frances Ellen Watkins

**Harper, Frances Ellen Watkins**
1825-1911 ................. **BLC 1:2; PC 21; TCLC 14, 217**
See also AFAW 1, 2; BW 1, 3; CA 111; 125; CANR 79; DAM MULT, POET; DLB 50, 221; MBL; PFS 44; RGAL 4

**Harper, Michael S.** 1938- .............. **BLC 2:2; CLC 7, 22; PC 130**
See also AFAW 2; BW 1; CA 33-36R, 224; CAAE 224; CANR 24, 108, 212; CP 2, 3, 4, 5, 6, 7; DLB 41; RGAL 4; TCLE 1:1

**Harper, Michael Steven**
See Harper, Michael S.

**Harper, Mrs. F. E. W.**
See Harper, Frances Ellen Watkins

**Harpur, Charles** 1813-1868 ......... **NCLC 114**
See also DLB 230; RGEL 2

**Harriot, Thomas** c. 1560-1621 ......... **LC 278**
See also DLB 136

**Harris, Charlaine** 1951- ................. **CLC 409**
See also CA 105; CANR 99, 155, 197, 246; SATA 263

**Harris, Christie**
See Harris, Christie (Lucy) Irwin

**Harris, Christie (Lucy) Irwin**
1907-2002 ................................. **CLC 12**
See also CA 5-8R; CANR 6, 83; CLR 47; DLB 88; JRDA; MAICYA 1, 2; SAAS 10; SATA 6, 74; SATA-Essay 116

**Harris, E. Lynn** 1955-2009 ........... **CLC 299**
See also CA 164; 288; CANR 111, 163, 206; MTFW 2005

**Harris, Everett Lynn**
See Harris, E. Lynn

**Harris, Everette Lynn**
See Harris, E. Lynn

**Harris, Frank** 1856-1931 .............. **TCLC 24**
See also CA 109; 150; CANR 80; DLB 156, 197; RGEL 2

**Harris, George Washington**
1814-1869 ...................... **NCLC 23, 165**
See also DLB 3, 11, 248; RGAL 4

**Harris, Joel Chandler** 1848-1908 .... **SSC 19, 103; TCLC 2**
See also CA 104; 137; CANR 80; CLR 49, 128; DLB 11, 23, 42, 78, 91; LAIT 2; MAICYA 1, 2; RGSF 2; SATA 100; WCH; YABC 1

**Harris, John (Wyndham Parkes Lucas) Beynon** 1903-1969 ................... **CLC 19**
See also BRWS 13; CA 102; 89-92; CANR 84; CLR 190; DLB 255; SATA 118; SCFW 1, 2; SFW 4

**Harris, MacDonald**
See Heiney, Donald (William)

**Harris, Mark** 1922-2007 ................. **CLC 19**
See also CA 5-8R; 260; CAAS 3; CANR 2, 55, 83; CN 1, 2, 3, 4, 5, 6, 7; DLB 2; DLBY 1980

**Harris, Norman** ............................... **CLC 65**

**Harris, (Theodore) Wilson** 1921- ... **BLC 2:2; CLC 25, 159, 297**
See also BRWS 5; BW 2, 3; CA 65-68; CAAS 16; CANR 11, 27, 69, 114; CDWLB 3; CN 1, 2, 3, 4, 5, 6, 7; CP 1, 2, 3, 4, 5, 6, 7; DLB 117; EWL 3; MTCW 1; RGEL 2

**Harris, Thomas** 1940- ................... **CLC 356**
See also AAYA 34; BPFB 2; CMTFW; CA 113; CANR 35, 73, 106; CMW 4; CPW; CSW; DAM POP; HGG; MTFW

**Harrison, Barbara Grizzuti**
1934-2002 ................................. **CLC 144**
See also CA 77-80; 205; CANR 15, 48; INT CANR-15

**Harrison, Elizabeth (Allen) Cavanna**
1909-2001 ................................. **CLC 12**
See also CA 9-12R; 200; CANR 6, 27, 85, 104, 121; JRDA; MAICYA 1; SAAS 4; SATA 1, 30; YAW

**Harrison, Harry** 1925- ..................... **CLC 42**
See also CA 1-4R; CANR 5, 21, 84, 225; DLB 8; SATA 4; SCFW 2; SFW 4

**Harrison, Harry Max**
See Harrison, Harry

**Harrison, James**
See Harrison, Jim

**Harrison, James Thomas**
See Harrison, Jim

**Harrison, Jim** 1937- ............. **CLC 6, 14, 33, 66, 143, 348; SSC 19**
See also AMWS 8; CA 13-16R; CANR 8, 51, 79, 142, 198, 229; CN 5, 6; CP 1, 2, 3, 4, 5, 6; DLBY 1982; INT CANR-8; RGAL 4; TCWW 2; TUS

**Harrison, Kathryn** 1961- ......... **CLC 70, 151**
See also CA 144; CANR 68, 122, 194

**Harrison, Tony** 1937- .............. **CLC 43, 129; PC 168**
See also BRWS 5; CA 65-68; CANR 44, 98; CBD; CD 5, 6; CP 2, 3, 4, 5, 6, 7; DLB 40, 245; MTCW 1; RGEL 2

**Harriss, Will(ard Irvin)** 1922- ....... **CLC 34**
See also CA 111

**Hart, Ellis**
See Ellison, Harlan

**Hart, Josephine** 1942-2011 ............. **CLC 70**
See also CA 138; CANR 70, 149, 220; CPW; DAM POP

**Hart, Moss** 1904-1961 ..................... **CLC 66**
See also CA 109; 89-92; CANR 84; DAM DRAM; DFS 1; DLB 7, 266; RGAL 4

**Harte, Bret** 1836-1902 ........ **SSC 8, 59, 207; TCLC 1, 25; WLC 3**
See also AMWS 2; CA 104; 140; CANR 80; CDALB 1865-1917; DA; DA3; DAC; DAM MST; DLB 12, 64, 74, 79, 186; EXPS; LAIT 2; RGAL 4; RGSF 2; SATA 26; SSFS 3; TUS

**Harte, Francis Brett**
See Harte, Bret

**Hartley, L(eslie) P(oles)**
1895-1972 ............. **CLC 2, 22; SSC 125**
See also BRWS 7; CA 45-48; 37-40R; CANR 33; CN 1; DLB 15, 139; EWL 3; HGG; MTCW 1, 2; MTFW 2005; RGEL 2; RGSF 2; SUFW 1

**Hartman, Geoffrey H.** 1929- ......... **CLC 27**
See also CA 117; 125; CANR 79, 214; DLB 67

**Hartmann, Sadakichi** 1869-1944 ... **TCLC 73**
See also CA 157; DLB 54

**Hartmann von Aue**
c. 1170-c. 1210 ............. **CMLC 15, 131**
See also CDWLB 2; DLB 138; RGWL 2, 3

**Hartog, Jan de**
See de Hartog, Jan

**Haruf, Kent** 1943- ......................... **CLC 34**
See also AAYA 44; CA 149; CANR 91, 131

**Harvey, Caroline**
See Trollope, Joanna

**Harvey, Gabriel** 1550(?)-1631 ........... **LC 88**
See also DLB 167, 213, 281

**Harvey, Jack**
See Rankin, Ian

**Harwood, Gwen** 1920-1995 .............. **PC 160**
See also CA 97-100; CP 1, 2, 3, 4, 5, 6; DLB 289

**Harwood, Ronald** 1934- ................... **CLC 32**
See also CA 1-4R; CANR 4, 55, 150; CBD; CD 5, 6; DAM DRAM, MST; DLB 13

**Hasegawa Tatsunosuke**
See Futabatei, Shimei

**Hasek, Jaroslav** 1883-1923 ............. **SSC 69; TCLC 4, 261**
See also CA 104; 129; CDWLB 4; DLB 215; EW 9; EWL 3; MTCW 1, 2; RGSF 2; RGWL 2, 3

**Hasek, Jaroslav Matej Frantisek**
See Hasek, Jaroslav

**Hasenclever, Walter** 1890-1940 ......... **DC 57**
See also IDTP

**Haslett, Adam** 1970- ...................... **CLC 334**
See also CA 216; SSFS 24

**Hass, Robert**
1941- ....... **CLC 18, 39, 99, 287; PC 16**
See also AMWS 6; CA 111; CANR 30, 50, 71, 187; CP 3, 4, 5, 6, 7; DLB 105, 206; EWL 3; MAL 5; MTFW 2005; PFS 37; RGAL 4; SATA 94; TCLE 1:1

**Hassan, Ihab** 1925- ........................ **CLC 365**
See also CA 5-8R; CAAS 12; CANR 3, 19, 41

**Hassler, Jon** 1933-2008 ................... **CLC 263**
See also CA 73-76; 270; CANR 21, 80, 161; CN 6, 7; INT CANR-21; SATA 19; SATA-Obit 191

**Hassler, Jon Francis**
See Hassler, Jon

**Hastings, Hudson**
See Kuttner, Henry

**Hastings, Selina** 1945- ..................... **CLC 44**
See also CA 257; CANR 225

**Hastings, Selina Shirley**
See Hastings, Selina

**Hastings, Lady Selina Shirley**
See Hastings, Selina

**Hastings, Victor**
See Disch, Thomas M.

**Hathorne, John** 1641-1717 ................. **LC 38**

**Hatteras, Amelia**
See Mencken, H. L.

**Hatteras, Owen**
See Mencken, H. L.; Nathan, George Jean

**Hatton, G. Noel**
See Caird, Mona

**Hauff, Wilhelm** 1802-1827 ......... **NCLC 185**
See also CLR 155; DLB 90; SUFW 1

**Hauptmann, Gerhart** 1862-1946 ... **DC 34, 52; SSC 37; TCLC 4, 300**

See also CA 104; 153; CDWLB 2; DAM
DRAM; DLB 66, 118, 330; EW 8; EWL 3;
RGSF 2; RGWL 2, 3; TWA

**Hauptmann, Gerhart Johann Robert**
See Hauptmann, Gerhart

**Hauser, Kaspar**
See Tucholsky, Kurt

**Havel, Vaclav** 1936-2011 ........... **CLC 25, 58,
65, 123, 314; DC 6**
See also CA 104; CANR 36, 63, 124, 175;
CDWLB 4; CWW 2; DA3; DAM DRAM;
DFS 10; DLB 232; EWL 3; LMFS 2;
MTCW 1, 2; MTFW 2005; RGWL 3

**Haviaras, Stratis**
See Chaviaras, Strates

**Hawes, Stephen** 1475(?)-1529(?) ........ **LC 17**
See also DLB 132; RGEL 2

**Hawk, Alex**
See Kelton, Elmer

**Hawkes, John** 1925-1998 ..... **CLC 1, 2, 3, 4,
7, 9, 14, 15, 27, 49**
See also BPFB 2; CA 1-4R; 167; CANR 2,
47, 64; CN 1, 2, 3, 4, 5, 6; DLB 2, 7, 227;
DLBY 1980, 1998; EWL 3; MAL 5;
MTCW 1, 2; MTFW 2005; RGAL 4

**Hawkesworth, John** 1715?-1773 ...... **LC 254**
See also DLB 142

**Hawking, S. W.**
See Hawking, Stephen W.

**Hawking, Stephen W.** 1942- ... **CLC 63, 105**
See also AAYA 13; BEST 89:1; CA 126;
129; CANR 48, 115; CPW; DA3; MTCW
2; MTFW 2005

**Hawking, Stephen William**
See Hawking, Stephen W.

**Hawkins, Anthony Hope**
See Hope, Anthony

**Hawthorne, Julian** 1846-1934 ....... **TCLC 25**
See also CA 165; HGG

**Hawthorne, Nathaniel** 1804-1864 ........ **NCLC
2, 10, 17, 23, 39, 79, 95, 158, 171, 191,
226; SSC 3, 29, 39, 89, 130, 166, 176,
185, 190, 195, 214, 227, 232, 257, 269;
WLC 3**
See also AAYA 18; AMW; AMWC 1;
AMWR 1; BPFB 2; BYA 3; CDALB
1640-1865; CLR 103, 163; DA; DA3;
DAB; DAC; DAM MST, NOV; DLB 1,
74, 183, 223, 269; EXPN; EXPS; GL 2;
HGG; LAIT 1; NFS 1, 20; RGAL 4; RGSF
2; SSFS 1, 7, 11, 15, 30, 35; SUFW 1;
TUS; WCH; YABC 2

**Hawthorne, Sophia Peabody**
1809-1871 ............................... **NCLC 150**
See also DLB 183, 239

**Haxton, Josephine Ayres** 1921-
See Douglas, Ellen

**Hayaseca y Eizaguirre, Jorge**
See Echegaray (y Eizaguirre), Jose
(Maria Waldo)

**Hayashi, Fumiko** 1904-1951 .......... **TCLC 27**
See also CA 161; DLB 180; EWL 3

**Hayashi Fumiko**
See Hayashi, Fumiko

**Haycraft, Anna** 1932-2005 .............. **CLC 40**
See also CA 122; 237; CANR 90, 141; CN
4, 5, 6; DLB 194; MTCW 2; MTFW 2005

**Haycraft, Anna Margaret**
See Haycraft, Anna

**Hayden, Robert**
See Hayden, Robert Earl

**Hayden, Robert E.**
See Hayden, Robert Earl

**Hayden, Robert Earl** 1913-1980 ... **BLC 1:2;
CLC 5, 9, 14, 37; PC 6, 123**
See also AFAW 1, 2; AMWS 2; BW 1, 3;
CA 69-72; 97-100; CABS 2; CANR 24,
75, 82; CDALB 1941-1968; CP 1, 2, 3;
DA; DAC; DAM MST, MULT, POET;
DLB 5, 76; EWL 3; EXPP; MAL 5;

MTCW 1, 2; PFS 1, 31; RGAL 4; SATA
19; SATA-Obit 26; WP

**Haydon, Benjamin Robert**
1786-1846 ............................... **NCLC 146**
See also DLB 110

**Hayek, F(riedrich) A(ugust von)**
1899-1992 ............................ **TCLC 109**
See also CA 93-96; 137; CANR 20; MTCW
1, 2

**Hayford, J(oseph) E(phraim) Casely**
See Casely-Hayford, J(oseph) E(phraim)

**Hayley, William** 1745-1820 ......... **NCLC 286**
See also DLB 142

**Hayman, Ronald** 1932- .................... **CLC 44**
See also CA 25-28R; CANR 18, 50, 88; CD
5, 6; DLB 155

**Hayne, Paul Hamilton**
1830-1886 ............................... **NCLC 94**
See also DLB 3, 64, 79, 248; RGAL 4

**Haynes, Todd** 1961- ...................... **CLC 313**
See also CA 220

**Hays, Mary** 1760-1843 ................. **NCLC 114**
See also DLB 142, 158; RGEL 2

**Haywood, Eliza (Fowler)**
1693(?)-1756 ................... **LC 1, 44, 177**
See also BRWS 12; DLB 39; RGEL 2

**Hazlitt, William** 1778-1830 ..... **NCLC 29, 82**
See also BRW 4; DLB 110, 158; RGEL 2; TEA

**Hazzard, Shirley** 1931- ... **CLC 18, 218, 325**
See also BRWS 19; CA 9-12R; CANR 4, 70,
127, 212; CN 1, 2, 3, 4, 5, 6, 7; DLB 289;
DLBY 1982; MTCW 1

**Head, Bessie** 1937-1986 ......... **BLC 1:2, 2:2;
CLC 25, 67; SSC 52; TCLC 337**
See also AFW; BW 2, 3; CA 29-32R; 119;
CANR 25, 82; CDWLB 3; CN 1, 2, 3, 4;
DA3; DAM MULT; DLB 117, 225; EWL
3; EXPS; FL 1:6; FW; MTCW 1, 2; MTFW
2005; NFS 31; RGSF 2; SSFS 5, 13, 30,
33; WLIT 2; WWE 1

**Headley, Elizabeth**
See Harrison, Elizabeth (Allen) Cavanna

**Headon, (Nicky) Topper** 1956(?)- ... **CLC 30**

**Heaney, Seamus** 1939-2013 ....... **CLC 5, 7, 14,
25, 37, 74, 91, 171, 225, 309, 370; PC 18,
100; WLCS**
See also AAYA 61; BRWR 1; BRWS 2; CA
85-88; CANR 25, 48, 75, 91, 128, 184,
241; CDBLB 1960 to Present; CP 1, 2, 3,
4, 5, 6, 7; DA3; DAB; DAM POET; DLB
40, 330; DLBY 1995; EWL 3; EXPP;
MTCW 1, 2; MTFW 2005; PAB; PFS 2,
5, 8, 17, 30, 41; RGEL 2; TEA; WLIT 4

**Heaney, Seamus Justin**
See Heaney, Seamus

**Hearn, Lafcadio**
1850-1904 ....... **SSC 158; TCLC 9, 263**
See also AAYA 79; CA 105; 166; DLB 12,
78, 189; HGG; MAL 5; RGAL 4

**Hearn, Patricio Lafcadio Tessima Carlos**
See Hearn, Lafcadio

**Hearne, Samuel** 1745-1792 ................ **LC 95**
See also DLB 99

**Hearne, Vicki** 1946-2001 ................ **CLC 56**
See also CA 139; 201

**Hearon, Shelby** 1931- ...................... **CLC 63**
See also AITN 2; AMWS 8; CA 25-28R;
CAAS 11; CANR 18, 48, 103, 146; CSW

**Heat-Moon, William Least** 1939- ... **CLC 29**
See also AAYA 9, 66; ANW; CA 115; 119;
CANR 47, 89, 206; CPW; INT CA-119

**Hebbel, Friedrich** 1813-1863 ............ **DC 21;
NCLC 43, 287**
See also CDWLB 2; DAM DRAM; DLB
129; EW 6; RGWL 2, 3

**Hébert, Anne** 1916-2000 ...... **CLC 4, 13, 29,
246; PC 126**
See also CA 85-88; 187; CANR 69, 126;
CCA 1; CWP; CWW 2; DA3; DAC; DAM

MST, POET; DLB 68; EWL 3; GFL 1789
to the Present; MTCW 1, 2; MTFW 2005;
PFS 20

**Hebreo, Leon** c. 1460-1520 .............. **LC 193**
See also DLB 318

**Hecht, Anthony (Evan)**
1923-2004 ........ **CLC 8, 13, 19; PC 70**
See also AMWS 10; CA 9-12R; 232; CANR
6, 108; CP 1, 2, 3, 4, 5, 6, 7; DAM POET;
DLB 5, 169; EWL 3; MTFW 2005; WP

**Hecht, Ben** 1894-1964 ... **CLC 8; TCLC 101**
See also CA 85-88; DFS 9; DLB 7, 9, 25,
26, 28, 86; FANT; IDFW 3, 4; RGAL 4

**Hedayat, Sadeq** 1903-1951 ............ **SSC 131;
TCLC 21, 345**
See also CA 120; EWL 3; RGSF 2

**Hegel, Georg Wilhelm Friedrich**
1770-1831 ...................... **NCLC 46, 151**
See also DLB 90, 366; TWA

**Heidegger, Martin** 1889-1976 .......... **CLC 24**
See also CA 81-84; 65-68; CANR 34; DLB
296; MTCW 1, 2; MTFW 2005

**Heidenstam, (Carl Gustaf) Verner von**
1859-1940 ............................... **TCLC 5**
See also CA 104; DLB 330

**Heidi Louise**
See Erdrich, Louise

**Heifner, Jack** 1946- ......................... **CLC 11**
See also CA 105; CANR 47

**Heijermans, Herman** 1864-1924 ... **TCLC 24**
See also CA 123; EWL 3

**Heilbrun, Carolyn G.** 1926-2003 ... **CLC 25,
173, 303**
See also BPFB 1; CA 45-48; 220; CANR 1, 28,
58, 94; CMW; CPW; DLB 306; FW; MSW

**Heilbrun, Carolyn Gold**
See Heilbrun, Carolyn G.

**Hein, Christoph** 1944- .......... **CLC 154, 401**
See also CA 158; CANR 108, 210; CDWLB
2; CWW 2; DLB 124

**Heine, Heinrich** 1797-1856 ...... **NCLC 4, 54,
147, 249; PC 25**
See also CDWLB 2; DLB 90; EW 5; PFS
37; RGWL 2, 3; TWA

**Heinemann, Larry** 1944- ................ **CLC 50**
See also CA 110; CAAS 21; CANR 31, 81,
156; DLBD 9; INT CANR-31

**Heinemann, Larry Curtiss**
See Heinemann, Larry

**Heiney, Donald (William)** 1921-1993 .. **CLC 9**
See also CA 1-4R; 142; CANR 3, 58; FANT

**Heinlein, Robert A.** 1907-1988 ........ **CLC 1,
3, 8, 14, 26, 55; SSC 55; TCLC 337, 339**
See also AAYA 17; BPFB 2; BYA 4, 13; CA
1-4R; 125; CANR 1, 20, 53; CLR 75; CN
1, 2, 3, 4; CPW; DA3; DAM POP; DLB 8;
EXPS; JRDA; LAIT 5; LMFS 2; MAICYA
1, 2; MTCW 1, 2; MTFW 2005; NFS 40;
RGAL 4; SATA 9, 69; SATA-Obit 56;
SCFW 1, 2; SFW 4; SSFS 7; YAW

**Heinrich von dem Tuerlin**
fl. c. 1230- .......................... **CMLC 133**
See also DLB 138

**Heinse, Wilhelm** 1746-1803 ........ **NCLC 289**
See also DLB 94

**Hejinian, Lyn** 1941- .......................... **PC 108**
See also CA 153; CANR 85, 214; CP 4, 5, 6,
7; CWP; DLB 165; PFS 27; RGAL 4

**Held, Peter**
See Vance, Jack

**Heldris of Cornwall** fl. 13th cent. ... **CMLC 97**

**Helforth, John**
See Doolittle, Hilda

**Heliodorus** fl. 3rd cent. ................. **CMLC 52**
See also WLIT 8

**Helisenne de Crenne**
See Crenne, Helisenne de

**Hellenhofferu, Vojtech Kapristian z**
See Hasek, Jaroslav

**Heller, Joseph** 1923-1999 ......... **CLC 1, 3, 5, 8, 11, 36, 63; TCLC 131, 151; WLC 3**
See also AAYA 24; AITN 1; AMWS 4; BPFB 2; BYA 1; CA 5-8R; 187; CABS 1; CANR 8, 42, 66, 126; CN 1, 2, 3, 4, 5, 6; CPW; DA; DA3; DAB; DAC; DAM MST, NOV, POP; DLB 2, 28, 227; DLBY 1980, 2002; EWL 3; EXPN; INT CANR-8; LAIT 4; MAL 5; MTCW 1, 2; MTFW 2005; NFS 1; RGAL 4; TUS; YAW

**Heller, Peter** 1959- .......................... **CLC 354**
See also CA 276; CANR 256

**Hellman, Lillian** 1905-1984 ....... **CLC 2, 4, 8, 14, 18, 34, 44, 52; DC 1; TCLC 119**
See also AAYA 47; AITN 1, 2; AMWS 1; CA 13-16R; 112; CAD; CANR 33; CWD; DA3; DAM DRAM; DFS 1, 3, 14; DLB 7, 228; DLBY 1984; EWL 3; FL 1:6; FW; LAIT 3; MAL 5; MBL; MTCW 1, 2; MTFW 2005; RGAL 4; TUS

**Hellman, Lillian Florence**
See Hellman, Lillian

**Heloise** c. 1095-c. 1164 ............... **CMLC 122**

**Helprin, Mark** 1947- ....... **CLC 7, 10, 22, 32**
See also CA 81-84; CANR 47, 64, 124, 222; CDALBS; CN 7; CPW; DA3; DAM NOV, POP; DLB 335; DLBY 1985; FANT; MAL 5; MTCW 1, 2; MTFW 2005; SSFS 25; SUFW 2

**Helvetius, Claude-Adrien** 1715-1771 ... **LC 26**
See also DLB 313

**Helyar, Jane Penelope Josephine**
1933- ....................................... **CLC 17**
See also CA 21-24R; CANR 10, 26; CWRI 5; SAAS 2; SATA 5; SATA-Essay 138

**Hemans, Felicia** 1793-1835 ......... **NCLC 29, 71, 291; PC 170**
See also DLB 96; RGEL 2

**Hemingway, Ernest** 1899-1961 ........ **CLC 1, 3, 6, 8, 10, 13, 19, 30, 34, 39, 41, 44, 50, 61, 80; SSC 1, 25, 36, 40, 63, 117, 137, 168, 189, 190, 212, 229, 232, 234, 244, 263; TCLC 115, 203; WLC 3**
See also AAYA 19; AMW; AMWC 1; AMWR 1; BPFB 2; BYA 2, 3, 13, 15; CA 77-80; CANR 34; CDALB 1917-1929; CLR 168, 201; DA; DA3; DAB; DAC; DAM MST, NOV; DLB 4, 9, 102, 210, 308, 316, 330; DLBD 1, 15, 16; DLBY 1981, 1987, 1996, 1998; EWL 3; EXPN; EXPS; LAIT 3, 4; LATS 1:1; MAL 5; MTCW 1, 2; MTFW 2005; NFS 1, 5, 6, 14, 48; RGAL 4; RGSF 2; SSFS 1, 6, 8, 9, 11, 17, 26, 35; TUS; WYA

**Hemingway, Ernest Miller**
See Hemingway, Ernest

**Hempel, Amy** 1951- ......................... **CLC 39**
See also AMWS 21; CA 118; 137; CANR 70, 166; DA3; DLB 218; EXPS; MTCW 2; MTFW 2005; SSFS 2

**Henderson, Eleanor** ...................... **CLC 334**
See also CA 324

**Henderson, F. C.**
See Mencken, H. L.

**Henderson, Mary**
See Mavor, Osborne Henry

**Henderson, Smith** 1972- ............... **CLC 389**

**Henderson, Sylvia**
See Ashton-Warner, Sylvia (Constance)

**Henderson, Zenna (Chlarson)**
1917-1983 ................................. **SSC 29**
See also CA 1-4R; 133; CANR 1, 84; DLB 8; SATA 5; SFW 4

**Henisch, Peter** 1943- ...................... **CLC 385**
See also CA 177; DLB 85

**Henkin, Joshua** 1964- ..................... **CLC 119**
See also CA 161; CANR 186; DLB 350

**Henley, Beth** 1952- .................. **CLC 23, 255; DC 6, 14**
See also AAYA 70; CA 107; CABS 3; CAD; CANR 32, 73, 140; CD 5, 6; CSW; CWD;

DA3; DAM DRAM, MST; DFS 2, 21, 26; DLBY 1986; FW; MTCW 1, 2; MTFW 2005

**Henley, Elizabeth Becker**
See Henley, Beth

**Henley, William Ernest**
1849-1903 .................. **PC 127; TCLC 8**
See also CA 105; 234; DLB 19; PFS 43; RGEL 2

**Hennissart, Martha** 1929- ................ **CLC 2**
See also BPFB 2; CA 85-88; CANR 64; CMW 4; DLB 306

**Henry VIII** 1491-1547 ....................... **LC 10**
See also DLB 132

**Henry, O.** 1862-1910 .......... **SSC 5, 49, 117; TCLC 1, 19, 338; WLC 3**
See also AAYA 41; AMWS 2; CA 104; 131; CDALB 1865-1917; DA; DA3; DAB; DAC; DAM MST; DLB 12, 78, 79; EXPS; MAL 5; MTCW 1, 2; MTFW 2005; RGAL 4; RGSF 2; SSFS 2, 18, 27, 31; TCWW 1, 2; TUS; YABC 2

**Henry of Ghent** c. 1217-1293 .... **CMLC 199**
See also DLB 115

**Henry, Oliver**
See Henry, O.

**Henry, Patrick** 1736-1799 .......... **LC 25, 225**
See also LAIT 1

**Henry, Robert**
See MacDonald, John D.

**Henryson, Robert** 1430(?)-1506(?) .... **LC 20, 110; PC 65**
See also BRWS 7; DLB 146; RGEL 2

**Henschke, Alfred**
See Klabund

**Henson, Lance** 1944- ......................... **NNAL**
See also CA 146; DLB 175

**Hentoff, Nat(han Irving)** 1925- ...... **CLC 26**
See also AAYA 4, 42; BYA 6; CA 1-4R; CAAS 6; CANR 5, 25, 77, 114; CLR 1, 52; DLB 345; INT CANR-25; JRDA; MAICYA 1, 2; SATA 42, 69, 133; SATA-Brief 27; WYA; YAW

**Hentz, Caroline Lee** 1800-1856 .... **NCLC 281**
See also DLB 3, 248

**Heppenstall, (John) Rayner**
1911-1981 ................................. **CLC 10**
See also CA 1-4R; 103; CANR 29; CN 1, 2; CP 1, 2, 3; EWL 3

**Heraclitus** c. 540 BCE-c. 450 BCE .... **CMLC 22**
See also DLB 176

**Herber, William**
See Everson, William

**Herbert, Edward** 1583-1648 ............ **LC 177**
See also DLB 121, 151, 252; RGEL 2

**Herbert, Frank** 1920-1986 ........ **CLC 12, 23, 35, 44, 85**
See also AAYA 21; BPFB 2; BYA 4, 14; CA 53-56; 118; CANR 5, 43; CDALBS; CPW; DAM POP; DLB 8; INT CANR-5; LAIT 5; MTCW 1, 2; MTFW 2005; NFS 17, 31; SATA 9, 37; SATA-Obit 47; SCFW 1, 2; SFW 4; YAW

**Herbert, George** 1593-1633 ....... **LC 24, 121, 259; PC 4, 145, 194**
See also BRW 2; BRWR 2; CDBLB Before 1660; DAB; DAM POET; DLB 126; EXPP; PFS 25, 43; RGEL 2; TEA; WP

**Herbert, Zbigniew** 1924-1998 .... **CLC 9, 43; PC 50; TCLC 168**
See also CA 89-92; 169; CANR 36, 74, 177; CDWLB 4; CWW 2; DAM POET; DLB 232; EWL 3; MTCW 1; PFS 22

**Herbert of Cherbury, Lord**
See Herbert, Edward

**Herbst, Josephine (Frey)**
1897-1969 .................. **CLC 34; TCLC 243**
See also CA 5-8R; 25-28R; DLB 9

**Herder, Johann Gottfried von**
1744-1803 ........................ **NCLC 8, 186**

See also DLB 97; EW 4; TWA

**Heredia, Jose Maria** 1803-1839 ..... **HLCS 2; NCLC 209**
See also LAW

**Hergesheimer, Joseph**
1880-1954 ................................. **TCLC 11**
See also CA 109; 194; DLB 102, 9; RGAL 4

**Herlihy, James Leo** 1927-1993 ......... **CLC 6**
See also CA 1-4R; 143; CAD; CANR 2; CN 1, 2, 3, 4, 5

**Herman, William**
See Bierce, Ambrose

**Hermogenes** fl. c. 175 .................... **CMLC 6**

**Hernandez, Felisberto** 1902-1964 ... **SSC 152**
See also CA 213; EWL 3; LAWS 1

**Hernandez, Gilbert** 1957- ............. **CLC 378**
See also CA 37-40R; 171; 224; CANR 134, 211, 221, 268

**Hernandez, Jaime** 1959- ............... **CLC 378**
See also CA 37-40R; 171; 224; CANR 134, 211, 221, 268

**Hernandez, Jose** 1834-1886 ......... **NCLC 17, 269; PC 141**
See also LAW; RGWL 2, 3; WLIT 1

**Hernandez, Mario** 1953- ............... **CLC 378**
See also CA 37-40R; 171; 224; CANR 134, 211, 221, 268

**Herodotus** c. 484 BCE-c. 420 BCE ......... **CMLC 17, 163**
See also AW 1; CDWLB 1; DLB 176; RGWL 2, 3; TWA; WLIT 8

**Heron, Lili**
See Mansfield, Katherine

**Herr, Michael** 1940(?)- ................... **CLC 231**
See also CA 89-92; CANR 68, 142; DLB 185; MTCW 1

**Herrera, Fernando de** c. 1534-1597 ... **PC 180**
See also DLB 318

**Herrick, Robert**
1591-1674 ........ **LC 13, 145; PC 9, 138**
See also BRW 2; BRWC 2; DA; DAB; DAC; DAM MST, POP; DLB 126; EXPP; PFS 13, 29, 39; RGAL 4; RGEL 2; TEA; WP

**Herring, Guilles**
See Somerville, Edith Oenone

**Herriot, James** 1916-1995 .............. **CLC 12**
See also AAYA 1, 54; BPFB 2; CA 77-80; 148; CANR 40; CLR 80; CPW; DAM POP; LAIT 3; MAICYA 2; MAICYAS 1; MTCW 2; SATA 86, 135; SATA-Brief 44; TEA; YAW

**Herris, Violet**
See Hunt, Violet

**Herrmann, Dorothy** 1941- .............. **CLC 44**
See also CA 107

**Herrmann, Taffy**
See Herrmann, Dorothy

**Hersey, John** 1914-1993 ....... **CLC 1, 2, 7, 9, 40, 81, 97**
See also AAYA 29; BPFB 2; CA 17-20R; 140; CANR 33; CDALBS; CN 1, 2, 3, 4, 5; CPW; DAM POP; DLB 6, 185, 278, 299, 364; MAL 5; MTCW 1, 2; MTFW 2005; NFS 41; RGHL; SATA 25; SATA-Obit 76; TUS

**Hersey, John Richard**
See Hersey, John

**Hervent, Maurice**
See Grindel, Eugene

**Herzen, Aleksandr Ivanovich**
1812-1870 ................ **NCLC 10, 61, 323**
See also DLB 277

**Herzen, Alexander**
See Herzen, Aleksandr Ivanovich

**Herzl, Theodor** 1860-1904 ............. **TCLC 36**
See also CA 168

**Herzog, Werner** 1942- ............ **CLC 16, 236**
See also AAYA 85; CA 89-92; CANR 215

**Hesiod** fl. 8th cent. BCE .......... **CMLC 5, 102**
See also AW 1; DLB 176; RGWL 2, 3; WLIT 8

**Hesse, Hermann** 1877-1962 ..... **CLC 1, 2, 3, 6, 11, 17, 25, 69; SSC 9, 49; TCLC 148, 196; WLC 3**
See also AAYA 43; BPFB 2; CA 17-18; CAP 2; CDWLB 2; DA; DA3; DAB; DAC; DAM MST, NOV; DLB 66, 330; EW 9; EWL 3; EXPN; LAIT 1; MTCW 1, 2; MTFW 2005; NFS 6, 15, 24; RGWL 2, 3; SATA 50; TWA

**Hewes, Cady**
See De Voto, Bernard (Augustine)

**Heyen, William** 1940- ................ **CLC 13, 18**
See also CA 33-36R, 220; CAAE 220; CAAS 9; CANR 98, 188; CP 3, 4, 5, 6, 7; DLB 5; RGHL

**Heyerdahl, Thor** 1914-2002 ............ **CLC 26**
See also CA 5-8R; 207; CANR 5, 22, 66, 73; LAIT 4; MTCW 1, 2; MTFW 2005; SATA 2, 52

**Heym, Georg (Theodor Franz Arthur)** 1887-1912 ................................. **TCLC 9**
See also CA 106; 181

**Heym, Stefan** 1913-2001 ................ **CLC 41**
See also CA 9-12R; 203; CANR 4; CWW 2; DLB 69; EWL 3

**Heyse, Paul (Johann Ludwig von)** 1830-1914 ................................. **TCLC 8**
See also CA 104; 209; DLB 129, 330

**Heyward, (Edwin) DuBose** 1885-1940 ... **HR 1:2; TCLC 59**
See also CA 108; 157; DLB 7, 9, 45, 249; MAL 5; SATA 21

**Heywood, John** 1497(?)-1580(?) ......... **LC 65**
See also DLB 136; RGEL 2

**Heywood, Thomas** 1573(?)-1641 ....... **DC 29; LC 111**
See also DAM DRAM; DLB 62; LMFS 1; RGEL 2; TEA

**Hiaasen, Carl** 1953- ...................... **CLC 238**
See also CA 105; CANR 22, 45, 65, 113, 133, 168; CMW 4; CPW; CSW; DA3; DLB 292; LNFS 2, 3; MTCW 2; MTFW 2005; SATA 208

**Hibbert, Eleanor Alice Burford** 1906-1993 .................................... **CLC 7**
See also BEST 90:4; BPFB 2; CA 17-20R; 140; CANR 9, 28, 59; CMW 4; CPW; DAM POP; MTCW 2; MTFW 2005; RHW; SATA 2; SATA-Obit 74

**Hichens, Robert (Smythe)** 1864-1950 .................................. **TCLC 64**
See also CA 162; DLB 153; HGG; RHW; SUFW

**Higden, Ranulf** c. 1280-1364 ..... **CMLC 179**

**Higgins, Aidan** 1927- ...................... **SSC 68**
See also CA 9-12R; CANR 70, 115, 148; CN 1, 2, 3, 4, 5, 6, 7; DLB 14

**Higgins, George V(incent)** 1939-1999 .................. **CLC 4, 7, 10, 18**
See also BPFB 2; CA 77-80; 186; CAAS 5; CANR 17, 51, 89, 96; CMW 4; CN 2, 3, 4, 5, 6; DLB 2; DLBY 1981, 1998; INT CANR-17; MSW; MTCW 1

**Higginson, Thomas Wentworth** 1823-1911 ................................. **TCLC 36**
See also CA 162; DLB 1, 64, 243

**Higgonet, Margaret** ........................ **CLC 65**

**Highet, Helen**
See MacInnes, Helen (Clark)

**Highsmith, Mary Patricia**
See Highsmith, Patricia

**Highsmith, Patricia** 1921-1995 ..... **CLC 2, 4, 14, 42, 102**
See also AAYA 48; BRWS 5; CA 1-4R; 147; CANR 1, 20, 48, 62, 108; CMW 4; CN 1, 2, 3, 4, 5; CPW; DA3; DAM NOV, POP;

DLB 306; GLL 1; MSW; MTCW 1, 2; MTFW 2005; NFS 27; SSFS 25

**Highwater, Jamake (Mamake)** 1942(?)-2001 ............................... **CLC 12**
See also AAYA 7, 69; BPFB 2; BYA 4; CA 65-68; 199; CAAS 7; CANR 10, 34, 84; CLR 17; CWRI 5; DLB 52; DLBY 1985; JRDA; MAICYA 1, 2; SATA 32, 69; SATA-Brief 30

**Highway, Tomson** 1951- ......... **CLC 92, 333; DC 33; NNAL**
See also CA 151; CANR 75; CCA 1; CD 5, 6; CN 7; DAC; DAM MULT; DFS 2; DLB 334; MTCW 2

**Hijuelos, Oscar** 1951-2013 ... **CLC 65; HLC 1**
See also AAYA 25; AMWS 8; BEST 90:1; CA 123; CANR 50, 75, 125, 205, 239; CPW; DA3; DAM MULT, POP; DLB 145; HW 1, 2; LLW; MAL 5; MTCW 2; MTFW 2005; NFS 17; RGAL 4; WLIT 1

**Hikmet, Nazim** 1902-1963 ............... **CLC 40**
See also CA 141; 93-96; EWL 3; PFS 38, 41; WLIT 6

**Hilbig, Wolfgang** 1941-2007 .......... **CLC 445**

**Hildegard von Bingen** 1098-1179 ..................... **CMLC 20, 118**
See also DLB 148

**Hildesheimer, Wolfgang** 1916-1991 ... **CLC 49**
See also CA 101; 135; DLB 69, 124; EWL 3; RGHL

**Hill, Aaron** 1685-1750 ...................... **LC 148**
See also DLB 84; RGEL 2

**Hill, Geoffrey** 1932- .............. **CLC 5, 8, 18, 45, 251; PC 125**
See also BRWR 3; BRWS 5; CA 81-84; CANR 21, 89; CDBLB 1960 to Present; CP 1, 2, 3, 4, 5, 6, 7; DAM POET; DLB 40; EWL 3; MTCW 1; RGEL 2; RGHL

**Hill, George Roy** 1921-2002 ........... **CLC 26**
See also CA 110; 122; 213

**Hill, John**
See Koontz, Dean

**Hill, Susan** 1942- ........................ **CLC 4, 113**
See also BRWS 14; CA 33-36R; CANR 29, 69, 129, 172, 201; CN 2, 3, 4, 5, 6, 7; DAB; DAM MST, NOV; DLB 14, 139; HGG; MTCW 1; RHW; SATA 183

**Hill, Susan Elizabeth**
See Hill, Susan

**Hill, Thomas**
See Ainsworth, William Harrison

**Hillard, Asa G. III** ........................ **CLC 70**

**Hillerman, Anthony Grove**
See Hillerman, Tony

**Hillerman, Tony** 1925-2008 ..... **CLC 62, 170**
See also AAYA 40; BEST 89:1; BPFB 2; CA 29-32R; 278; CANR 21, 42, 65, 97, 134; CMW 4; CPW; DA3; DAM POP; DLB 206, 306; MAL 5; MSW; MTCW 2; MTFW 2005; RGAL 4; SATA 6; SATA-Obit 198; TCWW 2; YAW

**Hillesum, Etty** 1914-1943 .............. **TCLC 49**
See also CA 137; RGHL

**Hilliard, Noel (Harvey)** 1929-1996 ... **CLC 15**
See also CA 9-12R; CANR 7, 69; CN 1, 2, 3, 4, 5, 6

**Hillis, Rick** 1956- ........................ **CLC 66**
See also CA 134

**Hilsenrath, Edgar** 1926- ............... **CLC 441**
See also CA 49-52; DLB 299; RGHL

**Hilton, James** 1900-1954 ............... **TCLC 21**
See also AAYA 76; CA 108; 169; DLB 34, 77; FANT; SATA 34

**Hilton, Walter** 1343-1396(?) ... **CMLC 58, 141**
See also DLB 146; RGEL 2

**Himes, Chester (Bomar)** 1909-1984 ....... **BLC 1:2; CLC 2, 4, 7, 18, 58, 108; TCLC 139**

See also AFAW 2; AMWS 16; BPFB 2; BW 2; CA 25-28R; 114; CANR 22, 89; CMW 4; CN 1, 2, 3; DAM MULT; DLB 2, 76, 143, 226; EWL 3; MAL 5; MSW; MTCW 1, 2; MTFW 2005; RGAL 4

**Himmelfarb, Gertrude** 1922- ........ **CLC 202**
See also CA 49-52; CANR 28, 66, 102, 166

**Hinde, Thomas** 1926- .................. **CLC 6, 11**
See also CA 5-8R; CN 1, 2, 3, 4, 5, 6; EWL 3

**Hine, (William) Daryl** 1936- .......... **CLC 15**
See also CA 1-4R; CAAS 15; CANR 1, 20; CP 1, 2, 3, 4, 5, 6, 7; DLB 60

**Hinkson, Katharine Tynan**
See Tynan, Katharine

**Hinojosa, Rolando** 1929- .................. **HLC 1**
See also CA 131; CAAS 16; CANR 62; DAM MULT; DLB 82; EWL 3; HW 1, 2; LLW; MTCW 2; MTFW 2005; RGAL 4

**Hinton, S. E.** 1950- .................. **CLC 30, 111**
See also AAYA 2, 33; BPFB 2; BYA 2, 3; CA 81-84; CANR 32, 62, 92, 133; CDALBS; CLR 3, 23; CPW; DA; DA3; DAB; DAC; DAM MST, NOV; JRDA; LAIT 5; MAICYA 1, 2; MTCW 1, 2; MTFW 2005; NFS 5, 9, 15, 16, 35; SATA 19, 58, 115, 160; WYA; YAW

**Hinton, Susan Eloise**
See Hinton, S. E.

**Hippius, Zinaida**
See Gippius, Zinaida

**Hiraoka, Kimitake** 1925-1970 ...... **CLC 2, 4, 6, 9, 27; DC 1; SSC 4; TCLC 161; WLC 4**
See Mishima, Yukio
See also AAYA 50; BPFB 2; CA 97-100; 29-32R; DA3; DAM MULT; DLB 182; EWL 3; GLL 1; MJW; MTCW 1, 2; RGSF 2; RGWL 2, 3; SSFS 5, 12

**Hirsch, E.D., Jr.** 1928- .................... **CLC 79**
See also CA 25-28R; CANR 27, 51, 146, 181; DLB 67; INT CANR-27; MTCW 1

**Hirsch, Edward** 1950- ............... **CLC 31, 50**
See also CA 104; CANR 20, 42, 102, 167, 229; CP 6, 7; DLB 120; PFS 22

**Hirsch, Eric Donald, Jr.**
See Hirsch, E.D., Jr.

**Hitchcock, Alfred (Joseph)** 1899-1980 ............. **CLC 16; TCLC 331**
See also AAYA 22; CA 159; 97-100; SATA 27; SATA-Obit 24

**Hitchens, Christopher** 1949-2011 ... **CLC 157**
See also CA 152; CANR 89, 155, 191

**Hitchens, Christopher Eric**
See Hitchens, Christopher

**Hitler, Adolf** 1889-1945 ................. **TCLC 53**
See also CA 117; 147

**Holderlin, (Johann Christian) Friedrich** 1770-1843 ... **NCLC 16, 187, 263; PC 4**
See also CDWLB 2; DLB 90; EW 5; RGWL 2, 3

**Hoagland, Edward (Morley)** 1932- ......................................... **CLC 28**
See also ANW; CA 1-4R; CANR 2, 31, 57, 107; CN 1, 2, 3, 4, 5, 6, 7; DLB 6; SATA 51; TCWW 2

**Hoban, Russell** 1925-2011 ........... **CLC 7, 25**
See also BPFB 2; CA 5-8R; CANR 23, 37, 66, 114, 138, 218; CLR 3, 69, 139; CN 4, 5, 6, 7; CWRI 5; DAM NOV; DLB 52; FANT; MAICYA 1, 2; MTCW 1, 2; MTFW 2005; SATA 1, 40, 78, 136; SFW 4; SUFW 4; TCLE 1:1

**Hoban, Russell Conwell**
See Hoban, Russell

**Hobbes, Thomas** 1588-1679 ... **LC 36, 142, 199**
See also DLB 151, 252, 281; RGEL 2

**Hobbs, Perry**
See Blackmur, R(ichard) P(almer)

**Hobson, Laura Z(ametkin)** 1900-1986 ............................ **CLC 7, 25**
See also BPFB 2; CA 17-20R; 118; CANR 55; CN 1, 2, 3, 4; DLB 28; SATA 52

**Hoccleve, Thomas** c. 1368-c. 1437 ... **LC 75; PC 146**
See also DLB 146; RGEL 2

**Hoch, Edward D.** 1930-2008 .......... **SSC 119**
See also CA 29-32R; CANR 11, 27, 51, 97; CMW 4; DLB 306; SFW 4

**Hoch, Edward Dentinger**
See Hoch, Edward D.

**Hochhuth, Rolf** 1931- .......... **CLC 4, 11, 18**
See also CA 5-8R; CANR 33, 75, 136; CWW 2; DAM DRAM; DLB 124; EWL 3; MTCW 1, 2; MTFW 2005; RGHL

**Hochman, Sandra** 1936- .............. **CLC 3, 8**
See also CA 5-8R; CP 1, 2, 3, 4, 5; DLB 5

**Hochwaelder, Fritz** 1911-1986 ........ **CLC 36**
See also CA 29-32R; 120; CANR 42; DAM DRAM; EWL 3; MTCW 1; RGWL 2, 3

**Hochwalder, Fritz**
See Hochwaelder, Fritz

**Hocking, Mary** 1921- ...................... **CLC 13**
See also CA 101; CANR 18, 40

**Hocking, Mary Eunice**
See Hocking, Mary

**Hodge, Merle** 1944- ......................... **BLC 2:2**
See also EWL 3

**Hodgins, Jack** 1938- ........ **CLC 23; SSC 132**
See also CA 93-96; CN 4, 5, 6, 7; DLB 60

**Hodgson, William Hope**
1877(?)-1918 ............................ **TCLC 13**
See also CA 111; 164; CMW 4; DLB 70, 153, 156, 178; HGG; MTCW 2; SFW 4; SUFW 1

**Hoeg, Peter**
See Høeg, Peter

**Høeg, Peter** 1957- ............. **CLC 95, 156, 398**
See also CA 151; CANR 75, 202; CMW 4; DA3; DLB 214; EWL 3; MTCW 2; MTFW 2005; NFS 17; RGWL 3; SSFS 18

**Hoffman, Alice** 1952- ...................... **CLC 51**
See also AAYA 37; AMWS 10; CA 77-80; CANR 34, 66, 100, 138, 170, 237; CN 4, 5, 6, 7; CPW; DAM NOV; DLB 292; MAL 5; MTCW 1, 2; MTFW 2005; TCLE 1:1

**Hoffman, Daniel (Gerard)**
1923-2013 ....... **CLC 6, 13, 23; PC 190**
See also CA 1-4R; CANR 4, 142; CP 1, 2, 3, 4, 5, 6, 7; DLB 5; TCLE 1:1

**Hoffman, Eva** 1945- ........................ **CLC 182**
See also AMWS 16; CA 132; CANR 146, 209

**Hoffman, Stanley** 1944- .................... **CLC 5**
See also CA 77-80

**Hoffman, William** 1925-2009 ........ **CLC 141**
See also AMWS 18; CA 21-24R; CANR 9, 103; CSW; DLB 234; TCLE 1:1

**Hoffman, William M.**
See Hoffman, William M(oses)

**Hoffman, William M(oses)** 1939- ... **CLC 40**
See also CA 57-60; CAD; CANR 11, 71; CD 5, 6

**Hoffmann, E(rnst) T(heodor) A(madeus)**
1776-1822 ...... **NCLC 2, 183, 364; SSC 13, 92**
See also CDWLB 2; CLR 133; DLB 90; EW 5; GL 2; RGSF 2; RGWL 2, 3; SATA 27; SUFW 1; WCH

**Hofmann, Gert** 1931-1993 .............. **CLC 54**
See also CA 128; CANR 145; EWL 3; RGHL

**Hofmannsthal, Hugo von**
1874-1929 ................... **DC 4; TCLC 11**
See also CA 106; 153; CDWLB 2; DAM DRAM; DFS 17; DLB 81, 118; EW 9; EWL 3; RGWL 2, 3

**Hoffmannswaldau, Christian Hoffmann von**
1616-1679 ................................... **LC 237**
See also DLB 168

**Hogan, Linda** 1947- ................. **CLC 73, 290; NNAL; PC 35**
See also AMWS 4; ANW; BYA 12; CA 120, 226; CAAE 226; CANR 45, 73, 129, 196; CWP; DAM MULT; DLB 175; SATA 132; TCWW 2

**Hogarth, Charles**
See Creasey, John

**Hogarth, Emmett**
See Polonsky, Abraham (Lincoln)

**Hogarth, William** 1697-1764 ............. **LC 112**
See also AAYA 56

**Hogg, James** 1770-1835 ................. **NCLC 4, 109, 260, 361; SSC 130**
See also BRWS 10; DLB 93, 116, 159; GL 2; HGG; RGEL 2; SUFW 1

**Holbach, Paul-Henri Thiry** 1723-1789 .. **LC 14**
See also DLB 313

**Holberg, Ludvig** 1684-1754 ......... **LC 6, 208**
See also DLB 300; RGWL 2, 3

**Holbrook, John**
See Vance, Jack

**Holcroft, Thomas** 1745-1809 ......... **NCLC 85**
See also DLB 39, 89, 158; RGEL 2

**Holden, Ursula** 1921- ...................... **CLC 18**
See also CA 101; CAAS 8; CANR 22

**Holdstock, Robert** 1948-2009 .......... **CLC 39**
See also CA 131; CANR 81, 207; DLB 261; FANT; HGG; SFW 4; SUFW 2

**Holdstock, Robert P.**
See Holdstock, Robert

**Holinshed, Raphael** fl. 1580 ....... **LC 69, 217**
See also DLB 167; RGEL 2

**Holland, Isabelle (Christian)**
1920-2002 .................................. **CLC 21**
See also AAYA 11, 64; CA 21-24R; 205; CAAE 181; CANR 10, 25, 47; CLR 57; CWRI 5; JRDA; LAIT 4; MAICYA 1, 2; SATA 8, 70; SATA-Essay 103; SATA-Obit 132; WYA

**Holland, Marcus**
See Caldwell, (Janet Miriam) Taylor (Holland)

**Hollander, John** 1929-2013 ..... **CLC 2, 5, 8, 14; PC 117**
See also CA 1-4R; CANR 1, 52, 136; CP 1, 2, 3, 4, 5, 6, 7; DLB 5; MAL 5; SATA 13

**Hollander, Paul**
See Silverberg, Robert

**Holleran, Andrew** 1943(?)- .............. **CLC 38**
See also CA 144; CANR 89, 162; GLL 1

**Holley, Marietta** 1836(?)-1926 ....... **TCLC 99**
See also CA 118; DLB 11; FL 1:3

**Hollinghurst, Alan** 1954- ... **CLC 55, 91, 329**
See also BRWS 10; CA 114; CN 5, 6, 7; DLB 207, 326; GLL 1

**Hollis, Jim**
See Summers, Hollis (Spurgeon, Jr.)

**Holly, Buddy** 1936-1959 ................ **TCLC 65**
See also CA 213

**Holmes, Gordon**
See Shiel, M. P.

**Holmes, John**
See Souster, (Holmes) Raymond

**Holmes, John Clellon** 1926-1988 .... **CLC 56**
See also BG 1:2; CA 9-12R; 125; CANR 4; CN 1, 2, 3, 4; DLB 16, 237

**Holmes, Oliver Wendell, Jr.**
1841-1935 .................................. **TCLC 77**
See also CA 114; 186

**Holmes, Oliver Wendell**
1809-1894 ........... **NCLC 14, 81; PC 71**
See also AMWS 1; CDALB 1640-1865; DLB 1, 189, 235; EXPP; PFS 24; RGAL 4; SATA 34

**Holmes, Raymond**
See Souster, (Holmes) Raymond

**Holt, Elliott** 1974- ........................... **CLC 370**
See also CA 351

**Holt, Samuel**
See Westlake, Donald E.

**Holt, Victoria**
See Hibbert, Eleanor Alice Burford

**Holub, Miroslav** 1923-1998 ............... **CLC 4**
See also CA 21-24R; 169; CANR 10; CDWLB 4; CWW 2; DLB 232; EWL 3; RGWL 3

**Holz, Detlev**
See Benjamin, Walter

**Homer** c. 8th cent. BCE ........... **CMLC 1, 16, 61, 121, 166; PC 23; WLCS**
See also AW 1; CDWLB 1; DA; DA3; DAB; DAC; DAM MST, POET; DLB 176; EFS 1:1, 2:1,2; LAIT 1; LMFS 1; RGWL 2, 3; TWA; WLIT 8; WP

**Hong, Maxine Ting Ting**
See Kingston, Maxine Hong

**Hongo, Garrett Kaoru** 1951- ............. **PC 23**
See also CA 133; CAAS 22; CP 5, 6, 7; DLB 120, 312; EWL 3; EXPP; PFS 25, 33, 43; RGAL 4

**Honig, Edwin** 1919-2011 ................. **CLC 33**
See also CA 5-8R; CAAS 8; CANR 4, 45, 144; CP 1, 2, 3, 4, 5, 6, 7; DLB 5

**Hood, Hugh (John Blagdon)**
1928- .......... **CLC 15, 28, 273; SSC 42**
See also CA 49-52; CAAS 17; CANR 1, 33, 87; CN 1, 2, 3, 4, 5, 6, 7; DLB 53; RGSF 2

**Hood, Thomas** 1799-1845 ............. **NCLC 16, 242; PC 93**
See also BRW 4; DLB 96; RGEL 2

**Hooft, Pieter Corneliszoon**
1581-1647 ................................ **LC 214**
See also RGWL 2, 3

**Hooker, (Peter) Jeremy** 1941- ........ **CLC 43**
See also CA 77-80; CANR 22; CP 2, 3, 4, 5, 6, 7; DLB 40

**Hooker, Richard** 1554-1600 ............. **LC 95**
See also BRW 1; DLB 132; RGEL 2

**Hooker, Thomas** 1586-1647 ............. **LC 137**
See also DLB 24

**hooks, bell** 1952(?)- ............ **BLCS; CLC 94**
See also BW 2; CA 143; CANR 87, 126, 211; DLB 246; MTCW 2; MTFW 2005; SATA 115, 170

**Hooper, Johnson Jones**
1815-1862 ............................. **NCLC 177**
See also DLB 3, 11, 248; RGAL 4

**Hope, A(lec) D(erwent)**
1907-2000 ................ **CLC 3, 51; PC 56**
See also BRWS 7; CA 21-24R; 188; CANR 33, 74; CP 1, 2, 3, 4, 5; DLB 289; EWL 3; MTCW 1, 2; MTFW 2005; PFS 8; RGEL 2

**Hope, Anthony** 1863-1933 ................ **TCLC 83**
See also CA 157; DLB 153, 156; RGEL 2; RHW

**Hope, Brian**
See Creasey, John

**Hope, Christopher** 1944- ................. **CLC 52**
See also AFW; CA 106; CANR 47, 101, 177; CN 4, 5, 6, 7; DLB 225; SATA 62

**Hope, Christopher David Tully**
See Hope, Christopher

**Hopkins, Gerard Manley**
1844-1889 ........ **NCLC 17, 189; PC 15; WLC 3**
See also BRW 5; BRWR 2; CDBLB 1890-1914; DA; DA3; DAB; DAC; DAM MST, POET; DLB 35, 57; EXPP; PAB; PFS 26, 40; RGEL 2; TEA; WP

**Hopkins, John (Richard)** 1931-1998 ... **CLC 4**
See also CA 85-88; 169; CBD; CD 5, 6

**Hopkins, Pauline Elizabeth**
1859-1930 ..... **BLC 1:2; TCLC 28, 251**
See also AFAW 2; BW 2, 3; CA 141; CANR 82; DAM MULT; DLB 50

**Hopkinson, Francis** 1737-1791 ......... **LC 25**
See also DLB 31; RGAL 4

**Hopkinson, Nalo** 1960- ................... **CLC 316**
See also AAYA 40; CA 196, 219; CAAE 219; CANR 173; DLB 251

**Hopley, George**
See Hopley-Woolrich, Cornell George

**Hopley-Woolrich, Cornell George**
1903-1968 ................................... **CLC 77**
See also CA 13-14; CANR 58, 156; CAP 1;
CMW 4; DLB 226; MSW; MTCW 2

**Horace** 65 BCE-8 BCE ............ **CMLC 39, 125;
PC 46**
See also AW 2; CDWLB 1; DLB 211;
RGWL 2, 3; WLIT 8

**Horatio**
See Proust, Marcel

**Horgan, Paul (George Vincent O'Shaughnessy)**
1903-1995 ................................. **CLC 9, 53**
See also BPFB 2; CA 13-16R; 147; CANR
9, 35; CN 1, 2, 3, 4, 5; DAM NOV; DLB
102, 212; DLBY 1985; INT CANR-9;
MTCW 1, 2; MTFW 2005; SATA 13;
SATA-Obit 84; TCWW 1, 2

**Horkheimer, Max** 1895-1973 ...... **TCLC 132**
See also CA 216; 41-44R; DLB 296

**Horn, Peter**
See Kuttner, Henry

**Hornby, Nicholas Peter John**
See Hornby, Nick

**Hornby, Nick** 1957(?)- ................... **CLC 243**
See also AAYA 74; BRWS 15; CA 151;
CANR 104, 151, 191; CN 7; DLB 207, 352

**Horne, Frank** 1899-1974 ................... **HR 1:2**
See also BW 1; CA 125; 53-56; DLB 51; WP

**Horne, Richard Henry Hengist**
1802(?)-1884 ......................... **NCLC 127**
See also DLB 32; SATA 29

**Hornem, Horace Esq.**
See Lord Byron

**Horne Tooke, John** 1736-1812 .... **NCLC 195**

**Horney, Karen (Clementine Theodore
Danielsen)** 1885-1952 .......... **TCLC 71**
See also CA 114; 165; DLB 246; FW

**Hornung, E(rnest) W(illiam)**
1866-1921 ................................ **TCLC 59**
See also CA 108; 160; CMW 4; DLB 70

**Horovitz, Israel** 1939- ................... **CLC 56**
See also CA 33-36R; CAD; CANR 46, 59; CD
5, 6; DAM DRAM; DLB 7, 341; MAL 5

**Horton, George Moses**
1797(?)-1883(?) ....................... **NCLC 87**
See also DLB 50

**Horvath, Oedoen von**
See Horvath, Odon von

**Horvath, Odon von** 1901-1938 ..... **TCLC 45**
See also CA 118; 184, 194; DLB 85, 124;
EWL 3; RGWL 2, 3

**Horwitz, Julius** 1920-1986 .............. **CLC 14**
See also CA 9-12R; 119; CANR 12

**Horwitz, Ronald**
See Harwood, Ronald

**Hospital, Janette Turner**
1942- ........................... **CLC 42, 145, 321**
See also CA 108; CANR 48, 166, 200; CN
5, 6, 7; DLB 325; DLBY 2002; RGSF 2

**Hosseini, Khaled** 1965- ................. **CLC 254**
See also CA 225; LNFS 1, 3; SATA 156

**Hostos, E. M. de**
See Hostos (y Bonilla), Eugenio Maria de

**Hostos, Eugenio M. de**
See Hostos (y Bonilla), Eugenio Maria de

**Hostos, Eugenio Maria**
See Hostos (y Bonilla), Eugenio Maria de

**Hostos (y Bonilla), Eugenio Maria de**
1839-1903 ............................... **TCLC 24**
See also CA 123; 131; HW 1

**Hou Hsiao-hsien** 1947- ................... **CLC 402**

**Hou, Lei**
See Hou Hsiao-hsien

**Houdini**
See Lovecraft, H. P.

**Houellebecq, Michel** 1958- .... **CLC 179, 311**
See also CA 185; CANR 140, 231; MTFW
2005

**Hougan, Carolyn** 1943-2007 .......... **CLC 34**
See also CA 139; 257

**Hour, Shiaw Shyann**
See Hou Hsiao-hien

**Household, Geoffrey** 1900-1988 ...... **CLC 11**
See also BRWS 17; CA 77-80; 126; CANR
58; CMW 4; CN 1, 2, 3, 4; DLB 87; SATA
14; SATA-Obit 59

**Housman, A. E.** 1859-1936 .......... **PC 2, 43;
TCLC 1, 10; WLCS**
See also AAYA 66; BRW 6; CA 104; 125;
DA; DA3; DAB; DAC; DAM MST, POET;
DLB 19, 284; EWL 3; EXPP; MTCW 1, 2;
MTFW 2005; PAB; PFS 4, 7, 40; RGEL 2;
TEA; WP

**Housman, Alfred Edward**
See Housman, A. E.

**Housman, Laurence** 1865-1959 ...... **TCLC 7**
See also CA 106; 155; DLB 10; FANT;
RGEL 2; SATA 25

**Houston, Jeanne Wakatsuki** 1934- ....... **AAL**
See also AAYA 49; CA 103, 232; CAAE
232; CAAS 16; CANR 29, 123, 167; LAIT
4; SATA 78, 168; SATA-Essay 168

**Houth, Eduardo**
See Barker, Howard

**Hove, Chenjerai** 1956- ................... **BLC 2:2**
See also CP 7; DLB 360

**Howard, E. J.**
See Howard, Elizabeth Jane

**Howard, Elizabeth Jane** 1923- ... **CLC 7, 29**
See also BRWS 11; CA 5-8R; CANR 8, 62,
146, 210; CN 1, 2, 3, 4, 5, 6, 7

**Howard, Maureen** 1930- ........... **CLC 5, 14,
46, 151**
See also CA 53-56; CANR 31, 75, 140, 221;
CN 4, 5, 6, 7; DLBY 1983; INT CANR-
31; MTCW 1, 2; MTFW 2005

**Howard, Richard** 1929- ....... **CLC 7, 10, 47;
PC 168**
See also AITN 1; CA 85-88; CANR 25, 80,
154, 217; CP 1, 2, 3, 4, 5, 6, 7; DLB 5;
INT CANR-25; MAL 5

**Howard, Robert E.** 1906-1936 ...... **SSC 202;
TCLC 8**
See also AAYA 80; BPFB 2; BYA 5; CA
105; 157; CANR 155; FANT; SUFW 1;
TCWW 1, 2

**Howard, Robert Ervin**
See Howard, Robert E.

**Howard, Sidney (Coe)** 1891-1939 ..... **DC 42**
See also CA 198; DFS 29; DLB 7, 26, 249;
IDFW 3, 4; MAL 5; RGAL 4

**Howard, Warren F.**
See Pohl, Frederik

**Howe, Fanny** 1940- ........... **CLC 47; PC 197**
See also CA 117; 187; CAAE 187; CAAS
27; CANR 70, 116, 184, 240; CP 6, 7;
CWP; SATA-Brief 52

**Howe, Fanny Quincy**
See Howe, Fanny

**Howe, Irving** 1920-1993 ................. **CLC 85**
See also AMWS 6; CA 9-12R; 141; CANR
21, 50; DLB 67; EWL 3; MAL 5; MTCW
1, 2; MTFW 2005

**Howe, Julia Ward** 1819-1910 .......... **PC 81;
TCLC 21**
See also CA 117; 191; DLB 1, 189, 235; FW

**Howe, Susan** 1937- ..... **CLC 72, 152; PC 54**
See also AMWS 4; CA 160; CANR 209; CP
5, 6, 7; CWP; DLB 120; FW; RGAL 4

**Howe, Tina** 1937- ............... **CLC 48; DC 43**
See also CA 109; CAD; CANR 125; CD 5,
6; CWD; DLB 341

**Howell, James** 1594(?)-1666 .............. **LC 13**
See also DLB 151

**Howells, W. D.**
See Howells, William Dean

**Howells, William D.**
See Howells, William Dean

**Howells, William Dean** 1837-1920 ... **SSC 36,
TCLC 7, 17, 41**
See also AMW; CA 104; 134; CDALB 1865-
1917; DLB 12, 64, 74, 79, 189; LMFS 1;
MAL 5; MTCW 2; NFS 43; RGAL 4; TUS

**Howes, Barbara** 1914-1996 ............. **CLC 15**
See also CA 9-12R; 151; CAAS 3; CANR
53; CP 1, 2, 3, 4, 5, 6; SATA 5; TCLE 1:1

**Hrabal, Bohumil** 1914-1997 ..... **CLC 13, 67;
TCLC 155**
See also CA 106; 156; CAAS 12; CANR 57;
CWW 2; DLB 232; EWL 3; RGSF 2

**Hrabanus Maurus** 776(?)-856 ...... **CMLC 78**
See also DLB 148

**Hroswitha of Gandersheim**
See Hrotsvit of Gandersheim

**Hrotsvit of Gandersheim**
c. 935-c. 1000 ............... **CMLC 29, 123**
See also DLB 148

**Hsi, Chu** 1130-1200 ....................... **CMLC 42**

**Hsun, Lu**
See Shu-Jen, Chou

**Huan Yue**
See Shen Congwen

**Huang Chunming** 1935- ............... **CLC 438**

**Hubbard, L. Ron** 1911-1986 ........... **CLC 43**
See also AAYA 64; CA 77-80; 118; CANR
52; CPW; DA3; DAM POP; FANT;
MTCW 2; MTFW 2005; SFW 4

**Hubbard, Lafayette Ronald**
See Hubbard, L. Ron

**Huber, L. F.**
See Huber, Therese

**Huber, Therese** 1764-1829 ........... **NCLC 320**
See also DLB 90

**Huch, Ricarda (Octavia)**
1864-1947 ................................ **TCLC 13**
See also CA 111; 189; DLB 66; EWL 3

**Huddle, David** 1942- ....................... **CLC 49**
See also CA 57-60, 261; CAAS 20; CANR
89; DLB 130

**Hudgins, Andrew** 1951- .................... **PC 175**
See also CA 21, 132; CANR 90, 151, 266;
CSW; DLB 120, 282; PFS 14

**Hudson, Jeffery**
See Crichton, Michael

**Hudson, Jeffrey**
See Crichton, Michael

**Hudson, W(illiam) H(enry)**
1841-1922 ................................. **TCLC 29**
See also CA 115; 190; DLB 98, 153, 174;
RGEL 2; SATA 35

**Hueffer, Ford Madox**
See Ford, Ford Madox

**Hugh of Saint Victor**
c. 1096-1141 ......................... **CMLC 186**
See also DLB 208

**Hughart, Barry** 1934- ..................... **CLC 39**
See also CA 137; FANT; SFW 4; SUFW 2

**Hughes, Colin**
See Creasey, John

**Hughes, David (John)** 1930-2005 ... **CLC 48**
See also CA 116; 129; 238; CN 4, 5, 6, 7;
DLB 14

**Hughes, Edward James**
See Hughes, Ted

**Hughes, James Langston**
See Hughes, Langston

**Hughes, Langston** 1902-1967 ........ **BLC 1:2;
CLC 1, 5, 10, 15, 35, 44, 108; DC 3; HR
1:2; PC 1, 53; SSC 6, 90, 235; WLC 3**
See also AAYA 12; AFAW 1, 2; AMWR 1;
AMWS 1; BW 1, 3; CA 1-4R; 25-28R;
CANR 1, 34, 82; CDALB 1929-1941; CLR
17; DA; DA3; DAB; DAC; DAM DRAM,
MST, MULT, POET; DFS 6, 18; DLB 4, 7,
48, 51, 86, 228, 315; EWL 3; EXPP;

**Idris, Yusuf** 1927-1991 .................... **SSC 74;**
  **TCLC 232**
    See also AFW; DLB 346; EWL 3; RGSF 2,
    3; RGWL 3; WLIT 2

**Ignatieff, Michael** 1947- ................. **CLC 236**
    See also CA 144; CANR 88, 156; CN 6, 7;
    DLB 267

**Ignatieff, Michael Grant**
    See Ignatieff, Michael

**Ignatius of Antioch, Saint**
    c. 35-108 ............................. **CMLC 187**

**Ignatius of Loyola, Saint** 1491-1556 ... **LC 252**

**Ignatow, David** 1914-1997 ..... **CLC 4, 7, 14,**
  **40; PC 34**
    See also CA 9-12R; 162; CAAS 3; CANR
    31, 57, 96; CP 1, 2, 3, 4, 5, 6; DLB 5;
    EWL 3; MAL 5

**Ignotus**
    See Strachey, (Giles) Lytton

**Ihimaera, Witi (Tame)** 1944- .... **CLC 46, 329**
    See also CA 77-80; CANR 130; CN 2, 3, 4,
    5, 6, 7; RGSF 2; SATA 148

**Il'f, Il'ia**
    See Fainzilberg, Ilya Arnoldovich

**Ilf, Ilya**
    See Fainzilberg, Ilya Arnoldovich

**Illyes, Gyula** 1902-1983 ....................... **PC 16**
    See also CA 114; 109; CDWLB 4; DLB 215;
    EWL 3; RGWL 2, 3

**Imalayan, Fatima-Zohra**
    See Djebar, Assia

**Imalayène, Fatima-Zohra**
    See Djebar, Assia

**Imalayène, Fatma-Zohra**
    See Djebar, Assia

**Imalhayène, Fatma-Zohra**
    See Djebar, Assia

**Immermann, Karl (Lebrecht)**
    1796-1840 ......................... **NCLC 4, 49**
    See also DLB 133

**Ince, Thomas H.** 1882-1924 ......... **TCLC 89**
    See also IDFW 3, 4

**Inchbald, Elizabeth** 1753-1821 .... **NCLC 62,**
  **276**
    See also BRWS 15; DLB 39, 89; RGEL 2

**Inclan, Ramon del Valle**
    See Valle-Inclan, Ramon del

**Incogniteau, Jean-Louis**
    See Kerouac, Jack

**Infante, Guillermo Cabrera**
    See Cabrera Infante, G.

**Ingalls, Rachel** 1940- ....................... **CLC 42**
    See also CA 123; 127; CANR 154

**Ingalls, Rachel Holmes**
    See Ingalls, Rachel

**Ingamells, Reginald Charles**
    See Ingamells, Rex

**Ingamells, Rex** 1913-1955 ............. **TCLC 35**
    See also CA 167; DLB 260

**Inge, William (Motter)** 1913-1973 ... **CLC 1,**
  **8, 19; DC 37; TCLC 283**
    See also CA 9-12R; CAD; CDALB 1941-
    1968; DA3; DAM DRAM; DFS 1, 3, 5, 8;
    DLB 7, 249; EWL 3; MAL 5; MTCW 1, 2;
    MTFW 2005; RGAL 4; TUS

**Ingelow, Jean** 1820-1897 ...... **NCLC 39, 107;**
  **PC 119**
    See also DLB 35, 163; FANT; SATA 33

**Ingram, Willis J.**
    See Harris, Mark

**Innaurato, Albert (F.)** 1948(?)- ... **CLC 21, 60**
    See also CA 115; 122; CAD; CANR 78; CD
    5, 6; INT CA-122

**Innes, Michael**
    See Stewart, J(ohn) I(nnes) M(ackintosh)

**Innis, Harold Adams** 1894-1952 ... **TCLC 77**
    See also CA 181; DLB 88

**Insluis, Alanus de**
    See Alain de Lille

**Iola**
    See Wells-Barnett, Ida B(ell)

**Ion**
    See Günderrode, Karoline von

**Ionesco, Eugene** 1909-1994 ... **CLC 1, 4, 6, 9,**
  **11, 15, 41, 86; DC 12; TCLC 232; WLC 3**
    See also CA 9-12R; 144; CANR 55, 132;
    CWW 2; DA; DA3; DAB; DAC; DAM
    DRAM, MST; DFS 4, 9, 25; DLB 321;
    EW 13; EWL 3; GFL 1789 to the Present;
    LMFS 2; MTCW 1, 2; MTFW 2005;
    RGWL 2, 3; SATA 7; SATA-Obit 79; TWA

**Iqbal, Muhammad** 1877-1938 ....... **TCLC 28**
    See also CA 215; EWL 3

**Ireland, Patrick**
    See O'Doherty, Brian

**Irenaeus St.** 130- ......................... **CMLC 42**

**Irigaray, Luce** 1930- ................. **CLC 164, 326**
    See also CA 154; CANR 121; FW

**Irish, William**
    See Hopley-Woolrich, Cornell George

**Irland, David**
    See Green, Julien

**Iron, Ralph**
    See Schreiner, Olive

**Ironside, Nestor**
    See Addison, Joseph

**Irving, John** 1942- ............. **CLC 13, 23, 38,**
  **112, 175**
    See also AAYA 8, 62; AMWS 6; BEST 89:3;
    BPFB 2; CA 25-28R; CANR 28, 73, 112,
    133, 223; CN 3, 4, 5, 6, 7; CPW; DA3;
    DAM NOV, POP; DLB 6, 278; DLBY
    1982; EWL 3; MAL 5; MTCW 1, 2;
    MTFW 2005; NFS 12, 14; RGAL 4; TUS

**Irving, John Winslow**
    See Irving, John

**Irving, Washington** 1783-1859 ......... **NCLC 2,**
  **19, 95, 242; SSC 2, 37, 104, 197, 210, 211;**
  **WLC 3**
    See also AAYA 56; AMW; CDALB 1640-
    1865; CLR 97; DA; DA3; DAB; DAC;
    DAM MST; DLB 3, 11, 30, 59, 73, 74,
    183, 186, 250, 254; EXPS; GL 2; LAIT 1;
    RGAL 4; RGSF 2; SSFS 1, 8, 16; SUFW
    1; TUS; WCH; YABC 2

**Irwin, P. K.**
    See Page, P.K.

**Isaacs, Jorge Ricardo** 1837-1895 .. **NCLC 70**
    See also LAW

**Isaacs, Susan** 1943- ......................... **CLC 32**
    See also BEST 89:1; BPFB 2; CA 89-92;
    CANR 20, 41, 65, 112, 134, 165, 226;
    CPW; DA3; DAM POP; INT CANR-20;
    MTCW 1, 2; MTFW 2005

**Isherwood, Christopher** 1904-1986 ... **CLC 1,**
  **9, 11, 14, 44; SSC 56; TCLC 227**
    See also AMWS 14; BRW 7; CA 13-16R;
    117; CANR 35, 97, 133; CN 1, 2, 3; DA3;
    DAM DRAM, NOV; DLB 15, 195; DLBY
    1986; EWL 3; IDTP; MTCW 1, 2; MTFW
    2005; RGAL 4; RGEL 2; TUS; WLIT 4

**Isherwood, Christopher William Bradshaw**
    See Isherwood, Christopher

**Ishiguro, Kazuo** 1954- ....... **CLC 27, 56, 59,**
  **110, 219, 439**
    See also AAYA 58; BEST 90:2; BPFB 2;
    BRWR 3; BRWS 4; CA 120; CANR 49, 95,
    133, 299; CMTFW; CN 5, 6, 7; DA3; DAM
    NOV; DLB 194, 326, 377; EWL 3; MTCW
    1, 2; MTFW 2005; MBL; NFS 13, 35, 39;
    WLIT 4; WWE 1

**Ishikawa, Hakuhin**
    See Ishikawa, Takuboku

**Ishikawa, Takuboku** 1886(?)-1912 .... **PC 10;**
  **TCLC 15**
    See Ishikawa Takuboku
    See also CA 113; 153; DAM POET

**Isidore of Seville** c. 560-636 ....... **CMLC 101**

**Iskander**
    See Herzen, Aleksandr Ivanovich

**Iskander, Fazil (Abdulovich)** 1929- ... **CLC 47**
    See also CA 102; DLB 302; EWL 3

**Iskander, Fazil' Abdulevich**
    See Iskander, Fazil (Abdulovich)

**Islas, Arturo** 1938-1991 ............... **TCLC 321**
    See also CA 131, 140; DLB 122; HW 1

**Isler, Alan (David)** 1934- ................. **CLC 91**
    See also CA 156; CANR 105

**Ivan IV** 1530-1584 ............................. **LC 17**

**Ivanov, V.I.**
    See Ivanov, Vyacheslav

**Ivanov, Vyacheslav** 1866-1949 ...... **TCLC 33**
    See also CA 122; EWL 3

**Ivanov, Vyacheslav Ivanovich**
    See Ivanov, Vyacheslav

**Ivask, Ivar Vidrik** 1927-1992 ......... **CLC 14**
    See also CA 37-40R; 139; CANR 24

**Ives, Morgan**
    See Bradley, Marion Zimmer

**Ivo of Chartres** c. 1040-1115 ..... **CMLC 116**

**Izumi Shikibu** c. 973-c. 1034 ....... **CMLC 33**

**J. R. S.**
    See Gogarty, Oliver St. John

**Jabès, Edmond** 1912-1991 .......... **TCLC 304**
    See also CA 127, 133; EWL 3; RGHL

**Jabran, Kahlil**
    See Gibran, Kahlil

**Jabran, Khalil**
    See Gibran, Kahlil

**Jaccottet, Philippe** 1925- ..................... **PC 98**
    See also CA 116; 129; CWW 2; GFL 1789
    to the Present

**Jackson, Charles R.** 1903-1968 .. **TCLC 347**
    See also CA 25-28R; DLB 234

**Jackson, Daniel**
    See Wingrove, David

**Jackson, Helen Hunt**
    1830-1885 ...................... **NCLC 90, 256**
    See also DLB 42, 47, 186, 189; RGAL 4

**Jackson, Jesse** 1908-1983 ............... **CLC 12**
    See also BW 1; CA 25-28R; 109; CANR 27;
    CLR 28; CWRI 5; MAICYA 1, 2; SATA 2,
    29; SATA-Obit 48

**Jackson, Laura** 1901-1991 .......... **CLC 3, 7;**
  **PC 44; TCLC 240**
    See also CA 65-68; 135; CANR 28, 89; CP
    1, 2, 3, 4, 5; DLB 48; RGAL 4

**Jackson, Laura Riding**
    See Jackson, Laura

**Jackson, Sam**
    See Trumbo, Dalton

**Jackson, Sara**
    See Wingrove, David

**Jackson, Shirley** 1916-1965 ...... **CLC 11, 60,**
  **87; SSC 9, 39, 213; TCLC 187; WLC 3**
    See also AAYA 9; AMWS 9; BPFB 2; CA
    1-4R; 25-28R; CANR 4, 52; CDALB
    1941-1968; DA; DA3; DAC; DAM MST;
    DLB 6, 234; EXPS; HGG; LAIT 4; MAL
    5; MTCW 2; MTFW 2005; NFS 37;
    RGAL 4; RGSF 2; SATA 2; SSFS 1, 27,
    30, 37; SUFW 1, 2

**Jacob, (Cyprien-)Max** 1876-1944 ... **TCLC 6**
    See also CA 104; 193; DLB 258; EWL 3;
    GFL 1789 to the Present; GLL 2; RGWL
    2, 3

**Jacobs, Harriet A.**
    1813(?)-1897 ................... **NCLC 67, 162**
    See also AFAW 1, 2; DLB 239; FL 1:3; FW;
    LAIT 2; RGAL 4

**Jacobs, Harriet Ann**
    See Jacobs, Harriet A.

**Jacobs, Jim** 1942- ........................... **CLC 12**
    See also CA 97-100; INT CA-97-100

DAB; DAM NOV; DLB 139, 194, 323, 326; EWL 3; IDFW 3, 4; INT CANR-29; MTCW 1, 2; MTFW 2005; RGSF 2; RGWL 2; RHW; TEA

**Jia Pingwa** 1952- ........................... **CLC 437**

**Jibran, Kahlil**
See Gibran, Kahlil

**Jibran, Khalil**
See Gibran, Kahlil

**Jiles, Paulette** 1943- ................... **CLC 13, 58**
See also CA 101; CANR 70, 124, 170; CP 5; CWP

**Jimenez, Juan Ramon** 1881-1958 ... **HLC 1; PC 7; TCLC 4, 183**
See also CA 104; 131; CANR 74; DAM MULT, POET; DLB 134, 330; EW 9; EWL 3; HW 1; MTCW 1, 2; MTFW 2005; NFS 36; RGWL 2, 3

**Jimenez, Ramon**
See Jimenez, Juan Ramon

**Jimenez Mantecon, Juan**
See Jimenez, Juan Ramon

**Jimenez Mantecon, Juan Ramon**
See Jimenez, Juan Ramon

**Jin, Ba** 1904-2005 ............................ **CLC 18**
See Cantu, Robert Clark
See also CA 105; 244; CWW 2; DLB 328; EWL 3

**Jin, Ha** 1956- ................. **CLC 109, 262, 424**
See also AMWS 18; CA 152; CANR 91, 130, 184; DLB 244, 292; MTFW 2005; NFS 25; SSFS 17, 32

**Jin, Xuefei**
See Jin, Ha

**Jin Ha**
See Jin, Ha

**Jin Yong** 1924- ............................... **CLC 358**
See also DLB 370

**Junger, Ernst**
See Juenger, Ernst

**Jobbry, Archibald**
See Galt, John

**Jodelle, Etienne** 1532-1573 ............... **LC 119**
See also DLB 327; GFL Beginnings to 1789

**Joel, Billy** 1949- ................................. **CLC 26**
See also CA 108

**Joel, William Martin**
See Joel, Billy

**John, St.**
See John of Damascus, St.

**John of Damascus, St.**
c. 675-749 ...................... **CMLC 27, 95**

**John of Salisbury**
c. 1120-1180 ................. **CMLC 63, 128**

**John of the Cross, St.**
1542-1591 ......................... **LC 18, 146**
See also RGWL 2, 3

**John Paul II, Pope** 1920-2005 ...... **CLC 128**
See also CA 106; 133; 238

**Johnson, B(ryan) S(tanley William)**
1933-1973 ............................... **CLC 6, 9**
See also CA 9-12R; 53-56; CANR 9; CN 1; CP 1, 2; DLB 14, 40; EWL 3; RGEL 2

**Johnson, Benjamin F., of Boone**
See Riley, James Whitcomb

**Johnson, Charles (Richard)**
1948- ........... **BLC 1:2, 2:2; CLC 7, 51, 65, 163; SSC 160**
See also AFAW 2; AMWS 6; BW 2, 3; CA 116; CAAS 18; CANR 42, 66, 82, 129; CN 5, 6, 7; DAM MULT; DLB 33, 278; MAL 5; MTCW 2; MTFW 2005; NFS 43; RGAL 4; SSFS 16

**Johnson, Charles S(purgeon)**
1893-1956 ............................. **HR 1:3**
See also BW 1, 3; CA 125; CANR 82; DLB 51, 91

**Johnson, Denis** 1949-2017 ...... **CLC 52, 160, 444; SSC 56**

See also CA 117, 121; CANR 71, 99, 178, 290; CN 4, 5, 6, 7; DLB 120

**Johnson, Diane** 1934- .... **CLC 5, 13, 48, 244**
See also BPFB 2; CA 41-44R; CANR 17, 40, 62, 95, 155, 198; CN 4, 5, 6, 7; DLB 350; DLBY 1980; INT CANR-17; MTCW 1

**Johnson, E(mily) Pauline**
1861-1913 ...................... **NNAL; PC 199**
See also CA 150; CCA 1; DAC; DAM MULT; DLB 92, 175; TCWW 2

**Johnson, Eyvind (Olof Verner)**
1900-1976 ................................. **CLC 14**
See also CA 73-76; 69-72; CANR 34, 101; DLB 259, 330; EW 12; EWL 3

**Johnson, Fenton** 1888-1958 ........... **BLC 1:2**
See also BW 1; CA 118; 124; DAM MULT; DLB 45, 50

**Johnson, Georgia Douglas (Camp)**
1880-1966 ................................. **HR 1:3**
See also BW 1; CA 125; DLB 51, 249; WP

**Johnson, Helene** 1907-1995 ............... **HR 1:3**
See also CA 181; DLB 51; WP

**Johnson, J. R.**
See James, C.L.R.

**Johnson, James Weldon** 1871-1938 ...... **BLC 1:2; HR 1:3; PC 24; TCLC 3, 19, 175**
See also AAYA 73; AFAW 1, 2; BW 1, 3; CA 104; 125; CANR 82; CDALB 1917-1929; CLR 32; DA3; DAM MULT, POET; DLB 51; EWL 3; EXPP; LMFS 2; MAL 5; MTCW 1, 2; MTFW 2005; NFS 22; PFS 1; RGAL 4; SATA 31; TUS

**Johnson, Joyce** 1935- ......................... **CLC 58**
See also BG 1:3; CA 125; 129; CANR 102

**Johnson, Judith** 1936- .................. **CLC 7, 15**
See also CA 25-28R, 153; CANR 34, 85; CP 2, 3, 4, 5, 6, 7; CWP

**Johnson, Judith Emlyn**
See Johnson, Judith

**Johnson, Lionel (Pigot)**
1867-1902 ............................. **TCLC 19**
See also CA 117; 209; DLB 19; RGEL 2

**Johnson, Marguerite Annie**
See Angelou, Maya

**Johnson, Mel**
See Malzberg, Barry N(athaniel)

**Johnson, Pamela Hansford**
1912-1981 ........................ **CLC 1, 7, 27**
See also CA 1-4R; 104; CANR 2, 28; CN 1, 2, 3; DLB 15; MTCW 1, 2; MTFW 2005; RGEL 2

**Johnson, Paul** 1928- ......................... **CLC 147**
See also BEST 89:4; CA 17-20R; CANR 34, 62, 100, 155, 197, 241

**Johnson, Paul Bede**
See Johnson, Paul

**Johnson, Robert** ............................... **CLC 70**

**Johnson, Robert** 1911(?)-1938 ...... **TCLC 69**
See also BW 3; CA 174

**Johnson, Samuel** 1709-1784 ........ **LC 15, 52, 128, 249, 250, 252, 267; PC 81; WLC 3**
See also BRW 3; BRWR 1; CDBLB 1660-1789; DA; DAB; DAC; DAM MST; DLB 39, 95, 104, 142, 213; LMFS 1; RGEL 2; TEA

**Johnson, Stacie**
See Myers, Walter Dean

**Johnson, Uwe** 1934-1984 ..... **CLC 5, 10, 15, 40; TCLC 249**
See also CA 1-4R; 112; CANR 1, 39; CDWLB 2; DLB 75; EWL 3; MTCW 1; RGWL 2, 3

**Johnston, Basil H.** 1929- ................... **NNAL**
See also CA 69-72; CANR 11, 28, 66; DAC; DAM MULT; DLB 60

**Johnston, George (Benson)**
1913- ....................................... **CLC 51**
See also CA 1-4R; CANR 5, 20; CP 1, 2, 3, 4, 5, 6, 7; DLB 88

**Johnston, Jennifer (Prudence)**
1930- ........................... **CLC 7, 150, 228**
See also CA 85-88; CANR 92; CN 4, 5, 6, 7; DLB 14

**Joinville, Jean de** 1224(?)-1317 ... **CMLC 38, 152**

**Jolley, Elizabeth** 1923-2007 .... **CLC 46, 256, 260; SSC 19**
See also CA 127; 257; CAAS 13; CANR 59; CN 4, 5, 6, 7; DLB 325; EWL 3; RGSF 2

**Jolley, Monica Elizabeth**
See Jolley, Elizabeth

**Jones, Arthur Llewellyn**
1863-1947 ......... **SSC 20, 206; TCLC 4**
See also CA 104; 179; DLB 36; HGG; RGEL 2; SUFW 1

**Jones, D(ouglas) G(ordon)** 1929- ... **CLC 10**
See also CA 29-32R; CANR 13, 90; CP 1, 2, 3, 4, 5, 6, 7; DLB 53

**Jones, David (Michael)** 1895-1974 ... **CLC 2, 4, 7, 13, 42; PC 116**
See also BRW 6; BRWS 7; CA 9-12R; 53-56; CANR 28; CDBLB 1945-1960; CP 1, 2; DLB 20, 100; EWL 3; MTCW 1; PAB; RGEL 2

**Jones, David Robert**
See Bowie, David

**Jones, Diana Wynne** 1934-2011 ..... **CLC 26**
See also AAYA 12; BYA 6, 7, 9, 11, 13, 16; CA 49-52; CANR 4, 26, 56, 120, 167; CLR 23, 120; DLB 161; FANT; JRDA; MAI-CYA 1, 2; MTFW 2005; SAAS 7; SATA 9, 70, 108, 160, 234; SFW 4; SUFW 2; YAW

**Jones, Edward P.** 1950- ................. **BLC 2:2; CLC 76, 223**
See also AAYA 71; BW 2, 3; CA 142; CANR 79, 134, 190; CSW; LNFS 2; MTFW 2005; NFS 26

**Jones, Edward Paul**
See Jones, Edward P.

**Jones, Ernest Charles**
1819-1869 ............................. **NCLC 222**
See also DLB 32

**Jones, Everett LeRoi**
See Baraka, Amiri

**Jones, Gail** 1955- ........................... **CLC 386**
See also CA 188; CANR 193

**Jones, Gayl** 1949- ........ **BLC 1:2; CLC 6, 9, 131, 270**
See also AFAW 1, 2; BW 2, 3; CA 77-80; CANR 27, 66, 122; CN 4, 5, 6, 7; CSW; DA3; DAM MULT; DLB 33, 278; MAL 5; MTCW 1, 2; MTFW 2005; RGAL 4

**Jones, James** 1921-1977 ..... **CLC 1, 3, 10, 39**
See also AITN 1, 2; AMWS 11; BPFB 2; CA 1-4R; 69-72; CANR 6; CN 1, 2; DLB 2, 143; DLBD 17; DLBY 1998; EWL 3; MAL 5; MTCW 1; RGAL 4

**Jones, John J.**
See Lovecraft, H. P.

**Jones, LeRoi**
See Baraka, Amiri

**Jones, Louis B.** 1953- ...................... **CLC 65**
See also CA 141; CANR 73

**Jones, Madison** 1925- ......................... **CLC 4**
See also CA 13-16R; CAAS 11; CANR 7, 54, 83, 158; CN 1, 2, 3, 4, 5, 6, 7; CSW; DLB 152

**Jones, Madison Percy, Jr.**
See Jones, Madison

**Jones, Mervyn** 1922-2010 .......... **CLC 10, 52**
See also CA 45-48; CAAS 5; CANR 1, 91; CN 1, 2, 3, 4, 5, 6, 7; MTCW 1

**Jones, Mick** 1956(?)- ......................... **CLC 30**

**Jones, Nettie (Pearl)** 1941- ............. **CLC 34**
See also BW 2; CA 137; CAAS 20; CANR 88

**Kaniuk, Yoram** 1930- ...................... **CLC 19**
See also CA 134; DLB 299; RGHL

**Kant, Immanuel** 1724-1804 .......... **NCLC 27, 67, 253**
See also DLB 94

**Kant, Klerk**
See Copeland, Stewart

**Kantor, MacKinlay** 1904-1977 .......... **CLC 7**
See also CA 61-64; 73-76; CANR 60, 63; CN 1, 2; DLB 9, 102; MAL 5; MTCW 2; RHW; TCWW 1, 2

**Kanze Motokiyo**
See Zeami

**Kaplan, David Michael** 1946- ......... **CLC 50**
See also CA 187

**Kaplan, James** 1951- ....................... **CLC 59**
See also CA 135; CANR 121, 228

**Karadzic, Vuk Stefanovic**
1787-1864 ............................. **NCLC 115**
See also CDWLB 4; DLB 147

**Karageorge, Michael**
See Anderson, Poul

**Karamzin, Nikolai Mikhailovich**
1766-1826 ................. **NCLC 3, 173, 331**
See also DLB 150; RGSF 2

**Karapanou, Margarita** 1946- ......... **CLC 13**
See also CA 101

**Karinthy, Frigyes** 1887-1938 ........ **TCLC 47**
See also CA 170; DLB 215; EWL 3

**Karl, Frederick R(obert)** 1927-2004 .. **CLC 34**
See also CA 5-8R; 226; CANR 3, 44, 143

**Karnad, Girish** 1938- ..................... **CLC 367**
See also CA 65-68; CD 5, 6; DLB 323

**Karr, Mary** 1955- ........................... **CLC 188**
See also AMWS 11; CA 151; CANR 100, 191, 241; MTFW 2005; NCFS 5

**Kastel, Warren**
See Silverberg, Robert

**Kataev, Evgeny Petrovich**
1903-1942 ............................... **TCLC 21**
See also CA 120; DLB 272

**Kataphusin**
See Ruskin, John

**Katz, Steve** 1935- ............................. **CLC 47**
See also CA 25-28R; CAAS 14, 64; CANR 12; CN 4, 5, 6, 7; DLBY 1983

**Kauffman, Janet** 1945- .................... **CLC 42**
See also CA 117; CANR 43, 84; DLB 218; DLBY 1986

**Kaufman, Bob (Garnell)**
1925-1986 ..................... **CLC 49; PC 74**
See also BG 1:3; BW 1; CA 41-44R; 118; CANR 22; CP 1; DLB 16, 41

**Kaufman, George S.** 1889-1961 .... **CLC 38; DC 17**
See also CA 108; 93-96; DAM DRAM; DFS 1, 10; DLB 7; INT CA-108; MTCW 2; MTFW 2005; RGAL 4; TUS

**Kaufman, Moises** 1963- ..................... **DC 26**
See also AAYA 85; CA 211; DFS 22; MTFW 2005

**Kaufman, Sue**
See Barondess, Sue K.

**Kavafis, Konstantinos Petrov**
See Cavafy, Constantine

**Kavan, Anna** 1901-1968 ....... **CLC 5, 13, 82**
See also BRWS 7; CA 5-8R; CANR 6, 57; DLB 255; MTCW 1; RGEL 2; SFW 4

**Kavanagh, Dan**
See Barnes, Julian

**Kavanagh, Julie** 1952- .................. **CLC 119**
See also CA 163; CANR 186

**Kavanagh, Patrick (Joseph)**
1904-1967 ............ **CLC 22; PC 33, 105**
See also BRWS 7; CA 123; 25-28R; DLB 15, 20; EWL 3; MTCW 1; RGEL 2

**Kawabata, Yasunari** 1899-1972 ... **CLC 2, 5, 9, 18, 107; SSC 17**

See also CA 93-96; 33-36R; CANR 88; DAM MULT; DLB 180, 330; EWL 3; MJW; MTCW 2; MTFW 2005; NFS 42; RGSF 2; RGWL 2, 3; SSFS 29, 37

**Kawabata Yasunari**
See Kawabata, Yasunari

**Kaye, Mary Margaret**
See Kaye, M.M.

**Kaye, M.M.** 1908-2004 .................... **CLC 28**
See also CA 89-92; 223; CANR 24, 60, 102, 142; MTCW 1, 2; MTFW 2005; RHW; SATA 62; SATA-Obit 152

**Kaye, Mollie**
See Kaye, M.M.

**Kaye-Smith, Sheila** 1887-1956 ...... **TCLC 20**
See also CA 118; 203; DLB 36

**Kaymor, Patrice Maguilene**
See Senghor, Leopold Sedar

**Kazakov, Iurii Pavlovich**
See Kazakov, Yuri Pavlovich

**Kazakov, Yuri Pavlovich** 1927-1982 ... **SSC 43**
See also CA 5-8R; CANR 36; DLB 302; EWL 3; MTCW 1; RGSF 2

**Kazakov, Yury**
See Kazakov, Yuri Pavlovich

**Kazan, Elia** 1909-2003 .......... **CLC 6, 16, 63**
See also AAYA 83; CA 21-24R; 220; CANR 32, 78

**Kazanjoglou, Elia**
See Kazan, Elia

**Kazantzakis, Nikos** 1883(?)-1957 .... **PC 126; TCLC 2, 5, 33, 181**
See also AAYA 83; BPFB 2; CA 105; 132; DA3; EW 9; EWL 3; MTCW 1, 2; MTFW 2005; RGWL 2, 3

**Kazin, Alfred** 1915-1998 ... **CLC 34, 38, 119**
See also AMWS 8; CA 1-4R; CAAS 7; CANR 1, 45, 79; DLB 67; EWL 3

**Koda Rohan**
See Koda Shigeyuki

**Keane, Mary Nesta** 1904-1996 ....... **CLC 31**
See also CA 108; 114; 151; CN 5, 6; INT CA-114; RHW; TCLE 1:1

**Keane, Mary Nesta Skrine**
See Keane, Mary Nesta

**Keane, Molly**
See Keane, Mary Nesta

**Keates, Jonathan** 1946(?)- .............. **CLC 34**
See also CA 163; CANR 126

**Keaton, Buster** 1895-1966 .............. **CLC 20**
See also AAYA 79; CA 194

**Keats, John** 1795-1821 .... **NCLC 8, 73, 121, 225, 337; PC 1, 96, 157, 211, 213; WLC 3**
See also AAYA 58; BRW 4; BRWR 1; CDBLB 1789-1832; DA; DA3; DAB; DAC; DAM MST, POET; DLB 96, 110; EXPP; LMFS 1; PAB; PFS 1, 2, 3, 9, 17, 32, 36; RGEL 2; TEA; WLIT 3; WP

**Keble, John** 1792-1866 ................... **NCLC 87**
See also DLB 32, 55; RGEL 2

**Keene, Donald** 1922- ...................... **CLC 34**
See also CA 1-4R; CANR 5, 119, 190

**Kees, Weldon** 1914-1955? .................. **PC 166**
See also AMWS 15

**Keiller, Patrick** 1950- ..................... **CLC 428**

**Keillor, Garrison** 1942- ... **CLC 40, 115, 222**
See also AAYA 2, 62; AMWS 16; BEST 89:3; BPFB 2; CA 111; 117; CANR 36, 59, 124, 180; CPW; DA3; DAM POP; DLBY 1987; EWL 3; MTCW 1, 2; MTFW 2005; SATA 58; TUS

**Keillor, Gary Edward**
See Keillor, Garrison

**Keith, Carlos**
See Lewton, Val

**Keith, Michael**
See Hubbard, L. Ron

**Kell, Joseph**
See Burgess, Anthony

**Keller, Gottfried** 1819-1890 ... **NCLC 2, 277; SSC 26, 107**
See also CDWLB 2; DLB 129; EW; RGSF 2; RGWL 2, 3

**Keller, Nora Okja** 1965- ........ **CLC 109, 281**
See also CA 187

**Kellerman, Jonathan** 1949- ............. **CLC 44**
See also AAYA 35; BEST 90:1; CA 106; CANR 29, 51, 150, 183, 236; CMW 4; CPW; DA3; DAM POP; INT CANR-29

**Kelley, William Melvin** 1937- ....... **BLC 2:2; CLC 22**
See also BW 1; CA 77-80; CANR 27, 83; CN 1, 2, 3, 4, 5, 6, 7; DLB 33; EWL 3

**Kellock, Archibald P.**
See Mavor, Osborne Henry

**Kellogg, Marjorie** 1922-2005 ........... **CLC 2**
See also CA 81-84; 246

**Kellow, Kathleen**
See Hibbert, Eleanor Alice Burford

**Kelly, Lauren**
See Oates, Joyce Carol

**Kelly, M(ilton) T(errence)** 1947- .... **CLC 55**
See also CA 97-100; CAAS 22; CANR 19, 43, 84; CN 6

**Kelly, Robert** 1935- ........................... **SSC 50**
See also CA 17-20R; CAAS 19; CANR 47; CP 1, 2, 3, 4, 5, 6, 7; DLB 5, 130, 165

**Kelman, James** 1946- ........ **CLC 58, 86, 292**
See also BRWS 5; CA 148; CANR 85, 130, 199; CN 5, 6, 7; DLB 194, 319, 326; RGSF 2; WLIT 4

**Kelton, Elmer** 1926-2009 .............. **CLC 299**
See also AAYA 78; AITN 1; BYA 9; CA 21-24R; 289; CANR 12, 36, 85, 149, 173, 209; DLB 256; TCWW 1, 2

**Kelton, Elmer Stephen**
See Kelton, Elmer

**Kemal, Yasar**
See Kemal, Yashar

**Kemal, Yashar** 1923(?)- ............. **CLC 14, 29**
See also CA 89-92; CANR 44; CWW 2; EWL 3; WLIT 6

**Kemble, Fanny** 1809-1893 ............. **NCLC 18**
See also DLB 32

**Kemelman, Harry** 1908-1996 ........... **CLC 2**
See also AITN 1; BPFB 2; CA 9-12R; 155; CANR 6, 71; CMW 4; DLB 28

**Kempe, Margery**
1373(?)-1440(?) .............. **LC 6, 56, 224**
See also BRWS 12; DLB 146; FL 1:1; RGEL 2

**Kempis, Thomas a** 1380-1471 .......... **LC 11**

**Kenan, Randall (G.)** 1963- ............. **BLC 2:2**
See also BW 2, 3; CA 142; CANR 86; CN 7; CSW; DLB 292; GLL 1

**Kendall, Henry** 1839-1882 ............. **NCLC 12**
See also DLB 230

**Keneally, Thomas** 1935- ........ **CLC 5, 8, 10, 14, 19, 27, 43, 117, 279**
See also BRWS 4; CA 85-88; CANR 10, 50, 74, 130, 165, 198, 240; CN 1, 2, 3, 4, 5, 6, 7; CPW; DA3; DAM NOV; DLB 289, 299, 326; EWL 3; MTCW 1, 2; MTFW 2005; NFS 17, 38; RGEL 2; RGHL; RHW

**Keneally, Thomas Michael**
See Keneally, Thomas

**Keneally, Tom**
See Keneally, Thomas

**Kenkō, Yoshida** c. 1283-c. 1352 ... **CMLC 193**
See also DLB 203; RGWL 3

**Kennedy, A. L.** 1965- .............. **CLC 188, 432**
See also CA 168, 213; CAAE 213; CANR 108, 193, 285; CD 5, 6; CN 6, 7; DLB 271; RGSF 2

**Kennedy, Adrienne (Lita)**
1931- .... **BLC 1:2; CLC 66, 308; DC 5**

See also AAYA 15; AMWS 7; CA 129; 134; CANR 60, 96, 133, 179; CDALBS; CN 7; CPW; CSW; DA3; DAM POP; DLB 206; INT CA-134; LAIT 5; MTCW 2; MTFW 2005; NFS 5, 10, 12, 24; RGAL 4; TCLE 1:1

**Kingston, Maxine Hong** 1940- ... **AAL; CLC 12, 19, 58, 121, 271; SSC 136; WLCS**
See also AAYA 8, 55; AMWS 5; BPFB 2; CA 69-72; CANR 13, 38, 74, 87, 128, 239; CDALBS; CN 6, 7; DA3; DAM MULT, NOV; DLB 173, 212, 312; DLBY 1980; EWL 3; FL 1:6; FW; INT CANR-13; LAIT 5; MAL 5; MBL; MTCW 1, 2; MTFW 2005; NFS 6; RGAL 4; SATA 53; SSFS 3; TCWW 2

**Kingston, Maxine Ting Ting Hong**
See Kingston, Maxine Hong

**Kinnell, Galway** 1927-2014 ...... **CLC 1, 2, 3, 5, 13, 29, 129, 395; PC 26, 202**
See also AMWS 3; CA 9-12R; CANR 10, 34, 66, 116, 138, 175; CP 1, 2, 3, 4, 5, 6, 7; DLB 5, 342; DLBY 1987; EWL 3; INT CANR-34; MAL 5; MTCW 1, 2; MTFW 2005; PAB; PFS 9, 26, 35; RGAL 4; TCLE 1:1; WP

**Kinsella, John** 1963- ...................... **CLC 384**
See also CA 189; CP 7; DLB 325; WWE 1

**Kinsella, Thomas** 1928- ..... **CLC 4, 19, 138, 274; PC 69**
See also BRWS 5; CA 17-20R; CANR 15, 122; CP 1, 2, 3, 4, 5, 6, 7; DLB 27; EWL 3; MTCW 1, 2; MTFW 2005; RGEL 2; TEA

**Kinsella, William Patrick**
See Kinsella, W.P.

**Kinsella, W.P.** 1935- .......... **CLC 27, 43, 166**
See also AAYA 7, 60; BPFB 2; CA 97-100, 222; CAAE 222; CAAS 7; CANR 21, 35, 66, 75, 129; CN 4, 5, 6, 7; CPW; DAC; DAM NOV, POP; DLB 362; FANT; INT CANR-21; LAIT 5; MTCW 1, 2; MTFW 2005; NFS 15; RGSF 2; SSFS 30

**Kinsey, Alfred C(harles)** 1894-1956 ...................... **TCLC 91**
See also CA 115; 170; MTCW 2

**Kipling, Joseph Rudyard**
See Kipling, Rudyard

**Kipling, Rudyard** 1865-1936 ........ **PC 3, 91; SSC 5, 54, 110, 207, 217, 222; TCLC 8, 17, 167; WLC 3**
See also AAYA 32; BRW 6; BRWC 1, 2; BRWR 3; BYA 4; CA 105; 120; CANR 33; CDBLB 1890-1914; CLR 39, 65, 83, 199, 212; CWRI 5; DA; DA3; DAB; DAC; DAM MST, POET; DLB 19, 34, 141, 156, 330; EWL 3; EXPS; FANT; LAIT 3; LMFS 1; MAICYA 1, 2; MTCW 1, 2; MTFW 2005; NFS 21; PFS 22; RGEL 2; RGSF 2; SATA 100; SFW 4; SSFS 8, 21, 22, 32, 42; SUFW 1; TEA; WCH; WLIT 4; YABC 2

**Kircher, Athanasius** 1602-1680 ........ **LC 121**
See also DLB 164

**Kirk, Richard**
See Holdstock, Robert

**Kirk, Russell (Amos)** 1918-1994 ... **TCLC 119**
See also AITN 1; CA 1-4R; 145; CAAS 9; CANR 1, 20, 60; HGG; INT CANR-20; MTCW 1, 2

**Kirkham, Dinah**
See Card, Orson Scott

**Kirkland, Caroline M.** 1801-1864 ........................... **NCLC 85, 309**
See also DLB 3, 73, 74, 250, 254; DLBD 13

**Kirkup, James** 1918-2009 ................. **CLC 1**
See also CA 1-4R; CAAS 4; CANR 2; CP 1, 2, 3, 4, 5, 6, 7; DLB 27; SATA 12

**Kirkwood, James** 1930(?)-1989 ........ **CLC 9**
See also AITN 2; CA 1-4R; 128; CANR 6, 40; GLL 2

**Kirsch, Sarah** 1935- ...................... **CLC 176**
See also CA 178; CWW 2; DLB 75; EWL 3

**Kirshner, Sidney**
See Kingsley, Sidney

**Kissinger, Henry A.** 1923- ............. **CLC 137**
See also CA 1-4R; CANR 2, 33, 66, 109; MTCW 1

**Kissinger, Henry Alfred**
See Kissinger, Henry A.

**Kittel, Frederick August**
See Wilson, August

**Kivi, Aleksis** 1834-1872 ........ **NCLC 30, 328**

**Kizer, Carolyn** 1925- .. **CLC 15, 39, 80; PC 66**
See also CA 65-68; CAAS 5; CANR 24, 70, 134; CP 1, 2, 3, 4, 5, 6, 7; CWP; DAM POET; DLB 5, 169; EWL 3; MAL 5; MTCW 2; MTFW 2005; PFS 18; TCLE 1:1

**Klabund** 1890-1928 ...................... **TCLC 44**
See also CA 162; DLB 66

**Klappert, Peter** 1942- ...................... **CLC 57**
See also CA 33-36R; CSW; DLB 5

**Klausner, Amos**
See Oz, Amos

**Klay, Phil** 1983- ............................. **CLC 389**
See also CA 358

**Klein, A. M.** 1909-1972 ................... **CLC 19**
See also CA 101; 37-40R; CP 1; DAB; DAC; DAM MST; DLB 68; EWL 3; RGEL 2; RGHL

**Klein, Abraham Moses**
See Klein, A. M.

**Klein, Joe**
See Klein, Joseph

**Klein, Joseph** 1946- ...................... **CLC 154**
See also CA 85-88; CANR 55, 164

**Klein, Norma** 1938-1989 ................. **CLC 30**
See also AAYA 2, 35; BPFB 2; BYA 6, 7, 8; CA 41-44R; 128; CANR 15, 37; CLR 2, 19, 162; INT CANR-15; JRDA; MAICYA 1, 2; SAAS 1; SATA 7, 57; WYA; YAW

**Klein, T.E.D.** 1947- ......................... **CLC 34**
See also CA 119; CANR 44, 75, 167; HGG

**Klein, Theodore Eibon Donald**
See Klein, T.E.D.

**Kleinzahler, August** 1949- ............ **CLC 320**
See also CA 125; CANR 51, 101, 153, 210

**Kleist, Heinrich von** 1777-1811 ........ **DC 29; NCLC 2, 37, 222, 293, 313, 342; SSC 22**
See also CDWLB 2; DAM DRAM; DLB 90; EW 5; RGSF 2; RGWL 2, 3

**Klima, Ivan** 1931- ...................... **CLC 56, 172**
See also CA 25-28R; CANR 17, 50, 91; CDWLB 4; CWW 2; DAM NOV; DLB 232; EWL 3; RGWL 3

**Klimentov, Andrei Platonovich**
See Klimentov, Andrei Platonovich

**Klimentov, Andrei Platonovich** 1899-1951 ............... **SSC 42; TCLC 14**
See also CA 108; 232; DLB 272; EWL 3

**Kline, T. F.**
See Harwood, Gwen

**Klinger, Friedrich Maximilian von** 1752-1831 ........................ **NCLC 1, 325**
See also DLB 94

**Klingsor the Magician**
See Hartmann, Sadakichi

**Klopstock, Friedrich Gottlieb** 1724-1803 ...................... **NCLC 11, 225**
See also DLB 97; EW 4; RGWL 2, 3

**Kluge, Alexander** 1932- ...................... **SSC 61**
See also CA 81-84; CANR 163; DLB 75

**Knapp, Caroline** 1959-2002 .... **CLC 99, 309**
See also CA 154; 207

**Knebel, Fletcher** 1911-1993 ............ **CLC 14**
See also AITN 1; CA 1-4R; 140; CAAS 3; CANR 1, 36; CN 1, 2, 3, 4, 5; SATA 36; SATA-Obit 75

**Kung, Hans** 1928- ......................... **CLC 130**
See also CA 53-56; CANR 66, 134; MTCW 1, 2; MTFW 2005

**Knickerbocker, Diedrich**
See Irving, Washington

**Knight, Etheridge** 1931-1991 ........ **BLC 1:2; CLC 40; PC 14**
See also BW 1, 3; CA 21-24R; 133; CANR 23, 82; CP 1, 2, 3, 4, 5; DAM POET; DLB 41; MTCW 2; MTFW 2005; PFS 36; RGAL 4; TCLE 1:1

**Knight, Sarah Kemble** 1666-1727 ....... **LC 7**
See also DLB 24, 200

**Knister, Raymond** 1899-1932 ........ **TCLC 56**
See also CA 186; DLB 68; RGEL 2

**Knoff, Artur**
See Grass, Günter

**Knowles, John** 1926-2001 .. **CLC 1, 4, 10, 26**
See also AAYA 10, 72; AMWS 12; BPFB 2; BYA 3; CA 17-20R; 203; CANR 40, 74, 76, 132; CDALB 1968-1988; CLR 98; CN 1, 2, 3, 4, 5, 6, 7; DA; DAC; DAM MST, NOV; DLB 6; EXPN; MTCW 1, 2; MTFW 2005; NFS 2; RGAL 4; SATA 8, 89; SATA-Obit 134; YAW

**Knox, Calvin M.**
See Silverberg, Robert

**Knox, John** c. 1505-1572 ................... **LC 37**
See also DLB 132

**Knye, Cassandra**
See Disch, Thomas M.

**Koch, C(hristopher) J(ohn)** 1932- ... **CLC 42**
See also CA 127; CANR 84; CN 3, 4, 5, 6, 7; DLB 289

**Koch, Christopher**
See Koch, C(hristopher) J(ohn)

**Koch, Kenneth** 1925-2002 ..... **CLC 5, 8, 44; PC 80**
See also AMWS 15; CA 1-4R; 207; CAD; CANR 6, 36, 57, 97, 131; CD 5, 6; CP 1, 2, 3, 4, 5, 6, 7; DAM POET; DLB 5; INT CANR-36; MAL 5; MTCW 2; MTFW 2005; PFS 20; SATA 65; WP

**Kochanowski, Jan** 1530-1584 ..... **LC 10, 229**
See also RGWL 2, 3

**Kock, Charles Paul de** 1794-1871 ... **NCLC 16**

**Koda Rohan**
See Koda Shigeyuki

**Koda Shigeyuki** 1867-1947 ............ **TCLC 22**
See also CA 121; 183; DLB 180

**Koeppen, Wolfgang** 1906-1996 ... **TCLC 324**
See also CA 183; DLB 69; EWL 3; RGHL

**Koestler, Arthur** 1905-1983 ..... **CLC 1, 3, 6, 8, 15, 33; TCLC 283**
See also BRWS 1; CA 1-4R; 109; CANR 1, 33; CDBLB 1945-1960; CN 1, 2, 3; DLBY 1983; EWL 3; MTCW 1, 2; MTFW 2005; NFS 19; RGEL 2

**Kogawa, Joy** 1935- ... **CLC 78, 129, 262, 268**
See also AAYA 47; CA 101; CANR 19, 62, 126; CN 6, 7; CP 1; CWP; DAC; DAM MST, MULT; DLB 334; FW; MTCW 2; MTFW 2005; NFS 3; SATA 99

**Kogawa, Joy Nozomi**
See Kogawa, Joy

**Kohout, Pavel** 1928- ........................ **CLC 13**
See also CA 45-48; CANR 3

**Koizumi, Yakumo**
See Hearn, Lafcadio

**Kolmar, Gertrud** 1894-1943 .......... **TCLC 40**
See also CA 167; EWL 3; RGHL

**Komunyakaa, Yusef** 1947- ............ **BLC 2:2; BLCS; CLC 86, 94, 207, 299; PC 51**
See also AFAW 2; AMWS 13; CA 147; CANR 83, 164, 211, 241; CP 6, 7; CSW; DLB 120; EWL 3; PFS 5, 20, 30, 37; RGAL 4

**Kong Shangren** 1648-1718 .............. **LC 210**

**Konigsberg, Alan Stewart**
See Allen, Woody

**Konrad, George**
See Konrad, Gyorgy

**Konrad, George**
See Konrad, Gyorgy

**Konrad, Gyorgy** 1933- .......... **CLC 4, 10, 73**
See also CA 85-88; CANR 97, 171; CDWLB 4; CWW 2; DLB 232; EWL 3

**Konwicki, Tadeusz** 1926- ............ **CLC 8, 28, 54, 117**
See also CA 101; CAAS 9; CANR 39, 59; CWW 2; DLB 232; EWL 3; IDFW 3; MTCW 1

**Koontz, Dean** 1945- ............ **CLC 78, 206**
See Koontz, Dean R.
See also AAYA 9, 31; BEST 89:3, 90:2; CA 108; CANR 19, 36, 52, 95, 138, 176; CMW 4; CPW; DA3; DAM NOV, POP; DLB 292; HGG; MTCW 1; MTFW 2005; SATA 92, 165; SFW 4; SUFW 2; YAW

**Koontz, Dean R.**
See Koontz, Dean
See also SATA 225

**Koontz, Dean Ray**
See Koontz, Dean

**Kooser, Ted** 1939- ...................... **PC 162, 211**
See also AAYA 69; CMTFW; CA 33-36R; CANR 15, 136, 220, 292; CP 7; DLB 105, 380; LNFS 2; PFS 8, 24; SATA 306

**Kopernik, Mikolaj**
See Copernicus, Nicolaus

**Kopit, Arthur** 1937- ............ **CLC 1, 18, 33; DC 37**
See also AITN 1; CA 81-84; CABS 3; CAD; CD 5, 6; DAM DRAM; DFS 7, 14, 24; DLB 7; MAL 5; MTCW 1; RGAL 4

**Kopit, Arthur Lee**
See Kopit, Arthur

**Kopitar, Jernej (Bartholomaus)**
1780-1844 .......................... **NCLC 117**

**Kops, Bernard** 1926- .......................... **CLC 4**
See also CA 5-8R; CANR 84, 159; CBD; CN 1, 2, 3, 4, 5, 6, 7; CP 1, 2, 3, 4, 5, 6, 7; DLB 13; RGHL

**Kornbluth, C(yril) M.** 1923-1958 ... **TCLC 8**
See also CA 105; 160; DLB 8; SCFW 1, 2; SFW 4

**Korolenko, V.G.**
See Korolenko, Vladimir G.

**Korolenko, Vladimir**
See Korolenko, Vladimir G.

**Korolenko, Vladimir G.** 1853-1921 ... **TCLC 22**
See also CA 121; DLB 277

**Korolenko, Vladimir Galaktionovich**
See Korolenko, Vladimir G.

**Korzybski, Alfred (Habdank Skarbek)**
1879-1950 ............................ **TCLC 61**
See also CA 123; 160

**Kosinski, Jerzy** 1933-1991 ... **CLC 1, 2, 3, 6, 10, 15, 53, 70**
See also AMWS 7; BPFB 2; CA 17-20R; 134; CANR 9, 46; CN 1, 2, 3, 4; DA3; DAM NOV; DLB 2, 299; DLBY 1982; EWL 3; HGG; MAL 5; MTCW 1, 2; MTFW 2005; NFS 12; RGAL 4; RGHL; TUS

**Kostelanetz, Richard** 1940- ............ **CLC 28**
See also CA 13-16R; CAAS 8; CANR 38, 77; CN 4, 5, 6; CP 2, 3, 4, 5, 6, 7

**Kostelanetz, Richard Cory**
See Kostelanetz, Richard

**Kostrowitzki, Wilhelm Apollinaris de**
1880-1918
See Apollinaire, Guillaume

**Kotlowitz, Robert** 1924- ................... **CLC 4**
See also CA 33-36R; CANR 36

**Kotzebue, August (Friedrich Ferdinand) von**
1761-1819 ........ **DC 51; NCLC 25, 260**
See also DLB 94

**Kotzwinkle, William** 1938- ... **CLC 5, 14, 35**
See also BPFB 2; CA 45-48; CANR 3, 44, 84, 129; CLR 6; CN 7; DLB 173; FANT; MAICYA 1, 2; SATA 24, 70, 146; SFW 4; SUFW 2; YAW

**Kourouma, Ahmadou** 1927-2003 .. **CLC 347**
See also BW 2; CA 143; 224; CA 128; DLB 360; EWL 3; RGWL 3

**Kowna, Stancy**
See Szymborska, Wislawa

**Kozol, Jonathan** 1936- ..................... **CLC 17**
See also AAYA 46; CA 61-64; CANR 16, 45, 96, 178; MTFW 2005

**Kozoll, Michael** 1940(?)- .................. **CLC 35**

**Krakauer, Jon** 1954- ........................ **CLC 248**
See also AAYA 24; AMWS 18; BYA 9; CA 153; CANR 131, 212; MTFW 2005; SATA 108

**Kramer, Kathryn** 19(?)- ................... **CLC 34**

**Kramer, Larry** 1935- ............ **CLC 42; DC 8**
See also CA 124; 126; CANR 60, 132; DAM POP; DLB 249; GLL 1

**Krasicki, Ignacy** 1735-1801 ............. **NCLC 8**

**Krasinski, Zygmunt** 1812-1859 ....... **NCLC 4**
See also RGWL 2, 3

**Kraus, Karl** 1874-1936 .......... **TCLC 5, 263**
See also CA 104; 216; DLB 118; EWL 3

**Kraynay, Anton**
See Gippius, Zinaida

**Kreve (Mickevicius), Vincas**
1882-1954 .......................... **TCLC 27**
See also CA 170; DLB 220; EWL 3

**Kripke, Saul** 1940- ......................... **CLC 430**
See also CA 130; DLB 279

**Kristeva, Julia** 1941- .. **CLC 77, 140, 340, 367**
See also CA 154; CANR 99, 173; DLB 242; EWL 3; FW; LMFS 2

**Kristofferson, Kris** 1936- ................. **CLC 26**
See also CA 104

**Krizanc, John** 1956- ........................ **CLC 57**
See also CA 187

**Krleza, Miroslav** 1893-1981 ...... **CLC 8, 114**
See also CA 97-100; 105; CANR 50; CDWLB 4; DLB 147; EW 11; RGWL 2, 3

**Kroetsch, Robert** 1927-2011 ...... **CLC 5, 23, 57, 132, 286; PC 152**
See also CA 17-20R; CANR 8, 38; CCA 1; CN 2, 3, 4, 5, 6, 7; CP 6, 7; DAC; DAM POET; DLB 53; MTCW 1

**Kroetsch, Robert Paul**
See Kroetsch, Robert

**Kroetz, Franz**
See Kroetz, Franz Xaver

**Kroetz, Franz Xaver** 1946- ............. **CLC 41**
See also CA 130; CANR 142; CWW 2; EWL 3

**Krog, Antjie** 1952- ........................ **CLC 373**
See also CA 194

**Kroker, Arthur (W.)** 1945- ............. **CLC 77**
See also CA 161

**Kroniuk, Lisa**
See Berton, Pierre (Francis de Marigny)

**Kropotkin, Peter** 1842-1921 ......... **TCLC 36**
See also CA 119; 219; DLB 277

**Kropotkin, Peter Alekseevich**
See Kropotkin, Peter

**Kropotkin, Petr Alekseevich**
See Kropotkin, Peter

**Krotkov, Yuri** 1917-1981 ................ **CLC 19**
See also CA 102

**Krumb**
See Crumb, R.

**Krumgold, Joseph (Quincy)**
1908-1980 ........................... **CLC 12**
See also BYA 1, 2; CA 9-12R; 101; CANR 7; MAICYA 1, 2; SATA 1, 48; SATA-Obit 23; YAW

**Krumwitz**
See Crumb, R.

**Krutch, Joseph Wood** 1893-1970 ... **CLC 24**
See also ANW; CA 1-4R; 25-28R; CANR 4; DLB 63, 206, 275

**Krutzch, Gus**
See Eliot, T. S.

**Krylov, Ivan Andreevich**
1768(?)-1844 .......................... **NCLC 1**
See also DLB 150

**Kubin, Alfred (Leopold Isidor)**
1877-1959 ............................ **TCLC 23**
See also CA 112; 149; CANR 104; DLB 81

**Kubrick, Stanley** 1928-1999 .......... **CLC 16; TCLC 112**
See also AAYA 30; CA 81-84; 177; CANR 33; DLB 26

**Kueng, Hans**
See Kung, Hans

**Kumin, Maxine** 1925- .......... **CLC 5, 13, 28, 164; PC 15**
See also AITN 2; AMWS 4; ANW; CA 1-4R; 271; CAAE 271; CAAS 8; CANR 1, 21, 69, 115, 140; CP 2, 3, 4, 5, 6, 7; CWP; DA3; DAM POET; DLB 5; EWL 3; EXPP; MTCW 1, 2; MTFW 2005; PAB; PFS 18, 38; SATA 12

**Kumin, Maxine Winokur**
See Kumin, Maxine

**Kundera, Milan** 1929- ..... **CLC 4, 9, 19, 32, 68, 115, 135, 234; SSC 24**
See also AAYA 2, 62; BPFB 2; CA 85-88; CANR 19, 52, 74, 144, 223; CDWLB 4; CWW 2; DA3; DAM NOV; DLB 232; EW 13; EWL 3; MTCW 1, 2; MTFW 2005; NFS 18, 27; RGSF 2; RGWL 3; SSFS 10

**Kunene, Mazisi** 1930-2006 ............. **CLC 85**
See also BW 1, 3; CA 125; 252; CANR 81; CP 1, 6, 7; DLB 117

**Kunene, Mazisi Raymond**
See Kunene, Mazisi

**Kunene, Mazisi Raymond Fakazi Mngoni**
See Kunene, Mazisi

**Kunert, Günter** 1929- ................... **CLC 377**
See also CA 178; CANR 149; CWW 2; DLB 75; EWL 3

**Kung, Hans**
See Kung, Hans

**K'ung Shang-jen**
See Kong Shangren

**Kunikida, Tetsuo**
See Kunikida Doppo

**Kunikida Doppo** 1869(?)-1908 ...... **TCLC 99**
See also DLB 180; EWL 3

**Kunikida Tetsuo**
See Kunikida Doppo

**Kunitz, Stanley** 1905-2006 ... **CLC 6, 11, 14, 148, 293; PC 19, 181**
See also AMWS 3; CA 41-44R; 250; CANR 26, 57, 98; CP 1, 2, 3, 4, 5, 6, 7; DA3; DLB 48; INT CANR-26; MAL 5; MTCW 1, 2; MTFW 2005; PFS 11; RGAL 4

**Kunitz, Stanley Jasspon**
See Kunitz, Stanley

**Kunt, Klerk**
See Copeland, Stewart

**Kunze, Reiner** 1933- ...................... **CLC 10**
See also CA 93-96; CWW 2; DLB 75; EWL 3

**Kunzru, Hari** 1969- ....................... **CLC 419**
See also BRWS 14; CA 204; CANR 146, 188

**Kuprin, Aleksander Ivanovich**
1870-1938 ............................ **TCLC 5**
See also CA 104; 182; DLB 295; EWL 3

**Kuprin, Aleksandr Ivanovich**
See Kuprin, Aleksander Ivanovich

**Kuprin, Alexandr Ivanovich**
See Kuprin, Aleksander Ivanovich

**Kureishi, Hanif** 1954- .... **CLC 64, 135, 284, 406; DC 26**
See also BRWS 11; CA 139; CANR 113, 197; CBD; CD 5, 6; CN 6, 7; DLB 194,

245, 352; GLL 2; IDFW 4; WLIT 4; WWE
1

**Kurosawa, Akira** 1910-1998 ... **CLC 16, 119**
See also AAYA 11, 64; CA 101; 170; CANR
46; DAM MULT

**Kushner, Tony** 1956- ...... **CLC 81, 203, 297;
DC 10, 50**
See also AAYA 61; AMWS 9; CA 144;
CAD; CANR 74, 130; CD 5, 6; DA3;
DAM DRAM; DFS 5; DLB 228; EWL
3; GLL 1; LAIT 5; MAL 5; MTCW 2;
MTFW 2005; RGAL 4; RGHL; SATA 160

**Kuttner, Henry** 1915-1958 ............. **TCLC 10**
See also CA 107; 157; DLB 8; FANT;
SCFW 1, 2; SFW 4

**Kutty, Madhavi**
See Das, Kamala

**Kuzma, Greg** 1944- ............................. **CLC 7**
See also CA 33-36R; CANR 70

**Kuzmin, Mikhail (Alekseevich)**
1872(?)-1936 ............................. **TCLC 40**
See also CA 170; DLB 295; EWL 3

**Kyd, Thomas**
1558-1594 ........... **DC 3, 55; LC 22, 125**
See also BRW 1; DAM DRAM; DFS 21;
DLB 62; IDTP; LMFS 1; RGEL 2; TEA;
WLIT 3

**Kyōka, Izumi** 1873-1939 ............. **TCLC 334**
See also CA 191; DLB 180; EWL 3; MJW

**Kyprianos, Iossif**
See Samarakis, Antonis

**L. S.**
See Stephen, Sir Leslie

**Labé, Louise**
1521-1566 ........... **LC 120, 222; PC 154**
See also DLB 327

**L'abeille**
See Riccoboni, Marie-Jeanne

**Labeo, Notker**
See Notker Labeo

**Labou Tansi, Sony** 1947?-1995 ... **TCLC 331**
See also DLB 360; EWL 3

**Labrunie, Gerard**
See Nerval, Gerard de

**La Bruyere, Jean de** 1645-1696 .... **LC 17, 168**
See also DLB 268; EW 3; GFL Beginnings
to 1789

**LaBute, Neil** 1963- ......................... **CLC 225**
See also CA 240

**La Calprenede, Gautier de Costes** 1610
(?)-1663 ...................................... **LC 215**
See also DLB 268; GFL Beginnings to 1789

**Lacan, Jacques (Marie Emile)**
1901-1981 ............................. **CLC 75**
See also CA 121; 104; DLB 296; EWL 3; TWA

**La Ceppède, Jean de** c. 1550-1623 ... **LC 249**
See also DLB 327

**Laclos, Pierre-Ambroise Francois**
1741-1803 ............ **NCLC 4, 87, 239**
See also DLB 313; EW 4; GFL Beginnings
to 1789; RGWL 2, 3

**Lacolere, Francois**
See Aragon, Louis

**La Colere, Francois**
See Aragon, Louis

**Lactantius** c. 250-c. 325 ............. **CMLC 118**

**La Deshabilleuse**
See Simenon, Georges

**Lady Gregory**
See Gregory, Lady Isabella Augusta (Persse)

**Lady of Quality, A**
See Bagnold, Enid

**La Fayette, Marie-(Madelaine Pioche de la
Vergne)** 1634-1693 ................ **LC 2, 144**
See also DLB 268; GFL Beginnings to 1789;
RGWL 2, 3

**Lafayette, Marie-Madeleine**
See La Fayette, Marie-(Madelaine Pioche de
la Vergne)

**Lafayette, Rene**
See Hubbard, L. Ron

**La Flesche, Francis** 1857(?)-1932 ...... **NNAL**
See also CA 144; CANR 83; DLB 175

**La Fontaine, Jean de**
1621-1695 ............................. **LC 50, 184**
See also DLB 268; EW 3; GFL Beginnings
to 1789; MAICYA 1, 2; RGWL 2, 3;
SATA 18

**LaForet, Carmen** 1921-2004 ......... **CLC 219**
See also CA 246; CWW 2; DLB 322; EWL 3

**LaForet Diaz, Carmen**
See LaForet, Carmen

**Laforgue, Jules** 1860-1887 ...... **NCLC 5, 53,
221; PC 14; SSC 20**
See also DLB 217; EW 7; GFL 1789 to the
Present; RGWL 2, 3

**Lagerkvist, Paer** 1891-1974 ........ **CLC 7, 10,
13, 54; SSC 12; TCLC 144**
See also CA 85-88; 49-52; DA3; DAM
DRAM, NOV; DLB 259, 331; EW 10;
EWL 3; MTCW 1, 2; MTFW 2005; RGSF
2; RGWL 2, 3; SSFS 33; TWA

**Lagerkvist, Paer Fabian**
See Lagerkvist, Paer

**Lagerkvist, Par**
See Lagerkvist, Paer

**Lagerlof, Selma** 1858-1940 ....... **TCLC 4, 36**
See also CA 108; 188; CLR 7; DLB 259,
331; MTCW 2; RGWL 2, 3; SATA 15; SSFS
18, 35

**Lagerloef, Selma**
See Lagerlof, Selma

**Lagerloef, Selma Ottiliana Lovisa**
See Lagerlof, Selma

**Lagerlof, Selma Ottiliana Lovisa**
See Lagerlof, Selma

**La Calprènede, Gautier de Costes**
1609/1610-1663 ........................ **LC 215**
See also DLB 268, GFL

**La Guma, Alex** 1925-1985 ................ **BLCS;
CLC 19; TCLC 140**
See also AFW; BW 1, 3; CA 49-52; 118;
CANR 25, 81; CDWLB 3; CN 1, 2, 3; CP 1;
DAM NOV; DLB 117, 225; EWL 3; MTCW
1, 2; MTFW 2005; WLIT 2; WWE 1

**La Guma, Justin Alexander**
See La Guma, Alex

**Lahiri, Jhumpa** 1967- .......... **CLC 282, 335;
SSC 96, 251**
See also AAYA 56; AMWS 21; CA 193;
CANR 134, 184; DLB 323; MTFW 2005;
NFS 31; SSFS 19, 27, 37

**Lahontan, Louis-Armand de Lom d'Arce**
1666-1715? ............................. **LC 280**
See also DLB 99

**Laidlaw, A. K.**
See Grieve, C. M.

**Lainez, Manuel Mujica**
See Mujica Lainez, Manuel

**Laing, B. Kojo** 1946-2017 .............. **CLC 446**
See also CA 185; CP 7; DLB 157

**Laing, R(onald) D(avid)** 1927-1989 .. **CLC 95**
See also CA 107; 129; CANR 34; MTCW 1

**Laishley, Alex**
See Booth, Martin

**Lalage**
See Palmer, Nettie

**Lamartine, Alphonse de** 1790-1869 ... **NCLC
11, 190; PC 16**
See also DAM POET; DLB 217; GFL 1789
to the Present; RGWL 2, 3

**Lamartine, Alphonse Marie Louis Prat de**
See Lamartine, Alphonse de

**Lamb, Charles** 1775-1834 ... **NCLC 10, 113,
298; SSC 112; WLC 3**
See also BRW 4; CDBLB 1789-1832; DA;
DAB; DAC; DAM MST; DLB 93, 107,
163; RGEL 2; SATA 17; TEA

**Lamb, Lady Caroline**
1785-1828 ...................... **NCLC 38, 261**
See also DLB 116

**Lamb, Mary Ann** 1764-1847 ..... **NCLC 125,
285; SSC 112**
See also DLB 163; SATA 17

**Lame Deer** 1903(?)-1976 .................... **NNAL**
See also CA 69-72

**La Mettrie, Julien Offroy de**
1709-1751 ................................. **LC 202**
See also DLB 313

**Lamming, George** 1927- ........ **BLC 1:2, 2:2;
CLC 2, 4, 66, 144**
See also BW 2, 3; CA 85-88; CANR 26,
76; CDWLB 3; CN 1, 2, 3, 4, 5, 6, 7; CP
1; DAM MULT; DLB 125; EWL 3; MTCW
1, 2; MTFW 2005; NFS 15; RGEL 2

**Lamming, George William**
See Lamming, George

**L'Amour, Louis** 1908-1988 ........ **CLC 25, 55**
See also AAYA 16; AITN 2; BEST 89:2;
BPFB 2; CA 1-4R; 125; CANR 3, 25, 40;
CPW; DA3; DAM NOV, POP; DLB 206;
DLBY 1980; MTCW 1, 2; MTFW 2005;
RGAL 4; TCWW 1, 2

**Lampedusa, Giuseppe di**
1896-1957 ...................... **TCLC 13, 351**
See also CA 111; 164; DLB 177; EW 11;
EWL 3; MTCW 2; MTFW 2005; RGWL
2, 3; WLIT 7

**Lampman, Archibald**
1861-1899 ...................... **NCLC 25, 194**
See also DLB 92; RGEL 2; TWA

**Lancaster, Bruce** 1896-1963 ............. **CLC 36**
See also CA 9-10; CANR 70; CAP 1; SATA 9

**Lanchester, John** 1962- ........... **CLC 99, 280**
See also CA 194; DLB 267

**Landau, Mark Alexandrovich**
See Aldanov, Mark (Alexandrovich)

**Landau-Aldanov, Mark Alexandrovich**
See Aldanov, Mark (Alexandrovich)

**Lande, Jean de La**
See Sorel, Charles

**Landis, Jerry**
See Simon, Paul

**Landis, John** 1950- ............................. **CLC 26**
See also CA 112; 122; CANR 128

**Landolfi, Tommaso** 1908-1979 ... **CLC 11, 49**
See also CA 127; 117; DLB 177; EWL 3

**Landon, Letitia Elizabeth**
1802-1838 ....... **NCLC 15, 266; PC 163**
See also DLB 96

**Landor, Walter Savage** 1775-1864 ... **NCLC 14**
See also BRW 4; DLB 93, 107; RGEL 2

**Landwirth, Heinz**
See Lind, Jakov

**Lane, John**
See MacDonald, John D.

**Lane, Patrick** 1939- ........................... **CLC 25**
See also CA 97-100; CANR 54; CP 3, 4, 5, 6,
7; DAM POET; DLB 53; INT CA-97-100

**Lane, Rose Wilder**
1887-1968 ................................. **TCLC 177**
See also CA 102; CANR 63; SATA 29;
SATA-Brief 28; TCWW 2

**Lang, Andrew** 1844-1912 .............. **TCLC 16**
See also CA 114; 137; CANR 85; CLR 101,
174, 227; DLB 98, 141, 184; FANT; MAI-
CYA 1, 2; MBL 2; RGEL 2; SATA 16;
WCH

**Lang, Fritz** 1890-1976 ............. **CLC 20, 103**
See also AAYA 65; CA 77-80; 69-72; CANR 30

**Lange, John**
See Crichton, Michael

**Langer, Elinor** 1939- ......... **CLC 34**
See also CA 121

**Langland, William**
1332(?)-1400(?) .................... **LC 19, 120**

**Lennon, John** 1940-1980 .......... **CLC 12, 35**
    See also CA 102; SATA 114
**Lennon, John Ono**
    See Lennon, John
**Lennox, Charlotte**
    1729(?)-1804 .......... **NCLC 23, 134, 263**
    See also BRWS 17; DLB 39; RGEL 2
**Lentricchia, Frank, Jr.**
    See Lentricchia, Frank
**Lentricchia, Frank** 1940- ......... **CLC 34, 387**
    See also CA 25-28R; CANR 19, 106, 148;
    DLB 246
**Lenz, Gunter** .................................. **CLC 65**
**Lenz, Jakob Michael Reinhold**
    1751-1792 .......................... **LC 100, 226**
    See also DLB 94; RGWL 2, 3
**Lenz, Siegfried** 1926- ........ **CLC 27; SSC 33**
    See also CA 89-92; CANR 80, 149; CWW
    2; DLB 75; EWL 3; RGSF 2; RGWL 2, 3
**Leo Africanus, Johannes**
    c. 1490-1550(?) .......................... **LC 215**
**Leon, David**
    See Jacob, (Cyprien-)Max
**Leonard, Dutch**
    See Leonard, Elmore
**Leonard, Elmore** 1925-2013 ..... **CLC 28, 34,**
    **71, 120, 222, 370**
    See also AAYA 22, 59; AITN 1; BEST 89:1,
    90:4; BPFB 2; CA 81-84; CANR 12, 28, 53,
    76, 96, 133, 176, 219; CMW 4; CN 5, 6, 7;
    CPW; DA3; DAM POP; DLB 173, 226;
    INT CANR-28; MSW; MTCW 1, 2; MTFW
    2005; RGAL 4; SATA 163; TCWW 1, 2
**Leonard, Elmore John, Jr.**
    See Leonard, Elmore
**Leonard, Hugh** 1926-2009 .............. **CLC 19**
    See also CA 102; 283; CANR 78, 140;
    CBD; CD 5, 6; DFS 13, 24; DLB 13; INT
    CA-102
**Leonard, Tom** 1944- ....................... **CLC 289**
    See also CA 77-80; CANR 13, 31; CP 2, 3,
    4, 5, 6, 7
**Leonov, Leonid** 1899-1994 .............. **CLC 92**
    See also CA 129; CANR 76; DAM NOV; DLB
    272; EWL 3; MTCW 1, 2; MTFW 2005
**Leonov, Leonid Maksimovich**
    See Leonov, Leonid
**Leonov, Leonid Maximovich**
    See Leonov, Leonid
**Leopardi, (Conte) Giacomo**
    1798-1837 ......... **NCLC 22, 129; PC 37**
    See also EW 5; RGWL 2, 3; WLIT 7; WP
**Leprince de Beaumont, Marie**
    1711-1780? ............................... **SSC 260**
**Le Prince D. B.**
    See Leprince de Beaumont, Marie
**Le Reveler**
    See Artaud, Antonin
**Lerman, Eleanor** 1952- ...................... **CLC 9**
    See also CA 85-88; CANR 69, 124, 184
**Lerman, Rhoda** 1936- ...................... **CLC 56**
    See also CA 49-52; CANR 70
**Lermontov, Mikhail Iur'evich**
    See Lermontov, Mikhail Yuryevich
**Lermontov, Mikhail Yuryevich**
    1814-1841 ....... **NCLC 5, 47, 126, 288;**
    **PC 18**
    See also DLB 205; EW 6; RGWL 2, 3; TWA
**Leroux, Gaston** 1868-1927 .............. **TCLC 25**
    See also CA 108; 136; CANR 69; CMW 4;
    MTFW 2005; NFS 20; SATA 65
**Lesage, Alain-René** 1668-1747 ...... **LC 2, 28,**
    **233**
    See also DLB 313; EW 3; GFL Beginnings
    to 1789; RGWL 2, 3
**Lesbia**
    See Robinson, Mary
**Leskov, N(ikolai) S(emenovich)**
    See Leskov, Nikolai Semenovich

**Leskov, Nikolai (Semyonovich)**
    See Leskov, Nikolai Semenovich
**Leskov, Nikolai Semenovich**
    1831-1895 ...... **NCLC 25, 174; SSC 34,**
    **96, 247**
    See also DLB 238
**Leskov-Stebnitskiy, M.**
    See Leskov, Nikolai Semenovich
**Lesser, Milton**
    See Marlowe, Stephen
**Lessing, Doris** 1919-2013 ..... **CLC 1, 2, 3, 6,**
    **10, 15, 22, 40, 94, 170, 254, 370; SSC 6,**
    **61, 160, 229, 260; WLCS**
    See also AAYA 57; AFW; BRWS 1; CA 9-
    12R; CAAS 14; CANR 33, 54, 76, 122, 179;
    CBD; CD 5, 6; CDBLB 1960 to Present; CN
    1, 2, 3, 4, 5, 6, 7; CWD; DA; DA3; DAB;
    DAC; DAM MST, NOV; DFS 20; DLB 15,
    139; DLBY 1985; EWL 3; EXPS; FL 1:6;
    FW; LAIT 4; MTCW 1, 2; MTFW 2005;
    NFS 27, 38; RGEL 2; RGSF 2; SFW 4;
    SSFS 1, 12, 20, 26, 30, 35; TEA; WLIT 2, 4
**Lessing, Doris May**
    See Lessing, Doris
**Lessing, Gotthold Ephraim**
    1729-1781 ........ **DC 26; LC 8, 124, 162**
    See also CDWLB 2; DLB 97; EW 4; RGWL
    2, 3
**Lester, Julius** 1939- ......................... **BLC 2:2**
    See also AAYA 12, 51; BW 2; BYA 3, 9, 11,
    12; CA 17-20R; CANR 8, 23, 43, 129,
    174; CLR 2, 41, 143; JRDA; MAICYA 1,
    2; MAICYAS 1; MTFW 2005; SATA 12,
    74, 112, 157; YAW
**Lester, Richard** 1932- ...................... **CLC 20**
**Lethem, Jonathan** 1964- ............... **CLC 295**
    See also AAYA 43; AMWS 18; CA 150;
    CANR 80, 138, 165; CN 7; MTFW 2005;
    SFW 4
**Lethem, Jonathan Allen**
    See Lethem, Jonathan
**Letts, Tracy** 1965- ........................... **CLC 280**
    See also CA 223; CANR 209
**Levenson, Jay** ................................. **CLC 70**
**Lever, Charles (James)**
    1806-1872 .............................. **NCLC 23**
    See also DLB 21; RGEL 2
**Leverson, Ada Esther**
    1862(?)-1933(?) ....................... **TCLC 18**
    See also CA 117; 202; DLB 153; RGEL 2
**Levertov, Denise** 1923-1997 ..... **CLC 1, 2, 3,**
    **5, 8, 15, 28, 66; PC 11, 164**
    See also AMWS 3; CA 1-4R, 178; 163;
    CAAE 178; CAAS 19; CANR 3, 29, 50,
    108; CDALBS; CP 1, 2, 3, 4, 5, 6; CWP;
    DAM POET; DLB 5, 165, 342; EWL 3;
    EXPP; FW; INT CANR-29; MAL 5;
    MTCW 1, 2; PAB; PFS 7, 17, 31, 42;
    RGAL 4; RGHL; TUS; WP
**Levi, Carlo** 1902-1975 .................. **TCLC 125**
    See also CA 65-68; 53-56; CANR 10; EWL
    3; RGWL 2, 3
**Levi, Jonathan** ............................... **CLC 76**
    See also CA 197
**Levi, Peter (Chad Tigar)**
    1931-2000 .................................. **CLC 41**
    See also CA 5-8R; 187; CANR 34, 80; CP 1,
    2, 3, 4, 5, 6, 7; DLB 40
**Levi, Primo** 1919-1987 .............. **CLC 37, 50;**
    **SSC 12, 122, 239; TCLC 109**
    See also CA 13-16R; 122; CANR 12, 33, 61,
    70, 132, 171; DLB 177, 299; EWL 3;
    MTCW 1, 2; MTFW 2005; RGHL; RGWL
    2, 3; WLIT 7
**Levin, Ira** 1929-2007 ..................... **CLC 3, 6**
    See also CA 21-24R; 266; CANR 17, 44, 74,
    139; CMW 4; CN 1, 2, 3, 4, 5, 6, 7; CPW;
    DA3; DAM POP; HGG; MTCW 1, 2;
    MTFW 2005; SATA 66; SATA-Obit 187;
    SFW 4

**Levin, Ira Marvin**
    See Levin, Ira
**Levin, Meyer** 1905-1981 ................... **CLC 7**
    See also AITN 1; CA 9-12R; 104; CANR
    15; CN 1, 2, 3; DAM POP; DLB 9, 28;
    DLBY 1981; MAL 5; RGHL; SATA 21;
    SATA-Obit 27
**Levine, Albert Norman**
    See Levine, Norman
**Levine, Norman** 1923-2005 ............. **CLC 54**
    See also CA 73-76; 240; CAAS 23; CANR
    14, 70; CN 1, 2, 3, 4, 5, 6, 7; CP 1; DLB 88
**Levine, Norman Albert**
    See Levine, Norman
**Levine, Philip** 1928- ...... **CLC 2, 4, 5, 9, 14,**
    **33, 118; PC 22**
    See also AMWS 5; CA 9-12R; CANR 9, 37,
    52, 116, 156; CP 1, 2, 3, 4, 5, 6, 7; DAM
    POET; DLB 5; EWL 3; MAL 5; PFS 8
**Levinson, Deirdre** 1931- ................. **CLC 49**
    See also CA 73-76; CANR 70
**Levitin, Sonia** 1934- ....................... **CLC 17**
    See also AAYA 13, 48; CA 29-32R; CANR
    14, 32, 79, 182; CLR 53; JRDA; MAICYA
    1, 2; SAAS 2; SATA 4, 68, 119, 131, 192;
    SATA-Essay 131; YAW
**Levon, O. U.**
    See Kesey, Ken
**Levy, Amy** 1861-1889 .......... **NCLC 59, 203,**
    **PC 126**
    See also DLB 156, 240
**Levy, Andrea** 1956- ....................... **CLC 420**
    See also CA 236; CANR 225; DLB 347
**Lewald, Fanny** 1811-1889 .......... **NCLC 275**
    See also DLB 129
**Lewees, John**
    See Stockton, Francis Richard
**Lewes, George Henry**
    1817-1878 ..................... **NCLC 25, 215**
    See also DLB 55, 144
**Lewis, Alun** 1915-1944 .... **SSC 40; TCLC 3**
    See also BRW 7; CA 104; 188; DLB 20,
    162; PAB; RGEL 2
**Lewis, C. S.** 1898-1963 ...... **CLC 1, 3, 6, 14,**
    **27, 124; WLC 4**
    See also AAYA 3, 39; BPFB 2; BRWS 3;
    BYA 15, 16; CA 81-84; CANR 33, 71,
    132; CDBLB 1945-1960; CLR 3, 27, 109,
    173; CWRI 5; DA; DA3; DAB; DAC;
    DAM MST, NOV, POP; DLB 15, 100,
    160, 255; EWL 3; FANT; JRDA; LMFS
    2; MAICYA 1, 2; MTCW 1, 2; MTFW
    2005; NFS 24; RGEL 2; SATA 13, 100;
    SCFW 1, 2; SFW 4; SUFW 1; TEA;
    WCH; WYA; YAW
**Lewis, Clive Staples**
    See Lewis, C. S.
**Lewis, Harry Sinclair**
    See Lewis, Sinclair
**Lewis, Janet** 1899-1998 ................... **CLC 41**
    See also CA 9-12R; 172; CANR 29, 63;
    CAP 1; CN 1, 2, 3, 4, 5, 6; DLBY 1987;
    RHW; TCWW 2
**Lewis, Matthew Gregory**
    1775-1818 ...................... **NCLC 11, 62, 320**
    See also DLB 39, 158, 178; GL 3; HGG;
    LMFS 1; RGEL 2; SUFW
**Lewis, Sinclair** 1885-1951 ........ **TCLC 4, 13,**
    **23, 39, 215; WLC 4**
    See also AMW; AMWC 1; BPFB 2; CA 104;
    133; CANR 132; CDALB 1917-1929; DA;
    DA3; DAB; DAC; DAM MST, NOV; DLB
    9, 102, 284, 331; DLBD 1; EWL 3; LAIT
    3; MAL 5; MTCW 1, 2; MTFW 2005; NFS
    15, 19, 22, 34; RGAL 4; TUS
**Lewis, (Percy) Wyndham**
    1884(?)-1957 ........ **SSC 34; TCLC 2, 9,**
    **104, 216**

See also AAYA 77; BRW 7; CA 104; 157;
DLB 15; EWL 3; FANT; MTCW 2;
MTFW 2005; RGEL 2

**Lewisohn, Ludwig** 1883-1955 ....... **TCLC 19**
See also CA 107; 203; DLB 4, 9, 28, 102;
MAL 5

**Lewton, Val** 1904-1951 ................. **TCLC 76**
See also CA 199; IDFW 3, 4

**Leyner, Mark** 1956- ....................... **CLC 92**
See also CA 110; CANR 28, 53; DA3; DLB
292; MTCW 2; MTFW 2005

**Leyton, E. K.**
See Campbell, Ramsey

**Lezama Lima, Jose** 1910-1976 ... **CLC 4, 10,
101; HLCS 2; TCLC 371**
See also CA 77-80; CANR 71; DAM MULT;
DLB 113, 283; EWL 3; HW 1, 2; LAW;
RGWL 2, 3

**L'Heureux, John (Clarke)** 1934- .... **CLC 52**
See also CA 13-16R; CANR 23, 45, 88; CP
1, 2, 3, 4; DLB 244

**Li Ang** 1952- .................................. **CLC 413**
See also DLB 370; EWL 3; RGWL 3

**Li Ch'ing-chao** 1081(?)-1141(?) ... **CMLC 71**

**Li, Fei-kan**
See Jin, Ba

**Lichtenberg, Georg Christoph**
1742-1799 ................................... **LC 162**
See also DLB 94

**Liddell, C. H.**
See Kuttner, Henry

**Lie, Jonas (Lauritz Idemil)**
1833-1908(?) ............................... **TCLC 5**
See also CA 115

**Lieber, Joel** 1937-1971 ..................... **CLC 6**
See also CA 73-76; 29-32R

**Lieber, Stanley Martin**
See Lee, Stan

**Lieberman, Laurence (James)**
1935- ........................................ **CLC 4, 36**
See also CA 17-20R; CANR 8, 36, 89; CP 1,
2, 3, 4, 5, 6, 7

**Lieh Tzu** fl. 7th cent. BCE-5th cent.
BCE ........................................... **CMLC 27**

**Lieksman, Anders**
See Haavikko, Paavo Juhani

**Lifton, Robert Jay** 1926- ................. **CLC 67**
See also CA 17-20R; CANR 27, 78, 161,
239; INT CANR-27; SATA 66

**Lightfoot, Gordon** 1938- ................. **CLC 26**
See also CA 109; 242

**Lightfoot, Gordon Meredith**
See Lightfoot, Gordon

**Lightman, Alan P.** 1948- ................. **CLC 81**
See also CA 141; CANR 63, 105, 138, 178;
MTFW 2005; NFS 29

**Lightman, Alan Paige**
See Lightman, Alan P.

**Ligotti, Thomas** 1953- ....... **CLC 44; SSC 16**
See also CA 123; CANR 49, 135; HGG;
SUFW 2

**Ligotti, Thomas Robert**
See Ligotti, Thomas

**Li Ho** 791-817 ..................................... **PC 13**

**Li Ju-chen** c. 1763-c. 1830 ......... **NCLC 137**

**Liking, Werewere** 1950- ............... **BLC 2:2**
See also CA 293; DLB 360; EWL 3

**Lilar, Francoise**
See Mallet-Joris, Francoise

**Liliencron, Detlev**
See Liliencron, Detlev von

**Liliencron, Detlev von** 1844-1909 ... **TCLC 18**
See also CA 117

**Liliencron, Friedrich Adolf Axel Detlev von**
See Liliencron, Detlev von

**Liliencron, Friedrich Detlev von**
See Liliencron, Detlev von

**Lille, Alain de**
See Alain de Lille

**Lillo, George** 1691-1739 ..... **DC 54; LC 131**
See also DLB 84; RGEL 2

**Lilly, William** 1602-1681 .................... **LC 27**

**Lima, Jose Lezama**
See Lezama Lima, Jose

**Lima Barreto, Afonso Henrique de**
1881-1922 .............................. **TCLC 23**
See also CA 117; 181; DLB 307; LAW

**Lima Barreto, Afonso Henriques de**
See Lima Barreto, Afonso Henrique de

**Limonov, Eduard**
See Limonov, Edward

**Limonov, Edward** 1944- .................. **CLC 67**
See also CA 137; DLB 317

**Lin, Frank**
See Atherton, Gertrude (Franklin Horn)

**Lin, Yutang** 1895-1976 ................ **TCLC 149**
See also CA 45-48; 65-68; CANR 2; RGAL 4

**Lincoln, Abraham** 1809-1865 ... **NCLC 18, 201**
See also LAIT 2

**Lincoln, Geoffrey**
See Mortimer, John

**Lind, Jakov**
1927-2007 ............. **CLC 1, 2, 4, 27, 82**
See also CA 9-12R; 257; CAAS 4; CANR 7;
DLB 299; EWL 3; RGHL

**Lindbergh, Anne Morrow**
1906-2001 ................................. **CLC 82**
See also BPFB 2; CA 17-20R; 193; CANR
16, 73; DAM NOV; MTCW 1, 2; MTFW
2005; SATA 33; SATA-Obit 125; TUS

**Lindbergh, Anne Spencer Morrow**
See Lindbergh, Anne Morrow

**Lindgren, Astrid** 1907-2002 .......... **CLC 361**
See also BYA 5; CLR 1, 39, 119; CA 13-16R;
204; CANR 39, 80, 117; CWW 2; DLB
257; MAICYA 1, 2; SATA 2, 38, 118; TWA

**Lindholm, Anna Margaret**
See Haycraft, Anna

**Lindsay, David** 1878(?)-1945 ......... **TCLC 15**
See also CA 113; 187; DLB 255; FANT;
SFW 4; SUFW 1

**Lindsay, Nicholas Vachel**
See Lindsay, Vachel

**Lindsay, Vachel** 1879-1931 ........ **PC 23, 139;
TCLC 17; WLC 4**
See also AMWS 1; CA 114; 135; CANR 79;
CDALB 1865-1917; DA; DA3; DAC;
DAM MST, POET; DLB 54; EWL 3;
EXPP; MAL 5; RGAL 4; SATA 40; WP

**Linke Poot**
See Döblin, Alfred

**Linney, Romulus** 1930-2011 ........... **CLC 51**
See also CA 1-4R; CAD; CANR 40, 44, 79;
CD 5, 6; CSW; RGAL 4

**Linton, Eliza Lynn**
1822-1898 ........................... **NCLC 41, 362**
See also DLB 18

**Li Po** 701-763 ............. **CMLC 2, 86; PC 29**
See also PFS 20, 40; WP

**Lippard, George** 1822-1854 ........ **NCLC 198**
See also AMWS 23; DLB 202

**Lipsius, Justus** 1547-1606 .......... **LC 16, 207**

**Lipsyte, Robert** 1938- ..................... **CLC 21**
See also AAYA 7, 45; CA 17-20R; CANR 8,
57, 146, 189; CLR 23, 76; DA; DAC;
DAM MST, NOV; JRDA; LAIT 5; MAI-
CYA 1, 2; NFS 35; SATA 5, 68, 113, 161,
198; WYA; YAW

**Lipsyte, Robert Michael**
See Lipsyte, Robert

**Lish, Gordon** 1934- .......... **CLC 45; SSC 18**
See also CA 113; 117; CANR 79, 151; DLB
130; INT CA-117

**Lish, Gordon Jay**
See Lish, Gordon

**Lispector, Clarice** 1920-1977 .......... **CLC 43;
HLCS 2; SSC 34, 96, 215; TCLC 305**
See also CA 139; 116; CANR 71; CDWLB 3;
DLB 113, 307; DNFS 1; EWL 3; FW; HW
2; LAW; RGSF 2; RGWL 2, 3; WLIT 1

**Liszt, Franz** 1811-1886 ................ **NCLC 199**

**Littell, Jonathan** 1967- ................. **CLC 383**
See also CA 259; CANR 207

**Littell, Robert** 1935(?)- ................... **CLC 42**
See also CA 109; 112; CANR 64, 115, 162,
217; CMW 4

**Little, Malcolm**
See Malcolm X

**Littleton, Mark**
See Pendleton, John Kennedy

**Littlewit, Humphrey Gent.**
See Lovecraft, H. P.

**Litwos**
See Sienkiewicz, Henryk (Adam
Alexander Pius)

**Liu, E.** 1857-1909 ......................... **TCLC 15**
See also CA 115; 190; DLB 328

**Liu Xiaobo** 1955-2017 .................. **CLC 439**

**Liu Xie** c. 465-c. 523 ................. **CMLC 185**
See also DLB 358

**Liu Yiqing** 403-444 ..................... **CMLC 190**
See also DLB 358

**Lively, Penelope** 1933- ...... **CLC 32, 50, 306**
See also BPFB 2; CA 41-44R; CANR 29,
67, 79, 131, 172, 222; CLR 7, 159; CN 5,
6, 7; CWRI 5; DAM NOV; DLB 14, 161,
207, 326; FANT; JRDA; MAICYA 1, 2;
MTCW 1, 2; MTFW 2005; SATA 7, 60,
101, 164; TEA

**Lively, Penelope Margaret**
See Lively, Penelope

**Livesay, Dorothy (Kathleen)**
1909-1996 ....................... **CLC 4, 15, 79**
See also AITN 2; CA 25-28R; CAAS 8;
CANR 36, 67; CP 1, 2, 3, 4, 5; DAC;
DAM MST, POET; DLB 68; FW; MTCW
1; RGEL 2; TWA

**Livius Andronicus**
c. 284 BCE-c. 204 BCE .......... **CMLC 102**

**Livy** c. 59 BCE-c. 12 CE ......... **CMLC 11, 154**
See also AW 2; CDWLB 1; DLB 211;
RGWL 2, 3; WLIT 8

**Li Yaotang**
See Jin, Ba

**Liyong, Taban lo**
1939- ....................................... **CLC 359**
See also BW 2; CA 105; CANR 79; CP 2, 3,
4, 5, 6, 7; DLB 125

**Li-Young, Lee**
See Lee, Li-Young

**Lizardi, José Joaquín Fernández de**
1776-1827 ....................... **NCLC 30, 320**
See also LAW

**Llewellyn, Richard**
See Llewellyn Lloyd, Richard Dafydd Vivian

**Llewellyn Lloyd, Richard Dafydd Vivian**
1906-1983 ............................. **CLC 7, 80**
See also CA 53-56; 111; CANR 7, 71; DLB
15; NFS 30; SATA 11; SATA-Obit 37

**Llosa, Jorge Mario Pedro Vargas**
See Vargas Llosa, Mario

**Llosa, Mario Vargas**
See Vargas Llosa, Mario

**Lloyd, Manda**
See Mander, (Mary) Jane

**Lloyd Webber, Andrew** 1948- ........ **CLC 21**
See also AAYA 1, 38; CA 116; 149; DAM
DRAM; DFS 7; SATA 56

**Llull, Ramon**
c. 1235-c. 1316 ............. **CMLC 12, 114**

**Lonnbohm, Armas Eino Leopold**
1878-1926 ............................. **TCLC 24**
See also CA 123; EWL 3

**Lobb, Ebenezer**
See Upward, Allen
**Lochhead, Liz** 1947- ..................... **CLC 286**
See also BRWS 17; CA 81-84; CANR 79;
CBD; CD 5, 6; CP 2, 3, 4, 5, 6, 7; CWD;
CWP; DLB 310
**Lock, Anne** c. 1530-c. 1595 ............. **PC 135**
**Locke, Alain Leroy** 1885-1954 ... **BLCS; HR
1:3; TCLC 43**
See also AMWS 14; BW 1, 3; CA 106; 124;
CANR 79; DLB 51; LMFS 2; MAL 5;
RGAL 4
**Locke, John** 1632-1704 ... **LC 7, 35, 135, 281**
See also DLB 31, 101, 213, 252; RGEL 2;
WLIT 3
**Locke-Elliott, Sumner**
See Elliott, Sumner Locke
**Lockhart, John Gibson**
1794-1854 ......................... **NCLC 6, 324**
See also DLB 110, 116, 144
**Lockridge, Ross (Franklin), Jr.**
1914-1948 ............................... **TCLC 111**
See also CA 108; 145; CANR 79; DLB 143;
DLBY 1980; MAL 5; RGAL 4; RHW
**Lockwood, Robert**
See Johnson, Robert
**Lodge, David** 1935- ......... **CLC 36, 141, 293**
See also BEST 90:1; BRWS 4; CA 17-20R;
CANR 19, 53, 92, 139, 197, 243; CN 1, 2,
3, 4, 5, 6, 7; CPW; DAM POP; DLB 14,
194; EWL 3; INT CANR-19; MTCW 1, 2;
MTFW 2005
**Lodge, David John**
See Lodge, David
**Lodge, Thomas** 1558-1625 ................. **LC 41**
See also DLB 172; RGEL 2
**Loewinsohn, Ron(ald William)**
1937- ......................................... **CLC 52**
See also CA 25-28R; CANR 71; CP 1, 2, 3, 4
**Logan, Jake**
See Smith, Martin Cruz
**Logan, John (Burton)** 1923-1987 ..... **CLC 5**
See also CA 77-80; 124; CANR 45; CP 1, 2,
3, 4; DLB 5
**Lohenstein, Daniel Casper von**
1635-1683 ................................... **LC 240**
See also DLB 168
**Lo-Johansson, (Karl) Ivar**
1901-1990 ................................. **TCLC 216**
See also CA 102; 131; CANR 20, 79, 137;
DLB 259; EWL 3; RGWL 2, 3
**Lo Kuan-chung**
See Luo Guanzhong
**Lomax, Pearl**
See Cleage, Pearl
**Lomax, Pearl Cleage**
See Cleage, Pearl
**Lombard, Nap**
See Johnson, Pamela Hansford
**Lombard, Peter** 1100(?)-1160(?) ... **CMLC 72**
**Lombino, Salvatore**
See Hunter, Evan
**London, Jack** 1876-1916 ............. **SSC 4, 49,
133, 241; TCLC 9, 15, 39; WLC 4**
See also AAYA 13, 75; AITN 2; AMW;
BPFB 2; BYA 4, 13; CA 110; 119; CANR
73; CDALB 1865-1917; CLR 108; DA;
DA3; DAB; DAC; DAM MST, NOV; DLB
8, 12, 78, 212; EWL 3; EXPS; JRDA;
LAIT 3; MAICYA 1, 2,; MAL 5; MTCW
1, 2; MTFW 2005; NFS 8, 19, 35; RGAL
4; RGSF 2; SATA 18; SFW 4; SSFS 7, 35;
TCWW 1, 2; TUS; WYA; YAW
**London, John Griffith**
See London, Jack
**Long, Emmett**
See Leonard, Elmore
**Longbaugh, Harry**
See Goldman, William

**Longfellow, Henry Wadsworth**
1807-1882 ................ **NCLC 2, 45, 101,
103, 235, 344; PC 30, 196, 199; WLCS**
See also AMW; AMWR 2; CDALB 1640-
1865; CLR 99; DA; DA3; DAB; DAC;
DAM MST, POET; DLB 1, 59, 235;
EXPP; PAB; PFS 2, 7, 17, 31, 39; RGAL
4; SATA 19; TUS; WP
**Longinus** c. 1st cent. .................... **CMLC 27**
See also AW 2; DLB 176
**Longley, Michael** 1939- ..... **CLC 29; PC 118**
See also BRWS 8; CA 102; CP 1, 2, 3, 4, 5,
6, 7; DLB 40
**Longstreet, Augustus Baldwin**
1790-1870 .................... **NCLC 159, 355**
See also DLB 3, 11, 74, 248; RGAL 4
**Longus** fl. c. 2nd cent. .......... **CMLC 7, 182**
**Longway, A. Hugh**
See Lang, Andrew
**Lonnbohm, Armas Eino Leopold**
See Lonnbohm, Armas Eino Leopold
**Lonsdale, Roger** ............................ **CLC 65**
**Lopate, Phillip** 1943- ....................... **CLC 29**
See also CA 97-100; CANR 88, 157, 196;
DLBY 1980; INT CA-97-100
**Lopez, Barry** 1945- .................. **CLC 70, 359**
See also AAYA 9, 63; ANW; CA 65-68;
CANR 7, 23, 47, 68, 92; DLB 256, 275,
335; INT CANR-7, CANR-23; MTCW 1;
RGAL 4; SATA 67
**Lopez, Barry Holstun**
See Lopez, Barry
**Lopez y Fuentes, Gregorio**
1897(?)-1966 .............................. **CLC 32**
See also CA 131; EWL 3; HW 1
**Lorca, Federico Garcia**
See Garcia Lorca, Federico
**Lord, Audre**
See Lorde, Audre
**Lord, Bette Bao** 1938- .......... **AAL; CLC 23**
See also BEST 90:3; BPFB 2; CA 107; CANR
41, 79; CLR 151; INT CA-107; SATA 58
**Lord Auch**
See Bataille, Georges
**Lord Brooke**
See Greville, Fulke
**Lord Byron** 1788-1824 .... **DC 24; NCLC 2,
12, 109, 149, 256; PC 16, 95, 189; WLC 1**
See also AAYA 64; BRW 4; BRWC 2;
CDBLB 1789-1832; DA; DA3; DAB;
DAC; DAM MST, POET; DLB 96, 110;
EXPP; LMFS 1; PAB; PFS 1, 14, 29, 35;
RGEL 2; TEA; WLIT 3; WP
**Lord Dunsany** 1878-1957 ........ **TCLC 2, 59**
See also CA 104; 148; DLB 10, 77, 153,
156, 255; FANT; MTCW 2; RGEL 2; SFW
4; SUFW 1
**Lorde, Audre** 1934-1992 ........ **BLC 1:2, 2:2;
CLC 18, 71; PC 12, 141; TCLC 173, 300**
See also AFAW 1, 2; BW 1, 3; CA 25-28R;
142; CANR 16, 26, 46, 82; CP 2, 3, 4, 5;
DA3; DAM MULT, POET; DLB 41; EWL
3; FW; GLL 1; MAL 5; MTCW 1, 2;
MTFW 2005; PFS 16, 32; RGAL 4
**Lorde, Audre Geraldine**
See Lorde, Audre
**Lord Houghton**
See Milnes, Richard Monckton
**Lord Jeffrey**
See Jeffrey, Francis
**Loreaux, Nichol** ............................ **CLC 65**
**Lorenzo, Heberto Padilla**
See Padilla (Lorenzo), Heberto
**Loris**
See Hofmannsthal, Hugo von
**Loti, Pierre**
See Viaud, Julien
**Lottie**
See Grimke, Charlotte L. Forten

**Lou, Henri**
See Andreas-Salome, Lou
**Louie, David Wong** 1954- .............. **CLC 70**
See also CA 139; CANR 120
**Louis, Adrian C.** ............................... **NNAL**
See also CA 223
**Louis, Father M.**
See Merton, Thomas
**Louise, Heidi**
See Erdrich, Louise
**Lounsbury, Ruth Ozeki**
See Ozeki, Ruth L.
**Lovecraft, H. P.** 1890-1937 ......... **SSC 3, 52,
165, 200; TCLC 4, 22**
See also AAYA 14; BPFB 2; CA 104; 133;
CANR 106; DA3; DAM POP; HGG;
MTCW 1, 2; MTFW 2005; RGAL 4;
SCFW 1, 2; SFW 4; SUFW
**Lovecraft, Howard Phillips**
See Lovecraft, H. P.
**Lovelace, Earl** 1935- ....... **CLC 51; SSC 141**
See also BW 2; CA 77-80; CANR 41, 72,
114; CD 5, 6; CDWLB 3; CN 1, 2, 3, 4, 5,
6, 7; DLB 125; EWL 3; MTCW 1
**Lovelace, Richard**
1618-1658 .............. **LC 24, 158; PC 69**
See also BRW 2; DLB 131; EXPP; PAB;
PFS 32, 34; RGEL 2
**Low, Penelope Margaret**
See Lively, Penelope
**Lowe, Pardee** 1904- ............................. **AAL**
**Lowell, Amy** 1874-1925 ............ **PC 13, 168;
TCLC 1, 8, 259**
See also AAYA 57; AMW; CA 104; 151;
DAM POET; DLB 54, 140; EWL 3; EXPP;
LMFS 2; MAL 5; MBL; MTCW 2; MTFW
2005; PFS 30, 42; RGAL 4; TUS
**Lowell, James Russell**
1819-1891 ................. **NCLC 2, 90, 347**
See also AMWS 1; CDALB 1640-1865;
DLB 1, 11, 64, 79, 189, 235; RGAL 4
**Lowell, Robert**
1917-1977 .................... **CLC 1, 2, 3, 4,
5, 8, 9, 11, 15, 37, 124; PC 3, 132; WLC 4**
See also AMW; AMWC 2; AMWR 2; CA 9-
12R; 73-76; CABS 2; CAD; CANR 26, 60;
CDALBS; CP 1, 2; DA; DA3; DAB; DAC;
DAM MST, NOV; DLB 5, 169; EWL 3;
MAL 5; MTCW 1, 2; MTFW 2005; PAB;
PFS 6, 7, 36; RGAL 4; WP
**Lowell, Robert Trail Spence, Jr.**
See Lowell, Robert
**Lowenthal, Michael** 1969- ............. **CLC 119**
See also CA 150; CANR 115, 164
**Lowenthal, Michael Francis**
See Lowenthal, Michael
**Lowndes, Marie Adelaide (Belloc)**
1868-1947 ................................. **TCLC 12**
See also CA 107; CMW 4; DLB 70; RHW
**Lowry, (Clarence) Malcolm**
1909-1957 ... **SSC 31; TCLC 6, 40, 275**
See also BPFB 2; BRWS 3; CA 105; 131;
CANR 62, 105; CDBLB 1945-1960; DLB
15; EWL 3; MTCW 1, 2; MTFW 2005;
RGEL 2
**Lowry, Mina Gertrude**
1882-1966 .................... **CLC 28; PC 16**
See also CA 113; DAM POET; DLB 4, 54;
PFS 20
**Lowry, Sam**
See Soderbergh, Steven
**Loxsmith, John**
See Brunner, John (Kilian Houston)
**Loy, Mina**
See Lowry, Mina Gertrude
**Loyson-Bridet**
See Schwob, Marcel (Mayer Andre)

**Mallon, Thomas** 1951- .................. **CLC 172**
  See also CA 110; CANR 29, 57, 92, 196;
  DLB 350
**Mallowan, Agatha Christie**
  See Christie, Agatha
**Maloff, Saul** 1922- ............................. **CLC 5**
  See also CA 33-36R
**Malone, Louis**
  See MacNeice, (Frederick) Louis
**Malone, Michael** 1942- .................... **CLC 43**
  See also CA 77-80; CANR 14, 32, 57, 114, 214
**Malone, Michael Christopher**
  See Malone, Michael
**Malory, Sir Thomas**
  1410(?)-1471(?) .......... **LC 11, 88, 229;**
  **WLCS**
  See also BRW 1; BRWR 2; CDBLB Before
  1660; DA; DAB; DAC; DAM MST; DLB
  146; EFS 1:2, 2:2; RGEL 2; SATA 59;
  SATA-Brief 33; TEA; WLIT 3
**Malouf, David**
  1934- ......... **CLC 28, 86, 245; SSC 234**
  See also BRWS 12; CA 124; CANR 50, 76,
  180, 224; CN 3, 4, 5, 6, 7; CP 1, 3, 4, 5, 6,
  7; DLB 289; EWL 3; MTCW 2; MTFW
  2005; SSFS 24
**Malouf, George Joseph David**
  See Malouf, David
**Malraux, Andre** 1901-1976 ..... **CLC 1, 4, 9,**
  **13, 15, 57; TCLC 209**
  See also BPFB 2; CA 21-22; 69-72; CANR
  34, 58; CAP 2; DA3; DAM NOV; DLB 72;
  EW 12; EWL 3; GFL 1789 to the Present;
  MTCW 1, 2; MTFW 2005; RGWL 2, 3;
  TWA
**Malraux, Georges-Andre**
  See Malraux, Andre
**Malthus, Thomas Robert**
  1766-1834 .............................. **NCLC 145**
  See also DLB 107, 158; RGEL 2
**Malzberg, Barry N(athaniel)** 1939- ... **CLC 7**
  See also CA 61-64; CAAS 4; CANR 16;
  CMW 4; DLB 8; SFW 4
**Mamet, David** 1947- ....... **CLC 9, 15, 34, 46,**
  **91, 166; DC 4, 24**
  See also AAYA 3, 60; AMWS 14; CA 81-84;
  CABS 3; CAD; CANR 15, 41, 67, 72, 129,
  172; CD 5, 6; DA3; DAM DRAM; DFS 2,
  3, 6, 12, 15; DLB 7; EWL 3; IDFW 4; MAL
  5; MTCW 1, 2; MTFW 2005; RGAL 4
**Mamet, David Alan**
  See Mamet, David
**Mamoulian, Rouben (Zachary)**
  1897-1987 ................................. **CLC 16**
  See also CA 25-28R; 124; CANR 85
**Man in the Cloak, The**
  See Mangan, James Clarence
**Mandel, Eli**
  1922-1992 ................................... **PC 208**
  See also CA 73-76; CANR 15, 43; CP 1, 2,
  3, 4, 5; DLB 53
**Mandela, Nelson** 1918-2013 ........... **CLC 425**
  See also BW 2, 3; CA 125; CANR 43, 59,
  82, 151, 238; DAM MULT; WLIT 2
**Mandelshtam, Osip**
  See Mandelstam, Osip
**Mandel'shtam, Osip Emil'evich**
  See Mandelstam, Osip
**Mandelstam, Osip** 1891(?)-1943(?) ... **PC 14;**
  **TCLC 2, 6, 225**
  See also CA 104; 150; DLB 295; EW 10;
  EWL 3; MTCW 2; RGWL 2, 3; TWA
**Mandelstam, Osip Emilievich**
  See Mandelstam, Osip
**Mander, (Mary) Jane** 1877-1949 ... **TCLC 31**
  See also CA 162; RGEL 2
**Mandeville, Bernard** 1670-1733 ........ **LC 82**
  See also DLB 101
**Mandeville, Sir John** fl. 1350 .. **CMLC 19, 184**
  See also DLB 146

**Mandiargues, Andre Pieyre de**
  See Pieyre de Mandiargues, Andre
**Mandrake, Ethel Belle**
  See Thurman, Wallace (Henry)
**Manea, Norman** 1936- .................... **CLC 445**
  See also CA 142; CANR 97, 174; DLB 232
**Mangan, James Clarence**
  1803-1849 ....... **NCLC 27, 316; PC 203**
  See also BRWS 13; RGEL 2
**Maniere, J. E.**
  See Giraudoux, Jean
**Mankell, Henning** 1948-2015 ... **CLC 292, 408**
  See also CA 187; CANR 163, 200
**Mankiewicz, Herman (Jacob)**
  1897-1953 .............................. **TCLC 85**
  See also CA 120; 169; DLB 26; IDFW 3, 4
**Manley, (Mary) Delariviere**
  1672(?)-1724 ........................... **LC 1, 42**
  See also DLB 39, 80; RGEL 2
**Mann, Abel**
  See Creasey, John
**Mann, Emily** 1952- ............................. **DC 7**
  See also CA 130; CAD; CANR 55; CD 5, 6;
  CWD; DFS 28; DLB 266
**Mann, Erica**
  See Jong, Erica
**Mann, Klaus** 1906-1949 .............. **TCLC 333**
  See also CA 204; DLB 56
**Mann, (Luiz) Heinrich**
  1871-1950 ........................ **TCLC 9, 279**
  See also CA 106; 164, 181; DLB 66, 118;
  EW 8; EWL 3; RGWL 2, 3
**Mann, Mary Tyler Peabody**
  1806-1887 ........................... **NCLC 317**
  See also DLB 239
**Mann, Paul Thomas**
  See Mann, Thomas
**Mann, Thomas** 1875-1955 .... **SSC 5, 80, 82,**
  **170, 172, 174; TCLC 2, 8, 14, 21, 35, 44,**
  **60, 168, 236, 292, 293, 303, 312; WLC 4**
  See also BPFB 2; CA 104; 128; CANR 133;
  CDWLB 2; DA; DA3; DAB; DAC; DAM
  MST, NOV; DLB 66, 331; EW 9; EWL 3;
  GLL 1; LATS 1:1; LMFS 1; MTCW 1, 2;
  MTFW 2005; NFS 17; RGSF 2; RGWL 2,
  3; SSFS 4, 9; TWA
**Mannheim, Karl** 1893-1947 ......... **TCLC 65**
  See also CA 204
**Manning, David**
  See Faust, Frederick
**Manning, Frederic** 1882-1935 ....... **TCLC 25**
  See also CA 124; 216; DLB 260
**Manning, Olivia** 1915-1980 ......... **CLC 5, 19**
  See also CA 5-8R; 101; CANR 29; CN 1, 2;
  EWL 3; FW; MTCW 1; RGEL 2
**Mannyng, Robert** c. 1264-c. 1340 **CMLC 83**
  See also DLB 146
**Mano, D. Keith** 1942- ................. **CLC 2, 10**
  See also CA 25-28R; CAAS 6; CANR 26,
  57; DLB 6
**Mansfield, Katherine** 1888-1923 ........ **SSC 9,**
  **23, 38, 81, 223, 224, 235; TCLC 2, 8, 39,**
  **164; WLC 4**
  See also BPFB 2; BRW 7; CA 104; 134;
  DA; DA3; DAB; DAC; DAM MST; DLB
  162; EWL 3; EXPS; FW; GLL 1; MTCW
  2; RGEL 2; RGSF 2; SSFS 2, 8, 10, 11,
  29; TEA; WWE 1
**Mansfield, Kathleen**
  See Mansfield, Katherine
**Manso, Peter** 1940- ......................... **CLC 39**
  See also CA 29-32R; CANR 44, 156
**Mantecon, Juan Jimenez**
  See Jimenez, Juan Ramon
**Mantel, Hilary** 1952- ..... **CLC 144, 309, 354**
  See also CA 125; CANR 54, 101, 161, 207;
  CN 5, 6, 7; DLB 271; RHW
**Mantel, Hilary Mary**
  See Mantel, Hilary

**Manto, Saadat Hasan** 1912-1955 ... **SSC 208**
  See also RGEL 2; SSFS 15
**Manton, Peter**
  See Creasey, John
**Man Without a Spleen, A**
  See Chekhov, Anton
**Manzano, Juan Franciso**
  1797(?)-1854 ........................ **NCLC 155**
**Manzoni, Alessandro**
  1785-1873 ........ **NCLC 29, 98, 319, 329**
  See also EW 5; RGWL 2, 3; TWA; WLIT 7
**Mao Dun** 1896-1981 ...................... **TCLC 299**
  See also CA 103; DLB 328; EWL 3; RGSF 3
**Mao Lin**
  See Shen Congwen
**Mao Tun**
  See Mao Dun
**Map, Walter** 1140-1209 ....... **CMLC 32, 147**
**Mapanje, Jack** 1944- ..................... **CLC 399**
  See also BW 3; CA 166; CP 5, 6, 7; DLB
  157; WWE 1
**Mapu, Abraham (ben Jekutiel)**
  1808-1867 .............................. **NCLC 18**
**Mara, Sally**
  See Queneau, Raymond
**Maracle, Lee** 1950- ........................... **NNAL**
  See also CA 149
**Maraini, Dacia** 1936- .................... **CLC 436**
  See also CA 5-8R; CANR 11, 91; CWW 2;
  DLB 196; EWL 3; WLIT 7
**Marat, Jean Paul** 1743-1793 ............. **LC 10**
**Marcabru** fl. 1129-1150 ............. **CMLC 172**
**Marcel, Gabriel Honore** 1889-1973 **CLC 15**
  See also CA 102; 45-48; EWL 3; MTCW 1, 2
**March, Anne**
  See Woolson, Constance Fenimore
**March, Ausiàs** 1400-1459 ................. **PC 179**
**March, William** 1893-1954 ........... **TCLC 96**
  See also CA 108; 216; DLB 9, 86, 316;
  MAL 5
**Marchbanks, Samuel**
  See Davies, Robertson
**Marchi, Giacomo**
  See Bassani, Giorgio
**Marcus Aurelius**
  See Aurelius, Marcus
**Marcuse, Herbert** 1898-1979 ...... **TCLC 207**
  See also CA 188; 89-92; DLB 242
**Marechera, Dambudzo**
  1952-1987 .............................. **TCLC 335**
  See also BW 3; CA 166; CN 4; DLB 157;
  EWL 3
**Marguerite**
  See de Navarre, Marguerite
**Marguerite d'Angouleme**
  See de Navarre, Marguerite
**Marguerite de Navarre**
  See de Navarre, Marguerite
**Margulies, Donald** 1954- ................ **CLC 76**
  See also AAYA 57; CA 200; CD 6; DFS 13;
  DLB 228
**Marias, Javier** 1951- ..................... **CLC 239**
  See also CA 167; CANR 109, 139, 232;
  DLB 322; HW 2; MTFW 2005
**Marie de France** c. 12th cent. ....... **CMLC 8,**
  **111; PC 22**
  See also DLB 208; FW; RGWL 2, 3
**Marie de l'Incarnation** 1599-1672 ... **LC 10, 168**
**Marier, Captain Victor**
  See Griffith, D.W.
**Mariner, Scott**
  See Pohl, Frederik
**Marinetti, Filippo Tommaso**
  1876-1944 .............................. **TCLC 10**
  See also CA 107; DLB 114, 264; EW 9;
  EWL 3; WLIT 7

**Mason, Hunni B.**
See Sternheim, (William Adolf) Carl

**Mason, Lee W.**
See Malzberg, Barry N(athaniel)

**Mason, Nick** 1945- .......................... **CLC 35**

**Mason, Tally**
See Derleth, August (William)

**Mass, Anna** ...................................... **CLC 59**

**Mass, William**
See Gibson, William

**Massinger, Philip** 1583-1640 ............. **DC 39;
LC 70**
See also BRWS 11; DLB 58; RGEL 2

**Master Lao**
See Lao Tzu

**Masters, Edgar Lee** 1868-1950 ..... **PC 1, 36;
TCLC 2, 25; WLCS**
See also AMWS 1; CA 104; 133; CDALB
1865-1917; DA; DAC; DAM MST, POET;
DLB 54; EWL 3; EXPP; MAL 5; MTCW
1, 2; MTFW 2005; PFS 37; RGAL 4; TUS;
WP

**Masters, Hilary** 1928- ...................... **CLC 48**
See also CA 25-28R, 217; CAAE 217; CANR
13, 47, 97, 171, 221; CN 6, 7; DLB 244

**Masters, Hilary Thomas**
See Masters, Hilary

**Mastretta, Ángeles** 1949- ............... **CLC 428**
See also CA 254

**Mastrosimone, William** 1947- ......... **CLC 36**
See also CA 186; CAD; CD 5, 6

**Mathe, Albert**
See Camus, Albert

**Mather, Cotton** 1663-1728 .......... **LC 38, 265**
See also AMWS 2; CDALB 1640-1865;
DLB 24, 30, 140; RGAL 4; TUS

**Mather, Increase** 1639-1723 ....... **LC 38, 161**
See also DLB 24

**Mathers, Marshall**
See Eminem

**Mathers, Marshall Bruce**
See Eminem

**Matheson, Richard** 1926-2013 .. **CLC 37, 267**
See also AAYA 31; CA 97-100; CANR 88,
99, 236; DLB 8, 44; HGG; INT CA-97-
100; SCFW 1, 2; SFW 4; SUFW 2

**Matheson, Richard Burton**
See Matheson, Richard

**Mathews, Harry** 1930- ................. **CLC 6, 52**
See also CA 21-24R; CAAS 6; CANR 18,
40, 98, 160; CN 5, 6, 7

**Mathews, John Joseph**
1894-1979 ................... **CLC 84; NNAL**
See also CA 19-20; 142; CANR 45; CAP 2;
DAM MULT; DLB 175; TCWW 1, 2

**Mathias, Roland** 1915-2007 ........... **CLC 45**
See also CA 97-100; 263; CANR 19, 41; CP
1, 2, 3, 4, 5, 6, 7; DLB 27

**Mathias, Roland Glyn**
See Mathias, Roland

**Matshoba, Mtutuzeli** 1950- ............. **SSC 173**
See also CA 221

**Matsuo Basho** 1644(?)-1694 ............. **LC 62;
PC 3, 125**
See also DAM POET; PFS 2, 7, 18; RGWL
2, 3; WP

**Mattheson, Rodney**
See Creasey, John

**Matthew, James**
See Barrie, J. M.

**Matthew of Vendome**
c. 1130-c. 1200 ...................... **CMLC 99**
See also DLB 208

**Matthew Paris**
See Paris, Matthew

**Matthews, (James) Brander**
1852-1929 ............................. **TCLC 95**
See also CA 181; DLB 71, 78; DLBD 13

**Matthews, Greg** 1949- ..................... **CLC 45**
See also CA 135

**Matthews, William (Procter III)**
1942-1997 ................................. **CLC 40**
See also AMWS 9; CA 29-32R; 162; CAAS
18; CANR 12, 57; CP 2, 3, 4, 5, 6; DLB 5

**Matthias, John (Edward)** 1941- ....... **CLC 9**
See also CA 33-36R; CANR 56; CP 4, 5, 6, 7

**Matthiessen, F(rancis) O(tto)**
1902-1950 ............................... **TCLC 100**
See also CA 185; DLB 63; MAL 5

**Matthiessen, Francis Otto**
See Matthiessen, F(rancis) O(tto)

**Matthiessen, Peter** 1927-2014 ...... **CLC 5, 7,
11, 32, 64, 245, 395**
See also AAYA 6, 40; AMWS 5; ANW;
BEST 90:4; BPFB 2; CA 9-12R; CANR
21, 50, 73, 100, 138; CN 1, 2, 3, 4, 5, 6, 7;
DA3; DAM NOV; DLB 6, 173, 275; MAL
5; MTCW 1, 2; MTFW 2005; SATA 27

**Maturin, Charles Robert**
1780(?)-1824 ........... **NCLC 6, 169, 347**
See also BRWS 8; DLB 178; GL 3; HGG;
LMFS 1; RGEL 2; SUFW

**Matute (Ausejo), Ana Maria** 1925- .. **CLC 11,
352**
See also CA 89-92; CANR 129; CWW 2;
DLB 322; EWL 3; MTCW 1; RGSF 2

**Maufrigneuse**
See Maupassant, Guy de

**Maugham, W. S.**
See Maugham, W. Somerset

**Maugham, W. Somerset**
1874-1965 ......... **CLC 1, 11, 15, 67, 93;
SSC 8, 94, 164; TCLC 208; WLC 4**
See also AAYA 55; BPFB 2; BRW 6; CA 5-
8R; 25-28R; CANR 40, 127; CDBLB 1914-
1945; CMW 4; DA; DA3; DAB; DAC;
DAM DRAM, MST, NOV; DFS 22; DLB
10, 36, 77, 100, 162, 195; EWL 3; LAIT 3;
MTCW 1, 2; MTFW 2005; NFS 23, 35;
RGEL 2; RGSF 2; SATA 54; SSFS 17

**Maugham, William S.**
See Maugham, W. Somerset

**Maugham, William Somerset**
See Maugham, W. Somerset

**Maupassant, Guy de** 1850-1893 .... **NCLC 1,
42, 83, 234; SSC 1, 64, 132, 225; WLC 4**
See also BYA 14; DA; DA3; DAB; DAC;
DAM MST; DLB 123; EW 7; EXPS; GFL
1789 to the Present; LAIT 2; LMFS 1;
RGSF 2; RGWL 2, 3; SSFS 4, 21, 28, 31;
SUFW; TWA

**Maupassant, Henri Rene Albert Guy de**
See Maupassant, Guy de

**Maupin, Armistead** 1944- .............. **CLC 95**
See also CA 125; 130; CANR 58, 101, 183;
CPW; DA3; DAM POP; DLB 278; GLL 1;
INT CA-130; MTCW 2; MTFW 2005

**Maupin, Armistead Jones, Jr.**
See Maupin, Armistead

**Maurhut, Richard**
See Traven, B.

**Mauriac, Claude** 1914-1996 ............. **CLC 9**
See also CA 89-92; 152; CWW 2; DLB 83;
EWL 3; GFL 1789 to the Present

**Mauriac, Francois (Charles)**
1885-1970 ........ **CLC 4, 9, 56; SSC 24;
TCLC 281**
See also CA 25-28; CAP 2; DLB 65, 331;
EW 10; EWL 3; GFL 1789 to the Present;
MTCW 1, 2; MTFW 2005; RGWL 2, 3;
TWA

**Mavor, Osborne Henry** 1888-1951 ... **TCLC 3**
See also CA 104; DLB 10; EWL 3

**Maxwell, Glyn** 1962- ..................... **CLC 238**
See also CA 154; CANR 88, 183; CP 6, 7;
PFS 23

**Maxwell, William (Keepers, Jr.)**
1908-2000 ................................. **CLC 19**

See also AMWS 8; CA 93-96; 189; CANR
54, 95; CN 1, 2, 3, 4, 5, 6, 7; DLB 218,
278; DLBY 1980; INT CA-93-96; MAL 5;
SATA-Obit 128

**May, Elaine** 1932- ........................... **CLC 16**
See also CA 124; 142; CAD; CWD; DLB 44

**Mayakovski, Vladimir**
1893-1930 ......................... **TCLC 4, 18**
See also CA 104; 158; EW 11; EWL 3;
IDTP; MTCW 2; MTFW 2005; RGWL 2,
3; SFW 4; TWA; WP

**Mayakovski, Vladimir Vladimirovich**
See Mayakovski, Vladimir

**Mayakovsky, Vladimir**
See Mayakovski, Vladimir

**Mayhew, Henry** 1812-1887 ... **NCLC 31, 328**
See also BRWS 16; DLB 18, 55, 190

**Mayle, Peter** 1939(?)- ...................... **CLC 89**
See also CA 139; CANR 64, 109, 168, 218

**Maynard, Joyce** 1953- ..................... **CLC 23**
See also CA 111; 129; CANR 64, 169, 220

**Mayne, William** 1928-2010 ............. **CLC 12**
See also AAYA 20; CA 9-12R; CANR 37,
80, 100; CLR 25, 123; FANT; JRDA;
MAICYA 1, 2; MAICYAS 1; SAAS 11;
SATA 6, 68, 122; SUFW 2; YAW

**Mayne, William James Carter**
See Mayne, William

**Mayo, Jim**
See L'Amour, Louis

**Maysles, Albert** 1926- ..................... **CLC 16**
See also CA 29-32R

**Maysles, David** 1932-1987 .............. **CLC 16**
See also CA 191

**Mazer, Norma Fox** 1931-2009 ........ **CLC 26**
See also AAYA 5, 36; BYA 1, 8; CA 69-72;
292; CANR 12, 32, 66, 129, 189; CLR 23;
JRDA; MAICYA 1, 2; SAAS 1; SATA 24,
67, 105, 168, 198; WYA; YAW

**Mažuranić, Ivan** 1814-1890 ........ **NCLC 259**
See also DLB 147

**Mazzini, Guiseppe** 1805-1872 ....... **NCLC 34**

**M'Baye, Mariètou**
See Bugul, Ken

**Mbue, Imbolo** 1982- ..................... **CLC 421**

**McAlmon, Robert (Menzies)**
1895-1956 ............................. **TCLC 97**
See also CA 107; 168; DLB 4, 45; DLBD
15; GLL 1

**McAuley, James Phillip** 1917-1976 ... **CLC 45**
See also CA 97-100; CP 1, 2; DLB 260;
RGEL 2

**McBain, Ed**
See Hunter, Evan

**McBride, James** 1957- .................. **CLC 370**
See also BW 3; CA 153; CANR 113, 194,
266; CMTFW; MTFW

**McBrien, William** 1930- ................. **CLC 44**
See also CA 107; CANR 90

**McBrien, William Augustine**
See McBrien, William

**McCabe, Pat**
See McCabe, Patrick

**McCabe, Patrick** 1955- .................. **CLC 133**
See also BRWS 9; CA 130; CANR 50, 90,
168, 202; CN 6, 7; DLB 194

**McCaffrey, Anne** 1926-2011 .......... **CLC 17**
See also AAYA 6, 34; AITN 2; BEST 89:2;
BPFB 2; BYA 5; CA 25-28R, 227; CAAE
227; CANR 15, 35, 55, 96, 169, 234; CLR
49, 130; CPW; DA3; DAM NOV, POP;
DLB 8; JRDA; MAICYA 1, 2; MTCW 1,
2; MTFW 2005; SAAS 11; SATA 8, 70,
116, 152; SATA-Essay 152; SFW 4;
SUFW 2; WYA; YAW

**McCaffrey, Anne Inez**
See McCaffrey, Anne

**McCall, Nathan** 1955(?)- ................ **CLC 86**
See also AAYA 59; BW 3; CA 146; CANR
88, 186

**Mortimer, John** 1923-2009 ........ **CLC 28, 43**
See Morton, Kate
See also CA 13-16R; 282; CANR 21, 69, 109, 172; CBD; CD 5, 6; CDBLB 1960 to Present; CMW 4; CN 5, 6, 7; CPW; DA3; DAM DRAM, POP; DLB 13, 245, 271; INT CANR-21; MSW; MTCW 1, 2; MTFW 2005; RGEL 2

**Mortimer, John C.**
See Mortimer, John

**Mortimer, John Clifford**
See Mortimer, John

**Mortimer, Penelope (Ruth)**
1918-1999 ................................. **CLC 5**
See also CA 57-60; 187; CANR 45, 88; CN 1, 2, 3, 4, 5, 6

**Mortimer, Sir John**
See Mortimer, John

**Morton, Anthony**
See Creasey, John

**Morton, Thomas** 1579(?)-1647(?) ...... **LC 72**
See also DLB 24; RGEL 2

**Mosca, Gaetano** 1858-1941 .......... **TCLC 75**

**Moses, Daniel David** 1952- ............... **NNAL**
See also CA 186; DLB 334

**Mosher, Howard Frank** 1943- ........ **CLC 62**
See also CA 139; CANR 65, 115, 181

**Mosley, Nicholas** 1923- ............. **CLC 43, 70**
See also CA 69-72; CANR 41, 60, 108, 158; CN 1, 2, 3, 4, 5, 6, 7; DLB 14, 207

**Mosley, Walter** 1952- ........ **BLCS; CLC 97, 184, 278**
See also AAYA 57; AMWS 13; BPFB 2; BW 2; CA 142; CANR 57, 92, 136, 172, 201, 239; CMW 4; CN 7; CPW; DA3; DAM MULT, POP; DLB 306; MSW; MTCW 2; MTFW 2005

**Moss, Howard** 1922-1987 .......... **CLC 7, 14, 45, 50**
See also CA 1-4R; 123; CANR 1, 44; CP 1, 2, 3, 4; DAM POET; DLB 5

**Mossgiel, Rab**
See Burns, Robert

**Motion, Andrew** 1952- .................... **CLC 47**
See also BRWS 7; CA 146; CANR 90, 142; CP 4, 5, 6, 7; DLB 40; MTFW 2005

**Motion, Andrew Peter**
See Motion, Andrew

**Motley, Willard (Francis)** 1909-1965 .. **CLC 18**
See also AMWS 17; BW 1; CA 117; 106; CANR 88; DLB 76, 143

**Motoori, Norinaga** 1730-1801 ... **NCLC 45, 329**

**Mott, Michael (Charles Alston)**
1930- .................................. **CLC 15, 34**
See also CA 5-8R; CAAS 7; CANR 7, 29

**Moulinet, Nicolas, sieur Du Parc**
See Sorel, Charles

**Moulsworth, Martha** 1577-1646 ...... **LC 168**

**Mountain Wolf Woman**
1884-1960 ................... **CLC 92; NNAL**
See also CA 144; CANR 90

**Moure, Erin** 1955- ........................... **CLC 88**
See also CA 113; CP 5, 6, 7; CWP; DLB 60

**Mourning Dove**
1888-1936 ................ **NNAL; TCLC 304**
See also CA 144; CANR 90; DAM MULT; DLB 175, 221

**Mowat, Farley** 1921- ........................ **CLC 26**
See also AAYA 1, 50; BYA 2; CA 1-4R; CANR 24, 42, 68, 108; CLR 20; CPW; DAC; DAM MST; DLB 68; INT CANR-24; JRDA; MAICYA 1, 2; MTCW 1, 2; MTFW 2005; SATA 3, 55; YAW

**Mowat, Farley McGill**
See Mowat, Farley

**Mowatt, Anna Cora** 1819-1870 .... **NCLC 74**
See also RGAL 4

**Moye, Guan**
See Yan, Mo

**Mo Yen**
See Yan, Mo

**Moyers, Bill** 1934- .......................... **CLC 74**
See also AITN 2; CA 61-64; CANR 31, 52, 148

**Mpe, Phaswane** 1970-2004 ........... **CLC 338**

**Mphahlele, Es'kia** 1919-2008 ........ **BLC 1:3; CLC 25, 133, 280**
See also AFW; BW 2, 3; CA 81-84; 278; CANR 26, 76; CDWLB 3; CN 4, 5, 6; DA3; DAM MULT; DLB 125, 225; EWL 3; MTCW 2; MTFW 2005; RGSF 2; SATA 119; SATA-Obit 198; SSFS 11

**Mphahlele, Ezekiel**
See Mphahlele, Es'kia

**Mphahlele, Zeke**
See Mphahlele, Es'kia

**Mqhayi, S(amuel) E(dward) K(rune Loliwe)**
1875-1945 ............. **BLC 1:3; TCLC 25**
See also CA 153; CANR 87; DAM MULT

**Mrozek, Slawomir** 1930- ............. **CLC 3, 13**
See also CA 13-16R; CAAS 10; CANR 29; CDWLB 4; CWW 2; DLB 232; EWL 3; MTCW 1

**Mrs. Belloc-Lowndes**
See Lowndes, Marie Adelaide (Belloc)

**Mrs. Fairstar**
See Horne, Richard Henry Hengist

**Mrs. K. P.**
See Philips, Katherine

**Mrs. K. Philips**
See Philips, Katherine

**M'Taggart, John M'Taggart Ellis**
See McTaggart, John McTaggart Ellis

**Mtwa, Percy** (?)- ............................. **CLC 47**
See also CD 6

**Mudrooroo** 1938- ........................... **CLC 396**
See also CA 154; CANR 172; CN 4, 5, 6, 7; CP 6, 7; DLB 289

**Mueenuddin, Daniyal** 1963- .......... **CLC 299**
See also CA 292

**Mueller, Lisel** 1924- ...... **CLC 13, 51; PC 33**
See also CA 93-96; CP 6, 7; DLB 105; PFS 9, 13

**Muggeridge, Malcolm (Thomas)**
1903-1990 ............................. **TCLC 120**
See also AITN 1; CA 101; CANR 33, 63; MTCW 1, 2

**Muggins**
See Twain, Mark

**Muhammad** 570-632 ......................... **WLCS**
See also DA; DAB; DAC; DAM MST; DLB 311

**Mugo, Micere Githae** 1942- .......... **CLC 446**
See also CA 164; DLB 360

**Muir, Edwin**
1887-1959 ............. **PC 49; TCLC 2, 87**
See also BRWS 6; CA 104; 193; DLB 20, 100, 191; EWL 3; RGEL 2

**Muir, John** 1838-1914 .................... **TCLC 28**
See also AMWS 9; ANW; CA 165; DLB 186, 275

**Mujica Lainez, Manuel** 1910-1984 .. **CLC 31**
See also CA 81-84; 112; CANR 32; EWL 3; HW 1

**Mukherjee, Bharati** 1940- ... **AAL; CLC 53, 115, 235; SSC 38, 173**
See also AAYA 46; BEST 89:2; CA 107, 232; CAAE 232; CANR 45, 72, 128, 231; CN 5, 6, 7; DAM NOV; DLB 60, 218, 323; DNFS 1, 2; EWL 3; FW; MAL 5; MTCW 1, 2; MTFW 2005; NFS 37; RGAL 4; RGSF 2; SSFS 7, 24, 32; TUS; WWE 1

**Muldoon, Paul** 1951- ......... **CLC 32, 72, 166, 324; PC 143**
See also BRWS 4; CA 113; 129; CANR 52, 91, 176; CP 2, 3, 4, 5, 6, 7; DAM POET; DLB 40; INT CA-129; PFS 7, 22; TCLE 1:2

**Mulisch, Harry** 1927-2010 ...... **CLC 42, 270**
See also CA 9-12R; CANR 6, 26, 56, 110; CWW 2; DLB 299; EWL 3

**Mulisch, Harry Kurt Victor**
See Mulisch, Harry

**Mull, Martin** 1943- .......................... **CLC 17**
See also CA 105

**Mullen, Harryette** 1953- ................. **CLC 321**
See also CA 218; CP 7

**Mullen, Harryette Romell**
See Mullen, Harryette

**Muller, Heiner** 1929-1995 ................... **DC 47**
See also CA 193; CWW 2; EWL 3

**Müller, Herta** 1953- ....................... **CLC 299**

**Muller, Wilhelm** ........................... **NCLC 73**

**Mulock, Dinah Maria**
See Craik, Dinah Maria (Mulock)

**Multatuli** 1820-1881 ...................... **NCLC 165**
See also RGWL 2, 3

**Munday, Anthony** 1560-1633 ............. **LC 87**
See also DLB 62, 172; RGEL 2

**Munford, Robert** 1737(?)-1783 ........... **LC 5**
See also DLB 31

**Mungo, Raymond** 1946- ................... **CLC 72**
See also CA 49-52; CANR 2

**Munnings, Clare**
See Conway, Jill K.

**Munro, Alice** 1931- ........ **CLC 6, 10, 19, 50, 95, 222, 370; SSC 3, 95, 208, 268; WLCS**
See also AAYA 82; AITN 2; BPFB 2; CA 33-36R; CANR 33, 53, 75, 114, 177, 256, 296; CCA 1; CMTFW; CN 1, 2, 3, 4, 5, 6, 7; DA3; DAC; DAM MST, NOV; DLB 53; EWL 3; LNFS 3; MTCW 1, 2; MTFW 2005; NFS 27; RGEL 2; RGSF 2; SATA 29; SSFS 5, 13, 19, 28, 36, 43; TCLE 1:2; WWE 1

**Munro, Alice Anne**
See Munro, Alice

**Munro, H. H.**
See Saki

**Munro, Hector H.**
See Saki

**Munro, Hector Hugh**
See Saki

**Murakami, Haruki** 1949- ..... **CLC 150, 274; SSC 204**
See also CA 165; CANR 102, 146, 212; CWW 2; DLB 182; EWL 3; LNFS 2; MJW; RGWL 3; SFW 4; SSFS 23, 36

**Murakami Haruki**
See Murakami, Haruki

**Murasaki, Lady**
See Murasaki Shikibu

**Murasaki Shikibu**
978(?)-1014(?) .......... **CMLC 1, 79, 160**
See also EFS 1:2, 2:2; LATS 1:1; RGWL 2, 3

**Murdoch, Iris** 1919-1999 ..... **CLC 1, 2, 3, 4, 6, 8, 11, 15, 22, 31, 51; TCLC 171**
See also BRWS 1; CA 13-16R; 179; CANR 8, 43, 68, 103, 142; CBD; CDBLB 1960 to Present; CN 1, 2, 3, 4, 5, 6; CWD; DA3; DAB; DAC; DAM MST, NOV; DLB 14, 194, 233, 326; EWL 3; INT CANR-8; MTCW 1, 2; MTFW 2005; NFS 18; RGEL 2; TCLE 1:2; TEA; WLIT 4

**Murdoch, Jean Iris**
See Murdoch, Iris

**Murfree, Mary Noailles**
1850-1922 ............. **SSC 22; TCLC 135**
See also CA 122; 176; DLB 12, 74; RGAL 4

**Murglie**
See Murnau, F.W.

**Murnane, Gerald** 1939- ................. **CLC 362**
See also CA 164; CN 5, 6, 7; DLB 289; SFW 4

**Murnau, Friedrich Wilhelm**
See Murnau, F.W.

**Murnau, F.W.** 1888-1931 .............. **TCLC 53**
See also CA 112

**Murphy, Arthur** 1727-1805 ......... **NCLC 229**
See also DLB 89, 142; RGEL 2

**Murphy, Dennis Jasper**
See Maturin, Charles Robert

Author Index

**Norris, Benjamin Franklin, Jr.**
See Norris, Frank

**Norris, Frank** 1870-1902 ............... **SSC 28;
   TCLC 24, 155, 211**
See also AAYA 57; AMW; AMWC 2; BPFB
   2; CA 110; 160; CDALB 1865-1917; DLB
   12, 71, 186; LMFS 2; MAL 5; NFS 12;
   RGAL 4; TCWW 1, 2; TUS

**Norris, Kathleen** 1947- ................. **CLC 248**
See also CA 160; CANR 113, 199

**Norris, Leslie** 1921-2006 .......... **CLC 14, 351**
See also CA 11-12; 251; CANR 14, 117;
   CAP 1; CP 1, 2, 3, 4, 5, 6, 7; DLB 27, 256

**North, Andrew**
See Norton, Andre

**North, Anthony**
See Koontz, Dean

**North, Captain George**
See Stevenson, Robert Louis

**North, Milou**
See Erdrich, Louise

**Northrup, B. A.**
See Hubbard, L. Ron

**North Staffs**
See Hulme, T(homas) E(rnest)

**Northup, Solomon** 1808-1863 ..... **NCLC 105**

**Nortje, Arthur** 1942-1970 ............ **TCLC 375**
See also BW 2; CA 141; CANR 93; DLB
   125, 225; WWE 1

**Norton, Alice Mary**
See Norton, Andre

**Norton, Andre** 1912-2005 ................ **CLC 12**
See also AAYA 83; BPFB 2; BYA 4, 10, 12;
   CA 1-4R; 237; CANR 2, 31, 68, 108, 149;
   CLR 50, 184; DLB 8, 52; JRDA; MAI-
   CYA 1, 2; MTCW 1; SATA 1, 43, 91;
   SUFW 1, 2; YAW

**Norton, Caroline** 1808-1877 ... **NCLC 47, 205**
See also DLB 21, 159, 199

**Norway, Nevil Shute**
See Shute, Nevil

**Norwid, Cyprian Kamil** 1821-1883 .. **NCLC 17**
See also RGWL 3

**Nosille, Nabrah**
See Ellison, Harlan

**Nossack, Hans Erich** 1901-1977 ....... **CLC 6**
See also CA 93-96; 85-88; CANR 156; DLB
   69; EWL 3

**Nostradamus** 1503-1566 ...................... **LC 27**

**Nosu, Chuji**
See Ozu, Yasujiro

**Notenburg, Eleanora (Genrikhovna) von**
See Guro, Elena (Genrikhovna)

**Nothomb, Amélie** 1967- ................. **CLC 344**
See also CA 205; CANR 154, 205

**Notker Labeo** c. 950-1022 .......... **CMLC 181**
See also DLB 148

**Nova, Craig** 1945- ........................ **CLC 7, 31**
See also CA 45-48; CANR 2, 53, 127, 223

**Novak, Joseph**
See Kosinski, Jerzy

**Novalis** 1772-1801 ......... **NCLC 13, 178, 341;
   PC 120**
See also CDWLB 2; DLB 90; EW 5; RGWL
   2, 3

**Novick, Peter** 1934-2012 ............... **CLC 164**
See also CA 188

**Novis, Emile**
See Weil, Simone

**Nowlan, Alden (Albert)** 1933-1983 ... **CLC 15**
See also CA 9-12R; CANR 5; CP 1, 2, 3;
   DAC; DAM MST; DLB 53; PFS 12

**Nowra, Louis** 1950- ....................... **CLC 372**
See also CA 195; CD 5, 6; DLB 325; IDTP

**Noyes, Alfred** 1880-1958 .... **PC 27; TCLC 7**
See also CA 104; 188; DLB 20; EXPP;
   FANT; PFS 4; RGEL 2

**Nugent, Richard Bruce** 1906(?)-1987 ... **HR 1:3**
See also BW 1; CA 125; CANR 198; DLB
   51; GLL 2

**Nunez, Elizabeth** 1944- ................... **BLC 2:3**
See also CA 223; CANR 220

**Nunn, Kem** ...................................... **CLC 34**
See also CA 159; CANR 204

**Nussbaum, Martha** 1947- .............. **CLC 203**
See also CA 134; CANR 102, 176, 213, 241

**Nussbaum, Martha Craven**
See Nussbaum, Martha

**Nwapa, Flora (Nwanzuruaha)**
   1931-1993 ................. **BLCS; CLC 133**
See also BW 2; CA 143; CANR 83;
   CDWLB 3; CLR 162; CWRI 5; DLB
   125; EWL 3; WLIT 2

**Nye, Robert** 1939- ..................... **CLC 13, 42**
See also BRWS 10; CA 33-36R; CANR 29,
   67, 107; CN 1, 2, 3, 4, 5, 6, 7; CP 1, 2, 3, 4,
   5, 6, 7; CWRI 5; DAM NOV; DLB 14, 271;
   FANT; HGG; MTCW 1; RHW; SATA 6

**Nyro, Laura** 1947-1997 ................... **CLC 17**
See also CA 194

**O. Henry**
See Henry, O.

**Oates, Joyce Carol** 1938- ............. **CLC 1, 2,
   3, 6, 9, 11, 15, 19, 33, 52, 108, 134, 228;
   SSC 6, 70, 121, 234; WLC 4**
See also AAYA 15, 52; AITN 1; AMWS 2;
   BEST 89:2; BPFB 2; BYA 11; CA 5-8R;
   CANR 25, 45, 74, 113, 129, 165; CDALB
   1968-1988; CN 1, 2, 3, 4, 5, 6, 7; CP 5, 6,
   7; CPW; CWP; DA; DA3; DAB; DAC;
   DAM MST, NOV, POP; DLB 2, 5, 130;
   DLBY 1981; EWL 3; EXPS; FL 1:6; FW;
   GL 3; HGG; INT CANR-25; LAIT 4;
   MAL 5; MBL; MTCW 1, 2; MTFW
   2005; NFS 8, 24; RGAL 4; RGSF 2; SATA
   159; SSFS 1, 8, 17, 32; SUFW 2; TUS

**Oberon**
See Robinson, Mary

**Obradovic, Dositej** 1740(?)-1811 .. **NCLC 254**
See also DLB 147

**O'Brian, E.G.**
See Clarke, Arthur C.

**O'Brian, Patrick** 1914-2000 ......... **CLC 152**
See also AAYA 55; BRWS 12; CA 144; 187;
   CANR 74, 201; CPW; MTCW 2; MTFW
   2005; RHW

**O'Brien, Darcy** 1939-1998 .............. **CLC 11**
See also CA 21-24R; 167; CANR 8, 59

**O'Brien, Edna** 1930- ............... **CLC 3, 5, 8,
   13, 36, 65, 116, 237; SSC 10, 77, 192**
See also BRWS 5; CA 1-4R; CANR 6, 41,
   65, 102, 169, 213; CDBLB 1960 to Present;
   CN 1, 2, 3, 4, 5, 6, 7; DA3; DAM NOV;
   DLB 14, 231, 319; EWL 3; FW; MTCW 1,
   2; MTFW 2005; RGSF 2; WLIT 4

**O'Brien, E.G.**
See Clarke, Arthur C.

**O'Brien, Fitz-James** 1828-1862 .... **NCLC 21**
See also DLB 74; RGAL 4; SUFW

**O'Brien, Flann**
See O Nuallain, Brian

**Ono no Komachi** fl. c. 850- ....... **CMLC 134**

**O'Brien, Richard** 1942- ................... **CLC 17**
See also CA 124

**O'Brien, Tim** 1946- ...... **CLC 7, 19, 40, 103,
   211, 305; SSC 74, 123, 239**
See also AAYA 16; AMWS 5; CA 85-88;
   CANR 40, 58, 133; CDALBS; CN 5, 6, 7;
   CPW; DA3; DAM POP; DLB 152; DLBD
   9; DLBY 1980; LATS 1:2; MAL 5;
   MTCW 2; MTFW 2005; NFS 37; RGAL
   4; SSFS 5, 15, 29, 32; TCLE 1:2

**O'Brien, William Timothy**
See O'Brien, Tim

**Obstfelder, Sigbjorn** 1866-1900 .... **TCLC 23**
See also CA 123; DLB 354

**Ocampo, Silvina** 1906-1993 ............. **SSC 175**
See also CA 131; CANR 87, CWW 2, HW
   1, RGSF 2

**O'Casey, Brenda**
See Haycraft, Anna

**O'Casey, Sean** 1880-1964 ........ **CLC 1, 5, 9,
   11, 15, 88; DC 12; WLCS**
See also BRW 7; CA 89-92; CANR 62;
   CBD; CDBLB 1914-1945; DA3; DAB;
   DAC; DAM DRAM, MST; DFS 19; DLB
   10; EWL 3; MTCW 1, 2; MTFW 2005;
   RGEL 2; TEA; WLIT 4

**O'Cataract, Jehu**
See Neal, John

**O'Cathasaigh, Sean**
See O'Casey, Sean

**Occom, Samson** 1723-1792 ... **LC 60; NNAL**
See also DLB 175

**Occomy, Marita (Odette) Bonner**
   1899(?)-1971 ................ **HR 1:2; PC 72;
   TCLC 179**
See also BW 2; CA 142; DFS 13; DLB 51, 228

**Ochs, Phil(ip David)** 1940-1976 ...... **CLC 17**
See also CA 185; 65-68

**O'Connor, Edwin (Greene)**
   1918-1968 ................................. **CLC 14**
See also CA 93-96; 25-28R; MAL 5

**O'Connor, Flannery** 1925-1964 ....... **CLC 1,
   2, 3, 6, 10, 13, 15, 21, 66, 104; SSC 1, 23,
   61, 82, 111, 168, 173, 190, 195, 196, 199,
   230, 262; TCLC 132, 305; WLC 4**
See also AAYA 7; AMW; AMWR 2; BPFB
   3; BYA 16; CA 1-4R; CANR 3, 41;
   CDALB 1941-1968; DA; DA3; DAB;
   DAC; DAM MST, NOV; DLB 2, 152;
   DLBD 12; DLBY 1980; EWL 3; EXPS;
   LAIT 5; MAL 5; MAWW; MTCW 1, 2;
   MTFW 2005; NFS 3, 21; RGAL 4; RGSF
   2; SSFS 2, 7, 10, 19, 34, 41; TUS

**O'Connor, Frank** 1903-1966 .... **CLC 14, 23;
   SSC 5, 109, 177, 226**
See also BRWS 14; CA 93-96; CANR 84;
   DLB 162; EWL 3; RGSF 2; SSFS 5, 34

**O'Connor, Mary Flannery**
See O'Connor, Flannery

**O'Dell, Scott** 1898-1989 ................... **CLC 30**
See also AAYA 3, 44; BPFB 3; BYA 1, 2, 3,
   5; CA 61-64; 129; CANR 12, 30, 112;
   CLR 1, 16, 126; DLB 52; JRDA; MAI-
   CYA 1, 2; SATA 12, 60, 134; WYA; YAW

**Odets, Clifford** 1906-1963 ............... **CLC 2,
   28, 98; DC 6; TCLC 244**
See also AMWS 2; CA 85-88; CAD; CANR
   62; DAM DRAM; DFS 3, 17, 20; DLB 7,
   26, 341; EWL 3; MAL 5; MTCW 1, 2;
   MTFW 2005; RGAL 4; TUS

**O'Doherty, Brian** 1928- ................... **CLC 76**
See also CA 105; CANR 108

**O'Donnell, K. M.**
See Malzberg, Barry N(athaniel)

**O'Donnell, Lawrence**
See Kuttner, Henry

**O'Donovan, Michael Francis**
See O'Connor, Frank

**Oe, Kenzaburo** 1935- ......... **CLC 10, 36, 86,
   187, 303; SSC 20, 176**
See also CA 97-100; CANR 36, 50, 74, 126;
   CWW 2; DA3; DAM NOV; DLB 182,
   331; DLBY 1994; EWL 3; LATS 1:2;
   MJW; MTCW 1, 2; MTFW 2005; RGSF
   2; RGWL 2, 3

**Oe Kenzaburo**
See Oe, Kenzaburo

**O'Faolain, Julia** 1932- ... **CLC 6, 19, 47, 108**
See also CA 81-84; CAAS 2; CANR 12, 61;
   CN 2, 3, 4, 5, 6, 7; DLB 14, 231, 319; FW;
   MTCW 1; RHW

**O'Faolain, Sean** 1900-1991 ... **CLC 1, 7, 14,
   32, 70; SSC 13, 194; TCLC 143**
See also CA 61-64; 134; CANR 12, 66; CN
   1, 2, 3, 4; DLB 15, 162; MTCW 1, 2;
   MTFW 2005; RGEL 2; RGSF 2

**O'Flaherty, Liam** 1896-1984 ...... **CLC 5, 34;**
**SSC 6, 116**
See also CA 101; 113; CANR 35; CN 1, 2, 3;
DLB 36, 162; DLBY 1984; MTCW 1, 2;
MTFW 2005; RGEL 2; RGSF 2; SSFS 5, 20

**Ogai**
See Mori Ogai

**Ogilvy, Gavin**
See Barrie, J. M.

**O'Grady, Standish (James)**
1846-1928 ............................... **TCLC 5**
See also CA 104; 157

**O'Grady, Timothy** 1951- ................. **CLC 59**
See also CA 138

**O'Hagan, Howard** 1902-1982 ..... **TCLC 328**
See also CA 1-4R; DLB 68

**O'Hara, Frank** 1926-1966 ..... **CLC 2, 5, 13,**
**78; PC 45**
See also AMWS 23; CA 9-12R; 25-28R;
CANR 33; DA3; DAM POET; DLB 5, 16,
193; EWL 3; MAL 5; MTCW 1, 2; MTFW
2005; PFS 8, 12, 34, 38; RGAL 4; WP

**O'Hara, John** 1905-1970 ..... **CLC 1, 2, 3, 6,**
**11, 42; SSC 15**
See also AMW; BPFB 3; CA 5-8R; 25-28R;
CANR 31, 60; CDALB 1929-1941; DAM
NOV; DLB 9, 86, 324; DLBD 2; EWL 3;
MAL 5; MTCW 1, 2; MTFW 2005; NFS
11; RGAL 4; RGSF 2

**O'Hara, John Henry**
See O'Hara, John

**O'Hara, Scott**
See MacDonald, John D.

**O'Hehir, Diana** 1929- ...................... **CLC 41**
See also CA 245; CANR 177

**O'Hehir, Diana F.**
See O'Hehir, Diana

**Ohiyesa**
See Eastman, Charles A(lexander)

**Okada, John** 1923-1971 ........................ **AAL**
See also BYA 14; CA 212; DLB 312; NFS 25

**O'Kelly, Seamus** 1881(?)-1918 ........ **SSC 136**

**Okigbo, Christopher** 1930-1967 ... **BLC 1:3;**
**CLC 25, 84; PC 7, 128; TCLC 171**
See also AFW; BW 1, 3; CA 77-80; CANR
74; CDWLB 3; DAM MULT, POET; DLB
125; EWL 3; MTCW 1, 2; MTFW 2005;
RGEL 2

**Okigbo, Christopher Ifenayichukwu**
See Okigbo, Christopher

**Okri, Ben** 1959- ............. **BLC 2:3; CLC 87,**
**223, 337; SSC 127**
See also AFW; BRWS 5; BW 2, 3; CA 130;
138; CANR 65, 128; CN 5, 6, 7; DLB 157,
231, 319, 326; EWL 3; INT CA-138;
MTCW 2; MTFW 2005; RGSF 2; SSFS
20; WLIT 2; WWE 1

**Old Boy**
See Hughes, Thomas

**Olds, Sharon** 1942- ....... **CLC 32, 39, 85, 361;**
**PC 22**
See also AMWS 10; CA 101; CANR 18, 41,
66, 98, 135, 211; CP 5, 6, 7; CPW; CWP;
DAM POET; DLB 120; MAL 5; MTCW 2;
MTFW 2005; PFS 17

**Oldstyle, Jonathan**
See Irving, Washington

**Olesha, Iurii**
See Olesha, Yuri (Karlovich)

**Olesha, Iurii Karlovich**
See Olesha, Yuri (Karlovich)

**Olesha, Yuri (Karlovich)** 1899-1960 ... **CLC 8;**
**SSC 69; TCLC 136**
See also CA 85-88; DLB 272; EW 11; EWL
3; RGWL 2, 3

**Olesha, Yury Karlovich**
See Olesha, Yuri (Karlovich)

**Oliphant, Laurence** 1829(?)-1888 .. **NCLC 47**
See also DLB 18, 166

**Oliphant, Margaret (Oliphant Wilson)**
1828-1897 ......... **NCLC 11, 61, 221, 344;**
**SSC 25**
See also BRWS 10; DLB 18, 159, 190;
HGG; RGEL 2; RGSF 2; SUFW

**Oliphant, Mrs.**
See Oliphant, Margaret (Oliphant Wilson)

**Oliver, Mary** 1935- .... **CLC 19, 34, 98, 364;**
**PC 75**
See also AMWS 7; CA 21-24R; CANR 9,
43, 84, 92, 138, 217; CP 4, 5, 6, 7; CWP;
DLB 5, 193, 342; EWL 3; MTFW 2005;
PFS 15, 31, 40

**Olivi, Peter** 1248-1298 ................ **CMLC 114**

**Olivier, Laurence (Kerr)** 1907-1989 ... **CLC 20**
See also CA 111; 150; 129

**Olivieri, David**
See Wharton, Edith

**O.L.S.**
See Russell, George William

**Olsen, Tillie** 1912-2007 ...... **CLC 4, 13, 114;**
**SSC 11, 103, 242**
See also AAYA 51; AMWS 13; BYA 11; CA
1-4R; 256; CANR 1, 43, 74, 132; CDALBS;
CN 2, 3, 4, 5, 6, 7; DA; DA3; DAB; DAC;
DAM MST; DLB 28, 206; DLBY 1980;
EWL 3; EXPS; FW; MAL 5; MTCW 1, 2;
MTFW 2005; RGAL 4; RGSF 2; SSFS 1,
32; TCLE 1:2; TCWW 2; TUS

**Olson, Charles** 1910-1970 ........ **CLC 1, 2, 5,**
**6, 9, 11, 29; PC 19**
See also AMWS 2; CA 13-16; 25-28R;
CABS 2; CANR 35, 61; CAP 1; CP 1;
DAM POET; DLB 5, 16, 193; EWL 3;
MAL 5; MTCW 1, 2; RGAL 4; WP

**Olson, Charles John**
See Olson, Charles

**Olson, Merle Theodore**
See Olson, Toby

**Olson, Toby** 1937- ............................ **CLC 28**
See also CA 65-68; CAAS 11; CANR 9, 31,
84, 175; CP 3, 4, 5, 6, 7

**Olyesha, Yuri**
See Olesha, Yuri (Karlovich)

**Olympiodorus of Thebes**
c. 375-c. 430 .......................... **CMLC 59**

**Omar Khayyam**
See Khayyam, Omar

**Ondaatje, Michael** 1943- ................. **CLC 14,**
**29, 51, 76, 180, 258, 322; PC 28**
See also AAYA 66; CA 77-80; CANR 42,
74, 109, 133, 172; CN 5, 6, 7; CP 1, 2, 3,
4, 5, 6, 7; DA3; DAB; DAC; DAM MST;
DLB 60, 323, 326; EWL 3; LATS 1:2;
LMFS 2; MTCW 2; MTFW 2005; NFS 23;
PFS 8, 19; TCLE 1:2; TWA; WWE 1

**Ondaatje, Philip Michael**
See Ondaatje, Michael

**Oneal, Elizabeth** 1934- ..................... **CLC 30**
See also AAYA 5, 41; BYA 13; CA 106;
CANR 28, 84; CLR 13, 169; JRDA; MAI-
CYA 1, 2; SATA 30, 82; WYA; YAW

**Oneal, Zibby**
See Oneal, Elizabeth

**O'Neill, Eugene** 1888-1953 ................ **DC 20;**
**TCLC 1, 6, 27, 49, 225; WLC 4**
See also AAYA 54; AITN 1; AMW; AMWC
1; CA 110; 132; CAD; CANR 131;
CDALB 1929-1941; DA; DA3; DAB;
DAC; DAM DRAM, MST; DFS 2, 4, 5,
6, 9, 11, 12, 16, 20, 26, 27; DLB 7, 331;
EWL 3; LAIT 3; LMFS 2; MAL 5;
MTCW 1, 2; MTFW 2005; RGAL 4; TUS

**O'Neill, Eugene Gladstone**
See O'Neill, Eugene

**O'Neill, Owen Roe**
See Palmer, Nettie

**Onetti, Juan Carlos** 1909-1994 ... **CLC 7, 10;**
**HLCS 2; SSC 23; TCLC 131**
See also CA 85-88; 145; CANR 32, 63;
CDWLB 3; CWW 2; DAM MULT, NOV;

DLB 113; EWL 3; HW 1, 2; LAW;
MTCW 1, 2; MTFW 2005; RGSF 2

**Lonnrot, Elias** 1802-1884 .............. **NCLC 53**
See also EFS 1:1, 2:1

**O'Nolan, Brian**
See O Nuallain, Brian

**O Nuallain, Brian** 1911-1966 ....... **CLC 1, 4,**
**5, 7, 10, 47**
See also BRWS 2; CA 21-22; 25-28R; CAP 2;
DLB 231; EWL 3; FANT; RGEL 2; TEA

**Ophuls, Max** 1902-1957 ................. **TCLC 79**
See also CA 113

**Opie, Amelia** 1769-1853 ....... **NCLC 65, 317**
See also DLB 116, 159; RGEL 2

**Opitz, Martin** 1597-1639 ................. **LC 207**
See also DLB 164

**Oppen, George** 1908-1984 ... **CLC 7, 13, 34;**
**PC 35; TCLC 107**
See also CA 13-16R; 113; CANR 8, 82; CP
1, 2, 3; DLB 5, 165

**Oppenheim, E(dward) Phillips**
1866-1946 ............................... **TCLC 45**
See also CA 111; 202; CMW 4; DLB 70

**Oppenheimer, Max**
See Ophuls, Max

**Opuls, Max**
See Ophuls, Max

**Ophuls, Max**
See Ophuls, Max

**Orage, A(lfred) R(ichard)**
1873-1934 ............................ **TCLC 157**
See also CA 122

**Oresme, Nicole**
1320/1325?-1382 .................. **CMLC 163**

**Origen** c. 185-c. 254 ..................... **CMLC 19**

**Orinda**
See Philips, Katherine

**Orlovitz, Gil** 1918-1973 ................. **CLC 22**
See also CA 77-80; 45-48; CN 1; CP 1, 2;
DLB 2, 5

**Orosius** c. 385-c. 420 ..................... **CMLC 100**

**O'Rourke, P. J.** 1947- ................... **CLC 209**
See also CA 77-80; CANR 13, 41, 67, 111,
155, 217; CPW; DAM POP; DLB 185

**O'Rourke, Patrick Jake**
See O'Rourke, P.J.

**Orrery**
See Boyle, Roger

**Orris**
See Ingelow, Jean

**Ortega y Gasset, Jose** 1883-1955 .... **HLC 2;**
**TCLC 9**
See also CA 106; 130; DAM MULT; EW 9;
EWL 3; HW 1, 2; MTCW 1, 2; MTFW 2005

**Ortese, Anna Maria** 1914-1998 ...... **CLC 89**
See also DLB 177; EWL 3

**Ortiz, Fernando** 1881-1969 ......... **TCLC 340**

**Ortiz, Simon**
See Ortiz, Simon J.

**Ortiz, Simon J.** 1941- ............. **CLC 45, 208;**
**NNAL; PC 17; SSC 213**
See also AMWS 4; CA 134; CANR 69, 118,
164; CP 3, 4, 5, 6, 7; DAM MULT, POET;
DLB 120, 175, 256, 342; EXPP; MAL 5;
PFS 4, 16; RGAL 4; SSFS 22; TCWW 2

**Ortiz, Simon Joseph**
See Ortiz, Simon J.

**Ortiz Cofer, Judith** 1952- ................. **PC 185**
See also AAYA 30; BYA 12; CA115; CANR
32, 72, 130, 254; CSW; DNFS 1, 2; HW 1,
2; LLW; PFS 37, 46; RGAL 4; SATA 110,
164, 282; SSFS 27, 29, 34; YAW

**Orton, Joe**
See Orton, John Kingsley

**Orton, John Kingsley** 1933-1967 ..... **CLC 4,**
**13, 43; DC 3; TCLC 157**
See also BRWS 5; CA 85-88; CANR 35, 66;
CBD; CDBLB 1960 to Present; DAM
DRAM; DFS 3, 6; DLB 13, 310; GLL

1; MTCW 1, 2; MTFW 2005; RGEL 2;
TEA; WLIT 4

**Orwell, George** 1903-1950 ............... **SSC 68;
TCLC 2, 6, 15, 31, 51, 123, 128, 129,
276; WLC 4**
See also BPFB 3; BRW 7; BYA 5; CA 104;
132; CDBLB 1945-1960; CLR 68, 171,
196; DA; DA3; DAB; DAC; DAM MST,
NOV; DLB 15, 98, 195, 255; EWL 3;
EXPN; LAIT 4, 5; LATS 1:1; MTCW 1,
2; MTFW 2005; NFS 3, 7; RGEL 2; SATA
29; SCFW 1, 2; SFW 4; SSFS 4; TEA;
WLIT 4; YAW X

**Osborne, David**
See Silverberg, Robert

**Osborne, Dorothy** 1627-1695 ........... **LC 141**

**Osborne, George**
See Silverberg, Robert

**Osborne, John** 1929-1994 ........ **CLC 1, 2, 5,
11, 45; DC 38; TCLC 153; WLC 4**
See also BRWS 1; CA 13-16R; 147; CANR
21, 56; CBD; CDBLB 1945-1960; DA;
DAB; DAC; DAM DRAM, MST; DFS
4, 19, 24; DLB 13; EWL 3; MTCW 1,
2; MTFW 2005; RGEL 2

**Osborne, Lawrence** 1958- ............... **CLC 50**
See also CA 189; CANR 152

**Osbourne, Lloyd** 1868-1947 .......... **TCLC 93**

**Osceola**
See Blixen, Karen

**Osgood, Frances Sargent**
1811-1850 .............................. **NCLC 141**
See also DLB 250

**Oshima, Nagisa** 1932- ...................... **CLC 20**
See also CA 116; 121; CANR 78

**Oskison, John Milton** 1874-1947 ...... **NNAL;
TCLC 35**
See also CA 144; CANR 84; DAM MULT;
DLB 175

**Osofisan, Femi** 1946- ....... **CLC 307; DC 52**
See also AFW; BW 2; CA 142; CANR 84;
CD 5, 6; CDWLB 3; DLB 125; EWL 3

**Ossian** c. 3rd cent.
See Macpherson, James

**Ossoli, Sarah Margaret**
See Fuller, Margaret

**Ossoli, Sarah Margaret Fuller**
See Fuller, Margaret

**Ostriker, Alicia** 1937- ..................... **CLC 132**
See also CA 25-28R; CAAS 24; CANR 10,
30, 62, 99, 167; CWP; DLB 120; EXPP;
PFS 19, 26

**Ostriker, Alicia Suskin**
See Ostriker, Alicia

**Ostrovsky, Aleksandr Nikolaevich**
See Ostrovsky, Alexander

**Ostrovsky, Alexander**
1823-1886 ......................... **NCLC 30, 57**
See also DLB 277

**Osundare, Niyi** 1947- ..................... **BLC 2:3**
See also AFW; BW 3; CA 176; CDWLB 3;
CP 7; DLB 157

**Oswald von Wolkenstein**
1377(?)-1455 .............................. **LC 208**

**Otero, Blas de** 1916-1979 ............... **CLC 11**
See also CA 89-92; DLB 134; EWL 3

**O'Trigger, Sir Lucius**
See Horne, Richard Henry Hengist

**Otto, Rudolf** 1869-1937 ................ **TCLC 85**

**Otto, Whitney** 1955- ........................ **CLC 70**
See also CA 140; CANR 120

**Otway, Thomas** 1652-1685 ............... **DC 24;
LC 106, 170**
See also DAM DRAM; DLB 80; RGEL 2

**Ouida**
See De La Ramee, Marie Louise

**Ouologuem, Yambo** 1940- ..... **CLC 146, 293**
See also CA 111; 176

**Ousmane, Sembene** 1923-2007 ..... **BLC 1:3,
2:3; CLC 66**
See also AFW; BW 1, 3; CA 117; 125; 261;
CANR 81; CWW 2; DLB 360; EWL 3;
MTCW 1; WLIT 2

**Out and Outer, An**
See Mangan, James Clarence

**Ovid** 43 BCE-17 CE ... **CMLC 7, 53, 108, 178;
PC 2, 135**
See also AW 2; CDWLB 1; DA3; DAM
POET; DLB 211; PFS 22; RGWL 2, 3;
WLIT 8; WP

**Owen, Hugh**
See Faust, Frederick

**Owen, Wilfred (Edward Salter)**
1893-1918 .......... **PC 19, 102; TCLC 5,
27; WLC 4**
See also BRW 6; CA 104; 141; CDBLB 1914-
1945; DA; DAB; DAC; DAM MST, POET;
DLB 20; EWL 3; EXPP; MTCW 2; MTFW
2005; PFS 10, 37; RGEL 2; WLIT 4

**Owens, Louis (Dean)**
1948-2002 ................. **CLC 321; NNAL**
See also CA 137; 179; 207; CAAE 179;
CAAS 24; CANR 71

**Owens, Rochelle** 1936- ....................... **CLC 8**
See also CA 17-20R; CAAS 2; CAD; CANR
39; CD 5, 6; CP 1, 2, 3, 4, 5, 6, 7; CWD;
CWP

**Owenson, Sydney**
See Morgan, Lady

**Oyeyemi, Helen** 1984- .................... **CLC 410**
See also CA 243; CANR 249, 280

**Oyono, Ferdinand** 1929-2010 ........ **CLC 399**
See also AFW; CANR 360; EWL 3; WLIT 2

**Oz, Amos** 1939- ......... **CLC 5, 8, 11, 27, 33,
54; SSC 66**
See also AAYA 84; CA 53-56; CANR 27,
47, 65, 113, 138, 175, 219; CWW 2; DAM
NOV; EWL 3; MTCW 1, 2; MTFW 2005;
RGHL; RGSF 2; RGWL 3; WLIT 6

**Özdamar, Emine Sevgi** 1946- ....... **CLC 420**
See also DLB 379

**Ozeki, Ruth L.** 1956- .................... **CLC 307**
See also CA 181

**Ozick, Cynthia** 1928- ....... **CLC 3, 7, 28, 62,
155, 262; SSC 15, 60, 123, 241**
See also AMWS 5; BEST 90:1; CA 17-20R;
CANR 23, 58, 116, 160, 187; CN 3, 4, 5,
6, 7; CPW; DA3; DAM NOV; DLB
28, 152, 299; DLBY 1982; EWL 3; EXPS;
INT CANR-23; MAL 5; MTCW 1, 2;
MTFW 2005; RGAL 4; RGHL; RGSF
2; SSFS 3, 12, 22

**Ozu, Yasujiro** 1903-1963 ................. **CLC 16**
See also CA 112

**Pabst, G. W.** 1885-1967 ............... **TCLC 127**

**Pacheco, C.**
See Pessoa, Fernando

**Pacheco, José Emilio**
1939- ........................ **CLC 376; HLC 2**
See also CA 111; 131; CANR 65; CWW 2;
DAM MULT; DLB 290; EWL 3; HW 1, 2;
RGSF 2

**Pa Chin**
See Jin, Ba

**Pack, Robert** 1929- ......................... **CLC 13**
See also CA 1-4R; CANR 3, 44, 82; CP 1, 2,
3, 4, 5, 6, 7; DLB 5; SATA 118

**Packard, Mrs. Clarissa**
See Caroline Gilman

**Packer, Vin**
See Meaker, Marijane

**Padgett, Lewis**
See Kuttner, Henry

**Padilla (Lorenzo), Heberto**
1932-2000 .............................. **CLC 38**
See also AITN 1; CA 123; 131; 189; CWW
2; EWL 3; HW 1

**Padura, Leonardo** 1955- ............... **CLC 365**
See also CA 256; CANR 218

**Paerdurabo, Frater**
See Crowley, Edward Alexander

**Page, James Patrick** 1944- ............. **CLC 12**
See also CA 204

**Page, Jimmy** 1944-
See Page, James Patrick

**Page, Louise** 1955- ......................... **CLC 40**
See also CA 140; CANR 76; CBD; CD 5, 6;
CWD; DLB 233

**Page, Patricia Kathleen**
See Page, P.K.

**Page, P.K.** 1916-2010 ..... **CLC 7, 18; PC 12**
See also CA 53-56; CANR 4, 22, 65; CCA
1; CP 1, 2, 3, 4, 5, 6, 7; DAC; DAM MST;
DLB 68; MTCW 1; RGEL 2

**Page, Stanton**
See Fuller, Henry Blake

**Page, Thomas Nelson** 1853-1922 ...... **SSC 23**
See also CA 118; 177; DLB 12, 78; DLBD
13; RGAL 4

**Pagels, Elaine**
See Pagels, Elaine Hiesey

**Pagels, Elaine Hiesey** 1943- .......... **CLC 104**
See also CA 45-48; CANR 2, 24, 51, 151;
FW; NCFS 4

**Paget, Violet** 1856-1935 .... **SSC 33, 98, 216;
TCLC 5**
See also CA 104; 166; DLB 57, 153, 156,
174, 178; GLL 1; HGG; SUFW 1

**Paget-Lowe, Henry**
See Lovecraft, H. P.

**Paglia, Camille** 1947- ..................... **CLC 68**
See also CA 140; CANR 72, 139; CPW;
FW; GLL 2; MTCW 2; MTFW 2005

**Pagnol, Marcel (Paul)** 1895-1974 ... **TCLC 208**
See also CA 128; 49-52; DLB 321; EWL 3;
GFL 1789 to the Present; MTCW 1;
RGWL 2, 3

**Paige, Richard**
See Koontz, Dean

**Paine, Thomas** 1737-1809 ............. **NCLC 62,
248, 354**
See also AMWS 1; CDALB 1640-1865;
DLB 31, 43, 73, 158; LAIT 1; RGAL 4;
RGEL 2; TUS

**Pakenham, Antonia**
See Fraser, Antonia

**Palahniuk, Chuck** 1962- ................. **CLC 359**
See also AAYA 59; CA 198; CANR 140,
171, 223; CMTFW; MTFW

**Palamas, Costis**
See Palamas, Kostes

**Palamas, Kostes** 1859-1943 ............ **TCLC 5**
See also CA 105; 190; EWL 3; RGWL 2, 3

**Palamas, Kostis**
See Palamas, Kostes

**Palazzeschi, Aldo** 1885-1974 .......... **CLC 11;
TCLC 316**
See also CA 89-92; 53-56; DLB 114, 264;
EWL 3

**Pales Matos, Luis** 1898-1959 ......... **HLCS 2**
See Pales Matos, Luis
See also DLB 290; HW 1; LAW

**Paley, Grace** 1922-2007 ........ **CLC 4, 6, 37,
140, 272; SSC 8, 165, 237**
See also AMWS 6; CA 25-28R; 263; CANR
13, 46, 74, 118; CN 2, 3, 4, 5, 6, 7; CPW;
DA3; DAM POP; DLB 28, 218; EWL 3;
EXPS; FW; INT CANR-13; MAL 5; MBL;
MTCW 1, 2; MTFW 2005; RGAL 4;
RGSF 2; SSFS 3, 20, 27

**Paley, Grace Goodside**
See Paley, Grace

**Palin, Michael** 1943- ....................... **CLC 21**
See also CA 107; CANR 35, 109, 179, 229;
DLB 352; SATA 67

**Palin, Michael Edward**
See Palin, Michael

See also BW 1; CA 65-68; CANR 27, 84;
CN 1, 2, 3, 4, 5, 6

**Patton, George S(mith), Jr.**
1885-1945 ................................ **TCLC 79**
See also CA 189

**Paulding, James Kirke**
1778-1860 ............................ **NCLC 2, 355**
See also DLB 3, 59, 74, 250; RGAL 4

**Paulhan, Jean** 1884-1968 ............. **TCLC 313**
See also CA 25-28R, 249; EWL 3

**Paulin, Thomas Neilson**
See Paulin, Tom

**Paulin, Tom** 1949- .................... **CLC 37, 177**
See also CA 123; 128; CANR 98; CP 3, 4, 5,
6, 7; DLB 40

**Paulinus of Nola** 353?-431 ......... **CMLC 156**

**Pausanias** c. 1st cent. .................... **CMLC 36**

**Paustovsky, Konstantin (Georgievich)**
1892-1968 ................................ **CLC 40**
See also CA 93-96; 25-28R; DLB 272;
EWL 3

**Pavese, Cesare** 1908-1950 ................. **PC 13;**
**SSC 19; TCLC 3, 240**
See also CA 104; 169; DLB 128, 177; EW
12; EWL 3; PFS 20; RGSF 2; RGWL 2, 3;
TWA; WLIT 7

**Pavic, Milorad** 1929-2009 ................. **CLC 60**
See also CA 136; CDWLB 4; CWW 2; DLB
181; EWL 3; RGWL 3

**Pavlov, Ivan Petrovich** 1849-1936 ... **TCLC 91**
See also CA 118; 180

**Pavlova, Karolina Karlovna**
1807-1893 ............................... **NCLC 138**
See also DLB 205

**Payne, Alan**
See Jakes, John

**Payne, John Howard** 1791-1852 ... **NCLC 241**
See also DLB 37; RGAL 4

**Payne, Rachel Ann**
See Jakes, John

**Paz, Gil**
See Lugones, Leopoldo

**Paz, Octavio** 1914-1998 ..... **CLC 3, 4, 6, 10,**
**19, 51, 65, 119; HLC 2; PC 1, 48; TCLC**
**211; WLC 4**
See also AAYA 50; CA 73-76; 165; CANR
32, 65, 104; CWW 2; DA; DA3; DAB;
DAC; DAM MST, MULT, POET; DLB
290, 331; DLBY 1990, 1998; DNFS 1;
EWL 3; HW 1, 2; LAW; LAWS 1; MTCW
1, 2; MTFW 2005; PFS 18, 30, 38; RGWL
2, 3; SSFS 13; TWA; WLIT 1

**p'Bitek, Okot** 1931-1982 ................ **BLC 1:3;**
**CLC 96; TCLC 149**
See also AFW; BW 2, 3; CA 124; 107;
CANR 82; CP 1, 2, 3; DAM MULT; DLB
125; EWL 3; MTCW 1, 2; MTFW 2005;
RGEL 2; WLIT 2

**Peabody, Elizabeth Palmer**
1804-1894 ............................... **NCLC 169**
See also DLB 1, 223

**Peacham, Henry** 1578-1644(?) ......... **LC 119**
See also DLB 151

**Peacock, Molly** 1947- ...................... **CLC 60**
See also CA 103, 262; CAAE 262; CAAS
21; CANR 52, 84, 235; CP 5, 6, 7; CWP;
DLB 120, 282

**Peacock, Thomas Love**
1785-1866 ................... **NCLC 22; PC 87**
See also BRW 4; DLB 96, 116; RGEL 2;
RGSF 2

**Peake, Mervyn** 1911-1968 ............ **CLC 7, 54**
See also CA 5-8R; 25-28R; CANR 3; DLB
15, 160, 255; FANT; MTCW 1; RGEL 2;
SATA 23; SFW 4

**Pearce, Ann Philippa**
See Pearce, Philippa

**Pearce, Philippa** 1920-2006 ............ **CLC 21**
See also BRWS 19; BYA 5; CA 5-8R; 255;
CANR 4, 109; CLR 9; CWRI 5; DLB 161;

FANT; MAICYA 1; SATA 1, 67, 129;
SATA-Obit 179

**Pearl, Eric**
See Elman, Richard (Martin)

**Pearson, Jean Mary**
See Gardam, Jane

**Pearson, Thomas Reid**
See Pearson, T.R.

**Pearson, T.R.** 1956- ........................ **CLC 39**
See also CA 120; 130; CANR 97, 147, 185;
CSW; INT CA-130

**Peck, Dale** 1967- .............................. **CLC 81**
See also CA 146; CANR 72, 127, 180; GLL 2

**Peck, John (Frederick)** 1941- ........... **CLC 3**
See also CA 49-52; CANR 3, 100; CP 4, 5, 6, 7

**Peck, Richard** 1934- ......................... **CLC 21**
See also AAYA 1, 24; BYA 1, 6, 8, 11; CA
85-88; CANR 19, 38, 129, 178; CLR 15,
142; INT CANR-19; JRDA; MAICYA 1,
2; SAAS 2; SATA 18, 55, 97, 110, 158,
190, 228; SATA-Essay 110; WYA; YAW

**Peck, Richard Wayne**
See Peck, Richard

**Peck, Robert Newton** 1928- ............ **CLC 17**
See also AAYA 3, 43; BYA 1, 6; CA 81-84,
182; CAAE 182; CANR 31, 63, 127; CLR
45, 163; DA; DAC; DAM MST; JRDA;
LAIT 3; MAICYA 1, 2; NFS 29; SAAS 1;
SATA 21, 62, 111, 156; SATA-Essay 108;
WYA; YAW

**Peckinpah, David Samuel**
See Peckinpah, Sam

**Peckinpah, Sam** 1925-1984 ............. **CLC 20**
See also CA 109; 114; CANR 82

**Pedersen, Knut** 1859-1952 ....... **TCLC 2, 14,**
**49, 151, 203**
See also AAYA 79; CA 104; 119; CANR 63;
DLB 297, 330; EW 8; EWL 8; MTCW 1,
2; RGWL 2, 3

**Peele, George** 1556-1596 ..... **DC 27; LC 115**
See also BRW 1; DLB 62, 167; RGEL 2

**Peeslake, Gaffer**
See Durrell, Lawrence

**Péguy, Charles (Pierre)**
1873-1914 ............................ **TCLC 10, 323**
See also CA 107; 193; DLB 258; EWL 3;
GFL 1789 to the Present

**Penninc** fl. 13th cent. .................... **CMLC 173**

**Peirce, Charles Sanders**
1839-1914 ....................... **TCLC 81, 374**
See also CA 194; DLB 270

**Pelagius** c. 350-c. 418 .................. **CMLC 118**

**Pelecanos, George P.** 1957- ........... **CLC 236**
See also CA 138; CANR 122, 165, 194, 243;
DLB 306

**Pelevin, Victor** 1962- ...................... **CLC 238**
See also CA 154; CANR 88, 159, 197;
DLB 285

**Pelevin, Viktor Olegovich**
See Pelevin, Victor

**Pellicer, Carlos** 1897(?)-1977 .......... **HLCS 2**
See also CA 153; 69-72; DLB 290; EWL 3;
HW 1

**Pena, Ramon del Valle y**
See Valle-Inclan, Ramon del

**Pendennis, Arthur Esquir**
See Thackeray, William Makepeace

**Penn, Arthur**
See Matthews, (James) Brander

**Penn, William** 1644-1718 .................... **LC 25**
See also DLB 24

**Penny, Carolyn**
See Chute, Carolyn

**PEPECE**
See Prado (Calvo), Pedro

**Pepetela** 1941- ................................. **CLC 391**
See also AW; DLB 367; EWL 3; WLIT 2

**Pepys, Samuel** 1633-1703 .......... **LC 11, 58;**
**WLC 4**

See also BRW 2; CDBLB 1660-1789; DA;
DA3; DAB; DAC; DAM MST; DLB 101,
213; NCFS 4; RGEL 2; TEA; WLIT 3

**Percy, Thomas** 1729-1811 ............. **NCLC 95**
See also DLB 104

**Percy, Walker** 1916-1990 ..... **CLC 2, 3, 6, 8,**
**14, 18, 47, 65**
See also AMWS 3; BPFB 3; CA 1-4R; 131;
CANR 1, 23, 64; CN 1, 2, 3, 4; CPW;
CSW; DA3; DAM NOV, POP; DLB 2;
DLBY 1980, 1990; EWL 3; MAL 5;
MTCW 1, 2; MTFW 2005; RGAL 4; TUS

**Percy, William Alexander**
1885-1942 ................................ **TCLC 84**
See also CA 163; MTCW 2

**Perdurabo, Frater**
See Crowley, Edward Alexander

**Perec, Georges** 1936-1982 ....... **CLC 56, 116;**
**TCLC 352**
See also CA 141; DLB 83, 299; EWL 3;
GFL 1789 to the Present; RGHL; RGWL 3

**Pereda (y Sanchez de Porrua), Jose Maria de**
1833-1906 ................................ **TCLC 16**
See also CA 117

**Pereda y Porrua, Jose Maria de**
See Pereda (y Sanchez de Porrua), Jose
Maria de

**Peregoy, George Weems**
See Mencken, H. L.

**Perelman, Bob** 1947- ........................ **PC 132**
See also CA 154; CANR 85, 160; CP 5, 6, 7;
DLB 193; RGAL 4

**Perelman, Robert**
See Perelman, Bob

**Perelman, S(idney) J(oseph)**
1904-1979 ...... **CLC 3, 5, 9, 15, 23, 44,**
**49; SSC 32**
See also AAYA 79; AITN 1, 2; BPFB 3; CA
73-76; 89-92; CANR 18; DAM DRAM;
DLB 11, 44; MTCW 1, 2; MTFW 2005;
RGAL 4

**Perets, Yitskhok Leybush**
See Peretz, Isaac Loeb

**Peretz, Isaac Leib** (?)-
See Peretz, Isaac Loeb

**Peretz, Isaac Loeb** 1851-1915 ......... **SSC 26;**
**TCLC 16**
See also Peretz, Isaac Leib
See also CA 109; 201; DLB 333

**Peretz, Yitzkhok Leibush**
See Peretz, Isaac Loeb

**Peri Rossi, Cristina** 1941- ........... **CLC 156;**
**HLCS 2**
See also CA 131; CANR 59, 81; CWW 2;
DLB 145, 290; EWL 3; HW 1, 2

**Perkins, W. Epaminondas Adrastus**
See Twain, Mark

**Perlata**
See Peret, Benjamin

**Perloff, Marjorie G(abrielle)** 1931- ... **CLC 137**
See also CA 57-60; CANR 7, 22, 49, 104

**Perrault, Charles** 1628-1703 ........ **LC 2, 56;**
**SSC 144**
See also BYA 4; CLR 79, 134, 203; DLB
268; GFL Beginnings to 1789; MAICYA
1, 2; RGWL 2, 3; SATA 25; WCH

**Perrotta, Tom** 1961- ........................ **CLC 266**
See also CA 162; CANR 99, 155, 197

**Perry, Anne** 1938- ............................ **CLC 126**
See also CA 101; CANR 22, 50, 84, 150, 177,
238; CMW 4; CN 6, 7; CPW; DLB 276

**Perry, Brighton**
See Sherwood, Robert E(mmet)

**Perse, St.-John**
See Leger, Alexis Saint-Leger

**Perse, Saint-John**
See Leger, Alexis Saint-Leger

**Persius** 34-62 ................................. **CMLC 74**
See also AW 2; DLB 211; RGWL 2, 3

**Perutz, Leo(pold)** 1882-1957 ......... **TCLC 60**
　See also CA 147; DLB 81

**Peseenz, Tulio F.**
　See Lopez y Fuentes, Gregorio

**Pesetsky, Bette** 1932- ...................... **CLC 28**
　See also CA 133; DLB 130

**Peshkov, Alexei Maximovich**
　See Gorky, Maxim

**Pessoa, Fernando** 1888-1935 ............ **HLC 2;**
　**PC 20, 165; TCLC 27, 257, 368**
　See also CA 125, 183; CANR 182; DAM
　MULT; DLB 287; EW 10; EWL 3; RGWL
　2, 3; WP

**Pessoa, Fernando António Nogueira**
　See Pessoa, Fernando

**Pestana dos Santos, Artur Carlos Maurício**
　See Pepetela

**Peterkin, Julia Mood** 1880-1961 .... **CLC 31**
　See also CA 102; DLB 9

**Peter of Blois** c. 1135-c. 1212 .... **CMLC 127**

**Peters, Joan K(aren)** 1945- ............ **CLC 39**
　See also CA 158; CANR 109

**Peters, Robert L(ouis)** 1924- ............ **CLC 7**
　See also CA 13-16R; CAAS 8; CP 1, 5, 6, 7;
　DLB 105

**Peters, S. H.**
　See Henry, O.

**Petofi, Sandor** 1823-1849 ...... **NCLC 21, 264**
　See also RGWL 2, 3

**Petrakis, Harry Mark** 1923- ............. **CLC 3**
　See also CA 9-12R; CANR 4, 30, 85, 155;
　CN 1, 2, 3, 4, 5, 6, 7

**Petrarch** 1304-1374 ... **CMLC 20; PC 8, 187**
　See also DA3; DAM POET; EW 2; LMFS 1;
　PFS 42; RGWL 2, 3; WLIT 7

**Petrarch, Francesco**
　See Petrarch

**Petronius** c. 20-66 ................. **CMLC 34, 170**
　See also AW 2; CDWLB 1; DLB 211;
　RGWL 2, 3; WLIT 8

**Petrov, Eugene**
　See Kataev, Evgeny Petrovich

**Petrov, Evgenii**
　See Kataev, Evgeny Petrovich

**Petrov, Evgeny**
　See Kataev, Evgeny Petrovich

**Petrovsky, Boris**
　See Mansfield, Katherine

**Petrushevskaia, Liudmila** 1938- ... **CLC 387**
　See also CWW 2; DLB 285; EWL 3

**Petry, Ann** 1908-1997 ........... **CLC 1, 7, 18;**
　**SSC 161; TCLC 112**
　See also AFAW 1, 2; BPFB 3; BW 1, 3; BYA
　2; CA 5-8R; 157; CAAS 6; CANR 4, 46;
　CLR 12, 214; CN 1, 2, 3, 4, 5, 6; DLB 76;
　EWL 3; JRDA; LAIT 1; MAICYA 1, 2;
　MAICYAS 1; MTCW 1; NFS 33; RGAL 4;
　SATA 5; SATA-Obit 94; TUS

**Petry, Ann Lane**
　See Petry, Ann

**Petursson, Halligrimur** 1614-1674 ....... **LC 8**

**Peychinovich**
　See Vazov, Ivan (Minchov)

**Phaedrus** c. 15 BCE-c. 50 CE .... **CMLC 25, 171**
　See also DLB 211

**Phelge, Nanker**
　See Richards, Keith

**Phelps (Ward), Elizabeth Stuart**
　See Phelps, Elizabeth Stuart

**Phelps, Elizabeth Stuart**
　1844-1911 .................... **TCLC 113, 296**
　See also CA 242; DLB 74; FW

**Pheradausi**
　See Ferdowsi, Abu'l Qasem

**Philip, M(arlene) Nourbese**
　1947- ................................... **CLC 307, 360**
　See also BW 3; CA 163; CWP; DLB 157, 334

**Philippe de Remi**
　c. 1247-1296 ......................... **CMLC 102**

**Philips, Katherine**
　1632-1664 ...... **LC 30, 145; PC 40, 180**
　See also DLB 131; RGEL 2

**Philipson, Ilene J.** 1950- ................. **CLC 65**
　See also CA 219

**Philipson, Morris H.** 1926-2011 ..... **CLC 53**
　See also CA 1-4R; CANR 4

**Phillips, Caryl**
　1958- ................. **BLCS; CLC 96, 224**
　See also BRWS 5; BW 2; CA 141; CANR
　63, 104, 140, 195; CBD; CD 5, 6; CN 5, 6,
　7; DA3; DAM MULT; DLB 157; EWL 3;
　MTCW 2; MTFW 2005; WLIT 4; WWE 1

**Phillips, David Graham** 1867-1911 **TCLC 44**
　See also CA 108; 176; DLB 9, 12, 303;
　RGAL 4

**Phillips, Jack**
　See Sandburg, Carl

**Phillips, Jayne Anne** 1952- ...... **CLC 15, 33,**
　**139, 296; SSC 16**
　See also AAYA 57; BPFB 3; CA 101;
　CANR 24, 50, 96, 200; CN 4, 5, 6, 7;
　CSW;　DLBY　1980;　INT　CANR-24;
　MTCW 1, 2; MTFW 2005; RGAL 4;
　RGSF 2; SSFS 4

**Phillips, Richard**
　See Dick, Philip K.

**Phillips, Robert (Schaeffer)** 1938- ... **CLC 28**
　See also CA 17-20R; CAAS 13; CANR 8;
　DLB 105

**Phillips, Ward**
　See Lovecraft, H. P.

**Philo** c. 20 BCE-c. 50 CE .............. **CMLC 100**
　See also DLB 176

**Philostratus, Flavius**
　c. 179-c. 244 ................. **CMLC 62, 171**

**Phiradausi**
　See Ferdowsi, Abu'l Qasem

**Piccolo, Lucio** 1901-1969 ................. **CLC 13**
　See also CA 97-100; DLB 114; EWL 3

**Pickthall, Marjorie L(owry) C(hristie)**
　1883-1922 .............................. **TCLC 21**
　See also CA 107; DLB 92

**Pico della Mirandola, Giovanni**
　1463-1494 .......................... **LC 15, 268**
　See also LMFS 1

**Piercy, Marge** 1936- ......... **CLC 3, 6, 14, 18,**
　**27, 62, 128, 347; PC 29**
　See also BPFB 3; CA 21-24R; 187; CAAE
　187; CAAS 1; CANR 13, 43, 66, 111; CN 3,
　4, 5, 6, 7; CP 1, 2, 3, 4, 5, 6, 7; CWP; DLB
　120, 227; EXPP; FW; MAL 5; MTCW 1, 2;
　MTFW 2005; PFS 9, 22, 32, 40; SFW 4

**Pineau, Gisèle** 1956- ........................ **CLC 444**
　See also CA 259; EWL 3

**Pinero, Miguel (Antonio Gomez)**
　1946-1988 ............................. **CLC 4, 55**
　See also CA 61-64; 125; CAD; CANR 29,
　90; DLB 266; HW 1; LLW

**Piers, Robert**
　See Anthony, Piers

**Pieyre de Mandiargues, Andre**
　1909-1991 ............................. **CLC 41**
　See also CA 103; 136; CANR 22, 82; DLB
　83; EWL 3; GFL 1789 to the Present

**Piglia, Ricardo** 1941- .................... **CLC 395**
　See also CA 230; EWL 3; LAWS 1

**Pilkington, Laetitia** 1709?-1750 ....... **LC 211**

**Pil'niak, Boris**
　See Vogau, Boris Andreyevich

**Pil'niak, Boris Andreevich**
　See Vogau, Boris Andreyevich

**Pilnyak, Boris** 1894-1938
　See Vogau, Boris Andreyevich

**Pinchback, Eugene**
　See Toomer, Jean

**Pincherle, Alberto** 1907-1990 ....... **CLC 2, 7,**
　**11, 27, 46; SSC 26**
　See also CA 25-28R; 132; CANR 33, 63,
　142; DAM NOV; DLB 127; EW 12; EWL
　3; MTCW 2; MTFW 2005; RGSF 2;
　RGWL 2, 3; WLIT 7

**Pinckney, Darryl** 1953- ................... **CLC 76**
　See also BW 2, 3; CA 143; CANR 79

**Pindar** 518(?) BCE-438(?) BCE ....... **CMLC 12,**
　**130; PC 19**
　See also AW 1; CDWLB 1; DLB 176;
　RGWL 2

**Pineda, Cecile** 1942- ....................... **CLC 39**
　See also CA 118; DLB 209

**Piñera, Virgilio** 1912-1979 ........... **TCLC 348**
　See also CA 131; EWL 3, HW 1

**Pinero, Arthur Wing** 1855-1934 ... **TCLC 32**
　See also CA 110; 153; DAM DRAM; DLB
　10, 344; RGEL 2

**Pinget, Robert** 1919-1997 ..... **CLC 7, 13, 37**
　See also CA 85-88; 160; CWW 2; DLB 83;
　EWL 3; GFL 1789 to the Present

**Pink Floyd**
　See Barrett, Syd; Gilmour, David; Mason,
　Nick; Waters, Roger; Wright, Rick

**Pinkney, Edward** 1802-1828 ......... **NCLC 31**
　See also DLB 248

**Pinkwater, D. Manus**
　See Pinkwater, Daniel

**Pinkwater, Daniel** 1941- ................... **CLC 35**
　See also AAYA 1, 46; BYA 9; CA 29-32R;
　CANR 12, 38, 89, 143; CLR 4, 175; CSW;
　FANT; JRDA; MAICYA 1, 2; SAAS 3;
　SATA 8, 46, 76, 114, 158, 210, 243; SFW
　4; YAW

**Pinkwater, Daniel M.**
　See Pinkwater, Daniel

**Pinkwater, Daniel Manus**
　See Pinkwater, Daniel

**Pinkwater, Manus**
　See Pinkwater, Daniel

**Pinsky, Robert** 1940- ...... **CLC 9, 19, 38, 94,**
　**121, 216; PC 27**
　See also AMWS 6; CA 29-32R; CAAS 4;
　CANR 58, 97, 138, 177; CP 3, 4, 5, 6, 7;
　DA3; DAM POET; DLBY 1982, 1998;
　MAL 5; MTCW 2; MTFW 2005; PFS
　18, 44; RGAL 4; TCLE 1:2

**Pinta, Harold**
　See Pinter, Harold

**Pinter, Harold** 1930-2008 ........ **CLC 1, 3, 6,**
　**9, 11, 15, 27, 58, 73, 199; DC 15; WLC 4**
　See also BRWR 1; BRWS 1; CA 5-8R; 280;
　CANR 33, 65, 112, 145; CBD; CD 5, 6;
　CDBLB 1960 to Present; CP 1; DA; DA3;
　DAB; DAC; DAM DRAM; DFS 3,
　5, 7, 14, 25; DLB 13, 310, 331; EWL 3;
　IDFW 3, 4; LMFS 2; MTCW 1, 2; MTFW
　2005; RGEL 2; RGHL; TEA

**Piozzi, Hester Lynch (Thrale)**
　1741-1821 ...................... **NCLC 57, 294**
　See also DLB 104, 142

**Pirandello, Luigi** 1867-1936 ............... **DC 5;**
　**SSC 22, 148; TCLC 4, 29, 172; WLC 4**
　See also CA 104; 153; CANR 103; DA;
　DA3; DAB; DAC; DAM DRAM, MST;
　DFS 4, 9; DLB 264, 331; EW 8; EWL 3;
　MTCW 2; MTFW 2005; RGSF 2; RGWL
　2, 3; SSFS 30, 33; WLIT 7

**Pirdousi**
　See Ferdowsi, Abu'l Qasem

**Pirdousi, Abu-l-Qasim**
　See Ferdowsi, Abu'l Qasem

**Pirsig, Robert M(aynard)**
　1928-2017 ................ **CLC 4, 6, 73, 443**
　See also CA 53-56; CANR 42, 74; CPW 1;
　DA3; DAM POP; MTCW 1, 2; MTFW
　2005; NFS 31; SATA 39

**Pisan, Christine de**
　See Christine de Pizan

**Portia**
See Robinson, Mary

**Portillo (y Pacheco), Jose Lopez**
See Lopez Portillo (y Pacheco), Jose

**Portillo Trambley, Estela** 1927-1998 ... **HLC 2; SSC 180; TCLC 163**
See also CA 77-80; CANR 32; DAM MULT; DLB 209; HW 1; RGAL 4

**Posey, Alexander (Lawrence)**
1873-1908 ...................................... **NNAL**
See also CA 144; CANR 80; DAM MULT; DLB 175

**Posse, Abel** ............................... **CLC 70, 273**
See also CA 252

**Post, Melville Davisson** 1869-1930 **TCLC 39**
See also CA 110; 202; CMW 4

**Postl, Carl**
See Sealsfield, Charles

**Postman, Neil** 1931(?)-2003 ........... **CLC 244**
See also CA 102; 221

**Potocki, Jan** 1761-1815 ................ **NCLC 229**

**Potok, Chaim** 1929-2002 ....... **CLC 2, 7, 14, 26, 112, 325**
See also AAYA 15, 50; AITN 1, 2; BPFB 3; BYA 1; CA 17-20R; 208; CANR 19, 35, 64, 98; CLR 92; CN 4, 5, 6; DA3; DAM NOV; DLB 28, 152; EXPN; INT CANR-19; LAIT 4; MTCW 1, 2; MTFW 2005; NFS 4, 34, 38; RGHL; SATA 33, 106; SATA-Obit 134; TUS; YAW

**Potok, Herbert Harold**
See Potok, Chaim

**Potok, Herman Harold**
See Potok, Chaim

**Potter, Dennis (Christopher George)**
1935-1994 ................... **CLC 58, 86, 123**
See also BRWS 10; CA 107; 145; CANR 33, 61; CBD; DLB 233; MTCW 1

**Poulin, Jacques** 1937- ................... **CLC 390**
See also CA 165; CNAR 216; DLB 60

**Pound, Ezra** 1885-1972 ........ **CLC 1, 2, 3, 4, 5, 7, 10, 13, 18, 34, 48, 50, 112; PC 4, 95, 160; WLC 5**
See also AAYA 47; AMW; AMWR 1; CA 5-8R; 37-40R; CANR 40; CDALB 1917-1929; CP 1; DA; DA3; DAB; DAC; DAM MST, POET; DLB 4, 45, 63; DLBD 15; EFS 1:2, 2:1; EWL 3; EXPP; LMFS 2; MAL 5; MTCW 1, 2; MTFW 2005; PAB; PFS 2, 8, 16, 44; RGAL 4; TUS; WP

**Pound, Ezra Weston Loomis**
See Pound, Ezra

**Povod, Reinaldo** 1959-1994 ............. **CLC 44**
See also CA 136; 146; CANR 83

**Powell, Adam Clayton, Jr.**
1908-1972 ................ **BLC 1:3; CLC 89**
See also BW 1, 3; CA 102; 33-36R; CANR 86; DAM MULT; DLB 345

**Powell, Anthony** 1905-2000 ..... **CLC 1, 3, 7, 9, 10, 31**
See also BRW 7; CA 1-4R; 189; CANR 1, 32, 62, 107; CDBLB 1945-1960; CN 1, 2, 3, 4, 5, 6; DLB 15; EWL 3; MTCW 1, 2; MTFW 2005; RGEL 2; TEA

**Powell, Dawn** 1896(?)-1965 ............. **CLC 66**
See also CA 5-8R; CANR 121; DLBY 1997

**Powell, Padgett** 1952- ..................... **CLC 34**
See also CA 126; CANR 63, 101, 215; CSW; DLB 234; DLBY 01; SSFS 25

**Power, Susan** 1961- .......................... **CLC 91**
See also BYA 14; CA 160; CANR 135; NFS 11

**Powers, J(ames) F(arl)** 1917-1999 ... **CLC 1, 4, 8, 57; SSC 4**
See also CA 1-4R; 181; CANR 2, 61; CN 1, 2, 3, 4, 5, 6; DLB 130; MTCW 1; RGAL 4; RGSF 2

**Powers, John**
See Powers, John R.

**Powers, John R.** 1945- ..................... **CLC 66**
See also CA 69-72

**Powers, Kevin** 1980- ...................... **CLC 354**

**Powers, Richard** 1957- ............. **CLC 93, 292**
See also AMWS 9; BPFB 3; CA 148; CANR 80, 180, 221; CN 6, 7; DLB 350; MTFW 2005; TCLE 1:2

**Powers, Richard S.**
See Powers, Richard

**Pownall, David** 1938- ....................... **CLC 10**
See also CA 89-92, 180; CAAS 18; CANR 49, 101; CBD; CD 5, 6; CN 4, 5, 6, 7; DLB 14

**Powys, John Cowper** 1872-1963 ..... **CLC 7, 9, 15, 46, 125**
See also CA 85-88; CANR 106; DLB 15, 255; EWL 3; FANT; MTCW 1, 2; MTFW 2005; RGEL 2; SUFW

**Powys, T(heodore) F(rancis)**
1875-1953 ................................ **TCLC 9**
See also BRWS 8; CA 106; 189; DLB 36, 162; EWL 3; FANT; RGEL 2; SUFW

**Pozzo, Modesta**
See Fonte, Moderata

**Prado (Calvo), Pedro** 1886-1952 ... **TCLC 75**
See also CA 131; DLB 283; HW 1; LAW

**Praed, Rosa** 1851-1935 ................ **TCLC 319**
See also DLB 230; HGG

**Prager, Emily** 1952- ......................... **CLC 56**
See also CA 204

**Pratchett, Terence David John**
See Pratchett, Terry

**Pratchett, Terry** 1948-2015 ........... **CLC 197**
See also AAYA 19, 54; BPFB 3; CA 143; CANR 87, 126, 170, 248, 281; CLR 64, 225; CN 6, 7; CPW; CWRI 5; FANT; MTFW 2005; SATA 82, 139, 185, 253, 291; SFW 4; SUFW 2

**Pratolini, Vasco** 1913-1991 ......... **TCLC 124**
See also CA 211; DLB 177; EWL 3; RGWL 2, 3

**Pratt, E(dwin) J(ohn)** 1883(?)-1964 ... **CLC 19**
See also CA 141; 93-96; CANR 77; DAC; DAM POET; DLB 92; EWL 3; RGEL 2; TWA

**Premacanda**
See Srivastava, Dhanpat Rai

**Premchand**
See Srivastava, Dhanpat Rai

**Prem Chand, Munshi**
See Srivastava, Dhanpat Rai

**Premchand, Munshi**
See Srivastava, Dhanpat Rai

**Prescott, William Hickling**
1796-1859 ............................ **NCLC 163**
See also DLB 1, 30, 59, 235

**Preseren, France** 1800-1849 ........ **NCLC 127**
See also CDWLB 4; DLB 147

**Preston, Thomas** 1537-1598 ............. **LC 189**
See also DLB 62

**Peret, Benjamin** 1899-1959 .. **PC 33; TCLC 20**
See also CA 117; 186; GFL 1789 to the Present

**Preussler, Otfried** 1923- ................... **CLC 17**
See also CA 77-80; SATA 24

**Perez Galdos, Benito** 1843-1920 .... **HLCS 2; TCLC 27**
See also CA 125; 153; EW 7; EWL 3; HW 1; RGWL 2, 3

**Price, Edward Reynolds**
See Price, Reynolds

**Price, Reynolds** 1933-2011 .... **CLC 3, 6, 13, 43, 50, 63, 212, 341; SSC 22**
See also AMWS 6; CA 1-4R; CANR 1, 37, 57, 87, 128, 177, 217; CN 1, 2, 3, 4, 5, 6, 7; CSW; DAM NOV; DLB 2, 218, 278; EWL 3; INT CANR-37; MAL 5; MTFW 2005; NFS 18

**Price, Richard** 1949- ........... **CLC 6, 12, 299**
See also CA 49-52; CANR 3, 147, 190; CN 7; DLBY 1981

**Prichard, Katharine Susannah**
1883-1969 ................................ **CLC 46**
See also CA 11-12; CANR 33; CAP 1; DLB 260; MTCW 1; RGEL 2; RGSF 2; SATA 66

**Priestley, J(ohn) B(oynton)**
1894-1984 ............ **CLC 2, 5, 9, 34**
See also BRW 7; CA 9-12R; 113; CANR 33; CDBLB 1914-1945; CN 1, 2, 3; DA3; DAM DRAM, NOV; DLB 10, 34, 77, 100, 139; DLBY 1984; EWL 3; MTCW 1, 2; MTFW 2005; RGEL 2; SFW 4

**Prince** 1958- ..................................... **CLC 35**
See also CA 213

**Prince, F(rank) T(empleton)**
1912-2003 ................. **CLC 22, PC 122**
See also CA 101; 219; CANR 43, 79; CP 1, 2, 3, 4, 5, 6, 7; DLB 20

**Prince Kropotkin**
See Kropotkin, Peter

**Prince, Mary** c. 1788-1833? ........ **NCLC 282**
See also AAYA 71

**Prior, Matthew**
1664-1721 ........ **LC 4, 52, 274; PC 102**
See also DLB 95; RGEL 2

**Prior, Capt. Samuel**
See Galt, John

**Prishvin, Mikhail** 1873-1954 ......... **TCLC 75**
See also DLB 272; EWL 3

**Prishvin, Mikhail Mikhailovich**
See Prishvin, Mikhail

**Pritchard, William H(arrison)**
1932- ......................................... **CLC 34**
See also CA 65-68; CANR 23, 95; DLB 111

**Pritchett, V(ictor) S(awdon)** 1900-1997 .. **CLC 5, 13, 15, 41; SSC 14, 126**
See also BPFB 3; BRWS 3; CA 61-64; 157; CANR 31, 63; CN 1, 2, 3, 4, 5, 6; DA3; DAM NOV; DLB 15, 139; EWL 3; MTCW 1, 2; MTFW 2005; RGEL 2; RGSF 2; TEA

**Private 19022**
See Manning, Frederic

**Probst, Mark** 1925- ......................... **CLC 59**
See also CA 130

**Procaccino, Michael**
See Cristofer, Michael

**Proclus** c. 412-c. 485 ..................... **CMLC 81**

**Procopius of Caesarea**
500?-560? ............................. **CMLC 161**

**Procter, Adelaide Anne**
1825-1864 ............................. **NCLC 305**
See also DLB 32, 199

**Prokosch, Frederic** 1908-1989 .... **CLC 4, 48**
See also CA 73-76; 128; CANR 82; CN 1, 2, 3, 4; CP 1, 2, 3, 4; DLB 48; MTCW 2

**Propertius, Sextus**
c. 50 BCE-c. 16 BCE ....... **CMLC 32, 140**
See also AW 2; CDWLB 1; DLB 211; RGWL 2, 3; WLIT 8

**Prophet, The**
See Dreiser, Theodore

**Prose, Francine** 1947- .............. **CLC 45, 231**
See also AMWS 16; CA 109; 112; CANR 46, 95, 132, 175, 218; DLB 234; MTFW 2005; SATA 101, 149, 198

**Protagoras** c. 490 BCE-420 BCE ...... **CMLC 85**
See also DLB 176

**Proteus**
See Blunt, Wilfrid Scawen

**Proudhon**
See Cunha, Euclides (Rodrigues Pimenta) da

**Proulx, Annie** 1935- ....... **CLC 81, 158, 250, 331; SSC 128, 168**
See also AAYA 81; AMWS 7; BPFB 3; CA 145; CANR 65, 110, 206; CN 6, 7; CPW 1; DA3; DAM POP; DLB 335, 350; MAL

5; MTCW 2; MTFW 2005; NFS 38; SSFS 18, 23

**Proulx, E. Annie**
See Proulx, Annie

**Proulx, Edna Annie**
See Proulx, Annie

**Proust, Marcel** 1871-1922 .............. **SSC 75; TCLC 7, 13, 33, 220; WLC 5**
See also AAYA 58; BPFB 3; CA 104; 120; CANR 110; DA; DA3; DAB; DAC; DAM MST, NOV; DLB 65; EW 8; EWL 3; GFL 1789 to the Present; MTCW 1, 2; MTFW 2005; RGWL 2, 3; TWA

**Proust, Valentin-Louis-George-Eugene Marcel**
See Proust, Marcel

**Prowler, Harley**
See Masters, Edgar Lee

**Prudentius, Aurelius Clemens** 348-c. 405 ............................... **CMLC 78**
See also EW 1; RGWL 2, 3

**Prudhomme, Rene Francois Armand**
See Sully Prudhomme, Rene-Francois-Armand

**Prus, Boleslaw** 1845-1912 .............. **TCLC 48**
See also RGWL 2, 3

**Prevert, Jacques** 1900-1977 ............. **CLC 15**
See also CA 77-80; 69-72; CANR 29, 61, 207; DLB 258; EWL 3; GFL 1789 to the Present; IDFW 3, 4; MTCW 1; RGWL 2, 3; SATA-Obit 30

**Prevert, Jacques Henri Marie**
See Prevert, Jacques

**Prevost, (Antoine Francois)** 1697-1763 ................................. **LC 1, 174**
See also DLB 314; EW 4; GFL Beginnings to 1789; RGWL 2, 3

**Prunier, Joseph**
See Maupassant, Guy de

**Prynne, William** 1600-1669 .............. **LC 148**

**Prynne, Xavier**
See Hardwick, Elizabeth

**Pryor, Aaron Richard**
See Pryor, Richard

**Pryor, Richard** 1940-2005 ............... **CLC 26**
See also CA 122; 152; 246

**Pryor, Richard Franklin Lenox Thomas**
See Pryor, Richard

**Przybyszewski, Stanislaw** 1868-1927 ................................ **TCLC 36**
See also CA 160; DLB 66; EWL 3

**Pseudo-Dionysius the Areopagite** fl. c. 5th cent. .......................... **CMLC 89**
See also DLB 115

**Pteleon**
See Grieve, C. M.

**Puckett, Lute**
See Masters, Edgar Lee

**Puff, Peter, Secundus**
See Mangan, James Clarence

**Puig, Manuel** 1932-1990 ... **CLC 3, 5, 10, 28, 65, 133; HLC 2; TCLC 227, 366**
See also BPFB 3; CA 45-48; CANR 2, 32, 63; CDWLB 3; CMTFW; DA3; DAM MULT; DLB 113; DNFS 1; EWL 3; GLL 1; HW 1, 2; LAW; MTCW 1, 2; MTFW 2005; RGWL 2, 3; TWA; WLIT 1

**Pulci, Luigi** 1432-1484 .................... **LC 246**

**Pulitzer, Joseph** 1847-1911 ............ **TCLC 76**
See also CA 114; DLB 23

**Pullman, Philip** 1946- ..................... **CLC 245**
See also AAYA 15, 41; BRWS 13; BYA 8, 13; CA 127; CANR 50, 77, 105, 134, 190; CLR 20, 62, 84, 202; JRDA; MAICYA 1, 2; MAICYAS 1; MTFW 2005; SAAS 17; SATA 65, 103, 150, 198; SUFW 2; WYAS 1; YAW

**Purchas, Samuel** 1577(?)-1626 .......... **LC 70**
See also DLB 151

**Purdy, A(lfred) W(ellington)** 1918-2000 ... **CLC 3, 6, 14, 50; PC 171**
See also CA 81-84; 189; CAAS 17; CANR 42, 66; CP 1, 2, 3, 4, 5, 6, 7; DAC; DAM MST, POET; DLB 88; PFS 5; RGEL 2

**Purdy, James** 1914-2009 ........ **CLC 2, 4, 10, 28, 52, 286**
See also AMWS 7; CA 33-36R; 284; CAAS 1; CANR 19, 51, 132; CN 1, 2, 3, 4, 5, 6, 7; DLB 2, 218; EWL 3; INT CANR-19; MAL 5; MTCW 1; RGAL 4

**Purdy, James Amos**
See Purdy, James

**Purdy, James Otis**
See Purdy, James

**Pure, Simon**
See Swinnerton, Frank Arthur

**Pushkin, Aleksandr Sergeevich**
See Pushkin, Alexander

**Pushkin, Alexander** 1799-1837 ...... **NCLC 3, 27, 83, 278; PC 10; SSC 27, 55, 99, 189; WLC 5**
See also DA; DA3; DAB; DAC; DAM DRAM, MST, POET; DLB 205; EW 5; EXPS; PFS 28, 34; RGSF 2; RGWL 2, 3; SATA 61; SSFS 9; TWA

**Pushkin, Alexander Sergeyevich**
See Pushkin, Alexander

**P'u Sung-ling** 1640-1715 .... **LC 49; SSC 31**

**Putnam, Arthur Lee**
See Alger, Horatio, Jr.

**Puttenham, George** 1529(?)-1590 .... **LC 116**
See also DLB 281

**Puzo, Mario** 1920-1999 ........... **CLC 1, 2, 6, 36, 107**
See also BPFB 3; CA 65-68; 185; CANR 4, 42, 65, 99, 131; CN 1, 2, 3, 4, 5, 6; CPW; DA3; DAM NOV, POP; DLB 6; MTCW 1, 2; MTFW 2005; NFS 16; RGAL 4

**Pygge, Edward**
See Barnes, Julian

**Pyle, Ernest Taylor**
See Pyle, Ernie

**Pyle, Ernie** 1900-1945 .................... **TCLC 75**
See also CA 115; 160; DLB 29, 364; MTCW 2

**Pyle, Howard** 1853-1911 ............... **TCLC 81**
See also AAYA 57; BYA 2, 4; CA 109; 137; CLR 22, 117; DLB 42, 188; DLBD 13; LAIT 1; MAICYA 1, 2; SATA 16, 100; WCH; YAW

**Pym, Barbara (Mary Crampton)** 1913-1980 ........... **CLC 13, 19, 37, 111; TCLC 279**
See also BPFB 3; BRWS 2; CA 13-14; 97-100; CANR 13, 34; CAP 1; DLB 14, 207; DLBY 1987; EWL 3; MTCW 1, 2; MTFW 2005; RGEL 2; TEA

**Pynchon, Thomas** 1937- ...... **CLC 2, 3, 6, 9, 11, 18, 33, 62, 72, 123, 192, 213; SSC 14, 84; WLC 5**
See also AMWS 2; BEST 90:2; BPFB 3; CA 17-20R; CANR 22, 46, 73, 142, 198; CN 1, 2, 3, 4, 5, 6, 7; CPW 1; DA; DA3; DAB; DAC; DAM MST, NOV, POP; DLB 2, 173; EWL 3; MAL 5; MTCW 1, 2; MTFW 2005; NFS 23, 36; RGAL 4; SFW 4; TCLE 1:2; TUS

**Pynchon, Thomas Ruggels, Jr.**
See Pynchon, Thomas

**Pynchon, Thomas Ruggles**
See Pynchon, Thomas

**Pythagoras** c. 582 BCE-c. 507 BCE .. **CMLC 22, 177**
See also DLB 176

**Q**
See Quiller-Couch, Sir Arthur (Thomas)

**Qian, Chongzhu**
See Qian, Zhongshu

**Qian, Sima**
See Sima Qian

**Qian, Zhongshu** 1910-1998 ............. **CLC 22**
See also CA 130; CANR 73, 216; CWW 2; DLB 328; MTCW 1, 2

**Qroll**
See Dagerman, Stig (Halvard)

**Quarles, Francis** 1592-1644 .............. **LC 117**
See also DLB 126; RGEL 2

**Quarrington, Paul** 1953-2010 ......... **CLC 65**
See also CA 129; CANR 62, 95, 228

**Quarrington, Paul Lewis**
See Quarrington, Paul

**Quasimodo, Salvatore** 1901-1968 ..................... **CLC 10; PC 47**
See also CA 13-16; 25-28R; CAP 1; DLB 114, 332; EW 12; EWL 3; MTCW 1; RGWL 2, 3

**Quatermass, Martin**
See Carpenter, John

**Quay, Stephen** 1947- ....................... **CLC 95**
See also CA 189

**Quay, Timothy** 1947- ....................... **CLC 95**
See also CA 189

**Queen, Ellery**
See Dannay, Frederic; Hoch, Edward D.; Lee, Manfred B.; Marlowe, Stephen; Sturgeon, Theodore (Hamilton); Vance, Jack

**Queneau, Raymond** 1903-1976 .... **CLC 2, 5, 10, 42; TCLC 233**
See also CA 77-80; 69-72; CANR 32; DLB 72, 258; EW 12; EWL 3; GFL 1789 to the Present; MTCW 1, 2; RGWL 2, 3

**Quevedo, Francisco de** 1580-1645 ... **LC 23,160**

**Quiller-Couch, Sir Arthur (Thomas)** 1863-1944 ................................ **TCLC 53**
See also CA 118; 166; DLB 135, 153, 190; HGG; RGEL 2; SUFW 1

**Quin, Ann** 1936-1973 ....................... **CLC 6**
See also CA 9-12R; 45-48; CANR 148; CN 1; DLB 14, 231

**Quin, Ann Marie**
See Quin, Ann

**Quinault, Philippe** 1635-1688 .......... **LC 229**
See also DLB 268; IDTP

**Quincey, Thomas de**
See De Quincey, Thomas

**Quindlen, Anna** 1953- ..................... **CLC 191**
See also AAYA 35; AMWS 17; CA 138; CANR 73, 126; DA3; DLB 292; MTCW 2; MTFW 2005

**Quinn, Martin**
See Smith, Martin Cruz

**Quinn, Peter** 1947- ......................... **CLC 91**
See also CA 197; CANR 147, 239

**Quinn, Peter A.**
See Quinn, Peter

**Quinn, Simon**
See Smith, Martin Cruz

**Quintana, Leroy V.** 1944- .... **HLC 2; PC 36**
See also CA 131; CANR 65, 139; DAM MULT; DLB 82; HW 1, 2

**Quintasket, Christal**
See Mourning Dove

**Quintasket, Christine**
See Mourning Dove

**Quintilian** c. 40-c. 100 ................. **CMLC 77**
See also AW 2; DLB 211; RGWL 2, 3

**Quiroga, Horacio (Sylvestre)** 1878-1937 .................. **HLC 2; SSC 89; TCLC 20**
See also CA 117; 131; DAM MULT; EWL 3; HW 1; LAW; MTCW 1; RGSF 2; SSFS 37; WLIT 1

**Quoirez, Francoise**
See Sagan, Francoise

**Raabe, Wilhelm (Karl)** 1831-1910 ... **TCLC 45**
See also CA 167; DLB 129

**Rabe, David** 1940- .......................... **CLC 4, 8, 33, 200; DC 16**
See also CA 85-88; CABS 3; CAD; CANR 59, 129, 218; CD 5, 6; DAM DRAM; DFS 3, 8, 13; DLB 7, 228; EWL 3; MAL 5

**Rabe, David William**
See Rabe, David

**Rabelais, Francois** 1494-1553 ....... **LC 5, 60, 186; WLC 5**
See also DA; DAB; DAC; DAM MST; DLB 327; EW 2; GFL Beginnings to 1789; LMFS 1; RGWL 2, 3; TWA

**Rabi`a al-`Adawiyya**
c. 717-c. 801 ................. **CMLC 83, 145**
See also DLB 311

**Rabinovitch, Sholem**
See Aleichem, Sholom

**Rabinovitsh, Sholem Yankev**
See Aleichem, Sholom

**Rabinowitz, Sholem Yakov**
See Rabinovitch, Sholem

**Rabinyan, Dorit** 1972- ................... **CLC 119**
See also CA 170; CANR 147

**Rachilde**
See Vallette, Marguerite Eymery; Vallette, Marguerite Eymery

**Racine, Jean** 1639-1699 ..................... **DC 32; LC 28, 113**
See also DA3; DAB; DAM MST; DFS 28; DLB 268; EW 3; GFL Beginnings to 1789; LMFS 1; RGWL 2, 3; TWA

**Radcliffe, Ann** 1764-1823 ........ **NCLC 6, 55, 106, 223, 326**
See also BRWR 3; DLB 39, 178; GL 3; HGG; LMFS 1; RGEL 2; SUFW; WLIT 3

**Radclyffe-Hall, Marguerite**
See Hall, Radclyffe

**Radiguet, Raymond** 1903-1923 ..... **TCLC 29**
See also CA 162; DLB 65; EWL 3; GFL 1789 to the Present; RGWL 2, 3

**Radishchev, Aleksandr Nikolaevich**
1749-1802 ............................. **NCLC 190**
See also DLB 150

**Radishchev, Alexander**
See Radishchev, Aleksandr Nikolaevich

**Radnoti, Miklos** 1909-1944 .......... **TCLC 16**
See also CA 118; 212; CDWLB 4; DLB 215; EWL 3; RGHL; RGWL 2, 3

**Rado, James** 1939- ........................... **CLC 17**
See also CA 105

**Radvanyi, Netty**
1900-1983 ............... **CLC 7; TCLC 330**
See also CA 85-88; 110; CANR 82; CDWLB 2; DLB 69; EWL 3

**Rae, Ben**
See Griffiths, Trevor

**Raeburn, John (Hay)** 1941- ............ **CLC 34**
See also CA 57-60

**Ragni, Gerome** 1942-1991 .............. **CLC 17**
See also CA 105; 134

**Rahv, Philip**
See Greenberg, Ivan

**Rai, Navab**
See Srivastava, Dhanpat Rai

**Raimund, Ferdinand Jakob**
1790-1836 ............................. **NCLC 69**
See also DLB 90

**Raine, Craig** 1944- ................... **CLC 32, 103**
See also BRWS 13; CA 108; CANR 29, 51, 103, 171; CP 3, 4, 5, 6, 7; DLB 40; PFS 7

**Raine, Craig Anthony**
See Raine, Craig

**Raine, Kathleen (Jessie)**
1908-2003 ............................. **CLC 7, 45**
See also CA 85-88; 218; CANR 46, 109; CP 1, 2, 3, 4, 5, 6, 7; DLB 20; EWL 3; MTCW 1; RGEL 2

**Rainis, Janis** 1865-1929 ................. **TCLC 29**
See also CA 170; CDWLB 4; DLB 220; EWL 3

**Rakosi, Carl**
See Rawley, Callman

**Ralegh, Sir Walter**
See Raleigh, Sir Walter

**Raleigh, Richard**
See Lovecraft, H. P.

**Raleigh, Sir Walter** 1554(?)-1618 ..... **LC 31, 39, 255; PC 31**
See also BRW 1; CDBLB Before 1660; DLB 172; EXPP; PFS 14; RGEL 2; TEA; WP

**Rallentando, H. P.**
See Sayers, Dorothy L(eigh)

**Ramal, Walter**
See de la Mare, Walter (John)

**Ramana Maharshi** 1879-1950 ....... **TCLC 84**

**Ramírez, Sergio** 1942- ................... **CLC 398**
See also CA 184; CWW 2; DLB 145; EWL 3; HW 2

**Ramon, Juan**
See Jimenez, Juan Ramon

**Ramoacn y Cajal, Santiago**
1852-1934 ................................. **TCLC 93**

**Ramos, Graciliano** 1892-1953 ....... **TCLC 32**
See also CA 167; DLB 307; EWL 3; HW 2; LAW; WLIT 1

**Rampersad, Arnold** 1941- .............. **CLC 44**
See also BW 2, 3; CA 127; 133; CANR 81; DLB 111; INT CA-133

**Rampling, Anne**
See Rice, Anne

**Ramsay, Allan** 1686(?)-1758 ............... **LC 29**
See also DLB 95; RGEL 2

**Ramsay, Jay**
See Campbell, Ramsey

**Ramus, Peter**
See La Ramee, Pierre de

**Ramus, Petrus**
See La Ramee, Pierre de

**Ramuz, Charles-Ferdinand**
1878-1947 ............................. **TCLC 33**
See also CA 165; EWL 3

**Rand, Ayn** 1905-1982 .......... **CLC 3, 30, 44, 79; SSC 116; TCLC 261; WLC 5**
See also AAYA 10; AMWS 4; BPFB 3; BYA 12; CA 13-16R; 105; CANR 27, 73; CDALBS; CN 1, 2, 3; CPW; DA; DA3; DAC; DAM MST, NOV, POP; DLB 227, 279; MTCW 1, 2; MTFW 2005; NFS 10, 16, 29; RGAL 4; SFW 4; TUS; YAW

**Randall, Anne Frances**
See Robinson, Mary

**Randall, Dudley** 1914-2000 .......... **BLC 1:3; CLC 1, 135; PC 86**
See also BW 1, 3; CA 25-28R; 189; CANR 23, 82; CP 1, 2, 3, 4, 5; DAM MULT; DLB 41; PFS 5

**Randall, Dudley Felker**
See Randall, Dudley

**Randall, Robert**
See Silverberg, Robert

**Randolph, Thomas** 1605-1635 ......... **LC 195**
See also DLB 58, 126; RGEL 2

**Ranger, Ken**
See Creasey, John

**Rank, Otto** 1884-1939 ................. **TCLC 115**

**Rankin, Ian** 1960- .......................... **CLC 257**
See also BRWS 10; CA 148; CANR 81, 137, 171, 210; DLB 267; MTFW 2005

**Rankin, Ian James**
See Rankin, Ian

**Ransom, John Crowe** 1888-1974 ..... **CLC 2, 4, 5, 11, 24; PC 61**
See also AMW; CA 5-8R; 49-52; CANR 6, 34; CDALBS; CP 1, 2; DA3; DAM POET;

DLB 45, 63; EWL 3; EXPP; MAL 5; MTCW 1, 2; MTFW 2005; RGAL 4; TUS

**Rao, Raja** 1908-2006 ........ **CLC 25, 56, 255; SSC 99**
See also CA 73-76; 252; CANR 51; CN 1, 2, 3, 4, 5, 6; DAM NOV; DLB 323; EWL 3; MTCW 1, 2; MTFW 2005; RGEL 2; RGSF 2

**Raphael, Frederic** 1931- .............. **CLC 2, 14**
See also CA 1-4R; CANR 1, 86, 223; CN 1, 2, 3, 4, 5, 6, 7; DLB 14, 319; TCLE 1:2

**Raphael, Frederic Michael**
See Raphael, Frederic

**Raphael, Lev** 1954- ....................... **CLC 232**
See also CA 134; CANR 72, 145, 217; GLL 1

**Rastell, John** c. 1475(?)-1536(?) ....... **LC 183**
See also DLB 136, 170; RGEL 2

**Ratcliffe, James P.**
See Mencken, H. L.

**Rathbone, Julian** 1935-2008 ............ **CLC 41**
See also CA 101; 269; CANR 34, 73, 152, 221

**Rathbone, Julian Christopher**
See Rathbone, Julian

**Rattigan, Terence** 1911-1977 ............ **CLC 7; DC 18**
See also BRWS 7; CA 85-88; 73-76; CBD; CDBLB 1945-1960; DAM DRAM; DFS 8; DLB 13; IDFW 3, 4; MTCW 1, 2; MTFW 2005; RGEL 2

**Rattigan, Terence Mervyn**
See Rattigan, Terence

**Ratushinskaya, Irina** 1954- ............ **CLC 54**
See also CA 129; CANR 68; CWW 2

**Raven, Simon (Arthur Noel)**
1927-2001 ................................. **CLC 14**
See also CA 81-84; 197; CANR 86; CN 1, 2, 3, 4, 5, 6; DLB 271

**Ravenna, Michael**
See Welty, Eudora

**Rawley, Callman**
1903-2004 ................... **CLC 47; PC 126**
See also CA 21-24R; 228; CAAS 5; CANR 12, 32, 91; CP 1, 2, 3, 4, 5, 6, 7; DLB 193

**Rawlings, Marjorie Kinnan**
1896-1953 ........................... **TCLC 4, 248**
See also AAYA 20; AMWS 10; ANW; BPFB 3; BYA 3; CA 104; 137; CANR 74; CLR 63; DLB 9, 22, 102; DLBD 17; JRDA; MAICYA 1, 2; MAL 5; MTCW 2; MTFW 2005; RGAL 4; SATA 100; WCH; YABC 1; YAW

**Raworth, Thomas Moore** 1938- ....... **PC 107**
See also CA 29-32R; CAAS 11; CANR 46; CP 1, 2, 3, 4, 5, 7; DLB 40

**Raworth, Tom**
See Raworth, Thomas Moore

**Ray, Satyajit** 1921-1992 ............. **CLC 16, 76**
See also CA 114; 137; DAM MULT

**Read, Herbert Edward**
1893-1968 ............... **CLC 4; TCLC 348**
See also BRW 6; CA 85-88; 25-28R; DLB 20, 149; EWL 3; PAB; RGEL 2

**Read, Piers Paul** 1941- ......... **CLC 4, 10, 25**
See also CA 21-24R; CANR 38, 86, 150; CN 2, 3, 4, 5, 6, 7; DLB 14; SATA 21

**Reade, Charles** 1814-1884 ... **NCLC 2, 74, 275**
See also DLB 21; RGEL 2

**Reade, Hamish**
See Gray, Simon

**Reading, Peter** 1946-2011 ............... **CLC 47**
See also BRWS 8; CA 103; CANR 46, 96; CP 5, 6, 7; DLB 40

**Reaney, James** 1926-2008 ............... **CLC 13**
See also CA 41-44R; CAAS 15; CANR 42; CD 5, 6; CP 1, 2, 3, 4, 5, 6, 7; DAC; DAM MST; DLB 68; RGEL 2; SATA 43

**Reaney, James Crerar**
See Reaney, James

**Richard, Keith**
  See Richards, Keith

**Richards, David Adams** 1950- ........ **CLC 59**
  See also CA 93-96; CANR 60, 110, 156;
  CN 7; DAC; DLB 53; TCLE 1:2

**Richards, I(vor) A(rmstrong)**
  1893-1979 ........................ **CLC 14, 24**
  See also BRWS 2; CA 41-44R; 89-92;
  CANR 34, 74; CP 1, 2; DLB 27; EWL
  3; MTCW 2; RGEL 2

**Richards, Keith** 1943- ..................... **CLC 17**
  See also CA 107; CANR 77

**Richards, Scott**
  See Card, Orson Scott

**Richardson, Anne**
  See Roiphe, Anne

**Richardson, Dorothy Miller**
  1873-1957 ........................ **TCLC 3, 203**
  See also BRWS 13; CA 104; 192; DLB 36;
  EWL 3; FW; RGEL 2

**Richardson, Ethel Florence Lindesay**
  1870-1946 ........................ **TCLC 4, 327**
  See also CA 105; 190; DLB 197, 230; EWL
  3; RGEL 2; RGSF 2; RHW

**Richardson, Henrietta**
  See Richardson, Ethel Florence Lindesay

**Richardson, Henry Handel**
  See Richardson, Ethel Florence Lindesay

**Richardson, John** 1796-1852 ......... **NCLC 55**
  See also CCA 1; DAC; DLB 99

**Richardson, Samuel** 1689-1761 ..... **LC 1, 44,**
  **138, 204; WLC 5**
  See also BRW 3; CDBLB 1660-1789; DA;
  DAB; DAC; DAM MST, NOV; DLB 154;
  RGEL 2; TEA; WLIT 3

**Richardson, Willis** 1889-1977 .......... **HR 1:3**
  See also BW 1; CA 124; DLB 51; SATA 60

**Richardson Robertson, Ethel Florence**
  **Lindesay**
  See Richardson, Ethel Florence Lindesay

**Richler, Mordecai** 1931-2001 ....... **CLC 3, 5,**
  **9, 13, 18, 46, 70, 185, 271**
  See also AITN 1; CA 65-68; 201; CANR 31,
  62, 111; CCA 1; CLR 17; CN 1, 2, 3, 4, 5,
  7; CWRI 5; DAC; DAM MST, NOV; DLB
  53; EWL 3; MAICYA 1, 2; MTCW 1, 2;
  MTFW 2005; RGEL 2; RGHL; SATA 44,
  98; SATA-Brief 27; TWA

**Richter, Conrad (Michael)**
  1890-1968 .......................... **CLC 30**
  See also AAYA 21; AMWS 18; BYA 2; CA
  5-8R; 25-28R; CANR 23; DLB 9, 212;
  LAIT 1; MAL 5; MTCW 1, 2; MTFW
  2005; NFS 43; RGAL 4; SATA 3; TCWW
  1, 2; TUS; YAW

**Ricostranza, Tom**
  See Ellis, Trey

**Riddell, Charlotte** 1832-1906 ........ **TCLC 40**
  See also CA 165; DLB 156; HGG; SUFW

**Riddell, Mrs. J. H.**
  See Riddell, Charlotte

**Ridge, John Rollin** 1827-1867 .... **NCLC 82;**
  **NNAL**
  See also CA 144; DAM MULT; DLB 175

**Ridgeway, Jason**
  See Marlowe, Stephen

**Ridgway, Keith** 1965- ..................... **CLC 119**
  See also CA 172; CANR 144

**Riding, Laura**
  See Jackson, Laura

**Riefenstahl, Berta Helene Amalia**
  See Riefenstahl, Leni

**Riefenstahl, Leni** 1902-2003 .... **CLC 16, 190**
  See also CA 108; 220

**Riefenstahl, Leni**
  See Riefenstahl, Berta Helene Amalia

**Riera, Carme** 1948- ....... **CLC 368; SSC 177**
  See also CA 254, DLB 322, EWL 3

**Rieser, Henry**
  See MacDonald, John D.

**Rifaat, Alifa** 1930-1996 ................ **TCLC 346**
  See also CA 123; CANR 50

**Rif'at, Fatima**
  See Rifaat, Alifa

**Riffaterre, Michael** 1924-2006
  See also CA 183, 250; DLB 67

**Riffe, Ernest**
  See Bergman, Ingmar

**Riffe, Ernest Ingmar**
  See Bergman, Ingmar

**Riggs, (Rolla) Lynn** 1899-1954 ......... **NNAL;**
  **TCLC 56**
  See also CA 144; DAM MULT; DLB 175

**Riis, Jacob A(ugust)** 1849-1914 .... **TCLC 80**
  See also CA 113; 168; DLB 23

**Rikki**
  See Ducornet, Erica

**Riley, James Whitcomb** 1849-1916 ... **PC 48;**
  **TCLC 51**
  See also CA 118; 137; DAM POET; MAI-
  CYA 1, 2; RGAL 4; SATA 17

**Riley, Tex**
  See Creasey, John

**Rilke, Rainer Maria** 1875-1926 .. **PC 2, 140;**
  **TCLC 1, 6, 19, 195, 310**
  See also CA 104; 132; CANR 62, 99;
  CDWLB 2; DA3; DAM POET; DLB 81;
  EW 9; EWL 3; MTCW 1, 2; MTFW 2005;
  PFS 19, 27; RGWL 2, 3; TWA; WP

**Rimbaud, Arthur** 1854-1891 ... **NCLC 4, 35,**
  **82, 227; PC 3, 57; WLC 5**
  See also DA; DA3; DAB; DAC; DAM MST,
  POET; DLB 217; EW 7; GFL 1789 to the
  Present; LMFS 2; PFS 28; RGWL 2, 3;
  TWA; WP

**Rimbaud, Jean Nicholas Arthur**
  See Rimbaud, Arthur

**Rinehart, Mary Roberts** 1876-1958 .. **TCLC 52**
  See also BPFB 3; CA 108; 166; RGAL 4;
  RHW

**Ringmaster, The**
  See Mencken, H. L.

**Ringwood, Gwen(dolyn Margaret) Pharis**
  1910-1984 .............................. **CLC 48**
  See also CA 148; 112; DLB 88

**Rio, Michel** 1945(?)- ........................ **CLC 43**
  See also CA 201

**Rios, Alberto** 1952- ............................ **PC 57**
  See also AAYA 66; AMWS 4; CA 113;
  CANR 34, 79, 137; CP 6, 7; DLB 122;
  HW 2; MTFW 2005; PFS 11

**Rios, Alberto Alvaro**
  See Rios, Alberto

**Ritchie, Anne Thackeray**
  1837-1919 ............................ **TCLC 297**
  See also CA 180; DLB 18

**Ritson, Joseph** 1752-1803 ........... **NCLC 333**
  See also DLB 356

**Ritsos, Giannes**
  See Ritsos, Yannis

**Ritsos, Yannis** 1909-1990 ...... **CLC 6, 13, 31**
  See also CA 77-80; 133; CANR 39, 61; EW
  12; EWL 3; MTCW 1; RGWL 2, 3

**Ritter, Erika** 1948- .......................... **CLC 52**
  See also CA 318; CD 5, 6; CWD; DLB 362

**Rivera, Jose Eustasio** 1889-1928 ... **TCLC 35**
  See also CA 162; EWL 3; HW 1, 2; LAW

**Rivera, Tomás** 1935-1984 .............. **HLCS 2;**
  **SSC 160, 242**
  See also CA 49-52; CANR 32; DLB 82; HW
  1; LLW; RGAL 4; SSFS 15; TCWW 2;
  WLIT 1

**Rivers, Conrad Kent** 1933-1968 ....... **CLC 1**
  See also BW 1; CA 85-88; DLB 41

**Rivers, Elfrida**
  See Bradley, Marion Zimmer

**Riverside, John**
  See Heinlein, Robert A.

**Rizal, Jose** 1861-1896 ..................... **NCLC 27**
  See also DLB 348

**Rolaag, Ole Edvart**
  See Rolvaag, O.E.

**Rolvaag, O.E.**
  See Rolvaag, O.E.

**Rolvaag, O.E.** 1876-1931 ...... **TCLC 17, 207**
  See also AAYA 75; CA 117; 171; DLB 9,
  212; MAL 5; NFS 5; RGAL 4; TCWW 1, 2

**Roa Bastos, Augusto** 1917-2005 .... **CLC 45,**
  **316, 355; HLC 2; SSC 174**
  See also CA 131; 238; CWW 2; DAM
  MULT; DLB 113; EWL 3; HW 1; LAW;
  RGSF 2; WLIT 1

**Roa Bastos, Augusto Jose Antonio**
  See Roa Bastos, Augusto

**Robbe-Grillet, Alain** 1922-2008 ....... **CLC 1,**
  **2, 4, 6, 8, 10, 14, 43, 128, 287**
  See also BPFB 3; CA 9-12R; 269; CANR
  33, 65, 115; CWW 2; DLB 83; EW 13;
  EWL 3; GFL 1789 to the Present; IDFW 3,
  4; MTCW 1, 2; MTFW 2005; RGWL 2, 3;
  SSFS 15

**Robbins, Harold** 1916-1997 .............. **CLC 5**
  See also BPFB 3; CA 73-76; 162; CANR
  26, 54, 112, 156; DA3; DAM NOV;
  MTCW 1, 2

**Robbins, Thomas Eugene**
  See Robbins, Tom

**Robbins, Tom** 1936- ...... **CLC 9, 32, 64, 362**
  See also AAYA 32; AMWS 10; BEST 90:3;
  BPFB 3; CA 81-84; CANR 29, 59, 95,
  139; CN 3, 4, 5, 6, 7; CPW; CSW; DA3;
  DAM NOV, POP; DLBY 1980; MTCW 1,
  2; MTFW 2005

**Robbins, Trina** 1938- ..................... **CLC 21**
  See also AAYA 61; CA 128; CANR 152

**Robert de Boron** fl. 12th cent. ...... **CMLC 94**

**Roberts, Charles G(eorge) D(ouglas)**
  1860-1943 ................... **SSC 91; TCLC 8**
  See also CA 105; 188; CLR 33; CWRI 5;
  DLB 92; RGEL 2; RGSF 2; SATA 88;
  SATA-Brief 29

**Roberts, Elizabeth Madox**
  1881-1941 ....................... **TCLC 68, 349**
  See also CA 111; 166; CLR 100; CWRI 5;
  DLB 9, 54, 102; RGAL 4; RHW; SATA
  33; SATA-Brief 27; TCWW 2; WCH

**Roberts, Kate** 1891-1985 ................ **CLC 15**
  See also CA 107; 116; DLB 319

**Roberts, Keith (John Kingston)**
  1935-2000 .............................. **CLC 14**
  See also BRWS 10; CA 25-28R; CANR 46;
  DLB 261; SFW 4

**Roberts, Kenneth (Lewis)**
  1885-1957 ............................ **TCLC 23**
  See also CA 109; 199; DLB 9; MAL 5;
  RGAL 4; RHW

**Roberts, Michele** 1949- ........... **CLC 48, 178**
  See also BRWS 15; CA 115; CANR 58, 120,
  164, 200; CN 6, 7; DLB 231; FW

**Roberts, Michele Brigitte**
  See Roberts, Michele

**Robertson, Ellis**
  See Ellison, Harlan; Silverberg, Robert

**Robertson, Thomas William**
  1829-1871 .............................. **NCLC 35**
  See also DAM DRAM; DLB 344; RGEL 2

**Robertson, Tom**
  See Robertson, Thomas William

**Robeson, Kenneth**
  See Dent, Lester

**Robinson, Eden** 1968- ................... **CLC 301**
  See also CA 171

**Robinson, Edwin Arlington**
  1869-1935 ....... **PC 1, 35; TCLC 5, 101**
  See also AAYA 72; AMW; CA 104; 133;
  CDALB 1865-1917; DA; DAC; DAM
  MST, POET; DLB 54; EWL 3; EXPP;

MAL 5; MTCW 1, 2; MTFW 2005; PAB;
PFS 4, 35; RGAL 4; WP

**Robinson, Henry Crabb**
1775-1867 ...................... **NCLC 15, 239**
See also DLB 107

**Robinson, Jill** 1936- ......................... **CLC 10**
See also CA 102; CANR 120; INT CA-102

**Robinson, Kim Stanley**
1952- ........................... **CLC 34, 248, 417**
See also AAYA 26; CA 126; CANR 113,
139, 173; CN 6, 7; MTFW 2005; SATA
109; SCFW 2; SFW 4

**Robinson, Lloyd**
See Silverberg, Robert

**Robinson, Marilynne**
1943- .......................... **CLC 25, 180, 276**
See also AAYA 69; AMWS 21; CA 116;
CANR 80, 140, 192, 240; CN 4, 5, 6, 7;
DLB 206, 350; MTFW 2005; NFS 24, 39

**Robinson, Mary**
1756/7-1800 ................... **NCLC 142, 329**
See also BRWS 13; DLB 158; FW

**Robinson, Smokey** 1940- ................. **CLC 21**
See also CA 116

**Robinson, William, Jr.**
See Robinson, Smokey

**Robison, Christopher**
See Burroughs, Augusten

**Robison, Mary** 1949- ................. **CLC 42, 98**
See also CA 113; 116; CANR 87, 206; CN
4, 5, 6, 7; DLB 130; INT CA-116; RGSF
2; SSFS 33

**Roche, Regina Maria** 1764-1845 ... **NCLC 308**

**Rochester**
See Wilmot, John

**Rod, Edouard** 1857-1910 ............... **TCLC 52**

**Rodo, Jose Enrique** 1871(?)-1917 ... **HLCS 2**
See also CA 178; EWL 3; HW 2; LAW

**Roddenberry, Eugene Wesley**
See Roddenberry, Gene

**Roddenberry, Gene** 1921-1991 ....... **CLC 17**
See also AAYA 5; CA 110; 135; CANR 37;
SATA 45; SATA-Obit 69

**Rodgers, Mary** 1931- ..................... **CLC 12**
See also BYA 5; CA 49-52; CANR 8, 55, 90;
CLR 20; CWRI 5; DFS 28; INT CANR-8;
JRDA; MAICYA 1, 2; SATA 8, 130

**Rodgers, W(illiam) R(obert)**
1909-1969 ..................................... **CLC 7**
See also CA 85-88; DLB 20; RGEL 2

**Rodman, Eric**
See Silverberg, Robert

**Rodman, Howard** 1920(?)-1985 ...... **CLC 65**
See also CA 118

**Rodman, Maia**
See Wojciechowska, Maia (Teresa)

**Rodolph, Utto**
See Ouologuem, Yambo

**Rodoreda, Mercè** 1908-1983 ........... **SSC 221**
See also CA 243; DLB 322; EWL 3; RGSF 2

**Rodriguez, Claudio** 1934-1999 ........ **CLC 10**
See also CA 188; DLB 134

**Rodriguez, Richard** 1944- .... **CLC 155, 321;**
**HLC 2**
See also AMWS 14; CA 110; CANR 66,
116; DAM MULT; DLB 82, 256; HW 1, 2;
LAIT 5; LLW; MTFW 2005; NCFS 3;
WLIT 1

**Roethke, Theodore** 1908-1963 ..... **CLC 1, 3,**
**8, 11, 19, 46, 101; PC 15, 137, 205**
See also AMW; CA 81-84; CABS 2; CDALB
1941-1968; DA3; DAM POET; DLB 5,
206; EWL 3; EXPP; MAL 5; MTCW 1,
2; PAB; PFS 3, 34, 40; RGAL 4; WP

**Roethke, Theodore Huebner**
See Roethke, Theodore

**Rogers, Carl R(ansom)**
1902-1987 ............................. **TCLC 125**
See also CA 1-4R; 121; CANR 1, 18;
MTCW 1

**Rogers, Samuel** 1763-1855 ............ **NCLC 69**
See also DLB 93; RGEL 2

**Rogers, Thomas** 1927-2007 ............ **CLC 57**
See also CA 89-92; 259; CANR 163; INT
CA-89-92

**Rogers, Thomas Hunton**
See Rogers, Thomas

**Rogers, Will(iam Penn Adair)**
1879-1935 ............. **NNAL; TCLC 8, 71**
See also CA 105; 144; DA3; DAM MULT;
DLB 11; MTCW 2

**Rogin, Gilbert** 1929- ..................... **CLC 18**
See also CA 65-68; CANR 15

**Rohan, Koda**
See Koda Shigeyuki

**Rohlfs, Anna Katharine Green**
See Green, Anna Katharine

**Rohmer, Eric** 1920-2010 ................. **CLC 16**
See also CA 110

**Rohmer, Sax**
See Ward, Arthur Henry Sarsfield

**Roiphe, Anne** 1935- ..................... **CLC 3, 9**
See also CA 89-92; CANR 45, 73, 138, 170,
230; DLBY 1980; INT CA-89-92

**Roiphe, Anne Richardson**
See Roiphe, Anne

**Rojas, Fernando de** 1475-1541 ...... **HLCS 1,**
**2; LC 23, 169**
See also DLB 286; RGWL 2, 3

**Rojas, Gonzalo** 1917-2011 ............... **HLCS 2**
See also CA 178; HW 2; LAWS 1

**Rojas Zorrilla, Francisco de**
1607-1648 .............................. **LC 204**

**Roland (de la Platiere), Marie-Jeanne**
1754-1793 ............................. **LC 98, 258**
See also DLB 314

**Rolfe, Frederick (William Serafino Austin**
**Lewis Mary)** 1860-1913 ........ **TCLC 12**
See also CA 107; 210; DLB 34, 156; GLL 1;
RGEL 2

**Rolland, Romain** 1866-1944 ......... **TCLC 23**
See also CA 118; 197; DLB 65, 284,
332; EWL 3; GFL 1789 to the Present;
RGWL 2, 3

**Rolle, Richard**
c. 1300-c. 1349 ............. **CMLC 21, 165**
See also DLB 146; LMFS 1; RGEL 2

**Rolvaag, O.E.**
See Rolvaag, O.E.

**Romain Arnaud, Saint**
See Aragon, Louis

**Romains, Jules** 1885-1972 ................. **CLC 7**
See also CA 85-88; CANR 34; DLB 65, 321;
EWL 3; GFL 1789 to the Present; MTCW 1

**Romero, Jose Ruben** 1890-1952 ... **TCLC 14**
See also CA 114; 131; EWL 3; HW 1; LAW

**Ronsard, Pierre de** 1524-1585 ..... **LC 6, 54;**
**PC 11, 105**
See also DLB 327; EW 2; GFL Beginnings
to 1789; RGWL 2, 3; TWA

**Rooke, Leon** 1934- ..................... **CLC 25, 34**
See also CA 25-28R; CANR 23, 53; CCA 1;
CPW; DAM POP

**Rooney, Sally** 1991- ..................... **CLC 439**

**Roosevelt, Franklin Delano**
1882-1945 ............................. **TCLC 93**
See also CA 116; 173; LAIT 3

**Roosevelt, Theodore** 1858-1919 .... **TCLC 69**
See also CA 115; 170; DLB 47, 186, 275

**Roper, Margaret** c. 1505-1544 ......... **LC 147**

**Roper, William** 1498-1578 ................. **LC 10**

**Roquelaure, A. N.**
See Rice, Anne

**Rorty, Richard** 1931-2007 ............. **CLC 441**
See also CA 21-24R; 261; CANR 9, 135;
DLB 246, 279

**Rosa, Joao Guimaraes**
See Guimaraes Rosa, Joao

**Rose, Wendy** 1948- ............ **CLC 85; NNAL;**
**PC 13**
See also CA 53-56; CANR 5, 51; CWP;
DAM MULT; DLB 175; PFS 13; RGAL 4;
SATA 12

**Rosen, R.D.** 1949- ......................... **CLC 39**
See also CA 77-80; CANR 62, 120, 175;
CMW 4; INT CANR-30

**Rosen, Richard**
See Rosen, R.D.

**Rosen, Richard Dean**
See Rosen, R.D.

**Rosenberg, Isaac** 1890-1918 ........... **PC 146;**
**TCLC 12; 314**
See also BRW 6; CA 107; 188; DLB 20,
216; EWL 3; PAB; RGEL 2

**Rosenblatt, Joe**
See Rosenblatt, Joseph

**Rosenblatt, Joseph** 1933- ................. **CLC 15**
See also CA 89-92; CP 3, 4, 5, 6, 7; INT
CA-89-92

**Rosenfeld, Samuel**
See Tzara, Tristan

**Rosenstock, Sami**
See Tzara, Tristan

**Rosenstock, Samuel**
See Tzara, Tristan

**Rosenthal, M(acha) L(ouis)**
1917-1996 ................................. **CLC 28**
See also CA 1-4R; 152; CAAS 6; CANR 4,
51; CP 1, 2, 3, 4, 5, 6; DLB 5; SATA 59

**Ross, Barnaby**
See Dannay, Frederic; Lee, Manfred B.

**Ross, Bernard L.**
See Follett, Ken

**Ross, J. H.**
See Lawrence, T. E.

**Ross, John Hume**
See Lawrence, T. E.

**Ross, Martin** 1862-1915
See Martin, Violet Florence
See also DLB 135; GLL 2; RGEL 2; RGSF 2

**Ross, (James) Sinclair** 1908-1996 ... **CLC 13;**
**SSC 24**
See also CA 73-76; CANR 81; CN 1, 2, 3, 4,
5, 6; DAC; DAM MST; DLB 88; RGEL 2;
RGSF 2; TCWW 1, 2

**Rossetti, Christina** 1830-1894 ........ **NCLC 2,**
**50, 66, 186, 333; PC 7, 119; WLC 5**
See also AAYA 51; BRW 5; BRWR 3; BYA
4; CLR 115; DA; DA3; DAB; DAC; DAM
MST, POET; DLB 35, 163, 240; EXPP; FL
1:3; LATS 1:1; MAICYA 1, 2; PFS 10, 14,
27, 34; RGEL 2; SATA 20; TEA; WCH

**Rossetti, Christina Georgina**
See Rossetti, Christina

**Rossetti, Dante Gabriel**
1828-1882 ... **NCLC 4, 77, 325; PC 44;**
**WLC 5**
See also AAYA 51; BRW 5; CDBLB 1832-
1890; DA; DAB; DAC; DAM MST, POET;
DLB 35; EXPP; RGEL 2; TEA

**Rossi, Cristina Peri**
See Peri Rossi, Cristina

**Rossi, Jean-Baptiste** 1931-2003 .... **CLC 90, 406**
See also CA 201; 215; CMW 4; NFS 18

**Rossner, Judith** 1935-2005 ....... **CLC 6, 9, 29**
See also AITN 2; BEST 90:3; BPFB 3; CA
17-20R; 242; CANR 18, 51, 73; CN 4, 5,
6, 7; DLB 6; INT CANR-18; MAL 5;
MTCW 1, 2; MTFW 2005

**Rossner, Judith Perelman**
See Rossner, Judith

**Rostand, Edmond** 1868-1918 ........... **DC 10;**
**TCLC 6, 37**
See also CA 104; 126; DA; DA3; DAB;
DAC; DAM DRAM, MST; DFS 1; DLB
192; LAIT 1; MTCW 1; RGWL 2, 3; TWA

**Rostand, Edmond Eugene Alexis**
See Rostand, Edmond

See also BW 2, 3; CA 33-36R; CANR 24, 49, 74, 115; CLR 18; CP 2, 3, 4, 5, 6, 7; CSW; CWP; DA3; DAM MULT; DLB 41; DLBD 8; EWL 3; MAICYA 1, 2; MAL 5; MTCW 1, 2; MTFW 2005; PFS 26; SATA 22, 136; WP

**Sancho, Ignatius** 1729-1780 .............. **LC 84**

**Sand, George** 1804-1876 **DC 29; NCLC 2, 42, 57, 174, 234; WLC 5**
See also DA; DA3; DAB; DAC; DAM MST, NOV; DLB 119, 192; EW 6; FL 1:3; FW; GFL 1789 to the Present; RGWL 2, 3; TWA

**Sandburg, Carl** 1878-1967 .......... **CLC 1, 4, 10, 15, 35; PC 2, 41; WLC 5**
See also AAYA 24; AMW; BYA 1, 3; CA 5-8R; 25-28R; CANR 35; CDALB 1865-1917; CLR 67; DA; DA3; DAB; DAC; DAM MST, POET; DLB 17, 54, 284; EWL 3; EXPP; LAIT 2; MAICYA 1, 2; MAL 5; MTCW 1, 2; MTFW 2005; PAB; PFS 3, 6, 12, 33, 36; RGAL 4; SATA 8; TUS; WCH; WP; WYA

**Sandburg, Carl August**
See Sandburg, Carl

**Sandburg, Charles**
See Sandburg, Carl

**Sandburg, Charles A.**
See Sandburg, Carl

**Sanders, Ed** 1939- ............................ **CLC 53**
See also BG 1:3; CA 13-16R; CAAS 21; CANR 13, 44, 78; CP 1, 2, 3, 4, 5, 6, 7; DAM POET; DLB 16, 244

**Sanders, Edward**
See Sanders, Ed

**Sanders, James Edward**
See Sanders, Ed

**Sanders, Lawrence** 1920-1998 ........ **CLC 41**
See also BEST 89:4; BPFB 3; CA 81-84; 165; CANR 33, 62; CMW 4; CPW; DA3; DAM POP; MTCW 1

**Sanders, Noah**
See Blount, Roy, Jr.

**Sanders, Winston P.**
See Anderson, Poul

**Sandoz, Mari(e Susette)** 1900-1966 .... **CLC 28**
See also CA 1-4R; 25-28R; CANR 17, 64; DLB 9, 212; LAIT 2; MTCW 1, 2; SATA 5; TCWW 1, 2

**Sandys, George** 1578-1644 ................. **LC 80**
See also DLB 24, 121

**Saner, Reg(inald Anthony)** 1931- ..... **CLC 9**
See also CA 65-68; CP 3, 4, 5, 6, 7

**Sankara** 788-820 ................... **CMLC 32, 149**

**Sannazaro, Jacopo** 1456(?)-1530 ... **LC 8, 254**
See also RGWL 2, 3; WLIT 7

**Sansom, William** 1912-1976 ......... **CLC 2, 6; SSC 21**
See also CA 5-8R; 65-68; CANR 42; CN 1, 2; DAM NOV; DLB 139; EWL 3; MTCW 1; RGEL 2; RGSF 2

**Santayana, George** 1863-1952 ...... **TCLC 40**
See also AMW; CA 115; 194; DLB 54, 71, 246, 270; DLBD 13; EWL 3; MAL 5; RGAL 4; TUS

**Santiago, Danny**
See James, Daniel (Lewis)

**Santiago, Esmeralda** 1948- ........... **CLC 363**
See also AAYA 43; BYA 12; CA 179; CANR 130, 235; LLW; SATA 129

**Santillana, Inigo Lopez de Mendoza, Marques de** 1398-1458 ............. **LC 111**
See also DLB 286

**Santmyer, Helen Hooven** 1895-1986 ............. **CLC 33; TCLC 133**
See also CA 1-4R; 118; CANR 15, 33; DLBY 1984; MTCW 1; RHW

**Santoka, Taneda** 1882-1940 .......... **TCLC 72**

**Santos, Bienvenido N(uqui)** 1911-1996 ...................... **AAL; CLC 22; TCLC 156**
See also CA 101; 151; CANR 19, 46; CP 1; DAM MULT; DLB 312, 348; EWL; RGAL 4; SSFS 19

**Santos, Miguel**
See Mihura, Miguel

**Sapir, Edward** 1884-1939 ........... **TCLC 108**
See also CA 211; DLB 92

**Sapper**
See McNeile, Herman Cyril

**Sapphire** 1950- ................................ **CLC 99**
See also CA 262

**Sapphire, Brenda**
See Sapphire

**Sappho** c. 630 bce-c. 570 bce ........ **CMLC 3, 67, 160; PC 5, 117**
See also CDWLB 1; DA3; DAM POET; DLB 176; FL 1:1; PFS 20, 31, 38, 44; RGWL 2, 3; WLIT 8; WP

**Sappho**
See Robinson, Mary

**Saramago, Jose** 1922-2010 ... **CLC 119, 275; HLCS 1**
See also CA 153; CANR 96, 164, 210, 242; CWW 2; DLB 287, 332; EWL 3; LATS 1:2; NFS 27; SSFS 23

**Sarduy, Severo** 1937-1993 ......... **CLC 6, 97; HLCS 2; TCLC 167**
See also CA 89-92; 142; CANR 58, 81; CWW 2; DLB 113; EWL 3; HW 1, 2; LAW

**Sargeson, Frank** 1903-1982 ............ **CLC 31; SSC 99**
See also CA 25-28R; 106; CANR 38, 79; CN 1, 2, 3; EWL 3; GLL 2; RGEL 2; RGSF 2; SSFS 20

**Sarmiento, Domingo Faustino** 1811-1888 ............ **HLCS 2; NCLC 123**
See also LAW; WLIT 1

**Sarmiento, Felix Ruben Garcia**
See Dario, Ruben

**Saro-Wiwa, Ken(ule Beeson)** 1941-1995 ........... **CLC 114; TCLC 200**
See also BW 2; CA 142; 150; CANR 60; DLB 157, 360

**Saroyan, William** 1908-1981 ........ **CLC 1, 8, 10, 29, 34, 56; DC 28; SSC 21; TCLC 137; WLC 5**
See also AAYA 66; CA 5-8R; 103; CAD; CANR 30; CDALBS; CN 1, 2; DA; DA3; DAB; DAC; DAM DRAM, MST, NOV; DFS 17; DLB 7, 9, 86; DLBY 1981; EWL 3; LAIT 4; MAL 5; MTCW 1, 2; MTFW 2005; NFS 39; RGAL 4; RGSF 2; SATA 23; SATA-Obit 24; SSFS 14; TUS

**Sarraute, Nathalie** 1900-1999 ...... **CLC 1, 2, 4, 8, 10, 31, 80; TCLC 145**
See also BPFB 3; CA 9-12R; 187; CANR 23, 66, 134; CWW 2; DLB 83, 321; EW 12; EWL 3; GFL 1789 to the Present; MTCW 1, 2; MTFW 2005; RGWL 2, 3

**Sarton, May** 1912-1995 ....... **CLC 4, 14, 49, 91; PC 39; TCLC 120**
See also AMWS 8; CA 1-4R; 149; CANR 1, 34, 55, 116; CN 1, 2, 3, 4, 5, 6; CP 1, 2, 3, 4, 5, 6; DAM POET; DLB 48; DLBY 1981; EWL 3; FW; INT CANR-34; MAL 5; MTCW 1, 2; MTFW 2005; RGAL 4; SATA 36; SATA-Obit 86; TUS

**Sartre, Jean-Paul** 1905-1980 ... **CLC 1, 4, 7, 9, 13, 18, 24, 44, 50, 52; DC 3; SSC 32; TCLC 354; WLC 5**
See also AAYA 62; CA 9-12R; 97-100; CANR 21; DA; DA3; DAB; DAC; DAM DRAM, MST, NOV; DFS 5, 26; DLB 72, 296, 321, 332; EW 12; EWL 3; GFL 1789

to the Present; LMFS 2; MTCW 1, 2; MTFW 2005; NFS 21; RGHL; RGSF 2; RGWL 2, 3; SSFS 9; TWA

**Sassoon, Siegfried** 1886-1967 ......... **CLC 36, 130; PC 12**
See also BRW 6; CA 104; 25-28R; CANR 36; DAB; DAM MST, NOV, POET; DLB 20, 191; DLBD 18; EWL 3; MTCW 1, 2; MTFW 2005; PAB; PFS 28; RGEL 2; TEA

**Sassoon, Siegfried Lorraine**
See Sassoon, Siegfried

**Satrapi, Marjane** 1969- ................. **CLC 332**
See also AAYA 55; CA 246

**Satterfield, Charles**
See Pohl, Frederik

**Satyremont**
See Peret, Benjamin

**Saul, John** 1942- ............................. **CLC 46**
See also AAYA 10, 62; BEST 90:4; CA 81-84; CANR 16, 40, 81, 176, 221; CPW; DAM NOV, POP; HGG; SATA 98

**Saul, John W.**
See Saul, John

**Saul, John Woodruff III**
See Saul, John

**Saunders, Abel**
See Pound, Ezra

**Saunders, Caleb**
See Heinlein, Robert A.

**Saunders, George** 1958- ........ **CLC 325, 439**
See also CA 164; CANR 98, 157, 197, 255; DLB 335

**Saunders, George W.**
See Saunders, George

**Saunders, Richard**
See Franklin, Benjamin

**Saura (Atares), Carlos** 1932-1998 ................................. **CLC 20**
See also CA 114; 131; CANR 79; HW 1

**Sauser, Frederic Louis**
See Sauser-Hall, Frederic

**Sauser-Hall, Frederic** 1887-1961 .......... **CLC 18, 106; PC 179**
See also CA 102; 93-96; CANR 36, 62; DLB 258; EWL 3; GFL 1789 to the Present; MTCW 1; WP

**Saussure, Ferdinand de** 1857-1913 ............................... **TCLC 49**
See also DLB 242

**Savage, Catharine**
See Brosman, Catharine Savage

**Savage, Richard** 1697(?)-1743 ........... **LC 96**
See also DLB 95; RGEL 2

**Savage, Thomas** 1915-2003 ............. **CLC 40**
See also CA 126; 132; 218; CAAS 15; CN 6, 7; INT CA-132; SATA-Obit 147; TCWW 2

**Savan, Glenn** 1953-2003 ................. **CLC 50**
See also CA 225

**Savonarola, Girolamo** 1452-1498 ............................. **LC 152**
See also LMFS 1

**Sax, Robert**
See Johnson, Robert

**Saxo Grammaticus** c. 1150-c. 1222 ............. **CMLC 58, 141**

**Saxton, Robert**
See Johnson, Robert

**Sayers, Dorothy L(eigh)** 1893-1957 ... **SSC 71; TCLC 2, 15, 237**
See also BPFB 3; BRWS 3; CA 104; 119; CANR 60; CDBLB 1914-1945; CMW 4; DAM POP; DLB 10, 36, 77, 100; MSW; MTCW 1, 2; MTFW 2005; RGEL 2; SSFS 12; TEA

**Sayers, Valerie** 1952- ................. **CLC 50, 122**
See also CA 134; CANR 61; CSW

**Sayles, John** 1950- ...................... **CLC 7, 10, 14, 198**
See also CA 57-60; CANR 41, 84; DLB 44

Servius c. 370-c. 431 ................... **CMLC 120**

**Seth, Vikram** 1952- ......... **CLC 43, 90, 277; PC 118**
See also BRWS 10; CA 121; 127; CANR 50, 74, 131; CN 6, 7; CP 5, 6, 7; DA3; DAM MULT; DLB 120, 271, 282, 323; EWL 3; INT CA-127; MTCW 2; MTFW 2005; WWE 1

**Setien, Miguel Delibes**
See Delibes Setien, Miguel

**Seton, Cynthia Propper** 1926-1982 .. **CLC 27**
See also CA 5-8R; 108; CANR 7

**Seton, Ernest (Evan) Thompson**
1860-1946 ............................... **TCLC 31**
See also ANW; BYA 3; CA 109; 204; CLR 59; DLB 92; DLBD 13; JRDA; SATA 18

**Seton-Thompson, Ernest**
See Seton, Ernest (Evan) Thompson

**Settle, Mary Lee** 1918-2005 ........... **CLC 19, 61, 273**
See also BPFB 3; CA 89-92; 243; CAAS 1; CANR 44, 87, 126, 182; CN 6, 7; CSW; DLB 6; INT CA-89-92

**Seuphor, Michel**
See Arp, Jean

**Seventeenth Earl of Oxford**
See de Vere, Edward

**Sewall, Samuel** 1652-1730 ................. **LC 38**
See also DLB 24; RGAL 4

**Seward, Anna** 1742-1809 ............. **NCLC 265**
See also BRWS 17; RGEL 2

**Sexton, Anne** 1928-1974 ........... **CLC 2, 4, 6, 8, 10, 15, 53, 123; PC 2, 79; TCLC 252; WLC 5**
See also AMWS 2; CA 1-4R; 53-56; CABS 2; CANR 3, 36; CDALB 1941-1968; CP 1, 2; DA; DA3; DAB; DAC; DAM MST, POET; DLB 5, 169; EWL 3; EXPP; FL 1:6; FW; MAL 5; MBL; MTCW 1, 2; MTFW 2005; PAB; PFS 4, 14, 30, 36, 40; RGAL 4; RGHL; SATA 10; TUS

**Sexton, Anne Harvey**
See Sexton, Anne

**Sexton, Margaret Wilkerson**
1983- ....................................... **CLC 439**

**Shaara, Jeff** 1952- ........................ **CLC 119**
See also AAYA 70; CA 163; CANR 109, 172; CN 7; MTFW 2005

**Shaara, Michael** 1929-1988 ............. **CLC 15**
See also AAYA 71; AITN 1; BPFB 3; CA 102; 125; CANR 52, 85; DAM POP; DLBY 1983; MTFW 2005; NFS 26

**Shackleton, C.C.**
See Aldiss, Brian W.

**Shacochis, Bob**
See Shacochis, Robert G.

**Shacochis, Robert G.** 1951- ............ **CLC 39**
See also CA 119; 124; CANR 100; INT CA-124

**Shadwell, Thomas** 1641(?)-1692 ...... **LC 114**
See also DLB 80; IDTP; RGEL 2

**Shaffer, Anthony** 1926-2001 ............ **CLC 19**
See also CA 110; 116; 200; CBD; CD 5, 6; DAM DRAM; DFS 13; DLB 13

**Shaffer, Anthony Joshua**
See Shaffer, Anthony

**Shaffer, Peter** 1926- ........ **CLC 5, 14, 18, 37, 60, 291; DC 7**
See also BRWS 1; CA 25-28R; CANR 25, 47, 74, 118; CBD; CD 5, 6; CDBLB 1960 to Present; DA3; DAB; DAM DRAM, MST; DFS 5, 13; DLB 13, 233; EWL 3; MTCW 1, 2; MTFW 2005; RGEL 2; TEA

**Shakespeare, William** 1564-1616 ....... **PC 84, 89, 98, 101, 128; WLC 5**
See also AAYA 35; BRW 1; BRWR 3; CDBLB Before 1660; DA; DA3; DAB; DAC; DAM DRAM, MST, POET; DFS 20, 21; DLB 62, 172, 263; EXPP; LAIT 1; LATS 1:1; LMFS 1; PAB; PFS 1, 2, 3, 4,

5, 8, 9, 35; RGEL 2; TEA; WLIT 3; WP; WS; WYA

**Shakey, Bernard**
See Young, Neil

**Shalamov, Varlam (Tikhonovich)**
1907-1982 ................. **CLC 18; SSC 205**
See also CA 129; 105; DLB 302; RGSF 2

**Shalott**
See Palmer, Nettie

**Shamloo, Ahmad**
See Shamlu, Ahmad

**Shamlou, Ahmad**
See Shamlu, Ahmad

**Shamlu, Ahmad** 1925-2000 ............. **CLC 10**
See also CA 216; CWW 2

**Shammas, Anton** 1951- ................... **CLC 55**
See also CA 199; DLB 346

**Shamsie, Kamila** 1973- ................... **CLC 432**
See also CA 208; CANR 213, 293

**Shandling, Arline**
See Berriault, Gina

**Shange, Ntozake** 1948- ......... **BLC 1:3, 2:3; CLC 8, 25, 38, 74, 126; DC 3**
See also AAYA 9, 66; AFAW 1, 2; BW 2; CA 85-88; CABS 3; CAD; CANR 27, 48, 74, 131, 208; CD 5, 6; CP 5, 6, 7; CWD; CWP; DA3; DAM DRAM, MULT; DFS 2, 11; DLB 38, 249; FW; LAIT 4, 5; MAL 5; MTCW 1, 2; MTFW 2005; NFS 11; RGAL 4; SATA 157; YAW

**Shanley, John Patrick** 1950- ........... **CLC 75**
See also AAYA 74; AMWS 14; CA 128; 133; CAD; CANR 83, 154; CD 5, 6; DFS 23, 28

**Shapcott, Thomas W(illiam)** 1935- .... **CLC 38**
See also CA 69-72; CANR 49, 83, 103; CP 1, 2, 3, 4, 5, 6, 7; DLB 289

**Shapiro, Jane** 1942- ........................ **CLC 76**
See also CA 196

**Shapiro, Karl** 1913-2000 ....... **CLC 4, 8, 15, 53; PC 25**
See also AMWS 2; CA 1-4R; 188; CAAS 6; CANR 1, 36, 66; CP 1, 2, 3, 4, 5, 6; DLB 48; EWL 3; EXPP; MAL 5; MTCW 1, 2; MTFW 2005; PFS 3; RGAL 4

**Sharp, William** 1855-1905 ............. **TCLC 39**
See also CA 160; DLB 156; RGEL 2; SUFW

**Sharpe, Thomas Ridley** 1928- ........ **CLC 36**
See also CA 114; 122; CANR 85; CN 4, 5, 6, 7; DLB 14, 231; INT CA-122

**Sharpe, Tom**
See Sharpe, Thomas Ridley

**Shatrov, Mikhail** ............................ **CLC 59**

**Shaw, Bernard**
See Shaw, George Bernard

**Shaw, G. Bernard**
See Shaw, George Bernard

**Shaw, George Bernard** 1856-1950 ... **DC 23; TCLC 3, 9, 21, 45, 205, 293; WLC 5**
See also AAYA 61; BRW 6; BRWC 1; BRWR 2; CA 104; 128; CDBLB 1914-1945; DA; DA3; DAB; DAC; DAM DRAM, MST; DFS 1, 3, 6, 11, 19, 22, 30; DLB 10, 57, 190, 332; EWL 3; LAIT 3; LATS 1:1; MTCW 1, 2; MTFW 2005; RGEL 2; TEA; WLIT 4

**Shaw, Henry Wheeler**
1818-1885 ............................... **NCLC 15**
See also DLB 11; RGAL 4

**Shaw, Irwin** 1913-1984 ......... **CLC 7, 23, 34**
See also AITN 1; BPFB 3; CA 13-16R; 112; CANR 21; CDALB 1941-1968; CN 1, 2, 3; CPW; DAM DRAM, POP; DLB 6, 102; DLBY 1984; MAL 5; MTCW 1, 21; MTFW 2005

**Shaw, Robert (Archibald)** 1927-1978 ... **CLC 5**
See also AITN 1; CA 1-4R; 81-84; CANR 4; CN 1, 2; DLB 13, 14

**Shaw, T. E.**
See Lawrence, T. E.

**Shawn, Wallace** 1943- ..................... **CLC 41**
See also CA 112; CAD; CANR 215; CD 5, 6; DLB 266

**Shaykh, Hanan al-** 1945- ............. **CLC 218**
See also CA 135; CANR 111, 220; CWW 2; DLB 346; EWL 3; WLIT 6

**Shchedrin, N.**
See Saltykov, Mikhail Evgrafovich

**Shea, Lisa** 1953- ............................... **CLC 86**
See also CA 147

**Sheed, Wilfrid** 1930-2011 ............. **CLC 2, 4, 10, 53**
See also CA 65-68; CANR 30, 66, 181; CN 1, 2, 3, 4, 5, 6, 7; DLB 6; MAL 5; MTCW 1, 2; MTFW 2005

**Sheed, Wilfrid John Joseph**
See Sheed, Wilfrid

**Sheehy, Gail** 1937- ......................... **CLC 171**
See also CA 49-52; CANR 1, 33, 55, 92; CPW; MTCW 1

**Sheldon, Alice Hastings Bradley**
1915(?)-1987 ........................ **CLC 48, 50**
See also CA 108; 122; CANR 34; DLB 8; INT CA-108; MTCW 1; SCFW 1, 2; SFW 4

**Sheldon, John**
See Bloch, Robert (Albert)

**Sheldon, Raccoona**
See Sheldon, Alice Hastings Bradley

**Shelley, Mary**
See Shelley, Mary Wollstonecraft

**Shelley, Mary Wollstonecraft**
1797-1851 ...... **NCLC 14, 59, 103, 170; SSC 92; WLC 5**
See also AAYA 20; BPFB 3; BRW 3; BRWC 2; BRWR 3; BRWS 3; BYA 5; CDBLB 1789-1832; CLR 133; DA; DA3; DAB; DAC; DAM MST, NOV; DLB 110, 116, 159, 178; EXPN; FL 1:3; GL 3; HGG; LAIT 1; LMFS 1, 2; NFS 1, 37; RGEL 2; SATA 29; SCFW 1, 2; SFW 4; TEA; WLIT 3

**Shelley, Percy Bysshe**
1792-1822 ...... **NCLC 18, 93, 143, 175; PC 14, 67, 158, 161; WLC 5**
See also AAYA 61; BRW 4; BRWR 1; CDBLB 1789-1832; DA; DA3; DAB; DAC; DAM MST, POET; DLB 96, 110, 158; EXPP; LMFS 1; PAB; PFS 2, 27, 32, 36; RGEL 2; TEA; WLIT 3; WP

**Shen Cong Wen**
See Shen Congwen

**Shen Congwen** 1902-1988 .......... **TCLC 301**
See also CA 125; 303; DLB 328; RGSF 2

**Shen Ts'ung-Wen**
See Shen Congwen

**Shenstone, William** 1714-1763 ......... **LC 262**
See also DLB 95; RGEL 2

**Shepard, James R.**
See Shepard, Jim

**Shepard, Jim** 1956- .......................... **CLC 36**
See also AAYA 73; CA 137; CANR 59, 104, 160, 199, 231; SATA 90, 164

**Shepard, Lucius** 1947- ..................... **CLC 34**
See also CA 128; 141; CANR 81, 124, 178; HGG; SCFW 2; SFW 4; SUFW 2

**Shepard, Sam** 1943-2017 ....... **CLC 4, 6, 17, 34, 41, 44, 169, 443; DC 5, 55**
See also AAYA 1, 58; AMWS 3; CA 69-72; CABS 3; CAD; CANR 22, 120, 140, 223; CD 5, 6; CMTFW; DA3; DAM DRAM; DFS 3, 6, 7, 14; DLB 7, 212, 341; EWL 3; IDFW 3, 4; MAL 5; MTCW 1, 2; MTFW 2005; RGAL 4

**Shepherd, Jean (Parker)**
1921-1999 ............................... **TCLC 177**
See also AAYA 69; AITN 2; CA 77-80; 187

**Shepherd, Michael**
See Ludlum, Robert

**Sherburne, Zoa (Lillian Morin)**
1912-1995 ................................. **CLC 30**

See also AAYA 13; CA 1-4R; 176; CANR 3, 37; MAICYA 1, 2; SAAS 18; SATA 3; YAW

**Sheridan, Frances** 1724-1766 .............. **LC 7**
See also DLB 39, 84

**Sheridan, Richard Brinsley**
1751-1816 ..... **DC 1; NCLC 5, 91, 323; WLC 5**
See also BRW 3; CDBLB 1660-1789; DA; DAB; DAC; DAM DRAM, MST; DFS 15; DLB 89; WLIT 3

**Sherman, Jonathan Marc** 1968- ..... **CLC 55**
See also CA 230

**Sherman, Martin** 1941(?)- .............. **CLC 19**
See also CA 116; 123; CAD; CANR 86; CD 5, 6; DFS 20; DLB 228; GLL 1; IDTP; RGHL

**Sherwin, Judith Johnson**
See Johnson, Judith

**Sherwood, Frances** 1940- ................ **CLC 81**
See also CA 146, 220; CAAE 220; CANR 158

**Sherwood, Mary Martha**
1775-1851 .............................. **NCLC 301**
See also DLB 163

**Sherwood, Robert E(mmet)**
1896-1955 ................... **DC 36; TCLC 3**
See also CA 104; 153; CANR 86; DAM DRAM; DFS 11, 15, 17; DLB 7, 26, 249; IDFW 3, 4; MAL 5; RGAL 4

**Shestov, Lev** 1866-1938 .................. **TCLC 56**

**Shevchenko, Taras** 1814-1861 ........... **NCLC 54, 281**

**Shiel, M. P.** 1865-1947 ..................... **TCLC 8**
See also CA 106; 160; DLB 153; HGG; MTCW 2; MTFW 2005; SCFW 1, 2; SFW 4; SUFW

**Shiel, Matthew Phipps**
See Shiel, M. P.

**Shields, Carol** 1935-2003 ........ **CLC 91, 113, 193, 298; SSC 126**
See also AMWS 7; CA 81-84; 218; CANR 51, 74, 98, 133; CCA 1; CN 6, 7; CPW; DA3; DAC; DLB 334, 350; MTCW 2; MTFW 2005; NFS 23

**Shields, David** 1956- ......................... **CLC 97**
See also CA 124; CANR 48, 99, 112, 157

**Shields, David Jonathan**
See Shields, David

**Shiga, Naoya** 1883-1971 ................. **CLC 33; SSC 23; TCLC 172**
See also CA 101; 33-36R; DLB 180; EWL 3; MJW; RGWL 3

**Shiga Naoya**
See Shiga, Naoya

**Shih Shu-tuan**
See Li Ang

**Shilts, Randy** 1951-1994 ................. **CLC 85**
See also AAYA 19; CA 115; 127; 144; CANR 45; DA3; GLL 1; INT CA-127; MTCW 2; MTFW 2005

**Shimazaki, Haruki** 1872-1943 ........ **TCLC 5**
See also CA 105; 134; CANR 84; DLB 180; EWL 3; MJW; RGWL 3

**Shimazaki Toson**
See Shimazaki, Haruki

**Shi Mo**
See Bei Dao

**Shirley, James** 1596-1666 ..... **DC 25; LC 96**
See also DLB 58; RGEL 2

**Shklovsky, Viktor** 1893-1984 ..... **TCLC 295**
See also CA 114, 144

**Sholokhov, Mikhail** 1905-1984 .... **CLC 7, 15**
See also CA 101; 112; DLB 272, 332; EWL 3; MTCW 1, 2; MTFW 2005; RGWL 2, 3; SATA-Obit 36

**Sholokhov, Mikhail Aleksandrovich**
See Sholokhov, Mikhail

**Shone, Patric**
See Hanley, James

**Showalter, Elaine** 1941- ................ **CLC 169**
See also CA 57-60; CANR 58, 106, 208; DLB 67; FW; GLL 2

**Shreve, Susan**
See Shreve, Susan Richards

**Shreve, Susan Richards** 1939- ........ **CLC 23**
See also CA 49-52; CAAS 5; CANR 5, 38, 69, 100, 159, 199; MAICYA 1, 2; SATA 46, 95, 152; SATA-Brief 41

**Shteyngart, Gary** 1972- ................ **CLC 319**
See also AAYA 68; CA 217; CANR 175

**Shteyngart, Igor**
See Shteyngart, Gary

**Shue, Larry** 1946-1985 .................... **CLC 52**
See also CA 145; 117; DAM DRAM; DFS 7

**Shu-Jen, Chou** 1881-1936 ... **SSC 20; TCLC 3**
See also CA 104; EWL 3

**Shukshin, Vasily** 1929-1974 ............... **SSC 203**
See also CA 135; CANR 87; DLB 302; EWL 3

**Shulman, Alix Kates** 1932- ......... **CLC 2, 10**
See also CA 29-32R; CANR 43, 199; FW; SATA 7

**Shuster, Joe** 1914-1992 ................... **CLC 21**
See also AAYA 50

**Shute, Nevil** 1899-1960 ................... **CLC 30**
See also BPFB 3; CA 102; 93-96; CANR 85; DLB 255; MTCW 2; NFS 9, 38; RHW 4; SFW 4

**Shuttle, Penelope (Diane)** 1947- ....... **CLC 7**
See also CA 93-96; CANR 39, 84, 92, 108; CP 3, 4, 5, 6, 7; CWP; DLB 14, 40

**Shvarts, Elena** 1948-2010 ................... **PC 50**
See also CA 147

**Sībawayhi** 750?-796? ................ **CMLC 161**
See also DLB 311

**Sidhwa, Bapsi** 1939-
See Sidhwa, Bapsy (N.)

**Sidhwa, Bapsy (N.)** 1938- .............. **CLC 168**
See also CA 108; CANR 25, 57; CN 6, 7; DLB 323; FW

**Sidney, Mary** 1561-1621 ...... **LC 19, 39, 182**
See also DLB 167

**Sidney, Sir Philip** 1554-1586 ....... **LC 19, 39, 131, 197, 240, 241; PC 32**
See also BRW 1; BRWR 2; CDBLB Before 1660; DA; DA3; DAB; DAC; DAM MST, POET; DLB 167; EXPP; PAB; PFS 30; RGEL 2; TEA; WP

**Sidney Herbert, Mary**
See Sidney, Mary

**Siegel, Jerome** 1914-1996 ................ **CLC 21**
See also AAYA 50; CA 116; 169; 151

**Siegel, Jerry**
See Siegel, Jerome

**Sienkiewicz, Henryk (Adam Alexander Pius)**
1846-1916 ................................ **TCLC 3**
See also CA 104; 134; CANR 84; DLB 332; EWL 3; RGSF 2; RGWL 2, 3

**Sierra, Gregorio Martinez**
See Martinez Sierra, Gregorio

**Sierra, Maria de la O'LeJarraga Martinez**
See Martinez Sierra, Maria

**Sigal, Clancy** 1926- .......................... **CLC 7**
See also CA 1-4R; CANR 85, 184; CN 1, 2, 3, 4, 5, 6, 7

**Siguenza y Gongora, Carlos de**
1645-1700 ...................... **HLCS 2; LC 8**
See also LAW

**Siger of Brabant** 1240(?)-1284(?) ... **CMLC 69**
See also DLB 115

**Sigourney, Lydia H.**
See Sigourney, Lydia Howard

**Sigourney, Lydia Howard**
1791-1865 ................ **NCLC 21, 87, 358**
See also DLB 1, 42, 73, 183, 239, 243

**Sigourney, Lydia Howard Huntley**
See Sigourney, Lydia Howard

**Sigourney, Lydia Huntley**
See Sigourney, Lydia Howard

**Sigurjonsson, Johann**
See Sigurjonsson, Johann

**Sigurjonsson, Johann** 1880-1919 ... **TCLC 27**
See also CA 170; DLB 293; EWL 3

**Sikelianos, Angelos** 1884-1951 ......... **PC 29; TCLC 39**
See also EWL 3; RGWL 2, 3

**Silkin, Jon** 1930-1997 ............. **CLC 2, 6, 43**
See also CA 5-8R; CAAS 5; CANR 89; CP 1, 2, 3, 4, 5, 6; DLB 27

**Silko, Leslie** 1948- .... **CLC 23, 74, 114, 211, 302; NNAL; SSC 37, 66, 151; WLCS**
See also AAYA 14; AMWS 4; ANW; BYA 12; CA 115; 122; CANR 45, 65, 118, 226; CN 4, 5, 6, 7; CP 4, 5, 6, 7; CPW 1; CWP; DA; DA3; DAC; DAM MST, MULT, POP; DLB 143, 175, 256, 275; EWL 3; EXPP; EXPS; LAIT 4; MAL 5; MTCW 2; MTFW 2005; NFS 4; PFS 9, 16; RGAL 4; RGSF 2; SSFS 4, 8, 10, 11; TCWW 1, 2

**Silko, Leslie Marmon**
See Silko, Leslie

**Sillanpaa, Frans Eemil** 1888-1964 .. **CLC 19**
See also CA 129; 93-96; DLB 332; EWL 3; MTCW 1

**Sillitoe, Alan** 1928-2010 ........... **CLC 1, 3, 6, 10, 19, 57, 148, 318; SSC 228**
See also AITN 1; BRWS 5; CA 9-12R, 191; CAAE 191; CAAS 2; CANR 8, 26, 55, 139, 213; CDBLB 1960 to Present; CN 1, 2, 3, 4, 5, 6; CP 1, 2, 3, 4, 5; DLB 14, 139; EWL 3; MTCW 1, 2; MTFW 2005; RGEL 2; RGSF 2; SATA 61

**Silone, Ignazio** 1900-1978 ... **CLC 4; TCLC 340**
See also CA 25-28; 81-84; CANR 34; CAP 2; DLB 264; EW 12; EWL 3; MTCW 1; RGSF 2; RGWL 2, 3

**Silone, Ignazione**
See Silone, Ignazio

**Siluriensis, Leolinus**
See Jones, Arthur Llewellyn

**Silva, José Asunción**
1865-1896 .................... **NCLC 114, 280**
See also DLB 283; LAW

**Silver, Joan Micklin** 1935- .............. **CLC 20**
See also CA 114; 121; INT CA-121

**Silver, Nicholas**
See Faust, Frederick

**Silverberg, Robert** 1935- ........... **CLC 7, 140**
See also AAYA 24; BPFB 3; BYA 7, 9; CA 1-4R; 186; CAAE 186; CAAS 3; CANR 1, 20, 36, 85, 140, 175, 236; CLR 59; CN 6, 7; CPW; DAM POP; DLB 8; INT CANR-20; MAICYA 1, 2; MTCW 1, 2; MTFW 2005; SATA 13, 91; SATA-Essay 104; SCFW 1, 2; SFW 4; SUFW 2

**Silverstein, Alvin** 1933- .................... **CLC 17**
See also CA 49-52; CANR 2; CLR 25; JRDA; MAICYA 1, 2; SATA 8, 69, 124

**Silverstein, Shel** 1932-1999 ................. **PC 49**
See also AAYA 40; BW 3; CA 107; 179; CANR 47, 74, 81; CLR 5, 96; CWRI 5; JRDA; MAICYA 1, 2; MTCW 2; MTFW 2005; SATA 33, 92; SATA-Brief 27; SATA-Obit 116

**Silverstein, Sheldon Allan**
See Silverstein, Shel

**Silverstein, Virginia B.** 1937- .......... **CLC 17**
See also CA 49-52; CANR 2; CLR 25; JRDA; MAICYA 1, 2; SATA 8, 69, 124

**Silverstein, Virginia Barbara Opshelor**
See Silverstein, Virginia B.

**Sim, Georges**
See Simenon, Georges

**Sima Qian** 145 BCE-c. 89 BCE .... **CMLC 72, 146**
See also DLB 358

**Simak, Clifford D(onald)**
1904-1988 ........................... **CLC 1, 55**
See also CA 1-4R; 125; CANR 1, 35; DLB 8; MTCW 1; SATA-Obit 56; SCFW 1, 2; SFW 4

**Small, David** 1945- .......................... **CLC 299**
See also CLR 53; MAICYA 2; SATA 50, 95,
126, 183, 216; SATA-Brief 46

**Smart, Christopher** 1722-1771 ... **LC 3, 134;**
**PC 13**
See also DAM POET; DLB 109; RGEL 2

**Smart, Elizabeth** 1913-1986 ........... **CLC 54;**
**TCLC 231**
See also CA 81-84; 118; CN 4; DLB 88

**Smiley, Jane** 1949- ..................... **CLC 53, 76,**
**144, 236**
See also AAYA 66; AMWS 6; BPFB 3; CA
104; CANR 30, 50, 74, 96, 158, 196, 231;
CN 6, 7; CPW 1; DA3; DAM POP; DLB
227, 234; EWL 3; INT CANR-30; MAL 5;
MTFW 2005; NFS 32; SSFS 19

**Smiley, Jane Graves**
See Smiley, Jane

**Smith, A(rthur) J(ames) M(arshall)**
1902-1980 .................................. **CLC 15**
See also CA 1-4R; 102; CANR 4; CP 1, 2, 3;
DAC; DLB 88; RGEL 2

**Smith, Adam** 1723(?)-1790 ................. **LC 36**
See also DLB 104, 252, 336; RGEL 2

**Smith, Alexander** 1829-1867 ......... **NCLC 59**
See also DLB 32, 55

**Smith, Alexander McCall** 1948- ... **CLC 268**
See also CA 215; CANR 154, 196; SATA
73, 179

**Smith, Anna Deavere** 1950- .... **CLC 86, 241**
See also CA 133; CANR 103; CD 5, 6; DFS
2, 22; DLB 341

**Smith, Betty** 1904-1972 ................... **CLC 19**
See also AAYA 72; AMWS 23; BPFB 3;
BYA 3; CA 5-8R; 33-36R; CLR 202;
DLBY 1982; LAIT 3; NFS 31; RGAL
4; SATA 6

**Smith, Charlotte Turner**
1749-1806 ....... **NCLC 23, 115; PC 104**
See also BRWS 19; DLB 39, 109; RGEL 2;
TEA

**Smith, Clark Ashton** 1893-1961 ..... **CLC 43**
See also AAYA 76; CA 143; CANR 81;
FANT; HGG; MTCW 2; SCFW 1, 2; SFW
4; SUFW

**Smith, Dave**
See Smith, David (Jeddie)

**Smith, David (Jeddie)** 1942- ..... **CLC 22, 42**
See also CA 49-52; CAAS 7; CANR 1, 59, 120;
CP 3, 4, 5, 6, 7; CSW; DAM POET; DLB 5

**Smith, Iain Crichton** 1928-1998 ..... **CLC 64**
See also BRWS 9; CA 21-24R; 171; CN 1,
2, 3, 4, 5, 6; CP 1, 2, 3, 4, 5, 6; DLB 40,
139, 319, 352; RGSF 2

**Smith, John** 1580(?)-1631 ..................... **LC 9**
See also DLB 24, 30; TUS

**Smith, Johnston**
See Crane, Stephen

**Smith, Joseph, Jr.** 1805-1844 .. **NCLC 53, 321**

**Smith, Kevin** 1970- ....................... **CLC 223**
See also AAYA 37; CA 166; CANR 131, 201

**Smith, Lee** 1944- ............. **CLC 25, 73, 258;**
**SSC 142**
See also CA 114; 119; CANR 46, 118, 173,
225; CN 7; CSW; DLB 143; DLBY 1983;
EWL 3; INT CA-119; RGAL 4

**Smith, Martin**
See Smith, Martin Cruz

**Smith, Martin Cruz** 1942- ... **CLC 25; NNAL**
See Smith, Martin Cruz
See also BEST 89:4; BPFB 3; CA 85-88;
CANR 6, 23, 43, 65, 119, 184; CMW 4;
CPW; DAM MULT, POP; HGG; INT
CANR-23; MTCW 2; MTFW 2005; RGAL 4

**Smith, Patti** 1946- ..................... **CLC 12, 318**
See also CA 93-96; CANR 63, 168, 232

**Smith, Pauline (Urmson)**
1882-1959 .............................. **TCLC 25**
See also DLB 225; EWL 3

**Smith, R. Alexander McCall**
See Smith, Alexander McCall

**Smith, Rosamond**
See Oates, Joyce Carol

**Smith, Seba** 1792-1868 ................ **NCLC 187**
See also DLB 1, 11, 243

**Smith, Sheila Kaye**
See Kaye-Smith, Sheila

**Smith, Sosthenes**
See Wells, H. G.

**Smith, Stevie** 1902-1971 ......... **CLC 3, 8, 25,**
**44; PC 12, 172**
See also BRWR 3; BRWS 2; CA 17-18; 29-
32R; CANR 35; CAP 2; CP 1; DAM
POET; DLB 20; EWL 3; MTCW 1, 2;
PAB; PFS 3; RGEL 2; TEA

**Smith, Wilbur** 1933- ....................... **CLC 33**
See also CA 13-16R; CANR 7, 46, 66, 134,
180, 236; CPW; MTCW 1, 2; MTFW 2005

**Smith, Wilbur Addison**
See Smith, Wilbur

**Smith, William Jay**
1918-2015 ..................... **CLC 6; PC 212**
See also AMWS 13; CA 5-8R; CANR 44,
106, 211; CP 1, 2, 3, 4, 5, 6, 7; CSW; CWRI
5; DLB 5; MAICYA 1, 2; SAAS 22; SATA
2, 68, 154; SATA-Essay 154; TCLE 1:2

**Smith, Woodrow Wilson**
See Kuttner, Henry

**Smith, Zadie** 1975- ................ **CLC 158, 306**
See also AAYA 50; CA 193; CANR 204;
DLB 347; MTFW 2005; NFS 40

**Smolenskin, Peretz** 1842-1885 ....... **NCLC 30**

**Smollett, Tobias (George)**
1721-1771 ....... **LC 2, 46, 188, 247, 248**
See also BRW 3; CDBLB 1660-1789; DLB
39, 104; RGEL 2; TEA

**Snodgrass, Quentin Curtius**
See Twain, Mark

**Snodgrass, Thomas Jefferson**
See Twain, Mark

**Snodgrass, W. D.** 1926-2009 ........ **CLC 2, 6,**
**10, 18, 68; PC 74**
See also AMWS 6; CA 1-4R; 282; CANR 6,
36, 65, 85, 185; CP 1, 2, 3, 4, 5, 6, 7; DAM
POET; DLB 5; MAL 5; MTCW 1, 2;
MTFW 2005; PFS 29; RGAL 4; TCLE 1:2

**Snodgrass, W. de Witt**
See Snodgrass, W. D.

**Snodgrass, William de Witt**
See Snodgrass, W. D.

**Snodgrass, William De Witt**
See Snodgrass, W. D.

**Snorri Sturluson** 1179-1241 **CMLC 56, 134**
See also RGWL 2, 3

**Snow, C(harles) P(ercy)**
1905-1980 ......... **CLC 1, 4, 6, 9, 13, 19**
See also BRW 7; CA 5-8R; 101; CANR 28;
CDBLB 1945-1960; CN 1, 2; DAM NOV;
DLB 15, 77; DLBD 17; EWL 3; MTCW 1,
2; MTFW 2005; RGEL 2; TEA

**Snow, Frances Compton**
See Adams, Henry

**Snyder, Gary** 1930- ............. **CLC 1, 2, 5, 9,**
**32, 120; PC 21**
See also AAYA 72; AMWS 8; ANW; BG
1:3; CA 17-20R; CANR 30, 60, 125; CP 1,
2, 3, 4, 5, 6, 7; DA3; DAM POET; DLB 5,
16, 165, 212, 237, 275, 342; EWL 3; MAL
5; MTCW 2; MTFW 2005; PFS 9, 19;
RGAL 4; WP

**Snyder, Gary Sherman**
See Snyder, Gary

**Snyder, Zilpha Keatley** 1927- ......... **CLC 17**
See also AAYA 15; BYA 1; CA 9-12R, 252;
CAAE 252; CANR 38, 202; CLR 31, 121;
JRDA; MAICYA 1, 2; SAAS 2; SATA 1,
28, 75, 110, 163, 226; SATA-Essay 112,
163; YAW

**Soares, Bernardo**
See Pessoa, Fernando

**Sobh, A.**
See Shamlu, Ahmad

**Sobh, Alef**
See Shamlu, Ahmad

**Sobol, Joshua** 1939- ....................... **CLC 60**
See also CA 200; CWW 2; RGHL

**Sobol, Yehoshua** 1939-
See Sobol, Joshua

**Socrates** 470 BCE-399 BCE ..... **CMLC 27, 178**

**Soderberg, Hjalmar** 1869-1941 ..... **TCLC 39**
See also DLB 259; EWL 3; RGSF 2

**Soderbergh, Steven** 1963- .............. **CLC 154**
See also AAYA 43; CA 243

**Soderbergh, Steven Andrew**
See Soderbergh, Steven

**Sodergran, Edith** 1892-1923 ......... **TCLC 31**
See also CA 202; DLB 259; EW 11; EWL 3;
RGWL 2, 3

**Soedergran, Edith Irene**
See Sodergran, Edith

**Softly, Edgar**
See Lovecraft, H. P.

**Softly, Edward**
See Lovecraft, H. P.

**Sokolov, Alexander V.** 1943- ........... **CLC 59**
See also CA 73-76; CWW 2; DLB 285;
EWL 3; RGWL 2, 3

**Sokolov, Alexander Vsevolodovich**
See Sokolov, Alexander V.

**Sokolov, Raymond** 1941- ................... **CLC 7**
See also CA 85-88

**Sokolov, Sasha**
See Sokolov, Alexander V.

**Soleather**
See Twain, Mark

**Soli, Tatjana** ............................... **CLC 318**
See also CA 307

**Solo, Jay**
See Ellison, Harlan

**Sologub, Fedor**
See Teternikov, Fyodor Kuzmich

**Sologub, Feodor**
See Teternikov, Fyodor Kuzmich

**Sologub, Fyodor**
See Teternikov, Fyodor Kuzmich

**Solomons, Ikey Esquir**
See Thackeray, William Makepeace

**Solomos, Dionysios** 1798-1857 ...... **NCLC 15**

**Solon** c. 630-c. 560 BCE .............. **CMLC 175**

**Solwoska, Mara**
See French, Marilyn

**Solzhenitsyn, Aleksandr** 1918-2008 ... **CLC 1,**
**2, 4, 7, 9, 10, 18, 26, 34, 78, 134, 235; SSC**
**32, 105; WLC 5**
See also AAYA 49; AITN 1; BPFB 3; CA
69-72; CANR 40, 65, 116; CWW 2; DA;
DA3; DAB; DAC; DAM MST, NOV; DLB
302, 332; EW 13; EWL 3; EXPS; LAIT 4;
MTCW 1, 2; MTFW 2005; NFS 6; PFS
38; RGSF 2; RGWL 2, 3; SSFS 9; TWA

**Solzhenitsyn, Aleksandr I.**
See Solzhenitsyn, Aleksandr

**Solzhenitsyn, Aleksandr Isayevich**
See Solzhenitsyn, Aleksandr

**Somebody, M. D. C.**
See Neal, John

**Somers, Jane**
See Lessing, Doris

**Somerville, Edith Oenone**
1858-1949 ................ **SSC 56; TCLC 51**
See also CA 196; DLB 135; RGEL 2; RGSF 2

**Somerville & Ross**
See Martin, Violet Florence; Somerville,
Edith Oenone

**Sommer, Scott** 1951- ....................... **CLC 25**
See also CA 106

**Sommers, Christina Hoff** 1950- .... **CLC 197**
See also CA 153; CANR 95

**Sondheim, Stephen** 1930- ......... **CLC 30, 39, 147; DC 22**
See also AAYA 11, 66; CA 103; CANR 47, 67, 125; DAM DRAM; DFS 25, 27, 28; LAIT 4

**Sondheim, Stephen Joshua**
See Sondheim, Stephen

**Sone, Monica** 1919- ................................ **AAL**
See also DLB 312

**Song, Cathy** 1955- .................... **AAL; PC 21**
See also CA 154; CANR 118; CWP; DLB 169, 312; EXPP; FW; PFS 5, 43

**Sontag, Susan** 1933-2004 .............. **CLC 1, 2, 10, 13, 31, 105, 195, 277**
See also AMWS 3; CA 17-20R; 234; CANR 25, 51, 74, 97, 184; CN 1, 2, 3, 4, 5, 6, 7; CPW; DA3; DAM POP; DLB 2, 67; EWL 3; MAL 5; MBL; MTCW 1, 2; MTFW 2005; RGAL 4; RHW; SSFS 10

**Sophocles** 496(?) BCE-406(?) BCE .... **CMLC 2, 47, 51, 86, 184; DC 1; WLCS**
See also AW 1; CDWLB 1; DA; DA3; DAB; DAC; DAM DRAM, MST; DFS 1, 4, 8, 24; DLB 176; LAIT 1; LATS 1:1; LMFS 1; RGWL 2, 3; TWA; WLIT 8

**Sor Juana**
See Juana Inés de la Cruz, Sor

**Sordello** 1189-1269 ........................ **CMLC 15**

**Sorel, Charles** c. 1600-1674 ............. **LC 273**
See also DLB 268; GFL

**Sorel, Georges** 1847-1922 .............. **TCLC 91**
See also CA 118; 188

**Sorel, Julia**
See Drexler, Rosalyn

**Sorokin, Vladimir** 1955- ........... **CLC 59, 374**
See also CA 258; CANR 233; DLB 285

**Sorokin, Vladimir Georgievich**
See Sorokin, Vladimir

**Sorrentino, Gilbert** 1929-2006 ..... **CLC 3, 7, 14, 22, 40, 247**
See also AMWS 21; CA 77-80; 250; CANR 14, 33, 115, 157; CN 3, 4, 5, 6, 7; CP 1, 2, 3, 4, 5, 6, 7; DLB 5, 173; DLBY 1980; INT CANR-14

**Soto, Gary** 1952- ....... **CLC 32, 80; HLC 2; PC 28**
See also AAYA 10, 37; BYA 11; CA 119; 125; CANR 50, 74, 107, 157, 219; CLR 38; CP 4, 5, 6, 7; DAM MULT; DFS 26; DLB 82; EWL 3; EXPP; HW 1, 2; INT CA-125; JRDA; LLW; MAICYA 2; MAICYAS 1; MAL 5; MTCW 2; MTFW 2005; PFS 7, 30; RGAL 4; SATA 80, 120, 174; SSFS 33; WYA; YAW

**Soupault, Philippe** 1897-1990 ......... **CLC 68**
See also CA 116; 147; 131; EWL 3; GFL 1789 to the Present; LMFS 2

**Souster, (Holmes) Raymond** 1921- ................................ **CLC 5, 14**
See also CA 13-16R; CAAS 14; CANR 13, 29, 53; CP 1, 2, 3, 4, 5, 6, 7; DA3; DAC; DAM POET; DLB 88; RGEL 2; SATA 63

**South, Nim**
See Surtees, Robert Smith

**Southern, Terry** 1924(?)-1995 ........... **CLC 7**
See also AMWS 11; BPFB 3; CA 1-4R; 150; CANR 1, 55, 107; CN 1, 2, 3, 4, 5, 6; DLB 2; IDFW 3, 4

**Southerne, Thomas** 1660-1746 .......... **LC 99**
See also DLB 80; RGEL 2

**Southey, Robert** 1774-1843 ........... **NCLC 8, 97, 332; PC 111**
See also BRW 4; DLB 93, 107, 142; RGEL 2; SATA 54

**Southwell, Robert** 1561(?)-1595 .. **LC 108, 258**
See also DLB 167; RGEL 2; TEA

**Southworth, Emma Dorothy Eliza Nevitte** 1819-1899 ................. **NCLC 26, 367**
See also DLB 239

**Souza, Ernest**
See Scott, Evelyn

**Sow Fall, Aminata** 1941- ............... **CLC 413**
See also CWW 2; EWL 3

**Soyinka, Wole** 1934- .............. **BLC 1:3, 2:3; CLC 3, 5, 14, 36, 44, 179, 331; DC 2; PC 118; WLC 5**
See also AFW; BW 2, 3; CA 13-16R; CANR 27, 39, 82, 136; CD 5, 6; CDWLB 3; CN 6, 7; CP 1, 2, 3, 4, 5, 6 ,7; DA; DA3; DAB; DAC; DAM DRAM, MST, MULT; DFS 10, 26; DLB 125, 332; EWL 3; MTCW 1, 2; MTFW 2005; PFS 27, 40; RGEL 2; TWA; WLIT 2; WWE 1

**Spackman, W(illiam) M(ode)** 1905-1990 ................................ **CLC 46**
See also CA 81-84; 132

**Spacks, Barry (Bernard)** 1931- ...... **CLC 14**
See also CA 154; CANR 33, 109; CP 3, 4, 5, 6, 7; DLB 105

**Spanidou, Irini** 1946- ...................... **CLC 44**
See also CA 185; CANR 179

**Spark, Muriel** 1918-2006 ..... **CLC 2, 3, 5, 8, 13, 18, 40, 94, 242, 440; PC 72; SSC 10, 115**
See also BRWS 1; CA 5-8R; 251; CANR 12, 36, 76, 89, 131; CDBLB 1945-1960; CMTFW; CN 1, 2, 3, 4, 5, 6, 7; CP 1, 2, 3, 4, 5, 6, 7; DA3; DAB; DAC; DAM MST, NOV; DLB 15, 139; EWL 3; FW; INT CANR-12; LAIT 4; MBL; MTCW 1, 2; MTFW 2005; NFS 22; RGEL 2; SSFS 28, 41; TEA; WLIT 4; YAW

**Spark, Muriel Sarah**
See Spark, Muriel

**Spaulding, Douglas**
See Bradbury, Ray

**Spaulding, Leonard**
See Bradbury, Ray

**Spectator, Mr.**
See Addison, Joseph

**Speght, Rachel** 1597-c. 1630 .............. **LC 97**
See also DLB 126

**Spence, J. A. D.**
See Eliot, T. S.

**Spencer, Anne** 1882-1975 .... **HR 1:3; PC 77**
See also BW 2; CA 161; DLB 51, 54

**Spencer, Elizabeth** 1921- ................ **CLC 22; SSC 57**
See also CA 13-16R; CANR 32, 65, 87; CN 1, 2, 3, 4, 5, 6, 7; CSW; DLB 6, 218; EWL 3; MTCW 1; RGAL 4; SATA 14

**Spencer, Leonard G.**
See Silverberg, Robert

**Spencer, Scott** 1945- ......................... **CLC 30**
See also CA 113; CANR 51, 148, 190; DLBY 1986

**Spender, Stephen** 1909-1995 ........ **CLC 1, 2, 5, 10, 41, 91; PC 71**
See also BRWS 2; CA 9-12R; 149; CANR 31, 54; CDBLB 1945-1960; CP 1, 2, 3, 4, 5, 6; DA3; DAM POET; DLB 20; EWL 3; MTCW 1, 2; MTFW 2005; PAB; PFS 23, 36; RGEL 2; TEA

**Spender, Stephen Harold**
See Spender, Stephen

**Spengler, Oswald (Arnold Gottfried)** 1880-1936 ................................ **TCLC 25**
See also CA 118; 189

**Spenser, Edmund** c. 1552-1599 ..... **LC 5, 39, 117, 233, 261; PC 8, 42, 170; WLC 5**
See also AAYA 60; BRW 1; CDBLB Before 1660; DA; DA3; DAB; DAC; DAM MST, POET; DLB 167; EFS 1:2, 2:1; EXPP; PAB; PFS 32; RGEL 2; TEA; WLIT 3; WP

**Spicer, Jack** 1925-1965 ........ **CLC 8, 18, 72**
See also BG 1:3; CA 85-88; DAM POET; DLB 5, 16, 193; GLL 1; WP

**Spiegelman, Art** 1948- ............. **CLC 76, 178**
See also AAYA 10, 46; CA 125; CANR 41, 55, 74, 124; DLB 299; MTCW 2; MTFW 2005; NFS 35; RGHL; SATA 109, 158; YAW

**Spielberg, Peter** 1929- ....................... **CLC 6**
See also CA 5-8R; CANR 4, 48; DLBY 1981

**Spielberg, Steven** 1947- ........... **CLC 20, 188**
See also AAYA 8, 24; CA 77-80; CANR 32; SATA 32

**Spillane, Frank Morrison**
See Spillane, Mickey

**Spillane, Mickey** 1918-2006 ............. **CLC 3, 13, 241**
See also BPFB 3; CA 25-28R; 252; CANR 28, 63, 125, 238; CMW 4; DA3; DLB 226; MSW; MTCW 1, 2; MTFW 2005; SATA 66; SATA-Obit 176

**Spinoza, Benedictus de** 1632-1677 ...................... **LC 9, 58, 177**

**Spinrad, Norman (Richard)** 1940- ... **CLC 46**
See also BPFB 3; CA 37-40R, 233; CAAE 233; CAAS 19; CANR 20, 91; DLB 8; INT CANR-20; SFW 4

**Spiotta, Dana** 1966- .......................... **CLC 328**
See also CA 246; CANR 238

**Spitteler, Carl** 1845-1924 .............. **TCLC 12**
See also CA 109; DLB 129, 332; EWL 3

**Spitteler, Karl Friedrich Georg**
See Spitteler, Carl

**Spivack, Kathleen (Romola Drucker)** 1938- ............................................. **CLC 6**
See also CA 49-52

**Spivak, Gayatri Chakravorty** 1942- .. **CLC 233**
See also CA 110; 154; CANR 91; FW; LMFS 2

**Spofford, Harriet (Elizabeth) Prescott** 1835-1921 .................................... **SSC 87**
See also CA 201; DLB 74, 221

**Spoto, Donald** 1941- ......................... **CLC 39**
See also CA 65-68; CANR 11, 57, 93, 173, 212

**Springsteen, Bruce** 1949- ................. **CLC 17**
See also CA 111

**Springsteen, Bruce F.**
See Springsteen, Bruce

**Spurling, Hilary** 1940- ..................... **CLC 34**
See also CA 104; CANR 25, 52, 94, 157, 224

**Spurling, Susan Hilary**
See Spurling, Hilary

**Spyker, John Howland**
See Elman, Richard (Martin)

**Squared, A.**
See Abbott, Edwin A.

**Squires, (James) Radcliffe** 1917-1993 ................................ **CLC 51**
See also CA 1-4R; 140; CANR 6, 21; CP 1, 2, 3, 4, 5

**Surdas** c. 1478-c. 1583 ...................... **LC 163**
See also RGWL 2, 3

**Srivastav, Dhanpat Ray**
See Srivastava, Dhanpat Rai

**Srivastav, Dheanpatrai**
See Srivastava, Dhanpat Rai

**Srivastava, Dhanpat Rai** 1880(?)-1936 ............................ **TCLC 21**
See also CA 118; 197; EWL 3

**Soseki Natsume** 1867-1916 ............ **TCLC 2, 10, 271**
See also CA 104; 195; DLB 180; EWL 3; MJW; RGWL 2, 3; TWA

**Ssu-ma Ch'ien** c. 145 BCE-c. 86 BCE .............. **CMLC 96**

**Ssu-ma T'an** (?)-c. 110 BCE ........... **CMLC 96**

**Stacy, Donald**
See Pohl, Frederik

**Stafford, Jean** 1915-1979 ....... **CLC 4, 7, 19, 68; SSC 26, 86**
See also CA 1-4R; 85-88; CANR 3, 65; CN 1, 2; DLB 2, 173; MAL 5; MTCW 1, 2; MTFW 2005; RGAL 4; RGSF 2; SATA-Obit 22; SSFS 21; TCWW 1, 2; TUS

**Stafford, William** 1914-1993 ........ **CLC 4, 7, 29; PC 71**

See also AMWS 11; CA 5-8R; 142; CAAS 3;
CANR 5, 22; CP 1, 2, 3, 4, 5; DAM POET;
DLB 5, 206; EXPP; INT CANR-22; MAL 5;
PFS 2, 8, 16; RGAL 4; WP

**Stafford, William Edgar**
See Stafford, William

**Stagnelius, Eric Johan** 1793-1823 ... **NCLC 61**

**Staines, Trevor**
See Brunner, John (Kilian Houston)

**Stairs, Gordon**
See Austin, Mary Hunter

**Stael**
See Stael-Holstein, Anne Louise Germaine
Necker

**Stael, Germaine de**
See Stael-Holstein, Anne Louise Germaine
Necker

**Stael-Holstein, Anne Louise Germaine Necker**
1766-1817 ......................... **NCLC 3, 91**
See also DLB 119, 192; EW 5; FL 1:3; FW;
GFL 1789 to the Present; RGWL 2, 3; TWA

**Stalin, Joseph** 1879-1953 ............... **TCLC 92**

**Stampa, Gaspara** 1524?-1554 ......... **LC 114,
262; PC 43**
See also RGWL 2, 3; WLIT 7

**Stampflinger, K.A.**
See Benjamin, Walter

**Stancykowna**
See Szymborska, Wislawa

**Standing Bear, Luther**
1868(?)-1939(?) ........................... **NNAL**
See also CA 113; 144; DAM MULT

**Stanhope, Philip Dormer, Fourth Earl of
Chesterfield** 1694-1773 ............. **LC 259**
See also DLB 104

**Stanhope, William**
See Walpole, Horace

**Stanislavsky, Constantin**
1863(?)-1938 ......................... **TCLC 167**
See also CA 118

**Stanislavsky, Konstantin**
See Stanislavsky, Constantin

**Stanislavsky, Konstantin Sergeievich**
See Stanislavsky, Constantin

**Stanislavsky, Konstantin Sergeivich**
See Stanislavsky, Constantin

**Stanislavsky, Konstantin Sergeyevich**
See Stanislavsky, Constantin

**Stanley, Elizabeth**
See Mansfield, Katherine

**Stannard, Martin** 1947- ................... **CLC 44**
See also CA 142; CANR 229; DLB 155

**Stanton, Elizabeth Cady**
1815-1902 ............................... **TCLC 73**
See also CA 171; DLB 79; FL 1:3; FW

**Stanton, Maura** 1946- ....................... **CLC 9**
See also CA 89-92; CANR 15, 123; DLB 120

**Stanton, Schuyler**
See Baum, L. Frank

**Stapledon, (William) Olaf**
1886-1950 ............................... **TCLC 22**
See also CA 111; 162; DLB 15, 255; SCFW
1, 2; SFW 4

**Starbuck, George (Edwin)**
1931-1996 ............................... **CLC 53**
See also CA 21-24R; 153; CANR 23; CP 1,
2, 3, 4, 5, 6; DAM POET

**Stark, Richard**
See Westlake, Donald E.

**Statius** c. 45-c. 96 ......................... **CMLC 91**
See also AW 2; DLB 211

**Staunton, Schuyler**
See Baum, L. Frank

**Stead, Christina (Ellen)** 1902-1983 ..... **CLC 2,
5, 8, 32, 80; TCLC 244**
See also BRWS 4; CA 13-16R; 109; CANR
33, 40; CN 1, 2, 3; DLB 260; EWL 3; FW;
MTCW 1, 2; MTFW 2005; NFS 27; RGEL
2; RGSF 2; WWE 1

**Stead, Robert J(ames) C(ampbell)**
1880-1959 ............................... **TCLC 225**
See also CA 186; DLB 92; TCWW 1, 2

**Stead, William Thomas** 1849-1912 .. **TCLC 48**
See also BRWS 13; CA 167

**Stebnitsky, M.**
See Leskov, Nikolai Semenovich

**Stedman, M. L.** 19??- .................... **CLC 354**

**Steele, Richard** 1672-1729 ................. **LC 18,
156, 159**
See also BRW 3; CDBLB 1660-1789; DLB
84, 101; RGEL 2; WLIT 3

**Steele, Timothy (Reid)** 1948- .......... **CLC 45**
See also CA 93-96; CANR 16, 50, 92; CP 5,
6, 7; DLB 120, 282

**Steffens, (Joseph) Lincoln**
1866-1936 ............................... **TCLC 20**
See also CA 117; 198; DLB 303; MAL 5

**Stegner, Wallace** 1909-1993 ........ **CLC 9, 49,
81; SSC 27; TCLC 281**
See also AITN 1; AMWS 4; ANW; BEST
90:3; BPFB 3; CA 1-4R; 141; CAAS 9;
CANR 1, 21, 46; CN 1, 2, 3, 4, 5; DAM
NOV; DLB 9, 206, 275; DLBY 1993;
EWL 3; MAL 5; MTCW 1, 2; MTFW
2005; RGAL 4; TCWW 1, 2; TUS

**Stegner, Wallace Earle**
See Stegner, Wallace

**Stein, Gertrude** 1874-1946 ................ **DC 19;
PC 18, 175; SSC 42, 105; TCLC 1, 6, 28,
48, 276; WLC 5**
See also AAYA 64; AMW; AMWC 2; CA
104; 132; CANR 108; CDALB 1917-1929;
DA; DA3; DAB; DAC; DAM MST, NOV,
POET; DLB 4, 54, 86, 228; DLBD 15;
EWL 3; EXPS; FL 1:6; GLL 1; MAL 5;
MBL; MTCW 1, 2; MTFW 2005; NCFS 4;
NFS 27; PFS 38; RGAL 4; RGSF 2; SSFS
5; TUS; WP

**Steinbeck, John** 1902-1968 ...... **CLC 1, 5, 9,
13, 21, 34, 45, 75, 124; DC 46; SSC 11,
37, 77, 135, 265; TCLC 135, 369; WLC 5**
See also AAYA 12; AMW; BPFB 3; BYA 2, 3,
13; CA 1-4R, 25-28R; CANR 1, 35; CDALB
1929-1941; CLR 172, 194, 195; DA; DA3;
DAB; DAC; DAM DRAM, MST, NOV;
DLB 7, 9, 212, 275, 309, 332, 364; DLBD
2; EWL 3; EXPS; LAIT 3; MAL 5; MTCW
1, 2; MTFW 2005; NFS 1, 5, 7, 17, 19, 28,
34, 37, 39, 46, 53; RGAL 4; RGSF 2; RHW;
SATA 9; SSFS 3, 6, 22; TCWW 1, 2; TUS;
WYA; YAW

**Steinbeck, John Ernst**
See Steinbeck, John

**Steinem, Gloria** 1934- ...................... **CLC 63**
See also CA 53-56; CANR 28, 51, 139; DLB
246; FL 1:1; FW; MTCW 1, 2; MTFW 2005

**Steiner, George** 1929- ............... **CLC 24, 221**
See also CA 73-76; CANR 31, 67, 108, 212;
DAM NOV; DLB 67, 299; EWL 3; MTCW
1, 2; MTFW 2005; RGHL; SATA 62

**Steiner, K. Leslie**
See Delany, Samuel R., Jr.

**Steiner, Rudolf** 1861-1925 ............. **TCLC 13**
See also CA 107

**Stendhal** 1783-1842 ....... **NCLC 23, 46, 178,
292; SSC 27; WLC 5**
See also DA; DA3; DAB; DAC; DAM MST,
NOV; DLB 119; EW 5; GFL 1789 to the
Present; RGWL 2, 3; TWA

**Stephen, Adeline Virginia**
See Woolf, Virginia

**Stephen, Sir Leslie** 1832-1904 ....... **TCLC 23**
See also BRW 5; CA 123; DLB 57, 144, 190

**Stephen, Sir Leslie**
See Stephen, Sir Leslie

**Stephen, Virginia**
See Woolf, Virginia

**Stephens, Ann Sophia** 1810-1886 .. **NCLC 303**
See also DLB 3, 73, 250

**Stephens, James** 1882(?)-1950 ........ **SSC 50;
TCLC 4**
See also CA 104; 192; DLB 19, 153, 162;
EWL 3; FANT; RGEL 2; SUFW

**Stephens, Reed**
See Donaldson, Stephen R.

**Stephenson, Neal** 1959- ................. **CLC 220**
See also AAYA 38; CA 122; CANR 88, 138,
195; CN 7; MTFW 2005; SFW 4

**Steptoe, Lydia**
See Barnes, Djuna

**Sterchi, Beat** 1949- ........................... **CLC 65**
See also CA 203

**Sterling, Brett**
See Bradbury, Ray; Hamilton, Edmond

**Sterling, Bruce** 1954- ....................... **CLC 72**
See also AAYA 78; CA 119; CANR 44, 135,
184; CN 7; MTFW 2005; SCFW 2; SFW 4

**Sterling, George** 1869-1926 ............. **TCLC 20**
See also CA 117; 165; DLB 54

**Stern, Gerald** 1925- ... **CLC 40, 100; PC 115**
See also AMWS 9; CA 81-84; CANR 28,
94, 206; CP 3, 4, 5, 6, 7; DLB 105; PFS
26; RGAL 4

**Stern, Richard (Gustave)** 1928- ... **CLC 4, 39**
See also CA 1-4R; CANR 1, 25, 52, 120;
CN 1, 2, 3, 4, 5, 6, 7; DLB 218; DLBY
1987; INT CANR-25

**Sternberg, Josef von** 1894-1969 ..... **CLC 20**
See also CA 81-84

**Sterne, Laurence** 1713-1768 ......... **LC 2, 48,
156; WLC 5**
See also BRW 3; BRWC 1; CDBLB 1660-
1789; DA; DAB; DAC; DAM MST, NOV;
DLB 39; RGEL 2; TEA

**Sternheim, (William Adolf) Carl**
1878-1942 ......................... **TCLC 8, 223**
See also CA 105; 193; DLB 56, 118; EWL
3; IDTP; RGWL 2, 3

**Stesichorus** 630?-555? BCE .......... **CMLC 167**

**Stetson, Charlotte Perkins**
See Gilman, Charlotte Perkins

**Stevens, Margaret Dean**
See Aldrich, Bess Streeter

**Stevens, Mark** 1951- ....................... **CLC 34**
See also CA 122

**Stevens, R. L.**
See Hoch, Edward D.

**Stevens, Wallace** 1879-1955 ......... **PC 6, 110;
TCLC 3, 12, 45; WLC 5**
See also AMW; AMWR 1; CA 104; 124;
CANR 181; CDALB 1929-1941; DA;
DA3; DAB; DAC; DAM MST, POET;
DLB 54, 342; EWL 3; EXPP; MAL 5;
MTCW 1, 2; PAB; PFS 13, 16, 35, 41;
RGAL 4; TUS; WP

**Stevenson, Anne (Katharine)**
1933- ..................................... **CLC 7, 33**
See also BRWS 6; CA 17-20R; CAAS 9;
CANR 9, 33, 123; CP 3, 4, 5, 6, 7; CWP;
DLB 40; MTCW 1; RHW

**Stevenson, Robert Louis** 1850-1894 ... **NCLC 5,
14, 63, 193, 274, 289, 292, 308; PC 84; SSC
11, 51, 126, 228, 235; WLC 5**
See also AAYA 24; BPFB 3; BRW 5; BRWC
1; BRWR 1; BYA 1, 2, 4, 13; CDBLB
1890-1914; CLR 10, 11, 107, 180, 204,
210, 221; DA; DA3; DAB; DAC; DAM
MST, NOV; DLB 18, 57, 141, 156, 174;
DLBD 13; GL 3; HGG; JRDA; LAIT 1, 3;
MAICYA 1, 2; NFS 11, 20, 33; RGEL 2;
RGSF 2; SATA 100; SUFW; TEA; WCH;
WLIT 4; WYA; YABC 2; YAW

**Stevenson, Robert Louis Balfour**
See Stevenson, Robert Louis

**Stewart, Douglas** 1913-1985 ........ **TCLC 317**
See also CA 81-84; CP 1, 2, 3, 4; DLB 260;
RGEL 2

**Sturges, Preston** 1898-1959 ........... **TCLC 48**
See also CA 114; 149; DLB 26

**Styron, William** 1925-2006 ...... **CLC 1, 3, 5,
   11, 15, 60, 232, 244; SSC 25**
See also AMW; AMWC 2; BEST 90:4;
   BPFB 3; CA 5-8R; 255; CANR 6, 33,
   74, 126, 191; CDALB 1968-1988; CN 1,
   2, 3, 4, 5, 6, 7; CPW; CSW; DA3; DAM
   NOV, POP; DLB 2, 143, 299; DLBY 1980;
   EWL 3; INT CANR-6; LAIT 2; MAL 5;
   MTCW 1, 2; MTFW 2005; NCFS 1; NFS
   22; RGAL 4; RGHL; RHW; TUS

**Styron, William C.**
See Styron, William

**Styron, William Clark**
See Styron, William

**Su, Chien** 1884-1918 ...................... **TCLC 24**
See also CA 123; EWL 3

**Suarez Lynch, B.**
See Bioy Casares, Adolfo; Borges, Jorge Luis

**Suassuna, Ariano Vilar** 1927- ......... **HLCS 1**
See also CA 178; DLB 307; HW 2; LAW

**Suckert, Kurt Erich**
See Malaparte, Curzio

**Suckling, Sir John** 1609-1642 .......... **LC 75;
   PC 30**
See also BRW 2; DAM POET; DLB 58, 126;
   EXPP; PAB; RGEL 2

**Suckow, Ruth** 1892-1960 ................. **SSC 18;
   TCLC 257**
See also CA 193; 113; DLB 9, 102; RGAL
   4; TCWW 2

**Sudan, Ali Kamal Kadir**
See Clarke, Arthur C.

**Sudermann, Hermann** 1857-1928 ... **TCLC 15**
See also CA 107; 201; DLB 118

**Sue, Eugene** 1804-1857 ................... **NCLC 1**
See also DLB 119

**Sueskind, Patrick**
See Suskind, Patrick

**Suetonius** c. 70-c. 130 .................. **CMLC 60**
See also AW 2; DLB 211; RGWL 2, 3;
   WLIT 8

**Su Hsuan-ying**
See Su, Chien

**Su Hsuean-ying**
See Su, Chien

**Sui Sin Far**
See Eaton, Edith Maude

**Sukenick, Ronald** 1932-2004 ........ **CLC 3, 4,
   6, 48**
See also CA 25-28R, 209; 229; CAAE 209;
   CAAS 8; CANR 32, 89; CN 3, 4, 5, 6, 7;
   DLB 173; DLBY 1981

**Suknaski, Andrew** 1942- ................. **CLC 19**
See also CA 101; CP 3, 4, 5, 6, 7; DLB 53

**Sullivan, Vernon**
See Vian, Boris

**Sully Prudhomme, Rene-Francois-Armand**
   1839-1907 ................................ **TCLC 31**
See also CA 170; DLB 332; GFL 1789 to the
   Present

**Sulpicius Severus** c. 363-c. 425 ... **CMLC 120**

**Su Man-shu**
See Su, Chien

**Sumarokov, Aleksandr Petrovich**
   1717-1777 .................................. **LC 104**
See also DLB 150

**Summerforest, Ivy B.**
See Kirkup, James

**Summers, Andrew James**
See Summers, Andy

**Summers, Andy** 1942- ..................... **CLC 26**
See also CA 255

**Summers, Hollis (Spurgeon, Jr.)**
   1916- ........................................ **CLC 10**
See also CA 5-8R; CANR 3; CN 1, 2, 3; CP
   1, 2, 3, 4; DLB 6; TCLE 1:2

**Summers, (Alphonsus Joseph-Mary
   Augustus) Montague**
   1880-1948 ................................ **TCLC 16**
See also CA 118; 163

**Sumner, Charles** 1811-1874 ...... **NCLC 364**
See also DLB 235

**Sumner, Gordon Matthew**
See Sting

**Sun Tzu** c. 400 BCE-c. 320 BCE ..... **CMLC 56**

**Supervielle, Jules** 1884-1960 ....... **TCLC 328**
See also CA 114; DLB 258; EWL 3; GFL

**Surayya, Kamala**
See Das, Kamala

**Surayya Kamala**
See Das, Kamala

**Surrey, Henry Howard**
   1517-1574 ............. **LC 121; PC 59, 167**
See also BRW 1; RGEL 2

**Surtees, R. S.**
See Surtees, Robert Smith

**Surtees, Robert Smith**
   1805-1864 ...................... **NCLC 14, 357**
See also DLB 21; RGEL 2

**Susann, Jacqueline** 1921-1974 .......... **CLC 3**
See also AITN 1; BPFB 3; CA 65-68; 53-56;
   MTCW 1, 2

**Su Shi** 1037-1101 ................... **CMLC 15, 139**
See also RGWL 2, 3

**Su Shih** 1037-1101 ................ **CMLC 15, 139**
See also RGWL 2, 3

**Suskind, Patrick**
   1949- ........................... **CLC 44, 182, 339**
See also BPFB 3; CA 145; CWW 2

**Suso, Heinrich** c. 1295-1366 ... **CMLC 87, 150**

**Sutcliff, Rosemary** 1920-1992 ......... **CLC 26**
See also AAYA 10; BRWS 16; BYA 1, 4;
   CA 5-8R; 139; CANR 37; CLR 1, 37, 138;
   CPW; DAB; DAC; DAM MST, POP;
   JRDA; LATS 1:1; MAICYA 1, 2; MAI-
   CYAS 1; RHW; SATA 6, 44, 78; SATA-
   Obit 73; WYA; YAW

**Sutherland, Efua (Theodora Morgue)**
   1924-1996 ................................ **BLC 2:3**
See also AFW; BW 1; CA 105; CWD; DLB
   117; EWL 3; IDTP; SATA 25

**Sutro, Alfred** 1863-1933 .................. **TCLC 6**
See also CA 105; 185; DLB 10; RGEL 2

**Sutton, Henry**
See Slavitt, David R.

**Su Yuan-ying**
See Su, Chien

**Su Yuean-ying**
See Su, Chien

**Suzuki, D. T.**
See Suzuki, Daisetz Teitaro

**Suzuki, Daisetz T.**
See Suzuki, Daisetz Teitaro

**Suzuki, Daisetz Teitaro**
   1870-1966 ........................... **TCLC 109**
See also CA 121; 111; MTCW 1, 2; MTFW
   2005

**Suzuki, Teitaro**
See Suzuki, Daisetz Teitaro

**Suzunoya**
See Motoori, Norinaga

**Svareff, Count Vladimir**
See Crowley, Edward Alexander

**Svevo, Italo**
See Schmitz, Aron Hector

**Sevigne, Marie (de Rabutin-Chantal)**
   1626-1696 ........................... **LC 11, 144**
See also DLB 268; GFL Beginnings to 1789;
   TWA

**Sevigne, Marie de Rabutin Chantal**
See Sevigne, Marie (de Rabutin-Chantal)

**Swados, Elizabeth** 1951- .................. **CLC 12**
See also CA 97-100; CANR 49, 163; INT
   CA-97-100

**Swados, Elizabeth A.**
See Swados, Elizabeth

**Swados, Harvey** 1920-1972 .............. **CLC 5**
See also CA 5-8R; 37-40R; CANR 6; CN 1;
   DLB 2, 335; MAL 5

**Swados, Liz**
See Swados, Elizabeth

**Swan, Gladys** 1934- ........................ **CLC 69**
See also CA 101; CANR 17, 39; TCLE 1:2

**Swanson, Logan**
See Matheson, Richard

**Swarthout, Glendon (Fred)**
   1918-1992 ................................ **CLC 35**
See also AAYA 55; CA 1-4R; 139; CANR 1,
   47; CN 1, 2, 3, 4, 5; LAIT 5; NFS 29;
   SATA 26; TCWW 1, 2; YAW

**Swedenborg, Emanuel** 1688-1772 .... **LC 105**

**Sweet, Sarah O.**
See Jewett, Sarah Orne

**Swenson, May** 1919-1989 .... **CLC 4, 14, 61,
   106; PC 14**
See also AMWS 4; CA 5-8R; 130; CANR
   36, 61, 131; CP 1, 2, 3, 4; DA; DAB; DAC;
   DAM MST, POET; DLB 5; EXPP; GLL 2;
   MAL 5; MTCW 1, 2; MTFW 2005; PFS
   16, 30, 38; SATA 15; WP

**Swift, Augustus**
See Lovecraft, H. P.

**Swift, Graham** 1949- .. **CLC 41, 88, 233, 353**
See also BRWC 2; BRWS 5; CA 117; 122;
   CANR 46, 71, 128, 181, 218; CN 4, 5, 6,
   7; DLB 194, 326; MTCW 2; MTFW 2005;
   NFS 18; RGSF 2

**Swift, Jonathan** 1667-1745 ............. **LC 1, 42,
   101, 202; PC 9, 133, 210; WLC 6**
See also AAYA 41; BRW 3; BRWC 1; BRWR
   1; BYA 5, 14; CDBLB 1660-1789; CLR 53,
   161; DA; DA3; DAB; DAC; DAM MST,
   NOV, POET; DLB 39, 95, 101; EXPN;
   LAIT 1; NFS 6; PFS 27, 37; RGEL 2;
   SATA 19; TEA; WCH; WLIT 3

**Swinburne, Algernon Charles** 1837-1909 ... **PC
   24, 196; TCLC 8, 36; WLC 6**
See also BRW 5; CA 105; 140; CDBLB 1832-
   1890; DA; DA3; DAB; DAC; DAM MST,
   POET; DLB 35, 57; PAB; RGEL 2; TEA

**Swinfen, Ann** .................................. **CLC 34**
See also CA 202

**Swinnerton, Frank (Arthur)**
   1884-1982 ................................ **CLC 31**
See also CA 202; 108; CN 1, 2, 3; DLB 34

**Swinnerton, Frank Arthur**
   1884-1982 ................................ **CLC 31**
See also CA 108; DLB 34

**Swithen, John**
See King, Stephen

**Syjuco, Miguel** 1976- .................... **CLC 318**
See also CA 305

**Sylphid**
See Robinson, Mary

**Sylvia**
See Ashton-Warner, Sylvia (Constance)

**Symmes, Robert Edward**
See Duncan, Robert

**Symonds, John Addington**
   1840-1893 ...................... **NCLC 34, 367**
See also BRWS 14; DLB 57, 144

**Symons, Arthur** 1865-1945 ............. **PC 119;
   TCLC 11, 243**
See also BRWS 14; CA 107; 189; DLB 19,
   57, 149; RGEL 2

**Symons, Julian (Gustave)**
   1912-1994 ...................... **CLC 2, 14, 32**
See also CA 49-52; 147; CAAS 3; CANR 3,
   33, 59; CMW 4; CN 1, 2, 3, 4, 5; CP 1, 3,
   4; DLB 87, 155; DLBY 1992; MSW;
   MTCW 1

**Synge, Edmund John Millington**
See Synge, John Millington

**Telles, Lygia Fagundes** 1923- ........ **CLC 390**
See also CA 157; CWW 2; DLB 113, 307;
EWL 3; HW 2; LAW; RGSF 2

**Temple, Ann**
See Mortimer, Penelope (Ruth)

**Tennant, Emma** 1937- ............... **CLC 13, 52**
See also BRWS 9; CA 65-68; CAAS 9;
CANR 10, 38, 59, 88, 177; CN 3, 4, 5,
6, 7; DLB 14; EWL 3; SFW 4

**Tenneshaw, S.M.**
See Silverberg, Robert

**Tenney, Tabitha Gilman**
1762-1837 .................... **NCLC 122, 248**
See also DLB 37, 200

**Tennyson, Alfred** 1809-1892 ......... **NCLC 30,
65, 115, 202; PC 6, 101; WLC 6**
See also AAYA 50; BRW 4; BRWR 3;
CDBLB 1832-1890; DA; DA3; DAB;
DAC; DAM MST, POET; DLB 32; EXPP;
PAB; PFS 1, 2, 4, 11, 15, 19, 44; RGEL 2;
TEA; WLIT 4; WP

**Teran, Lisa St. Aubin de**
See St. Aubin de Teran, Lisa

**Terence** c. 184 BCE-c. 159 BCE ...... **CMLC 14,
132; DC 7**
See also AW 1; CDWLB 1; DLB 211;
RGWL 2, 3; TWA; WLIT 8

**Teresa de Jesus, St.** 1515-1582 ... **LC 18, 149**

**Teresa of Avila, St.**
See Teresa de Jesus, St.

**Terkel, Louis**
See Terkel, Studs

**Terkel, Studs** 1912-2008 .................. **CLC 38**
See also AAYA 32; AITN 1; CA 57-60; 278;
CANR 18, 45, 67, 132, 195; DA3; MTCW
1, 2; MTFW 2005; TUS

**Terkel, Studs Louis**
See Terkel, Studs

**Terry, C. V.**
See Slaughter, Frank G(ill)

**Terry, Megan** 1932- ............ **CLC 19; DC 13**
See also CA 77-80; CABS 3; CAD; CANR
43; CD 5, 6; CWD; DFS 18; DLB 7, 249;
GLL 2

**Tertullian** c. 160-c. 240 ....... **CMLC 29, 177**

**Tertz, Abram**
See Sinyavsky, Andrei (Donatevich)

**Tesich, Steve** 1943(?)-1996 ......... **CLC 40, 69**
See also CA 105; 152; CAD; DLBY 1983

**Tesla, Nikola** 1856-1943 ................ **TCLC 88**
See also CA 157

**Teternikov, Fyodor Kuzmich**
1863-1927 ........................ **TCLC 9, 259**
See also CA 104; DLB 295; EWL 3

**Tevis, Walter** 1928-1984 .................. **CLC 42**
See also CA 113; SFW 4

**Tey, Josephine**
See Mackintosh, Elizabeth

**Thackeray, William Makepeace**
1811-1863 ............ **NCLC 5, 14, 22, 43,
169, 213, 294; WLC 6**
See also BRW 5; BRWC 2; CDBLB 1832-
1890; DA; DA3; DAB; DAC; DAM MST,
NOV; DLB 21, 55, 159, 163; NFS 13;
RGEL 2; SATA 23; TEA; WLIT 3

**Thakura, Ravindranatha**
See Tagore, Rabindranath

**Thalmayr, Andreas**
See Enzensberger, Hans Magnus

**Thames, C. H.**
See Marlowe, Stephen

**Tharoor, Shashi** 1956- ..................... **CLC 70**
See also CA 141; CANR 91, 201; CN 6, 7

**Thaxter, Celia** 1835-1894 ............. **NCLC 308**
See also ANW; DLB 239

**The Coen Brothers**
See Coen, Ethan; Coen, Joel

**Thelwall, John** 1764-1834 ........... **NCLC 162**
See also DLB 93, 158

**Thelwell, Michael Miles** 1939- ........ **CLC 22**
See also BW 2; CA 101

**Theo, Ion**
See Arghezi, Tudor

**Theobald, Lewis, Jr.**
See Lovecraft, H. P.

**Theocritus** c. 310 BCE .......... **CMLC 45, 167**
See also AW 1; DLB 176; RGWL 2, 3

**Theodorescu, Ion N.**
See Arghezi, Tudor

**Theodoret of Cyrrhus** 393-457? .... **CMLC 165**

**Therion, Master**
See Crowley, Edward Alexander

**Theroux, Alexander** 1939- ........... **CLC 2, 25**
See also CA 85-88; CANR 20, 63, 190; CN
4, 5, 6, 7

**Theroux, Alexander Louis**
See Theroux, Alexander

**Theroux, Paul** 1941- ........ **CLC 5, 8, 11, 15,
28, 46, 159, 303**
See also AAYA 28; AMWS 8; BEST 89:4;
BPFB 3; CA 33-36R; CANR 20, 45, 74,
133, 179, 233; CDALBS; CN 1, 2, 3, 4, 5, 6,
7; CP 1; CPW 1; DA3; DAM POP; DLB 2,
218; EWL 3; HGG; MAL 5; MTCW 1, 2;
MTFW 2005; RGAL 4; SATA 44, 109; TUS

**Theroux, Paul Edward**
See Theroux, Paul

**Thesen, Sharon** 1946- ..................... **CLC 56**
See also CA 163; CANR 125; CP 5, 6, 7;
CWP

**Thespis** fl. 6th cent. BCE ................. **CMLC 51**
See also LMFS 1

**Thevenin, Denis**
See Duhamel, Georges

**Thibault, Jacques Anatole Francois**
See France, Anatole

**Thiele, Colin** 1920-2006 ................... **CLC 17**
See also CA 29-32R; CANR 12, 28, 53, 105;
CLR 27; CP 1, 2; DLB 289; MAICYA 1,
2; SAAS 2; SATA 14, 72, 125; YAW

**Thiong'o, Ngugi Wa**
See Ngugi wa Thiong'o

**Thistlethwaite, Bel**
See Wetherald, Agnes Ethelwyn

**Thomas, Audrey (Callahan)** 1935- ... **CLC 7,
13, 37, 107, 289; SSC 20**
See also AITN 2; CA 21-24R; 237; CAAE
237; CAAS 19; CANR 36, 58; CN 2, 3, 4,
5, 6, 7; DLB 60; MTCW 1; RGSF 2

**Thomas, Augustus** 1857-1934 ....... **TCLC 97**
See also MAL 5

**Thomas, D.M.** 1935- ... **CLC 13, 22, 31, 132**
See also BPFB 3; BRWS 4; CA 61-64; 303;
CAAE 303; CAAS 11; CANR 17, 45, 75;
CDBLB 1960 to Present; CN 4, 5, 6, 7; CP
1, 2, 3, 4, 5, 6, 7; DA3; DLB 40, 207, 299;
HGG; INT CANR-17; MTCW 1, 2;
MTFW 2005; RGHL; SFW 4

**Thomas, Donald Michael**
See Thomas, D.M.

**Thomas, Dylan** 1914-1953 ............. **PC 2, 52;
SSC 3, 44; TCLC 1, 8, 45, 105; WLC 6**
See also AAYA 45; BRWR 3; BRWS 1; CA
104; 120; CANR 65; CDBLB 1945-1960;
DA; DA3; DAB; DAC; DAM DRAM,
MST, POET; DLB 13, 20, 139; EWL 3;
EXPP; LAIT 3; MTCW 1, 2; MTFW 2005;
PAB; PFS 1, 3, 8; RGEL 2; RGSF 2; SATA
60; TEA; WLIT 4; WP

**Thomas, Dylan Marlais**
See Thomas, Dylan

**Thomas, (Philip) Edward**
1878-1917 ................. **PC 53; TCLC 10**
See also BRW 6; BRWS 3; CA 106; 153;
DAM POET; DLB 19, 98, 156, 216; EWL
3; PAB; RGEL 2

**Thomas, J. F.**
See Fleming, Thomas

**Thomas, Joyce Carol** 1938- ............ **CLC 35**
See also AAYA 12, 54; BW 2, 3; CA 113;
116; CANR 48, 114, 135, 206; CLR 19;
DLB 33; INT CA-116; JRDA; MAICYA 1,
2; MTCW 1, 2; MTFW 2005; SAAS 7;
SATA 40, 78, 123, 137, 210; SATA-Essay
137; WYA; YAW

**Thomas, Lewis** 1913-1993 .............. **CLC 35**
See also ANW; CA 85-88; 143; CANR 38,
60; DLB 275; MTCW 1, 2

**Thomas, M. Carey** 1857-1935 ...... **TCLC 89**
See also FW

**Thomas, Paul**
See Mann, Thomas

**Thomas, Piri** 1928-2011 .... **CLC 17; HLCS 2**
See also CA 73-76; HW 1; LLW; SSFS 28

**Thomas, R(onald) S(tuart)**
1913-2000 ........ **CLC 6, 13, 48; PC 99**
See also BRWS 12; CA 89-92; 189; CAAS
4; CANR 30; CDBLB 1960 to Present; CP
1, 2, 3, 4, 5, 6, 7; DAB; DAM POET; DLB
27; EWL 3; MTCW 1; RGEL 2

**Thomas, Ross (Elmore)**
1926-1995 ................................. **CLC 39**
See also CA 33-36R; 150; CANR 22, 63;
CMW 4

**Thompson, Francis (Joseph)**
1859-1907 ................................. **TCLC 4**
See also BRW 5; CA 104; 189; CDBLB
1890-1914; DLB 19; RGEL 2; TEA

**Thompson, Francis Clegg**
See Mencken, H. L.

**Thompson, Hunter S.** 1937(?)-2005 ... **CLC 9,
17, 40, 104, 229**
See also AAYA 45; BEST 89:1; BPFB 3; CA
17-20R; 236; CANR 23, 46, 74, 77, 111,
133; CPW; CSW; DA3; DAM POP; DLB
185; MTCW 1, 2; MTFW 2005; TUS

**Thompson, Hunter Stockton**
See Thompson, Hunter S.

**Thompson, James Myers**
See Thompson, Jim

**Thompson, Jim** 1906-1977 ............. **CLC 69**
See also BPFB 3; CA 140; CMW 4; CPW;
DLB 226; MSW

**Thompson, Judith (Clare Francesca)**
1954- ....................................... **CLC 39**
See also CA 143; CD 5, 6; CWD; DFS 22;
DLB 334

**Thomson, James** 1700-1748 .............. **LC 16,
29, 40; PC 193**
See also BRWS 3; DAM POET; DLB 95;
RGEL 2

**Thomson, James** 1834-1882 .......... **NCLC 18**
See also DAM POET; DLB 35; RGEL 2

**Thoreau, Henry David**
1817-1862 .................... **NCLC 7, 21, 61,
138, 207; PC 30; WLC 6**
See also AAYA 42; AMW; ANW; BYA 3;
CDALB 1640-1865; DA; DA3; DAB;
DAC; DAM MST; DLB 1, 183, 223,
270, 298, 366; LAIT 2; LMFS 1; NCFS
3; RGAL 4; TUS

**Thorndike, E. L.**
See Thorndike, Edward L(ee)

**Thorndike, Edward L(ee)**
1874-1949 ............................ **TCLC 107**
See also CA 121

**Thornton, Hall**
See Silverberg, Robert

**Thorpe, Adam** 1956- ..................... **CLC 176**
See also CA 129; CANR 92, 160; DLB 231

**Thorpe, Thomas Bangs**
1815-1878 ............................. **NCLC 183**
See also DLB 3, 11, 248; RGAL 4

**Theriault, Yves** 1915-1983 ............. **CLC 79**
See also CA 102; CANR 150; CCA 1; DAC;
DAM MST; DLB 88; EWL 3

**Thubron, Colin** 1939- .................... **CLC 163**
See also CA 25-28R; CANR 12, 29, 59, 95, 171, 232; CN 5, 6, 7; DLB 204, 231

**Thubron, Colin Gerald Dryden**
See Thubron, Colin

**Thucydides**
c. 455 BCE-c. 399 BCE ..... **CMLC 17, 117**
See also AW 1; DLB 176; RGWL 2, 3; WLIT 8

**Thumboo, Edwin Nadason**
1933- ........................... **CLC 360; PC 30**
See also CA 194; CP 1

**Thurber, James** 1894-1961 ......... **CLC 5, 11, 25, 125; SSC 1, 47, 137**
See also AAYA 56; AMWS 1; BPFB 3; BYA 5; CA 73-76; CANR 17, 39; CDALB 1929-1941; CWRI 5; DA; DA3; DAB; DAC; DAM DRAM, MST, NOV; DLB 4, 11, 22, 102; EWL 3; EXPS; FANT; LAIT 3; MAICYA 1, 2; MAL 5; MTCW 1, 2; MTFW 2005; RGAL 4; RGSF 2; SATA 13; SSFS 1, 10, 19, 37; SUFW; TUS

**Thurber, James Grover**
See Thurber, James

**Thurman, Wallace (Henry)**
1902-1934 ................ **BLC 1:3; HR 1:3; TCLC 6**
See also BW 1, 3; CA 104; 124; CANR 81; DAM MULT; DLB 51

**Tian**
See Günderrode, Karoline von

**Tibullus** c. 54 BCE-c. 18 BCE .......... **CMLC 36**
See also AW 2; DLB 211; RGWL 2, 3; WLIT 8

**Ticheburn, Cheviot**
See Ainsworth, William Harrison

**Ticknor, George**
1791-1871 ............................. **NCLC 255**
See also DLB 1, 59, 140, 235

**Tieck, (Johann) Ludwig** 1773-1853 ... **DC 53; NCLC 5, 46; SSC 31, 100**
See also CDWLB 2; DLB 90; EW 5; IDTP; RGSF 2; RGWL 2, 3; SUFW

**Tiger, Derry**
See Ellison, Harlan

**Tiger, Theobald**
See Tucholsky, Kurt

**Tighe, Mary** 1772-1810 ................ **NCLC 330**

**Tighe, Mrs. Henry**
See Tighe, Mary

**Tilghman, Christopher** 1946- .......... **CLC 65**
See also CA 159; CANR 135, 151; CSW; DLB 244

**Tillich, Paul (Johannes)**
1886-1965 ............................. **CLC 131**
See also CA 5-8R; 25-28R; CANR 33; MTCW 1, 2

**Tillinghast, Richard (Williford)**
1940- ........................................ **CLC 29**
See also CA 29-32R; CAAS 23; CANR 26, 51, 96; CP 2, 3, 4, 5, 6, 7; CSW

**Tillman, Lynne** (?)- ................ **CLC 231, 312**
See also CA 173; CANR 144, 172, 238

**Timoneda, Juan de** 1518/1520?-1583 ... **LC 250**
See also DLB 318

**Timrod, Henry** 1828-1867 ............. **NCLC 25**
See also DLB 3, 248; RGAL 4

**Tindall, Gillian (Elizabeth)** 1938- ..... **CLC 7**
See also CA 21-24R; CANR 11, 65, 107; CN 1, 2, 3, 4, 5, 6, 7

**Ting Ling**
See Chiang, Pin-chin

**Tiny Tim**
See Harwood, Gwen

**Tiptree, James, Jr.**
See Sheldon, Alice Hastings Bradley

**Tirone Smith, Mary-Ann** 1944- ...... **CLC 39**
See also CA 118; 136; CANR 113, 210; SATA 143

**Tirso de Molina** 1580(?)-1648 .......... **DC 13; HLCS 2; LC 73**
See also RGWL 2, 3

**Titania**
See Robinson, Mary

**Titmarsh, Michael Angelo**
See Thackeray, William Makepeace

**Tiutchev, Fedor**
See Tyutchev, Fyodor

**Tjutčev, Fedor**
See Tyutchev, Fyodor

**Tocqueville, Alexis (Charles Henri Maurice Clerel Comte) de**
1805-1859 .................. **NCLC 7, 63, 267**
See also EW 6; GFL 1789 to the Present; TWA

**Toe, Tucker**
See Westlake, Donald E.

**Toer, Pramoedya Ananta**
1925-2006 .............................. **CLC 186**
See also CA 197; 251; CANR 170; DLB 348; RGWL 3

**Toffler, Alvin** 1928- ....................... **CLC 168**
See also CA 13-16R; CANR 15, 46, 67, 183; CPW; DAM POP; MTCW 1, 2

**Toibin, Colm** 1955- ................. **CLC 162, 285**
See also CA 142; CANR 81, 149, 213; CN 7; DLB 271

**Tolkien, J. R. R.** 1892-1973 ......... **CLC 1, 2, 3, 8, 12, 38; SSC 156; TCLC 137, 299; WLC 6**
See also AAYA 10; AITN 1; BPFB 3; BRWC 2; BRWS 2; CA 17-18; 45-48; CANR 36, 134; CAP 2; CDBLB 1914-1945; CLR 56, 152; CN 1; CPW 1; CWRI 5; DA; DA3; DAB; DAC; DAM MST, NOV, POP; DLB 15, 160, 255; EFS 1:2, 2:1; EWL 3; FANT; JRDA; LAIT 1; LATS 1:2; LMFS 2; MAICYA 1, 2; MTCW 1, 2; MTFW 2005; NFS 8, 26; RGEL 2; SATA 2, 32, 100; SATA-Obit 24; SFW 4; SUFW; TEA; WCH; WYA; YAW

**Tolkien, John Ronald Reuel**
See Tolkien, J. R. R.

**Toller, Ernst** 1893-1939 ......... **TCLC 10, 235**
See also CA 107; 186; DLB 124; EWL 3; RGWL 2, 3

**Tolson, M. B.**
See Tolson, Melvin B(eaunorus)

**Tolson, Melvin B(eaunorus)**
1898(?)-1966 .......... **BLC 1:3; CLC 36, 105; PC 88**
See also AFAW 1, 2; BW 1, 3; CA 124; 89-92; CANR 80; DAM MULT, POET; DLB 48, 76; MAL 5; RGAL 4

**Tolstaya, Tatyana** 1951- .................. **SSC 263**
See also CA 130; CANR 145, 170; CWW 2; DLB 285; EWL 3; RGSF 2; RGWL 3; SSFS 14

**Tolstoi, Aleksei Nikolaevich**
See Tolstoy, Alexey Nikolaevich

**Tolstoi, Lev**
See Tolstoy, Leo

**Tolstoy, Aleksei Nikolaevich**
See Tolstoy, Alexey Nikolaevich

**Tolstoy, Alexey Nikolaevich**
1882-1945 ................................. **TCLC 18**
See also CA 107; 158; DLB 272; EWL 3; SFW 4

**Tolstoy, Leo** 1828-1910 ............... **SSC 9, 30, 45, 54, 131, 267; TCLC 4, 11, 17, 28, 44, 79, 173, 260; WLC 6**
See also AAYA 56; CA 104; 123; DA; DA3; DAB; DAC; DAM MST, NOV; DLB 238; EFS 1:2, 2:2; EW 7; EXPS; IDTP; LAIT 2; LATS 1:1; LMFS 1; NFS 10, 28; RGSF 2; RGWL 2, 3; SATA 26; SSFS 5, 28, 37; TWA

**Tolstoy, Count Leo**
See Tolstoy, Leo

**Tolstoy, Leo Nikolaevich**
See Tolstoy, Leo

**Tomalin, Claire** 1933- .................... **CLC 166**
See also CA 89-92; CANR 52, 88, 165; DLB 155

**Tomasi di Lampedusa, Giuseppe**
See Lampedusa, Giuseppe di

**Tomlin, Lily** 1939(?)- ........................ **CLC 17**
See also CA 117

**Tomlin, Mary Jane**
See Tomlin, Lily

**Tomlin, Mary Jean**
See Tomlin, Lily

**Tomline, F. Latour**
See Gilbert, W(illiam) S(chwenck)

**Tomlinson, (Alfred) Charles**
1927- ........ **CLC 2, 4, 6, 13, 45; PC 17**
See also CA 5-8R; CANR 33; CP 1, 2, 3, 4, 5, 6, 7; DAM POET; DLB 40; TCLE 1:2

**Tomlinson, H(enry) M(ajor)**
1873-1958 ............................. **TCLC 71**
See also CA 118; 161; DLB 36, 100, 195

**Tomlinson, Mary Jane**
See Tomlin, Lily

**Tomson, Graham R.**
See Watson, Rosamund Marriott

**Tonna, Charlotte Elizabeth**
1790-1846 ............................. **NCLC 135**
See also DLB 163

**Tonson, Jacob** fl. 1655(?)-1736 .......... **LC 86**
See also DLB 170

**Toole, John Kennedy** 1937-1969 ... **CLC 19, 64**
See also BPFB 3; CA 104; DLBY 1981; MTCW 2; MTFW 2005

**Toomer, Eugene**
See Toomer, Jean

**Toomer, Eugene Pinchback**
See Toomer, Jean

**Toomer, Jean** 1894-1967 ............... **BLC 1:3; CLC 1, 4, 13, 22; HR 1:3; PC 7; SSC 1, 45, 138, 233; TCLC 172, 288; WLCS**
See also AFAW 1, 2; AMWS 3, 9; BW 1; CA 85-88; CDALB 1917-1929; DA3; DAM MULT; DLB 45, 51; EWL 3; EXPP; EXPS; LMFS 2; MAL 5; MTCW 1, 2; MTFW 2005; NFS 11; PFS 31, 43; RGAL 4; RGSF 2; SSFS 5

**Toomer, Nathan Jean**
See Toomer, Jean

**Toomer, Nathan Pinchback**
See Toomer, Jean

**Torley, Luke**
See Blish, James

**Tornimparte, Alessandra**
See Ginzburg, Natalia

**Toro, Guillermo del**
See del Toro, Guillermo

**Torre, Raoul della**
See Mencken, H. L.

**Torrence, Ridgely** 1874-1950 ........ **TCLC 97**
See also DLB 54, 249; MAL 5

**Torrente Ballester, Gonzalo**
1910-1999 ............................. **TCLC 323**
See also DLB 322; EWL 3

**Torrey, E. Fuller** 1937- .................... **CLC 34**
See also CA 119; CANR 71, 158

**Torrey, Edwin Fuller**
See Torrey, E. Fuller

**Torsvan, Ben Traven**
See Traven, B.

**Torsvan, Benno Traven**
See Traven, B.

**Torsvan, Berick Traven**
See Traven, B.

**Torsvan, Berwick Traven**
See Traven, B.

**Torsvan, Bruno Traven**
See Traven, B.

**Torsvan, Traven**
See Traven, B.

**Tourneur, Cyril** 1575(?)-1626 ..... **LC 66, 181**
See also BRW 2; DAM DRAM; DLB 58;
RGEL 2

**Tournier, Michel** 1924- ................ **CLC 6, 23, 36, 95, 249, 426; SSC 88**
See also CA 49-52; CANR 3, 36, 74, 149;
CWW 2; DLB 83; EWL 3; GFL 1789 to
the Present; MTCW 1, 2; SATA 23

**Tournier, Michel Edouard**
See Tournier, Michel

**Tournimparte, Alessandra**
See Ginzburg, Natalia

**Towers, Ivar**
See Kornbluth, C(yril) M.

**Towne, Robert (Burton)**
1936(?)- ........................... **CLC 87**
See also CA 108; DLB 44; IDFW 3, 4

**Townsend, Sue** 1946- ...................... **CLC 61**
See also AAYA 28; CA 119; 127; CANR 65,
107, 202; CBD; CD 5, 6; CPW; CWD;
DAB; DAC; DAM MST; DLB 271, 352;
INT CA-127; SATA 55, 93; SATA-Brief
48; YAW

**Townsend, Susan Lilian**
See Townsend, Sue

**Townshend, Pete**
See Townshend, Peter

**Townshend, Peter** 1945- ............. **CLC 17, 42**
See also CA 107

**Townshend, Peter Dennis Blandford**
See Townshend, Peter

**Tozzi, Federigo** 1883-1920 ............. **TCLC 31**
See also CA 160; CANR 110; DLB 264;
EWL 3; WLIT 7

**Trafford, F. G.**
See Riddell, Charlotte

**Traherne, Thomas**
1637(?)-1674 ........... **LC 99; PC 70, 174**
See also BRW 2; BRWS 11; DLB 131; PAB;
RGEL 2

**Traill, Catharine Parr**
1802-1899 .......................... **NCLC 31, 317**
See also DLB 99

**Trakl, Georg** 1887-1914 ..................... **PC 20; TCLC 5, 239**
See also CA 104; 165; EW 10; EWL 3;
LMFS 2; MTCW 2; RGWL 2, 3

**Trambley, Estela Portillo**
See Portillo Trambley, Estela

**Tranquilli, Secondino**
See Silone, Ignazio

**Transtromer, Tomas**
1931- .................... **CLC 52, 65, 334**
See also CA 117; 129; CAAS 17; CANR
115, 172; CWW 2; DAM POET; DLB 257;
EWL 3; PFS 21, 44

**Transtromer, Tomas Goesta**
See Transtromer, Tomas

**Transtromer, Tomas Gosta**
See Transtromer, Tomas

**Transtromer, Tomas Gosta**
See Transtromer, Tomas

**Traven, B.** 1882(?)-1969 ............... **CLC 8, 11**
See also CA 19-20; 25-28R; CAP 2; DLB 9,
56; EWL 3; MTCW 1; RGAL 4

**Trediakovsky, Vasilii Kirillovich**
1703-1769 ..................................... **LC 68**
See also DLB 150

**Treitel, Jonathan** 1959- .................... **CLC 70**
See also CA 210; DLB 267

**Trelawny, Edward John**
1792-1881 ................................. **NCLC 85**
See also DLB 110, 116, 144

**Tremain, Rose** 1943- ....................... **CLC 42**
See also CA 97-100; CANR 44, 95, 186,
232; CN 4, 5, 6, 7; DLB 14, 271; RGSF 2;
RHW

**Tremblay, Michel**
1942- ............ **CLC 29, 102, 225; DC 58**
See also CA 116; 128; CCA 1; CWW 2;
DAC; DAM MST; DLB 60; EWL 3; GLL
1; MTCW 1, 2; MTFW 2005

**Tressell, Robert** 1870-1911 .......... **TCLC 370**
See also CA 186; DLB 197; RGEL 2

**Trethewey, Natasha** 1966- ............. **CLC 340**
See also AMWS 21; CA 203; PFS 29, 39

**Trevanian**
See Whitaker, Rod

**Trevisa, John** c. 1342-c. 1402 .......... **LC 139**
See also BRWS 9; DLB 146

**Trevor, Frances**
See Teasdale, Sara

**Trevor, Glen**
See Hilton, James

**Trevor, William** 1928- ...... **CLC 7, 9, 14, 25, 71, 116, 266, 376; SSC 21, 58**
See also BRWS 4; CA 9-12R; CANR 4, 37,
55, 76, 102, 139, 195, 236; CBD; CD 5, 6;
DAM NOV; DLB 14, 139; EWL 3; INT
CANR-37; LATS 1; MTCW 1, 2;
MTFW 2005; RGEL 2; RGSF 2; SSFS
10, 33; TCLE 1:2; TEA

**Triana, Jose** 1931(?)- .......................... **DC 39**
See also CA 131; DLB 305; EWL 3; HW 1;
LAW

**Trifonov, Iurii (Valentinovich)**
See Trifonov, Yuri (Valentinovich)

**Trifonov, Yuri (Valentinovich)**
1925-1981 ............................. **CLC 45**
See also CA 126; 103; DLB 302; EWL 3;
MTCW 1; RGWL 2, 3

**Trifonov, Yury Valentinovich**
See Trifonov, Yuri (Valentinovich)

**Trilling, Diana (Rubin)**
1905-1996 ............................ **CLC 129**
See also CA 5-8R; 154; CANR 10, 46; INT
CANR-10; MTCW 1, 2

**Trilling, Lionel** 1905-1975 ............... **CLC 9, 11, 24; SSC 75**
See also AMWS 3; CA 9-12R; 61-64;
CANR 10, 105; CN 1, 2; DLB 28, 63;
EWL 3; INT CANR-10; MAL 5; MTCW
1, 2; RGAL 4; TUS

**Trimball, W. H.**
See Mencken, H. L.

**Triolet, Elsa** 1896-1970 ................ **TCLC 322**
See also CA 25-28R, 247; DLB 72

**Tristan**
See Gomez de la Serna, Ramon

**Tristram**
See Housman, A. E.

**Trogdon, William**
See Heat-Moon, William Least

**Trogdon, William Lewis**
See Heat-Moon, William Least

**Trollope, Anthony** 1815-1882 ........ **NCLC 6, 33, 101, 215, 269, 274, 275, 360; SSC 28, 133; WLC 6**
See also BRW 5; CDBLB 1832-1890; DA;
DA3; DAB; DAC; DAM MST, NOV; DLB
21, 57, 159, 366; NFS 42; RGEL 2; RGSF
2; SATA 22

**Trollope, Frances** 1779-1863 ... **NCLC 30, 360**
See also DLB 21, 166

**Trollope, Joanna** 1943- .................. **CLC 186**
See also CA 101; CANR 58, 95, 149, 191;
CN 7; CPW; DLB 207; RHW

**Trotsky, Leon** 1879-1940 ............... **TCLC 22**
See also CA 118; 167

**Trotter, Catharine** 1679-1749 ....... **LC 8, 165**
See also BRWS 16; DLB 84, 252

**Trotter, Wilfred** 1872-1939 ........... **TCLC 97**

**Troupe, Quincy** 1943- ..................... **BLC 2:3**
See also BW 2; CA 113; 124; CANR 43, 90,
126, 213; DLB 41

**Trout, Kilgore**
See Farmer, Philip Jose

**Trow, George William Swift**
See Trow, George W.S.

**Trow, George W.S.** 1943-2006 ........ **CLC 52**
See also CA 126; 255; CANR 91

**Troyat, Henri**
1911-2007 ................................ **CLC 23**
See also CA 45-48; 258; CANR 2, 33, 67,
117; GFL 1789 to the Present; MTCW 1

**Trudeau, Garretson Beekman**
See Trudeau, Garry

**Trudeau, Garry** 1948- ..................... **CLC 12**
See also AAYA 10, 60; AITN 2; CA 81-84;
CANR 31; SATA 35, 168

**Trudeau, Garry B.**
See Trudeau, Garry

**Trudeau, G. B.** 1948- ..................... **CLC 12**
See also AAYA 10, 60; AITN 2; CA 81-84;
CANR 31; SATA 35, 168

**Truffaut, Francois**
1932-1984 .......................... **CLC 20, 101**
See also AAYA 84; CA 81-84; 113; CANR 34

**Trumbo, Dalton**
1905-1976 ................................ **CLC 19**
See also CA 21-24R; 69-72; CANR 10; CN
1, 2; DLB 26; IDFW 3, 4; YAW

**Trumbull, John**
1750-1831 .............................. **NCLC 30**
See also DLB 31; RGAL 4

**Trundlett, Helen B.**
See Eliot, T. S.

**Truong, Monique** 1968- ................. **CLC 438**
See also CA 224; CANR 225

**Truth, Sojourner** 1797(?)-1883 ..... **NCLC 94**
See also DLB 239; FW; LAIT 2

**Tryon, Thomas** 1926-1991 .......... **CLC 3, 11**
See also AITN 1; BPFB 3; CA 29-32R; 135;
CANR 32, 77; CPW; DA3; DAM POP;
HGG; MTCW 1

**Tryon, Tom**
See Tryon, Thomas

**Tryphê**
See Barney, Natalie Clifford

**Ts'ao Hsueh-ch'in** 1715(?)-1763 .......... **LC 1**

**Toson**
See Shimazaki, Haruki

**Tsurayuki Ed.** fl. 10th cent. ................ **PC 73**

**Tsvetaeva, Marina** 1892-1941 .......... **PC 14; TCLC 7, 35**
See also CA 104; 128; CANR 73; DLB 295;
EW 11; MTCW 1, 2; PFS 29; RGWL 2, 3

**Tsvetaeva Efron, Marina Ivanovna**
See Tsvetaeva, Marina

**Tucholsky, Kurt** 1890-1935 ......... **TCLC 338**
See also CA 189; DLB 56; EWL 3

**Tuck, Lily** 1938- ............................. **CLC 70**
See also AAYA 74; CA 139; CANR 90, 192

**Tuckerman, Frederick Goddard**
1821-1873 ................................. **PC 85**
See also DLB 243; RGAL 4

**Tu Fu** 712-770 ........................................ **PC 9**
See also DAM MULT; PFS 32; RGWL 2, 3;
TWA; WP

**Tulsidas, Gosvami** 1532(?)-1623 ...... **LC 158**
See also RGWL 2, 3

**Tunis, John R(oberts)** 1889-1975 ... **CLC 12**
See also BYA 1; CA 61-64; CANR 62; DLB
22, 171; JRDA; MAICYA 1, 2; SATA 37;
SATA-Brief 30; YAW

**Tuohy, Frank**
See Tuohy, John Francis

**Tuohy, John Francis** 1925- ............... **CLC 37**
See also CA 5-8R; 178; CANR 3, 47; CN 1,
2, 3, 4, 5, 6, 7; DLB 14, 139

**Turco, Lewis** 1934- ..................... **CLC 11, 63**
See also CA 13-16R; CAAS 22; CANR 24,
51, 185; CP 1, 2, 3, 4, 5, 6, 7; DLBY 1984;
TCLE 1:2

**Turco, Lewis Putnam**
See Turco, Lewis

**Turgenev, Ivan** 1818-1883 ................. **DC 7;**
**NCLC 21, 37, 122, 269; SSC 7, 57, 240;**
**WLC 6**
See also AAYA 58; DA; DAB; DAC; DAM
MST, NOV; DFS 6; DLB 238, 284; EW 6;
LATS 1:1; NFS 16; RGSF 2; RGWL 2, 3;
TWA

**Turgenev, Ivan Sergeevich**
See Turgenev, Ivan

**Turgot, Anne-Robert-Jacques**
1727-1781 ..................................... **LC 26**
See also DLB 314

**Turlin, Heinrich von dem**
See Heinrich von dem Tuerlin

**Turner, Frederick** 1943- ................... **CLC 48**
See also CA 73-76, 227; CAAE 227; CAAS
10; CANR 12, 30, 56; DLB 40, 282

**Turrini, Peter** 1944- .......................... **DC 49**
See also CA 209; DLB 124

**Turton, James**
See Crace, Jim

**Tutu, Desmond M.** 1931- .............. **BLC 1:3;**
**CLC 80**
See also BW 1, 3; CA 125; CANR 67, 81,
242; DAM MULT

**Tutu, Desmond Mpilo**
See Tutu, Desmond M.

**Tutuola, Amos** 1920-1997 ...... **BLC 1:3, 2:3;**
**CLC 5, 14, 29; TCLC 188**
See also AAYA 76; AFW; BW 2, 3; CA 9-
12R; 159; CANR 27, 66; CDWLB 3; CN
1, 2, 3, 4, 5, 6; DA3; DAM MULT; DLB
125; DNFS 2; EWL 3; MTCW 1, 2;
MTFW 2005; RGEL 2; WLIT 2

**Twain, Mark** 1835-1910 ....... **SSC 6, 26, 34,**
**87, 119, 210, 234, 258; TCLC 6, 12, 19,**
**36, 48, 59, 161, 185, 260; WLC 6**
See also AAYA 20; AMW; AMWC 1; BPFB
3; BYA 2, 3, 11, 14; CA 104, 135; CDALB
1865-1917; CLR 58, 60, 66, 156, 187; DA;
DA3; DAB; DAC; DAM MST, NOV; DLB
11, 12, 23, 64, 74, 186, 189, 343; EXPN;
EXPS; JRDA; LAIT 2; LMFS 1; MAICYA
1, 2; MAL 5; NCFS 4; NFS 1, 6; RGAL 4;
RGSF 2; SATA 100; SFW 4; SSFS 1, 7,
16, 21, 27, 33, 42; SUFW; TUS; WCH;
WYA; YABC 2; YAW

**Twohill, Maggie**
See Angell, Judie

**Tyard, Pontus de** 1521?-1605 .......... **LC 243**
See also DLB 327

**Tyler, Anne** 1941- .... **CLC 7, 11, 18, 28, 44,**
**59, 103, 205, 265, 443**
See also AAYA 18, 60; AMWS 4; BEST
89:1; BPFB 3; BYA 12; CA 9-12R; CANR
11, 33, 53, 109, 132, 168, 251, 292, 326;
CDALBS; CMTFW; CN 1, 2, 3, 4, 5, 6, 7;
CPW; CSW; DAM NOV, POP; DLB 6,
143; DLBY 1982; EWL 3; EXPN; LATS
1:2; MAL 5; MAWW; MTCW 1, 2; MTFW
2005; NFS 2, 7, 10, 38; RGAL 4; SATA 7,
90, 173; SSFS 1, 31, 39; TCLE 1:2; TUS;
YAW

**Tyler, Royall** 1757-1826 ......... **NCLC 3, 244**
See also DLB 37; RGAL 4

**Tynan, Katharine**
1861-1931 ........ **PC 120; TCLC 3, 217**
See also CA 104; 167; DLB 153, 240; FW

**Tyndale, William** c. 1484-1536 ........ **LC 103**
See also DLB 132

**Tyrtaeus** 7th cent. BCE .................. **CMLC 178**

**Tyutchev, Fyodor**
1803-1873 ....................... **NCLC 34, 291**

**Tzara, Tristan**
1896-1963 ............................... **CLC 47;**
**PC 27; TCLC 168**
See also CA 153; 89-92; DAM POET; EWL
3; MTCW 2

**Uc de Saint Circ**
c. 1190-13th cent. ...................... **CMLC 102**

**Uchida, Yoshiko** 1921-1992 ................... **AAL**
See also AAYA 16; BYA 2, 3; CA 13-16R;
139; CANR 6, 22, 47, 61; CDALBS; CLR
6, 56; CWRI 5; DLB 312; JRDA; MAI-
CYA 1, 2; MTCW 1, 2; MTFW 2005; NFS
26; SAAS 1; SATA 1, 53; SATA-Obit 72;
SSFS 31

**Udall, Nicholas** 1504-1556 ................. **LC 84**
See also DLB 62; RGEL 2

**Ueda Akinari**
1734-1809 ............................. **NCLC 131**

**Ugrešić, Dubravka** 1949- ................ **CLC 375**
See also CA 136, CANR 90, 159, 198;
CWW 2; DLC 181

**Uhry, Alfred** 1936- ............. **CLC 55; DC 28**
See also CA 127; 133; CAD; CANR 112;
CD 5, 6; CSW; DA3; DAM DRAM, POP;
DFS 11, 15; INT CA-133; MTFW 2005

**Ulf, Haerved**
See Strindberg, August

**Ulf, Harved**
See Strindberg, August

**Ulibarri, Sabine R(eyes)**
1919-2003 ................. **CLC 83; HLCS 2**
See also CA 131; 214; CANR 81; DAM
MULT; DLB 82; HW 1, 2; RGSF 2

**Ulyanov, V. I.**
See Lenin, Vladimir

**Ulyanov, Vladimir Ilyich**
See Lenin, Vladimir

**Ulyanov-Lenin**
See Lenin, Vladimir

**Unamuno, Miguel de**
1864-1936 .................................... **DC 45;**
**HLC 2; SSC 11, 69; TCLC 2, 9, 148, 237**
See also CA 104; 131; CANR 81; DAM
MULT, NOV; DLB 108, 322; EW 8; EWL
3; HW 1, 2; MTCW 1, 2; MTFW 2005;
RGSF 2; RGWL 2, 3; SSFS 20; TWA

**Unamuno y Jugo, Miguel de**
See Unamuno, Miguel de

**Uncle Shelby**
See Silverstein, Shel

**Undercliffe, Errol**
See Campbell, Ramsey

**Underwood, Miles**
See Glassco, John

**Undset, Sigrid** 1882-1949 ...... **TCLC 3, 197;**
**WLC 6**
See also AAYA 77; CA 104; 129; DA; DA3;
DAB; DAC; DAM MST, NOV; DLB 293,
332; EW 9; EWL 3; FW; MTCW 1, 2;
MTFW 2005; RGWL 2, 3

**Ungaretti, Giuseppe** 1888-1970 ........ **CLC 7,**
**11, 15; PC 57; TCLC 200**
See also CA 19-20; 25-28R; CAP 2; DLB
114; EW 10; EWL 3; PFS 20; RGWL 2, 3;
WLIT 7

**Unger, Douglas** 1952- ...................... **CLC 34**
See also CA 130; CANR 94, 155

**Unsworth, Barry** 1930-2012 .... **CLC 76, 127**
See also BRWS 7; CA 25-28R; CANR 30,
54, 125, 171, 202; CN 6, 7; DLB 194, 326

**Unsworth, Barry Forster**
See Unsworth, Barry

**Updike, John** 1932-2009 .............. **CLC 1, 2,**
**3, 5, 7, 9, 13, 15, 23, 34, 43, 70, 139,**
**214, 278; PC 90; SSC 13, 27, 103, 236;**
**WLC 6**
See also AAYA 36; AMW; AMWC 1;
AMWR 1; BPFB 3; BYA 12; CA 1-4R;
282; CABS 1; CANR 4, 33, 51, 94, 133,
197, 229; CDALB 1968-1988; CN 1, 2, 3,
4, 5, 6, 7; CP 1, 2, 3, 4, 5, 6, 7; CPW 1;
DA; DA3; DAB; DAC; DAM MST, NOV,
POET, POP; DLB 2, 5, 143, 218, 227;
DLBD 3; DLBY 1980, 1982, 1997; EWL
3; EXPP; HGG; MAL 5; MTCW 1, 2;

MTFW 2005; NFS 12, 24; RGAL 4; RGSF
2; SSFS 3, 19, 37; TUS

**Updike, John Hoyer**
See Updike, John

**Upshaw, Margaret Mitchell**
See Mitchell, Margaret

**Upton, Mark**
See Sanders, Lawrence

**Upward, Allen** 1863-1926 ............. **TCLC 85**
See also CA 117; 187; DLB 36

**Urdang, Constance (Henriette)**
1922-1996 .................................... **CLC 47**
See also CA 21-24R; CANR 9, 24; CP 1, 2,
3, 4, 5, 6; CWP

**Urfé, Honoré d'**
1567(?)-1625 ...................... **LC 132, 232**
See also DLB 268; GFL Beginnings to 1789;
RGWL 2, 3

**Uriel, Henry**
See Faust, Frederick

**Uris, Leon**
1924-2003 ............................. **CLC 7, 32**
See also AITN 1, 2; AMWS 20; BEST 89:2;
BPFB 3; CA 1-4R; 217; CANR 1, 40, 65,
123; CN 1, 2, 3, 4, 5, 6; CPW 1; DA3;
DAM NOV, POP; MTCW 1, 2; MTFW
2005; RGHL; SATA 49; SATA-Obit 146

**Urista, Alberto**
See Alurista

**Urmuz**
See Codrescu, Andrei

**Urquhart, Guy**
See McAlmon, Robert (Menzies)

**Urquhart, Jane** 1949- ............... **CLC 90, 242**
See also CA 113; CANR 32, 68, 116, 157;
CCA 1; DAC; DLB 334

**Usigli, Rodolfo** 1905-1979 ............... **HLCS 1;**
**TCLC 347**
See also CA 131; DLB 305; EWL 3; HW 1;
LAW

**Usk, Thomas** (?)-1388 ................... **CMLC 76**
See also DLB 146

**Ustinov, Peter (Alexander)**
1921-2004 ....................................... **CLC 1**
See also AITN 1; CA 13-16R; 225; CANR 25,
51; CBD; CD 5, 6; DLB 13; MTCW 2

**U Tam'si, Gerald Felix Tchicaya**
See Tchicaya, Gerald Felix

**U Tam'si, Tchicaya**
See Tchicaya, Gerald Felix

**Vachss, Andrew** 1942- .................. **CLC 106**
See also CA 118, 214; CAAE 214; CANR
44, 95, 153, 197, 238; CMW 4

**Vachss, Andrew H.**
See Vachss, Andrew

**Vachss, Andrew Henry**
See Vachss, Andrew

**Vaculik, Ludvik**
1926- ........................................... **CLC 7**
See also CA 53-56; CANR 72; CWW 2;
DLB 232; EWL 3

**Vaihinger, Hans**
1852-1933 ................................. **TCLC 71**
See also CA 116; 166

**Valdez, Luis (Miguel)** 1940- .......... **CLC 84;**
**DC 10; HLC 2**
See also CA 101; CAD; CANR 32, 81; CD
5, 6; DAM MULT; DFS 5, 29; DLB 122;
EWL 3; HW 1; LAIT 4; LLW

**Valenzuela, Luisa** 1938- .......... **CLC 31, 104;**
**HLCS 2; SSC 14, 82**
See also CA 101; CANR 32, 65, 123;
CDWLB 3; CWW 2; DAM MULT; DLB
113; EWL 3; FW; HW 1, 2; LAW; RGSF
2; RGWL 3; SSFS 29

**Valera y Alcala-Galiano, Juan**
1824-1905 ................................. **TCLC 10**
See also CA 106

**Verus, Marcus Annius**
See Aurelius, Marcus

**Very, Jones** 1813-1880 ....... **NCLC 9; PC 86**
See also DLB 1, 243; RGAL 4

**Very, Rev. C.**
See Crowley, Edward Alexander

**Vesaas, Tarjei** 1897-1970 ................ **CLC 48**
See also CA 190; 29-32R; DLB 297; EW 11; EWL 3; RGWL 3

**Vialis, Gaston**
See Simenon, Georges

**Vian, Boris** 1920-1959(?) ....... **TCLC 9, 283**
See also CA 106; 164; CANR 111; DLB 72, 321; EWL 3; GFL 1789 to the Present; MTCW 2; RGWL 2, 3

**Viator, Vacuus**
See Hughes, Thomas

**Viaud, Julien** 1850-1923 ....... **TCLC 11, 239**
See also CA 107; DLB 123; GFL 1789 to the Present

**Viaud, Louis Marie Julien**
See Viaud, Julien

**Vicar, Henry**
See Felsen, Henry Gregor

**Vicente, Gil** 1465-c. 1536 ................... **LC 99**
See also DLB 318; IDTP; RGWL 2, 3

**Vicker, Angus**
See Felsen, Henry Gregor

**Vico, Giambattista**
See Vico, Giovanni Battista

**Vico, Giovanni Battista** 1668-1744 .. **LC 138**
See also EW 3; WLIT 7

**Vidal, Eugene Luther Gore**
See Vidal, Gore

**Vidal, Gore** 1925-2012 ......... **CLC 2, 4, 6, 8, 10, 22, 33, 72, 142, 289**
See also AAYA 64; AITN 1; AMWS 4; BEST 90:2; BPFB 3; CA 5-8R; CAD; CANR 13, 45, 65, 100, 132, 167; CD 5, 6; CDALBS; CN 1, 2, 3, 4, 5, 6, 7; CPW; DA3; DAM NOV, POP; DFS 2; DLB 6, 152; EWL 3; GLL 1; INT CANR-13; MAL 5; MTCW 1, 2; MTFW 2005; RGAL 4; RHW; TUS

**Vieira, António** 1608-1697 ................ **LC 263**
See also DLB 307

**Viereck, Peter** 1916-2006 ...... **CLC 4; PC 27**
See also CA 1-4R; 250; CANR 1, 47; CP 1, 2, 3, 4, 5, 6, 7; DLB 5; MAL 5; PFS 9, 14

**Viereck, Peter Robert Edwin**
See Viereck, Peter

**Vigny, Alfred de** 1797-1863 ........... **NCLC 7, 102, 278; PC 26**
See also DAM POET; DLB 119, 192, 217; EW 5; GFL 1789 to the Present; RGWL 2, 3

**Vigny, Alfred Victor de**
See Vigny, Alfred de

**Vilakazi, Benedict Wallet** 1906-1947 ................................ **TCLC 37**
See also CA 168

**Vile, Curt**
See Moore, Alan

**Villa, Jose Garcia** 1914-1997 ............... **AAL; PC 22; TCLC 176**
See also CA 25-28R; CANR 12, 118; CP 1, 2, 3, 4; DLB 312; EWL 3; EXPP

**Villard, Oswald Garrison** 1872-1949 ........................ **TCLC 160**
See also CA 113; 162; DLB 25, 91

**Villarreal, Jose Antonio** 1924- ......... **HLC 2**
See also CA 133; CANR 93; DAM MULT; DLB 82; HW 1; LAIT 4; RGAL 4

**Villaurrutia, Xavier** 1903-1950 ..... **TCLC 80**
See also CA 192; EWL 3; HW 1; LAW

**Villaverde, Cirilo** 1812-1894 ....... **NCLC 121**
See also LAW

**Villedieu, Madame de** 1640?-1683 ... **LC 231**
See also DLB 268

**Villehardouin, Geoffroi de** 1150(?)-1218(?) ...................... **CMLC 38**

**Villiers, George** 1628-1687 .............. **LC 107**
See also DLB 80; RGEL 2

**Villiers de l'Isle-Adam, Auguste de**
See Villiers de l'Isle Adam, Jean Marie Mathias Philippe-Auguste

**Villiers de l'Isle Adam, Jean-Marie Mathias Philippe-Auguste** 1838-1889 ... **NCLC 3, 237; SSC 14, 252**
See also DLB 123, 192; GFL 1789 to the Present; RGSF 2

**Villon, Francois** 1431-1463(?) .......... **LC 62, 166; PC 13**
See also DLB 208; EW 2; RGWL 2, 3; TWA

**Vine, Barbara**
See Rendell, Ruth

**Vinge, Joan (Carol) D(ennison)** 1948- .......................... **CLC 30; SSC 24**
See also AAYA 32; BPFB 3; CA 93-96; CANR 72; SATA 36, 113; SFW 4; YAW

**Viola, Herman J(oseph)** 1938- ........ **CLC 70**
See also CA 61-64; CANR 8, 23, 48, 91; SATA 126

**Violis, G.**
See Simenon, Georges

**Viramontes, Helena Maria** 1954- .............. **HLCS 2; SSC 149**
See also CA 159; CANR 182; CLR 285; DLB 122, 350; HW 2; LLW

**Virgil**
See Vergil

**Virilio, Paul** 1932- ......................... **CLC 358**

**Visconti, Luchino** 1906-1976 .......... **CLC 16**
See also CA 81-84; 65-68; CANR 39

**Vitry, Jacques de**
See Jacques de Vitry

**Vittorini, Elio** 1908-1966 ........ **CLC 6, 9, 14**
See also CA 133; 25-28R; DLB 264; EW 12; EWL 3; RGWL 2, 3

**Vivekananda, Swami** 1863-1902 ... **TCLC 88**

**Vives, Juan Luis** 1493-1540 ............. **LC 170**
See also DLB 318

**Vivien, Renée** 1877-1909 ................... **PC 205**
See also CA 212; DLB 217; GLL 1

**Vizenor, Gerald Robert** 1934- ..... **CLC 103, 263; NNAL; SSC 179**
See also CA 13-16R, 205; CAAE 205; CAAS 22; CANR 5, 21, 44, 67, 233; DAM MULT; DLB 175, 227; MTCW 2; MTFW 2005; TCWW 2

**Vizinczey, Stephen** 1933- ................. **CLC 40**
See also CA 128; CCA 1; INT CA-128

**Vladislavic, Ivan** 1957- ................... **SSC 178**
See also CA 259

**Vliet, R(ussell) G(ordon)** 1929-1984 ................................ **CLC 22**
See also CA 37-40R; 112; CANR 18; CP 2, 3

**Vogau, Boris Andreevich**
See Vogau, Boris Andreyevich

**Vogau, Boris Andreyevich** 1894-1938 ... **SSC 48; TCLC 23**
See also CA 123; 218; DLB 272; EWL 3; RGSF 2; RGWL 2, 3

**Vogel, Paula A.** 1951- ............. **CLC 76, 290; DC 19**
See also CA 108; CAD; CANR 119, 140; CD 5, 6; CWD; DFS 14; DLB 341; MTFW 2005; RGAL 4

**Vogel, Paula Anne**
See Vogel, Paula A.

**Vogelweide, Walther von der**
See Walther von der Vogelweide

**Voigt, Cynthia** 1942- ....................... **CLC 30**
See also AAYA 3, 30; BYA 1, 3, 6, 7, 8; CA 106; CANR 18, 37, 40, 94, 145; CLR 13, 48, 141; INT CANR-18; JRDA; LAIT 5; MAICYA 1, 2; MAICYAS 1; MTFW 2005; SATA 48, 79, 116, 160; SATA-Brief 33; WYA; YAW

**Voigt, Ellen Bryant** 1943- .............. **CLC 54**
See also CA 69-72; CANR 11, 29, 55, 115, 171; CP 5, 6, 7; CSW; CWP; DLB 120; PFS 23, 33

**Voinovich, Vladimir** 1932- ............. **CLC 10, 49, 147**
See also CA 81-84; CAAS 12; CANR 33, 67, 150; CWW 2; DLB 302; MTCW 1

**Voinovich, Vladimir Nikolaevich**
See Voinovich, Vladimir

**Vollmann, William T.** 1959- .................................. **CLC 89, 227**
See also AMWS 17; CA 134; CANR 67, 116, 185; CN 7; CPW; DA3; DAM NOV, POP; DLB 350; MTCW 2; MTFW 2005

**Voloshinov, V. N.**
See Bakhtin, Mikhail Mikhailovich

**Voltaire** 1694-1778 .............. **LC 14, 79, 110; SSC 12, 112, 167; WLC 6**
See also BYA 13; DA; DA3; DAB; DAC; DAM DRAM, MST; DLB 314; EW 4; GFL Beginnings to 1789; LATS 1:1; LMFS 1; NFS 7; RGWL 2, 3; TWA

**von Aschendrof, Baron Ignatz**
See Ford, Ford Madox

**von Chamisso, Adelbert**
See Chamisso, Adelbert von

**von Daeniken, Erich** 1935- ............. **CLC 30**
See also AITN 1; CA 37-40R; CANR 17, 44

**von Daniken, Erich**
See von Daeniken, Erich

**von dem Turlin, Heinrich**
See Heinrich von dem Tuerlin

**von der Vogelweide, Walther**
See Walther von der Vogelweide

**von Eschenbach, Wolfram** c. 1170-c. 1220 ..... **CMLC 5, 145, 153; PC 131**
See also CDWLB 2; DLB 138; EW 1; RGWL 2, 3

**von Hartmann, Eduard** 1842-1906 ................................ **TCLC 96**

**von Hayek, Friedrich August**
See Hayek, F(riedrich) A(ugust von)

**von Heidenstam, (Carl Gustaf) Verner**
See Heidenstam, (Carl Gustaf) Verner von

**von Heyse, Paul (Johann Ludwig)**
See Heyse, Paul (Johann Ludwig von)

**von Hofmannsthal, Hugo**
See Hofmannsthal, Hugo von

**von Horvath, Oedoen**
See Horvath, Odon von

**von Horvath, Odon**
See Horvath, Odon von

**von Kleist, Heinrich**
See Kleist, Heinrich von

**von Reuental, Neidhart**
See Neidhart von Reuental

**Vonnegut, Kurt, Jr.**
See Vonnegut, Kurt

**Vonnegut, Kurt** 1922-2007 ...... **CLC 1, 2, 3, 4, 5, 8, 12, 22, 40, 60, 111, 212, 254, 387; SSC 8, 155; WLC 6**
See also AAYA 6, 44; AITN 1; AMWS 2; BEST 90:4; BPFB 3; BYA 3, 14; CA 1-4R; 259; CANR 1, 25, 49, 75, 92, 207; CDALB 1968-1988; CN 1, 2, 3, 4, 5, 6, 7; CPW 1; DA; DA3; DAB; DAC; DAM MST, NOV, POP; DLB 2, 8, 152; DLBD 3; DLBY 1980; EWL 3; EXPN; EXPS; LAIT 4; LMFS 2; MAL 5; MTCW 1, 2; MTFW 2005; NFS 3, 28; RGAL 4; SCFW; SFW 4; SSFS 5; TUS; YAW

**Von Rachen, Kurt**
See Hubbard, L. Ron

**von Sternberg, Josef**
See Sternberg, Josef von

**Vondel, Joost van den** 1587-1679 .... **LC 261**
**Vorster, Gordon** 1924- ..................... **CLC 34**
   See also CA 133
**Vosce, Trudie**
   See Ozick, Cynthia
**Vostaert, Pieter** fl. 13th cent. ...... **CMLC 173**
**Voznesensky, Andrei** 1933-2010 ....... **CLC 1,**
   **15, 57**
   See also CA 89-92; CANR 37; CWW 2;
   DAM POET; DLB 359; EWL 3; MTCW 1
**Voznesensky, Andrei Andreievich**
   See Voznesensky, Andrei
**Voznesensky, Andrey**
   See Voznesensky, Andrei
**Wace, Robert** c. 1100-c. 1175 ...... **CMLC 55**
   See also DLB 146
**Waddington, Miriam** 1917-2004 ..... **CLC 28**
   See also CA 21-24R; 225; CANR 12, 30;
   CCA 1; CP 1, 2, 3, 4, 5, 6, 7; DLB 68
**Wade, Alan**
   See Vance, Jack
**Wagman, Fredrica** 1937- .................. **CLC 7**
   See also CA 97-100; CANR 166; INT CA-
   97-100
**Wagner, Linda W.**
   See Wagner-Martin, Linda (C.)
**Wagner, Linda Welshimer**
   See Wagner-Martin, Linda (C.)
**Wagner, Richard** 1813-1883 .......... **NCLC 9,**
   **119, 258**
   See also DLB 129; EW 6
**Wagner-Martin, Linda (C.)** 1936- ... **CLC 50**
   See also CA 159; CANR 135
**Wagoner, David (Russell)** 1926- ...... **CLC 3,**
   **5, 15; PC 33**
   See also AMWS 9; CA 1-4R; CAAS 3; CANR
   2, 71; CN 1, 2, 3, 4, 5, 6, 7; CP 1, 2, 3, 4, 5,
   6, 7; DLB 5, 256; SATA 14; TCWW 1, 2
**Wah, Fred(erick James)**
   1939- ................. **CLC 44, 338; PC 172**
   See also CA 107; 141; CP 1, 6, 7; DLB 60
**Wahloo, Per** 1926-1975 ..................... **CLC 7**
   See also BPFB 3; CA 61-64; CANR 73;
   CMW 4; MSW
**Wahloo, Peter**
   See Wahloo, Per
**Wain, John** 1925-1994 .... **CLC 2, 11, 15, 46**
   See also BRWS 16; CA 5-8R; 145; CAAS 4;
   CANR 23, 54; CDBLB 1960 to Present;
   CN 1, 2, 3, 4, 5; CP 1, 2, 3, 4, 5; DLB 15,
   27, 139, 155; EWL 3; MTCW 1, 2;
   MTFW 2005
**Wajda, Andrzej** 1926- .............. **CLC 16, 219**
   See also CA 102
**Wakefield, Dan** 1932- ....................... **CLC 7**
   See also CA 21-24R, 211; CAAE 211;
   CAAS 7; CN 4, 5, 6, 7
**Wakefield, Herbert Russell**
   1888-1965 ............................. **TCLC 120**
   See also CA 5-8R; CANR 77; HGG; SUFW
**Wakoski, Diane** 1937- ......... **CLC 2, 4, 7, 9,**
   **11, 40; PC 15**
   See also CA 13-16R, 216; CAAE 216;
   CAAS 1; CANR 9, 60, 106; CP 1, 2, 3,
   4, 5, 6, 7; CWP; DAM POET; DLB 5; INT
   CANR-9; MAL 5; MTCW 2; MTFW
   2005; PFS 43
**Wakoski-Sherbell, Diane**
   See Wakoski, Diane
**Walcott, Derek** 1930-2017 ..... **BLC 1:3, 2:3;**
   **CLC 2, 4, 9, 14, 25, 42, 67, 76, 160, 282,**
   **439; DC 7; PC 46**
   See also BW 2; CA 89-92; CANR 26, 47,
   75, 80, 130, 230; CBD; CD 5, 6; CDWLB
   3; CMTFW; CP 1, 2, 3, 4, 5, 6, 7; DA3;
   DAB; DAC; DAM MST, MULT, POET;
   DLB 117, 332; DLBY 1981; DNFS 1; EFS
   1:1, 2:2; EWL 3; LMFS 2; MTCW 1, 2;
   MTFW 2005; PFS 6, 34, 39; RGEL 2;
   TWA; WWE 1

**Walcott, Derek Alton**
   See Walcott, Derek
**Waldman, Anne** 1945- ....................... **CLC 7**
   See also BG 1:3; CA 37-40R; CAAS 17;
   CANR 34, 69, 116, 219; CP 1, 2, 3, 4, 5, 6,
   7; CWP; DLB 16
**Waldman, Anne Lesley**
   See Waldman, Anne
**Waldo, E. Hunter**
   See Sturgeon, Theodore (Hamilton)
**Waldo, Edward Hamilton**
   See Sturgeon, Theodore (Hamilton)
**Waldrop, Rosmarie** 1935- ................. **PC 109**
   See also CA 101; CAAS 30; CANR 18, 39,
   67; CP 6, 7; CWP; DLB 169
**Walker, Alice** 1944- ...... **BLC 1:3, 2:3; CLC**
   **5, 6, 9, 19, 27, 46, 58, 103, 167, 319, 381,**
   **424; PC 30; SSC 5; WLCS**
   See also AAYA 3, 33; AFAW 1, 2; AMWS 3;
   BEST 89:4; BPFB 3; BW 2, 3; CA 37-40R;
   CANR 9, 27, 49, 66, 82, 131, 191, 238;
   CDALB 1968-1988; CN 4, 5, 6, 7; CLR
   198; CPW; CSW; DA; DA3; DAB; DAC;
   DAM MST, MULT, NOV, POET, POP;
   DLB 6, 33, 143; EWL 3; EXPN; EXPS;
   FL 1:6; FW; INT CANR-27; LAIT 3; MAL
   5; MBL; MTCW 1, 2; MTFW 2005; NFS
   5; PFS 30, 34; RGAL 4; RGSF 2; SATA
   31; SSFS 2, 11; TUS; YAW
**Walker, Alice Malsenior**
   See Walker, Alice
**Walker, David Harry** 1911-1992 .... **CLC 14**
   See also CA 1-4R; 137; CANR 1; CN 1, 2;
   CWRI 5; SATA 8; SATA-Obit 71
**Walker, Edward Joseph**
   1934-2004 ................................. **CLC 13**
   See also CA 21-24R; 226; CANR 12, 28, 53;
   CP 1, 2, 3, 4, 5, 6, 7; DLB 40
**Walker, George F(rederick)**
   1947- ................................... **CLC 44, 61**
   See also CA 103; CANR 21, 43, 59; CD 5,
   6; DAB; DAC; DAM MST; DLB 60
**Walker, Joseph A.** 1935-2003 ........ **CLC 19**
   See also BW 1, 3; CA 89-92; CAD; CANR
   26, 143; CD 5, 6; DAM DRAM, MST;
   DFS 12; DLB 38
**Walker, Margaret** 1915-1998 ........ **BLC 1:3;**
   **CLC 1, 6; PC 20; TCLC 129**
   See also AFAW 1, 2; BW 2, 3; CA 73-76;
   172; CANR 26, 54, 76, 136; CN 1, 2, 3, 4,
   5, 6; CP 1, 2, 3, 4, 5, 6; CSW; DAM MULT;
   DLB 76, 152; EXPP; FW; MAL 5; MTCW
   1, 2; MTFW 2005; PFS 31; RGAL 4; RHW
**Walker, Ted**
   See Walker, Edward Joseph
**Wallace, David Foster** 1962-2008 ... **CLC 50,**
   **114, 271, 281, 403; SSC 68**
   See also AAYA 50; AMWS 10; CA 132;
   277; CANR 59, 133, 190, 237; CN 7;
   DA3; DLB 350; MTCW 2; MTFW 2005
**Wallace, Dexter**
   See Masters, Edgar Lee
**Wallace, (Richard Horatio) Edgar**
   1875-1932 ................................. **TCLC 57**
   See also CA 115; 218; CMW 4; DLB 70;
   MSW; RGEL 2
**Wallace, Irving** 1916-1990 .......... **CLC 7, 13**
   See also AITN 1; BPFB 3; CA 1-4R; 132;
   CAAS 1; CANR 1, 27; CPW; DAM NOV,
   POP; INT CANR-27; MTCW 1, 2
**Wallace-Crabbe, Chris** 1934- ........ **CLC 394**
   See also BRWS 8; CA 77-80; CANR 14; CP
   1, 2, 3, 4, 5, 6, 7; DLB 289
**Wallant, Edward Lewis**
   1926-1962 .............................. **CLC 5, 10**
   See also CA 1-4R; CANR 22; DLB 2, 28,
   143, 299; EWL 3; MAL 5; MTCW 1, 2;
   RGAL 4; RGHL

**Wallas, Graham** 1858-1932 .......... **TCLC 91**
**Waller, Edmund** 1606-1687 ... **LC 86; PC 72**
   See also BRW 2; DAM POET; DLB 126;
   PAB; RGEL 2
**Walley, Byron**
   See Card, Orson Scott
**Walls, Jeannette** 1960(?)- .............. **CLC 299**
   See also CA 242; CANR 220
**Walpole, Horace** 1717-1797 .......... **LC 2, 49,**
   **152, 266**
   See also BRW 3; DLB 39, 104, 213; GL 3;
   HGG; LMFS 1; RGEL 2; SUFW 1; TEA
**Walpole, Hugh** 1884-1941 ............... **TCLC 5**
   See also CA 104; 165; DLB 34; HGG;
   MTCW 2; RGEL 2; RHW
**Walpole, Hugh Seymour**
   See Walpole, Hugh
**Walrond, Eric (Derwent)**
   1898-1966 ................................... **HR 1:3**
   See also BW 1; CA 125; DLB 51
**Walser, Martin** 1927- ............... **CLC 27, 183**
   See also CA 57-60; CANR 8, 46, 145;
   CWW 2; DLB 75, 124; EWL 3
**Walser, Robert** 1878-1956 .............. **SSC 20;**
   **TCLC 18, 267**
   See also CA 118; 165; CANR 100, 194;
   DLB 66; EWL 3
**Walsh, Gillian Paton**
   See Paton Walsh, Jill
**Walsh, Jill Paton**
   See Paton Walsh, Jill
**Walter, Villiam Christian**
   See Andersen, Hans Christian
**Walter of Chatillon**
   c. 1135-c. 1202 .................... **CMLC 111**
**Walters, Anna L(ee)** 1946- ................. **NNAL**
   See also CA 73-76
**Walther von der Vogelweide**
   c. 1170-1228 ......................... **CMLC 56**
**Walther von der Vogelweide** c. 1170-c.
   1230 ................................. **CMLC 147**
   See also DLB 138; EW 1; RGWL 2, 3
**Walton, Izaak** 1593-1683 ................. **LC 72**
   See also BRW 2; CDBLB Before 1660; DLB
   151, 213; RGEL 2
**Walzer, Michael** 1935- .................. **CLC 238**
   See also CA 37-40R; CANR 15, 48,
   127, 190
**Walzer, Michael Laban**
   See Walzer, Michael
**Wambaugh, Joseph, Jr.**
   1937- ...................................... **CLC 3, 18**
   See also AITN 1; BEST 89:3; BPFB 3; CA
   33-36R; CANR 42, 65, 115, 167, 217;
   CMW 4; CPW 1; DA3; DAM NOV, POP;
   DLB 6; DLBY 1983; MSW; MTCW 1, 2
**Wambaugh, Joseph Aloysius**
   See Wambaugh, Joseph, Jr.
**Wang Meng** 1934- .......................... **CLC 416**
   See also CA 169; DLB 370
**Wang Shuo** 1958- .......................... **CLC 408**
   See also CA 171; DLB 370
**Wang Wei** 699(?)-761(?) .......... **CMLC 100;**
   **PC 18**
   See also TWA
**Wang Wenxing** 1939- .................... **CLC 411**
   See also DLB 370
**Warburton, William** 1698-1779 ......... **LC 97**
   See also DLB 104
**Ward, Arthur Henry Sarsfield**
   1883-1959 ............................... **TCLC 28**
   See also AAYA 80; CA 108; 173; CMW 4;
   DLB 70; HGG; MSW; SUFW
**Ward, Douglas Turner** 1930- .......... **CLC 19**
   See also BW 1; CA 81-84; CAD; CANR 27;
   CD 5, 6; DLB 7, 38
**Ward, E. D.**
   See Lucas, E(dward) V(errall)

**Wharton, William**
1925-2008 .......................... **CLC 18, 37**
See also CA 93-96; 278; CN 4, 5, 6, 7; DLBY 1980; INT CA-93-96

**Whately, Richard** 1787-1863 ....... **NCLC 299**
See also DLB 190

**Wheatley, Phillis**
1753(?)-1784 ........................... **BLC 1:3; LC 3, 50, 183; PC 3, 142, 201; WLC 6**
See also AFAW 1, 2; AMWS 20; CDALB 1640-1865; DA; DA3; DAC; DAM MST, MULT, POET; DLB 31, 50; EXPP; FL 1:1; PFS 13, 29, 36; RGAL 4

**Wheatley Peters, Phillis**
See Wheatley, Phillis

**Wheelock, John Hall** 1886-1978 ..... **CLC 14**
See also CA 13-16R; 77-80; CANR 14; CP 1, 2; DLB 45; MAL 5

**Whim-Wham**
See Curnow, (Thomas) Allen (Monro)

**Whisp, Kennilworthy**
See Rowling, J.K.

**Whitaker, Rod** 1931-2005 ................. **CLC 29**
See also CA 29-32R; 246; CANR 45, 153; CMW 4

**Whitaker, Rodney**
See Whitaker, Rod

**Whitaker, Rodney William**
See Whitaker, Rod

**White, Babington**
See Braddon, Mary Elizabeth

**White, E. B.** 1899-1985 ...... **CLC 10, 34, 39**
See also AAYA 62; AITN 2; AMWS 1; CA 13-16R; 116; CANR 16, 37; CDALBS; CLR 1, 21, 107; CPW; DA3; DAM POP; DLB 11, 22; EWL 3; FANT; MAICYA 1, 2; MAL 5; MTCW 1, 2; MTFW 2005; NCFS 5; RGAL 4; SATA 2, 29, 100; SATA-Obit 44; TUS

**White, Edmund** 1940- .............. **CLC 27, 110**
See also AAYA 7; CA 45-48; CANR 3, 19, 36, 62, 107, 133, 172, 212; CN 5, 6, 7; DA3; DAM POP; DLB 227; MTCW 1, 2; MTFW 2005

**White, Edmund Valentine III**
See White, Edmund

**White, Elwyn Brooks**
See White, E. B.

**White, Hayden V.** 1928- ................. **CLC 148**
See also CA 128; CANR 135; DLB 246

**White, Patrick** 1912-1990 ........ **CLC 3, 4, 5, 7, 9, 18, 65, 69; SSC 39; TCLC 176, 326**
See also BRWS 1; CA 81-84; 132; CANR 43; CN 1, 2, 3, 4; DLB 260, 332; EWL 3; MTCW 1; RGEL 2; RGSF; RHW; TWA; WWE 1

**White, Patrick Victor Martindale**
See White, Patrick

**White, Phyllis Dorothy James**
See James, P. D.

**White, T(erence) H(anbury)**
1906-1964 ............................... **CLC 30**
See also AAYA 22; BPFB 3; BYA 4, 5; CA 73-76; CANR 37; CLR 139; DLB 160; FANT; JRDA; LAIT 1; MAICYA 1, 2; NFS 30; RGEL 2; SATA 12; SUFW 1; YAW

**White, Terence de Vere** 1912-1994 .... **CLC 49**
See also CA 49-52; 145; CANR 3

**White, Walter**
See White, Walter F(rancis)

**White, Walter F(rancis)**
1893-1955 ............... **BLC 1:3; HR 1:3; TCLC 15**
See also BW 1; CA 115; 124; DAM MULT; DLB 51

**White, William Hale** 1831-1913 ... **TCLC 25**
See also CA 121; 189; DLB 18; RGEL 2

**Whitehead, Alfred North**
1861-1947 ............................... **TCLC 97**
See also CA 117; 165; DLB 100, 262

**Whitehead, Colson**
1969- ..... **BLC 2:3; CLC 232, 348, 421**
See also CA 202; CANR 162, 211

**Whitehead, E(dward) A(nthony)**
1933- .......................................... **CLC 5**
See also CA 65-68; CANR 58, 118; CBD; CD 5, 6; DLB 310

**Whitehead, Ted**
See Whitehead, E(dward) A(nthony)

**White-Liver, Richard**
See Walpole, Horace

**Whiteman, Roberta J. Hill** 1947- ...... **NNAL**
See also CA 146

**Whitemore, Hugh (John)**
1936- .......................................... **CLC 37**
See also CA 132; CANR 77; CBD; CD 5, 6; INT CA-132

**Whitman, Sarah Helen (Power)**
1803-1878 ............................... **NCLC 19**
See also DLB 1, 243

**Whitman, Walt**
1819-1892 ...... **NCLC 4, 31, 81, 205, 268, 343; PC 3, 91, 200; WLC 6**
See also AAYA 42; AMW; AMWR 1; CDALB 1640-1865; DA; DA3; DAB; DAC; DAM MST, POET; DLB 3, 64, 224, 250; EXPP; LAIT 2; LMFS 1; PAB; PFS 2, 3, 13, 22, 31, 39; RGAL 4; SATA 20; TUS; WP; WYAS 1

**Whitman, Walter**
See Whitman, Walt

**Whitney, David**
See Malick, Terrence

**Whitney, Isabella**
fl. 1565-fl. 1575 ......... **LC 130; PC 116**
See also DLB 136

**Whitney, Phyllis A.** 1903-2008 ....... **CLC 42**
See also AAYA 36; AITN 2; BEST 90:3; CA 1-4R; 269; CANR 3, 25, 38, 60; CLR 59; CMW 4; CPW; DA3; DAM POP; JRDA; MAICYA 1, 2; MTCW 2; RHW; SATA 1, 30; SATA-Obit 189; YAW

**Whitney, Phyllis Ayame**
See Whitney, Phyllis A.

**Whittemore, Edward Reed**
See Whittemore, Reed, Jr.

**Whittemore, Reed, Jr.** 1919-2012 ..... **CLC 4**
See also CA 9-12R, 219; CAAE 219; CAAS 8; CANR 4, 119; CP 1, 2, 3, 4, 5, 6, 7; DLB 5; MAL 5

**Whittier, John Greenleaf**
1807-1892 ................ **NCLC 8, 59, 339; PC 93, 207**
See also AMWS 1; CDALB 1640-1865; DLB 1, 243; PFS 36; RGAL 4

**Whittlebot, Hernia**
See Coward, Noel

**Wicker, Thomas Grey**
See Wicker, Tom

**Wicker, Tom** 1926-2011 ..................... **CLC 7**
See also CA 65-68; CANR 21, 46, 141, 179

**Wickham, Anna** 1883-1947 .............. **PC 110**
See also DLB 240

**Wicomb, Zoe** 1948- ........................ **BLC 2:3**
See also CA 127; CANR 106, 167; DLB 225

**Wideman, John Edgar** 1941- ....... **BLC 1:3, 2:3; CLC 5, 34, 36, 67, 122, 316; SSC 62**
See also AFAW 1, 2; AMWS 10; BPFB 4; BW 2, 3; CA 85-88; CANR 14, 42, 67, 109, 140, 187; CN 4, 5, 6, 7; DAM MULT; DLB 33, 143; MAL 5; MTCW 2; MTFW 2005; RGAL 4; RGSF 2; SSFS 6, 12, 24; TCLE 1:2

**Wiebe, Rudy** 1934- .............. **CLC 6, 11, 14, 138, 263**
See also CA 37-40R; CANR 42, 67, 123, 202; CN 1, 2, 3, 4, 5, 6, 7; DAC; DAM MST; DLB 60; RHW; SATA 156

**Wiebe, Rudy Henry**
See Wiebe, Rudy

**Wieland, Christoph Martin**
1733-1813 .............. **NCLC 17, 177, 335**
See also DLB 97; EW 4; LMFS 1; RGWL 2, 3

**Wiene, Robert** 1881-1938 .............. **TCLC 56**

**Wieners, John** 1934- .......... **CLC 7; PC 131**
See also BG 1:3; CA 13-16R; CP 1, 2, 3, 4, 5, 6, 7; DLB 16; WP

**Wiesel, Elie** 1928-2016 ..... **CLC 3, 5, 11, 37, 165, 421; WLCS**
See also AAYA 7, 54; AITN 1; CA 5-8R; CAAS 4; CANR 8, 40, 65, 125, 207; CDALBS; CLR 192; CWW 2; DA; DA3; DAB; DAC; DAM MST, NOV; DLB 83, 299; DLBY 1987; EWL 3; INT CANR-8; LAIT 4; MTCW 1, 2; MTFW 2005; NCFS 4; NFS 4; RGHL; RGWL 3; SATA 56; YAW

**Wiesel, Eliezer**
See Wiesel, Elie

**Wiggins, Marianne** 1947- ................ **CLC 57**
See also AAYA 70; BEST 89:3; CA 130; CANR 60, 139, 180; CN 7; DLB 335

**Wigglesworth, Michael** 1631-1705 ... **LC 106**
See also DLB 24; RGAL 4

**Wiggs, Susan** ................................. **CLC 70**
See also CA 201; CANR 173, 217

**Wight, James Alfred**
See Herriot, James

**Wilbur, Richard** 1921- ....... **CLC 3, 6, 9, 14, 53, 110; PC 51**
See also AAYA 72; AMWS 3; CA 1-4R; CABS 3; CANR 2, 29, 76, 93, 139, 237; CDALBS; CP 1, 2, 3, 4, 5, 6, 7; DA; DAB; DAC; DAM MST, POET; DLB 5, 169; EWL 3; EXPP; INT CANR-29; MAL 5; MTCW 1, 2; MTFW 2005; PAB; PFS 11, 12, 16, 29; RGAL 4; SATA 9, 108; WP

**Wilbur, Richard Purdy**
See Wilbur, Richard

**Wild, Peter** 1940- ............................. **CLC 14**
See also CA 37-40R; CP 1, 2, 3, 4, 5, 6, 7; DLB 5

**Wilde, Oscar** 1854-1900 ............. **DC 17, 57; PC 111; SSC 11, 77, 208; TCLC 1, 8, 23, 41, 175, 272, 349; WLC 6**
See also AAYA 49; BRW 5; BRWC 1, 2; BRWR 2; BYA 15; CA 104; 119; CANR 112; CDBLB 1890-1914; CLR 114; DA; DA3; DAB; DAC; DAM DRAM, MST, NOV; DFS 4, 8, 9, 21; DLB 10, 19, 34, 57, 141, 156, 190, 344; EXPS; FANT; GL 3; LATS 1:1; NFS 20; RGEL 2; RGSF 2; SATA 24; SSFS 7; SUFW; TEA; WCH; WLIT 4

**Wilde, Oscar Fingal O'Flahertie Wills**
See Wilde, Oscar

**Wilder, Billy** 1906-2002 .................... **CLC 20**
See also AAYA 66; CA 89-92; 205; DLB 26

**Wilder, Laura Ingalls** 1867-1957 ... **TCLC 344**
See also AAYA 26; BYA 2; CA 111, 137; CLR 2, 11, 229; CWRI 5; DA3; DLB 22, 256; MAICYA 1, 2; MTCW 2; MTFW; SATA 15, 29, 100; TCWW; WCH; WYA

**Wilder, Samuel**
See Wilder, Billy

**Wilder, Samuel** 1906-2002 .............. **CLC 20**
See also AAYA 66; CA 89-92; 205; DLB 26

**Wilder, Stephen**
See Marlowe, Stephen

**Wilder, Thornton** 1897-1975 ........ **CLC 1, 5, 6, 10, 15, 35, 82; DC 1, 24; TCLC 284; WLC 6**
See also AAYA 29; AITN 2; AMW; CA 13-16R; 61-64; CAD; CANR 40, 132; CDALBS; CN 1, 2; DA; DA3; DAB; DAC; DAM DRAM, MST, NOV; DFS 1, 4, 16; DLB 4, 7, 9, 228; DLBY 1997; EWL 3; LAIT 3; MAL 5; MTCW 1, 2; MTFW 2005; NFS 24; RGAL 4; RHW; WYAS 1

**Wilder, Thornton Niven**
See Wilder, Thornton

**Wright, Charles**
1932-2008 ................ **BLC 1:3; CLC 49**
See also BW 1; CA 9-12R; 278; CANR 26;
CN 1, 2, 3, 4, 5, 6, 7; DAM MULT, POET;
DLB 33

**Wright, Charles** 1935- ......... **CLC 6, 13, 28,
119, 146; PC 142**
See also AMWS 5; CA 29-32R; CAAS 7;
CANR 23, 36, 62, 88, 135, 180; CP 3, 4, 5,
6, 7; DLB 165; DLBY 1982; EWL 3;
MTCW 1, 2; MTFW 2005; PFS 10, 35

**Wright, Charles Penzel, Jr.**
See Wright, Charles

**Wright, Charles Stevenson**
See Wright, Charles

**Wright, Frances** 1795-1852 ........... **NCLC 74**
See also DLB 73

**Wright, Frank Lloyd**
1867-1959 ............................. **TCLC 95**
See also AAYA 33; CA 174

**Wright, Harold Bell** 1872-1944 .. **TCLC 183**
See also BPFB 3; CA 110; DLB 9; TCWW 2

**Wright, Jack R.**
See Harris, Mark

**Wright, James (Arlington)**
1927-1980 ..... **CLC 3, 5, 10, 28; PC 36**
See also AITN 2; AMWS 3; CA 49-52; 97-
100; CANR 4, 34, 64; CDALBS; CP 1, 2;
DAM POET; DLB 5, 169, 342; EWL 3;
EXPP; MAL 5; MTCW 1, 2; MTFW 2005;
PFS 7, 8; RGAL 4; TUS; WP

**Wright, Judith** 1915-2000 ........ **CLC 11, 53,
327; PC 14**
See also CA 13-16R; 188; CANR 31, 76, 93;
CP 1, 2, 3, 4, 5, 6, 7; CWP; DLB 260;
EWL 3; MTCW 1, 2; MTFW 2005; PFS 8;
RGEL 2; SATA 14; SATA-Obit 121

**Wright, Judith Arundell**
See Wright, Judith

**Wright, L(auralie) R.** 1939- ............. **CLC 44**
See also CA 138; CMW 4

**Wright, Richard** 1908-1960 ......... **BLC 1:3;
CLC 1, 3, 4, 9, 14, 21, 48, 74; SSC 2, 109,
253, 260; TCLC 136, 180; WLC 6**
See also AAYA 5, 42; AFAW 1, 2; AMW;
BPFB 3; BW 1; BYA 2; CA 108; CANR
64; CDALB 1929-1941; DA; DA3; DAB;
DAC; DAM MST, MULT, NOV; DLB 76,
102; DLBD 2; EWL 3; EXPN; LAIT 3, 4;
MAL 5; MTCW 1, 2; MTFW 2005; NCFS
1; NFS 1, 7; RGAL 4; RGSF 2; SSFS 3, 9,
15, 20; TUS; YAW

**Wright, Richard B.** 1937- ................. **CLC 6**
See also CA 85-88; CANR 120; DLB 53

**Wright, Richard Bruce**
See Wright, Richard B.

**Wright, Richard Nathaniel**
See Wright, Richard

**Wright, Rick** 1945- ........................... **CLC 35**

**Wright, Rowland**
See Wells, Carolyn

**Wright, Stephen** 1946- ..................... **CLC 33**
See also CA 237; DLB 350

**Wright, Willard Huntington**
1888-1939 ............................... **TCLC 23**
See also CA 115; 189; CMW 4; DLB 306;
DLBD 16; MSW

**Wright, William** 1930- ..................... **CLC 44**
See also CA 53-56; CANR 7, 23, 154

**Wrobel, Ignaz**
See Tucholsky, Kurt

**Wroblewski, David** 1959- ............. **CLC 280**
See also CA 283

**Wroth, Lady Mary** 1587-1653(?) ..... **LC 30,
139, 253; PC 38**
See also DLB 121

**Wu Ch'eng-en** 1500(?)-1582(?) .... **LC 7, 213**

**Wu Ching-tzu**
1701-1754 ...................................... **LC 2**

**Wulfstan**
c. 10th cent. -1023 ............ **CMLC 59, 135**

**Wurlitzer, Rudolph** 1938(?)- ..... **CLC 2, 4, 15**
See also CA 85-88; CN 4, 5, 6, 7; DLB 173

**Wyatt, Sir Thomas** c. 1503-1542 ...... **LC 70;
PC 27, 169**
See also BRW 1; DLB 132; EXPP; PFS 25;
RGEL 2; TEA

**Wycherley, William** 1640-1716 ......... **DC 41;
LC 8, 21, 102, 136**
See also BRW 2; CDBLB 1660-1789; DAM
DRAM; DLB 80; RGEL 2

**Wyclif, John**
c. 1330-1384 ................. **CMLC 70, 143**
See also DLB 146

**Wyld, Evie** 1980- ........................... **CLC 334**
See also CA 299

**Wylie, Elinor (Morton Hoyt)**
1885-1928 .................... **PC 23; TCLC 8**
See also AMWS 1; CA 105; 162; DLB 9,
45; EXPP; MAL 5; RGAL 4

**Wylie, Philip (Gordon)**
1902-1971 ................................ **CLC 43**
See also CA 21-22; 33-36R; CAP 2; CN 1;
DLB 9; SFW 4

**Wyndham, John**
See Harris, John (Wyndham Parkes Lucas)
Beynon

**Wyss, Johann David Von**
1743-1818 ............................... **NCLC 10**
See also CLR 92; JRDA; MAICYA 1, 2;
SATA 29; SATA-Brief 27

**X, Malcolm**
See Malcolm X

**Xenophon**
c. 430 BCE-c. 354 BCE ...... **CMLC 17, 137**
See also AW 1; DLB 176; RGWL 2, 3; WLIT 8

**Xiao Tong** 501-531 ...................... **CMLC 203**

**Xie Lingyun** 385-433 ................... **CMLC 187**
See also DLB 358

**Xingjian, Gao** 1940- ...... **CLC 167, 315, 409**
See also CA 193; DFS 21; DLB 330; MTFW
2005; RGWL 3

**Xu Nancun**
See Chen Yingzhen

**Xuan Zhu**
See Mao Dun

**Yakamochi** 718-785 ......... **CMLC 45; PC 48**

**Yakumo Koizumi**
See Hearn, Lafcadio

**Yamada, Mitsuye (May)** 1923- ........... **PC 44**
See also CA 77-80

**Yamamoto, Hisaye**
1921-2011 ..... **AAL; CLC 343; SSC 34**
See also CA 214; DAM MULT; DLB 312;
LAIT 4; SSFS 14

**Yamashita, Karen Tei**
1951- ............................ **AAL; CLC 382**
See also CA 166; CANR 129, 223; DLB 312

**Yamauchi, Wakako** 1924- .................... **AAL**
See also CA 214; DLB 312

**Yan, Mo** 1956(?)- ................... **CLC 257, 354**
See also CA 201; CANR 192; EWL 3;
RGWL 3

**Yanez, Jose Donoso**
See Donoso, Jose

**Yang Xiong** 53 BCE-18 CE ........... **CMLC 192**
See also DLB 358

**Yanovsky, Basile S.**
See Yanovsky, V(assily) S(emenovich)

**Yanovsky, V(assily) S(emenovich)**
1906-1989 ............................ **CLC 2, 18**
See also CA 97-100; 129

**Yates, Richard**
1926-1992 ........................ **CLC 7, 8, 23**
See also AMWS 11; CA 5-8R; 139; CANR
10, 43; CN 1, 2, 3, 4, 5; DLB 2, 234; DLBY
1981, 1992; INT CANR-10; SSFS 24

**Yau, John** 1950- ................................. **PC 61**
See also CA 154; CANR 89; CP 4, 5, 6, 7;
DLB 234, 312; PFS 26

**Yearsley, Ann** 1753-1806 ........ **NCLC 174, 346;
PC 149**
See also DLB 109

**Yeats, W. B.**
See Yeats, William Butler

**Yeats, William Butler**
1865-1939 ................................... **DC 33;
PC 20, 51, 129; TCLC 1, 11, 18, 31, 93,
116; WLC 6**
See also AAYA 48; BRW 6; BRWR 1; CA
104; 127; CANR 45; CDBLB 1890-1914;
DA; DA3; DAB; DAC; DAM DRAM,
MST, POET; DLB 10, 19, 98, 156, 332;
EWL 3; EXPP; MTCW 1, 2; MTFW 2005;
NCFS 3; PAB; PFS 1, 2, 5, 7, 13, 15, 34,
42; RGEL 2; TEA; WLIT 4; WP

**Yehoshua, A. B.**
1936- ........................... **CLC 13, 31, 243**
See also CA 33-36R; CANR 43, 90, 145,
202; CWW 2; EWL 3; RGHL; RGSF 2;
RGWL 3; WLIT 6

**Yehoshua, Abraham B.**
See Yehoshua, A. B.

**Yellow Bird**
See Ridge, John Rollin

**Yep, Laurence** 1948- ........................ **CLC 35**
See also AAYA 5, 31; BYA 7; CA 49-52;
CANR 1, 46, 92, 161; CLR 3, 17, 54, 132;
DLB 52, 312; FANT; JRDA; MAICYA 1,
2; MAICYAS 1; SATA 7, 69, 123, 176,
213, 242; WYA; YAW

**Yep, Laurence Michael**
See Yep, Laurence

**Yerby, Frank G(arvin)**
1916-1991 ....... **BLC 1:3; CLC 1, 7, 22**
See also BPFB 3; BW 1, 3; CA 9-12R; 136;
CANR 16, 52; CN 1, 2, 3, 4, 5; DAM
MULT; DLB 76; INT CANR-16; MTCW
1; RGAL 4; RHW

**Yesenin, Sergei Aleksandrovich**
See Esenin, Sergei

**Yevtushenko, Yevgeny Alexandrovich**
See Yevtushenko, Yevgenyn

**Yevtushenko, Yevgenyn** 1933- ...... **CLC 1, 3,
13, 26, 51, 126; PC 40**
See also CA 81-84; CANR 33, 54; CWW 2;
DAM POET; DLB 359; EWL 3; MTCW 1;
PFS 29; RGHL; RGWL 2, 3

**Yezierska, Anzia** 1885(?)-1970 ....... **CLC 46;
SSC 144, 271; TCLC 205**
See also CA 89-92; 126; DLB 28, 221; FW;
MTCW 1; NFS 29; RGAL 4; SSFS 15, 43

**Yglesias, Helen** 1915-2008 ........... **CLC 7, 22**
See also CA 37-40R; 272; CAAS 20; CANR
15, 65, 95; CN 4, 5, 6, 7; INT CANR-15;
MTCW 1

**Y.O.**
See Russell, George William

**Yokomitsu, Riichi** 1898-1947 ......... **TCLC 47**
See also CA 170; EWL 3

**Yolen, Jane** 1939- ........................... **CLC 256**
See also AAYA 4, 22, 85; BPFB 3; BYA 9,
10, 11, 14, 16; CA 13-16R; CANR 11, 29,
56, 91, 126, 185; CLR 4, 44, 149; CWRI 5;
DLB 52; FANT; INT CANR-29; JRDA;
MAICYA 1, 2; MTFW 2005; NFS 30;
SAAS 1; SATA 4, 40, 75, 112, 158,
194, 230; SATA-Essay 111; SFW 4; SSFS
29; SUFW 2; WYA; YAW

**Yolen, Jane Hyatt**
See Yolen, Jane

**Yonge, Charlotte** 1823-1901 ... **TCLC 48, 245**
See also BRWS 17; CA 109; 163; CLR 210;
DLB 18, 163; RGEL 2; SATA 17; WCH

**Yonge, Charlotte Mary**
See Yonge, Charlotte

# Literary Criticism Series
# Cumulative Topic Index

This index lists all topic entries in Gale's *Children's Literature Review* (CLR), *Classical and Medieval Literature Criticism* (CMLC), *Contemporary Literary Criticism* (CLC), *Drama Criticism* (DC), *Literature Criticism from 1400 to 1800* (LC), *Nineteenth-Century Literature Criticism* (NCLC), *Poetry Criticism* (PC), *Short Story Criticism* (SSC), and *Twentieth-Century Literary Criticism* (TCLC). The index also lists topic entries in the Gale Critical Companion Collection, which includes the following publications: *The Beat Generation* (BG), *Feminism in Literature* (FL), *Gothic Literature* (GL), and *Harlem Renaissance* (HR).

Topic Index

Topic Index

Topic Index

Topic Index

Topic Index

**Topic Index**

# *TCLC* Cumulative Nationality Index

Borges, Jorge Luis **109, 320**
Cortazar, Julio **252**
Güiraldes, Ricardo (Guillermo) **39**
Hudson, W(illiam) H(enry) **29**
Lugones, Leopoldo **15**
Pizarnik, Alejandra **318**
Puig, Manuel **227, 366**
Storni, Alfonsina **5, 281**

## AUSTRALIAN

Baynton, Barbara **57, 211**
Campbell, David **325**
Franklin, (Stella Maria Sarah) Miles (Lampe) **7**
Furphy, Joseph **25**
Hanrahan, Barbara **219**
Ingamells, Rex **35**
Lawson, Henry (Archibald Hertzberg) **27**
Neilson, John Shaw **325**
Palmer, Nettie **325**
Palmer, Vance **326**
Paterson, A(ndrew) B(arton) **32**
Praed, Rosa **319**
Richardson, Henry Handel **4, 327**
Stead, Christina **244**
Warung, Price **45**
Webb, Francis **329**
White, Patrick **176, 326**

## AUSTRIAN

Améry, Jean **342**
Bachmann, Ingeborg **192**
Beer-Hofmann, Richard **60**
Bernhard, Thomas **165**
Broch, Hermann **20, 304, 307**
Brod, Max **115, 305**
Ebner-Eschenbach, Marie von **345**
Eisler, Hanns **361**
Franzos, Karl Emil **339**
Freud, Sigmund **52**
Hayek, F(riedrich) A(ugust von) **109**
Hofmannsthal, Hugo von **11**
Kafka, Franz **2, 6, 13, 29, 47, 53, 112, 179, 288**
Kraus, Karl **5, 263**
Kubin, Alfred (Leopold Isidor) **23**
Meyrink, Gustav **21**
Musil, Robert (Edler von) **12, 68, 213, 291**
Pabst, G. W. **127**
Perutz, Leo(pold) **60**
Rank, Otto **115**
Rilke, Rainer Maria **1, 6, 19, 195, 310**
Roth, (Moses) Joseph **33, 277**
Schnitzler, Arthur **4, 275**
Steiner, Rudolf **13**
Stroheim, Erich von **71**
Trakl, Georg **5, 239**
Weininger, Otto **84**
Werfel, Franz (Viktor) **8, 248**
Zweig, Stefan **17, 290**

## BELGIAN

Bosschere, Jean de **19**
Ghelderode, Michel de **187**
Lemonnier, (Antoine Louis) Camille **22**
Maeterlinck, Maurice **3, 251**
Sarton, May (Eleanor) **120**
van Ostaijen, Paul **33**
Verhaeren, Émile (Adolphe Gustave) **12**
Yourcenar, Marguerite **193**

## BOTSWANAN

Head, Bessie **337, 341**

## BRAZILIAN

Cunha, Euclides (Rodrigues Pimenta) da **24**
Drummond de Andrade, Carlos **139**
Lima Barreto, Afonso Henrique de **23**
Lispector, Clarice **305**

Machado de Assis, Joaquim Maria **10, 269**
Ramos, Graciliano **32**
Veríssimo, Érico **341**

## BULGARIAN

Vazov, Ivan (Minchov) **25**

## CANADIAN

Aquin, Hubert **342**
Callaghan, Morley **292**
Campbell, Wilfred **9**
Carman, (William) Bliss **7**
Carr, Emily **32, 260**
Connor, Ralph **31**
Drummond, William Henry **25**
Duncan, Sara Jeannette **60**
Engel, Marian **137**
Frye, Northrop **165**
Garneau, (Hector de) Saint-Denys **13**
Grove, Frederick Philip **248**
Innis, Harold Adams **77**
Knister, Raymond **56**
Leacock, Stephen (Butler) **2, 263**
Lewis, (Percy) Wyndham **2, 9, 104, 216**
McCrae, John **12**
Montgomery, L(ucy) M(aud) **51, 140**
Nelligan, Emile **14**
O'Hagan, Howard **328**
Pickthall, Marjorie L(owry) C(hristie) **21**
Roberts, Charles G(eorge) D(ouglas) **8**
Roy, Gabrielle **256**
Scott, Duncan Campbell **6**
Service, Robert W(illiam) **15**
Seton, Ernest (Evan) Thompson **31**
Smart, Elizabeth **231**
Stead, Robert J. C. **225**
Stringer, Arthur **37**
Sui Sin Far **232**
Wetherald, Agnes Ethelwyn **81**

## CHILEAN

Bombal, María Luisa **296**
Donoso, José **133**
Mistral, Gabriela **2, 277**
Huidobro Fernandez, Vicente Garcia **31**
Prado (Calvo), Pedro **75**

## CHINESE

Chang, Eileen **184**
Lin, Yutang **149**
Liu, E. **15**
Lu Hsun **3, 289**
Mao Dun **299**
Shen Congwen **301**
Su Man-shu **24**
Wen I-to **28**

## COLOMBIAN

Rivera, José Eustasio **35**

## CONGOLESE (KINSHASA)

Labou Tansi, Sony **331**

## CUBAN

Arenas, Reinaldo **191**
Cabrera, Lydia **223**
Carpentier, Alejo **201, 294, 316**
Lezama Lima, José **371**
Ortiz, Fernando **340**
Piñera, Virgilio **348**
Sarduy, Servero **167**

## CZECH

Brod, Max **115, 305**
Čapek, Karel **6, 37, 192**
Freud, Sigmund **52**
Hašek, Jaroslav (Matej Frantisek) **4, 261**

Hrabal, Bohumil **155**
Kafka, Franz **2, 6, 13, 29, 47, 53, 112, 288**
Nezval, Vitezslav **44**

## DANISH

Brandes, Georg (Morris Cohen) **10, 264**
Dinesen, Isak (Karen Blixen) **255**
Hansen, Martin A(lfred) **32**
Jensen, Johannes V. **41**
Nexo, Martin Andersen **43**
Pontoppidan, Henrik **29**

## DUTCH

Bok, Edward W. **101**
Couperus, Louis (Marie Anne) **15**
Heijermans, Herman **24**
Hillesum, Etty **49**
van Schendel, Arthur(-François-Émile) **56**

## ECUADORIAN

Aguilera Malta, Demetrio **353**

## EGYPTIAN

Idris, Yusuf **232**
Jabès, Edmond **304**
Rifaat, Alifa **346**

## ENGLISH

Abbott, Edwin **139**
Abercrombie, Lascelles **141**
Aldington, Richard **296**
Alexander, Samuel **77**
Amis, Kingsley **330**
Auden, W(ystan) H(ugh) **223**
Barbellion, W. N. P. **24**
Barfield, Owen **332**
Baring, Maurice **8**
Baring-Gould, Sabine **88**
Beerbohm, (Henry) Max(imilian) **1, 24**
Bell, Gertrude (Margaret Lowthian) **67**
Belloc, (Joseph) Hilaire (Pierre Sebastien
    Rene Swanton) **7, 18**
Bennett, (Enoch) Arnold **5, 20, 197**
Benson, A. C. **123**
Benson, E(dward) F(rederic) **27**
Benson, Stella **17**
Bentley, E(dmund) C(lerihew) **12**
Beresford, J(ohn) D(avys) **81**
Besant, Annie (Wood) **9**
Blackmore, R(ichard) D(oddridge) **27**
Blackwood, Algernon (Henry) **5**
Blunt, Wilfrid Scawen **365**
Bolt, Robert **175**
Bottomley, Gordon **107**
Bowen, Elizabeth **148**
Braddon, Mary Elizabeth **111, 366**
Bramah, Ernest **72**
Bridges, Robert (Seymour) **1**
Brittain, Vera **228**
Brooke, Rupert (Chawner) **2, 7**
Buchanan, Robert **107**
Burgess, Anthony **316, 319**
Burke, Thomas **63**
Burnett, Frances Hodgson **375**
Butler, Samuel **1, 33, 329, 331, 350**
Butts, Mary **77**
Byron, Robert **67**
Caine, Hall **97**
Caird, Mona **361**
Carpenter, Edward **88**
Carter, Angela **139, 321**
Cary, (Arthur) Joyce (Lunel) **1, 29, 196**
Chesterton, G(ilbert) K(eith) **1, 6, 64, 284**
Childers, (Robert) Erskine **65**
Christie, Agatha **333**
Churchill, Winston (Leonard Spencer) **113**
Clark, Kenneth Mackenzie **147**

Nationality Index

# *TCLC*-377 Title Index

Title Index